ISBN 978-0-260-93244-0
PIBN 10989876

1995

Illinois Register

Rules of Governmental Agencies

Volume 19, Issue 12— Mar. 24, 1995

Pages 3601-4782

published by

George H. Ryan
Secretary of State

Index Department
Administrative Code Div.
111 East Monroe Street
Springfield, IL 62756
(217) 782-7017

 Printed on recycled paper

PROPOSED RULES

ii

NOTICE OF PROPOSED AMENDMENTS

1) Heading of the Part: Access to and Eligibility for Child Welfare Services

2) Code Citation: 89 Ill. Adm. Code 304

3) Section Numbers: Proposed Action:
   304.2   Amend

4) Statutory Authority: The Children and Family Services Act [20 ILCS 505].

5) A Complete Description of the Subjects and Issues Involved: The Department is amending Section 304.2, Definitions, by adding definitions of "Biological Parent", "Family" and "Relative Caregiver". It is also correcting the definitions of "Abused child", "Neglected child", "Dependent minor", "Minimum parenting standards" and "Minor requiring authoritative intervention (MRAI)" to either make them agree with the statutes in which they are found or with other Department rules.

6) Will this proposed amendment replace an emergency rule currently in effect? No

7) Does this rulemaking contain an automatic repeal date? No

8) Does this proposed amendment contain incorporations by reference? No

9) Are there any other amendments pending on this Part? No

10) Statement of Statewide Policy Objectives: These amendments do not create or expand a state mandate as defined in Section 3(b) of the State Mandates Act [30 ILCS 805/3(b)].

11) Time, Place, and Manner in which interested persons may comment on this proposed rulemaking:

Comments on this proposed rulemaking may be submitted in writing for a period of 45 days following publication of this notice. Comments should be submitted to:

Jacqueline Bottingham, Chief
Office of Rules and Procedures
Department of Children and Family Services
406 East Monroe - Station #222
Springfield, Illinois 62701-1498
Telephone: (217) 524-1983
TTY: (217) 524-3715

The Department will consider fully all written comments on this proposed rulemaking submitted during the 45-day comment period. Comments submitted

NOTICE OF PROPOSED AMENDMENTS

by small businesses should be identified as such. Public hearings have been scheduled on these proposed amendments in the following areas:

April 11, 1995
7:00 p.m.
Quality Inn at Halsted
One South Halsted
Chicago, Illinois
(312) 829-5000

April 13, 1995
7:00 p.m.
State House
Room 212
Springfield, Illinois
(217) 782-1095

Persons are asked to limit their testimony to a maximum of 15 minutes per person. We will gladly accept written testimony at the public hearings. Persons who need translation or interpretation services to enable their community should request assistance by contacting the Office of Rules and Procedures.

12) Initial Regulatory Flexibility Analysis: The Department has determined that the proposed amendment does not have an effect on small businesses.

13) State reason(s) for this rulemaking if it was not included in either of the two most recent regulatory agendas. The need for this rulemaking was not foreseen at the time the Department filed its regulatory agenda. A major management initiative affecting home or relative care has prompted the Department to file these amendments at the present time in order to implement them at the start of the next fiscal year.

The full text of the proposed amendment begins on the next page.

DEPARTMENT OF CHILDREN AND FAMILY SERVICES

NOTICE OF PROPOSED AMENDMENTS

TITLE 89: SOCIAL SERVICES
CHAPTER III: DEPARTMENT OF CHILDREN AND FAMILY SERVICES
SUBCHAPTER a: SERVICE DELIVERY

PART 304
ACCESS TO AND ELIGIBILITY FOR CHILD WELFARE SERVICES

Section
304.1   Purpose
304.2   Definitions
304.3   Introduction to Child Welfare Services
304.4   Eligibility for Child Welfare Services
304.5   Access to Child Welfare Services
304.6   Decision Concerning Case Opening

AUTHORITY: Implementing and authorized by Section 5 of the Children and Family Services Act [20 ILCS 505/5]; Sections 2 and 2.1 of the Abused and Neglected Child Reporting Act [325 ILCS 5/2 and 2.1]; Section 1-2 of the Juvenile Court Act of 1987 [705 ILCS 405/1-2]; Section 1-103 of the Illinois Alcoholism and Other Drug Dependency Act [20 ILCS 305/1-103]; and Public Law 96-272, The Adoption Assistance and Child Welfare Act of 1980, which amends Section 471 of the Social Security Act (42 U.S.C.A. 671(a)(14)).

SOURCE: Adopted and codified at 5 Ill. Reg. 13117, effective November 30, 1981; amended at 8 Ill. Reg. 12118, effective July 9, 1984; amended at 17 Ill. Reg. 251, effective December 31, 1992; amended at 19 Ill. Reg. _____, effective _____.

Section 304.2 Definitions

"Abused child" means a child whose parent or immediate family member, or any person responsible for the child's welfare, or any individual residing in the same home as the child, or a paramour of the child's parent:

  inflicts, causes to be inflicted, or allows to be inflicted upon such child physical or mental injury, by other than accidental means, which causes death, disfigurement, impairment of physical or emotional health, or loss or impairment of any bodily function;

  creates a substantial risk of physical or mental injury to such child by other than accidental means which would be likely to cause death, disfigurement, impairment of physical or emotional health, or loss of or impairment of any bodily function;

  commits or allows to be committed any sex offense against such child, as such sex offenses are defined in the Criminal Code of

DEPARTMENT OF CHILDREN AND FAMILY SERVICES

NOTICE OF PROPOSED AMENDMENTS

  1961 as amended, and extending those definitions of sex offenses to include children under 18 years of age;

  commits or allows to be committed an act or acts of torture upon such child; or

  inflicts excessive corporal punishment. [Ill. Rev. Stat. 1991, ch. 23, par. 2053] [325 ILCS 5/3].

"Addicted Minor" includes any minor who is an addict or an alcoholic as defined in the Illinois Alcoholism and Other Drug Dependence Act [Ill. Rev. Stat. 1991, ch. 111-1/2, par. 6351.3] [20 ILCS 305/1-103].

"Adjudicated" as used in these rules means that the Juvenile Court has entered an order declaring that a child is neglected, dependent, a minor requiring authoritative intervention, a delinquent minor or an addicted minor.

"Biological father" means a man who has acknowledged his paternity via a notarized statement or whose paternity is adjudicated in court. When paternity has been acknowledged or adjudicated, the relatives of the biological father as well as those of the mother may be considered for the placement of related children.

"Child welfare services" means public social services which are directed toward the accomplishment of the following purposes:

  protecting and promoting the welfare of all children, including homeless, dependent, or neglected children; preventing or remedying, or assisting in the solution of problems which may result in, the neglect, abuse exploitation, or delinquency of children;

  preventing the unnecessary separation of children from their families by identifying family problems, assisting families in resolving their problems, and preventing breakup of the family where the prevention of child removal is desirable and possible;

  restoring to their families children who have been removed, by the provision of services to the child and the families;

  placing children in suitable adoptive homes, in cases where restoration to the biological family is not possible or appropriate;

  assuring adequate care of children away from their homes, in cases where the child cannot be returned home or cannot be placed for adoption;

DEPARTMENT OF CHILDREN AND FAMILY SERVICES

NOTICE OF PROPOSED AMENDMENTS

*providing supportive services and living maintenance which
contribute to the physical, emotional and social well-being of
children who are pregnant and unmarried;*

*providing shelter and independent living services for homeless
youth; and*

*placing and maintaining children in facilities that provide
separate living quarters for children under the age of 18 and for
children 18 years of age and older, unless a child 18 years of
age is in the last year of high school education or vocational
training, in an approved individual or group treatment program,
or in a licensed shelter facility. The Department is not
required to place or maintain children:*

who are in a foster home;

*who are developmentally disabled, as defined in the Mental
Health and Developmental Disabilities Code;*

*who are female children who are pregnant, pregnant and
parenting or parenting; or*

who are siblings,

*in facilities that provide separate living quarters for children
18 years of age and older and for children under 18 years of age.*
~~(Ill. Rev. Stat. 1991, ch. 23, par. 5005)~~ [20 ILCS 505/5]

"Delinquent minor" means a minor who before his 17th birthday violated
or attempted to violate a Federal or State law or municipal ordinance.
Delinquent minor is further defined in the Juvenile Court Act of 1987.

"Department client" means a child or a family who is receiving child
welfare services either directly from the Department or through the
Department's purchase of service providers.

"Dependent minor" means ~~a child under 18 years of age who as a result
of physical or mental disability of a parent or other legal guardian
is not receiving proper medical remedial or other care necessary for
his or her well being or whose parent wishes to release the child for
adoption. "Dependent minor" is further defined in the Juvenile Court
Act of 1987.~~ any minor under 18 years of age:

who is without a parent, guardian or legal custodian;

who is without proper care because of the physical or mental
disability of his parent, guardian or custodian;

DEPARTMENT OF CHILDREN AND FAMILY SERVICES

NOTICE OF PROPOSED AMENDMENTS

who is without proper medical or other remedial care recognized
under State law or other care necessary for his or her well being
through no fault, neglect or lack of concern by his parents,
guardian or custodian, provided that no order may be made
terminating parental rights, nor may a minor be removed from the
custody of his or her parents for longer than 6 months, pursuant
to an adjudication as a dependent minor under Section 2-4(c) of
the Juvenile Court Act of 1987, unless it is found to be in his
or her best interest by the court or the case automatically
closes as provided under Section 2-31 of the Act; or

who has a parent, guardian or legal custodian who with good cause
wishes to be relieved of all residual parental rights and
responsibilities, guardianship or custody, and who desires the
appointment of a guardian of the person with power to consent to
the adoption of the minor under Section 2-29 of the Act.

This definition does not apply to a minor who would be included herein
solely for the purpose of qualifying for financial assistance for
himself, his parents, guardian or custodian. [705 ILCS 405/2.4] This
definition does not apply to a minor whose parent or guardian has left
the minor in the care of an adult relative for any period of time.

"Family" means one or more adults and children, related by blood,
marriage or adoption and residing in the same household.

"Minimum parenting standards" means that a parent or other person
responsible for the child's welfare sees that the child is adequately
fed, clothed appropriately for the weather conditions, provided with
adequate shelter, protected from physical, mental and emotional harm,
and provided with necessary medical care ~~and education required by
law~~. A parent who has abandoned a child, deserted a child for three
months, or failed to demonstrate ~~an a reasonable degree of interest,
concern, or responsibility as to the welfare of~~ in a newborn child for
30 days after birth is deemed to have failed to have met the minimum
parenting standards, unless the parent has arranged for the child's
care in the home of a relative. In addition, a parent who is addicted
to alcohol or who is a drug addict, as defined in Section 1-10] of the
Illinois Alcoholism and Other Drug Dependency Act ~~(Ill. Rev. Stat.
1991, ch. 111 1/2, par. 6351-1-3)~~ [20 ILCS 305/1-103] and who has
consistently failed to cooperate in a rehabilitation program for a
period of at least six months is deemed to have failed to have met the
minimum parenting standards unless the parent has arranged for the
child's safety and well being despite the parent's addiction.

"Minor Requiring Authoritative Intervention (MRAI)" means any minor
under 18 years of age (1) who is (a) absent from home without consent
of parent, guardian or custodian, or (b) beyond the control of his or

DEPARTMENT OF CHILDREN AND FAMILY SERVICES

NOTICE OF PROPOSED AMENDMENTS

her parent, guardian or custodian, or circumstances which constitute a substantial or immediate danger to the minor's physical safety; and (2) who, after being taken into limited custody for the period provided for in this Section and offered interim crisis intervention services, where available, refuses to return home after the minor and his or her parent, guardian or custodian cannot agree to an arrangement for an alternative voluntary residential placement or to the continuation of such placement. Any minor taken into limited custody for the reasons specified in this Section may not be adjudicated a minor requiring authoritative intervention until the following number of days have elapsed from his or her having been taken into limited custody: 21 days for the first instance of being taken into limited custody and 5 days for the second, third, or fourth instances of being taken into limited custody. For the fifth or any subsequent instance of being taken into limited custody for the reasons specified in this Section, the minor may be adjudicated as requiring authoritative intervention without any specified period of time expiring after his or her being taken into limited custody, without the minor's being offered interim crisis intervention services and without the minor's being offered interim crisis intervention services, and without the minor's being afforded an opportunity to agree to an arrangement for an alternative voluntary residential placement. Notwithstanding any other provision for of this Section, for the first instance in which a minor is taken into limited custody where one year has elapsed from the last instance of his having been taken into limited custody, the minor may not be adjudicated a minor requiring authoritative intervention until 21 days have passed since being taken into limited custody. [705 ILCS 405/3-3] {111. Rev. Stat. 1991, ch. 37, par. 803-3}

"Neglected child" means any child whose parent or other person responsible for the child's welfare withholds or denies nourishment or medically indicated treatment subject to food or care denied solely on the basis of present or anticipated mental or physical impairment as determined by a physician acting alone or in consultation with other physicians or otherwise is not receiving proper support, or medical or other remedial care recognized under State law as necessary for a child's well being including adequate food, clothing, and shelter, or who is abandoned by his or her parents or other person responsible for the child's welfare or who is a newborn infant whose blood or urine contains any amount of a controlled substance as defined in subsection (f) of Section 102 of the Illinois Controlled Substances Act or a metabolite thereof, with the exception of a controlled substance or metabolite thereof whose presence in the newborn infant is the result of medical treatment administered to the mother or the newborn infant. A child shall not be considered neglected for the sole reason that such child's parent or other person responsible for his or her welfare depends upon spiritual

DEPARTMENT OF CHILDREN AND FAMILY SERVICES

NOTICE OF PROPOSED AMENDMENTS

means through prayer alone for the treatment or cure of disease or remedial care. {111. Rev. Stat. 1991, ch. 23, par. 2053} means any child who is not receiving the proper or necessary nourishment or medically indicated treatment including food or care not provided solely on the basis of present or anticipated mental or physical impairment as determined by a physician acting alone or in consultation with other physicians or otherwise is not receiving the proper or necessary support or medical or other remedial care recognized under State law as necessary for a child's well-being (including where there is harm or substantial risk of harm to the child's health or welfare), or other care necessary for a child's well-being, including adequate food, clothing and shelter; or who is abandoned by his or her parents or other person responsible for the child's welfare without a proper plan of care; or who is a newborn infant whose blood and urine contains any amount of controlled substance as defined in subsection (f) of Section 102 of the Illinois Controlled Substance Act or a metabolite thereof, with the exception of a controlled substance or metabolite thereof whose presence in the newborn infant is the result of medical treatment administered to the mother or newborn infant. A child shall not be considered neglected for the sole reason that the child's parent or other person responsible for his or her welfare has left the child in the care of an adult relative for any period of time. A child shall not be considered neglected or abused for the sole reason that such child's parent or other person responsible for his or her welfare depends upon spiritual means through prayer alone for the treatment or cure of disease or remedial cure under Section 4 of the Abused and Neglected Child Reporting Act. [325 ILCS 5/3] Where the circumstances indicate harm or substantial risk of harm to the child's health or welfare and necessary medical care is not being provided to treat or prevent that harm or risk of harm because such parent or other person responsible for the child's welfare depends upon spiritual means alone for treatment or cure, such child is subject to the requirements of the Abused and Neglected Child Reporting Act for the reporting of, investigation of, and provision of protective services with respect to such child and his health needs, and in such cases spiritual means through prayer alone for the treatment or cure of disease or for remedial medical care will not be recognized as a substitute for such necessary medical care, if the Department or, a juvenile court determines that medical care is necessary. A child shall not be considered neglected or abused solely because the child is not attending school in accordance with the requirements of Article 26 of the School Code. [325 ILCS 5/3]

"Purchase of services provider" means an agency or individual offering services to a Department client through a signed contract with the Department.

DEPARTMENT OF CHILDREN AND FAMILY SERVICES

NOTICE OF PROPOSED AMENDMENTS

"Relative caregiver" means a person 21 years of age or older, other than the parent, who has physical custody of the child and to whom the child has any of the following currently existing relationships by blood or adoption: grandparent, sibling, great grandparent, uncle, aunt, nephew, niece, first cousin, great uncle, great aunt, or who is the spouse of such a relative or who is the child's step-father, step-mother, step-brother or step-sister.

"Services delivered by the Department" means those social services provided either directly by Department of Children and Family Services staff or by purchase of service providers.

"Voluntary placement agreement" means a time-limited written request and consent from a parent, guardian or legal custodian of a child for placement of the child out of the home. When signed by designated Department staff, the Department agrees to provide child welfare services which include placement.

(Source: Amended at 19 Ill. Reg. _____, effective _____)

DEPARTMENT OF CHILDREN AND FAMILY SERVICES

NOTICE OF PROPOSED AMENDMENTS

1) Heading of the Part: Authorized Child Care Payments

2) Code Citation: 89 Ill. Adm. Code 359

3) Section Numbers: Proposed Action:

    359.2   Amend
    359.4   Amend

4) Statutory Authority: The Children and Family Services Act [20 ILCS 505].

5) A Complete Description of the Subjects and Issues Involved: References to approved relative homes have been deleted, since the Department is terminating the approval process effective July 1, 1995. The Department will pay the foster care board rate only to relative caregivers who are licensed in accordance with 89 Ill. Adm Code 402, Licensing Standards for Foster Family Homes. When the Department places children with relative caregivers who are not licensed but meet the pre-placement conditions of 89 Ill. Adm. Code 301.80, Relative Home Placement, relative caregivers who choose this option will be referred to the Department of Public Aid to apply for Aid to Families with Dependent Children (AFDC) for the related children placed with them. The Department of Children and Family Services will provide a supplement for children for whom the Department is legally responsible to bring the total income for the related children placed with the relative caregiver to the child only standard of need established for that number of children by the Illinois Department of Public Aid. Relatives who are licensed will be paid more because licensed homes represent a higher level of training and standard of care.

In addition the Department has added a definition of "Relative caregiver" to Section 359.2, Definitions.

6) Will this proposed amendment replace an emergency rule currently in effect? No

7) Does this rulemaking contain an automatic repeal date? No

8) Does this proposed amendment contain incorporations by reference? No

9) Are there any other amendments pending on this Part? No

10) Statement of Statewide Policy Objectives: These amendments do not create or expand a State mandate as defined in Section 3(b) of the State Mandates Act [30 ILCS 805/3(b)].

11) Time, Place, and Manner in which interested persons may comment on this proposed rulemaking:

DEPARTMENT OF CHILDREN AND FAMILY SERVICES

NOTICE OF PROPOSED AMENDMENTS

Comments on this proposed rulemaking may be submitted in writing for a period of 45 days following publication of this notice. Comments should be submitted to:

Jacqueline Nottingham, Chief
Office of Rules and Procedures
Department of Children and Family Services
406 East Monroe - Station 222
Springfield, Illinois 62701-1498
Telephone: (217) 524-1983
TTY: (217) 524-3715

The Department will consider fully all written comments on this proposed rulemaking submitted during the 45-day comment period. Comments submitted by small businesses should be identified as such. Public hearings have been scheduled on these proposed amendments in the following areas:

April 11, 1995
7:00 p.m.
Quality Inn at Halsted
One South Halsted
Chicago, Illinois
(312) 829-5000

April 13, 1995
7:00 p.m.
State House
Room 212
Springfield, Illinois
(217) 782-2099

Persons are asked to limit their testimony to a maximum of 15 minutes per person. We will gladly accept written testimony at the public hearings. Persons who need translation or interpretation services to enable their commentary should request assistance by contacting the Office of Rules and Procedures.

12) Initial Regulatory Flexibility Analysis: The Department has determined that the proposed amendment does not have an affect on small businesses.

13) State reason(s) for this rulemaking if it was not included in either of the two most recent regulatory agendas. The need for this rulemaking was not foreseen at the time the Department filed its regulatory agendas. A major management initiative affecting home of relative care, has prompted the Department to file these amendments at the present time in order to implement them at the start of the next fiscal year.

The full text of the proposed amendment begins on the next page.

DEPARTMENT OF CHILDREN AND FAMILY SERVICES

NOTICE OF PROPOSED AMENDMENTS

TITLE 89: SOCIAL SERVICES
CHAPTER III: DEPARTMENT OF CHILDREN AND FAMILY SERVICES
SUBCHAPTER c: FISCAL ADMINISTRATION

PART 359
AUTHORIZED CHILD CARE PAYMENTS

Section
359.1   Purpose
359.2   Definitions
359.3   Introduction
359.4   Payments for Substitute Care Services
359.5   Payments for Family Preservation and Auxiliary Services
359.6   Payments for Independent Living Arrangements
359.7   Payments for Children's Personal and Physical Maintenance
359.8   Payments for Unmarried Mothers
359.9   Payments for Medical Care
359.10   Overpayments and Repayments

AUTHORITY: Implementing and authorized by Section 5 of the Children and Family Services Act [20 ILCS 505/5].

SOURCE: Adopted and codified at 5 Ill. Reg. 13129, effective November 30, 1981; amended at 9 Ill. Reg. 19705, effective December 16, 1985; amended at 10 Ill. Reg. 15575, effective September 19, 1986; amended at 19 Ill. Reg. _____, effective _____.

Section 359.2 Definitions

"Auxiliary services" means those services provided by the Department to children in their own homes as well as to children in placement which supplement or complement the primary service. For example, when advocacy services are provided to children in substitute care, this is an auxiliary service.

"Children for whom the Department has legal responsibility" means children for whom the Department has temporary protective custody, custody or guardianship via court order, or whose parent(s) has signed an adoptive surrender or voluntary placement agreement with the Department.

"Family preservation services" means those services provided to children and families who require social services to maintain the family unit intact.

"Overpayment" means an amount paid for a service in excess of the actual incurred expenses or rate for that service or a payment for a service that is not rendered. This includes board payments for a

DEPARTMENT OF CHILDREN AND FAMILY SERVICES

NOTICE OF PROPOSED AMENDMENTS

child that continue after the child is no longer in the placement for which the payment is made.

"Relative caregiver" means a person 21 years of age or older, other than the parent, who has physical custody of the child and to whom the child has any of the following currently existing relationships by blood or adoption: grandparent, sibling, great grandparent, uncle, aunt, nephew, niece, first cousin, great uncle, great aunt, or who is the spouse of such a relative or who is the child's step-father, step-mother, step-brother or step-sister.

"Substitute care services" means those services provided to children who require placement away from their families.

(Source: Amended at 19 Ill. Reg. _____, effective _____)

Section 359.4 Payments for Substitute Care Services

Payments are made for children for whom the Department has legal responsibility in the following types of substitute care living arrangements if the placements meet the requirements established via the purchase of service contracts and the applicable licensing rules as specified in 89-Ill.-Adm.-Code-355,-Relative-Home Placement, 89 Ill. Adm. Code 357, Purchase of Service, 89 Ill. Adm. Code 401, Licensing Standards for Child Welfare Agencies, 89 Ill. Adm. Code 402, Licensing Standards for Foster Family Homes, 89 Ill. Adm. Code 403, Licensing Standards for Group Homes, and 89 Ill. Adm. Code 404, Licensing Standards for Child Care Institutions and Maternity Centers:

    a) Foster family care is provided in licensed foster family homes or approved-homes-of-relative-caretakers. The Department recognizes the following types of foster family care:

        1) Specialized foster family homes and intensive service foster homes receive additional monthly compensation because they accept children with medical, behavioral and/or psychological problems or because they accept pregnant girls or young mothers who are in need of specialized training in parenting skills, child development, money management, and self sufficiency.

        2) Emergency foster homes may be paid a flat rate for days of service provided or may receive retainer fees to assure that emergency beds are available 24 hours per day.

        3) Department boarding homes are licensed foster family homes operated by foster parents supervised by the Department.

        4) Private agency foster homes are licensed foster homes supervised by licensed child welfare agencies.

        5) Relative---boarding--homes--are--those--homes--approved--by--the Department-in-which-relatives-(excluding--parents)--provide--care for---related---children---for--whom--the--Department--has--legal responsibility.

DEPARTMENT OF CHILDREN AND FAMILY SERVICES

NOTICE OF PROPOSED AMENDMENTS

        5)6) Deaf foster care is a unique service provided in Department boarding homes for children for whom the Department is not legally responsible who require placement for educational reasons.

    b) Relative home care may be provided by relative caregivers, as defined in Section 359.2. If a relative caregiver does not wish to apply for licensure as a foster family home or has applied for licensure and been denied, the relative may provide care to children for whom the Department is legally responsible if the relative family home meets the placement pre-conditions in Section 301.80 of 89 Ill. Adm. Code 301, Placement and Visitation Services. Relative caregivers who choose this option will be referred to the Department of Public Aid to apply for Aid to Families with Dependent Children (AFDC) for the related children placed with them. The Department of Children and Family Services will provide a supplement for children for whom the Department is legally responsible to bring the total income for the related children placed with the relative caregiver to the child only standard of need established for that number of children by the Illinois Department of Public Aid.

    b)c) Institution and group home care is provided in licensed institutions and group homes. Rates are established for these facilities via a purchase of service contract with the Department.

    c)d) Subsidized adoptive homes are adoptive homes to which the Department provides financial assistance when a special needs child for whom the Department was legally responsible is adopted.

        1) Special service subsidy is special help given to handle an anticipated expense when no other resource is available. It may include:

            A) legal fees related to the consummation of the adoption;

            B) medical costs, not covered by the adopting family's medical insurance or by the Division of Services--for-Crippled Children Specialized Care for Children;

            C) other special services, such as physical therapy, counseling, prosthesis, special education a child may require due to a physical or mental handicap.

        2) Regular adoption assistance payments are monthly payments beyond the legal consummation of the adoption and may continue until the child reaches age 18 (for children adopted after the-effective date-of-this-Part November 30, 1981) unless the child has a mental or physical handicap. When other assistance is not available for a child adopted after the-effective--date--of--this Part November 30, 1981 with a mental or physical handicap, adoption assistance may be provided to age 21.

        3) The purpose, amount, and duration of the adoption assistance will be mutually agreed to by the Department and the adopting parents prior to completion of the adoption in the form of a written agreement. The amount of financial assistance shall be less than the cost of maintaining the child in an appropriate foster family

DEPARTMENT OF CHILDREN AND FAMILY SERVICES

NOTICE OF PROPOSED AMENDMENTS

home. Special service fees shall cost no more than such services
would cost the Department.

4) The Department shall annually review with the adoptive parent(s)
the continuing needs of the child for adoption assistance. There
shall be an annual written reapplication for adoption assistance
prior to the anniversary date of the finalization of the
adoption.

e)[e] Related services are not substitute care services but are provided to
enhance the care provided to children who require substitute care
services.

1) In an effort to upgrade the quality of foster family care, the
Department may pay for foster parent training and costs
associated with training. These payments are provided as funding
allows.

2) Permanent planning and adoption contracts may be negotiated with
licensed child welfare agencies. These contracts are negotiated
to develop plans for children in substitute care and to secure
adoptive resources for special needs children.

(Source: Amended at 19 Ill. Reg. _____, effective
_____)

DEPARTMENT OF CHILDREN AND FAMILY SERVICES

NOTICE OF PROPOSED AMENDMENTS

1) **Heading of the Part:**   Background Check of Foster Family Home Applicants

2) **Code Citation:**   89 Ill. Adm. Code 380

3) **Section Numbers:**   Proposed Action:

   380.1   Amend
   380.2   Amend
   380.3   Amend
   380.4   Amend
   380.5   Amend
   380.6   Amend
   380.7   Amend
   380.8   Amend
   380.12   Amend
   380.13   Amend
   380.14   Amend
   380.Appendix A   New

4) **Statutory Authority:**   Section 4 of the Child Care Act of 1969 [225 ILCS
   10/4]

5) **A Complete Description of the Subjects and Issues Involved:** The Child
Care Act of 1969 requires criminal background checks of all applicants for
licensure as a foster family home and gives the Department the authority
to require by rule criminal background checks of other adult members of
the household. In addition, the Child Care Act of 1969 requires that
persons who have been convicted of committing or attempting to commit
certain serious crimes may not be granted a foster parent license and
allows the Department to establish standards for how to consider crimes
not specifically identified in the Child Care Act. The Department has
identified the crimes in Appendix A as sufficiently serious to prevent
licensure as a foster family home.

Nearly one fourth of child abuse and neglect reports involve other members
of the foster family's household, rather than the foster parents
themselves. Therefore, the Department is proposing that criminal
background investigations be completed for all adult members of the foster
parent(s)' household and that a check of the State Central Registry be
completed for any member of the household age 13 or older. This will
increase the safety of children placed in foster care and insure that all
the safety of the foster home has been thoroughly evaluated.

6) **Will these proposed amendments replace an emergency rule currently in
effect?** / Yes

7) **Does this rulemaking contain an automatic repeal date?** No

DEPARTMENT OF CHILDREN AND FAMILY SERVICES

NOTICE OF PROPOSED AMENDMENTS

8) Do these proposed amendments contain incorporations by reference? No

9) Are there any other amendments pending on this part? Yes

Section	Proposed Action	Illinois Register Citation
380.1	Repeal	June 17, 1994 (18 Ill. Reg. 8779)
380.2	Repeal	June 17, 1994 (18 Ill. Reg. 8779)
380.3	Repeal	June 17, 1994 (18 Ill. Reg. 8779)
380.4	Repeal	June 17, 1994 (18 Ill. Reg. 8779)
380.5	Repeal	June 17, 1994 (18 Ill. Reg. 8779)
380.6	Repeal	June 17, 1994 (18 Ill. Reg. 8779)
380.7	Repeal	June 17, 1994 (18 Ill. Reg. 8779)
380.8	Repeal	June 17, 1994 (18 Ill. Reg. 8779)
380.9	Repeal	June 17, 1994 (18 Ill. Reg. 8779)
380.10	Repeal	June 17, 1994 (18 Ill. Reg. 8779)
380.11	Repeal	June 17, 1994 (18 Ill. Reg. 8779)
380.12	Repeal	June 17, 1994 (18 Ill. Reg. 8779)
380.13	Repeal	June 17, 1994 (18 Ill. Reg. 8779)
380.14	Repeal	June 17, 1994 (18 Ill. Reg. 8779)

10) State of Statewide Policy Objectives: These rules do not create or expand
     a State mandate as defined in Section 3(b) of the State Mandates Act [30
     ILCS 805/3(b)].

11) Time, Place, and Manner in which interested persons may comment on this
     proposed rulemaking:

     Comments on this proposed rulemaking may be submitted in writing for a
     period of 45 days following publication of this notice. Comments should
     be submitted to:

          Jacqueline Nottingham, Chief
          Office of Rules and Procedures
          Department of Children and Family Services
          406 East Monroe Street, Station # 222
          Springfield, Illinois 62701-1498

          Telephone: (217) 524-1983
          TTY: (217) 524-3715

     The Department will consider fully all written comments on this proposed
     rulemaking submitted during the 45-day comment period. Comments submitted
     by small businesses should be identified as such. Public hearings have
     been scheduled on these proposed amendments as follows;

          April 11, 1995
          7:00 p.m.

DEPARTMENT OF CHILDREN AND FAMILY SERVICES

NOTICE OF PROPOSED AMENDMENTS

          Quality Inn at Halsted
          One South Halsted
          Chicago, Illinois
          (312) 829-5000

          April 13, 1995
          7:00 p.m.
          State House
          Room 212
          Springfield, Illinois
          (217) 782-2099

     Persons are asked to limit their testimony to a maximum of 15 minutes per
     person. We will gladly accept written testimony at the public hearings.
     Persons who need translation or interpretation services to enable their
     commentary should request assistance by contacting the Office of Rules and
     Procedures at least five days prior to the public hearing.

12) Initial Regulatory Flexibility Analysis: The proposed amendments do not
     affect small businesses.

13) State reason(s) for this rulemaking if it was not included in either of
     the two (2) most recent regulatory agendas: The Department has proposed
     amendments to 89 Ill. Adm. Code 385, Background Checks, to impose similar
     requirements on all child care facilities subject to licensure by the
     Department. Those proposed amendments continue to undergo review and
     refinement in response to the public comments received. There has been an
     alarming number of tragedies in foster family and relative home care
     within the past few months. Therefore, the Department is proceeding with
     amendments to this Part, which is limited to foster family care, until the
     issues in 89 Ill. Adm. Code 385 can be resolved fully.

     The full text of the proposed amendments are identical to the text of the
     emergency amendments on page 4755.

DEPARTMENT OF CHILDREN AND FAMILY SERVICES

NOTICE OF PROPOSED AMENDMENTS

1) Heading of the Part: Client Service Planning

2) Code Citation: 89 Ill. Adm. Code 305

3) Section Numbers: Proposed Action:

    305.20   Amend
    305.30   Amend
    305.40   Amend

4) Statutory Authority: Section 4 of the Children and Family Services Act [20 ILCS 505/4].

5) A Complete Description of the Subjects and Issues Involved: These changes are necessary in order to make Part 305 consistent with other Department rules regarding home of relative care. When children are living apart from their parents but with other related caregivers, they will no longer be considered as neglected for that reason alone. The Department may work to maintain the child with the relative caregiver.

6) Will this proposed amendment replace an emergency rule currently in effect? No

7) Does this rulemaking contain an automatic repeal date? No

8) Does this proposed amendment contain incorporations by reference? No

9) Are there any other amendments pending on this Part? Yes

    Section Proposed Action   Illinois Register Citation

    305.80   Amend   December 30, 1995 (18 Ill. Reg. 18164)

10) Statement of Statewide Policy Objectives: These amendments do not create or expand a state mandate as defined in Section 3(b) of the State Mandates Act [30 ILCS 805/3].

11) Time, place, and manner in which interested persons may comment on this proposed rulemaking:

    Comments on this proposed rulemaking may be submitted in writing for a period of 45 days following publication of this Notice. Comments should be submitted to:

        Jacqueline Nottingham, Chief
        Office of Rules and Procedures
        Department of Children and Family Services
        406 East Monroe - Station 222

DEPARTMENT OF CHILDREN AND FAMILY SERVICES

NOTICE OF PROPOSED AMENDMENTS

        Springfield, Illinois 62701-1498
    Telephone: (217)524-1983
    TTY: (217)524-3715

The Department will consider fully all written comments on this proposed rulemaking submitted during the 45-day comment period. Comments submitted by small businesses should be identified as such. Public hearings have been scheduled on these proposed amendments in the following areas:

        April 11, 1995
        7:00 p.m.
        Quality Inn at Halsted
        One South Halsted
        Chicago, Illinois
        (312) 829-5000

        April 13, 1995
        7:00 p.m.
        State House
        Room 212
        Springfield, Illinois
        (217) 782-2099

Persons are asked to limit their testimony to a maximum of 15 minutes per person. We will gladly accept written testimony at the public hearings. Persons who need translation or interpretation services to enable their commentary should request assistance by contacting the Office of Rules and Procedures.

12) Initial Regulatory Flexibility Analysis: The Department has determined that the proposed amendment does not have an affect on small businesses.

13) State reason(s) for this rulemaking if it was not included in either of the two most recent regulatory agendas. The need for this rulemaking was not foreseen at the time the Department filed its regulatory agendas. A major management initiative affecting home of relative care has prompted the Department to file these amendments at the present time in order to implement them at the start of the next fiscal year.

The full text of the proposed amendment begins on the next page.

DEPARTMENT OF CHILDREN AND FAMILY SERVICES

NOTICE OF PROPOSED AMENDMENTS

TITLE 89: SOCIAL SERVICES
CHAPTER III: DEPARTMENT OF CHILDREN AND FAMILY SERVICES
SUBCHAPTER a: SERVICE DELIVERY

PART 305
CLIENT SERVICE PLANNING

Section
305.10   Purpose
305.20   Definitions
305.30   Introduction to Client Service Planning
305.40   Types of Permanency Goals and Alternative Permanency Options
305.50   Service Plan
305.60   Case Review System
305.70   Roles and Responsibilities of the Administrative Case Reviewer
305.80   Decision Review
305.90   Parent-Child Visitation (Recodified)
305.100   Evaluating Whether Children in Placement Should Be Returned Home
305.110   Termination of Parental Rights
305.120   Planning for the Termination of Services
305.130   The Department's Role in the Juvenile Court
305.140   Compliance With the Client Service Planning Requirements

AUTHORITY: Implementing and authorized by the Children and Family Services Act
[20 ILCS 505], the Abused and Neglected Child Reporting Act [325 ILCS 5], the
Adoption Assistance and Child Welfare Act of 1980, amending Section 475 of the
Social Security Act [42 U.S.C. 675 (1991)], the Juvenile Court Act [705 ILCS
405], and the Adoption Act [750 ILCS 50].

SOURCE: Adopted and codified at 5 Ill. Reg. 14456, effective December 29,
1981; amended at 8 Ill. Reg. 21570, effective November 1, 1984; amended at 9
Ill. Reg. 7920, effective May 31, 1985; recodified at 16 Ill. Reg. 12772;
amended at 16 Ill. Reg. 16552, effective October 19, 1992; amended at 18 Ill.
Reg. 17200, effective December 1, 1994; Section 305.90 recodified to 89 Ill.
Adm. Code 301.210 at 19 Ill. Reg. _____; amended at 19 Ill. Reg.
_____, effective _____.

Section 305.20 Definitions

    "Abandonment" means parental conduct which demonstrates the purpose of
    relinquishing all parental rights and claims to the child.

    "Administrative case review" means a review open to the participation
    of the parents of the child, conducted by a panel of appropriate
    persons at least one of whom is not responsible for the case
    management of, or the delivery of services to, either the child or the
    parents who are the subjects of the review.

DEPARTMENT OF CHILDREN AND FAMILY SERVICES

NOTICE OF PROPOSED AMENDMENTS

    "Biological father" means a man who has acknowledged his paternity via
    a notarized statement or whose paternity is adjudicated in court.
    When paternity has been acknowledged or adjudicated, the relatives of
    the biological father as well as those of the mother may be considered
    for the placement of related children.

    "Children for whom the Department is legally responsible" means
    children for whom the Department has temporary protective custody,
    custody or guardianship via court order, or children whose parent(s)
    have signed an adoptive surrender or voluntary placement agreement
    with the Department.

    "Delegated relative authority" means the Department has selected a
    relative caregiver, in accordance with Section 305.40(d), as a
    continuous, stable living arrangement for related children and has
    delegated day to day decision making on behalf of those children to
    the relative caregiver. The Department would retain guardianship of
    the children and continue to exercise authority over all major
    decisions which affect their lives and health.

    "Department client" means a child or a family who is receiving child
    welfare services either directly from the Department or through a
    purchase of service provider.

    "Desertion" means parental conduct which evidences an intention to
    permanently terminate custody of a child but not to relinquish all
    parental rights, claims and responsibilities.

    "Discharge planning" means service planning which focuses on providing
    a smooth transition from Department guardianship or custody and the
    receipt of child welfare services to discharge from guardianship or
    custody and the termination of child welfare services.

    "Family" means one or more adults and children, related by blood,
    marriage or adoption and residing in the same household.

    "Individual treatment plan (ITP)" or "treatment plan" as defined in 59
    Ill. Adm. Code 132, Medicaid Community Mental Health Services, means a
    written document developed by the appropriate service provider staff
    with the participation of the client with a mental illness and, if
    applicable, the client's guardian, which specifies the client's
    diagnosis, problems, and service needs to be addressed, the
    intermediate objectives and long-term goals for the services and the
    planned interventions for achieving these goals.

    "Individualized Education Plan/Program (IEP)" means the document
    prepared by the local school district, as a result of a
    Multidisciplinary Conference, that identifies the specific special

DEPARTMENT OF CHILDREN AND FAMILY SERVICES

NOTICE OF PROPOSED AMENDMENTS

1) **Heading of the Part**: Client Service Planning

2) **Code Citation**: 89 Ill. Adm. Code 305

3) **Section Numbers**:   Proposed Action:

   305.20   Amend
   305.30   Amend
   305.40   Amend

4) **Statutory Authority**: Section 4 of the Children and Family Services Act [20 ILCS 505/4].

5) **A Complete Description of the Subjects and Issues Involved**: These changes are necessary in order to make Part 305 consistent with other Department rules regarding home of relative care. When children are living apart from their parents but with other related caregivers, they will no longer be considered as neglected for that reason alone. The Department may work to maintain the child with the relative caregiver.

6) **Will this proposed amendment replace an emergency rule currently in effect?** No

7) **Does this rulemaking contain an automatic repeal date?** No

8) **Does this proposed amendment contain incorporations by reference?** No

9) **Are there any other amendments pending on this Part?** Yes

   Section Proposed Action Illinois Register Citation

   305.80   Amend   December 30, 1995 (18 Ill. Reg. 18164)

10) **Statement of Statewide Policy Objectives**: These amendments do not create or expand a state mandate as defined in Section 3(b) of the State Mandates Act [30 ILCS 805/3].

11) **Time, place, and manner in which interested persons may comment on this proposed rulemaking**:

   Comments on this proposed rulemaking may be submitted in writing for a period of 45 days following publication of this Notice. Comments should be submitted to:

   Jacqueline Nottingham, Chief
   Office of Rules and Procedures
   Department of Children and Family Services
   406 East Monroe - Station 222

DEPARTMENT OF CHILDREN AND FAMILY SERVICES

NOTICE OF PROPOSED AMENDMENTS

   Springfield, Illinois 62701-1498
   Telephone: (217)524-1983
   TTY: (217)524-3715

The Department will consider fully all written comments on this proposed rulemaking submitted during the 45-day comment period. Comments submitted by small businesses should be identified as such. Public hearings have been scheduled on these proposed amendments in the following areas:

   April 11, 1995
   7:00 p.m.
   Quality Inn at Halsted
   One South Halsted
   Chicago, Illinois
   (312) 829-5000

   April 13, 1995
   7:00 p.m.
   State House
   Room 212
   Springfield, Illinois
   (217) 782-2099

Persons are asked to limit their testimony to a maximum of 15 minutes per person. We will gladly accept written testimony at the public hearings. Persons who need translation or interpretation services to enable their commentary should request assistance by contacting the Office of Rules and Procedures.

12) **Initial Regulatory Flexibility Analysis**: The Department has determined that the proposed amendment does not have an affect on small businesses.

13) **State reason(s) for this rulemaking if it was not included in either of the two most recent regulatory agendas**. The need for this rulemaking was not foreseen at the time the Department filed its regulatory agendas. A major management initiative affecting home of relative care has prompted the Department to file these amendments at the present time in order to implement them at the start of the next fiscal year.

The full text of the proposed amendment begins on the next page.

DEPARTMENT OF CHILDREN AND FAMILY SERVICES

NOTICE OF PROPOSED AMENDMENTS

TITLE 89: SOCIAL SERVICES
CHAPTER III: DEPARTMENT OF CHILDREN AND FAMILY SERVICES
SUBCHAPTER a: SERVICE DELIVERY

PART 305
CLIENT SERVICE PLANNING

Section
305.10   Purpose
305.20   Definitions
305.30   Introduction to Client Service Planning
305.40   Types of Permanency Goals and Alternative Permanency Options
305.50   Service Plan
305.60   Case Review System
305.70   Roles and Responsibilities of the Administrative Case Reviewer
305.80   Decision Review
305.90   Parent-Child Visitation (Recodified)
305.100   Evaluating Whether Children in Placement Should Be Returned Home
305.110   Termination of Parental Rights
305.120   Planning for the Termination of Services
305.130   The Department's Role in the Juvenile Court
305.140   Compliance With the Client Service Planning Requirements

AUTHORITY: Implementing and authorized by the Children and Family Services Act
[20 ILCS 505], the Abused and Neglected Child Reporting Act [325 ILCS 5], the
Adoption Assistance and Child Welfare Act of 1980, amending Section 475 of the
Social Security Act (42 U.S.C. 675 (1991)), the Juvenile Court Act [705 ILCS
405], and the Adoption Act [750 ILCS 50].

SOURCE: Adopted and codified at 5 Ill. Reg. 14456, effective December 29,
1981; amended at 8 Ill. Reg. 21570, effective November 1, 1984; amended at 9
Ill. Reg. 7920, effective May 31, 1985; recodified at 16 Ill. Reg. 12772;
amended at 16 Ill. Reg. 16552, effective October 19, 1992; amended at 18 Ill.
Reg. 17200, effective December 1, 1994; Section 305.90 recodified to 89 Ill.
Adm. Code 301.210 at 19 Ill. Reg. _____; amended at 19 Ill. Reg.
_____, effective _____.

Section 305.20 Definitions

"Abandonment"-means-parental-conduct-which-demonstrates-the-purpose-of
relinquishing-all-parental-rights-and-claims-to-the-child.

"Administrative case review" means a review open to the participation
of the parents of the child, conducted by a panel of appropriate
persons at least one of whom is not responsible for the case
management of, or the delivery of services to, either the child or the
parents who are the subjects of the review.

DEPARTMENT OF CHILDREN AND FAMILY SERVICES

NOTICE OF PROPOSED AMENDMENTS

"Biological father" means a man who has acknowledged his paternity via
a notarized statement or whose paternity is adjudicated in court.
When paternity has been acknowledged or adjudicated, the relatives of
the biological father as well as those of the mother may be considered
for the placement of related children.

"Children for whom the Department is legally responsible" means
children for whom the Department has temporary protective custody,
custody or guardianship via court order, or children whose parent(s)
have signed an adoptive surrender or voluntary placement agreement
with the Department.

"Delegated relative authority" means the Department has selected a
relative caregiver, in accordance with Section 305.40(d), as a
continuous, stable living arrangement for related children and has
delegated day to day decision making on behalf of those children to
the relative caregiver. The Department would retain guardianship of
the children and continue to exercise authority over all major
decisions which effect their lives and health.

"Bepartment---client"--means-a-child-or-a-family-who-is-receiving-child
welfare-services-either-directly-from--the--Department--or--through--a
purchase-of-service-provider.

"Desertion"--means--parental--conduct--which-evidences-an-intention-to
permanently-terminate-custody-of-a-child,-but-not--to--relinquish--all
parental-rights,-claims-and-responsibilities.

"Discharge planning" means service planning which focuses on providing
a smooth transition from Department guardianship or custody and the
receipt of child welfare services to discharge from guardianship or
custody and the termination of child welfare services.

"Family" means one or more adults and children, related by blood,
marriage or adoption and residing in the same household.

"Individual treatment plan (ITP)" or "treatment plan" as defined in 59
Ill. Adm. Code 132, Medicaid Community Mental Health Services, means a
written document developed by the appropriate service provider staff
with the participation of the client with a mental illness and, if
applicable, the client's guardian, which specifies the client's
diagnosis, problems, and service needs to be addressed, the
intermediate objectives and long-term goals for the services and the
planned interventions for achieving these goals.

"Individualized Education Plan/Program (IEP)" means the document
prepared by the local school district, as a result of a
Multidisciplinary Conference, that identifies the specific special

DEPARTMENT OF CHILDREN AND FAMILY SERVICES

NOTICE OF PROPOSED AMENDMENTS

education services that will be provided to the child. The IEP also includes education goals, services, frequency, quantity and duration. IEP is further defined in 23 Ill. Adm. Code 226, Special Education.

"Individualized Family Service Plan (IFSP)" means a written working document developed for each child in order to facilitate the provisions of Early Intervention (EI) services. The IFSP is created by the family, an inter-disciplinary team, the core EI agency, and the case manager (service coordinator). The EI agency is responsible for coordinating the IFSP implementation.

"Minimum parenting standards" means that a parent or other person responsible for the child's welfare sees that the child is adequately fed, clothed appropriately for the weather conditions, provided with adequate shelter, protected from severe physical, mental and emotional harm, and provided with necessary medical care and education required by law. A parent who has abandoned a child, deserted a child for three months, or failed to demonstrate a reasonable degree of interest, concern, or responsibility as to the welfare of a newborn child for 30 days after birth is deemed to have failed to have met the minimum parenting standards, unless the parent has arranged for the child's care in the home of a relative. In addition, a parent who is addicted to alcohol or who is a drug addict, as defined in the Illinois Alcoholism and Other Drug Dependency Act [20 ILCS 305] and who has consistently failed to cooperate in a rehabilitation program for a period of at least twelve months is deemed to have failed to have met the minimum parenting standards unless the parent has arranged for the child's safety and well-being have been ensured despite the parent's addiction.

"Parents" means the child's legal parents whose rights have not been terminated and adoptive parents. Putative Biological fathers are considered legal parents when paternity has been acknowledged in writing or adjudicated in court.

"Permanency goal" means the continuous living arrangement which the Department deems desirable for and available to the child. A permanent legal status is usually a component of the permanency goal. The means for attaining a permanency goal as well as the goal itself can change as the child's developmental and emotional needs change or as the child's and family's circumstances change.

"Permanency option" means a placement which provides a continuous, stable living arrangement for the child, but does not necessarily provide a permanent living arrangement or a permanent legal status for the child. Permanency options may serve as steps to the ultimate achievement of a permanency goal.

DEPARTMENT OF CHILDREN AND FAMILY SERVICES

NOTICE OF PROPOSED AMENDMENTS

"Permanent family placement" means placement in a foster family home or a relative home which is intended to last until the child reaches age 21 or until the child is capable of self-sufficiency. The Department may retain guardianship of the child, or the foster parent or relative may take guardianship of the child.

"Permanent legal status" means a legally binding relationship between a child and a family as established by birth or by a court of law.

"Rehabilitative services plan." A written plan developed in accordance with 59 Ill. Adm. Code 132.155, Medicaid Community Mental Health Services, which includes identification of the problems to be addressed, the rehabilitative services to be provided and the outcomes to be achieved for eligible clients served by the Department pursuant to the Abused and Neglected Child Reporting Act, the Children and Family Services Act or the Juvenile Court Act of 1987.

"Relative caregiver" means a person 21 years of age or older, other than the parent, who has physical custody of the child and to whom the child has any of the following currently existing relationships by blood or adoption: grandparent, sibling, great grandparent, uncle, aunt, nephew, niece, first cousin, great uncle, great aunt, or who is the spouse of such a relative or who is the child's step-father, step-mother, step-brother or step-sister.

"Service plan" means a written plan on a form prescribed by the Department which guides all participants in the plan toward the permanency goals for the children.

"Substitute care" means the care of children who require placement away from their families. Substitute care includes foster family care, care provided in a an approved relative home placement as defined in 89 Ill. Adm. Code 301, Placement and Visitation Services, Section 301.80, care provided in a group home, and care provided in a child care or other institution.

"Termination of parental rights" means a court order which relieves the legal parents of parental responsibility for the child and revokes all legal rights with respect to the child. The termination order also frees the child from all obligations of maintenance and obedience with respect to the legal parents.

(Source: Amended at 19 Ill. Reg. _____, effective _____)

Section 305.30 Introduction to Client Service Planning

a) Principles of Client Service Planning

DEPARTMENT OF CHILDREN AND FAMILY SERVICES

NOTICE OF PROPOSED AMENDMENTS

1) Client service planning is an on-going process that must begin with an assessment of client need in relation to Department service mandates and must include periodic reassessment of such needs in light of the services provided, the permanency goal or an alternative permanency option, and the progress toward achieving the goal or option.

2) Case planning must ensure accountability on the part of clients, the Department and other service providers through written documentation of expectations and obligations. This documentation should include:

   A) a desired permanent living arrangement for each child served that is recorded in the service plan as a permanency goal or permanency option;

   B) identification of problems that must be resolved to achieve this status, including, when applicable, achievement of minimum parenting standards;

   C) identification of measurable changes or outcomes that will signify problem resolution;

   D) identification of what the Department and other service providers will provide toward achieving the desired permanent living arrangement;

   E) identification of applicable timeframes; and

   F) identification of any consequences to the client if the timeframes are not met.

3) Although the Department maintains ultimate responsibility for the service plan, case planning must be an inclusive process in which all of the participants in a case (parents, children, service providers) are given the opportunity to have input.

4) Case planning activities, including development of the service plan and case review, reflect and must be consistent with federal and State requirements, e.g., 42 U~S~C~ 675 (1991) U.S.C.A. 670 et seq. and the Children and Family Services Act (20 ILCS 505).

b) The Need For a Permanent, Secure and Nurturing Home

   1) The Department recognizes that children need permanent, secure, and nurturing homes for healthy psychological development in order to mature to stable adulthood. Therefore, Whenever it is in the best interests of the child, the Department strives to preserve family life and to stabilize children's homes whenever possible, and to assist in the solution of problems which are likely to result in the abuse, neglect, or exploitation of children.

   2) When children and families parents must be separated to reduce or prevent harm to the children, the Department strives to reunite families as quickly as is consistent with the children's best interests, safety and well-being. Sometimes, When children and families parents cannot be reunited because the parents are unable or unwilling to care for the children and therefore cannot achieve the minimum parenting standards, When this

DEPARTMENT OF CHILDREN AND FAMILY SERVICES

NOTICE OF PROPOSED AMENDMENTS

occurs, the Department strives to find other permanent homes for children.

c) The Child's Sense of Time and The Importance of Aggressive Planning

   1) The Department recognizes that children have a different sense of time than adults. What seems like a short family disruption or a brief separation to adults may be a very painful and intolerably long period for children. In general, younger children are less able to tolerate periods of separation than older children. For this reason, the Department shall act promptly using the best information available when dealing with children and their families.

   2) The Department believes that aggressive planning with an emphasis on decision making, followed by the actions needed to carry out those decisions, will secure permanent homes for children. Therefore, the Department requires service planning directed toward a permanency goal beginning from the earliest contacts with children and families. Through service planning the Department strives to assure that children are in permanent homes as quickly as is consistent with their safety and well-being while recognizing the urgency caused by the child's sense of time.

d) The Use of Outside Consultation

   1) The Department recognizes the gravity of the decisions that must be made and, recognizing the urgency caused by the child's sense of time, the importance of acting deliberatively, yet promptly, on each case. Therefore, the Department strives to consult professionals and agencies outside the Department and to seek a balance of opinions from the following public and private agencies, when appropriate:

      A) health, education and social service agencies;

      B) law enforcement agencies; and

      C) other agencies, organizations, or programs which provide or are concerned with human services.

   2) This consultation allows Department staff to attain a broad perspective on the alternatives available to children and families and on the potential impact of these alternatives on the lives of the children and families served.

e) The Critical Decisions

   1) Although all Department decisions affecting children and families are important, the Department identifies the following decisions as the most critical ones affecting children and families:

      A) deciding whether to remove children from the home of their parents or relative caregiver or whether services can prevent placement away from their parents or relative caregiver;

      B) deciding whether to return children to the home of their parents or relative caregiver from a placement away from their parents or relative caregiver;

DEPARTMENT OF CHILDREN AND FAMILY SERVICES

NOTICE OF PROPOSED AMENDMENTS

C) deciding whether to decrease the frequency or the duration of parent-child parent and/or sibling visits with the child and whether the visits should be supervised;

D) deciding whether to change children's placements;

E) deciding whether parental rights should be terminated and an alternate permanent home sought; and

F) deciding if children are prepared for partial or total independence; or

G) deciding whether children shall be placed apart from siblings who are also placed in substitute care.

2) When making a critical decision, any opinions or recommendations from professionals or agencies outside the Department shall be carefully weighed. In addition, the Department requires the participation of children and families in service planning and decision-making to the greatest extent possible.

(Source: Amended At 19 Ill. Reg. _____, effective _____)

Section 305.40 Types of Permanency Goals and Alternative Permanency Options

a) The Department shall consider the recommendations of the purchase of service providers, if any, and shall select permanency goals or alternative permanency options for the children and families it serves in order to guide service planning and achieve permanent homes for children. The Department shall ensure that services provided to children and families move them toward the permanency goals or alternative permanency options. The permanency goals are:

1) Remaining at Home;

2) Returning Home;

3) Adoption;

4) Permanent Family Placement

A) with an unrelated foster family;

B) with relatives;

5) Independence;

6) Long Term Care in a Residential Facility; and

7) Substitute Care Pending Court Decision Regarding Termination of Parental Rights.

b) When selecting a permanency goal, the Department shall use the criteria in this Section.

1) Remaining at Home

Remaining home with their parents or private guardian is the preferred goal when the child's safety and well-being are not clearly endangered if allowed to remain at home. This permanency goal is consistent with the Department's service goal of family preservation. It emphasizes the importance of keeping families together and also stresses that the family is primarily responsible for caring for the child. In addition, this

DEPARTMENT OF CHILDREN AND FAMILY SERVICES

NOTICE OF PROPOSED AMENDMENTS

permanency goal is usually the least disruptive to family life.

2) Returning Home

A) Returning children to their parent's parent(s)' or private guardian(s)' homes is the preferred goal for children who have been placed in substitute care away from their parents. This permanency goal is consistent with the Department's service goal of family reunification. It reinforces the family's responsibility to care for their children and maintain the family relationship. Furthermore, this permanency goal is usually the least traumatic alternative for both the families and children. Returning home should be established as the permanency goal:

i) when the parents appear to have the capability to attain the minimum parenting standards with the aid of family reunification services; and

ii) when the parents are cooperative with the Department and its purchase of service providers, if any, and want to resolve the problems.

B) Returning home should be continued as the permanency goal as long as the parents are substantially complying with the requirements of the service plan and are progressing satisfactorily toward the permanency goal.

3) Adoption

Adoption is the preferred permanency goal when parental rights have been terminated on a child. This permanency goal is to be established only:

A) after both parents have signed adoptive surrenders; or

B) after a court has terminated the parental rights of both parents and has designated the Department as guardian with the power to consent to the child's adoption; or

C) after one parent has signed an adoptive surrender and parental rights have been terminated on the remaining parent through court action; or

D) when one parent has signed an adoptive surrender and the identity and/or the whereabouts of the remaining parent is unknown, and the Department expects the parental rights of the remaining parent to be terminated through court action; and

E) the child, if 14 years of age or over, consents to the adoption.

4) Permanent Family Placement

A) Although a permanent family placement is more desirable than a series of short-term placements, it is not a preferred permanency goal for the child. Without the legal safeguards offered by a permanent legal guardian, a permanent family placement may fail to provide the child with a sense of belonging and permanency. A permanent family placement is the permanency goal only:

DEPARTMENT OF CHILDREN AND FAMILY SERVICES

NOTICE OF PROPOSED AMENDMENTS

    i)   when to return the child home is not consistent with ensuring the child's safety and well-being; and

    ii) when the child, if 14 years of age or older, clearly does not want to be adopted or the child, if under age 14, has been provided counseling to help him accept another family, but continues to be unable to accept another family; or

    iii) the child is otherwise deemed unadoptable.

B) The Department shall strive to assure continuity of care, a sense of permanency, and emotional support for the child by establishing the child's permanent caretaker caregiver as the legal guardian of the child. However, taking legal guardianship is not required for the placement to be considered permanent.

C) When weighing the advantages of a permanent family placement with relatives against the advantages of a permanent family placement with an unrelated foster family, the quality of the relationship between the relatives, the child, the child's parents, and the child's foster parents, if any, shall be a factor. In addition, other factors shall be the likelihood of establishing a permanent legal relationship between the child and the relative as compared to the likelihood of establishing a permanent legal relationship between the child and the unrelated foster parents.

5) Independence

Independence may be a goal for adolescents 16 years of age or older who have demonstrated the ability to care for themselves, who do not wish to be adopted, who are becoming economically self-sufficient, or who are establishing a family of their own. When the child becomes 18, the child must cooperate according to his service plan. If the child 18 years of age or over does not cooperate, the Department may seek to terminate services and seek to end its legal relationship with the child.

6) Long-Term Care in a Residential Facility

A) A very small percentage of children served by the Department are determined severely physically, mentally, or emotionally handicapped by a physician, psychiatrist, or other professional qualified by education or experience to make this judgment. These children require long term care, usually in an intermediate or skilled nursing facility, or in a child care institution. They are expected to continue to need this care in the foreseeable future. For these children, long-term care in a residential facility is the permanency goal.

B) These severely physically, mentally, or emotionally handicapped children who require long-term care should not be confused with children who are in group homes or institutions in order to receive intensive, short-term

DEPARTMENT OF CHILDREN AND FAMILY SERVICES

NOTICE OF PROPOSED AMENDMENTS

treatment directed toward correcting problems which significantly interfere with life outside the institution. Long-term care in a residential facility is not an appropriate permanency goal for children who are receiving short-term, intensive services in a group home or institution.

7) Substitute Care Pending Court Decision Regarding Termination of Parental Rights

A) Substitute care pending court decision regarding termination of parental rights is the preferred permanency goal when a decision has been made to pursue termination of parental rights. This goal is to be established only when:

    i)   Efforts to reunite the child and biological or legal family have been unsuccessful as documented in the case record; or

    ii) The evaluations of at least two professionals must find the parent(s) have a chronic incapacity which will not respond to rehabilitation and which makes it clearly improbable that the parents will attain minimum parenting standards. These professionals must be qualified by their education or experience in the fields of psychiatry, psychology, social work, developmental disabilities, chemical dependency, or other specialized areas of knowledge relevant to the pending issue. These evaluations shall weigh whether the parents can attain the minimum parenting standards (established by the Department) after considering the public, private and extended family resources which can assist the parents with caring for the children; and

    iii) The child, if 14 years of age or older, is in agreement with the plan to pursue termination of parental rights; and

    iv) Department legal staff determine if there is sufficient evidence to pursue termination of parental rights in accordance with Section 1 (D) of the Adoption Act [750 ILCS 50/1].

B) This goal shall continue as the permanency goal until such time as the court has granted or denied termination of parental rights, or until such time as a degree of progress is noted in the parent(s) situation which would require an evaluation of, and possible change in the established permanency goal pursuant to Sections 305.50 and 305.60.

C) If the court grants termination of parental rights, this goal shall be changed to adoption. If the termination of parental rights petition is denied, another permanency goal shall be selected.

c) Permanency Options

DEPARTMENT OF CHILDREN AND FAMILY SERVICES

NOTICE OF PROPOSED AMENDMENTS

In addition to the permanency goals identified in subsection (b) above, the Department also recognizes delegated relative authority as an alternative permanency option which does not provide the legal status of a permanency goal, but does allow the child to be placed in a stable, continuous living arrangement. When delegated relative authority is selected as a permanency option, the relative caregiver shall continue to receive payments for the care of the child which shall equal the ~~foster care rate~~ payment in effect when authority for the child's care was delegated to the relative. Administrative case reviews shall continue to be conducted at least every six months, permanency review hearings shall continue to be held as required by law, and parent/child visits shall continue, as appropriate. The Department retains guardianship of the child and the authority to make all major medical consents and other major decisions which affect the related children's lives and health.

d) Delegated relative authority may be selected as a permanency option for the following types of cases:

1) the children have been living with a ~~related~~ relative caregiver who has been ~~approved under 89 Ill. Adm. Code 335, Relative Home Placement, or~~ licensed under 89 Ill. Adm. Code 402, Licensing Standards for Foster Family Homes, or who has met the placement preconditions prescribed in 89 Ill. Adm. Code 301, Placement and Visitation Services, Section 301.80 Relative Home Placement, and the children have remained with the ~~related~~ relative caregiver for a minimum of one year immediately prior to establishing delegated relative authority;

2) the children ~~have been~~ are in the guardianship of the Department ~~for at least six months~~ immediately prior to establishing delegated relative authority;

3) the children do not have extraordinary medical, mental health, or educational needs which require ~~targeted case management~~ additional casework services;

4) the relative caregivers have demonstrated the willingness and ability to protect the children from persons who may harm them;

5) the relative caregivers have demonstrated the willingness and ability to appropriately control and supervise visits and contacts between the children and their biological or legal parents, in accordance with the service plan developed by the Department;

6) the relative caregivers have a safe and stable home environment which poses no danger to the related children;

7) the Department has documented that reunification with the biological or legal parents within a one year period is highly unlikely for reasons such as:
   A) long-term parental incarceration; or
   B) chronic and serious mental illness; or
   C) serious physical or mental incapacity; or
   D) addiction to drugs or alcohol which is not responding

DEPARTMENT OF CHILDREN AND FAMILY SERVICES

NOTICE OF PROPOSED AMENDMENTS

   successfully to treatment; or
   E) other significant barriers to returning the children home within one year;

8) adoption [unless adoption by the relative caregiver is pending] or private guardianship as a permanency goal has been determined to be not in the best interests of the related children; or

9) other circumstances as the Department may determine to be appropriate.

(Source: Amended at 19 Ill. Reg. _____, effective _____)

DEPARTMENT OF CHILDREN AND FAMILY SERVICES

NOTICE OF PROPOSED AMENDMENTS

1) <u>Heading of the Part</u>: Foster Care Placement Goal

2) <u>Code Citation</u>: 89 Ill. Adm. Code 301

3) <u>Section Numbers</u>:   Proposed Action:

    301.1   Renumbered to 301.310, Amend
    301.2   Repealed
    301.3   Renumbered to 301.320, Amend
    301.4   Renumbered to 301.330, Amend
    301.10   New Section
    301.20   New Section
    301.30   New Section
    301.40   New Section
    301.50   New Section
    301.60   New Section
    301.80   New Section
    301.90   New Section
    301.100   New Section
    301.110   New Section
    301.120   New Section
    301.130   New Section
    301.140   New Section

4) <u>Statutory Authority</u>: Section 4 of the Children and Family Services Act (20
    ILCS 505/4].

5) <u>A Complete Description of the Subjects and Issues Involved</u>: This Part is
    being amended to add Department rules on placement services formerly
    contained in 89 Ill. Adm. Code 302, Services Delivered by the Department,
    Section 302.390, Placement Services. At a later date the Department will
    add rules on sibling visitation to create Subpart B. The result of these
    changes will be that Department policy governing placement and visitation
    services will be brought together into one set of rules. The current
    content of Part 301, which is Foster Care Placement Goal, has been
    renumbered to Subpart C.

    In addition to these reformatting changes, the Department is amending its
    policy regarding the selection of a placement for a child. Although
    relatives will be considered when seeking a placement for a child, the
    primary factors will be the child's best interests and special needs. When
    the Department does place a child in the home of a relative, the home must
    either be licensed as a foster family home or meet certain pre-placement
    conditions which are specified in 89 Ill. Adm. Code 301.80, Relative Home
    Placement. The pre-placement conditions replace and improve upon the
    pre-placement conditions found in 89 Ill. Adm. Code 335, Relative Home
    Placement, which is being repealed.

DEPARTMENT OF CHILDREN AND FAMILY SERVICES

NOTICE OF PROPOSED AMENDMENTS

6) <u>Will this proposed amendment replace an emergency rule currently in
    effect?</u> No

7) <u>Does this rulemaking contain an automatic repeal date?</u> No

8) <u>Does this proposed amendment contain incorporations by reference?</u> No

9) <u>Are there any other amendments pending on this Part?</u> No

10) <u>Statement of Statewide Policy Objectives</u>: These amendments do not create
    or expand a State mandate as defined in Section 3(b) of the State Mandates
    Act (30 ILCS 805/3(b)].

11) <u>Time, Place, and Manner in which interested persons may comment on this
    proposed rulemaking</u>:

    Comments on this proposed rulemaking may be submitted in writing for a
    period of 45 days following publication on this notice. Comments should
    be submitted to:

        Jacqueline Nottingham, Chief
        Office of Rules and Procedures
        Department of Children and Family Services
        406 East Monroe - Station #222
        Springfield, Illinois 62701-1498
        Telephone:(217) 524-1983
        TTY:(217) 524-3715

    The Department will consider fully all written comments on this proposed
    rulemaking submitted during the 45-day comment period. Comments submitted
    by small businesses should be identified as such. Public hearings have
    been scheduled on these proposed amendments in the following areas:

        April 11, 1995
        7:00 p.m.
        Quality Inn at Halsted
        One South Halsted
        Chicago, Illinois
        (312) 829-5000

        April 13, 1995
        7:00 p.m.
        State House
        Room 212
        Springfield, Illinois
        (217) 782-2099

    Persons are asked to limit their testimony to a maximum of 15 minutes per

DEPARTMENT OF CHILDREN AND FAMILY SERVICES

NOTICE OF PROPOSED AMENDMENTS

person. We will gladly accept written testimony at the public hearings. Persons who need translation or interpretation services to enable their commentary should request assistance by contacting the Office of Rules and Procedures.

12) Initial Regulatory Flexibility Analysis: The Department has determined that the proposed amendment does not have an effect on small businesses.

13) State reason(s) for this rulemaking if it was not included in either of the two most recent regulatory agendas. The transfer of the rules on placement and visitation to this Part was announced in the Regulatory Agenda published in the January 13,1995 Illinois Register. The amendments regarding relative home placements were not foreseen at the time the Department filed its regulatory agendas. A major management initiative affecting home of relative care has prompted the Department to file these amendments at the present time in order to implement them at the start of the next fiscal year.

The full text of the proposed amendment begins on the next page.

DEPARTMENT OF CHILDREN AND FAMILY SERVICES

NOTICE OF PROPOSED AMENDMENTS

TITLE 89: SOCIAL SERVICES
CHAPTER III: DEPARTMENT OF CHILDREN AND FAMILY SERVICES
SUBCHAPTER a: SERVICE DELIVERY

PART 301
FOSTER-CARE-PLACEMENT-GOAL PLACEMENT AND VISITATION SERVICES

Section
301.1   Purpose (Renumbered)
301.2   Definition (Repealed)
301.3   Foster Care Placement Goal (Renumbered)
301.4   Plans to Achieve This Goal (Renumbered)

SUBPART A: PLACEMENT SERVICES

SUBPART C: FOSTER CARE PLACEMENT GOAL

AUTHORITY: Implementing and authorized by the Children and Family Services Act (20 ILCS 505); Section 3-6-2(g) of the Unified Code of Corrections (730 ILCS 5/3-6-2(g)); Section 1-103 of the Illinois Alcoholism and Dangerous Drug Dependency Act (20 ILCS 305/1-103); Public Law 96-272, the Adoption Assistance and Child Welfare Act of 1980 (42 U.S.C.A. 670 et seq.); 45 CFR 1356.40 and 1356.41; the Juvenile Court Act of 1987 (705 ILCS 405); and the Adoption Act (750 ILCS 50).

SOURCE: Adopted and codified at 7 Ill. Reg. 861, effective January 12, 1983; amended at 9 Ill. Reg. 9904, effective July 1, 1985; amended at 19 Ill. Reg. _____, effective _____.

DEPARTMENT OF CHILDREN AND FAMILY SERVICES

NOTICE OF PROPOSED AMENDMENTS

Section 301.1   Purpose (Renumbered)

(Source: Section 301.1 renumbered to Section 301.310 at 19 Ill. Reg.
_____, effective _____)

Section 301.2   Definition (Repealed)

~~"Federally-funded-foster-care"-means-foster-care-maintenance-payments-made
in--accordance--with--Title--IV-E-of-the-Social-Security-Act-for-which
Federal-matching-grants-are-received.~~

(Source: Repealed   at   19   Ill.   Reg.   _____,   effective
_____)

Section 301.3   Foster Care Placement Goal (Renumbered)

(Source: Section   301.3   renumbered   to   Section   301.320 at 19 Ill. Reg.
_____, effective _____)

Section 301.4   Plans to Achieve This Goal (Renumbered)

(Source: Section 301.4 renumbered to Section 301.330 at 19 Ill. Reg.
_____, effective _____)

SUBPART A: PLACEMENT SERVICES

Section 301.10   Purpose

The purpose of this Subpart is to describe the substitute care services
provided by the Department or its contractual agencies when it is in the best
interests of children to be placed apart from their parents or guardians.
Included in this Subpart is an explanation of:
    a)   the conditions under which children are placed in substitute care;
    b)   the types of substitute care settings in which children are placed;
    c)   the criteria used for selecting a placement; and
    d)   other legal and service requirements that must be fulfilled when
         placing children.

(Source: Added   at   19   Ill.   Reg.   _____,   effective
_____)

Section 301.20   Definitions

"Administrative case review" or "ACR" means case reviews required by
42 U.S.C.A. 675(1) and 20 ILCS 505/6a.

"Biological father" means a man who has acknowledged his paternity via
a notarized statement or whose paternity is adjudicated in court. When

DEPARTMENT OF CHILDREN AND FAMILY SERVICES

NOTICE OF PROPOSED AMENDMENTS

paternity has been acknowledged or adjudicated, the relatives of the
biological father as well as those of the mother may be considered for
the placement of related children.

"Children for whom the Department is legally responsible" means
children for whom the Department has temporary protective custody,
custody or guardianship via court order, or children whose parent(s)
signed an adoptive surrender or voluntary placement agreement with the
Department.

"Department" as used in this Part, means the Department of Children
and Family Services.

"Family" means one or more adults and children, related by blood,
marriage, or adoption and residing in the same household.

"Federally-funded foster care" means foster care maintenance payments
made in accordance with Title IV-E of the Social Security Act for
which federal matching grants are received.

"LEADS" means Law Enforcement Agency Data System.

"Parents" means the child's legal parents whose parental rights have
not been terminated and adoptive parents. Biological fathers are
considered legal parents when paternity has been acknowledged via a
notarized written statement or adjudicated in court.

"Permanency goal" means the continuous living arrangement which the
Department deems desirable for and available to the child. A
permanent legal status is usually a component of the permanency goal.
The means for attaining a permanency goal as well as the goal itself
can change as the child's developmental and emotional needs change or
as the child's and family's circumstances change.

"Permanent family placement" means placement in a foster family home
or a relative home which is intended to last until the child reaches
age 21 or until the child is capable of self-sufficiency. The
Department may retain guardianship of the child, or the foster parent
or relative may assume guardianship of the child.

"Permanent legal status" means a legally binding relationship between
a child and a family as established by birth or a matter of law.

"Relative" means a person 21 years of age or over, other than the
parent, to whom the child has any of the following currently existing
relationships by blood or adoption: grandparent, sibling, great
grandparent, uncle, aunt, nephew, niece, first cousin, great uncle,
great aunt, or who is the spouse of such a relative or who is the

DEPARTMENT OF CHILDREN AND FAMILY SERVICES

NOTICE OF PROPOSED AMENDMENTS

child's step-father, step-mother, step-brother or step-sister.

"Substitute care" means the care of children who require placement away from their families. Substitute care includes foster family care, care of a child for whom the Department is legally responsible provided in a relative family home, care provided in a group home, and care provided in a child care or other institution.

"Voluntary placement agreement" means a time-limited written request and consent from a parent, guardian or legal custodian of a child for placement of the child out of the home. When signed by designated Department staff, the Department agrees to provide child welfare services which include placement.

(Source: Added at 19 Ill. Reg. _____, effective _____)

Section 301.30 Introduction

Placement or substitute care services means the care of children for whom the Department is legally responsible who require a living arrangement away from their families due to abuse, neglect, dependency, voluntary surrender of parental rights, or voluntary placement agreement. Placement services include foster family or relative home care, care provided in a group home or child care institution or other institution. Placement is intended to be a temporary situation for the children during the time that the parents' ability to care for the child is being evaluated or the parents are receiving services to alleviate the problems in the home so the family can be reunited. However, there may be times when it is in the best interests of the child to seek a permanent placement away from the child's family. In these instances a permanency goal other than family reunification is sought. The complete range of permanency goals is described in 89 Ill. Adm. Code 305, Client Service Planning.

(Source: Added at 19 Ill. Reg. _____, effective _____)

Section 301.40 Legal Authority to Place

The Department shall not place children until it has the appropriate legal authority to do so. Such legal authority includes:

a) temporary protective custody in accordance with the Abused and Neglected Child Reporting Act [325 ILCS 5];
b) adoptive surrender in accordance with the Adoption Act [750 ILCS 50];
c) custody or guardianship in accordance with the Juvenile Court Act of 1987 [705 ILCS 405]; or
d) temporary custody with written consent of the parent(s) or, if the child is not in the custody of either parent, written consent of the

DEPARTMENT OF CHILDREN AND FAMILY SERVICES

NOTICE OF PROPOSED AMENDMENTS

guardian or custodian of the child, in accordance with the Children and Family Services Act [20 ILCS 505]. A written consent from a parent, guardian or legal custodian requesting temporary placement services for their child(ren) is known as a voluntary placement agreement. A voluntary placement agreement may be entered into for a maximum of 60 days when it is in the best interests of the children. A voluntary placement agreement requires prior written approval of the administrator in charge of the Department region or his designee. A voluntary placement agreement may be renewed for an additional 60 days only with the prior non-delegable written approval of the administrator in charge of the Department region.

(Source: Added at 19 Ill. Reg. _____, effective _____)

Section 301.50 Emergency Placement

Emergency placement services shall be provided immediately when the provision of other services are not in the child's best interests or will not ensure the safety of the child and the Department has reason to believe:

a) that leaving the child in the home of his or her caregiver would present an imminent danger to the child's life or health; or
b) that a child has been left unsupervised for an unreasonable period of time without regard for the mental or physical health, safety, or welfare of the child and the child's parents cannot be readily located; or
c) that services directed toward keeping the family together would not be in the child's best interests or would not sufficiently protect the child from harm, thus endangering the child's safety and well-being; or
d) that the child appears to be severely ill or injured and the parent or caregiver is unable to care for the child in this situation; or
e) the child is abandoned; or
f) the child is a runaway in accordance with 89 Ill. Adm. Code 329, Return of Runaway Children.

(Source: Added at 19 Ill. Reg. _____, effective _____)

Section 301.60 Placement Selection Criteria

All placement decisions will be made consistent with the best interests and special needs of the child. When a child is removed from the care of a custodial parent, the placing worker shall explore whether the non-custodial parent would be a suitable caregiver for the child. If placement with the non-custodial parent is not consistent with the best interests and special needs of the child or if the non-custodial parent is not a suitable caregiver for the child, placement in substitute care shall be considered. Substitute

DEPARTMENT OF CHILDREN AND FAMILY SERVICES

NOTICE OF PROPOSED AMENDMENTS

care placement decisions consistent with the best interests and special needs
of the child shall be made in consideration of the following:

a) the least restrictive setting appropriate for the child which most
   closely approximates a family;

b) placement within reasonable proximity to the child's home when the
   permanency goal is return home, and within the child's school
   district, whenever possible, taking into account any special needs of
   the child and family, the importance of maintaining continuity of the
   children's educational and social relationships, and the availability
   of the service resources needed for the child and family;

c) a home that, if possible, most closely approximates the religious,
   racial, ethnic and cultural background of the child; and

d) placement, if the child is of American Indian heritage, according to
   criteria described in 89 Ill. Adm. Code 307, Indian Child Welfare
   Services.

(Source: Added   at   19   Ill.   Reg.   _____,   effective
_____)

Section 301.80 Relative Home Placement

a) A child for whom the Department is legally responsible may be placed
   in the home of a relative when the Department has reason to believe
   that the relative can safely and adequately care for the child in the
   absence of formal licensing, including training. In determining
   whether relative home placement is in the best interests of the child,
   the placing worker shall consider the child's prior relationship with
   the relative, the comfort level of the child with the relative, and
   the extent to which the relative complies with the placement selection
   criteria of Section 301.60.

b) No child under age 18 for whom the Department is legally responsible
   shall be placed with a relative unless the pre-conditions specified in
   this Section have been met prior to placement of the child with the
   relative. Staff of the placing agency shall meet with the relative
   and ascertain that the relative meets the following preconditions and
   signs an agreement to that effect. The relative:

   1) will accept for care no more than the number of children
      consistent with the number and ages of children permitted in a
      licensed foster family home (89 Ill. Adm. Code 402, Licensing
      Standards for Foster Family Homes);

   2) is willing and capable of protecting the child(ren) from harm by
      the parent(s) or any other person whose actions or inactions
      allegedly threatened the child(ren)'s safety or well-being as
      determined by a child abuse or neglect investigation pursuant to
      the Abused and Neglected Child Reporting Act [325 ILCS 5];

   3) agrees not to transfer physical custody of the child(ren) to
      anyone, including parent(s) or other relative(s), unless
      previously authorized in writing by the Department;

DEPARTMENT OF CHILDREN AND FAMILY SERVICES

NOTICE OF PROPOSED AMENDMENTS

   4) agrees not to allow the indicated or alleged perpetrators of
      abuse or neglect to reside in the relative's home unless
      previously authorized in writing by the Department;

   5) agrees to notify the Department of any changes in the household
      composition;

   6) agrees to notify the Department of any change of address;

   7) agrees to seek the prior written consent of the Department for
      non-emergency medical, psychological, or psychiatric testing or
      treatment;

   8) agrees to take the child(ren) out of state only if previously
      authorized in writing by the Department;

   9) agrees to abide by any conditions or limitations on the
      parent-child visitation plan which have been imposed by the court
      or are contained in the client service plan;

   10) is willing to cooperate with the agency, the child(ren)'s
       parent(s) and other resource persons to help develop and achieve
       the permanency goal recorded in the child(ren)'s service plan;
       and

   11) agrees to adequately supervise the children so they are not left
       in situations or circumstances which are likely to require
       judgment or actions greater than the child's level of maturity,
       physical condition, and/or mental abilities would reasonably
       dictate.

c) Prior to placement with a relative, staff of the placing agency shall
   visit the home of the proposed caregiver and shall determine whether
   the following placement pre-conditions are met:

   1) background checks of the Child Abuse Neglect Tracking System
      (CANTS) as required by 89 Ill. Adm. Code 385 (Background Checks),
      have been completed on all adult members of the household and
      children age 13 and over, communicated to the supervising agency
      prior to placement, and appropriate decisions made as required by
      89 Ill. Adm. Code 385, Background Checks.

   2) a check of the Law Enforcement Agency Data System (LEADS) on all
      adult members of the household is completed prior to placement of
      the related child(ren). If the results of the LEADS check
      identify prior criminal convictions or any pending criminal
      charges listed in Appendix A of 89 Ill. Adm. Code 380, Background
      Check of Foster Family Home Applicants, for any adult member of
      the household, child(ren) shall not be placed in the relative's
      home;

   3) the home is free from observable hazards;

   4) prescription and non-prescription drugs, dangerous household
      supplies, dangerous tools, weapons, guns and ammunition are
      stored in places inaccessible to children;

   5) basic utilities -- water, heat, electricity -- are in operation;

   6) sleeping arrangements are suitable to the age and sex of the
      child(ren);

   7) meals can be provided daily to the related child(ren) in

DEPARTMENT OF CHILDREN AND FAMILY SERVICES

NOTICE OF PROPOSED AMENDMENTS

sufficient quantities to meet the child(ren)'s nutritional needs;
8) supervision of the related child(ren) can be assured at all times
    including times when the relative is employed or otherwise
    engaged in activity outside of the home;
9) the relative can provide basic necessities for themselves and
    their own child(ren);
10) the relative can access health care and provide necessary in-home
    support for any health care needs of the related child(ren);
11) no member of the household appears to have a communicable disease
    which could pose a threat to the health of the related child(ren)
    or an emotional or physical impairment which could affect the
    ability of the caregiver to provide routine daily care to the
    related child(ren) or to evacuate them safely in an emergency;
12) there is no evidence of current drug or alcohol abuse by any
    household member as determined by the placing agency's
    observations and statements provided by the relative;
13) the relative has the ability to contact the agency, if necessary,
    and the ability to be contacted;
14) the relative has immediate access to a telephone when the related
    child has medical or other special needs; and
15) the relative shall cooperate with the supervising agency's
    educational and service plan for the child.
d) Prior to or concurrent with placement in a relative's home, staff of
    the placing agency shall document, on the form prescribed by the
    Department, that the pre-conditions prescribed by this Section have
    been met.
e) The Department shall reassess the appropriateness of the relative home
    placement prior to each administrative case review and at any point
    the Department has reason to believe the caregiver can no
    longer safely or adequately care for the child(ren) as measured by the
    conditions described in subsection (c).
f) The Department will advise relatives that the Department will assist
    them in applying to the Illinois Department of Public Aid for Aid to
    Families with Dependent Children (AFDC) for related children placed
    with them and that the Department will provide a supplement to bring
    the total income for the related children placed with them to the
    child only standard of need established for that number of children by
    the Illinois Department of Public Aid.
g) Relatives who care for children for whom the Department is legally
    responsible may, but need not, apply for licensure as a foster family
    home in accordance with the requirements of 89 Ill. Adm. Code 402,
    Licensing Standards for Foster Family Homes. When a relative is
    licensed under Part 402, the relative will receive the established
    foster care payment rate appropriate for the number and ages of foster
    children placed in care.

(Source: Added   at   19   Ill.   Reg.   _____,   effective
    _____)

DEPARTMENT OF CHILDREN AND FAMILY SERVICES

NOTICE OF PROPOSED AMENDMENTS

Section 301.90 Foster Family Home Care

a) Foster family home care is provided in licensed foster family homes
    for children who cannot remain home and who can benefit from a family
    structure of care. The Department shall have legal responsibility for
    the child before the child is placed in a foster family home and the
    home shall have received a license or permit to receive children for
    foster care.
b) Although foster family home care is generally provided to children
    whose parents are unable or unwilling to protect or care for them, it
    is also available for hearing impaired children who require special
    education not available in their home communities. The Department is
    not legally responsible for the children receiving this unique
    placement service. Care is provided in cooperation with the Illinois
    State Board of Education.

(Source: Added   at   19   Ill.   Reg.   _____,   effective
    _____)

Section 301.100 Residential Care

Residential care is provided in licensed group homes and residential care
facilities (child care institutions). Group home care is provided for youth
unable to adjust to family living who need a less structured living situation
than is provided in residential care facilities. Placement in a residential
care facility shall be made only when no other less restrictive setting is
appropriate for children requiring intensive services to change behaviors which
significantly interfere with their ability to cope with daily life or which
preclude placement in a family setting.

(Source: Added   at   19   Ill.   Reg.   _____,   effective
    _____)

Section 301.110 Care in a Medical/Psychiatric Facility

Care in a medical or psychiatric facility is provided for:
    a) children who require long term care on an ongoing basis in an
        intermediate or skilled nursing care facility because of a severe
        physical or mental disability;
    b) children who require acute or long term care on an ongoing basis
        because of a severe emotional handicap.

(Source: Added   at   19   Ill.   Reg.   _____,   effective
    _____)

Section 301.120 Sharing Appropriate Information with the Caregiver

    a) At the time the Department places a child in foster care or other

DEPARTMENT OF CHILDREN AND FAMILY SERVICES

NOTICE OF PROPOSED AMENDMENTS

substitute care setting, the Department shall provide available information about the child necessary for the proper care of the child to the foster parent or other caregiver.

b) This information includes:

1) The medical history of the child including known medical problems or communicable diseases, information concerning the immunization status of the child, and insurance and medical card information;

2) The school history of the child, including any special educational needs;

3) A copy of the child's portion of the client service plan, case history of the child, including how the child came into care, the child's legal status, the permanency goal for the child and a history of the child's previous placements, criminal history, if any, and reasons for placement changes, excluding information that identifies or reveals the location of any previous foster or relative home caregiver;

4) Other background information of the child, including behavior problems, any prior criminal history, habits, likes, dislikes, etc.

5) Information subject to the Mental Health and Developmental Disabilities Confidentiality Act shall be shared only in accordance with 89 Ill. Adm. Code 431, Confidentiality of Personal Information of Persons Served by the Department, Section 431.100.

6) Information regarding Acquired Immunodeficiency Syndrome (AIDS), AIDS Related Complex (ARC) or Human Immunodeficiency Virus (HIV) test results, shall be shared only in accordance with 89 Ill. Adm. Code 431, Confidentiality of Personal Information of Persons Served by the Department, Section 431.110.

7) When the above information is not available at the time of placement, the caregiver shall be given what information is available and advised that additional information will be provided when it is received.

(Source: Added at 19 Ill. Reg. _____, effective _____)

Section 301.130 Medical Examinations for Children in Placement

The Department shall ensure that:

a) all children entering substitute care receive an initial health screening within 24 hours of the Department assuming legal custody of a child, preferably, before placement, regardless of the type of custody (i.e., protective custody, temporary custody, or voluntary placement agreement);

b) all children for whom the Department is awarded temporary custody receive a comprehensive health evaluation which meets the requirements of the Department of Public Aid's Early and Periodic Screening,

DEPARTMENT OF CHILDREN AND FAMILY SERVICES

NOTICE OF PROPOSED AMENDMENTS

Diagnosis and Treatment (EPSDT) schedule within 21 days of the date on which the Department was given temporary custody of a child; and

c) all children entering substitute care via a voluntary placement agreement receive a comprehensive health evaluation within 21 days of the date on which the Department accepted custody of the child via the voluntary placement agreement.

(Source: Added at 19 Ill. Reg. _____, effective _____)

Section 301.140 Education of Children While in Placement

When children are placed in substitute care, the Department shall ensure that they are enrolled in school in accordance with the provisions of 89 Adm. Code 314, Educational Services and that they receive the educational services required by that Part.

(Source: Added at 19 Ill. Reg. _____, effective _____)

SUBPART C: FOSTER CARE PLACEMENT GOAL

Section 301.1 301.310 Purpose

The purpose of this Part Subpart is to comply with Federal requirements by establishing the Department's goal for the maximum number of children who will remain in Federally funded foster care after having been in such care for a period in excess of 24 months. In addition, this Part Subpart explains the Department's plans to achieve this goal.

(Source: Section 301.310 renumbered from Section 301.1 and amended at 19 Ill. Reg. _____, effective _____)

Section 301.3 301.320 Foster Care Placement Goal

The Department of Children and Family Services has set the following percentage goal which is applicable at any time during each Federal Fiscal Year. A maximum of 60% of all children receiving Aid to Families With Dependent Children - Foster Care (AFDC-FC) under Title IV-E during a Federal Fiscal Year will remain in foster care if they have been in such care for a period in excess of 24 months.

(Source: Section 301.320 renumbered from Section 301.3 and amended at 19 Ill. Reg. _____, effective _____)

Section 301.4 301.330 Plans to Achieve This Goal

a) In order to achieve this goal, the Department shall observe the

DEPARTMENT OF CHILDREN AND FAMILY SERVICES

NOTICE OF PROPOSED AMENDMENTS

necessary prerequisites of client service planning set forth in 89 Ill. Adm. Code 305, Client Service Planning, in providing the child welfare services described in 89 Ill. Adm. Code 302, Services Delivered By The Department. Such planning and service delivery shall:

1) assure that parental visits with children who are to be returned home are arranged as scheduled and agreed upon in the service plan;

2) acquire or provide appropriate services to the family and/or child;

3) contact the family and/or child on a regular basis to provide supportive casework services;

4) develop and implement service plans, as provided for in 89 Ill. Adm. Code 305, Client Service Planning, which can be understood by the participating family members; and

5) conduct reviews of these cases as required by State law, consistent with the program guidelines in P.L. 96-272 [42 U.S.C.A. 670 et seq.].

b) If it is determined that children cannot be returned home and an adoptive family must be sought, the Department shall:

1) seek the termination of the biological family's parental rights,

2) conduct an extensive search for an appropriate adoptive family, and

3) provide supportive casework services to the adoptive family, if appropriate.

(Source: Section 301.330 renumbered from Section 301.4 and amended at 19 Ill. Reg. _____, effective _____)

DEPARTMENT OF CHILDREN AND FAMILY SERVICES

NOTICE OF PROPOSED AMENDMENTS

1) **Heading of the Part:**   Licensing Standards for Foster Family Homes

2) **Code Citation:**   89 Ill. Adm. Code 402

3) **Section Numbers:**   **Proposed Action:**

402.2	Amend
402.3	Amend
402.4	Amend
402.6	Renumber
402.7	Renumber, Amend
402.8	Amend
402.9	Amend
402.12	Amend
402.13	Amend
402.15	Amend
402.Appendix A	New

4) **Statutory Authority:**   The Child Care Act of 1969 (225 ILCS 10)

5) **A Complete Description of the Subjects and Issues Involved:**   The Department intends to end the approval process for relative family homes effective July 1, 1995. Relatives may apply to be licensed as a foster family home under Part 402 or may choose to serve as a relative caregiver in accordance with the requirements of Section 301.80, Relative Home Placement (89 Ill. Adm. Code 301, Placement and Visitation Services).

The Department reviewed the current licensing standards for foster family homes and the recommendations of the Licensing Reform Panel created under the auspices of the B.H. Consent Decree. The Department determined that some licensing requirements may exclude otherwise qualified applicants from seeking licensure because of the expenses associated with compliance. These amendments reflect many of the recommendations of the Licensing Reform Panel and intend to modify those standards that may unnecessarily screen out licensed applicants for reasons unrelated to the safety and welfare of children place in the home.

6) **Will these proposed amendments replace an emergency rule currently in effect?** No

7) **Does this rulemaking contain an automatic repeal date?** Yes

8) **Do these proposed amendments contain incorporations by reference?** No

9) **Are there any other amendments pending on this part?** No

10) **State of Statewide Policy Objectives:** These rules do not create or expand a State mandate as defined in Section 3(b) of the State Mandates Act (30

DEPARTMENT OF CHILDREN AND FAMILY SERVICES

NOTICE OF PROPOSED AMENDMENTS

ILCS 805/3(b)].

11) Time, Place, and Manner in which interested persons may comment on this proposed rulemaking:

Comments on this proposed rulemaking may be submitted in writing for a period of 45 days following publication of this notice. Comments should be submitted to:

Jacqueline Nottingham, Chief
Office of Rules and Procedures
Department of Children and Family Services
406 East Monroe Street, Station # 222
Springfield, Illinois 62701-1498

Telephone: (217) 524-1983
TTY: (217) 524-3715

The Department will consider fully all written comments on this proposed rulemaking submitted during the 45-day comment period. Comments submitted by small businesses should be identified as such. Public hearings have been scheduled on these proposed amendments as follows:

April 11, 1995
7:00 p.m.
Quality Inn at Halsted
One South Halsted
Chicago, Illinois
(312) 829-5000

April 13, 1995
7:00 p.m.
State House
Room 212
Springfield, Illinois
(217) 782-2099

Persons are asked to limit their testimony to a maximum of 15 minutes per person. We will gladly accept written testimony at the public hearings. Persons who need translation or interpretation services to enable their commentary should request assistance by contacting the Office of Rules and Procedures.

12) Initial Regulatory Flexibility Analysis: The Department has determined that these proposed amendments do not have an affect on small businesses.

13) State reason(s) for this rulemaking if it was not included in either of the two (2) most recent regulatory agendas: This rulemaking was included

---

DEPARTMENT OF CHILDREN AND FAMILY SERVICES

NOTICE OF PROPOSED AMENDMENTS

in the Regulatory Agenda published in the January 13, 1995 Illinois Register.

The full text of the proposed amendments begins on the next page:

DEPARTMENT OF CHILDREN AND FAMILY SERVICES

NOTICE OF PROPOSED AMENDMENTS

TITLE 89: SOCIAL SERVICES
CHAPTER III: DEPARTMENT OF CHILDREN AND FAMILY SERVICES
SUBCHAPTER e: REQUIREMENTS FOR LICENSURE

PART 402
LICENSING STANDARDS FOR FOSTER FAMILY HOMES

Section
402.1   Purpose
402.2   Definitions
402.3   Effective Date of Standards
402.4   Application for License
402.5   Application for Renewal of License
402.6   Provisions Pertaining to ~~the License~~ Permits
402.7   Provisions Pertaining to ~~Permits~~ the License
402.8   General Requirements for the Foster Home
402.9   Requirements for Sleeping Arrangements
402.10   Nutrition and Meals
402.11   Business and Employment of Foster Parents
402.12   Qualifications of Foster Parents
402.13   Background Inquiry
402.14   Health of Foster Family
402.15   Number and Ages of Children Served
402.16   Meeting Basic Needs of Children
402.17   Health Care of Children
402.18   Religion
402.19   Recreation and Leisure Time
402.20   Education
402.21   Discipline of Children
402.22   Emergency Care of Children
402.23   Release of Children
402.24   Confidentiality of Information
402.25   Required Written Consents
402.26   Records to be Maintained
402.27   Licensing Supervision
402.28   Adoptive Homes
402.29   Severability of This Part

APPENDIX A   Criminal Convictions Which Prevent Licensure

AUTHORITY: Implementing and authorized by the Child Care Act of 1969 (225 ILCS 10).

SOURCE: Adopted and codified at 5 Ill. Reg. 9548, effective October 1, 1981;
emergency amendment at 6 Ill. Reg. 15580, effective December 15, 1982, for a
maximum of 150 days; amended at 7 Ill. Reg. 3439, effective April 4, 1983;
amended at 7 Ill. Reg. 13858, effective November 1, 1983; amended at 8 Ill.
Reg. 23197, effective December 3, 1984; amended at 11 Ill. Reg. 4292, effective

DEPARTMENT OF CHILDREN AND FAMILY SERVICES

NOTICE OF PROPOSED AMENDMENTS

March 1, 1987; emergency amendment at 16 Ill. Reg. 11879, effective July 13,
1992, for a maximum of 150 days; amended at 17 Ill. Reg. 267, effective
December 21, 1992; emergency amendment at 18 Ill. Reg. 8481, effective May 20,
1994, for a maximum of 150 days; emergency expired on October 17, 1994; amended
at 19 Ill. Reg. 1801, effective February 1, 1995; amended at 19 Ill. Reg.
_____, effective _____.

Section 402.2 Definitions

"Child" means any person under 18 years of age.

~~"Child--care--facility"--means--any--person--group-of-persons--agency--
association-or-corporation-which-arranges-for-or--cares--for--children
unrelated--to--the--operator--of-the-facility-apart-from-the-parents.
Child-care-facilities-may-be-established-for-profit-or-not-for-profit.~~

*"Child care facility" means any person, group of persons, agency,
association or organization, whether established for gain or
otherwise, who or which receives or arranges for care or placement of
one or more children, unrelated to the operator of the facility, apart
from the parents, with or without the transfer of the right of custody
in any facility as defined in the Child Care Act of 1969, established
and maintained for the care of children. [225 ILCS 10/2.05] Child
care facility includes a relative who is licensed as a foster family
home pursuant to Section 4 of the Child Care Act of 1969 [225 ILCS
10/4].*

"Classifiable fingerprints" means fingerprints have been obtained
through an electronic or ink printing process which were determined to
provide sufficiently clear impressions to identify the individual from
whom the prints were obtained.

*"Common parentage" means having the same biological or adoptive
father, the same biological or adoptive mother, or the same biological
or adoptive father and mother.*

"Department" means the Department of Children and Family Services.

~~"Foster--family-home"-means-the-residence-of-the-family-which-provides
full-time-family-care-and-training--to--children--unrelated--to--them.
Foster--family--homes-are-limited-to-a-maximum-of-8-children-including
the-foster-family's-children-unless-all-of-the-children--unrelated--to
the--foster--family--are--of--common--parentage-or-the-Director-of-the
Department-of-Children-and-Family-Services-has-waived-the-limit--of--8
unrelated--children--for-good-cause-pursuant-to-Section-402.15-(b)-and
only-to-facilitate-an-adoptive-placement.~~

"Foster family home" means a facility for child care in residences of

DEPARTMENT OF CHILDREN AND FAMILY SERVICES

NOTICE OF PROPOSED AMENDMENTS

families who receive no more than 8 children unrelated to them, unless all the children are of common parentage, or residences of relatives who receive related children for the purpose of providing family care and training for the children on a full-time basis, except the Director of Children and Family Services, pursuant to Department regulations, may waive the limit of 8 children unrelated to an adoptive family for good cause to facilitate an adoptive placement. The family's own children, under 18 years of age, shall be included in determining the maximum number of children served. [225 ILCS 10/2.17]

"Full-time care" means the child is a resident of the household, whether on a temporary, emergency, or permanent basis, and is receiving family care usually provided by a parent or guardian.

"LEADS" means the Law Enforcement Agency Data System.

"License" means a document issued by the Department of Children and Family Services which authorizes child care facilities to operate in accordance with applicable standards and the provisions of the Child Care Act.

"Licensee" means those individuals, agencies, or organizations who hold a license or permit issued by the Department of Children and Family Services.

"Licensing applicant" means those individuals, agencies, or organizations who applied for a license from the Department of Children and Family Services.

"Licensing representative" means those Department staff or other persons authorized under the Child Care Act to examine facilities for licensure.

"Minor traffic violation", as used in this Part, means a traffic violation under the laws of the State of Illinois or any municipal authority therein or another state or municipal authority which resulted in a fine of $100.00 or less without other penalty such as license suspension or revocation, probation, jail sentence or community service work.

"Permit" means a one-time only document issued by the Department of Children and Family Services for a two month period to allow the individual(s) to become eligible for a license.

"Relative" means a person 21 years of age or over, other than the parent, to whom the child has any of the following currently existing relationships by blood or adoption: grandparent, sibling, great grandparent, uncle, aunt, nephew, niece, first cousin, great uncle,

DEPARTMENT OF CHILDREN AND FAMILY SERVICES

NOTICE OF PROPOSED AMENDMENTS

great aunt, or who is the spouse of such a relative or who is the child's step-father, step-mother, step-brother or step-sister.

"Supervising agency", for the purpose of this part, means a licensed child welfare agency, a license-exempt agency, or the Department of Children and Family Services.

(Source: Amended at 19 Ill. Reg. _____, effective _____)

Section 402.3 Effective Date of Standards

The standards prescribed in this part shall become effective upon the date they are officially adopted and published and shall apply immediately to all facilities foster family homes. which are not currently licensed. Foster family homes licensed at the time this rule is officially adopted and published shall have 6 months from that date to comply with the new or revised standards.

(Source: Amended at 19 Ill. Reg. _____, effective _____)

Section 402.4 Application for License

a) Application for license as a foster family home shall be completed, signed by the foster parent applicant(s), and filed with the Department of Children and Family Services by the supervising agency on forms prescribed by the Department. Any relative who receives a child or children for placement on a full-time basis may apply for a license to operate a foster family home as defined in Section 2.17 of the Child Care Act of 1969 [225 ILCS 10/2.17].

b) As part of the application process, each foster family home applicant and adult member of the household shall authorize fingerprinting in accordance with Part 89 Ill. Adm. Code 380, Background Check of Foster Family Home Applicants, to determine if the applicant individual has ever been charged with a crime, and if so, the disposition of the charges. In addition, each foster family home applicant and member of the household 13 years of age or older shall authorize a check of the Child Abuse Neglect Tracking System to determine if the individual has been indicated as the perpetrator of child abuse or neglect.

c) The supervising agency shall study each foster home under its supervision before recommending issuance of a license. The licensing study shall be conducted by a qualified licensing representative and shall be reviewed and approved by his the assigned supervisor. Supervisory approval indicates recommendation for license or denial of a license and compliance with the standards. The study shall be in writing and shall be signed by the licensing representative performing the study and by his the assigned supervisor.

DEPARTMENT OF CHILDREN AND FAMILY SERVICES

NOTICE OF PROPOSED AMENDMENTS

d) A new application shall be filed when any of the following occurs:
1) when an application for license has been withdrawn, and the licensee or agency seeks to reapply; or
2) when there is a change in the name of the licensee, the address location of the foster home, the supervising agency, or the area in the home used to children; or
3) when there is a change in the status of joint licensees, such as separation, divorce, or death; or
4) when the Department has revoked or refused to renew a license, and a new license is sought.
e) A new application may be submitted at any time except that when a license has been revoked or the Department has refused to renew a license, the licensee may not reapply for licensure as a foster family home for a period of one year after revocation or refusal to renew.

(Source: Amended at 19 Ill. Reg. _____, effective _____)

Section 402.7402.6 Provisions Pertaining to Permits

a) A two month permit may be issued only with the personal written approval of the Director of the Department when:
1) The application for license has been completed and signed by the foster parent applicant(s) and submitted to the Department;
2) The required background check forms have been completed in accordance with 89 Ill. Adm. Code 380, Background Check of Foster Family Home Applicants, classifiable fingerprints, as defined in this Part, have been obtained, and a LEADS check has been completed which finds no history of criminal activities for the foster home applicants;
3) A complete licensing study has been conducted by the licensing representative and it has been determined that the family is in reasonable compliance with all applicable standards except for receipt, review, and disposition of the criminal background check required by 89 Ill. Adm. Code 380, Background Check of Foster Family Home Applicants;
4) furnishing, equipment and space sufficient for the children have been acquired; and
5) the applicants have signed:
A) affidavits indicating that they have not been convicted or charged with a crime other than a minor traffic violation;
B) acknowledgments that, by virtue of being a foster parent, they are mandated to report suspected child abuse or neglect;
C) acknowledgements that the permit is time limited and issuance of a license is contingent upon the results of the criminal background check;
D) acknowledgements that the permit may be cancelled and the

DEPARTMENT OF CHILDREN AND FAMILY SERVICES

NOTICE OF PROPOSED AMENDMENTS

Department will refuse to issue a license if the results of the criminal background check are unfavorable; and
E) acknowledgements that any children placed in their care will be removed without prior notice if information provided during the application process has been falsified or the applicants have a prior criminal history, other than for a minor traffic violation.
b) A permit shall not be issued retroactively.
c) Permits shall not be transferred to another person, organization or supervising agency.
d) Permits shall not be valid for a name or address different from the name and address shown on the issued permit.
e) Permits shall not be renewable.
f) A current permit shall be available in the foster home at all times.
g) A license shall be issued at any time within the two month period covered by the permit provided that the foster family home achieves compliance with the Department's licensing standards.
h) The foster family shall adhere to the provisions or restrictions specified on the permit.
i) There shall be no fee or charge for the permit.

(Source: Renumbered from Section 402.7 to Section 402.6 at 19 Ill. Reg. _____, effective _____)

Section 402.6403.7 Provisions Pertaining to the License

a) A foster family home license is valid for 2 four years unless revoked by the Department or voluntarily given up by the licensee.
b) The number of children cared for in the foster family home shall not exceed the license capacity and must conform with the requirements for the number and ages of children who may reside in a foster family home.
c) The foster parents' biological and adopted children under 18 years of age shall be counted when determining license capacity.
d) The license shall not be transferred to another person.
e) The license shall not be valid for a name or an address location other than the name and address location on the license.
f) A current license shall be available in the foster home at all times.
g) There shall be no fee or charge for the license.
h) The foster family shall adhere to the provisions or restrictions specified on the license in accordance with these rules.

(Source: Renumbered from Section 402.6 to Section 402.7 and amended at 19 Ill. Reg. _____, effective _____)

Section 402.8 General Requirements for the Foster Home

a) The foster home shall be clean, well ventilated, free from observable

DEPARTMENT OF CHILDREN AND FAMILY SERVICES

NOTICE OF PROPOSED AMENDMENTS

hazards, properly lighted and heated, and free of fire hazards.

b) The water supply of the foster family home shall comply with the requirements of the local and state health departments. If well water is used, a copy of the Inspection Report and Compliance with Regulations shall be on file with the supervising agency.

c) Portable space heaters may be used as a supplementary source of heat if they meet safety approval standards (Underwriters Laboratories) and are used in accordance with local and State building and fire codes. Portable space heaters may not be used in rooms where children are sleeping. ~~Portable~~ and fixed space heaters in areas occupied by children shall be separated by fire resistant partitions or barriers to prevent contact with the heater.

d) Prescription and nonprescription drugs, dangerous household supplies, dangerous tools, weapons, guns, and ammunition shall be kept in a safe place. Loaded guns shall not be kept in a foster home unless required by law enforcement officers and in accordance with their law enforcement agency's safety procedures.

e) The foster home shall comply with all requirements of the state laws and municipal codes for household pets. Certificates of inoculation for rabies shall be available for inspection.

f) ~~The foster home shall have an operating telephone on the premises unless the supervising agency has approved a written plan detailing the immediate and unrestricted access to such an instrument.~~ The foster home shall have access to a telephone in case of an emergency. In cases where the children in care require special services or frequent medical attention, the foster family shall have immediate access to a telephone.

g) The foster home shall have fire and emergency evacuation plans which are to be discussed and routinely rehearsed with the children.

h) Adequate closet and dresser space comparable to that provided to the other children of the household shall be provided for each foster child to accomodate personal belongings.

i) Foster parents shall respect childrens' rights to privacy while sleeping, toileting and dressing.

(Source: Amended at 19 Ill. Reg. _____, effective _____)

Section 402.9 Requirements for Sleeping Arrangements

a) Each foster child shall be provided his own separate bed or crib, except that two children up to age 10 of the same sex with no more than two years difference in their ages may share a double-sized (or larger) bed.

b) Child(ren) who have been victims of sexual abuse or who are sexually aggressive shall not share a bedroom with another child or adult unless sharing a bedroom has been approved in writing by the supervising agency. Such approvals shall contain the name(s) and

DEPARTMENT OF CHILDREN AND FAMILY SERVICES

NOTICE OF PROPOSED AMENDMENTS

birth date(s) of the child(ren) for whom the approval was issued. The approval shall be reviewed and reapproved annually and whenever there is any change in the behaviors of the child(ren).

b) ~~Children under six years of age may share a room with children of the opposite sex provided sharing the room is approved by the supervising agency. The additional child(ren) is/are related, as defined in Section 2.24 of the Child Care Act; the oldest child is no older than 10 years of age and each child is provided with his/her own separate crib or bed.~~

c) Child(ren) under six years of age may share a bedroom with related child(ren) of the opposite sex who are also under age six if each child is provided with a separate bed or crib.

c)d) A foster child shall not share the bedroom with an adult except under emergency conditions for a brief period of time, ~~or~~ when a child under six years of age is ill or needs frequent attention or as allowed in Section 402.9(e) through (h) below.

e) When adulthood (age 18) is reached by a foster, biological or adopted child for whom sharing the bedroom with a foster child under eighteen years of age has been determined appropriate ~~by the supervising agency~~ to be in the best interests of the foster child, the supervising agency shall approve such arrangements in accordance with the provisions of this Section.

f) Female foster children under six years of age may share a bedroom with one related female adult or a related married couple if provided with their own beds or cribs.

g) Male foster children under six years of age may share a bedroom with a related adult (male or female) or a related married couple if provided with their own beds or cribs.

h) Foster children over six years of age may share a bedroom with one related adult of the same sex if provided with their own beds or cribs.

d)i) There shall be a minimum of 40 square feet, excluding the closet and wardrobe area, for the first child occupying a bedroom and a minimum of 35 square feet for each additional child sharing the room bedroom. However, the supervising agency may approve a smaller bedroom size on an individual case basis when such approval is in the best interests of the children. Such approvals shall be in writing and shall contain the names and birth dates of the children for whom the approval was issued. These approvals shall be reviewed at each license renewal.

e)j) The room bedroom shall be exposed to an outside window or shall have auxiliary means of ventilation.

f)k) The springs and mattresses on each bed requiring such shall be level, clean, unsoiled with no rips, tears or sags in the mattress or mattress cover, and not infested with insects. The bedding shall be suitable for the season.

g)l) Linens shall be changed at least weekly for all children and as frequently as needed for children not toilet trained and for those who are enuretic.

h)m) Waterproof mattress covers shall be provided for all beds or cribs for enuretic children.

i)n) Sleeping rooms shall be comfortable and shall be furnished suitably for the age and sex of the child.

j)o)

1) Basements and attics may be used for sleeping for children who are mobile, capable of self preservation, and able to understand and follow directions with minimal assistance in an emergency.

2) Children for whom basement or attic sleeping arrangements may be provided shall be individually evaluated and approved by the supervising agency in accordance with the above cited requirements.

3) To be used for sleeping, basements and attics shall have two exits with one exit leading directly to the outside with means to safely reach the ground level. The second exit may be an easily accessible outside window which provides an unobstructed opening, operable from the inside without the use of tools, and large enough to accomodate an adult. The sleeping area shall be separated from the furnace and utility areas.

4) No basement or attic shall be used for sleeping without the approval of the supervising agency after consultation with the appropriate safety authority(ies).

(Source: Amended at 19 Ill. Reg. _____, effective _____)

Section 402.12 Qualifications of Foster Parents

a) The licensee(s) shall be either a single foster parent or a man and woman married to each other. A married foster parent who has been physically separated from his or her spouse for a period of at least one year may be considered a single person at the discretion of the supervising agency. Each foster parent shall be willing and able to assume appropriate responsibilities for the child or children received for care.

b) Foster parents shall be stable, law abiding, responsible, mature individuals, at least 21 years of age, who shall have passed the background check required for foster parents and adult members of the household, as required in Part 380, Background Check of Foster Family Homes Applicants and shall be able to accept agency supervision.

c) Foster parents shall adequately supervise children in their care to assure compliance with laws including, but not limited to, criminal laws.

d) Foster home applicants shall provide the names and addresses of at least three unrelated references who can attest to the applicant's moral character.

e) Unless parental rights have been terminated, foster parents shall respect and support a child's ties to his or her biological family and

shall cooperate with the supervising agency and the service plan for the child and his/her family.

f) The foster family shall have sufficient financial resources to provide basic necessities for themselves and their own children and the foster children).

g) Foster parents shall complete, as a condition of initial licensure, at least six clock hours of training on content approved by the Department. Relative caregivers who had been approved under 89 Ill. Adm. Code 335, Relative Home Placement, prior to July 1, 1995, and who are in compliance with all other licensing requirements shall be granted a conditional foster home license pending completion of this training. Relatives who receive conditional licensure under this subsection shall be given 90 days from the effective date of these amendments to complete the required training.

(Source: Amended at 19 Ill. Reg. _____, effective _____)

Section 402.13 Background Inquiry

a) As a condition of issuance or renewal of a license by the Department, foster parents shall furnish information of any offenses (other than minor traffic violations) for which they have been charged. The Department shall make a determination concerning their suitability in working with the child in accordance with this part and Part 89 Ill. Adm. Code 380, Background Check of Foster Family Home Applicants.

b) Persons who have been convicted of an offense shall not be automatically rejected as foster parents. However, the Department shall consider the following:

1) the type of crime for which the individual was convicted;
2) the number of crimes for which the individual was convicted;
3) the nature of the offense(s);
4) the age of the individual at the time of conviction;
5) the length of time that has elapsed since the last conviction;
6) the relationship of the crime and the capacity to care for children;
7) evidence of rehabilitation; and
8) opinions of community members concerning the individual in question.

(Source: Amended at 19 Ill. Reg. _____, effective _____)

Section 402.15 Number and Ages of Children Served

a) The maximum number of children permitted in foster family home is 8, unless all of the foster children are of common parentage, as defined in Section 402.2, or a waiver has been granted in accordance with

DEPARTMENT OF CHILDREN AND FAMILY SERVICES

NOTICE OF PROPOSED AMENDMENTS

subsection ~~(b)~~(c) below. This maximum number includes the foster parents' own children and all other children under the age of 18, cared for on a full-time basis.

b) When determining how many children the foster family home shall serve, children who have special needs due to physical, mental, or emotional disabilities shall be considered at the level at which they function.

~~b)~~ ~~The Director of the Department of Children and Family Services shall waive in writing the maximum number of 8 children to effect an adoptive placement provided the following criteria are met:~~

~~1)~~ ~~a licensed child welfare agency or the Department proposes to place an additional child or children, in the home, for the purpose of adoption;~~

~~2)~~ ~~the child welfare agency or the Department has documented in the child's case record that this home is the most appropriate choice consistent with the best interest of the child or children;~~

~~3)~~ ~~the foster family is otherwise in compliance with the licensing requirements of this Part, and could meet standards for the additional child or children; and~~

~~4)~~ ~~the foster family has requested, in writing, that the Director waive the limit of 8 children under the age of 18 so that an additional child or children may be placed in their home for purposes of adoption.~~

c) The Director of the Department of Children and Family Services shall waive in writing the maximum number of 8 children to effect an adoptive placement provided the following criteria are met:

1) a licensed child welfare agency or the Department proposes to place an additional child or children, in the home, for the purpose of adoption;

2) the child welfare agency or the Department has documented in the child's case record that this home is the most appropriate choice consistent with the best interest of the child or children;

3) the foster family is otherwise in compliance with the licensing requirements of this Part, and could meet standards for the additional child or children; and

4) the foster family has requested, in writing, that the Director waive the limit of 8 children under the age of 18 so that an additional child or children may be placed in their home for purposes of adoption.

~~c)~~ ~~No more than 4 children under the age of 6, including the foster parents' own children, shall receive full-time care at any one time. No more than 2 children, including the family's own children, shall be under the age of 2, unless the foster parent(s) is aided by a child care assistant at least 16 years of age other than a foster child. The Director of the Department of Children and Family Services may waive the age requirements in this subsection, if necessary, to place a child in an adoptive home provided the criteria in subsections (b)(1) through (4) are met.~~

~~d)~~ ~~Independent foster homes receive children by independent arrangement.~~

DEPARTMENT OF CHILDREN AND FAMILY SERVICES

NOTICE OF PROPOSED AMENDMENTS

~~These homes are not subject to direct and regular supervision by a child welfare agency. These homes shall not be licensed for more than a maximum of 4 children unless all of the unrelated children are of common parentage. No more than 2 of these children, including the family's own children, shall be under the age of 2 unless of common parentage.~~

d) No more than 4 children under the age of 6, including the foster parent(s)' own children, shall receive full-time care at any one time. No more than 2 children, including the family's own children, shall be under the age of 2, unless the foster parent(s) is aided by a child care assistant at least 16 years of age other than a foster child. The supervising agency may place children whose ages do not comply with this subsection in a foster family home when all of the foster children are of common parentage and the supervising agency's approval of the placement is documented in writing. Such approval shall include the name(s), birth date(s), and the common parent(s)' of the foster child(ren).

e) The Director of the Department of Children and Family Services may waive in writing the age requirements in subsection (d), if necessary, to place a child in an adoptive home provided the criteria in subsections (c)(1) through (4) are met and there are a sufficient number of suitable adult caregivers or child care assistants to insure that the children receive proper care and supervision.

f) A foster child who is the parent of another child placed in the same foster home may serve as a child care assistant in relation to the care of his or her own child. Child care assistants shall meet health requirements as specified in Section 402.14.

g) Independent foster homes receive children by independent arrangement. These homes are not subject to direct and regular supervision by a child welfare agency. These homes shall not be licensed for more than a maximum of 4 children unless all of the unrelated children are of common parentage. No more than 2 of these children, including the family's own children, shall be under the age of 2 unless of common parentage.

(Source: Amended at 19 Ill. Reg. _____, effective _____)

DEPARTMENT OF CHILDREN AND FAMILY SERVICES

NOTICE OF PROPOSED AMENDMENTS

Section 402.APPENDIX A Criminal Convictions Which Prevent Licensure

If the foster parent applicant(s) or any adult member of the household has been convicted of committing or attempting to commit one or more of the following serious criminal offenses under the Criminal Code of 1961 [720 ILCS 5] or under any earlier Illinois criminal law or code or an offense in another state, the elements of which are similar and bear a substantial relation to any of the criminal offenses specified below, this conviction will serve as a bar to receiving a foster home license or permit.

OFFENSES DIRECTED AGAINST THE PERSON

HOMICIDE

Murder
Solicitation of murder
Solicitation of murder for hire
Intentional homicide of an unborn child
Voluntary manslaughter of an unborn child
Involuntary manslaughter
Reckless homicide
Concealment of a homicidal death
Involuntary manslaughter of an unborn child
Reckless homicide of an unborn child

KIDNAPPING AND RELATED OFFENSES

Drug induced kidnapping
Kidnapping
Aggravated kidnapping
Unlawful restraint
Aggravated unlawful restraint
Forcible detention
Child abduction
Aiding and abetting child abduction

SEX OFFENSES

Indecent solicitation of a child
Sexual exploitation of a child
Sexual relations within families
Prostitution
Soliciting for a prostitute
Soliciting for a juvenile prostitute
Pandering
Felony keeping a place of prostitution
Patronizing a juvenile prostitute
Felony pimping

DEPARTMENT OF CHILDREN AND FAMILY SERVICES

NOTICE OF PROPOSED AMENDMENTS

Juvenile pimping
Exploitation of a child
Felony obscenity
Child pornography
Felony harmful material

BODILY HARM

Felony aggravated assault
Vehicular endangerment
Felony domestic battery
Aggravated battery
Heinous battery
Aggravated battery with a firearm
Aggravated battery of a child or institutionalized mentally retarded person
Aggravated battery of an unborn child
Tampering with food, drugs, or cosmetics
Aggravated battery of a senior citizen
Drug induced infliction of great bodily harm
Intimidation
Compelling organization membership of persons
Hate crime
Stalking
Aggravated stalking
Threatening public officials
Home invasion
Vehicular invasion
Criminal sexual assault
Aggravated sexual assault
Felony criminal sexual abuse
Aggravated sexual abuse
Criminal transmission of HIV
Abuse and gross neglect of a long term care facility resident
Criminal neglect of an elderly or disabled person
Child abandonment
Endangering the life or health of a child
Felony violation of an order of protection
Ritual Mutilation
Ritualized abuse of a child

OFFENSES DIRECTED AGAINST PROPERTY

Felony theft
Robbery
Aggravated robbery
Aggravated vehicular hijacking
Burglary

DEPARTMENT OF CHILDREN AND FAMILY SERVICES

NOTICE OF PROPOSED AMENDMENTS

Possession of burglary tools
Residential burglary
Criminal fortification of a residence or building
Arson
Aggravated arson

OFFENSES AFFECTING PUBLIC HEALTH, SAFETY AND DECENCY

Felony unlawful use of weapons
Aggravated discharge of a firearm
Reckless discharge of a firearm
Unlawful use of metal piercing bullets
Unlawful sale or delivery of firearms on the premises of any
  school
Disarming a police officer
Obstructing justice
Concealing or aiding a fugitive
Armed violence
Felony contributing to the criminal delinquency of a juvenile

DRUG OFFENSES

Possession of more than thirty grams of cannabis
Manufacture of more than 10 grams of cannabis
Cannabis trafficking
Delivery of cannabis on school grounds
Unauthorized production of more than five cannabis sativa plants
Calculated criminal cannabis conspiracy
Unauthorized manufacture or delivery of controlled substances
Controlled substance trafficking
Manufacture, distribution, advertisement of look-alike substances
Calculated criminal drug conspiracy
Permitting unlawful use of a building
Delivery of controlled, counterfeit or look-alike substances to
  persons under age 18, or at truck stops, rest stops, safety rest
  areas, or on school property
Using, engaging, or employing persons under 18 to deliver
  controlled, counterfeit or look-alike substances
Delivery of controlled substances
Sale or delivery of drug paraphernalia
Felony possession, sale or exchange of instruments adapted for use
  of controlled substance or cannabis by subcutaneous injection

(Source: Added   at   19   Ill. Reg. _____,   effective
_____.)

DEPARTMENT OF CHILDREN AND FAMILY SERVICES

NOTICE OF PROPOSED REPEALER

1) Heading of the Part: Relative Home Placement

2) Code Citation: 89 Ill. Adm. Code 335

3) Section Numbers: Proposed Action:

Section Numbers:	Proposed Action:
335.100	Repeal
335.102	Repeal
335.200	Repeal
335.202	Repeal
335.204	Repeal
335.206	Repeal
335.300	Repeal
335.302	Repeal
335.304	Repeal
335.306	Repeal
335.310	Repeal
335.312	Repeal
335.314	Repeal
335.316	Repeal
335.318	Repeal
335.320	Repeal
335.322	Repeal
335.324	Repeal
335.326	Repeal
335.328	Repeal
335.330	Repeal
335.332	Repeal
335.334	Repeal
335.336	Repeal
335.338	Repeal
335.340	Repeal

4) Statutory Authority: Section 5 of the Children and Family Services Act
    [20 ILCS 505/5]

5) A Complete Description of the Subjects and Issues Involved: The
    Department is proposing a change in the legal definition of neglected
    child so that children who are receiving adequate care and supervision
    from a related adult are no longer considered neglected for the sole
    reason that such care was provided by a person other than the child's
    parent.   The Department has concluded that state custody and the approval
    process is not the appropriate response for a majority of relative care.

    Effective July 1, 1995, the Department is discontinuing its process of
    approving relative homes using standards comparable to the licensing
    standards for foster homes.   The Department has initiated legislation and
    proposed changes to 89 Ill. Adm. Code 102, Licensing Standards for Foster

DEPARTMENT OF CHILDREN AND FAMILY SERVICES

NOTICE OF PROPOSED REPEALER

Family Homes, which will allow relative families to be licensed under the Child Care Act of 1969 and to receive the foster care rate for related children who have been placed with them by the Department of Children and Family Services. Relatives who do not seek to become licensed foster family homes may continue to provide care to related children, but will receive the AFDC rate for these children plus special add-on payments to assist with the extra costs associated with providing care to a foster child, thus bringing the amount received by the foster parent up to the child only standard of need established for that number of children by the Illinois Department of Public Aid.

The Department will continue with its requirement that relatives who provide care to children for whom the Department is legally responsible must meet certain placement pre-conditions with regard to the safety of the home and the adequacy of the related caregivers. These requirements are being transferred to 89 Ill. Adm. Code 301, Foster Care Placement Goal, which is being retitled Placement and Visitation Services.

6) Will these proposed amendments replace an emergency rule currently in effect? No

7) Does this rulemaking contain an automatic repeal date? No

8) Do these proposed amendments contain incorporations by reference? No

9) Are there any other amendments pending on this part? Yes

Section Numbers	Proposed Action	Illinois Register Citation
335.204	Amend	18 Ill. Reg. 16892, 11/28/94
335.206	Amend	18 Ill. Reg. 16892, 11/28/94
335.208	Repeal	18 Ill. Reg. 16892, 11/28/94
335.300	Amend	18 Ill. Reg. 16892, 11/28/94
Appendix A	New	18 Ill. Reg. 16892, 11/28/94

10) State of Statewide Policy Objectives: These rules do not create or expand a State mandate as defined in Section 3(b) of the State Mandates Act [30 ILCS 805/3(b)].

11) Time, Place, and Manner in which interested persons may comment on this proposed rulemaking:

Comments on this proposed rulemaking may be submitted in writing for a period of 45 days following publication of this notice. Comments should be submitted to:

Jacqueline Nottingham, Chief
Office of Rules and Procedures
Department of Children and Family Services

DEPARTMENT OF CHILDREN AND FAMILY SERVICES

NOTICE OF PROPOSED REPEALER

406 East Monroe Street, Station # 222
Springfield, Illinois 62701-1498

Telephone: (217) 524-1983
TTY: (217) 524-3715

The Department will consider fully all written comments on this proposed repealer submitted during the 45-day comment period. Comments submitted by small businesses should be identified as such. Public hearings have been scheduled on these proposed amendments as follows:

April 11, 1995
7:00 p.m.
Quality Inn at Halsted
One South Halsted
Chicago, Illinois
(312) 829-5000

April 13, 1995
7:00 p.m.
State House
Room 212
Springfield, Illinois
(217) 782-2099

Persons are asked to limit their testimony to a maximum of 15 minutes per person. We will gladly accept written testimony at the public hearings. Persons who need translation or interpretation services to enable their commentary should request assistance by contacting the Office of Rules and Procedures.

12) Initial Regulatory Flexibility Analysis: These amendments do not affect small businesses.

13) State reason(s) for this rulemaking if it was not included in either of the two (2) most recent regulatory agendas: The need for this rulemaking was not foreseen at the time the Department filed its regulatory agendas. A major management initiative affecting home of relative care has prompted the Department to file these amendments at the present time in order to implement them at the start of the next fiscal year.

The full text of the proposed amendments begins on the next page:

DEPARTMENT OF CHILDREN AND FAMILY SERVICES

NOTICE OF PROPOSED REPEALER

TITLE 89: SOCIAL SERVICES
CHAPTER III: DEPARTMENT OF CHILDREN AND FAMILY SERVICES
SUBCHAPTER b: PROGRAM AND TECHNICAL SUPPORT

PART 335
RELATIVE HOME PLACEMENT (REPEALED)

SUBPART A: GENERAL PROVISIONS

AUTHORITY: Implementing and Authorized by Section 5 of the Children and
Family Services Act (Ill. Rev. Stat. 1991, ch. 23, par. 5005) [20 ILCS 505/5].

SOURCE: Adopted at 10 Ill. Reg. 4513, effective April 1, 1986; amended at 16

DEPARTMENT OF CHILDREN AND FAMILY SERVICES

NOTICE OF PROPOSED REPEALER

Ill. Reg. 7633, effective April 30, 1992; amended at 17 Ill. Reg. 13420,
effective July 31, 1993; amended at 18 Ill. Reg. 7744, effective September 1,
1994; emergency amendment at 18 III. Reg. 14436, effective August 31, 1994, for
a maximum of 150 days; emergency expired January 30, 1995; repealed at 19 Ill.
Reg. _____, effective _____.

SUBPART A: GENERAL PROVISIONS

Section 335.100   Purpose

The purpose of this Part is to specify that related caregivers of children for
whom the Department of Children and Family Services is legally responsible must
meet the standards prescribed by this Part, which are prescribed to ensure the
safety, health, and welfare of related children.

Section 335.102   Definitions

"Approval" or "Approved" means that a relative family home wherein the
caregiver is related to the child(ren) in care has met the standards
prescribed by this Part. A relative home is approved on the effective
date entered on the approval recommendation. Such standards are
substantially the same with regard to the safety, health and welfare
of children as those promulgated for licensure of unrelated foster
family homes pursuant to the Child Care Act of 1969 (Ill. Rev. Stat.
1991, ch. 23, par. 2211 et seq.) [225 ILCS 10] and codified at 89 Ill.
Adm. Code 402, Licensing Standards for Foster Family Homes.

"Biological or putative father" means a man who has acknowledged his
paternity via a notarized written statement or whose paternity is
adjudicated in court. When paternity has been acknowledged or
adjudicated, the relatives of the biological father as well as those
of the mother may be considered for the placement of related children.

"Children for whom the Department is legally responsible" means
children for whom the Department has temporary protective custody,
custody or guardianship via court order, or whose parent(s) has signed
an adoptive surrender or voluntary placement agreement with the
Department in accordance with 89 Ill. Adm. Code 302, Services
Delivered by the Department.

"Department" means the Department of Children and Family Services.

"Director" means the Director of the Department of Children and Family
Services.

"Placing agency", as used in this Part, means a child welfare agency
licensed in accordance with 89 Ill. Adm. Code 401, Licensing Standards
For Child Welfare Agencies, a license-exempt agency in accordance with

DEPARTMENT OF CHILDREN AND FAMILY SERVICES

NOTICE OF PROPOSED REPEALER

89 Ill. Adm. Code 382. Agencies Exempt From Licensing, or the Department of Children and Family Services, which places children in a relative family home.

"Related or Relative Caregiver" means a person who provides care for a child or children for whom the Department is legally responsible by reason of temporary protective custody, court ordered custody or guardianship, or an adoptive surrender or voluntary placement agreement signed by the parent(s) and to whom the child or children or members of a sibling group have any of the following currently existing relationships by blood, marriage, or adoption: grandfather, grandmother, great-grandfather, great-grandmother, step-grandfather, step-grandmother, great-uncle, great-aunt, brother, sister, stepfather, stepmother, stepbrother, stepsister, uncle, aunt, nephew, niece or first cousin.

"Relative family home" or "home" means the home of a related caregiver approved in accordance with the standards prescribed by this Part.

"Specified relative" means any of those relatives who have first preference and consideration in the placement of related children in the home. Specified relatives include the following currently existing relationships by blood or adoption: grandfather, grandmother, great-grandfather, great-grandmother, great-uncle, great-aunt, brother, sister, uncle, aunt, nephew, niece, or first cousin.

"Supervising Agency" as used in this Part, means a licensed child welfare agency, a license-exempt agency, or the Department of Children and Family Services, which has responsibility for the day-to-day supervision, approval and monitoring of a relative family home.

SUBPART B: PLACEMENT

Section 335.200 Identification and Selection of Relative Placements

Department and private agency staff shall make reasonable attempts to locate relatives who may be willing to serve as a placement to children related to them. The Department or private agency shall identify relatives of the children, contact the relatives, and assess their suitability to serve as relative caregivers for the children. When children must be placed apart from their parents, specified relatives as defined in Section 335.102, shall have preference and first consideration over more distant relatives and over non-relatives. Department or private agency staff shall refer relatives for approval when their home meets the placement preconditions in Section 335.202, when the relative caregivers will not pose an obstacle to permanency for the children, and when the placement is consistent with the best interests and special needs of the children in accordance with the criteria of 89 Ill.

DEPARTMENT OF CHILDREN AND FAMILY SERVICES

NOTICE OF PROPOSED REPEALER

Adm. Code 302.390(e), Placement Selection Criteria.

Section 335.202 Placement Pre-conditions

a) Effective with the adoption of these rules, no child for whom the Department is legally responsible shall be placed with a relative unless the pre-conditions specified in this Section have been met. When a child is already in the care of a relative when the Department assumes legal responsibility, the pre-conditions of this Section shall be met within forty-eight (48) hours of the Department's assuming legal responsibility for the child.

b) Staff of the placing agency shall meet with the proposed related caregiver and ascertain that the relative, in accordance with the Department's rules at 89 Ill. Adm. Code 300 (Reports of Child Abuse and Neglect), 302 (Services Delivered by the Department), 305 (Client Service Planning), 307 (Indian Child Welfare Services), and 327 (Permanency Advocacy Services):

   1) is capable of protecting the child(ren) from further harm by the parent(s) or others whose action or inaction allegedly threatened the child(ren)'s safety or well-being as determined by a child abuse or neglect investigation pursuant to the Abused and Neglected Child Reporting Act (Ill. Rev. Stat. 1991, ch. 23, par. 2051 et seq.) [325 ILCS 5];

   2) agrees not to release the child to anyone, including parent(s) or other relative(s), unless previously authorized by the Department;

   3) agrees not to allow the child's parents to reside in the relative's home unless previously authorized in writing by the Department;

   4) agrees not to move the child to another home or give the child to another caregiver unless previously authorized in writing by the Department;

   5) agrees not to arrange for medical, psychological, or psychiatric testing or treatment unless previously authorized in writing by the Department;

   6) agrees not to take the child out of state unless previously authorized in writing by the Department;

   7) agrees to abide by any conditions or limitations on the parent-child visitation plan which have been imposed by the court or are contained in the client service plan; and

   8) is willing to cooperate with the agency, the child(ren)'s parent(s) and other resource persons to help develop and achieve the permanency goal recorded in the child(ren)'s service plan.

c) Prior to placement with a related caregiver (or within 48 hours of the Department's assuming legal responsibility for a child already in the care of a related caregiver), staff of the placing agency shall visit the home of the proposed caregiver and shall determine whether the following standards are met:

1) background checks as required by 89 Ill. Adm. Code 385 (Background Checks) have been completed on all adult members of the household and communicated to the supervising agency prior to placement;

2) the home is free from observable hazards;

3) prescription and non-prescription drugs, dangerous household supplies, dangerous tools, weapons, guns and ammunition are stored in places inaccessible to children;

4) basic utilities -- water, heat, electricity -- are in operation;

5) sleeping arrangements are suitable to the age and sex of the child(ren);

6) meals can be provided daily to the related child(ren) in sufficient quantities to meet the child(ren)'s nutritional needs as required by Section 335.306;

7) supervision of the related child(ren) can be assured at all times including times when the related caregiver is employed or otherwise engaged in activity outside of the home;

8) the related caregiver can provide basic necessities, as defined by Section 335.310 (e), for themselves and their own child(ren);

9) the medical needs of the related child(ren) can be met;

10) no member of the household appears to have a communicable disease which could pose a threat to the health of the related child(ren) or an emotional or physical impairment which could affect the ability of the caregiver to provide routine daily care to the related child(ren) or to evacuate them safely in an emergency;

11) there is no evidence of current drug or alcohol abuse by any household member as determined by the placing agency's observations and statements provided by the related caregiver(s);

12) the related caregiver has the ability to contact the agency, if necessary, and the ability to be contacted;

13) the related caregiver has immediate access to a telephone when the related child has medical or other special needs; and

14) the related caregiver shall cooperate with the supervising agency's educational plan for the child.

d) Prior to or concurrent with placement in a related caregiver's home, staff of the placing agency shall document, on the form prescribed by the Department, that the pre-conditions prescribed by this Section have been met.

e) Children for whom the Department is legally responsible who are in the care of related caregivers approved in accordance with this Part shall receive the same care and services as children in the care of unrelated caregivers unless otherwise required by this Part.

Section 335.204 Continuation of Placement

a) Related caregivers shall meet the standards prescribed in Subpart C of this Part within 90 days of the initial placement.

b) Placement staff of the supervising agency shall assure that no child

for whom the Department is legally responsible remains in the care of a related caregiver in excess of 90 days unless:

1) the related caregiver has been approved as meeting standards prescribed by Subpart C of this Part; or

2) the related caregiver is awaiting the results of a medical examination completed within 90 days of the child's initial placement; or

3) a waiver as specified in subsection (c) below has been requested and granted.

c) The Director of the Department or designee shall waive specific Approval Standards For Relative Family Homes except for those requirements in Sections 335.302, 335.310 (a) and (b), and 335.312 where a waiver of the particular standard(s) would endanger the health, safety or welfare of the child(ren) involved, or where the waiver would result in a placement for which the federal government refuses to provide funding to the Department or would result in a placement that would pose an obstacle to achieving permanency for the child. Requests for waivers shall be in writing, on a form prescribed by the Department.

d) Waivers granted in accordance with subsection (c) above shall be valid for the duration of approvals granted pursuant to Subpart C of this Part.

Section 335.206 Required Notices and Information

a) The Department shall provide written information to relative caregivers at the time children are placed in their home and to relatives who are being assessed as a placement resource. The information shall explain the difference between private and public guardianship and shall advise the relatives that they have 90 days from the date of placement to come into compliance with the approval standards for relative home caregivers or to be granted a waiver of specific approval standards.

b) The Department shall provide a notice to specified relatives which explains that they may seek a waiver of any approval standards which they have failed to meet, except the standards in Sections 335.302, 335.310(a) and (b) and 335.312 and the Department shall grant waivers of those standards unless the granting of a waiver would:

1) endanger the health, safety, or welfare of the related child; or

2) result in a placement for which the federal government refuses to provide funding to the Department; or

3) pose an obstacle to achieving permanency for the related child.

c) If the Department concludes that a relative home cannot be approved, or a waiver has been requested and denied, or if, as a result of the relative's failure to cooperate with the approval process, the approval review cannot be completed within 90 days, the Department shall send a written notice to the relative caregiver, the child's parent or parents, the child (if over age 7), and the child's attorney

DEPARTMENT OF CHILDREN AND FAMILY SERVICES

NOTICE OF PROPOSED REPEALER

and guardian ad litem which explains that the relative caregiver's home has not met the approval standards for a relative home and that the child will be placed in another home. The notice shall meet the requirements of 89 Ill. Adm. 337, Service Appeals Process, and shall advise the relative that all appeals regarding the move of related children to another placement will be combined.

SUBPART C: APPROVAL STANDARDS FOR RELATIVE FAMILY HOMES

Section 335.300 Provisions Pertaining To Approval

a) Approval of a relative family home shall be valid for four years unless one of the following occurs:
   1) The family moves to an address other than that for which approval was granted;
   2) The related caregiver(s) substantially violates the requirements of this Part so as to endanger the health, safety or welfare of the child(ren). Refusal to cooperate with the supervising agency is a factor taken into consideration in determining whether the violation is substantial;
   3) The specific related children for whom the home was approved no longer reside with the relative caregiver.
b) The related caregiver shall notify the supervising agency within thirty (30) days of a change of address or a change in the family composition. Whenever any of the events specified in subsection (a) above occur, the home shall be submitted for re-evaluation.
c) Ninety days prior to the expiration date of the most recent approval, the home shall be submitted for re-evaluation.
d) The child(ren) shall remain in the home during the re-evaluation provided the requirements of Section 335.200 continue to be met.

Section 335.302 Safety Requirements for the Relative Family Home

a) The home shall be clean, well-ventilated, free from observable hazards, properly lighted and heated, and free of fire hazards.
b) The water supply for the home shall comply with requirements of the local and state health departments. If well water is used, a copy of the Inspection Report and Compliance with Regulations shall be on file with the supervising agency.
c) Portable space heaters may be used as a supplementary source of heat if they meet safety approval standards (Underwriters (Laboratories)) and are used in accordance with local and state building and fire codes. Portable space heaters may not be used in rooms where children are sleeping. Portable and fixed space heaters in areas occupied by children shall be separated by fire resistant partitions or barriers to prevent contact with the heater.
d) Prescription and non-prescription drugs, dangerous household supplies, dangerous tools, weapons, guns, and ammunition shall be kept in a safe

DEPARTMENT OF CHILDREN AND FAMILY SERVICES

NOTICE OF PROPOSED REPEALER

place. Loaded guns shall not be kept in the home unless required by law enforcement officers and maintained and stored in accordance with their safety procedures.
e) Healthy household pets which present no danger to children are permitted. Household pets must be inoculated in accordance with local requirements. There shall be careful supervision of children who are permitted to care for and handle animals.
f) The home shall have access to a telephone in case of an emergency. In cases where the child in care requires special services or frequent medical attention, the related family shall have immediate access to a telephone.
g) The home shall be equipped with a minimum of one operable smoke detector on every floor level, including attic and basement.
h) The home shall have fire and emergency evacuation plans which are to be discussed and routinely rehearsed with the child(ren).
i) None of the standards in this Section may be waived under any circumstances.

Section 335.304 Requirements For Sleeping Arrangements

a) Each child for whom the home is approved shall be provided his or her own bed or crib, except that two related children up to age 10 of the same sex with no more than two years difference in their ages may share a double-sized (or larger) bed.
b) Female children under six years of age may share a sleeping room with one related female adult or a related married couple if provided with their own beds or cribs.
c) Male children under six years of age may share a room with a related adult (male or female) or related married couple if provided with their own beds or cribs.
d) Children over six years of age may share a sleeping room with one related adult of the same sex if provided with their own beds or cribs.
e) Children under six years of age may share a sleeping room with related children of the opposite sex who are also under age 6 if each child is provided with a separate bed or crib.
f) Basements and attics may be used as separate sleeping quarters for children who are mobile, capable of self-preservation, and able to understand and follow directions with minimal assistance in an emergency.
   1) To be used for separate sleeping quarters, basements and attics shall have two exits with one exit leading directly to the outside with means to safely reach ground level. The second exit can be an easily accessible exterior window, operable from the inside without the use of tools, and large enough to accommodate an adult.
   2) Children for whom basement or attic separate sleeping quarters are allowed shall be individually evaluated and approved by the

DEPARTMENT OF CHILDREN AND FAMILY SERVICES

NOTICE OF PROPOSED REPEALER

supervising agency in accordance with the above-cited requirements.

g) The room shall be exposed to an outside window or shall have auxiliary means of ventilation.

h) The springs and mattresses on each bed requiring such shall be level. The bedding shall be suitable for the season.

i) Linens shall be changed at least weekly for all children and as frequently as needed for children not toilet trained, and for those who are enuretic.

j) Waterproof mattress covers shall be provided for all beds or cribs for enuretic children.

k) Any child who is ill or suspected of having a contagious disease shall be isolated from other children until a medical determination has been received that the disease is not contagious or is no longer contagious.

l) Sleeping room shall be comfortable and shall be furnished suitably for the age and sex of the child.

m) Storage space shall be provided to accommodate the personal belongings of each child.

Section 335.306 Nutrition and Meals

a) Meals shall be provided daily to the related children in sufficient quantities to meet the children's nutritional needs.

b) A child requiring a special diet due to medical reasons, allergic reactions, or religious beliefs shall be provided meals in accordance with the child's needs.

c) The home shall consider the child's nutritional needs in relationship to the sex, age, religious beliefs and cultural background of the child. Otherwise, meals served to the child(ren) shall be substantially the same as those served to other family members.

Section 335.310 Qualifications of Relative Family Home

a) The related caregivers shall be related to the child(ren) as defined by this Part, and shall be willing to assume appropriate responsibilities for the child or children for whom care is provided.

b) Related caregivers shall be stable, law abiding, responsible, mature individuals, at least 21 years of age. All adult members of the household age 18 or over shall have authorized the background check required for foster parents in 89 Ill. Adm. Code 380, Background Check of Foster Family Home Applicants, and shall be able to accept agency supervision.

c) Related caregivers shall provide the names and addresses of at least three unrelated references who can attest to their parenting ability and moral character or shall provide the names of school officials where their own children attended school.

d) Unless parental rights are terminated, the related caregivers shall

DEPARTMENT OF CHILDREN AND FAMILY SERVICES

NOTICE OF PROPOSED REPEALER

respect and support the child(ren)'s ties to his or her biological parent(s) and shall cooperate with the supervising agency in this regard.

e) The relative family shall demonstrate an ability to manage their financial resources (income, governmental benefits, other assets) so as to provide basic necessities (shelter, food, clothing, utilities and essential medical care) for themselves and their own child(ren).

f) The conduct or behavior of members of the household shall not endanger the health, safety, or welfare of the child(ren) in care.

g) The operation of other legal business enterprises on the premises, such as beauty shops, tailoring businesses, pet grooming, or 'cottage' industries, is permitted, but shall not interfere with the care of the child(ren) or endanger the health, safety, and welfare of the child(ren).

Section 335.312 Background Inquiry

a) As a condition of approval by the Department, the related caregivers and each adult member of the household shall furnish information of any offenses (other than minor traffic violations) for which they have been charged. The Department shall make a determination concerning their suitability for working with the child(ren) in accordance with this Part, 89 Ill. Adm. Code 380, Background Check of Foster Home Applicants, and Sections 4.1-4.4 of the Child Care Act of 1969 (Ill. Rev. Stat. 1991, ch. 23, par. 2214.1-2214.4) [225 ILCS 10/4.1-4.4].

b) Persons who have been convicted of an offense or who allow persons convicted of an offense to reside in their home shall be automatically rejected as related caregivers. When a person with such a criminal history is present in the home, Department employees designated by the Director of the Department shall review the materials focusing on the relationship between the offense which was the basis for the conviction and the children's health, safety and welfare in that relative family home. The following shall be considered in addition to the criteria in Section 4.2 of the Child Care Act of 1969:

1) The type of crime for which the individual was convicted;
2) The number of crimes for which the individual was convicted;
3) The nature of the offense(s);
4) The age of the individual at the time of the conviction;
5) The length of time that has elapsed since the last conviction;
6) The relationship of the crime and the capacity to care for children;
7) Evidence of rehabilitation; and
8) Opinions of community members concerning the individual in question.

c) If any adult member of the household has been convicted of one of the crimes identified in items (1) through (11) of Section 4.2 of the Child Care Act of 1969, any request for a waiver of this conviction

DEPARTMENT OF CHILDREN AND FAMILY SERVICES

NOTICE OF PROPOSED REPEALER

must be submitted in writing to the Director of the Department for his or her personal approval.

Section 335.314 Health of Relative Family

a) Medical examinations of related caregivers or other members of the household shall be required when, through personal observation of the relative family, the supervising agency has reason to believe that the related caregiver or a member of the household has a disease or physical impairment which would affect the ability to provide care for the child(ren). Medical examinations shall be at the expense of the related caretaker(s) or member of the household.

b) If the supervising agency has a question regarding whether the mental or emotional health of the related caregiver(s) or other member of the household may endanger a child or children in care or there is a concern about a member of the household's use of drugs or alcohol, the supervising agency shall require clinical or medical evaluations and reports to assess the condition. Clinical or medical evaluations shall be at the expense of the Department of Children and Family Services.

Section 335.316 Number of Children Served

The maximum number of children for which a relative family home shall be approved for full-time care shall be eight (including the family's own children and other members of the household under 18 years of age whose parent(s) or guardian does not reside in the home) unless all of the related children for whom the home is approved are of common parentage. The maximum number of eight shall not include other children whose parent(s) or guardian is/are members of the household and assume full responsibility for their care. Nor shall the maximum of eight include children born to or adopted by the related caregivers after the home is initially approved.

Section 335.318 Meeting Basic Needs of Related Children

a) Children in the home shall be treated equitably.

b) Children in the home shall be protected from exploitation, neglect, and abuse. Suspected child abuse or neglect shall be reported to the supervising agency and to the Department immediately.

c) Children under the age of 10 shall not be left in the home without supervision by a responsible person age 15 or over.

d) When the related caregiver(s) is employed or otherwise engaged in activities inside or outside the home, age-appropriate supervision of the children shall be provided. Children shall receive responsible supervision appropriate to their needs, developmental stage, and maturity. When supervision by other than the related caregiver(s) will occur on a regular basis, the plan shall be in writing, and shall be approved by the supervising agency. The supervising agency shall

DEPARTMENT OF CHILDREN AND FAMILY SERVICES

NOTICE OF PROPOSED REPEALER

review and approve the plan only when the health, safety or welfare of the child(ren) is ensured.

e) Each child shall be encouraged to visit his or her parent(s) and other family members in accordance with the provisions of the client service plan unless such visitation has been restricted by court order.

f) Each child shall be given the opportunity to develop social relationships through participation in schools, and other community and group activities. Each child shall have the opportunity to invite friends to the home and to visit in the home of friends.

g) Related caregivers shall assist the child(ren) in the proper handling of money by providing a personal allowance based upon the child(ren)'s age. Personal allowances for the child shall not be less than the amount provided by the child's parent, guardian, or legal custodian.

h) Adolescents may be allowed to earn additional spending money.

i) A reasonable amount of the child's spending money may be saved for future expenditures. Savings over $100 are to be held in a separate account in the child's name.

j) Each child shall have the opportunity to learn to assume some responsibility for himself or herself and for household duties in accordance with his or her age, health, and ability. No child shall be permitted to do tasks which are hazardous, dangerous, or risk harm to the child.

k) Each child shall be provided with his or her own clothing for health, comfort, and physical well-being. Clothing shall be properly fitted and appropriate for the season.

l) Related caregivers shall encourage the child(ren) to engage in appropriate indoor and outdoor recreation.

m) Related caregivers shall cooperate with the supervising agency in providing information about related children in their care, and shall notify the supervising agency of incidents that affect the care of the child, including but not limited to death, serious illness, incarceration, or any other significant occurrence.

Section 335.320 Health Care of Related Children

a) Each child shall have medical and dental check-ups in accordance with the Illinois Department of Public Aid's early periodic screening, diagnosis and treatment program, 89 Ill. Adm. Code 140.485, Healthy Kids Program, or upon medical or dental recommendation.

b) In case of sickness or accident, immediate medical care shall be secured for the child in accordance with the supervising agency's directions.

c) Related caregivers shall keep the supervising agency informed of the child(ren)'s health problems, including alcoholism and drug abuse.

d) No prescription drugs or medicines shall be given to a related child without a physician's prescription or authorization.

e) Related caregivers shall thoroughly acquaint anyone caring for the child(ren) in their absence with the foregoing health requirements.

Section 335.322 Religion

a) Each child shall be given religious instruction in his or her own faith, or that of his or her parent(s), unless there is written consent of the parent(s) or guardian [if residual parental rights have been legally terminated] for the child to participate in religious instruction and to attend the facility of another faith. This shall include consent to baptism or confirmation.

c) Children shall be permitted to participate in religious services either singly or in groups.

Section 335.324 Education

c) Foster parents shall encourage each child to complete high school or vocational training in accordance with his or her aptitude. Foster parent(s) shall cooperate with the supervising agency in the children's educational plan(s).
   The supervising agency shall encourage to participate in extra-curricular activities including sports, art and music to the extent of their interests, abilities, and talents.
   1) Child(ren) is/are placed in appropriate grades and program(s) that maintain contact with those serving the educational needs of the child(ren) and seek their cooperation to assure that
   2) There is periodic evaluation of individual children.
   The supervising agency shall ensure that each child is provided with the necessary school supplies, materials and equipment.

Section 335.326 Discipline of Related Children

a) Discipline shall be appropriate to the age of the child, related to the child's act, and shall not be out of proportion to the particular inappropriate behavior. Discipline shall be handled without prolonged delay.
b) The related caregiver(s) shall never be delegated to the discipline of the child. Discipline shall never be delegated to the child's peer or the child, nor to persons who are strangers to the child.
c) No child shall be subjected to corporal (physical) punishment, verbal abuse, threats or derogatory remarks about the child or his or her family.
d) No child shall be deprived of a meal or part of a meal as punishment.
e) No child shall be deprived of visits with family or other persons with whom he or she has established a parenting bond as punishment.
f) No child shall be deprived of clothing or sleep as punishment.
g) A child may be restricted to an unlocked bedroom for a reasonable period of time. While restricted, the child shall have full access to

sanitary facilities.

h) A child may be temporarily restrained by a person physically holding the child if the child poses a danger to him or herself or to others.
i) The personal spending money of a child may be used as a constructive disciplinary measure to teach the child about responsibility and the consequences of his or her behavior. However, no more than 50% of the child's monthly personal spending money (as provided by parent(s), guardian or supervising agency) shall be withheld for any reason.
   1) Withholding a child's monthly personal spending money shall occur only under the following circumstances:
   A) For reasonable restitution for damages done by the child; or
   B) for breaking the family's rules if the child has been given an oral warning that his or her spending money will be reduced for this infraction.
   2) When a child's spending money has been reduced because he or she has broken a rule, the related caregiver(s) shall keep the withheld money for the child and shall not use it for any other purpose. The related caregiver(s) shall give the child opportunities to earn the money back and shall explain to the child how the spending money can be restored.
   3) Special or additional chores may be assigned as a disciplinary measure.
   k) Privileges may be temporarily removed as a disciplinary measure.

Section 335.328 Emergency Care of Related Children

In the case of an emergency requiring the absence of the related caregiver(s) from the home for a period of 24 hours or longer, the supervising agency must be notified so that appropriate arrangements may be made for the care of the child(ren).

Section 335.330 Release of Children

The related caregiver(s) shall not release a related child to anyone (including the child's own parent or parents) except as authorized by the supervising agency.

Section 335.332 Confidentiality of Information

Information concerning a related child, his or her family and background shall be treated as confidential by all persons involved with the child.

Section 335.334 Required Written Consents

a) The supervising agency shall ensure that written consents from legally responsible persons (parent, court, or other legal custodian or guardian) are obtained for certain acts of a child or performance of certain acts on his or her behalf as required by law, including but

DEPARTMENT OF CHILDREN AND FAMILY SERVICES

NOTICE OF PROPOSED REPEALER

not limited to:
1) health care and treatment, including medical, surgical, psychiatric, psychological, and dental;
2) use of psychoactive drugs;
3) religious instruction and/or church attendance in a different faith than that of the parent(s) or guardian;
4) work programs, induction into the armed services, driving a car and car ownership;
5) visits, trips, or excursions which include out-of-state travel;
6) use of photographs for publicity or other purposes; and
7) consent to marriage for a child under the age of 18.
b) Written consents shall be dated and limited to a specific period of time.
c) Any written or verbal consent or authorization given by persons referred or referenced in paragraph a) above or by others which conflict with any of the requirements of this Part is not valid.

Section 335.336   Records To Be Maintained

a) Records to be maintained by the relative family shall include:
1) the name and date of birth of the child, the legal guardian of the child, religion of the child, and arrangements for education of the child;
2) a record of immunizations the child has received; any physical problems, limitations, or allergies the child has; any current recommendations for special medical care;
3) the name, address, and telephone number of the child's physician, guardian, and supervising agency;
4) the names, addresses, and telephone numbers of persons to contact in case of emergency; and
5) the name(s) of person(s) to whom the child may be released.
b) Records maintained by the family shall be kept current and shall be open to inspection by the supervising agency. All persons who have access to the records shall respect their confidential nature.

Section 335.338   Cooperation With the Supervising Agency and the Department

Authorized representatives of the supervising agency or the Department shall be admitted to the relative family home (during reasonable hours) to determine compliance with these rules and any conditions issued pursuant to these rules accompanying approval of the home.

Section 335.340   Severability of This Part

If any court of competent jurisdiction finds that any rule, clause, phrase, or provision of this Part is unconstitutional or invalid for any reason whatsoever, this finding shall not affect the validity of the remaining portions of this Part.

DEPARTMENT OF CHILDREN AND FAMILY SERVICES

NOTICE OF PROPOSED AMENDMENTS

1) Heading of the Part: Reports of Child Abuse and Neglect

2) Code Citation: 89 Ill. Adm. Code 300

3) Section Numbers: Proposed Action:

300.20	Amend
300.40	Amend
300.80	Amend
300.120	Amend
300.130	Amend
300.150	Amend
300.Appendix B	Amend

4) Statutory Authority: The Abused and Neglected Child Reporting Act [325 ILCS 5]

5) A Complete Description of the Subjects and Issues Involved: Children, who are left in the care of a relative, will not be considered neglected for that reason alone. When services would be beneficial to maintain the child with the relative caregiver, the relative caregiver and the child will be provided services.

In addition Section 300.130, Notices Whether Child Abuse or Neglect Occurred, has been revised to comply with provisions of the B.H. Consent Decree' regarding notifications of child abuse and neglect reports concerning children who are in substitute care settings.

6) Will this proposed amendment replace an emergency rule currently in effect?   No

7) Does this rulemaking contain an automatic repeal date?   No

8) Does this proposed amendment contain incorporations by reference?   No

9) Are there any other amendments pending on this Part?   No

10) Statement of Statewide Policy Objectives   These amendments do not create or expand a State mandate as defined in Section 3(b) of the State Mandates Act [30 ILCS 805/3(b)].

11) Time, Place, and Manner in which interested persons may comment on this proposed rulemaking: Comments on this proposed rulemaking may be submitted in writing for a period of 45 days following publication of this notice. Comments should be submitted to:

Jacqueline Nottingham, Chief
Office of Rules and Procedures

DEPARTMENT OF CHILDREN AND FAMILY SERVICES

NOTICE OF PROPOSED AMENDMENTS

Department of Children and Family Services
406 East Monroe
Springfield, Illinois 62701-1498
Telephone: (217) 524-1983
TTY: (217) 524-3715

The Department will consider fully all written comments on this proposed rulemaking submitted during the 45-day comment period. Comments submitted by small businesses should be identified as such. Public hearings have been scheduled on these proposed amendments in the following areas:

April 11, 1995
7:00 p.m.
Quality Inn at Halsted
One South Halsted
Chicago, Illinois
(312)829-5000

April 13, 1995
7:00 p.m.
State House
Room 212
Springfield, Illinois
(217) 782-2099

Persons are asked to limit their testimony to a maximum of 15 minutes per person. We will gladly accept written testimony at the public hearings. Persons who need translation or interpretation services to enable their commentary should request assistance by contacting the Office of Rules and Procedures.

12) Initial Regulatory Flexibility Analysis: The Department has determined that these proposed amendments do not have an affect on small businesses.

13) State reason(s) for this rulemaking if it was not included in either of the two most recent regulatory agendas. The need for this rulemaking was not foreseen at the time the Department filed its regulatory agendas. A major management initiative affecting home of relative care has prompted the Department to file these amendments at the present time in order to implement them at the start of the next fiscal year.

The full text of the proposed amendment begins on the next page.

DEPARTMENT OF CHILDREN AND FAMILY SERVICES

NOTICE OF PROPOSED AMENDMENTS

TITLE 89: SOCIAL SERVICES
CHAPTER III: DEPARTMENT OF CHILDREN AND FAMILY SERVICES
SUBCHAPTER a: SERVICE DELIVERY

PART 300
REPORTS OF CHILD ABUSE AND NEGLECT

AUTHORITY: Implementing and authorized by the Abused and Neglected Child Reporting Act (325 ILCS 5) and Section 3 of the Consent by Minors to Medical Procedures Act (410 ILCS 210/3].

SOURCE: Adopted and codified as 89 Ill. Adm. Code 302 at 5 Ill. Reg. 13188, effective November 30, 1981; amended at 6 Ill. Reg. 15529, effective January 1, 1983; recodified at 8 Ill. Reg. 992; peremptory amendment at 8 Ill. Reg. 5373, effective April 12, 1984; amended at 8 Ill. Reg. 12143, effective July 9, 1984; amended at 9 Ill. Reg. 2467, effective March 1, 1985; amended at 9 Ill. Reg. 9104, effective June 14, 1985; amended at 9 Ill. Reg. 15820, effective November 1, 1985; amended at 10 Ill. Reg. 5915, effective April 15, 1986; amended at II Ill. Reg. 1390, effective January 13, 1987; amended at 11 Ill. Reg. 1151, effective January 14, 1987; amended at 11 Ill. Reg. 1829, effective January 15, 1987; recodified from 89 Ill. Adm. Code 302.20, 302.100, 302.110, 302.120, 302.130, 302.140, 302.150, 302.160, 302.170, 302.180, 302.190, and Appendix A at 11 Ill. Reg. 3492; emergency amendments at 11 Ill. Reg. 4058, effective February 20, 1987, for a maximum of 150 days; amended at 11 Ill. Reg. 12619, effective July 20, 1987; recodified at 11 Ill. Reg. 13405; amended at 13 Ill. Reg. 2419, effective March 1, 1989; emergency amendment at 14 Ill. Reg. 11356, effective July 1, 1990, for a maximum of 150 days; amended at 14 Ill. Reg.

DEPARTMENT OF CHILDREN AND FAMILY SERVICES

NOTICE OF PROPOSED AMENDMENTS

17558, effective October 15, 1990; amended at 14 Ill. Reg. 19827, effective November 28, 1990; emergency amendment at 15 Ill. Reg. 14285, effective September 25, 1991; amended at 15 Ill. Reg. 17986, effective December 1, 1991; emergency amendment at 17 Ill. Reg. 15658, effective September 10, 1993, for a maximum of 150 days; emergency amendment expired February 7, 1994; amended at 18 Ill. Reg. 8377, effective May 31, 1994; amended at 18 Ill. Reg. 8601, effective June 1, 1994; amended at 19 Ill. Reg. 3469, effective March 15, 1995; amended at 19 Ill. Reg. _____, effective _____.

Section 300.20 Definitions

"Abused Child" means a child whose parent or immediate family member, or any person responsible for the child's welfare, or any individual residing in the same home as the child, or a paramour of the child's parent:

> inflicts, causes to be inflicted, or allows to be inflicted upon such child physical or mental injury, by other than accidental means, which causes death, disfigurement, impairment of physical or emotional health, or loss or impairment of any bodily function;
> creates a substantial risk of physical or mental injury to such child by other than accidental means which would be likely to cause death, disfigurement, impairment of physical or emotional health, or loss of or impairment of any bodily function;
> commits or allows to be committed any sex offense against such child, as such sex offenses are defined in the Criminal Code of 1961, as amended, and extending those definitions of sex offenses to include children under 18 years of age;
> commits or allows to be committed an act or acts of torture upon such child; or
> inflicts excessive corporal punishment. [~~111~~--~~Rev~~--~~Stat~~--~~1991~~,~~ch.~~~~23~~,~~par.~~~~2053~~] [325 ILCS 5/3]

"~~Caretaker~~" "Caregiver" means the child's parent(s), guardian, or custodian or relative caregiver with whom the child lives and who has primary responsibility for the care and supervision of the child.

"Child" means any person under the age of 18 years, unless legally emancipated by reason of marriage or entry into a branch of the United States armed services.

~~"Child care facility" means any person, group of persons, agency, association, or organization which arranges for or cares for children unrelated to the operator of the facility, apart from the parents. Child care facilities may be established for profit or non-for-profit. "Child care facility" is further defined in Section 2.05 of the Child Care Act and includes foster family homes and day care homes.~~

DEPARTMENT OF CHILDREN AND FAMILY SERVICES

NOTICE OF PROPOSED AMENDMENTS

"Child care facility" means any person, group of persons, agency, association or organization, whether established for gain or otherwise, who or which receives or arranges for care or placement of one or more children, unrelated to the operator of the facility, apart from the parents, with or without the transfer of the right of custody in any facility as defined in the Child Care Act of 1969, established *and maintained for the care of children [225 ILCS 10/2.05]. Child care facility includes a relative who is licensed as a foster family home pursuant to Section 4 of the Child Care Act of 1969 [225 ILCS 10/4].*

"Child Protective Service Unit" (CPS) means certain specialized State employees of the Department assigned by the Director or his designee to perform the duties and responsibilities as provided under this Part. They are also known as investigative staff. [~~Ill.--Rev.--Stat.~~ ~~1991,--ch.--23,--par.--2053~~] [325 ILCS 5/3]

"Children for whom the Department is legally responsible" means children for whom the Department has temporary protective custody, custody or guardianship via court order, or children whose parent(s) has signed an adoptive surrender or voluntary placement agreement with the Department.

"Collateral contact" means obtaining information concerning a child, parent, or other person responsible for the child from a person who has knowledge of the family situation but was not directly involved in referring the child or family to the Department for services.

"Credible evidence of child abuse or neglect" means that the available facts when viewed in light of surrounding circumstances would cause a reasonable person to believe that a child was abused or neglected.

"Delegation of an investigation" means the decision whether a report of child abuse or neglect was "indicated" or "unfounded" has been deferred to another authority. The Department maintains responsibility for entering information about the report in the State Central Register and for notifying the subjects of the report and mandated reporters of the results of the investigation.

"Department," as used in this Part, means the Department of Children and Family Services.

"Determination" means a final Department decision about whether there is credible evidence that child abuse or neglect occurred. A determination must be either "indicated" or "unfounded."

"Disfigurement" means a serious or protracted blemish, scar, or deformity that spoils a person's appearance or limits bodily

DEPARTMENT OF CHILDREN AND FAMILY SERVICES

NOTICE OF PROPOSED AMENDMENTS

functions.

"Formal investigation" means those activities conducted by Department investigative staff necessary to make a determination as to whether a report of suspected child abuse or neglect is indicated or unfounded. Such activities shall include: an evaluation of the environment of the child named in the report and any other children in the same environment; a determination of the risk to such children if they continue to remain in the existing environments, as well as a determination of the nature, extent and cause of any condition enumerated in such report, the name, age and condition of other children in the environment; and an evaluation as to whether there would be an immediate and urgent necessity to remove the child from the environment if appropriate family preservation services were provided. After seeing to the safety of the child or children, the Department shall forthwith notify the subjects of the report in writing, of the existence of the report and their rights existing under this Act in regard to amendment or expungement. [Ill. Rev. Stat. 1991, ch. 23, par. 2053] [325 ILCS 5/3]

"Indicated Report" means any report of child abuse or neglect made to the Department for which it is determined, after an investigation, that credible evidence of the alleged abuse or neglect exists.

"Initial Investigation" means those activities conducted by Department investigative staff to determine whether a report of suspected child abuse or neglect is a good faith indication of abuse or neglect and, therefore, requires a formal investigation. Good faith in this context means that the report was made with the honest intention to identify actual child abuse or neglect.

"Initial Oral Report" means a report alleging child abuse or neglect for which the State Central Register has no prior records on the family.

"Involved Subject" means a child who is the alleged victim of child abuse or neglect or a person who is the alleged perpetrator of the child abuse or neglect.

"Local law enforcement agency" means the police of a city, town, village or other incorporated area or the sheriff of an unincorporated area or any sworn officer of the Illinois Department of State Police.

"Mandated reporters" means those individuals required to report suspected child abuse or neglect to the Department. A list of these persons and their associated responsibilities is provided in Section 300.30 of this Part.

DEPARTMENT OF CHILDREN AND FAMILY SERVICES

NOTICE OF PROPOSED AMENDMENTS

"Neglected child" means any child who is not receiving the proper or necessary nourishment or medically indicated treatment including food or care not provided solely on the basis of present or anticipated mental or physical impairment as determined by a physician acting alone or in consultation with other physicians or otherwise is not receiving the proper or necessary support, or medical or other remedial care recognized under State law as necessary for a child's well-being (including where there is harm or substantial risk of harm to the child's health or welfare), or other care necessary for a child's well-being, including adequate food, clothing and shelter; or who is abandoned by his or her parents or other person responsible for the child's welfare without a proper plan of care; or who is a newborn infant whose blood and urine contains any amount of controlled substance as defined in subsection (f) of Section 102 of the Illinois Controlled Substances Act or a metabolite thereof, with the exception of a controlled substance or metabolite thereof whose presence in the newborn infant is the result of medical treatment administered to the mother or newborn infant. A child shall not be considered neglected for the sole reason that the child's parent or other person responsible for his or her welfare has left the child in the care of an adult relative for any period of time-as-a-plan-of-care. A child shall not be considered neglected or abused for the sole reason that such child's parent or other person responsible for his or her welfare depends upon spiritual means through prayer alone for the treatment or cure of disease or remedial care under Section 4 of the Abused and Neglected Child Reporting Act. Where the circumstances indicate harm or substantial risk of harm to the child's health or welfare and necessary medical care is not being provided to treat or prevent that harm or risk of harm because such parent or other person responsible for the child's welfare depends upon spiritual means alone for treatment or cure, such child is subject to the requirements of this Act for the reporting of, investigation of, and provision of protective services with respect to such child and his health needs, and in such cases spiritual means through prayer alone for the treatment or cure of disease or for remedial care will not be recognized as a substitute for such necessary medical care, if the Department or, as necessary, a juvenile court determines that medical care is necessary. A child shall not be considered neglected or abused solely because the child is not attending school in accordance with the requirements of Article 26 of the School Code. [Ill. Rev. Stat. 1991, ch. 23, par. 2053] [325 ILCS 5/3]

"Perpetrator" means a person who, as a result of investigation, has been determined by the Department to have caused child abuse or neglect.

"Person responsible for the child's welfare" means the child's parent, relative caregiver, guardian, custodian, foster parent, an operator,

DEPARTMENT OF CHILDREN AND FAMILY SERVICES

NOTICE OF PROPOSED AMENDMENTS

supervisor, or employee of a public or private residential agency or institution or public or private profit or not-for-profit child care facility; or any other person responsible for the child's welfare at the time of the alleged abuse or neglect, or any person who came to know the child through an official capacity or position of trust, including but not limited to health care professionals, educational personnel, recreational supervisors, and volunteers or support personnel in any setting where children may be subject to abuse or neglect. [Ill. Rev. Stat. 1991, ch. 23, par. 2059] (325 ILCS 5/3)

"Relative caregiver" means a person 21 years of age or older, other than the parent, who has physical custody of the child and to whom the child has any of the following currently existing relationships by blood or adoption: grandparent, sibling, great grandparent, uncle, aunt, nephew, niece, first cousin, great uncle, great aunt, or who is the spouse of such a relative or who is the child's step-father, step-mother, step-brother or step-sister.

"Subject of a report" means any child reported to the child abuse/neglect State Central Register, and his or her parent, personal guardian or other person responsible for the child's welfare who is named in the report.

"Temporary protective custody" means custody within a hospital or other medical facility or a place previously designated by the Department, subject to review by the Court. Temporary protective custody cannot exceed 48 hours excluding Saturdays, Sundays and holidays.

"Undetermined report" means any report of child abuse or neglect made to the Department in which it was not possible to complete an investigation within 60 days on the basis of information provided to the Department.

"Unfounded report" means any report of child abuse or neglect for which it is determined, after an investigation, that no credible evidence of the alleged abuse or neglect exists.

(Source: Amended at 19 Ill. Reg. _____, effective _____)

Section 300.40 Content of Child Abuse or Neglect Reports

The State Central Register or the local report-taker shall attempt to secure the following information from the reporter:
  a) family composition, including the name, age, sex, race, ethnicity, and address of the children named in the report and any other children in the environment;

DEPARTMENT OF CHILDREN AND FAMILY SERVICES

NOTICE OF PROPOSED AMENDMENTS

  b) name, age, sex, race, ethnicity and address of the children's parents, caregiver, if different from the parent(s), and if different, the relationship of the caregiver to the child(ren), and of the alleged perpetrator and his/her relationship to the child subjects;
  c) the physical harm to the involved children and an estimation of the children's present physical, medical, and environmental condition. This estimation should include information concerning any previous incidents of suspected child abuse or neglect; and
  d) the reporter's name, occupation and relationship to the children, actions taken by the reporter, where the reporter can be reached, and other information the reporter believes will be of assistance.

(Source: Amended at 19 Ill. Reg. _____, effective _____)

Section 300.80 Delegation of the Investigation

The Department may delegate the investigation of the child abuse or neglect report to:
  a) the local police, sheriff's office, other law enforcement agency, or the State's Attorney, when they are concurrently conducting a criminal investigation of the same incidents and allegations; or
  b) a coroner or medical examiner who is investigating the cause of death of a child who may have been the victim of child abuse or neglect; or
  c) a licensed child welfare agency or private social service agency agencies which had been designated for this purpose by the Department prior to July 1, 1986; or
  d) the Department of State Police, when the investigation involves suspected child abuse or neglect perpetrated by State employees acting in their official capacity or in State facilities or institutions.

(Source: Amended at 19 Ill. Reg. _____, effective _____)

Section 300.120 Taking Children Into Temporary Protective Custody

  a) Local law enforcement officers, Department investigative staff, and physicians treating a child may take temporary protective custody of a child without the consent of the person(s) responsible for the child's welfare, if they have reason to believe that:
    1) leaving the child in the home or in the care and custody of the child's caretaker caregiver presents an imminent danger to the child's life or health. The child shall not be taken into protective custody for the sole reason that the child was left with a relative, the relative is willing to keep the child, and the Department has reason to believe that the relative can adequately and safely care for the child; and
    2) there is insufficient time to obtain a Juvenile Court order

authorizing temporary custody.

b) In addition to the above requirements, Department investigative staff shall have decided that in-home services would not sufficiently protect the child before Department staff take temporary protective custody of a child.

c) Local law enforcement officers or physicians who take temporary protective custody of a child must immediately notify the Department of their action.

d) When taking temporary protective custody of a child or receiving a child who was taken into temporary protective custody by the local law enforcement officer or by a physician, Department investigative staff shall:

1) immediately notify the State Central Register of this action;

2) make every reasonable effort to notify the child's parents, personal guardian, or legal custodian <u>or relative caregiver</u> of the action;

3) request that the Guardianship Administrator or designee authorize any ordinary medical care or treatment necessary for those children taken into temporary protective custody;

4) if the child needs treatment of an emergency nature and the parent or guardian is unavailable or unwilling to provide consent, the physician or hospital shall be asked to proceed under ~~"AN ACT in relation to the performance of medical, dental or surgical procedures on and counseling for minors" (Ill. Rev. Stat. 1989, ch. 111, par. 4501 et seq.)~~ <u>the Consent by Minors to Medical Procedures Act [410 ILCS 210]</u>, which allows treatment to be given to minors without consent; and

5) obtain a shelter care hearing under the provisions of the Juvenile Court Act within 48 hours, excluding Saturdays, Sundays, and holidays, in order to retain custody for more than 48 hours.

(Source: Amended   at   19   Ill.   Reg.   _____,   effective _____)

Section 300.130 Notices Whether Child Abuse or Neglect Occurred

a) Written Notices of Decision

The Department provides a written notice to mandated reporters who reported suspected child abuse or neglect as well as to the child's parent, personal guardian, ~~or~~ legal custodian, <u>or relative caregiver;</u> the Juvenile Court Judge (when a State ward is involved); and the alleged perpetrator concerning the final determination of the report.

b) Mandated Reporters

1) Mandated reporters who have reported suspected child abuse or neglect are informed via a written notice that a formal investigation was conducted. The written notice also provides an explanation of how further information on an indicated report may be secured. Department staff will notify them in writing:

A) ~~whether~~ <u>of the name of</u> the child <u>who</u> was the subject of a report of abuse or neglect;

B) whether the report was indicated or unfounded;

C) whether the Department took temporary protective custody.

2) Requests for additional information must be directed, in writing, to the State Central Register and must include:

A) the identity of the requestor;

B) the subject(s) name for whom the record is requested;

C) a notary public's attestation as to the identity of the requestor;

D) the purpose of the request.

3) Upon receipt of an appropriate request, only the following information will be disclosed to the mandated reporter:

A) whether a Department case has been opened for the family or children; and

B) what Department services are being provided to the family or children.

4) All requested information is sent in writing through certified mail and is deliverable only to the mandated reporter who made the request.

c) Parents, Personal Guardians, Legal Custodians, <u>Relative Caregivers,</u> and Alleged Perpetrators

1) Custodial and non-custodial parents, personal guardians, or legal custodians, <u>or relative caregivers</u> of child subjects, and alleged perpetrators shall receive notification within ~~5~~ <u>five</u> calendar days after the report has been indicated or unfounded which indicate that the allegations were either:

A) unfounded, and that all identifying information in the computer and local index files will be ~~destroyed unless the subjects request that they be retained~~ <u>retained in accordance with 89 Ill. Adm. Code 431, Confidentiality of Information of Persons Served by the Department;</u> or

B) indicated, and all Department records will be maintained intact.

2) In addition, written notices shall explain that:

A) the subjects of the report have access to the Department's records on the report, with the exception of the identity of the reporter or other persons who cooperated in the investigation;

B) the subjects of the report have the right to request a review of the determination that the report was indicated including the decision to maintain a record of the report in the Department's computer and local index files. 89 Ill. Adm. Code 336, Appeal of Child Abuse and Neglect Investigation Findings, fully explains the Department's review and appeal process; and

C) the subjects of the report may request, within 10 days of the date on the written notice, that an unfounded report be

DEPARTMENT OF CHILDREN AND FAMILY SERVICES

NOTICE OF PROPOSED AMENDMENTS

retained in the Department's computer and local index files,
if the subjects of the report believe the report was not
made in good faith. All such requests will be honored.

d) Other Parties
The Department shall notify, in writing, those supervisors or
administrators referenced in Section 300.100(1) of this Part whether a
report involving the person(s) they supervise was indicated or
unfounded and, if unfounded, that Section 13 of the Personnel Record
Review Act (Ill. Rev. Stat. 1991, ch. 48, par. 2013) [820 ILCS 40/13]
requires that any record of the investigation must be expunged from
the employee's personnel records. The Department shall also notify
the employee, in writing, that notification has been sent to the
employer informing the employer that the Department's investigation
has resulted in an unfounded report. The notice to the employee shall
also contain a statement of the employee's right to take the notice to
the employer to have any record of the investigation expunged from the
employee's record.

e) Child Abuse and Neglect Reports on Children in Department Custody
1) When a child is reported to the Department as being abused or
neglected while in a foster home or relative home placement,
whether by the foster parent, caregiver, or any other person in
the placement, the Department shall promptly notify the following
persons when the report has been made, when an investigation is
pending, an investigation has been initiated and when the report
has been indicated or unfounded:
A) the parent(s) or private guardian(s) of the alleged abuse or
neglect victim;
B) all Department caseworkers or case managers responsible for
the alleged victim and for any other children in the same
foster home or relative home placement;
C) the Department's Bureau of Quality Assurance which shall be
those persons designated by the Director as responsible for
evaluating the investigation and the disposition of the
report;
D) Department staff responsible for licensing and making
placements with the facility.
2) When a child is reported to the Department as being abused or
neglected while in residential placement, the Department shall
promptly notify the following persons when the report has been
made, an investigation is pending, and when the report has been
indicated or unfounded:
A) the parent(s) or private guardian(s) of the alleged abuse or
neglect victim;
B) those Department caseworkers or case managers responsible
for the alleged victim, for each child alleged to be a
witness to the incident, and for each child alleged to be a
perpetrator of the incident;
C) those persons designated by the Director responsible for

DEPARTMENT OF CHILDREN AND FAMILY SERVICES

NOTICE OF PROPOSED AMENDMENTS

evaluating the investigation and the disposition of the
report;
D) Department staff responsible for licensing and making
placements with the facility.
2)3) The Department shall notify the following when a report
involving a child in Department custody is indicated:
A) the Juvenile Court. If services are being provided by the
Department or its providers, the notice shall also give the
name and location of the Department office serving the
children;
B) the Department's administrative case reviewer responsible
for reviewing the case plans of the children involved.
3)4) The Department shall transmit a copy of the report to the
guardian ad litem appointed under the Juvenile Court Act of 1987
when a report has been indicated, unfounded, or undetermined and
the minor who is the subject of the report is also the minor for
whom the guardian ad litem has been appointed.

(Source: Amended at 19 Ill. Reg. _____, effective
_____)

Section 300.150 Referral for Services

a) When an investigative worker determines that a report is indicated,
the parents or caretakers caregivers may be given the opportunity to
cooperate with the Department through services provided or arranged
for by the Department. When the parents or caretakers caregivers are
unwilling or unable to cooperate, or when legal custody or
guardianship through the Department is necessary to protect the child,
the worker may seek court intervention.
b) When the investigative worker determines that a report is unfounded
but the family, including a relative caregiver, may need services, the
worker shall:
1) inform the family of available child welfare services and refer
the family for services, if requested; or
2) provide information regarding other community resources.
c) If the report is unfounded and the family does not want services, the
worker shall make no recommendation for additional services.
d) The Department will may offer services to any child or family,
including a relative caregiver, who is the subject of the report of
child abuse or neglect prior to making a determination of indicated or
unfounded when the family is in immediate need of services or there is
an imminent danger to the child's life or health. However, the
child's or family's willingness to accept services shall not be
considered in making the determination of indicated or unfounded.
e) When the State Central Register does not accept a report of abuse or
neglect because the sole reason for the report was that a child was
left in the care of a relative, the State Central Register may:

DEPARTMENT OF CHILDREN AND FAMILY SERVICES

NOTICE OF PROPOSED AMENDMENTS

1) Inform the relative of available child welfare services and refer the relative for services, if requested; or

2) Provide information to the relative regarding other community resources.

(Source: Amended at 19 Ill. Reg. _____, effective _____

DEPARTMENT OF CHILDREN AND FAMILY SERVICES

NOTICE OF PROPOSED AMENDMENTS

Section 300.APPENDIX B Child Abuse and Neglect Allegations

This Appendix describes the specific incidents of harm which must be alleged to have been caused by the acts or omissions of the persons identified in Section 3 of the Abused and Neglected Child Reporting Act before the Department will accept a report of child abuse or neglect. The allegation definitions focus upon the harm or the risk of harm to the child. Many of the allegations of harm can be categorized as resulting from either abuse or neglect. All abuse allegations of harm are coded with a one or two digit number under thirty. All neglect allegations of harm are coded with a two digit number greater than fifty. In addition each allegation is coded with a priority number, either I, II or III. This priority number ranges from the most serious, Level I, to the least serious, Level III. The allegations of harm, with their assigned priority number in parenthesis, are defined as follows:

Allegation #	Definition
1/51	Death (Priority 1)

Permanent cessation of all vital functions.

The following definitions of death are also commonly used:

- Total, irreversible cessation of cerebral function, spontaneous function of the respiratory system, and spontaneous function of the circulatory system.
- The final and irreversible cessation of perceptible heart beat and respiration.

Verification of death must come from a physician or coroner.

2/52	Brain Damage/Skull Fracture (Priority 1)

Brain damage means injury to the large, soft mass of nerve tissue contained within the cranium skull. Skull fracture means a broken bone in the skull.

Verification of brain damage or skull fracture must come from a physician, preferably a neurosurgeon or radiologist.

3/53	Subdural Hematoma (Priority 1)

Hematoma

A swelling or mass of blood (usually clotted) confined to an organ, tissue or space and caused by a break in a blood vessel.

DEPARTMENT OF CHILDREN AND FAMILY SERVICES

NOTICE OF PROPOSED AMENDMENTS

Allegation #	Definition

Subdural

Beneath the dura mater (the outer membrane covering the spinal cord and brain).

A subdural hematoma is located beneath the membrane covering the brain and is usually the result of head injuries or the shaking of a small child or infant. It may result in loss of consciousness, seizures, mental or physical damage, or death.

Verification of subdural hematoma must come from a physician.

4/54   Internal Injuries (Priority I)

An internal injury is an injury which is not visible from the outside, e.g. an injury to the organs occupying the thoracic or abdominal cavities. Such injury may result from a direct blow. A person so injured may be pale, cold, perspiring freely, have an anxious expression, or may seem semicomatose. Pain is usually intense at first, and may continue or gradually diminish as patient grows worse.

Verification of internal injuries must come from a physician.

5/55   Burns/Scalding (Priority II)

Burns

Tissue injury resulting from excessive exposure to thermal, chemical, electrical or radioactive agents. The effects vary according to the type, duration and intensity of the agent and the part of the body involved. Burns are usually classified as:

First Degree

Superficial burns, damage being limited to the outer layer of skin. Scorching or painful redness of the skin.

Second Degree

DEPARTMENT OF CHILDREN AND FAMILY SERVICES

NOTICE OF PROPOSED AMENDMENTS

Allegation #	Definition

The damage extends through the outer layer of the skin into the inner layers. Blistering will be present within 24 hours.

Third Degree

Burns in which the skin is destroyed with damage extending into underlying tissues, which may be charred or coagulated.

Scalding

A burn to the skin or flesh caused by moist heat and hot vapors, as steam.

All emersion burns (scalds) must be confirmed by a physician unless the alleged perpetrator has admitted to scalding the child.

6/56   Poison/Noxious Substances (Priority II)

Poison

Any substance, other than mood altering chemicals or alcohol, taken into the body by ingestion, inhalation, injection, or absorption that interferes with normal physiological functions. (Virtually any substance can be poisonous if consumed in sufficient quantity; therefore, the term poison more often implies an excessive amount rather than a specific group of substances.)

Noxious

Harmful, injurious, not wholesome.

Verification must come from a physician or by a direct admission from the alleged perpetrator.

7/57   Wounds (Priority I)

A gunshot or stabbing injury.

Verification must come from a physician, a law enforcement officer or by a direct admission from the alleged perpetrator.

DEPARTMENT OF CHILDREN AND FAMILY SERVICES

NOTICE OF PROPOSED AMENDMENTS

Allegation #	Definition

8   No allegation.

9/59   Bone Fractures (Priority II)

A fracture is a broken bone. There are ten types of
fractures, the most common being:

Chip Fracture

A small piece of bone is flaked from the major part of the
bone.

Simple Fracture

The bone is broken, but there is no external wound.

Complicated Fractures

   Compound
   The bone is broken, and there is an external wound
   leading down to the site of fracture or fragments
   of bone protrude through the skin.
   Comminuted
   The bone is broken or splintered into pieces.
   Spiral
   Twisting causes the line of the fracture to
   encircle the bone in the form of a spiral.

Verification must come from a physician or radiologist.

10   No allegation.

11/61   Cuts, Bruises and Welts (Priority II)

Cut

An opening, incision or break in the skin made by some
external agent.

Bruise

An injury which results in bleeding within the skin, where
the skin is discolored but not broken.

Welt

DEPARTMENT OF CHILDREN AND FAMILY SERVICES

NOTICE OF PROPOSED AMENDMENTS

Allegation #	Definition

An elevation on the skin produced by a lash, blow, or
allergic stimulus. The skin is not broken and the mark is
reversible.

Factors to be Considered

Not every cut, bruise, or welt constitutes an allegation of
harm. The following factors should be considered when
determining whether an injury which resulted in cuts,
bruises or welts constitute an allegation of harm:

-   the child's age (children aged 6 and under are at a
    much greater risk of harm).
-   child's medical condition, behavioral, mental, or
    emotional problems, developmental disability, or
    physical handicap, particularly as they relate to the
    child's ability to protect himself or herself.
-   pattern or chronicity of similar incidents.
-   severity of the cuts, bruises, or welts (size, number,
    depth, extent of discoloration).
-   location of the cuts, bruises, or welts.
-   whether an instrument was used on the child.
-   previous history of indicated abuse or neglect.

12/62   Human Bites (Priority II)

A bruise, cut or indentation in the skin caused by seizing,
piercing, or cutting the skin with human teeth.

13/63   Sprains/Dislocations (Priority II)

Sprain

Trauma to a joint which causes pain and disability
depending upon the degree of injury to ligaments. In a
severe sprain, ligaments may be completely torn. The signs
are rapid swelling, heat and disability, often
discoloration and limitation of function.

Dislocation

The displacement of any part, especially the temporary
displacement of a bone from its normal position in a joint.
Types include:

   Complicated

DEPARTMENT OF CHILDREN AND FAMILY SERVICES

NOTICE OF PROPOSED AMENDMENTS

Allegation #	Definition

A dislocation associated with other major injuries.
Compound
    Dislocation in which the joint is exposed to the
    external air.
Closed
    A simple dislocation.
Complete
    A dislocation which completely separates the
    surfaces of a joint.

Verification must come from a physician, registered nurse,
licensed practical nurse or by a direct admission from the
alleged perpetrator.

14   Tying/Close Confinement (Priority II)

Unreasonable restriction of a child's mobility, actions or
physical functioning by tying the child to a fixed (or
heavy) object, tying limbs together or forcing the child to
remain in a closely confined area which restricts physical
movement. Examples include, but are not limited to:

-   locking a child in a closet.
-   tying one or more limbs to a bed, chair, or other
    object except as authorized by a licensed physician.
-   tying a child's hands behind his back.

15/65   Substance Misuse (Priority II)

The consumption of a mood altering chemical capable of
intoxication to the extent that it harmfully affects the
child's health, behavior, motor coordination, judgment, or
intellectual capability. Mood altering chemicals include
cannabis (marijuana), hallucinogens, stimulants (including
cocaine), sedatives (including alcohol and Valium),
narcotics, or inhalants.

Fetal alcohol syndrome or drug withdrawal at birth caused
by the mother's addiction to drugs is included in this
definition and is considered child neglect. Also included
is any amount of a controlled substance or a metabolite
thereof, found in the blood , urine or meconium (newborn's
first stool) of a newborn infant. A controlled substance
is defined in subsection (f) of Section 102 of the Illinois
Controlled Substances Act [720 ILCS 570/102]. The
presence of such substances shall not be considered as

DEPARTMENT OF CHILDREN AND FAMILY SERVICES

NOTICE OF PROPOSED AMENDMENTS

Allegation #	Definition

child neglect if the presence is due to medical treatment
of the mother or infant.

NOTE: Methadone withdrawal or other withdrawal verified as
under the auspices of a drug treatment program is not
included under drug withdrawal at birth.

Examples of substance misuse include, but are not limited
to:

-   giving a minor (unless prescribed by a physician) any
    amount of heroin, giving a minor (unless prescribed by
    a physician) any amount of heroin, cocaine, morphine,
    peyote, LSD, PCP, pentazocine, or methaqualone or
    encouraging, insisting, or permitting a minor's
    consumption of the above substances.
-   giving any mood altering substance, including alcohol
    or sedatives, unless prescribed by a physician, to an
    infant or toddler.
-   encouraging, insisting or permitting a child who has
    not reached puberty to consume alcohol, drugs, or
    another mood altering substance on a regular or
    frequent basis.
-   encouraging, insisting or permitting an adolescent to
    consume alcohol, drugs, or another mood altering
    substance on a daily basis.
-   encouraging, insisting or permitting any minor to
    become intoxicated by alcohol, drugs, or another mood
    altering substance even if on an infrequent basis.

Factors to be Considered

The following factors should be considered when determining
whether a child is involved in substance misuse.

-   age of the child.
-   frequency of substance misuse.
-   amount of substance consumption.
-   whether the substance is illegal.
-   degree of behavioral dysfunction, or physical
    impairment linked to substance misuse.
-   the child's culture, particularly as it relates to use
    of alcohol in religious ceremonies or on special
    occasions.

DEPARTMENT OF CHILDREN AND FAMILY SERVICES

NOTICE OF PROPOSED AMENDMENTS

Allegation #   Definition

- whether the parent or ~~caretaker's~~ caregiver's attempts
  to control an older child's substance misuse or to seek
  help for the child's substance misuse were reasonable
  under the circumstances.
- whether the parent or ~~caretaker~~ caregiver knew or
  should have known of the child's substance misuse.

16   Torture (Priority I)

Deliberately and/or systematically inflicting unusual or
cruel treatment which results in physical or mental
suffering.

17/67   Mental Injury (Priority II)

Injury to the intellectual, emotional or psychological
development of a child as evidenced by observable and
substantial impairment in the child's ability to function
within a normal range of performance and behavior, with due
regard to his or her culture.

Verification that a child has been mentally injured must
come from a medical doctor, registered psychologist,
certified social worker, registered nurse or professional
employee of a community mental health agency.

18   Sexually Transmitted Diseases (Priority I)

A disease which was acquired originally as a result of
sexual penetration or sexual conduct with an individual who
is afflicted. The diseases may include, but are not
limited to:

    Gonorrhea
    Nonspecific Urethritis
    Syphilis
    Chancroid
    Genital Candidiasis
- Lymphogranuloma Venereum
    Granuloma Inguinale
    Genital Herpes
    Genital Warts
    Balanoposthitis
    Proctitis
    Neisseria Gonorrhea
    Chlamydia Trachomatis

DEPARTMENT OF CHILDREN AND FAMILY SERVICES

NOTICE OF PROPOSED AMENDMENTS

Allegation #   Definition

    Treponema Pallidum
    Haemophilus Ducreyi
    Calymmatobacterium Granulomatis
- Trichomonas Vaginalis (Symptomatic)
    AIDS

Sexual penetration is defined in the Illinois Criminal
Sexual Assault Act as "any contact, however slight, between
the sex organ or anus of one person by an object, the sex
organ, mouth or anus of another person, or any intrusion,
however slight, of any part of the body of one person or
any animal or object into the sex organ or anus of another
person, including but not limited to cunnilingus, fellatio
or anal penetration."

Sexual conduct is defined in the Act as "any intentional or
knowing touching or fondling of the victim or the
perpetrator, either directly or through clothing of the sex
organs, anus or breast of the victim or the accused, or any
part of the body of a child . . . for the purpose of sexual
gratification or arousal of the victim or the accused."

Verification of sexually transmitted diseases must come
from a medical source.

19   Sexual Penetration (Priority I)

Any contact, however slight, between the sex organ or anus
of one person by an object, the sex organ, mouth or anus
of another person, or any intrusion, however slight, of any
part of the body of one person or any animal or object into
the sex organ or anus of another person. This includes
acts commonly known as oral sex (cunnilingus, fellatio),
anal penetration, coition, coitus, and copulation.

20   Sexual Exploitation (Priority I)

Sexual use of a child for sexual arousal, gratification,
advantage, or profit. This includes but is not limited to:

- indecent solicitation of a child/explicit verbal
  enticement.
    child pornography.
- exposing sexual organs to a child for the purpose of
  sexual arousal or gratification.
- forcing the child to watch sexual acts.

DEPARTMENT OF CHILDREN AND FAMILY SERVICES

NOTICE OF PROPOSED AMENDMENTS

Allegation #   Definition

- self-masturbation in the child's presence.

NOTE: Sexual penetration and molestation are excluded
        from this allegation. They are listed as separate
        allegations.

21   Sexual Molestation (Priority I)

Sexual conduct with a child when such contact, touching or
interaction is used for arousal or gratification of sexual
needs or desires. Examples include, but are not limited
to:

        fondling.
-   the alleged perpetrator inappropriately touching or
    pinching parts of the child's body generally associated
    with sexual activity.
-   encouraging, forcing, or permitting the child to
    inappropriately   touch   parts   of   the   alleged
    perpetrator's body generally associated with sexual
    activity.

22   Substantial Risk of Physical Injury (Priority II)

Substantial risk of physical injury means that the parent,
~~caretaker~~ caregiver, immediate family member aged 16 or
over, other person residing in the home aged 16 or over, or
the parent's paramour has created a real and significant
danger of physical injury or sexual abuse to the child.

This allegation of harm is to be used when the type or
extent of harm is undefined but the total circumstances
lead a reasonable person to believe that the child is in
substantial risk of physical injury or sexual abuse.

This allegation of harm also includes incidents of violence
or intimidation directed toward the child which have not
yet resulted in injury or impairment but which clearly
threaten such injury or impairment.

Examples of incidents or circumstances which place the
child in substantial risk of physical injury include, but
are not limited to, the following:

Incidents

DEPARTMENT OF CHILDREN AND FAMILY SERVICES

NOTICE OF PROPOSED AMENDMENTS

Allegation #   Definition

        choking the child.
        smothering the child.
-   pulling the child's hair out.
-   violently pushing or shoving the child into fixed or
    heavy objects.
-   throwing or shaking a smaller child.
-   other violent or intimidating acts directed toward the
    child which cause excessive pain or fear.

Circumstances

-   domestic violence in the home when the child has been
    threatened and the threat is believable, as evidenced
    by a past history of violence, or uncontrolled
    behavior.
-   a perpetrator of child abuse who has been ordered to
    remain out of the home returns home and has access to
    the abused child.
-   the non-accidental death of one child provides reason
    to believe that another child is at risk.
-   past sexual abuse, when confirmed by the victim,
    provides reason to believe that another child is at
    risk.

Factors to be Considered

Whether there is a real and significant danger is
determined by the following factors:

-   the child's age, (children aged 6 and under are at a
    much greater risk of harm).
-   the child's medical condition, behavioral, mental, or
    emotional problems, developmental disability, or
    physical handicap, particularly related to his or her
    ability to protect himself or herself.
-   the severity of the occurrence.
-   the frequency of the occurrence.
-   the alleged perpetrator's physical, mental and/or
    emotional abilities, particularly related to his or her
    ability to control his or her actions.
-   the dynamics of the relationship between the alleged
    perpetrator and the child.
-   the alleged perpetrator's access to the child.
-   the previous history of indicated abuse or neglect.
-   the current stresses/crisis in the home.
-   the presence of other supporting persons in the home.

DEPARTMENT OF CHILDREN AND FAMILY SERVICES

NOTICE OF PROPOSED AMENDMENTS

Allegation #   Definition

74   Inadequate Supervision (Priority II)

The child has been placed in a situation or circumstances
which are likely to require judgment or actions greater
than the child's level of maturity, physical condition,
and/or mental abilities would reasonably dictate. A child
shall not be considered neglected for the sole reason that
the child's parent or other person responsible for his or
her welfare has left the child in the care of an adult
relative for any period of time. Examples include, but are
not limited to:

- leaving children alone when they are too young to care
  for themselves.
- leaving children alone who have a condition that
  requires close supervision. Such conditions may
  include medical conditions, behavioral, mental, or
  emotional problems, or developmental or physical
  disabilities or physical handicaps.
- leaving children in the care of an inadequate or
  inappropriate caretaker caregiver.
- being present but unable to supervise because of the
  caretaker's caregiver's condition (This includes (1)
  the parent or caretaker who repeatedly uses drugs or
  alcohol to the extent that it has the effect of
  producing a substantial state of stupor,
  unconsciousness, intoxication or irrationality and (2)
  the parent or caretaker who cannot adequately supervise
  the child because of his or her medical condition,
  behavioral, mental, or emotional problems, or a
  developmental or physical disability, or physical
  handicap.)
- leaving children unattended in a place which is unsafe
  for them when their maturity, physical condition, and
  mental abilities are considered.

Factors to be Considered

The following factors should be considered when determining
whether a child is inadequately supervised.

Child Factors

- child's age and developmental stage, particularly
  related to the ability to make sound judgments in the
  event of an emergency.

DEPARTMENT OF CHILDREN AND FAMILY SERVICES

NOTICE OF PROPOSED AMENDMENTS

Allegation #   Definition

- child's physical condition, particularly related to the
  child's ability to care for or protect himself or
  herself. Is the child physically or mentally
  handicapped, or otherwise in need of ongoing prescribed
  medical treatment such as periodic doses of insulin or
  other medications?
- child's mental abilities, particularly as related to
  the ability to comprehend the situation.
- was the child's movement restricted or was the child
  otherwise locked within a room or other structure?

Caretaker Caregiver Factors

- presence or accessibility of caretaker caregiver.

  o How long does it take the caretaker caregiver to
     reach the child?
  o Can the caretaker caregiver see and hear the child?
  o Is the caretaker caregiver accessible by telephone?
  o Has the child been given phone numbers to call in
     the event of an emergency?

- caretaker's caregiver's age.

  o Is the caretaker caregiver mature enough to assume
     responsibility for the situation?

- caretaker's caregiver's physical and mental condition.

  o Is the caretaker caregiver able to make appropriate
     judgments on the child's behalf?

Incident Factors

- frequency of occurrence.
- duration of the occurrence (as related to the "child
  factors" above).
- time of the day or night when the incident occurs.
- child's location (the condition and location of
  the place where the minor was left without
  supervision).
- the weather conditions, including whether the minor was
  left in a location with adequate protection from the
  natural elements such as adequate heat or light.

DEPARTMENT OF CHILDREN AND FAMILY SERVICES

NOTICE OF PROPOSED AMENDMENTS

Allegation #   Definition

- other supporting persons who are overseeing the child.
  (Was the child given a phone number of a person or
  location to call in the event of an emergency and
  whether the child was capable of making an emergency
  call?).
- whether food and other provisions were left for the
  child.
- other factors that may endanger the health and safety
  of the child.

'5   Abandonment/Desertion (Priority II)

Abandonment

Abandonment is parental or--caretaker conduct which
demonstrates the purpose of relinquishing all parental
rights and claims to the child. Abandonment is also
defined as any parental or-caretaker conduct which evinces
a settled purpose to forego all parental duties and
relinquish all parental claims to the child.

Examples of abandonment include, but are not limited to,
parents who:

- leave a baby on a doorstep.
- leave a baby in a garbage can.

Desertion

Desertion is any conduct on the part of a parent or
caretaker whith indicates an intention to terminate
custody of the child but not to relinquish all duties
to and claims on the child. Desertion includes leaving
a child with no apparent intention to return, unless
the child has been left in the care of a relative.

Examples-of-abandonment/desertion-include,-but-are--not
limited-to,-parents-or-caretakers-who:

- leave-a-baby-on-a-doorstep.
- leave-a-baby-in-a-garbage-can.
- leave-a-child-with-no-apparent-intention-to-return.
- leave-a-child-with-an-appropriate-caretaker-but-fail-to
  resume--care--of--the--child,-as-agreed,-for-a-period-of
  three-months-or-more;-and-the-caretaker-cannot-or--will
  not-continue-to-care-for-the-child.

DEPARTMENT OF CHILDREN AND FAMILY SERVICES

NOTICE OF PROPOSED AMENDMENTS

Allegation #   Definition

76   Inadequate Food (Priority III)

Lack of food adequate to sustain normal functioning. It is
not as severe as Malnutrition or Failure to Thrive, both of
which require a medical diagnosis.

Examples include:

- the child who frequently and repeatedly misses meals or
  who is frequently and repeatedly fed insufficient
  amounts of food.
- the child who frequently and repeatedly asks neighbors
  for food and other information substantiates that the
  child is not being fed.
- the child who is frequently and repeatedly fed
  unwholesome foods when his age, developmental stage,
  and physical condition are considered.

Factors to be Considered

    Child Factors

    - child's age.
    - child's developmental stage.
    - child's physical condition, particularly related to the
      need for a special diet.
    - child's mental abilities, particularly related to his
      ability to obtain and prepare his own food.

    Incident Factors

    - frequency of the occurrence.
    - duration of the occurrence.
    - pattern or chronicity of occurrence.
    - previous history of occurrences.
    - availability of adequate food.

77   Inadequate Shelter (Priority III)

Lack of shelter which is safe and which protects the
child(ren) from the elements.

Examples of inadequate shelter include, but are not limited
to:

    no housing or shelter.

DEPARTMENT OF CHILDREN AND FAMILY SERVICES

NOTICE OF PROPOSED AMENDMENTS

Allegation #   Definition

condemned housing.
- exposed, frayed wiring.
- housing with structural defects which endanger the
  health or safety of a child.
- housing with indoor temperatures consistently below 50°
  F.
- housing with broken windows in sub-zero weather.
- housing which is a fire hazard obvious to the
  reasonable person.
- housing with an unsafe heat source which poses a fire
  hazard or threat of asphyxiation.

Factors to be Considered

    Child Factors

    - child's age.
    - child's developmental stage.
    - child's physical condition, particularly when it may be
      aggravated by the inadequate shelter.
    - child's mental abilities, particularly related to the
      child's ability to comprehend the dangers posed by the
      inadequate shelter.

    Shelter Factors

    - seriousness of the problem.
    - frequency of the problem.
    - duration of the problem.
    - pattern or chronicity of the problem.
    - previous history of shelter-related problems.

78   Inadequate Clothing (Priority III)

Lack of appropriate clothing to protect the child from the
elements.

Factors to be Considered

    Child Factors

    - child's age.
    - child's developmental stage.
    - child's physical condition, particularly related to
      conditions which may be aggravated by exposure to the
      elements.

DEPARTMENT OF CHILDREN AND FAMILY SERVICES

NOTICE OF PROPOSED AMENDMENTS

Allegation #   Definition

    - child's mental abilities, particularly related to his
      or her ability to obtain appropriate clothing.

    Incident Factors

    - frequency of the incident.
    - duration of the incident.
    - chronicity or pattern of similar incidents.
    - weather conditions such as extreme heat or extreme
      cold.

79   Medical Neglect (Priority II)

Medical or Dental Treatment

Lack of medical or dental treatment for a health problem or
condition which, if untreated, could become severe enough
to constitute a serious or long-term harm to the child;
lack of follow-through on a prescribed treatment plan for a
condition which could become serious enough to constitute
serious or long-term harm to the child if the plan goes
unimplemented.

Immunizations

Lack of immunizations required by Section I of the
Communicable Disease Prevention Act [410 ILCS 315] which
states:

    It is declared to be the public policy of this State
    that all children shall be protected, as soon after
    birth as medically indicated, by the appropriate
    vaccines and immunizing procedures to prevent
    communicable diseases which are or which may in the
    future become preventable by immunization.

The Department of Public Health has specified that the
following immunizations are required unless there is a
medical or religious reason why these immunizations should
not be administered. The judgment of the family's
physician with regard to whether there is a medical reason
why immunization should not be administered shall be
respected.

    Diphtheria
    Pertussis

DEPARTMENT OF CHILDREN AND FAMILY SERVICES

NOTICE OF PROPOSED AMENDMENTS

Allegation #   Definition

        Tetanus
        Poliomyelitis
        Measles
        Rubella
        Mumps

The investigative worker shall give the parents 30 days to
begin the required immunization series.

Factors to be Considered

        -   child's age, particularly as it relates to the ability
            to obtain treatment.
        -   child's developmental stage..
        -   child's physical condition.
        -   seriousness of the current health problem.
        -   probable outcome if the current health problem is not
            treated and the seriousness of that outcome.
        -   generally accepted medical benefits of the prescribed
            treatment.
        -   generally recognized side effects/harms associated with
            the prescribed treatment.

        It must be verified that the child has/had an untreated
        health problem, or that a prescribed treatment plan was
        implemented, or that the child has not started to receive
        immunizations required by State law within the 30-day
        period. Such verification must come from a physician,
        registered nurse, dentist, or by a direct admission from
        the alleged perpetrator. It must further be verified by a
        physician, registered nurse or dentist that the problem or
        condition, if untreated, could result in serious or
        long-term harm to the child.

80   No Allegation

81   Failure to Thrive (Priority I)
                            (Non-Organic)

A serious medical condition most often seen in children
under one year of age. The child's weight, height and
motor development fall significantly short of the average
growth rates of normal children (i.e., below the fifth
percentile). In about 10% of these cases, there is an
organic cause such as a serious kidney, heart, or

DEPARTMENT OF CHILDREN AND FAMILY SERVICES

NOTICE OF PROPOSED AMENDMENTS

Allegation #   Definition

intestinal disease, a genetic error of metabolism or brain
damage. All other cases are a result of a disturbed
parent-child relationship manifested in severe physical and
emotional neglect of the child. Non-organic failure to
thrive requires a medical diagnosis before it may be
indicated.

Verification of failure to thrive must come from a
physician.

82   Environmental Neglect (Priority III)

The child's person, clothing, or living conditions are
unsanitary to the point that the child's health may be
impaired. This may include infestations of rodents,
spiders, insects, snakes, etc., human or animal feces,
rotten or spoiled food or rotten or spoiled garbage which
the child can reach.

Factors to be Considered

Special attention should be paid to the child's physical
condition and the living conditions in the home in order to
determine whether the report constitutes an allegation of
harm. In addition, the following factors should be
considered.

        Child Factors

        -   child's age (children aged 6 and under are more likely
            to be harmed).
        -   child's developmental stage.
        -   child's physical condition.
        -   child's mental abilities.

        Incident Factors

        -   severity of the conditions.
        -   frequency of the conditions.
        -   duration of the conditions.
        -   chronicity or pattern of similar conditions.

83   Malnutrition (Priority I)
                            (Non-Organic)

DEPARTMENT OF CHILDREN AND FAMILY SERVICES

NOTICE OF PROPOSED AMENDMENTS

Allegation #   Definition

Lack of necessary or proper food substances in the body caused by inadequate food, lack of food, or insufficient amounts of vitamin or minerals. (Also known as marasmus or kwashiorkor.) Non-organic malnutrition requires a medical diagnosis before it may be indicated. There are various physical signs of malnutrition:

- A decrease in lean body mass or fat; very prominent ribs; the child may often be referred to as skin and bones.
- The hair is often sparse, thin, dry, and is easily pulled out or falls out spontaneously.
- The child is often pale and suffers from anemia.
- Excessive perspiration, especially about the head.
- The face appear lined and aged, often with a pinched and sharp appearance.
- The skin has an old, wrinkled look with poor turgor. (Classically, skin folds hang loose on the inner thigh and buttock.)
- The abdomen is often protuberant.
- There are abnormal pulses, blood pressure, stool patterns, intercurrent infections, abnormal sleep patterns and a decreased level of physical and mental activity.

Verification of malnutrition must come from a physician.

84   Lock-Out (Priority II)

The parent or caretaker caregiver has denied the child access to the home and has refused or failed to make provisions for another living arrangement for the child.

85   Medical Neglect of Disabled Infants (Priority I)

The withholding of appropriate nutrition, hydration, medication or other medically indicated treatment from a disabled Infant with a life-threatening condition. Medically Indicated treatment includes medical care which is most likely to relieve or correct all life-threatening conditions and evaluations or consultations necessary to assure that sufficient information has been gathered to make informed medical decisions. Nutrition, hydration, and medication, as appropriate for the infant's needs, is medically indicated for all disabled infants. Other types of treatment are not medically indicated when:

DEPARTMENT OF CHILDREN AND FAMILY SERVICES

NOTICE OF PROPOSED AMENDMENTS

Allegation #   Definition

- the infant is chronically and irreversibly comatose.
- the provision of the treatment would be futile and would merely prolong dying.
- the provision of the treatment would be virtually futile and the treatment itself would be inhumane under the circumstances.

In determining whether treatment will be medically indicated, reasonable medical judgments, such as those made by a prudent physician knowledgeable about the case and its treatment possibilities, will be respected. However, opinions about the infant's future "quality of life" are not to bear on whether a treatment is judged to be medically indicated.

Factors to be Considered

- infant's physical condition.
- seriousness of the current health problem.
- probable medical outcome if the current health problem is not treated and the seriousness of that outcome.
- generally accepted medical benefits of the prescribed treatment.
- generally recognized side effects/harms associated with the prescribed treatment.
- the opinions of the Infant Care Review Committee (ICRC), (if the hospital has an ICRC).
- the judgment of the Perinatal Coordinator regarding whether treatment is medically indicated and whether there is credible evidence of medical neglect.
- the parent's knowledge and understanding of the treatment and the probable medical outcome.

Verification that treatment was medically indicated must come from a physician and may come from experts in the field of neonatal pediatrics.

(Source: Amended at 19 Ill. Reg. _____, effective _____)

DEPARTMENT OF CHILDREN AND FAMILY SERVICES

NOTICE OF PROPOSED AMENDMENTS

1) <u>Heading of the Part</u>: Service Appeal Process

2) <u>Code Citation</u>: 89 Ill. Adm. Code 337

3) <u>Section Numbers</u>:   <u>Proposed Action</u>:

        337.10   Amend
        337.20   Amend
        337.60   Amend
        337.70   Amend

4) <u>Statutory Authority</u>: The Children and Family Services Act [20 ILCS 505].

5) <u>A Complete Description of the Subjects and Issues Involved</u>: The
   Department is proposing relative home placement reforms that remove the
   presumption that relatives will receive preference when the Department
   seeks to place a child in substitute care. The primary consideration in
   placing children will be the best interests of the child. Therefore,
   language in this Part which allows relatives to appeal the denial of
   placement of a related child is being deleted.

6) <u>Will this proposed amendment replace an emergency rule currently in
   effect</u>? No

7) <u>Does this rulemaking contain an automatic repeal date</u>? No

8) <u>Does this proposed amendment contain incorporations by reference</u>? No

9) <u>Are there any other amendments pending on this Part</u>? Yes

   <u>Section</u> <u>Proposed Action</u> <u>Illinois Register Citation</u>

   337.30   Amend   December 23, 1994 (18 Ill. Reg. 18168)
   337.70   Amend   December 23, 1994 (18 Ill. Reg. 18168)
   337.100   Amend   December 23, 1994 (18 Ill. Reg. 18168)
   337.210   Amend   December 23, 1994 (18 Ill. Reg. 18168)
   337.230   Amend   December 23, 1994 (18 Ill. Reg. 18168)

10) <u>Statement of Statewide Policy Objectives</u>: These amendments do not create
    or expand a state mandate as defined in Section 3(b) of the State Mandates
    Act [30 ILCS 805/3(b)].

11) <u>Time, Place, and Manner in which interested persons may comment on this
    proposed rulemaking</u>: Comments on this proposed rulemaking may be
    submitted in writing for a period of 45 days following publication of this
    notice. Comments should be submitted to:

        Jacqueline Nottingham, Chief

DEPARTMENT OF CHILDREN AND FAMILY SERVICES

NOTICE OF PROPOSED AMENDMENTS

        Office of Rules and Procedures
        Department of Children and Family Services
        406 East Monroe - Station 222
        Springfield, Illinois 62701-1498
        Telephone: (217)524-1983
        TTY: (217)524-3715

   The Department will consider fully all written comments on this proposed
   rulemaking submitted during the 45-day comment period. Comments submitted
   by small businesses should be identified as such. Public hearings have
   been scheduled on these proposed amendments in the following areas:

        April 11, 1995
        7:00 p.m.
        Quality Inn at Halsted
        One South Halsted
        Chicago, Illinois
        (312)829-5000

        April 13, 1995
        7:00 p.m.
        State House
        Room 212
        Springfield, Illinois
        (217)782-2099

   Persons are asked to limit their testimony to a maximum of 15 minutes per
   person. We will gladly accept written testimony at the public hearings.
   Persons who need translation or interpretation services to enable their
   commentary should request assistance by contacting the Office of Rules and
   Procedures.

12) <u>Initial Regulatory Flexibility Analysis</u>: The Department has determined
    that the proposed amendment does not have an affect on small businesses.

13) <u>State reason(s) for this rulemaking if it was not included in either of
    the two most recent regulatory agendas.</u> The need for this rulemaking was
    not foreseen at the time the Department filed its regulatory agendas. A
    major management initiative affecting home of relative care has prompted
    the Department to file these amendments at the present time in order to
    implement them at the start of the next fiscal year.

<u>The full text of the proposed amendment begins on the next page.</u>

DEPARTMENT OF CHILDREN AND FAMILY SERVICES

NOTICE OF PROPOSED AMENDMENTS

TITLE 89: SOCIAL SERVICES
CHAPTER III: DEPARTMENT OF CHILDREN AND FAMILY SERVICES
SUBCHAPTER a: SERVICE DELIVERY

PART 337
SERVICE APPEAL PROCESS

AUTHORITY: Implementing and authorized by Sections 4 and 5 of the Children and
Family Services Act [20 ILCS 505/4 and 5].

SOURCE: Adopted at 17 Ill. Reg. 1046, effective January 15, 1993; amended at
19 Ill. Reg. _____, effective _____.

Section 337.10   Purpose

These rules govern the service appeal process for child welfare services
provided either directly or through a provider agency. Persons who may appeal
through this process may include persons requesting or receiving services, and
as governed by this Part, foster parents, and relative caregivers--and
relatives-denied-the-placement-of-a-related-child.

DEPARTMENT OF CHILDREN AND FAMILY SERVICES

NOTICE OF PROPOSED AMENDMENTS

(Source: Amended   at   19   Ill. Reg. _____,   effective
_____)

Section 337.20   Definitions

"Adequate Notice" means a notice which contains all of the elements
identified in Section 337.90 (c) of this Part.

"Administrative Hearings Unit" means the Department's unit responsible
for receiving requests for and acting upon a service appeal and
conducting fair hearings on appeal.

"Administrative law judge" means an attorney who is appointed by the
Director of the Department and who is responsible for conducting the
fair hearing.

"Administrator of the Administrative Hearings Unit" means the person
who is responsible for receiving requests for a service appeal and for
coordinating the fair hearings.

"Appellant" means the person who requests a service appeal, or on
whose behalf a service appeal is requested.

"Authorized representative" means a person authorized in writing by
the appellant to assist the appellant in the appeal process. If the
appellant is unable to reduce such authorization to writing, the
Department shall assist the appellant in doing so. The representative
may be legal counsel or other spokesperson.

"Child welfare services" means public social services which are
directed toward the accomplishment of the following purposes:

protecting and promoting the welfare of all children, including
homeless, dependent, or neglected children;

preventing or remedying, or assisting in the solution of problems
which may result in, the neglect, abuse, exploitation, or
delinquency of children;

preventing the unnecessary separation of children from their
families by identifying family problems, and preventing breakup
of the family where the prevention of child removal is desirable
and possible;

restoring to their families children who have been removed by the
provision of services to the child and the families;

placing children in suitable adoptive homes, in cases where

DEPARTMENT OF CHILDREN AND FAMILY SERVICES

NOTICE OF PROPOSED AMENDMENTS

restoration to the biological family is not possible or appropriate;

assuring adequate care of children away from their homes, in cases where the child cannot be returned home or cannot be placed for adoption;

providing supportive services and living maintenance which contributes to the physical, emotional and social well-being of children who are pregnant and unmarried;

providing shelter and independent living services for homeless youth; and

placing and maintaining children in facilities that provide separate living quarters for children under the age of 18 and for children 18 years of age and older, unless a child 18 years of age is in the last year of high school education or vocational training, in an approved individual or group treatment program, or in a licensed shelter facility. The Department is not required to place or maintain children:

who are in a foster home; or

who are developmentally disabled, as defined in the Mental Health and Developmental Disabilities Code; or

who are female children who are pregnant, pregnant and parenting or parenting; or

who are siblings,

in facilities that provide separate living quarters for children 18 years of age and older and for children under 18 years of age. ↑↑↓↓↓-Rev.-Stat.↓-1991,-ch.-23,-par.-5005↑ [20 ILCS 505/5].

These services include but are not limited to: counseling, advocacy, day care, homemaker, emergency caregiver, family planning, adoption, visitation, placement, child protection and information and referral.

"Date of action" means the effective date of the action or proposed action by the Department or provider agency which resulted in the appeal.

"Date of appeal" means the postmark date or date of receipt of appellant's written request for an appeal, whichever is earlier, at the address specified in the notice.

DEPARTMENT OF CHILDREN AND FAMILY SERVICES

NOTICE OF PROPOSED AMENDMENTS

"Date of notice" means the date on which the appellant receives written notice of the Department's intended action or decision or the date on which the appellant learns of the intended action or decision, if a written notice was not provided.

"Day care services" means care provided to children for less than 24 hours per day in facilities requiring licensure under the Child Care Act of 1969 ↑↑↓↓↓-Rev.-Stat.↓-1991,-ch.-23,-par.-2211-et--seq.↑ [225 ILCS 10] in facilities exempt from licensure, in the home(s) of relatives, or in their own home.

"Department representative" means the designated individual responsible for presenting the Department's position in an emergency review and fair hearing.

"Emergency review" means a limited review of the actions or decisions of the Department or provider agency which may adversely affect an individual or individuals served by the Department. An emergency review provides for an interim decision pending a fair hearing.

"Fair hearing", as used in this Part, means a formal review of the action or decision of the Department or provider agency to determine whether such action or decision was in compliance with applicable laws and rules and in the best interests of the child.

"Family" means the biological or adoptive parents (provided a court has not terminated parental rights), legal guardian, or any relative who has assumed custody and control of the child in the absence of the child's biological or adoptive parents.

"Final administrative decision" means the Department's final decision, order, or determination on an appealed issue rendered by the Director in a particular case which affects the legal rights, duties or privileges of appellants and which may be appealed in a circuit court under the Administrative Review Law ↑↑↓↓-Rev.-Stat.↓-1991,-ch.-110, par.-3-101↑ [735 ILCS 5/Art. III].

"Imminent risk of harm" means that individuals' actions, omissions or conditions endanger the life, or seriously jeopardize the physical or mental health or safety of themselves or others, if protective action would not be taken immediately.

"Individual legally acting on a person's behalf" means an individual who has been appointed by a court to act on behalf of a person when the person is incompetent, incapacitated, or otherwise unable to speak for himself or herself.

"Mediation" means a meeting open to all parties affected by the

DEPARTMENT OF CHILDREN AND FAMILY SERVICES

NOTICE OF PROPOSED AMENDMENTS

decision being appealed to attempt agreement on the issue in dispute with a mediator, who assists the parties in resolving issues and drawing up an agreement.

"Mediator" means a neutral third party appointed by the Director of the Department who conducts the mediation and assists the parties in resolving issues and drawing up an agreement.

"Parties" means the Department or its agents and those persons who have appealed the service decision(s) made by the Department or its agents.

"Preponderance of the evidence" means the greater weight of the evidence or evidence which renders a fact more likely than not.

"Provider agency" means an agency offering case management and/or casework services through a signed contract with the Department for paid services.

"Relative" means any person who has any of the following currently existing relations to a child by blood or adoption: grandfather, grandmother, great-grandfather, great-grandmother, great-uncle, great-aunt, brother, sister, uncle, aunt, nephew, niece or first cousin.

"Relative caregiver" means a person 21 years of age or older, other than the parent, who has physical custody of the child and to whom the child has any of the following currently existing relationships by blood or adoption: grandparent, sibling, great grandparent, uncle, aunt, nephew, niece, first cousin, great uncle, great aunt, or who is the spouse of such a relative or who is the child's step-father, step-mother, step-brother or step-sister.

"Request for an appeal" means the written request by an appellant for a fair hearing to review an action taken or a decision made by the Department or a provider agency on behalf of the Department. If the appellant is unable to request an appeal in writing, the Department or provider agency shall help the appellant put the request in writing.

"Reviewer" means the person appointed by the Department to conduct an emergency review.

"Service appeal process" means the appeal system offered by the Department to review appealable service issues raised by appellants.

"Services" means child welfare or day care services, including placement services or benefits provided by the Department or its provider agencies under Titles IV and XX of the Social Security Act

DEPARTMENT OF CHILDREN AND FAMILY SERVICES

NOTICE OF PROPOSED AMENDMENTS

(42 U.S.C. Section 601 et seq. and 1397 et seq.) or the laws of the State of Illinois.

"Stay of action" means the action or decision made by the Department or its provider agency will not be implemented pending an emergency review or final administrative decision by the Department.

"Timely written notice" means a notice which complies with the requirements of Section 337.90 (b) of this Part.

(Source: Amended at 19 Ill. Reg. _____, effective
_____)

Section 337.60 Who May Appeal

a) The following persons may appeal decisions made by or on behalf of the Department in accordance with Section 337.70 of this Part:
    1) families and children who receive child welfare services, either directly from the Department or through its provider agency;
    2) families and children requesting child welfare services from the Department; or
    3) foster parents or relative caregivers who have care and custody of a child for whom the Department is legally responsible; or.
    4) relatives denied placement of a related child for whom the Department is legally responsible.
b) The appeal may be requested by:
    1) families and children who receive child welfare services, either directly from the Department or through its provider agency;
    2) families and children requesting child welfare services from the Department;
    3) foster parents or relative caregivers who have care and custody of a child for whom the Department is legally responsible;
    4) relatives denied placement of a related child for whom the Department is legally responsible;
    5)4) the authorized representative of any of the above persons:
    6)5) an individual who has been appointed by a court to legally act on behalf of the above parties including the guardian ad litem for a child; when monetary claims are at issue, an individual appointed by the court as administrator of the estate or a person acting in a similar capacity may appeal for the deceased person. A certified copy of the court's order must be provided as authorization to represent such persons unless the appointment is as a Guardian Ad Litem in Juvenile Court.
c) If an appellant has an authorized representative or an individual legally acting on the appellant's behalf, that representative or individual may exercise the rights of the party in the mediation and emergency review and the fair hearing. These rights include the right to review and copy case materials pursuant to 89 Ill. Adm. Code 431.

DEPARTMENT OF CHILDREN AND FAMILY SERVICES

NOTICE OF PROPOSED AMENDMENTS

Confidentiality of Personal Information of Persons Served by the
Department, to receive Department notices, to speak in the mediation
or emergency review and the fair hearing, and to take any other
actions permitted an appellant in this Part.

(Source: Amended   at   19   Ill.   Reg. _____ , effective
_____)

Section 337.70 What May Be Appealed

a) By Families and Children
   Families and children may appeal the following issues:
   1) the denial, in whole or in part, of child welfare or day care
      services in accordance with 89 Ill. Adm. Code 303, Access to and
      Eligibility for Day Care Services, requested by families,
      children, or an individual legally appointed to represent a
      minor, incompetent or incapacitated person or the failure of the
      Department or its provider agency to decide, within 30 calendar
      days of the date of the request, whether to grant or deny
      services requested by the parents or children;
   2) a decision to reduce, suspend or terminate services;
   3) the choice of a permanency goal or the denial of a request for a
      change in permanency goal;
   4) the failure to complete a service plan within 30 calendar days of
      case opening or the failure to review the service plan within the
      Department's specified time frames;
   5) the failure to provide services as specified in the service plan
      with reasonable promptness or within the time frames as provided
      in the service plan;
   6) the frequency or length of family visitation, or failure to
      arrange parent-child visits when the child is placed out of the
      home and parental rights have not been terminated, and the
      frequency or length of sibling visits when children are placed
      apart;
   7) a change in the placement of the child;
   8) the imposition of unnecessary services or conditions as part of a
      service plan.
   9) a denial of a relative's request for placement with that relative
      of a child for whom the Department is legally responsible.
b) By Foster Parents and Relative Caregivers
   1) Foster parents may appeal the following issues:
      A) decisions made by the Department or its provider agency
         which directly affect the foster parent, such as payment
         issues, as defined in 89 Ill. Adm. Code 359, Authorized
         Child Care Payments;
      B) decisions made by the Department or its provider agency
         regarding services provided for the benefit of foster
         children in their care, such as day care, medical,

DEPARTMENT OF CHILDREN AND FAMILY SERVICES

NOTICE OF PROPOSED AMENDMENTS

         educational, and psychological services;
      C) failure to provide services as specified in the service plan
         for the benefit of the foster children in their care. This
         does not include services provided to the biological family,
         such as family therapy or family counseling; and
      D) a change in the child's substitute care placement. This
         does not include placement with the biological or adoptive
         parent(s), relative(s), or sibling(s), placements for
         purposes of adoption as ordered by the court, or return to
         an unrelated individual(s) with whom the child resided prior
         to entering substitute care.
   2) Relative caregivers may appeal the following issues:
      A) decisions made by the Department or its provider agency that
         directly affect the relative caregiver, such as payment
         issues as defined in 89 Ill. Adm. Code 359, Authorized Child
         Care Payments;
      B) decisions made by the Department or its provider agency
         regarding services provided for the benefit of foster
         children in their care, such as day care, medical,
         educational, and psychological services;
      C) failure to provide services as specified in the service plan
         for the benefit of the foster children in their care. This
         does not include services provided to the biological family,
         such as family therapy or family counseling; and
      D) a change in the child's substitute care placement. This
         does not include placement with the biological or adoptive
         parent(s), placements for purposes of adoption as ordered by
         the court, or return to an unrelated individual(s) with whom
         the child resided prior to entering substitute care.
   3) Foster parents and relative caregivers have the right to be heard
      by the Bureau of Quality Assurance on issues specified in 89 Ill.
      Adm. Code 305, Client Service Planning, Section 305.80, Decision
      Review, which issues are not appealable under this Part.
      However, they will not be considered a party to the service
      appeal on issues which may affect residual parental rights and
      responsibilities. These include, but are not limited to, issues
      regarding the child's return home, family visitation, the right
      to consent to adoption, the right to determine the minor's
      religious affiliation and other issues which do not directly
      affect the foster parents themselves or their roles as caregivers
      of the child. The residual rights and responsibilities of
      parents are further defined in Section 801-3 1-3 of the Juvenile
      Court Act of 1987 (Ill. Rev. Stat. 1991, ch. 37, par. 801-3 [705
      ILCS 1-3].
   c) By Relatives
      Relatives who are denied placement of a related child may appeal the
      denial.

DEPARTMENT OF CHILDREN AND FAMILY SERVICES

NOTICE OF PROPOSED AMENDMENTS

(Source: Amended at 19 Ill. Reg. _____, effective _____)

DEPARTMENT OF CHILDREN AND FAMILY SERVICES

NOTICE OF PROPOSED AMENDMENTS

1) Heading of the Part: Services Delivered by the Department

2) Code Citation: 89 Ill. Adm. Code 302

3) Section Numbers: Proposed Action:

   302.20   Amend
   302.40   Amend
   302.320   Amend
   302.330   Amend
   302.340   Amend
   302.370   Amend
   302.390   Repeal

4) Statutory Authority: The Children and Family Services Act [20 ILCS 505].

5) A Complete Description of the Subjects and Issues Involved: These changes are necessary in order to make Part 302 consistent with other Department rules regarding home of relative care. When children are living apart from their parents but with other related caregivers, they will no longer be considered as neglected for that reason alone. The Department will work to preserve and strengthen appropriate relative family arrangements by providing services to maintain the child with the relative caregiver and avoid placing children in State custody. The effect of these proposed rule changes will be to support and stabilize an increased number of children in family homes, rather than placing them in substitute care.

6) Will these proposed amendments replace an emergency rule currently in effect? No

7) Does this rulemaking contain an automatic repeal date? No

8) Does this proposed amendment contain incorporations by reference? No

9) Are there any other amendments pending on this Part? Yes

   Section   Proposed Action   Illinois Register Citation

   302.310   Amend   February 17, 1995 (19 Ill. Reg. 1372)

10) Statement of Statewide Policy Objectives These amendments do not create or expand a State mandate as defined in Section 3(b) of the State Mandates Act [30 ILCS 805/3(b)].

11) Time, Place, and Manner in which interested persons may comment on this proposed rulemaking: Comments on this proposed rulemaking may be submitted in writing for a period of 45 days following publication of this notice. Comments should be submitted to:

DEPARTMENT OF CHILDREN AND FAMILY SERVICES

NOTICE OF PROPOSED AMENDMENTS

Jacqueline Nottingham, Chief
Office of Rules and Procedures
Department of Children and Family Services
406 East Monroe - Station #222
Springfield, Illinois 62701-1498
Telephone: (217)524-1983
TTY: (217)524-3715

The Department will consider fully all written comments on this proposed rulemaking submitted during the 45-day comment period. Comments submitted by small businesses should be identified as such. Public hearings have been scheduled on these proposed amendments in the following areas:

April 11, 1995
7:00 p.m.
Quality Inn at Halsted
One South Halsted
Chicago, Illinois
(312) 829-5000

April 13, 1995
7:00 p.m.
State House
Room 212
Springfield, Illinois
(217) 782-2099

Persons are asked to limit their testimony to a maximum of 15 minutes per person. We will gladly accept written testimony at the public hearings. Persons who need translation or interpretation services to enable their commentary should request assistance by contacting the Office of Rules and Procedures.

12) Initial Regulatory Flexibility Analysis: The Department has determined that the proposed amendment does not have an affect on small businesses.

13) State reason(s) for this rulemaking if it was not included in either of the two most recent regulatory agendas: The need for this rulemaking was not foreseen at the time the Department filed its regulatory agendas. A major management initiative affecting home of relative care has prompted the Department to file these amendments at the present time in order to implement them at the start of the next fiscal year.

The full text of the proposed amendment begins on the next page.

DEPARTMENT OF CHILDREN AND FAMILY SERVICES

NOTICE OF PROPOSED AMENDMENTS

TITLE 89: SOCIAL SERVICES
CHAPTER III: DEPARTMENT OF CHILDREN AND FAMILY SERVICES
SUBCHAPTER a: SERVICE DELIVERY

PART 302
SERVICES DELIVERED BY THE DEPARTMENT

SUBPART A: GENERAL PROVISIONS

SUBPART B: REPORTS OF SUSPECTED CHILD ABUSE OR NEGLECT (RECODIFIED)

SUBPART C: DEPARTMENT CHILD WELFARE SERVICES

DEPARTMENT OF CHILDREN AND FAMILY SERVICES

NOTICE OF PROPOSED AMENDMENTS

302.400   Successor Guardianship

SUBPART D: INTENSIVE FAMILY PRESERVATION SERVICES

Section
302.500   Purpose
302.510   Implementation of the Family Preservation Act
302.520   Types of Intensive Family Preservation Services
302.530   Phase In Plan for Statewide Family Preservation Services
302.540   Time Frames

Appendix A   Acknowledgement of Mandated Reporter Status (Recodified)

AUTHORITY: Implementing and authorized by the Children and Family Services Act
[20 ILCS 505]; Section 3-6-2(g) of the Unified Code of Corrections [730 ILCS
5/3-6-2(g)]; the Illinois Alcoholism and Dangerous Drug Dependency Act [20 ILCS
305]; the Adoption Assistance and Child Welfare Act of 1980 [42 U.S.C.A. 670 et
seq.); 45 CFR 1356.40 and 1356.41; the Juvenile Court Act of 1987 [705 ILCS
405]; and the Adoption Act [750 ILCS 50].

SOURCE: Adopted and codified at 5 Ill. Reg. 13188, effective November 30,
1981; amended at 6 Ill. Reg. 15529, effective January 1, 1983; recodified at 8
Ill. Reg. 992; peremptory amendment at 8 Ill. Reg. 5373, effective April 12,
1984; amended at 8 Ill. Reg. 12143, effective July 9, 1984; amended at 9 Ill.
Reg. 2467, effective March 1, 1985; amended at 9 Ill. Reg. 9104, effective June
14, 1985; amended at 9 Ill. Reg. 15820, effective November 1, 1985; amended at
10 Ill. Reg. 5557, effective April 15, 1986; amended at 11 Ill. Reg. 1390,
effective January 13, 1987; amended at 11 Ill. Reg. 1551, effective January 14,
1987; amended at 11 Ill. Reg. 1829, effective January 15, 1987; recodified to
89 Ill. Adm. Code 300 at 11 Ill. Reg. 3492, Sections 302.20, 302.100, 302.110,
302.120, 302.130, 302.140, 302.150, 302.160, 302.170, 302.180, 302.190,
Appendix A; amended at 13 Ill. Reg. 18847, effective November 15, 1989; amended
at 14 Ill. Reg. 3438, effective March 1, 1990; amended at 14 Ill. Reg. 16430,
effective September 25, 1990; amended at 14 Ill. Reg. 19010, effective November
15, 1990; amended at 16 Ill. Reg. 274, effective December 31, 1992; emergency
amendment   at 17 Ill. Reg. 2513, effective February 10, 1993, for a maximum of
150 days; emergency expired on July 9, 1993; amended at 17 Ill. Reg. 13438,
effective July 31, 1993; amended at 19 Ill. Reg. _____, effective
_____.

SUBPART A: GENERAL PROVISIONS

Section 302.20   Definitions

        "Adoption assistance" or "adoption subsidy" means financial assistance
from the Department which is provided to the adoptive parents after
the finalization of an adoption.

DEPARTMENT OF CHILDREN AND FAMILY SERVICES

NOTICE OF PROPOSED AMENDMENTS

"Adoption placement" means a living arrangement with a family which is
directed toward establishing that family as the child's new legal
parents.

"Biological father" means a man who has acknowledged his paternity via
a notarized statement or whose paternity is adjudicated in court.
When paternity has been acknowledged or adjudicated, the relatives of
the biological father as well as those of the mother may be considered
for the placement of related children.

"Child welfare services" means public social services which are
directed toward the accomplishment of the following purposes:

        protecting and promoting the welfare of all children, including
        homeless, dependent, or neglected children;

        preventing or remedying, or assisting in the solution of problems
        which may result in, the neglect, abuse, exploitation, or
        delinquency of children;

        preventing the unnecessary separation of children from their
        families by identifying family problems, assisting families in
        resolving their problems, and preventing breakup of the family
        where the prevention of child removal is desirable and possible;

        restoring to their families children who have been removed, by
        the provision of services to the child and the families;

        placing children in suitable adoptive homes, in cases where
        restoration to the biological family is not possible or
        appropriate;

        assuring adequate care of children away from their homes, in
        cases where the child cannot be returned home or cannot be placed
        for adoption;

        providing supportive services and living maintenance which
        contributes to the physical, emotional and social well-being of
        children who are pregnant and unmarried;

        providing shelter and independent living services for homeless
        youth; and

        placing and maintaining children in facilities that provide
        separate living quarters for children under the age of 18 and for
        children 18 years of age and older, unless a child 18 years of
        age is in the last year of high school education or vocational
        training, in an approved individual or group treatment program,

DEPARTMENT OF CHILDREN AND FAMILY SERVICES

NOTICE OF PROPOSED AMENDMENTS

or in a licensed shelter facility. The Department is not
required to place or maintain children:

who are in a foster home; or

who are developmentally disabled, as defined in the Mental
Health and Developmental Disabilities Code; or

who are female children who are pregnant, pregnant and
parenting or parenting; or

who are siblings,

in facilities that provide separate living quarters for children
18 years of age and older and for children under 18 years of age.
†Ill.-Rev.-Stat.-1991,-ch.-23,-par.-5005† [20 ILCS 505/5]

These services include but are not limited to: counseling, advocacy,
day care, homemaker, emergency caretaker, family planning, adoption,
placement, child protection and information and referral.

"Children for whom the Department is legally responsible" means
children for whom the Department has temporary protective custody,
custody or guardianship via court order, or children whose parent(s)
has signed an adoptive surrender or voluntary placement agreement with
the Department.

"Department" as used in this Part, means the Department of Children
and Family Services.

"Family" means one or more adults and children, related by blood,
marriage, or adoption and residing in the same household.

"Minimum parenting standards" means that a parent or other person
responsible for the child's welfare sees that the child is adequately
fed, clothed appropriately for the weather conditions, provided with
adequate shelter, protected from severe physical, mental and emotional
harm, and provided with necessary medical care and--education--as
required--by--law--. A parent who has abandoned a child, deserted a
child for three months, or failed to demonstrate an a reasonable
degree of interest, concern, or responsibility as to the welfare of an
a newborn child for 30 days after birth is deemed to have failed to
have met the minimum parenting standards, unless the parent has
arranged for the child's care in the home of a relative. In addition,
a parent who is addicted to alcohol, or who is a drug addict, as
defined in Section 1-103 of the Illinois Alcoholism and Other Drug
Dependency Act †Ill.--Rev.--Stat.--1991,--ch.--111-1/2,--par.--6351-3† [20
ILCS 305/1-103] and who has consistently failed to cooperate in a

DEPARTMENT OF CHILDREN AND FAMILY SERVICES

NOTICE OF PROPOSED AMENDMENTS

rehabilitation program for a period of at least twelve months is
deemed to have failed to have met the minimum parenting standards
unless the parent has arranged for the child's safety and well-being
have-been-ensured despite the parent's addiction.

"Parents" means the child's legal parents whose rights have not been
terminated and adoptive parents. Biological fathers are considered
legal parents when paternity has been acknowledged in writing or
adjudicated in court.

"Permanency goal" means the continuous living arrangement which the
Department deems desirable for and available to the child. A
permanent legal status is usually a component of the permanency goal.
The means for attaining a permanency goal as well as the goal itself
can change as the child's developmental and emotional needs change or
as the child's and family's circumstances change.

"Permanent legal status" means a legally binding relationship between
a child and a family as established by birth or a court of law.

"Relative caregiver" means a person 21 years of age or older, other
than the parent, who has physical custody of the child and to whom the
child has any of the following currently existing relationships by
blood or adoption: grandparent, sibling, great grandparent, uncle,
aunt, nephew, niece, first cousin, great uncle, great aunt, or who is
the spouse of such a relative or who is the child's step-father,
step-mother, step-brother or step-sister.

"Service constellation" means a variety of services provided to a
child and his/her family.

"Service plan" means a written plan on a form prescribed by the
Department in the plan toward the permanency goal for the children.

"Successor guardianship" means the judicial transfer under Section
802-27, 803-28, 804-25, or 805-29 of the Juvenile Court Act of 1987 of
the Department's guardianship duties and responsibilities for a minor
to a related or unrelated person whom the child has lived with for a
continuous period of a year or more before transfer of guardianship.

"Voluntary placement agreement" means a time-limited written request
and consent from a parent, guardian or legal custodian of a child for
placement of the child out of the home. When signed by designated
Department staff, the Department agrees to provide child welfare
services which include placement.

(Source: Amended at 19 Ill. Reg. _____, effective
_____)

DEPARTMENT OF CHILDREN AND FAMILY SERVICES

NOTICE OF PROPOSED AMENDMENTS

Section 302.40 Department Service Goals

a) The Department provides, directly or through purchase, a number of services for children and families which are individually planned to meet the needs of each child and family. These services are directed toward four service goals which are:
   1) family preservation
   2) family reunification
   3) adoption or attainment of a permanent living arrangement
   4) youth development

b) Family Preservation
   When family preservation is the goal, services are directed toward ensuring the child's children's development, safety and well-being in the home of their family his-parents'-home and preventing placement of the child children away from the their family. Such families may have been reported to the Department for alleged child abuse or neglect or referred to the Department for services. The service constellation for these children and families may include:
   1) counseling/advocacy
   2) emergency caretaker
   3) homemaker
   4) day care and child development
   5) family planning
   6) parent education
   7) self-help groups
   8) emergency family shelter
   9) intensive family preservation services
   10) other placement prevention services
   11) referral for substance abuse treatment services

c) Family Reunification
   When family reunification is the goal, services are directed toward returning a child to his parent's or private guardian's home when the child was removed because of alleged child abuse or neglect or other reasons. Family reunification services are directed toward helping the child's children's parents parent(s) or private guardian(s) achieve minimum parenting standards and ensuring the-child's their safety and well-being upon his return home. The service constellation for these children and families may include:
   1) counseling/advocacy
   2) homemaker
   3) day care and child development
   4) foster family home care
   5) relative home care
   6) residential care
   7) family planning
   8) parent education
   9) intensive family preservation services
   10) referral for substance abuse treatment services

DEPARTMENT OF CHILDREN AND FAMILY SERVICES

NOTICE OF PROPOSED AMENDMENTS

d) Adoption or Attainment of a Permanent Living Arrangement
   When adoption or attainment of a permanent living arrangement is the goal, services are directed at securing a new legal status in a permanent living situation for children who cannot return to their legal families. A goal of permanent living arrangement means that the child is to remain with a relative or foster family permanently and the Department intends to transfer legal guardianship to the family. The service constellation for these children may include:
   1) counseling
   2) adoption
   3) relative home care
   4) foster family home care
   5) intensive family preservation services

e) Youth Development
   1) When youth development is the goal, services are directed at helping youth live independently or assisting unmarried youth with planning for the birth or care of their child. Such services may be provided by the Department to:
      A) Youth 16 years of age or older for whom the Department has legal responsibility, to help them live independently of adult caretaker caregiver supervision and achieve economic self-sufficiency; and
      B) Youth who are high school graduates and have been awarded scholarships in accordance with "AN--ACT--creating--the Department-of-Children-and-Family--Services,--codifying--its powers--and--duties,-and-repealing-certain-Acts-and-Sections herein-named"-[Ill.--Rev.-Stat.-1989,-ch.-23,-par.--5005] the Children and Family Services Act [20 ILCS 505]; and
      C) Unmarried pregnant youth for whom the Department has legal responsibility; and
      D) Unmarried pregnant youth under age 18 for whom the Department is not legally responsible.
   2) The service constellation for youth for whom the Department is legally responsible may include:
      A) counseling/advocacy
      B) day care for the children of unmarried youth
      C) homemaker
      D) family planning
      E) maintenance payments or foster family home, relative home or residential care payment except that maternity home payment shall be limited to a maximum of ninety (90) days.
   3) The only purchased service for unmarried youth for whom the Department is not legally responsible for which the Department will make payment is a maximum of ninety (90) days of maternity home care for unmarried pregnant youth under age 18 at the time of anticipated delivery.

(Source: Amended at 19 Ill. Reg. _____, effective

DEPARTMENT OF CHILDREN AND FAMILY SERVICES

NOTICE OF PROPOSED AMENDMENTS

_____)

SUBPART C: DEPARTMENT CHILD WELFARE SERVICES

Section 302.320 Counseling or Casework Services

a) Counseling or casework services are provided to children and families
   to assist them in resolving or coping with problems as well as to
   identify, obtain and use community resources and services. Problems
   addressed include, but are not limited to: unsatisfactory parent
   caregiver-child relationships; marital discord; inadequate home
   management, housekeeping or child care practices; parental illness,
   handicap, desertion or absence; and, physical or mental handicap, or
   behavior of the child which adversely affects his ability to adjust to
   his family, school or community.
b) Counseling provided to children in need of a one-to-one relationship
   with an adult is referred to as advocacy and offered to:
   1) help children in institutional settings prepare for and adjust to
      post-institutional care;
   2) prevent unnecessary out-of-home placement of children when
      placement is likely; or
   3) help adolescents move toward independent functioning and
      self-sufficiency.

(Source: Amended at 19 Ill. Reg. _____, effective
_____)

Section 302.330 Day Care Services

Day care services are provided to children in licensed or license exempt day or
night care facilities, in their own homes or in the homes of relatives:
a) when parents or relative caregivers are away from home during part of
   the day due to employment or training; or
b) when parents or relative caregivers are unable to care for the child
   due to illness; or
c) when care away from the home for part of the day is essential for the
   safety and well-being of children and the welfare of the parents or
   relative caregivers; or
d) when the parent's or relative caregiver's ability to care for the
   children at home during certain hours of the day is impaired; or
e) when a child with special developmental needs will benefit from day
   care services; or
f) when a child in foster family care or relative home placement can
   benefit from day care services.

(Source: Amended at 19 Ill. Reg. _____, effective
_____)

DEPARTMENT OF CHILDREN AND FAMILY SERVICES

NOTICE OF PROPOSED AMENDMENTS

Section 302.340 Emergency Caretaker Services

Emergency caretaker services are provided when the parents or caretakers
caregivers are absent from the home and there would be no risk if the child
remains in the home with adequate supervision. The intent of this service is
to maintain the child in familiar surroundings and reduce inappropriate
out-of-home placement. The Department may provide an emergency caretaker for
up to 12 hours without taking temporary custody of the child.

(Source: Amended at 19 Ill. Reg. _____, effective
_____)

Section 302.370 Homemaker Services

Homemaker services are provided primarily as an in-home, protective service to
maintain and strengthen the ability of the parent(s) or relative caregiver to
provide adequate child care and to improve their parenting skills.
Additionally, homemaker services may be provided to ease the reunification of
families, or to assist foster parents during times of family crisis as well as
during pre-planned relief time. Service activities may include teaching and
provision of home management, including meal planning and preparation,
budgeting, shopping and child care; health care; teaching parenting skills;
observation of family interaction; and assessment of client's needs.

(Source: Amended at 19 Ill. Reg. _____, effective
_____)

Section 302.390 Placement Services (Repealed)

a) When Placement is Appropriate
   1) Placement services are not offered unless appropriate family
      preservation services have been provided to the family, or have
      been offered to and refused by the family. However, when the
      children's safety and well-being are endangered as defined in
      subsection (d) below and other services are deemed insufficient
      to ensure their safety and well-being, placement services shall
      be provided even though other appropriate services have not been
      offered.
   2) Other than situations where emergency placement is necessary, the
      family shall be offered an appropriate mix of services directed
      at family preservation to supplement their parenting skills or to
      resolve or alleviate family problems which threaten to harm the
      child. Services directed toward family preservation shall be
      offered and will be identified in the service plan. When
      services are unsuccessful or are offered to and refused by the
      family, the child may be placed in accordance with applicable
      legal procedures.
   3) When efforts toward achieving family reunification fail to result

DEPARTMENT OF CHILDREN AND FAMILY SERVICES

NOTICE OF PROPOSED AMENDMENTS

~~in--a-home-environment-that-is-consistent-with-the-child's-safety
and-well-being-a-new-permanent-legal-status-and-permanent-living
situation-shall-be-sought-in-accordance-with-the-child's-needs~~

~~b) Placement-is-Temporary
Placement-is-intended-to-be-a-temporary--situation--for--the--children
during--the--time--that--the-parents'-ability-to-care-for-the-child-is
being-evaluated-or-the-parents-are-receiving-services-to-alleviate-the
problems-in-the-home-so-the-family-can-be-reunited~~

~~c) Legal-Authority-to-Place
The-Department-shall-not-place-children-until-it-has--the--appropriate
legal--authority--to-do-so---Such-legal-authority-includes:--temporary
protective-custody-in-accordance-with-the-Abused-or--Neglected--Child
Reporting--Act--[Ill.-Rev.-Stat.-1991,-ch.-23,-par.-2051-et-seq.]-[325
ILCS-5],-an-adoptive-surrender[s]-in-accordance-with-the-Adoption--Act
[Ill.--Rev.--Stat.--1991,--ch.--40,--par.-1500-et-seq.]-[750-ILCS-50];
custody-or-guardianship-in-accordance-with-the-Juvenile-Court--Act--of
1987--[Ill.--Rev.--Stat.--1991,--ch.-37,-par.-801-1-et-seq.]-[705-ILCS
405],-or-temporary-custody-with-written-consent-of-the--parent(s)--or;
if--the--child-is-not-in-the-custody-of-either-parent;-written-consent
of-the-guardian-or-custodian-of-the--child--in--accordance--with--the
Children--and-Family-Services-Act-[Ill.-Rev.-Stat.-1991,-ch.-23,-par.-
5001-et-seq.]-[20-ILCS-505]-A-written-consent-from-a-parent;-guardian
or--legal--custodian--requesting-temporary-placement-services-for-their
children-is-known-as-a-voluntary-placement-agreement.--A--voluntary
placement--agreement--may-be-entered-into-for-a-maximum-of-60-days-and
requires-prior-written-approval-of-the-administrator-in-charge-of--the
Department--region--or--his-designee.--A-voluntary-placement-agreement
may-be--renewed--for--an--additional--60--days--only--with--the--prior
non-delegable--written--approval-of-the-administrator-in-charge-of-the
Department-region~~

~~d) Emergency-Placement
Emergency-placement-services-shall-be-provided-immediately-when--other
services--will--not-ensure-the-safety-of-the-child-when-the-Department
has-reason-to-believe:~~

~~1) that-leaving-the-child-in-the-home-of-his-caretaker-would-present
an-imminent-danger-to-the-child's-safety-and-well-being;-or~~

~~2) that-the-parent(s)-of-a-child-who-has-been-left-unsupervised--and
is--unable--to--care--for--himself--cannot-be-readily-located-and
emergency-caretaker-services-are-not-available;-or~~

~~3) that--services-directed-toward-keeping-the-family--together--would
not--sufficiently--protect--the--child--from--life-threatening-or
severe-physical-injury-and-would;-therefore;-endanger--the--child's
safety-and-well-being;-or~~

~~4) that-the-child-appears-to-be-severely--ill--or--injured--and--the
parent--or--caretaker--is--unable--to--care-for-the-child-in-this
situation;-or~~

~~5) the-child-is-abandoned;-or~~

~~6) the-child-is-a-runaway-in-accordance-with-89-Ill.-Adm.-Code--329.~~

DEPARTMENT OF CHILDREN AND FAMILY SERVICES

NOTICE OF PROPOSED AMENDMENTS

~~Return-of-Runaway-Children.~~

~~e) Placement-Selection
All--placement--decisions--will--be--made---consistent---with--the--best
interests--and--special--needs-of-the-child.-When-children-are-removed
from-the-care-of-a-custodial--parent,--the--Department--shall--explore
whether--the--non-custodial-parent-would-be-a-suitable-caregiver-to-the
children.---If---placement---with---the--non-custodial--parent--is--not
consistent--with--the-best-interests-and-special-needs-of-the-children
or-if-the-non-custodial-parent-is-not-a--suitable--caregiver--for--the
children;-placement-in-substitute-care-shall-be-considered.
Children-who-need-placement-shall:~~

~~1) be-placed,-if-possible-and-appropriate,-with-a-specified-relative
in--accordance--with--the--provisions--of--89--Ill.-Adm.-Code-335
(Relative-Home-Placement);~~

~~2) be-placed-in-the-least-restrictive--setting--which--most--closely
approximates--a--family--and--which--is--consistent-with-the-best
interest-of-the-children;-and~~

~~3) be-placed-within-reasonable-proximity-to--their--homes--when--the
permanency--goal--is--to--return--home-and-within-the-same-school
district;-whenever-possible.--taking--into--account--any--special
needs--of--the--child--and--family,-the-importance-of-maintaining
continuity--of--the--children's--educational---and---social
relationships--and--the--availability--of--the--service-resources
needed-for-the-child-and-family;-and~~

~~4) be-placed,-if-of-American-Indian-heritage;-according-to--criteria
described--in--89--Ill.--Adm.--Code--307,--Indian--Child--Welfare
Services.~~

~~f) Relative-Home-Care
1) Specified--relatives,--as-defined-in-89-Ill.-Adm.-Code-335,-shall
be-given-preference-and-first--consideration--over--more--distant
relatives--and--non-relatives--when--selecting--the--placement-for
children--for--whom--the--Department--is--legally---responsible.
Department-or-private-agency-staff-shall-make-reasonable-attempts
to--identify--contact,--and--assess--relatives--who-can-meet-the
requirements-of-89-Ill.-Adm.-Code-335,-Relative--Home--Placement;
and-who-are-willing-to-provide-care-to-related-children.~~

~~2) When-more-than-one-relative-has-been-identified-who-is-willing-to
act--as--a--caregiver--to-the-related-children,-the-Department-or
private-agency-provider--shall--select--the--relative--who--most
closely--meets--the--placement-selection-criteria-in-89-Ill.-Adm.-
Code-307;-Section-307.190(e).-Placement-Selection,--and--89--Ill.-
Adm.--Code--335.250,--Identification--and--Selection--of-Relative
Placements.~~

~~g) Foster-Family-Home-Care
1) Foster-family-home-care-is-provided--in--licensed--foster--family
homes--for--children--who--cannot-remain-home-and-who-can-benefit
from-a-family-structure-of-care.--The-Department-shall-have-legal
responsibility-for-the-child-before-the--child--is--placed--in--a~~

DEPARTMENT OF CHILDREN AND FAMILY SERVICES

NOTICE OF PROPOSED AMENDMENTS

foster-family-home.

g) Although--foster--family--home--care--is--generally--provided--to
children-whose-parents-are-unable-or-unwilling-to-protect-or-care
for--them,-it-is-also-available-for-hearing-impaired-children-who
require--special--education---not---available---in---their---home
communities.---The--Department-is-not-legally-responsible-for-the
children--receiving--this--unique--placement--service.---Care--is
provided--in--cooperation--with--the--Illinois--State--Board---of
Education.

h) Residential-Care
Residential--care--is-provided-in-licensed-group-homes-and-residential
care-facilities-(child-care-institutions-and-intermediate--or--skilled
nursing--care--facilities).---Group--homes-are-considered-to-be-a-less
restrictive-environment-than-an--institutional--setting.---Group--home
care--is--provided-for-teenagers-unable-to-adjust-to-family-living-who
need--a--less--structured--living--situation--than--is---provided---in
residential-care-facilities.--Placement-in-a-residential-care-facility
shall--be--made--only--when--no--other--less--restrictive--setting--is
appropriate-for:

1) children---requiring--intensive-services-to-change-behaviors-which
significantly-interfere-with-their-ability--to--cope--with--daily
life-or-which-preclude-placement-in-a-family-setting;-or

2) children-who--require--long--term-care-on-an-ongoing-basis-in-an
intermediate--or--skilled-nursing-care-facility-because-of-a-severe
physical-or-mental-handicap;-or

3) children-who-require-long-term-care-on-an-ongoing--basis--because
of-a-severe-emotional-handicap.

i) Sharing-Appropriate-Information-with-the-Caretaker

1) At-the-time-the-Department-places-a-child-in-foster-care-or-other
substitute--care--setting,-the-Department-shall-provide-available
information-about-the-child-necessary-for-the-proper-care-of--the
child-to-the-foster-parent-or-other-caretaker.

2) This-information-includes:

A) The--medical--history--of---the--child-including-known-medical
problems-or-communicable-diseases;

B) The-school-history--of---the--child;--including--any--special
educational-needs;

C) The--case-history-of-the-child,-including-how-the-child-came
into-care,-the-child's-legal-status-and-the-permanency--goal
for-the-child;

D) Other---background---information--of--the--child,--including
behavior-problems,-habits,-likes,-and-dislikes,-etc.

3) Information--subject--to--the--Mental--Health---and--Developmental
Disabilities-Code,-shall-be-shared-only--in--accordance--with--89
Ill.--Adm.--Code--411,-Confidentiality-of-Personal-Information-of
Persons-Served-by-the-Department,-Section-411.7.

4) Information--regarding--the--Acquired--Immunodeficiency--Syndrome
(AIDS),-AIDS-Related--Complex--(ARC)--or--Human--Immunodeficiency

DEPARTMENT OF CHILDREN AND FAMILY SERVICES

NOTICE OF PROPOSED AMENDMENTS

Virus--(HIV)--test-results,-shall-be-shared-only-in-accordance-with
89-Ill.--Adm.--Code-411,-Confidentiality-of-Personal-Information-of
Persons-Served-By-the-Department,-Section-411.11.

5) When--the--above--information--is--not--available--at-the-time-of
placement,-the-caretaker--shall--be--given--what--information--is
available--and--advised--that--additional--information--will--be
provided-when-it-is-received.

(Source: Repealed at 19 Ill. Reg. _____, effective
_____)

DEPARTMENT OF CONSERVATION

NOTICE OF PROPOSED AMENDMENTS

1) Heading of the Part: Designation of Restricted Waters in the State of
   Illinois

2) Code Citation: 17 Ill. Adm. Code 2030

3) Section Numbers: Proposed Action:

   2030.10   New Section
   2030.15   Amendments
   2030.20   Amendments
   2030.30   Amendments
   2030.40   Amendments
   2030.50   Amendments
   2030.60   Repealed
   2030.70   New Section

4) Statutory Authority: Implementing and authorized by Sections 5-7 and 5-12
   of the Boat Registration and Safety Act [625 ILCS 45/5-7 and 5-12].

5) A complete description of the subjects and issues involved: Amendments
   include adding language concerning the Uniform State Waterway Marking
   System, establishing minimum requirements for markers, establishing a
   process for designation, outlining designated areas and adding language
   regarding Riverboat Gambling Casinos.

6) Will this proposed rule replace an emergency rule currently in effect? No

7) Does this rulemaking contain an automatic repeal date? No

8) Do these proposed amendments contain incorporations by reference? No

9) Are there any other proposed amendments pending on this Part? No

10) Statement of statewide policy objectives: This rule has no impact on
    local governments.

11) Time, place and manner in which interested persons may comment on this
    proposed rulemaking: Comments on the proposed rule may be submitted in
    writing for a period of 45 days following publication of this notice to:

                  Jack Price
                  Department of Conservation
                  524 S. Second Street, Room 485
                  Springfield, IL 62701-1787
                  Phone 217/782-1809

12) Initial regulatory flexibility analysis: This rule does not affect small
    businesses.

DEPARTMENT OF CONSERVATION

NOTICE OF PROPOSED AMENDMENTS

13) State reason(s) for this rulemaking if it was not included in either of
    the two (2) most recent regulatory agendas: The Department neglected to
    submit an agency agenda for this Part.

The full text of the proposed amendments begins on the next page.

DEPARTMENT OF CONSERVATION

NOTICE OF PROPOSED AMENDMENTS

TITLE 17: CONSERVATION
CHAPTER I: DEPARTMENT OF CONSERVATION
SUBCHAPTER e: LAW ENFORCEMENT

PART 2030
DESIGNATION OF RESTRICTED WATERS IN THE STATE OF ILLINOIS

AUTHORITY: Implementing and authorized by Sections 5-7 and 5-12 of the Boat Registration and Safety Act [625 ILCS 45/5-7 and 5-12].

SOURCE: Adopted at 5 Ill. Reg. 8763, effective August 25, 1981; codified at 5 Ill. Reg. 10617; amended at 9 Ill. Reg. 4789, effective April 2, 1985; amended at 11 Ill. Reg. 9519, effective May 5, 1987; emergency amendments at 12 Ill. Reg. 8765, effective May 15, 1988, for a maximum of 150 days; emergency expired September 20, 1988; emergency amendments at 12 Ill. Reg. 12111, effective July 6, 1988, for a maximum of 150 days; emergency expired December 12, 1988; amended at 12 Ill. Reg. 16707, effective September 30, 1988; amended at 12 Ill. Reg. 20472, effective November 28, 1988; corrected at 13 Ill. Reg. 967; emergency amendments at 13 Ill. Reg. 2878, effective February 21, 1989, for a maximum of 150 days; amended at 13 Ill. Reg. 12814, effective July 21, 1989; amended at 16 Ill. Reg. 8483, effective May 26, 1992; amended at 19 Ill. Reg. _____, effective _____.

Section 2030.10 General Regulations

a) All waters designated as Restricted Boating Areas shall be posted in accordance with the United States Coast Guard's Uniform Waterway Marking System, contained in 33 CFR 66, Subpart 66.10, except as provided in subsections (b) and (c).

b) The use of regulatory markers prescribed by the Uniform State Waterway Marking System shall be further restricted as follows:

1) Where a sign is used as a marker, the sign shall be of square or rectangular shape. The sign shall be white, with an international orange border and an international orange geometric shape centered on the signboard.

2) The minimum size of any sign used as a marker shall be 24 inches on each side.

DEPARTMENT OF CONSERVATION

NOTICE OF PROPOSED AMENDMENTS

3) The minimum size of any buoy used as a marker shall be 9 inches in diameter.

4) The minimum size of any alpha or numeric characters used on any sign or buoy shall be 1 inch of height for every 50 feet of intended visibility, provided that in no case shall the height of the characters be less than 3 inches.

5) The minimum height of any geometric shape used on any sign or buoy shall be 12 inches.

6) The minimum band width of any border or geometric shape used on a sign or buoy shall be 2 inches.

c) No existing Restricted Boating Areas designated prior to July 1, 1995 shall be required to comply with the provisions of subsection (a) until July 1, 1995.

(Source: Former Section 2030.10 repealed at 16 Ill. Reg. 8483, effective May 26, 1992; new Section added at 19 Ill. Reg. _____, effective _____)

Section 2030.15 Designation of Restricted Waters by the Department of Conservation

a) Areas will be considered for designation, modification or elimination as restricted when the request for establishing a restricted area is made from outside the Department. Requests from outside the Department must meets the following criteria:

1) Be accompanied by a minimum of 25 signatures of interested persons over the age of 18 who would be directly affected by the restrictions.

2) Contain a detailed description of the area proposed for restriction with appropriate maps and other supporting data.

b) All requests for the restricting of areas shall meet the following criteria:

1) Evidence indicates that a boating safety hazard presently exists; or

2) Evidence indicates a public safety concern exists relative to other water uses (e.g. swimming, skiing, etc.); or

3) Evidence indicates that a boating user conflict exists.

c) Consideration for protection of private property shall not be considered as appropriate criteria for restriction.

d) Procedures for processing requests for restrictions.:

1) All requests will be forwarded to the Department of Conservation, Office of Law Enforcement Division.

2) The Department of Conservation, Office of Law Enforcement Division will investigate and validity of the request in accordance with subsection (b) Section 2030.15(b) and forward a report and recommendation to the Director for action by the Department.

DEPARTMENT OF CONSERVATION

NOTICE OF PROPOSED AMENDMENTS

(Source: Amended at 19 Ill. Reg. _____, effective
_____)

Section 2030.20 Region I - Designated Restricted Boating Areas.

a) The following portions of the Rock River are designated as Slow, No Wake areas:

1) An area of the Rock River located at Moonlite Bay, 4 miles east of Sterling and 6 miles west of Dixon, Illinois.

2) The portion of the Rock River 1/4 mile above the dam at Oregon, Illinois, at the docking area at Lowden Memorial Park.

3) An-area-of-the-Rock-River-located--at--Joe's--Marina,--NY--Second Street,-Rockford,-Illinois;

4) An-area--of--the--Rock-River-located-at-Martin-Park,-Love-Park, Illinois;

5) An-area-at-the-Rock-River-Boat-Club,-Oslonay,-Illinois;

b) The following portions of the Fox River are designated as Slow, No Wake areas:

The portion of the Fox River between the Main Street bridge of the City of Ottawa and the mouth of the Fox River at the confluence of the Illinois River.

c) The following portions of the Illinois River are designated as Slow, No Wake areas:

1) The portion of the Illinois River from the Burlington Northern R.R. bridge in the City of Ottawa to the upstream side of the mouth of the Fox River.

2) The area of the Illinois River near the Spring Bay boat harbor at Spring Bay, Illinois.

3) An area of the Illinois River at the Woodford County Conservation area, 7 miles north of Spring Bay off Route 87.

4) An area of the Illinois River located at the Detweiller Marina, Peoria, Illinois.

5) An area of the Illinois River at Alfresco Harbor, Peoria Heights, Illinois.

6) An area located at the Sobowski Marina, Peoria Heights, Illinois.

7) An area located at the Illinois Valley Yacht Club, Peoria Heights, Illinois.

8) An area at Henry, Illinois, on the west side of the River from Browns Landing to 300 yards north of the bridge.

9) The Lacon Boat Club Dock, Lacon, Illinois.

10) The boat harbor at Lacon, Illinois.

11) An-area-at-the-town-of-Hennepin-and-Spring-Valley,-Illinois;

12) 11) The-launching-area-at-Starved-Rock-State-Park;

13) The-launching-area-at-Starved-Rock-State-Park;

14) 12) The harbor of Starved Rock Marina, Ottawa, Illinois.

15) An-area-at-the-Starved-Rock-Yacht-Club-at-Ottawa,-Illinois;

16) 13) The waters of the Illinois River beginning in front of the Pekin Boat Club launching ramp.

DEPARTMENT OF CONSERVATION

NOTICE OF PROPOSED AMENDMENTS

d) The following portions of the Mississippi River are designated as Slow, No Wake areas:

1) An area bordering the Savanna Park waterfront, extending from a jetty south of the Ritchie Boat Dock, north to a jetty north of the Kindell Marina.

2) An--area--in--the-vicinity-of-the-boat-dock-and-launching-ramp-at boud-Thunder-Forest-Preserve-located-3-miles-west-of-Andalusia;

3) 2) An area in Vaely Chute which runs through the Andalusia Islands located 4 miles west of Andalusia.

4) 3) An area at the launching ramp and harbor of the Rock Island Boat Club located at the foot of 18th Avenue in Rock Island.

5) 4) An area at the harbor and boat ramp in front of the Legion Hall at Cordova, Illinois.

6) 5) An area located at the boat ramps, City of Moline, between 26th Street and 34th Street and River Drive.

7) 6) An area near the launching ramp and bathing beach at Keithsburg, Illinois.

8) 7) An area in the chute connecting Sturgeon Bay and the Mississippi River at New Boston, Illinois.

9) 8) An area near the boat ramp and floating gas station at the end of Route 17 at New Boston.

10) 9) An area at Shokohon, Illinois.

11) 10) An area in the fish preserve lock and dam 19 at Hamilton, Illinois.

12) 11) The public launching area 3 miles north above the dam at Hamilton.

13) An-area-6-1/2-miles-north-of-Hamilton,-Illinois;

14) 12) The waters of Harris Slough Mississippi River backwaters at the Galena Boat Club, 3 miles south of Galena, Illinois.

15) 13) The waters encompassing the cut starting at the mouth of the cut on Deadman's Slough, then northward approximately 250 feet to the confluence of the Harris and Reohough Sloughs.

16) 14) The backwater section of the Mississippi River (river mile marker 479.8) that starts at the Harbor opening of Potter's Lake, Sunset Park, Rock Island and covers the entire lake area.

17) 15) The area of Cattail Slough off the Mississippi River, located south of Fulton, Whiteside County, 7/10 mile in length, 150 yards wide, starting on the north at the Chicago and Northwestern R.R. bridge and extending south 7/10 of a mile to the first narrows.

18) 16) The waters of the south entrance to Chandler Slough lying upstream from the north boundary of the U.S. Fish and Wildlife Service property up to and including the Bent Prop Marina harbor area.

19) 17) The waters of Frentress Lake lying upstream from the boat ramp at Charlies Boat Dock, including the adjacent sand pit harbor area.

20) 18) An area of the Mississippi River in the vicinity of the Lazy River Marina at Savanna, Illinois, extending from the upper limit

DEPARTMENT OF CONSERVATION

NOTICE OF PROPOSED AMENDMENTS

of the dredge cut at Miller's Lake to a point north of the Miller's Hollow public launching ramp.

2) ~~An area located at the Albany Marina, Albany Township, Whiteside County~~

2) ~~An area located at the Fulton Sandbar in Fulton Township, Whiteside County.~~

e) The following waters of ~~Region 1~~ shall be designated as restricted waters as described below:

1) NO BOATS

   A) The swimming area at Martin Park, Loves Park, Illinois.

   B) The swimming area at Albany Beach located in Albany Township.

   C) The swimming area at the Santa Fe Island bar, approximately 4 miles north of Savanna.

   D) The head of Big Island and 1 1/2 miles north of Oquawka, Illinois.

   E) The Boy Scout Camp located on Lake Cooper, Mississippi River.

   F) ~~The swimming area located at Mississippi River Mile Marker 580, at the East Dubuque Sand Bar, East Dubuque, Illinois.~~

   6)F) The waters of the four chutes of Argyle Lake, approximately 2 miles north of Colchester, Illinois.

   H)G) The water 600 feet above and 150 feet below dams 12, 13, 14, 15, 16, 17 and 18 on the Mississippi River.

2) NO SKI - It shall be unlawful to water ski in the following designated waters:

   That area of the inside cut of the Mississippi River, opening directly into Frentress Lake, includes the area from the north to the south entrances from the river slough, inclusive, east of Mile Post 576.

(Source: Amended at 19 Ill. Reg. _____, effective _____)

Section 2030.30 Region II - Designated Restricted Boating Areas

a) The following portions of the Calumet and Little Calumet Rivers ~~waters located in Region II shall be~~ are designated as Slow, No Wake areas:

   1) ~~On the waters of the Little Calumet River in an area around the Forest Preserve launching Ramp at 31st Street and Ashland Avenue, Blue Island, Illinois, extending 150 feet from the launching ramp.~~ An area from the O'Brien Locks to the Michigan Central Railroad Bridge (approximately mile 326.5 to 325.3).

   2) ~~An area around the Bay Hill Marina, Wilmington, Illinois (approximately mile 273.7), extending 150 feet out into the river and 300 feet both upstream and downstream from the center of the Marina.~~ An area around the Pier 11 Marina and the Lake Calumet Boat and Gun Club (approximately mile 323.2 to 323.1).

DEPARTMENT OF CONSERVATION

NOTICE OF PROPOSED AMENDMENTS

3) ~~On the Des Plaines River in an area around the Three Rivers Yacht Club, Wilmington, Illinois (approximately mile 273.7), extending 150 feet from the harbor entrance.~~ An area around the Maryland Manor Boat Club, Skipper's Marina, and Rentner Marina (approximately mile 323.0 to 322.5).

4) ~~On the Kankakee River in an area around the launching camp at Des Plaines Conservation Area, extending 150 feet from the launching ramp.~~ An Area around Triplex Marina (approximately mile 319.9 to 319.8).

5) ~~On the Illinois River in an area around the launching ramp at Wm. G. Stratton Access Area (approximately mile 263.5), extending 150 feet from the launching ramp.~~

b) ~~It shall be unlawful to operate any watercraft with a motor larger than ten (10) horsepower on the waters of Griswold Lake in McHenry County.~~ The following portions of the Des Plaines River are designated as Slow, No Wake areas:

   1) An area around the Bay Hill Marina, Wilmington, Illinois (approximately mile 273.7), extending 150 feet out into the river and 300 feet both upstream and downstream from the center of the Marina.

   2) An area around the Three Rivers Yacht Club, Wilmington, Illinois (approximately mile 273.7), extending 150 feet from the harbor entrance.

c) The following portion of the Fox River is designated as a Slow, No Wake area:

   An area within 150 feet upstream and downstream of the I-90 bridge.

d) The following portions of Lake Michigan are designated as No Boat areas:

   1) An area at Worth Point Marina, located off the nothern breakwater, running 200 yards parallel to the shoreline and 100 yards out into the lake.

   2) An area at Illinois Beach State Park, located between the park office and the #3 bathhouse, running parallel to the shoreline and 70 yards out into the lake.

(Source: Amended at 19 Ill. Reg. _____, effective _____)

Section 2030.40 Region III - Designated Restricted Boating Areas

The following areas are designated as Slow, No Wake areas:

a) ~~These~~ portions Posted areas of Lake Decatur ~~listed below,~~ Decatur, Illinois.

   Big Creek Area

   Rea's Bridge Area

   Sand Creek Area

   West's Landing Area

DEPARTMENT OF CONSERVATION

NOTICE OF PROPOSED AMENDMENTS

b) Posted areas of East and West Lakes, north of Paris, Illinois.
c) Posted areas of Lake Vermilion, Danville, Illinois.
d) Posted areas of Waterworks Lake, Little Vermilion River, Georgetown, Illinois.
e) Posted areas of Lake Shelbyville.
f) Posted areas of Lake Mattoon in Cumberland, Coles and Shelby Counties.
g) Posted areas of Charleston Side Channel Lake, Charleston, Illinois.
h) Posted areas of Mill Creek Lake, Clark County Park District, Clarksville, Illinois.
i) Posted areas of Clinton Lake, Clinton, Illinois.

(Source: Amended at 19 Ill. Reg. _____, effective
_____)

Section 2030.50 Region IV - Designated Restricted Boating Areas

a) The following portions of the Illinois River are designated as Slow, No Wake areas:
   1) In the area designated on the west side of Diamond Island in the waters known as Dark Chute.
   2) The designated portion of the river in the vicinity of "The Boats" at Hapley, Illinois.
   3)1) The designated area in the vicinity of the boat launching ramp at Havana, Illinois.
   4)2) The mouth of Patterson Bay.
   5)3) The waters of Bath Chute at head of Island, at the foot of Island, above the town of Bath, Illinois, and below the town of Bath, Illinois.
   6) Designated areas of Pulnam Lake in Calhoun County.
   9)4) Designated areas of Silver Lake in Calhoun County.
b) The following portion of the Mississippi River is designated as No Boats:
   The water 600 feet above and 150 feet below dams 19, 20, 21 and 22 on the Mississippi River.
c) The following portions of Quincy Bay in Adams County are designated as Slow, No Wake Areas:
   1) Designated area at the entrance to Broad Lake.
   2) Designated area at the "River Channel Cut-Through."
   3) Quincy Bay Harbor area from the Railroad Bridge south to the southern tip of Quinsippi Island.
d) Piasa Creek in Jersey County from its mouth at the Mississippi River upstream to Illinois Route 100 bridge.
e) Otter Creek in Jersey County from its mouth at the Mississippi Illinois River upstream to Illinois Route 100 bridge.
f) The following portions of Sangchris Lake in Christian County---the buoyed areas of the areas containing the east and west boat launches: are designated as No Boat areas:
   1) The power plant intake arm beyond the buoy line.

DEPARTMENT OF CONSERVATION

NOTICE OF PROPOSED AMENDMENTS

   2) The power plant discharge arm beyond the buoy line.
   3) The designated South Waterfowl Refuge or Rest Area.
   4) The designated North Waterfowl Refuge or Rest Area.
g) Macoupin Creek from its mouth at the Illinois River upstream to Reddish Ford bridge.
h) The following portions of Coffeen Lake in Montgomery County---the buoyed areas surrounding all boat launches: are designated as No Boats and No Fishing areas:
   1) The power plant intake arm beyond the buoy line.
   2) The power plant discharge arm beyond the buoy line.
   3) The buoyed area of the spillway.
i) The following portions of the Kaskaskia River are designated as Slow, No Wake Areas:
   1) All backwaters and/or side channels below Fayetteville, Illinois.
   2) All waters between the Illinois Route 3 Bridge and the Northern boundary of the public boat ramp in Evansville, Illinois.
   3) All waters between the ICG Railroad Bridge and the entrance to the public boat launching ramp known as "Baldwin Ramp."
   4) River Mile 24 to 25.
   5) 100 yards upstream and 100 yards downstream from the Kaskaskia River Lock and Dam.
   6) 100 yards upstream and 100 yards downstream from the New Athens boat launching ramp.
   j) The following portion of the Mississippi River is designated as a Slow, No Wake area:
      An area 6 1/2 miles north of Hamilton, Illinois.
   k) Those portions of Carlyle Lake, as posted, are designated No Entry, No Boats, No Fishing, or otherwise restricted areas.

(Source: Amended at 19 Ill. Reg. _____, effective
_____)

Section 2030.60 Region V - Designated Restricted Boating Areas (Repealed)

That portion of Big Grand Pierre Creek in Pope County from its mouth at the Ohio River to a point one half mile upstream is designated Slow No Wake from January 1 through August 31.

(Source: Repealed at 19 Ill. Reg. _____, effective
_____)

Section 2030.70 Riverboat Gambling Casinos - Designated Restricted Boating Areas

It shall be unlawful to operate any watercraft at greater than a No Wake speed within 150 feet of any moored, licensed Riverboat Gambling Casino on the waters of this State.

DEPARTMENT OF CONSERVATION

NOTICE OF PROPOSED AMENDMENTS

(Source: Added at 19 Ill. Reg. _____, effective _____)

ENVIRONMENTAL PROTECTION AGENCY

NOTICE OF PROPOSED AMENDMENT(S)

1) Heading of the Part: Annual Testing Fees For Analytical Services

2) Code Citation: 35 Ill. Adm. Code 691

3) Section Numbers: Proposed Action:

691.102	Amend
691.103	Amend
691.104	Amend
691.105	Amend
691.106	Amend
691.201	Amend
691.202	Repeal
691.203	Amend
691.301	Amend
691.303	Amend
691.304	Amend
691.305	Amend
691.306	Amend
691.401	New Section
691.403	New Section
691.Appendix A	Repeal

4) Statutory Authority: Implementing and authorized by Section 17.7 of the Illinois Environmental Protection Act (415 ILCS 5/17.7) as added by P.A. 86-670, effective January 1, 1990 and as amended by Public Act 88-488, effective September 10, 1993.

5) A Complete Description of the Subjects and Issues Involved: This rulemaking proposes amendments to the Testing Fees for Analytical Services rules. These rules establish procedures for the determination and the collection of fees from community water supplies ("CWS") for analytical services to show compliance with the drinking water regulations established pursuant to the federal Safe Drinking Water Act (42 U.S.C. 300f (1991)) and the Illinois Environmental Protection Act ("Act") (415 ILCS 5). The proposed amendments to these rules reflect the changes resulting from the enactment of Public Act 88-488, effective September 10, 1993. In accordance with Section 17.7(e) of the Act (415 ILCS 5/17.7(e)), the Agency has submitted these amendments to the Community Water Testing Council ("Council") for review prior to submission of these rules for rulemaking and the Council voted its concurrence with these amendments on December 7, 1994.

6) Will this proposed rule replace an emergency rule currently in effect? No

7) Does this rulemaking contain an automatic repeal date? No

8) Does this proposed rule (amendment, repealer) contain incorporations by

ENVIRONMENTAL PROTECTION AGENCY

NOTICE OF PROPOSED AMENDMENT(S)

reference? No

9) Are there any other proposed amendments pending on this Part? No

10) Statement of Statewide Policy Objectives: This rulemaking does not create or expand a mandate under Section 3 of the State Mandates Act [930 ILCS 805/3].

11) Time, Place, and Manner in which interested persons may comment on this proposed rulemaking:

Stephen C. Ewart, Deputy Counsel
Division of Legal Counsel
Illinois Environmental Protection Agency
2200 Churchill Road, P.O. Box 19276
Springfield, IL 62794-9276
(217) 782-5544

12) Initial Regulatory Flexibility Analysis:

A) Date rule was submitted to the Business Assistance Office of the Department of Commerce and Community Affairs: January 25, 1995

B) Types of small businesses affected: The proposed amendments provide an updated fee-based voluntary program for analytical services to municipalities, small businesses, and other entities that furnish drinking water to the public as CWSs.

C) Reporting, bookkeeping or other procedures required for compliance: A CWS must submit samples and maintain records in the same fashion as required by the sampling, analytical, and recordkeeping requirements established for each CWS by State and federal regulations pursuant to the federal Safe Drinking Water Act (42 U.S.C. 300f (1991)).

D) Types of professional skills necessary for compliance: The proposed amendments require same sampling and recordkeeping skills that are required by the existing rules.

13) State reasons for this rulemaking if it was not included in either of the two most recent regulatory agendas: This proposed rulemaking was included in the last regulatory agenda that was published in the Illinois Register on January 6, 1995 (19 Ill. Reg. 90).

The full text of the Proposed Rule begins on the next page:

ENVIRONMENTAL PROTECTION AGENCY

NOTICE OF PROPOSED AMENDMENT(S)

TITLE 35: ENVIRONMENTAL PROTECTION
SUBTITLE F: PUBLIC WATER SUPPLIES
CHAPTER II: ENVIRONMENTAL PROTECTION AGENCY

PART 691
ANNUAL TESTING FEES FOR ANALYTICAL SERVICES

SUBPART A: GENERAL

Section
691.101   Purpose and Applicability
691.102   Definitions
691.103   Payment of Annual the Testing Fee Required Prior to Laboratory Testing by the Agency
691.104   Analytical Service Period
691.105   Reduced Participation in the Annual Testing Fee Program
691.106   Relation to Other Fee Systems
691.107   Severability

SUBPART B: PROCEDURES FOR ESTABLISHING ANNUAL TESTING FEES

Section
691.201   Annual Testing Fee For Calendar Year 1990
691.202   Annual Testing Fee After Calendar Year 1990 (Repealed)
691.203   Determining the Number of Service Connections

SUBPART C: PROCEDURES FOR BILLING AND COLLECTING ANNUAL THE TESTING FEES

Section
691.301   Billing Statements
691.302   Due Date of Payment
691.303   Form of Payment
691.304   Prohibition Against Refund
691.305   Overpayment or Underpayment of Annual Testing Fee
691.306   Audit and Access to Records

SUBPART D: DISPUTE RESOLUTION PROCEDURES

Section
691.401   Council's Non-Concurrence With the Agency Fee Determination
691.403   Dispute Resolution of Testing Fee Issues Between the Agency and the Council
APPENDIX A   Agreement for Reduced Participation in Sample Analysis (Repealed)

AUTHORITY: Implementing and authorized by Section 17.7 of the Environmental Protection Act [415 ILCS 5/17.7] (see Public Act 88-489, effective September

ENVIRONMENTAL PROTECTION AGENCY

NOTICE OF PROPOSED AMENDMENT(S)

10, 1993).

SOURCE: Adopted at 14 Ill. Reg. 2045, effective January 18, 1990; amended at
19 Ill. Reg. _____, effective _____.

SUBPART A: GENERAL

Section 691.102 Definitions

a) Unless specified otherwise, all terms shall have the meaning set forth
    in the Act.

b) For purposes of this Part, the following definitions apply:

    "Act" means the Environmental Protection Act [Ill.--Rev.--Stat.--1987,
    ch.--111-1/2,--pars.--1001-et-seq.] [415 ILCS 5].

    "Agency" means the Illinois Environmental Protection Agency.

    "Annual testing Testing fee" or "fee" means the amount due from the
    community water supply for analytical services as prescribed by
    Section 17.7 of the Act.

    "Board" means the Illinois Pollution Control Board.

    "Certified laboratory" means any laboratory approved by the Agency
    pursuant to 35 Ill. Adm. Code 183, or other department or agency of
    State government if such authority is delegated for the specific
    parameters to be examined, pursuant to Section 4(n) or (o) of the Act.

    "Community water supply" or "supply" means a public water supply which
    serves or is intended to serve at least 25 service connections used by
    residents or regularly serves at least 25 residents. (Section 3.05 of
    the Act)

    "Council" means the Community Water Supply Testing Council established
    by Section 17.7(g) of the Act.

    "Laboratory testing" means the analysis of drinking water by the
    Agency required under Section 4(p)-of-the-Act;-other--than--analytical
    work--described--in--Section--691.103(b)(1)--or--(2) 35 Ill. Adm. Code
    Subtitle F and regulations established under the federal Safe Drinking
    Water Act (42 U.S.C. 300 f).

    "Parent community water supply" or "Parent supply" is a community
    water supply that uses or sells potable water derived from its own
    sources or receives only a portion of its potable water from other
    potable water sources.

ENVIRONMENTAL PROTECTION AGENCY

NOTICE OF PROPOSED AMENDMENT(S)

"Public water supply" or "PWS" means all mains, pipes and structures
through which water is obtained and distributed to the public,
including wells and well structures. Intakes and cribs, pumping
stations, treatment plants, reservoirs, storage tanks and
appurtenances, collectively or severally, actually used or intended
for use for the purpose of furnishing water for drinking or general
domestic use and which serve at least 25 service connections or which
regularly serve at least 25 persons at least 60 days per year. A
public water supply is either a "community water supply" or a
"non-community water supply". (Section 3.28 of the Act)

"Purchase community water supply" or "Purchase supply" is a community
water supply that purchases or receives its potable water entirely
from another potable water source.

"Service connection" means the opening, including all fittings and
appurtenances at the water main through which water is supplied to the
user.

(Source: Amended   at   19   Ill.   Reg.   _____,   effective
_____)

Section 691.103 Payment of Annual the Testing Fee Required Prior to Laboratory
Testing by the Agency

a) Community water supplies must pay all annual testing fees due under
    this Part prior to the initiation of any laboratory testing by the
    Agency.

b) Unless all fees due from a community water supply under this Part have
    been paid to the Agency, the Agency shall have the duty under Section
    4(p) of the Act to analyze samples from such community water supply
    only for:

    1) Up to six total coliform samples per sampling period as required
        under Section 4(p) of the Act; and

    2) Contaminants for which a maximum allowable concentration in
        finished drinking water has been established by Board regulation
        in 35 Ill. Adm. Code: Subtitle F prior to January 1, 1988.

(Source: Amended   at   19   Ill.   Reg.   _____,   effective
_____)

Section 691.104 Analytical Service Period

a) Except as provided otherwise in subsection (b), upon payment of the
    annual testing fee by a community water supply in accordance with this
    Part, the Agency shall perform laboratory testing commencing no later
    than July 1 of the year in which payment is received by the Agency,
    and ending on the following June 30.

ENVIRONMENTAL PROTECTION AGENCY

NOTICE OF PROPOSED AMENDMENT(S)

b) For a new community water supply that receives a billing statement after the Agency's annual billing cycle, the Agency shall perform laboratory testing for a period of time which shall commence on the first day of the first calendar quarter after fee payment is received by the Agency, and shall end on the following June 30.

(Source: Amended at 19 Ill. Reg. _____, effective _____)

Section 691.105 Reduced Participation in the Annual Testing Fee Program

a) Except as provided otherwise in subsection (b), an annual testing fee shall be due from each community water supply.

b) No annual testing fee shall be due from any community water supply that both 1) Signs and returns to the Agency the Agreement set forth in Appendix A notifies the Agency in writing within 45 days after issuance of the billing statement to the community water supply of its decision not to participate in the testing fee program; and 2) Submits no samples to the Agency for analytical testing during the analytical service period for which the signed Agreement submitted pursuant to subsection (b)(1) applies; or other than samples for the analyses described in Section 691.103(b).

c) If no annual testing fee is due received from a community water supply pursuant to subsection (b), the Agency shall not perform any laboratory testing for the supply during the analytical service period unless revenues from other sources are provided for which the signed Agreement submitted under subsection (b)(1) applies; other than the testing described in Section 691.103(b).

d) The Agency with the concurrence of the Council shall establish testing fees pursuant to Section 17.7 of the Act for community water supplies which shall consider but not be limited to the following criteria:

1) number of service connections of the community water supply;

2) maximum and minimum testing fees for all community water supplies;

3) single or multiple payment plans for the annual or multi-year testing fee; or

4) testing requirement differences among community water supplies based on considerations including but not limited to the following:

A) the potable water is derived from a groundwater or surface water source;

B) the community water supply is a parent or purchase supply; or

C) the differences in required analytical services.

(Source: Amended at 19 Ill. Reg. _____, effective _____)

ENVIRONMENTAL PROTECTION AGENCY

NOTICE OF PROPOSED AMENDMENT(S)

Section 691.106 Relation to Other Fee Systems

Payment of fees under this Part shall not include any fees due to the Agency for any purpose other than the annual testing fees.

(Source: Amended at 19 Ill. Reg. _____, effective _____)

SUBPART B: PROCEDURES FOR ESTABLISHING ANNUAL TESTING FEES

Section 691.201 Annual Testing Fee For Calendar Year 1990

For calendar year 1990, the fee from each community water supply shall be determined by multiplying $0.75 by the number of service connections; subject to a minimum fee of $90 and a maximum fee of $2,500. (Section 17.7(a) of the Act)

a) The Agency shall collect an annual nonrefundable testing fee from each community water supply for participating in the laboratory fee program for analytical services to determine compliance with contaminant levels specified in State or federal drinking water regulations. A community water supply may commit to participation in the laboratory fee program. If the community water supply makes such a commitment, it shall commit for a period consistent with the participation requirements established by the Agency and the Community Water Supply Testing Council (Council). If a community water supply elects not to participate, it must annually notify the Agency in writing of its decision not to participate in the laboratory fee program.

b) The Agency, with the concurrence of the Council, shall determine the fee for participating in the laboratory fee program for analytical services. The Agency, with the concurrence of the Council, may establish multi-year participation requirements for community water supplies and establish fees accordingly. The Agency shall base its annual fee determination upon the actual and anticipated costs for testing under State and federal drinking water regulations and the associated administrative costs of the Agency and the Council. By October 1 of each year, the Agency shall submit its fee determination and supporting documentation for the forthcoming year to the Council. Before the following January 1, the Council shall hold at least one regular meeting to consider the Agency's determination. If the Council concurs with the Agency's determination, it shall thereupon take effect. The Agency and the Council may establish procedures for resolution of disputes in the event the Council does not concur with the Agency's fee determination.

c) Community water supplies that choose not to participate in the laboratory fee program or do not pay the fees shall have the duty to analyze all drinking water samples as required by State or federal safe drinking water regulations established after the federal Safe

ENVIRONMENTAL PROTECTION AGENCY

NOTICE OF PROPOSED AMENDMENT(S)

Drinking Water Act Amendments of 1986. (Section 17.7 of the Act)

(Source: Amended at 19 Ill. Reg. _____, effective
_____)

Section 691.202 Annual Testing Fee After Calendar Year 1990 (Repealed)

a) The-annual-fees-for-calendar-years-after-1990-shall-be--determined--by
the--Agency--in--accordance-with-this-Section,-and-shall-be-within-the
following-ranges:
1) The-basic-testing-fee-shall-be-at-least-$0.65-and-not--more--than
$0.95-per-service-connection:
2) The--minimum-fee-per-community-water-supply-shall-be-at-least-$75
and-not-more-than-$110;-and
3) The-maximum-fee-per-community-water--supply--shall--be--at--least
$7,000-and-not-more-than-$3200.
b) The-Agency-shall-base-its-annual-fee-determination-upon-the-actual-and
anticipated--costs--of--the--additional-testing-provided-for-under-the
Federal-Safe-Drinking-Water-Act-amendments-of-1986;-and-the-appropriate
administrative-costs-of-the-Agency--and--the--Community--Water--Supply
Testing-Council.
c) For--each-calendar-year,-the-Agency-shall-submit-its-fee-determination
and-supporting-documentation-to-the-Council-by-the--preceding--October
1;-and-the-council-shall-hold-at-least-one-regular-meeting-to-consider
the-Agency's-determination-prior-to-January-1.
d) If--the--Council--concurs--with--the--Agency's-determination,-it-shall
thereupon-take-effect.
e) If-the-Council-does-not-concur-with-an--Agency--fee--determination--by
January--1--of--the--calendar-year-in-which-the-fee-was-intended-to-be
applicable,-the-prior-year's-fees--shall--remain--in--effect--for--one
additional--year.--During--this-additional-year,-the-Director-and-the
Chairman-shall-make-every-reasonable-effort-to-resolve-any-outstanding
concerns.--Failure-to-resolve--such--concerns--by--January--1--of--the
following--year--shall--result--in--the--Agency--having-the-duty-under
subsection-(p)-of-Section--4--of--the--Act--to--analyze--samples--from
community--water-supplies-only-for-total-coliform-and-contaminants-for
which--a--maximum--allowable--concentration--in--finished--water---was
established-by-Board-regulation-prior-to-January-1,-1988.

(Source: Repealed at 19 Ill. Reg. _____, effective
_____)

Section 691.203 Determining the Number of Service Connections

a) In-determining-the-number-of-service-connections-for-For purposes of
calculating determining the annual testing fee under Sections 691.201
or-691.202, the community water supply shall include only those
service connections for which the community water supply is:

ENVIRONMENTAL PROTECTION AGENCY

NOTICE OF PROPOSED AMENDMENT(S)

1) Directly metering or collecting revenue; or
2) Otherwise providing delivery of potable water.
b) When finished water is sold to another community water supply, the
selling community water supply shall not include the service
connections of the purchasing community water supply for purposes of
calculating the annual testing fee under Sections 691.201 or--691.202. .
The purchasing community water supply shall include its service
connections for purposes of calculating the annual testing fee under
Sections 691.201 or-691.202.

(Source: Amended at 19 Ill. Reg. _____, effective
_____)

SUBPART C: PROCEDURES FOR BILLING AND COLLECTING ANNUAL THE TESTING
FEES

Section 691.301 Billing Statements

Commencing-in-1990,-the The Agency shall send a billing statement for the
annual testing fee to each community water supply in January of each calendar
year.

(Source: Amended at 19 Ill. Reg. _____, effective
_____)

Section 691.303 Form of Payment

a) Payment must be by check or money order payable to "Treasurer, State
of Illinois" and shall be accompanied by the name of the community
water supply and the facility identification number assigned by the
Agency's Division of Public Water Supplies.
b) Payment and all supporting documentation must be mailed together in a
single package to:
Illinois Environmental Protection Agency
Data Entry and Cash Receipts Unit
Fiscal Services Section
2200-Churchill-Road
P.O. Box 19276
Springfield, Illinois 62794-9276
c) Payment shall not include any fees due to the Agency for any purpose
other than the annual testing fee.

(Source: Amended at 19 Ill. Reg. _____, effective
_____)

Section 691.304 Prohibition Against Refund

Any annual testing fee remitted to the Agency shall not be refunded at any time

ENVIRONMENTAL PROTECTION AGENCY

NOTICE OF PROPOSED AMENDMENT(S)

or for any reason, either in whole or in part.

(Source: Amended   at   19   Ill.   Reg.   _____,   effective
_____)

Section 691.305 Overpayment or Underpayment of Annual Testing Fee

    a) If the amount remitted is more than the amount due under this Part,
the community water supply's account shall be credited by the amount
of the overpayment.

    b) If the amount remitted is less than the amount due under this Part,
the community water supply will be billed for the balance due.

(Source: Amended   at   19   Ill.   Reg.   _____,   effective
_____)

Section 691.306 Audit and Access to Records

    a) Each community water supply for which an annual testing fee is
required under this Part shall preserve and maintain all records
relating to the number of service connections used in calculating the
fee for at least 5 years after the close of the analytical service
period.

    b) The records described in subsection (a) shall be available to the
Agency or its authorized representative for examination during normal
business hours.

(Source: Amended   at   19   Ill.   Reg.   _____,   effective
_____)

SUBPART D: DISPUTE RESOLUTION PROCEDURES

Section 691.401 Council's Non-Concurrence With the Agency Fee Determination

If the Council does not concur with the Agency fee determination by January 1
of the calendar year in which the testing fee was intended to be effective, or
if the Agency and the Council do not agree on any other issue related to the
testing fee program by January 1 of the same calendar year, the Agency and the
Council shall make every effort to resolve the dispute in question within the
time frame established in Section 691.403 below.

(Source: Added   at   19   Ill.   Reg.   _____,   effective
_____)

Section 691.403 Dispute Resolution of Testing Fee Issues Between the Agency and the Council

ENVIRONMENTAL PROTECTION AGENCY

NOTICE OF PROPOSED AMENDMENT(S)

    a) Where the Agency and the Council cannot agree on issues related to the
testing fee program, the Council shall initiate procedures for an
external audit of the testing fee program.

    b) The results of the external audit including the recommendation shall
serve as the basis for the Agency and the Council deliberations
regarding the testing fee in dispute.

    c) If the conclusions of the external audit will not be completed by
January 1 of the calendar year in which the testing fee was intended
to take effect, the Agency shall issue billing statements to community
water supplies in amounts that are derived from the Agency fee
determination.

    d) If the Agency and the Council deliberations conclude that, based upon
the external audit, the testing fee should be different from the
Agency fee determination amount, the Agency shall make the necessary
adjustments in the subsequent fiscal year's Agency fee determination
amount.

(Source: Added   at   19   Ill.   Reg.   _____,   effective
_____)

ENVIRONMENTAL PROTECTION AGENCY

NOTICE OF PROPOSED AMENDMENT(S)

Section 691.APPENDIX A Agreement for Reduced Participation in Sample Analysis (Repealed)

AGREEMENT-TO-PROVIDE-FOR-REDUCED-PARTICIPATION-IN-SAMPLE-ANALYSIS

FACILITY-#   FOR-SAMPLING-FROM --------,-19--*,-THROUGH-JUNE-30,-19--*
NAME
ADDRESS

Pursuant-to-Section-17.9-of-the-Environmental-Protection-Act-(Ill.--Rev.--Stat.
1987,--ch.--111-1/2,--par.-1017.9,--as-added-by-P.A.-85-678,-effective-January-1,
1989),-the-above-referenced-community-water--supply--elects--not--to--have--the
Illinois---Environmental---Protection---Agency---analyze--drinking--water--for
contaminants-other-than-total-coliform-and-contaminants--for--which--a--maximum
allowable--concentration--in-finished-water-was-established-by-Board-regulation
prior-to-January-1,-1988.

It-is-understood-that--all--laboratory--analyses--must--be--carried--out--by--a
laboratory--which--has--been--certified-by-the-Agency-and-that-all-test-results
must-be-forwarded-to-the-Agency-in-accordance-with-35-Ill.-Adm.-Code:--Subtitle
F.

It-is-further-understood-that-failure-by-the-community-water-supply-to--perform
laboratory-analyses-will-result-in-enforcement-action-by-the-Agency.

It-is-further-understood-that-the-Agency-will-continue-to-perform-laboratory
analyses-only-for-up-to-six-total-coliform-samples--and--for--contaminants--for
which--a--maximum-allowable-concentration-in-finished-water-has-been-established
by-Board-regulation-prior-to-January-1,-1988.

It-is-further-understood-that-this-Agreement-will-expire-on-June-30,-19--*,-and
that-this-Agreement-is-irrevocable.

Owner-or-Official-Custodian------------------Date
F-------------
*The-Agency-will-enter-the-correct--year--for--the--annual--analytical--service
period-(as-described-in-Section-691.404).

(Source: Repealed at 19 Ill. Reg. _____, effective
_____)

POLLUTION CONTROL BOARD

NOTICE OF PROPOSED AMENDMENTS

1) **Heading of the Part:** Hazardous Waste Injection Restrictions

2) **Code Citation:** 35 Ill. Adm. Code 738

3) **Section numbers:** Proposed Action

   738.117   Amended

4) **Statutory Authority:** 415 ILCS 5/13, 22.4 and 27

5) **A complete description of the subjects and issues involved:**

A more detailed description is contained in the Board's proposed opinion of March 2, 1995, in R95-4 and R95-6 (consolidated), which opinion is available from the address below. Sections 13(c) and 22.4(a) of the Environmental Protection Act (415 ILCS 5/13(c) & 22.4(a)) provides that Section 5-35 of the Administrative Procedure Act [5 ILCS 100/5-35] shall not apply. Because this rulemaking is not subject to Section 5-35 of the APA, it is not subject to first notice or to second notice review by JCAR.

This rulemaking updates Parts 700, 702, 703, 705, 720, 721, 722, 723, 724, 725, 726, 728, 730, 738, and 739 of the Illinois RCRA Subtitle C hazardous waste and underground injection control (UIC) rules to correspond with amendments adopted by U.S. EPA that appeared in the Federal Register during the period July 1 through December 31, 1994. During this period, U.S. EPA amended its regulations as follows:

Federal Action	Summary
59 Fed. Reg. 38536, July 28, 1994	Exclusion from definition of solid waste for certain in-process recycled secondary materials used by the petroleum refining industry
59 Fed. Reg. 43496, August 24, 1994	Withdrawal of exemption from Subtitle C regulation of slag residues from high temperature metal recovery (HTMR) of electric arc furnace dust (K061), steel finishing pickle liquor (K062), and electroplating sludges (F006) that are used in a manner constituting disposal
59 Fed. Reg. 47980, September 19, 1994	Restoration of text from 40 CFR 268.7(a) inadvertently omitted in the amendments of August 31, 1993, at 58 Fed. Reg. 46040

59 Fed. Reg. 47982,   Phase II land disposal restrictions (LDRs);
September 19, 1994   toxicity wastes and newly-listed wastes
   (including underground injection control
   (UIC) amendments)

59 Fed. Reg. 62896,   Organic material air emission standards for
December 6, 1994   tanks, surface impoundments, and containers

60 Fed. Reg. 242,   Corrections to the Phase II land disposal
January 3, 1995   restrictions (universal treatment standards)

In addition to these principal amendments that occurred during the update period, the Board has included an additional, later action:

This January 3 action was an amendment of the September 19, 1994 Phase II LDRs (universal waste rule). U.S. EPA corrected errors and clarified language in the universal treatment standards. The Board did not delay in adding these amendments for three reasons:

1) the January 3, 1995 amendments are corrections and clarifications of the September 19, 1994 regulations, and not new substantive amendments;

2) the January 3, 1995 amendments will facilitate implementation of the Phase II LDRs; and

3) prompt action on the January 3, 1995 amendments will allow us to add the January 3, 1995 amendments to those of September 19, 1994. (See "Expedited Consideration," below.)

The Board also notes that the later amendments occurred within six months of the earliest amendments included in this docket, even if they occurred outside the nominal time-frame of the docket.

In addition to the federally-derived amendments, the Board used this opportunity to undertake a number of housekeeping and corrective amendments. We have effected the removal of all cross-references for effective dates and repealed Part 700. We have corrected equations and language and structure of various provisions, including correcting formulae to the standard scientific format. We have tried to improve the effective dates and spelling where necessary.

Specifically, the segment of the amendments involved in Part 738 incorporates the UIC-related aspects of the newly-listed hazardous waste (wastes listed by U.S. EPA since 1984) land disposal restrictions of the September 19, 1994 federal Phase II LDRs.

---

6) Will this proposed rule replace an emergency rule currently in effect? No

7) Does this rulemaking contain an automatic repeal date? No

8) Do these proposed amendments contain incorporations by reference? No

9) Are there any other proposed amendments pending on this Part? No

10) Statement of statewide policy objectives: This rulemaking is mandated by Sections 13(c) and 22.4(a) of the Environmental Protection Act [415 ILCS 5/13(c) & 22.4(a)]. The statewide policy objectives are set forth in Section 10 of that Act. This rulemaking imposes mandates on units of local government only to the extent that they may be involved in the generation, transportation, treatment, storage, or disposal of hazardous waste or they engage in underground injection of waste.

11) Time, place and manner in which interested persons may comment on this proposed rulemaking: The Board will accept written public comment on this proposal for a period of 45 days after the date of this publication. Comments should reference Docket R95-4/R95-6 and be addressed to:

Ms. Dorothy M. Gunn, Clerk
Illinois Pollution Control Board
State of Illinois Center, Suite 11-500
100 W. Randolph St.
Chicago, IL 60601
(312) 814-6931

12) Initial regulatory flexibility analysis:

A) Date rule was submitted to the Small Business Office of the Department of Commerce and Community Affairs: March 6, 1995.

B) Types of small businesses affected: The existing rules and proposed amendments affect small businesses that generate, treat, store, or dispose of hazardous waste or engage in underground injection of waste.

C) Reporting, bookkeeping or other procedures required for compliance: The existing rules and proposed amendments require extensive reporting, bookkeeping, and other procedures, including the preparation of manifests and annual reports, waste analyses, and maintenance of operating records.

D) Types of professional skills necessary for compliance: Compliance with the existing rules and proposed amendments may require

POLLUTION CONTROL BOARD

NOTICE OF PROPOSED AMENDMENTS

services of an attorney, certified public accountant, chemist, and registered professional engineer.

The full text of the proposed amendments begins on the next page:

POLLUTION CONTROL BOARD

NOTICE OF PROPOSED AMENDMENTS

TITLE 35: ENVIRONMENTAL PROTECTION
SUBTITLE G: WASTE DISPOSAL
CHAPTER I: POLLUTION CONTROL BOARD
SUBCHAPTER d: UNDERGROUND INJECTION CONTROL AND
UNDERGROUND STORAGE TANK PROGRAMS

PART 738
HAZARDOUS WASTE INJECTION RESTRICTIONS

SUBPART A: GENERAL

AUTHORITY: Implementing Section 13 and 22.4 and authorized by Section 27 of the Environmental Protection Act [415 ILCS 5/13, 22.4 and 27].

SOURCE: Adopted in R89-2 at 14 Ill. Reg. 3059, effective February 20, 1990; amended in R89-11 at 14 Ill. Reg. 11948, effective July 9, 1990; amended in R90-14 at 15 Ill. Reg. 11425, effective July 24, 1991; amended in R92-13 at 17 Ill. Reg. 6190, effective April 5, 1993; amended in R93-6 at 17 Ill. Reg. 15641, effective September 14, 1993; amended in R95-6 at 19 Ill. Rev. _____, effective _____.

POLLUTION CONTROL BOARD

NOTICE OF PROPOSED AMENDMENTS

SUBPART B: PROHIBITIONS ON INJECTION

Section 738.117 Waste Specific Prohibitions - Newly-Listed Wastes

a) The wastes specified in 35 Ill. Adm. Code 721.Subpart D by the following U.S. EPA Hazardous hazardous Waste waste numbers are prohibited from underground injection:

F037
F038
K107
K108
K109
K110
K111
K117
K123
K124
K125
K126
K131
K136
U328
U353
U359

b) The wastes specified in 35 Ill. Adm. Code 721.Subpart D by the following U.S. EPA hazardous waste numbers are prohibited from underground injection:

K141
K142
K143
K144
K145
K147
K148
K149
K150
K151

c) Effective September 19, 1995, the wastes specified in 35 Ill. Adm. Code 721.Subpart C by the following U.S. EPA hazardous waste numbers are prohibited from underground injection:

D001 (high TOC subcategory, as specified at 35 Ill. Adm. Code 728.140)
D012
D013
D014
D015

POLLUTION CONTROL BOARD

NOTICE OF PROPOSED AMENDMENTS

D016
D017

b)d) Effective June 30, 1995, the wastes specified in 35 Ill. Adm. Code 721.Subpart D by the following U.S. EPA Hazardous hazardous Waste waste numbers are prohibited from underground injection:

K117
K118
K131
K132

c)e) The requirements of subsections (a) and (b) above do not apply:

1) If the wastes meet or are treated to meet the applicable standards specified in 35 Ill. Adm. Code 728.Subpart D; or

2) If an adjusted standard has been granted in response to a petition under 728.Subpart C of this Part; or

3) During the period of extension of the applicable effective date, if an extension is granted under Section 738.104.

BOARD NOTE: Derived from 40 CFR 148.17, as added at 57 Fed. Reg. 37263 (Aug. 18, 1992).

(Source: Amended at 19 Ill. Reg. _____, effective _____)

POLLUTION CONTROL BOARD

NOTICE OF PROPOSED AMENDMENTS

1) **Heading of the Part:** Hazardous Waste Management System: General

2) **Code Citation:** 35 Ill. Adm. Code 720

3) **Section numbers:**   **Proposed Action:**

720.111	Amended
720.121	Amended
720.130	Amended
720.131	Amended

4) **Statutory Authority:** 415 ILCS 5/22.4 and 27.

5) **A complete description of the subjects and issues involved:**

A more detailed description is contained in the Board's proposed opinion of March 2, 1995, in R95-4 and R95-6 (consolidated), which opinion is available from the address below. Section 22.4(a) of the Environmental Protection Act [415 ILCS 5/22.4(a)] provides that Section 5-35 of the Administrative Procedure Act [5 ILCS 100/5-35] shall not apply. Because this rulemaking is not subject to Section 5-35 of the APA, it is not subject to first notice or to second notice review by JCAR.

This rulemaking updates Parts 700, 702, 703, 705, 720, 721, 722, 723, 724, 725, 726, 728, 730, 738, and 739 of the Illinois RCRA Subtitle C hazardous waste and underground injection control (UIC) rules to correspond with amendments adopted by U.S. EPA that appeared in the Federal Register during the period July 1 through December 31, 1994. During this period, U.S. EPA amended its regulations as follows:

Federal Action	Summary
59 Fed. Reg. 38536, July 28, 1994	Exclusion from definition of solid waste for certain in-process recycled secondary materials used by the petroleum refining industry
59 Fed. Reg. 43496, August 24, 1994	Withdrawal of exemption from Subtitle C regulation of slag residues from high temperature metal recovery (HTMR) of electric arc furnace dust (K061), steel finishing pickle liquor (K062), and electroplating sludges (F006) that are used in a manner constituting disposal
59 Fed. Reg. 47980, September 19, 1994	Restoration of text from 40 CFR 268.7(a) inadvertently omitted in the amendments of August 31, 1993, at 58 Fed. Reg. 46040

POLLUTION CONTROL BOARD

NOTICE OF PROPOSED AMENDMENTS

| 59 Fed. Reg. 47982, September 19, 1994 | Phase II land disposal restrictions (LDRs): universal treatment standards for organic toxicity wastes and newly-listed wastes (including underground injection control (UIC) amendments) |
| 59 Fed. Reg. 62896, December 6, 1994 | Organic material air emission standards for tanks, surface impoundments, and containers |

In addition to these principal amendments that occurred during the update period, the Board has included an additional, later action:

| 60 Fed. Reg. 242, January 3, 1995 | Corrections to the Phase II land disposal restrictions (universal treatment standards) |

This January 3 action was an amendment of the September 19, 1994 Phase II LDRs (universal waste rule). U.S. EPA corrected errors and clarified language in the universal treatment standards. The Board did not delay in adding these amendments for three reasons:

1) The January 3, 1995 amendments are corrections and clarifications of the September 19, 1994 regulations, and not new substantive amendments;

2) Prompt action on the January 3, 1995 amendments will facilitate implementation of the Phase II LDRs; and

3) The Board has received a request from the regulated community that we add the January 3, 1995 amendments to those of September 19, 1994. (See "Expedited Consideration" below.)

The Board also notes that the later amendments occurred within six months of the earliest amendments included in this docket, even if they occurred outside the nominal time-frame of the docket.

In addition to the federally-derived amendments, the Board used this opportunity to undertake a number of housekeeping and corrective amendments. We have effected the removal of all cross-references for effective dates and repealed Part 700. We have converted equations and formulae to the standard scientific format. We have tried to improve the language and structure of various provision, including correcting grammar, punctuation, and spelling where necessary.

Specifically, the segment of the amendments involved in Part 720 update incorporations by reference to reflect new and revised methods required by U.S. EPA as part of the December 6, 1994 air emissions requirements. Other amendments to Part 720 incorporate certain revisions made by U.S. EPA as part of the September 19, 1994 Phase II LDR amendments. These

POLLUTION CONTROL BOARD

NOTICE OF PROPOSED AMENDMENTS

The amendments relate to the removal of the "primary production process" limitation to the conditions under which a variance is available from the classification as a solid waste for materials that are recycled or accumulated speculatively.

6) Will this proposed rule replace an emergency rule currently in effect? No

7) Does this rulemaking contain an automatic repeal date? No

8) Do these proposed amendments contain incorporations by reference? Yes. Section 720.111 is the central listing of all documents incorporated by reference throughout the text of 35 Ill. Adm. Code 703 through 705, 721 through 726, 728, 730, 738, and 739. The present amendments update existing and incorporate new incorporations to reflect changes in methods and procedures required by U.S. EPA.

9) Are there any other amendments pending on this Part? No

10) Statement of statewide policy objectives: This rulemaking is mandated by Section 22.4(a) of the Environmental Protection Act [415 ILCS 5/22.4(a)]. The statewide policy objectives are set forth in Section 20 of that Act. This rulemaking imposes mandates on units of local government only to the extent that they may be involved in the generation, transportation, treatment, storage, or disposal of hazardous waste or they engage in underground injection of waste.

11) Time, place and manner in which interested persons may comment on this proposed rulemaking: The Board will accept written public comment on this proposal for a period of 45 days after the date of this publication. Comments should reference Docket R95-4/R95-6 and be addressed to:

Ms. Dorothy M. Gunn, Clerk
Illinois Pollution Control Board
State of Illinois Center, Suite 11-500
100 W. Randolph St.
Chicago, IL 60601
(312) 814-6931

Address all questions to Michael J. McCambridge, at 312-814-6924.

12) Initial regulatory flexibility analysis:

A) Date rule was submitted to the Small Business Office of the Department of Commerce and Community Affairs: March 6, 1995.

B) Types of small businesses affected: The existing rules and proposed amendments affect small businesses that generate, transport, treat,

---

POLLUTION CONTROL BOARD

NOTICE OF PROPOSED AMENDMENTS

store, or dispose of hazardous waste or engage in underground injection of waste.

C) Reporting, bookkeeping or other procedures required for compliance: The existing rules and proposed amendments require extensive reporting, bookkeeping, and other procedures, including the preparation of manifests and annual reports, waste analyses, and maintenance of operating records.

D) Types of professional skills necessary for compliance: Compliance with the existing rules and proposed amendments may require the services of an attorney, certified public accountant, chemist, and registered professional engineers.

The full text of the proposed amendments begins on the next page.

POLLUTION CONTROL BOARD

NOTICE OF PROPOSED AMENDMENTS

TITLE 35: ENVIRONMENTAL PROTECTION
SUBTITLE G: WASTE DISPOSAL
CHAPTER I: POLLUTION CONTROL BOARD
SUBCHAPTER c: HAZARDOUS WASTE OPERATING REQUIREMENTS

PART 720
HAZARDOUS WASTE MANAGEMENT SYSTEM: GENERAL

SUBPART A: GENERAL PROVISIONS

AUTHORITY: Implementing Section 22.4 and authorized by Section 27 of the
Environmental Protection Act [415 ILCS 5/22.4 and 27].

SOURCE: Adopted in R81-22, 43 PCB 427, at 5 Ill. Reg. 9781, effective May 17,
1982; amended and codified in R81-22, 45 PCB 317, at 6 Ill. Reg. 4828,
effective May 17, 1982; amended in R82-19 at 7 Ill. Reg. 14015, effective Oct.
12, 1983; amended in R84-9, 53 PCB 131 at 9 Ill. Reg. 11819, effective July
24, 1985; amended in R85-22 at 10 Ill. Reg. 968, effective January 2, 1986;
amended in R86-1 at 10 Ill. Reg. 13998, effective August 12, 1986; amended in
R86-19 at 10 Ill. Reg. 20630, effective December 2, 1986; amended in R86-28 at

POLLUTION CONTROL BOARD

NOTICE OF PROPOSED AMENDMENTS

11 Ill. Reg. 6017, effective March 24, 1987; amended in R86-46 at 11 Ill. Reg.
13435, effective August 4, 1987; amended in R87-5 at 11 Ill. Reg. 19280,
effective November 12, 1987; amended in R87-26 at 12 Ill. Reg. 2450, effective
January 15, 1988; amended in R87-39 at 12 Ill. Reg. 12999, effective July 29,
1988; amended in R88-16 at 13 Ill. Reg. 362, effective December 27, 1988;
amended in R89-1 at 13 Ill. Reg. 18278, effective November 13, 1989; amended in
R89-2 at 14 Ill. Reg. 3075, effective February 20, 1990; amended in R89-9 at 14
Ill. Reg. 6229, effective April 16, 1990; amended in R90-10 at 14 Ill. Reg.
16450, effective September 25, 1990; amended in R90-17 at 15 Ill. Reg. 7934,
effective May 9, 1991; amended in R90-11 at 15 Ill. Reg. 9323, effective June
17, 1991; amended in R91-1 at 15 Ill. Reg. 14446, effective September 30, 1991;
amended in R91-13 at 16 Ill. Reg. 9489, effective June 9, 1992; amended in
R92-1 at 16 Ill. Reg. 17636, effective November 6, 1992; amended in R92-10 at
17 Ill. Reg. 5625, effective March 26, 1993; amended in R93-4 at 17 Ill. Reg.
20545, effective November 22, 1993; amended in R93-16 at 18 Ill. Reg. 6720,
effective April 26, 1994; amended in R94-7 at 18 Ill. Reg. 12160, effective
July 29, 1994; amended in R94-17 at 18 Ill. Reg. 17480, effective November 23,
1994; amended in R95-6 at 19 Ill. Reg. _____, effective _____, effective

SUBPART B: DEFINITIONS

Section 720.111 References

a)   The following publications are incorporated by reference:

ANSI. Available from the American National Standards Institute,
1430 Broadway, New York, New York 10018, 212-354-3300:

ANSI B31.3 and B31.4. See ASME/ANSI B31.3 and B31.4

ACI. Available from the American Concrete Institute, Box 19150,
Redford Station, Detroit, Michigan 48219:

ACI 318-83: "Building Code Requirements for Reinforced
Concrete", adopted September, 1983.

API. Available from the American Petroleum Institute, 1220 L
Street, N.W., Washington, D.C. 20005, 202-682-8000:

"Cathodic Protection of Underground Petroleum Storage Tanks
and Piping Systems", API Recommended Practice 1632, Second
Edition, December, 1987.

"Evaporative Loss from External Floating-Roof Tanks", API
Publication 2517, Third Edition, February, 1989.

"Guide for Inspection of Refinery Equipment. Chapter XIII,

POLLUTION CONTROL BOARD

NOTICE OF PROPOSED AMENDMENTS

Atmospheric and Low Pressure Storage Tanks," 4th Edition, 1981, reaffirmed December, 1987.

~~"Cathodic Protection of Underground Petroleum Storage Tanks and Piping Systems," API Recommended Practice 1632, Second Edition, December, 1987.~~

"Installation of Underground Petroleum Storage Systems," API Recommended Practice 1615, Fourth Edition, November, 1987.

APTI. Available from the Air and Waste Management Association, Box 2861, Pittsburgh, PA 15230, 412-232-3444:

   APTI Course 415: Control of Gaseous Emissions, EPA Publication EPA-450/2-81-005, December, 1981.

ASME. Available from the American Society of Mechanical Engineers, 345 East 47th Street, New York, NY 10017, 212-705-7722:

   "Chemical Plant and Petroleum Refinery Piping", ASME/ANSI B31.3 - 1987, as supplemented by B31.3a - 1988 and B31.3b - 1988. Also available from ANSI.

   "Liquid Transportation Systems for Hydrocarbons, Liquid Petroleum Gas, Anhydrous Ammonia, and Alcohols", ASME/ANSI B31.4 - 1986, as supplemented by B31.4a - 1987. Also available from ANSI.

ASTM. Available from American Society for Testing and Materials, 1916 Race Street, Philadelphia, PA 19103, 215-299-5400:

   ASTM C94-90, Standard Specification for Ready-Mixed Concrete, approved March 30, 1990.

   ASTM D88-87, Standard Test Method for Saybolt Viscosity, April 24, 1981, reapproved January, 1987.

   ASTM D93-85, Standard Test Methods for Flash Point by Pensky - Martens Closed Tester, approved October 25, 1985.

   ASTM D1946-90, Standard Practice for Analysis of Reformed Gas by Gas Chromatography, approved March 30, 1990.

   ASTM D2161-87, Standard Practice for Conversion of Kinematic Viscosity to Saybolt Universal or to Saybolt Furol Viscosity, March 27, 1987.

POLLUTION CONTROL BOARD

NOTICE OF PROPOSED AMENDMENTS

ASTM D2267-88, Standard Test Method for Aromatics in Light Naphthas and Aviation Gasolines by Gas Chromatography, approved November 17, 1988.

ASTM D2382-88, Standard Test Method for Heat of Combustion of Hydrocarbon Fuels by Bomb Calorimeter (High Precision Method), approved October 31, 1988.

ASTM D2879-86, Standard Test Method for Vapor Pressure-Temperature Relationship and Initial Decomposition Temperature of Liquids by Isoteniscope, approved October 31, 1986.

ASTM D 2879-92, Standard Test Method for Vapor Pressure-Temperature Relationship and Initial Decomposition Temperature of Liquids by Isoteniscope, approved 1992.

ASTM D3828-87, Standard Test Method for Flash Point of Liquids by Setaflash Closed Tester, approved December 14, 1988.

ASTM E168-88, Standard Practices for General Techniques of Infrared Quantitative Analysis, approved May 27, 1988.

ASTM E169-87, Standard Practices for General Techniques of Ultraviolet-Visible Quantitative Analysis, approved February 1, 1987.

ASTM E260-85, Standard Practice for Packed Column Gas Chromatography, approved June 28, 1985.

ASTM E926-88 C, Standard Test Methods for Preparing Refuse-Derived Fuel (RDF) Samples for Analysis of Metals, Bomb-Acid Digestion Method, approved March 35, 1988.

ASTM Method G21-70 (1984a) -- Standard Practice for Determining Resistance of Synthetic Polymer Materials to Fungi

ASTM Method G22-76 (1984b) -- Standard Practice for Determining Resistance of Plastics to Bacteria.

GPO. Available from the Superintendent of Documents, U.S. Government Printing Office, Washington, D.C. 20402, 202-783-3238:

   Standard Industrial Classification Manual (1972), and 1977 Supplement, republished in 1983

POLLUTION CONTROL BOARD

NOTICE OF PROPOSED AMENDMENTS

"Test Methods for Evaluating Solid Waste, Physical/Chemical Methods," U.S. EPA Publication number SW-846 (Third Edition, November, 1986), as amended by Updates I and IIA (Document Number 955-001-00000-1) (contact U.S. EPA, Office of Solid Waste, or MICE, as indicated below, for Update IIA).

MICE. Available from Methods Information Communication Service, at 703-821-4789:

"Test Methods for Evaluating Solid Waste, Physical/Chemical Methods," U.S. EPA Publication number SW-846 (Third Edition, November, 1986), Update IIA (Document Number 955-001-00000-1) (contact GPO, as indicated above, for SW-846 and Update I).

NACE. Available from the National Association of Corrosion Engineers, 1400 South Creek Dr., Houston, TX 77084, 713-492-0535:

"Control of External Corrosion on Metallic Buried, Partially Buried, or Submerged Liquid Storage Systems", NACE Recommended Practice RP0285-85, approved March, 1985.

NFPA. Available from the National Fire Protection Association, Batterymarch Park, Boston, MA 02269, 617-770-3000 or 800-344-3555:

"Flammable and Combustible Liquids Code" NFPA 30, issued July 17, 1987. Also available from ANSI.

NTIS. Available from the U.S. Department of Commerce, National Technical Information Service, 5285 Port Royal Road, Springfield, VA 22161, 703-487-4600:

"Generic Quality Assurance Project Plan for Land Disposal Restrictions Program", EPA/530-SW-87-011, March 15, 1987. (Document number PB 88-170766.)

"Guidance on Air Quality Models", Revised 1986. (Document number PB86-245-248 (Guideline) and PB88-150-958 (Supplement)).

"Methods for Chemical Analysis of Water and Wastes", Third Edition, March, 1983. (Document number PB 84-128677).

"Methods Manual for Compliance with BIF Regulations", December, 1990. (Document number PB91-120-006).

POLLUTION CONTROL BOARD

NOTICE OF PROPOSED AMENDMENTS

"Petitions to Delist Hazardous Wastes--A Guidance Manual", EPA/530-SW-85-003, April, 1985. (Document Number PB 85-194488).

"Procedures Manual for Ground Water Monitoring at Solid Waste Disposal Facilities", EPA-530/SW-611, 1977. (Document number PB 84-174820).

"Screening Procedures for Estimating the Air Quality Impact of Stationary Sources", October, 1992, Publication Number EPA-450/R-92-019.

STI. Available from the Steel Tank Institute, 728 Anthony Trail, Northbrook, IL 60062, 708-498-1980:

"Standard for Dual Wall Underground Steel Storage Tanks" (1986).

U.S. EPA. Available from United States Environmental Protection Agency, Office of Drinking Water, State Programs Division, WH 550 E, Washington, D.C. 20460:

"Technical Assistance Document: Corrosion, Its Detection and Control in Injection Wells", EPA 570/9-87-002, August, 1987.

U.S. EPA. Available from U.S. EPA, Office of Solid Waste (Mail Code 5304), 401 M Street SW, Washington, D.C. 20460:

"Test Methods for Evaluating Solid Waste, Physical/Chemical Methods," U.S. EPA Publication number SW-846 (Third Edition, November, 1986), Update IIA (Document Number 955-001-00000-1) (contact GPO, as indicated above, for SW-846 and Update I).

U.S. EPA. Available from U.S. EPA, Number F-90-WPWF-FFFFF, Room M2427, 401 M Street SW, Washington, D.C. 20460, 202-475-9327:

"Test Method 8290: Procedures for the Detection and Measurement of PCDDs and PCDFs", EPA/530-SW-91-019 (January, 1991)).

U.S. EPA Available from Receptor Analysis Branch, U.S. EPA (MD-14), Research Triangle Park, NC 27711:

"Screening Procedures for Estimating the Air Quality Impact of Stationary Sources, Revised", October, 1992, Publication Number EPA-450/R-92-019.

POLLUTION CONTROL BOARD

NOTICE OF PROPOSED AMENDMENTS

b) "Code of Federal Regulations. Available from the Superintendent of Documents, U.S. Government Printing Office, Washington, D.C. 20401, 202-783-3338:

10 CFR 20, Appendix B (1992 1994)

40 CFR 52.100(ii) (1992 1994)

40 CFR 81, Subpart W, as added at 58 Fed. Reg. 30822 (July 20, 1993 1994)

40 CFR 60 (1993) (1994), as amended at 59 Fed. Reg. 62924 (Dec. 6, 1994)

40 CFR 61, Subpart V (1993) (1994)

40 CFR 136 (1993) (1994)

40 CFR 142 (1993) (1994)

40 CFR 220 (1992) (1994)

40 CFR 260.20 (1992) (1994)

40 CFR 264 (1992) (1994)

40 CFR 268.Appendix IX (1992) (1994)

40 CFR 302.4, 302.5 and 302.6 (1992) (1994)

40 CFR 761 (1993) (1994)

49 CFR 178 (1994)
c) Federal Statutes

Section 3004 of the Resource Conservation and Recovery Act (42 U.S.C. 6901 et seq.), as amended through December 31, 1987.

d) This Section incorporates no later editions or amendments.

(Source: Amended at 19 Ill. Reg. _____, effective _____)

SUBPART C: RULEMAKING PETITIONS AND OTHER PROCEDURES

Section 720.121 Alternative Equivalent Testing Methods

a) The Agency has no authority to alter the universe of regulated wastes.

POLLUTION CONTROL BOARD

NOTICE OF PROPOSED AMENDMENTS

Modification of testing methods which that are stated in Part 35 Ill. Adm. Code 721 requires rulemaking pursuant to Section 720.120. However, deviation from these methods is allowed under the express provisions of Part 35 Ill. Adm. Code 721, as for example in Section by 35 Ill. Adm. Code 721.120(c).
b) The Agency may approve alternative equivalent testing methods to be for a particular person's used-by-a-certain-person use to determine whether specified types of wastestreams are subject to these regulations. This shall be done by permit condition or by a letter directed to the person.
c) The Board does not intend to require that either the testing methods specified in Part 35 Ill. Adm. Code 721 or the alternative equivalent testing methods approved by the Agency should need not be applied to identify or distinguish waste streams which that are known, admitted, or assumed to be subject to these regulations. In this case, any method may be used, subject to the Agency's authority over testing procedures (Section 725.133).
d) Any petition to the Board or request to the Agency concerning alternative equivalent testing methods shall must include the information required by 40 CFR Section 260.21(b).
e) Alternative equivalent testing methods will not be approved if the result of the approval would make the Illinois RCRA Subtitle C program less than substantially equivalent to the federal.

(Source: Amended at 19 Ill. Reg. _____, effective _____)

Section 720.130 Procedures for Solid Waste Determination

In accordance with the standards and criteria in Section 720.131 and the procedures in Section 720.133, the Board will determine on a case-by-case basis that the following recycled materials are not solid wastes:
a) Materials that are accumulated speculatively without sufficient amounts being recycled (as defined in Section 721.101(c)(8));
b) Materials that are reclaimed and then reused within the original primary production process in which they were generated; and
c) Materials that have been reclaimed but must be reclaimed further before the materials are completely recovered.

(Source: Amended at 19 Ill. Reg. _____, effective _____)

Section 720.131 Solid Waste Determinations

a) The Board will determine that those materials that are accumulated speculatively without sufficient amounts being recycled are not solid wastes if the applicant demonstrates that sufficient amounts of the material will be recycled or transferred for recycling in the

POLLUTION CONTROL BOARD

NOTICE OF PROPOSED AMENDMENTS

following year. Such a determination is valid only for the following
year, but can be renewed, on an annual basis, by filing a new
application. This determination will be based on the following
criteria:

   1) The manner in which the material is expected to be recycled, when
      the material is expected to be recycled, and whether this
      expected disposition is likely to occur (for example, because of
      past practice, market factors, the nature of the material or
      contractual arrangements for recycling);
   2) The reason that the applicant has accumulated the material for
      one or more years without recycling 75 percent of the volume
      accumulated at the beginning of the year;
   3) The quantity of material already accumulated and the quantity
      expected to be generated and accumulated before the material is
      recycled;
   4) The extent to which the material is handled to minimize loss; and
   5) Other relevant factors.
b) The Board will determine that those materials that are reclaimed and
   then reused as feedstock within the original primary production
   process in which the materials were generated are not solid wastes if
   the reclamation operation, is an essential part of the production
   process. This determination will be based on the following criteria:
   1) How economically viable the production process would be if it
      were to use virgin materials, rather than reclaimed materials;
   2) The prevalence of the practice on an industry-wide basis;
   3) The extent to which the material is handled before reclamation to
      minimize loss;
   4) The time periods between generating the material and its
      reclamation, and between reclamation and return to the original
      primary production process;
   5) The location of the reclamation operation in relation to the
      production process;
   6) Whether the reclaimed material is used for the purpose for which
      it was originally produced when it is returned to the original
      process, and whether it is returned to the process in
      substantially its original form;
   7) Whether the person who that generates the material also reclaims
      it; and
   8) Other relevant factors.
c) The Board will determine that those materials that have been reclaimed
   but must be reclaimed further before recovery is completed are not
   solid wastes if, after initial reclamation, the resulting material is
   commodity-like (even though it is not yet a commercial product, and
   has to be reclaimed further). This determination will be based on the
   following criteria:
   1) The degree of processing the material has undergone and the
      degree of further processing that is required;
   2) The value of the material after it has been reclaimed;

POLLUTION CONTROL BOARD

NOTICE OF PROPOSED AMENDMENTS

   3) The degree to which the reclaimed material is like an analogous
      raw material;
   4) The extent to which an end market for the reclaimed material is
      guaranteed;
   5) The extent to which the reclaimed material is handled to minimize
      loss; and
   6) Other relevant factors.

(Source: Amended at 19 Ill. Reg. _____, effective
_____)

POLLUTION CONTROL BOARD

NOTICE OF PROPOSED AMENDMENTS

1) Heading of the Part: Identification and Listing of Hazardous Waste

2) Code citation: 35 Ill. Adm. Code 721

3) Section numbers: Proposed Action:

    721.102, 721.103, 721.104   Amended
    721.106, 721.App. I, Tab. A   Amended
    721.App. I, Tab. B, 721.App. I, Tab. C   Amended
    721.App. I, Tab. D   Amended

4) Statutory authority: 415 ILCS 5/22.4 and 27.

5) A complete description of the subjects and issues involved:

A more detailed description is contained in the Board's proposed opinion
of March 2, 1995, in R95-4 and R95-6 (consolidated), which opinion is
available from the address below. Section 22.4(a) of the Environmental
Protection Act [415 ILCS 5/22.4(a)] provides that Section 5 of the
Administrative Procedure Act [5 ILCS 100/5-35 and 5-40] shall not apply.
Because this rulemaking is not subject to Section 5 of the APA, it is not
subject to first notice or to second notice review by JCAR.

This rulemaking updates Parts 700, 702, 703, 705, 720, 721, 722, 723, 724,
725, 726, 728, 730, 738, and 739 of the Illinois RCRA Subtitle C hazardous
waste and underground injection control (UIC) rules to correspond with
amendments adopted by U.S. EPA that appeared in the Federal Register
during the period July 1 through December 31, 1994. During this period,
U.S. EPA amended its regulations as follows:

Federal Action	Summary
59 Fed. Reg. 38536, July 28, 1994	Exclusion from definition of solid waste for certain in-process recycled secondary materials used by the petroleum refining industry
59 Fed. Reg. 43496, August 24, 1994	Withdrawal of exemption from Subtitle C regulation of slag residues from high temperature metal recovery (HTMR) of electric arc furnace dust (K061), steel finishing pickle liquor (K062), and electroplating sludges (F006) that are used in a manner constituting disposal
59 Fed. Reg. 47980, September 19, 1994	Restoration of text from 40 CFR 268.7(a) inadvertently omitted in the amendments of August 31, 1993, at 58 Fed. Reg. 46040

POLLUTION CONTROL BOARD

NOTICE OF PROPOSED AMENDMENTS

59 Fed. Reg. 47982, September 19, 1994	Phase II land disposal restrictions (LDRs): universal treatment standards for organic toxicity wastes and newly-listed wastes (including underground injection control (UIC) amendments)
59 Fed. Reg. 62896, December 6, 1994	Organic material air emission standards for tanks, surface impoundments, and containers

In addition to these principal amendments that occurred during the update
period, the Board has included an additional, later action:

60 Fed. Reg. 242, January 3, 1995	Corrections to the Phase II land disposal restrictions (universal treatment standards)

This January 3 action was an amendment of the September 19, 1994 Phase II
LDRs (universal waste rule). U.S. EPA corrected errors and clarified
language in the universal treatment standards. The Board did not delay in
adding these amendments for three reasons:

1) The January 3, 1995 amendments are corrections and clarifications of
    the September 19, 1994 regulations, and not new substantive
    amendments;

2) Prompt action on the January 3, 1995 amendments will facilitate
    implementation of the Phase II LDRs; and

3) The Board has received a request from the regulated community that we
    add the January 3, 1995 amendments to those of September 19, 1994.
    (See "Expedited Consideration" below.)

The Board also notes that the later amendments occurred within six months
of the earliest amendments included in this docket, even if they occurred
outside the nominal time-frame of the docket.

In addition to the federally-derived amendments, the Board used this
opportunity to undertake a number of housekeeping and corrective
amendments. We have effected the removal of all cross-references for
effective dates and repealed Part 700. We have converted equations and
formulae to the standard scientific format. We have tried to improve the
language and structure of various provision, including correcting grammar,
punctuation, and spelling where necessary.

Specifically, the segment of the amendments involved in Part 721
incorporate various changes. First, the amendments incorporate certain
revisions made by U.S. EPA as part of the September 19, 1994 Phase II LDR
amendments. These amendments relate to the removal of the "primary
production process" limitation to the conditions under which a variance is

POLLUTION CONTROL BOARD

NOTICE OF PROPOSED AMENDMENTS

available from the classification as a solid waste for materials that are recycled or accumulated speculatively. Second, the amendments implement the July 28, 1994 revisions that exclude certain in-process recycled secondary materials used by the petroleum refining industry from the definition of solid waste. Finally, the amendments incorporate changes in Section 721.Appendix I to reflect hazardous waste delistings (adjusted standards) granted by the Board since the last update.

6) Will this proposed rule replace an emergency rule currently in effect? No

7) Does this rulemaking contain an automatic repeal date? No

8) Do these proposed amendments contain incorporations by reference?

   Yes. 35 Ill. Adm. Code 720.111 is the central listing of all documents incorporated by reference throughout the text of 35 Ill. Adm. Code 702 through 705, 721 through 726, 728, 730, 738, and 739. Although the present amendments do not update the documents incorporated by reference, they change one reference by removing the edition from the text of Section 721.103(a)(2)(E). That edition is given in the central incorporation at 35 Ill. Adm. Code 720.111, and removing it from Section 721.103(a)(2)(E) will facilitate any future amendment to this edition.

9) Are there any other amendments pending on this Part? No

10) Statement of statewide policy objectives: This rulemaking is mandated by Section 22.4(a) of the Environmental Protection Act [415 ILCS 5/22.4(a)]. The statewide policy objectives are set forth in Section 20 of that Act. This rulemaking imposes mandates on units of local government only to the extent that they may be involved in the generation, transportation, treatment, storage, or disposal of hazardous waste or they engage in underground injection of waste.

11) Time, place and manner in which interested persons may comment on this proposed rulemaking: The Board will accept written public comment on this proposal for a period of 45 days after the date of this publication. Comments should reference Docket R95-4/R95-6 and be addressed to:

   Ms. Dorothy M. Gunn, Clerk
   Illinois Pollution Control Board
   State of Illinois Center, Suite 11-500
   100 W. Randolph St.
   Chicago, IL 60601
   (312) 814-6931

   Address all questions to Michael J. McCambridge, at (312) 814-6924.

12) Initial regulatory flexibility analysis:

POLLUTION CONTROL BOARD

NOTICE OF PROPOSED AMENDMENTS

A) Date rule was submitted to the Small Business Office of the Department of Commerce and Community Affairs: March 6, 1995.

B) Types of small businesses affected: The existing rules and proposed amendments affect small businesses that generate, transport, treat, store, or dispose of hazardous waste or engage in underground injection of waste.

C) Reporting, bookkeeping or other procedures required for compliance: The existing rules and proposed amendments require extensive reporting, bookkeeping, and other procedures, including the preparation of manifests and annual reports, waste analyses, and maintenance of operating records.

D) Types of professional skills necessary for compliance: Compliance with the existing rules and proposed amendments may require the services of an attorney, certified public accountant, chemist, and registered professional engineer.

The full text of the proposed amendments begins on the next page:

POLLUTION CONTROL BOARD

NOTICE OF PROPOSED AMENDMENTS

TITLE 35: ENVIRONMENTAL PROTECTION
SUBTITLE G: WASTE DISPOSAL
CHAPTER I: POLLUTION CONTROL BOARD
SUBCHAPTER c: HAZARDOUS WASTE OPERATING REQUIREMENTS

PART 721
IDENTIFICATION AND LISTING OF
HAZARDOUS WASTE

SUBPART A: GENERAL PROVISIONS

SUBPART B: CRITERIA FOR IDENTIFYING THE
CHARACTERISTICS OF HAZARDOUS WASTE
AND FOR LISTING HAZARDOUS WASTES

SUBPART C: CHARACTERISTICS OF HAZARDOUS WASTE

SUBPART D: LISTS OF HAZARDOUS WASTE

POLLUTION CONTROL BOARD

NOTICE OF PROPOSED AMENDMENTS

AUTHORITY: Implementing Section 22.4 and authorized by Section 27 of the Environmental Protection Act [415 ILCS 5/22.4 and 27].

SOURCE: Adopted in R81-22, 43 PCB 427, at 5 Ill. Reg. 9781, effective May 17, 1982; amended and codified in R81-22, 45 PCB 317, at 6 Ill. Reg. 4828, effective May 17, 1982; amended in R82-18, 51 PCB 31, at 7 Ill. Reg. 2518, effective February 22, 1983; amended in R82-19, 53 PCB 131, at 7 Ill. Reg. 13999, effective October 12, 1983; amended in R84-34, 61 PCB 247, at 8 Ill. Reg. 24562, effective December 11, 1984; amended in R84-9, at 9 Ill. Reg. 11834, effective July 24, 1985; amended in R85-22 at 10 Ill. Reg. 998, effective January 2, 1986; amended in R85-2 at 10 Ill. Reg. 8112, effective May 2, 1986; amended in R86-1 at 10 Ill. Reg. 14002, effective August 12, 1986; amended in R86-19 at 10 Ill. Reg. 20647, effective December 2, 1986; amended in R86-28 at 11 Ill. Reg. 6035, effective March 24, 1987; amended in R86-46 at 11 Ill. Reg. 13466, effective August 4, 1987; amended in R87-32 at 11 Ill. Reg. 16698, effective September 30, 1987; amended in R87-5 at 11 Ill. Reg. 19303, effective November 12, 1987; amended in R87-26 at 12 Ill. Reg. 2456, effective January 15, 1988; amended in R87-30 at 12 Ill. Reg. 12070, effective July 12, 1988; amended in R87-39 at 12 Ill. Reg. 13006, effective July 29, 1988; amended in R88-16 at 13 Ill. Reg. 382, effective December 27, 1988; amended in R89-1 at 13 Ill. Reg. 18300, effective November 13, 1989; amended in R90-2 at 14 Ill. Reg. 14401, effective August 22, 1990; amended in R90-10 at 14 Ill. Reg. 16472, effective September 25, 1990; amended in R90-17 at 15 Ill. Reg. 7950, effective May 9, 1991; amended in R90-II at 15 Ill. Reg. 9332, effective June 17, 1991; amended in R91-1 at 15 Ill. Reg. 14473, effective September 30, 1991; amended in R91-12 at 16 Ill. Reg. 2155, effective January 27, 1992; amended in R91-26

POLLUTION CONTROL BOARD

NOTICE OF PROPOSED AMENDMENTS

at 16 Ill. Reg. 2600, effective February 3, 1992; amended in R91-13 at 16 Ill.
Reg. 9619, effective June 9, 1992; amended in R92-1 at 16 Ill. Reg. 17666,
effective November 6, 1992; amended in R92-10 at 17 Ill. Reg. 5650, effective
March 26, 1993; amended in R93-4 at 17 Ill. Reg. 20568, effective November 22,
1993; amended in R93-16 at 18 Ill. Reg. 6741, effective April 26, 1994; amended
in R94-7 at 18 Ill. Reg. 12175, effective July 29, 1994; amended in R94-17 at
18 Ill. Reg. 17490, effective November 23, 1994; amended in R95-6 at 19 Ill.
Reg. _____, effective _____.

SUBPART A: GENERAL PROVISIONS

Section 721.102 Definition of Solid Waste

a) Solid waste.

   1) A solid waste is any discarded material that is not excluded by
       Section 721.104(a) or that is not excluded pursuant to 35 Ill.
       Adm. Code 720.130 and 720.131.

   2) A discarded material is any material which that is:

       A) Abandoned, as explained in subsection (b)y below; or
       B) Recycled, as explained in subsection (c)y below; or
       C) Considered inherently waste-like, as explained in subsection
           (d)y below.

,) Materials are solid waste if they are abandoned by being:

   1) Disposed of; or
   2) Burned or incinerated; or
   3) Accumulated, stored or treated (but not recycled) before or in
       lieu of being abandoned by being disposed of, burned or
       incinerated.

.) Materials are solid wastes if they are recycled -- or accumulated,
    stored or treated before recycling -- as specified in subsections
    (c)(1) through (c) (4)y below if they are:

   1) Used in a manner constituting disposal.

       A) Materials noted with a "yes" in column 1 of table in
           Appendix I are solid wastes when they are:
           i)   Applied to or placed on the land in a manner that
                constitutes disposal; or
           ii) Used to produce products that are applied to or placed
                on the land or are otherwise contained in products that
                are applied to or placed on the land (in which cases
                the product itself remains a solid waste).

       B) However, commercial chemical products listed in Section
           721.133 are not solid wastes if they are applied to the land
           and that is their ordinary manner of use.

   2) Burned for energy recovery.

       A) Materials noted with a "yes" in column 2 of table in
           Appendix I are solid wastes when they are:
           i)   Burned to recover energy;
           ii) Used to produce a fuel or are otherwise contained in

POLLUTION CONTROL BOARD

NOTICE OF PROPOSED AMENDMENTS

           fuels (in which case the fuel itself remains a solid
           waste);
           iii) Contained in fuels (in which case the fuel itself
                remains a solid waste).

       B) However, commercial chemical products listed in Section
           721.133 are not solid wastes when reclaimed.

   3) Reclaimed. Materials noted with a "yes" in column 3 of table in
       Appendix I are solid wastes when reclaimed.

   4) Accumulated speculatively. Materials noted with "yes" in column
       4 of table in Appendix I are solid wastes when accumulated
       speculatively.

d) Inherently waste-like materials. The following materials are solid
    wastes when they are recycled in any manner:

   1) Hazardous waste numbers F020, F021 (unless used as an ingredient
       to make a product at the site of generation), F022, F023, F026,
       and F028.

   2) Secondary materials fed to a halogen acid furnace that exhibit a
       characteristic of a hazardous waste or are listed as a hazardous
       waste as defined in 721. Subparts C or D, except for brominated
       material which that meets the following criteria:
       A) The material must contain a bromine concentration of at
           least 45%; and
       B) The material must contain less than a total of 1% of toxic
           organic compounds listed in Appendix H; and
       C) The material is processed continually on-site in the halogen
           acid furnace via direct conveyance (hard piping).

   3) The following criteria are used to add wastes to the list:
       A) Disposal method or toxicity
           i)   The materials are ordinarily disposed of, burned, or
                incinerated; or
           ii) The materials contain toxic constituents listed in
                Appendix H and these constituents are not ordinarily
                found in raw materials or products for which the
                materials substitute (or are found in raw materials or
                products in smaller concentrations) and are not used or
                reused during the recycling process; and
       B) The material may pose a substantial hazard to human health
           and the environment when recycled.

e) Materials that are not solid waste when recycled.

   1) Materials are not solid wastes when they can be shown to be
       recycled by being:
       A) Used or reused as ingredients in an industrial process to
           make a product, provided the materials are not being
           reclaimed; or
       B) Used or reused as effective substitutes for commercial
           products; or
       C) Returned to the original process from which they are
           generated, without first being reclaimed. The materials

POLLUTION CONTROL BOARD

NOTICE OF PROPOSED AMENDMENTS

must be returned as a substitute for raw--materials feedstock
materials--and--the--process--must--use--raw--materials--as
principal--feedstock. In cases where the original process
to which the material is returned is a secondary process,
the materials must be managed so there is no placement on
the land.

2) The following materials are solid wastes, even if the recycling
involves use, reuse, or return to the original process (described
in subsections (e)(1)(A) through (e)(1)(C)y above):

A) Materials used in a manner constituting disposal, or used to
produce products that are applied to the land; or

B) Materials burned for energy recovery; used to produce a
fuel, or contained in fuels; or

C) Materials accumulated speculatively; or

D) Materials listed in subsections (d)(1) and (d)(2); above.

f) Documentation of claims that materials are not solid wastes or are
conditionally exempt from regulation. Respondents in actions to
enforce regulations implementing Subtitle C of the Resource
Conservation Recovery Act or Section 21 of the Environmental
Protection Act who that raise a claim that a certain material is not
solid wastey or that the material is conditionally exempt from
regulation must demonstrate that there is a known market or
disposition for the materialy and that they meet the terms of the
exclusion or exemption. In doing so, they the person must provide
appropriate documentation (such as contracts showing that a second
person used the material as an ingredient in a production process) to
demonstrate that the material is not a waste or that the material is
exempt from regulation. In addition, owners or operators of
facilities claiming that they actually are recycling materials must
show that they have the necessary equipment to do so.

(Source: Amended at   19   Ill. Reg. _____,   effective

Section 721.103 Definition of Hazardous Waste

a) A solid waste, as defined in Section 721.102, is a hazardous waste if:

I) It is not excluded from regulation as a hazardous waste under
Section 721.104(b); and

2) It meets any of the following criteria:

A) It exhibits any of the characteristics of hazardous waste
identified in 721.Subpart C of--this--Part.

i) Except that any mixture of a waste from the extraction,
beneficiation, or processing of ores or minerals
excluded under Section 721.104(b)(7) and any other
solid waste exhibiting a characteristic of hazardous
waste under 721.Subpart C of--this--Part is a hazardous
waste only: if it exhibits a characteristic that would

POLLUTION CONTROL BOARD

NOTICE OF PROPOSED AMENDMENTS

not have been exhibited by the excluded waste alone if
such mixture had not occurred, ory if it continues to
exhibit any of the characteristics exhibited by the
non-excluded wastes prior to mixture.

ii) Further, for the purposes of applying the toxicity
characteristic to such mixtures under subsection
(a)(2)(A)(i) above, the mixture is also a hazardous
waste: if it exceeds the maximum concentration for any
contaminant listed in Section 721.124 that would not
have been exceeded by the excluded waste alone if the
mixture had not occurred, ory if it continues to
exceed the maximum concentration for any contaminant
exceeded by the nonexempt waste prior to mixture.

B) It is listed in 721.Subpart D of--this--Part and has not been
excluded from the lists in 721.Subpart D of--this--Part under
35 Ill. Adm. Code 720.120 and 720.122.

C) It is a mixture of a solid waste and a hazardous waste that
is listed in 721.Subpart D of--this--Part solely because it
exhibits one or more of the characteristics of hazardous
waste identified in 721.Subpart C of--this--Part, unless:

i) the resultant mixture no longer exhibits any
characteristic of hazardous waste identified in
721.Subpart C of--this--Part, or unless

ii) the solid waste: is excluded from regulation under
Section 721.104(b)(7)y and; the resultant mixture no
longer exhibits any characteristic of hazardous waste
identified in 721.Subpart C of--this--Part for which the
hazardous waste listed in 721.Subpart D of--this--Part
was listed.

iii) (However,--nonwastewater Nonwastewater mixtures are
still subject to the requirements of 35 III. Adm. Code
728, even if they no longer exhibit a characteristic at
the point of land disposal.

D) It is a mixture of solid waste and one or more hazardous
wastes listed in 721.Subpart D of--this--Part and has not been
excluded from this subsection (a)(2) under 35 Ill. Adm. Code
720.120 and 720.122; however, the following mixtures of
solid wastes and hazardous wastes listed in 721.Subpart D of
this--Part are not hazardous wastes (except by application of
subsection (a)(2)(A) or (a)(2)(B) above) If the generator
demonstrates that the mixture consists of wastewater the
discharge of which is subject to regulation under either 35
III. Adm. Code 309 or 310 (including wastewater at
facilities which that have eliminated the discharge of
wastewater) and:

I) One or more of the following solvents listed in Section
721.131: - carbon tetrachloride, tetrachloroethylene,
trichloroethylene, - provided that the maximum total

POLLUTION CONTROL BOARD

NOTICE OF PROPOSED AMENDMENTS

weekly usage of these solvents (other than the amounts that can be demonstrated not to be discharged to wastewater) divided by the average weekly flow of wastewater into the headworks of the facility's wastewater treatment or pretreatment system does not exceed 1 part per million; or

ii) One or more of the following spent solvents listed in Section 721.131; - methylene chloride, 1,1,1 - trichloroethane, chlorobenzene, o-dichlorobenzene, cresols, cresylic acid, nitrobenzene, toluene, methyl ethyl ketone, carbon disulfide, isobutanol, pyridine, spent chlorofluorocarbon solvents, - provided that the maximum total weekly usage of these solvents (other than the amounts that can be demonstrated not to be discharged to wastewater) divided by the average weekly flow of wastewater into the headworks of the facility's wastewater treatment or pretreatment system does not exceed 25 parts per million; or

iii) One of the following wastes listed in Section 721.132; - heat exchanger bundle cleaning sludge from the petroleum refining industry (U.S. EPA Hazardous hazardous Waste—No waste no. K050); or

iv) A discarded commercial chemical product; or chemical intermediate listed in Section 721.133, arising from de minimis losses of these materials from manufacturing operations in which these materials are used as raw materials or are produced in the manufacturing process. For purposes of this subsection, "de minimis" losses include those from normal material handling operations (e.g., spills from the unloading or transfer of materials from bins or other containers, leaks from pipes, valves, or other devices used to transfer materials); minor leaks of process equipment, storage tanks, or containers; leaks from well-maintained pump packings and seals; sample purgings; relief device discharges; discharges from safety showers and rinsing and cleaning of personal safety equipment; and rinsate from empty containers or from containers that are rendered empty by that rinsing; or

v) Wastewater resulting from laboratory operations containing toxic (T) wastes listed in 721.Subpart D of this Part, provided that the annualized average flow of laboratory wastewater does not exceed one percent of total wastewater flow into the headworks of the facility's wastewater treatment or pretreatment system, or provided that the wastes combined annualized average concentration does not exceed one part per million in the headworks of the facility's wastewater treatment or

POLLUTION CONTROL BOARD

NOTICE OF PROPOSED AMENDMENTS

pretreatment facility. Toxic (T) wastes used in laboratories that are demonstrated not to be discharged to wastewater are not to be included in this calculation.

E) Rebuttable presumption for used oil. Used oil containing more than 1,000 ppm total halogens is presumed to be a hazardous waste because it has been mixed with halogenated hazardous waste listed in 721.Subpart D of this Part. Persons may rebut this presumption by demonstrating that the used oil does not contain hazardous waste (for example, by using an analytical method from SW-846, SW-edr; incorporated by reference at 35 Ill. Adm. Code 720.111, to show that the used oil does not contain significant concentrations of halogenated hazardous constituents listed in 721.Appendix H).

i) The rebuttable presumption does not apply to metalworking oils or fluids containing chlorinated paraffins; if they are processed, through a tolling arrangement as described in 35 Ill. Adm. Code 739.124(c); to reclaim metalworking oils or fluids. The presumption does apply to metalworking oils or fluids if such oils or fluids are recycled in any other manner; or disposed.

ii) The rebuttable presumption does not apply to used oils contaminated with chlorofluorocarbons (CFCs) removed from refrigeration units where the CFCs are destined for reclamation. The rebuttable presumption does apply to used oils contaminated with CFCs that have been mixed with used oil from sources other than refrigeration units.

b) A solid waste which that is not excluded from regulation under subsection (a)(1) above becomes a hazardous waste when any of the following events occur:

1) In the case of a waste listed in 721.Subpart D of this Part, when the waste first meets the listing description set forth in 721.Subpart D of this Part.

2) In the case of a mixture of solid waste and one or more listed hazardous wastes, when a hazardous waste listed in 721.Subpart D of this Part is first added to the solid waste.

3) In the case of any other waste (including a waste mixture), when the waste exhibits any of the characteristics identified in 721.Subpart C of this Part.

c) Unless and until it meets the criteria of subsection (d) below, a hazardous waste will remain a hazardous waste.
BOARD NOTE: This subsection corresponds with 40 CFR 261.3(c)(1). The Board has codified 40 CFR 261.3(c)(2) at subsection (e) below.
1) A hazardous waste will remain a hazardous waste.
2) Specific inclusions and exclusions.

POLLUTION CONTROL BOARD

NOTICE OF PROPOSED AMENDMENTS

A) Except-as-otherwise-provided-in-subsection-(c)(2)(B)--below,
any--solid--waste--generated--from-the-treatment,-storage-or
disposal-of-a-hazardous-waste,-including-any--sludge,--spill
residue,--ash,--emission--control--dust-or-leachate-(but--not
including-precipitation--run-off),--is--a--hazardous--waster
(However,-materials-that-are-reclaimed-from-solid-wastes-and
that--are--used--beneficially-are-not-solid-wastes-and-hence
are-not-hazardous-wastes-under--this--provision--unless--the
reclaimed--material-is-burned-for-energy-recovery-or-used-in
a-manner-constituting-disposal.)

B) The-following-solid-wastes-are--not--hazardous--even--though
they--are--generated-from-the-treatment,-storage-or-disposal
of-a-hazardous-waste,-unless-they-exhibit-one-or-more-of-the
characteristics-of-hazardous-waster

   i) Waste--pickle--liquor---sludge---generated---by---lime
      stabilization--of-spent-pickle-liquor-from-the-iron-and
      steel--industry--(SIC--Codes--331--and--332)--(Standard
      Industrial--Codes,--as--defined--and--incorporated--by
      reference-in-35-Ill,-Adm.-Code-720,110-and-720,111);

   ii) Wastes--from-burning-any-of-the-materials-exempted-from
       regulation-by-Section-72b,106(a)(2)(B),(F),(G)-or-(H);

   iii) Nonwastewater-residues,-such-as-slag,--resulting--from
        high--temperature--metal--recovery-(HTMR)-processing-of
        K061,--K062-or-F006--wastes,-in-units-identified,-that-are
        disposed-of-in-non-hazardous--waste-units;-provided-that
        these--residues--meet--the--generic--exclusion---levels
        identified--in--the--tables--in-this-subsection-for-all
        constituents,--and--exhibit--no--characteristics---of
        hazardous--waste.---The--types--of--units--are--rotary
        kilns,--flame--reactors,--electric-furnaces,-plasma-arc
        furnaces,--slag--reactors,--rotary-hearth-furnace/electric
        furnace--combinations--or--the--following--types---of
        industrial--furnaces,--(as--defined-in-35-Ill.-Adm.-Code
        720,111):--blast--furnaces---smelting,--melting---and
        refining--furnaces-including-pyrometallurgical-devices
        such--as--cupolas,--reverberator--furnaces,--sintering
        machines,--roasters--and--foundry--furnaces);--and-other
        furnaces-designated-by--the--Agency--pursuant--to--that
        definition.---Testing-requirements-must-be-incorporated
        in-a-facility's-waste-analysis-plan--or--a--generator's
        self-implementing--waste--analysis--plan-at-a-minimum,
        composite-samples-of-residues,-must--be--collected--and
        analyzed--quarterly--and--when-the-process-or-operation
        generating-the-waste-changes.--Persons--claiming--this
        exclusion-in-an-enforcement-action-will-have-the-burden
        of--proving-by--clear-and-convincing-evidence-that-the
        material-meets-all-of-the-exclusion--requirements.--The
        generic-exclusion-levels-are:

POLLUTION CONTROL BOARD

NOTICE OF PROPOSED AMENDMENTS

Constituent	Maximum-for-any-single composite-sample-(mg/l)

Generic-exclusion-levels
for-K061-and-K062
nonwastewater--HTMR
residues

Antimony,,,,,,,,,,,,,,,,,,	0,10
Arsenic,,,,,,,,,,,,,,,,,,,	0,50
Barium,,,,,,,,,,,,,,,,,,,,	7,6
Beryllium,,,,,,,,,,,,,,,,,	0,010
Cadmium,,,,,,,,,,,,,,,,,,,	0,050
Chromium-(total),,,,,,,,,,	0,33
Lead,,,,,,,,,,,,,,,,,,,,,,	0,15
Mercury,,,,,,,,,,,,,,,,,,,	0,009
Nickel,,,,,,,,,,,,,,,,,,,,	1,0
Selenium,,,,,,,,,,,,,,,,,,	0,16
Silver,,,,,,,,,,,,,,,,,,,,	0,30
Thallium,,,,,,,,,,,,,,,,,,	0,020
Vanadium,,,,,,,,,,,,,,,,,,	1,26
Zinc,,,,,,,,,,,,,,,,,,,,,,	70,

Generic--exclusion--levels-for--F006--nonwastewater--HTMR
residues

Antimony,,,,,,,,,,,,,,,,,,	0,10
Arsenic,,,,,,,,,,,,,,,,,,,	0,50
Barium,,,,,,,,,,,,,,,,,,,,	7,6
Beryllium,,,,,,,,,,,,,,,,,	0,010
Cadmium,,,,,,,,,,,,,,,,,,,	0,050
Chromium-(total),,,,,,,,,,	0,33
Cyanide-(total)-(mg/kg),,,	1,8
Lead,,,,,,,,,,,,,,,,,,,,,,	0,15
Mercury,,,,,,,,,,,,,,,,,,,	0,009
Nickel,,,,,,,,,,,,,,,,,,,,	1,0
Selenium,,,,,,,,,,,,,,,,,,	0,16
Silver,,,,,,,,,,,,,,,,,,,,	0,30
Thallium,,,,,,,,,,,,,,,,,,	0,020
Zinc,,,,,,,,,,,,,,,,,,,,,,	70

A--one-time--notification--and--certification--must-be
placed--in-the-facility's-files-and-sent-to--the--Agency
(or,--for--out-of-State--shipments,--to-the-appropriate
Regional--Administrator--of--USEPA--or---state---agency
authorized--to--implement--40-CFR-268-requirements)-for
K061,-K062-or-F006-HTMR-residues-that-meet-the--generic
exclusion--levels--for--all-constituents--and--do--not
exhibit--any--characteristics--that--are--sent--to-RCRA
Subtitle-D-units.--The-notification--and--certification

POLLUTION CONTROL BOARD

NOTICE OF PROPOSED AMENDMENTS

that-is-placed-in-the-generators-or-treaters-files-must
be--updated--if-the-process-or-operation-generating-the
waste-changes-or-if-the-RCRA-Subtitle-D-unit--receiving
the--waste--changes---However-the-generator-or-treater
need-only-notify-the-Agency-on-an-annual-basis-if--such
changes--occur---Such--notification--and-certification
should-be-sent-to-the-Agency-by-the-end-of-the-calendar
year-but-no-later-than-December-31---The--notification
must--include--the-following-information---The-name-and
address--of--the--nonhazardous--waste--management--unit
receiving-the-waste-shipment-The-USHPA-hazardous-waste
number-and-treatability-group-at-the-initial--point--of
generation---The--treatment-standards-applicable-to-the
waste--at--the--initial--point--of--generation----The
certification--must--be---signed--by--an--authorized
representative-and-must-state-as-follows-
"I-certify--under--penalty--of--law--that--the--generic
exclusion--levels--for--all--constituents-have-been-met
without--impermissible---dilution----and----that----no
characteristic--of--hazardous-waste-is-exhibited---I-am
aware--that--there--are---significant---penalties--for
submitting---a---false---certification--including--the
possibility-of-fine-and-imprisonment"
BOARD-NOTE:--The-generic-exclusion-levels--for--arsenic
and--zinc--are--higher--than-the-HTMR-based-alternative
treatment-standards-for-K062-and-F006-and--HTMR--based
treatment-standards-for-K061-specified-in-35-Ill.-Adm-
Code-728.143---However-the-HTMR-residues-must-meet--the
applicable---treatment--standards--prior--to--generic
exclusion---Therefore-to-be--eligible--for--a--generic
exclusion---the-treated-residues-must-meet-the-lower-of
either-the-treatment-standards-or-the-generic-exclusion
levels-for-each-constituent-

d) Any solid waste described in subsection (c) above is not a hazardous
waste if it meets the following criteria:
   1) In the case of any solid waste, it does not exhibit any of the
      characteristics of hazardous waste identified in 721.Subpart C of
      this-Part. (However, wastes which that exhibit a characteristic
      at the point of generation may still be subject to the
      requirements of 35 Ill. Adm. Code 728, even if they no longer
      exhibit a characteristic at the point of land disposal.)
   2) In the case of a waste which that is a listed waste under
      721.Subpart D of-this-Part, a waste that contains a waste listed
      under 721.Subpart D of-this-Part, or a waste that is a derived
      from a waste listed in 721.Subpart D of-this-Part, it also has
      been excluded from subsection (c) above under 35 Ill. Adm. Code
      720.120 and 720.122.

e) This-subsection-corresponds-with-40-CFR-261.3(e),-a--subsection--which

POLLUTION CONTROL BOARD

NOTICE OF PROPOSED AMENDMENTS

has--been--deleted--from--the--federal--regulations.---This--statement
maintains-structural-consistency-with-USEPA-rules Specific inclusions
and exclusions.
   1) Except as otherwise provided in subsection (e)(2) below, any
      solid waste generated from the treatment, storage, or disposal of
      a hazardous waste, including any sludge, spill residue, ash,
      emission control dust, or leachate (but not including
      precipitation run-off), is a hazardous waste. (However,
      materials that are reclaimed from solid wastes and that are used
      beneficially are not solid wastes and hence are not hazardous
      wastes under this provision unless the reclaimed material is
      burned for energy recovery or used in a manner constituting
      disposal.)
   2) The following solid wastes are not hazardous even though they are
      generated from the treatment, storage, or disposal of a hazardous
      waste unless they exhibit one or more of the characteristic of
      hazardous waste:
      A) Waste pickle liquor sludge generated by lime stabilization
         of spent pickle liquor from the iron and steel industry (SIC
         Codes 331 and 332).
      B) Wastes from burning any of the materials exempted from
         regulation by any of Section 721.106(a)(3)(D)
         through(a)(3)(F).
      C) Nonwastewater residues, such as slag, resulting from high
         temperature metal recovery (HTMR) processing of K061, K062,
         or F006 waste in the units identified in this subsection
         that are disposed of in non-hazardous waste units, provided
         that these residues meet the generic exclusion levels
         identified in the tables in this subsection for all
         constituents and the residues exhibit no characteristics of
         hazardous waste. The types of units identified are rotary
         kilns, flame reactors, electric furnaces, plasma arc
         furnaces, slag reactors, rotary hearth furnace/electric
         furnace combinations, or the following types of industrial
         furnaces (as defined in 35 Ill. Adm. Code 720.110): blast
         furnaces, smelting, melting and refining furnaces (including
         pyrometallurgical devices such as cupolas, reverberator
         furnaces, sintering machines, roasters, and foundry
         furnaces), and other furnaces designated by the Agency
         pursuant to that definition.
         (i) Testing requirements must be incorporated in a
             facility's waste analysis plan or a generator's
             self-implementing waste analysis plan; at a minimum,
             composite samples of residues must be collected and
             analyzed quarterly and when the process or operation
             generating the waste changes.
         (ii) Persons claiming this exclusion in an enforcement
              action will have the burden of proving by clear and

POLLUTION CONTROL BOARD

NOTICE OF PROPOSED AMENDMENTS

convincing evidence that the material meets all of the exclusion requirements. The generic exclusion levels are:

Constituent	Maximum for any single composite sample (mg/L)

Generic exclusion levels for K061 and K062 nonwastewater HTMR residues.

Antimony	0.10
Arsenic	0.50
Barium	7.6
Beryllium	0.010
Cadmium	0.050
Chromium (total)	0.33
Lead	0.15
Mercury	0.009
Nickel	1.0
Selenium	0.16
Silver	0.30
Thallium	0.020
Vanadium	1.26
Zinc	70.0

Generic exclusion levels for F006 nonwastewater HTMR residues

Antimony	0.10
Arsenic	0.50
Barium	7.6
Beryllium	0.010
Cadmium	0.050
Chromium (total)	0.33
Cyanide (total) (mg/kg)	1.8
Lead	0.15
Mercury	0.009
Nickel	1.0
Selenium	0.16
Silver	0.30
Thallium	0.020
Zinc	70.0

(iii) A one-time notification and certification must be placed in the facility's files and sent to the Agency (or, for out-of-State shipments, to the appropriate Regional Administrator of U.S. EPA or the state agency authorized to implement 40 CFR 268 requirements) for

POLLUTION CONTROL BOARD

NOTICE OF PROPOSED AMENDMENTS

K061, K062, or F006 HTMR residues that meet the generic exclusion levels for all constituents and do not exhibit any characteristics and which are sent to RCRA Subtitle D (municipal solid waste landfill) units. The notification and certification that is placed in the generator's or treater's files must be updated if the process or operation generating the waste changes or if the RCRA Subtitle D unit receiving the waste changes. However, the generator or treater need only notify the Agency on an annual basis if such changes occur. Such notification and certification should be sent to the Agency by the end of the calendar year, but no later than December 31. The notification must include the following information: the name and address of the nonhazardous waste management unit receiving the waste shipment; the U.S. EPA hazardous waste number and treatability group at the initial point of generation; and the treatment standards applicable to the waste at the initial point of generation. The certification must be signed by an authorized representative and must state as follows:

"I certify under penalty of law that the generic exclusion levels for all constituents have been met without impermissible dilution and that no characteristic of hazardous waste is exhibited. I am aware that there are significant penalties for submitting a false certification, including the possibility of fine and imprisonment."

BOARD NOTE: This subsection would normally correspond with 40 CFR 261.3(e), a subsection which has been deleted and marked "reserved" by U.S. EPA. Rather, this subsection corresponds with 40 CFR 261.3(c)(2), which the Board codified here to comport with codification requirements and enhance clarity.

f) Notwithstanding subsections (a) through ~~(d)~~ (e) above and provided the debris, as defined in 35 Ill. Adm. Code 728.102, does not exhibit a characteristic identified at 721.Subpart D ~~of this Part~~, the following materials are not subject to regulation under 35 Ill. Adm. Code 720, 721 to 726, 728, or 730:

1) Hazardous debris as defined in 35 Ill. Adm. Code 728.102 that has been treated using one of the required extraction or destruction technologies specified in ~~Table--A--of~~ 35 Ill. Adm. Code 728.~~44~~Table F; persons claiming this exclusion in an enforcement action will have the burden of proving by clear and convincing evidence that the material meets all of the exclusion requirements; or

2) Debris as defined in 35 Ill. Adm. Code 728.102 that the Agency, considering the extent of contamination, has determined is no

POLLUTION CONTROL BOARD

NOTICE OF PROPOSED AMENDMENTS

longer contaminated with hazardous waste.

(Source: Amended in at 19 Ill. Reg. _____, effective
_____)

Section 721.104 Exclusions

a) Materials that are not solid wastes. The following materials are not
solid wastes for the purpose of this Part:

1) Sewage:
A) Domestic sewage; and
B) Any mixture of domestic sewage and other waste that passes
through a sewer system to publicly-owned treatment works for
treatment.
C) "Domestic sewage" means untreated sanitary wastes that pass
through a sewer system.

2) Industrial wastewater discharges that are point source discharges
with NPDES permits issued by the Agency pursuant to Section 12(f)
of the Environmental Protection Act and 35 Ill. Adm. Code 309.
BOARD NOTE: This exclusion applies only to the actual point
source discharge. It does not exclude industrial wastewaters
while they are being collected, stored, or treated before
discharge, nor does it exclude sludges that are generated by
industrial wastewater treatment.

3) Irrigation return flows.

4) Source, special nuclear, or by-product material as defined by the
Atomic Energy Act of 1954, as amended (42 U.S.C. 2011 et seq.)

5) Materials subjected to in-situ mining techniques that are not
removed from the ground as part of the extraction process.

6) Pulping liquors (i.e., black liquor) that are reclaimed in a
pulping liquor recovery furnace and then reused in the pulping
process, unless accumulated speculatively, as defined in Section
721.101(c).

7) Spent sulfuric acid used to produce virgin sulfuric acid, unless
it is accumulated speculatively, as defined in Section
721.101(c).

8) Secondary materials that are reclaimed and returned to the
original process or processes in which they were generated where
they are reused in the production process, provided:
A) Only tank storage is involved, and the entire process
through completion of reclamation is closed by being
entirely connected with pipes or other comparable enclosed
means of conveyance;
B) Reclamation does not involve controlled flame combustion
(such as occurs in boilers, industrial furnaces or
incinerators);
C) The secondary materials are never accumulated in such tanks
for over twelve months without being reclaimed; and

POLLUTION CONTROL BOARD

NOTICE OF PROPOSED AMENDMENTS

D) The reclaimed material is not used to produce a fuel, or
used to produce products that are used in a manner
constituting disposal.

9) Wood preserving wastes.
A) Spent wood preserving solutions that have been used and
which are reclaimed and reused for their original intended
purpose; and
B) Wastewaters from the wood preserving process that have been
reclaimed and which are reused to treat wood.

10) Hazardous waste number numbers K060, K087, K141, K142, K143,
K144, K145, K147, and K148, and any wastes from the coke
by-products processes that are hazardous only because they
exhibit the toxicity characteristic specified in Section 721.124,
when subsequent to generation these materials are recycled to
coke ovens, to the tar recovery process as a feedstock to produce
coal tar, or are mixed with coal tar prior to the tar's sale or
refining. This exclusion is conditioned on there being no land
disposal of the wastes waste from the point they it are is
generated to the point they it are is recycled to coke ovens, to
or tar recovery, to or the tar refining processes, or prior to
when it is mixed with coal.

11) Nonwastewater splash condenser dross residue from the treatment
of hazardous waste number K061 in high temperature metals
recovery units, provided it is shipped in drums (if shipped) and
not land disposed before recovery.

12) Recovered oil from petroleum refining, exploration, and
production and from transportation incident thereto that is to be
inserted into the petroleum refining process (SIC Code 2911)
along with normal process streams prior to crude distillation or
catalytic cracking. This exclusion applies to recovered oil
stored or transported prior to insertion, except that the oil
must not be stored in a manner involving placement on the land
and the oil must not be accumulated speculatively before being
recycled. Recovered oil is oil that has been reclaimed from
secondary materials (such as wastewater) generated from normal
petroleum refining, exploration and production, and
transportation practices. Recovered oil includes oil that is
recovered from refinery wastewater collection and treatment
systems, oil recovered from oil and gas drilling operations, and
oil recovered from waste removed from crude oil storage tanks.
Recovered oil does not include (among other things) oil-bearing
hazardous waste listed in 721.Subpart D (e.g., K048 through K052,
F037, and F038). However, oil recovered from such wastes may be
considered recovered oil. Recovered oil also does not include
used oil as defined in 35 Ill. Adm. Code 739.100.

b) Solid wastes that are not hazardous wastes. The following solid
wastes are not hazardous wastes:

1) Household waste, including household waste that has been

POLLUTION CONTROL BOARD

NOTICE OF PROPOSED AMENDMENTS

collected, transported, stored, treated, disposed, recovered (e.g., refuse-derived fuel), or reused. "Household waste" means any waste material (including garbage, trash, and sanitary wastes in septic tanks) derived from households (including single and multiple residences, hotels, and motels, bunkhouses, ranger stations, crew quarters, campgrounds, picnic grounds, and day-use recreation areas). A resource recovery facility managing municipal solid waste shall not be deemed to be treating, storing, disposing of, or otherwise managing hazardous wastes for the purposes of regulation under this Part, if such facility:

A) Receives and burns only:

   1) Household waste (from single and multiple dwellings, hotels, motels, and other residential sources); and

   ii) Solid waste from commercial or industrial sources that does not contain hazardous waste; and

B) Such facility does not accept hazardous waste and the owner or operator of such facility has established contractual requirements or other appropriate notification or inspection procedures to assure that hazardous wastes are not received at or burned in such facility.

BOARD NOTE: The U.S. Supreme Court determined, in City of Chicago v. Environmental Defense Fund, Inc., no, 92-1639 (May 2, 1994), that this exclusion and RCRA section 3001(i) (42 U.S.C. 6921(i)) do not exclude the ash from facilities covered by this subsection from regulation as a hazardous waste. At 59 Fed. Reg. 29372 (June 7, 1994), U.S. EPA granted facilities managing ash from such facilities that is determined a hazardous waste under 721.Subpart C Until December 7, 1994 to file a Part A permit application pursuant to 35 III. Adm. Code 703.181.

2) Solid wastes generated by any of the following that are returned to the soil as fertilizers:

A) The growing and harvesting of agricultural crops, or

B) The raising of animals, including animal manures.

3) Mining overburden returned to the mine site.

4) Fly ash waste, bottom ash waste, slag waste, and flue gas emission control waste generated primarily from the combustion of coal, or other fossil fuels, except as provided in 35 Ill. Adm. Code 726.212 for facilities that burn or process hazardous waste.

5) Drilling fluids, produced waters, and other wastes associated with the exploration, development, or production of crude oil, natural gas, or geothermal energy.

6) Chromium

A) Wastes that fail the test for the toxicity characteristic (Section 721.124 and Appendix B) because chromium is present or which are are listed in 721.Subpart D of this Part due to the presence of chromium, that do not fail the test for the toxicity characteristic for any other constituent or which

POLLUTION CONTROL BOARD

NOTICE OF PROPOSED AMENDMENTS

are not listed due to the presence of any other constituent, and that do not fail the test for any other characteristic, if it is shown by a waste generator or by waste generators that:

i) The chromium in the waste is exclusively (or nearly exclusively) trivalent chromium; and

ii) The waste is generated from an industrial process that uses trivalent chromium exclusively (or nearly exclusively) and the process does not generate hexavalent chromium; and

iii) The waste is typically and frequently managed in non-oxidizing environments.

B) Specific wastes that meet the standard in subsection subsections (b)(6)(A)(i)--(b)(6)(A)--(iii)--and--(b)(6)(A) (iii) above (so long as they do not fail the test for the toxicity characteristic for any other constituent and do not exhibit any other characteristic) are:

i) Chrome (blue) trimmings generated by the following subcategories of the leather tanning and finishing industry: hair pulp/chrome tan/ retan/wet finish, hair save/chrome tan/retan/wet finish, retan/wet finish, no beamhouse, through-the-blue, and shearling;

ii) Chrome (blue) shavings generated by the following subcategories of the leather tanning and finishing industry: hair pulp/chrome tan/retan/wet finish, hair save/chrome tan/retan/wet finish, retan/wet finish, no beamhouse, through-the-blue, and shearling;

iii) Buffing dust generated by the following subcategories of the leather tanning and finishing industry: hair pulp/chrome tan/retan/wet finish, retan/wet finish, no beamhouse, through-the-blue;

iv) Sewer screenings generated by the following subcategories of the leather tanning and finishing industry: hair pulp/chrome tan/retan/wet finish, hair save/chrome tan/retan/wet finish, retan/wet finish, no beamhouse, through-the-blue, and shearling;

v) Wastewater treatment sludges generated by the following subcategories of the leather tanning and finishing industry: hair pulp/chrome tan/retan/wet finish, hair save/chrome tan/retan/wet finish, retan/wet finish, no beamhouse, through-the-blue, and shearling;

vi) Wastewater treatment sludges generated by the following subcategories of the leather tanning and finishing industry: hair pulp/chrome tan/retan/wet finish, hair save/chrome tan/retan/wet finish, and through-the-blue;

POLLUTION CONTROL BOARD

NOTICE OF PROPOSED AMENDMENTS

vii) Waste scrap leather from the leather tanning industry, the shoe manufacturing industry, and other leather product manufacturing industries; and

viii) Wastewater treatment sludges from the production of titanium dioxide pigment using chromium-bearing ores by the chloride process.

7) Solid waste from the extraction, beneficiation, and processing of ores and minerals (including coal, phosphate rock, and overburden from the mining of uranium ore), except as provided by 35 Ill. Adm. Code 726.212 for facilities that burn or process hazardous waste. For purposes of this subsection, beneficiation of ores and minerals is restricted to the following activities: crushing, grinding, washing, dissolution, crystallization, filtration, sorting, sizing, drying, sintering, pelletizing, briquetting, calcining to remove water or carbon dioxide, roasting, autoclaving or chlorination in preparation for leaching (except where the roasting or autoclaving or chlorination and leaching sequence produces a final or intermediate product that does not undergo further beneficiation or processing), gravity concentration, magnetic separation, electrostatic separation, floatation, ion exchange, solvent extraction, electrowinning, precipitation, amalgamation, and heap, dump, vat tank, and in situ leaching. For the purposes of this subsection, solid waste from the processing of ores and minerals includes only the following wastes:

A) Slag from primary copper processing;

B) Slag from primary lead processing;

C) Red and brown muds from bauxite refining;

D) Phosphogypsum from phosphoric acid production;

E) Slag from elemental phosphorus production;

F) Gasifier ash from coal gasification;

G) Process wastewater from coal gasification;

H) Calcium sulfate wastewater treatment plant sludge from primary copper processing;

I) Slag tailings from primary copper processing;

J) Fluorogypsum from hydrofluoric acid production;

K) Process wastewater from hydrofluoric acid production;

L) Air pollution control dust or sludge from iron blast furnaces;

M) Iron blast furnace slag;

N) Treated residue from roasting and leaching of chrome ore;

O) Process wastewater from primary magnesium processing by the anhydrous process;

P) Process wastewater from phosphoric acid production;

Q) Basic oxygen furnace and open hearth furnace air pollution control dust or sludge from carbon steel production;

R) Basic oxygen furnace and open hearth furnace slag from carbon steel production;

POLLUTION CONTROL BOARD

NOTICE OF PROPOSED AMENDMENTS

S) Chloride processing waste solids from titanium tetrachloride production; andy

T) Slag from primary zinc smelting.

8) Cement kiln dust waste, except as provided by 35 Ill. Adm. Code 726.213 for facilities that burn or process hazardous waste. *

9) Solid waste that consists of discarded arsenical-treated wood or wood products which that fails the test for the toxicity characteristic for hazardous waste codes D004 through D017 and that which is not a hazardous waste for any other reason if the waste is generated by persons who that utilize the arsenical-treated wood and wood products for these materials' intended end use.

10) Petroleum-contaminated media and debris that fail the test for the toxicity characteristic of Section 721.124 (hazardous waste codes D018 through D043 only) and which are subject to corrective action regulations under 35 Ill. Adm. Code 721.

11) Injected groundwater that is hazardous only because it exhibits the toxicity characteristic (U.S. EPA hazardous waste codes D018 through D024 only) in Section 721.124 that is reinjected through an underground injection well pursuant to free phase hydrocarbon recovery operations undertaken at petroleum refineries, petroleum marketing terminals, petroleum bulk plants, petroleum pipelines, and petroleum spill sites until January 25, 1993. This extension applies to recovery operations in existence or for which contracts have been issued, on or before March 25, 1991. For groundwater returned through infiltration galleries from such at petroleum refineries, marketing terminals, and bulk plants until October 31, 1991. New operations involving injection wells (beginning after March 25, 1991) will qualify for this compliance date extension (until January 25, 1993) only if This subsection corresponds with 40 CFR 261.4(b)(11), which expired by its own terms on January 25, 1993. This statement maintains structural parity with U.S. EPA regulations.

A) Operations are performed pursuant to a "free product removal report" pursuant to 35 Ill. Adm. Code 731.164; and

B) A copy of the "free product removal report" has been submitted to:

Characteristics Section (OS-333)
U.S. EPA
401 M Street, SW
Washington, D.C. 20460

12) Used chlorofluorocarbon refrigerants from totally enclosed heat transfer equipment, including mobile air conditioning systems, mobile refrigeration, and commercial and industrial air conditioning and refrigeration systems that use uses chlorofluorocarbons as the heat transfer fluid in a refrigeration cycle, provided the refrigerant is reclaimed for further use.

13) Non-terne plated used oil filters that are not mixed with wastes

POLLUTION CONTROL BOARD

NOTICE OF PROPOSED AMENDMENTS

listed in 721.Subpart D ~~of this Part~~, if these oil filters have been gravity hot-drained using one of the following methods:

    A) Puncturing the filter anti-drain back valve or the filter dome end and hot-draining;

    B) Hot-draining and crusing;

    C) Dismantling and hot-draining; or

    D) Any other equivalent hot-draining method that will remove used oil.

14) Used oil re-refining distillation bottoms that are used as feedstock to manufacture asphalt products.

c) Hazardous wastes that are exempted from certain regulations. A hazardous waste that is generated in a product or raw material storage tank, a product or raw material transport vehicle or vessel, a product or raw material pipeline, or in a manufacturing process unit, or an associated non-waste-treatment manufacturing unit, is not subject to regulation under 35 Ill. Adm. Code 702, 703, 705, and 722 through 725, and 728 or to the notification requirements of Section 3010 of RCRA until it exits the unit in which it was generated, unless the unit is a surface impoundment, or unless the hazardous waste remains in the unit more than 90 days after the unit ceases to be operated for manufacturing; or for storage or transportation of product or raw materials.

d) Samples.

  1) Except as provided in subsection (d)(2) below, a sample of solid waste or a sample of water, soil, or air that is collected for the sole purpose of testing to determine its characteristics or composition is not subject to any requirements of this Part or 35 Ill. Adm. Code 702, 703, 705 and 722 through 728. The sample qualifies when:

    A) The sample is being transported to a laboratory for the purpose of testing; or

    B) The sample is being transported back to the sample collector after testing; or

    C) The sample is being stored by the sample collector before transport to a laboratory for testing; or

    D) The sample is being stored in a laboratory before testing; or

    E) The sample is being stored in a laboratory for testing but before it is returned to the sample collector; or

    F) The sample is being stored temporarily in the laboratory after testing for a specific purpose (for example, until conclusion of a court case or enforcement action where further testing of the sample may be necessary).

  2) In order to qualify for the exemption in ~~subsections~~ subsection (d)(1)(A) ~~and~~ or (d)(1)(B) above, a sample collector shipping samples to a laboratory and a laboratory returning samples to a sample collector shall:

    A) Comply with U.S. Department of Transportation (DOT), U.S.

POLLUTION CONTROL BOARD

NOTICE OF PROPOSED AMENDMENTS

Postal Service (USPS), or any other applicable shipping requirements; or

    B) Comply with the following requirements if the sample collector determines that DOT, USPS, or other shipping requirements do not apply to the shipment of the sample:

      i) Assure that the following information accompanies the sample: The sample collector's name, mailing address, and telephone number; the laboratory's name, mailing address, and telephone number; the quantity of the sample; the date of the shipment; and a description of the sample.

      ii) Package the sample so that it does not leak, spill, or vaporize from its packaging.

  3) This exemption does not apply if the laboratory determines that the waste is hazardous but the laboratory is no longer meeting any of the conditions stated in subsection (d)(1) above.

e) Treatability study samples.

  1) Except as is provided in subsection (e)(2) below, a person ~~persons who~~ that generates ~~generate~~ or collects ~~collect~~ samples for the purpose of conducting treatability studies, as defined in 35 Ill. Adm. Code 721.110, are not subject to any requirement of 35 Ill. Adm. Code 721 through 723 or to the notification requirements of Section 3010 of the Resource Conservation and Recovery Act. Nor are such samples included in the quantity determinations of Section 721.105 and 35 Ill. Adm. Code 722.134(d) when:

    A) The sample is being collected and prepared for transportation by the generator or sample collector; or

    B) The sample is being accumulated or stored by the generator or sample collector prior to transportation to a laboratory or testing facility; or

    C) The sample is being transported to the laboratory or testing facility for the purpose of conducting a treatability study.

  2) The exemption in subsection (e)(1) above is applicable to samples of hazardous waste being collected and shipped for the purpose of conducting treatability studies provided that:

    A) The generator or sample collector uses (in "treatability studies") no more than 10,000 kg of media contaminated with non-acute hazardous waste, 1000 kg of non-acute hazardous waste other than contaminated media, 1 kg of acute hazardous waste, or 2500 kg of media contaminated with acute hazardous waste for each process being evaluated for each generated wastestream; and

    B) The mass of each shipment does not exceed 10,000 kg; the 10,000 kg quantity may be all media contaminated with non-acute hazardous waste, or may include 2500 kg of media contaminated with acute hazardous waste, 1000 kg of hazardous waste, and 1 kg of acute hazardous waste; and

POLLUTION CONTROL BOARD

NOTICE OF PROPOSED AMENDMENTS

C) The sample must be packaged so that it does not leak, spill, or vaporize from its packaging during shipment and the requirements of subsections (e)(2)(C)(i) or (e)(2)(C)(ii), below, are met.

   i) The transportation of each sample shipment complies with U.S. Department of Transportation (DOT), U.S. Postal Service (USPS), or any other applicable shipping requirements; or

   ii) If the DOT, USPS, or other shipping requirements do not apply to the shipment of the sample, the following information must accompany the sample: The name, mailing address, and telephone number of the originator of the sample; the name, address, and telephone number of the facility that will perform the treatability study; the quantity of the sample; the date of the shipment; and, a description of the sample, including its U.S. EPA hazardous waste number;

D) The sample is shipped to a laboratory or testing facility that is exempt under subsection (f) below, or has an appropriate RCRA permit or interim status;

E) The generator or sample collector maintains the following records for a period ending 9 three years after completion of the treatability study:

   i) Copies of the shipping documents;

   ii) A copy of the contract with the facility conducting the treatability study;

   iii) Documentation showing: The amount of waste shipped under this exemption; the name, address, and U.S. EPA identification number of the laboratory or testing facility that received the waste; the date the shipment was made; and, whether or not unused samples and residues were returned to the generator;

F) The generator reports the information required in subsection (e)(2)(E)(iii) above in its report under 35 Ill. Adm. Code 722.141.

3) The Agency may grant requests on a case-by-case basis for up to an additional two years for treatability studies involving bioremediation. The Agency may grant requests, on a case-by-case basis, for quantity limits in excess of those specified in subsection (e)(2)(A) and (e)(2)(B) above and (f)(4) below, for up to an additional 5000 kg of media contaminated with non-acute hazardous waste, 500 kg of non-acute hazardous waste, 2500 kg of media contaminated with acute hazardous waste, and 1 kg of acute hazardous waste:

A) In response to requests for authorization to ship, store, and conduct further treatability studies in advance of commencing treatability studies. Factors to be considered in reviewing such requests include the nature of the

POLLUTION CONTROL BOARD

NOTICE OF PROPOSED AMENDMENTS

technology, the type of process (e.g., batch versus continuous), the size of the unit undergoing testing (particularly in relation to scale-up considerations), the time or quantity of material required to reach steady-state operating conditions, or test design considerations, such as mass balance calculations.

B) In response to requests for authorization to ship, store, and conduct treatability studies on additional quantities after initiation or completion of initial treatability studies when: There has been an equipment or mechanical failure during the conduct of the treatability study; there is need to verify the results of a previously-conducted treatability study; there is a need to study and analyze alternative techniques within a previously-evaluated treatment process; or there is a need to do further evaluation of an ongoing treatability study to determine final specifications for treatment.

C) The additional quantities allowed and timeframes allowed in subsections (e)(3)(A) and (e)(3)(B) above are subject to all the provisions in subsections (e)(1) and (e)(2)(B) through (e)(2)(F) above. The generator or sample collector shall apply to the Agency and provide in writing the following information:

   i) The reason why the generator or sample collector requires additional time or quantity of sample for the treatability study evaluation and the additional time or quantity needed;

   ii) Documentation accounting for all samples of hazardous waste from the wastestream that have been sent for or undergone treatability studies, including the date each previous sample from the waste stream was shipped, the quantity of each previous shipment, the laboratory or testing facility to which it was shipped, what treatability study processes were conducted on each sample shipped, and the available results of each treatability study;

   iii) A description of the technical modifications or change in specifications that will be evaluated and the expected results;

   iv) If such further study is being required due to equipment or mechanical failure, the applicant shall include information regarding the reason for the failure or breakdown and also include what procedures or equipment improvements have been made to protect against further breakdowns; and

   v) Such other information as the Agency determines is necessary.

4) Final Agency determinations pursuant to this subsection may be

POLLUTION CONTROL BOARD

NOTICE OF PROPOSED AMENDMENTS

appealed to the Board.

f) Samples undergoing treatability studies at laboratories or testing facilities. Samples undergoing treatability studies and the laboratory or testing facility conducting such treatability studies (to the extent such facilities are not otherwise subject to RCRA requirements) are not subject to any requirement of this Part, or of 35 Ill. Adm. Code 702, 703, 705, 722 through 726, and 728, or to the notification requirements of Section 3010 of the Resource Conservation and Recovery Act, provided that the requirements of subsections (f)(1) through (f)(11)r below are met. A mobile treatment unit may qualify as a testing facility subject to subsections (f)(1) through (f)(11)r below. Where a group of mobile treatment units are located at the same site, the limitations specified in subsections (f)(1) through (f)(11)r below apply to the entire group of mobile treatment units collectively as if the group were one mobile treatment unit.

1) No less than 45 days before conducting treatability studies, the facility notifies the Agency in writing that it intends to conduct treatability studies under this subsection.

2) The laboratory or testing facility conducting the treatability study has a U.S. EPA identification number.

3) No more than a total of 10,000 kg of "as received" media contaminated with non-acute hazardous waste, 2500 kg of media contaminated with acute hazardous waste, or 250 kg of other "as received" hazardous waste is subject to initiation of treatment in all treatability studies in any single day. "As received" waste refers to the waste as received in the shipment from the generator or sample collector.

4) The quantity of "as received" hazardous waste stored at the facility for the purpose of evaluation in treatability studies does not exceed 10,000 kg, the total of which can include 10,000 kg of media contaminated with non-acute hazardous waste, 2500 kg of media contaminated with acute hazardous waste, 1000 kg of non-acute hazardous wastes other than contaminated media, and 1 kg of acute hazardous waste. This quantity limitation does not include treatment materials (including nonhazardous solid waste) added to "as received" hazardous waste.

5) No more than 90 days have elapsed since the treatability study for the sample was completed, or no more than one year (two years for treatability studies involving bioremediation) has elapsed since the generator or sample collector shipped the sample to the laboratory or testing facility, whichever date first occurs. Up to 500 kg of treated material from a particular waste stream from treatability studies may be archived for future evaluation up to five years from the date of initial receipt. Quantities of materials archived are counted against the total storage limit for the facility.

6) The treatability study does not involve the placement of hazardous waste on the land or open burning of hazardous waste.

POLLUTION CONTROL BOARD

NOTICE OF PROPOSED AMENDMENTS

7) The facility maintains records θ three years following completion of each study that show compliance with the treatment rate limits and the storage time and quantity limits. The following specific information must be included for each treatability study conducted:
   A) The name, address, and U.S. EPA identification number of the generator or sample collector of each waste sample;
   B) The date the shipment was received;
   C) The quantity of waste accepted;
   D) The quantity of "as received" waste in storage each day;
   E) The date the treatment study was initiated and the amount of "as received" waste introduced to treatment each day;
   F) The date the treatability study was concluded;
   G) The date any unused sample or residues generated from the treatability study were returned to the generator or sample collector or, if sent to a designated facility, the name of the facility and the U.S. EPA identification number.

8) The facility keeps, on-site, a copy of the treatability study contract and all shipping papers associated with the transport of treatability study samples to and from the facility for a period ending θ three years from the completion date of each treatability study.

9) The facility prepares and submits a report to the Agency by March 15 of each year that estimates the number of studies and the amount of waste expected to be used in treatability studies during the current year, and includes the following information for the previous calendar year:
   A) The name, address, and U.S. EPA identification number of the facility conducting the treatability studies;
   B) The types (by process) of treatability studies conducted;
   C) The names and addresses of persons for whom studies have been conducted (including their U.S. EPA identification numbers);
   D) The total quantity of waste in storage each day;
   E) The quantity and types of waste subjected to treatability studies;
   F) When each treatability study was conducted; and
   G) The final disposition of residues and unused sample from each treatability study.

10) The facility determines whether any unused sample or residues generated by the treatability study are hazardous waste under Section 721.103 and, if so, are subject to 35 Ill. Adm. Code 702, 703, and 721 through 728, unless the residues and unused samples are returned to the sample originator under the subsection (e) exemption above.

11) The facility notifies the Agency by letter when the facility is no longer planning to conduct any treatability studies at the site.

POLLUTION CONTROL BOARD

NOTICE OF PROPOSED AMENDMENTS

(Source: Amended   at   19   Ill.   Reg.   _____,   effective
_____)

Section 721.106 Requirements for Recyclable Materials

a) Recyclable materials:

   1) Hazardous   wastes   that   are   recycled   are   subject   to   the
       requirements for generators, transporters, and storage facilities
       of subsections (b) and (c)+ below, except for the materials
       listed in subsections (a)(2) and (a)(3)+ below. Hazardous wastes
       that are recycled will be known as "recycleable materials".

   2) The following recycleable materials are not subject to the
       requirements of this Section but are regulated under 35 Ill. Adm.
       Code 726.Subparts C through H and all applicable provisions in 35
       Ill. Adm. Code 702, 703, and 705.

       A) Recyclable materials used in a manner constituting disposal
           (35 Ill. Adm. Code 726.Subpart C);

       B) Hazardous wastes burned for energy recovery in boilers and
           industrial furnaces that are not regulated under 35 Ill.
           Adm. Code 724._Subpart O or 725.Subpart O (35 Ill. Adm. Code
           726.Subpart H);

       C) Recyclable   materials   from   which   precious   metals   are
           reclaimed (35 Ill. Adm. Code 726.Subpart F);

       D) Spent lead-acid batteries that are being reclaimed (35 Ill.
           Adm. Code 726.Subpart G).

   3) The following recycleable materials are not subject to regulation
       under 35 Ill. Adm. Code 722 through 726, 728, or 702, 703, or 705
       and are not subject to the notification requirements of Section
       3010 of the Resource Conservation and Recovery Act:

       A) Industrial ethyl alcohol that is reclaimed except that,
           unless provided otherwise in an international agreement as
           specified in 35 Ill. Adm. Code 722.158;

           i) A person initiating a shipment for reclamation in a
               foreign country and any intermediary arranging for the
               shipment shall comply with the requirements applicable
               to a primary exporter in 35 Ill. Adm. Code 722.153,;
               722.156(a)(1) through (a)(4), (a)(6), and (b);, and
               722.157,, shall export such materials only upon consent
               of the receiving country and in conformance with the
               U.S. EPA Acknowledgement of Consent, as defined in 35
               Ill. Adm. Code 722.Subpart E;, and shall provide a copy
               of the U.S. EPA Acknowledgement of Consent to the
               shipment to the transporter transporting the shipment
               for export;

           ii) Transporters transporting a shipment for export shall
               not accept a shipment if the transporter knows that the
               shipment does not conform to the U.S. EPA
               Acknowledgement of Consent, shall ensure that a copy of

POLLUTION CONTROL BOARD

NOTICE OF PROPOSED AMENDMENTS

       the U.S. EPA Acknowlegdement of Consent accompanies the
       shipment, and shall ensure that is is delivered to the
       facility designated by the person initiating the
       shipment.

   B) Used batteries (or used battery cells) returned to a battery
       manufacturer for regeneration;

   C) Scrap metal;

   D) Fuels produced from the refining of oil-bearing hazardous
       wastes along with normal process streams at a petroleum
       refining facility if such wastes result from normal
       petroleum refining, production, and transportation practices
       [this exemption does not apply to fuels produced from oil
       recovered   from   oil-bearing   hazardous   waste   where   such
       recovered   oil   is   already   excluded   under   Section
       721.104(a)(12)];

   E) Oil reclaimed from hazardous waste resulting from normal
       petroleum refining, production and transportation practices,
       which oil is to be refined along with normal process streams
       at a petroleum refining facility;

   E) Petroleum refining wastes.

       i) Hazardous waste fuel produced from oil-bearing
           hazardous wastes from petroleum refining, production,
           or transportation practices, or produced from oil
           reclaimed from such hazardous wastes, where such
           hazardous wastes are reintroduced into a process that
           does not use distillation or does not produce products
           from crude oil, so long as the resulting fuel meets the
           used oil specification under 35 Ill. Adm. Code
           726.140(e) and so long as no other hazardous wastes are
           used to produce the hazardous waste fuel;

       ii) Hazardous waste fuel produced from oil-bearing
           hazardous waste from petroleum refining production, and
           transportation practices, where such hazardous wastes
           are reintroduced into a refining process after a point
           at which contaminants are removed, so long as the fuel
           meets the used oil fuel specification under 35 Ill.
           Adm. Code 726.140(e); and

       iii) Oil reclaimed from oil-bearing hazardous wastes from
            petroleum refining, production, and transportation
            practices, which reclaimed oil is burned as a fuel
            without reintroduction to a refining process, so long
            as the reclaimed oil meets the used oil fuel
            specification under 35 Ill. Adm. Code 726.140(e); and

   F) Petroleum coke produced from petroleum refinery hazardous
       wastes containing oil at the same facility at which such by
       the same person that generated the wastes were generated,
       unless the resulting coke product exceeds one or more of the
       characteristics of hazardous waste in 721.Subpart D of this

POLLUTION CONTROL BOARD

NOTICE OF PROPOSED AMENDMENTS

Part.

4) Used oil that is recycled and is also a hazardous waste solely because it exhibits a hazardous characteristic is not subject to the requirements of 35 Ill. Adm. Code 720 through 728, but it is regulated under 35 Ill. Adm Code 739. Used oil that is recycled includes any used oil which that is reused for any purpose following its original use, for any purpose (including the purpose for which the oil was originally used). Such term includes, but is not limited to, oil which that is re-refined, reclaimed, burned for energy recovery, or reprocessed.

b) Generators and transporters of recyclable materials are subject to the applicable requirements of 35 Ill. Adm. Code 722 and 723 and the notification requirements under Section 3010 of the Resource Conservation and Recovery Act, except as provided in subsection (a), above.

c) Storage and recycling:

1) Owners or operators of facilities that store recyclable materials before they are recycled are regulated under all applicable provisions of 35 Ill. Adm. Code 702, 703, and 705; 724.Subparts A through L, AA, and BB; and 725.Subparts A through L, AA, and BB; 726, 728, 702, 703 and 705 and the notification requirement under Section 3010 of the Resource Conservation and Recovery Act, except as provided in subsection (a), above. (The recycling process itself is exempt from regulation, except as provided in subsection (d), below.)

2) Owners or operators of facilities that recycle recycleable materials without storing them before they are recycled are subject to the following requirements, except as provided in subsection (a), above;

A) Notification requirements under Section 3010 of the Resource Conservation and Recovery Act, ;

B) 35 Ill. Adm. Code 725.171 and 725.172 (dealing with the use of the manifest and manifest discrepancies), and

C) Subsection (d), below.

d) Owners or operators of facilities required to have a RCRA permit pursuant to 35 Ill. Adm. Code 703 with hazardous waste management units which that recycle hazardous wastes are subject to 35 Ill. Adm. Code 724.Subpart Subparts AA and BB and 725.Subpart Subparts AA and BB.

(Source: Amended at 19 Ill. Reg. _____, effective _____)

POLLUTION CONTROL BOARD

NOTICE OF PROPOSED AMENDMENTS

ltm;10=0,0;11=5,9;12=10,14;13=15,19;14=20,24;15=25,29

Section 721.APPENDIX I Wastes Excluded under Section 720, 120 and 720.122 by Administrative Action

Section 721.TABLE A Wastes Excluded by U.S. EPA under 40 CFR 260.20 and 260.22 from From Non-specific Sources

Facility Address	Waste Description
Envirite--------Corp. Harvey, Illinois	Dewatered--wastewater--sludges (EPA-Hazardous-Waste-NO. F006) generated-from-electroplating--operations; spent cyanide--plating--solutions--(EPA--Hazardous--Waste-No. F007) generated-from-electroplating-operations; plating bath-residues-from-the-bottom-of--plating--baths--(EPA Hazardous--Waste-No-F008) generated-from-the-bottom-of plating-baths-(EPA-Hazardous-Waste-No--F008) generated from--electroplating-operations-where-cyanides-are-used in-the--process; spent--stripping--and--cleaning--bath solutions-(EPA-Hazardous-Waste-No--F009)-generated-from electroplating--operations--where--cyanides-are-used-in the-process; spent-cyanide-solutions-from-salt-bath-pot cleaning-(EPA-Hazardous-Waste-No--F011)-generated--from metal--heat--treating--operations; quenching-wastewater treatment--sludges--(EPA--Hazardous--Waste--No---F012) generated--from--metal-heat-treating-where-cyanides-are used-in-the-process; wastewater-treatment-sludges--(EPA Hazardous--Waste--No--F019)-generated-from-the-chemical conversion-coating-of-aluminum-after-November-14,-1986; To-ensure-that-hazardous-constituents-are--not--present in--the--waste--at--levels--of--regulatory-concern; the facility-must-implement-a-contingency--testing--program for--the--petitioned-wastes. This-testing-program-must meet-the-following-conditions-for-the-exclusions-to--be valid:
	1) Each---batch---of---treatment---residue---must--be representatively-sampled-and-tested-using--the--EP Toxicity--test--for--arsenic; barium; cadmium; chromium; lead; selenium; silver; mercury; and nickel. If--the--extract--concentration--for chromium; lead; arsenic-and--silver--exceed--5 ppm; barium-levels-exceed--G.3-ppm; cadmium-and selenium-exceed-0.663-ppm; mercury-exceeds--0.026 ppm; or-nickel-levels-exceed-2.705-ppm; the-waste must-be-re-treated-or-managed-and--disposed--as--a

POLLUTION CONTROL BOARD

NOTICE OF PROPOSED AMENDMENTS

hazardous--waste--under--35--Ill.--Adm.--Code--722--to--725
and--the--permitting--standards--of--35--Ill.--Adm.--Code
702,--703,--and--705.

2) Each-batch-of-treatment-residue-must-be-tested-for
reactive-and-leachable-cyanide.--If--the--reactive
cyanide-levels-exceed-250-ppm-or-leachable-cyanide
levels--(using-the-EP-Toxicity-test-without-acetic
acid-adjustment)-exceed-1.26-ppm,-the--waste---must
be---retreated---or--managed--and--disposed--as--a
hazardous-waste-under-35-Ill.-Adm.-Code-722-to-725
and-the-permitting-standards-of-35-Ill.-Adm.--Code
702,-703,-and-705.

3) Each--batch---of--waste--must-be-tested-for-the-total
content-of-specific--organic--contents.--If--the
total--content--of--anthracene--exceeds--76.8--ppm,
1,2-diphenyl---hydrazine---exceeds---0.001----ppm,
methylene--chloride-exceeds-8.18-ppm,-methyl-ethyl
ketone--exceeds--326--ppm,--n-nitrosodiphenylamine
exceeds--11.9--ppm,--phenol--exceeds--1.566---ppm,
tetrachloroethylene----exceeds---0.188---ppm,---or
trichloroethylene-exceeds--0.592--ppm,--the--waste
must--be-managed-and-disposed-as-a-hazardous-waste
under-35--Ill.--Adm.--Code--722--to--725--and--the
permitting--standards--of--35--Ill.-Adm.-Code-702,
703,-and-705.

4) A-grab-sample-must-be-collected-from-each-batch-to
form-one-monthly-composite-sample--which--must--be
tested-using-gas-chromatography-mass-spectrometry
analysis--for--the-compounds-listed-in-No.-3-above
as-well-as-the-remaining-organics-on-the--Priority
Pollutant--list-(incorporated-by-reference,-see-40
CFR-423-App.-A-(1983)-(as-adopted-at-47-Fed.--Reg.
52,309--(Nov.--19,---1982)))--not--including--later
amendments).

5) The---data-from-conditions-1-4-must-be-kept-on-file
at-the-facility-for-inspection-purposes--and--must
be--compiled,--summarized,--and--submitted--to--the
Administrator---of---USEPA---by---certified---mail
semi-annually.--The--USEPA---will---review---this
information--and--if-needed-will-propose-to-modify
or-withdraw-the-exclusion.--Should--USEPA--propose
to--modify--or--withdraw--the--exclusion,-Envirite
shall--promptly--provide--notice--thereof--to--the
Board.--The-decision-to-conditionally-exclude--the
treatment--residue--generated--from--the--wastewater
treatment-systems-at-Envirite's--Harvey,--Illinois
facility-applies-only-to-the-wastewater-and-solids
treatment--systems--as--they--presently--exist--as
described--in--the-delisting-petition-submitted-to
the-USEPA.--The-exclusion-does-not--apply--to--the
proposed---process---additions---described--in--the
petition-submitted-to-USEPA-as-recovery--including
crystallization,--electrolytic--metals--recovery,
evaporative-recovery-and-ion-exchange.

(Source: Amended   at   19   Ill.   Reg. _____, effective
          _____)

POLLUTION CONTROL BOARD

NOTICE OF PROPOSED AMENDMENTS

Section 721.TABLE B Wastes Excluded by U.S. EPA under 40 CFR 260.20 and 260.22
from From Non-specific Sources

Facility Address	Waste Description
Amoco Oil Company Wood River, Illinois	150 million gallons of DAF float from petroleum refining contained in four surge ponds after treatment with the Chemfix stabilization process. This waste contains U.S. EPA hazardous waste number K048. This exclusion applies to the 150 million gallons of waste after chemical stabilization as long as the mixing ratios of the reagent with the waste are monitored continuously and do not vary outside of the limits presented in the demonstration sample; and one grab sample is taken each hour from each treatment unit, composited, and EP toxicity tests performed on each sample. If the levels of lead or total chromium exceed 0.5 ppm in the EP extract, then the waste that was processed during the compositing period is considered hazardous; the treatment residue shall be pumped into bermed cells to ensure that the waste is identifiable in the event that removal is necessary.
~~Envirite------Corp~ Harvey,-Illinois~~	~~Spent-pickle-liquor--(EPA--Hazardous--Waste--No.--K062) generated-from-steel-finishing-operations-of-facilities within--the--iron-and-steel-industry-(SIC-Codes-331-and 332);-wastewater-treatment-sludge-(EPA-Hazardous--Waste No.--K002)--generated--from--the--production--of-chrome yellow-and-orange-pigments;-wastewater-treatment-sludge (EPA--Hazardous--Waste--No.--K003)--generated--from--the production-of--molybdate--orange--pigments;--wastewater treatment---sludge--(EPA--Hazardous--Waste--No.--K004) generated-from-the-production-of-zinc-yellow--pigments; wastewater--treatment--sludge--(EPA-Hazardous--Waste-No. K005)-generated-from-the--production--of--chrome--green pigments;--wastewater--treatment--sludge-(EPA-Hazardous Waste-No.--K006)-generated-from-the-production-of-chrome oxide--green--pigments--(anhydrous---and----hydrated); wastewater--treatment--sludge--(EPA-Hazardous-Waste-No. K007)--generated--from--the--production--of--iron--blue pigments;-oven-residues-(EPA-Hazardous--Waste-No.--K008) generated--from--the--production--of-chrome-oxide-green pigments-after--November--14,--1986;---To--ensure--that hazardous--constituents-are-not-present-in-the-waste-at levels--of--regulatory--concern,--the--facility---must implement---a--contingency--testing--program--for--the~~

POLLUTION CONTROL BOARD

NOTICE OF PROPOSED AMENDMENTS

~~petitioned--wastes.--This-testing-program-must-meet--the following-conditions-for-the-evaluations-to-be-valid:~~

~~1) Each---batch---of---treatment---residue---must--be representatively-sampled-and-tested-using--the--EP Toxicity--test---for--arsenic--barium--cadmium, chromium,-lead,--selenium,--silver,--mercury---and nickel;---If---the---extract--concentrations--for chromium,-lead,-arsenic,-and-silver--exceed--0.315 ppm;--barium--levels--exceed--6.3-ppm--cadmium-and selenium-exceed-0.063-ppm;-or-nickel-levels-exceed 2.205-ppm,-the-waste-must-be-re-treated-or-managed and-disposed-of--a-hazardous-waste--under--35--Ill. Adm:--Code--722-to-725-and-the-permitting-standards of-35-Ill.-Adm:-Code-702,-703,-and-705.~~

~~2) Each-batch-of-treatment-residue-must-be-tested-for reactive-and-leachable-cyanide.--If--the--reactive cyanide---levels---exceed--250--ppm;--or--leachable cyanide-levels-(using-the-EP-Toxicity-test--without acetic-acid-adjustment)-exceed-1.26-ppm;-the-waste must-be-re-treated--or--managed--and--disposed--as hazardous-waste-under-35-Ill.-Adm:-Code-722-to-725 and--the-permitting-standards-of-35-Ill.-Adm:-Code 702,-703,-and-705.~~

~~3) Each-batch-of-waste-must-be-tested-for--the--total content--of--specific--organic--toxicants;--If--the total-content--of--anthracene--exceeds--76.8--ppm; 1,2-diphenyl---hydrazine---exceeds--2.081---ppm; methylene-chloride-exceeds-0.18-ppm;-methyl--ethyl ketone--exceeds--326--ppm;-n-nitrosodiphenylamine exceeds---11.9--ppm;--phenol--exceeds--1,566--ppm; tetrachloroethylene---exceeds---9.188---ppm,----or trichloroethylene--exceeds--0.592--ppm;-the-waste must-be-managed-and-disposed-as-a-hazardous--waste under--35--Ill.--Adm:--Code--722--to--725-and-the permitting-standards-of-35-Ill.--Adm:--Code--702, 703,-nad-705.~~

~~4) A-grab-sample-must-be-collected-from-each-batch-to form--one--monthly--composite-sample-which-must-be tested-using-gas-chromatography--mass-spectrometry analysis-for-the-compounds-listed-in-No.--3--above as--well-as-the-remaining-organics-on-the-Priority Pollutant-List-(incorporated-by-reference;-see--40 CFR-423-App.-A-(1983)-(as-adopted-at-47-Fed.-Reg. 52,309--(Nov.--19,--1982)),--not--including--later 703,-nad-705.~~

POLLUTION CONTROL BOARD

NOTICE OF PROPOSED AMENDMENTS

amendments~

6) ~The~data~from~conditions~1-4~must~be~kept~on~file
    at~the~facility~for~inspection~purposes~and~must
    be~compiled,~summarized,~and~submitted~to~the
    USEPA---Administrator----by---certified---mail
    semi-annually.--The--USEPA--will--review--this
    information--and--if-needed-will-propose-to-modify
    or~withdraw~the~exclusion.~~Should~USEPA~propose
    to~modify~or~withdraw~the~exclusion,~Envirite
    shall--promptly--provide--notice--thereof--to--the
    Board.~~The~decision~to~conditionally~exclude~the
    treatment~residue~generated~from~the~wastewater
    treatment~systems~at~Envirite's~Harvey,~Illinois
    facility~applies~only~to~the~wastewater~and~solids
    treatment~systems~as~they~presently~exist~as
    described~in~the~delisting~petition~submitted~to
    the~USEPA.~~The~exclusion~does~not~apply~to~the
    proposed--process--additions--described--in--the
    petition-submitted-to-USEPA-as-recovery-including
    crystallization,~electrolytic~metals~recovery,
    evaporative-recovery,-and-ion-exchange~

USX Steel   Full-cured chemically stabilized electric arc furnace
Corporation,   dust/sludge (CSEAFD) treatment residue (U.S. EPA
Chicago, Illinois ~Hazardous~ ~hazardous~ ~Waste~ waste ~No.~ number K061)
               generated from the primary production of steel after
               April 29, 1991. This exclusion (for 35,000 tons of
               CSEAFD per year) is conditioned upon on the data
               obtained from USX's full-scale CSEAFD treatment
               facility. To ensure that hazardous constituents are
               not present in the waste at levels of regulatory
               concern once the full-scale treatment facility is in
               operation, USX shall implement a testing program for
               the petitioned waste. This testing program must meet
               the following conditions for the exclusion to be valid:

               1. Testing: Sample collection and analyses
                   (including quality control (QC) procedures) must
                   be performed according to SW-846 methodologies,
                   SW-846-is, incorporated by reference in 35 Ill.
                   Adm. Code 720.111.

                   A. Initial Testing: During the first four weeks
                       of operation of the full scale treatment
                       system, USX shall collect representative grab
                       samples of each treated batch of the CSEAFD
                       and composite the grab samples daily. The

POLLUTION CONTROL BOARD

NOTICE OF PROPOSED AMENDMENTS

daily composites, prior to disposal, must be
analyzed for the EP leachate concentrations
of all the EP toxic metals, nickel and
cyanide (using distilled water in the cyanide
extractions), and the total concentrations of
reactive sulfide and reactive cyanide. USX
shall report the analytical test data,
including quality control information,
obtained during this initial period no later
than 90 days after the treatment of the first
full-scale batch.

B. Subsequent Testing: USX shall collect
    representative grab samples from every
    treated batch of CSEAFD generated daily and
    composite all of the grab samples to produce
    a weekly composite sample. USX then shall
    analyze each weekly composite sample for all
    of the EP toxic metals and nickel. The
    analytical data, including quality control
    information, must be compiled and maintained
    on site for a minimum of three years. These
    data must be furnished upon request and made
    available for inspection by any employee or
    representative of U₅E, EPA or the Agency.

2. Delisting levels: If the EP extract
    concentrations for chromium, lead, arsenic, or
    silver exceed 0.315 mg/l; for barium exceeds 6.3
    mg/l; for cadmium or selenium exceed 0.063 mg/l;
    for mercury exceeds 0.0126 mg/l; for nickel
    exceeds 3.15 mg/l; or for cyanide exceeds 4.42
    mg/l; or total reactive cyanide or total reactive
    sulfide levels exceed 250 mg/kg and 500 mg/kg,
    respectively, the waste must either be re-treated
    until it meets these levels or managed and
    disposed of in accordance with Subpart C of the
    Resource Conservation and Recovery Act (42 U.S.C.
    6901 et seq.).

3. Data submittal to and enforcement by U₅E,
    EPA: Within one week of system start-up USX shall
    notify the Section Chief, Delisting Section (see
    address below) when its full-scale stabilization
    system is on-line and waste treatment has begun.
    The data obtained through condition (1)(A) shall
    be submitted to the Section Chief, Delisting
    Section, CAD/OSM (OS-333), U.S. EPA, 401 M Street,

POLLUTION CONTROL BOARD

NOTICE OF PROPOSED AMENDMENTS

S.W., Washington, DC 20460 within the time period specified. At the U.S. EPA's request, USX must submit any other analytical data obtained through conditions (1)(A) or (1)(B) within the time period specified by the Section Chief. Failure to submit the required data obtained from conditions (1)(A) or (1)(B) within the specified time period or maintain the required records for the specified time will be considered by U.S. EPA, at its decision, sufficient basis to revoke USX's federal exclusion to the extent directed by U.S. EPA. All data must be accompanied by the following certification statement: "Under civil and criminal penalty of law for the making or submission of false or fraudulent statements or representations (pursuant to the applicable provisions of the Federal Code which include, but may not be limited to, 18 U.S.C. Section 6928), I certify that the information contained in or accompanying this document is true, accurate and complete. As to the (those) identified section(s) of this document for which I cannot personally verify its (their) truth and accuracy, I certify as the company official having supervisory responsibility for the persons who, acting under my direct instructions, made the verification that this information is true, accurate and complete. In the event that any of this information is determined by U.S. EPA in its sole discretion to be false, inaccurate or incomplete, and upon conveyance of this fact to the company, I recognize and agree that this federal exclusion of wastes will be void as if it never had effect or to the extent directed by U.S. EPA and that the company will be liable for any actions taken in contravention of the company's RCRA and CERCLA obligations premised upon the company's reliance on the void exclusion."

4.   Data Submittal to Agency: The data obtained through condition (1)(A) must be submitted to the Illinois Environmental Protection Agency, Planning and Reporting Section, 2200 Churchill Road, P.O. Box 19276, Springfield, IL 62794-9276 within the time period specified. At Agency's request, USX must submit any other analytical data obtained through conditions (1)(A) or (1) (B) within the time period specified by the Agency. All data

POLLUTION CONTROL BOARD

NOTICE OF PROPOSED AMENDMENTS

must be accompanied by the following certification statement: "Under civil and criminal penalty of law for the making or submission of false or fraudulent statements or representations (pursuant to the applicable provisions of Illinois' Environmental Protection Act), I certify that the information contained in or accompanying this document is true, accurate and complete. As to the (those) identified section(s) of this document for which I cannot personally verify its (their) truth and accuracy, I certify as the company official having supervisory responsibility for the persons who, acting under my direct instructions, made the verification that this information is true, accurate and complete."

5.   Enforcement by the Agency: Whenever the Agency finds that USX has violated the standards in this exclusion, has failed to submit the required data obtained from conditions (1)(A) or (1)(B) within the specified time period, has failed to maintain the required records for the specified time or has submitted false, inaccurate or incomplete data, the Agency may take such action as is allowed by Title VIII of the Act.

6.   Notification to the Board: Upon modification, termination, revocation, or other alteration of this exemption by U.S. EPA, USX shall file a petition, pursuant to Part 102, with this Board requesting that the Board follow the U.S. EPA action.

(Source: Amended at   19   Ill.   Reg.   _____ ,   effective
_____)

POLLUTION CONTROL BOARD

NOTICE OF PROPOSED AMENDMENTS

Section 721.TABLE C Wastes Excluded by U.S. EPA under 40 CFR 260.20 and 260.22
from From Commercial Chemical Products, Off-Specification Species, Container
Residues, and Soil Residues Thereof

Facility Address	Waste Description

(Source: Amended at 19 Ill. Reg. _____, effective
_____)

POLLUTION CONTROL BOARD

NOTICE OF PROPOSED AMENDMENTS

Section 721.TABLE D Wastes Excluded by the Board by Adjusted Standard

The Board has entered the following orders on petitions for adjusted standards
for delisting, pursuant to 35 Ill. Adm. Code 720.122.

AS91-1   Petition of Keystone Steel and Wire Co. for Hazardous
            Waste Delisting, February 6, 1992, and modified at 133 PCB
            189, April 23, 1992. (treated K061 waste)

AS91-3   Petition of Peoria Disposal Co. for an Adjusted Standard
            from 35 Ill. Adm. Code 721.Subpart D, February 6 and March
            11, 1993. (treated F006 waste)

AS93-7   Petition of Keystone Steel & Wire Co. for an Adjusted
            Standard from 35 Ill. Adm. Code 721.Subpart D, February
            17, 1994, as modified March 17, 1994. (treated K062 waste)

(Source: Amended at   19   Ill. Reg.   _____,   effective

POLLUTION CONTROL BOARD

NOTICE OF PROPOSED AMENDMENTS

1) Heading of the Part: Interim Status Standards for Owners and Operators of
   Hazardous Waste Treatment, Storage, and Disposal Facilities

2) Code Citation: 35 Ill. Adm. Code 725

3) Section Numbers: Proposed Action:

   725.101, 725.113, 725.114   Amended
   725.115, 725.117, 725.150   Amended
   725.156, 725.171, 725.173   Amended
   725.177, 725.192, 725.194   Amended
   725.271, 725.272, 725.274   Amended
   725.278   New Section
   725.301   Amended
   725.302   New Section
   725.325   Amended
   725.331   New Section
   725.352, 725.378, 725.477   Amended
   725.501, 725.502, 725.503   Amended
   725.504, 725.505, 725.506   Amended
   725.933, 725.963   Amended
   725.980, 725.981, 725.982   New Section
   725.983, 725.984, 725.985   New Section
   725.986, 725.987, 725.988   New Section
   725.989, 725.990, 725.991   New Section
   725.1102   Amended

4) Statutory Authority: 415 ILCS 5/22.4 and 27.

5) A complete description of the subjects and issues involved:

   A more detailed description is contained in the Board's proposed opinion
   of March 2, 1995, in R95-4 and R95-6 (consolidated), which opinion is
   available from the address below. Section 22.4(a) of the Environmental
   Protection Act (415 ILCS 5/22.4(a)) provides that Section 5-35 of the
   Administrative Procedure Act (5 ILCS 100/5-35) shall not apply. Because
   this rulemaking is not subject to Section 5-35 of the APA, it is not
   subject to first notice or to second notice review by JCAR.

   This rulemaking updates Parts 700, 702, 703, 705, 720, 721, 722, 723, 724,
   725, 726, 728, 730, 738, and 739 of the Illinois RCRA Subtitle G hazardous
   waste and underground injection control (UIC) rules to correspond with
   amendments adopted by U.S. EPA that appeared in the Federal Register
   during the period July 1 through December 31, 1994. During this period,
   U.S. EPA amended its regulations as follows:

   Federal Action   Summary

POLLUTION CONTROL BOARD

NOTICE OF PROPOSED AMENDMENTS

59 Fed. Reg. 38536, July 28, 1994	Exclusion from definition of solid waste for certain in-process recycled secondary materials used by the petroleum refining industry
59 Fed. Reg. 43496, August 24, 1994	Withdrawal of exemption from Subtitle C regulation of slag residues from high temperature metal recovery (HTMR) of electric arc furnace dust (K061), steel finishing pickle liquor (K062), and electroplating sludges (F006) that are used in a manner constituting disposal
59 Fed. Reg. 47980,	September 19, 1994 Restoration of text from 40 CFR 268.7(a) inadvertently omitted in the amendments of August 31, 1993, at 58 Fed. Reg. 46040
59 Fed. Reg. 47982, September 19, 1994	Phase II land disposal restrictions (LDRs): universal treatment standards for organic toxicity wastes and newly-listed wastes (including underground injection control (UIC) amendments)
59 Fed. Reg. 62896, December 6, 1994	Organic material air emission standards for tanks, surface impoundments, and containers

In addition to these principal amendments that occurred during the update
period, the Board has included an additional, later action:

60 Fed. Reg. 242, January 3, 1995	Corrections to the Phase II land disposal restrictions (universal treatment standards)

This January 3 action was an amendment of the September 19, 1994 Phase II
LDRs (universal waste rule). U.S. EPA corrected errors and clarified
language in the universal treatment standards. The Board did not delay in
adding these amendments for three reasons:

1) The January 3, 1995 amendments are corrections and clarifications of
   the September 19, 1994 regulations, and not new substantive
   amendments;

2) Prompt action on the January 3, 1995 amendments will facilitate
   implementation of the Phase II LDRs; and

3) The Board has received a request from the regulated community that we
   add the January 3, 1995 amendments to those of September 19, 1994.
   (See "Expedited Consideration" below.)

POLLUTION CONTROL BOARD

NOTICE OF PROPOSED AMENDMENTS

The Board also notes that the later amendments occurred within six months of the earliest amendments included in this docket, even if they occurred outside the nominal time-frame of the docket.

In addition to the federally-derived amendments, the Board used this opportunity to undertake a number of housekeeping and corrective amendments. We have effected the removal of all cross-references for effective dates and repealed Part 700. We have converted equations and formulae to the standard scientific format. We have tried to improve the language and structure of various provisions, including correcting grammar, punctuation, and spelling where necessary.

Specifically, the segment of the amendments involved in Part 725 incorporate the major requirements of the federal air emissions regulations of December 6, 1994 and one federal correction. The bulk of the air emissions requirements for tanks, containers, and surface impoundments is in new 725.Subpart CC. The federal correction, made as part of the September 19, 1994 Phase II LDRs, is the correction at Section 725.101(e)(10) of the type of waste that is exempt from regulation if managed in an elementary neutralization unit from corrosive to reactive waste.

6) Will this proposed rule replace an emergency rule currently in effect? No

7) Does this rulemaking contain an automatic repeal date? No

8) Do these proposed amendments contain incorporations by reference?

    Yes. 35 Ill. Adm. Code 720.111 is the central listing of all documents incorporated by reference throughout the text of 35 Ill. Adm. Code 702 through 705, 721 through 726, 728, 730, 738, and 739. The present amendments update the documents incorporated by reference in a few ways. First, the Board has added the year code to the references to ASTM methods at Sections 725.933(e)(2) and 725.963(d)(1) and (h). We then add the methods references in 725.Subpart CC used by U.S. EPA in the December 6, 1994 air emissions requirements: the U.S. DOT hazardous materials transportation regulations of 49 CFR 178; Methods 21, 25D, 25E, and 27 of 40 CFR 60, appendix A; sampling methods and Method 9095 from SW-846; Method 301 from 40 CFR 63, appendix A; API 2517; ASTM D 2879-92; and the 40 CFR 60, subpart VV and 61, subpart V equipment leaks air requirements.

9) Are there any other amendments pending on this Part? No

10) Statement of statewide policy objectives:

    This rulemaking is mandated by Section 22.4(a) of the Environmental Protection Act [415 ILCS 5/22.4(a)]. The statewide policy objectives are set forth in Section 20 of that Act. This rulemaking imposes mandates on

POLLUTION CONTROL BOARD

NOTICE OF PROPOSED AMENDMENTS

units of local government only to the extent that they may be involved in the generation, transportation, treatment, storage, or disposal of hazardous waste or they engage in underground injection of waste.

11) Time, place and manner in which interested persons may comment on this proposed rulemaking:

    The Board will accept written public comment on this proposal for a period of 45 days after the date of this publication. Comments should reference Docket R95-4/R95-6 and be addressed to:

        Ms. Dorothy M. Gunn, Clerk
        Illinois Pollution Control Board
        State of Illinois Center, Suite 11-500
        100 W. Randolph St.
        Chicago, IL 60601
        312-814-6931

    Address all questions to Michael J. McCambridge, at 312-814-6924.

12) Initial regulatory flexibility analysis:

    A) Date rule was submitted to the Small Business Office of the Department of Commerce and Community Affairs: March 6, 1995.

    B) Types of small businesses affected:

        The existing rules and proposed amendments affect small businesses that generate, transport, treat, store, or dispose of hazardous waste or engage in underground injection of waste.

    C) Reporting, bookkeeping or other procedures required for compliance:

        The existing rules and proposed amendments require extensive reporting, bookkeeping, and other procedures, including the preparation of manifests and annual reports, waste analyses, and maintenance of operating records.

    D) Types of professional skills necessary for compliance:

        Compliance with the existing rules and proposed amendments may require the services of an attorney, certified public accountant, chemist, and registered professional engineer.

The full text of the proposed amendments begins on the next page:

POLLUTION CONTROL BOARD

NOTICE OF PROPOSED AMENDMENTS

TITLE 35: ENVIRONMENTAL PROTECTION
SUBTITLE G: WASTE DISPOSAL
CHAPTER I: POLLUTION CONTROL BOARD
SUBCHAPTER c: HAZARDOUS WASTE OPERATING REQUIREMENTS

PART 725
INTERIM STATUS STANDARDS FOR OWNERS AND
OPERATORS OF HAZARDOUS WASTE TREATMENT,
STORAGE, AND DISPOSAL FACILITIES

SUBPART A: GENERAL PROVISIONS

SUBPART B: GENERAL FACILITY STANDARDS

SUBPART C: PREPAREDNESS AND PREVENTION

SUBPART D: CONTINGENCY PLAN AND EMERGENCY PROCEDURES

POLLUTION CONTROL BOARD

NOTICE OF PROPOSED AMENDMENTS

SUBPART E: MANIFEST SYSTEM, RECORDKEEPING AND REPORTING

SUBPART F: GROUNDWATER MONITORING

SUBPART G: CLOSURE AND POST-CLOSURE

SUBPART H: FINANCIAL REQUIREMENTS

POLLUTION CONTROL BOARD

NOTICE OF PROPOSED AMENDMENTS

POLLUTION CONTROL BOARD

NOTICE OF PROPOSED AMENDMENTS

POLLUTION CONTROL BOARD

NOTICE OF PROPOSED AMENDMENTS

SUBPART O: INCINERATORS

SUBPART P: THERMAL TREATMENT

SUBPART Q: CHEMICAL, PHYSICAL AND BIOLOGICAL TREATMENT

SUBPART R: UNDERGROUND INJECTION

SUBPART W: DRIP PADS

POLLUTION CONTROL BOARD

NOTICE OF PROPOSED AMENDMENTS

SUBPART AA: AIR EMISSION STANDARDS FOR PROCESS VENTS

SUBPART BB: AIR EMISSION STANDARDS FOR EQUIPMENT LEAKS

SUBPART DD: CONTAINMENT BUILDINGS

POLLUTION CONTROL BOARD

NOTICE OF PROPOSED AMENDMENTS

Section
725.1100   Applicability
725.1101   Design and operating standards
725.1102   Closure and ~~post-closure-care~~ Post-closure Care

APPENDIX A   Recordkeeping Instructions
APPENDIX B   EPA Report Form and Instructions (Repealed)
APPENDIX C   EPA Interim Primary Drinking Water Standards
APPENDIX D   Tests for Significance
APPENDIX E   Examples of Potentially Incompatible Waste

AUTHORITY: Implementing Section 22.4 and authorized by Section 27 of the
Environmental Protection Act [415 ILCS 5/22.4 and 27].

SOURCE: Adopted in R81-22, 43 PCB 427, at 5 Ill. Reg. 9781, effective May 17,
1982; amended and codified in R81-22, 45 PCB 317, at 6 Ill. Reg. 4828,
effective May 17, 1982; amended in R82-18, 51 PCB 831, at 7 Ill. Reg. 2518,
effective February 22, 1983; amended in R82-19, 53 PCB 131, at 7 Ill. Reg.
14034, effective October 12, 1983; amended in R84-9, at 9 Ill. Reg. 11869,
effective July 24, 1985; amended in R85-22 at 10 Ill. Reg. 1085, effective
January 2, 1986; amended in R86-1 at 10 Ill. Reg. 14069, effective August 12,
1986; amended in R86-28 at 11 Ill. Reg. 6044, effective March 24, 1987; amended
in R86-46 at 11 Ill. Reg. 13489, effective August 4, 1987; amended in R87-5 at
11 Ill. Reg. 19338, effective November 10, 1987; amended in R87-26 at 12 Ill.
Reg. 2485, effective January 15, 1988; amended in R87-39 at 12 Ill. Reg. 13027,
effective July 29, 1988; amended in R88-16 at 13 Ill. Reg. 437, effective
December 28, 1988; amended in R89-1 at 13 Ill. Reg. 18354, effective November
13, 1989; amended in R90-2 at 14 Ill. Reg. 14447, effective August 22, 1990;
amended in R90-10 at 14 Ill. Reg. 16498, effective September 25, 1990; amended
in R90-11 at 15 Ill. Reg. 9398, effective June 17, 1991; amended in R91-1 at 15
Ill. Reg. 14534, effective October 1, 1991; amended in R93-13 at 16 Ill. Reg.
9578, effective June 9, 1992; amended in R92-1 at 16 Ill. Reg. 17672, effective
November 6, 1992; amended in R92-10 at 17 Ill. Reg. 5681, effective March 26,
1993; amended in R93-4 at 17 Ill. Reg. 20620, effective November 22, 1993;
amended in R93-16 at 18 Ill. Reg. 6771, effective April 26, 1994; amended in
R94-7 at 18 Ill. Reg. 12190, effective July 29, 1994; amended in R94-17 at 18
Ill. Reg. 17548, effective November 23, 1994; amended in R95-6 at 19 Ill. Reg.
_____, effective _____.

SUBPART A: GENERAL PROVISIONS

Section 725.101 Purpose, Scope and Applicability

    a) The purpose of this Part is to establish minimum standards ~~which~~ that
        define the acceptable management of hazardous waste during the period
        of interim status and until certification of final closure or, if the
        facility is subject to post-closure requirements, until post-closure
        responsibilities are fulfilled.

POLLUTION CONTROL BOARD

NOTICE OF PROPOSED AMENDMENTS

    b) Except as provided in Section 725.980(b), the ~~The~~ standards in this
        Part and ~~of~~ 35 Ill. Adm. Code 724.652 and 724.653 apply to owners and
        operators of facilities ~~which~~ that treat, store, or dispose of
        hazardous waste ~~who~~ that have fully complied with the requirements for
        interim status under Section 3005(e) of the Resource Conservation and
        Recovery Act (RCRA) (42 U.S.C. 6901 et seq.) and 35 Ill. Adm. Code
        703, until either a permit is issued under Section 3005 of the
        Resource Conservation and Recovery Act or Section 21(f) of the
        Environmental Protection Act, or until applicable closure and
        post-closure responsibilities under this Part are fulfilled, and to
        those owners and operators of facilities in existence on November 19,
        1980, ~~who~~ that have failed to provide timely notification as required
        by Section 3010(a) of RCRA, or that have failed to file Part A of the
        Permit Application, as required by 40 CFR 270.10(e) and (g) or 35 Ill.
        Adm. Code 703.150 and 703.152. These standards apply to all
        treatment, storage, or disposal of hazardous waste after November 19,
        1980, except as specifically provided otherwise in
        this Part or 35 Ill. Adm. Code 721.
        BOARD NOTE: As stated in Section 3005(a) of RCRA, after the effective
        date of regulations under that Section, [i.e., 40 CFR 270 and 124],
        the treatment, storage, or disposal of hazardous waste is prohibited
        except in accordance with a permit. Section 3005(e) of RCRA provides
        for the continued operation of an existing facility ~~which~~ that meets
        certain conditions until final administrative disposition of the
        owner's and operator's permit application is made. 35 Ill. Adm. Code
        703.140 et seq. provide that a permit is deemed issued under Section
        21(f)(1) of the Environmental Protection Act under conditions similar
        to federal interim status.

    c) The requirements of this Part do not apply to:
        1) A person disposing of hazardous waste by means of ocean disposal
            subject to a permit issued under the Marine Protection, Research
            and Sanctuaries Act (16 U.S.C. 1431-1434; 33 U.S.C. 1401).
            BOARD NOTE: This Part applies to the treatment or storage of
            hazardous waste before it is loaded into an ocean vessel for
            incineration or disposal at sea, as provided in subsection (b).
        3) The owner or operator of a POTW (publicly owned treatment works)
            which that treats, stores or disposes of hazardous waste;
            BOARD NOTE: The owner or operator of a facility under
            subsections (c)(1) through (c)(3) is subject to the requirements
            of 35 Ill. Adm. Code 724 to the extent they are included in a
            permit by rule granted to such a person under 35 Ill. Adm. Code
            702 and 703 or are required by 35 Ill. Adm. Code 704.Subpart F.
        5) The owner or operator of a facility permitted, licensed, or
            registered by Illinois to manage municipal or industrial solid
            waste, if the only hazardous waste the facility treats, stores,
            or disposes of is excluded from regulation under this Part by 35
            Ill. Adm. Code 721.105;
        6) The owner or operator of a facility managing recyclable materials

POLLUTION CONTROL BOARD

NOTICE OF PROPOSED AMENDMENTS

described in 35 Ill. Adm. Code 721.106(a)(2), through (a)(4), +except to the extent that requirements of this Part are referred to in 35 Ill. Adm. Code 726.Subparts C, F, G, or H or 35 Ill. Adm. Code 739;

7) A generator accumulating waste on-site in compliance with 35 Ill. Adm. Code 722.134, except to the extent the requirements are included in 35 Ill. Adm. Code 722.134;

8) A farmer disposing of waste pesticides from the farmer's own use in compliance with 35 Ill. Adm. Code 722.170;

9) The owner or operator of a totally enclosed treatment facility, as defined in 35 Ill. Adm. Code 720.110;

10) The owner or operator of an elementary neutralization unit or a wastewater treatment unit as defined in 35 Ill. Adm. Code 720.110, provided that if the owner or operator is diluting hazardous ignitable (D001) wastes (other than the D001 High TOC Subcategory defined in 35 Ill. Adm. Code 728.Table B, or corrosive (D002) waste, in order to remove the characteristic before land disposal, the owner or operator must comply with the requirements set out in Section 725.117(b);

11) Immediate response:

A) Except as provided in subsection (c)(11)(B), below, a person engaged in treatment or containment activities during immediate response to any of the following situations:

i) A discharge of a hazardous waste;

ii) An imminent and substantial threat of a discharge of a hazardous waste;

iii) A discharge of a material which, when discharged, that becomes a hazardous waste when discharged.

B) An owner or operator of a facility otherwise regulated by this Part must comply with all applicable requirements of 725.Subparts C and D.

C) Any person who that is covered by subsection (c)(11)(A), above and who that continues or initiates hazardous waste treatment or containment activities after the immediate response is over is subject to all applicable requirements of this Part and 35 Ill. Adm. Code 702, 703, and 705 for those activities.

12) A transporter storing manifested shipments of hazardous waste in containers meeting the requirements of 35 Ill. Adm. Code 722.130 at a transfer facility for a period of ten days or less.

13) The addition of absorbent material to waste in a container (as defined in 35 Ill. Adm. Code 720.110), or the addition of waste to the absorbent material in a container, provided that these actions occur at the time that the waste is first placed in the container; and Sections 725.117(b), 725.271, and 725.272 are complied with.

d) The following hazardous wastes must not be managed at facilities subject to regulation under this Part: hazardous waste numbers F020,

POLLUTION CONTROL BOARD

NOTICE OF PROPOSED AMENDMENTS

F021, F022, F023, F026, or F027 unless:

1) The wastewater treatment sludge is generated in a surface impoundment as part of the plant's wastewater treatment system;

2) The waste is stored in tanks or containers;

3) The waste is stored or treated in waste piles that meet the requirements of 35 Ill. Adm. Code 724.350(c) as well as and all other applicable requirements of 725.Subpart L;

4) The waste is burned in incinerators that are certified pursuant to the standards and procedures in Section 725.452; or

5) The waste is burned in facilities that thermally treat the waste in a device other than an incinerator and that are certified pursuant to the standards and procedures in Section 725.483.

e) This Part applies to owners and operators of facilities which that treat, store, or dispose of hazardous wastes referred to in 35 Ill. Adm. Code 728, and the 35 Ill. Adm. Code 728 standards are considered material conditions or requirements of the interim status standards of this Part.

f) 35 Ill. Adm. Code 700 contains rules concerning application of other Board regulations, Other bodies of regulations may apply to a person, facility, or activity, such as 35 Ill. Adm. Code 809 (special waste hauling), 35 Ill. Adm. Code 807 or 810 through 817 (solid waste landfills), 35 Ill. Adm. Code 848 or 849 (used and scrap tires), or 35 Ill. Adm. Code 1420 through 1422 (potentially infectious medical waste), depending on the provisions of those other regulations.

(Source: Amended at 19 Ill. Reg. _____, effective _____)

SUBPART B: GENERAL FACILITY STANDARDS

Section 725.113 General Waste Analysis

a) Waste analysis:

1) Before an owner or operator treats, stores, or disposes of any hazardous waste, or non-hazardous waste if applicable under Section 725.213(d), the owner or operator shall obtain a detailed chemical and physical analysis of a representative sample of the waste. At a minimum, the analysis must contain all the information which that must be known to treat, store, or dispose of the waste in accordance with this Part and 35 Ill. Adm. Code 728.

2) The analysis may include data developed under 35 Ill. Adm. Code 721 and existing published or documented data on the hazardous waste or on waste generated from similar processes.

BOARD NOTE: For example, the facility's record of analyses performed on the waste before the effective date of these regulations or studies conducted on hazardous waste generated from processes similar to that which generated the waste to be

POLLUTION CONTROL BOARD

NOTICE OF PROPOSED AMENDMENTS

managed at the facility may be included in the data base required to comply with subsection (a)(1) above, except as otherwise specified in 35 Ill. Adm. Code 728.107(b) and (c). The owner or operator of an off-site facility may arrange for the generator of the hazardous waste to supply part or all of the information required by subsection (a)(1), above. If the generator does not supply the information and the owner or operator chooses to accept a hazardous waste, the owner or operator is responsible for obtaining the information required to comply with this Section.

3) The analysis must be repeated as necessary to ensure that it is accurate and up to date. At a minimum, the analysis must be repeated:

A) When the owner or operator is notified, or has reason to believe that the process or operation generating the hazardous waste, or non-hazardous waste if applicable under Section 725.213(d), has changed; and

B) For off-site facilities, when the results of the inspection required in subsection (a)(4), below indicate that the hazardous waste received at the facility does not match the waste designated on the accompanying manifest or shipping paper.

4) The owner or operator of an off-site facility shall inspect and, if necessary, analyze each hazardous waste movement received at the facility to determine whether it matches the identity of the waste specified on the accompanying manifest or shipping paper.

b) The owner or operator shall develop and follow a written waste analysis plan which that describes the procedures which that the owner or operator will carry out to comply with subsection (a), above. The owner or operator shall keep this plan at the facility. At a minimum, the plan must specify:

1) The parameters for which each hazardous waste, or non-hazardous waste if applicable under Section 725.213(d), will be analyzed and the rationale for the selection of these parameters (i.e., how analysis on the waste's properties will provide sufficient information on the waste's properties to comply with subsection (a), above.

2) The test methods which that will be used to test for these parameters.

3) The sampling method which that will be used to obtain a representative sample of the waste to be analyzed. A representative sample may be obtained using either:

A) One of the sampling methods described in 35 Ill. Adm. Code 721.Appendix A, or

B) An equivalent sampling method.

BOARD NOTE: See 35 Ill. Adm. Code 720.120(c) for related discussion.

4) The frequency with which the initial analysis of the waste will

POLLUTION CONTROL BOARD

NOTICE OF PROPOSED AMENDMENTS

be reviewed or repeated to ensure that the analysis is accurate and up-to-date.

5) For off-site facilities, the waste analysis that hazardous waste generators have agreed to supply.

6) Where applicable, the methods which that will be used to meet the additional waste analysis requirements for specific waste management methods, as specified in Sections 725.300, 725.325, 725.352, 725.373, 725.414, 725.441, 725.475, 725.502, 725.934(d), and 725.963(d), and 725.984, and 35 Ill. Adm. Code 728.107. And,

7) For surface impoundments exempted from land disposal restrictions under 35 Ill. Adm. Code 728.104(a), the procedures and schedules for:

A) The sampling of impoundment contents;

B) The analysis of test data; and,

C) The annual removal of residues which that are not delisted under 35 Ill. Adm. Code 720.122 or which that exhibit a characteristic of hazardous waste; and either:

i) Do not meet the applicable standards of 35 Ill. Adm. Code 728.Subpart D; or

ii) Where no treatment standards have been established; Such residues are prohibited from land disposal under 35 Ill. Adm. Code 728.132 or 728.139; or such residues are prohibited from land disposal under 35 Ill. Adm. Code 728.133.

8) For owners and operators seeking an exemption to the air emission standards of 724.Subpart CC of this Part in accordance with Section 725.983:

A) The procedures and schedules for waste sampling and analysis; and the analysis of test data to verify the exemption.

B) Each generator's notice and certification of the volatile organic concentration in the waste if the waste is received from offsite.

c) For off-site facilities, the waste analysis plan required in subsection (b), above must also specify the procedures which that will be used to inspect and, if necessary, analyze each movement of hazardous waste received at the facility to ensure that it matches the identity of the waste designated on the accompanying manifest or shipping paper. At a minimum, the plan must Describe:

1) The procedures which that will be used to determine the identity of each movement of waste managed at the facility; and

2) The sampling method which that will be used to obtain a representative sample of the waste to be identified, if the identification method includes sampling.

3) The procedures that the owner or operator of an off-site landfill receiving containerized hazardous waste will use to determine whether a hazardous waste generator or treater has added a biodegradable sorbent to the waste in the container.

POLLUTION CONTROL BOARD

NOTICE OF PROPOSED AMENDMENTS

(Source: Amended at 19 Ill. Reg. _____, effective
_____)

Section 725.114 Security

a) The owner or operator must prevent the unknowing entry and minimize
the possibility for the unauthorized entry of persons or livestock
onto the active portion of his facility, unless:
I) Physical contact with the waste, structures, or equipment of the
active portion of the facility will not injure unknowing or
unauthorized persons or livestock which that may enter the active
portion of a the facility; and
2) Disturbance of the waste or equipment by the unknowing or
unauthorized entry of persons or livestock onto the active
portion of a facility will not cause a violation of the
requirements of this part Part.
b) Unless exempt under paragraphs subsections (a)(1) and (a)(2) of--this
section above, a facility must have:
I) A 24-hour surveillance system (e.g., television monitoring or
surveillance by guards or facility personnel) which that
continuously monitors and controls entry into the active portion
of the facility; or
2)
2) Controlled access, including the following minimum elements:
A) An artificial or natural barrier (e.g., a fence in good
repair or a fence combined with a cliff)--which that
completely surrounds the active portion of the facility; and
B) A means to control entry at all times through the gates or
other entrances to the active portion of the facility (e.g.,
an attendant, television monitors, locked entrance, or
controlled roadway access to the facility).
BOARD NOTE: The requirements of paragraph subsection (b) of
this--section above are satisfied if the facility or plant
within which the active portion is located itself has a
surveillance system or a barrier and a means to control
entry which that complies with the requirements of paragraph
subsection (b)(1) or (b)(2) of-this-section.
c) Unless exempt under paragraphs subsection (a)(1) and Or (a)(2) of--this
section above, a sign with the legend, "Danger--Unauthorized Personnel
Keep Out," must be posted at each entrance to the active portion of a
facility and at other locations, in sufficient numbers to be seen from
any approach to this active portion. The sign must be legible from a
distance of at least 25 feet. Existing signs with a legend other than
"Danger--Unauthorized Personnel Keep Out" may be used if the legend on
the sign indicates that only authorized personnel are allowed to enter
the active portion and that entry onto the active portion can be
dangerous.
BOARD NOTE: See Section 725.217(b) for discussion of security

POLLUTION CONTROL BOARD

NOTICE OF PROPOSED AMENDMENTS

requirements at disposal facilities during the post-closure care
period.

(Source: Amended at 19 Ill. Reg. _____, effective
_____)

Section 725.115 General Inspection Requirements

a) The owner or operator shall inspect the facility for malfunctions and
deterioration, operator errors and discharges which that may be
causing -- or may lead to -- the conditions listed below. The owner
or operator shall conduct these inspections often enough to identify
problems in time to correct them before they harm human health or the
environment.
1) Release of hazardous waste constituents to the environment, or
2) A threat to human health.
b) Written schedule.
1) The owner or operator shall develop and follow a written schedule
for inspecting all monitoring equipment, safety and emergency
equipment, security devices, and operating and structural
equipment (such as dikes and sump pumps) that are important to
preventing, detecting, or responding to environmental or human
health hazards.
2) The owner or operator shall keep this schedule at the facility.
3) The schedule must identify the types of problems (e.g.,
malfunctions or deterioration) which that are to be looked for
during the inspection (e.g., inoperative sump pump, leaking
fitting, eroding dike, etc.).
4) The frequency of inspection may vary for the items on the
schedule. However, it should be based on the rate of
deterioration, of the equipment and the probability of an
environmental or human health incident if the deterioration,
malfunction, or any operator error goes undetected between
inspections. Areas subject to spills, such as loading and
unloading areas, must be inspected daily when in use. At a
minimum, the inspection schedule must include the items and
frequencies called for in Sections 725.274, 725.293, 725.295,
725.326, 725.360, 725.378, 725.404, 725.447, 725.477, 725.503,
725.933, 725.952, 725.953, and 725.958, 725.989, and 725.991(b),
where applicable.
c) The owner or operator shall remedy any deterioration or malfunction of
equipment or structure which that the inspection reveals on a schedule
which ensures that the problem does not lead to an environmental or
human health hazard. Where a hazard is imminent or has already
occurred, remedial action must be taken immediately.
d) The owner or operator shall record inspections in an inspection log or
summary. The owner or operator shall keep these records for at least
three years from the date of inspection. At a minimum, these records

POLLUTION CONTROL BOARD

NOTICE OF PROPOSED AMENDMENTS

must include the date and time of the inspection, the name of the inspector, a notation of the observations made and the date, and nature of any repairs or other remedial actions.

(Source: Amended at 19 Ill. Reg. _____, effective _____)

Section 725.117 General Requirements for Ignitable, Reactive, or Incompatible Wastes

a) The owner or operator must take precautions to prevent accidental ignition or reaction of ignitable or reactive waste. This waste must be separated and protected from sources of ignition or reaction, including, but not limited to,: open flames, smoking, cutting and welding, hot surfaces, frictional heat, sparks (static, electrical or mechanical), spontaneous ignition (e.g. from heat-producing chemical reactions), and radiant heat. While ignitable or reactive waste is being handled, the owner or operator must confine smoking and open flame to specially designated locations. "No Smoking" signs must be conspicuously placed wherever there is a hazard from ignitable or reactive waste.

b) Where specifically required by other ~~sections~~ Sections of this part Part, the treatment, storage, or disposal of ignitable or reactive waste and the mixture or commingling of incompatible waste or incompatible wastes and materials, must be conducted so that it does not:

1) Generate extreme heat or pressure, fire or explosion, or violent reaction;

2) Produce uncontrolled toxic mists, fumes, dusts, or gases in sufficient quantities to threaten human health;

3) Produce uncontrolled flammable fumes or gases in sufficient quantities to pose a risk of fire or explosions;

4) Damage the structural integrity of the device or facility containing the waste; or

5) Through other like means, threaten human health or the environment.

(Source: Amended at 19 Ill. Reg. _____, effective _____)

SUBPART D: CONTINGENCY PLAN AND EMERGENCY PROCEDURES

Section 725.150 Applicability

The regulations in this ~~subpart~~ Subpart apply to owners and operators of all hazardous waste facilities, except as Section 725.101 provides otherwise.

(Source: Amended at 19 Ill. Reg. _____, effective

POLLUTION CONTROL BOARD

NOTICE OF PROPOSED AMENDMENTS

_____)

Section 725.156 Emergency Procedures

a) Whenever there is an imminent or actual emergency situation, the emergency coordinator (or his designee when the emergency coordinator is on call) shall immediately:

1) Activate internal facility alarms or communication systems, where applicable, to notify all facility personnel; and

2) Notify appropriate state or local agencies with designated response roles if their help is needed.

b) Whenever there is a release, fire, or explosion, the emergency coordinator shall immediately identify the character, exact source, amount, and areal extent of any released materials. He or she may do this by observation or review of facility records or manifests and, if necessary, by chemical analysis.

c) Concurrently, the emergency coordinator shall assess possible hazards to human health or the environment that may result from the release, fire, or explosion. This assessment must consider both direct and indirect effects of the release, fire, or explosion (e.g., the effects of any toxic, irritating, or asphyxiating gases that are generated, or the effects of any hazardous surface water runoffs from water or chemical agents used to control fire and heat-induced explosions).

d) If the emergency coordinator determines that the facility has had a release, fire, or explosion that could threaten human health or the environment outside the facility, he or she shall report his findings as follows:

1) If his assessment indicates that evacuation of local areas may be advisable, he or she shall immediately notify appropriate local authorities. He or she must be available to help appropriate officials decide whether local areas should be evacuated; and

2) He or she shall immediately notify either the government official designated as the on-scene coordinator for that geographical area (in the applicable regional contingency plan under 40 CFR Part 300), or the National Response Center (using their 24-hour toll free number 800-424-8802). The report must include:

A) Name and telephone number of reporter;

B) Name and address of facility;

C) Time and type of incident (e.g., release, fire);

D) Name and quantity of ~~materials~~ materials involved, to the extent known;

E) The extent of injuries, if any; and

F) The possible hazards to human health or the environment outside the facility.

e) During an emergency the emergency coordinator shall take all reasonable measures necessary to ensure that fires, explosions, and releases do not occur, recur, or spread to other hazardous waste at the facility. These measures must include, where applicable, stopping

POLLUTION CONTROL BOARD

NOTICE OF PROPOSED AMENDMENTS

processes and operations, collecting and containing released waste, and removing or isolating containers.

f) If the facility stops operations in response to a fire, explosion or release, the emergency coordinator shall monitor for leaks, pressure buildup, gas generation or ruptures in valves, pipes, or other equipment, wherever this is appropriate.

g) Immediately after an emergency, the emergency coordinator shall provide for treating, storing, or disposing of recovered waste, contaminated soil, or surface water, or any other material that results from a release, fire, or explosion at the facility.
Comment BOARD NOTE: Unless the owner or operator can demonstrate: in accordance with Section 721.103(e̶d̶) or (d̶e̶) that the recovered material is not a hazardous waste, the owner or operator becomes a generator of hazardous waste and shall manage it in accordance with all applicable requirements of Parts 722, 723, and 725.

h) The emergency coordinator shall ensure that, in the affected area(s) of the facility:

1) No waste that may be incompatible with the released material is treated, stored, or disposed of until cleanup procedures are completed; and

2) All emergency equipment listed in the contingency plan is cleaned and fit for its intended use before operations are resumed.

i) The owner or operator shall notify the Director and other appropriate state and local authorities that the facility is in compliance with p̶a̶r̶a̶g̶r̶a̶p̶h̶ subsection (h) o̶f̶ ̶t̶h̶i̶s̶ ̶s̶e̶c̶t̶i̶o̶n̶ above before operations are resumed in the affected a̶r̶e̶a̶(̶s̶)̶ areas of the facility.

j) The owner or operator shall note in the operating record the time, date, and details of any incident that requires implementing the contingency plan. Within 15 days after the incident, it shall submit a written report on the incident to the Director. The report must include:

1) Name, address, and telephone number of the owner or operator;

2) Name, address, and telephone number of the facility;

3) Date, time, and type of incident (e.g., fire, explosion);

4) Name and quantity of m̶a̶t̶e̶r̶i̶a̶l̶(̶s̶)̶ materials involved;

5) The extent of injuries, if any;

6) An assessment of actual or potential hazards to human health or the environment, where this is applicable; and

7) Estimated quantity and disposition of recovered material that resulted from the incident.

(Source: Amended at 19 Ill. Reg. _____, effective _____)

SUBPART E: MANIFEST SYSTEM, RECORDKEEPING AND REPORTING

Section 725.171 Use of Manifest System

POLLUTION CONTROL BOARD

NOTICE OF PROPOSED AMENDMENTS

a) If a facility receives hazardous waste accompanied by a manifest, the owner or operator or his agent must:

1) Sign and date each copy of the manifest to certify that the hazardous waste covered by the manifest was received;

2) Note any significant discrepancies in the manifest, ǂ as defined in Section 725.172(a)ǂ, on each copy of the manifest:
Comment BOARD NOTE: T̶h̶e̶ ̶B̶o̶a̶r̶d̶ ̶d̶o̶e̶s̶ ̶n̶o̶t̶ ̶i̶n̶t̶e̶n̶d̶ ̶t̶h̶a̶t̶ ̶t̶h̶e̶ An owner or operator of a facility whose procedures under Section 725.113(c) include waste analysis m̶u̶s̶t̶ need not perform that analysis before signing the manifest and giving it to the transporter. Section 725.172(b), however, requires the owner or operator to r̶e̶p̶o̶r̶t̶i̶n̶g̶ report an̶ any unreconciled discrepancy discovered during later analysis.

3) Immediately give the transporter at least one copy of the signed manifest;

4) W̶i̶t̶h̶i̶n̶ ̶3̶0̶ ̶d̶a̶y̶s̶ ̶a̶f̶t̶e̶r̶ ̶t̶h̶e̶ ̶d̶e̶l̶i̶v̶e̶r̶y̶,̶ ̶s̶e̶n̶d̶ Send a copy of the manifest to e̶a̶c̶h̶ of the generator and t̶o̶ the Agency within 30 days of the date of delivery; and

5) Retain at the facility a copy of each manifest for at least three years from the date of delivery.

b) If a facility receives from a rail or water (bulk shipment) transporter hazardous waste w̶h̶i̶c̶h̶ that is accompanied by a shipping paper containing all the information required on the manifest (excluding the U.S. EPA identification numbers, generator's certification and signatures), the owner or operator or h̶i̶s̶ its agent must:

1) Sign and date each copy of the manifest or shipping paper (if the manifest has not been received) to certify that the hazardous waste covered by the manifest or shipping paper was received;

2) Note any significant discrepancies, ǂ as defined in Section 725.172(a)ǂ, in the manifest or shipping paper (if the manifest has not been received) on each copy of the manifest or shipping paper;
Comment BOARD NOTE: T̶h̶e̶ ̶B̶o̶a̶r̶d̶ ̶d̶o̶e̶s̶ ̶n̶o̶t̶ ̶i̶n̶t̶e̶n̶d̶ ̶t̶h̶a̶t̶ ̶t̶h̶e̶ An owner or operator of a facility whose procedures under Section 725.113(c) include waste analysis m̶u̶s̶t̶ need not perform that analysis before signing the shipping paper and giving it to the transporter. Section 725.172(b), however, requires reporting an unreconciled discrepancy discovered during later analysis.

3) Immediately give the rail or water (bulk shipment) transporter at least one copy of the manifest or shipping paper (if the manifest has not been received);

4) W̶i̶t̶h̶i̶n̶ ̶3̶0̶ ̶d̶a̶y̶s̶ ̶a̶f̶t̶e̶r̶ ̶d̶e̶l̶i̶v̶e̶r̶y̶,̶ ̶s̶e̶n̶d̶ Send a copy of the signed and dated manifest to the generator and to the Agency within 30 days after the delivery; however, if the manifest has not been received within 30 days after delivery, the owner or operator, or his agent, must send a copy of the shipping paper signed and dated to the generator; and

POLLUTION CONTROL BOARD

NOTICE OF PROPOSED AMENDMENTS

~~Comment~~BOARD NOTE: ~~Section~~ 35 Ill. Adm. Code 722.123(c) requires the generator to send three copies of the manifest to the facility when hazardous waste is sent by rail or water (bulk shipment).

5) Retain at the facility a copy of the manifest and shipping paper (if signed in lieu of the manifest at the time of delivery) for at least three years from the date of delivery.

c) Whenever a shipment of hazardous waste is initiated from a facility, the owner or operator of that facility must comply with the requirements of ~~Part~~ 35 Ill. Adm. Code 722.

~~Comment~~BOARD NOTE: The provisions of ~~Section~~ 35 Ill. Adm. Code 722.134 are applicable to the on-site accumulation of hazardous wastes by generators. Therefore, the provisions of ~~Section~~ 35 Ill. Adm. Code 722.134 ~~only~~ apply only to owners or operators ~~who~~ that are shipping hazardous waste ~~which~~ that they generated at that facility.

(Source: Amended at 19 Ill. Reg. _____, effective _____)

Section 725.173 Operating Record

a) The owner or operator shall keep a written operating record at the facility.

b) The following information must be recorded as it becomes available and maintained in the operating record until closure of the facility.

1) A description and the quantity of each hazardous waste received and the method or methods and date or dates of its treatment, storage, or disposal at the facility as required by Section 725.Appendix A;

2) The location of each hazardous waste within the facility and the quantity at each location. For disposal facilities the location and quantity of each hazardous waste must be recorded on a map or diagram of each cell or disposal area. For all facilities this information must include cross-references to specific manifest document numbers if the waste was accompanied by a manifest;
BOARD NOTE: See Sections 725.219, 725.379, and 725.409 for related requirements.

3) Records and results of waste analysis, waste determinations, and trial tests performed as specified in Sections 725.113, 725.300, 725.325, 725.352, 725.373, 725.414, 725.441, 725.475, 725.502, 725.934, ~~and~~ 725.963, and 725.984 and 35 Ill. Adm. Code 728.104(a) and 728.107;

4) Summary reports and details of all incidents that require implementing the contingency plan as specified in Section 725.156(j);

5) Records and results of inspections as required by Sections 725.15(d) (except these data need be kept only three years);

6) Monitoring, testing or analytical data ~~and corrective action data~~

POLLUTION CONTROL BOARD

NOTICE OF PROPOSED AMENDMENTS

where required by 725.Subpart F or Sections 725.119, 725.190, 725.194, 725.291, 725.293, 725.295, 725.322, 725.323, 725.326, 725.395, 725.359, 725.360, 725.376, 725.378, 725.380(d)(1), 725.402 through 725.404, 725.447, 725.477, 725.934(c) through (f), 725.935, 725.963(d) through (i), or 725.964, 725.989 through 725.991;
BOARD NOTE: As required by Section 725.194, monitoring data at disposal facilities must be kept throughout the post-closure period.

7) All closure cost estimates under Section 725.242 and, for disposal facilities, all post-closure cost estimates under Section 725.244;

8) Records of the quantities (and date of placement) for each shipment of hazardous waste placed in land disposal units under restriction pursuant to 35 Ill. Adm. Code 728.105, a petition pursuant to 35 Ill. Adm. Code 728.106, or a certification under 35 Ill. Adm. 728.108, and the applicable notice required of a generator under 35 Ill. Adm. Code 728.107(a):

9) For an off-site treatment facility, a copy of the notice, and the certification and demonstration, if applicable, required of the generator or the owner or operator under 35 Ill. Adm. Code 728.107 or 728.108;

10) For an on-site treatment facility, the information contained in the notice (except the manifest number) and the certification and demonstration, if applicable, required of the generator or the owner or operator under 35 Ill. Adm. Code 728.107 or 728.108;

11) For an off-site land disposal facility, a copy of the notice r and the certification and demonstration, if applicable, required of the generator or the owner or operator of a treatment facility under 35 Ill. Adm. Code 728.107 or 728.108~~--whichever is applicable~~;

12) For an on-site land disposal facility, the information contained in the notice required of the generator or owner or operator of a treatment facility under 35 Ill. Adm. Code 728.107, except for the manifest number, and the certification and demonstration, if applicable, required under 35 Ill. Adm. Code 728.107 or 728.108~~--whichever is applicable~~;

13) For an off-site storage facility, a copy of the notice, and the certification and demonstration, if applicable, required of the generator or the owner or operator under 35 Ill. Adm. Code 728.107 or 728.108; and

14) For an on-site storage facility, the information contained in the notice (except the manifest number), and the certification and demonstration if applicable, required of the generator or the owner or operator under 35 Ill. Adm. Code 728.107 or 728.108.

POLLUTION CONTROL BOARD

NOTICE OF PROPOSED AMENDMENTS

(Source: Amended at 19 Ill. Reg. _____, effective _____)

Section 725.177' Additional Reports

In addition to submitting the annual report and unmanifested waste reports described in Sections 725.175 and 725.176, the owner or operator shall also report to the Agency:

a) Releases, fires, and explosions, as specified in Section 725.156(j);
b) Groundwater contamination and monitoring data, as specified in Section 725.193 and 725.194;
c) Facility closure, as specified in Section 725.215; and
d) As otherwise required by 725 Subparts AA, and BB, and CC.

(Source: Amended at 19 Ill. Reg. _____, effective _____)

SUBPART F: GROUNDWATER MONITORING

Section 725.192 Sampling and Analysis

a) The owner or operator must shall obtain and analyze samples from the installed groundwater monitoring system. The owner or operator must shall develop and follow a groundwater sampling and analysis plan. HeThe owner or operator must shall keep this plan at the facility. The plan must include procedures and techniques for:
1) Sample collection;
2) Sample preservation and shipment;
3) Analytical procedures; and
4) Chain of custody control.
CommentBOARD NOTE: See "Procedures Manual For Groundwater Monitoring At Solid Waste Disposal Facilities" EPA-530/SW-611, August 1977 and "Methods for Chemical Analysis of Water and Wastes", EPA-600/4-79--020, March 1979 incorporated by reference in 35 Ill. Adm. Code 720.111, for discussions of sampling and analysis procedures.

b) The owner or operator must shall determine the concentration or value of the following parameters in groundwater samples in accordance with paragraph subsections (c) and (d) of this section below:
1) Parameters characterizing the suitability of the groundwater as a drinking water supply, as specified in Section 725.Appendix IIIC.
2) Parameters establishing groundwater quality:
A) Chloride,
B) Iron,
C) Manganese,
D) Phenols,
E) Sodium, and
F) Sulfate,

POLLUTION CONTROL BOARD

NOTICE OF PROPOSED AMENDMENTS

CommentBOARD NOTE: These parameters are to be used as a basis for comparison in the event a groundwater quality assessment is required under Section 725.193(d).
3) Parameters used as indicators of groundwater contamination:
A) pH,
B) Specific Conductance,
C) Total Organic Carbon, and
D) Total Organic Halogen,

c) Establishing background concentrations:
1) For all monitoring wells, the owner or operator must shall establish initial background concentrations or values of all parameters specified in paragraph subsection (b) of this section above. HeThe owner or operator must shall do this quarterly for one year.
2) For each of the indicator parameters specified in paragraph subsection (b)(3) above, the owner or operator shall obtain at least four replicate measurements must be obtained for each sample and determine the initial background arithmetic mean and variance must be determined by pooling the replicate measurements for the respective parameter concentrations or values in samples obtained from upgradient wells during the first year.

d) After the first year, the owner or operator shall sample all monitoring wells must be sampled and analyze the samples analyzed with the following frequencies:
1) Samples collected to establish groundwater quality must be obtained and analyzed for the parameters specified in paragraph subsection (b)(2) of this section above at least annually.
2) Samples collected to indicate groundwater contamination must be obtained and analyzed for the parameters specified in paragraph subsection (b)(3) of this section above at least semi-annually.

e) The owner or operator shall determine the elevation Elevation of the groundwater surface at each monitoring well must be determined each time a sample is obtained.

(Source: Amended at 19 Ill. Reg. _____, effective _____)

Section 725.194 Recordkeeping and Reporting

a) Unless the groundwater is monitored to satisfy the requirements of Section 725.193(d)(4), the owner or operator must shall:
1) Keep records of the analyses required in Section 725.192(c) and (d), the associated groundwater surface elevations required in Section 725.192(e), and the evaluations required in Section 725.193(b) throughout the active life of the facility and, for disposal facilities, also throughout the post-closure care period as well; and
2) Report the following groundwater monitoring information to the

POLLUTION CONTROL BOARD

NOTICE OF PROPOSED AMENDMENTS

~~Director~~ Agency:

A) During the first year when initial background concentrations are being established for the facility: concentrations or values of the parameters listed in Section 725.192(b)(1) for each groundwater monitoring well, within 15 days after completing each quarterly analysis. The owner or operator ~~must~~ shall separately identify for each monitoring well any parameters whose concentration or value has been found to exceed the maximum contaminant levels listed in Section 725.Appendix ~~III~~C.

B) Annually: concentrations or values of the parameters listed in Section 725.192(b)(3) for each groundwater monitoring well. along with the required evaluations for these parameters under Section 725.193(b). The owner or operator ~~must~~ shall separately identify any significant differences from initial background found in the upgradient wells. in accordance with Section 725.193(c)(1). During the active life of the facility, the owner or operator shall submit this information ~~must be submitted~~ as part of the annual report required under Section 725.175.

C) As part of the annual report required under Section 725.175: results of the evaluation of groundwater surface elevations under Section 725.193(f) and a description of the response to the evaluation. where applicable.

b) If the groundwater is monitored to satisfy the requirements of Section 725.193(d)(4), the owner or operator must shall:

1) ~~Keep~~ records of the analyses and evaluations specified in the plan~~which~~ that ~~satisfies~~ satisfy the requirements of Section 725.193(d)(3) throughout the active life of the facility and, for disposal facilities, ~~also~~ throughout the post-closure care period ~~as well~~; and

2) Annually. until final closure of the facility, submit to the ~~Director~~ Agency a report containing the results of ~~his~~ the groundwater quality assessment program ~~which~~ that includes, but is not limited to, the calculated (or measured) rate of migration of hazardous waste or hazardous waste constituents in the groundwater during the reporting period. The owner or operator shall submit this ~~This~~ report ~~must be submitted~~ as part of the annual report required under Section 725.175.

(Source: Amended at 19 Ill. Reg. _____, effective _____.)

SUBPART I: USE AND MANAGEMENT OF CONTAINERS

Section 725.271 Condition of Containers

If a container holding hazardous waste is not in good condition or if it begins

POLLUTION CONTROL BOARD

NOTICE OF PROPOSED AMENDMENTS

to leak. the owner or operator ~~must~~ shall transfer the hazardous waste from this container to a container that is in good condition or manage the waste in some other way that it complies with the requirements of this Part.

(Source: Amended at 19 Ill. Reg. _____, effective _____.)

Section 725.272 Compatibility of Waste with Container

The owner or operator ~~must~~ shall use a container made of or lined with materials ~~which~~ that will not react with and are otherwise compatible with the hazardous waste to be stored, so that the ability of the container to contain the waste is not impaired.

(Source: Amended at 19 Ill. Reg. _____, effective _____.)

Section 725.274 Inspections

The owner or operator ~~must~~ shall inspect areas where containers are stored at least weekly, looking for leaks and for deterioration caused by corrosion or other factors.

~~Comment:~~BOARD NOTE: See Section 725.271 for remedial action required if deterioration or leaks are detected.

(Source: Amended at 19 Ill. Reg. _____, effective _____.)

Section 725.278 Air Emission Standards

The owner or operator shall manage all hazardous waste placed in a container in accordance with the requirements of 724.Subpart CC.

(Source: Added at 19 Ill. Reg. _____, effective _____.)

SUBPART J: TANK SYSTEMS

Section 725.301 Generators of 100 to 1000 kg/mo*

a) The requirements of this Section apply to small quantity generators of that generate more than 100 kg but less than 1000 kg of hazardous waste in a calendar month, that accumulate hazardous waste in tanks for less than 180 days (or 270 days if the generator must ship the waste greater than 200 miles), and that do not accumulate over 6,000 kg on-site at any time.

b) A generator Generators of between 100 and 1000 kg/mo hazardous waste shall comply with the following general operating requirements:

POLLUTION CONTROL BOARD

NOTICE OF PROPOSED AMENDMENTS

1) Treatment or storage of hazardous waste in tanks must comply with Section 725.117(b)~;

2) Hazardous wastes or treatment reagents must not be placed in a tank if they could cause the tank or its inner liner to rupture, leak, corrode, or otherwise fail before the end of its intended life~;

3) Uncovered tanks must be operated to ensure at least 60 centimeters (2 feet) of freeboard; unless the tank is equipped with a containment structure (e.g. dike or trench), a drainage control system, or a diversion structure (e.g., standby tank) with a capacity that equals or exceeds the volume of the top 60 centimeters (2 feet) of the tank~; and

4) Where hazardous waste is continuously fed into a tank, the tank must be equipped with a means to stop this inflow (e.g., waste feed cutoff system or by-pass system to a stand-by tank).

BOARD NOTE: These systems are intended to be used in the event of a leak or overflow from the tank due to a system failure (e.g., a malfunction in the treatment process, a crack in the tank, etc.).

c) A generator Generators of between 100 and 1000 kg/mo accumulating hazardous waste in tanks shall inspect, where present:

1) Discharge control equipment (e.g., waste feed cutoff systems, by-pass systems, and drainage systems) at least once each operating day, to ensure that it is in good working order;

2) Data gathered from monitoring equipment (e.g., pressure and temperature gauges) at least once each operating day to ensure that the tank is being operated according to its design;

3) The level of waste in the tank at least once each operating day to ensure compliance with subsection (b)(3) above;

4) The construction materials of the tank at least weekly to detect corrosion or leaking of fixtures or seams; and

5) The construction materials of, and the area immediately surrounding, discharge confinement structures (e.g., dikes) at least weekly to detect erosion or obvious signs of leakage (e.g., wet spots or dead vegetation).

BOARD NOTE: As required by Section 725.115(c), the owner or operator must remedy any deterioration or malfunction the owner or operator finds.

d) A generator Generators of between 100 and 1000 kg/mo accumulating hazardous waste in tanks shall, upon closure of the facility, remove all hazardous waste from tanks, discharge control equipment and discharge confinement structures.

BOARD NOTE: At closure, as throughout the operating period, unless the owner or operator demonstrates, in accordance with 35 Ill. Adm. Code 721.103(eg) or (df), that any solid waste removed from the tank is not a hazardous waste, the owner or operator becomes a generator of hazardous waste and must manage it in accordance with all applicable requirements of 35 Ill. Adm. Code 722, 723, and 725.

POLLUTION CONTROL BOARD

NOTICE OF PROPOSED AMENDMENTS

e) A generator Generators of between 100 and 1000 kg/mo shall comply with the following special requirements for ignitable or reactive waste:

1) Ignitable or reactive waste must not be placed in a tank, unless:

A) The waste is treated, rendered, or mixed before or immediately after placement in a tank so that:

i) The resulting waste, mixture, or dissolution of material no longer meets the definition of ignitable or reactive waste under 35 Ill. Adm. Code 721.121 or 721.123, and

ii) Section 725.117(b) is complied with; or

B) The waste is stored or treated in such a way that it is protected from any material or conditions that may cause the waste to ignite or react; or

C) The tank is used solely for emergencies.

2) The owner or operator of a facility which that treats or stores ignitable or reactive waste in covered tanks shall comply with the buffer zone requirements for tanks contained in Tables 2-1 through 2-6 of the National Fire Protection Association's "Flammable and Combustible Liquids Code," incorporated by reference in 35 Ill. Adm. Code 720.111.

f) A generator Generators of between 100 and 1000 kg/mo shall comply with the following special requirements for incompatible wastes:

1) Incompatible wastes, or incompatible wastes and materials (see Appendix E for examples) must not be placed in the same tank, unless Section 725.117(b) is complied with.

2) Hazardous waste must not be place placed in an unwashed tank which that previously held an incompatible waste or material, unless Section 725.117(b) is complied with.

(Source: Amended at   19   Ill.   Reg. _____,   effective _____)

Section 725.302 Air Emission Standards

The owner or operator shall manage all hazardous waste placed in a tank in accordance with the requirements of 724.Subparts AA, BB, and CC.

(Source: Added at   19   Ill.   Reg. _____,   effective _____)

SUBPART K: SURFACE IMPOUNDMENTS

Section 725.325 Waste Analysis and Trial Tests

In addition to the waste analyses required by Section 725.113, whenever a surface impoundment is to be used to:

a) Chemically treat a hazardous waste which that is substantially different from waste previously treated in that impoundment; or

b) Chemically treat hazardous waste with a substantially different process than and previously used in that impoundment, the owner or operator must, before treating the different waste or using the different process:

   1) Conduct waste analyses and trial treatment tests (e.g., bench scale or pilot plant scale tests); or

   2) Obtain written, documented information on similar treatment of similar waste under similar operating conditions, to show that this treatment will comply with Section 725.117(b).

   ~~Comment~~BOARD NOTE: As required by Section 725.113, the waste analyses plan must include analyses needed to comply with Sections 725.329 and 725.330. As required by Section 725.173, the owner or operator ~~must~~shall place the results from each waste analysis and trial test, or the documented information in the operating record of the facility.

(Source: Amended at 19 Ill. Reg. _____, effective _____)

Section 725.331 Air Emission Standards

The owner or operator shall manage all hazardous waste placed in a surface impoundment in accordance with the requirements of 724.Subpart CC.

(Source: Added at 19 Ill. Reg. _____, effective _____)

SUBPART L: WASTE FILES

Section 725.352 Waste Analysis

a) In addition to the waste analyses required by Section 725.113, the owner or operator ~~must~~shall analyze a representative sample of waste from each incoming movement before adding the waste to any existing pile unless:

   1) The only wastes the facility receives ~~which~~ that are amenable to piling are compatible with each other, or

   2) The waste received is compatible with the waste in the pile to which it is to be added.

b) The analysis conducted must be capable of differentiating between the types of hazardous waste the owner or operator places in piles, so that mixing of incompatible waste does not inadvertently occur. The analysis must include a visual comparison of color and texture. ~~Comment~~BOARD NOTE: As required by Section 725.113, the waste analysis plan must include analyses needed to comply with Sections 725.356 and 725.357. As required by Section 725.173, the owner or operator must place the results of this analysis in the operating record of the facility.

(Source: Amended at 19 Ill. Reg. _____, effective _____)

SUBPART M: LAND TREATMENT

Section 725.378 Unsaturated Zone (Zone of Aeration) Monitoring

a) The owner or operator ~~must~~ shall have in writing and ~~must~~ shall implement, an unsaturated zone monitoring plan which ~~that~~ is designed to:

   1) Detect the vertical migration of hazardous waste and hazardous waste constituents under the active portion of the land treatment facility, and

   2) Provide information on the background concentrations of the hazardous waste and hazardous waste constituents in similar but untreated soil nearby, ~~this~~ This background monitoring must be conducted before or in conjunction with the monitoring required under ~~paragraph~~ subsection (a)(1) ~~of this section~~ above.

b) The unsaturated zone monitoring plan must include, at a minimum:

   1) Soil monitoring using soil cores, and

   2) Soil-pore water monitoring using devices, such as lysimeters.

c) To comply with ~~paragraph~~ subsection (a)(1) ~~of this section~~ above, the owner or operator must demonstrate in his unsaturated zone monitoring plan that:

   1) The depth at which soil and soil-pore water samples are to be taken is below the depth to which the waste is incorporated into the soil;

   2) The number of soil and soil-pore water samples to be taken is based on the variability of:

      A) The hazardous waste constituents (as identified in Section 725.373(a) and(b)) in the waste and in the soil, and

      B) The soil type; and

   3) The frequency and timing of soil and soil-pore water sampling is based on the frequency, time, and rate of waste application, proximity to ground water, and soil permeability.

d) The owner or operator ~~must~~shall keep at the facility ~~his~~its unsaturated zone monitoring plan and the rationale used in developing this plan.

e) The owner or operator ~~must~~ shall analyze the soil and soil-pore water samples for the hazardous waste constituents that were found in the waste during the waste analysis under Section 725.373(a) and (b). ~~Comment~~BOARD NOTE: As required by Section 725.173, the owner or operator must place all data and information developed ~~by the owner or operator~~ under this ~~section~~ Section ~~must be placed~~ in the operating record of the facility.

(Source: Amended at 19 Ill. Reg. _____, effective _____)

POLLUTION CONTROL BOARD

NOTICE OF PROPOSED AMENDMENTS

SUBPART P: THERMAL TREATMENT

Section 725.477 Monitoring and Inspections

The owner or operator ~~must~~ shall conduct, as a minimum, the following monitoring and inspections when thermally treating hazardous waste:

a) Existing instruments ~~which~~ that relate to temperature and emission control (if an emission control device is present) must be monitored at least every 15 minutes. Appropriate corrections to maintain steady state or other appropriate thermal treatment conditions must be made immediately either automatically or by the operator. Instruments ~~which~~ that relate to temperature and emission control would normally include those measuring waste feed, auxiliary fuel feed, treatment process temperature and relevant process flow and level controls.

b) The stack plume (emissions), where present, must be observed visually at least hourly for normal appearance (color and opacity). The operator must immediately make any indicated operating corrections necessary to return any visible emissions to their normal appearance.

c) The complete thermal treatment process and associated equipment (pumps, valves, conveyors, pipes, etc.) must be inspected at least daily for leaks, spills and fugitive emissions, and all emergency shutdown controls and system alarms must be checked to assure proper operation.

(Source: Amended at 19 Ill. Reg. _____, effective _____)

SUBPART Q: CHEMICAL, PHYSICAL AND BIOLOGICAL TREATMENT

Section 725.501 General Operating Requirements

a) Chemical, physical or biological treatment of hazardous waste must comply with Section 725.117(b).

b) Hazardous waste or treatment reagents must not be placed in the treatment process or equipment if they could cause the treatment process or equipment to rupture, leak, corrode, or otherwise fail before the end of its intended life.

c) Where hazardous waste is continuously fed into a treatment process or equipment, the process or equipment must be equipped with a means to stop this inflow (e.g., a waste feed cutoff system or bypass system to a standby containment device).
    ~~Comment:~~BOARD NOTE: These systems are intended to be used in the event of a malfunction in the treatment process or equipment.

(Source: Amended at 19 Ill. Reg. _____, effective _____)

Section 725.502 Waste Analysis and Trial Tests

POLLUTION CONTROL BOARD

NOTICE OF PROPOSED AMENDMENTS

a) In addition to the waste analysis required by Section 725.113, ~~paragraph~~ subsection (b) above applies whenever:

1) A hazardous waste ~~which~~ that is substantially different from waste previously treated in a treatment process or equipment at the facility is to be treated in that process or equipment, or

2) A substantially different process from any previously used at the facility is to be used to chemically treat hazardous waste.

b) To show that this proposed treatment will meet all applicable requirements of Section 725.501(a) and (b), the owner or operator must, before treating the different waste or using the different process or equipment:

1) Conduct waste analyses and trial treatment tests (e.g., bench scale or pilot plant scale tests), or

2) Obtain written, documented information on similar treatment of similar waste under similar operating conditions.
    ~~Comment:~~BOARD NOTE: As required by Section 725.113, the waste analysis plan must include analyses needed to comply with Sections 725.505 and 725.506. As required by Section 725.173, the owner or operator must shall place the results from each waste analysis and trial test, or the documented information, in the operating record of the facility.

(Source: Amended at 19 Ill. Reg. _____, effective _____)

Section 725.503 Inspections

The owner operator of a treatment facility must shall inspect, where present:

a) Discharge control and safety equipment (e.g., waste feed cutoff systems, bypass systems, drainage systems and pressure relief systems) at least once each operating day to ensure that it is in good working order;

b) Data gathered from monitoring equipment (e.g., pressure and temperature gauges) at least once each operating day to ensure that the treatment process or equipment is being operated according to its design;

c) The construction materials of the treatment process or equipment at least weekly to detect corrosion or leaking of fixtures or seams; and

d) The construction materials of, and the area immediately surrounding, discharge confinement structures (e.g., dikes) at least weekly to detect erosion or obvious signs of leakage (e.g., wet spots or dead vegetation).
    ~~Comment:~~BOARD NOTE: As required by Section 725.115(c), the owner or operator must remedy any deterioration or malfunction ~~he~~ it finds.

(Source: Amended at 19 Ill. Reg. _____, effective _____)

POLLUTION CONTROL BOARD

NOTICE OF PROPOSED AMENDMENTS

Section 725.504 Closure

At closure, all hazardous waste and hazardous waste residues must be removed from treatment processes or equipment, discharge control equipment, and discharge confinement structures.
~~Comment~~BOARD NOTE: At closure, as throughout the operating period, unless the owner or operator can demonstrate, in accordance with ~~Section~~ 35 Ill. Adm. Code 721.103 (c) or (d), that any solid waste removed from his treatment process or equipment is not a hazardous waste, the owner or operator becomes a generator of hazardous waste and must manage it in accordance with all applicable requirements of ~~Parts~~ 35 Ill. Adm. Code 722, 723, and 725.

(Source: Amended at 19 Ill. Reg. _____, effective
_____)

Section 725.505 Special Requirements for Ignitable or Reactive Waste

Ignitable or reactive waste must not be placed in a treatment process or equipment unless:
  a) The waste is treated, rendered or mixed before or immediately after placement in the treatment process or equipment so that
    1) The resulting waste, mixture or dissolution of material no longer meets the definition of ignitable or reactive waste under Section 721.121 or 721.123, and
    2) Section 725.117(b) is complied with; or
  b) The waste is treated in such a way that it is protected from any material or conditions ~~which~~ that may cause the waste to ignite or react.

(Source: Amended at 19 Ill. Reg. _____, effective
_____)

Section 725.506 Special Requirements for Incompatible Wastes

  a) An owner or operator shall not place incompatible ~~Incompatible~~ wastes or incompatible wastes and materials (see Section 725.Appendix V5 for examples) ~~must not be placed~~ in the same treatment process or equipment unless it complies with Section 725.117(b) ~~is complied with~~.
  b) An owner, operator shall not place hazardous ~~Hazardous~~ waste ~~must not be placed~~ in unwashed treatment equipment ~~which~~ that previously held an incompatible waste or material, unless it complies with Section 725.117(b) ~~is complied with~~.

(Source: Amended at 19 Ill. Reg. _____, effective
_____)

SUBPART AA: AIR EMISSION STANDARDS FOR PROCESS VENTS

POLLUTION CONTROL BOARD

NOTICE OF PROPOSED AMENDMENTS

Section 725.933 Standards: Closed-vent Systems and Control Devices

  a) Compliance Required.
    1) Owners or operators of closed-vent systems and control devices used to comply with provisions of this Part shall comply with the provisions of this Section.
    2) The owner or operator of an existing facility ~~who~~ that cannot install a closed-vent system and control device to comply with the provisions of this Subpart on the effective date that the facility becomes subject to the provisions of this Subpart shall prepare an implementation schedule that includes dates by which the closed-vent system and control device will be installed and in operation. The controls must be installed as soon as possible, but the implementation schedule may allow up to 18 months after the effective date that the facility becomes subject to this Subpart for installation and startup. All units that begin operation after December 21, 1990, must comply with the rules immediately (i.e., must have control devices installed and operating on startup of the affected unit); the 2-year implementation schedule does not apply to these units.
  b) A control device involving vapor recovery (e.g., a condenser or adsorber) must be designed and operated to recover the organic vapors vented to it with an efficiency of 95 weight percent or greater unless the total organic emission limits of Section 725.932(a)(1) for all affected process vents is attained at an efficiency less than 95 weight percent.
  c) An enclosed combustion device (e.g., a vapor incinerator, boiler, or process heater) must be designed and operated to reduce the organic emissions vented to it by 95 weight percent or greater; to achieve a total organic compound concentration of 20 ppmv, expressed as the sum of the actual compounds, not carbon equivalents, on a dry basis corrected to 3 percent oxygen; or to provide a minimum residence time of 0.50 seconds at a minimum temperature of 760° C. If a boiler or process heater is used as the control device, then the vent stream must be introduced into the flame combustion zone of the boiler or process heater.
  d) Flares
    1) A flare must be designed for and operated with no visible emissions as determined by the methods specified in subsection (e)(1) below except for periods not to exceed a total of 5 minutes during any 2 consecutive hours.
    2) A flare must be operated with a flame present at all times, as determined by the methods specified in subsection below.
    3) A flare must be used only if the net heating value of the gas being combusted is 11.2 MJ/scm (300 Btu/scf) or greater if the flare is steam-assisted or air-assisted, or if the net heating value of the gas being combusted is 7.45 MJ/scm (200Btu/scf) or

POLLUTION CONTROL BOARD

NOTICE OF PROPOSED AMENDMENTS

greater if the flare is nonassisted. The net heating value of the gas being combusted must be determined by the methods specified in subsection (e)(2) below.

4) Exit Velocity.

A) A steam-assisted or nonassisted flare must be designed for an operated with an exit velocity, as determined by the methods specified in subsection (e)(3) below, less than 18.3 m/s (60 ft/s), except as provided in subsections (d)(4)(B) and (d)(4)(C) below.

B) A steam-assisted or nonassisted flare designed for and operated with an exit velocity, as determined by the methods specified in subsection (e)(3) below, equal to or greater than 18.3 m/s (60 ft/s) but less than 122 m/s (400 ft/s) is allowed if the net heating value of the gas being combusted is greater than 37.3 MJ/scm (1000 Btu/scf).

C) A steam-assisted or nonassisted flare designed for and operated with an exit velocity, as determined by the methods specified in subsection (e)(3) below, less than the velocity, V as determined by the method specified in subsection (e)(4) and less than 122 m/s (400 ft/s) is allowed.

5) An air-assisted flare must be designed and operated with an exit velocity less than the velocity, V as determined by the method specified in subsection (e)(5) below.

6) A flare used to comply with this Section must be steam-assisted, air-assisted, or nonassisted.

e)

1) Reference Method 22 in 40 CFR 60, incorporated by reference in 35 Ill. Adm. Code 720.111, must be used to determine the compliance of a flare with the visible emission provisions of this Subpart. The observation period is 2 hours and must be used according to Method 22.

2) The net heating value of the gas being combusted in a flare must be calculated using the following equation:

$$H[T] = K' \times \text{SUM} \ (C[i] \times H[i])$$
$$i=1 \ \text{to} \ n$$

H = K' × SUM(Ci × Hi)

Where:

H[T] is the net heating value of the sample in MJ/scm; where the net enthalpy per mole of offgas is based on combustion at 25° C and 760 mm Hg, but the standard temperature for determining the volume corresponding to 1 mole is 20° C.

POLLUTION CONTROL BOARD

NOTICE OF PROPOSED AMENDMENTS

K = 1.74 x 10(-7) 8--7 (1/ppm) (g mol/scm) (MJ/kcal) where standard temperature for a (g mol/scm) 20° C.

SUM (Xi) SUM (X[i]) means the sum of the values of X for each component i, from i=1 to n.

C[i] is the concentration of sample component i in ppm on a wet basis, as measured for organics by Reference Method 18 in 40 CFR 60, and for carbon monoxide, by ASTM D 1946-90, incorporated by reference in 35 Ill. Adm. Code 720.111.

H[i] is the net heat of combustion of sample component i, kcal/gmol at 25° C and 760 mm Hg. The heats of combustion must be determined using ASTM D 2382-88, incorporated by reference in 35 Ill. Adm. Code 720.111, if published values are not available or cannot be calculated.

3) The actual exit velocity of a flare must be determined by dividing the volumetric flow rate (in units of standard temperature and pressure), as determined by Reference Methods 2, 2A, 2C, or 2D in 40 CFR 60, incorporated by reference in 35 Ill. Adm. Code 720.111, as appropriate, by the unobstructed (free) cross-sectional area of the flare tip.

4) The maximum allowed velocity in m/s, V for a flare complying with subsection (d)(4)(C) above must be determined by the following equation:

$$\text{Log}(10) \ V[max] = \frac{H[T] + 28.8}{31.7}$$

LOG(V) = (H + 28.8) / 31.7

Where:

LOG Log[10] means logarithm to the base 10

H is the net heating value as determined in subsection (e)(2) above.

5) The maximum allowed velocity in m/s, V for an air-assisted flare must be determined by the following equation:

$$V = 8.706 + 0.7084 \ H[T]$$

V = 8.706 + 0.7084 H

Where:

POLLUTION CONTROL BOARD

NOTICE OF PROPOSED AMENDMENTS

H is the net heating value as determined in subsection
(e)(2) above.

f) The owner or operator shall monitor and inspect each control device
    required to comply with this Section to ensure proper operation and
    maintenance of the control device by implementing the following
    requirements:
    1) Install, calibrate, maintain, and operate according to the
        manufacturer's specifications a flow indicator that provides a
        record of vent stream flow from each affected process vent to the
        control device at least once every hour. The flow indicator
        sensor must be installed in the vent stream at the nearest
        feasible point to the control device inlet but before being
        combined with other vent streams.
    2) Install, calibrate, maintain, and operate according to the
        manufacturer's specifications a device to continuously monitor
        control device operation as specified below:
        A) For a thermal vapor incinerator, a temperature monitoring
            device equipped with a continuous recorder. The device must
            have accuracy of +-+ ± 1 percent of the temperature being
            monitored in °C or + ± 0.5° C, whichever is greater. the The
            temperature sensor must be installed at a location in the
            combustion chamber downstream of the combustion zone.
        B) For a catalytic vapor incinerator, a temperature monitoring
            device equipped with a continuous recorder. The device must
            be capable of monitoring temperature at two locations and
            have an accuracy of +-+ ± 1 percent of the temperature being
            monitored in C° or +-0+5-0 ± 0.5° C, whichever is greater.
            One temperature sensor must be installed in the vent stream
            at the nearest feasible point to the catalyst bed inlet and
            a second temperature sensor must be installed in the vent
            stream at the nearest feasible point to the catalyst bed
            outlet.
        C) For a flare, a heat sensing monitoring device equipped with
            a continuous recorder that indicates the continuous ignition
            of the pilot flame.
        D) For a boiler or process heater having a design heat input
            capacity less than 44 MW, a temperature monitoring device
            equipped with a continuous recorder. The device must have an
            accuracy of + ± 1 percent of the temperature being monitored
            in °C or +-0+5--0 ± 0.5° C, whichever is greater. The
            temperature sensor must be installed at a location in the
            furnace downstream of the combustion zone.
        E) For a boiler or process heater having a design heat input
            capacity greater than or equal to 44 MW, a monitoring device
            equipped with a continuous recorder to measure a
            parameter(s) parameters that indicates good combustion
            operating practices are being used.

POLLUTION CONTROL BOARD

NOTICE OF PROPOSED AMENDMENTS

        F) For a condenser, either:
            i)   A monitoring device equipped with a continuous
                 recorder to measure the concentration level of the
                 organic compounds in the exhaust vent stream from the
                 condenser; or
            ii) A temperature monitoring device equipped with a
                 continuous recorder. The device must be capable of
                 monitoring temperature at two locations and have an
                 accuracy of + ± 1 percent of the temperature being
                 monitored in °C or +-0+5-0 ± 0.5° C, whichever is
                 greater. One temperature sensor must be installed at a
                 location in the exhaust vent stream from the
                 condenser, and a second temperature sensor must be
                 installed at a location in the coolant fluid exiting
                 the condenser.
        G) For a carbon adsorption system such as a fixed-bed carbon
            adsorber that regenerates the carbon bed directly in the
            control device, either:
            i)   A monitoring device equipped with a continuous
                 recorder to measure the concentration level of the
                 organic compounds in the exhaust vent stream from the
                 carbon bed; or
            ii) A monitoring device equipped with a continuous
                 recorder to measure a parameter that indicates the
                 carbon bed is regenerated on a regular, predetermined
                 time cycle.
    3) Inspect the reading from each monitoring device required by
        subsection (f)(1) and (f)(2) above at least once each operating
        day to check control device operation and, if necessary,
        immediately implement the corrective measure necessary to ensure
        the control device operates in compliance with the requirements
        of this Section.
g) An owner or operator using a carbon adsorption system such as a
    fixed-bed carbon adsorber that regenerates the carbon bed directly
    onsite in the control device shall replace the existing carbon in the
    control device with fresh carbon at a regular, predetermined time
    interval that is no longer than the carbon service life established as
    a requirement of Section 725.935(b)(4)(C)(vi).
h) An owner or operator using a carbon adsorption system such as a carbon
    canister that does not regenerate the carbon bed directly onsite in
    the control device shall replace the existing carbon in the control
    device with fresh carbon on a regular basis by using one of the
    following procedures:
    1) Monitor the concentration level of the organic compounds in the
        exhaust vent stream from the carbon adsorption system on a
        regular schedule, and replace the existing carbon with fresh
        carbon immediately when carbon breakthrough is indicated. The
        monitoring frequency must be daily or at an interval no greater

POLLUTION CONTROL BOARD

NOTICE OF PROPOSED AMENDMENTS

        than 20 percent of the time required to consume the total carbon
        working capacity established as a requirement of Section
        725.935(b)(4)(C)(vii), whichever is longer.
    2) Replace the existing carbon with fresh carbon at a regular,
        predetermined time interval that is less than the design carbon
        replacement interval established as a requirement of Section
        725.935(b)(4)(C)(vii).
i) An owner or operator of an affected facility seeking to comply with
    the provisions of this Part by using a control device other than a
    thermal vapor incinerator, catalytic vapor incinerator, flare, boiler,
    process heater, condenser, or carbon adsorption system is required to
    develop documentation including sufficient information to describe the
    control device operation and identify the process parameter or
    parameters that indicate proper operation and maintenance of the
    control device.
j) Closed vent systems.
    1) Closed-vent systems must be designed for and operated with no
        detectable emissions, as indicated by an instrument reading of
        less than 500 ppm above background and by visual inspections, as
        determined by the methods specified in Section 725.934(b).
    2) Closed-vent systems must be monitored to determine compliance
        with this Section during the initial leak detection monitoring,
        which must be conducted by the date that the facility becomes
        subject to the provisions of this Section annually, and at other
        times as specified by the Agency pursuant to Section 725.930(c).
        For the annual leak detection monitoring after the initial leak
        detection monitoring, the owner or operator is not required to
        monitor those closed-vent system components that continuously
        operate in vacuum service or those closed vent system joints,
        seams, or other connections that are permanently or
        semi-permanently sealed (e.g., a welded joint between two
        sections of metal pipe or a bolted and gasketed pipe flange).
    3) Detectable emissions, as indicated by an instrument reading
        greater than 500 ppm and visual inspections, must be controlled
        as soon as practicable, but not later than 15 calendar days after
        the emission is detected.
    4) A first attempt at repair must be made no later than 5 calendar
        days after the emission is detected.v
k) Closed-vent systems and control devices used to comply with provisions
    of this Subpart must be operated at all times when emissions may be
    vented to them.
l) The owner or operator using a carbon adsorption system shall document
    that all carbon removed from the control device is managed in one of
    the following manners:
    1) It is regenerated or reactivated in a thermal treatment unit that
        is permitted under 35 Ill. Adm. Code 724.Subpart X or 725.Subpart
        P;
    2) It is incinerated by a process that is permitted under 35 Ill.

POLLUTION CONTROL BOARD

NOTICE OF PROPOSED AMENDMENTS

        Adm. Code 724.Subpart O or 725.Subpart O; or
    3) It is burned in a boiler or industrial furnace that is permitted
        under 35 Ill. Adm. Code 726.Subpart H.

(Source: Amended   at   19   Ill.   Reg.   _____,   effective
          _____)

    SUBPART BB: AIR EMISSION STANDARDS FOR EQUIPMENT LEAKS

Section 725.963 Test Methods and Procedures

    a) Each owner or operator subject to the provisions of this Subpart shall
        comply with the test methods and procedures requirements provided in
        this Section.
    b) Leak detection monitoring, as required in Sections 725.952 through
        725.962, must comply with the following requirements:
        1) Monitoring must comply with Reference Method 21 in 40 CFR 60,
            incorporated by reference in 35 Ill. Adm. Code 720.111.
        2) The detection instrument must meet the performance criteria of
            Reference Method 21.
        3) The instrument must be calibrated before use on each day of its
            use by the procedures specified in Reference Method 21.
        4) Calibration gases must be:
            A) Zero air (less than 10 ppm of hydrocarbon in air).
            B) A mixture of methane or n-hexane and air at a concentration
                of approximately, but less than, 10,000 ppm methane or
                n-hexane.
        5) The instrument probe must be traversed around all potential leak
            interfaces as close to the interface as possible as described in
            Reference Method 21.
    c) When equipment is tested for compliance with no detectable emissions,
        as required in Sections 725.952(e), 725.953(i), 725.954, and
        725.957(f), the test must comply with the following requirements:
        1) The requirements of subsections (b)(1) through (b)(4) above
            apply.
        2) The background level must be determined as set forth in Reference
            Method 21.
        3) The instrument probe must be traversed around all potential leak
            interfaces as close to the interface as possible as described in
            Reference Method 21.
        4) This arithmetic difference between the maximum concentration
            indicated by the instrument and the background level is compared
            with 500 ppm for determining compliance.
    d) In accordance with the waste analysis plan required by Section
        725.113(b), an owner or operator of a facility shall determine, for
        each piece of equipment, whether the equipment contains or contacts a
        hazardous waste with organic concentration that equals or exceeds 10
        percent by weight using the following:

POLLUTION CONTROL BOARD

NOTICE OF PROPOSED AMENDMENTS

1) Methods described in ASTM Methods D 2267-<u>88</u>, E 168-<u>88</u>, E 169-<u>87</u>, or E 260-<u>85</u>, incorporated by reference in 35 Ill. Adm. Code 720.111;

2) Method 9060 or 8240 of SW-846, incorporated by reference in 35 Ill. Adm. Code 720.111; or

3) Application of the knowledge of the nature of the hazardous wastestream or the process by which it was produced. Documentation of a waste determination by knowledge is required. Examples of documentation that must be used to support a determination under this provision include production process information documenting that no organic compounds are used, information that the waste is generated by a process that is identical to a process at the same or another facility that has previously been demonstrated by direct measurement to have a total organic content less than 10 percent, or prior speciation analysis results on the same wastestream where it is also documented that no process changes have occurred since that analysis that could affect the waste total organic concentration.

e) If an owner or operator determines that a piece of equipment contains or contacts a hazardous waste with organic concentrations at least 10 percent by weight, the determination can be revised only after following the procedures in subsection (d)(1) or (d)(2) above.

f) When an owner or operator and the Agency do not agree on whether a piece of equipment contains or contacts a hazardous waste with organic concentrations at least 10 percent by weight, the procedures in subsection (d)(1) or (d)(2) above must be used to resolve the dispute.

g) Samples used in determining the percent organic content must be representative of the highest total organic content hazardous waste that is expected to be contained in or contact the equipment.

h) To determine if pumps or valves are in light liquid service, the vapor pressures of constituents must either be obtained from standard reference texts or be determined by ASTM D- 2879-<u>86</u>, incorporated by reference in 35 Ill. Adm. Code 720.111.

i) Performance tests to determine if a control device achieves 95 weight percent organic emission reduction must comply with the procedures of Section 725.934(c)(1) through (c)(4).

(Source: Amended at 19 Ill. Reg. _____, effective _____)

SUBPART CC: AIR EMISSION STANDARDS FOR TANKS, SURFACE IMPOUNDMENTS, AND CONTAINERS

Section 725.980 Applicability

a) The requirements of this Subpart apply to owners and operators of all facilities that treat, store, or dispose of hazardous waste in tanks, surface impoundments, or containers subject to either 725.Subparts I,

J, or K, except as Section 725.1 and subsection (b) below provide otherwise.

b) The requirements of this Subpart do not apply to the following waste management units at the facility:

1) A waste management unit that holds hazardous waste placed in the unit before June 5, 1995 and in which no hazardous waste is added to the unit on or after June 5, 1995.

2) A container that has a design capacity less than or equal to 0.1 m(3) (3.5 ft(3) or 26.4 gal).

3) A tank in which an owner or operator has stopped adding hazardous waste and the owner or operator has begun implementing or completed closure pursuant to an approved closure plan.

4) A surface impoundment in which an owner or operator has stopped adding hazardous waste (except to implement an approved closure plan) and the owner or operator has begun implementing or completed closure pursuant to an approved closure plan.

5) A waste management unit that is used solely for on-site treatment or storage of hazardous waste that is generated as the result of implementing remedial activities required pursuant to the Act or Board regulations or under the corrective action authorities of RCRA sections 3004(u), 3004(v) or 3008(h); CERCLA authorities; or similar federal or state authorities.

6) A waste management unit that is used solely for the management of radioactive mixed waste in accordance with all applicable regulations under the authority of the Atomic Energy Act (42 U.S.C. 2011 et seq.) and the Nuclear Waste Policy Act.

c) For the owner and operator of a facility subject to this Subpart who has received a final RCRA permit prior to June 5, 1995, the following requirements apply:

1) The requirements of 35 Ill. Adm. Code 724.Subpart CC must be incorporated into the permit when the permit is reissued, renewed, or modified in accordance with the requirements of 35 Ill. Adm. Code 703 and 705.

2) Until the date when the permit is reissued, renewed, or modified in accordance with the requirements of 35 Ill. Adm. Code 703 and 705, the owner and operator is subject to the requirements of this Subpart.

(Source: Added at 19 Ill. Reg. _____, effective _____)

Section 725.981 Definitions

As used in this Subpart and in 35 Ill. Adm. Code 724, all terms not defined herein shall have the meaning given to them in the Act and 35 Ill. Adm. Code 720 through 726.

"Average volatile organic concentration" or "average VO concentration"

POLLUTION CONTROL BOARD

NOTICE OF PROPOSED AMENDMENTS

POLLUTION CONTROL BOARD

NOTICE OF PROPOSED AMENDMENTS

means the mass-weighted average volatile organic concentration of a hazardous waste, as determined in accordance with the requirements of Section 725.984.

"Cover" means a device or system that is placed on or over a hazardous waste such that the entire hazardous waste surface area is enclosed and sealed to reduce air emissions to the atmosphere. A cover may have openings such as access hatches, sampling ports, and gauge wells that are necessary for operation, inspection, maintenance, or repair of the unit on which the cover is installed provided that each opening is closed and sealed when not in use. Examples of covers include a fixed roof installed on a tank, a floating membrane cover installed on a surface impoundment, a lid installed on a drum, or an enclosure in which an open container is placed during waste treatment.

"External floating roof" means a pontoon-type or double-deck type floating roof that rests on the surface of the hazardous waste being managed in a tank that has no fixed roof.

"Fixed roof" means a rigid cover that is installed in a stationary position so that it does not move with fluctuations in the level of the hazardous waste placed in a tank.

"Floating membrane cover" means a cover consisting of a synthetic flexible membrane material that rests upon and is supported by the hazardous waste being managed in a surface impoundment.

"Floating roof" means a pontoon-type or double-deck-type cover that rests upon and is supported by the hazardous waste being managed in a tank.

"Internal floating roof" means a floating roof that rests on or floats on the surface of the hazardous waste being managed in a tank that has a fixed roof.

"Liquid-mounted seal" means a foam or liquid-filled primary seal mounted in contact with the hazardous waste between the tank wall and the floating roof, continuously around the circumference of the tank.

"Maximum organic vapor pressure" means the equilibrium partial pressure exerted by the hazardous waste contained in a tank, determined at the temperature equal to either:

The local maximum monthly average temperature as reported by the National Weather Service, when the hazardous waste is stored or treated at ambient temperatures; or

POLLUTION CONTROL BOARD

NOTICE OF PROPOSED AMENDMENTS

The highest calendar-month average temperature of the hazardous waste, when the hazardous waste is stored at temperatures above the ambient temperature; or when the hazardous waste is stored or treated at temperatures below the ambient temperature.

"No detectable organic emissions" means no escape of organics from a device or system below the ambient temperature, as determined at the device or system below the atmosphere, as determined:

By an instrument reading less than 500 parts per million by volume (ppmv) above the background level, at each joint, fitting, and seal, when measured in accordance with the requirements of method 21 in 40 CFR Part 60, Appendix A, and

By no visible opening or defects in the device or system such as flaps, tears, or gaps.

"Point of waste origination" means as follows:

When the facility owner or operator is the generator of the hazardous waste, the "point of waste origination" means the point where a solid waste is produced by a system, process, or waste management unit is determined to be a hazardous waste, as defined in 40 CFR Part 261.

BOARD NOTE: In this case, this term is being used in a manner similar to the use of the term "point of generation" in all standards established for waste management operations under authority of the federal Clean Air Act in 40 CFR Parts 60, 61, and 63.

When the owner or operator accepts delivery or takes possession of the hazardous waste, "point of waste origination" means the point where the owner or operator accepts delivery or takes possession of the hazardous waste.

"Point of waste treatment" means the point where a hazardous waste exits a waste management unit that used to destroy, degrade, or remove organics in the hazardous waste.

"Vapor-mounted seal" means a foam-filled primary seal mounted continuously around the circumference of the tank so that there is an annular vapor space underneath the seal. The annular vapor space is bounded by the bottom of the primary seal, the tank wall, the hazardous waste surface, and the floating roof.

"Volatile organic concentration" or "VO concentration" means the fraction by weight of organic compounds in a hazardous waste expressed in terms of parts per million (ppmw), as determined by direct measurement, using Method 25D, or by knowledge of the waste, in accordance with the requirements of Section 725.984.

POLLUTION CONTROL BOARD

NOTICE OF PROPOSED AMENDMENTS

"Waste determination" means performing all applicable procedures in accordance with the requirements of Section 725.984 to determine whether a hazardous waste meets standards specified in this Subpart. Examples of a waste determination include performing the procedures in accordance with the requirements of Section 725.984 to determine the average VO concentration of a hazardous waste at the point of waste origination, determining the average VO concentration of a hazardous waste at the point of waste treatment and comparing the results to the exit concentration limit specified for the process used to treat the hazardous waste, determining the organic reduction efficiency and the organic biodegradation efficiency for a biological process used to treat a hazardous waste and comparing the results to the applicable standards, or determining the maximum volatile organic vapor pressure for a hazardous waste in a tank and comparing the results to the applicable standards.

"Waste stabilization process" means any physical or chemical process used to either reduce the mobility of hazardous constituents in a hazardous waste or eliminate free liquids as determined by Test Method 9095 (Paint Filter Liquids Test) in "Test Methods for Evaluating Solid Waste, Physical/Chemical Methods", incorporated by reference in Section 720.111. A waste stabilization process includes mixing the hazardous waste with binders or other materials and curing the resulting hazardous waste and binder mixture. Other synonymous terms used to refer to this process are "waste fixation" or "waste solidification".

(Source: Added at 19 Ill. Reg. _____, effective _____)

Section 725.982 Schedule for Implementation of Air Emission Standards

a) Owners or operators of facilities existing on June 5, 1995 and subject to 725.Subparts I, J, and K shall meet the following requirements:
1) The owner or operator shall install and begin operation of all control equipment required by this Subpart by June 5, 1995, except as provided in subsection (a)(2) below.
2) When control equipment required by this Subpart cannot be installed and in operation by June 5, 1995, the owner or operator shall:
A) Install and begin operation of the control equipment as soon as possible, but in no case later than December 8, 1997.
B) Prepare an implementation schedule that includes the following information: specific calendar dates for award of contracts or issuance of purchase orders for the control equipment, initiation of on-site installation of the control equipment, completion of the control equipment installation, and performance of any testing to demonstrate that the

POLLUTION CONTROL BOARD

NOTICE OF PROPOSED AMENDMENTS

installed equipment meets the applicable standards of this Subpart.
C) For facilities subject to the recordkeeping requirements of Section 725.173, the owner or operator shall enter the implementation schedule specified in subsection (a)(2)(B) above in the operating record no later than June 5, 1995.
D) For facilities not subject to Section 725.173 above, the owner or operator shall enter the implementation schedule specified in subsection (a)(2)(B) of this section in a permanent, readily available file located at the facility no later than June 5, 1995.

b) An owner or operator of facilities in existence on the effective date of statutory or regulatory amendments under the Act that render the facility subject to 725.Subparts I, J, or K shall meet the following requirements:
1) The owner or operator shall install and begin operation of all control equipment required by this Subpart by the effective date of the amendment, except as provided in subsection (b)(2) below.
2) When control equipment required by this Subpart cannot be installed and begin operation by the effective date of the amendment, the owner or operator shall:
A) Install and operate the control equipment as soon as possible, but in no case later than 30 months after the effective date of the amendment.
B) For facilities subject to the recordkeeping requirements of Section 725.173, enter and maintain the implementation schedule specified in subsection (a)(2)(B) above in the operating record no later than the effective date of the amendment, or
C) For facilities not subject to Section 725.173, the owner or operator shall enter and maintain the implementation schedule specified in subsection (a)(2)(B) above in a permanent, readily available file, located at the facility site, no later than the effective date of the amendment.

c) The Agency may elect to extend the implementation date for control equipment at a facility, on a case by case basis, to a date later than December 8, 1997:
1) When special circumstances that are beyond the facility owner's or operator's control delay installation or operation of control equipment, and
2) The owner or operator has made all reasonable and prudent attempts to comply with the requirements of this Subpart.

(Source: Added at 19 Ill. Reg. _____, effective _____)

Section 725.983 Standards: General

POLLUTION CONTROL BOARD

NOTICE OF PROPOSED AMENDMENTS

a) This Section applies to the management of hazardous waste in tanks, surface impoundments, and containers subject to this Subpart.

b) The owner or operator shall control air emissions from each waste management unit in accordance with standards specified in Sections 725.985 through Section 725.988, as applicable to the waste management unit, except as provided for in subsection (c) below.

c) A waste management unit is exempted from standards specified in Section 725.985 through Section 725.988, provided that all hazardous waste placed in the waste management unit is determined by the owner or operator to meet either of the following conditions:

   1) The average VO concentration of the hazardous waste at the point of waste origination is less than 100 parts per million by weight (ppmw). The average VO concentration must be determined by the procedures specified in Section 725.984(a).

   2) The organic content of the hazardous waste has been reduced by an organic destruction or removal process that achieves any one of the following conditions:

      A) The process removes or destroys the organics contained in the hazardous waste to such a level that the average VO concentration of the hazardous waste at the point of waste treatment is less than the exit concentration limit (Cti) established for the process. The average VO concentration of the hazardous waste at the point of waste treatment and the exit concentration limit for the process must be determined using the procedures specified in Section 725.984(b).

      B) The process removes or destroys the organics contained in the hazardous waste to such a level that the organic reduction efficiency (R) for the process is equal to or greater than 95 percent, and the average VO concentration of the hazardous waste at the point of waste treatment is less than 50 ppmw. The organic reduction efficiency for the process and the average VO concentration of the hazardous waste at the point of waste treatment must be determined using the procedures specified in Section 725.984(b).

      C) The process removes or destroys the organics contained in the hazardous waste to such a level that the actual organic mass removal rate (MR) for the process is greater than the required organic mass removal rate (RMR) established for the process. The required organic mass removal rate and the actual organic mass removal rate for the process must be determined using the procedures specified in Section 725.984(b).

      D) The process is a biological process that destroys or degrades the organics contained in the hazardous waste so that either of the following conditions is met:

         i) The organic reduction efficiency (R) for the process is equal to or greater than 95 percent, and the

POLLUTION CONTROL BOARD

NOTICE OF PROPOSED AMENDMENTS

organic biodegradation efficiency (R(bio)) for the process is equal to or greater than 95 percent. The organic reduction efficiency and the organic biodegradation efficiency for the process must be determined in accordance with the procedures specified in Section 725.984(b).

         ii) The total actual organic mass biodegradation rate (MR(bio)) for all hazardous waste treated by the process is equal to or greater than the required organic mass removal rate (RMR). The required organic mass removal rate and the actual organic mass biodegradation rate for the process must be determined using the procedures specified in Section 725.984(b).

   2) The process is one that removes or destroys the organics contained in the hazardous waste and meets all of the following conditions:

      i) All of the materials entering the process are hazardous wastes.

      ii) From the point of waste origination through the point where the hazardous waste enters the process, the hazardous waste is continuously managed in waste management units that use air emission controls in accordance with the standards specified in Section 725.985 through Section 725.988, as applicable to the waste management unit.

      iii) The average VO concentration of the hazardous waste at the point of waste treatment is less than the lowest average VO concentration at the point of waste origination determined for each of the individual hazardous waste streams entering the process or 100 ppmw, whichever value is lower. The average VO concentration of each individual hazardous waste stream at the point of waste origination must be determined using the procedure specified in Section 725.984(a). The average VO concentration of the hazardous waste at the point of waste treatment must be determined using the procedures specified in Section 725.984(b).

   F) A hazardous waste incinerator for which the owner or operator has either:

      i) Been issued a final permit under 35 Ill. Adm. Code 703 and 705, and the owner or operator designs and operates the unit in accordance with the requirements of 35 Ill. Adm. Code 724, Subpart O; or

      ii) The owner or operator has certified compliance for the unit with the interim status requirements of 725, Subpart O.

   G) A boiler or industrial furnace for which the owner or

operator has either:

    i)   Been issued a final permit under 35 Ill. Adm. Code 703 and 705, and the owner or operator designs and operates the unit in accordance with the requirements of 35 Ill. Adm. Code 726.Subpart M, or

    ii) The owner or operator has certified compliance for the unit with the interim status requirements of 35 Ill. Adm. Code 726.Subpart M.

d)   When a process is used for the purpose of treating a hazardous waste to meet one of the sets of conditions specified in subsections (c)(2)(A) through (c)(2)(E) above, each material removed from or exiting the process that is not a hazardous waste but which has an average VO concentration equal to or greater than 100 ppmw must be managed in a waste management unit in accordance with the requirements of subsection (b) above.

e)   The Agency may at any time perform or request that the owner or operator perform a waste determination for a hazardous waste managed in a tank, surface impoundment, or container that is exempted from using air emission controls under the provisions of this Section as follows:

    1) The waste determination for average VO concentration of a hazardous waste at the point of waste origination must be performed using direct measurement in accordance with the applicable requirements of Section 725.984(a). The waste determination for a hazardous waste at the point of waste treatment must be performed in accordance with the applicable requirements of Section 725.984(b).

    2) To perform the waste determination, the owner or operator is requested, the Agency may elect to have an authorized representative observe the collection of the hazardous waste samples used for the analysis.

    3) Where the results of the waste determination performed or requested by the Agency do not agree with the results of a waste determination performed by the owner or operator using knowledge of the waste, then the results of the waste determination performed in accordance with the requirements of subsection (e)(1) above must be used to establish compliance with the requirements of this Subpart.

    4) Where the owner or operator has used an averaging period greater than one hour for determining the average VO concentration of a hazardous waste at the point of waste origination, the Agency may elect to establish compliance with this Subpart by performing or requesting that the owner or operator perform a waste determination using direct measurement based on waste samples collected within a 1-hour period as follows:

        A) The average VO concentration of the hazardous waste at the point of waste origination must be determined by direct measurement in accordance with the requirements of Section

           725.984(a).

        B) Results of the waste determination performed or requested by the Agency showing that the average VO concentration of the hazardous waste at the point of waste origination is equal to or greater than 100 ppmw shall constitute noncompliance with this Subpart, except in a case as provided for in subsection (e)(4)(C) below.

        C) Where the average VO concentration of the hazardous waste at the point of waste origination previously has been determined by the owner or operator using an averaging period greater than one hour to be less than 100 ppmw but because of normal operating process variations the VO concentration of the hazardous waste determined by direct measurement for any given 1-hour period may be equal to or greater than 100 ppmw, information that was used by the owner or operator to determine the average VO concentration of the hazardous waste (e.g., test results, measurements, calculations, and other documentation) and recorded in the facility records in accordance with the requirements of Sections 725.984(a) and 725.990 must be considered by the Agency together with the results of the waste determination performed or requested by the Agency in establishing compliance with this Subpart.

(Source: Added at 19 Ill. Reg. _____, effective _____)

Section 725.984 Waste Determination Procedures

a)   Waste determination procedure for volatile organic (VO) concentration of a hazardous waste at the point of waste origination.

    1) An owner or operator shall determine the average VO concentration at the point of waste origination for each hazardous waste placed in a waste management unit exempted under the provisions of Section 725.983(c)(1) from using air emission controls in accordance with standards specified in Section 725.985 through Section 725.988, as applicable to the waste management unit.

    2) When the facility owner or operator is the generator of the hazardous waste, the owner or operator shall determine the average VO concentration of the hazardous waste using either direct measurement, as specified in subsection (a)(5) below, or knowledge of the waste, as specified in subsection (a)(6) below, for each hazardous waste generated as follows:

        A) When the hazardous waste is generated as part of a continuous process, the owner or operator shall:

           1) Perform an initial waste determination of the average VO concentration of the waste stream before the first time any portion of the material in the waste stream

POLLUTION CONTROL BOARD

NOTICE OF PROPOSED AMENDMENTS

is placed in a waste management unit subject to this
Subpart and thereafter update the information used for
the waste determination at least once every 12 months
following the date of the initial waste determination;
and

    ii)   Perform a new waste determination whenever changes to
the source generating the waste stream are reasonably
likely to cause the average VO concentration of the
hazardous waste to increase to a level that is equal
to or greater than the applicable VO concentration
limits specified in Section 725.983.

B)   When the hazardous waste is generated as part of a batch
process that is performed repeatedly but not necessarily
continuously, the owner or operator shall:

    i)   Perform an initial waste determination of the average
VO concentration for one or more representative waste
batches generated by the process, before the first
time any portion of the material in the batches is
placed in a waste management unit subject to this
Subpart, and thereafter update the information used
for the waste determination at least once every 12
months following the date of the initial waste
determination; and

    ii)   Perform a new waste determination whenever changes to
the process generating the waste batches are
reasonably likely to cause the average VO
concentration of the hazardous waste to increase to a
level that is equal to or greater than the applicable
VO concentration limits specified in Section 725.983.

3)   When the facility owner and operator is not the generator of the
hazardous waste, the owner or operator shall determine the
average VO concentration of the hazardous waste using either
direct measurement, as specified in subsection (a)(5) below, or
knowledge of the waste, as specified in subsection (a)(6) below,
for each hazardous waste entering the facility as follows:

A)   When the hazardous waste enters the facility as a continuous
flow of material through a pipeline or other means (e.g.,
wastewater stream), the owner or operator shall:

    i)   Perform an initial waste determination of the waste
stream before the first time any portion of the
material in the waste stream is placed in a waste
management unit subject to this Subpart, and
thereafter update the information used for the waste
determination at least once every 12 months following
the date of the initial waste determination; and

    ii)   Perform a new waste determination whenever changes to
the source generating the waste stream are reasonably
likely to cause the average VO concentration of the

POLLUTION CONTROL BOARD

NOTICE OF PROPOSED AMENDMENTS

hazardous waste to increase to a level that is equal
to or greater than the applicable VO concentration
limits specified in Section 725.983.

B)   When the hazardous waste enters the facility in a container,
the owner or operator shall perform a waste determination
for the material held in each container.

4)   Where the average VO concentration of the hazardous waste is
determined by the owner or operator to be less than 100 ppmw, but
because of normal operating variations in the source or process
generating the hazardous waste the VO concentration of the
hazardous waste may be equal to or greater than 100 ppmw at any
given time during the averaging period, the owner or operator
shall prepare and enter in the facility operating record
information that specifies the following:

A)   The maximum and minimum VO concentration values for the
hazardous waste that occur during that averaging period used
for the waste determination;

B)   The operating conditions or circumstances under which the VO
concentration of the hazardous waste will be equal to or
greater than 100 ppmw; and

C)   The information and calculations used by the owner or
operator to determine the average VO concentration of the
hazardous waste.

5)   Procedure for using direct measurement to determine average VO
concentration of a hazardous waste at the point of waste
origination.

A)   The owner or operator shall identify and record the point of
waste origination for the hazardous waste. All waste
samples used to determine the average VO concentration of
the hazardous waste must be collected at this point.

B)   The owner or operator shall designate and record the
averaging period to be used for determining the average VO
concentration for the hazardous waste. The averaging period
must not exceed one year. An initial waste determination
must be performed for each averaging period.

C)   The owner or operator shall identify each discrete quantity
of the material composing the hazardous waste represented by
the averaging period designated in subsection (a)(5)(B)
above. An example of a discrete quantity of material
composing a hazardous waste generated as part of a
continuous process is the quantity of material generated
during a process operating mode defined by a specific set of
operating conditions that are normal for the process. An
example of a discrete quantity of material composing a
hazardous waste generated as part of a batch process that is
performed repeatedly but not necessarily continuously is the
total quantity of material composing a single batch
generated by the process. An example of a discrete quantity

POLLUTION CONTROL BOARD

NOTICE OF PROPOSED AMENDMENTS

of material composing a hazardous waste delivered to a facility in a container is the total quantity of material held in the container.

D) The following procedure must be used measure the VO concentration for each discrete quantity of material identified in subsection (a)(5)(C) above:

i) A sufficient number of samples, but in no case fewer than four, must be collected to represent the organic composition for the entire discrete quantity of hazardous waste being tested. All of the samples must be collected within a 1-hour period. Sufficient information must be prepared and recorded to document the waste quantity represented by the samples and, as applicable, the operating conditions for the source or process generating the hazardous waste represented by the samples.

ii) Each sample must be collected in accordance with the requirements specified in "Test Methods for Evaluating Solid Waste, Physical/Chemical Methods", incorporated by reference in Section 720.111.

iii) Each collected sample must be prepared and analyzed in accordance with the requirements of Method 25D in 40 CFR Part 60, Appendix A, incorporated by reference in 35 Ill. Adm. Code 720.111.

iv) The measured VO concentration for the discrete quantity of hazardous waste must be determined by using the results for all samples analyzed in accordance with subsection (a)(5)(D)(iii) above and the following equation:

$$C = \frac{1}{n} \times \sum_{i=1}^{n} C[i]$$

Where:

C = Measured VO concentration of the discrete quantity of hazardous waste, in ppmw.

i = Individual sample "i" of the hazardous waste collected in accordance with the requirements of SW-846.

n = Total number of samples of hazardous waste collected (at least 4) within a 1-hour period.

C[i] = VO concentration measured by Method 25D for sample "i", in ppmw.

POLLUTION CONTROL BOARD

NOTICE OF PROPOSED AMENDMENTS

E) The average VO concentration of the hazardous waste must be determined using the following procedure:

i) When the facility owner or operator is the generator of the hazardous waste, a sufficient number of VO concentration measurements for the hazardous waste must be performed in accordance with the requirements of subsection (a)(5)(D) above to represent the complete range of hazardous waste organic compositions and quantities that occur during the entire averaging period due to normal variations in the operating conditions for each process operating mode identified for the source or process generating the hazardous waste.

ii) When the facility owner or operator is not the generator of the hazardous waste, a sufficient number of VO concentration measurements for the hazardous waste must be performed in accordance with the requirements of subsection (a)(5)(D) above to represent the complete range of hazardous waste organic compositions and quantities that occur in the hazardous waste as received at the facility during the entire averaging period.

iii) The average VO concentration of the hazardous waste at the point of waste origination must be calculated by using the results for all VO measurements performed in accordance with subsection (a)(5)(D) above and the following equation:

$$C[ave] = \frac{1}{Q[T]} \times \sum_{j=1}^{m} (Q[j] \times C[j])$$

Where:

C[ave] = Average VO concentration of the hazardous waste at the point of waste origination, in ppmw.

j = Individual discrete quantity "j" of hazardous waste for which a VO concentration measurement is determined in accordance with the requirements of subsection (a)(5)(D) above.

m = Total number of VO concentration measurements determined in accordance with the requirements of subsection (a)(5)(D) above for the averaging period.

Q[j] = Mass of the discrete quantity of the hazardous waste represented by C[j], in kg.

$Q(T)$ = Total mass of the hazardous waste for the averaging period, in kg.

$C(i)$ = Measured VO concentration of discrete quantity "i" for the hazardous waste determined in accordance with the requirements of subsection (a)(5)(D) above, in ppmw.

6) Procedure for using knowledge of the waste to determine the average VO concentration of a hazardous waste at the point of waste origination.

A) The owner or operator shall identify and record the point of waste origination for the hazardous waste. All information used to determine the average VO concentration of the hazardous waste must be based on the hazardous waste composition at this point.

B) The owner or operator shall designate and record the averaging period to be used for determining the average VO concentration for the hazardous waste. The averaging period must not exceed one year. An initial waste determination must be performed for each averaging period.

C) The owner or operator shall prepare and record sufficient information that documents the average VO concentration for the hazardous waste. Information may be used that is prepared by either the facility owner or operator or by the generator of the hazardous waste. Examples of information that may be used as the basis for knowledge of the waste include: organic material balances for the source or process generating the waste; VO concentration measurements for the same type of waste performed in accordance with the procedure specified in subsection (a)(5)(D) above; previous individual organic constituent test data for the waste that are still applicable to the current waste management practices; documentation that the waste is generated by a process for which no organics-containing materials are used; previous test data for other locations managing the same type of waste; or other knowledge based on manifests, shipping papers, or waste certification notices.

D) If test data other than VO concentration measurements performed in accordance with the procedure specified in subsection (a)(5)(D) above are used as the basis for knowledge of the waste, then the owner or operator shall document the test method, sampling protocol, and the means by which sampling variability and analytical variability are accounted for in the determination of the average VO concentration. For example, an owner or operator may use individual organic constituent concentration test data that are validated in accordance with Method 301 in 40 CFR Part 63, Appendix A, incorporated by reference in 35 Ill. Adm.

Code 720.111, as the basis for knowledge of the waste.

b) Waste determination procedures for treated hazardous waste.

1) An owner or operator shall perform the applicable waste determination for each treated hazardous waste placed in a waste management unit exempted under the provisions of Section 725.983(c)(2) from using air emission controls in accordance with standards specified in Section 725.985 through Section 725.988, as applicable to the waste management unit.

2) The owner or operator shall perform a waste determination for each discrete quantity of treated hazardous waste as follows:

A) When the hazardous waste is treated by a continuous process, the owner or operator shall:

i) Perform an initial waste determination for the treated waste stream before the first time any portion of the material in the waste stream is placed in a waste management unit subject to this Subpart, and thereafter update the information used for the waste determination at least once every 12 months following the date of the initial waste determination; and

ii) Perform a new waste determination whenever changes to the hazardous waste streams fed to the process are reasonably likely to cause the characteristics of the hazardous waste at the point of waste treatment to change to levels that fail to achieve the applicable conditions specified in Section 725.983(c)(2).

B) When the hazardous waste is treated by a batch process that is performed repeatedly but not necessarily continuously, the owner or operator shall:

i) Perform an initial waste determination for the treated hazardous waste in one or more representative batches treated by the process, and thereafter update the information used for the waste determination at least once every 12 months following the date of the initial waste determination; and

ii) Perform a new waste determination whenever changes to the hazardous waste treated by the process are reasonably likely to cause the characteristics of the hazardous waste at the point of waste treatment to change to levels that fail to achieve the applicable conditions specified in Section 725.983(c)(2).

3) The owner or operator shall designate and record the specific provision in Section 725.983(c)(2) for which the waste determination is being performed. The waste determination for the treated hazardous waste must be performed using the applicable procedures specified in subsections (b)(4) through (b)(10) below.

4) Procedure to determine the average VO concentration of a hazardous waste at the point of waste treatment.

POLLUTION CONTROL BOARD

NOTICE OF PROPOSED AMENDMENTS

A) The owner or operator shall identify and record the point of waste treatment for the hazardous waste. All waste samples used to determine the average VO concentration of the hazardous waste must be collected at this point.

B) The owner or operator shall designate and record the averaging period to be used for determining the average VO concentration for the hazardous waste. The averaging period must not exceed one year. An initial waste determination must be performed for each averaging period.

C) The owner or operator shall identify each discrete quantity of the material composing the hazardous waste represented by the averaging period designated in subsection (b)(4)(B) above.

D) The following procedure shall be used measure the VO concentration for each discrete quantity of material identified in subsection (b)(4)(C) above:

  i) A sufficient number of samples, but in no case fewer than four samples, must be collected to represent the organic composition for the entire discrete quantity of hazardous waste being tested. All of the samples must be collected within a 1-hour period. Sufficient information must be prepared and recorded to document the waste quantity represented by the samples and, as applicable, the operating conditions for the process treating the hazardous waste represented by the samples.

  ii) Each sample must be collected in accordance with the requirements specified in "Test Methods for Evaluating Solid Waste, Physical/Chemical Methods", incorporated by reference in 35 Ill. Adm. Code 720.111.

  iii) Each collected sample must be prepared and analysed in accordance with the requirements of Method 25D in 40 CFR Part 60, Appendix A, incorporated by reference in 35 Ill. Adm. Code 720.111.

  iv) The measured VO concentration for the discrete quantity of hazardous waste must be determined by using the results for all samples analyzed in accordance with subsection (b)(4)(E)(iii) above and the following equation:

$$C = \frac{1}{n} \times \sum_{i=1}^{n} C[i]$$

Where:

C = Measured VO concentration of the discrete quantity used to hazardous waste, in ppmw.

POLLUTION CONTROL BOARD

NOTICE OF PROPOSED AMENDMENTS

  i = Individual sample "i" of the hazardous waste collected in accordance with the requirements of SW-846.

  n = Total number of samples of hazardous waste collected (at least 4) within a 1-hour period.

  C[i] = VO concentration measured by Method 25D for sample "i", in ppmw.

E) The average VO concentration of the hazardous waste at the point of waste treatment must be determined using the following procedure:

  i) When the facility owner or operator is the generator of the hazardous waste, a sufficient number of VO concentration measurements for the hazardous waste must be performed in accordance with the requirements of subsection (b)(4)(D) above to represent the complete range of hazardous waste organic compositions and quantities treated by the process during the entire averaging period.

  ii) The average VO concentration of the hazardous waste at the point of waste treatment must be calculated by using the results for all VO measurements performed in accordance with subsection (b)(4)(D) above and the following equation:

$$C[ave] = \frac{1}{Q[T]} \times \sum_{j=1}^{m} (Q[j] \times C[j])$$

Where:

C[ave] = Average VO concentration of the hazardous waste at the point of waste origination, in ppmw.

j = Individual discrete quantity "j" of the hazardous waste for which a VO concentration measurement is determined in accordance with the requirements of subsection (b)(4)(D) above.

m = Total number of VO concentration measurements determined in accordance with the requirements of subsection (b)(4)(D) above for the averaging period.

Q[j] = Mass of the discrete quantity of hazardous waste represented by C[j], in kg.

NOTICE OF PROPOSED AMENDMENTS

Q[T] = Total mass of the hazardous waste for the averaging period, in kg.

C[i] = Measured VO concentration of discrete quantity "i" for the hazardous waste determined in accordance with the requirements of subsection (b)(4)(D) above, in ppmw.

5) Procedure to determine the exit concentration limit (C[t]) for a treated hazardous waste.
   A) The point of waste origination for each hazardous waste treated by the process at the same time must be identified.
   B) If a single hazardous waste stream is identified in subsection (b)(5)(A) above, then the exit concentration limit (C[t]) must be 100 ppmw.
   C) If more than one hazardous waste stream is identified in subsection (b)(5)(A) above, then the VO concentration of each hazardous waste stream at the point of waste origination must be determined in accordance with the requirements of subsection (a) above. The exit concentration limit (C[t]) must be calculated by using the results determined for each individual hazardous waste stream and the following equation:

$$C[t] = \frac{\sum_{x=1}^{m} (Q[x] \times C[x]) + \sum_{y=1}^{n} (Q[y] \times 100 \text{ ppmw})}{\sum_{x=1}^{m} Q[x] + \sum_{y=1}^{n} Q[y]}$$

Where:

C[t] = Exit concentration limit for treated hazardous waste, in ppmw.

x = Individual hazardous waste stream "x" that has a VO concentration less than 100 ppmw at the point of waste origination, as determined in accordance with the requirements of Section 725.984(a).

y = Individual hazardous waste stream "y" that has a VO concentration equal to or greater than 100 ppmw at the point of waste origination, as determined in accordance with the requirements of Section 725.984(a).

NOTICE OF PROPOSED AMENDMENTS

m = Total number of "x" hazardous waste streams treated by process.

n = Total number of "y" hazardous waste streams treated by process.

Q[x] = Annual mass quantity of hazardous waste stream "x", in kg/yr.

Q[y] = Annual mass quantity of hazardous waste stream "y", in kg/yr.

C[x] = Average VO concentration of hazardous waste stream "x" at the point of waste origination, as determined in accordance with the requirements of Section 725.984(a), in ppmw.

6) Procedure to determine the organic reduction efficiency (R) for a treated hazardous waste.
   A) The organic reduction efficiency for a treatment process must be determined based on results for a minimum of three consecutive runs. The sampling time for each run must be one hour.
   B) The point of each hazardous waste stream entering the process and each hazardous waste stream exiting the process that is to be included in the calculation of the organic reduction efficiency for the process must be identified.
   C) For each run, the following information must be determined for each hazardous waste stream identified in subsection (b)(6)(B) above, using the following procedures:
      i) The mass quantity of each hazardous waste stream entering the process (Q[b]) and the mass quantity of each hazardous waste stream exiting the process (Q[a]) must be determined.
      ii) The VO concentration of each hazardous waste stream entering the process (C[b]) during the run must be measured in accordance with the requirements of subsections (a)(5)(D)(i) through (a)(5)(D)(iv) below. The VO concentration of each hazardous waste stream exiting the process (C[a]) during the run must be determined in accordance with the requirements of subsection (b)(4)(D) below. Samples must be collected as follows: For a continuous process, the samples of the hazardous waste entering and samples of the hazardous waste exiting the process must be collected concurrently. For a batch process, the samples of the hazardous waste entering the process must be collected at the time that the hazardous waste is placed in the

process. The samples of the hazardous waste exiting the process must be collected as soon as practicable after the time when the process stops operation or the final treatment cycle ends.

D) The waste volatile organic mass flow entering the process (E[b]) and the waste volatile organic mass flow exiting the process (E[a]) must be calculated by using the results determined in accordance with subsection (b)(6)(C) above and the following equations:

$$E[b] = \frac{1}{10(6)} \sum_{i=1}^{m} (Q[bj] \times C[bj])$$

$$E[a] = \frac{1}{10(6)} \sum_{i=1}^{m} (Q[aj] \times C[aj])$$

Where:

E[a] = Waste volatile organic mass flow exiting process, in kg/hr.

E[b] = Waste volatile organic mass flow entering process, in kg/hr.

m = Total number of runs (at least 3)

j = Individual run "j"

Q[bj] = Mass quantity of hazardous waste entering process during run "j", in kg/hr.

Q[aj] = Average mass quantity of waste exiting process during run "j", in kg/hr.

C[aj] = Measured VO concentration of hazardous waste exiting process during run "j", as determined in accordance with the requirements of Section 725.984(b)(4)(D), in ppmw.

C[bj] = Measured VO concentration of hazardous waste entering process during run "j", as determined in accordance with the requirements of Section 725.984 (a)(5)(D)(i) through (a)(5)(D)(iv), in ppmw.

E) The organic reduction efficiency of the process must be calculated by using the results determined in accordance

with subsection (b)(6)(D) above and the following equation:

$$R = \frac{E[b] - E[a]}{E[b]} \times 100\%$$

Where:

R = Organic reduction efficiency, percent.

E[b] = Waste volatile organic mass flow entering process as determined in accordance with the requirements of subsection (b)(6)(D) above, in kg/hr.

E[a] = Waste volatile organic mass flow exiting process as determined in accordance with the requirements of subsection (b)(6)(D) above, in kg/hr.

7) Procedure to determine the organic biodegradation efficiency (R[bio]) for a treated hazardous waste.
A) The fraction of organics biodegraded (F[bio]) must be determined using the procedure specified in 40 CFR Part 63, Appendix C, incorporated by reference in 35 Ill. Adm. Code 70.111.
B) The organic biodegradation efficiency must be calculated by using the following equation:

$$R[bio] = F[bio] \times 100\%$$

Where:

R[bio] = Organic biodegradation efficiency, in percent.

F[bio] = Fraction of organic biodegraded as determined in accordance with the requirements of subsection (b)(7)(A) above.

8) Procedure to determine the required organic mass removal rate (RMR) for a treated hazardous waste.
A) The point of waste origination for each hazardous waste treated by the process at the same time must be identified.
B) For each hazardous waste stream identified in subsection (b)(8)(A) above, the VO concentration of the hazardous waste stream at the point of waste origination must be determined in accordance with the requirements of subsection (a) above.
C) For each individual hazardous waste stream that has a volatile organic concentration equal to or greater than 100 ppmw at the point of waste origination as determined in

POLLUTION CONTROL BOARD

NOTICE OF PROPOSED AMENDMENTS

accordance with the requirements of subsection (b)(8)(B)
above, the average volumetric flow rate of hazardous waste
at the point of waste origination and the density of the
hazardous waste stream must be determined.

D) The required organic mass removal rate for the hazardous
waste must be calculated by using the results determined for
each individual hazardous waste stream in accordance with
the requirements of subsections (b)(8)(B) and (b)(8)(C)
above and the following equation:

$$RMR = \sum_{y=1}^{n} [\ V[y] \times K[y] \times \frac{(\overline{G}[y] - 100\ ppmw)}{10(6)}\ ]$$

Where:

RMR = Required organic mass removal rate, in kg/hr.

y = Individual hazardous waste stream "y" that has a
volatile organic concentration equal to or greater
than 100 ppmw at the point of waste origination, as
determined in accordance with the requirements of
Section 725.984(a).

n = Total number of "y" hazardous waste streams
treated by process.

V[y] = Average volumetric flow rate of hazardous waste
stream "y" at the point of waste origination, in
m(3)/hr.

K[y] = Density of hazardous waste stream "y", in
kg/m(3)

$\overline{y}$ = Average VO concentration of hazardous waste stream
"y" at the point of waste origination as determined in
accordance with the requirements of Section
725.984(a), in ppmw.

9) Procedure to determine the actual organic mass removal rate (MR)
for a treated hazardous waste.

A) The actual organic mass removal rate must be determined
based on results for a minimum of three consecutive runs.
The sampling time for each run must be one hour.

B) The waste volatile organic mass flow entering the process
(E[b]) and the waste volatile organic mass flow exiting the

POLLUTION CONTROL BOARD

NOTICE OF PROPOSED AMENDMENTS

process (E[a]) must be determined in accordance with the
requirements of subsection (b)(6)(D) above.

C) The actual organic mass removal rate must be calculated by
using the results determined in accordance with the
requirements of subsection (b)(9)(B) above and the following
equation:

$$MR = E[b] - A[b]$$

Where:

MR = Actual organic mass removal rate, in kg/hr.

E[b] = Waste volatile organic mass flow entering
process, as determined in accordance with the
requirements of subsection (b)(6)(D) above, in kg/hr.

E[a] = Waste volatile organic mass flow exiting
process, as determined in accordance with the
requirements of subsection (b)(6)(D) above, in kg/hr.

10) Procedure to determine the actual organic mass biodegradation
rate (MR[bio]) for a treated hazardous waste.

A) The actual organic mass biodegradation rate must be
determined based on results for a minimum of three
consecutive runs. The sampling time for each run must be
one hour.

B) The waste organic mass flow entering the process (E[b]) must
be determined in accordance with the requirements of
subsection (b)(6)(D) above.

C) The fraction of organic biodegraded (F[bio]) must be
determined using the procedure specified in 40 CFR Part 63,
Appendix C, incorporated by reference in 35 Ill. Adm. Code
720.111.

D) The actual organic mass biodegradation rate must be
calculated by using the mass flow rates and fraction of
organic biodegraded determined in accordance with the
requirements of subsections (b)(10)(B) and (b)(10)(C) above
and the following equation:

$$MR[bio] = E[b] \times F[bio]$$

Where:

MR[bio] = Actual organic mass biodegradation rate,
in kg/hr.

E[b] = Waste organic mass flow entering process, as
determined in accordance with the requirements of

POLLUTION CONTROL BOARD

NOTICE OF PROPOSED AMENDMENTS

subsection (b)(6)(D) above, in kg/hr.

P[bio] = Fraction of organic biodegraded, as
determined in accordance with the requirements of
subsection (b)(10)(C) above.

c) Procedure to determine the maximum organic vapor pressure of a
hazardous waste in a tank.

1) An owner or operator shall determine the maximum organic vapor
pressure for each hazardous waste placed in a tank using air
emission controls in accordance with standards specified in
Section 725.985(c).

2) An owner or operator shall use either direct measurement, as
specified in subsection (c)(3) above, or knowledge of the waste,
as specified by subsection (c)(4) above, to determine the maximum
organic vapor pressure that is representative of the hazardous
waste composition stored or treated in the tank.

3) To determine the maximum organic vapor pressure of the hazardous
waste by direct measurement, the following procedure must be
used:

A) Representative samples of the waste contained in the tank
must be collected. Sampling must be conducted in accordance
with the requirements specified in "Test Methods for
Evaluating Solid Waste, Physical/Chemical Methods",
incorporated by references in 35 Ill. Adm. Code 720.111.

B) Any of the following methods may be used to analyze the
samples and compute the maximum organic vapor pressure, as
appropriate:

i) Method 25E in 40 CFR Part 60, Appendix A, incorporated
by reference in 35 Ill. Adm. Code 720.111;

ii) Methods described in American Petroleum Institute
Publication 2517, incorporated by reference in 35 Ill.
Adm. Code 720.111;

iii) Methods obtained from standard reference texts;

iv) ASTM Method D 2879-92, incorporated by reference in 35
Ill. Adm. Code 720.111; or

v) Any other method approved by the Agency for this use
by the owner or operator.

4) To determine the maximum organic vapor pressure of the hazardous
waste by knowledge, sufficient information must be prepared and
recorded that documents the maximum organic vapor pressure of the
hazardous waste in the tank. Examples of information that may be
used include: documentation that the waste is generated by a
process for which no organics-containing materials are used or
that the waste is generated by a process for which at other
locations it previously has been determined by direct measurement
that the waste maximum organic vapor pressure is less than the
maximum vapor pressure limit for the appropriate design capacity

POLLUTION CONTROL BOARD

NOTICE OF PROPOSED AMENDMENTS

category specified for the tank.

(Source: Added at 19 Ill. Reg. _____, effective
_____)

Section 725.985 Standards: Tanks

a) This Section applies to owners and operators of tanks subject to this
Subpart into which any hazardous waste is placed except for the
following tanks:

1) A tank in which all hazardous waste entering the tank meets the
conditions specified in Section 725.983(c); or

2) A tank used for biological treatment of hazardous waste in
accordance with the requirements of Section 725.983(c)(2)(D).

b) The owner or operator shall place the hazardous waste into one of the
following tanks:

1) A tank equipped with a cover (e.g., a fixed roof) that is vented
through a closed-vent system to a control device in accordance
with the requirements specified in subsection (d) below;

2) A tank equipped with a fixed roof and internal floating roof in
accordance with the requirements of Section 725.991;

3) A tank equipped with an external floating roof in accordance with
the requirements of Section 725.991; or

4) A pressure tank that is designed to operate as a closed system
such that the tank operates with no detectable organic emissions
at all times that hazardous waste is in the tank except as
provided for in subsection (g) below.

c) As an alternative to complying with subsection (b) above, an owner or
operator may place hazardous waste in a tank equipped with a cover
(e.g., a fixed roof) meeting the requirements specified in subsection
(d)(1) below when the hazardous waste is determined to meet all of the
following conditions:

1) The hazardous waste is neither mixed, stirred, agitated, nor
circulated within the tank by the owner or operator using a
process that results in splashing, frothing, or visible turbulent
flow on the waste surface during normal process operations;

2) The hazardous waste in the tank is not heated by the owner or
operator except during conditions requiring that the waste be
heated to prevent the waste from freezing or to maintain adequate
waste flow conditions for continuing normal process operations;

3) The hazardous waste in the tank is not treated by the owner or
operator using a waste stabilization process or a process that
produces an exothermic reaction; and

4) The maximum organic vapor pressure of the hazardous waste in the
tank as determined using the procedure specified in Section
725.984(c) is less than the following applicable value:

A) If the tank design capacity is equal to or greater than 151
m[3] (5333 ft[3] or 39,887 gal), then the maximum organic

POLLUTION CONTROL BOARD

NOTICE OF PROPOSED AMENDMENTS

vapor pressure must be less than 5.2 kPa (0.75 psia or 39 mm Hg);

B) If the tank design capacity is equal to or greater than 75 m(3) but less than 151 m(3) (5333 ft(3) or 39,887 gal), then the maximum organic vapor pressure must be less than 27.6 kPa (4.0 psia or 207 mm Hg); or

C) If the tank design capacity is less than 75 m(3) (2649 ft(3) or 19,810 gal), then the maximum organic vapor pressure must be less than 76.6 kPa (11.1 psia or 574 mm Hg).

d) To comply with subsection (b)(1) above, the owner or operator shall design, install, operate, and maintain a cover that vents the organic vapors emitted from hazardous waste in the tank through a closed-vent system connected to a control device.

1) The cover must be designed and operated to meet the following requirements:

A) The cover and all cover openings (e.g., access hatches, sampling ports, and gauge wells) must be designed to operate with no detectable organic emissions when all cover openings are secured in a closed, sealed position.

B) Each cover opening must be secured in a closed, sealed position (e.g., covered by a gasketed lid or cap) at all times that hazardous waste is in the tank except as provided for in subsection (f) below.

2) The closed-vent system and control device must be designed and operated in accordance with the requirements of Section 725.988.

e) The owner and operator shall install, operate, and maintain enclosed pipes or other closed systems for the transfer of hazardous waste as described in subsection (e)(1) or (e)(2) below. BOARD NOTE: U.S. EPA considers a drain system that meets the requirements of 40 CFR 61.346(a)(1) or (b)(1) through (b)(3) to be a "closed-system". The Board intends that this meaning be included in the use of that term for the purposes of this Subpart.

1) Transfer all hazardous waste to the tank from another tank, surface impoundment, or container subject to this Subpart, except for those hazardous wastes that meet the conditions specified in Section 725.983(c); and

2) Transfer all hazardous waste from the tank to another tank, surface impoundment, or container subject to this Subpart, except for those hazardous wastes that meet the conditions specified in Section 725.983(c).

f) Each cover opening must be secured in a closed, sealed position (e.g., covered by a gasketed lid) at all times that hazardous waste is in the tank except when it is necessary to use the cover opening to:

1) Add, remove, inspect, or sample the material in the tank;

2) Inspect, maintain, repair, or replace equipment located inside the tank; or

3) Vent gases or vapors from the tank to a closed-vent system connected to a control device that is designed and operated in

POLLUTION CONTROL BOARD

NOTICE OF PROPOSED AMENDMENTS

accordance with the requirements of Section 725.988.

g) One or more safety devices that vent directly to the atmosphere may be used on the tank, cover, closed-vent system, or control device provided each safety device meets all of the following conditions:

1) The safety device is not used for planned or routine venting of organic vapors from the tank or the closed-vent system connected to a control device; and

2) The safety device remains in a closed, sealed position at all times except when an unplanned event requires that the device open for the purpose of preventing physical damage or permanent deformation of the tank, cover, closed-vent system, or control device in accordance with good engineering and safety practices for handling flammable, combustible, explosive, or other hazardous materials. An example of an unplanned event is a sudden power outage.

(Source: Added at 19 Ill. Reg. _____, effective _____)

Section 725.986 Standards: Surface Impoundments

a) This Section applies to owners and operators of surface impoundments subject to this Subpart into which any hazardous waste is placed except for the following surface impoundments:

1) A surface impoundment in which all hazardous waste entering the surface impoundment meets the conditions specified in Section 725.983(c); or

2) A surface impoundment used for biological treatment of hazardous waste in accordance with the requirements of Section 725.983(c)(2)(iv).

b) The owner or operator shall place the hazardous waste into a surface impoundment equipped with a cover (e.g., an air-supported structure or a rigid cover) that is vented through a closed-vent system to a control device meeting the requirements specified in subsection (d) below.

c) As an alternative to complying with subsection (b) above, an owner or operator may place hazardous waste in a surface impoundment equipped with a floating membrane cover meeting the requirements specified in subsection (e) below when the hazardous waste is determined to meet all of the following conditions:

1) The hazardous waste is neither mixed, stirred, agitated, nor circulated within the surface impoundment by the owner or operator using a process that results in splashing, frothing, or visible turbulent flow on the waste surface during normal process operations;

2) The hazardous waste in the surface impoundment is not heated by the owner or operator; and

3) The hazardous waste in the surface impoundment is not treated by

POLLUTION CONTROL BOARD

NOTICE OF PROPOSED AMENDMENTS

the owner or operator using a waste stabilization process or a
process that produces an exothermic reaction.

d) To comply with subsection (b)(1) above, the owner or operator shall
design, install, operate, and maintain a cover that vents the organic
vapors emitted from hazardous waste in the surface impoundment through
a closed-vent system connected to a control device.

1) The cover must be designed, installed, operated, and maintained
to meet the following requirements:

A) The cover and all cover openings (e.g., access hatches,
sampling ports, and gauge wells) must be designed to operate
with no detectable organic emissions when all cover openings
are secured in a closed, sealed position.

B) Each cover opening must be secured in the closed, sealed
position (e.g., covered by a gasketed lid or cap) at all
times that hazardous waste is in the surface impoundment,
except as provided for in subsection (g) below.

C) The closed-vent system and control device must be designed
and operated in accordance with Section 725.988.

e) To comply with subsection (c) above, the owner or operator shall
design, install, operate, and maintain a floating membrane cover the
meets all of the following requirements:

1) The floating membrane cover must be designed, installed, and
operated such that at all times when hazardous waste is in the
surface impoundment, the entire surface area of the hazardous
waste is enclosed by the cover, and any air spaces underneath the
cover are not vented to the atmosphere except during conditions
specified in subsection (h) below.

2) The floating membrane cover and all cover openings (e.g., access
hatches, sampling ports, and gauge wells) must be designed to
operate with no detectable organic emissions when all cover
openings are secured in a closed, sealed position.

3) Each cover opening must be secured in a closed, sealed position
(e.g., covered by a gasketed lid or cap) at all times that
hazardous waste is in the surface impoundment except as provided
for in subsections (g)(1) through (g)(3) below.

4) The synthetic membrane material used for the floating membrane
cover must be either:

A) High density polyethylene with a thickness no less than 2.5
mm; or

B) A material or a composite of different materials determined
to have the following properties:

i) Organic permeability properties that are equivalent to
those of the material specified in subsection
(e)(4)(A) above; and

ii) Chemical and physical properties that maintain the
material integrity for as long as the cover is in use.
Factors that must be considered in selecting the
material include: the effects of contact with the

POLLUTION CONTROL BOARD

NOTICE OF PROPOSED AMENDMENTS

waste managed in the impoundment, weather exposure,
and cover installation and operation practices.

f) The owner or operator shall install, operate, and maintain enclosed
pipes or other closed systems for the transfer of hazardous waste as
described in subsection (f)(1) or (f)(2) below. BOARD NOTE: U.S. EPA
considers a drain system that meets the requirements of 40 CFR
61.346(a)(1) or (b)(1) through (b)(3) to be a "closed-system". The
Board intends that this meaning be included in the use of that term
for the purposes of this Subpart.

1) Transfer all hazardous waste to the surface impoundment from
another tank, surface impoundment, or container subject to this
Subpart, except for those hazardous wastes that meet the
conditions specified in Section 725.983(c); or

2) Transfer all hazardous waste from the surface impoundment to
another tank, surface impoundment, or container subject to this
Subpart, except for those hazardous wastes that meet the
conditions specified in Section 725.983(c).

g) Each cover opening must be secured in the closed, sealed position
(e.g., covered by a gasketed lid or cap) at all times that hazardous
waste is in the surface impoundment except when it is necessary to use
the cover opening to:

1) Add, remove, inspect, or sample the material in the surface
impoundment;

2) Inspect, maintain, repair, or replace equipment located
underneath the cover;

3) Remove treatment residues from the surface impoundment in
accordance with the requirements of 35 Ill. Adm. Code 728.104; or

4) Vent gases or vapors from the surface impoundment to a
closed-vent system connected to a control device that is designed
and operated in accordance with the requirements of Section
725.988.

h) One or more safety devices that vent directly to the atmosphere may be
installed on the cover, closed-vent system, or control device provided
each device meets all of the following conditions:

1) The safety device is not used for planned or routine venting of
organic vapors from the surface impoundment or the closed-vent
system connected to a control device; and

2) The safety device remains in a closed, sealed position at all
times except when an unplanned event requires that the device
open for the purpose of preventing physical damage or permanent
deformation of the cover, closed-vent system, or control device
in accordance with good engineering and safety practices for
handling flammable, combustible, explosive, or other hazardous
materials. An example of an unplanned event is a sudden power
outage.

(Source: Added at 19 Ill. Reg. _____, effective
_____)

Section 725.987 Standards: Containers

a) This Section applies to the owners and operators of containers having design capacities greater than 0.1 m(3) (3.5 ft(3) or 26.4 gal) subject to this Subpart into which any hazardous waste is placed, except for a container in which all hazardous waste entering the container meets the conditions specified in Section 725.983(c).

b) An owner or operator shall manage hazardous waste in containers using the following procedures:

   1) The owner or operator shall place the hazardous waste into one of the following containers, except when a container is used for hazardous waste treatment as required by subsection (b)(2) below:

   A) A container that is equipped with a cover that operates with no detectable organic emissions when all container openings (e.g., lids, bungs, hatches, and sampling ports) are secured in a closed, sealed position. The owner or operator shall determine that a container operates with no detectable emissions by testing each opening on the container for leaks in accordance with Method 21 in 40 CFR Part 60, Appendix A, incorporated by reference in 35 Ill. Adm. Code 720.111, the first time any portion of the hazardous waste is placed into the container. If a leak is detected and cannot be repaired immediately, the hazardous waste must be removed from the container and the container not used to meet the requirements of this subsection until the leak is repaired and the container is retested.

   B) A container having a design capacity less than or equal to 0.46 m(3) (16.2 ft(3) or 121.5 gal) that is equipped with a cover and complies with all applicable U.S. Department of Transportation regulations on packaging hazardous waste for transport under 49 CFR Part 178, incorporated by reference in 35 Ill. Adm. Code 720.111.

   i) A container that is managed in accordance with the requirements of 49 CFR Part 178 for the purpose of complying with this Subpart is not subject to any exceptions to the 49 CFR Part 178 regulations, except as noted in subsection (b)(1)(B)(ii) above.

   ii) A lab pack that is managed in accordance with the requirements of 49 CFR Part 178 for the purpose of complying with this Subpart may comply with the exceptions for combination packagings specified in 49 CFR 173.12(b).

   C) A container that is attached to or forms a part of any truck, trailer, or railcar and that has been demonstrated within the preceding 12 months to be organic vapor tight when all container openings are in a closed, sealed position (e.g., the container hatches or lids are gasketed and latched). For the purpose of meeting the requirements of

this subsection, a container is organic vapor tight if the container sustains a pressure change of not more than 0.75 kPa (0.11 psig or 5.6 mm Hg) within 5 minutes after it is pressurized to a minimum of 4.9 kPa (0.65 psig or 33.7 mm Hg). This condition is to be demonstrated using the pressure test specified in Method 27 of 40 CFR Part 60, Appendix A, incorporated by reference in 35 Ill. Adm. Code 720.111, and a pressure measurement device that has a precision of ± 2.5 mm water and that is capable of measuring above the atmospheric pressure at which the container is to be tested for vapor tightness.

   2) An owner or operator treating hazardous waste in a container by either a waste stabilization process, any process that requires the addition of heat to the waste, or any process that produces an exothermic reaction must meet the following requirements:

   A) Whenever it is necessary for the container to be open during the treatment process, the container must be located inside an enclosure that is vented through a closed-vent system to a control device.

   B) The enclosure must be a structure that is designed and operated in accordance with the following requirements:

   i) The enclosure must be a structure that is designed and operated with sufficient airflow into the structure to capture the organic vapors emitted from the hazardous waste in the container and vent the vapors through the closed-vent system to the control device.

   ii) The enclosure may have permanent or temporary openings to allow worker access, passage of containers through the enclosure by conveyor or other mechanical means, entry of permanent mechanical or electrical equipment, or to direct airflow into the enclosure. The pressure drop across each opening in the enclosure must be maintained at a pressure below atmospheric pressure such that whenever an open container is placed inside the enclosure no organic vapors released from the container exit the enclosure through the opening. The owner or operator shall determine that an enclosure achieves this condition by measuring the pressure drop across each opening in the enclosure. If the pressure within the enclosure is equal to or greater than atmospheric pressure then the enclosure does not meet the requirements of this Section.

   C) The closed-vent system and control device must be designed and operated in accordance with the requirements of Section 725.988.

   3) An owner or operator transferring hazardous waste into a container having a design capacity greater than 0.46 m(3) (16.2 ft(3) or 121.5 gal) shall meet the following requirements:

POLLUTION CONTROL BOARD

NOTICE OF PROPOSED AMENDMENTS

A) Hazardous waste transfer by pumping must be performed using a conveyance system that uses a tube (e.g., pipe, hose) to add the waste into the container. During transfer of the waste into the container, the cover must remain in place and all container openings must be maintained in a closed, sealed position except for those openings through which the tube enters the container and as provided for in subsection (c) below. The tube must be positioned in a manner such that either the:

   i) Tube outlet continuously remains submerged below the waste surface at all times waste is flowing through the tube;

   ii) Lower bottom edge of the tube outlet is located at a distance no greater than two inside diameters of the tube or 15.25 cm (0.50 ft or 6.0 in), whichever distance is greater, from the bottom of the container at all times waste is flowing through the tube; or

   iii) Tube is connected to a permanent port mounted on the bottom of the container so that the lower edge of the port opening inside the container is located at a distance equal to or less than 15.25 cm (0.50 ft or 6.0 in) from the container bottom.

B) Hazardous waste transferred by a means other than pumping must be performed such that during transfer of the waste into the container, the cover remains in place and all container openings are maintained in a closed, sealed position except for those openings through which the hazardous waste is added and as provided for in subsection (d) below.

c) Each container opening must be maintained in a closed, sealed position (e.g., covered by a gasketed lid) at all times that hazardous waste is in the container; except when it is necessary to use the opening to:

   Add, remove, inspect, or sample the material in the container;

   Inspect, maintain, repair, or replace equipment located inside the container; or

   3) Vent gases or vapors from a cover located over or enclosing an open container to a closed-vent system connected to a control device that is designed and operated in accordance with the requirements of Section 725.988.

d) One or more safety devices that vent directly to the atmosphere may be used on the container, cover, enclosure, closed-vent system, or control device provided each device meets all of the following conditions:

   1) The safety device is not used for planned or routine venting of organic vapors from the container, cover, enclosure, or closed-vent system connected to a control device; and

   2) The safety device remains in a closed, sealed position at all times except when an unplanned event requires that the device

POLLUTION CONTROL BOARD

NOTICE OF PROPOSED AMENDMENTS

open for the purpose of preventing physical damage or permanent deformation of the container, cover, enclosure, closed-vent system, or control device in accordance with good engineering and safety practices for handling flammable, combustible, explosive, or other hazardous materials. An example of an unplanned event is a sudden power outage.

(Source: Added at 19 Ill. Reg. _____, effective _____)

Section 725.988 Standards: Closed-vent Systems and Control Devices

a) This Section applies to each closed-vent system and control device installed and operated by the owner or operator to control air emissions in accordance with standards of this Subpart.

b) The closed-vent system must meet the following requirements:

   1) The closed-vent system must route the gases, vapors, and fumes emitted from the hazardous waste in the waste management unit to a control device that meets the requirements specified in subsection (c) below.

   2) The closed-vent system must be designed and operated in accordance with the requirements specified in Section 725.933(1).

   3) If the closed-vent system contains one or more bypass devices that could be used to divert all or a portion of the gases, vapors, or fumes from entering the control device, the owner or operator shall meet the following requirements:

     A) For each bypass device except as provided for in subsection (b)(3)(B) below, the owner or operator shall either:

       i) Install, calibrate, maintain, and operate a flow indicator at the inlet to the bypass device that indicates at least once every 15 minutes whether gas, vapor, or fume flow is present in the bypass device; or

       ii) Secure the valve installed at the inlet to the bypass device in the closed position using a car-seal or a lock-and-key type configuration. The owner or operator shall visually inspect the seal or closure mechanism at least once every month to verify that the valve is maintained in the closed position.

     B) Low leg drains, high point bleeds, analyzer vents, open-ended valves or lines, and safety devices are not subject to the requirements of subsection (b)(3)(A) above.

c) The control device must meet the following requirements:

   1) The control device must be one of the following devices:

     A) A control device designed and operated to reduce the total organic content of the inlet vapor stream vented to the control device by at least 95 percent by weight;

     B) An enclosed combustion device designed and operated in

POLLUTION CONTROL BOARD

NOTICE OF PROPOSED AMENDMENTS

accordance with the requirements of Section 725.933(g); or

C) A flare designed and operated in accordance with the requirements of Section 725.933(d).

2) The control device must be operating at all times when gases, vapors, or fumes are vented from the waste management unit through the closed-vent system to the control device.

3) The owner or operator using a carbon adsorption system to comply with subsection (c)(1) above shall operate and maintain the control device in accordance with the following requirements:

A) Following the initial startup of the control device, all activated carbon in the control device must be replaced with fresh carbon on a regular basis in accordance with the requirements of Section 725.933(g) or 725.933(h);

B) All carbon removed from the control device must be managed in accordance with the requirements of Section 725.933(i).

4) An owner or operator using a control device other than a thermal vapor incinerator, flare, boiler, process heater, condenser, or carbon adsorption system to comply with subsection (c)(1) above shall operate and maintain the control device in accordance with the requirements of Section 725.933(i).

5) The owner or operator shall demonstrate that a control device achieves the performance requirements of subsection (c)(1) above as follows:

A) An owner or operator shall demonstrate using either a performance test, as specified in subsection (c)(5)(C) below, or a design analysis, as specified in subsection (c)(5)(D) below, the performance of each control device except for the following:

i) A flare;

ii) A boiler or process heater with a design heat input capacity of 44 megawatts or greater;

iii) A boiler or process heater into which the vent stream is introduced with the primary fuel;

iv) A boiler or process heater burning hazardous waste for which the owner or operator has been issued a final permit 35 Ill. Adm. Code 703 and 705 and that is designed and operated in accordance with the requirements of 35 Ill. Adm. Code 726.Subpart H; or

v) A boiler or process heater burning hazardous waste for which the owner or operator has certified compliance with the interim status requirements of 35 Ill. Adm. Code 726.Subpart H.

B) An owner or operator shall demonstrate the performance of each flare in accordance with the requirements specified in Section 725.933(e).

C) For a performance test conducted to meet the requirements of subsection (c)(5)(A) above, the owner or operator shall use the test methods and procedures specified in Section

POLLUTION CONTROL BOARD

NOTICE OF PROPOSED AMENDMENTS

725.934(c)(1) through (c)(4).

D) For a design analysis conducted to meet the requirements of subsection (c)(5)(A) above, the design analysis must meet the requirements specified in Section 725.935(b)(4)(C).

E) The owner or operator shall demonstrate that a carbon adsorption system achieves the performance requirements of subsection (c)(1) above based on the total quantity of organics vented to the atmosphere from all carbon adsorption system equipment that is used for organic adsorption, organic desorption or carbon regeneration, organic recovery, and carbon disposal.

6) If the owner or operator and the Agency do not agree on a demonstration of control device performance using a design analysis, then the disagreement must be resolved using the results of a performance test performed by the owner or operator in accordance with the requirements of subsection (c)(5)(C) above. The Agency may choose to have an authorized representative observe the performance test.

(Source: Added at 19 Ill. Reg. _____, effective _____)

Section 725.989 Inspection and Monitoring Requirements

a) This Section applies to an owner or operator using air emission controls in accordance with the requirements of Sections 725.985 through 725.988.

b) Each cover used in accordance with requirements of Sections 725.985 through 725.987 must be visually inspected and monitored for detectable organic emissions by the owner or operator using the procedure specified in subsection (f) below, except as follows:

1) An owner or operator is exempted from performing the cover inspection and monitoring requirements specified in subsection (f) below for the following tank covers:

A) A tank internal floating roof that is inspected and monitored in accordance with the requirements of Section 725.991; or

B) A tank external floating roof that is inspected and monitored in accordance with the requirements of Section 725.991.

2) If a tank is buried partially or entirely underground, an owner or operator is required to perform the cover inspection and monitoring requirements specified in subsection (f) below only for those portions of the tank cover and those connections to the tank cover or tank body (e.g., fill ports, access hatches, gauge wells, etc.) that extend to or above the ground surface and can be opened to the atmosphere.

3) An owner or operator is exempted from performing the cover

POLLUTION CONTROL BOARD

NOTICE OF PROPOSED AMENDMENTS

inspection and monitoring requirements specified in subsection
(f) below for a container that meets all requirements specified
in either Section 725.987(b)(1)(B) or 725.987(b)(1)(C).

4) An owner or operator is exempted from performing the cover
inspection and monitoring requirements specified in subsection
(f) below for an enclosure used to control all emissions from
containers in accordance with the requirements of Section
725.987(b)(2).

c) Each closed-vent system used in accordance with the requirements of
Section 725.988 must be inspected and monitored by the owner or
operator in accordance with the procedure specified in Section
725.933(1).

d) Each control device used in accordance with the requirements of
Section 725.988 must be inspected and monitored by the owner or
operator in accordance with the procedure specified in Section
725.933(f).

e) The owner or operator shall develop and implement a written plan and
schedule to perform all inspection and monitoring requirements of this
section. The owner or operator shall incorporate this plan and
schedule into the facility inspection plan required under 35 Ill. Adm.
Code 725.115.

f) Inspection and monitoring of a cover in accordance with the
requirements of subsection (b) above must be performed as follows:

1) The cover and all cover openings must be initially visually
inspected and monitored for detectable organic emissions on or
before the date that the tank, surface impoundment, or container
using the cover becomes subject to the provisions of this Subpart
and at other times as requested by the Agency.

2) At least once every 6 months following the initial visual
inspection and monitoring for detectable organic emissions
required under subsection (f)(1) above, the owner and operator
shall visually inspect and monitor the cover and each cover
opening except for following cover openings:

A) A cover opening that has continuously remained in a closed,
sealed position for the entire period since the last time
the cover opening was visually inspected and monitored for
detectable emissions;

B) A cover opening that is designated as unsafe to inspect and
monitor in accordance with subsection (f)(5) below;

C) A cover opening on a cover installed and placed in operation
before December 6, 1994 that is designated as difficult to
inspect and monitor in accordance with subsection (f)(6)
below.

3) To visually inspect a cover, the owner or operator shall view the
entire cover surface and each cover opening in a closed, sealed
position for evidence of any defect that may affect the ability
of the cover or cover opening to continue to operate with no
detectable organic emissions. A visible hole, gap, tear, or

POLLUTION CONTROL BOARD

NOTICE OF PROPOSED AMENDMENTS

split in the cover surface or a cover opening is defined as a
leak that must be repaired in accordance with subsection (f)(7)
below.

4) To monitor a cover for detectable organic emissions, the owner or
operator shall use the following procedure:

A) Method 21 in 40 CFR Part 60, Appendix A, incorporated by
reference in 35 Ill. Adm. Code 720.111, to test each cover
seal and cover connection for detectable organic emissions.
Seals on floating membrane covers must be monitored around
the entire perimeter of the cover at locations spaced no
greater than 2 meters apart.

B) For all cover connections and seals except for the seals
around a rotating shaft that passes through a cover opening,
if the monitoring instrument indicates detectable organic
emissions (i.e., an instrument concentration reading greater
than 500 ppmv plus the background level), then a leak is
detected. Each detected leak must be repaired in accordance
with subsection (f)(7) below.

C) For the seals around a rotating shaft that passes through a
cover opening, if the monitoring instrument indicates a
concentration reading greater than 10,000 ppmv, then a leak
is detected. Each detected leak must be repaired in
accordance with subsection (f)(7) below.

5) An owner or operator may designate a cover as an unsafe to
inspect and monitor cover if all of the following conditions are
met:

A) The owner or operator determines that inspection or
monitoring of the cover would expose a worker to dangerous,
hazardous, or other unsafe conditions.

B) The owner or operator develops and implements a written plan
and schedule to inspect the cover using the procedure
specified in subsection (f)(3) above and monitor the cover
using the procedure specified in subsection (f)(4) below as
frequently as practicable during those times when a worker
can safely access the cover.

6) An owner or operator may designate a cover installed and placed
in operation before December 6, 1994, as a difficult to inspect
and monitor cover if all of the following conditions are met:

A) The owner or operator determines that inspection or
monitoring the cover requires elevating a worker to a height
greater than 2 meters (6.6 ft) above a support surface; and

B) The owner and operator develops and implements a written
plan and schedule to inspect the cover using the procedure
specified in subsection (f)(3) above, and to monitor the
cover using the procedure specified in subsection (f)(4)
above at least once per calendar year.

7) When a leak is detected by either of the methods specified in
subsection (f)(3) or (f)(4) above, the owner or operator shall

repair the leak in the following manner:

A) The owner or operator shall make a first attempt at repairing the leak no later than 5 calendar days after the leak is detected. Repair of the leak must be completed as soon as practicable, but no later than 15 calendar days after the leak is detected. If repair of the leak cannot be completed within the 15-day period, except as provided in subsection (f)(7)(B) below, then the owner or operator shall not add hazardous waste to the tank, surface impoundment, or container on which the cover is installed until the repair of the leak is completed.

B) Repair of a leak detected on a cover installed on a tank or surface impoundment may be delayed beyond 15 calendar days if the owner or operator determines that both of the following conditions occur:

i) Repair of the leak requires first emptying the contents of the tank or surface impoundment; and

ii) Temporary removal of the tank or surface impoundment from service will result in the unscheduled cessation of production from the process unit or operation of the waste management unit that is generating the hazardous waste managed in the tank or surface impoundment.

C) Repair of a leak determined by the owner or operator to meet the conditions specified in subsection (f)(7)(B) above must be performed at the next time the process, system, or waste management unit that is generating the hazardous waste managed in the tank or surface impoundment stops operation for any reason.

(Source: Added at 19 Ill. Reg. _____, effective _____.)

Section 725.990 Recordkeeping Requirements

a) Each owner or operator of a facility subject to requirements in this Subpart shall record and maintain the following information as applicable:

1) Documentation for each cover installed on a tank in accordance with the requirements of Section 725.985(b)(2) or 725.985(b)(3) that includes information prepared by the owner or operator or provided by the cover manufacturer or vendor describing the cover design, and certification by the owner or operator that the cover meets the applicable design specifications as listed in Section 725.985(c).

2) Documentation for each floating membrane cover installed on a surface impoundment in accordance with the requirements of Section 725.986(c) that includes information prepared by the

owner or operator or provided by the cover manufacturer or vendor describing the cover design, and certification by the owner or operator that the cover meets the specifications listed in Section 725.986(e).

3) Documentation for each enclosure used to control air emissions from containers in accordance with the requirements of Section 725.987(b)(2)(A) that includes information prepared by the owner or operator or provided by the manufacturer or vendor describing the enclosure design, and certification by the owner or operator that the enclosure meets the specifications listed in Section 725.987(b)(2)(B).

4) Documentation for each closed-vent system and control device installed in accordance with the requirements of Section 725.988 that includes:

A) Certification that is signed and dated by the owner or operator stating that the control device is designed to operate at the performance level documented by a design analysis, as specified in subsection (a)(4)(B) below, or by performance tests, as specified in subsection (a)(4)(C) below, when the tank, surface impoundment, or container is or would be operating at capacity or the highest level reasonably expected to occur.

B) If a design analysis is used, then design documentation as specified in Section 725.935(b)(4). The documentation must include information prepared by the owner or operator or provided by the control device manufacturer or vendor that describes the control device design in accordance with Section 725.935(b)(4)(C) and certification by the owner or operator that the control equipment meets the applicable specifications.

C) If performance tests are used, then a performance test plan as specified in Section 725.935(b)(3) and all test results.

D) Information as required by Sections 725.935(c)(1) and 725.935(c)(2).

5) Records for all Method 27 tests performed by the owner or operator for each container used to meet the requirements of Section 725.987(b)(1)(C).

6) Records for all visual inspections conducted in accordance with the requirements of Section 725.989.

7) Records for all monitoring for detectable organic emissions conducted in accordance with the requirements of Section 725.989.

8) Records of the date of each attempt to repair a leak, repair methods applied, and the date of successful repair.

9) Records for all continuous monitoring conducted in accordance with the requirements of Section 725.988.

10) Records of the management of carbon removed from a carbon adsorption system conducted in accordance with Section 725.988(c)(3)(B).

POLLUTION CONTROL BOARD

NOTICE OF PROPOSED AMENDMENTS

11) Records for all inspections of each cover installed on a tank in accordance with the requirements of Section 725.985(b)(2) or Section 725.985(b)(3) that includes information as listed in Section 725.991(c).

b) An owner or operator electing to use air emission controls for a tank in accordance with the conditions specified in Section 725.985(c) shall record the following information:

1) The date and time each waste sample is collected for direct measurement of maximum organic vapor pressure in accordance with Section 725.984(c).

2) The results of each determination for the maximum organic vapor pressure of the waste in the tank performed in accordance with Section 725.984(c).

3) The records specifying the tank dimensions and design capacity.

c) An owner or operator electing to use air emission controls for a tank in accordance with the requirements of Section 725.991 shall record the information required by Section 725.991(c).

d) An owner or operator electing not to use air emission controls for a particular tank, surface impoundment, or container subject to this Subpart in accordance with the conditions specified in Section 725.983(c) shall record the information used by the owner or operator for each waste determination (e.g., test results, measurements, calculations, and other documentation) in the facility operating log. If analysis results for waste samples are used for the waste determination, then the owner or operator shall record the date, time, and location that each waste sample is collected in accordance with applicable requirements of Section 725.984.

e) An owner or operator electing to comply with requirements in accordance with Section 725.983(c)(2)(F) or 725.983(c)(2)(B) shall record the identification number for the incinerator, boiler, or industrial furnace in which the hazardous waste is treated.

f) An owner or operator designating a cover as unsafe to inspect and monitor pursuant to Section 725.989(f)(5) or difficult to inspect and monitor pursuant to Section 725.989(f)(6) shall record in a log that is kept in the facility operating record the following information:

1) A list of identification numbers for tanks with covers that are designated as unsafe to inspect and monitor in accordance with the requirements of Section 725.989(f)(5), an explanation for each cover stating why the cover is unsafe to inspect and monitor, and the plan and schedule for inspecting and monitoring each cover.

2) A list of identification numbers for tanks with covers that are designated as difficult to inspect and monitor in accordance with the requirements of Section 725.989(f)(6), an explanation for each cover stating why the cover is difficult to inspect and monitor, and the plan and schedule for inspecting and monitoring each cover.

g) All records required by subsections (a) through (f) above, except as

POLLUTION CONTROL BOARD

NOTICE OF PROPOSED AMENDMENTS

required in subsections (a)(1) through (a)(4) above, must be maintained in the operating record for a minimum of 3 years. All records required by subsections (a)(1) through (a)(4) above must be maintained in the operating record until the air emission control equipment is replaced or otherwise no longer in service.

h) The owner or operator of a facility that is subject to this Subpart and to the control device standards in 40 CFR Part 60, Subpart VV, or 40 CFR Part 61, Subpart V, incorporated by reference in 35 Ill. Adm. Code 270.111, may elect to demonstrate compliance with the applicable Sections of this Subpart by documentation either pursuant to this Subpart, or pursuant to the provisions of 40 CFR Part 60, Subpart VV or 40 CFR Part 61, Subpart V, to the extent that the documentation required by 40 CFR Parts 60 or 61 duplicates the documentation required by this Section.

(Source: Added at 19 Ill. Reg. _____, effective _____)

Section 725.991 Alternative Tank Emission Control Requirements

a) This Section applies to owners and operators of tanks electing to comply with Section 725.985(b)(2) or (b)(3).

1) The owner or operator electing to comply with Section 725.985(b)(2) shall design, install, operate, and maintain a fixed roof and internal floating roof that meet the following requirements.

A) The fixed roof must comply with the requirements of Section 725.985(d)(1). The internal floating roof must rest or float on the waste surface (but not necessarily in complete contact with it) inside a tank that has a fixed roof. The internal floating roof must be floating on the waste surface at all times, except during initial fill and during those intervals when the tank is completely emptied or subsequently emptied and refilled. When the roof is resting on the leg supports, the process of filling, emptying, or refilling must be continuous and must be accomplished as rapidly as possible.

B) Each internal floating roof must be equipped with one of the following closure devices between the wall of the tank and the edge of the internal floating roof:

i) A foam- or liquid-filled seal mounted in contact with the waste (liquid-mounted seal). A liquid-mounted seal means a foam- or liquid-filled seal mounted in contact with the waste between the wall of the tank and the floating roof continuously around the circumference of the tank.

ii) Two seals mounted one above the other so that each forms a continuous closure that completely covers the

POLLUTION CONTROL BOARD

NOTICE OF PROPOSED AMENDMENTS

space between the wall of the tank and the edge of the
internal floating roof. The lower seal may be
vapor-mounted, but both must be continuous.

iii) A mechanical shoe seal. A mechanical shoe seal is a
metal sheet held vertically against the wall of the
tank by springs or weighted levers and is connected by
braces to the floating roof. A flexible coated fabric
(envelope) spans the annular space between the metal
sheet and the floating roof.

C) Each opening in a noncontact internal floating roof except
for automatic bleeder vents (vacuum breaker vents) and the
rim space vents is to provide a projection below the waste
surface.

D) Each opening in the internal floating roof except for leg
sleeves, automatic bleeder vents, rim space vents, column
wells, ladder wells, sample wells, and stub drains is to be
equipped with a cover or lid that is to be maintained in a
closed position at all times (i.e., no visible gap), except
when the device is in actual use. The cover or lid must be
equipped with a gasket. Covers on each access hatch and
automatic gauge float well must be bolted, except when they
are in use.

E) Automatic bleeder vents must be equipped with a gasket and
are to be closed at all times when the roof is floating,
except when the roof is being floated off or is being landed
on the roof leg supports.

F) Rim space vents must be equipped with a gasket and are to be
set to open only when the internal floating roof is not
floating or at the manufacturer's recommended setting.

G) Each penetration of the internal floating roof for the
purpose of sampling must be a sample well. The sample well
must have a slit fabric cover that covers at least 90
percent of the opening.

H) Each penetration of the internal floating roof that allows
for passage of a column supporting the fixed roof must have
a flexible fabric sleeve seal or a gasketed sliding cover.

I) Each penetration of the internal floating roof that allows
for passage of a ladder must have a gasketed sliding cover.

2) The owner or operator electing to comply with Section
725.985(b)(3) shall design, install, operate, and maintain an
external floating roof that meets the following requirements:

A) Each external floating roof must be equipped with a closure
device between the wall of the tank and the roof edge. The
closure device is to consist of two seals, one above the
other. The lower seal is referred to as the primary seal,
and the upper seal is referred to as the secondary seal.

i) The primary seal must be either a mechanical shoe seal
or a liquid-mounted seal. Except as provided in

POLLUTION CONTROL BOARD

NOTICE OF PROPOSED AMENDMENTS

subsection (b)(2)(D) below, the seal must completely
cover the annular space between the edge of the
floating roof and tank wall.

ii) The secondary seal must completely cover the annular
space between the external floating roof and the wall
of the tank in a continuous fashion except as allowed
in subsection (b)(2)(D) below.

B) Except for automatic bleeder vents and rim space vents, each
opening in a noncontact external floating roof must provide
a projection below the waste surface. Except for automatic
bleeder vents, rim space vents, roof drains, and leg
sleeves, each opening in the roof is to be equipped with a
gasketed cover, seal, or lid that is to be maintained in a
closed position at all times (i.e., no visible gap), except
when the device is in actual use. Automatic bleeder vents
are to be closed at all times when the roof is floating,
except when the roof is being floated off or is being landed
on the roof leg supports. Rim vents are to be set to open
when the roof is being floated off the roof leg supports or
at the manufacturer's recommended setting. Automatic
bleeder vents and rim space vents are to be gasketed. Each
emergency roof drain is to be provided with a slotted
membrane fabric cover that covers at least 90 percent of the
area of the opening.

C) The roof must be floating on the waste at all times (i.e.,
off the roof leg supports), except during initial fill until
the roof is lifted off leg supports and when the tank is
completely emptied and subsequently refilled. The process
of filling, emptying, or refilling when the roof is resting
on the leg supports must be continuous and must be
accomplished as rapidly as possible.

3) The owner or operator may elect to comply with Section
725.985(b)(2) or (b)(3) using an alternative means of emission
limitation for which U.S. EPA has published a Federal Register
notice in accordance with the requirements of 40 CFR 60.114b
permitting its use as an alternative means for the purpose of
compliance with 40 CFR 60.112b.

b) Monitoring and inspection of the control equipment described in
subsection (a) above must be conducted as follows:

1) After installation, owners and operators of internal floating
roofs shall:

A) Visually inspect the internal floating roof, the primary
seal, and the secondary seal (if one is in service), prior
to filling the tank with waste. If there are holes, tears,
or other openings in the primary seal, the secondary seal,
or the seal fabric, or defects in the internal floating
roof, or both, the owner or operator shall repair the items
before filling the tank.

POLLUTION CONTROL BOARD

NOTICE OF PROPOSED AMENDMENTS

B) For tanks equipped with a liquid-mounted or mechanical shoe primary seal, visually inspect the internal floating roof and the primary seal or the secondary seal (if one is in service) through manholes and roof hatches on the fixed roof at least once every 12 months after initial fill. If the internal floating roof is not resting on the surface of the waste inside the tank, or there is liquid accumulated on the roof, or the seal is detached, or there are holes or tears in the seal fabric, the owner or operator shall repair the items or empty and remove the tank from service within 45 days. If a failure that is detected during inspections required in this subsection cannot be repaired within 45 days and if the tank cannot be emptied within 45 days, the Agency may grant the owner or operator a provisional variance pursuant to Section 35(b) of the Act that extends this time for up to 30 days. Such a request for an extension must comply with 35 Ill. Adm. Code 180, and it must document that alternate capacity is unavailable and specify a schedule of actions the owner or operator will take that will assure that the control equipment will be repaired or the tank will be emptied as soon as possible.

C) For tanks equipped with a double-seal system as specified in subsection (a)(1)(A)(ii) above:
   i) Visually inspect the tank, as specified in subsection (b)(1)(D) below, at least every 5 years; or
   ii) Visually inspect the waste as specified in subsection (b)(1)(B) above.

D) Visually inspect the internal floating roof, the primary seal, the secondary seal (if one is in service), gaskets, slotted membranes, and sleeve seals (if any) each time the tank is emptied and degassed. If the internal floating roof has defects; the primary seal has holes, tears, or other openings in the seal or the seal fabric; the secondary seal has holes, tears, or other openings in the seal or the seal fabric; the gaskets no longer close off the waste surfaces from the atmosphere; or the slotted membrane has more than 10 percent open area, the owner or operator shall repair the items as necessary, so that none of the conditions specified in this subsection exist before refilling the tank with waste. In no event may inspections conducted in accordance with this provision occur at intervals greater than 10 years, in the case of tanks conducting the annual visual inspection as specified in subsection (b)(1)(B) above, or at intervals no greater than 5 years, in the case of tanks specified in subsection (b)(1)(C) above.

E) Notify the Agency in writing at least 30 days prior to the filling or refilling of each tank for which an inspection is required by subsections (b)(1)(A) and (b)(1)(D) above, to afford the Agency the opportunity to have an observer present. If the inspection required by subsection (b)(1)(D) above is not planned and the owner or operator could not have known about the inspection 30 days in advance of refilling the tank, the owner or operator shall notify the Agency at least 7 days prior to the refilling of the tank. Notification must be made by telephone immediately followed by written documentation demonstrating why the inspection was unplanned. Alternatively, this notification, including the written documentation, may be made in writing and sent by express mail so that it is received by the Agency at least 7 days prior to the refilling.

2) After installation, the owner or operator of an external floating roof shall:
   A) Determine the gap areas and maximum gap widths between the primary seal and the wall of the tank and between the secondary seal and the wall of the tank according to the following frequency:
      i) Measurements of gaps between the tank wall and the primary seal (seal gaps) must be performed during the hydrostatic testing of the tank or within 60 days of the initial fill with waste and at least once every five years thereafter.
      ii) Measurements of gaps between the tank wall and the secondary seal must be performed within 60 days of the initial fill with waste and at least once per year thereafter.
      iii) If any tank ceases to hold waste for a period of one year or more, subsequent introduction of waste into the tank must be considered an initial fill for the purposes of subsections (b)(2)(A)(i) and (b)(2)(A)(ii) above.
   B) Determine the gap widths and areas in the primary and secondary seals individually by the following procedures:
      i) Measure seal gaps, if any, at one or more floating roof levels when the roof is floating off the roof leg supports.
      ii) Measure seal gaps around the entire circumference of the tank in each place where a 0.32-cm diameter uniform probe passes freely (without forcing or binding against the seal) between the seal and the wall of the tank and measure the circumferential distance of each such location.
      iii) Determine the total surface area of each gap described in subsection (b)(2)(B)(ii) above by using probes of various widths to measure accurately the actual distance from the tank wall to the seal and multiplying each such width by its respective

POLLUTION CONTROL BOARD

NOTICE OF PROPOSED AMENDMENTS

circumferential distance.

C) Add the gap surface area of each gap location for the primary seal and the secondary seal individually and divide the sum for each seal by the nominal diameter of the tank and compare each ratio to the respective standards in subsection (b)(2)(D) below.

D) Make necessary repairs or empty the tank within 45 days of identification in any inspection for seals not meeting the following requirements:

i) The accumulated area of gaps between the tank wall and the mechanical shoe or liquid-mounted primary seal must not exceed 212 cm(2) per meter (10.0 in(2) per foot) of tank diameter, and the width of any portion of any gap must not exceed 3.81 cm (1.50 in). One end of the mechanical shoe is to extend into the waste contained in the tank, and the other end is to extend a minimum vertical distance of 61 cm (24.0 in) above the waste surface. There are to be no holes, tears, or other openings in the shoe, seal fabric, or seal envelope.

ii) The secondary seal is to meet the following requirements: The secondary seal is to be installed above the primary seal so that it completely covers the space between the roof edge and the tank wall except as provided in subsection (b)(2)(B)(iii) above. The accumulated area of gaps between the tank wall and the secondary seal must not exceed 21.2 cm(2) per meter (1.00 in(2) per foot) of tank diameter, and the width of any portion of any gap must not exceed 1.27 cm (0.500 in). There are to be no holes, tears, or other openings in the seal or seal fabric.

E) If a failure that is detected during inspections required in subsection (b)(2)(A) above cannot be repaired within 45 days and if the tank cannot be emptied within 45 days, the Agency may grant the owner or operator a provisional variance pursuant to Section 35(b) of the Act that extends this time for up to 30 days. Such a request for an extension must comply with 35 Ill. Adm. Code 180, and it must include a demonstration of the unavailability of alternate capacity and a specification of a schedule that will assure that the control equipment will be repaired or the tank will be emptied as soon as possible.

F) Notify the Agency 30 days in advance of any gap measurements required by subsection (b)(2)(A) above, to afford the Agency the opportunity to have an observer present.

G) Visually inspect the external floating roof, the primary seal, secondary seal, and fittings each time the vessel is emptied and degassed.

POLLUTION CONTROL BOARD

NOTICE OF PROPOSED AMENDMENTS

If the external floating roof has defects, the primary seal has holes, tears, or other openings in the seal or the seal fabric, or the secondary seal has holes, tears, or other openings in the seal or the seal fabric, the owner or operator shall repair the items as necessary so that none of the conditions specified in this subsection exist before filling or refilling the tank with waste.

ii) For all the inspections required by this subsection, the owner or operator shall notify the Agency in writing at least 30 days prior to the filling or refilling of each tank to afford the Agency the opportunity to inspect the tank prior to refilling. If the inspection required by this subsection is not planned and the owner or operator could not have known about the inspection 30 days in advance of refilling the tank, the owner or operator shall notify the Agency at least seven days prior to the refilling of the tank. Notification must be made by telephone immediately followed by written documentation demonstrating why the inspection was unplanned. Alternatively, this notification, including the written documentation, may be made in writing and sent by express mail so that it is received by the Agency at least seven days prior to the refilling.

c) Owners and operators that elect to install and operate the control equipment in subsection (a) above shall include the following information in the operating record in accordance with the requirements of Section 725.990(a)(1) and (a)(11):

1) Internal floating roof.

A) Documentation that describes the control equipment design and certifies that the control equipment meets the specifications of subsections (a)(1) and (b)(1) above.

B) Records of each inspection performed as required by subsections (b)(1)(A) through (b)(1)(D) above. Each record must identify the tank on which the inspection was performed and must contain the date the tank was inspected and the observed condition of each component of the control equipment (seals, internal floating roof, and fittings).

C) If any of the conditions described in subsection (b)(1)(B) above are detected during the annual visual inspection required by subsection (b)(1)(B) above, the records must identify the tank, the nature of the defects, and the date the tank was emptied or the nature of and date the repair was made.

D) After each inspection required by subsection (b)(1)(C) above that finds holes or tears in the seal or seal fabric, or defects in the internal floating roof, or other control

POLLUTION CONTROL BOARD

NOTICE OF PROPOSED AMENDMENTS

equipment defects listed in subsection (b)(1)(B) above, the records must identify the tank and the reason it did not meet the specifications of subsection (a)(1) or (b)(1)(C) above and describe each repair made.

2) External floating roof.

A) Documentation that describes the control equipment design and certifies that the control equipment meets the specifications of subsections (a)(2) and (b)(2)(B) through (b)(2)(D) above.

B) Records of each gap measurement performed as required by subsection (b)(2) above. Each record must identify the tank in which the measurement was performed, the date of measurement, the raw data obtained in the measurement, and the calculations described in subsections (b)(2)(B) and (b)(2)(C) above.

C) Records for each seal gap measurement that detects gaps exceeding the limitations specified by subsection (b)(2)(D) above that identifies the tank, the date the tank was emptied or the repairs made, and the nature of the repair.

(Source: Added at 19 Ill. Reg. _____, effective _____)

SUBPART DD: CONTAINMENT BUILDINGS

Section 725.1102 Closure and ~~post-closure care~~ Post-closure Care

a) At closure of a containment building, the owner or operator must remove or decontaminate all waste residues, contaminated containment system components (liners, etc.), contaminated subsoils, and structures and equipment contaminated with waste and leachate, and manage them as hazardous waste unless 35 Ill. Adm. Code 721.103(eg) applies. The closure plan, closure activities, cost estimates for closure, and financial responsibility for containment buildings must meet all of the requirements specified in 725.Subparts G and H.

b) If, after removing or decontaminating all residues and making all reasonable efforts to effect removal or decontamination of contaminated components, subsoils, structures, and equipment as required in subsection (a) above, the owner or operator finds that not all contaminated subsoils can be practicably removed or decontaminated, he must close the facility and perform post-closure care in accordance with the closure and post-closure requirements that apply to landfills (35 Ill. Adm. Code 725.310). In addition, for the purposes of closure, post-closure, and financial responsibility, such a containment building is then considered to be a landfill, and the owner or operator must meet all the requirements for landfills specified in 725.Subparts G and H.

POLLUTION CONTROL BOARD

NOTICE OF PROPOSED AMENDMENTS

(Source: Amended at 19 Ill. Reg. _____, effective _____)

POLLUTION CONTROL BOARD

NOTICE OF PROPOSED AMENDMENTS

1) Heading of the Part: Land Disposal Restrictions

2) Code citation: 35 Ill. Adm. Code 728

3) Section numbers:

	Proposed action:
728.101, 728.102, 728.107	Amended
728.109, 728.130, 728.133	Amended
728.138	New Section
728.140, 728.141, 728.142	Amended
728.143, 728.145, 728.146	Amended
728.148	New Section
728.App. D	Amended
728.App. E	Repealed
728.App. J	New Section
728.Tab. A, 728.Tab. B, 728.Tab. C	Amended
728.Tab. D, 728.Tab. E, 728.Tab. G	Amended
728.Tab. T, 728.Tab. U	New Section

4) Statutory authority: 415 ILCS 5/22.4 and 27.

5) A complete description of the subjects and issues involved:

A more detailed description is contained in the Board's proposed opinion of March 2, 1995, in R95-4 and R95-6 (consolidated), which opinion is available from the address below. Section 22.4(a) of the Environmental Protection Act (415 ILCS 5/22.4(a)) provides that Section 5-35 of the Administrative Procedure Act (5 ILCS 100/5-35) shall not apply. Because this rulemaking is not subject to Section 5-35 of the APA, it is not subject to first notice or to second notice review by JCAR.

This rulemaking updates Parts 700, 702, 703, 705, 720, 721, 722, 723, 724, 725, 726, 728, 730, 738, and 739 of the Illinois RCRA Subtitle C hazardous waste and underground injection control (UIC) rules to correspond with amendments adopted by U.S. EPA that appeared in the Federal Register during the period July 1 through December 31, 1994. During this period, U.S. EPA amended its regulations as follows:

Federal Action	Summary
59 Fed. Reg. 38536, July 28, 1994	Exclusion from definition of solid waste for certain in-process recycled secondary materials used by the petroleum refining industry
59 Fed. Reg. 43496, August 24, 1994	Withdrawal of exemption from Subtitle C regulation of slag residues from high

59 Fed. Reg. 47980, September 19, 1994	temperature metal recovery (HTMR) of electric arc furnace dust (K061), steel finishing pickle liquor (K062), and electroplating sludges (F006) that are used in a manner constituting disposal
59 Fed. Reg. 47980, September 19, 1994	Restoration of text from 40 CFR 268.7(a) inadvertently omitted in the amendments of August 31, 1993, at 58 Fed. Reg. 46040
59 Fed. Reg. 47982, September 19, 1994	Phase II land disposal restrictions (LDRs): universal treatment standards for organic toxicity wastes and newly-listed wastes (including underground injection control (UIC) amendments)
59 Fed. Reg. 62896, December 6, 1994	Organic material air emission standards for tanks, surface impoundments, and containers

In addition to these principal amendments that occurred during the update period, the Board has included an additional, later action:

| 60 Fed. Reg. 242, January 3, 1995 | Corrections to the Phase II land disposal Restrictions (universal treatment standards) |

This January 3 action was an amendment of the September 19, 1994 Phase II LDRs (universal waste rule). U.S. EPA corrected errors and clarified language in the universal treatment standards. The Board did not delay in adding these amendments for three reasons:

1) The January 3, 1995 amendments are corrections and clarifications of the September 19, 1994 regulations, and not new substantive amendments;

2) Prompt action on the January 3, 1995 amendments will facilitate implementation of the Phase II LDRs; and

3) The Board has received a request from the regulated community that we add the January 3, 1995 amendments to those of September 19, 1994. (See "Expedited Consideration" below.)

The Board also notes that the later amendments occurred within six months of the earliest amendments included in this docket, even if they occurred outside the nominal time-frame of the docket.

In addition to the federally-derived amendments, the Board used this opportunity to undertake a number of housekeeping and corrective amendments. We have effected the removal of all cross-references for

POLLUTION CONTROL BOARD

NOTICE OF PROPOSED AMENDMENTS

effective dates and repealed Part 700. We have converted equations and formulae to the standard scientific format. We have tried to improve the language and structure of various provisions, including correcting grammar, punctuation, and spelling where necessary.

Specifically, the segment of the amendments involved in Part 728 are based on the federal September 19, 1994 Phase II LDRs and the January 3, 1995 corrections and amendments to those September amendments. The Phase II LDRs establish universal treatment standards for wastewater and non-wastewater hazardous constituents that are independent of the type of waste in which they appear. A hazardous waste must either meet the established treatment technology or the wastewater or non-wastewater hazardous constituent standards before it is land disposed. The amendments also include new treatment standards for newly-listed wastes (wastes listed by U.S. EPA since 1984).

6) Will this proposed rule replace an emergency rule currently in effect? No.

7) Does this rulemaking contain an automatic repeal date? No.

8) Do these proposed amendments contain incorporations by reference?

Yes. 35 Ill. Adm. Code 720.111 is the central listing of all documents incorporated by reference throughout the text of 35 Ill. Adm. Code 702 through 705, 721 through 726, 728, 730, 738, and 739. The present amendments include the incorporation of prior U.S. EPA analytical methods from SW-846, and they delete a reference to 40 CFR 268.5(h)(2).

9) Are there any other amendments pending on this Part? No.

10) Statement of statewide policy objectives:

This rulemaking is mandated by Section 22.4(a) of the Environmental Protection Act [415 ILCS 5/22.4(a)]. The statewide policy objectives are set forth in Section 20 of that Act. This rulemaking imposes mandates on units of local government only to the extent that they may be involved in the generation, transportation, treatment, storage, or disposal of hazardous waste or they engage in underground injection of waste.

11) Time, place and manner in which interested persons may comment on this proposed rulemaking:

The Board will accept written public comment on this proposal for a period of 45 days after the date of this publication. Comments should reference Docket R95-4/R95-6 and be addressed to:

Ms. Dorothy M. Gunn, Clerk
Illinois Pollution Control Board

POLLUTION CONTROL BOARD

NOTICE OF PROPOSED AMENDMENTS

State of Illinois Center, Suite 11-500
100 W. Randolph St.
Chicago, IL 60601
312/814-6931

Address all questions to Michael J. McCambridge, at 312-814-6924.

12) Initial regulatory flexibility analysis:

A) Date rule was submitted to the Small Business Office of the Department of Commerce and Community Affairs: March 6, 1995.

B) Types of small businesses affected:

The existing rules and proposed amendments affect small businesses that generate, transport, treat, store, or dispose of hazardous waste or engage in underground injection of waste.

C) Reporting, bookkeeping or other procedures required for compliance:

The existing rules and proposed amendments require extensive reporting, bookkeeping, and other procedures, including the preparation of manifests and annual reports, waste analyses, and maintenance of operating records.

D) Types of professional skills necessary for compliance:

Compliance with the existing rules and proposed amendments may require the services of an attorney, certified public accountant, chemist, and registered professional engineer.

The full text of the proposed amendments begins on the next page:

POLLUTION CONTROL BOARD

NOTICE OF PROPOSED AMENDMENTS

TITLE 35: ENVIRONMENTAL PROTECTION
SUBTITLE G: WASTE DISPOSAL
CHAPTER I: POLLUTION CONTROL BOARD
SUBCHAPTER c: HAZARDOUS WASTE OPERATING REQUIREMENTS

PART 728
LAND DISPOSAL RESTRICTIONS

SUBPART A: GENERAL

POLLUTION CONTROL BOARD

NOTICE OF PROPOSED AMENDMENTS

SUBPART D: TREATMENT STANDARDS

AUTHORITY: Implementing Section 22.4 and authorized by Section 27 of the
Environmental Protection Act (415 ILCS 5/22.4 and 27).

SOURCE: Adopted in R87-5 at 11 Ill. Reg. 19354, effective November 12, 1987;
amended in R87-39 at 12 Ill. Reg.]3046, effective July 29, 1988; amended in
R89-1 at 13 Ill. Reg. 18403, effective November 13, 1989; amended in R89-9 at
14 Ill. Reg. 6232, effective April 16, 1990; amended in R90-2 at 14 Ill. Reg.
14470, effective August 22, 1990; amended in R90-10 at 14 Ill. Reg. 16508.

POLLUTION CONTROL BOARD

NOTICE OF PROPOSED AMENDMENTS

effective September 25, 1990; amended in R90-11 at 15 Ill. Reg. 9462, effective
June 17, 1991; amended in R90-11 at 15 Ill. Reg. 11937, effective August 12,
1991; amendment withdrawn at 15 Ill. Reg. 14716, October 11, 1991; amended in
R91-13 at 16 Ill. Reg. 9619, effective June 9, 1992; amended in R92-10 at 17
Ill. Reg. 5727, effective March 26, 1993; amended in R93-4 at 17 Ill. Reg.
20692, effective November 12, 1993; amended in R93-16 at 18 Ill. Reg. 6799,
effective April 26, 1994; amended in R94-7 at 18 Ill. Reg. 12203, effective
July 29, 1994; amended in R94-17 at 18 Ill. Reg. 17563, effective November 23,
1994; amended in R95-6 at 19 Ill. Reg. _____, effective
_____

SUBPART A: GENERAL

Section 728.101 Purpose, Scope and Applicability

a) This Part identifies hazardous wastes that are restricted from land
disposal and defines those limited circumstances under which an
otherwise prohibited waste may continue to be land disposed.

b) Except as specifically provided otherwise in this Part or 35 Ill. Adm.
Code 721, the requirements of this Part apply to persons who that
generate or transport hazardous waste treatment, storage, and disposal
facilities.

c) Restricted wastes may continue to be land disposed as follows:

1) Where persons have been granted an extension to the effective
date of a prohibition under Subpart C or pursuant to Section
728.105, with respect to those wastes covered by the extension;

2) Where persons have been granted an exemption from a prohibition
pursuant to a petition under Section 728.106, with respect to
those wastes and units covered by the petition;

3) Wastes that are hazardous only because they exhibit a hazardous
characteristic and which that are otherwise prohibited from land
disposal under this Part, are not prohibited from land disposal
if the wastes:

A) Are disposed into a nonhazardous or hazardous waste
injection well, as defined in 35 Ill. Adm. Code 704.106(a);
and

B) Do not exhibit any prohibited characteristic of hazardous
waste at the point of injection; and

C) If, at the point of generation, the injected wastes include
D001 High TOC subcategory wastes of D012-D017 pesticide
wastes that are prohibited under Section 728.117(c), those
wastes have been treated to meet the treatment standards of
Section 728.140 prior to injection.

d) This Part does not affect the availibility of a waiver under Section
121(d)(4) of the Comprehensive Environmental Response, Compensation,
and Liability Act of 1980 (CERCLA) (42 U.S.C. Sections 9601 et seq.).

e) The following hazardous wastes are not subject to any provision of
this Part:

POLLUTION CONTROL BOARD

NOTICE OF PROPOSED AMENDMENTS

1) Wastes generated by small quantity generators of less than 100 kg
of non-acute hazardous waste or less than 1 kg of acute hazardous
waste per month, as defined in 35 Ill. Adm. Code 721.105;

2) Waste pesticides that a farmer disposes of pursuant to 35 Ill.
Adm. Code 722.170;

3) Wastes identified or listed as hazardous after November 8, 1984,
for which USEPA U.S. EPA has not promulgated land disposal
prohibitions or treatment standards.

4) De minimis losses to wastewater treatment systems of commercial
chemical product or chemical intermediates that are ignitable
(D001); or corrosive (D002); or that are organic constituents
that exhibit the characteristic of toxicity (D012-D041) and that
contain underlying hazardous constituents, as defined in Section
728.102 of this Part, are not considered to be prohibited wastes.
"De minimis" is defined as losses from normal material handling
operations (e.g. spills from the unloading or transfer of
materials from bins or other containers; or leaks from pipes,
valves, or other devices used to transfer materials); minor leaks
of process equipment, storage tanks, or containers; leaks from
well-maintained pump packings and seals; sample purging; and
relief device discharges; discharges from safety showers and
rinsing and cleaning of personal safety equipment; and rinsate
from empty containers or from containers that are rendered empty
by that rinsing.

5) Land disposal prohibitions for hazardous characteristic wastes do
not apply to laboratory wastes displaying the characteristic of
ignitable ignitability (D001), and corrosive corrosivity (D002),
or organic toxicity (D012 through D043) laboratory wastes
containing underlying hazardous constituents from laboratory
operations, that are mixed with other plant wastewaters at
facilities whose ultimate discharge is subject to regulations
under the CWA (including wastewaters at facilities which that
have eliminated the discharge of wastewater); provided that the
annualized flow of laboratory wastewater into the facility's
headwork does not exceed one percent; or provided that the
laboratory wastes' combined annualized average concentration does
not exceed one part per million in the facility's headwork
headworks.

f) This part is cumulative with the land disposal restrictions of 35 Ill.
Adm. Code 729. The Environmental Protection Agency (Agency) shall not
issue a wastestream authorization pursuant to 35 Ill. Adm. Code 709 or
Sections 22.6 or 39(h) of the Environmental Protection Act (Ill. Rev.
Stat. 1987, ch. 111 1/2, pars. 1022.6 or 1039(h)) [415 ILCS 5/22.6 or
39.6] unless the waste meets the requirements of this Part as well as
35 Ill. Adm. Code 729.

(Source: Amended at 19 Ill. Reg. _____, effective

POLLUTION CONTROL BOARD

NOTICE OF PROPOSED AMENDMENTS

Section 728.102 Definitions

When used in this Part the following terms have the meanings given below. All other terms have the meanings given under 35 Ill. Adm. Code 702.110, 720.110, 720.102, or 721.103.

"Agency" means the Illinois Environmental Protection Agency.

"Board" means the Illinois Pollution Control Board.

"CERCLA" means the Comprehensive Environmental Response, Compensation, and Liability Act of 1980 (42 U.S.C. 9601 et seq.)

"Debris" means solid material exceeding a 60 mm particle size that is intended for disposal and that is: A _a_ manufactured object; or plant or animal matter; or natural geologic material. However, the following materials are not debris: Any _any_ material for which a specific treatment standard is provided in 728.Subpart D, _namely lead acid batteries, cadmium batteries, and radioactive lead solids;_ Process _process_ residuals, such as smelter slag and residues from the treatment of waste, wastewater, sludges, or air emission residues; and intact containers of hazardous waste that are not ruptured and that retain at least 75% of their original volume. A mixture of debris that has not been treated to the standards provided by Section 728.145 of this Part and other material is subject to regulation as debris if the mixture is comprised primarily of debris, by volume, based on visual inspection.

"Halogenated organic compounds" or "HOCs" means those compounds having a carbon-halogen bond which _that are_ listed under Appendix C.

"Hazardous constituent or constituents" means those constituents listed in 35 Ill. Adm. Code 721.Appendix H.

"Hazardous debris" means debris that contains a hazardous waste listed in 35 Ill. Adm. Code 721.Subpart D; or that exhibits a characteristic of hazardous waste identified in 35 Ill. Adm. Code 721.Subpart C.

Inorganic _solid_ Debris are nonfriable inorganic solids that are incapable of passing through a 9.5 mm standard sieve; and that require cutting or crushing or grinding; in mechanical sizing equipment prior to stabilization, limited to the following inorganic or metal materials:

Metal slags (either dross or scoria).

POLLUTION CONTROL BOARD

NOTICE OF PROPOSED AMENDMENTS

Glassified slag.

Glass.

Concrete (excluding cementitious or pozzolanic stabilized hazardous wastes).

Masonry and refractory bricks.

Metal cans, containers, drums, or tanks.

Metal nuts, bolts, pipes, pumps, valves, appliances, or industrial equipment.

Scrap metal, as defined in 35 Ill. Adm. Code 721.101(c)(6).

"Land disposal" means placement in or on the land, except in a corrective action management unit, and includes, but is not limited to, placement in a landfill, surface impoundment, waste pile, injection well, land treatment facility, salt dome formation, salt bed formation, underground mine, or cave; or placement in a concrete vault or bunker intended for disposal purposes.

"Nonwastewaters" are wastes that do not meet the criteria for "wastewaters" in this Section.

"Polychlorinated biphenyls" or "PCBs" are halogenated organic compounds defined in accordance with 40 CFR 761.3, incorporated by reference in 35 Ill. Adm. Code 720.111.

"ppm" means parts per million.

"RCRA corrective action" means corrective action taken under 35 Ill. Adm. Code 724.200 or 725.193, 40 CFR 264.100 or 265.93 (1992 _1994_), or similar regulations in other States with RCRA programs authorized by U.S. EPA pursuant to 40 CFR 271 (1992 _1994_).

"Underlying hazardous constituent" means any regulated constituent _listed in Section 728.Table U, "Universal Treatment Standards (UTS)", except vanadium and zinc, that can reasonably be expected to be present, at the point of generation of the hazardous waste,_ at levels _a concentration_ above the F039 constituent-specific UTS treatment standard at the point of generation of the hazardous waste.

"U.S. EPA" or "USEPA" means the United States Environmental Protection Agency.

POLLUTION CONTROL BOARD

NOTICE OF PROPOSED AMENDMENTS

"Wastewaters" are wastes that contain less than 1% by weight total organic carbon (TOC) and less than 1% by weight total suspended solids (TSS), with the following exceptions:

F001, F002, F003, F004, and F005 solvent-water mixtures that contain less than 1% by weight TOC or less than 1% by weight total F001, F002, F003, F004, and F005 solvent constituents listed in Table A.

K011, K013, and K014 wastewaters (as generated) that contain less than 5% by weight TOC and less than 1% by weight TSS.

K103 and K104 contain less than 4% by weight TOC and less than 1% by weight TSS.

(Source: Amended at 19 Ill. Reg. _____, effective
_____)

Section 728.107 Waste Analysis and Recordkeeping

a) Except as specified in Section 728.132, where a generator's waste is listed in 35 Ill. Adm. Code 721.Subpart D or if the waste exhibits one or more of the characteristics set out at 35 Ill. Adm. Code 721.Subpart C, the generator shall test its waste, or test an extract using the Toxicity Characteristic Leaching Procedure, Method 1311, in "Test Methods for Evaluating Solid Waste, Physical/Chemical Methods", U.S. EPA Publication SW-846, as incorporated by reference in 35 Ill. Adm. Code 720.111, or use knowledge of the waste to determine if the waste is restricted from land disposal under this Part. Except--as specified--in--Section-728.132,--if-a-generator's-waste-exhibits-one-or more-of-the-characteristics-set-out-at-35-Ill,-Adm,--Code--721,Subpart D,--the-generator--shall--test-an-extract-using-the-EP-Toxicity-Test, Method--1310,---in--"Test---Methods---for---Evaluating---Solid---Waste, Physical/Chemical---Methods",---U,S,---EPA---Publication---SW-846,--as incorporated-by-reference--in--35--Ill,--Adm,--Code--720,111,--or--use knowledge--of--the-waste,-to-determine-if-the-waste-is-restricted-from land-disposal-under-this-Part. If the generator determines that its waste displays the characteristic of ignitability (D001) (and is not in the High TOC Ignitable Liquids Subcategory or is not treated by IMERN,--FSUBS, CMBST or RORGS of Section 728.Table C of this Part), or the waste displays the characteristic or of corrosivity (D002), or is prohibited under Section 728.137, or the waste displays the characteristic of organic toxicity (D012-D043) and is prohibited under Section 728.138, the generator shall determine what underlying hazardous constituents (as defined in Section 728.102 of--this--Part), are reasonably expected to be present in the D001, or D002, or D012 through D043 waste.

    1) If a generator determines that the-generator it is managing a

POLLUTION CONTROL BOARD

NOTICE OF PROPOSED AMENDMENTS

restricted waste under this Part and determines-that the waste does not meet the applicable treatment set forth in 728.Subpart D of-this-Part or exceeds the applicable prohibition levels set forth in Section 728.132 or 728.139, with--each shipment--of--waste the generator shall notify the treatment or storage facility in writing of-the-appropriate-treatment-standard set--forth--in--Subpart--D-of--this--Part--and--any--applicable prohibition--levels--set-forth-in-Section-728.132-or-728.139 with each shipment of waste. The notice must include the following information:

    A) U.S. EPA hazardous waste number;
    B) The corresponding--treatment--standards waste constituents that the treater will monitor, if monitoring will not include all regulated constituents, for wastes F001 through F005, F039, D001, D002, D012 through D043, and wastes prohibited pursuant to Section 728.132 or Section 3004(d) of the Resource Conservation and Recovery Act, referenced in Section 728.139. Treatment--standards--for---all--other restricted--wastes-must-either-be-included--or-be-referenced by-including-on-the-notification-the--applicable--wastewater fas--defined--in--Section--728.102(f)--or-nonwastewater-fas defined-in--Section--728.102(d)--category,--the--applicable subcategory-made-within-a-waste-code-based-on-waste-specific criteria--(such--as-D003-reactive-cyanide)--and-the-Section and-subsections--where--the--applicable--treatment--standard appears;---Where--the--applicable--treatment--standards--are expressed-as-specified-technologies-in-Section-728.143,--the applicable--five-letter--treatment--code--found--in--Section 728.Table--C-(e.g.,-IMERN,-WETOX)-also-must-be-listed-on-the notification. The generator must also include whether the waste is a nonwastewater or wastewater (as defined in Section 728.102 (d) and (f)) and indicate the subcategory of the waste (such as "D003 reactive cyanide") if applicable;
    C) The manifest number associated with the shipment of waste; and
    D) For hazardous debris, the contaminants subject to treatment, as provided by Section 728.145(b), and the following statement: "This hazardous debris is subject to the alternative treatment standards of 35 Ill. Adm. code 728.145; and
    E) Waste analysis data, where available; and
    F) The date on which the waste is subject to the prohibitions.
    2) If a generator determines that the-generator it is managing a restricted waste under this Part, and determines that the waste can be land disposed without further treatment, with each shipment of waste the generator shall submit-to--the--treatment- storage--or--land-disposal-facility a notice and a certification to the treatment, storage, or land disposal facility stating that

POLLUTION CONTROL BOARD

NOTICE OF PROPOSED AMENDMENTS

the waste meets the applicable treatment standards set forth in 728.Subpart D ef--this--Part and setting forth the applicable prohibition levels set forth in Section 728.132 or RCRA Section 3004(d), referenced in Section 728.139. A Generators generator of hazardous debris that is excluded from the definition of hazardous waste under 35 III. Adm. Code 721.103(eg)(2), 35 Ill. Adm. Code 728.103(f)(2), and or 35 Ill. Adm. Code 720.122 (i.e. debris that is delisted), however, are is not subject to these notification and certification requirements.

A) The notice must include the following information:

  i) U.S. EPA hazardous waste number;

  ii) The eerrespending----treatment----standards waste constituents that the treater will monitor, if monitoring will not include all regulated constituents, for wastes F001 through F005, F039, D001, D002, D012 through D043, and wastes prohibited pursuant to Section 728.132 or Section 3004(d) of the Resource Conservation and Recovery Act, referenced in Section 728.139. Treatment-standards-for-all-other restricted--wastes--must---either--be---included---or referenced--by--including--on--the--notification--the applicable The generator must also include whether the waste is a wastewater or nonwastewater (as defined in Section 728.102(d) and (f)) category, and indicate the subcategory of the waste applicable-subdivisions-made within-a-waste-code-based-on-waste-specific--criteria (such as D003, reactive cyanides). and-the-Section-and subsection--where--the--applicable--treatment-standard appears if applicable. Where-the-applicable-treatment standards-are-expressed-as-specified--technologies--in Section--728.142;-the-applicable-five-letter-treatment code-found-in-Section-728;Table-G-(e.g.,-INEER;-WETOX) also-must-be-listed-on-the-notification;:

  iii) The manifest number associated with the shipment of waste; and

  iv) Waste analysis data, where available.

B) The certification must be signed by an authorized representative and must state the following:

  I certify under, penalty of law that I personally have examined and am familiar with the waste through analysis and testing or through knowledge of the waste to support this certification that the waste complies with the treatment standards specified in 35 Ill. Adm. Code 728.Subpart D and all applicable prohibitions set forth in 35 Ill. Adm. Code 728.132, 728.139, or Section 3004(d) of the Resource Conservation and Recovery Act. I believe that the information I submitted is true, accurate, and complete. I am aware

that there are significant penalties for submitting a false certification, including the possibility of a fine and imprisonment.

3) If a generator's waste is subject to an exemption from a prohibition on the type of land disposal method utilized for the waste (such as, but not limited to, a case-by-case extension under Section 728.105, an exemption under Section 728.106, an extension under Section 728.101(c)(3), or a nationwide capacity variance under 40 CFR 268.Subpart C (1991994)), with--each shipment--of--waste the generator shall submit a notice with each shipment of the waste to the facility receiving the generator's wastes stating that the waste is not prohibited from land disposal. The notice must include the following information:

  A) U.S. EPA hazardous waste number;

  B) The corresponding--treatment--standards waste constituents that the treater will monitor, if monitoring will not include all regulated constituents, for wastes F001 through F005, F039, D001, D002, and D012 through D043 and wastes prohibited-pursuant-to-Section-728.132-or-Section-3004(d)-of the-Resource-Conservation-and-Recovery--Act,--referenced--in Section--728.139.-----Treatment--standards--for--all--other restricted-wastes-must-either-be-included-or--be--referenced or-nonwastewater-(as-defined-in-Section--728.103)--category; the--applicable--subdivisions-made-within-a-waste-code-based on--waste-specific--criteria---(such---as---D003)---reactive cyanides);---and---the--Section--and--subsection--where--the applicable-treatment-standard-appears.--Where-the-applicable treatment-standards-are-expressed-as-specified--technologies in--Section--728.142;--the--applicable-five-letter-treatment code-found-in-Section-728;Table-G-(e.g.,-INEER;-WETOX)--also must-be-listed-on-the-notification. The generator must also include whether the waste is a nonwastewater or wastewater (as defined in Section 728.102(d) and (f)), and indicate the subcategory of the waste (such as "D003 (reactive cyanide"), if applicable;

  C) The manifest number associated with the shipment of waste;

  D) Waste analysis data, where available;

  E) For hazardous debris, the when using the alternative treatment technologies provided by Section 728.145:

    i) The containments contaminants subject to treatment, as provided by Section 728.145(b);

    ii) An indication that these contaminants are being treated to comply with Section 728.145 and--the following--statement:--"This--hazardous--debris--is subject--to--the-alternative-treatment-standards-of-35 Ill.-Adm-Code-728.145"; and

  F) For hazardous debris when using the treatment standards for

POLLUTION CONTROL BOARD

NOTICE OF PROPOSED AMENDMENTS

the contaminating waste(s) in Section 728.140; the
requirements described in subsections (a)(3)(A) through
(a)(3)(D) above and subsection (a)(3)(G) below; and,
PG) The date on which the waste is subject to the prohibitions.

4) If a generator is managing a prohibited waste in tanks, or
containers, or containment buildings regulated under 35 Ill. Adm.
Code 722.134r and is treating such waste in such tanks,
containers, or containment buildings to meet applicable treatment
standards under 728.Subpart D of this Part, the generator shall
develop and follow a written waste analysis plan that describes
the procedures the generator will carry out to comply with the
treatment standards. (A generator treating hazardous debris
under the alternative treatment standards of Section 728.Table F,
however, is not subject to these waste analysis requirements.)
The plan must be kept on-site in the generator's records, and the
following requirements must be met:

A) The waste analysis plan must be based on a detailed chemical
and physical analysis of a representative sample of the
prohibited wastes being treated and it must contain all
information necessary to treat the wastes in accordance with
the requirements of this Part, including the selected
testing frequency.

B) Such plan must be filed with the Agency a minimum of 30 days
prior to the treatment activity, with delivery verified.

C) Wastes shipped off-site pursuant to this subsection must
comply with the notification requirements of Section
728.107(a)(2).

5) If a generator determines whether the waste is restricted based
solely on the generator's knowledge of the waste, the generator
shall retain all supporting data used to make this determination
on-site in the generator's files. If a generator determines
whether the waste is restricted based on testing the waste or an
extract developed using the test method described in Appendix A,
the generator shall retain all waste analysis data on site in the
generator's its files.

6) If a generator determines, subsequent to the time of generation,
that the generator it is managing a restricted waste that is
excluded from the definition of hazardous or solid waste or
exempt from regulation as a RCRA hazardous waste under 35 Ill.
Adm. Code 712.102 through 721.106, the generator shall place, in
the facility's file, a one-time notice stating such generation,
the subsequent exclusion from the definition of hazardous or
solid waste or exemption from regulation as a RCRA hazardous
waste, and the disposition of the waste.

7) A generator Generators shall retain on-site a copy of all
notices, certifications, demonstrations, waste analysis data, and
other documentation produced pursuant to this Section for at
least five years from the date that the waste that is the subject

POLLUTION CONTROL BOARD

NOTICE OF PROPOSED AMENDMENTS

of such documentation was last sent to on-site or off-site
treatment, storage, or disposal. The five year record retention
period is automatically extended during the course of any
unresolved enforcement action regarding the regulated activity,
or as requested by the Agency. The requirements of this
subsection apply to solid wastes even when the hazardous
characteristic is removed prior to disposal, or when the waste is
excluded from the definition of hazardous or solid waste under 35
Ill. Adm. Code 721.102 through 721.106, or when the waste is
exempted from regulation as a RCRA hazardous waste subsequent to
the point of generation.

8) If a generator is managing a waste that contains wastes
identified in Appendix D and wishes to use the alternative
treatment standard under Section 728.142(c), with each shipment
of waste the generator shall submit a notice to the treatment
facility in accordance with subsection (a)(1) above, except that
underlying hazardous constituents need not be determined. The
generator shall also comply with the requirements in subsections
(a)(5) and (a)(6) above and shall submit the following
certification, which must be signed by an authorized
representative:

    I certify under penalty of law that I personally have
    examined and am familiar with the waste that the lab pack
    does not contains contain only any of the wastes specified
    identified in 35 Ill. Adm. Code 728.Appendix D or solid
    wastes not subject to regulation under 35 Ill. Adm. Code
    721. I am aware that there are significant penalties for
    submitting a false certification, including the possibility
    of fine or imprisonment.

9) If a generator is managing a lab pack that contains organic
wastes specified in Appendix B and wishes to use the alternate
treatment standards under Section 728.142, with each shipment of
waste the generator shall submit a notice to the treatment
facility in accordance with subsection (a)(1) above. The
generator also shall comply with the requirements in subsections
(a)(5) and (a)(6) above and shall submit the following
certification that must be signed by an authorized
representative. This subsection corresponds with 40 CFR
268.7(a)(9), marked "reserved" by U.S. EPA at 59 Fed. Reg. 48045
(Sept. 19, 1994). This statement maintains structural
consistency with federal regulations.

    I certify under penalty of law that I personally have
    examined and am familiar with the waste through analysis and
    testing or through knowledge of the waste and that the lab
    pack contains only organic waste specified in 35 Ill. Adm.
    Code 728.Appendix B or solid wastes not subject to
    regulation under 35 Ill. Adm. Code 721. I am aware that
    there are significant penalties for submitting a false

POLLUTION CONTROL BOARD

NOTICE OF PROPOSED AMENDMENTS

~~certification,---including---the---possibility--of--fine--or
imprisonment.~~

10) Small quantity generators with tolling agreements pursuant to 35
Ill. Adm. Code 722.120(e) shall comply with the applicable
notification and certification requirements of subsection (a)
above for the initial shipment of the waste subject to the
agreement. Such generators shall retain on-site a copy of the
notification and certification, together with the tolling
agreement, for at least three years after termination or
expiration of the agreement. The three-year record retention
period is automatically extended following notification pursuant
to Section 31(d) of the Environmental Protection Act, until
either any subsequent enforcement action is resolved, or __until__
the Agency notifies the generator documents need __be not not__ be
retained.

b) Treatment facilities shall test their wastes according to the
frequency specified in their waste analysis plans, as required by 35
Ill. Adm. Code 724.113 or 725.113. Such testing must be performed as
provided in subsections (b)(1), (b)(2), and (b)(3) below.

1) For wastes with treatment standards expressed as concentrations
in the waste extract (Section 728.141), the owner or operator of
the treatment facility shall test the treatment residues or an
extract of such residues developed using the test method
described in Appendix A to assure that the treatment residues or
extract meet the applicable treatment standards.

2) For wastes prohibited under Section 728.132 or 728.139 that are
not subject to any treatment standards under __728.__Subpart D ~~of
this-Part~~, the owner or operator of the treatment facility shall
test the treatment residues according to the generator testing
requirements specified in Section 728.132 to assure that the
treatment residues comply with the applicable prohibitions.

3) For wastes with treatment standards expressed as concentrations
in the waste (Section 728.143), the owner or operator of the
treatment facility shall test the treatment residues (not an
extract of such residues) to assure that the treatment residues
meet the applicable treatment standards.

4) A notice must be sent with each waste shipment to the land
disposal facility that includes the following information, except
that debris excluded from the definition of the hazardous waste
under ~~Section~~ 35 Ill. Adm. Code ~~728.103(f)(2)~~ 721.103(e) (i.e.,
debris treated by an extraction or destruction technology
provided by Section 728.Table F, and debris that is delisted) is
subject to the notification and certification requirements of
subsection (d) below rather than these notification requirements:

A) U.S. EPA hazardous waste number;

B) The ~~corresponding-treatment-standards__ waste constituents to
be monitored, if monitoring will not include all regulated
constituents,__ for wastes F001 through F005, F039, D001,

POLLUTION CONTROL BOARD

NOTICE OF PROPOSED AMENDMENTS

D002, D012 through D043, and__ wastes prohibited pursuant to
Section 728.132 or Section 3004(d) of the Resource
Conservation and Recovery Act, referenced in Section
728.135~~,---and--for--underlying--hazardous--constituents--(as
defined--in--Section-728.102-of-this-Part)--in-D001-and-D002
wastes-if-those-wastes-are-prohibited-under-Section--728.13?
of--this-Part. Treatment-standards-for-all-other-restricted
wastes--must--either--be--included,--or--be--referenced--by
including--on--the--notification--the--applicable~~ The generator
must also include whether the waste is a __nonwastewater or
wastewater__ (as defined in Section 728.102(d) or (f)), and
indicate the subcategory of the waste ~~or---nonwastewater--(as
defined--in--Section--728.102(d))--category--the-applicable
subdivisions--made--within--a---waste--code---based---on
waste-specific-criteria__ (such as D003 reactive cyanides),
and--the--Sections--and--subsections--where--the--applicable
treatment--standard--appears __if applicable.--Where--the
applicable-treatment-standards-are--expressed--as--specified
technologies--in-Section-728.142,-the-applicable-five-letter
treatment-code-found-in-Section-728.Table--C--or-g.,--INGEN,
NBPOK)-also-must-be-listed-on-the-notification.~~

C) The manifest number associated with the shipment of waste;
and

D) Waste analysis data, where available.

5) The treatment facility __owner or operator__ shall submit a
certification with each shipment of waste or treatment residue of
a restricted waste to the land disposal __facility__ stating that the
waste or treatment residue has been treated in compliance with
the treatment standards specified in __728.__Subpart D ~~of--this--Part~~
and the applicable prohibitions set forth in Section 728.132 or
728.139. Debris excluded from the definition of hazardous waste
under ~~Section~~ 35 Ill. Adm. Code ~~728.103(f)(2)~~ 721.103(e) (i.e.,
debris treated by an extraction or destruction technology
provided by Section 728.Table F, and debris that is delisted),
however, is subject to the notification and certification
requirements of subsection (d) below rather than the
certification requirements of subsection (b)(5).

A) For wastes with treatment standards expressed as
concentrations in the waste extract or in the waste
(Sections 728.141 or 728.143), or for wastes prohibited
under Section 728.132 or 728.139 that are not subject to any
treatment standards under __728.__Subpart D ~~of--this--Part~~, the
certification must be signed by an authorized representative
and must state the following:

    I certify under penalty of law that I have personally
examined and am familiar with the treatment technology
and operation of the treatment process used to support
this certification and that, based on my inquiry of

POLLUTION CONTROL BOARD

NOTICE OF PROPOSED AMENDMENTS

those individuals immediately responsible for obtaining this information. I believe that the treatment process has been operated and maintained properly, so as to comply with the performance levels specified in 35 Ill. Adm. Code 728.Subpart D and all applicable prohibitions set forth in 35 Ill. Adm. Code 728.132 or 728.139 or section 3004(d) of the Resource Conservation and Recovery Act without impermissible dilution of the prohibited waste. I am aware that there are significant penalties for submitting a false certification, including the possibility of fine and imprisonment.

B) For wastes with treatment standards expressed as technologies (Section 728.142), the certification must be signed by an authorized representative and must state the following:

I certify under penalty of law that the waste has been treated in accordance with the requirements of 35 Ill. Adm. Code 728.142. I am aware that there are significant penalties for submitting a false certification, including the possibility of fine and imprisonment.

C) For wastes with treatment standards expressed as concentrations in the waste pursuant to Section 728.143, if compliance with the treatment standards in 728.Subpart D of this Part is based in part or in whole on the analytical detection limit alternative specified in Section 728.143(c), the certification also must state the following:

I certify under penalty of law that I have personally examined and am familiar with the treatment technology and operation of the treatment process used to support this certification and that, based on my inquiry of those individuals immediately responsible for obtaining this information, I believe that the nonwastewater organic constituents have been treated by incineration in units operated in accordance with 35 Ill. Adm. Code 724.Subpart O or 35 Ill. Adm. Code 725.Subpart O, or by combustion in fuel substitution units operating in accordance with applicable technical requirements, and I have been unable to detect the nonwastewater organic constituents despite having used best good faith efforts to analyze for such constituents. I am aware that there are significant penalties for submitting a false certification, including the possibility of fine and imprisonment.

D) For characteristic wastes D001, D002, and D012 through D043 that are subject to the treatment standards in Section

POLLUTION CONTROL BOARD

NOTICE OF PROPOSED AMENDMENTS

728.140 (other than those expressed as a required method of treatment), that are reasonably expected to contain underlying hazardous constituents as defined in Section 728.102(l), that are treated on-site to remove the hazardous characteristic, and that are then sent off-site for treatment of underlying hazardous constituents, the certification must state the following:

I certify under penalty of law that the waste has been treated in accordance with the requirements of 35 Ill. Adm. Code 728.140 to remove the hazardous characteristic. This decharacterized waste contains underlying hazardous constituents that require further treatment to meet universal treatment standards. I am aware that there are significant penalties for submitting a false certification, including the possibility of fine and imprisonment.

6) If the waste or treatment residue will be further managed at a different treatment or storage facility, the treatment, storage, or disposal facility sending the waste or treatment residue off-site must comply with the notice and certification requirements applicable to generators under this Section.

7) Where the wastes are recyclable materials used in a manner constituting disposal subject to the provisions of 35 Ill. Adm. Code 726.120(b), regarding treatment standards and prohibition levels, the owner or operator of a treatment facility (i.e. the recycler) is not required to notify the receiving facility pursuant to subsection (b)(4) above. With each shipment of such wastes the owner or operator of the recycling facility shall submit a certification described in subsection (b)(5) above and a notice that includes the information listed in subsection (b)(4) above (except the name and number) to the Agency. The recycling facility also shall keep records of the name and location of each entity receiving the hazardous waste-derived product.

c) Except where the owner or operator is disposing of any waste that is a recyclable material used in a manner constituting disposal pursuant to 35 Ill. Adm. Code 726.120(b), the owner or operator of any land disposal facility disposing any waste subject to restrictions under this Part shall:

1) Have copies of the notice and certification specified in subsection (a) or (b) above and the certification specified in Section 728.107, if applicable.

2) Test the waste, or an extract of the waste or treatment residue developed using the test method described in Appendix A or using any methods required by generators under Section 728.132, to assure that the wastes or treatment residues are is in compliance with the applicable treatment standards set forth in 728.Subpart D of this Part and all applicable prohibitions set forth in Sections 728.132 or 728.139. Such testing must be performed according to the frequency specified in the facility's waste

POLLUTION CONTROL BOARD

NOTICE OF PROPOSED AMENDMENTS

analysis plan as required by 35 Ill. Adm. Code 724.113 or 725.113.

3) Where the owner or operator is disposing of any waste that is subject to the prohibitions under Section 728.133(f) but not subject to the prohibitions set forth in Section 728.132, the owner or operator shall ensure that such waste is the subject of a certification according to the requirements of Section 728.108 prior to disposal in a landfill or surface impoundment unit, and that such disposal is in accordance with the requirements of Section 728.105(h)(2). The same requirement applies to any waste that is subject to the prohibitions under Section 728.133(f) and also is subject to the statutory prohibitions in the codified prohibitions in Section 728.139 or Section 728.132.

4) Where the owner or operator is disposing of any waste that is a recyclable material used in a manner constituting disposal subject to the provisions of 35 Ill. Adm. Code 726.120(b), the owner or operator is not subject to subsections (c)(1) through (c)(3) above, with respect to such waste.

d) A ~~Generators~~ generator or treaters that first ~~claim~~ claims that hazardous debris is excluded from the definition of hazardous waste under 35 Ill. Adm. Code ~~728.103(f)(2)~~ 721.103(e) (i.e., debris treated by an extraction or destruction technology provided by Section 728.Table F, and debris that has been delisted) ~~are~~ is subject to the following notification and certification requirements:

I) A one-time notification must be submitted to the Agency including the following information:

A) The name and address of the RCRA Subtitle D (municipal solid waste landfill) facility receiving the treated debris;

B) A description of the hazardous debris as initially generated, including the applicable U.S. EPA hazardous waste numbers; and

C) For debris excluded under 35 Ill. Adm. Code 728.103(f)(2), the technology from Section 728.Table F used to treat the debris.

2) The notification must be updated if the debris is shipped to a different facility; and, for debris excluded 35 Ill. Adm. Code 721.2(d)(1), if a different type of debris is treated or if a different technology is used to treat the debris.

3) For debris excluded under 35 Ill. Adm. Code 728.103(f)(2), the owner or operator of the treatment facility shall document and certify compliance with the treatment standards of Section 728.Table F, as follows:

A) Records must be kept of all inspections, evaluations, and analyses of treated debris that are made to determine compliance with the treatment standards;

B) Records must be kept of any data or information the treater obtains during treatment of the debris that identifies key operating parameters of the treatment unit; and

POLLUTION CONTROL BOARD

NOTICE OF PROPOSED AMENDMENTS

C) For each shipment of treated debris, a certification of compliance with the treatment standards must be signed by an authorized representative and placed in the facility's files. The certification must state the following:
"I certify under penalty of law that the debris has been treated in accordance with the requirements of 35 Ill. Adm. Code 728.145. I am aware that there are significant penalties for making a false certification, including the possibility of fine and imprisonment."

(Source: Amended at 19 Ill. Reg. _____, effective _____)

Section 728.109 Special Rules for Characteristic Wastes

a) The initial generator of a solid waste shall determine each U.S. EPA hazardous waste number (waste code) applicable to the waste in order to determine the applicable treatment standards under 728.Subpart D of ~~this Part~~. For purposes of this Part, the waste must carry the waste code for any applicable listing under 35 Ill. Adm. Code 721.Subpart D. In addition, the waste must carry one or more of the waste codes under 35 Ill. Adm. Code 721.Subpart C where the waste exhibits the relevant characteristic, except in the case when the treatment standard for the waste code listed in 35 Ill. Adm. Code 721.Subpart D operates in lieu of the standard for the waste code under 35 Ill. Adm. Code 721.Subpart C, as specified in subsection (b) below. If the generator determines that its waste displays the characteristic of ignitability (D001) (and is not in the High TOC Ignitable Liquids Subcategory or is not treated by ~~INCIN, PSUBS, CMBST~~ or RORGS ~~of Section 728.Table C of this Part~~), or that its waste displays the characteristic of corrosivity (D002) and is prohibited under Section 728.137, that its waste displays the characteristic of toxicity (D012 through D043) and is prohibited under Section 728.438, the generator shall determine what underlying hazardous constituents (as defined in Section 728.102) are reasonably expected to be present in the D001, or D002, or D012 through D043 waste.

b) Where a prohibited waste is both listed under 35 Ill. Adm. Code 721.Subpart D and exhibits a characteristic under 35 Ill. Adm. Code 721.Subpart C, the treatment standard for the waste code listed in 35 Ill. Adm. Code 721.Subpart D will operate in lieu of the standard for the waste code under 35 Ill. Adm. Code 721.Subpart C, provided that the treatment standard for the listed waste includes a treatment standard for the constituent that causes the waste to exhibit the characteristic. Otherwise, the waste must meet the treatment standards for all prohibited listed and characteristic waste codes.

c) In addition to any applicable standards determined from the initial point of generation, no prohibited waste which that exhibits a characteristic under 35 Ill. Adm. Code 721.Subpart C shall be land

disposed unless the waste complies with the treatment standards under 728.Subpart D of-this-Part.

d) A Wastes waste that exhibit exhibits a characteristic are is also subject to Section 728.107 requirements. except that once the waste is no longer hazardous, one time notification and certification must be placed in the generators generator's or treaters treater's files and sent to the Agency. The notification and certification that is placed in the generators generator's or treaters' treater's files must be updated if the process or operation generating the waste changes or if the subtitle D facility receiving the waste changes. However, the generator or treater need only notify the Agency on an annual basis if such changes occur. Such notification and certification should be sent to the Agency by the end of the year, but no later than December 31.

1) The notification must include the following information:

A) The name and address of the non-hazardous--waste RCRA Subtitle D (municipal solid waste landfill) facility receiving the waste shipment; and

B) A description of the waste as initially generated, including the applicable U.S. EPA hazardous waste numbers, the applicable---wastewater---or---nonwastewater treatability group(s), and the underlying hazardous constituents (as defined in Section 728.102(i)) category---and---the subdivisions---made---within---a---waste---code---based---on waste-specific-criteria-(such-as-D003)--reactive--cyanides); in D001 and D002 wastes prohibited under Section 728.137 or D012 through D043 wastes prohibited under Section 728.136.

C) The-treatment-standards--applicable--to--the--waste--at--the initial-point-of-generation;

2) The certification must be signed by an authorized representative and must state the language found in Section 728.107(b)(5)(A). If treatment removes the characteristic but does not treat underlying hazardous constituents, then the certification found in Section 728.107(b)(5)(D) applies.

(Source: Amended at 19 Ill. Reg. _____, effective _____)

SUBPART C: PROHIBITION ON LAND DISPOSAL

Section 728.130 Waste Specific Prohibitions -- Solvent Wastes

a) The spent solvent wastes specified in 35 Ill. Adm. Code 721.131 as USEPA U.S. EPA Hazardous Waste Numbers F001, F002, F003, F004, and F005 are prohibited under this Part from land disposal (except in an injection well) unless one or more of the following conditions apply:

1) The generator of the solvent waste is a small quantity generator of 100 to 1000 kilograms of hazardous waste per month; or

2) The solvent waste is generated from any response action taken under CERCLA or from RCRA corrective action; except where the waste is solvent-contaminated soil or debris; or

3) The initial generator's solvent waste is a solvent-water mixture, solvent-containing sludge or solid, or solvent-contaminated soil (non-CERCLA or non-RCRA corrective action) containing less than 1 percent total F001 through F005 solvent constituents listed in Table A T; or

4) The solvent waste is a residue from treating a waste described in subsections subsection (a)(1), (a)(2), or (a)(3) above, or the solvent waste is a residue from treating a waste not described in subsections subsection (a)(1), (a)(2), or (a)(3) provided such residue belongs to a different treatability group than the waste as initially generated and wastes belonging to such treatability group are described in subsection (a)(3).

b) The F001 through F005 solvent wastes listed in subsections (a)(1), (a)(2), (a)(3), or (a)(4) above are prohibited from land disposal.

c) Effective--November--8;-1990;-the The F001 through F005 solvent wastes which that are contaminated soil and debris resulting from a CERCLA response or RCRA corrective action or the residue from treatment of these wastes are prohibited from land disposal. Until--November--8; 1990;-these-waste-may-be-disposed-in-a-landfill-or-surface-impoundment only--if-such-unit-is-in-compliance-with-the-requirements-specified-in 40-CFR-268.5(h)(2);-incorporated-by-reference-in-Section-728.105.

d) The requirements of subsections (a), (b), and (c) above do not apply if:

1) The wastes meet the standards of 728.Subpart D; or

2) Persons-have-been-granted-an An exemption (adjusted standard) was granted from a prohibition pursuant to a petition under Section 728.106, with respect to those wastes and units and the activity is covered by the petition; or

3) Persons have been granted an extension to the effective date of a prohibition by U.S. EPA pursuant to Section 728.105, with respect to those wastes and units and the activity is covered by the extension.

(Source: Amended at 19 Ill. Reg. _____, effective _____)

Section 728.133 Waste Specific Prohibitions;----First Third Wastes

a) The wastes specified in 35 Ill. Adm. Code 721.132 as USEPA U.S. EPA hazardous wastes numbers listed below are prohibited from land disposal (except in an injection well).

F006 (nonwastewater)
K001
K004 wastes specified in Section Sections 728.143(a) 728.140 and 728.Table B T

POLLUTION CONTROL BOARD

NOTICE OF PROPOSED AMENDMENTS

K008 wastes specified in ~~Section~~ Sections ~~728.143(a)~~ 728.140 and
728.Table B T
K015
K016
K018
K019
K020
K021 wastes specified in ~~Section~~ Sections ~~728.143(a)~~ 728.140 and
728.Table B T
K022 (nonwastewater)
K024
K025 nonwastewaters specified in ~~Section~~ Sections ~~728.143(a)~~
728.140 and 728.Table B T
K030
K036 (nonwastewater)
K037
K044
K045 (nonexplosive)
K046 (nonwastewater)
K047
K060 (nonwastewater)
K061 (nonwastewaters containing less than 15% zinc)
K062 (non CaSO4)
K069 (nonwastewater)
K083
K086 (solvent washes),
K087
K099
K100 nonwastewaters specified in ~~Section~~ Sections ~~728.143(a)~~
728.140 and 728.Table B T
K101 (wastewater)
K101 (nonwastewater, low arsenic subcategory--less than 1% total
    arsenic)
K102 (wastewater)
K102 (nonwastewater, low arsenic subcategory--less than 1% total
    arsenic)
K103
K104

b) The wastes specified in 35 Ill. Adm. Code 721.132 as ~~USEPA~~ U.S. EPA
   Hazardous Waste No K071 is prohibited from land disposal.
c) The wastes specified in Section 728.110 having a treatment standard in
   728.Subpart D based on incineration and which are contaminated soil
   and debris are prohibited from land disposal.
e) The requirements of subsection (a), (b), and (c) above, do not apply
   if:
   1) The ~~wastes~~ waste ~~meet~~ meets the applicable standards specified in
      728.Subpart D; or
   2) ~~Persons have been granted an~~ An exemption [adjusted standard] was

POLLUTION CONTROL BOARD

NOTICE OF PROPOSED AMENDMENTS

granted from a prohibition pursuant to a petition under Section
728.106, with respect to those wastes and units and the activity
is covered by the petition; or
3) Persons have been granted an extension to the effective date of a
prohibition by U.S. EPA pursuant to Section 728.105, with respect
to those wastes and units and the activity is covered by the
extension.
f) This subsection corresponds with 40 CFR 268.33(f), a provision whose
effectiveness has expired. This statement maintains structural
consistency with U.S. EPA regulations.
g) To determine whether a hazardous waste listed in Section 728.110
exceeds the applicable treatment standards specified in Sections
728.131, ~~and 728.143~~ 728.140, and 728.Table T, the initial generator
shall test a representative sample or the extract of the waste, or the
generator may use knowledge of the waste, or the generator shall test
the entire waste concentrations in the waste extract or the waste. If
the waste contains constituents in excess of the applicable
728.Subpart D levels, the waste is prohibited from land disposal and
all requirements of this Part are applicable except as otherwise
specified.

(Source: Amended at 19 Ill. Reg. _____, effective
_____)

Section 728.138 Waste - Specific Prohibitions: -- Newly-Identified Organic
Toxicity Characteristic Wastes and Newly-Listed Coke By-Product and
Chlorotoluene Production Wastes

a) The wastes specified in 35 Ill. Adm. Code 721.132 as U.S. EPA
hazardous waste numbers K141, K142, K143, K144, K145, K147, K148,
K149, K150, and K151 are prohibited from land disposal. In addition,
debris contaminated with U.S. EPA hazardous waste numbers F037, F038,
K107 through K112, K117, K118, K123 through K126, K131, K132, K136,
U328, U353, U359 and soil and debris contaminated with D012 through
D043, K141 through K145, and K147 through K151 are prohibited from
land disposal. The following wastes that are specified in the table
at 35 Ill. Adm. Code 721.124(b) as U.S. EPA hazardous waste numbers
D012, D013, D014, D015, D016, D017, D018, D019, D020, D021, D022,
D023, D024, D025, D026, D027, D028, D029, D030, D031, D012, D033,
D034, D035, D036, D037, D038, D039, D040, D041, D042, and D043 that
are not radioactive, that are managed in systems other than those
whose discharge is regulated under the federal Clean Water Act (CWA;
33 U.S.C. Sections 1251 et seq.), that are zero dischargers that do
not engage in CWA-equivalent treatment before ultimate land disposal,
or that are injected in Class I deep wells regulated under the Safe
Drinking Water Act (SDWA) are prohibited from land disposal.
"CWA-equivalent treatment", as used in this Section, means biological
treatment for organics, alkaline chlorination or ferrous sulfate

POLLUTION CONTROL BOARD

NOTICE OF PROPOSED AMENDMENTS

precipitation for cyanide; precipitation and sedimentation for metals;
reduction for hexavalent chromium, or another treatment technology
that can be demonstrated to perform equally to or better than these
technologies.

b) On September 19, 1996, radioactive wastes that are mixed with any of
U.S. EPA hazardous waste number D018 through D043 waste that are
managed in systems other than those whose discharge is regulated under
the Clean Water Act (CWA), in systems that inject in Class I deep
wells regulated under the Safe Drinking Water Act (SDWA), or in
systems that are zero discharges that engage in CWA-equivalent
treatment, as defined in subsection (a) above, before ultimate land
disposal are prohibited from land disposal. Radioactive wastes mixed
with any of U.S. EPA hazardous waste number K141 through K145 and K147
through K151 are also prohibited from land disposal. In addition,
soil and debris contaminated with these radioactive mixed wastes are
prohibited from land disposal.

c) Between December 19, 1994 and September 19, 1996, the wastes included
in subsection (b) above may be disposed in a landfill or surface
impoundment only if such unit is in compliance with the requirements
specified in Section 728.105(b)(2).

d) The requirements of subsections (a), (b), and (c) above do not apply
if:

1) The wastes meet the applicable treatment standards specified in
728.Subpart D;

2) Persons have been granted an exemption from a prohibition
pursuant to a petition under Section 728.106, with respect to
those waters and units covered by the petition;

3) The wastes meet the applicable alternate treatment standards
established pursuant to a petition granted under Section 728.144;

4) Persons have been granted an extension to the effective date of a
prohibition pursuant to Section 728.105, with respect to these
wastes covered by the extension.

e) To determine whether a hazardous waste identified in this Section
exceeds the applicable treatment standards specified in Sections
728.140 and 728.Table T, the initial generator must test a sample of
the waste extract or the entire waste, depending on whether the
treatment standards are expressed as concentrations in the waste
extract or the entire waste, or the generator may use knowledge of the
waste. If the waste contains constituents in excess of the applicable
728.Subpart D levels, the waste is prohibited from land disposal and
all requirements of this Part are applicable, except as otherwise
specified.

(Source: Added at 19 Ill. Reg. _____, effective
_____)

SUBPART D: TREATMENT STANDARDS

POLLUTION CONTROL BOARD

NOTICE OF PROPOSED AMENDMENTS

Section 728.140 Applicability of Treatment Standards

a) A-restricted-waste-identified-in-Section-728.141-may-be-land--disposed
only--if--an--extract--of-the-waste-or-of-the-treatment-residue-of-the
waste--developed--using--Method--1311,--the--Toxicity--Characteristic
Leaching--Procedure;--does--not--exceed--the--value--shown--in-Section
728.Table-A-for-any-hazardous-constituent-listed-in-Section--728.Table
A--for--that--waste,-with-the-following-exceptions:--D004,-D005,-D031;
D004,-K031,-K132,-K030,-P011,-P012,-P036,-P038-and-W136.--These-wastes
may-be-land-disposed-only-if--an--extract--of--the--waste--or--of--the
treatment-residue-of-the-waste-developed-using-either-Method-1310,-the
Extraction--Procedure--Toxicity--Test,--or--Method--1311,-the-Toxicity
Characteristic-Leaching-Procedure,--or--the--test--method--in--Section
728-Appendix--A--does--not--exceed--the-concentration-shown-in-Section
728.Table-B-for-any-hazardous-constituent-listed--in--Section--728.Table
A--for--that--waste.---Methods--1310--and-1311-are-both-found-in-"Test
Methods-for-Evaluating-Solid-Waste,-Physical/Chemical--Methods",--U.S.
EPA--Publication--SW-846-as-incorporated-by-reference-in-35-Ill.-Adm.
Code-720.111. A waste identified in Section 728.Table T, "Treatment
Standards for Hazardous Wastes", may be land disposed only if it meets
the requirements found in that Section. For each waste, Section
728.Table T identifies one of three types of treatment standard
requirements:

1) All hazardous constituents in the waste or in the treatment
residue must be at or below the values found in that Section for
that waste ("total waste standards");

2) The hazardous constituents in the extract of the waste or in the
extract of the treatment residue must be at or below the values
found in that Section ("waste extract standards"); or

3) The waste must be treated using the technology specified in that
Section ("technology standard"), which is described in detail in
Section 728.Table C, "Technology Codes and Description of
Technology-Based Standards".

b) A-restricted-waste-for-which-a-treatment-technology-is-specified-under
Section--728.142(a)--or--hazardous--debris--for--which--a--treatment
technology--is--specified--under-Section-728.145-may-be-land-disposed
after-it-is-treated-using-that-specified-technology-or--an--equivalent
treatment-method-approved-by-the-Agency-under-the-procedures-set-forth
in--Section--728.142(b).---For--waste-displaying-the-characteristic-of
ignitability-(D001)-and-reactivity-(D003),-that-are--disposed--to--meet
the--deactivation--treatment--standard--in-Section-728.Table-T-and-if
(BDAT?)-the-treater-shall--comply--with--the--precautionary--measures
specified--in--35--Ill.--Adm.--Code--724.117(b)--and-35-Ill.-Adm.-Code
725.117(b). For wastewaters, compliance with concentration level
standards is based on maximums for any one day, except for D004
through D011 wastes for which the previously promulgated treatment
standards based on grab samples remain in effect. For all
nonwastewaters, compliance with concentration level standards is based

POLLUTION CONTROL BOARD

NOTICE OF PROPOSED AMENDMENTS

on grab sampling. For wastes covered by the waste extract standards, the test Method 1311, the Toxicity Characteristic Leaching Procedure, found in "Test Methods for Evaluating Solid Waste, Physical/Chemical Methods", U.S. EPA Publication SW-846, incorporated by reference in Section 720.111, must be used to measure compliance. An exception is made for D004 and D008, for which either of two test methods may be used: Method 1311 or Method 1310, the Extraction Procedure Toxicity Test, found in "Test Methods for Evaluating Solid Waste, Physical/Chemical Methods", U.S. EPA Publication SW-846, incorporated by reference in Section 720.111. For wastes covered by a technology standard, the wastes may be land disposed after being treated using that specified technology or an equivalent treatment technology approved by the Agency pursuant to Section 728.142(b).

c) Except--as--otherwise--specifies--in--Section-728.143(c),--a-restricted waste-identified-in-Section-728.143-may-be-land-disposed-only--if--the constituent--concentrations--in--the--waste-or-treatment-residue-of-the waste-do-not-exceed-the-value-shown-in-Section--728.Table--B--for--any hazardous--constituent--listed--in-Section-728.Table-B-for-that-waster When wastes with differing treatment standards for a constituent of concern are combined for purposes of treatment, the treatment residue must meet the lowest treatment standard for the constituent of concern.

d) If--a--treatment--standard--has--been--established--in-Section-728.143 through-728.143-for--a-hazardous-waste-that-is-itself-subject--to--those standards-rather-than-the-standards-for-hazardous-debris-under-Section 728.145; Notwithstanding the prohibitions specified in subsection (a) above, treatment and disposal facilities may demonstrate compliance with the treatment standards for organic constituents specified by a footnote in Section 728.Table T, provided the following conditions are satisfied:

1) The treatment standards for the organic constituents were established based on incineration in units operated in accordance with the technical requirements of 35 Ill. Adm. Code 724.Subpart O, or based on combustion in fuel substitution units operating in accordance with applicable technical requirements;

2) The treatment or disposal facility has used the methods referenced in subsection (d)(1) above to treat the organic constituents; and

3) The treatment or disposal facility may demonstrate compliance with organic constituents if good-faith analytical efforts achieve detection limits for the regulated organic constituents that do not exceed the treatment standards specified in this Section and Section 728.Table T by an order of magnitude.

e) For characteristic wastes (U.S EPA hazardous waste numbers D001, D002, and D012 through D043 that are subject to treatment standards in Section 728.Table T, "Treatment Standards for Hazardous Wastes", all underlying hazardous constituents (as defined in Section 728.102(1))

POLLUTION CONTROL BOARD

NOTICE OF PROPOSED AMENDMENTS

must meet universal treatment standards, found in Sections 728.148 and 728.Table U prior to land disposal.

f) The treatment standards for U.S. EPA hazardous waste numbers F001 through F005 nonwastewater constituents carbon disulfide, cyclohexanone, or methanol apply to wastes that contain only one, two, or three of these constituents. Compliance is measured for these constituents in the waste extract from test Method 1311, the Toxicity Characteristic Leaching Procedure found in "Test Methods for Evaluating Solid Waste, Physical/Chemical Methods", U.S. EPA Publication SW-846, incorporated by reference in Section 720.111. If the waste contains any of these three constituents along with any of the other 25 constituents found in U.S. EPA hazardous waste numbers F001 through F005, then compliance with treatment standards for carbon disulfide, cyclohexanone, or methanol are not required.

(Source: Amended at 19 Ill. Reg. _____, effective _____)

Section 728.141 Treatment Standards expressed as Concentrations in Waste Extract

For the requirements previously found in this Section and for treatment standards in Section 728.Table A, "Table CCWE-Constituent Concentrations in Waste Extracts", refer to Section 728.140 and 728.Table T, "Treatment Standards for Hazardous Wastes".

a) Section--728.Table--A--identifies--the--restricted--wastes--and--the concentrations--of--their--associated--constituents--that--may--not-be exceeded-by-the--extract--of--a--waste--or--waste--treatment--residual extracted--using--Method--1311;--the--Toxicity-Characteristic-Leaching Procedure,-for-the-allowable-land-disposal-of-such-waste;--Compliance with--these-concentrations-is-required-based-upon-grab-samples,-unless otherwise-noted-in-Section-728.Table-A,--Method-1311-is-found-in-"Test Methods-for-Evaluating-Solid-Waste,-Physical/Chemical--Methods",--U.S. EPA--Publication--SW-846,-as-incorporated-by-reference-in-35-Ill.-Adm. Code-720.111.

b) When-wastes-with-differing-treatment-standards-for--a--constituent--of concern--are-combined-for-purposes-of-treatment,-the-treatment-residue must-meet--the--lowest--treatment--standard--for--the--constituent--of concern;--except-that-mixtures-of-high-and-low-zinc-nonwastewater-H062 are-subject-to-the-treatment-standard-for-high-zinc-H061;

c) The-treatment-standards-for-constituents-in-F001-through-F005-that are-listed-in-Section-728.Table-A-only-apply-to-wastes--which--contain one,--two--or-all-three-of-these-constituents;--If-the-waste-contains any-of-these-three-constituents--along--with--any--of--the--other--26 constituents--found--in--F001--through--F005,-then-only-the-treatments standards-in-728.Table-A-are-required;

(Source: Amended at 19 Ill. Reg. _____, effective

POLLUTION CONTROL BOARD

NOTICE OF PROPOSED AMENDMENTS

_____)

Section 728.142 Treatment Standards Expressed as Specified Technologies

a) The following wastes in subsections (a)(1) and (b)(2) below and
    Sections 728.Table B T, "Treatment Standards for Hazardous Wastes",
    for which standards are expressed as a treatment method rather than a
    concentration level, and 728.Table H must be treated using the
    technology or technologies specified in subsections (a)(1) and (a)(2)
    below and Section 728.Table C T.
    1) Liquid hazardous wastes containing PCBs at concentrations greater
        than or equal to 50 ppm but less than 500 ppm must be incinerated
        in accordance with the technical requirements of 40 CFR 761.70,
        incorporated by reference in 35 Ill. Adm. Code 720.111, or burned
        in high efficiency boilers in accordance with the technical
        requirements of 40 CFR 761.60. Liquid hazardous wastes
        containing PCBs at concentrations greater than or equal to 500
        ppm must be incinerated in accordance with the technical
        requirements of 40 CFR 761.70. Thermal treatment in accordance
        with this Section must be in compliance with applicable
        regulations in 35 Ill. Adm. Code 724, 725, and 726.
    2) Nonliquid hazardous wastes containing halogenated organic
        compounds (HOCs) in total concentrations greater than or equal to
        1000 mg/kg and liquid HOC-containing wastes that are prohibited
        under Section 728.132(a)(1) must be incinerated in accordance
        with the requirements of 35 Ill. Adm. Code 724.Subpart O or 35
        Ill. Adm. Code 725.Subpart O. These treatment standards do not
        apply where the waste is subject to a treatment standard codified
        in 728.Subpart C of this Part for a specific HOC (such as a
        hazardous waste chlorinated solvent for which a treatment
        standard is established under Section 728.141(a)).
    3) A mixture consisting of wastewater, the discharge of which is
        subject to regulation under 35 Ill. Adm. Code 309 or 310, and de
        minimis losses of materials from manufacturing operations in
        which these materials are used as raw materials or are produced
        as products in the manufacturing process, and that meets the
        criteria of the D001 ignitable liquids containing greater than
        10% total organic constituents (TOC) subcategory, is are subject
        to the DEACT treatment standard described in Section 728.Table C.
        For purposes of this subsection, "de minimis losses" include:
        A) Those from normal material handling operations (e.g., spills
            from the unloading or transfer of materials from bins or
            other containers, or leaks from pipes, valves, or other
            devices used to transfer materials);
        B) Minor leaks from process equipment, storage tanks, or
            containers;
        C) Leaks from well-maintained pump packings and seals;
        D) Sample purgings; and

POLLUTION CONTROL BOARD

NOTICE OF PROPOSED AMENDMENTS

        E) Relief device discharges.
b) Any person may submit an application to the Agency demonstrating that
    an alternative treatment method can achieve a level of performance
    equivalent to that achievable by methods specified in subsections (a)
    above and (c) and (d) below for wastes or specified in Section
    728.Table F for hazardous debris. The applicant shall submit
    information demonstrating that the applicant's treatment method is in
    compliance with federal and state requirements, including this Part,
    35 Ill. Adm. Code 709, 724, 725, 726, and 729; and Sections 22.6 and
    39(h) of the Environmental Protection Act [415 ILCS 5/22.6 and39(h)],
    and that it the treatment method is protective of human health or and
    the environment. On the basis of such information and any other
    available information, the Agency shall approve the use of the
    alternative treatment method if the Agency finds that the alternative
    treatment method provides a measure of performance equivalent to that
    achieved by methods specified in subsections (a) above and (c) and (d)
    below for hazardous debris. Any approval
    must be stated in writing and may contain such provisions and
    conditions as the Agency determines to be appropriate. The person to
    whom such approval is issued shall comply with all limitations
    contained in such determination.
c) As an alternative to the otherwise applicable treatment standards of
    728.Subpart D of this Part, lab packs are eligible for land disposal
    provided the following requirements are met:
    1) The lab packs comply with the applicable provisions of 35 Ill.
        Adm. Code 724.416 and 725.416;
        BOARD NOTE: 35 Ill. Adm. Code 729.301 and 729.312 include
        additional restrictions on the use of lab packs.
    2) All hazardous wastes contained in each lab packs are specified in
        Appendix B or Appendix B The lab pack does not contain any of the
        wastes listed in Section 728.Appendix D;
    3) The lab packs are incinerated in accordance with the requirements
        of 35 Ill. Adm. Code 724.Subpart O or 35 Ill. Adm. Code
        725.Subpart O; and
    4) Any incinerator residues from lab packs containing D004, D005,
        D006, D007, D008, D010, and D011 are treated in compliance with
        the applicable treatment standards specified from such wastes in
        728.Subpart D.
d) Radioactive hazardous mixed wastes with treatment standards specified
    in Section 728.Table H are not subject to any treatment standards
    specified in Section 728.141, 728.143, or 728.Table B. Radioactive
    hazardous mixed wastes not subject to treatment standards in Section
    728.Table H remain subject to all applicable treatment standards
    specified in Sections 728.141, 728.143, and 728.Table D. are subject
    to the treatment standards in Sections 728.140 and 728.Table T. Where
    treatment standards are specified for radioactive mixed wastes in
    Section 728.Table T, "Table of Treatment Standards", those treatment
    standards will govern. Where there is no specific treatment standard

POLLUTION CONTROL BOARD

NOTICE OF PROPOSED AMENDMENTS

for radioactive mixed waste, the treatment standard for the hazardous waste (as designated by EPA waste code) applies. Hazardous debris containing radioactive waste is not subject to the treatment standards specified in Section 728.Table F but is subject to the treatment standards specified in Section 728.145.

(Source: Amended at 19 Ill. Reg. _____, effective _____)

Section 728.143 Treatment Standards ~~expressed~~ Expressed as Waste Concentrations

For the requirements previously found in this Section and for treatment standards in Section 728.Table A, "CCW-Constituent Concentrations in Wastes", refer to Section 728.140 and 728.Table T, "Treatment Standards for Hazardous Wastes".

~~a) Table B identifies the restricted wastes and the concentrations of their associated hazardous constituents which must not be exceeded by the waste or treatment residual (not an extract of such waste or treatment residual) for the allowable land disposal of such waste or residual. Compliance with these concentrations is required upon grab samples, unless otherwise noted in Table B.~~

~~b) When wastes with different treatment standards for a constituent of concern are combined for purposes of treatment, the treatment residue must meet the lowest treatment standard for the constituent of concern.~~

~~c) Notwithstanding the prohibitions specified in subsection (a) and Table B, treatment and disposal facilities may demonstrate (and certify pursuant to Section 728.107(b)(1)) compliance with the treatment standards for organic constituents specified in this Section and Table B by satisfying the following conditions:~~

~~1) The treatment for the organic constituents were established based on incineration in units operated in accordance with the technical requirements of 35 Ill. Adm. Code 724.Subpart O or 35 Ill. Adm. Code 725.Subpart O or based on combustion in fuel substitution units operating in accordance with applicable technical requirements;~~

~~2) The organic constituents have been treated using the methods referenced in subsection (c)(1); and~~

~~3) The treatment or disposal facility has been unable to detect the organic constituents despite using its best good faith efforts as defined by applicable standards. Until such standards are developed by good faith efforts may be demonstrated by showing that the treatment or disposal facility has detected the organic constituents at levels less than ten times the treatment standard specified in this Section.~~

(Source: Amended at 19 Ill. Reg. _____, effective

POLLUTION CONTROL BOARD

NOTICE OF PROPOSED AMENDMENTS

_____)

Section 728.145 Treatment Standards for Hazardous Debris

a) Treatment standards. Hazardous debris must be treated prior to land disposal as follows unless the Board has determined, under 35 Ill. Adm. Code 721.103(d)(2), that the debris is no longer contaminated with hazardous waste or the debris is treated to the waste-specific treatment standard provided in this Subpart for the waste contaminating the debris:

1) General. Hazardous debris must be treated for each "contaminant subject to treatment", defined by subsection (b) of this Section below, using the technology or technologies identified in Section 728.Table F.

2) Characteristic debris. Hazardous debris that exhibits the characteristic of ignitability, corrosivity, or reactivity identified under 35 Ill. Adm. Code 721.121, 721.122, and or 721.123, respectively, must be deactivated by treatment using one of the technologies identified in Section 728.Table F.

3) Mixtures of debris types. The treatment standards of Section 728.Table F must be achieved for each type of debris contained in a mixture of debris types. If an immobilization technology is used in a treatment train, it must be the last treatment technology used.

4) Mixtures of contaminant types. Debris that is contaminated with two or more contaminants subject to treatment identified under subsection (b) of this Section below must be treated for each contaminant using one or more treatment technologies identified in Section 728.Table F. If an immobilization technology is used in a treatment train, it must be the last treatment technology used.

5) Waste PCBs. Hazardous debris that is also a waste PCB under 40 CFR 761 is subject to the requirements of either 40 CFR 761 or the requirements of this Section, whichever are more stringent.

b) Contaminants subject to treatment. Hazardous debris must be treated for each "contaminant subject to treatment". The contaminants subject to treatment must be determined as follows:

1) Toxicity characteristic debris. The contaminants subject to treatment for debris that exhibits the Toxicity Characteristic (TC) by 35 Ill. Adm. Code 721.124 are those EP constituents for which the debris exhibits the TC toxicity characteristic.

2) Debris contaminated with listed waste. The contaminants subject to treatment for debris that is contaminated with a prohibited listed hazardous waste are those constituents or wastes for which BDAT treatment standards are established for the waste under Sections 728.141 728.140 and 728.143 728.Table T.

3) Cyanide reactive debris. Hazardous debris that is reactive because of cyanide must be treated for cyanide.

POLLUTION CONTROL BOARD

NOTICE OF PROPOSED AMENDMENTS

c) Conditioned exclusion of treated debris. Hazardous debris that has been treated using one of the specified extraction or destruction technologies in Section 728.Table F and that does not exhibit a characteristic of hazardous waste identified under 35 Ill. Adm. Code 721.Subpart C after treatment is not a hazardous waste and need not be managed in a subtitle C facility. Hazardous debris contaminated with a listed waste that is treated by an immobilization technology specified in Section 728.Table F is a hazardous waste and must be managed in a RCRA Subtitle ~~subtitle~~ C treatment, storage, or disposal facility.

d) Treatment residuals

1) General requirements. Except as provided by subsections (d)(2) and (d)(4) below:

A) Residue from the treatment of hazardous debris must be separated from the treated debris using simple physical or mechanical means; and

B) Residue from the treatment of hazardous debris is subject to the waste-specific treatment standards provided by 728.Subpart D ~~of this Part~~ for the waste contaminating the debris.

2) Nontoxic debris. Residue from the deactivation of ignitable, corrosive, or reactive characteristic hazardous debris (other than cyanide-reactive) that is not contaminated with a contaminant subject to treatment defined by subsection (b) above, must be deactivated prior to land disposal and is not subject to the waste-specific treatment standards of 728.Subpart D ~~of this Part~~.

3) Cyanide-reactive debris. Residue from the treatment of debris that is reactive because of cyanide must meet the standards for U.S. EPA hazardous waste number D003 under Section 728.143.

4) Ignitable nonwastewater residue. Ignitable nonwastewater residue containing equal to or greater than 10% total organic carbon is subject to the technology-based standards for U.S. EPA hazardous waste number D001: "Ignitable Liquids based on 35 Ill. Adm. Code 721.121(a)(1)", under Section 728.142.

5) Residue from spalling. Layers of debris removed by spalling are hazardous debris that remain subject to the treatment standards of this Section.

(Source: Amended at 19 Ill. Reg. _____, effective _____)

Section 728.146 Alternative Treatment Standards Based on ~~HTMR~~

~~Section 728.Table G identifies alternative treatment standards for F006 and K062 nonwastewaters.~~ For the treatment standards previously found in Section 728.Table G, as formerly referenced in this Section, refer to Sections 728.140 and 728.Table T, "Treatment Standards for Hazardous Wastes".

POLLUTION CONTROL BOARD

NOTICE OF PROPOSED AMENDMENTS

(Source: Amended at 19 Ill. Reg. _____, effective _____)

Section 728.148 Universal Treatment Standards

Section 728.Table U, "Universal Treatment Standards (UTS)", identifies the hazardous constituents, along with the nonwastewater and wastewater treatment standard levels, that are used to regulate most prohibited hazardous wastes with numerical limits. For determining compliance with treatment standards for underlying hazardous constituents, as defined in Section 728.102(1), these treatment standards may not be exceeded. Compliance with these treatment standards is measured by analysis of grab samples, unless otherwise noted in Section 728.Table U.

(Source: Added at 19 Ill. Reg. _____, effective _____)

POLLUTION CONTROL BOARD

NOTICE OF PROPOSED AMENDMENTS

Section 728.APPENDIX D ~~Organometallic Lab Packs~~ Wastes Excluded from Lab Packs

Hazardous waste with the following U.S. EPA hazardous waste codes may not be placed in lab packs under the alternative lab pack treatment standards of Section 728.142(c): D009, F019, K003, K004, K005, K006, K062, K071, K100, K106, P010, P011, P012, P076, P078, U134, and U151.
~~Hazardous waste with the following EPA hazardous waste code numbers may be placed in an "organometallic" or "Appendix D lab pack:"~~

~~P001, P002, P003, P004, P005, P006, P007, P308, P009, P011, P014, P015, P016, P017, P018, P020, P021, P022, P023, P024, P026, P027, P028, P029, P030, P031, P033, P034, P036, P037, P038, P039, P040, P041, P042, P043, P044, P045, P046, P047, P048, P049, P050, P051, P054, P056, P057, P058, P059, P060, P062, P063, P064, P065, P066, P067, P068, P069, P070, P071, P072, P073, P074, P075, P077, P081, P082, P084, P085, P087, P088, P089, P092, P093, P094, P095, P076, P097, P098, P099, P101, P102, P103, P104, P105, P106, P108, P109, P110, P111, P112, P113, P114, P115, P116, P118, P119, P120, P121, P122, P123~~

~~U001, U002, U003, U004, U005, U006, U007, U008, U009, U010, U011, U012, U014, U015, U016, U017, U018, U019, U020, U021, U022, U023, U024, U025, U026, U028, U029, U030, U031, U032, U033, U035, U036, U037, U038, U039, U041, U042, U043, U044, U045, U046, U047, U048, U049, U050, U051, U052, U053, U055, U056, U057, U058, U059, U060, U061, U062, U063, U064, U066, U067, U068, U069, U070, U071, U073, U074, U075, U076, U077, U078, U079, U080, U081, U082, U083, U084, U085, U086, U088, U089, U090, U091, U092, U093, U094, U095, U096, U097, U098, U099, U101, U102, U103, U105, U106, U107, U108, U109, U110, U111, U122, U137, U141, U145, U146, U147, U151, U152, U153, U160, U161, U162, U135, U136, U139, U131, U138, U140, U143, U147, U143, U144, U145, U146, U147, U148, U149, U150, U152, U153, U154, U155, U156, U157, U158, U159, U161, U162, U163, U164, U165, U166, U167, U168, U169, U170, U173, U174, U176, U177, U178, U179, U180, U181, U182, U183, U184, U185, U186, U187, U180, U189, U190, U191, U192, U193, U194, U196, U197, U200, U201, U203, U204, U205, U206, U209, U230, U211, U213, U214, U215, U216, U217, U218, U219, U220, U221, U222, U203, U225, U226, U227, U228, U234, U235, U236, U238, U239, U240, U243, U244, U246, U247, U248, U249~~

~~F001, F002, F003, F004, F005, F006, F010, F020, F021, F022, F023, F024, F025, F026, F027, F028, F039~~

~~K001, K002, K008, K009, K010, K011, K013, K014, K015, K016, K017, K018, K019, K020, K021, K022, K023, K024, K025, K027, K028, K029, K031, K032, K033, K034, K035, K036, K037, K039, K040, K041, K042, K043, K044, K045, K046, K047, K048, K049, K050, K051, K052, K060, K061, K069, K071, K083, K084, K085, K086, K093, K094, K095, K096, K097, K098, K099, K101, K102, K103, K104, K105, K113, K114, K115, K116~~

~~D001, D002, D003, D004, D005, D006, D007, D008, D010, D011, D012, D013, D014~~

~~D015, D016, D017~~
BOARD NOTE: 35 Ill. Adm. Code 729.
limitations on the use of lab packs.

(Source: Amended at 19 Ill.
_____)

POLLUTION CONTROL BOARD

NOTICE OF PROPOSED AMENDMENTS

Section 728.APPENDIX E Organic Lab Packs (Repealed)

Hazardous--wastes-with-the-following-EPA-Hazardous-Code-Nov-may-be-placed
in-an-"organic"-or-"Appendix-B"-lab-pack:

P001,--P002,--P003,-P004,-P005,-P007,-P008,-P009,-P014,-P016,-P017,--P050,--P054,
P051,--P029,--P024,--P026,--P027,-P028,--P030,--P031,-P033,-P034,-P037,-P039,
P040,--P041,--P042,-P043,-P044,-P045,-P046,-P047,-P048,-P049,-P050,--P051,--P054,
P057,--P058,--P059,-P060,-P062,-P063,-P064,-P065,-P067,-P068,-P069,-P070,-P071,
P072,--P073,--P074,-P075,-P077,-P078,-P079,-P080,-P081,-P082,--P083,--P084,
P098--P101,-P103,-P105,-P106,-P108,-P109,-P111,-P112,-P116,-P118-P123

U001,--U002,--U003,-U004,--U005,-U006,-U007,-U008,-U009,-U010,-U011,-U012,--U014,
U015,--U016,--U017,-U019,-U020,-U021,-U022,-U023,-U024,-U025,--U026,--U027,
U028,--U029,--U030,-U031,-U032,-U034,-U035,-U036,-U037,-U038,-U039,-U041,-U042,
U043,--U044,--U045,-U046,-U047,-U048,-U049,-U050,-U052,-U053,-U055,--U056,--U057,
U058,--U059,--U060,-U061,-U062,-U063,-U064,-U066,-U067,-U068,-U069,-U070,-U071,
U072,--U073,--U074,-U075,-U077,-U078,-U079,-U080,-U081,-U082,--U083,--U084,
U085,--U086,--U087,-U088,-U089,-U090,-U091,-U092,-U093,-U094,-U095,-U096,-U097,
U098,--U099,--U101,-U103,-U105,-U106,-U107,-U108,-U109,-U110,--U111,--U112,
U113,--U114,--U115,-U116,-U117,-U118,-U119,-U120,-U122,-U123,-U124,-U125,
U126,--U127,--U129,-U130,-U131,-U132,-U133,-U135,-U137,--U138,--U140,--U141,
U142,--U143,--U147,-U148,-U149,-U150,-U151,-U153,-U154,-U155,-U156,-U157,-U158,
U159,--U160,--U161,-U162,-U164,-U165,-U166,-U167,-U168,-U169,--U170,--U171,
U172,--U173,--U174,-U176,-U177,-U178,-U179,-U180,-U181,-U183,-U183,-U184,-U185,
U186,--U187,--U188,-U189,-U190,-U191,-U192,-U193,-U194,-U196,-U197,--U200,--U201,
U202,--U203,--U206,-U207,-U208,-U209,-U210,-U211,-U213,-U218,-U219,-U220,-U221,
U222,--U223,--U225,-U227,-U228,-U234,-U235,-U236,-U237,--U238,--U239,--U240,
U243--U244--U246--U247--U248--U249

P001,---P002,---P003,-P004,-P005,-P010,-P020,-P021,-P022,-P023,-P025,-P026,-P027,
P008

N009,--N010,--N011,-N012,-P014,-N016,-N017,-N019,-N020,-N023,--N024,--N025,
N026,--N027,--N029,-N030,-N032,-N033,-N034,-N035,-N036,-N037,-N038,-N039,-N040,
N041,--N042,--N043,-N044,-N045,-N047,-N060,-N073,-N085,-N093,-N094,--N095,-N096,
N097--N098,-N099,-N100,-N104,-N105,-N113,-N114,-N116

D001,--D012,--D013,-D014,-D015,-D016,-D017
BOARD---NOTE:--35--Ill:--Adm:--Code--729.301--and--729.312--include--additional
limitations-on-the-use-of-lab-packs:

(Source: Repealed at 19 Ill. Reg. ____ ____, effective
_____)

POLLUTION CONTROL BOARD

NOTICE OF PROPOSED AMENDMENTS

Section 728.APPENDIX J Recordkeeping, Notification, and Certification
Requirements

Entity and Scenario	Frequency	Recipient of Notification	Recordkeeping, Notification, and Certification Requirements
I. Generator			
A. Waste does not meet applicable treatment standards or exceeds applicable prohibition levels (see Section 728.107(a)(1)).	Each shipment	Treatment or storage facility.	Notice must include: --U.S. EPA hazardous waste number. --Constituents of concern. --Treatability group. --Manifest number. --Waste analysis data (where available).
B. Waste can be disposed of without further treatment (meets applicable treatment standards or does not exceed prohibition levels upon generation) (see Section 728.107 (a)(2)).	Each shipment	Land disposal facility	Notice and certification statement that waste meets applicable treatment standards or applicable prohibition levels. Notice must include: --U.S. EPA hazardous waste number. --Constituents of concern. --Treatability group.

			--Manifest number.
			--Waste analysis data (where available).
			Certification statement required under Section 728.107(a)(2)(B) that waste complies with treatment standards and prohibitions.
C. Waste is subject to exemption from a prohibition on the type of land disposal utilized for the waste, such as a case-by-case extension under Section 728.105, an exemption under Section 728.106, or a nationwide capacity variance (see Section 728.107(a)(3)).	Each shipment	Receiving facility	Notice must include:
			--Statement that waste is not prohibited from land disposal.
			--U.S. EPA hazardous waste number.
			--Constituents of concern.
			--Treatability group.
			--Manifest number.
			--Waste analysis data (where available).
			--Date the waste is subject to the prohibitions.
D. Waste is being accumulated in tanks or containers regulated under 35 Ill. Adm. Code	Minimum of 30 days prior to treatment activity.	Agency, Delivery must be verified.	Generator must develop, keep on-site, and follow a written waste analysis plan describing

722.134 and is being treated in such tanks or containers to meet applicable treatment standards (see Section 728.107(a)(4)).			procedures used to comply with the treatment standards.
			If waste is shipped off-site, generator also must comply with notification notification requirement of Section 728.107(a)(2).
E. Generator is managing a lab pack containing certain wastes and wishes to use an alternative treatment standard (see Section 728.107(a)(8)).	Each shipment	Treatment facility	Notice in accordance with Section 728.107(a)(1), (a)(5), and (a)(6), where applicable.
			Certification in accordance with Section 728.107(a)(8).
F. Small quantity generators with tolling agreements (pursuant to 35 Ill. Adm. Code 722.120(e)) (see Section 728.107(a)(9)).	Initial shipment	Treatment facility	Must comply with applicable notification and certification requirements in Section 728.107(a). Generator also must retain copy of the notification and certification together with tolling agreement on-site for at least 3 years after termination or expiration of agreement.
G. Generator has determined waste is restricted based solely on his knowledge of	N/A	Generator's file	All supporting data must be retained on-site in generator's files.

POLLUTION CONTROL BOARD

NOTICE OF PROPOSED AMENDMENTS

the waste (see Section 728.107 (a)(5)).

H. Generator has determined waste is restricted based on testing waste or an extract (see Section 728.107(a)(5)).	N/A	Generator's file	All waste analysis data must be retained on-site in generator's files.
I. Generator has determined that waste is excluded from the definition of hazardous or solid waste or exempt from RCRA Subtitle C (hazardous waste) regulation (see Section 728.107(a)(6)).	One-time	Generator's file	Notice of generation and subsequent exclusion from the definition of hazardous or solid waste, or exemption from RCRA Subtitle C (hazardous waste) regulation, and information regarding the disposition of the waste.
J. Generator (or treater) claims that hazardous debris is excluded from the definition of hazardous waste under 35 Ill. Adm. Code 721.103(f)(1) (see Section 728.107(d)).	One-time	Agency. Notification must be updated as necessary under Section 728.107(d)(2).	Notice must include: --Name and address of RCRA Subtitle D (municipal solid waste landfill) facility receiving treated debris. --U.S. EPA hazardous waste number and description of debris as initially generated. --Technology used to treat the debris (Table 1 of Section 728.145).

POLLUTION CONTROL BOARD

NOTICE OF PROPOSED AMENDMENTS

Certification and recordkeeping in accordance with Section 728.107 (d)(3).

K. Generator (or treater) claims that characteristic wastes are no longer hazardous (see Section 728.109(d)).	One-time	Generator's (or treater's) files and Agency. Notification must be updated as necessary under Section 728.109(d).	Notice must include: --Name and address of RCRA Subtitle D (municipal solid waste landfill) facility receiving the waste. --U.S. EPA hazardous waste number and description of waste as initially generated. --Treatability group. --Underlying hazardous constituents. Certification in accordance with Section 728.109 (d)(2).
L. Other recordkeeping requirements (see Section 728.107 (a)(7)).	N/A	Generator's file	Generator must retain a copy of all notices, certifications, demonstrations, waste analysis data, and other documentation produced pursuant to Section 728.107 on-site for at least 5 years from the date that the waste was last sent

II. Treatment Facility

			to on-site or off-site treatment, storage, or disposal. This period is automatically extended during enforcement actions or as requested by the Agency.
A. Waste shipped from treatment facility to land disposal facility (see Sections 728.107(b)(4) and (b)(5)).	Each shipment	Land disposal facility	Notice must include: --U.S. EPA hazardous waste number. --Constituents of concern. --Treatability group. --Manifest number. --Waste analysis data (where available). Application certification, in accordance with Section 728.107 (b)(5)(A), (b)(5)(B) or (b)(5)(C), stating that the waste or treatment residue has been treated in compliance with applicable treatment standards and prohibitions.
B. Waste treatment residue from a	Each shipment	Receiving facility	Treatment, storage, or disposal

	treatment or storage facility will be further managed at a different treatment or storage facility (see Section 728.107(b)(6)).			facility must comply with all notice and certification requirements applicable to generators.
C. Where wastes are recyclable materials used in a manner constituting disposal subject to Section 726.120 (b) (see Section 728.107(b)(7)).	Each shipment	Agency.	No notification to receiving facility required pursuant to Section 728.107(b)(4). Certification as described in Section 728.107(b)(5) and notice with information listed in Section 728.107 (b)(4), except manifest number. Recycling facility must keep records of the name and location of each entity receiving hazardous waste-derived products.

III. Land Disposal Facility

A. Wastes accepted by land disposal facility (see Section 728.107 (c)).	N/A	N/A	Maintain copies of notice and certifications specified in Section 728.107(a) and (b).

Certification Statements

A. I certify under penalty of law that I personally have examined and am familiar with the waste through analysis and testing or through knowledge of the waste to support this certification that the waste complies with

POLLUTION CONTROL BOARD

NOTICE OF PROPOSED AMENDMENTS

the treatment standards specified in 35 Ill. Adm. Code 728.Subpart D and all applicable prohibitions set forth in 35 Ill. Adm. Code 728.132 or RCRA section 3004(d). I believe that the information I submitted is true, accurate and complete. I am aware that there are significant penalties for submitting a false certification, including the possibility of fine and imprisonment. (Section 728.107(a)(2)(B))

B. I certify under penalty of law that I personally have examined and am familiar with the waste and that the lab pack does not contain any wastes identified at Section 728.Appendix D. I am aware that there are significant penalties for submitting a false certification, including possibility of fine or imprisonment. (Section 728.107(a)(8))

C. I certify under penalty of law that I have personally examined and am familiar with the treatment technology and operation of the treatment process used to support this certification and that, based on my inquiry of those individuals immediately responsible for obtaining this information, I believe that the treatment process has been operated and maintained properly so as to comply with the performance levels specified in 35 Ill. Adm. Code 728.Subpart D, and all applicable prohibitions set forth in 35 Ill. Adm. Code 728.132 or RCRA section 3004(d) without impermissible dilution of the prohibited waste. I am aware that there are significant penalties for submitting a false certification, including the possibility of fine and imprisonment. (Section 728.107(b)(5)(A))

D. I certify under penalty of law that the waste has been treated in accordance with the requirements of 35 Ill. Adm. Code 728.142. I am aware that there are significant penalties for submitting a false certification, including the possibility of fine and imprisonment. (Section 728.107(b)(5)(B))

E. I certify under penalty of law that I have personally examined and am familiar with the treatment technology and operation of the treatment process used to support this certification and that, based on my inquiry of those individuals immediately responsible for obtaining this information, I believe that the nonwastewater organic constituents have been treated by incineration in units operated in accordance with 35 Ill. Adm. Code 724.Subpart O or 35 Ill. Adm. Code 725.Subpart O or by combustion in fuel substitution units operating in accordance with applicable technical requirements, and I have been unable to detect the nonwastewater organic constituents, despite having used best good faith efforts to analyze for such constituents. I am aware that there are significant penalties for submitting a false certification, including the possibility of fine and imprisonment. (Section 728.107(b)(5)(C))

F. I certify under penalty of law that the waste has been treated in accordance with the requirements of 35 Ill. Adm. Code 728.140 to remove the hazardous characteristic. This decharacterized waste contains

POLLUTION CONTROL BOARD

NOTICE OF PROPOSED AMENDMENTS

underlying hazardous constituents that require further treatment to meet universal treatment standards. I am aware that there are significant penalties for submitting a false certification, including the possibility of fine and imprisonment. (Section 728.107(b)(5)(D))

G. I certify under penalty of law that the debris have been treated in accordance with the requirements of 35 Ill. Adm. Code 728.145. I am aware that there are significant penalties for making a false certification, including the possibility of fine and imprisonment. (Section 728.107(d)(3)(C))

(Source: Added at 19 Ill. Reg. _____, effective _____)

POLLUTION CONTROL BOARD

NOTICE OF PROPOSED AMENDMENTS

Section 728.TABLE A Constituent Concentration in Waste Extract (CCWE)

For the requirements previously found in this Section and Section 728.141, refer to Section 728.140 and 728.Table T, "Treatment Standards for Hazardous Wastes".

D-, F-, and K-Listed Wastes

Waste Code	See Also	Regulated Hazardous Constituent	CAS No. for Regulated Hazardous Constituent	Concentration (mg/l) Wastewaters	Non-wastewaters
D004	Table B	Arsenic	7440-38-2	NA	5.0-#A
D005	Table B	Barium	7440-39-3	NA	100.
D006	Table B	Cadmium	7440-43-9	NA	1.0
D007	Table B	Chromium (Total)	7440-47-32	NA	5.0
D008	Table B	Lead	7439-92-1	NA	5.0-#A
D009	(Low-Mercury-Subcategory--less-than-260-mg/kg-Mercury) Tables B-A-B	Mercury	7439-97-6	NA	0.20
D010	Table B	Selenium	7782-49-2	NA	5.7
D011	Table B	Silver	7440-22-4	NA	5.0
F001-F005-spent-solvents	Table B	Carbon-disulfide	75-15-0	NA	4.0
		Cyclohexanone	108-94-1	NA	0.75
		Methanol	67-56-1	NA	0.75
F006	Table B	Cadmium	7440-43-9	NA	0.066
		Chromium (Total)	7440-47-32	NA	5.2
		Lead	7439-92-1	NA	0.51
		Nickel	7440-02-0	NA	0.32
		Silver	7440-22-4	NA	0.072
F007	Table B	Cadmium	7440-43-9	NA	0.066
		Chromium (Total	7440-47-32	NA	5.2
		Lead	7439-92-1	NA	0.51
		Nickel	7440-02-0	NA	0.32
		Silver	7440-22-4	NA	0.072

POLLUTION CONTROL BOARD

NOTICE OF PROPOSED AMENDMENTS

F008	Table B	Cadmium	7440-43-9	NA	0.066
		Chromium (Total)	7440-47-32	NA	5.2
		Lead	7439-92-1	NA	0.51
		Nickel	7440-02-0	NA	0.32
		Silver	7440-22-4	NA	0.072
F009	Table B	Cadmium	7440-43-9	NA	0.066
		Chromium (Total)	7440-47-32	NA	5.2
		Lead	7439-92-1	NA	0.51
		Nickel	7440-02-0	NA	0.32
		Silver	7440-22-4	NA	0.072
F011	Table B	Cadmium	7440-43-9	NA	0.066
		Chromium (Total)	7440-47-32	NA	5.2
		Lead	7439-92-1	NA	0.51
		Nickel	7440-02-0	NA	0.32
		Silver	7440-22-4	NA	0.072
F012	Table B	Cadmium	7440-43-9	NA	0.066
		Chromium (Total)	7440-47-32	NA	5.2
		Lead	7439-92-1	NA	0.51
		Nickel	7440-02-0	NA	0.32
		Silver	7440-22-4	NA	0.072
F019	Table B	Chromium (Total)	7440-47-32	NA	5.2
F020-F023-and-F026-F028-dioxin-containing-wastes*		HxCDD-All Hexachloro-dibenzo-p-dioxins		<1.-ppb	<1.-ppb
		HxCDF-All Hexachloro-dibenzofurans		<1.-ppb	<1.-ppb
		PeCDD-All Pentachloro-dibenzo-p-dioxins		<1.-ppb	<1.-ppb
		PeCDF-All-Penta-chlorodibenzo-furans		<1.-ppb	<1.-ppb
		TCDD-All-Tetra-chlorodibenzo-p-dioxins		<1.-ppb	<1.-ppb
		TCDF-All-Tetra-chlorodibenzo-furans			
		2,4,5-Trichloro-phenol	95-95-4	<1.-ppb	<1.-ppb

POLLUTION CONTROL BOARD

NOTICE OF PROPOSED AMENDMENTS

		2,4,6-Trichloro-phenol	88-06-2	-0.05-ppm	-0.05-ppm
		2,3,4,6-Tetra-chlorophenol	58-90-2	-0.05-ppm	-0.05-ppm
		Pentachloro-phenol	87-86-5	-0.01-ppm	-0.01-ppm
F024	Table-B	Chromium-(Total)	7440-47-32	NA	0.073
		Lead	7439-92-1	NA	-Reserved
		Nickel	7440-02-0	NA	0.000
F037	Table-B	Chromium-(Total)	7440-47-32	NA	1.7
		Nickel	7440-02-0	NA	0.20
F038	Table-B	Chromium-(Total)	7440-47-32	NA	1.7
		Nickel	7440-02-0	NA	0.20

F039-(and-D001-and-D002-wastes-prohibited-under-Section-728.137)

	Tables B-a-D	Antimony	7440-36-0	NA	0.23
		Arsenic	7440-38-2	NA	5.0
		Barium	7440-39-3	NA	52.
		Cadmium	7440-43-9	NA	0.066
		Chromium-(Total)	7440-47-32	NA	5.2
		Lead	7439-92-1	NA	0.51
		Mercury	7439-97-6	NA	0.025
		Nickel	7440-02-0	NA	0.32
		Selenium	7782-49-2	NA	5.7
		Silver	7440-02-4	NA	0.072
K001	Table-B	Lead	7439-92-1	NA	0.51
K002	Table-B	Chromium-(Total)	7440-47-32	NA	0.094
		Lead	7439-92-1	NA	0.37
K003	Table-B	Chromium-(Total)	7440-47-32	NA	0.094
		Lead	7439-92-1	NA	0.37
K004	Table-B	Chromium-(Total)	7440-47-32	NA	0.094
		Lead	7439-92-1	NA	0.37
K005	Table-B	Chromium-(Total)	7440-47-32	NA	0.094
		Lead	7439-92-1	NA	0.37
K006	(anhydrous)				
	Table-B	Chromium-(Total)	7440-47-32	NA	0.094
		Lead	7439-92-1	NA	0.37

POLLUTION CONTROL BOARD

NOTICE OF PROPOSED AMENDMENTS

K006	(hydrated)				
	Table-B	Chromium-(Total)	7440-47-32	NA	5.2
K007	Table-B	Chromium-(Total)	7440-47-32	NA	0.094
		Lead	7439-92-1	NA	0.37
K008	Table-B	Chromium-(Total)	7440-47-32	NA	00.094
		Lead	7439-92-1	NA	0.37
K015	Table-B	Chromium-(Total)	7440-47-32	NA	1.7
		Nickel	7440-02-0	NA	0.2
K021	Table-B	Antimony	7440-36-0	NA	0.23-1A
K022	Table-B	Chromium-(Total)	7440-47-32	NA	5.2
		Nickel	7440-02-0	NA	0.32
K028	Table-B	Chromium-(Total)	7440-47-32	NA	0.073
		Lead	7439-92-1	NA	0.51
		Nickel	7440-02-0	NA	0.000
K031	Table-B	Arsenic	7440-38-2	NA	5.6-1A
K046	Table-B	Lead	7439-92-1	NA	0.18
K048	Table-B	Chromium-(Total)	7440-47-32	NA	1.7
		Nickel	7440-02-0	NA	0.20
K049	Table-B	Chromium-(Total)	7440-47-32	NA	1.7
		Nickel	7440-02-0	NA	0.20
K050	Table-B	Chromium-(Total)	7440-47-32	NA	1.7
		Nickel	7440-02-0	NA	0.20
K051	Table-B	Chromium-(Total)	7440-47-32	NA	1.7
		Nickel	7440-02-0	NA	0.20
K052	Table-B	Chromium-(Total)	7440-47-32	NA	1.7
		Nickel	7440-02-0	NA	0.20
K061	Table-B	Antimony	7440-36-0	NA	2.1
		Arsenic	7440-38-2	NA	0.055
		Barium	7440-39-3	NA	7.6
		Beryllium	7440-41-7	NA	0.014
		Cadmium	7440-43-9	NA	0.19
		Chromium-(Total)	7440-47-32	NA	0.33
		Lead	7439-92-1	NA	0.37
		Mercury	7439-97-6	NA	0.009

POLLUTION CONTROL BOARD

NOTICE OF PROPOSED AMENDMENTS

		Nickel	7440-02-0	NA	5.
		Selenium	7782-49-2	NA	0.16
		Silver	7440-22-4	NA	0.3
		Thallium		NA	0.078
		Zinc	7440-66-6	NA	5.3
K062	Table-B	Chromium-(Total)	7440-47-32	NA	0.094
		lead	7439-92-1	NA	0.37
K069	(Calcium-Sulfate-Subcategory)				
	Table-B-a-B	Cadmium	7440-43-9	NA	0.14
		lead	7439-92-1	NA	0.24
K071	Table-B	Mercury	7439-97-6	NA	0.025
K083	Table-B	Nickel	7440-02-0	NA	0.088
K084	Table-B	Arsenic	7440-38-2	NA	5.6-8A
K086	Table-B	Chromium-(Total)	7440-47-32	NA	0.094
		lead	7439-92-1	NA	0.37
K087	Table-B	lead	7439-92-1	NA	0.51
K100	Table-B	Cadmium	7440-43-9	NA	0.066
		Chromium-(Total)	7440-47-32	NA	5.2
		lead	7439-92-1	NA	0.51
K101	Table-B	Arsenic	7440-38-2	NA	5.6-8A
K102	Table-B	Arsenic	7440-38-2	NA	5.6-8A
K106	(low-Mercury-Subcategory--less-than-260-mg/kg-Mercury--residues from-RMERC)				
	Table-B-a-B	Mercury	7439-97-6	NA	0.28
K106	(low-Mercury-Subcategory--less-than-260-mg/kg-Mercury--that-are not-residues-from-RMERC)				
	Table-B-a-B	Mercury	7439-97-6	NA	0.025
K115	Table-B	Nickel	7440-02-0	NA	0.32

P-and-U-Listed-Wastes

CAS-No--for

POLLUTION CONTROL BOARD

NOTICE OF PROPOSED AMENDMENTS

Commercial Waste Code	Chemical Name	See Also	Regulated Hazardous Constituent	Regulated Hazardous Constituent	Concentration (mg/l) Waste- waters	Non waste waters
P010 #A	Table B	Arsenic acid	Arsenic	7440-38-2	NA	5.6
P011 #A	Table B	Arsenic pentoxide	Arsenic	7440-38-2	NA	5.6
P012 #A	Table B	Arsenic trioxide	Arsenic	7440-38-2	NA	5.6
P013	Table B	Barium cyanide	Barium	7440-39-3	NA	52.
P036 #A	Table B	Dichloro- phenylar- sine	Arsenic	7440-38-2	NA	5.6
P038 #A	Table B	Diethyl- arsine	Arsenic	7440-38-2	NA	5.6
P065	(low-Mercury-Subcategory--less-than-260-mg/kg-Mercury--residues-from RMERC)					
	Table B-a-B	Mercury fulminate	Mercury	7439-97-6	NA	0.28
P065	(low-Mercury-Subcategory--less-than-260-mg/kg-Mercury--incinerator residues-(and-are-not-residues-from-RMERC))					
	Table B-a-B	Mercury fulminate	Mercury	7439-97-6	NA	0.025
P073	Table B	Nickel carbonyl	Nickel	7440-02-0	NA	0.32
P074	Table B	Nickel cyanide	Nickel	7440-02-0	NA	0.32
P092	(low-Mercury-Subcategory----less-than-260-mg/kg-Mercury--residues from RMERC)					
	Table B-a-B	Phenyl mercury acetate	Mercury	7439-97-6	NA	0.28
P092	(low-Mercury-Subcategory--less-than-260-mg/kg-Mercury--incinerator residues-(and-are-not-residues-from-RMERC))					
	Table B-a-B	Phenyl mercury acetate	Mercury	7439-97-6	NA	0.025
P099	Table B	Potassium silver	Silver	7440-22-4	NA	0.072

POLLUTION CONTROL BOARD

NOTICE OF PROPOSED AMENDMENTS

		cyanide				
P103	Table B	Selen-oures	Selenium	7782-49-2	NA	5.7
P104	Table B	Silver cyanide	Silver	7440-22-4	NA	0.072
P110	Table B	Tetra-ethyl lead	Lead	7439-92-1	NA	0.51
P114	Table B	Thallium selenite	Selenium	7782-49-2	NA	5.7
U032	Table B	Calcium chromate	Chromium (Total)	7440-47-33	NA	0.094
U051	Table B	Creosote	Lead	7439-92-1	NA	0.51
U136	Table B	Cacodylic acid	Arsenic	7440-38-2	NA	5.6
U144	Table B	Lead acetate	Lead	7439-92-1	NA	0.51
U145	Table B	Lead phosphate	Lead	7439-92-1	NA	0.51
U146	Table B	Lead subacetate	Lead	7439-92-1	NA	0.51

U151 (Low Mercury Subcategory—less than 260 mg/kg Mercury—residues form RMERC)

	Tables B-a-B	Mercury	Mercury	7439-97-6	NA	0.20

U151 (Low Mercury Subcategory—less than 260 mg/kg Mercury—that are not residues from RMERC)

	Tables B-a-B	Mercury dioxide	Mercury	7439-97-6	NA	0.025
U204	Table B	Selenium	Selenium	7782-49-2	NA	5.7
U205	Table B	Selenium sulfide	Selenium	7782-49-2	NA	5.7

#A—These treatment standards have been based on BP beathate analysis but this does not preclude the use of TULP analysis;

*B—These waste codes are not subcategorized into wastewaters and nonwastewaters;

NA—Not Applicable;

(Source: Amended at 19 Ill. Reg. _____, effective _____)

POLLUTION CONTROL BOARD

NOTICE OF PROPOSED AMENDMENTS

Section 728.TABLE B Constituent Concentrations in Waste (CCW)

For the requirements previously found in this Section and for treatment standards in Section 728.143, "Constituent Concentrations in Wastes (CCW)", refer to Section 728.140 and 728.Table T, "Treatment Standards for Hazardous Wastes".

By F and H listed Wastes

Waste Code	See Also	Regulated Hazardous Constituent	CAS No. for Regulated Hazardous Constituent	Concentration (mg/l) Wastewaters	Non-wastewaters

D003 (Reactive cyanides subcategory—based on 35 Ill. Adm. Code 721.123(a)(5))

	NA	Cyanides (Total)	57-12-5	Rsrv	0.590 - C
		Cyanides (Amendable)	57-12-5	0.86	-30.
D004	Table A	Arsenic	7440-38-2	5.0	NA
D005	Table A	Barium	7440-39-3	100.	NA
D006	Table A	Cadmium	7440-43-9	1.0	NA
D007	Table A	Chromium (Total)	7440-47-33	5.0	NA
D008	Table A	Lead	7439-92-1	5.0	NA
D009	Table A	Mercury	7439-97-6	0.20	NA
D010	Table A	Selenium	7782-49-2	1.0	NA
D011	Table A	Silver	7440-22-4	5.0	NA
D012	Table D	Endrin	720-20-8	NA	0.13 - A
D013	Table D	Lindane	58-89-9	NA	0.066 - A
D014	Table D	Methoxychlor	72-43-5	NA	0.18 - A
D015	Table D	Toxaphene	8001-35-1	NA	1.3 - A
D016	Table D	2,4-D	94-75-7	NA	10.0 - A
D017	Table D	2,4,5-TP (Silvex)	93-76-5	NA	7.9 - A

POLLUTION CONTROL BOARD

NOTICE OF PROPOSED AMENDMENTS

F001-F005 spent solvents

Acetone	67-64-1	0.28	160.
Benzene	71-43-2	0.070	3.7-A
n-Butyl alcohol	71-36-3	5.6	2.6
Carbon tetrachloride	56-23-5	0.057	5.6
Chlorobenzene	108-90-7	0.057	5.7
Cresol-(m- and p-isomers)		0.77	3.2
o-cresol		0.11	5.6
o-Dichlorobenzene	95-50-1	0.088	6.2
Ethyl acetate	141-7-6	0.34	33.
Ethyl benzene	100-41-4	0.057	6.0
Ethyl ether	60-29-7	0.12	160.
Isobutyl alcohol	78-83-1	5.6	170.
Methylene chloride	75-9-2	0.089	33.
Methyl ethyl ketone	78-93-3	0.28	36.
Methyl isobutyl ketone	108-10-1	0.14	33.
Nitrobenzene	98-95-3	0.068	14.
Pyridine	110-86-1	0.014	16.
Tetrachloroethylene	127-18-4	0.056	5.6
Toluene	108-88-3	0.08	28.
1,1,1-Trichloroethane	71-55-6	0.054	5.6
1,1,2-Trichloroethane	79-00-5	0.030	7.6-A
Trichloroethylene	79-01-6	0.054	5.6
1,1,2-Trichloro-1,2,2-trifluoroethane	76-13-1	0.057	28.
Trichloromonofluoromethane	75-69-4	0.02	33.
Xylenes-(total)		0.32	28.
F006 Table-A Cyanides-(Total)	57-12-5	1.2	590.
Cyanides (Amenable)	57-12-5	0.86	30.
Cadmium	7440-43-9	1.6	NA
Chromium	7440-47-32	0.32	NA

POLLUTION CONTROL BOARD

NOTICE OF PROPOSED AMENDMENTS

Lead	7439-92-1	0.040	NA
Nickel	7440-02-0	0.44	NA
F007 Table-A Cyanides-(Total)	57-12-5	1.9	590.
Cyanides (Amenable)	57-12-5	0.1	30.
Chromium-(Total)	7440-47-32	0.32	NA
Lead	7439-92-1	0.04	NA
Nickel	7440-02-0	0.44	NA
F008 Table-A Cyanides-(Total)	57-12-5	1.9	590.
Cyanides (Amenable)	57-12-5	0.1	30.
Chromium	7440-47-32	0.32	NA
Lead	7439-92-1	0.04	NA
Nickel	7440-02-0	0.44	NA
F009 Table-A Cyanides-(Total)	57-12-5	1.9	590.
Cyanides (Amenable)	57-12-5	0.1	30.
Chromium	7440-47-32	0.32	NA
Lead	7439-92-1	0.04	NA
Nickel	7440-02-0	0.44	NA
F010 NA Cyanides-(Total)	57-12-5	1.9	1.5
Cyanides (Amenable)	57-12-5	0.1	
F011 Table-A Cyanides-(Total)	57-12-5	1.9	110.
Cyanides (Amenable)	57-12-5	0.1	9.1
Chromium-(Total)	7440-47-32	0.32	NA
Lead	7439-92-1	0.04	NA
Nickel	7440-02-0	0.44	NA
F012 Table-A Cyanides-(Total)	57-12-5	1.9	110.
Cyanides (Amenable)	57-12-5	0.1	9.1
Chromium-(Total)	7440-47-32	0.32	NA
Lead	7439-92-1	0.04	NA
Nickel	7440-02-0	0.44	NA
F019 Table-A Cyanides-(Total)	57-12-5	1.2	590.-C
Cyanides (Amenable)	57-12-5	0.86	30.-C
Chromium-(Total)	7440-47-32	0.32	NA

F024 †Note:--F024 organic standards must be treated via incineration

POLLUTION CONTROL BOARD

NOTICE OF PROPOSED AMENDMENTS

((NEW)) Tables A-a-B	2-Chloro-1,3-butadiene	126-99-8	0.28-A	0.28-A
	3-Chloropropene	107-05-1	0.28-A	0.28-A
	1,1-Dichloro-ethane	75-34-3	0.014-A	0.014-A
	1,2-Dichloro-ethane	107-06-2	0.014-A	0.014-A
	1,2-Dichloroe-thane	78-87-5	0.014-A	0.014-A
	cis-1,3-Dichloropropene	10061-01-5	0.014-A	0.014-A
	trans-1,3-Dichloropropene	10061-02-6	0.014-A	0.014-A
	Bis(2-ethylhexyl) phthalate	117-81-7	0.036-A	1.8-A
	Hexachloroethane	67-72-1	0.036-A	a-1.8-A
	Chromium (Total)	7440-47-32	0.35	NA
	Nickel	7440-02-0	0.47	NA
P025	((Light-ends-subcategory))			
	Chloroform	67-66-3	0.046-B	6.2-A
	1,2-Dichloro-ethane	107-06-2	0.21-B	6.2-A
	1,1-Dichloro-ethylene	75-35-4	0.025-B	6.2-A
	Methylene chloride	75-9-2	0.089-B	33.-A
	Carbon-tetra-chloride	56-23-5	0.057-B	6.2-A
	1,1,2-Trichloro-ethane	79-00-5	0.054-B	6.2-A
	Trichloro-ethylene	79-01-6	0.054-B	5.6-A
	Vinyl chloride	75-01-4	0.27-B	33.-A
P025 NA	((Spent-filters-or-aids-and-desiccants-subcategory))			
	Chloroform	67-66-3	0.046-B	6.2-A
	Methylene chloride	75-9-2	0.089-B	33.-A
	Carbon tetrachloride	56-23-5	0.057-B	6.2-A
	1,1,2-Trichloro-ethane	79-00-5	0.054-B	6.2-A
	Trichloro ethylene	79-01-6	0.054-B	5.6-A
	Vinyl chloride	75-01-4	0.27-B	33.-A
	Hexachloro			

POLLUTION CONTROL BOARD

NOTICE OF PROPOSED AMENDMENTS

	benzene	118-74-1	0.055-B	37.-A
	Hexachloro-butadiene	87-68-3	0.055-B	28.-A
	Hexachloroethane	67-72-1	0.055-B	30.-A
P037	Table-A			
	Acenaphthene	208-96-8	0.059-B	NA
	Anthracene	120-12-7	0.059-B	28.-A
	Benzene	71-43-2	0.14-B	14.-A
	Benzo(a)anthracene	50-32-8	0.059-B	20.-A
	Benzo(a)pyrene	117-81-7	0.061-B	12.-A
	Bis(2-ethyl-hexyl) phthalate	75-15-0	0.28-B	7.3-A
	Chrysene	218-01-9	0.059-B	15.-A
	Di-n-butyl phthalate	105-67-9	0.057-B	3.6-A
	Ethylbenzene	100-41-4	0.057-B	14.-A
	Naphthalene	91-20-3	0.059-B	42.-A
	Phenanthrene	85-01-8	0.059-B	34.-A
	Phenol	108-95-2	0.039-B	3.6-A
	Pyrene	129-00-0	0.067-B	36.-A
	Toluene	108-00-3	0.08-B	14.-A
	Xylene(s)		0.32-B	28.-A
	Cyanides (Total)	57-12-5	0.028-B	1.8-A
	Chromium (Total)	7440-47-32	0.7	NA
	lead	7439-92-1	0.037	NA
P038	Table-A			
	Benzene	71-43-2	0.14-B	14.-A
	Benzo(a)pyrene	50-32-8	0.061-B	12.-A
	Bis(2-ethyl-hexyl) phthalate	117-81-7	0.28-B	7.3-A
	Chrysene	218-01-9	0.059-B	15.-A
	Di-n-butyl phthalate	84-74-2	0.057-B	3.6-A
	Ethylbenzene	100-41-4	0.057-B	14.-A
	Fluorene	86-73-7	0.059-B	NA
	Naphthalene	91-20-3	0.059-B	42.-A
	Phenanthrene	85-01-8	0.059-B	34.-A
	Phenol	108-95-2	0.039-B	3.6-A
	Pyrene	129-00-0	0.067-B	36.-A
	Toluene	108-00-3	0.080-B	14.-A
	Xylene(s)		0.32-B	22.-A
	Cyanides	57-12-5	0.028-A	1.8-A

POLLUTION CONTROL BOARD

NOTICE OF PROPOSED AMENDMENTS

	(Total) Chromium	7440-47-3	0.2	NA
	(Total) Lead	7439-92-1	0.037	NA
P099	(and D001 and D002 wastes prohibited under Section 728.137)			

Tables A-a-B

Acetone	67-64-1	0.28-B	160.-A
Acenaphthalene	208-96-8	0.059-B	3.4-A
Acenaphthene	83-32-9	0.059-B	4.0-A
Acetonitrile	75-05-8	0.17-B	NA
Acetophenone	96-86-2	0.010-B	9.7-A
2-Acetylamino-fluorene	853-96-3	0.059-B	140.-A
Acrolein	107-02-8	0.29-B	NA
Acrylonitrile	107-13-1	0.24-B	84.-A
Aldrin	309-00-2	0.021-B	0.066-A
4-Aminobiphenyl	92-67-1	0.13-B	NA
Aniline	62-53-3	0.81-B	14.-A
Anthracene	120-12-7	0.059-B	4.0-A
Aramite	140-57-8	0.36-B	NA
Aroclor-1016	12674-11-2	0.013-B	0.92-A
Aroclor-1221	11104-28-2	0.014-B	0.92-A
Aroclor-1232	11141-16-5	0.013-B	0.92-A
Aroclor-1242	53469-21-9	0.017-B	0.92-A
Aroclor-1248	12672-29-6	0.013-B	0.92-A
Aroclor-1254	11097-69-1	0.014-B	1.8-A
Aroclor-1260	11096-82-5	0.014-B	1.8-A
alpha-BHC	319-84-6	0.00014-B	0.066-A
beta-BHC	319-85-7	0.00014-B	0.066-A
delta-BHC	319-86-8	0.023-B	0.066-A
gamma-BHC	58-89-9	0.0017-B	0.066-A
Benzene	71-43-2	0.14-B	36.-A
Benzo(a)anthracene	56-55-3	0.059-B	8.2-A
Benzo(b)fluoranthene	205-99-2	0.055-B	3.4-A
Benzo(k)fluoranthene	207-08-9	0.059-B	3.4-A
Benzo(ghi)perylene	191-24-2	0.0055-B	1.8-A
Benzo(a)pyrene	50-32-8	0.061-B	8.2-A
Bromodichloromethane	75-27-4	0.35-B	15.-A
Bromoform (Tribromomethane)	75-25-2	0.63-B	15.-A
Bromomethane			

POLLUTION CONTROL BOARD

NOTICE OF PROPOSED AMENDMENTS

(methyl bromide)	74-83-9	0.11-B	15.-A
4-Bromophenyl phenyl ether	101-55-3	0.055-B	15.-A
n-Butyl alcohol	71-36-3	5.6-B	2.6-A
Butyl benzyl phthalate	85-68-7	0.017-B	7.9-A
2-sec-Butyl-4,6-dinitrophenol	88-85-7	0.066-B	2.5-A
Carbon tetrachloride	56-23-5	0.057-B	5.6-A
Carbon disulfide	75-15-0	0.014-B	NA
Chlordane	57-74-9	0.0033-B	0.13-A
p-Chloroaniline	106-47-8	0.46-B	16.-A
Chlorobenzene	108-90-7	0.057-B	5.7-A
Chlorobenzilate	510-15-6	0.10-B	NA
2-Chloro-1,3-butadiene	126-99-8	0.057-B	NA
Chlorodibromomethane	124-48-1	0.057-B	16.-A
Chloroethane	75-00-3	0.27-B	6.0-A
bis(2-Chloroethoxy)methane	111-91-1	0.036-B	7.2-A
bis(2-Chloroethyl)ether	111-44-4	0.033-B	7.2-A
Chloroform	67-66-3	0.046-B	5.6-A
bis(2-chloro-isopropyl)ether	39638-32-9	0.055-B	7.2-A
p-Chloro-m cresol	59-50-7	0.018-B	14.-A
Chloromethane (Methyl chloride)	74-87-3	0.19-B	33.-A
2-Chloronaphthalene	91-0-7	0.055-B	5.6-A
2-Chlorophenol	95-57-8	0.044-B	5.7-A
3-Chloropropene	107-05-1	0.036-B	28.-A
Chrysene	218-01-9	0.059-B	8.2-A
o-Cresol	95-48-7	0.11-B	5.6-A
Cresol-(m-and p-isomers)		0.77-B	3.2-A
Cyclohexanone	108-94-1	0.36-B	NA
1,2-Dibromo-3-chloropropane	96-12-8	0.11-B	15.-A
1,2-Dibromoethane (Ethylene dibromide)	106-93-4	0.028-B	15.-A
Dibromomethane	74-95-3	0.11-B	15.-A

POLLUTION CONTROL BOARD

NOTICE OF PROPOSED AMENDMENTS

2,4-Dichloro-			
phenoxyacetic			
acid (2,4-D)	94-75-7	0.72-B	10.-A
o,p'-DDD	53-19-0	0.023-B	9.007-A
p,p'-DDD	72-54-8	0.023-B	0.007-A
o,p'-DDE	3424-82-6	0.031-B	0.007-A
p,p'-DDE	72-55-9	0.031-B	0.007-A
o,p'-DDT	789-02-6	0.0039-B	0.007-A
p,p'-DDT	50-29-3	0.0039-B	0.007-A
Dibenz(a,h)			
anthracene	53-70-3	0.055-B	8.2-A
Dibenz(a,e)			
pyrene	192-65-4	0.061-B	NA
m-Dichloro-			
benzene	541-73-1	0.036-B	6.2-A
o-Dichloro-			
benzene	95-50-1	0.088-B	6.2-A
p-Dichloro			
benzene	106-46-7	0.090-B	6.2-A
Dichlorodifluoro-			
methane	75-71-8	0.23-B	7.2-A
1,1-Dichloroethane	75-34-3	0.059-B	7.2-A
1,2-Dichloroethane	107-06-2	0.21-B	7.2-A
1,1-Dichloroethy-			
lene	75-35-4	0.025-B	33.-A
trans-1,2-			
Dichloroethylene		0.054-B	33.-A
2,4-Dichloro-			
phenol	120-83-2	0.044-B	14.-A
2,6-Dichloro-			
phenol	87-65-0	0.044-B	14.-A
1,2-Dichloro-			
propane	0-87-5	0.85-B	18.-A
cis-1,3-Dichloro-			
propene	10061-01-5	0.036-B	18.-A
trans-1,3-Dichloro-			
propene	10061-02-6	0.036-B	18.-A
Dieldrin	60-57-1	0.017-B	0.13-A
Diethyl			
phthalate	84-66-2	0.20-B	28.-A
2,4-Dimethyl			
phenol	105-67-9	0.036-B	14.-A
Dimethyl			
phthalate	131-11-3	0.047-B	28.-A
Di-n-butyl			
phthalate	84-74-2	0.057-B	28.-A
1,4-Dinitro-			
benzene	100-25-4	0.32-B	2.3-A

POLLUTION CONTROL BOARD

NOTICE OF PROPOSED AMENDMENTS

4,6-Dinitro-o-			
cresol	534-52-1	0.28-B	160.-A
2,4-Dinitroph-			
enol	51-28-5	0.12-B	160.-A
2,4-Dinitro-			
toluene	121-14-2	0.32-B	140.-A
2,6-Dinitro-			
toluene	606-20-2	0.55-B	28.-A
Di-n-octyl			
phthalate	117-84-0	0.017-B	28.-A
Di-n-propylnitro-			
samine	621-64-7	0.40-B	14.-A
1,2-Diphenyl			
hydrazine	122-66-7	0.087-B	NA
Diphenylamine	122-39-4	0.92-B	NA
Diphenylnitro-			
samine	621-64-7	0.40-B	NA
1,4-Dioxane	123-91-1	0.12-B	170.-A
Disulfoton	298-04-4	0.017-B	6.2-A
Endosulfan-I	939-98-8	0.023-B	0.066-A
Endosulfan-II	33213-6-5	0.029-B	0.13-A
Endosulfan			
sulfate	1031-07-8	0.029-B	0.13-A
Endrin	72-20-8	0.0028-B	0.13-A
Endrin			
aldehyde	7421-93-4	0.025-B	0.13-A
Ethyl-acetate	141-78-6	0.34-B	33.-A
Ethyl-cyanide	107-12-0	0.24-B	360.-A
Ethyl-benzene	100-41-4	0.057-B	6.0-A
Ethyl-ether	60-29-7	0.12-B	160.-A
bis(2-Ethylhexyl)			
phthalate	117-81-7	0.28-B	28.-A
Ethyl			
methacrylate	97-63-2	0.14-B	160.-A
Ethylene-oxide	75-21-8	0.12-B	NA
Famphur	52-85-7	0.017-B	15.-A
Fluoranthene	206-44-0	0.068-B	3.7-A
Fluorene	86-73-7	0.059-B	4.0-A
Fluorotrichl-			
oromethane	75-69-4	0.020-B	33.-A
Heptachlor	76-44-8	0.0012-B	0.066-A
Heptachlor			
epoxide	1024-57-3	0.016-B	0.066-A
Hexachloro-			
benzene	118-74-1	0.055-B	37.-A
Hexachloro-			
butadiene	87-68-3	0.055-B	28.-A
Hexachlorocyc-			

POLLUTION CONTROL BOARD

NOTICE OF PROPOSED AMENDMENTS

Isopentadiene	79-47-4	0.057-B	9.6-A
Hexachlorodi-benzofurans		0.000063-B	8.001-A
Hexachloro-dibenzo-p-dioxins		0.000063-B	8.001-A
Hexachloro-ethane	67-72-1	8.055-B	28.-A
Hexachloro-propene	1888-71-7	0.035-B	28.-A
Indeno(1,2,3-cd)pyrene	193-39-5	0.0055-B	8.2-A
Iodomethane	74-88-4	0.019-B	65.-A
Isobutanol	78-83-1	5.6-B	170.-A
Isodrin	465-73-6	0.021-B	0.066-A
Isosafrole	120-58-1	0.081-B	2.6-A
Kepone	143-50-0	0.0011-B	0.13-A
Methacrylo-nitrile	126-98-7	0.24-B	84.-A
Methanol	67-56-1	5.6-B	NA
Methapyrilene	91-80-5	0.081-B	1.5-A
Methoxychlor	72-43-5	0.25-B	0.18-A
3-Methylchol-anthrene	56-49-5	0.0055-B	15.-A
4,4-Methylene-bis-(2-chloro-aniline)	101-14-4	0.90-B	35.-A
Methylene chloride	75-09-2	0.089-B	33.-A
Methyl-ethyl ketone	78-93-3	0.28-B	36.-A
Methyl-isobutyl ketone	108-10-1	0.14-B	33.-A
Methyl methacrylate	80-62-6	0.14-B	160.-A
Methyl methanesulfonate	66-27-3	0.018-B	NA
Methyl-parathion	298-00-40	0.014-B	4.6-B
Naphthalene	91-20-3	0.059-B	3.1-A
2-Naphthylamine	91-59-8	0.52-B	NA
p-Nitroaniline	100-01-6	0.028-B	28.-A
Nitrobenzene	98-95-3	0.068-B	14.-A
5-Nitro-o-toluidine	99-55-8	0.32-B	28.-A
4-Nitrophenol	100-02-7	0.12-B	29.-A
N-Nitrosodiethy-lamine	55-18-5	0.40-B	28.-A

POLLUTION CONTROL BOARD

NOTICE OF PROPOSED AMENDMENTS

N-Nitrosodimethy-lamine	62-75-9	0.40-B	NA
N-Nitroso-di-n-butylamine	924-16-3	0.40-B	17.-A
N-Nitrosomethyl-ethylamine	105-95-5	0.40-B	2.3-A
N-Nitrosomor-pholine	59-89-2	0.40-B	2.3-A
N-Nitrosopiperi-dine	100-75-4	0.013-B	35.-A
N-Nitrosopyr-rolidine	930-55-2	0.013-B	35.-A
Parathion	56-38-2	0.014-B	4.6-A
Pentachloro-benzene	608-93-5	0.055-B	37.-A
Pentachlorodi-benzo-furans		0.000063-B	0.001-A
Pentachloro-dibenzo-p-dioxins		0.000063-B	0.001-A
Pentachloro-nitrobenzene	82-68-8	0.055-B	4.8-A
Pentachloro-phenol	87-86-5	0.089-B	7.4-A
Phenacetin	62-44-2	0.081-B	16.-A
Phenanthrene	85-01-8	0.059-B	3.1-A
Phenol	108-95-2	0.039-B	6.8-A
Phorate	298-02-2	0.021-B	4.6-A
Phthalic anhydride	85-44-9	0.069-B	NA
Pronamide	23950-58-5	0.093-B	1.5-A
Pyrene	129-00-0	0.067-B	8.2-A
Pyridine	110-86-1	0.014-B	16.-A
Safrole	94-59-7	0.081-B	22.-A
Silvex-(2,4,5-TP)	93-72-1	0.72-B	7.9-A
2,4,5-T	93-76-5	0.72-B	7.9-A
1,2,4,5-Tetra-chlorobenzene	95-94-3	0.055-B	19.-A
Tetrachlorodi-benzofurans		0.000063-B	0.001-A
Tetrachloro-dibenzo-p-dioxins		0.000063-B	0.001-A
1,1,1,2-Tetra-chloroethane	630-20-6	0.057-B	42.-A
1,1,2,2-Tetra-			

POLLUTION CONTROL BOARD

NOTICE OF PROPOSED AMENDMENTS

chloroethane	79-34-6	0.057-B	42.-A
Tetrachloro-ethylene	127-18-4	0.056-B	5.6-A
2,3,4,6-Tetra-chlorophenol	58-90-2	0.030-B	37.-A
Toluene	108-88-3	0.080-B	28.-A
Toxaphene	8001-35-1	0.0095-B	1.3-A
1,2,4-Trichlor-obenzene	120-82-1	0.055-B	19.-A
1,1,1-Trichloro-ethane	71-55-6	0.054-B	5.6-A
1,1,2-Trichloro-ethane	79-00-5	0.054-B	5.6-A
Trichloro-ethylene	79-01-6	0.054-B	5.6-A
2,4,5-Trichlor-ophenol	95-95-4	0.18-B	37.-A
2,4,6-Trichlor-ophenol	88-06-2	0.035-B	37.-A
1,2,3-Trichloro-propane	96-18-4	0.85-B	28.-A
1,1,2-Trichloro-1,2,2-trifluoro-ethane	76-13-1	0.057-B	28.-A
Tris-(2,3-dibromo-propyl)-phosphate	126-72-7	.11-B	NA
Vinyl chloride	75-01-4	0.27-A	33.-A
Xylenes		0.32-B	28.-A
Cyanides (Total)	57-12-5	1.2-B	1.0-A
Fluoride	16964-48-8	35.-B	NA
Sulfide	8496-25-8	14.-B	NA
Antimony	7440-36-0	1.9-B	NA
Arsenic	7440-38-2	1.4-B	NA
Barium	7440-39-3	1.2-B	NA
Beryllium	7440-41-7	0.82-B	NA
Cadmium	7440-43-9	0.20-B	NA
Chromium (Total)	7440-47-32	0.37-B	NA
Copper	7440-50-8	1.3-B	NA
Lead	7439-92-1	0.28-B	NA
Mercury	7439-97-6	0.15-B	NA
Nickel	7440-02-0	0.55-B	NA
Selenium	7782-49-2	0.82-B	NA
Silver	7440-22-4	0.29-B	NA
Thallium	7440-28-0	1.4-B	NA
Vanadium	7440-62-2	0.042-B	NA
Zinc	7440-66-0	1.0-B	NA

POLLUTION CONTROL BOARD

NOTICE OF PROPOSED AMENDMENTS

R001	Table-A	Naphtha-lene	91-20-3	0.031-A	1.5-A
		Pentachlor-ophenol	87-86-5	0.001-A	1.5-A
		Phenanthrene	85-01-8	0.10-A	7.4-A
		Pyrene	129-00-0	0.028-A	1.5-A
		Toluene	108-88-3	0.020-A	28.-A
		Xylenes (Total)		0.032-A	33.-A
		Lead	7439-92-1	0.037-A	NA
R002	Table-A	Chromium (Total)	7440-47-32	2.9-B	NA
		Lead	7439-92-1	3.4-B	NA
R003	Table-A	Chromium (Total)	7440-47-32	0.9-B	NA
		Lead	7439-92-1	3.4-B	NA
R004	Table-A	Chromium (Total)	7440-47-32	0.9-B	NA
		Lead	7439-92-1	3.4-B	NA
R005	Table-A	Chromium (Total)	7440-47-32	0.9-B	NA
		Lead	7439-92-1	3.4-B	NA
		Cyanides (Total)	57-12-5	0.74-B	B
R006	Table-A	Chromium (Total)	7440-47-32	0.9-B	NA
		Lead	7439-92-1	3.4-B	NA
R007	Table-A	Chromium (Total)	7440-47-32	0.9-B	NA
		Lead	7439-92-1	3.4-B	NA-B
		Cyanides (Total)	57-12-5	0.74-B	
R008	Table-A	Chromium (Total)	7440-47-32	0.9-B	NA
		Lead	7439-92-1	3.4-B	NA
R009	NA	Chloroform	67-66-3	0.1	6.0-A
R010	NA	Chloroform	67-66-3	00.1	6.0
R011	NA	Acetonitrile	75-05-8	38.	1.0

POLLUTION CONTROL BOARD

NOTICE OF PROPOSED AMENDMENTS

		Acrylonitrile	107-13-1	0.06	1.4
		Acrylamide	79-06-1	19.	23.
		Benzene	71-43-2	0.02	0.03
		Cyanide			
		(Total)	57-12-5	21.	57.
K013	NA	Acetonitrile	75-05-8	38.	1.8-A
		Acrylonitrile	107-13-1	0.06	1.4-A
		Acrylamide	79-06-1		23.-A
		Benzene	71-43-2	0.02	0.03-A
		Cyanide			
		(Total)	57-12-5	21.	57.
K014	NA	Acetonitrile	75-05-8	38.	1.8-A
		Acrylonitrile	107-13-1	0.06	1.4-A
		Acrylamide	79-06-1	19.	23.-A
		Benzene	71-43-2	0.02	0.03-A
		Cyanide			
		(Total)	57-12-5	21.	57.
K015	Table-A	Anthracene	120-12-7	0.059	3.4-A
		Benzal-Chloride	98-87-3	0.28	6.2-A
		Sum-of-Benzo-(b)fluoranthene-and-Benzo-(k)fluoranthene	207-08-9	0.055	3.4
		Phenanthrene	85-01-8	0.05	3.4-A
		Toluene	108-88-3	0.08	6.0-A
		Chromium (Total)	7440-47-33	0.92	NA
		Nickel	7440-02-0	0.44	NA
K016	NA	Hexachlorobenzene	118-74-1	0.055	28.-A
		Hexachlorobutadiene	87-68-3	0.055	5.6-A
		Hexachlorocyclopentadiene	99-47-4	0.057	5.6-A
		Hexachloroethane	67-72-1	0.055	28.-A
		Tetrachloroethene	127-18-4	0.056	6.0-A
K017	NA	1,2-Dichloropropane	78-87	0.85-A-B	18.-A
		1,2,3-Trichloropropane	96-18	0.85-A-B	28.-A

POLLUTION CONTROL BOARD

NOTICE OF PROPOSED AMENDMENTS

		Bis(2-chloroethyl)ether	111-44	0.033-A-B	9.8-A
K018	NA	Chloroethane	75-00-3	0.27	6.0-A
		Chloromethane	74-87-3	0.19	NA
		1,2-Dichloroethane	75-34-3	0.069	6.0-A
		1,2-Dichloroethane	107-06-2	0.21	6.0-A
		Hexachlorobenzene	118-74-1	0.055	28.-A
		Hexachlorobutadiene	87-68-3	0.055	5.6-A
		Pentachloroethane	76-01-7	NA	5.6
		1,1,1-Trichloroethane	71-55-6	0.054	6.0
		Hexachloro-	67-72-1	0.055	28.-A
K019	NA	Bis(2-chloroethyl)ether	111-44-1	0.033	5.6-A
		Chlorobenzene	108-90-7	0.057	6.0-A
		Chloroform	67-66-3	0.046	6.0-A
		p-Dichlorobenzene	106-46-7	0.09	NA
		1,2-Dichloroethane	107-06-2	0.21	6.0-A
		Fluorene	86-73-7	0.059	NA
		Hexachloroethane	67-72-1	0.055	28.-A
		Naphthalene	91-20-3	0.059	5.6-A
		Phenanthrene	85-01-8	0.059	5.6-A
		1,2,4,5-Tetrachlorobenzene	95-94-3	0.055	NA
		Tetrachloroethene	127-18-4	0.056	6.0-A
		1,2,4-Trichlorobenzene	120-82-1	0.055	19.-A
		1,1,1-Trichloroethane	71-55-6	0.054	6.0-A
K020	NA	1,2-Dichloroethane	106-93-4	0.21	6.0-A
		1,1,2,2-Tetrachloroethane	99-34-6	0.057	5.6-A
		Tetrachloroethene	127-18-4	0.056	6.0-A

POLLUTION CONTROL BOARD

NOTICE OF PROPOSED AMENDMENTS

R021	Table-A	Chloroform	67-66-3	0.046-B	6.2-A
		Carbon tetrachloride	56-23-5	0.057-B	6.2-A
		Antimony	7440-36-0	0.60-B	6.2-A
R022	Table-A	Toluene	108-88-3	0.080-B	0.034-A
		Acetophenone	96-86-2	0.060-B	19.-A
		Diphenylamine	22-39-4	0.52-B	NA
		Diphenylnitrosamine	86-30-6	0.48	NA
		Sum of Diphenylamine and Diphenylnitrosamine		NA	19.-A
		Phenol	108-95-2	0.039	12.-A
		Chromium (Total)	7440-47-32	0.35	NA
		Nickel	7440-02-0	0.47	NA
R023	NA	Phthalic anhydride (measured as Phthalic acid)	85-44-9	0.069	28.-A
R024	NA	Phthalic anhydride (measured as Phthalic acid)	85-44-9	0.069	28.-A
R028	Table-A	1,1-Dichloroethane	75-34-3	0.059	6.0-A
		trans-1,2-Dichloroethene		0.054	6.0-A
		Hexachlorobutadiene	87-68-3	0.055	5.6-A
		Hexachloroethane	67-72-1	0.055	28.-A
		Pentachloroethane	76-01-7	NA	5.6-A
		1,1,1,2-Tetrachloroethane	630-20-6	0.057	5.6-A
		1,1,2,2-Tetrachloroethane	99-34-6	0.057	5.6-A
		1,1,1-Trichloroethane	71-55-6	0.054	6.0-A
		1,1,2-Trichloroethane	99-00-5	0.054	6.0-A
		Tetrachloro-			

POLLUTION CONTROL BOARD

NOTICE OF PROPOSED AMENDMENTS

		ethylene	127-18-4	0.056	6.0-A
		Cadmium	7440-43-9	0.4	NA
		Chromium (Total)	7440-47-32	0.35	NA
		Lead	7439-92-1	0.037	NA
		Nickel	7440-02-0	0.47	NA
R029	NA	Chloroform	67-66-3	0.46	6.0-A
		1,2-Dichloroethane	107-06-2	0.21	6.0-A
		1,1-Dichloroethylene	75-35-4	0.025	6.0-A
		1,1,1-Trichloroethane	71-55-6	0.054	6.0-A
		Vinyl chloride	75-01-4	0.27	6.0-A
R030	NA	o-Dichlorobenzene	95-50-1	0.088	NA
		p-Dichlorobenzene	106-46-7	0.09	NA
		Hexachlorobutadiene	87-68-3	0.055	5.6-A
		Hexachloroethane	67-72-1	0.055	28.-A
		Hexachloropropene	1888-71-7	NA	19.-A
		Pentachlorobenzene	608-93-5	NA	28.-A
		Pentachloroethane	76-01-7	NA	5.6-A
		1,2,4,5-Tetrachlorobenzene	95-94-3	0.055	14.-A
		Tetrachloroethene	127-18-4	0.056	6.0-A
		1,2,4-Trichlorobenzene	120-82-1	0.055	19.-A
R031	Table-A	Arsenic	7440-38-2	5N0.79	NA
R032	NA	Hexachlorocyclopentadiene	77-47-4	0.057-B	24.-A
		Chlordane	57-74-9	0.0033-B	0.26-A
		Heptachlor	76-44-8	0.0033-B	0.066-A
		Heptachlor epoxide	1024-57-3	0.016-B	0.066-A

POLLUTION CONTROL BOARD

NOTICE OF PROPOSED AMENDMENTS

R033	NA	Hexachloro-cyclopenta-diene	77-47-4	0.057-B	2.4-A
R034	NA	Hexachloro-cyclopenta-diene	77-47-4	0.057-B	2.4-A
R035	NA	Acenaphthene	83-32-9	NA	3.4-A
		Anthracene	120-12-7	NA	3.4-A
		Benz(a)an-thracene	56-55-3	0.59-B	3.4-A
		Benzo(a)-pyrene	50-32-8	NA	3.4-A
		Chrysene	218-01-9	0.059-B	3.4-A
		Dibenz(a,h)anthracene	53-70-3	NA	3.4-A
		Fluoranthene	206-44-0	0.068-B	3.4-A
		Fluorene	86-73-7	NA	3.4-A
		Indeno(1,2,3-cd)pyrene	193-39-5	NA	3.4-A
		Cresols (m-and p-isomers)		0.077-B	NA
		Naphthalene	91-20-3	0.59-B	3.4-A
		o-Cresol	95-48-7	0.11-B	3.4-A
		Phenanthrene	85-01-8	0.059-B	3.4-A
		Phenol	108-95-2	0.039	NA
		Pyrene	129-00-0	0.067-B	3.2-A
R036	NA	Disulfoton	298-04-4	0.025-B	0.1-A
R037	NA	Disulfoton	298-04-4	0.025-B	0.1-A
		Toluene	108-88-3	0.080-B	28.-A
R038	NA	Phorate	298-02-2	0.025	0.1-A
R040	NA	Phorate	298-02-2	0.025	0.1-A
R041	NA	Toxaphene	8001-35-1	0.0095-B	2.6-A
R042	NA	2,3,4,5-Tetra-chlorobenzene	95-94-3	0.055-B	4.4-A
		o-Dichloro-benzene	95-50-1	0.088-B	4.4-A
		p-Dichloro-benzene	106-46-7	0.090-B	4.4-A
		Pentachloro-benzene	608-93-5	0.055-B	4.4-A

ILLINOIS REGISTER 3998
95

POLLUTION CONTROL BOARD

NOTICE OF PROPOSED AMENDMENTS

		2,4,5-Trichloro-benzene	120-82-1	0.055-B	4.4-A
R043	NA	2,4-Dichloro-phenol	120-83-2	0.044	0.58-A
		3,6-Dichloro-phenol	187-65-0	0.044	0.74-A
		2,4,5-Trichloro-phenol	95-95-4	0.18	0.2-A
		2,4,6-Trichloro-phenol	88-06-2	0.035	7.4-A
		Tetrachloro-phenols-(Total)		NA	0.68-A
		Pentachloro-phenol	87-86-5	0.089	1.9-A
		Tetrachloro-ethene	79-01-6	0.056	1.7-A
		Hexachloro-dibenzo-p-dioxins		0.000063	0.001-A
		Hexachloro-dibenzofurans		0.000063	0.001-A
		Pentachloro-dibenzo-p-dioxins		0.000063	0.001-A
		Pentachloro-dibenzo-furans		0.000063	0.001-A
		Tetrachloro-dibenzo-p-dioxins		0.000063	0.001-A
		Tetrachloro-dibenzo-furans		0.000063	0.001-A
R046	Table-A	Lead	7439-92-1	0.037	NA
R048	Table-A	Benzene	71-43-2	0.14-B	14.-A
		Benzo(a)pyrene	50-32-8	0.061-B	12.-A
		Bis(2-ethyl-hexyl)phthalate	117-81-7	0.28-B	7.3-A
		Chrysene	218-01-9	0.059-B	15.-A
		Di-n-butyl phthalate	84-74-2	0.057-B	3.6-A
		Ethylbenzene	100-41-4	0.057-B	14.-B
		Fluorene	86-73-7	0.059-B	NA
		Naphthalene	91-20-3	0.059-B	42.-A
		Phenanthrene	85-01-8	0.059-B	34.-A

POLLUTION CONTROL BOARD

NOTICE OF PROPOSED AMENDMENTS

	Phenol	108-95-2	0.039-B	9.6-A
	Pyrene	1-29-00-0	0.067-B	36.-A
	Toluene	108-88-3	0.080-B	14.-A
	Xylene(s)		0.32-B	22.-A
	Cyanides-(Total)	57-12-5	0.028-B	1.8-A
	Chromium-(Total)	7440-47-32	0.2	NA
	Lead	7439-92-1	0.037	NA
R049 Table-A	Anthracene	120-12-7	0.059-B	28.-A
	Benzene	71-43-2	0.014-B	14.-A
	Benzo(a)pyrene	117-81-7	0.061-B	12.-A
	Bis(2-ethyl-hexyl) phthalate	75-150-9	0.28-B	7.3-A
	Carbon-disulfide	75-15-0	0.014-B	NA
	Chrysene	2218-01-9	0.059-B	15.-A
	2,4-Dimethyl phenol	105-67-9	0.036-B	NA
	Ethylbenzene	100-41-4	0.057-B	14.-A
	Napthalene	91-20-3	0.059-B	42.-A
	Phenanthrene	85-01-8	0.059-B	34.-A
	Phenol	108-95-2	0.039-B	9.6-A
	Pyrene	129-00-0	0.067-B	36.-A
	Toluene	108-88-3	0.080-B	14.-A
	Xylene(s)		0.32-B	22.-A
	Cyanides-(Total)	56-12-5	0.028-A	1.8-A
	Chromium-(Total)	7440-47-32	0.2	NA
R050 Table-A	Lead	7439-92-1	0.037	NA
	Benzo(a)pyrene	50-32-8	0.061-B	12.-A
	Phenol	108-95-2	0.039-B	9.6-A
	Cyanides-(Total)	57-12-5	0.028-A	1.8-A
	Chromium-(Total)	7440-47-32	0.2	NA
	Lead	7439-92-1	0.037	NA
R051 Table-A	Acenaphthene	200-96-8	0.059-B	NA
	Anthracene	120-12-7	0.059-B	28.-A
	Benzene	71-43-2	0.14-B	14.-A
	Benzo(a)-anthracene	117-81-7	0.059-B	28.-A
	Benzo(a)pyrene	117-81-7	0.061-B	12.-A
	Bis(2-ethyl-hexyl) phthalate	75-15-0	0.28-B	7.3-A
	Chrysene	2218-01-9	0.059-B	15.-A
	Di-n-butyl phthalate	105-67-9	0.057-B	3.6-A
	Ethylbenzene	100-41-4	0.057-B	14.-A

POLLUTION CONTROL BOARD

NOTICE OF PROPOSED AMENDMENTS

	Fluorene	86-73-7	0.059-B	NA
	Napthalene	91-20-3	0.059-B	42.-A
	Phenanthrene	85-01-8	0.059-B	34.-A
	Phenol	108-95-2	0.039-B	9.6-A
	Pyrene	129-00-0	0.067-B	36.-A
	Toluene	108-88-3	0.080-B	14.-A
	Xylene(s)		0.32-B	22.-A
	Cyanides (Total)	57-12-5	0.028-A	1.8-A
	Chromium-(Total)	7440-47-32	0.2	NA
	Lead	71-43-2	0.037	NA
	Benzene	71-43-2	0.14-B	14.-A
	Benzo(a)pyrene	50-32-8	0.061-B	12.-A
R052 Table-A	o-Cresol	95-48-7	0.11-B	6.2-A
	p-Cresol	106-44-5	0.77-B	6.2-A
	2,4-Dimethyl-phenol	105-67-9	0.036-B	NA
	Ethylbenzene	100-41-4	0.057-B	14.-A
	Napthalene	91-20-3	0.059-B	42.-A
	Phenanthrene	85-01-8	0.059-B	34.-A
	Phenol	108-95-2	0.039-B	9.6-A
	Toluene	108-88-3	0.080-B	14.-A
	Xylene(s)		0.32-B	22.-A
	Cyanides-(Total)	56-12-5	0.028-A	1.8-A
	Chromium-(Total)	7440-47-32	M0.2	NA
	Lead	7439-92-1	0.037	NA
R060 NA	Benzene	71-43-2	0.17-B	0.071-A
	Benzo(a)pyrene	50-32-8	0.035-B	3.6-A
	Napthalene	91-20-3	0.035-B	3.6-A
	Phenol	108-95-2	0.042-B	3.4-A
	Cyanides-(Total)	57-12-5	0.9	1.2
R061 Table-A	Cadmium	7440-43-9	1.61	NA
	Chromium-(Total)	7440-47-32	0.32	NA
	Lead	7439-92-1	0.51	NA
	Nickel	7440-02-0	0.44	NA
R062 Table-A (Total)7440-47-32	Chromium	0.32	NA	
	Lead	7439-92-1	0.04	NA
	Nickel	7440-02-0	0.44	NA
R069 Tables A-&-B	Cadmium	7440-43-9	1.6	NA
	Lead	7439-92-1	0.51	NA

POLLUTION CONTROL BOARD

NOTICE OF PROPOSED AMENDMENTS

R891	Table-A	Mercury	7439-97-6	0.030		NA
R892	NA	Carbon tetrachloride	56-23-5	0.057-B		6.2-A
		Chlordane	67-66-3	0.046-B		6.2-A
		Hexachloroethane	67-72-1	0.055-B		30.-A
		Tetrachloroethene	127-18-4	0.056-B		6.2-A
		1,1,1-Trichloroethane	71-55-6	0.054-B		6.2-A
R893	Table-A	Benzene	71-43-2	0.14-B		6.6-A
		Aniline	62-53-3	0.81-B		14.-A
		Diphenylamine	22-39-4	0.92-B		NA
		Diphenylnitrosamine	86-30-6	0.40-B	NA	
		Sum of Diphenylamine and Diphenylnitrosamine		NA		a-14r
		Nitrobenzene	98-95-3	0.068-B		14.-A
		Phenol	108-95-2	0.039		5.6-A
		Cyclohexanone	108-94-1	0.36		30.-A
		Nickel	7440-02-0	0.47		NA
R894	NA	Arsenic	7440-38-2	0.79		NA
R895	NA	Benzene	71-43-2	0.14-B		4.4-A
		Chlorobenzene	108-90-7	0.057-B		4.4-A
		o-Dichlorobenzene	95-50-1	0.088-B		4.4-A
		m-Dichlorobenzene	541-73-1	0.036-B		4.4-A
		p-Dichlorobenzene	106-46-7	0.090-B		4.4-A
		1,2,4-Trichlorobenzene	120-82-1	0.055-B		4.4-A
		1,2,4,5-Tetrachlorobenzene	95-94-3	0.055-B		4.4-A
		Pentachlorobenzene	608-93-5	SMO-055		4.4-A
		Hexachlorobenzene	118-74-1	0.055-B		4.4-A
		Aroclor-1016	12674-11-2	0.013-B		0.92-A
		Aroclor-1221	11104-28-2	0.014-B		0.92-A
		Aroclor-1232	11141-16-5	0.013-B		0.92-A
		Aroclor-1242	53469-21-9	0.017-B		0.92-A
		Aroclor-1248	12672-29-6	0.013-B		0.92-A

POLLUTION CONTROL BOARD

NOTICE OF PROPOSED AMENDMENTS

		Aroclor-1254	11097-69-1	0.014-B		1.8-A
		Aroclor-1260	11096-82-5	0.014-B		1.8-A
R896	Table-A	Acetone	67-64-1	0.28		160.-A
		Acetophenone	96-86-2	0.010		9.7-A
		Bis(2-ethylhexyl)phthalate	117-81-7	0.28-B		28.-A
		n-Butyl alcohol	71-36-3	5.6		2.6-A
		Butylbenzyl phthalate	85-68-7	0.017-B		7.9-A
		Cyclohexanone	108-94-1	0.36		NA
		1,2-Dichlorobenzene	95-50-1	0.088		6.0-A
		Diethyl phthalate	84-66-2	0.20		28.-A
		Dimethyl phthalate	131-11-3	0.047-B		28.-A
		Di-n-butyl phthalate	84-74-2	0.057-B		28.-A
		Di-n-octyl phthalate	117-84-0	0.017-B		28.-A
		Ethyl acetate	141-78-6	0.34-B		33.-A
		Ethylbenzene	100-41-4	0.057-B		6.0-A
		Methanol	67-56-1	5.6-B		NA
		Methyl isobutyl ketone	108-10-1	0.14		33.-A
		Methyl ethyl ketone	78-93-3	0.28		36.-A
		Methylene chloride	75-09-2	0.089-B		33.-A
		Naphthalene	91-20-3	0.059-B		3.1-A
		Nitrobenzene	98-95-3	0.068-B		14.-A
		Toluene	108-88-3	0.080-B		28.-A
		1,1,1-Trichloroethane	71-55-6	0.054-B		5.6-A
		Trichloroethylene	79-01-6	0.054-B		5.6-A
		Xylenes(Total)		0.32-B		28.-A
		Cyanides-(Total)	57-12-5	1.9		1.9
		Chromium-(Total)	7440-47-32	0.32		NA
		Lead	7439-92-1	0.037		NA
R897	Table-A	Acenaphthalene	208-96-8	0.059-B		3.4
		Benzene	71-43-2	0.014-B		0.071-A
		Chrysene	218-01-9	0.059-B		3.4-A
		Fluoranthene	206-44-0	0.068-B		3.4-A

POLLUTION CONTROL BOARD

NOTICE OF PROPOSED AMENDMENTS

		Indeno			
		(1,2,3-cd) pyrene	193-39-5	0.0055-B	3.4-A
		Naphthalene	91-20-3	0.059-B	3.4-A
		Phenanthrene	85-01-8	0.059-B	3.4-A
		Toluene	108-88-3	0.08-B	0.65-A
		Xylene(s)		0.32-B	0.07-A
		lead	7439-92-1	0.037	NA
R093	NA	Phthalic anhydride (measured as Phthalic acid)	85-44-9	0.69	28.-A
R094	NA	Phthalic anhydride (measured as Phthalic acid)	85-44-9	0.69	028.-A
R095	NA	1,1,1,2-Tetrachloroethane	630-20-6	0.057	5.6-A
		1,1,2,2-Tetrachloroethane	79-34-6	0.057	5.6-A
		Tetrachloroethene	127-18-4	0.056	6.0-A
		Trichloroethene	79-00-5	0.054	6.0-A
		Trichloroethylene	79-01-6	0.054	5.6-A
		Hexachloroethane	67-72-1	0.055	28.-A
		Pentachloroethane	76-01-7	0.055	5.5-A
R096	NA	1,1,1,2-Tetrachloroethane	630-20-6	0.057	5.6-A
		1,1,2,2-Tetrachloroethane	79-34-6	0.057	5.6-A
		Tetrachloroethene	127-18-4	0.056	6.0-A
		1,1,2-Trichloroethane	79-00-5	0.054	6.0-A
		Trichloroethene (Trichloroethylene) (Tri-chloroethylene)	79-01-6	0.054	5.6-A
		1,2-Dichlorobenzene	541-73-1	0.036	5.6-A
		Pentachloroethane	76-01-7	0.055	5.6-A

POLLUTION CONTROL BOARD

NOTICE OF PROPOSED AMENDMENTS

		1,1,4-Trichlorobenzene	120-82-1	0.055	19.-A
R097	NA	Hexachlorocyclopentadiene	77-47-4	0.057-B	2.4
		Chlordane	57-74-9	0.0033-B	0.26-A
		Heptachlor	76-44-8	0.0012-B	0.066-A
		Heptachlor epoxide	1024-57-3	0.016-B	0.066-A
R098	NA	Toxaphene	8001-35-1	0.0095-B	2.6-A
R099	NA	2,4-Dichlorophenoxyacetic-acid	94-75-7	1.0-A	1.0-A
		Hexachlorodibenzo-p-dioxins		0.001-A	0.001-A
		Hexachlorodibenzofurans		0.001-A	0.001-A
		Pentachlorodibenzo-p-dioxins		0.001-A	0.001-A
		Pentachlorodibenzofurans		0.001-A	0.001-A
		Tetrachlorodibenzo-p-dioxins		0.001-A	0.001-A
		Tetrachlorodibenzofurans		0.001-A	0.001-A
R100	Table-A	Cadmium	7440-43-9	1.6	NA
		Chromium (Total)	7440-47-3	0.32	NA
		lead	7439-92-1	0.51	NA
R101	NA	o-Nitroaniline	7440-38-2	0.27-A	14.-A
		Arsenic	7440-43-9	0.79	NA
		Cadmium	7439-92-1	0.74	NA
		lead	7439-97-6	0.17	NA
		Mercury		0.008	NA
R102	Table-A	o-Nitrophenol	7440-38-2	0.028-A	13.-A
		Arsenic	7440-43-9	0.79	NA
		Cadmium	7439-92-1	0.74	NA
		lead	7439-97-6	0.17	NA
		Mercury		0.008	NA
R103		Aniline	62-53-3	4.5-A	5.6
		Benzene	71-43-2	0.15-A	6.0-A
		2,4-Dinitro-	51-28-5	0.61-A	5.6-A

POLLUTION CONTROL BOARD

NOTICE OF PROPOSED AMENDMENTS

		phenol		
		Nitrobenzene	98-95-3	0.073-A	5.6-A
		Phenol	108-95-2	2.4-A	5.6-A
H104	NA	Aniline	62-53-3	4.5-A	5.6-A
		Benzene	71-43-2	0.15-A	5.6-A
		2,4-Dinitro-phenol	51-28-5	0.61-A	5.6-A
		Nitrobenzene	98-95-3	0.073-A	5.6-A
		Phenol	108-95-2	2.4-A	5.6-A
		Cyanides (Total)	57-12-5	2.7	2.7-A
H105	NA	Benzene	71-43-2	0.14	4.4-A
		Chlorobenzene	108-90-7	0.057	4.4-A
		o-Dichloro-benzene	95-50-1	0.088	4.4-A
		p-Dichloro-benzene	106-46-7	0.090	4.4-A
		2,4,5-Trichloro-phenol	95-95-4	0.18	4.4-A
		2,4,6-Trichloro-phenol	88-06-2	0.035	4.4-A
		2-Chlorophenol	95-57-8	0.044	4.4-A
		Phenol	108-95-2	0.039	4.4-A
H106	Tables A-a-B	Mercury	7439-97-6	0.030	NA
H115	Table A	Nickel	7440-02-0	0.47	NA
H111	NA	2,4-Dinitro-toluene	121-14-2	0.32	140
		2,6-Dinitro-toluene	606-20-2	0.55	28-A
H117	NA	Ethylene dibromide	106-93-4	0.028	15-A
		Methyl bromide	74-83-9	0.11	15-A
		Chloroform	67-66-3	0.046	5.6-A
H118	NA	Ethylene dibromide	106-93-4	0.028	15-A
		Methyl bromide	74-83-9	0.11	15-A
		Chloroform	67-66-3	0.046	5.6-A
H121	NA	Methyl bromide	74-83-9	0.11	15-A

POLLUTION CONTROL BOARD

NOTICE OF PROPOSED AMENDMENTS

H132	NA	Methyl bromide	74-83-9	0.11	15-A
H136	NA	Ethylene dibromide	106-93-4	0.028	15-A
		Methyl bromide	74-83-9	0.11	15-A
		Chloroform	67-66-3	0.046	5.6-A

TABLE B (CEW) -- P-AND-U-LISTED-WASTES

Waste Code	Commercial Chemical Name	See Also	Regulated Hazardous Constituent	CAS-No.-for Regulated Hazardous Constituent	Concentration (mg/l) Waste-waters	Non-waste waters
P004 A	Aldrin	NA	Aldrin	309-00-2	00.21-B	0.066
P010	Arsenic acid	Table A	Arsenic	7440-38-2	0.79	NA
P011	Arsenic pentoxide	Table A	Arsenic	7440-38-2	0.79	NA
P012	Arsenic trioxide	Table A	Arsenic	7440-38-2	0.79	NA
P013	Barium cyanide	Table A	Cyanides (Total)	57-12-5	1.9	110.
			Cyanides (Amenable)	57-12-5	0.1	9.1
P020 A	2-sec-Butyl-	NA	2-sec-Butyl-	88-85-7	0.066	7.5
	4,6-dinitro-phenol (Dinoseb)		4,6-dinitro-phenol (Dinoseb)			
P021	Calcium cyanide	NA	Cyanides (Total)	57-12-5	1.9	110.
			Cyanides (Amenable)	57-12-5	0.1	9.1
P022	Carbon-di-sulfide	Table D	Carbon-di-sulfide	75-15-0	0.014	NA
P024	p-Chloro-	NA	p-Chloro-	106-47-8	0.46	6.-A

POLLUTION CONTROL BOARD

NOTICE OF PROPOSED AMENDMENTS

			aniline	aniline		
P029	Copper cyanide	NA	Cyanides (Total)	57-12-5	1.9	110.
			Cyanides (Amenable)	57-12-5	0.1	9.1
P030	Cyanides (soluble salts and complexes)	NA	Cyanides (Total)	57-12-5	1.9	110.
			Cyanides (Amenable)	57-12-5	0.1	9.1
P036	Dichloro-phenylarsine	Table A	Arsenic	7440-38-2	0.79	NA
P037	Dieldrin	NA	Dieldrin	60-57-1	0.017-B	0.13
P038	Diethyl-arsine	Table A	Arsenic	7440-38-2	0.79	NA
P039	Disulfoton	NA	Disulfoton	298-04-4	0.017	1
P047	4,6-Dinitro-o-cresol	NA	4,6-Dinitro-o-cresol	534-52-1	28-B	1.0v
P048	2,4-Dinitro-phenol	NA	2,4-Dinitro-phenol	51-28-5	112-B	10v-B
P050	Endosulfan	NA	Endosulfan I	939-98-8	0.23-B	0.66
			Endosulfan II	33213-6-5	0.29-B	0.13-A
			Endosulfan sulfate	1031-07-8	0.29-B	0.13-A
P051	Endrin	NA	Endrin	72-20-8	.028-B	0.13-A
			Endrin aldehyde	7421-93-4	0.25-B	0.13-A
P056	Fluoride	Table B	Fluoride	16984-48-8	35v	NA
P059	Heptachlor	NA	Heptachlor	76-44-8	0.012-B	0.66
			Heptachlor epoxide	1024-57-3	0.016-B	0.66-A

POLLUTION CONTROL BOARD

NOTICE OF PROPOSED AMENDMENTS

P060	Isodrin	NA	Isodrin	465-73-6	0.021-B	0.66-A
P063	Hydrogen cyanide	NA	Cyanides (Total)	57-12-5	1.9	110.
			Cyanides (Amenable)	57-12-5	0.10	9.1
P065	Mercury fulminate	Tables A-a-B	Mercury	7439-97-6	0.030	NA
P071	Methyl parathion	NA	Methyl parathion	298-00-0	0.025	1.1-A
P073	Nickel carbonyl	Table A	Nickel	7440-02-0	0.22	NA
P074	Nickel cyanides	Table A	Cyanides (Total)	57-12-5	1.9	110.
			Cyanides (Amenable)	57-12-5	0.10	9.1
			Nickel	7440-02-0	0.44	NA
P077	p-Nitro-aniline	NA	p-Nitro-aniline	100-01-6	0.28-B	8v-A
P082	N-Nitroso-dimethyl-amine	Table B	N-Nitrosodi-methylamine	62-75-9	0.40	
P089	Parathion	NA	Parathion	56-38-2	0.025	1.1-A
P092	Phenyl-mercury acetate	Tables A-a-B	Mercury	7439-97-6	0.030	NA
P094	Phorate	NA	Phorate	298-02-2	0.025	1.1-A
P097	Famphur	NA	Famphur	52-85-7	0.025	1.1-A
P098	Potassium cyanide	NA	Cyanides (Total)	57-12-5	1.9	110.
			Cyanides (Amenable)	57-12-5	0.10	9.1
P099	Potassium silver	Table A	Cyanides (Total)	57-12-5	1.9	110.

POLLUTION CONTROL BOARD

NOTICE OF PROPOSED AMENDMENTS

cyanide		Cyanides (Amenable)	57-12-5	0.1	9.1	
		Silver	7440-22-4	0.29	NA	
P101	Ethyl cyanide (Propanenitrile)	NA	Ethyl cyanide (Propanenitrile)	107-12-0	0.24-B	360.-A
P103 B	Selenourea NA	Table A	Selenium	7782-49-2	.8	
P104	Silver cyanide	Table A	Cyanides (Total)	57-12-5	1.9	110.
			Cyanides (Amenable)	57-12-5	0.10	9.1
			Silver	7440-22-4	0.29	NA
P106	Sodium cyanide	NA	Cyanides (Total)	57-12-5	1.9	110.
			Cyanides (Amenable)	57-12-5	0.10	9.1
P110	Tetraethyl lead	Table A-1-B	Lead	7439-92-1	0.040	NA
P113	Thallic oxide	Table B	Thallium	7440-28-0	0.14-B	NA
P114	Thallium selenite	Table A	Selenium	7782-49-2	1.0	NA
P115 B	Thallium(I) sulfate	Table B	Thallium	7440-28-0	0.14	
P119	Ammonium vanadate	Table B	Vanadium	7440-62-2	8.-B	NA
P120	Vanadium pentoxide	Table B	Vanadium	7440-62-2	8.-B	NA
P121 Zinc cyanide NA		Cyanides (Total)	57-12-5	1.9	110.	
		Cyanides (Amenable)	57-12-5	0.10	9.1	

POLLUTION CONTROL BOARD

NOTICE OF PROPOSED AMENDMENTS

		(Amenable)				
P123	Toxaphene	NA	Toxaphene	8001-35-1	0.095-B	.2-A
U002	Acetone	NA	Acetone	67-64-1	0.28	18.
U003	Acetonitrile	Table B	Acetonitrile	75-05-8	0.17	.17
U004	Acetophenone	NA	Acetophenone	98-86-2	0.10-A	.9-A
U005	2-Acetylaminofluorene	NA	2-Acetylaminofluorene	53-96-3	0.59-B	140.-A
U009	Acrylonitrile	NA	Acrylonitrile	107-13-1	0.24-A	4.-A
U012	Aniline	NA	Aniline	62-53-3	0.81	4.-A
U018	Benz(a)anthracene	NA	Benz(a)anthracene	56-55-3	0.59-B	.2-A
U019	Benzene	NA	Benzene	71-43-2	14-B	6.-A
U022	Benzo(a)pyrene	NA	Benzo(a)pyrene	50-32-8	0.61-B	.2-A
U024 A	Bis(2-chloroethoxy)methane	NA	Bis(2-chloroethoxy)methane	111-91-1	0.036	.2
U025 A	Bis(2-chloroethyl)ether	NA	Bis(2-chloroethyl)ether	111-44-4	0.033	.2
U027	Bis(2-chloroisopropyl)ether	NA	Bis(2-chloroisopropyl)ether	39638-32-9	.055	.2-A

POLLUTION CONTROL BOARD

NOTICE OF PROPOSED AMENDMENTS

U028	Bis(2-ethyl-hexyl) phthalate	NA	Bis(2-ethyl-hexyl) phthalate	117-81-7	0.28	
U029	Bromo-methane (Methyl bromide)	NA	Bromomethane (Methyl bromide)	74-83-9	0.28-A	5.-A
U030	4-Bromophenyl phenyl-ether	NA	4-Bromo phenyl phenyl-ether	101-55-3	0.55-A	5.-A
U031	n-Butyl alcohol	NA	n-Butyl alcohol	71-36-3	5.6	.6-A
U032	Calcium chromate	Table A	Chromium (Total)	7440-47-32	0.32	NA
U036	Chlordane (alpha-and gamma)	NA	Chlordane (alpha-and gamma)	57-74-9	0.0033-B	13-A
U037	Chloro-benzene	NA	Chloro-benzene	108-90-9.	0.057-B	.9-A
U038	Chloro-benzilate	Table D	Chloro-benzilate	510-15-6	010-B	NA
U039	p-Chloro-m-cresol	NA	p-Chloro-m-cresol	59-50-7	0.18-B	4.-A
U043	Vinyl chloride	NA	Vinyl chloride	75-01-4	027-B	3.-A
U044	Chloroform	NA	Chloroform	67-66-3	0.46-B	.6-A
U045	Chloro-methane (Methyl chloride)	NA	Chloro-methane (Methyl chloride)	74-87-3	019-B.	3.-A
U047	2-Chloro-naphthalene	NA	2-Chloro-naphthalene	91-58-7	0.05-B-B	.6-A
U048	2-Chloro-phenol	NA	2-Chloro-phenol	95-57-8	0.44-B	.9-A

POLLUTION CONTROL BOARD

NOTICE OF PROPOSED AMENDMENTS

U050	Chrysene	NA	Chrysene	218-01-9	0.59-B	.8-A
U051	Creosote	Table A	Pentachloro-phenol	87-86-5	0.18	.9.4-A
			Phenanthrene	85-01-8	0.031	1.5-A
			Pyrene	129-00-0	0.088	28.-A
			Toluene	108-88-3	0.028	33.-A
			Xylenes (Total)		0.032	NA
			Lead	7439-92-6	0.037	NA
U052	Cresols (Cresylic acid)	NA	o-Cresol	95-48-7	011-B	5.6-A
			Cresols (m-and-p-isomers)		0.77-B	8.2
U057	Cyclo-hexanone	Table D	Cyclohexa none	108-94-1	0.36	NA
U060	DDD	NA	o,p'-DDD	53-19-0	0.023-B	0.87-A
			p,p'-DDD	72-54-8	0.023-B	0.87-A
U061	DDT	NA	o,p'-DDT	789-02-6	0.039-B	0.87-A
			p,p'-DDT	50-29-3	0.039-B	0.87-A
			o,p'-DDE	53-19-0	0.023-B	0.87-A
			p,p'-DDD	72-54-8	0.023-B	0.87-A
			o,p'-DDE	3424-82-6	0.31-B	0.87-A
			p,p'-DDE	72-55-9	0.31-B	0.87-A
U063	Dibenzo-(a,h)-anthracene	NA	Dibenzo (a,h)-anthracene	53-70-3	0.55-B	.8-A
U066	1,2-Dibromo-3-chloro-propane	NA	1,2-Dibromo-3-chloro-propane	96-12-8	0.11-B	5.
U067	1,2-Di-bromoethane (Ethylene dibromide)	NA	1,2-Dibromo ethane (Ethylene-di-bromide)	106-93-4	0.28-B	5.-A
U068	Di-	NA	Dibromo	74-95-3	0.11-B	15.-A

POLLUTION CONTROL BOARD

NOTICE OF PROPOSED AMENDMENTS

	bromoethane	ethane			
U869 A	Di-n-butyl phthalate	Di-n-butyl phthalate	84-74-2	0.057-A	20.
U870 A	o-Dichloro- benzene	o-Dichloro- benzene	95-50-1	0.088-B	6.2
U871 A	m-Dichloro- benzene	m-Dichloro- benzene	541-73-1	0.036	6.2
U872 A	p-Dichloro- benzene	p-Dichloro- benzene	184-46-7	0.090-B	6.2
U875 A	Dichlorodi- fluoro- methane	Dichlorodi- fluoro- methane	75-71-8	023-B	7.2
U876 A	1,1-Di- chloroethane	1,1-Di- chloro- ethane	75-34-3	0.59-B	7.2
U877 A	1,2-Di- chloroethane	1,2-Di- chloro- ethane	107-06-2	021-B	7.2
U878	1,1-Di- chloro- ethylene	1,1-Di- chloro- ethylene	75-35-4	0.025-B	33.-A
U879	1,2-Di- chloro- ethylene	trans-1,2- Dichloro- ethylene	156-60-5	0.54-B	33.-A
U880	Methylene chloride	Methylene chloride	75-09-2	0.89-B	33.-A
U881	2,4-Di- chlorophenol	2,4-Di- chloro- phenol	120-83-2	0.44-B	14.-A

POLLUTION CONTROL BOARD

NOTICE OF PROPOSED AMENDMENTS

U882	2,6-Di- chlorophenol	2,6-Di- chloro- phenol	87-65-0	0.44-B	14.-A
U883 A	1,2-Di- chloro- propane	1,2-Di- chloro- propane	78-87-5	0.85-B	18.
U084 A	1,3-Di- chloro- propene	cis-1,3- Dichloro- propylene trans-1,3- Dichloro- propylene	10061-01-5 10061-02-6	036-B 036-B	18. 18.-A
U088	Diethyl phthalate	Diethyl phthalate	84-66-2	0.2	28.-A
U093	p-Dimethyl- aminoaso- benzene	Table B	p-Dimethyl- aminoaso- benzene	60-11-7	0.13 B	NA
U101	2,4-Di- methyl phenol	2,4-Di- methyl- phenol	105-67-9	0.036-B	14.-A
U102	Dimethyl phthalate	Dimethyl phthalate	131-11-3	0.047	28.-A
U105	2,4-Di- nitro- toluene	2,4-Di- nitro- toluene	121-14-2	0.32-B	140.-A
U106	2,6-Di- nitro- toluene	2,6-Di- nitro- toluene	606-89-2	0.55-B	28.-A
U107	Di-n-octyl phthalate	Di-n- octyl phthalate	117-84-0	0.017	28.-A
U108	1,4-Dioxane	1,4-Di oxane	123-91-1	0.12-B	170.-A
U111	Di-n-pro	Di-n-pro	621-64-7	0.40-B	14.-A

POLLUTION CONTROL BOARD

NOTICE OF PROPOSED AMENDMENTS

	pri-nitrosoamine	pri-nitrosoamine			
#112	Ethyl acetate NA	Ethyl acetate	141-78-6	0.34-B	33.-A
#117	Ethyl-ether NA	Ethyl ether	60-29-7	0.12-B	160.-A
#118	Ethyl-meth-acrylate NA	Ethyl acrylate	97-63-2	0.14-B	160.-A
#120	Fluor-anthene NA	Fluor-anthene	206-44-0	0.060-B	0.2-A
#121	Trichloro-monofluoro-methane NA	Tri-chloro-monofluoro-methane	75-69-4	0.020-B	33.-A
#127 A	Hexachloro-benzene NA	Hexa-chloro-benzene	118-74-1	0.055-B	37.
#128	Hexachloro-butadiene NA	Hexa chloro-butadiene	87-68-3	0.055-B	28.-A
#129 A	Lindane NA	alpha-BHC	319-84-6	0.00011-B	0.66
		beta-BHC	319-85-7	0.00011-B	0.66-A
		Delta-BHC	319-86-8	0.023-B	0.66-A
		gamma-BHC (Lindane)	58-89-9	0.0017-B	0.66-A
#130 A	Hexachloro-cyclopenta-diene NA	Hexa-chloro-cyclo-pentadiene	77-47-7	0.057-B	3.6
#131	Hexachloro-ethane NA	Hexa-chloro-ethane	67-72-1	0.055-B	28.-A
#134	Hydrogen fluoride Table B	Fluoride	16964-48-8	35.	NA

POLLUTION CONTROL BOARD

NOTICE OF PROPOSED AMENDMENTS

#135	Cacodylic acid Table A	Arsenic	7440-38-2	0.79	NA
#137 A	Indeno (1,2,3-cyd) pyrene NA	Indeno (1,2,3-cyd) pyrene	193-39-5	0.0055-B	0.2
#138 A	Iodomethane NA	Iodo-methane	74-88-4	0.19-B	65.
#140	Isobutyl alcohol NA	Isobutyl alcohol	78-83-1	5.6	170.-A
#141 A	Isosafrole NA	Isosafrole	120-58-1	0.081	2.6
#142	Kepone NA	Kepone	143-50-0	0.0011	0.13-A
#144	Lead acetate Table A	Lead	7439-92-1	0.040	NA
#145	Lead phosphate Table A	Lead	7439-92-1	0.040	NA
#146	Lead subacetate Table A	Lead	7439-92-1	0.040	NA
#151	Mercury Table A-B	Mercury	7439-97-6	0.030	NA
#152 A	Methacrylo-nitrile NA	Metha-crylo-nitrile	126-98-7	0.24-B	84.
#154	Methanol NA	Methanol	67-56-1	5.6	NA
#155 A	Methapy-rilene NA	Methapy-rilene	91-80-5	0.081	1.5
#157 A	3-Methyl-cholanthrene NA	3-Methyl-cholanthrene	56-49-5	0.0055-B	15.
#158	4,4'- NA	Methylene-	101-14-4	0.50-B	35.

POLLUTION CONTROL BOARD

NOTICE OF PROPOSED AMENDMENTS

A	Methylene- bis(2- chloro aniline)		bis(2-chloro- aniline)		
U159	Methyl ethyl ketone	NA	Methyl ethyl ketone	78-93-3	0.20	36.-A
U161 A	Methyl isobutyl ketone	NA	Methyl isobutyl ketone	108-10-1	0.14	33.-A
U162	Methyl methacrylate	NA	Methyl methacrylate	80-62-6	0.14	160.-A
U165 A	Naphtha- lene		Naptha- lene	91-20-3	0.059-B	3.1
U168	2-Naph thylamine	Table B	2-Naph thylamine	91-59-8	0.52-B	NA
U169	Nitro- benzene	NA	Nitro- benzene	98-95-3	0.068-B	14.-A
U170 A	4-Nitro- phenol	NA	4-Nitro- phenol	100-02-7	0.12-B	29.
U172 A	N-Nitroso- di-n-butyl- amine	NA	N-Nitro- sodi--n- butylamine	924-16-3	0.40-B	17.
U174 A	N-Nitroso- diethylamine	NA	N-Nitro- sodi- ethylamine	55-18-5	0.40-B	28.
U179 B	N-Nitroso- 35.-A piperidine	NA	N-Nitro- so- piperidine	100-75-4	0.013	
U180 B	N-Nitroso- 35.-A	NA	N-Nitro-	930-55-2	0.013	

POLLUTION CONTROL BOARD

NOTICE OF PROPOSED AMENDMENTS

	pyrrolidine		so- pyrrolidine		
U181 A	5-Nitro-o- toluidine	NA	5-Nitro- o-toluidine	99-55-8	0.32-B	28.
U183 B	Pentachloro- 39.-A benzene	NA	Penta- chloro- benzene	608-93-5	0.055	
U185 A	Pentachloro- nitrobenzene	NA	Penta- chloro- nitrobenzene	82-68-8	0.055-B	4.8
U187 A	Phenacetin	NA	Phenacetin	62-44-2	0.081	16.
U188	Phenol	NA	Phenol	108-95-2	0.039	6.2-A
U190	Phthalic anhydride (measured-as Phthalic acid)		Phthalic anhydride (measured-as Phthalic acid)	85-44-9	0.069	28.-A
U192 A	Pronamide	NA	Pronamide	23950-58-5	0.093	1.5
U196	Pyridine	NA	Pyridine	110-86-1	0.014-B	16.
U203	Safrole	NA	Safrole	94-59-7	0.081	22.-A
U204	Selenium dioxide	Table A	Selenium	7783-49-2	1.0	NA
U205	Selenium sulfide	Table A	Selenium	7782-49-2	1.0	NA
U207 B	1,2,4,5- Tetra- chloro-		1,2,4,5- Tetra- chloro-	95-94-3	0.055 -19. A	

POLLUTION CONTROL BOARD

NOTICE OF PROPOSED AMENDMENTS

	benzene		benzene		
U208 A	1,1,1,2- Tetra- chloro- ethane	NA	1,1,1,2- Tetra- chloro- ethane	630-20-6	0.057	42.
U209	1,1,2,2- Tetra- chloro- ethane	NA	1,1,2,2- Tetra- chloro- ethane	79-34-5	0.057-B	42.-A
U210 B	Tetrachloro- 5,6-A ethylene	NA	Tetra- chloro- ethylene	127-18-4	0.056	
U211	Carbon tetra- chloride	NA	Carbon tetra- chloride	56-23-5	0.057-B	5.6-A
U214	Thall ium(I) acetate	Table B	Thall ium	7440-28-0	0.14-B	NA
U215	Thall ium(I) carbonate	Table B	Thall ium	7440-28-0	0.14-B	NA
U216	Thall ium(I) chloride	Table B	Thall ium	7440-28-0	0.14-B	NA
U217	Thall ium(I) nitrate	Table B	Thall ium	7440-28-0	0.14-B	NA
U220 A	Toluene	NA	Toluene	108-88-3	0.080-B	28.
U225 A	Tribromo- methane (Bromoform)	NA	Tribromo- methane (Bromoform)	75-25-2	0.63-B	15.
U226 B	1,1,1-Tri- 5,6-A	NA	1,1,1-Tri-	71-55-6	0.054	

POLLUTION CONTROL BOARD

NOTICE OF PROPOSED AMENDMENTS

	chloroethane		chloroethane		
U227	1,1,2- tri-chloroe- thane	NA	1,1,2- tri-chloroe- thane	79-00-5	0.054-B	5.6-A
U228	Tri- chloro- ethylene	NA	Tri- chloro- ethylene	79-01-6	0.054-B	5.6-A
U235 A	tris-(2,3- Dibromo- propyl)- phosphate	NA	tris-(2,3- Dibromo- propyl- phosphate	126-72-7	0.025	0.10
U239	Xylenes	NA	Xylene		0.32-B	28.-A
U240	2,4-Di- chloro- phenoxy- acetic acid	NA	2,4-Di- chloro- phenoxy- acetic acid	94-75-7	0.72	10.-A
U243 B	Hexachloro- 28. propene	NA	Hexa- chloro- propene	1888-71-7	0.035	
U247 A	Methoxy- chlor	NA	Methoxy- chlor	72-43-5	0.25-B	0.18

A Treatment standards for this organic constituent were established based upon incineration in units operated in accordance with the technical requirements of 35 Ill. Adm. Code 724 Subpart O, or 725 Subpart O, or based upon combustion in fuel substitution units operating in accordance with applicable technical requirements. A facility may certify compliance with these treatment standards according to provisions in Section 728.39.

B Based on analysis of composite samples.

C As analyzed using SW-846 Method 9010 or 9012, sample size 10g, distillation time one hour fifteen and minutes.

R Reserved.

NA Not Applicable.

POLLUTION CONTROL BOARD

NOTICE OF PROPOSED AMENDMENTS

Section 728.TABLE C Technology Codes and Description of Technology-Based Standards

Technology
code   Description of technology-based standard

ADGAS Venting of compressed gases into an absorbing or reacting media (i.e.,
       solid or liquid)--venting can be accomplished through physical release
       utilizing ~~valves/~~ valves or piping; physical penetration of the
       container; ~~and/~~ or penetration through detonation.

AMLGM Amalgamation of liquid, elemental mercury contaminated with radioactive
       materials utilizing inorganic reagents such as copper, zinc, nickel,
       gold, and sulfur that result in a nonliquid, semi-solid amalgam and
       thereby reducing potential emissions of elemental mercury vapors to the
       air.

BIODG Biodegradation of organics or non-metallic inorganics (i.e., degradable
       inorganics that contain the elements of phosphorus, nitrogen, and
       sulfur) in units operated under either aerobic or anaerobic conditions
       such that a surrogate compound or indicator parameter has been
       substantially reduced in concentration in the residuals (e.g., ~~Total
       Organic--Carbon~~ total organic carbon (TOC) can often be used as an
       indicator parameter for the biodegradation of many organic constituents
       that cannot be directly analyzed in wastewater residues).

CARBN Carbon adsorption (granulated or powdered) or non-metallic inorganics,
       organo-metallics, ~~and/~~or organic constituents, operated ~~such~~ so that a
       surrogate compound or indicator parameter has not undergone
       breakthrough (e.g., ~~Total--Organic--Carbon~~ total organic carbon (TOC) can
       often be used as an indicator parameter for the adsorption of many
       organic constituents that cannot be directly analyzed in wastewater
       residues). Breakthrough occurs when the carbon has become saturated
       with the constituent (or indicator parameter) and substantial change in
       adsorption rate associated with that constituent occurs.

CHOXD Chemical or electrolytic oxidation utilizing the following oxidation
       reagents (or waste reagents) or combinations or reagents:

       1) ~~Hypochlorite~~ hypochlorite (e.g. bleach);
       2) chlorine;
       3) chlorine dioxide;
       4) ozone or UV (ultraviolet light) assisted ozone;
       5) peroxides;
       6) persulfates;
       7) perchlorates;
       8) permanganates; ~~and/~~or

9) other oxidizing reagents of equivalent efficiency, performed in units operated such so that a surrogate compound or indicator parameter has been substantially reduced in concentration in the residuals (e.g., Total-Organic-Carbon total organic carbon (TOC) can often beused as an indicator parameter for the oxidation of many organic constituents that cannot be directly analyzed in wastewater residuals). Chemical oxidation specifically includes what is commonly referred to as alkaline chlorination.

CHRED Chemical reduction utilizing the following reducing reagents (or waste reagents) or combinations of reagents:

1) Sulfur sulfur dioxide;
2) sodium, potassium, or alkali salts of sulfites, bisulfites, metabisulfites, and polyethylene glycols (e.g., NaPEG and KPEG);
3) sodium hydrosulfide;
4) ferrous salts; and/or
6) other reducing reagents of equivalent efficiency, performed in units operated such that a surrogate compound or indicator parameter has been substantially reduced in concentration in the residuals (e.g., Total-Organic-Halogens total organic halogens (TOX) can often be used as an indicator parameter for the reduction of many halogenated organic constituents that cannot be directly analyzed in wastewater residuals). Chemical reduction is commonly used for the reduction of hexavalent chromium to the trivalent state.

CMBST Combustion in incinerators, boilers, or industrial furnaces operated in accordance with the applicable requirements of 35 Ill. Adm. Code 724.Subpart O or 35 Ill. Adm. Code 726.Subpart H.

DEACT Deactivation to remove the hazardous characteristics of a waste due to its ignitability, corrosivity, and/or reactivity.

FSUBS Fuel substitution in units operated in accordance with applicable technical operating requirements.

HLVIT Vitrification of high level mixed radioactive wastes in units in compliance with all applicable radioactive protection requirements under control of the federal Nuclear Regulatory Commission.

IMERC Incineration of wastes containing organics and mercury in units operated in accordance with the technical operating requirements of 35 Ill. Adm. Code 724.Subpart O or 725.Subpart O. All wastewater and nonwastewater residues derived from this process must then comply with the corresponding treatment standards per waste code with consideration of any applicable subcategories (e.g., High high or Low--Mercury Subcategories low mercury subcategories).

INCIN Incineration in units operated in accordance with the technical operating requirements of 35 Ill. Adm. Code 724.Subpart O or 725.Subpart O.

LLEXT Liquid-liquid extraction (often referred to as solvent extraction) of organics from liquid wastes into an immiscible solvent for which the hazardous constituents have a greater solvent affinity, resulting in an extract high in organics that must undergo either incineration, reuse as a fuel, or other recovery; or reuse and a raffinate (extracted liquid waste) proportionately low in organics that must undergo further treatment as specified in the standard.

MACRO Macroencapsulation with surface coating materials such as polymeric organics (e.g. resins and plastics) or with a jacket of inert inorganic materials to substantially reduce surface exposure to potential leaching media. Macroencapsulation specifically does not include any material that would be classified as a tank or container according to 35 Ill. Adm. Code 720.110.

NEUTR Neutralization with the following reagents (or waste reagents) or combinations of reagents:

1) Acids acids;
2) bases; or
3) water (including wastewaters) resulting in a pH greater than 2 but less than 12.5 as measured in the aqueous residuals.

NLDBR No land disposal based on recycling.

PRECP Chemical precipitation of metals and other inorganics as insoluble precipitates of oxides, hydroxides, carbonates, sulfides, sulfates, chlorides, fluorides, or phosphates. The following reagents (or waste reagents) are typically used alone or in combination:

1) lime lime (i.e., containing oxides and/or hydroxides of calcium and/or magnesium;
2) caustic (i.e., sodium and/or potassium hydroxides);
3) soda ash (i.e., sodium carbonate);
4) sodium sulfide;
5) ferric sulfate or ferric chloride;
6) alum; or
7) sodium sulfate. Additional flocculating, coagulation, or similar reagents; or processes that enhance sludge dewatering characteristics are not precluded from use.

RBERY Thermal recovery of Beryllium beryllium.

POLLUTION CONTROL BOARD

NOTICE OF PROPOSED AMENDMENTS

RCGAS Recovery/ or reuse of compressed gases including techniques such as reprocessing of the gases for reuse/ or resale; filtering/ or adsorption of impurities; remixing for direct reuse or resale; and use of the gas as a fuel source.

RCORR Recovery of acids or bases utilizing one or more of the following recover techniques:

1) Distillation distillation (i.e., thermal concentration);
2) ion exchange;
3) resin or solid adsorption;
4) reverse osmosis; and/or
5) incineration for the recover of acid--Note: this does not preclude the use of other physical phase separation or concentration techniques such as decantation, filtration (including ultrafiltration), and centrifugation, when used in conjunction with the above listed recovery technologies.

RLEAD Thermal recovery of lead in secondary lead smelters.

RMERC Retorting or roasting in a thermal processing unit capable of volatilizing mercury and subsequently condensing the volatilized mercury for recovery. The retorting or roasting unit (or facility) must be subject to one or more of the following:

a) A National--Emissions--Standard national emissions standard for Hazardous-Air-Pollutants hazardous air pollutants (NESHAP) for mercury (40 CFR 61, Subpart E);
b) A Best---Available--Control--Technology best available control technology (BACT) or a Lowest-Achievable lowest achievable Emission Rate emission rate (LAER) standard for mercury imposed pursuant to a Prevention prevention of Significant-Deterioration significant deterioration (PSD) permit (including 35 Ill. Adm. Code 201 through 203); or
c) A state permit that establishes emission limitations (within meaning of Section 302 of the Clean Air Act) for mercury, including a permit issued pursuant to 35 Ill. Adm. Code 201. All wastewater and nonwastewater residues derived from this process must then comply with consideration of any applicable subcategories (e.g., High high or low-Mercury-Subcategories low mercury subcategories).

RMETL Recovery of metals or inorganics utilizing one or more of the following direct physical/ or removal technologies:

1) Ion ion exchange;
2) resin or solid (i.e., zeolites) adsorption;
3) reverse osmosis;
4) chelation/ or solvent extraction;

POLLUTION CONTROL BOARD

NOTICE OF PROPOSED AMENDMENTS

5) freeze crystallization;
6) ultrafiltration; and/or
7) simple precipitation (i.e., crystallization)

Note: This does not preclude the use of other physical phase separation or concentration techniques such as decantation, filtration (including ultrafiltration), and centrifugation, when used in conjunction with the above listed recovery technologies.

RORGS Recovery of organics utilizing one or more of the following technologies:

1) Distillation;
2) thin film evaporation;
3) steam stripping;
4) carbon adsorption;
5) critical fluid extraction;
6) liquid-liquid extraction;
7) precipitation/ or crystallization (including freeze crystallization); or
8) chemical phase separation techniques (i.e., addition of acids, bases, demulsifiers, or similar chemicals);.

Note: This does not preclude the use of other physical phase separation techniques such as decantation, filtration (including ultrafiltration), and centrifugation, when used in conjunction with the above listed recovery technologies.

RTHRM Thermal recover of metals or inorganics from nonwastewaters in units defined as cement kilns, blast furnaces, smelting, melting and refining furnaces, combustion devices used to recover sulfur values from spent sulfuric acid and "other devices" determined by the Agency pursuant to 35 Ill. Adm. Code 720.110, the definition of "industrial furnace".

RZINC Resmelting in high temperature metal recovery units for the purpose of recovery of zinc.

STABL Stabilization with the following reagents (or waste reagents) or combinations of reagents:

1) Portland cement; or
2) lime/ or pozzolans (e.g., fly ash and cement kiln dust)--this does no preclude the addition of reagents (e.g., iron salts, silicates, and clays) designed to enhance the set/ or cure time and/or compressive strength, or to overall reduce the leachability of the metal or inorganic.

POLLUTION CONTROL BOARD

NOTICE OF PROPOSED AMENDMENTS

SSTRP Steam stripping of organics from liquid wastes utilizing direct application of steam to the wastes operated such that liquid and vapor flow rates, as well as, temperature and pressure ranges have been optimized, monitored, and maintained. These operating parameters are dependent upon the design parameters of the unit such as, the number of separation stages and the internal column design. Thus, resulting in a condensed extract high in organics that must undergo either incineration, reuse as a fuel, or other recovery/ or/ reuse and an extracted wastewater that must undergo further treatment as specified in the standard.

WETOX Wet air oxidation performed in units operated such that a surrogate compound or indicator parameter has been substantially reduced in concentration in the residuals (e.g., Total--Organic--Carbon total organic carbon (TOC) can often then be used as an indicator parameter for the oxidation of many organic constituents that cannot be directly analyzed in wastewater residues).

WTRRX Controlled reaction with water for highly reactive inorganic or organic chemicals with precautionary controls for protection of workers from potential violent reactions as well as precautionary controls for potential emissions of toxic/ or ignitable levels of gases released during the reaction.

Note 1: When a combination of these technologies (i.e., a treatment train) is specified as a single treatment standard, the order of application is specified in Section 728.Table D T by indicating the five letter technology code that must be applied first, then the designation "fb." (an abbreviation for "followed by"), then the five letter technology code for the technology that must be applied next, and so on.

Note 2: When more than one technology (or treatment train) are specified as alternative treatment standards, the five letter technology codes (or the treatment trains) are separated by a semicolon (;) with the last technology preceded by the word "OR". This indicates that any one of these BDAT technologies or treatment trains can be used for compliance with the standard.

(Source: Amended at 19 Ill. Reg. _____, effective _____)

POLLUTION CONTROL BOARD

NOTICE OF PROPOSED AMENDMENTS

Section 728.TABLE D Technology-Based Standards by RCRA Waste Code

BOARD NOTE: For the requirements previously found in this Section, refer to Sections 728.140 and 728.Table T.

WASTE CODES	SEE ALSO	CAS NO.	TECHNOLOGY CODE-WASTE-WATERS	TECHNOLOGY CODE-NON-WASTE-WATERS	WASTE DESCRIP-TIONS OR TREATMENT SUBCATEGORY
D001	Tables A & B	NA	BDACT, and meet FO39, or FSUBS, or RORGS, or INCIN	BDACT, and meet FO39, or FSUBS, or RORGS, or	All descriptions based--on--35 Ill. Adm.--Code 721.121(1) except for the Section 721.131 (a)(1) High TOC subcategory managed in non-CWA/non-CWA-equivalent/non-Class-I-SDWA systems
D001	NA	NA	BDACT	BDACT	All descriptions based--on--35 Ill. Adm.--Code 721.121--except for the Section 721.131(a)(1) High TOC sub-category managed in-CWA,-CWA-equivalent,-or Class-I-SDWA system
D001	NA	NA	NA	FSUBS, RORGS,-or INCIN	All descriptions based--on--35 Ill. Adm.--Code 721.121(a)(1)-

POLLUTION CONTROL BOARD

NOTICE OF PROPOSED AMENDMENTS

				High-THE Ignitable Liquids Sub-category-- Greater-than or-equal-to 10% total organic carbon		
as-A	NA	DEACT-and meet-F039	DEACT-and meet-F039	Acids-alkaline, and-other-sub- category-based on-35-Ill.-Adm. Code-721.122 managed-in-non- CWA,non-CWA- equivalent,non- Class-I-SDWA systems	D003	NA	NA	NA	DEACT	Water reactives based-on-35 Ill.-Adm. Code-721.123 (a)(2),(a)(3), and-(a)(4)
	NA	DEACT	DEACT	Acids-alkaline, and-other-sub- category--based on 35-Ill.-Adm. Code-721.122 managed-in-CWA, CWA-equivalent, or-Class-I SDWA-systems	D003	NA	NA	DEACT	DEACT	Other reactives-based on-35-Ill.- Adm.-Code 721.123(a) (4)
	NA	DEACT but-not including dilution as-a-sub- stitute for-ade- quate treat- ment,	DEACT but-not including dilution as-a-sub- stitute ade- quate treat- ment,	Reactive sulfides-based on-35-Ill.- Adm.-Code 721.123 (a)(5),	D006	NA	7440 -43-9	NA	RTHERM	Cadmium- containing batteries
	NA	DEACT	DEACT	Explosives based-on-35 Ill.-Adm. Code-721.123 (a)(6),-(a)(7), and-(a)(8),	D008	NA	7439 -92-1	NA	PLEAD	Lead-acid batteries (Note-- This-stand- ard-only applies-to lead-acid batteries that-are identified as-RCRA hazardous wastes-and that-are-not excluded-else- where-from regulation under-the-land disposal restrictions of-this-Part or-exempted under-other regulations (see-35-Ill.- Adm.-Code 726.100).),
					D009	Table-A	7439	NA	SMERC,-or	Mercury,

POLLUTION CONTROL BOARD

NOTICE OF PROPOSED AMENDMENTS

a-B	-97-6		RMHRG	(High-Mercury Subcategory-- greater-than or-equal-to 260-mg/kg total Mercury-- contains-mer- cury-and organics-(and are-not incinerator residues))	
D009	Tables-A a-B	7439 -07-6	NA	RMHRG	Mercury: (High-Mercury Subcategory-- greater-than or-equal-to 260-mg/kg total-Mer- cury-- inorganics (including incinerator residues-and residues-from RMHRG))
D012	Table-B	72-20 -8	DIOOG;-or INCIN	NA	Endrin
D013	Table-B	58-89 -9	CARBN;-or INCIN	NA	Lindane
D014	Table-B	72-43 -5	WETOX;-or INCIN	NA	Methoxychlor
D015	Table-B	8001 -35-2	DIOOG;-or INCIN	NA	Toxaphene
D016	Table-B	94-75 -7	CHOXD; DIOOG;-or INCIN	NA	2,4-D
D017	Table-B	93-72 -1	CHOXD;-or INCIN	NA	2,4,5-TP

POLLUTION CONTROL BOARD

NOTICE OF PROPOSED AMENDMENTS

P005	Tables-A a-B	75-46 -9	(WETOX-or CHOXD)-fb CARBN;-or INCIN	INCIN	2-Nitro- propane
P005	Tables-A aB	110-80 -5	DIOOG;-or INCIN	INCIN	2-Ethoxy ethanol
P024	Tables-A a-B	NA	INCIN	INCIN	---------
K025	NA	NA	LLEXT-fb SSTRIP-fb CARBN;-or INCIN	INCIN	Distillation bottoms-from the-production of-nitro- benzene-by-the nitration-of benzene
K026	NA	NA	INCIN	INCIN	Stripping still-tails from-the production-of methyl-ethyl pyridines
K027	NA	NA	CARBN;-or INCIN	FSUBS;-or INCIN	Centrifuge and distillation residues-from toluene-diiso- cyanate-pro- duction
K039	NA	NA	CARBN;-or INCIN	FSUBS;-or INCIN	Filter-cake from-the filtration-of diethylphospho rodithioic-acid in-the production-of phorate
K044	NA	NA	DEACT	DEACT	Wastewater treatment sludges-from the-manufac- turing-and

POLLUTION CONTROL BOARD

NOTICE OF PROPOSED AMENDMENTS

POLLUTION CONTROL BOARD

NOTICE OF PROPOSED AMENDMENTS

				processing of explosives	K168	NA	NA	~INCIN~ or CHEMD~fby CARBN~ or BIODG~fb CARBN	~INCIN~	Condensed column overheads from product sep- peration and condensed vent gases from the production of 1,1-dimethyl- hydrazine (UDMH) from carboxylic acid hydrazides
	NA	REACT	REACT	Spent carbon from the treatment of wastewater containing explosives						
	NA	REACT	REACT	Pink/red water from TNT operations						
A	NA	NA	RLEAD	Emission control dust/sludge from secondary lead smelting Non-Calcium Sulfate Subcategory	K169	NA	NA	~INCIN~ or CHEMD~fby CARBN~ or BIODG~fb CARBN	~INCIN~	Spent filter cake ridges from product purifi- cation from the production of 1,1- dimethylhydrazine (UDMH) from carboxylic acid hydrazides
A	NA	NA	RMERC	Wastewater treatment sludge from the mercury cell process in chlorine production: (High-Mercury Subcategory greater than or equal to 260 mg/kg total mercury)	K110	NA	NA	~INCIN~ or CHEMD~fby CARBN~ or BIODG~fb CARBN	~INCIN~	Condensed column overheads from intermediate separ- ation from the production of 1,1- dimethylhydrazine (UDMH) from car- boxylic acid hydrazides
	NA	~INCIN~ or CHEMD~fby CARBN~ or BIODG~fb CARBN	~INCIN~	Column bottoms from product separation from the production of						
				1,1-dimethyl- hydrazine (UDMH) from carboxylic acid hydrazides	K111	NA	NA	~INCIN~ or CHEMD~fby CARBN~ or BIODG~fb CARBN	~INCIN~	Reaction-by- product water from the drying column in the production of toluenediamine

POLLUTION CONTROL BOARD

NOTICE OF PROPOSED AMENDMENTS

POLLUTION CONTROL BOARD

NOTICE OF PROPOSED AMENDMENTS

			via hydrogenation of dinitrotoluene				the-solvent recovery-column in----------the production of-----toluene
NA	CARBN;-or INCIN	PSUBS;-or INCIN	Condensed liquid-light ends-from-the purification-of toluenediamine in----------the				diiso- cyanate-via phosgenation of-toluene- diamine
			production of toluenediamine via hydrogenation of dinitrotoluene	K123	NA	NA	INCIN;-or CHOXD-;b ;BIODG-or CARBN;	INCIN;	Process-waste- water (including supernatates filt- rates;-----and wash- waters;----from
NA	CARBN;-or INCIN	PSUBS;-or INCIN	Vicinals-from the purification of toluenediamine in----------the production of toluenediamine via hydrogenation of dinitrocarbamic	K124	NA	NA	INCIN;-or CHOXD-;b ;BIODG-or CARBN;	INCIN;	the production-of ethylenebis- dithiocarbamic acid-and its-salts
								Reactor-vent scrubber-water from-the-pro- duction-of ethylenebisdi- thiocarbamic acid and-its-salts
NA	CARBN;-or INCIN	PSUBS;-or INCIN	Heavy-ends from-the purification-of toluenediamine in----------the production of toluenediamine via-hydro- generation of-dinitro- toluene	K125	NA	NA	INCIN;-or CHOXD-;b ;BIODG-or CARBN;	INCIN;	Filtration; evapo- ration;-----and centri- fugation-solids from-the-pro- duction-of ethylenebisdi- thiocarbamic acid-and-its salts
NA	CARBN;-or INCIN	PSUBS;-or INCIN	Organic condensate-from	K126	NA	NA	INCIN;-or INCIN;		Baghouse-dust

POLLUTION CONTROL BOARD

NOTICE OF PROPOSED AMENDMENTS

			~~CHOKB~~-fb		and------floor sweepings in-milling-and packaging opera- tions--from-the produc- tion--------or formulation of-----ethylene bisdithio- carbamic---acid and its-salts
			~~{BIOOG-or CARBN}~~		
P001	NA	~~81-81 -2~~	~~{WRTOX-or CHOKD}-fb CARBN;-or INCIN~~	~~PSUBS;-or INCIN~~	Warfarin ~~(>-0.3%)~~
P002	NA	~~591-08 -2~~	~~{WRTOX-or CHOKD}-fb CARBN;-or INCIN~~	~~INCIN~~	1-Acetyl-2- thiourea
P003	NA	~~107-02 -8~~	~~{WRTOX-or CHOKD}-fb CARBN;-or INCIN~~	~~PSUBS;-or INCIN~~	Acrolein
P005	NA	~~107-18 -6~~	~~{WRTOX-or CHOKD}-fb CARBN;-or INCIN~~	~~PSUBS;-or INCIN~~	Allyl-alcohol
P006	NA	~~20859 -73-8~~	~~CHOKD; CHRED;-or INCIN~~	~~CHOKD; CHRED;-or INCIN~~	Aluminum phosphide
P007	NA	~~2763-96 -4~~	~~{WRTOX-or CHOKD}-fb CARBN;-or INCIN~~	~~INCIN~~	5-Aminoethyl 3-isoxazolol
P008	NA	~~504-24 -5~~	~~{WRTOX-or CHOKD}-fb CARBN;-or INCIN~~	~~INCIN~~	4- Aminopyridine

POLLUTION CONTROL BOARD

NOTICE OF PROPOSED AMENDMENTS

P009	NA	~~131-74 -8~~	~~CHOXD; CHRED; BIOGH;-or INCIN~~	~~PSUBS; CHOXD; CHRED;-or INCIN~~	Ammonium picrate
P014	NA	~~108-95 -5~~	~~{WRTOX-or CHOKD}-fb CARBN;-or INCIN~~	~~INCIN~~	Thiophenol {Benzene thiol}
P015	NA	~~7440-41 -7~~	~~RMETL;-or RTHRM~~	~~RMETL;-or RTHRM~~	Beryllium powder
P016	NA	~~542-88 -1~~	~~{WRTOX-or CHOKD}-fb CARBN;-or INCIN~~	~~INCIN~~	Bis{chloro- methyl}-ether
P017	NA	~~598-31 -2~~	~~{WRTOX-or CHOKD}-fb CARBN;-or INCIN~~	~~INCIN~~	Bromoacetone
P018	NA	~~357-57 -3~~	~~{WRTOX-or CHOKD}-fb CARBN;-or INCIN~~	~~INCIN~~	Brucine
P022	Table-B	~~75-15 -0~~	NA	~~INCIN~~	Carbon disulfide
P023	NA	~~107-20 -0~~	~~{WRTOX-or CHOKD}-fb CARBN;-or INCIN~~	~~INCIN~~	Chloro- acetaldehyde
P026	NA	~~5344-82 -1~~	~~{WRTOX-or CHOKD}-fb CARBN;-or INCIN~~	~~INCIN~~	1-{o-Chloro- phenyl}-thio- urea
P027	NA	~~542-76 -7~~	~~{WRTOX-or CHOKD}-fb CARBN;-or INCIN~~	~~INCIN~~	3-Chloro- propionitrile
P028	NA	~~100-44~~	~~{WRTOX-or~~	~~INCIN~~	Benzyl

POLLUTION CONTROL BOARD

NOTICE OF PROPOSED AMENDMENTS

		-7	CHOKD?-fb CARBN7-or INCIN		chloride
P031	NA	460-19 -5	CHOKD7 WHTOX7-or INCIN	CHOKD7 INCIN	Cyanogen
P033	NA	506-77 -4	CHOKD7 WHTOX7-or INCIN	CHOKD7-or INCIN	Cyanogen chloride
P034	NA	131-89 -5	7WHTOX-or CHOKD7-fb CARBN7-or INCIN	INCIN	2-Cyclohexyl-4,6-dinitro-phenol
P040	NA	297-97 -2	CARBN7-or INCIN	PSUBS7-or INCIN	0,0-Diethyl-O-pyrazinyl phosphoro-thioate
P041	NA	311-45 -5	CARBN7-or INCIN	PSUBS7-or INCIN	Diethyl-p-nitrophenyl phosphate
P042	NA	51-43 -4	7WHTOX-or CHOKD7-fb INCIN	INCIN	Epinephrine
P043	AN	55-91 -4	CARBN7-or INCIN	PSUBS7-or INCIN	Diisopropyl-fluoro-phosphate (DFP)
P044	NA	60-51 -5	CARBN7-or INCIN	PSUBS7-or INCIN	Dimethoate
P045	NA	39190-18 -4	7WHTOX-or CHOKD7-fb CARBN7-or INCIN	INCIN	Thiofanox
P046	NA	122-09 -8	7WHTOX-or CHOKD7-fb CARBN7-or INCIN	INCIN	alpha,alpha-Dimethylphen-ethylamine

POLLUTION CONTROL BOARD

NOTICE OF PROPOSED AMENDMENTS

P047	NA	534-52 -1	7WHTOX-or CHOKD7-fb CARBN7-or INCIN	INCIN	4,6-Dinitro-o-cresol-salts
P049	NA	541-53 -7	7WHTOX-or CHOKD7-fb CARBN7-or INCIN	INCIN	2,4-Dithio-biuret
P054	NA	151-56 -4	7WHTOX-or CARBN7-or INCIN	INCIN	Aziridine
P056	Table-B	7782-41 -4	NA	ADGAS-fb NEUTR	Fluorine
P057	NA	640-19 -7>	7WHTOX-or CHOKD7-fb CARBN7-or INCIN	INCIN	Fluoro-acetamide
P058	NA	62-74 -8	7WHTOX-or CHOKD7-fb INCIN	INCIN	Fluoroacetic acid,-sodium salt
P062	NA	757-58 -4	CARBN7-or INCIN	PSUBS-or INCIN	Hexaethyl-tetraphosphate
P064	NA	624-83 -9	7WHTOX-or CHOKD7-fb CARBN7-or INCIN	INCIN	Isocyanic acid,-methyl ester
P065	Tables-A a-B	628-86 4	NA	RMERC	Mercury fulminate (High-Mercury Subcategory--greater-than or-equal-to 260-mg/kg total-Mercury--either incinerator residues-or residues-from

POLLUTION CONTROL BOARD

NOTICE OF PROPOSED AMENDMENTS

					RMERG↑
P066	Tables-A & B	628-86 -4	NA	↓MERG	Mercury fulminate; (All non-wastewaters-- that-are-not incinerator residues or-are-not residues-from RMERG↑ regardless-of Mercury Content)
P066	NA	↓6758-77 -5	↑WETOX-or CHOXD↓-fb CARBN↑-or ↓NCIN	↓NCIN	Methomyl
P067	NA	75-55 -8	↑WETOX-or CHOXD↓-fb CARBN↑-or ↓NCIN	↓NCIN	2-Methyl-aziridine
P068	NA	60-34 -4	CHOXD↑ CHRED↑ CARBN↑ BIODG↑-or ↓NCIN	PSUBS↑ CHOXD↑ CHRED↓--OR	Methyl hydrazine
P069	NA	75-86 -5	↑WETOX-or CHOXD↓-fb CARBN↑-or ↓NCIN	↓NCIN	Methylacto-nitrile
P070	NA	116-06 -3	↑WETOX-or CHOXD↓-fb CARBN↑-or ↓NCIN	↓NCIN	Aldicarb
P072	NA	86-88 -4	↑WETOX-or CHOXD↓-fb CARBN↑-or ↓NCIN	↓NCIN	1-Naphthyl-2-thiourea
P075	NA	54-11	↑WETOX-or	↓NCIN	Nicotine-and

POLLUTION CONTROL BOARD

NOTICE OF PROPOSED AMENDMENTS

					salts
		-5	CHOXD↑-fb CARBN↑-or ↓NCIN		
P076	NA	↓0102-43 -9	ADGAS	ADGAS	Nitric-oxide
P078	NA	↓0102-44 -0	ADGAS	ADGAS	Nitrogen dioxide
P081	NA	55-63 -0	CHOXD↑ CHRED↑ CARBN↑ BIODG↑-or ↓NCIN	PSUBS↑ CHOXD↑ CHRED↑-or ↓NCIN	Nitroglycerin
P082	Table-B	62-75 -9	NA	↓NCIN	N-Nitrosodi-methylamine
P084	NA	4549-40 -0	↑WETOX-or CHOXD↑-fb CARBN↑-or ↓NCIN	↓NCIN	N-Nitroso-methylvinyl-amine
P085	NA	↓52-16 -9	CARBN↑-or ↓NCIN	PSUBS↑-or ↓NCIN	Octamethyl-pyrophosphor-amide
P087	NA	20816-12 -0	RMETL↑ or-RTIGRM	RMETL↑-or RTIGRM	Osmium tetroxide
P088	NA	145-73 -3	↑WETOX-or CHOXD↓-fb CARBN↑-or ↓NCIN	PSUBS↑-or ↓NCIN	Endothall
P092	Tables-A & B	62-38 -4	NA	RMERG	Phenyl-mercury acetate; (High-Mercury Subcategory-- greater-than or-equal-to 260-mg/kg total Mercury-- either incinerator residues-or

POLLUTION CONTROL BOARD

NOTICE OF PROPOSED AMENDMENTS

				residues-from RMERC†
P092	Tables-A a-B	62-38 -4	NA	†MERC†-or RMERC	Phenyl-mercury acetate- †All-non- wastewaters that-are-not incinerator residues-and are-not residues-and are-not residues-from RMERC, regardless-of Mercury Content†
P093	NA	103-85 -5	†WETOX-or CHOXD†-fb CARBN†-or INCIN	INCIN	N-Phenylthio- urea
P095	NA	75-44 -5	†WETOX-or CHOXD†-fb CARBN†-or INCIN	INCIN	Phosgene
P096	NA	7803-51 -2	CHOXD† CHRED†-or INCIN	CHOXD†-or INCIN	Phosphine
P102	NA	107-19 -7	†WETOX-or CHOXD†-fb CARBN†-or INCIN	PSUBS†-or INCIN	Propargyl alcohol
P105	NA	26628-22 -8	CHOXD† CHRED†-CARBN BIODG†-or INCIN	PSUBS† CHOXD†-or INCIN	Sodium-azide
P108	NA	57-24 -9-A	†WETOX-or CHOXD†-fb CARBN†-or INCIN	INCIN	Strychnine-and salts

POLLUTION CONTROL BOARD

NOTICE OF PROPOSED AMENDMENTS

P109	NA	3689-24 -5	CARBN†-or INCIN	PSUBS†-or INCIN	Tetraethyldi- thiopyro- phosphate
P112	NA	509-14 8	CHOXD† CHRED† CARBN† BIODG†-or INCIN	PSUBS† CHOXD† CHRED†-or INCIN	Tetranitro- methane
P113	Table-B	1314-32 -5	NA	RTHRM†-or STABL	Thallic-oxide
P115	Table-B	7446-18 -6	NA	RTHRM†-or STABL	Thallium-(I) sulfate
-P116	NA	79-19 -6	†WETOX-or CHOXD†-fb CARBN†-or INCIN	INCIN	Thiosemi- carbazide
P118	NA	75-70 -7	†WETOX-or CHOXD†-fb CARBN†-or INCIN	INCIN	Trichloro- methanethiol
P119	Table-B	7803-55 -6	NA	STABL	Ammonium vanadate
P120	Table-B	1314-62 -1	NA	STABL	Vanadium pentoxide
P122	NA	1314-84 -7	CHOXD† CHRED†-or INCIN	CHOXD† CHRED†-or INCIN	Zinc-Phosphide †-->-10%†
U001	NA	75-07 -0	†WETOX-or CHOXD†-fb CARBN†-or INCIN	INCIN	Acetaldehyde
U003	Table-B	75-05 -8	NA	INCIN	Acetonitrile
U006	NA	75-36 -5	†WETOX-or CHOXD†-fb CARBN†-or INCIN	INCIN	Acetyl chloride

POLLUTION CONTROL BOARD

NOTICE OF PROPOSED AMENDMENTS

U007	NA	79-06 -1	tWBTOX-or CHOKD-fb CARBN-or INCIN	INCIN	Acrylamide
U008	NA	79-10 -7	tWBTOX-or CHOKD-fb INCIN	PSUBS-or INCIN	Acrylic-acid
U010	NA	50-07 -7	tWBTOX-or CHOKD-fb CARBN-or INCIN	INCIN	Mitomycin-C
U011	NA	61-82 -5	tWBTOX-or CHOKD-fb INCIN	INCIN	Amitrole
U014	NA	492-80 -8	tWBTOX-or CHOKD-fb CARBN-or INCIN	INCIN	Auramine
U015	NA	115-02 -6	tWBTOX-or CHOKD-fb CARBN-or INCIN	INCIN	Azaserine
U016	NA	225-51 -4	tWBTOX-or CHOKD-fb INCIN	PSUBS-or INCIN	Benz(c)-acridine
U017	NA	98-07 -3	tWBTOX-or CHOKD-fb CARBN-or INCIN	INCIN	Benzal chloride
U020	NA	98-09 -9	tWBTOX-or CHOKD-fb CARBN-or INCIN	INCIN	Benzene-sulfonyl chloride
U021	NA	92-87 -5	tWBTOX-or CHOKD-fb CARBN-or	INCIN	Benzidine

POLLUTION CONTROL BOARD

NOTICE OF PROPOSED AMENDMENTS

			INCIN		
U023	NA	98-07 -7	CHOKD CHRBD CARBN BIODG-or INCIN	PSUBS CHOKD CHOKB-or INCIN	Benzotri-chloride
U026	NA	494-03 -1	tWBTOX-or CHOKD-fb CARBN-or INCIN	INCIN	Chlornaphazin
U033	NA	353-50 -4	tWBTOX-or CHOKD-fb CARBN-or INCIN	INCIN	Carbonyl fluoride
U034	NA	75-87 -6	tWBTOX-or CHOKD-fb CARBN-or INCIN	INCIN	Trichloroacet-aldehyde (Chloral)
U035	NA	305-03 -3	tWBTOX-or CHOKD-fb CARBN-or INCIN	INCIN	Chlorambucil
U038	Table-B	510-15 -6	NA	INCIN	Chloro-benzilate
U041	NA	106-89 -8	tWBTOX-or CHOKD-fb CARBN-or INCIN	INCIN	1-Chloro-2,3-epoxypropane (Epichloro-hydrin)
U042	Table-B	110-75 -8	NA	INCIN	2-Chloroethyl vinyl-ether
U046	NA	107-30 -2	tWBTOX-or CHOKD-fb INCIN	INCIN	Chloromethyl methyl-ether
U049	NA	3165-93 -3	tWBTOX-or CHOKD-fb CARBN-or INCIN	INCIN	4-Chloro-o-toluidine hydrochloride

POLLUTION CONTROL BOARD

NOTICE OF PROPOSED AMENDMENTS

U053	NA	4170-30 -3	~~TWETOX-or CHRED~-Fb CARBN~-or~~ INCIN	~~PSUBS~-or~~ INCIN	Crotonaldehyde
U055	NA	98-82 -8	~~TWETOX-or CHOXD~-Fb CARBN~-or~~ INCIN	~~PSUBS~-or~~ INCIN	Cumene
U056	NA	110-82 -7	~~TWETOX-or CHOXD~-Fb CARBN~-or~~ INCIN	~~PSUBS~-or~~ INCIN	Cyclohexane
U057	Table-B	108-94 -1	NA	~~PSUBS~-or~~ INCIN	Cyclohexanone
U058	NA	50-18 -0	~~CARBN~-or~~ INCIN	~~PSUBS~-or~~ INCIN	Cyclophosph- amide
U059	NA	20830-81 -3	~~TWETOX-or CHOXD~-Fb CARBN~-or~~ INCIN	INCIN	Daunomycin
U062	NA	2303-16 -4	~~TWETOX-or CHOXD~-Fb CARBN~-or~~ INCIN	INCIN	Diallate
U064	NA	189-55 -9	~~TWETOX-or CHOXD~-Fb CARBN~-or~~ INCIN	~~PSUBS~-or~~ INCIN	1,2,7,8-Di- benzopyrene
U073	NA	91-94 -1	~~TWETOX-or CHOXD~-Fb CARBN~-or~~ INCIN	INCIN	3,3'-Dichloro- benzidine
U074	NA	1476-11 -5	~~TWETOX-or CARBN~-or~~ INCIN	INCIN	cis-1,4-Di- chloro-2- butene-trans- 1,4-Dichloro- 2-butene
U086	NA	1464-53	~~TWETOX-or~~	~~PSUBS~-or~~	1,2,3,4-Di-

POLLUTION CONTROL BOARD

NOTICE OF PROPOSED AMENDMENTS

		-5	~~CHOXD~-Fb CARBN~-or~~ INCIN	INCIN	epoxybutane
U086	NA	1615-80 -1	~~CHOXD~ CHRED~-CARBN~ CARBN~-or~~ INCIN	~~PSUBS~ CHRED~-or~~ INCIN	N,N-Diethyl- hydrazine
U087	NA	3288-58 -2	~~CARBN~-or~~ INCIN	~~PSUBS~-or~~ INCIN	o,o-Diethyl-s- methyldithio- phosphate
U089	NA	56-53 -1	~~TWETOX-or CHOXD~-Fb CARBN~-or~~ INCIN	~~PSUBS~-or~~ INCIN	Diethyl stilbestrol
U090	NA	94-58 -6	~~TWETOX-or CHOXD~-Fb CARBN~-or~~ INCIN	~~PSUBS~-or~~ INCIN	Dihydrosafrole
U091	NA	119-90 -4	~~TWETOX-or CHOXD~-Fb CARBN~-or~~ INCIN	INCIN	3,3'-Di- methoxy- benzidine
U092	NA	124-40 -3	~~TWETOX-or CHOXD~-Fb~~ INCIN	INCIN	Dimethylamine
U093	Table-B	603-90 -9	NA	INCIN	p-Dimethyl- aminoazo- benzene
U094	NA	57-97 -6	~~TWETOX-or CHOXD~-Fb CARBN~-or~~ INCIN	~~PSUBS~-or~~ INCIN	7,12-Dimethyl- benz[a]- anthracene
U095	NA	119-93 -7	~~TWETOX-or CHOXD~-Fb CARBN~-or~~ INCIN	INCIN	3,3'-Dimethyl- benzidine
U096	NA	80-15	~~CHOXD~~	~~PSUBS~~	alpha,alpha-

POLLUTION CONTROL BOARD

NOTICE OF PROPOSED AMENDMENTS

		-9	~~CHRED~~, ~~CARBN~~, ~~BIODG~~,-or ~~INCIN~~	~~CHOXD~~, ~~CHRED~~,-or ~~INCIN~~	Dimethyl-benzyl-hydro-peroxide
U097	NA	99-44 -9	†~~WETOX~~-or ~~CHOXD~~,-fb ~~CARBN~~,-or ~~INCIN~~	~~INCIN~~	Dimethyl-carbamoyl chloride
U098	NA	57-14 -9	~~CHRED~~, ~~CHRED~~, ~~BIODG~~,-or ~~INCIN~~	~~PSUBS~~, ~~CHOXD~~, ~~CHRED~~,-or ~~INCIN~~	1,1-Dimethylhydrazine
U099	NA	540-73 -8	~~CHOXD~~, ~~CHRED~~, ~~CARBN~~, ~~BIODG~~,-or ~~INCIN~~	~~PSUBS~~, ~~CHRED~~, ~~CHRED~~,-or ~~INCIN~~	1,2-Dimethyl-hydrazine
U103	NA	77-78 -1	~~CHOXD~~, ~~CHRED~~, ~~CARBN~~, ~~BIODG~~,-or ~~INCIN~~	~~PSUBS~~, ~~CHOXD~~, ~~CHRED~~,-or ~~INCIN~~	Dimethyl sulfate
U109	NA	122-66 -9	~~CHOXD~~, ~~CHRED~~, ~~CARBN~~, ~~BIODG~~,-or ~~INCIN~~	~~PSUBS~~, ~~CHOXD~~, ~~CHRED~~,-or ~~INCIN~~	1,2-Diphenyl-hydrazine
U110	NA	142-84 -9	†~~WETOX~~-or ~~CHOXD~~,-fb ~~CARBN~~,-or ~~INCIN~~	~~INCIN~~	Dipropylamine
U113	NA	140-88 -5	†~~WETOX~~-or ~~CHOXD~~,-fb ~~CARBN~~,-or ~~INCIN~~	~~PSUBS~~,-or ~~INCIN~~	Ethyl-acrylate
U114	NA	111-54 6	†~~WETOX~~-or ~~CHOXD~~,-fb ~~CARBN~~,-or ~~INCIN~~	~~INCIN~~	Ethylenebis-dithiocarbamic acid

POLLUTION CONTROL BOARD

NOTICE OF PROPOSED AMENDMENTS

U115	NA	75-21 -8	†~~WETOX~~-or ~~CHOXD~~,-fb ~~CARBN~~,-or ~~INCIN~~	~~CHOXD~~,-or ~~INCIN~~	Ethylene-oxide
U116	NA	96-45 -7	†~~WETOX~~-or ~~CHOXD~~,-fb ~~CARBN~~,-or ~~INCIN~~	~~INCIN~~	Ethylene-thio-urea
U119	NA	62-50 -8	†~~WETOX~~-or ~~CHOXD~~,-fb ~~CARBN~~,-or ~~INCIN~~	~~INCIN~~	Ethyl-methane-sulfonate
U122	NA	50-00 -0	†~~WETOX~~-or ~~CHOXD~~,-fb ~~CARBN~~,-or ~~INCIN~~	~~PSUBS~~,-or ~~INCIN~~	Formaldehyde
U123	NA	64-18 -6	†~~WETOX~~-or ~~CHOXD~~,-fb ~~CARBN~~,-or ~~INCIN~~	~~PSUBS~~,-or ~~INCIN~~	Formic-acid
U124	NA	110-00 -9	†~~WETOX~~-or ~~CHOXD~~,-fb ~~CARBN~~,-or ~~INCIN~~	~~PSUBS~~,-or ~~INCIN~~	Furan
U125	NA	98-01 -1	†~~WETOX~~-or ~~CHOXD~~,-fb ~~CARBN~~,-or ~~INCIN~~	~~PSUBS~~,-or ~~INCIN~~	Furfural
U126	NA	765-34 -4	†~~WETOX~~-or ~~CHOXD~~,-fb ~~CARBN~~,-or ~~INCIN~~	~~PSUBS~~,-or ~~INCIN~~	Glycidyial-dehyde
U132	NA	70-30 -4	†~~WETOX~~-or ~~CHOXD~~,-fb ~~CARBN~~,-or ~~INCIN~~	~~INCIN~~	Hexachloro-phene
U133	NA	302-01 -2	~~CHOXD~~, ~~CHRED~~,-~~CARBN~~, ~~BIODG~~,-or	~~PSUBS~~, ~~CHOXD~~, ~~CHRED~~,-or	Hydrazine

POLLUTION CONTROL BOARD

NOTICE OF PROPOSED AMENDMENTS

				INGEN	INGEN	
U134	Table-B	7664-39-3	NA		ADGAS-fb NEUTR-or NEUTR	Hydrogen fluoride
U135	NA	7783-06-4	CHOXD-or CHRED-or INGEN	CHOXD-or CHRED-or INGEN		Hydrogen Sulfide
U143	NA	303-34-4	(WETOX-or CHOXD-fb CARBN-or INGEN	INGEN		lasiocarpine
U147	NA	108-31-6	(WETOX-or CHOXD-fb CARBN-or INGEN	PSUBS-or INGEN		Maleic anhydride
U148	NA	123-33-1	(WETOX-or CHOXD-fb CARBN-or INGEN	INGEN		Maleic hydrazide
U149	NA	109-77-3	(WETOX-or CHOXD-fb CARBN-or INGEN	INGEN		Malononitrile
U150	NA	148-82-3	(WETOX-or CHOXD-fb CARBN-or INGEN	INGEN		Melphalan
U151	Tables-A&B	7439-97-6	NA	RMERC		Mercury (High-Mercury Subcategory-- greater than or equal to 260 mg/kg total Mercury)
U153	NA	74-93-1	(WETOX-or CHOXD-fb CARBN-or INGEN	INGEN		Methanethiol

POLLUTION CONTROL BOARD

NOTICE OF PROPOSED AMENDMENTS

U154	NA	67-56-1	(WETOX-or CHOXD-fb CARBN-or INGEN	UFUBS-or INGEN	Methanol
U156	NA	79-22-1	(WETOX-or CHOXD-fb CARBN-or INGEN	INGEN	Methyl chloro- carbonate
U160	NA	1338-23-4	CHOXD-or CHRED--CARBN BIODG-or INGEN	PSUBS-or CHOXD-or INGEN	Methyl ethyl ketone peroxide
U163	NA	70-25-7	(WETOX-or CHOXD-fb CARBN-or INGEN	INGEN	N-Methyl-N'- nitro-N- Nitroso- guanidine
U164	NA	56-04-2	(WETOX-or CHOXD-fb CARBN-or INGEN	INGEN	Methylthio- uracil
U166	NA	130-15-4	(WETOX-or CHOXD-fb CARBN-or INGEN	PSUBS--or INGEN	1,4-Naphtho- quinone
U167	NA	134-32-7	(WETOX-or CHOXD-fb CARBN-or INGEN	INGEN	1-Naphthyl- amine
U168	Table-B	91-59-8	NA	INGEN	2-Naphthyl- amine
U171	NA	79-46-9	(WETOX-or CHOXD-fb CARBN-or INGEN	INGEN	2-Nitropropane
U173	NA	1116-54-7	(WETOX-or CHOXD-fb CARBN-or INGEN	INGEN	N-Nitroso-di- ethanolamine

POLLUTION CONTROL BOARD

NOTICE OF PROPOSED AMENDMENTS

U176	NA	759-73-9	(WETOX-or CHOXD)-fb CARBN)-or INCIN	INCIN	N-Nitroso-N-ethylurea
U177	NA	684-93-5	(WETOX-or CHOXD)-fb CARBN)-or INCIN	INCIN	N-Nitroso-N-methylurea
U178	NA	615-53-2	(WETOX-or CHOXD)-fb CARBN)-or INCIN	INCIN	N-Nitroso-N-methylurethane
U182	NA	123-63-9	(WETOX-or CHOXD)-fb CARBN)-or INCIN	PSUBS)-or INCIN	Paraldehyde
U184	NA	76-01-7	(WETOX-or CHOXD)-or CARBN)-or INCIN	INCIN	Pentachloro-ethane
U186	NA	504-60-9	(WETOX-or CHOXD)-fb CARBN)-or INCIN	PSUBS)-or INCIN	1,3-Pentadiene
U189	NA	1314-80-3	CHOXD) CHRED)-or INCIN	CHOXD) CHRED)-or INCIN	Phosphorus sulfide
U191	NA	109-06-8	(WETOX-or CHOXD)-fb CARBN)-or INCIN	INCIN	2-Picoline
U193	NA	1120-71-4	(WETOX-or CHOXD)-fb CARBN)-or INCIN	INCIN	1,3-Propane sultone
U194	NA	107-10-8	(WETOX-or CHOXD)-fb CARBN)-or INCIN	INCIN	n-Propylamine

POLLUTION CONTROL BOARD

NOTICE OF PROPOSED AMENDMENTS

U197	NA	106-51-4	(WETOX-or CHOXD)-fb CARBN)-or INCIN	PSUBS-or INCIN	p-Benzoquinone
U200	NA	50-55-5	(WETOX-or CHOXD)-fb CARBN)-or INCIN	INCIN	Reserpine
U201	NA	108-46-3	(WETOX-or CHOXD)-fb CARBN)-or INCIN	PSUBS)-fb INCIN	Resorcinol
U202	NA	81-07-2-A	(WETOX-or CHOXD)-fb CARBN)-or INCIN	INCIN	Saccharin and salts
U206	NA	18883-66-4	(WETOX-or CHOXD)-fb CARBN)-or INCIN	INCIN	Streptozotocin
U213	NA	109-99-9	(WETOX-or CHOXD)-fb CARBN)-or INCIN	PSUBS)-or INCIN	Tetrahydro-furan
U214	Table-B	563-68-8	NA	RTHRM)-or STABL	Thallium (I) acetate
U215	Table-B	6533-73-9	NA	RTHRM)-or STABL	Thallium (I) carbonate
U216	Table-B	7791-12-0	NA	RTHRM)-or STABL	Thallium (I) chloride
U217	Table-B	10102-45-1	NA	RTHRM)-or STABL	Thallium (I) nitrate
U218	NA	62-55-5	(WETOX-or CHOXD)-fb CARBN)-or INCIN	INCIN	Thioacetamide
U219	NA	62-56-6	(WETOX-or	INCIN	Thiourea

POLLUTION CONTROL BOARD

NOTICE OF PROPOSED AMENDMENTS

		-6	CHOXD₱-fb CARBN₱-or INCIN	PSUBS₱-or INCIN	
U221	NA	25376-45 -8	CARBN₱-or INCIN	PSUBS₱-or INCIN	Toluenediamine
U222	NA	636-21 -5	₱WETOX-or CHOXD₱-fb CARBN₱-or INCIN	INCIN	o-Toluidine hydrochloride
U223	NA	26471-62 -5	CARBN₱-or INCIN	PSUBS₱-or INCIN	Toluene-diiso-cynnate
U234	NA	99-35 -4	₱WETOX-or CHOXD₱-fb CARBN₱-or INCIN	INCIN	sym-Trinitro-benzene
U236	NA	72-57 -1	₱WETOX-or CHOXD₱-fb CARBN₱-or INCIN	INCIN	Trypan-Blue
U237	NA	66-75 -1	₱WETOX-or CHOXD₱-fb CARBN₱-or INCIN	INCIN	Uracil-mustard
U238	NA	51-79 -6	₱WETOX-or CHOXD₱-fb CARBN₱-or INCIN	INCIN	Ethyl carbamate
U240	NA	94-75 -7-*	₱WETOX-or CHOXD₱-fb CARBN₱-or INCIN	INCIN	2,4-Dichloro-phenoxyacetic acid-(salts and-esters)
U244	NA	137-26 -8	₱WETOX-or CHOXD₱-fb CARBN₱-or INCIN	INCIN	Thiram
U246	NA	506-68 -3	CHOXD₱ WETOX₱-or INCIN	CHOXD₱ WETOX₱-or INCIN	Cyanogen bromide

POLLUTION CONTROL BOARD

NOTICE OF PROPOSED AMENDMENTS

U248	NA	81-81 -2	₱WETOX-or CHOXD₱-fb CARBN₱-or INCIN	PSUBS₱-or INCIN	Warfarin (0.3%-or-less)
U249	NA	1314-84 -7	CHOXD₱ CHOXD₱-fb INCIN	CHOXD₱ CARBN₱-or INCIN	Zinc-Phosphide (<10%)
U328	NA	95-53-4	INCIN₱-or CHOXD-fb ₱BIODG-or BIODG-fb CARBN	INCIN₱-or Thermal Destructio nr	o-toluidine
U353	NA	106-49-0	INCIN₱-or CHOXD-fb ₱BIODG-or CARBN₱-or BIODG-fb CARBN	INCIN₱-or Thermal Destructio nr	p-toluidine
U359	NA	110-80-5	INCIN₱-or ₱BIODG-or CARBN₱₱-or CARBN	INCIN₱-or PSUBS₱	2-ethoxy-ethanol

A CAS-Number-given-for-parent-compound-only.

B This-waste-code-exists-in-gaseous-form-and-is-not-categorized--as--wastewater or-nonwastewater-former

NA--Not-Applicable.

BOARD-NOTE:--When-a-combination-of-these-technologies-(i.e.,-a-treatment-train) is--specified--as--a--single--treatment--standard,-the-order-of-application-is specified-in-this-Table-by-indicating-the-five-letter-technology-code-that-must be-applied-first;-then-the-designation--"fb"--(an--abbreviation--for--"followed by")--then--the--five-letter--technology--code-for-the-technology-that-must-be applied-next;-and-so-on.--When-more-than-one-technology--(or--treatment--train) are--specified--a--alternative--treatment-standards,-the-five-letter-technology codes-for-the-treatment-trains-are-separated-by-a-semicolon-(;)-with-the--last technology--preceded--by--the--word-"or".--This-indicates-that-any-one-of-these BDAT-technologies-or-treatment-trains-can--be--used--for--compliance--with--the standard.----See-Section-728-Table-C-for-a-listing-of-the-technology-codes-and

POLLUTION CONTROL BOARD

NOTICE OF PROPOSED AMENDMENTS

technology-based-treatment-standards.--Derived-from--40--CFR--260.42,--Table--2
(1991),-as-amended-at-57-Fed.-Reg.-37273-(Aug.-18,-1992)-and-59-Fed.-Reg.-31552
(June-20,-1994).

(Source: Amended at 19 Ill. Reg. _____, effective
_____.)

POLLUTION CONTROL BOARD

NOTICE OF PROPOSED AMENDMENTS

Section 728.TABLE E Standards for Radioactive Mixed Waste

BOARD NOTE: For the requirements previously found in this Section, refer to
Sections 728.140 and 728.Table T.

			Technology-Code	
Waste-code	Waste-descriptions and/or-treatment category	CAS-No.	Wastewaters	Nonwastewaters
D002	Radioactive-high level-wastes generated-during the-reprocessing of-fuel-rods subcategory	NA	NA	HLVIT
D004	Radioactive-high level-wastes generated-during the-reprocessing-of fuel-rods subcategory	NA	NA	HLVIT
D005	Radioactive-high level-wastes generated-during the-reprocessing of-fuel-rods -subcategory	NA	NA	HLVIT
D006	Radioactive-high level-wastes generated-during the-reprocessing-of fuel-rods subcategory	NA	NA	HLVIT
D007	Radioactive-high level-wastes generated-during the-reprocessing of-fuel-rods subcategory	NA	NA	HLVIT
D008	Radioactive-lead solids-subcategory (Note:--these-lead	9439-92-1	NA	MACRO

POLLUTION CONTROL BOARD

NOTICE OF PROPOSED AMENDMENTS

D002, D004, D005, D006, D007, D008, D009, D010, D011
Radioactive high level wastes generated during the reprocessing of fuel rods.
[Note: This subcategory consists of nonwastewaters only.]

Corrosivity (pH)	NA	NA	HLVIT
Arsenic	7440-38-2	NA	HLVIT
Barium	7440-39-3	NA	HLVIT
Cadmium	7440-43-9	NA	HLVIT
Chromium (Total)	7440-47-3	NA	HLVIT
Lead	7439-92-1	NA	HLVIT
Mercury	7439-87-6	NA	HLVIT
Selenium	7782-49-2	NA	HLVIT
Silver	7440-22-4	NA	HLVIT

D003
Reactive Sulfides Subcategory based on 35 Ill. Adm. Code 721.123(a)(5).

NA	NA	DEACT	DEACT

D003
Explosive subcategory based on 35 Ill. Adm. Code 721.123(a)(6), (a)(7), and (a)(8).

NA	NA	DEACT	DEACT

D003
Other Reactives Subcategory based on 35 Ill. Adm. Code 721.123(a)(1).

NA	NA	DEACT	DEACT

D003
Water Reactive Subcategory based on 35 Ill. Adm. Code 721.123(a)(2), (a)(3), and (a)(4).
[Note: This subcategory consists of nonwastewaters only.]

NA	NA	DEACT	DEACT

D003
Reactive Cyanides Subcategory based on 35 Ill. Adm. Code 721.123(a)(5).

Cyanides (Total)(7)	57-12-5	--	590
Cyanides (Amendable)(7)	57-12-5	0.86	30

D004
Wastes that exhibit, or are expected to exhibit, the characteristic of toxicity for arsenic based on the extraction procedure (EP) in SW-846 Method 1310.

Arsenic	7440-38-2	5.0	5.0mg/l EP

POLLUTION CONTROL BOARD

NOTICE OF PROPOSED AMENDMENTS

Arsenic: alternate(6) standard for nonwastewaters only.	7440-38-2	NA	5.0 mg/l TCLP

D005
Wastes that exhibit, or are expected to exhibit, the characteristic of toxicity for barium based on the extraction procedure (EP) in SW-846 Method 1310.

Barium	7440-39-3	100	100 mg/l TCLP

D006
Wastes that exhibit, or are expected to exhibit, the characteristic of toxicity for cadmium based on the extraction procedure (EP) in SW-846 Method 1310.

Cadmium	7440-43-9	1.0	1.0 mg/l TCLP

D006
Cadmium Containing Batteries Subcategory
[Note: This subcategory consists of nonwastewaters only.]

Cadmium	7440-43-9	NA	RTHRM

D007
Wastes that exhibit, or are expected to exhibit, the characteristic of toxicity for chromium based on the extraction procedure (EP) in SW-846 Method 1310.

Chromium (Total)	7440-47-3	5.0	5.0 mg/l TCLP

D008
Wastes that exhibit, or are expected to exhibit, the characteristic of toxicity for lead based on the extraction procedure (EP) in SW-846 Method 1310.

Lead	7439-92-1	5.0	5.0 mg/l EP
Lead: alternate(6) nonwastewaters only	7439-92-1	NA	5.0 mg/l TCLP

D008
Lead Acid Batteries Subcategory
[Note: This standard only applies to lead acid batteries that are identified as RCRA hazardous wastes and that are not excluded elsewhere from regulation under the land disposal restrictions of this Part or exempted under other regulations (see 35 Ill. Adm. Code 726.180).).
[Note: This subcategory consists of nonwastewaters only.]

Lead	7439-92-1	NA	RLEAD

D008
Radioactive Lead Solids Subcategory

POLLUTION CONTROL BOARD

NOTICE OF PROPOSED AMENDMENTS

technology-based-treatment-standards.--Derived-from--40--CFR--268.42,--Table--2
{1991},-as-amended-at-57-Fed.-Reg.-37272-(Aug.-18,-1992)-and-59-Fed.-Reg.-31552
{June-20,-1994}.

(Source: Amended at 19 Ill. Reg. _____, effective
_____)

POLLUTION CONTROL BOARD

NOTICE OF PROPOSED AMENDMENTS

Section 728.TABLE E Standards for Radioactive Mixed Waste

BOARD NOTE: For the requirements previously found in this Section, refer to
Sections 728.140 and 728.Table T.

Waste-code	Waste-descriptions and/or-treatment category	CAS-No.	Technology-Code	
			Wastewaters	Nonwastewaters
D002	Radioactive-high level-wastes generated-during the-reprocessing of-fuel-rods subcategory	NA	NA	HLVIT
D004	Radioactive-high level-wastes generated-during the-reprocessing-of fuel-rods subcategory	NA	NA	HLVIT
D005	Radioactive-high level-wastes generated-during the-reprocessing of-fuel-rods -subcategory	NA	NA	HLVIT
D006	Radioactive-high level-wastes generated-during the-reprocessing-of fuel-rods subcategory	NA	NA	HLVIT
D009	Radioactive-high level-wastes generated-during the-reprocessing of-fuel-rods subcategory	NA	NA	HLVIT
D008	Radioactive-lead solids-subcategory (Note:--these-lead	7439-92-1	NA	MACRO

POLLUTION CONTROL BOARD

NOTICE OF PROPOSED AMENDMENTS

solids-include,-but
are-not-limited-to,
all-forms-of-lead
shielding,-and-other
elemental-forms-of
lead.--These-lead
solids-do-not
include-treatment
residuals-such-as
hydroxide-sludges,
other-wastewater
treatment-residues,
or-incinerator-ashes
that-can-undergo
conventional-pozzolanic
stabilization,-nor-do
they-include
organolead-materials
that-can-be
incinerated-and
stabilized-as-ash,-

D008	Radioactive-high level-wastes generated-during the-reprocessing-of fuel-rods subcategory	NA	NA	HEW17
D009	Elemental-mercury contaminated-with radioactive-materials	7439-97-6	NA	AMLGM
D009	Hydraulic-oil contaminated-with mercury-radioactive materials-subcategory	7439-97-6	NA	IMERC
D009	Radioactive-high level-wastes generated-during the-reprocessing-of fuel-rods subcategory	NA	NA	HEW17
D010	Radioactive-high level-wastes generated-during	NA	NA	HEW17

POLLUTION CONTROL BOARD

NOTICE OF PROPOSED AMENDMENTS

the-reprocessing-of
fuel-rods
subcategory

| D011 | Radioactive-high level-wastes generated-during the-reprocessing-of fuel-rods subcategory | NA | NA | HEW17 |
| U151 | Mercury,--Elemental mercury-contaminated with-radioactive materials | 7439-97-6 | NA | AMLGM |

Note--NA-means-Not-Applicable.

(Source: Amended   at   19   Ill.   Reg. _____,   ef
_____.)

POLLUTION CONTROL BOARD

NOTICE OF PROPOSED AMENDMENTS

Section 728.TABLE G Alternative Treatment Standards Based on HMTR

For the treatment standards previously found in this Section and Section 728.146, refer to Sections 728.140 and 728.Table T, "Treatment Standards for Hazardous Wastes".

Waste code	See-Also	Regulated Hazardous Constituent	CAS-No.-for Regulated Hazardous Constituent	Nonwastewaters Concentration (mg/l)-TCLP
F006	Tables-A a-B	Antimony	7440-36-0	2.1
		Arsenic	7440-38-2	0.055
		Barium	7440-39-3	7.6
		Beryllium	7440-41-7	0.014
		Cadmium	7440-43-9	0.19
		Chromium (total)	7440-47-32	0.33
		Cyanide (mg/kg) (total)	57-12-5	1.8
		Lead	7439-92-1	0.37
		Mercury	7439-97-6	0.009
		Nickel	7440-02-0	5.0
		Selenium	7782-49-2	0.16
		Silver	7440-22-4	0.30
		Thallium		0.078
		Zinc	7440-66-6	5.3
K062	Tables-A a-B	Antimony	7440-36-0	2.1
		Arsenic	7440-38-2	0.055
		Barium	7440-39-3	7.6
		Beryllium	7440-41-7	0.014
		Cadmium	7440-43-9	0.19
		Chromium (total)	7440-47-32	0.33
		Lead	7439-92-1	0.37
		Mercury	7439-97-6	0.009
		Nickel	7440-02-0	5.0
		Selenium	7782-49-2	0.16
		Silver	7440-22-4	0.30
		Thallium		0.078
		Zinc	7440-66-6	5.3

(Source: Amended at 19 Ill. Reg. _____, effective _____)

POLLUTION CONTROL BOARD

NOTICE OF PROPOSED AMENDMENTS

Section 728.TABLE T Treatment Standards for Hazardous Wastes

Note: The treatment standards that heretofore appeared in tables in Sections 728.141, 728.142, and 728.143 have been consolidated into this table.

Regulated Hazardous Constituent		Wastewaters	Nonwastewaters
Common Name	CAS(2) Number	Concentration mg/l(3); or Technology Code(4)	Concentration in mg/kg(3) unless noted as "mg/l TCLP"; or Technology Code(4)

D001
Ignitable Characteristic Wastes, except for the Section 728.121(a)(1) High TOC Subcategory, that are managed in non-CWA or non-CWA-equivalent or non-Class I SDWA systems.

NA	NA	DEACT and meet Section 728.148 standards; or RORGS; or CMBST	DEACT and meet Section 728.148 standards; or RORGS; or CMBST

D001
Ignitable Characteristic Wastes, except for the Section 721.121(a)(1) High TOC Subcategory, that are managed in CWA or CWA-equivalent or Class I SDWA systems.

NA	NA	DEACT	DEACT

D001
High TOC Ignitable Characteristic Liquids Subcategory based on 35 Ill. Adm. Code 721.121(a)(1) - Greater than or equal to 10% total organic carbon. (Note: This subcategory consists of nonwastewaters only.)

NA	NA	NA	RORGS; or CMBST

D002
Corrosive Characteristic Wastes that are managed in non-CWA or non-CWA equivalent non-Class I SDWA systems.

NA	NA	DEACT and meet Section 728.148 standards	DEACT and meet Section 728.148 standards

POLLUTION CONTROL BOARD

NOTICE OF PROPOSED AMENDMENTS

D002, D004, D005, D006, D007, D008, D009, D010, D011
Radioactive high level wastes generated during the reprocessing of fuel rods.
(Note: This subcategory consists of nonwastewaters only.)

Corrosivity (pH)	NA	NA	NLVIT
Arsenic	7440-38-2	NA	NLVIT
Barium	7440-39-3	NA	NLVIT
Cadmium	7440-43-9	NA	NLVIT
Chromium (Total)	7440-47-3	NA	NLVIT
Lead	7439-92-1	NA	NLVIT
Mercury	7439-87-6	NA	NLVIT
Selenium	7782-49-2	NA	NLVIT
Silver	7440-22-4	NA	NLVIT

D003
Reactive Sulfides Subcategory based on 35 Ill. Adm. Code 721.123(a)(5).

NA	NA	DEACT	DEACT

D003
Explosive subcategory based on 35 Ill. Adm. Code 721.123(a)(6), (a)(7), and (a)(8).

NA	NA	DEACT	DEACT

D003
Other Reactives Subcategory based on 35 Ill. Adm. Code 721.123(a)(1).

NA	NA	DEACT	DEACT

D003
Water Reactive Subcategory based on 35 Ill. Adm. Code 721.123(a)(2), (a)(3), and (a)(4).
(Note: This subcategory consists of nonwastewaters only.)

NA	NA	DEACT	DEACT

D003
Reactive Cyanides Subcategory based on 35 Ill. Adm. Code 721.123(a)(5).

Cyanides (Total)(7)	57-12-5	--	590
Cyanides (Amendable)(7)	57-12-5	0.86	30

D004
Wastes that exhibit, or are expected to exhibit, the characteristic of toxicity for arsenic based on the extraction procedure (EP) in SW-846 Method 1310.

Arsenic	7440-38-2	5.0	5.0mg/l EP

POLLUTION CONTROL BOARD

NOTICE OF PROPOSED AMENDMENTS

Arsenic: alternate(6) standard for nonwastewaters only.	7440-38-2	NA	5.0 mg/l TCLP

D005
Wastes that exhibit, or are expected to exhibit, the characteristic of toxicity for barium based on the extraction procedure (EP) in SW-846 Method 1310.

Barium	7440-39-3	100	100 mg/l TCLP

D006
Wastes that exhibit, or are expected to exhibit, the characteristic of toxicity for cadmium based on the extraction procedure (EP) in SW-846 Method 1310.

Cadmium	7440-43-9	1.0	1.0 mg/l TCLP

D006
Cadmium Containing Batteries Subcategory
(Note: This subcategory consists of nonwastewaters only.)

Cadmium	7440-43-9	NA	RTHRM

D007
Wastes that exhibit, or are expected to exhibit, the characteristic of toxicity for chromium based on the extraction procedure (EP) in SW-846 Method 1310.

Chromium (Total)	7440-47-3	5.0	5.0 mg/l TCLP

D008
Wastes that exhibit, or are expected to exhibit, the characteristic of toxicity for lead based on the extraction procedure (EP) in SW-846 Method 1310.

Lead	7439-92-1	5.0	5.0 mg/l EP
Lead: alternate(6) nonwastewaters only	7439-92-1	NA	5.0 mg/l TCLP

D008
Lead Acid Batteries Subcategory
(Note: This standard only applies to lead acid batteries that are identified as RCRA hazardous wastes and that are not excluded elsewhere from regulation under the land disposal restrictions of this Part or exempted under other regulations (see 35 Ill. Adm. Code 726.180).).
(Note: This subcategory consists of nonwastewaters only.)

Lead	7439-92-1	NA	RLEAD

D008
Radioactive Lead Solids Subcategory

POLLUTION CONTROL BOARD

NOTICE OF PROPOSED AMENDMENTS

(Note: These lead solids include, but are not limited to, all forms of lead shielding and other elemental forms of lead. These lead solids do not include treatment residuals such as hydroxide sludges, other wastewater treatment residuals, or incinerator ashes that can undergo conventional pozzolanic stabilization, nor do they include organo-lead materials that can be incinerated and stabilized as ash.)
(Note: This subcategory consists of nonwastewaters only.)

| Lead | 7439-92-1 | NA | MACRO |

D009
Nonwastewaters that exhibit, or are expected to exhibit, the characteristic of toxicity for mercury based on the extraction procedure (EP) in SW-846 Method 1310; and contain greater than or equal to 260 mg/kg total mercury that also contain organics and are not incinerator residues.
(High Mercury-Organic Subcategory)

| Mercury | 7439-97-6 | NA | IMERC; or RMERC |

D009
Nonwastewaters that exhibit, or are expected to exhibit, the characteristic of toxicity for mercury based on the extraction procedure (EP) in SW-846 Method 1310; and contain greater than or equal to 260 mg/kg total mercury that are inorganic, including incinerator residues and residues from RMERC.
(High Mercury-Inorganic Subcategory)

| Mercury | 7439-97-6 | NA | RMERC |

D009
Nonwastewaters that exhibit, or are expected to exhibit, the characteristic of toxicity for mercury based on the extraction procedure (EP) in SW-846 Method 1310; and contain less than 260 mg/kg total mercury.
(Low Mercury Subcategory)

| Mercury | 7439-97-6 | NA | 0.20 mg/l TCLP |

All D009 wastewaters

| Mercury | 7439-97-6 | 0.20 | NA |

D009
Elemental mercury contaminated with radioactive materials.
(Note: This subcategory consists of nonwastewaters only.)

| Mercury | 7439-97-6 | NA | AMLGM |

D009

POLLUTION CONTROL BOARD

NOTICE OF PROPOSED AMENDMENTS

Hydraulic oil contaminated with Mercury Radioactive Materials Subcategory.
(Note: This subcategory consists of nonwastewaters only.)

| Mercury | 7439-97-6 | NA | IMERC |

D010
Wastes that exhibit, or are expected to exhibit, the characteristic or toxicity for selenium based on the extraction procedure (EP) in SW-846 Method 1310.

| Selenium | 7782-49-2 | 1.0 | 5.7 mg/l TCLP |

D011
Wastes that exhibit, or are expected to exhibit, the characteristic of toxicity for silver based on the extraction procedure (EP) in SW-846 Method 1310.

| Silver | 7440-22-4 | 5.0 | 5.0 mg/l TCLP |

D012
Wastes that are TC for Endrin based on the TCLP in SW-846 Method 1311.

| Endrin | 72-20-8 | BIODG; or INCIN | 0.13 and meet Section 728.148 standards |
| Endrin aldehyde | 7421-93-4 | BIODG; or INCIN | 0.13 and meet Section 728.148 standards |

D013
Wastes that are TC for Lindane based on the TCLP in SW-846 Method 1311.

alpha-BHC	319-84-6	CARBN; or INCIN	0.066 and meet Section 728.148 standards
beta-BHC	319-85-7	CARBN; or INCIN	0.066 and meet Section 728.148 standards
delta-BHC	319-86-8	CARBN; or INCIN	0.066 and meet Section

POLLUTION CONTROL BOARD

NOTICE OF PROPOSED AMENDMENTS

gamma-BHC (Lindane)	58-89-9	CARBN; or INCIN	728.148 standards 0.066 and meet Section 728.148 standards

D014
Wastes that are TC for Methoxychlor based on the TCLP in SW-846 Method 1311.

Methoxychlor	72-43-5	WETOX or INCIN	0.18 and meet Section 728.148 standards

D015
Wastes that are TC for Toxaphene based on the TCLP in SW-846 Method 1311.

Toxaphene	8001-35-2	BIODG or INCIN	2.6 and meet Section 728.148 standards

D016
Wastes that are TC for 2,4-D (2,4-Dichlorophenoxyacetic acid) based on the TCLP in SW-846 Method 1311.

2,4-D (2,4-Dichloro-phenoxyacetic acid)	94-75-7	CHOXD, BIODG, or INCIN	10 and meet Section 728.148 standards

D017
Wastes that are TC for 2,4,5-TP (Silvex) based on the TCLP in SW-846 Method 1311.

2,4,5-TP (Silvex)	93-72-1	CHOXD or INCIN	7.9 and meet Section 728.148 standards

D018
Wastes that are TC for Benzene based on the TCLP in SW-846 Method 1311 and that are managed in non-CWA or non-CWA equivalent or non-Class I SDWA systems only.

POLLUTION CONTROL BOARD

NOTICE OF PROPOSED AMENDMENTS

Benzene	71-43-2	0.14 and meet Section 728.148 standards	10 and meet Section 728.148 standards

D019
Wastes that are TC for Carbon tetrachloride based on the TCLP in SW-846 Method 1311 and that are managed in non-CWA or non-CWA equivalent or non-Class I SDWA systems only.

Carbon tetrachloride	56-23-5	0.05. and meet Section 728.148 standards	76.0 and meet Section 728.148 standards

D020
Wastes that are TC for Chlordane based on the TCLP in SW-846 Method 1311 and that are managed in non-CWA or non-CWA equivalent or non-Class I SDWA systems only.

Chlordane (alpha and gamma isomers)	57-74-9	0.0033 and meet Section 728.148 standards	0.26 and meet Section 728.148 standards

D021
Wastes that are TC for Chlorobenzene based on the TCLP in SW-846 Method 1311 and that are managed in non-CWA or non-CWA equivalent or non-Class I SDWA systems only.

Chlorobenzene	108-90-7	0.057 and meet Section 728.148 standards	6.0 and meet Section 728.148 standards

D022
Wastes that are TC for Chloroform based on the TCLP in SW-846 Method 1311 and that are managed in non-CWA or non-CWA equivalent or non-Class I SDWA systems only.

Chloroform	67-66-3	0.046 and meet Section 728.148	6.0 and meet Section 728.148

POLLUTION CONTROL BOARD

NOTICE OF PROPOSED AMENDMENTS

		standards	standards

D023
Wastes that are TC for o-Cresol based on the TCLP in SW-846 Method 1311 and that are managed in non-CWA or non-CWA equivalent or non-Class I SDWA systems only

o-Cresol	95-48-7	0.11 and meet Section 728.148 standards	5.6 and meet Section 728.148 standards

D024
Wastes that are TC for m-Cresol based on the TCLP in SW-846 Method 1311 and that are managed in non-CWA or non-CWA equivalent or non-Class I SDWA systems only.

m-Cresol (difficult to distinguish from p-cresol)	108-39-4	0.77 and meet Section 728.148 standards	5.6 and meet Section 728.148 standards

D025
Wastes that are TC for p-Cresol based on the TCLP in SW-846 Method 1311 and that are managed in non-CWA or non-CWA equivalent or non-Class I SDWA systems only.

p-Cresol (difficult to distinguish from m-cresol)	106-44-5	0.77 and meet Section 728.148 standards	5.6 and meet Section 728.148 standards

D026
Wastes that are TC for Cresols (Total) based on the TCLP in SW-846 Method 1311 and that are managed in non-CWA or non-CWA equivalent or non-Class I SDWA systems only.

Cresol-mixed isomers (Cresylic acid) (sum of o-, m-, and p-cresol concentrations)	1319-77-3	0.88 and meet Section 728.148 standards	11.2 and meet Section 728.148 standards

D027
Wastes that are TC for p-Dichlorobenzene based on the TCLP in SW-846 Method 1311 and that are managed in non-CWA or non-CWA equivalent or non-Class I SDWA

POLLUTION CONTROL BOARD

NOTICE OF PROPOSED AMENDMENTS

systems only.

p-Dichlorobenzene (1,4-Dichlorobenzene)	106-46-7	0.090 and meet Section 728.148 standards	6.0 and meet Section 728.148 standards

D028
Wastes that are TC for 1,2-Dichloroethane based on the TCLP in SW-846 Method 1311 and that are managed in non-CWA or non-CWA equivalent or non-Class I SDWA systems only.

1,2-Dichloroethane	107-06-2	0.2 and meet Section 728.148 standards	16.0 and meet Section 728.148 standards

D029
Wastes that are TC for 1,1-Dichloroethylene based on the TCLP in SW-846 Method 1311 and that are managed in non-CWA or non-CWA equivalent or non-Class I SDWA systems only.

1,1-Dichloroethylene	75-35-4	0.025 and meet Section 728.148 standards	6.0 and meet Section 728.148 standards

D030
Wastes that are TC for 2,4-Dinitrotoluene based on the TCLP in SW-846 Method 1311 and that are managed in non-CWA or non-CWA equivalent or non-Class I SDWA systems only.

2,4-Dinitrotoluene	121-14-2	0.32 and meet Section 728.148 standards	140 and meet Section 728.148 standards

D031
Wastes that are TC for Heptachlor based on the TCLP in SW-846 Method 1311 and that are managed in non-CWA or non-CWA equivalent or non-Class I SDWA systems only.

Heptachlor	76-44-8	0.0012	0.066 and meet

POLLUTION CONTROL BOARD

NOTICE OF PROPOSED AMENDMENTS

			Section 728.148 standards
Heptachlor epoxide	1024-57-3	0.016 and meet Section	0.066 and meet Section

D032
Wastes that are TC for Hexachlorobenzene based on the TCLP in SW-846 Method 1311 and that are managed in non-CWA or non-CWA equivalent or non-Class I SDWA systems only.

Hexachlorobenzene	118-74-1	0.055 and meet Section 728.148 standards	10 and meet Section 728.148 standards

D033
Wastes that are TC for Hexachlorobutadiene based on the TCLP in SW-846 Method 1311 and that are managed in non-CWA or non-Class I SDWA systems only.

Hexachlorobutadiene	67-68-3	0.055 and meet Section 728.148 standards	5.6 and meet Section 728.148 standards

D034
Wastes that are TC for Hexachloroethane based on the TCLP in SW-846 Method 1311 and that are managed in non-CWA or non-CWA equivalent or non-Class I SDWA systems only.

Hexachloroethane	67-72-1	0.055 and meet Section 728.148 standards	30 and meet Section 728.148 standards

D035
Wastes that are TC for Methyl ethyl ketone based on the TCLP in SW-846 Method 1311 and that are managed in non-CWA or non-CWA equivalent or non-Class I SDWA systems only.

Methyl ethyl ketone	78-93-3	0.28 and meet Section 728.148	36 and meet Section 728.148

POLLUTION CONTROL BOARD

NOTICE OF PROPOSED AMENDMENTS

		standards	standards

D036
Wastes that are TC for Nitrobenzene based on the TCLP in SW-846 Method 1311 and that are managed in non-CWA or non-CWA equivalent or non-Class I SDWA systems only.

Nitrobenzene	98-95-3	0.068 and meet Section 728.148 standards	14 and meet Section 728.148 standards

D037
Wastes that are TC for Pentachlorophenol based on the TCLP in SW-846 Method 1311 and that are managed in non-CWA or non-CWA equivalent or non-Class I SDWA systems only.

Pentachlorophenol	87-86-5	0.089 and meet Section 728.148 standards	7.4 and meet Section 728.148 standards

D038
Wastes that are TC for pyridine based on the TCLP in SW-846 Method 1311 and that are managed in non-CWA or non-CWA equivalent or non-Class I SDWA systems only.

Pyridine	110-86-1	0.014 and meet Section 728.148 standards	16 and meet Section 728.148 standards

D039
Wastes that are TC for Tetrachloroethylene based on the TCLP in SW-846 Method 1311 and that are managed in non-CWA or non-CWA equivalent or non-Class I SDWA systems only.

Tetrachloroethylene	127-18-4	0.056 and meet Section 728.148 standards	6.0 and meet Section 728.148 standards

D040
Wastes that are TC for Trichloroethylene based on the TCLP in SW-846 Method

POLLUTION CONTROL BOARD

NOTICE OF PROPOSED AMENDMENTS

1311 and that are managed in non-CWA or non-CWA equivalent or non-Class I SDWA systems only.

Trichloroethylene	79-01-6	0.054 and meet Section 728.148 standards	6.0 and meet Section 728.148 standards

D041
Wastes that are TC for 2,4,5-Trichlorophenol based on the TCLP in SW-846 Method 1311 and that are managed in non-CWA or non-CWA equivalent or non-Class I SDWA systems only.

2,4,5-Trichlorophenol	95-95-4	0.18 and meet Section 728.148 standards	7.4 and meet Section 728.148 standards

D042
Wastes that are TC for 2,4,6-Trichlorophenol based on the TCLP in SW-846 Method 1311 and that are managed in non-CWA or non-CWA equivalent or non-Class I SDWA systems only.

2,4,6-Trichlorophenol	88-06-2	0.035 and meet Section 728.148 standards	7.4 and meet Section 728.148 standards

D043
Wastes that are TC for Vinyl chloride based on the TCLP in SW-846 Method 1311 and that are managed in non-CWA or non-CWA equivalent or non-Class I SDWA systems only.

Vinyl chloride	75-01-4	0.27 and meet Section 728.148 standards	6.0 and meet Section 728.148 standards

F001, F002, F003, F004, & F005
F001, F002, F003, F004, or F005 solvent wastes that contain any combination of one or more of the following spent solvents: acetone, benzene, n-butyl alcohol, carbon disulfide, carbon tetrachloride, chlorinated fluorocarbons, chlorobenzene, o-cresol, m-cresol, p-cresol, cyclohexanone, o-dichlorobenzene, 2-ethoxyethanol, ethyl acetate, ethyl benzene, ethyl ether, isobutyl alcohol,

POLLUTION CONTROL BOARD

NOTICE OF PROPOSED AMENDMENTS

methanol, methylene chloride, methyl ethyl ketone, methyl isobutyl ketone, nitrobenzene, 2-nitropropane, pyridine, tetrachloroethylene, toluene, 1,1,1-trichloroethane, 1,1,2-trichloroethane, 1,1,2-trichloro-1,2,2-trifluoroethane, trichloroethylene, trichloromonofluoromethane, or xylenes (except as specifically noted in other subcategories). See further details of these listings in 35 Ill. Adm. Code 721.131

Acetone	67-64-1	0.28	160
Benzene	71-43-2	0.14	10
n-Butyl alcohol	71-36-3	5.6	2.6
Carbon disulfide	75-15-0	3.8	NA
Carbon tetrachloride	56-23-5	0.057	6.0
Chlorobenzene	108-90-7	0.057	6.0
o-Cresol	95-48-7	0.11	5.6
m-Cresol (difficult to distinguish from p-cresol	108-39-4	0.77	5.6
p-Cresol (difficult to distinguish from m-cresol)	106-44-5	0.77	5.6
Cresol-mixed isomers (Cresylic acid) (Sum of o-, m-, and p-cresol concentrations)	1319-77-3	0.88	11.2
Cyclohexanone	108-94-1	0.36	NA
o-Dichlorobenzene	95-50-1	0.088	6.0
Ethyl acetate	141-78-6	0.34	33
Ethyl benzene	100-41-4	0.057	10
Ethyl ether	60-29-7	0.12	160
Isobutyl alcohol	78-83-1	5.6	170
Methanol	67-56-1	5.6	NA
Methylene chloride	75-9-2	0.089	30
Methyl ethyl ketone	78-93-3	0.28	36
Methyl isobutyl ketone	108-10-1	0.14	33
Nitrobenzene	98-95-3	0.068	14
Pyridine	110-86-1	0.014	16
Tetrachloroethylene	127-18-4	0.056	6.0
Toluene	108-88-3	0.080	10
1,1,1-Trichloroethane	71-55-6	0.054	6.0
1,1,2-Trichloroethane	79-00-5	0.054	6.0
1,1,2-Trichloro-1,2,2-trifluoroethane	76-13-1	0.057	30
Trichloroethylene	70-01-6	0.054	6.0
Trichloromonofluoromethane	75-69-4	0.020	30
Xylenes-mixed isomers	1330-20-7	0.32	30

[sum of o-, m-, and p-xylene concentrations]

F001, F002, F003, F004 & F005
F003 and F005 solvent wastes that contain any combination of one or more of the following three solvents as the only listed F001 through F005 solvents: carbon disulfide, cyclohexanone, or methanol. (Formerly Section 728.141(c))

Carbon disulfide	75-15-0	3.8	4.8 mg/l TCLP
Cyclohexanone	108-94-1	0.36	0.75 mg/l TCLP
Methanol	67-56-1	5.6	0.75 mg/l TCLP

F001, F002, F003, F004 & F005
F005 solvent waste containing 2-Nitropropane as the only listed F001 through F005 solvent.

2-Nitropropane	79-46-9	(WETOX or CHOXD; fb CARBN; or INCIN	INCIN

F001, F002, F003, F004 & F005
F005 solvent waste containing 2-Ethoxyethanol as the only listed F001 through F005 solvent.

2-Ethoxyethanol	110-80-5	BIODG; or INCIN	INCIN

F006
Wastewater treatment sludges from electroplating operations except from the following processes: (1) Sulfuric acid anodizing of aluminum; (2) tin plating on carbon steel; (3) zinc plating (segrated basis) on carbon steel; (4) aluminum or zinc-aluminum plating on carbon steel; (5) cleaning or stripping associated with tin, zinc, and aluminum plating on carbon steel; and (6) chemical etching and milling of aluminum.

Cadmium	7440-43-9	0.69	0.19 mg/l TCLP
Chromium (Total)	7440-47-3	2.77	0.86 mg/l TCLP
Cyanides (Total)(7)	57-12-5	1.2	590
Cyanides (Amenable)(7)	57-12-5	0.86	30
Lead	7439-92-1	0.69	0.37 mg/l TCLP
Nickel	7440-02-0	3.98	5.0 mg/l TCLP
Silver	7440-22-4	NA	0.30 mg/l TCLP

F007
Spent cyanide plating bath solutions from electroplating operations.

Cadmium	7440-43-9	NA	0.19 mg/l TCLP
Chromium (Total)	7440-47-3	2.77	0.86 mg/l TCLP
Cyanides (Total)(7)	57-12-5	1.2	590
Cyanides (Amenable)(7)	57-12-5	0.86	30

Lead	7439-92-1	0.69	0.37 mg/l TCLP
Nickel	7440-02-0	3.98	5.0 mg/l TCLP
Silver	7440-22-4	NA	0.30 mg/l TCLP

F008
Plating bath residues from the bottom of plating baths from electroplating operations where cyanides are used in the process.

Cadmium	7440-43-9	NA	0.19 mg/l TCLP
Chromium (Total)	7440-47-3	2.77	0.86 mg/l TCLP
Cyanides (Total)(7)	57-12-5	1.2	590
Cyanides (Amenable)(7)	57-12-5	0.86	30
Lead	7439-92-1	0.69	0.37 mg/l TCLP
Nickel	7440-02-0	3.98	5.0 mg/l TCLP
Silver	7440-22-4	NA	0.30 mg/l TCLP

F009
Spent stripping and cleaning bath solutions from eletroplating operations where cyanides are used in the process.

Cadmium	7440-43-9	NA	0.19 mg/l TCLP
Chromium (Total)	7440-47-3	2.77	0.86 mg/l TCLP
Cyanides (Total)(7)	57-12-5	1.2	590
Cyanides (Amenable)(7)	57-12-5	0.86	30
Lead	7439-92-1	0.69	0.37 mg/l TCLP
Nickel	7440-02-0	3.98	5.0 mg/l TCLP
Silver	7440-22-4	NA	0.30 mg/l TCLP

F010
Quenching bath residues from oil baths from metal heat treating operations where cyanides are used in the process.

Cyanides (Total)(7)	57-12-5	1.2	590
Cyanides (Amendable)(7)	57-12-5	0.80	NA

F011
Spent cyanide solutions from salt bath pot cleaning from metal heat treating operations.

Cadmium	7440-43-9	NA	0.19 mg/l TCLP
Chromium (Total)	7440-47-3	2.77	0.86 mg/l TCLP
Cyanides (Total)(7)	57-12-5	1.2	590
Cyanides (Amenable)(7)	57-12-5	0.86	30
Lead	7439-92-1	0.69	0.37 mg/l TCLP
Nickel	7440-02-0	3.98	5.0 mg/l TCLP
Silver	7440-22-4	NA	0.30 mg/l TCLP

F012
Quenching wastewater treatment sludges from metal heat treating operations where cyanides are used in the process.

POLLUTION CONTROL BOARD

NOTICE OF PROPOSED AMENDMENTS

Cadmium	7440-43-9	NA	0.19 mg/l TCLP
Chromium (Total)	7440-47-3	2.77	0.86 mg/l TCLP
Cyanides (Total)(7)	57-12-5	1.2	590
Cyanides (Amenable)(7)	57-12-5	0.86	30
Lead	7439-92-1	0.69	0.37 mg/l TCLP
Nickel	7440-02-0	3.98	5.0 mg/l TCLP
Silver	7440-22-4	NA	0.30 mg/l TCLP

F019

Wastewater treatment sludges from the chemical conversion coating of aluminum except from zirconium phosphating in aluminum can washing when such phosphating is an exclusive conversion coating process.

Chromium (Total)	7440-47-3	2.77	0.86 mg/l TCLP
Cyanides (Total)(7)	57-12-5	1.2	590
Cyanides Amenable)(7)	57-12-5	0.86	30

F020, F021, F022, F023, F026

Wastes (except wastewater and spent carbon from hydrogen chloride purification) from the production or manufacturing use (as a reactant, chemical intermediate, or component in a formulating process) of: (1) tri- or tetrachlorophenol, or of intermediates used to produce their pesticide derivatives, excluding wastes from the production of Hexachlorophene from highly purified 2,4,5-trichlorophenol (i.e., F020); (2) pentachlorophenol, or of intermediates used to produce its derivatives (i.e., F021); (3) tetra-, penta-, or hexachlorobenzenes under alkaline conditions (i.e., F022). Wastes (except wastewater and spent carbon from hydrogen chloride purification) from the production of materials on equipment previously used for the production or manufacturing use (as a reactant, chemical intermediate, or component in a formulating process) of: (1) tri-or tetrachlorophenols, excluding wastes from equipment used only for the production of Hexachlorophene from highly purified 2,4,5-trichlorophenol (F023); (2) tetra-, penta-, or hexachlorobenzenes under alkaline conditions (i.e., F026).

HxCDDs (All Hexachloro-dibenzo-p-dioxins)	NA	0.000063	0.001
HxCDFs (All Hexachloro-dibenzofurans)	NA	0.000063	0.001
PeCDDs (All Penta-chloro-dibenzo-p-dioxins)	NA	0.000063	0.001
PeCDFs (All Pentachloro-dibenzofurans)	NA	0.000035	0.001
TCDDs (All Tetrachloro-dibenzo-p-dioxins)	NA	0.000063	0.001
TCDFs (All Tetrachloro-dibenzofurans)	NA	0.000063	0.001
2,4,5-Trichlorophenol	95-95-4	0.18	7.4

POLLUTION CONTROL BOARD

NOTICE OF PROPOSED AMENDMENTS

2,4,6-Trichlorophenol	88-06-2	0.035	7.4
2,3,4,6-Tetrachloro-phenol	58-90-2	0.030	7.4
Pentachlorophenol	87-86-5	0.089	7.4

F027

Discarded unused formulations containing tri-, tetra-, or pentachlorophenol or discarded unused formulations containing compounds derived from these chlorophenols. (This listing does not include formulations containing hexachlorophene synthesized from prepurified 2,4,5-trichlorophenol as the sole component.)

HxCDDs (All Hexachloro-dibenzo-p-dioxins)	NA	0.000063	0.001
HxCDFs (All Hexachloro-dibenzofurans)	NA	0.000063	0.001
PeCDDs (All Pentachloro-dibenzo-p-dioxins)	NA	0.000063	0.001
PeCDFs (All Pentachloro-dibenzofurans)	NA	0.000035	0.001
TCDDs (All Tetrachloro-dibenzo-p-dioxins)	NA	0.000063	0.001
TCDFs (All Tetrachloro-dibenzofurans)	NA	0.000063	0.001
2,4,5-Trichlorophenol	95-95-4	0.18	7.4
2,4,6-Trichlorophenol	88-06-2	0.035	7.4
2,3,4,6-Tetrachloro-phenol	58-90-2	0.030	7.4
Pentachlorophenol	87-86-5	0.089	7.4

F028

Residues resulting from the incineration or thermal treatment of soil contaminated with U.S. EPA hazardous waste numbers F020, F021, F022, F026, and F027.

HxCDDs (All Hexachloro-dibenzo-p-dioxins)	NA	0.000063	0.001
HxCDFs (All Hexachloro-dibenzofurans)	NA	0.000063	0.001
PeCDDs (All Pentachloro-dibenzo-p-dioxins)	NA	0.000063	0.001
PeCDFs (All Pentachloro-dibenzofurans)	NA	0.000035	0.001
TCDDs (All Tetrachloro-dibenzo-p-dioxins)	NA	0.000063	0.001
TCDFs (All Tetrachloro-dibenzofurans)	NA	0.000063	0.001
2,4,5-Trichlorophenol	95-95-4	0.18	7.4
2,4,6-Trichlorophenol	88-06-2	0.035	7.4
2,3,4,6-Tetrachloro-	58-90-2	0.030	7.4

POLLUTION CONTROL BOARD

NOTICE OF PROPOSED AMENDMENTS

phenol			
Pentachlorophenol	87-86-5	0.089	7.4

F024
Process wastes, including but not limited to, distillation residues, heavy ends, tars, and reactor clean-out wastes, from the production of certain chlorinated aliphatic hydrocarbons by free radical catalysed processes. These chlorinated aliphatic hydrocarbons are those having carbon chain lengths ranging from one to an including five, with varying amounts and positions of chlorine substitution. (This listing does not include wastewaters, wastewater treatment sludges, spent catalysts, and wastes listed in 35 Ill. Adm. Code 721.131 or 721.132.)

All F024 wastes	NA	INCIN	INCIN
2-Chloro-1,3-butadiene	126-99-8	0.057	0.28
3-Chloropropylene	107-05-1	0.036	30
1,1-Dichloroethane	75-34-3	0.059	6.0
1,2-Dichloroethane	107-06-2	0.21	6.0
1,2-Dichloropropane	78-87-5	0.85	18
cis-1,3-Dichloro-propylene	10061-01-5	0.036	18
trans-1,3-Dichloro-propylene	10061-02-6	0.036	18
bis(2-Ethylhexyl) phthalate	117-81-7	0.28	28
Hexachloroethane	67-72-1	0.055	30
Chromium (Total)	7440-47-3	2.77	0.86 mg/l TCLP
Nickel	7440-02-0	3.98	5.0 mg/l TCLP

F025
Condensed light ends from the production of certain chlorinated aliphatic hydrocarbons, by free radical catalysed processes. These chlorinated aliphatic hydrocarbons are those having carbon chain lengths ranging from one to and including five, with varying amounts and positions of chlorine substitution.

F025 - Light Ends Subcategory

Carbon tetrachloride	56-23-6	0.057	6.0
Chloroform	67-66-3	0.046	6.0
1,2-Dichloroethane	107-06-2	0.21	6.0
1,1-Dichloroethylene	75-35-4	0.025	6.0
Mthylene chloride	75-9-2	0.089	30
1,1,2-Trichloroethane	79-00-5	0.054	6.0
Trichloroethylene	79-01-6	0.054	6.0
Vinyl chloride	75-01-4	0.27	6.0

F025
Spent filters and filter aids, and spent desiccant wastes from the production

POLLUTION CONTROL BOARD

NOTICE OF PROPOSED AMENDMENTS

of certain chlorinated aliphatic hydrocarbons, by free radical catalysed processes. These chlorinated aliphatic hydrocarbons are those having carbon chain lengths ranging from one to and including five, with varying amounts and positions of chlorine substitution.

F025 - Spent Filters and Aids and Desiccants Subcategory

Carbon tetrachloride	56-23-5	0.057	6.0
Chloroform	67-66-3	0.046	6.0
Hexachlorobenzene	118-74-1	0.055	10
Hexachlorobutadiene	87-68-3	0.055	5.6
Hexachloroethane	67-72-1	0.055	30
Methylene chloride	75-9-2	0.089	30
1,1,2-Trichloroethane	79-00-5	0.054	6.0
Trichloroethylene	79-01-6	0.054	6.0
Vinyl chloride	75-01-4	0.27	6.0

F037
Petroleum refinery primary oil/water/solids separation sludge-Any sludge generated from the gravitational separation of oil/water/solids during the storage or treatment of process wastewaters and oily cooling wastewaters from petroleum refineries. Such sludges include, but are not limited to, those generated in: oil/water/solids separators; tanks and impoundments; ditches and other conveyances; sumps; and stormwater units receiving dry weather flow. Sludge generated in stormwater units that do not receive dry weather flow, sludges generated from non-contact once-through cooling waters segregated for treatment from other process or oily cooling waters, sludges generated in aggressive biological treatment units as defined in 35 Ill. Adm. Code 721.131(b)(2) (including sludges generated in one or more additional units after wastewaters have been treated in aggressive biological treatment units) and K051 wastes are not included in this listing.

Acenaphthene	83-32-_	0.059	NA
Anthracene	120-12-7	0.059	3.4
Benzene	71-43-2	0.14	10
Benz(a)anthracene	56-55-3	0.059	3.4
Benzo(a)pyrene	50-32-8	0.061	3.4
bis(2-Ethylhexyl) phthalate	117-81-7	0.28	28
Chrysene	218-01-9	0.059	3.4
Di-n-butyl phthalate	84-74-2	0.057	28
Ethylbenzene	100-41-4	0.057	10
Fluorene	86-73-7	0.059	NA
Naphthalene	91-20-3	0.059	5.6
Phenanthrene	85-01-8	0.059	5.6
Phenol	108-95-2	0.039	6.2
Pyrene	129-00-0	0.067	8.2
Toluene	108-88-3	0.080	10
Xylenes-mixed isomers (sum of O-, M-, and p-	1330-20-7	0.032	30

POLLUTION CONTROL BOARD

NOTICE OF PROPOSED AMENDMENTS

xylene concentrations)			
Chromium (Total)	7440-47-3	2.77	0.86 mg/l TCLP
Cyanides (Total)	57-12-5	1.2	590
Lead	7439-92-1	0.69	NA
Nickel	7440-02-0	NA	5.0 mg/l TCLP

F038

Petroleum refinery secondary (emulsified) oil/water/solids separation sludge or float generated from the physical or chemical separation of oil/water/solids in process wastewaters and oily cooling wastewaters from petroleum refineries. Such wastes include, but are not limited to, all sludges and floats generated in: induced air floatation (IAF) units, tanks and impoundments, and all sludges generated in DAF units. Sludges generated in stormwater units that do not receive dry weather flow, sludges generated from non-contact once-through cooling waters segregated for treatment from other process or oily cooling waters, sludges and floats generated in aggressive biological treatment units as defined in 35 Ill. Adm. Code 721.131(b)(2) (including sludges and floats generated in one or more additional units after wastewaters have been treated in aggressive biological units) and F037, K048, and K051 are not included in this list.

Benzene	71-43-2	0.14	10
Benzo(a)pyrene	50-32-8	0.061	3.4
bis(2-Ethylhexyl) phthalate	117-81-7	0.28	28
Chrysene	218-01-9	0.059	3.4
Di-n-butyl phthalate	84-74-2	0.057	28
Ethylbenzene	100-41-4	0.057	10
Fluorene	86-73-7	0.059	NA
Naphthalene	91-20-3	0.059	3.6
Phenanthrene	85-01-8	0.059	5.6
Phenol	108-95-2	0.039	6.2
Pyrene	129-00-0	0.067	8.2
Toluene	108-88-3	0.080	10
Xylenes-mixed isomers (sum of o-, m-, and p-xylene concentrations)	1330-20-7	0.32	30
Chromium (Total)	7440-47-3	2.77	0.86 mg/l TCLP
Cyanides (Total)(7)	57-12-5	1.2	590
Lead	7439-92-1	0.69	NA
Nickel	7440-02-0	NA	5.0 mg/l TCLP

F039

Leachate (liquids that have percolated through land disposed wastes) resulting from the disposal of more than one restricted waste classified as hazardous under 728.Subpart D. (Leachate resulting from the disposal of one or more of the following U.S. EPA hazardous wastes and no other hazardous wastes retains its U.S. EPA hazardous waste numbers: F020, F021, F022, F026, F027, or F028.

Acenaphthylene	208-96-8	0.059	3.4

POLLUTION CONTROL BOARD

NOTICE OF PROPOSED AMENDMENTS

Acenaphthene	83-32-9	0.059	3.4
Acetone	67-64-1	0.28	160
Acetonitrile	75-05-8	5.6	NA
Acetophenone	96-86-2	0.010	9.7
2-Acetylaminofluorene	53-96-3	0.059	140
Acrolein	107-02-8	0.29	NA
Acrylonitrile	107-13-1	0.24	84
Aldrin	309-00-2	0.021	0.066
4-Aminobiphenyl	92-67-1	0.13	NA
Aniline	62-53-3	0.81	14
Anthracene	120-12-7	0.059	3.4
Aramite	140-57-8	0.36	NA
alpha-BHC	319-84-6	0.00014	0.066
beta-BHC	319-85-7	0.00014	0.066
delta-BHC	319-86-8	0.023	0.066
gamma-BHC	58-89-9	0.0017	0.066
Benzene	71-43-2	0.14	10
Benz(a)anthracene	56-55-3	0.059	3.4
Benzo(b)fluoranthene (difficult to distinguish from benzo-(k)fluoranthene)	205-99-2	0.11	6.8
Benzo(k)fluoranthene (difficult to distinguish from benzo-b)fluoranthene)	207-08-9	0.11	6.8
Benzo(g,h,i)perylene	191-24-2	0.0055	1.8
Benzo(a)pyrene	50-32-8	0.061	3.4
Bromodichloromethane	75-27-4	0.35	15
Methyl bromide (Bromo-methane)	74-83-9	0.11	15
4-Bromophenyl phenyl ether	101-55-3	0.055	15
n-Butyl alcohol	71-36-3	5.6	2.6
Butyl benzyl phthalate	85-68-7	0.017	28
2-sec-Butyl-4,6-dinitro-phenol (Dinoseb)	88-85-7	0.066	2.5
Carbon disulfide	75-15-0	3.8	NA
Carbon tetrachloride	56-23-5	0.057	6.0
Chlordane (alpha and gamma isomers)	57-74-9	0.0033	0.26
p-Chloroaniline	106-47-8	0.46	16
Chlorobenzene	108-90-7	0.057	6.0
Chlorobenzilate	510-15-6	0.10	NA
2-Chloro-1,3-butadiene	126-99-8	0.057	NA
Chlorodibromomethane	124-48-1	0.057	15
Chloroethane	75-00-3	0.27	6.0
bis(2-Chloroethoxy)-	111-91-1	0.036	7.2

POLLUTION CONTROL BOARD

NOTICE OF PROPOSED AMENDMENTS

methane bis(2-Chloroethyl)ether	111-44-4	0.033	6.0
Chloroform	67-66-3	0.046	6.0
bis(2-Chloroisopropyl)-ether	108-60-1	0.055	7.2
p-Chloro-m-cresol	59-50-7	0.018	14
Chloromethane (Methyl chloride	74-87-3	0.19	30
2-Chloronaphthalene	91-58-7	0.055	5.6
2-Chlorophenol	95-57-8	0.044	5.7
3-Chloropropylene	107-05-1	0.036	30
Chrysene	218-01-9	0.059	3.4
o-Cresol	95-48-7	0.11	5.6
m-Cresol (difficult to distinguish from p-cresol)	108-39-4	0.77	5.6
p-Cresol (difficult to distinguish from m-cresol)	106-44-5	0.77	5.6
Cyclohexanone	108-94-1	0.36	NA
1,2-Dibromo-3-chloro-propane	96-12-8	0.11	15
Ethylene dibromide (1,2-Dibromoethane)	106-93-4	0.028	15
Dibromomethane	74-95-3	0.11	15
2,4-D (2,4-Dichloro-phenoxyacetic acid)	94-75-7	0.72	10
o,p'-DDD	53-19-0	0.023	0.087
p,p'-DDD	72-54-8	0.023	0.087
o,p'-DDE	3424-82-6	0.031	0.087
p,p'-DDE	72-55-9	0.031	0.087
o,p'-DDT	789-02-6	0.0039	0.087
p,p'-DDT	50-29-3	0.0039	0.087
Dibenz(a,h)anthracene	53-70-3	0.055	8.2
Dibenz(a,e)pyrene	192-65-4	0.061	NA
m-Dichlorobenzene	541-73-1	0.036	6.0
o-Dichlorobenzene	95-50-1	0.088	6.0
p-Dichlorobenzene	106-46-7	0.090	6.0
Dichlorodifluoromethane	75-71-8	0.23	7.2
1,1-Dichloroethane	75-34-3	0.059	6.0
1,2-Dichloroethane	107-06-2	0.21	6.0
1,1-Dichloroethylene	75-35-4	0.025	6.0
trans-1,2-Dichloro-ethylene	156-60-5	0.054	30
2,4-Dichlorophenol	120-83-2	0.044	14
2,6-Dichlorophenol	87-65-0	0.044	14

POLLUTION CONTROL BOARD

NOTICE OF PROPOSED AMENDMENTS

1,2-Dichloropropane	78-87-5	0.85	18
cis-1,3-Dichloro-propylene	10061-01-5	0.036	18
trans-1,3-Dichloro-propylene	10061-02-6	0.036	18
Dieldrin	60-57-1	0.017	0.13
Diethyl phthalate	84-66-2	0.20	28
2-4-Dimethyl phenol	105-67-9	0.036	14
Dimethyl phthalate	131-11-3	0.047	28
Di-n-butyl phthalate	84-74-2	0.057	28
1,4-Dinitrobenzene	100-25-4	0.32	2.3
4,6-Dinitro-o-cresol	534-52-1	0.28	160
2,4-Dinitrophenol	51-28-5	0.12	160
2,4-Dinitrotoluene	121-14-2	0.32	140
2,6-Dinitrotoluene	606-20-2	0.55	28
Di-n-octyl phthalate	117-84-0	0.017	28
Di-n-propylnitrosamine	621-64-7	0.40	14
1,4-Dioxane	123-91-1	NA	170
Diphenylamine (difficult to distinguish from diphenylnitrosamine)	122-39-4	0.92	NA
Diphenylnitrosamine (difficult to distinguish from diphenylamine)	86-30-6	0.92	NA
1,2-Diphenylhydrazine	122-66-7	0.087	NA
Disulfoton	298-04-4	0.017	6.2
Endosulfan I	939-98-8	0.023	0.066
Endosulfan II	33213-6-5	0.029	0.13
Endosulfan sulfate	1-31-07-8	0.029	0.13
Endrin	72-20-8	0.0028	0.13
Endrin aldehyde	7421-93-4	0.025	0.13
Ethyl acetate	141-78-6	0.34	33
Ethyl cyanide (Propane-nitrile)	107-12-0	0.24	360
Ethyl benzene	100-41-4	0.057	10
Ethyl ether	60-29-7	0.12	160
bis(2-Ethylhexyl) phthalate	117-81-7	0.28	28
Ethyl methacrylate	97-63-2	0.14	160
Ethylene oxide	75-21-8	0.12	NA
Famphur	52-85-7	0.017	15
Fluoranthene	206-44-0	0.068	3.4
Fluorene	86-73-7	0.059	3.4
Heptachlor	76-44-8	0.0012	0.066
Heptachlor epoxide	1024-57-3	0.016	0.066
Hexachlorobenzene	118-74-1	0.055	10
Hexachlorobutadiene	87-68-3	0.055	5.6

POLLUTION CONTROL BOARD

NOTICE OF PROPOSED AMENDMENTS

Hexachlorocyclopenta-diene	77-47-4	0.057	2.4
HxCDDs (All Hexachloro-dibenzo-p-dioxins)	NA	0.000063	0.001
HxCDFs (All Hexachloro-dibenzofurans)	NA	0.000063	0.001
Hexachloroethane	67-72-1	0.055	10
Hexachloropropylene	1888-71-7	0.023	30
Indeno (1,2,3-c,d) pyrene	193-39-5	0.0055	3.4
Iodomethane	74-88-4	0.19	65
Isobutyl alcohol	78-93-1	5.6	170
Isodrin	465-73-6	0.021	0.066
Isosafrole	120-58-1	0.081	2.6
Kepone	143-50-8	0.0011	0.13
Methacrylonitrile	126-98-7	0.24	84
Methanol	67-56-1	5.6	NA
Methapyrilene	91-80-5	0.081	1.5
Methoxychlor	72-43-5	0.25	0.18
3-Methylcholanthrene	56-49-5	0.0055	15
4,4-Methylene bis(2-chloroaniline)	101-14-4	0.50	30
Methylene chloride	75-09-2	0.089	30
Methyl ethyl ketone	78-93-1	0.28	36
Methyl isobutyl ketone	108-10-1	0.14	33
Methyl methacrylate	80-62-6	0.14	160
Methyl methansulfonate	66-27-3	0.018	NA
Methyl parathion	298-00-0	0.014	4.6
Naphthalene	91-20-3	0.059	5.6
2-Naphthylamine	91-59-8	0.52	NA
p-Nitroaniline	100-01-6	0.028	28
Nitrobenzene	98-95-3	0.068	14
5-Nitro-o-toluidine	99-55-8	0.32	28
p-Nitrophenol	100-02-7	0.12	29
N-Nitrosodiethylamine	55-18-5	0.40	28
N-Nitrosodimethylamine	62-75-9	0.40	NA
N-Nitroso-di-n-butyl-amine	924-16-3	0.40	17
N-Nitrosomethylethyl-amine	10595-95-6	0.40	2.3
N-Nitrosomorpholine	59-89-2	0.40	2.3
N-Nitrosopiperidine	100-75-4	0.013	35
N-Nitrosopyrrolidine	930-55-2	0.013	35
Parathion	56-38-2	0.014	4.6
Total PCBs (sum of all PCB isomers, or all Aroclors)	1336-36-3	0.10	10
Pentachlorobenzene	608-93-5	0.055	10

POLLUTION CONTROL BOARD

NOTICE OF PROPOSED AMENDMENTS

PeCdds (All Pentachloro-dibenzo-p-dioxins)	NA	0.000063	
PcCDFs (All Pentachloro-dibenzofurans)	NA	0.000035	
Pentachloronitrobenzene	82-68-8	0.055	4.8
Pentachlorophenol	87-86-5	0.089	7.4
Phenacetin	62-44-2	0.081	16
Phenanthrene	85-01-8	0.059	5.6
Phenol	108-95-2	0.039	6.2
Phorate	298-02-2	0.021	4.6
Phthalic anyhydride	85-44-9	0.055	NA
Pronamide	23950-58-5	0.093	1.5
Pyrene	129-00-0	0.067	8.2
Pyridine	110-86-1	0.014	16
Safrole	94-59-7	0.081	22
Silver (2,4,5-TP)	93-72-1	0.72	7.9
2,4,5-T	93-76-5	0.72	7.9
1,2,4,5-Tetrachloro-benzene	95-94-3	0.055	14
TCDDs (All Tetrachloro-dibenzo-p-dioxins)	NA	0.000063	0.00
TCDFs (All Tetrachloro-dibenzofurans)	NA	0.000063	
1,1,1,2-Tetrachloro-ethane	630-20-6	0.057	6.0
1,1,2,2-Tetrachloro-ethane	79-34-6	0.057	6.0
Tetrachloroethylene	127-18-4	0.056	6.0
2,3,4,6-Tetrachloro-phenol	58-90-2	0.030	7.4
Toluene	108-88-3	0.080	10
Toxaphene	8001-35-2	0.0095	2.6
Bromoform (Tribromo-methane)	75-25-2	0.63	15
1,2,4-Trichlorobenzene	120-82-1	0.055	19
1,1,1-Trichloroethane	71-55-6	0.054	6.0
1,1,2-Trichloroethane	79-00-5	0.054	6.0
Trichloroethylene	79-01-6	0.054	6.0
Trichloromonofluoro-methane	75-69-4	0.020	30
2,4,5-Trichlorophenol	95-95-4	0.18	7.4
2,4,6-Trichlorophenol	88-06-2	0.035	7.4
1,2,3-Trichloropropane	96-18-4	0.85	30
1,1,2-Trichloro-1,2,2-trifluoroethane	76-13-1	0.057	30
tris(2,3-Dibromopropyl) phosphate	126-72-7	0.11	NA
Vinyl chloride	75-01-4	0.27	6.0

POLLUTION CONTROL BOARD

NOTICE OF PROPOSED AMENDMENTS

Xylenes-mixed isomers (sum or o-, m-, and p-xylene concentrations)	1330-20-7	0.32	30
Antimony	7440-36-0	1.9	2.1 mg/l TCLP
Arsenic	7440-38-2	1.4	5.0 mg/l TCLP
Barium	7440-39-3	1.2	7.6 mg/l TCLP
Beryllium	7440-41-7	0.82	NA
Cadmium	7440-43-9	0.69	0.19 mg/l TCLP
Chromium (Total)	7440-47-3	2.77	0.86 mg/l TCLP
Cyanides (Total)(7)	57-12-5	1.2	590
Cyanides (Amenable)(7)	57-12-5	0.86	NA
Fluoride	16964-48-8	35	NA
Lead	7439-92-1	0.69	0.37 mg/l TCLP
Mercury	7439-97-6	0.15	0.025 mg/l TCLP
Nickel	7440-02-0	3.98	5.0 mg/l TCLP
Selenium	7782-49-2	0.82	0.16 mg/l TCLP
Silver	7440-22-4	0.43	0.30 mg/l TCLP
Sulfide	8496-23-8	14	NA
Thallium	7440-28-0	1.4	NA
Vanadium	7440-62-2	4.3	NA

K001
Bottom sediment sludge from the treatment of wastewaters from wood preserving processes that use creosote or penthachlorophenol.

Naphthalene	91-20-3	0.059	5.6
Pentachlorophenol	87-86-5	0.089	7.4
Phenanthrene	85-01-8	0.059	5.6
Pyrene	129-00-0	0.067	8.2
Toluene	108-88-3	0.080	10
Xylenes-mixed isomers (sum of o-, m-, and p-xylene concentrations)	1330-20-7	0.32	30
Lead	7439-92-1	0.69	0.37 mg/l TCLP

K002
Wastewater treatment sludge from the production of chrome yellow and orange pigments.

Chromium (Total)	7440-47-3	2.77	0.86 mg/l TCLP
Lead	7439-92-1	0.69	0.37 mg/l TCLP

K003
Wastewater treatment sludge from the production of molybdate orange pigments.

Chromium (Total)	7440-47-3	2.77	0.86 mg/l TCLP
Lead	7439-92-1	0.69	0.37 mg/l TCLP

K004
Wastewater treatment sludge from the production of zinc yellow pigments.

POLLUTION CONTROL BOARD

NOTICE OF PROPOSED AMENDMENTS

Chromium (Total)	7440-47-3	2.77	0.86 mg/l TCLP
Lead	7439-92-1	0.69	0.37 mg/l TCLP

K005
Wastewater treatment sludge from the production of chrome green pigments.

Chromium (Total)	7440-47-3	2.77	0.86 mg/l TCLP
Lead	7439-92-1	0.69	0.37 mg/l TCLP
Cyanides (Total)(7)	57-12-5	1.2	590

K006
Wastewater treatment sludge from the production of chrome oxide green pigments (anhydrous).

Chromium (Total)	7440-47-3	2.77	0.86 mg/l TCLP
Lead	7439-92-1	0.69	0.37 mg/l TCLP

K006
Wastewater treatment sludge from the production of chrome oxide green pigments (hydrated).

Chromium (Total)	7440-47-3	2.77	0.86 mg/l TCLP
Lead	7439-92-1	0.69	NA

K007
Wastewater treatment sludge from the production of iron blue pigments.

Chromium (Total)	7440-47-3	2.77	0.86 mg/l TCLP
Lead	7439-92-1	0.69	NA
Cyanides (Total)(7)	57-12-5	1.2	590

K008
Oven residue from the production of chrome oxide green pigments.

Chromium (Total)	7440-47-3	2.77	0.86 mg/l TCLP
Lead	7439-92-1	0.69	0.37 mg/l TCLP

K009
Distillation bottoms from the production of acetaldehyde from ethylene.

Chloroform	67-66-3	0.046	6.0

K010
Distillation side cuts from the production of acetaldehyde from ethylene.

Chloroform	67-66-3	0.046	6.0

K011
Bottom stream from the wastewater stripper in the production of acrylonitrile.

Acetonitrile	75-05-8	5.8	18
Acrylonitrile	107-13-1	0.24	84
Acrylamide	79-06-1	19	23
Benzene	71-43-2	0.14	10
Cyanide (Total)	57-12-5	1.2	590

POLLUTION CONTROL BOARD

NOTICE OF PROPOSED AMENDMENTS

K013
Bottom stream from the acetonitrile column in the production of acrylonitrile.

Acetonitrile	75-05-8	5.6	1.8
Acrylonitrile	107-13-1	0.24	84
Acrylamide	79-06-1	19	23
Benzene	71-43-2	0.14	10
Cyanide (Total)	57-12-5	1.2	590

K014
Bottoms from the acetonitrile purification column in the production of acrylonitrile.

Acetonitrile	75-05-8	5.6	1.8
Acrylonitrile	107-13-1	0.24	84
Acrylamide	79-06-1	19	23
Benzene	71-43-2	0.1410	
Cyanide (Total)	57-12-5	1.2	590

K015
Still bottoms from the distillation of benzyl chloride.

Anthracene	120-12-7	0.059	3.4
Benzal chloride	98-87-3	0.055	6.0
Benzo(b)fluoranthene (difficult to distinguish from benzo-(k)fluoranthene)	205-99-2	0.11	6.8
Benzo(k)fluoranthene (difficult to distinguish from benzo-(b)fluoranthene)	207-08-9	0.11	6.8
Phenanthrene	85-01-8	0.059	3.6
Toluene	108-88-3	0.080	10
Chromium (Total)	7440-47-3	2.77	0.86 mg/l TCLP
Nickel	7440-02-0	3.98	5.0 mg/l TCLP

K016
Heavy ends or distillation residues from the production of carbon tetrachloride.

Hexachlorobenzene	118-74-1	0.055	10
Hexachlorobutadiene	87-68-3	0.055	5.6
Hexachlorocyclopenta-diene	77-47-4	0.057	2.4
Hexachloroethane	67-72-1	0.055	30
Tetrachloroethylene	127-18-4	0.056	6.0

K017
Heavy ends (still bottoms) from the purification column in the production of epichlorohydrin.

bis(2-Chloroethyl)ether	111-44-4	0.033	6.0

POLLUTION CONTROL BOARD

NOTICE OF PROPOSED AMENDMENTS

1,2-Dichloropropane	78-87-5	0.85	18
1,2,3-Trichloropropane	96-18-4	0.85	30

K018
Heavy ends from the fractionation column in ethyl chloride production.

Chloroethane	75-00-3	0.27	6.0
Chloromethane	74-87-3	0.19	NA
1,1,-Dichloroethane	75-34-3	0.059	6.0
1,2-Dichloroethane	107-06-2	0.21	6.0
Hexachlorobenzene	118-74-1	0.055	10
Hexachlorobutadiene	87-68-3	0.055	5.6
Hexachloroethane	67-72-1	0.055	30
Pentachloroethane	76-01-7	NA	6.0
1,1,1-Trichloroethane	71-55-6	0.054	6.0

K019
Heavy ends from the distillation of ethylene dichloride in ethylene dichloride production.

bis(2-Chloroethyl) ether	111-44-1	0.033	6.0
Chlorobenzene	108-90-7	0.057	6.0
Chloroform	67-66-3	0.046	6.0
p-Dichlorobenzene	106-46-7	0.090	NA
1,2-Dichloroethane	107-06-2	0.21	6.0
Fluorene	86-73-7	0.059	NA
Hexachloroethane	67-72-1	0.055	30
Naphthalene	91-20-3	0.059	5.6
Phenanthrene	85-01-8	0.059	5.6
1,2,4,5-Tetrachloro-benzene	95-94-3	0.055	NA
Tetrachlorethylene	127-18-4	0.056	6.0
1,2,4-Trichlorobenzene	120-82-1	0.055	19
1,1,1-Trichloroethane	71-55-6	0.054	6.0

K020
Heavy ends from the distillation of vinyl chloride in vinyl chloride monomer production.

1,2-Dichloroethane	107-06-2	0.21	6.0
1,1,2,2-Tetrachloro-ethane	79-34-6	0.057	6.0
Tetrachloroethylene	127-18-4	0.056	6.0

K021
Aqueous spent antimony catalyst waste from fluoromethane production.

Carbon tetrachloride	56-23-5	0.057	6.0
Chloroform	67-66-3	0.046	6.0
Antimony	7440-36-0	1.9	2.1 mg/l TCLP

K022

POLLUTION CONTROL BOARD

NOTICE OF PROPOSED AMENDMENTS

Distillation bottom tars form the production of phenol or acetone from cumene.

Toluene	108-88-3	0.080	10
Acetophenone	98-86-2	0.010	9.7
Diphenylamine (difficult) to distinguish from diphenylnitrosamine)	122-39-4	0.92	13
Diphenylnitrosamine (difficult to distinguish from diphenylamine)	86-30-6	0.92	13
Phenol	108-95-2	0.039	6.2
Chromium (Total)	7440-47-3	2.77	0.86 mg/l TCLP
Nickel	7440-02-0	0.28	5.0 mg/l TCLP

K023
Distillation light ends from the production of phthalic anhydride from naphthalene.

Phthalic anhydride (measured as Phthalic acid or Terephthalic acid)	100-21-0	0.055	28
Phthalic anhydride	85-44-9	0.055	28

K024
Distillation bottoms from the production of phthalic anhydride from naphthalene.

Phthalic anhydride (measured as Phthalic acid or Terephthalic acid)	100-21-0	0.055	28
Phthalic anhydride	85-44-9	0.055	28

K025
Distillation bottoms from the production of nitrobenzene by the nitration of benzene.

NA	NA	LLEXT fb SSTRP fb CARBN; or INCIN	INCIN

K026
Stripping still tails from the production of methyl ethyl pyridines.

NA	NA	INCIN	INCIN

K027
Centrifuge and distillation residues from the toluene diisocyanate production.

NA	NA	CARBN; or INCIN	CMBST

POLLUTION CONTROL BOARD

NOTICE OF PROPOSED AMENDMENTS

K028
Spent catalyst from the hydrochlorinator reactor in the production of 1,1,1-trichloroethane.

1,1-Dichloroethane	75-34-3	0.059	6.0
trans-1,2-Dichloro-ethylene	156-60-5	0.054	30
Hexachlorobutadiene	87-68-3	0.055	5.6
Hexachloroethane	67-72-1	0.055	30
Pentachloroethane	76-01-7	NA	6.0
1,1,1,2-Tetrachloro-ethane	630-20-6	0.057	6.0
1,1,2,2-Tetrachloro-ethane	79-34-6	0.057	6.0
Tetrachloroethylene	127-18-4	0.056	6.0
1,1,1-Trichloroethane	71-55-6	0.054	6.0
1,1,2-Trichloroethane	79-00-5	0.054	6.0
Cadmium	7440-43-9	0.69	NA
Chromium (Total)	7440-47-3	2.77	0.86 mg/l TCLP
Lead	7439-92-1	0.69	0.37 mg/l TCLP
Nickel	7440-02-0	3.98	5.0 mg/l TCLP

K029
Waste from the product steam stripper in the production of 1,1,1-trichloroethane.

Chloroform	67-66-3	0.046	6.0
1,2-Dichloroethane	107-06-2	0.21	6.0
1,1-Dichloroethylene	75-35-4	0.025	6.0
1,1,1-Trichloroethane	71-55-6	0.054	6.0
Vinyl chloride	75-01-4	0.27	6.0

K030
Column bodies or heavy ends from the combined production of trichloroethylene and perchloroethylene.

o-Dichlorobenzene	95-50-1	0.088	NA
p-Dichlorobenzene	106-46-7	0.090	NA
Hexachlorobutadiene	87-68-3	0.055	5.6
Hexachloroethane	67-72-1	0.055	30
Hexachloropropylene	1888-71-7	NA	30
Pentachlorobenzene	608-93-5	NA	10
Pentachloroethane	76-01-7	NA	6.0
1,2,4,5-Tetrachloro-benzene	95-94-3	0.055	14
Tetrachloroethylene	127-18-4	0.056	6.0
1,2,4-Trichlorobenzene	120-82-1	0.055	19

K031
By-product salts generated in the production of MSMA and cacodylic acid.

Arsenic	7440-38-2	1.4	5.0 mg/l TCLP

POLLUTION CONTROL BOARD

NOTICE OF PROPOSED AMENDMENTS

K032
Wastewater treatment sludge from the production of chlordane.

Hexachlorocyclopenta-diene	77-48-4	0.057	2.4
Chlordane (alph and gamma isomers)	57-74-9	0.0033	0.26
Heptachlor	76-44-8	0.0012	0.066
Heptachlor epoxide	1024-57-3	0.016	0.066

K033
Wastewater and scrub water from the chlorination of cyclopentadiene in the production of chlordane.

Hexachlorocyclopenta-diene	77-47-4	0.057	2.4

K034
Filter solids from the filtration of hexachlorocyclopetadiene in the production of chlordane.

Hexachlorocyclopenta-diene	77-47-4	0.057	2.4

K035
Wastewater treatment sludges generated in the production of creosote.

Acenaphthene	83-32-9	NA	3.4
Anthracene	120-12-7	NA	3.4
Benz(a)anthracene	56-55-3	0.061	3.4
Benzo(a)pyrene	50-32-8	0.061	3.4
Chrysene	218-01-9	0.059	3.4
o-Cresol	95-48-7	0.11	5.6
m-Cresol (difficult to distinguish from p-cresol	108-39-4	0.77	5.6
p-Cresol (difficult to distinguish from m-cresol)	106-44-5	0.77	5.6
Dibenz(a,h)anthracene	53-70-3	NA	8.2
Fluoranthene	206-44-0	0.068	3.4
Fluorene	86-73-7	NA	3.4
Indeno(1,2,3-cd)pyrene	193-39-5	NA	3.4
Naphthalene	91-20-3	0.059	5.6
Phenanthrene	85-01-8	0.059	5.6
Phenol	108-95-2	0.039	6.2
Pyrene	129-00-0	0.067	8.2

K036
Still bottoms from toluene reclamation distillation in the production of

POLLUTION CONTROL BOARD

NOTICE OF PROPOSED AMENDMENTS

disulfoton.

Disulfoton	298-04-4	0.017	6.2

K037
Wastewater treatment sludges from the production of disulfoton.

Disulfoton	298-04-4	0.017	6.2
Toluene	108-88-3	0.080	10

K038
Wastewater from the washing and stripping of phorate production.

Phorate	298-02-2	0.021	4.6

K039
Filter cake form the filtration of diethylphosphorodithioic acid in the production of phorate.

NA	NA	CARBN; or INCIN	CMBST

K040
Wastewater treatment sludge from the production of phorate.

Phorate	298-02-2	0.021	4.6

K041
Wastewater treatment sludge from the production of toxaphene.

Toxaphene	8001-35-2	0.0095	2.6

K042
Heavy ends or distillation residues from the distillation of tetrachlorobenzene in the production of 2,4,5-T.

o-Dichlorobenzene	95-50-1	0.088	6.0
p-Dichlorobenzene	106-46-7	0.090	6.0
Pentachlorobenzene	608-93-5	0.055	10
1,2,4,5-Tetrachloro-benzene	95-94-3	0.055	14
1,2,4-Trichlorobenzene	120-82-1	0.055	19

K043
2,6-Dichlorophenol waste from the production of 2,4-D.

2,4-Dichlorophenol	120-83-2	0.044	14
2,6-Dichlorophenol	187-65-0	0.044	14
2,4,5-Trichlorophenol	95-95-4	0.18	7.4
2,4,6-Trichlorophenol	88-06-2	0.035	7.4
2,3,4,6-Tetrachloro-phenol	58-90-2	0.030	7.4
Pentachlorophenol	87-86-5	0.089	7.4
Tetrachloroethylene	127-18-4	0.056	6.0
HxCDDs (All Hexachloro-dibenzo-p-dioxins)	NA	0.000063	0.001

POLLUTION CONTROL BOARD

NOTICE OF PROPOSED AMENDMENTS

HxCDFs (All Hexachloro-dibenzofurans)	NA	0.000063	0.001
PeCDDs (All Pentachloro-dibenzo-p-dioxins)	NA	0.000063	0.001
PeCDFs (All Pentachloro-dibenzofurans)	NA	0.000035	0.001
TCDDs (All Tetrachloro-dibenzo-p-dioxins)	NA	0.00063	0.001
TCDFs (All Tetrachloro-dibenzofurans)	NA	0.00063	0.001

K044
Wastewater treatment sludges from the manufacturing and processing of explosives.

NA	NA	DEACT	DEACT

K045
Spent carbon from the treatment of wastewater containing explosives.

NA	NA	DEACT	DEACT

K046
Wastewater treatment sludges from the manufacturing, formulation and loading of lead-based initiating compounds.

Lead	7439-92-1	0.69	0.37 mg/l TCLP

K047
Pink or red water from TNT operations.

NA	NA	DEACT	DEACT

K048
Dissolved air flotation (DAF) float from the petroleum refining industry.

Benzene	71-43-2	0.14	10
Benzo(a)pyrene	50-32-8	0.061	3.4
bis(2-Ethylhexyl)phthalate	117-81-7	0.28	28
Chrysene	218-01-9	0.059	3.4
Di-n-butyl phthalate	84-74-2	0.057	28
Ethylbenzene	100-41-4	0.057	10
Fluorene	86-73-7	0.059	NA
Naphthalene	91-20-3	0.059	5.6
Phenanthrene	85-01-8	0.059	5.6
Phenol	108-95-2	0.039	6.2
Pyrene	129-00-0	0.067	8.2
Toluene	108-88-3	0.080	10
Xylenes-mixed isomers (sum of o-, m-, and p-xylene concentrations)	1330-20-7	0.32	30
Chromium (Total)	7440-47-3	2.77	0.86 mg/l TCLP

POLLUTION CONTROL BOARD

NOTICE OF PROPOSED AMENDMENTS

Cyanides (Total)(7)	57-12-5	1.2	590
Lead	7439-92-1	0.69	NA
Nickel	7440-02-0	NA	5.0 mg/l TCLP

K049
Slop oil emulsion solids from the petroleum refining industry.

Anthracene	120-12-7	0.059	3.4
Benzene	71-43-2	0.14	10
Benzo(a)pyrene	50-32-8	0.061	3.4
bis(2-Ethylhexyl)phthalate	117-81-7	0.28	28
Carbon disulfide	75-15-0	3.8	NA
Chrysene	218-01-9	0.059	3.4
2,4-Dimethylphenol	105-67-9	0.036	NA
Ethylbenzene	100-41-4	0.057	10
Naphthalene	91-20-3	0.059	5.6
Phenanthrene	85-01-8	0.059	5.6
Phenol	108-95-2	0.039	6.2
Pyrene	129-00-0	0.067	8.2
Toluene	108-88-3	0.080	10
Xylenes-mixed isomers (sum of o-, m-, and p-xylene concentrations)	1330-20-7	0.32	30
Cyanides (Total)(7)	57-12-5	1.2	590
Chromium (Total)	7440-47-3	2.77	0.86 mg/l TCLP
Lead	7439-92-1	0.69	NA
Nickel	7440-02-0	NA	5.0 mg/l TCLP

K050
Heat exchanger bundle cleaning sludge from the petroleum refining industry.

Benzo(a)pyrene	50-32-8	0.061	3.4
Phenol	108-95-2	0.039	6.2
Cyanides (Total)(7)	57-12-5	1.2	590
Chromium (Total)	7440-47-3	2.77	0.86 mg/l TCLP
Lead	7439-92-1	0.69	NA
Nickel	7440-02-0	NA	5.0 mg/l TCLP

K051
API separator sludge from the petroleum refining industry.

Acenaphthene	83-32-9	0.059	NA
Anthracene	120-12-7	0.059	3.4
Benz(a)anthracene	56-55-3	0.059	3.4
Benzene	71-43-2	0.14	10
Benzo(a)pyrene	50-32-8	0.061	3.4
bis(2-Ethylhexyl)phthalate	117-81-7	0.28	28
Chrysene	218-01-9	0.059	3.4
Di-n-butyl phthalate	105-67-9	0.057	28

POLLUTION CONTROL BOARD

NOTICE OF PROPOSED AMENDMENTS

Ethylbenzene	100-41-4	0.057	10
Fluorene	86-73-7	0.059	NA
Naphthalene	91-20-3	0.059	5.6
Phenanthrene	85-01-8	0.059	5.6
Phenol	108-95-2	0.039	6.2
Pyrene	129-00-0	0.067	8.2
Toluene	106-88-3	0.08	10
Xylenes-mixed isomers (sum of o-, m- and p-xylene concentrations)	1330-20-7	0.32	30
Cyanides (Total)(7)	57-12-5	1.2	590
Chromium (Total)	7440-47-3	2.77	0.86 mg/l TCLP
Lead	7439-92-1	0.69	NA
Nickel	7440-02-0	NA	5.0 mg/l TCLP

K052
Tank bottoms (leaded) from the petroleum refining industry.

Benzene	71-43-2	0.14	10
Benzo (a)pyrene	50-32-8	0.061	3.4
o-Cresol	95-48-7	0.11	5.6
m-Cresol (difficult to distinguish from p-cresol)	108-39-4	0.77	5.6
p-Cresol (difficult to distinguish from m-cresol)	106-44-5	0.77	5.6
2,4-Dimethylphenol	105-67-9	0.036	NA
Ethylbenzene	100-41-4	0.057	10
Naphthalene	91-20-3	0.059	5.6
Phenanthrene	85-01-8	0.059	5.6
Phenol	108-95-2	0.039	6.2
Toluene	108-88-3	0.08	10
Xylene-mixed isomers (sum of o-, m-, and p-xylene concentrations)	1330-20-7	0.32	30
Chromium (Total)	7440-47-3	2.77	0.86 mg/l TCLP
Cyanides (Total)(7)	57-12-5	1.2	590
Lead	7439-92-1	0.69	NA
Nickel	7440-02-0	NA	5.0 mg/l TCLP

K060
Ammonia still lime sludge from coking operations.

Benzene	71-43-2	0.14	10
Benzo(a) pyrene	50-32-8	0.061	3.4
Naphthalene	91-20-3	0.059	5.6
Phenol	108-95-2	0.039	6.2

POLLUTION CONTROL BOARD

NOTICE OF PROPOSED AMENDMENTS

Cyanides (Total)(7)	57-12-5	1.2	590

K061
Emission control dust or sludge from the primary production of steel in electric furnaces.

Antimony	7440-36-0	NA	2.1 mg/l TCLP
Arsenic	7440-38-2	NA	5.0 mg/l TCLP
Barium	7440-39-3	NA	7.6 mg/l TCLP
Beryllium	7440-41-7	NA	0.014 mg/l TCLP
Cadmium	7440-43-9	0.69	0.19 mg/l TCLP
Chromium (Total)	7440-47-3	2.77	0.86 mg/l TCLP
Lead	7439-92-1	0.69	0.37 mg/l TCLP
Mercury	7439-97-6	NA	0.025 mg/l TCLP
Nickel	7440-02-0	3.98	5.0 mg/l TCLP
Selenium	7782-49-2	NA	0.16 mg/l TCLP
Silver	7740-22-4	NA	0.30 mg/l TCLP
Thallium	NA	NA	0.078 mg/l TCLP
Zinc	7440-66-6	NA	5.3 mg/l TCLP

K062
Spent pickle liquor generated by steel finishing operations of facilities within the iron and steel industry (SIC Codes 331 and 332).

Chromium (Total)	7740-47-3	2.77	0.86 mg/l TCLP
Lead	7439-92-1	0.69	0.37 mg/l TCLP
Nickel	7440-02-0	NA	5.0 mg/l TCLP

K069
Emission control dust or sludge from secondary lead smelting. - Calcium sulfate (Low Lead) Subcategory

Cadmium	7440-43-9	0.69	0.19 mg/l TCLP
Lead	7439-92-1	0.69	0.37 mg/l TCLP

K069
Emission control dust or sludge from secondary lead smelting. - Non-Calcium sulfate (High Lead) Subcategory

NA	NA	NA	RLEAD

K071
K071 (Brine purification muds from the mercury cell process in chlorine production, where separately prepurified brine is not used) nonwastewaters that are residues from BMERC.

Mercury	7439-97-6	NA	0.20 mg/l TCLP

K071
K071 (Brine purification muds from the mercury cell process in chlorine production, where separately prepurified brine is to used) nonwastewaters that are not residues from BMERC.

POLLUTION CONTROL BOARD

NOTICE OF PROPOSED AMENDMENTS

Mercury	7439-97-6	NA	0.025 mg/l TCLP

K071
All K071 wastewaters.

Mercury	7439-97-6	0.015	NA

K073
Chlorinated hydrocarbon waste from the purification step of the diaphragm cell process using graphite anodes in chlorine production.

Carbon tetrachloride	56-23-5	0.057	6.0
Chloroform	67-66-3	0.046	6.0
Hexachloroethane	67-72-1	0.055	30
Tetrachloroethylene	127-18-4	0.056	6.0
1,1,1-Trichloroethane	71-55-6	0.054	6.0

K083
Distillation bottoms from aniline production.

Aniline	62-53-3	0.81	14
Benzene	71-43-2	0.14	10
Cyclohexanone	108-94-1	0.36	NA
Diphenylamine (difficult to distinguish from diphenylnitrosamine)	122-39-4	0.92	13
Diphenylnitrosamine (difficult to distinguish from diphenylamine)	86-30-6	0.92	13
Nitrobenzene	98-95-3	0.068	14
Phenol	108-95-2	0.039	6.2
Nickel	7440-02-0	3.98	5.0 mg/l TCLP

K084
Wastewater treatment sludges generated during the production of veterinary pharmaceuticals from arsenic or organo-arsenic compounds.

Arsenic	7440-38-2	1.4	5.0 mg/l TCLP

K085
Distillation or fractionation colum bottoms from the production of chlorobenzenes.

Benzene	71-43-2	0.014	10
Chlorobenzene	108-90-7	0.057	6.0
m-Dichlorobenzene	541-73-1	0.036	6.0
o-Dichlorobenzene	95-50-1	0.088	6.0
p-Dichlorobenzene	106-46-7	0.090	6.0
Hexachlorobenzene	118-74-1	0.055	10
Total PCBs	1336-36-3	0.10	10

POLLUTION CONTROL BOARD

NOTICE OF PROPOSED AMENDMENTS

(sum of all PCB isomers, or all Aroclors)			
Pentachlorobenzene	608-93-5	0.055	10
1,2,4,5-Tetrachloro-benzene	95-94-3	0.055	10
1,2,4-Trichlorobenzene	120-82-1	0.055	19

K086
Solvent wastes and sludges, caustic washes and sludges, or water washes and sludges from cleaning tubs and equipment used in the formulation of ink from pigments, driers, soaps, and stabilizers containing chromium and lead.

Acetone	67-64-1	0.28	160
Acetophenone	96-86-2	0.010	9.7
bis(2)Ethylhexyl) phthalate	117-81-7	0.28	28
n-Butyl alcohol	71-36-3	5.6	2.6
Butylbenzyl phthalate	85-68-7	0.017	28
Cyclohexanone	108-94-1	0.36	NA
o-Dichlorobenzene	95-50-1	0.088	6.0
Diethyl phthalate	84-66-2	0.20	28
Dimethyl phthalate	131-11-3	0.047	28
Di-n-butyl phthalate	84-74-2	0.057	28
Di-n-octyl phthalate	117-84-0	0.017	28
Ethyl acetate	141-78-6	0.34	33
Ethylbenzene	100-41-4	0.057	10
Methanol	67-56-1	5.6	NA
Methyl ethyl ketone	78-93-3	0.28	36
Methyl isobutyl ketone	108-10-1	0.14	33
Methylene chloride	75-09-2	0.089	30
Naphthalene	91-20-3	0.059	5.6
Nitrobenzene	98-95-3	0.068	14
Toluene	108-88-3	0.080	10
1,1,1-Trichloroethane	71-55-6	0.054	6.0
Trichloroethylene	79-01-6	0.054	6.0
Xylenes-mixed isomers (sum of o-, m-, and p-xylene concentrations)	1330-20-7	0.32	30
Chromium (Total)	7440-47-3	2.77	0.86 mg/l TCLP
Cyanides (Total)(7)	57-12-5	1.2	590
Lead	7439-92-1	0.69	0.37 mg/l TCLP

K087
Decanter tank tar sludge from coking operations.

Acenaphthylene	208-96-8	0.059	3.4
Benzene	71-43-2	0.14	10
Chrysene	218-01-9	0.059	3.4
Fluoranthene	206-44-0	0.068	3.4
Indeno(1,2,3-cd)pyrene	193-39-5	0.0055	3.4

POLLUTION CONTROL BOARD

NOTICE OF PROPOSED AMENDMENTS

Naphthalene	91-20-3	0.059	5.6
Phenanthrene	85-01-8	0.059	5.6
Toluene	108-88-3	0.080	10
Xylenes-mixed isomers	1330-20-7	0.32	30
(sum of o-, m-, and p-xylene concentrations)			
Lead	7439-92-1	0.069	0.37 mg/l TCLP

K093
Distillation light ends from the production of phthalic anhydride from orthoxylene.

Phthalic anhydride (measured as Phthalic acid or erephthalic acid)	100-21-0	0.055	28
Phthalic anhydride	85-44-9	0.055	28

K094
Distillation bottoms from the production of phthalic anhydride from orthoxylene.

Phthalic anhydride (measured as Phthalic acid or Terephthalic acid)	100-21-0	0.055	28
Phthalic anhydride	85-44-9	0.055	28

K095
Distillation bottoms from the production of 1,1,1-trichloroethane.

Hexachloroethane	67-72-1	0.055	30
Pentachloroethane	76-01-7	0.055	6.0
1,1,1,2-Tetrachloro-ethane	630-20-6	0.057	6.0
1,1,2,2-Tetrachloro-ethane	79-34-6	0.057	6.0
Tetrachloroethylene	127-18-4	0.056	6.0
1,1,2-Trichloroethane	79-00-5	0.054	6.0
Trichloroethylene	79-01-6	0.054	6.0

K096
Heavy ends from the heavy ends colum from the production of 1,1,1-trichloroethane.

o-Dichlorobenzene	541-73-1	0.036	6.0
Pentachloroethane	76-01-7	0.055	6.0
1,1,1,2-Tetrachloro-ethane	630-20-6	0.057	6.0
1,1,2,2-Tetrachloro-ethane	79-34-6	0.057	6.0
Tetrachloroethylene	127-18-4	0.056	6.0

POLLUTION CONTROL BOARD

NOTICE OF PROPOSED AMENDMENTS

1,2,4-Trichlorobenzene	120-82-1	0.055	19
1,1,2-Trichloroethane	79-00-5	0.054	6.0
Trichloroethylene	79-01-6	0.054	6.0

K097
Vacuum stripper discharge from the chlordane chlorinator in the production of chlordane.

Chlordane alpha and gamma isomers	57-74-9	0.0033	0.26
Heptachlor	76-44-8	0.0012	0.066
Heptachlor epoxide	1024-57-3	0.016	0.066
Hexachlorocyclopenta-diene	77-47-4	0.057	2.4

K098
Untreated process wastewater from the production of toxaphene.

Toxaphene	8001-35-2	0.0095	2.6

K099
Untreated wastewater from the production of 2,4-D.

2,4-Dichlorophenoxy-acetic acid	94-75-7	0.72	10
HxCDDs (All Hexachloro-dibenzo-p-dioxins)	NA	0.000063	0.001
HxCDFs (All) Hexachloro-dibenzofurans)	NA	0.000063	0.001
PeCDDs (All Pentachloro-dibenzo-p-dioxins)	NA	0.000063	0.001
PeCDFs (All Pentachloro-dibenzofurans)	NA	0.000035	0.001
TCDDs (All Tetrachloro-dibenzo-p-dioxins)	NA	0.000063	0.001
TCDFs (All Tetrachloro-dibenzofurans	NA	0.000063	0.001

K100
Waste leaching solution from acid leaching of emission control dust or sludge from secondary lead smelting.

Cadmium	7440-43-9	0.69	0.19 mg/l TCLP
Chromium (Total)	7440-47-3	2.77	0.86 mg/l TCLP
Lead	7439-92-1	0.69	0.37 mg/l TCLP

K101
Distillation tar residues from the distillation of aniline-based compounds in the production of veterinary pharmaceuticals from arsenic or organo-arsenic compounds.

o-Nitroaniline	88-74-4	0.27	14
Arsenic	7440-38-2	1.4	5.0 mg/l TCLP

POLLUTION CONTROL BOARD

NOTICE OF PROPOSED AMENDMENTS

Cadmium	7440-43-9	0.69	NA
Lead	7439-92-1	0.69	NA
Mercury	7439-97-6	0.15	NA

K102
Residue from the use of activated carbon f--decolorizatin in the production of veterinary pharmaceuticals from arsenic or organo-arsenic compounds.

o-Nitrophenol	88-75-5	0.028	13
Arsenic	7440-38-2	1.4	5.0 mg/l TCLP
Cadmium	7440-43-9	0.069	NA
Lead	7439-92-1	0.69	NA
Mercury	7439-97-6	0.15	NA

K103
Process residues from aniline extraction from the production of aniline.

Aniline	62-53-3	0.81	14
Benzene	71-43-2	0.14	10
2,4-Dinitrophenol	51-28-5	0.12	160
Nitrobenzene	98-95-3	0.068	14
Phenol	108-95-2	0.039	6.2

K104
Combined wastewater streams generated from nitrobenzene or aniline production.

Aniline	62-53-3	0.81	14
Benzene	71-43-2	0.14	10
2,4-Dinitrophenol	51-28-5	0.12	160
Nitrobenzene	98-95-3	0.068	14
Phenol	108-95-2	0.039	6.2
Cyanides (Total)(7)	57-12-5	1.2	590

K105
Separated aqueous stream from the reactor product washing step in the production of chlorobenzenes.

Benzene	71-43-2	0.14	10
Chlorobenzene	108-90-7	0.057	6.0
2-Chlorophenol	95-57-8	0.044	5.7
o-Dichlorobenzene	95-50-1	0.088	6.0
p-Dichlorobenzene	106-46-7	0.090	6.0
Phenol	108-95-2	0.039	6.2
2,4,5-Trichlorophenol	95-95-4	0.18	7.4
2,4,6-Trichlorophenol	88-06-2	0.035	7.4

K106
K106 (wastewater treatment sludge from the mercury cell process in chlorine production) nonwastewaters that contain greater than or equal to 260 mg/kg total mercury.

| Mercury | 7439-97-6 | NA | RMERC |

POLLUTION CONTROL BOARD

NOTICE OF PROPOSED AMENDMENTS

K106
K106 (wastewater treatment sludge from the mercury cell process in chlorine production) nonwastewaters that contain less than 260 mg/kg total mercury that are residues from RMERC.

| Mercury | 7439-97-6 | NA | 0.20 mg/l TCLP |

K106
Other K106 nonwastewaters that contain less than 260 mg/kg total mercury and are not residues from RMERC.

| Mercury | 7439-97-6 | NA | 0.025 mg/l TCLP |

K106
All K106 wastewaters.

| Mercury | 7439-97-6 | 0.15 | NA |

K107
Column bottoms from product separation from the production of 1,1-dimethylhydrazine (UDMH) from carboxylic acid hydrazides.

| NA | NA | INCIN; or CHOXD fb CARBN; or BIODG fb CARBN | INCIN |

K108
Condensed colum overheads from product separation and condensed reactor vent gases from the production of 1,1-dimethylhydrazine (UDMH) from carboxylic acid hydrazides.

| NA | NA | INCIN; or CHOXD fb CARBN; or BIODG fb CARBN | INCIN |

K109
Spent filter cartridges from product purification from the production of 1,1-dimethylhydrazine (UDMH) from carboxylic acid hydrazides.

| NA | NA | INCIN; or CHOXD fb CARBN; or BIODG fb CARBN | INCIN |

K110
Condensed column overheads from intermediate separation from the production of 1,1-dimethylhydrazine (UDMH) from carboxylic acid hydrazides.

| NA | NA | INCIN; or CHOXD fb CARBN; or BIODG fb CARBN | INCIN |

POLLUTION CONTROL BOARD

NOTICE OF PROPOSED AMENDMENTS

K111
Product washwaters from the production of dinitrotoluene via nitration of toluene.

| 2,4-Dinitrotoluene | 121-1-1 | 0.32 | 140 |
| 2,6-Dinitrotoluene | 606-20-2 | 0.55 | 28 |

K112
Reaction by-product water from the drying column in the production of toluenediamine via hydrogenation of dinitrotoluene.

| NA | NA | INCIN; or CHOXD fb CARBN; or BIODG fb CARBN | INCIN |

K113
Condensed liquid light ends from the purification of toluenediamine in the production of toluenediamine via hydrogenation of dinitrotoluene.

| NA | NA | CARBN; or INCIN | CMBST |

K114
Vicinals from the purification of toluenediamine in the production of toluenediamine via hydrogenation of dinitrotoluene.

| NA | NA | CARBN; or INCIN | CMBST |

K115
Heavy ends from the purification of toluenediamine in the production of toluenediamine via hydrogenation of dinitrotoluene.

| Nickel | 7440-02-0 | 1.98 | 5.0 mg/l TCLP |
| NA | NA | CARBN; or INCIN | CMBST |

K116
Organic condensate from the solvent recovery column in the production of toluene diisocyanate via phosgenation of toluenediamine.

| NA | NA | CARBN; or INCIN | CMBST |

K117
Wastewater from the reactor vent gas scrubber in the production of ethylene dibromide via bromination of ethene.

Methyl bromide (Bromo-methane)	74-83-90.11	15	
Chloroform	67-66-3	0.046	6.0
Ethylene-dibromide (1,2-Dibromoethane)	106-93-4	0.028	15

POLLUTION CONTROL BOARD

NOTICE OF PROPOSED AMENDMENTS

K118
Spent absorbent solids from purification of ethylene dibromide in the production of ethylene dibromide via bromination of ethene.

Methyl bromide (Bromo-methane)	74-83-9	0.11	15
Chloroform	67-66-3	0.046	6.0
Ethylene dibromide (1,2-Dibromoethane)	106-93-4	0.028	15

K123
Process wastewater (including supernates, filtrates, and washwaters) from the production of ethylenebisdithiocarbamic acid and its salts.

| NA | NA | INCIN; or CHOXD fb (BIODG or CARBN) | INCIN |

K124
Reactor vent scrubber water from the production of ethylenebisdithiocarbamic acid and it salts.

| NA | NA | INCIN; or CHOXD fb (BIODG or CARBN) | INCIN |

K125
Filtration, evaporation, and centrifugation solids from the production of ethylenebisdithiocarbamic acid and it salts.

| NA | NA | INCIN; or CHOXD fb (BIODG or CARBN) | INCIN |

K126
Baghouse dust and floor sweeping in milling and packaging operations from the production or formulation of ethylenebisdithiocarbamic acid and its salts.

| NA | NA | INCIN; or CHOXD fb (BIODG or CARBN) | INCIN |

K131
Wastewater from the reactor and spent sulfuric acid from the acid dryer from the production of methyl bromide.

| Methyl bromide (Bromo-methane) | 74-83-9 | 0.11 | 15 |

K132
Spent absorbent and wastewater separator solids from the production of methyl

POLLUTION CONTROL BOARD

NOTICE OF PROPOSED AMENDMENTS

bromide.

Methyl bromide (Bromo-methane)	74-83-9	0.11	15

K136
Still bottoms from the purification of ethylene dibromide in the production of ethylene dibromide via bromination of ethene.

Methyl bromide (Bromo-methane)	74-83-9	0.11	15
Chloroform	67-66-3	0.046	6.0
Ethylene dibromide (1,2-Dibromoethane)	106-93-4	0.028	15

K141
Process residues from the recovery of coal tar, including, but not limited to, collecting sump residues from the production of coke or the recovery of coke by-products produced from coal. This listing does not include K087 (decanter tank tar sludge from coking operations).

Benzene	71-43-2	0.14	10
Benz(a)anthracene	56-55-3	0.059	3.4
Benzo(a)pyrene	50-2-8	0.061	3.4
(difficult to distinguish from benzo-(k)fluoranthene)			
Benzo(k)fluoranthene (difficult to distinguish from benzo-(b)fluoranthene)	207-08-9	0.11	6.8
Chrysene	218-01-9	0.059	3.4
Dibenz(a,h)anthracene	53-70-3	0.055	8.2
Indeno(1,2,3-cd)pyrene	193-39-5	0.0055	3.4

K142
Tar storage tank residues from the production of coke from coal or from the recovery of coke by-products produced from coal.

Benzene	71-43-2	0.14	10
Benz(a)anthracene	56-55-3	0.059	3.4
Benzo(a)pyrene	50-32-8	0.061	3.4
Benzo(b)fluoranthene (difficult to distinguish from benzo-(k)fluoranthene)	205-99-2	0.11	6.8
Benzo(k)fluoranthene (difficult to distinguish from benzo-(b)fluoranthene)	207-08-9	0.11	6.8
Chrysene	218-01-9	0.059	3.4
Dibenz(a,h)anthracene	53-70-3	0.055	8.2

POLLUTION CONTROL BOARD

NOTICE OF PROPOSED AMENDMENTS

Ideno(1,2,3-cd)pyrene	193-39-5	0.0055	3.4

K143
Process residues from the recovery of light oil, including, but not limited to, those generated in stills, decanters, and wash oil recovery units from the recovery of coke by-products produced from coal.

Benzene	71-43-2	0.14	10
Benz(a)anthracene	56-55-3	0.059	3.4
Benzo(a)pyrene	50-32-8	0.061	3.4
Benzo(b)fluoranthene (difficult to distinguish from benzo-(k)fluoranthene)	205-99-2	0.11	6.8
Benzo(k)fluoranthene (difficult to distinguish from benzo-(b)fluoranthene)	207-08-9	0.11	6.8
Chrysene	218-01-9	0.059	3.4

K144
Wastewater sump residues from light oil refining, including, but not limited to, intercepting or contamination sump sludges from the recovery of coke by-products produced from coal.

Benzene	71-43-2	0.14	10
Benz(a)anthracene	56-55-3	0.059	3.4
Benzo(a)pyrene	50-32-8	0.061	3.4
Benzo(b)fluoranthene (difficult to distinguish from benzo-(k)fluoranthene)	205-99-2	0.11	6.8
Benzo(k)fluoranthene (difficult to distinguish from benzo-(b)fluoranthene)	207-08-9	0.11	6.8
Chrysene	218-01-9	0.059	3.4
Dibenz(a,h)anthracene	53-70-3	0.055	8.2

K145
Residues from naphthalene collection and recovery operations from the recovery of coke by-products produced from coal.

Benzene	71-43-2	0.14	10
Benz(a)anthracene	56-55-3	0.059	3.4
Benzo(a)pyrene	50-32-8	0.061	3.4
Chrysene	218-01-9	0.059	3.4
Dibenz(a,h)anthracene	53-70-3	0.055	8.2
Naphthalene	91-20-3	0.059	5.6

K147

POLLUTION CONTROL BOARD

NOTICE OF PROPOSED AMENDMENTS

Tar storage tank residues from coal tar refining.

Benzene	71-43-2	0.14	10
Benz(a)anthracene	56-55-3	0.059	3.4
Benz(a)pyrene	50-32-8	0.061	3.4
Benzo(b)fluoranthene	205-99-2	0.11	6.8
(difficult to			
distinguish from benzo-			
(k)fluoranthene)			
Benzo(k)fluoranthene	207-08-9	0.11	6.8
(difficult to			
distinguish from benzo-			
(b)fluoranthene)			
Chrysene	218-01-9	0.059	3.4
Dibenz(a,h)anthracene	53-70-3	0.055	8.2
Indeno(1,2,3-cd)pyrene	193-39-5	0.0055	3.4

K148
Residues from coal tar distillation, including, but not limited to, still bottoms.

Benz(a)anthracene	56-55-3	0.059	3.4
Benzo(a)pyrene	50-32-8	0.061	3.4
Benzo(b)fluoranthene	205-99-2	0.11	6.8
(difficult to			
distinguish from benzo-			
(k)fluoranthene)			
Benzo(k)fluoranthene	207-08-9	0.11	6.8
(difficult to			
distinguish from benzo-			
(b)fluoranthene)			
Chrysene	218-01-9	0.059	3.4
Dibenz(a,h)anthracene	53-70-3	0.055	8.2
Indeno(1,2,3-cd)pyrene	193-39-5	0.0055	3.4

K149
Distillation bottoms from the production of alpha- (or methyl-) chlorinated toluenes, ring-chlorinated toluenes, benzoyl chlorides, and compounds with mixtures of these functional groups. (This waste does not include still bottoms from the distillations of benzyl chloride.)

Chlorobenzene	108-90-7	0.057	6.0
Chloroform	67-66-3	0.046	6.0
Chloromethane	74-87-3	0.19	30
p-Dichlorobenzene	106-46-7	0.090	6.0
Hexachlorobenzene	118-74-1	0.055	10
Pentachlorobenzene	608-93-5	0.055	10
1,2,4,5-Tetrachloro-	95-94-3	0.055	14
benzene			
Toluene	108-88-3	0.080	10

POLLUTION CONTROL BOARD

NOTICE OF PROPOSED AMENDMENTS

K150
Organic residuals, excluding spent carbon adsorbent, from the spent chlorine gas and hydrochloric acid recovery processes associated with the production of alpha- (or methyl-) chlorinated toluenes, ring-chlorinated toluenes, benzoyl chlorides, and compounds with mixtures of these functional groups.

Carbon tetrachloride	56-23-5	0.057	6.0
Chloroform	67-66-3	0.046	6.0
Chloromethane	74-87-3	0.19	30
p-Dichlorobenzene	106-46-7	0.090	6.0
Hexachlorobenzene	118-74-1	0.055	10
Pentachlorobenzene	608-93-5	0.055	10
1,2,4,5-Tetrachloro-	95-94-3	0.055	14
benzene			
1,1,2,2-Tetrachloro-	79-34-5	0.057	6.0
ethane			
Tetrachloroethylene	127-18-4	0.056	6.0
1,2,4-Trichlorobenzene	120-82-1	0.055	19

K151
Wastewater treatment sludges, excluding neutralization and biological sludges, generated during the treatment of wastewaters from the production of alpha- (or methyl-) chlorinated toluenes, ring-chlorinated toluenes, benzoyl chlorides, and compounds with mixtures of these functional groups.

Benzene	71-43-2	0.14	10
Carbon tetrachloride	56-23-5	0.057	6.0
Chloroform	67-66-3	0.046	6.0
Hexachlorobenzene	118-74-1	0.055	10
Pentachlorobenzene	608-93-5	0.055	10
1,2,4,5-Tetrachloro-	95-94-3	0.055	14
benzene			
Tetrachloroethylene	127-18-4	0.056	6.0
Toluene	108-88-3	0.080	10

P001
Warfarin, & salts, when present at concentrations greater than 0.3%

Warfarin	81-81-2	(WETOX or	CMBST
		CHOXD) fb	
		CARBN; or	
		INCIN	

P002
1-Acetyl-2-thiourea

1-Acetyl-2-thiourea	591-08-2	(WETOX or	INCIN
		CHOXD) fb	
		CARBN; or	
		INCIN	

P003

POLLUTION CONTROL BOARD

NOTICE OF PROPOSED AMENDMENTS

Acrolein
Acrolein   107-02-6   0.29   CMBST

P004
Aldrin
Aldrin   309-00-2   0.021   0.06#

P005
Allyl alcohol
Allyl alcohol   107-18-6   (WETOX or CHOXD) fb CARBN; or INCIN   CMBST

P006
Aluminum phosphide
Aluminum phosphide   20859-73-8   CHOXD;CHRED; or INCIN   CHOXD;CHRED; or INCIN

P007
5-Aminomethyl-3-isoxazolol
5-Aminomethyl-3-isoxa-zolol   2763-96-4   (WETOX or CHOXD) fb CARBN; or INCIN   INCIN

P008
4-Aminopyridine
4-Aminopyridine   504-24-5   (WETOX or CHOXD) fb CARBN; or INCIN   INCIN

P009
Ammonium picrate
Ammonium picrate   131-74-8   CHOXD; CHRED; CARBN; BIODG; or INCIN   CHOXD; CHRED; or CMBST

P010
Arsenic acid
Arsenic   7440-38-2   1.4   5.0 mg/l TCLP

P011
Arsenic pentoxide
Arsenic   7440-38-2   1.4   5.0 mg/l TCLP

POLLUTION CONTROL BOARD

NOTICE OF PROPOSED AMENDMENTS

P012
Arsenic trioxide
Arsenic   7440-38-2   1.4   5.0 mg/l TCLP

013
Barium cyanide
Barium   7440-39-3   NA   7.6 mg/l TCLP
Cyanides (Total)(7)   57-12-5   A   590
Cyanides (Amendable)(7)   57-12-5   0.86   30

P014
Thiophenol (Benzene thiol)
Thiophenol (Benzene thiol)   108-98-5   (WETOX or CHOXD) fb CARBN; or INCIN   INCIN

P015
Beryllium dust
Beryllium   7440-41-7   RMETL; or RTHRM   RMETL; or RTHRM

P016
Dichloromethyl ether (Bis(chloromethyl)ether)
Dichloromethyl ether   542-88-1   (WETOX or CHOXD) fb CARBN; or INCIN   INCIN

P017
Bromoacetone
Bromoacetone   598-31-2   (WETOX or CHOXD) fb CARBN; or INCIN   INCIN

P018
Brucine
Brucine   357-57-3   (WETOX or CHOXD) fb CARBN; or INCIN   INCIN

P020
2-sec-Butyl-4,6-dinitrophenol (Dinoseb)
2-sec-Butyl-4,6-dinitro-phenol (Dinoseb)   88-85-7   0.066   2.5

POLLUTION CONTROL BOARD

NOTICE OF PROPOSED AMENDMENTS

P021
Calcium cyanide

Cyanides (Total)(7)	57-12-5	1.2	590
Cyanides (Amenable)(7)	57-12-5	0.86	30

P022
Carbon idisulfide

| Carbon disulfide | 75-15-0 | 3.8 | INCIN |
| Carbon disulfide; alternate(6) standard for nonwastewaters only | 75-15-0 | NA | 4.8 mg/l TCLP |

P023
Chloroacetaldehyde

| Chloroacetaldehyde | 107-20-0 | (WETOX or CHOXD) fb CARBN; or INCIN | INCIN |

P024
p-Chloroaniline

| p-Chloroaniline | 106-47-8 | .046 | 16 |

P026
1-(o-Chlorophenyl)thiourea

| 1-(o-Chlorophenyl)thio-urea | 5344-82-1 | (WETOX or CHOXD) fb CARBN; or INCIN | INCIN |

P027
3-Chloropropionitrile

| 3-Chloropropionitrile | 542-76-7 | (WETOX or CHOXD) fb CARBN; or INCIN | INCIN |

P028
Benzyl chloride

| Benzyl chloride | 100-44-7 | (WETOX or CHOXD) fb CARBN; or INCIN | INCIN |

P029
Copper cyanide

| Cyanides (Total)(7) | 57-12-5 | 1.2 | 590 |
| Cyanides (Amenable)(7) | 57-12-5 | 0.86 | 30 |

POLLUTION CONTROL BOARD

NOTICE OF PROPOSED AMENDMENTS

P030
Cyanides (soluble salts and complexes)

Cyanides (Total)(7)	57-12-5	1.2	590
Cyanides (Amenable)(7)	57-12-5	0.86	30

P031
Cyanogen

| Cyanogen | 460-19-5 | CHOXD; WETOX; or INCIN | CHOXD; WETOX; or INCIN |

P033
Cyanogen chloride

| Cyanogen chloride | 506-77-4 | CHOXD; WETOX; or INCIN | CHOXD; WETOX; or INCIN |

P034
2-Cyclohexyl-4,6-dinitrophenol

| 2-Cyclohexyl-4,6-dinitrophenol | 131-89-5 | (WETOX or CHOXD) fb CARBN; or INCIN | INCIN |

P036
Dichlorophenylarsine

| Arsenic | 7440-38-2 | 1.4 | 5.0 mg/l TCLP |

P037
Dieldrin

| Dieldrin | 60-57-1 | 0.017 | 0.13 |

P038
Diethylarsine

| Arsenic | 7440-38-2 | 1.4 | 5.0 mg/l TCLP |

P039
Disulfoton

| Disulfoton | 298-04-4 | 0.017 | 6.2 |

P040
o,o-Diethyl-o-pyraxinyl-phosphorothioate

| o,o-Diethyl-o-pyraxinyl-phosphorothioate | 297-97-2 | CARBN; or INCIN | CMBST |

P041
Diethyl-p-nitrophenyl phosphate

| Diethyl-p-nitrophenyl phosphate | 311-45-5 | CARBN; or INCIN | CMBST |

P042			
Epinephrine			
Epinephrine	51-43-4	(WETOX or CHOXD) fb CARBN; or INCIN	INCIN
P043			
Diisopropylfluorophosphate (DFP)			
Diisopropylfluoro-phosphate (DFP)	55-91-4	CARBN; or INCIN	CMBST
P044			
Dimethoate			
Dimethoate	60-51-5	CARBN; or INCIN	CMBST
P045			
Thiofanox			
Thiofanox	39196-18-4	(WETOX or CHOXD) fb CARBN; or INCIN	INCIN
P046			
alpha,alpha-Dimethylphenethylamine			
alpha,alpha-Dimethyl-phenethylamine	122-09-8	(WETOX or CHOXD) fb CARBN; or INCIN	INCIN
P047			
4,6-Dinitro-o-cresol			
4,6-Dinitro-o-cresol	543-52-1	0.28	160
P047			
4,6-Dinitro-o-cresol salts			
NA	NA	(WETOX or CHOXD) fb CARBN; or INCIN	INCIN
P048			
2,4-Dinitrophenol	51-28-5	0.12	160
P049			
Dithiobiuret			
Dithiobiuret	541-53-7	(WETOX or	INCIN

		CHOXD) fb CARBN; or INCIN	
P050			
Endosulfan			
Endosulfan I	939-98-8	0.023	0.066
Endosulfan II	33213-6-5	0.029	0.13
Endosulfan sulfate	1031-07-8	0.029	0.13
P051			
Endrin			
Endrin	72-20-8	0.0028	0.13
Endrin aldehyde	7421-93-4	0.025	0.13
P054			
Aziridine			
Aziridine	151-56-4	(WETOX or CHOXD) fb CARBN; or INCIN	INCIN
P056			
Fluorine			
Fluoride (measured in wastewaters only)	16964-48-8	35	ADGAS fb NEUT
P057			
Fluoroacetamide			
Fluoroacetamide	640-19-7	(WETOX or CHOXD) fb CARBN; or INCIN	INCIN
P058			
Fluoroacetic acid, sodium salt			
Fluoroacetic acid, sodium salt	62-74-8	(WETOX or CHOXD) fb CARBN; or INCIN	INCIN
P059			
Heptachlor			
Heptachlor	76-44-8	0.0012	0.066
Heptachlor epoxide	1024-57-3	0.016	0.066
P060			

POLLUTION CONTROL BOARD

NOTICE OF PROPOSED AMENDMENTS

Isodrin			
Isodrin	465-73-6	0.021	0.066
P062			
Hexaethyl tetraphosphate			
Hexaethyl tetraphosphate	757-58-4	CARBN; or INCIN	CMBST
P063			
Hydrogen cyanide			
Cyanides (Total)(7)	57-12-5	1.2	590
Cyanides (Amenable)(7)	57-12-5	0.86	30
P064			
Isocyanic acid, ethyl ester			
Isocyanic acid, ethyl ester	624-83-9	(WETOX or CHOXD) fb CARBN; or INCIN	INCIN

P065 (mercury fulminate)) nonwastewaters, regardless of their total mercury content, that are not incinerator residues or are not residues from RMERC.

Mercury	7439-97-6	NA	IMERC

P065 (mercury fulminate) nonwastewaters that are either incinerator residues or are residues from RMERC; and contain greater than or equal to 260 mg/kg total mercury.

Mercury	7339-97-6	RMERC	

P065 (mercury fulminate) nonwastewaters that are residues from RMERC and contain less than 260 mg/kg total mercury.

Mercury	7439-97-6	NA	0.20 mg/l TCLP

P065 (mercury fulminate) nonwastewaters that ar incinerator residues and contain less than 260 mg/kg total mercury.

Mercury	7439-97-6	NA	0.025 mg/l TCLP

P065 All P065 (mercury fulminate) wastewaters.

Mercury	7439-97-6	0.15	NA

P066

POLLUTION CONTROL BOARD

NOTICE OF PROPOSED AMENDMENTS

Methomyl			
Methomyl	16752-77-5	(WETOX or CHOXD) fb CARBN; or INCIN	INCIN
P067			
2-Methyl-aziridine			
2-Methyl-aziridine	75-55-8	(WETOX or CHOXD fb CARBN; or INCIN	INCIN
P068			
Methyl hydrazine			
Methyl hydrazine	60-34-4	CHOXD; CHRED; CARBN; BIODG; or INCIN	CHOXD; CHRED; or CMBST
P069			
2-Methyllactonitrile			
2-Methyllactonitrile	75-86-5	(WETOX or CHOXD) fb CARBN; or INCIN	INCIN
P070			
Aldicarb			
Aldicarb	116-06-2	(WETOX or CHOXD) fb CARBN; or INCIN	INCIN
P071			
Methyl parathion			
Methyl parathion	298-00-0	0.014	4.6
P072			
1-Naphthyl-2-thiourea			
1-Naphthyl-2-thiourea	86-88-4	(WETOX or CHOXD) fb CARBN; or INCIN	INCIN
P073			
Nickel carbonyl			
Nickel	7440-02-0	3.98	5.0 mg/l TCLP

POLLUTION CONTROL BOARD

NOTICE OF PROPOSED AMENDMENTS

P074
Nickel cyanide
Cyanides (Total)(7)	57-12-5	1.2	590
Cyanides (Amenable)(7)	57-12-5	0.86	30
Nickel	7440-02-0	3.98	5.0 mg/l TCLP

P075
Nicotine and salts
| Nicotine and salts | 54-11-5 | (WETOX or CHOXD) fb CARBN; or INCIN | INCIN |

P076
Nitric oxide
| Nitric oxide | 10102-43-9 | ADGAS | ADGAS |

P077
p-Nitroaniline
| p-Nitroaniline | 100-01-6 | 0.028 | 28 |

P078
Nitrogen dioxide
| Nitrogen dioxide | 10102-44-0 | ADGAS | ADGAS |

P081
Nitroglycerin
| Nitroglycerin | 55-63-0 | CHOXD; CHRED; CARBN; BIODG or INCIN | CHOXD; CHRED; or CMBST |

P082
N-Nitrosodimethylamine
| N-Nitrosodimethylamine | 62-75-9 | 0.40 | 2.3 |

P084
N-Nitrosomethylvinylamine
| N-Nitrosomethylvinyl-amine | 4549-40-0 | (WETOX or CHOXD) fb CARBN;or INCIN | INCIN |

P085
Octamethylpyrophosphoramide
| Octamethylpyrophosphor-amide | 152-16-9 | CARBN; or INCIN | CMBST |

P087

POLLUTION CONTROL BOARD

NOTICE OF PROPOSED AMENDMENTS

Osmium tetroxide
| Osmium tetroxide | 20816-12-0 | RMETL;or RTHRM | RMETL; or RTHRM |

P088
Endothall
| Endothall | 145-73-3 | (WETOX or CHOXD) fb CARBN; or INCIN | CMBST |

P089
Parathion
| Parathion | 56-38-2 | 0.014 | 4.6 |

P092
P092 (phenyl mercuric acetate) nonwastewaters, regardless of their total mercury content, that are not incinerator residues or are not residues from RMERC.
| Mercury | 7439-97-6 | NA | IMERC; or RMERC |

P092
P092 (phenyl mercuric acetate) nonwastewaters that are either incinerator residues or are residues from RMERC; and still contain greater than or equal to 260 mg/kg total mercury.
| Mercury | 7439-97-6 | NA | RMERC |

P092
P092 (phenyl mercuric acetate) nonwastewaters that are residues from RMERC and contain less than 260 mg/kg total mercury.
| Mercury | 7439-97-6 | NA | 0.20 mg/l TCLP |

P092
P092 (phenyl mercuric acetate) nonwastewaters that are incinerator residues and contain less than 260 mg/kg total mercury.
| Mercury | 7439-97-6 | NA | 0.025 mg/l TCLP |

P092
All P092 (phenyl mercuric acetate) wastewaters.
| Mercury | 7439-97-6 | 0.15 | NA |

P093
Phenylthiourea
| Phenylthiourea | 103-85-5 | (WETOX or CHOXD) fb CARBN; or | INCIN |

POLLUTION CONTROL BOARD

NOTICE OF PROPOSED AMENDMENTS

INCIN

P094
Phorate
| Phorate | 298-02-2 | 0.021 | 4.6 |

P095
Phosgene
| Phosgene | 75-44-5 | (WETOX or CHOXD) fb CARBN; or INCIN | INCIN |

P096
Phosphine
| Phosphine | 7803-51-2 | CHOXD; CHRED; or INCIN | CHOXD; CHRED; or INCIN |

P097
Famphur
| Famphur | 52-85-7 | 0.017 | 15 |

P098
Potassium cyanide
| Cyanides (Total)(7) | 57-12-5 | 1.2 | 590 |
| Cyanides (Amenable(7) | 57-12-5 | 0.86 | 30 |

P099
Potassium silver cyanide
Cyanides (Total)(7)	57-12-5	1.2	590
Cyanides (Amenable)(7)	57-12-5	0.86	30
Silver	7440-22-4	0.43	0.30mg/l TCLP

P101
Ethyl cyanide (Propanenitrile)
| Ethyl cyanide (Propanenitrile) | 107-12-0 | 0.24 | 360 |

P102
Propargyl alcohol
| Propargyl alcohol | 107-19-7 | (WETOX or CHOXD) fb CARBN; or INCIN | CMBST |

P103
Selenourea
| Selenium | 7782-49-2 | 0.82 | 0.16 mg/l TCLP |

POLLUTION CONTROL BOARD

NOTICE OF PROPOSED AMENDMENTS

P104
Silver cyanide
Cyanides (Total)(7)	57-12-5	1.2	590
Cyanides (Amenable)(7)	57-12-5	0.86	30
Silver	7440-22-4	0.43	0.30 mg/l TCLP

P105
Sodium azide
| Sodium azide | 26628-22-8 | CHOXD; CHRED; CARBN; BIODG; or INCIN | CHOXD; CHRED; or CMBST |

P106
Sodium cyanide
| Cyanides (Total)(7) | 57-12-5 | 1.2 | 590 |
| Cyanides (Amenable)(7) | 57-12-5 | 0.86 | 30 |

P108
Strychnine and salts
| Strychnine and salts | 57-24-9 | (WETOX or CHOXD) fb CARBN; or INCIN | INCIN |

P109
Tetraethyldithiopyrophosphate
| Tetraethyldithiopyro-phosphate | 3689-24-5 | CARBN; or INCIN | CMBST |

P110
Tetraethyl lead
| lead | 7439-92-1 | 0.69 | 0.37 mg/l TCLP |

P111
Tetraethylpyrophosphate
| Tetraethylpyrophosphate | 107-49-3 | CARBN; or INCIN | CMBST |

P112
Tetranitromethane
| Tetranitromethane | 509-14-8 | CHOXD; CHRED; CARBN; BIODG; or INCIN | CHOXD; CHRED; or CMBST |

P113
Thallic oxide
| Thallium (measured in wastewaters only) | 7440-28-0 | 1.4 | RTHRM; or STABL |

POLLUTION CONTROL BOARD

NOTICE OF PROPOSED AMENDMENTS

P114
Thallium selenite
Selenium   7782-49-2   0.82   0.16mg/l TCLP

P115
Thallium (I) sulfate
Thallium (measured in   7440-28-0   1.4   RTHRM; or
wastewaters only)   STABL

P116
Thiosemicarbazide
Thiosemicarbazide   79-19-6   (WETOX or   INCIN
                          CHOXD) fb
                          CARBN; or
                          INCIN

P118
Trichloromethanethiol
Trichloromethanethiol   75-70-7   (WETOX or   INCIN
                          CHOXD) fb
                          CARBN; or
                          INCIN

P119
Ammonium vanadate
Vanadium (measured in   7440-62-2   4.3   STABL
wastewaters only)

P120
Vanadium pentoxide
Vanadium (measured in   7440-62-2   4.3   STABL
wastewaters only)

P121
Zinc cyanide
Cyanides (Total)(7)   57-12-5   1.2   590
Cyanides (Amenable)(7)   57-12-5   0.86   30

P122
Zinc phosphide Zn[1]P[2], when present at concentrations greater than 10%
Zinc Phosphide   1314-84-7   CHOXD; CHRED;   CHOXD; CHRED;
                         or INCIN   or INCIN

P123
Toxaphene
Toxaphene   8001-35-2   0.0095   2.6

U001

POLLUTION CONTROL BOARD

NOTICE OF PROPOSED AMENDMENTS

Acetaldehyde
Acetaldehyde   75-07-0   (WETOX or   CMBST
                       CHOXD) fb
                       CARBN; or
                       INCIN

U002
Acetone
Acetone   67-64-1   0.28   160

U003
Acetonitrile
Acetonitrile   75-05-8   5.6   INCIN
Acetonitrile; alternate(6)u75-05-8   NA   1.8
standard for
nonwastewaters only

U004
Acetophenone
Acetophenone   98-86-2   0.010   9.7

U005
2-Acetylaminofluorene
2-Acetylaminofluorene   53-96-3   0.059   140

U006
Acetyl chloride
Acetyl chloride   75-36-5   (WETOX or   INCIN
                          CHOXD) fb
                          CARBN; or
                          INCIN

U007
Acrylamide
Acrylamide   79-06-1   (WETOX or   INCIN
                          CHOXD) fb
                          CARBN; or
                          INCIN

U008
Acrylic acid
Acrylic acid   79-10-7   (WETOX or   CMBST
                          CHOXD) fb
                          CARBN; or
                          INCIN

U009
Acrylonitrile

POLLUTION CONTROL BOARD

NOTICE OF PROPOSED AMENDMENTS

Acrylonitrile	107-13-1	0.24	84
U010 Mitomycin C Mitomycin C	50-07-7	(WETOX or CHOXD) fb CARBN; or INCIN	INCIN
U011 Amitrole Amitrole	61-82-5	(WETOX or CHOXD) fb CARBN; or INCIN	INCIN
U012 Aniline Aniline	62-53-3	0.81	14
U014 Auramine Auramine	492-80-8	(WETOX or CHOXD) fb CARBN; or INCIN	INCIN
U015 Azaserine Azaserine	115-02-6	(WETOX or CHOXD) fb CARBN; or INCIN	INCIN
U016 Benz(c)acridine Benz(c)acridine	225-51-4	(WETOX or CHOXD) fb CARBN; or INCIN	CMBST
U017 Benzal chloride Benzal chloride	98-87-3	(WETOX or CHOXD) fb CARBN; or INCIN	INCIN

POLLUTION CONTROL BOARD

NOTICE OF PROPOSED AMENDMENTS

U018 Benz(a)anthracene Benz(a)anthracene	56-55-3	0.059	3.4
U-19 Benzene Benzene	71-43-2	0.14	10
U020 Benzenesulfonyl chloride Benzenesulfonyl chloride	98-09-9	(WETOX or CHOXD) fb CARBN; or INCIN	INCIN
U021 Benzidine Benzidine	92-87-5	(WETOX or CHOXD) fb CARBN; or INCIN	INCIN
U022 Benzo(a)pyrene Benzo(a)pyrene	50-32-8	0.061	3.4
U023 Benzotrichloride Benzotrichloride	98-07-7	CHOXD; CHRED; CARBN; BIODG; or INCIN	CHOXD; CHRED; or CMBST
U024 bis(2-Chloroethoxy)methane bis(2-Chloroethoxy)-methane	111-91-1	0.036	7.2
U025 bis(2-Chloroethyl)ether bis(2-Chloroethyl)ether	111-44-4	0.033	6.0
U026 Chlornaphazine Chlornaphazine	494-03-1	(WETOX or CHOXD) fb CARBN; INCIN	INCIN

POLLUTION CONTROL BOARD

NOTICE OF PROPOSED AMENDMENTS

POLLUTION CONTROL BOARD

NOTICE OF PROPOSED AMENDMENTS

U027 bis(2-Chloroisopropyl)ether bis(2-Chloroisopropyl) ether	39638-32-9	0.055	7.2
U028 bis(2-Ethylhexyl)phthalate bis(2-Ethylhexyl)-phthalate	117-81-7	0.28	28
U029 Methyl bromide (Bromomethane) Methyl bromide (Bromo-methane)	74-83-9	0.11	15
U030 4-Bromophenyl phenyl ether 4-Bromophenyl phenyl ether	101-55-3	0.055	15
U031 n-Butyl alcohol n-Butyl alcohol	71-36-3	5.6	2.6
U032 Calcium chromate Chromium (Total)	7440-47-3	2.77	0.86 mg/l TCLP
U033 Carbon oxyfluoride Carbon oxyfluoride	353-50-4	(WETOX or CHOXD) fb CARBN; or INCIN	INCIN
U034 Trichloroacetaldehyde (Chloral) Trichloroacetaldehyde (Chloral)	75-87-6	(WETOX or CHOXD) fb CARBN; or INCIN	INCIN
U035 Chlorambucil Chlorambucil	305-03-3	(WETOX or CHOXD) fb CARBN; or INCIN	INCIN

U036 Chlordane Chlordane (alpha and gamma isomers)	57-74-9	0.0033	
U037 Chlorobenzene Chlorobenzene	108-90-7	0.057	
U038 Chlorobenzilate Chlorobenzilate	510-15-6	0.10	
U039 p-Chloro-m-cresol p-Chloro-m-cresol	59-50-7	0.018	
U041 Epichlorohydrin (1-Chloro-2,3-epoxypropane) Epichlorohydrin (1-Chloro-2,3-epoxypropane)	106-89-8	(WETOX or CHOXD) fb CARBN; or INCIN	
U042 2-Chloroethyl vinyl ether 2-Chloroethyl vinyl ether	110-75-8	0.062	
U043 Vinyl chloride Vinyl chloride	75-01-4	0.27	6.0
U044 Chloroform Chloroform	67-66-3	0.046	6.0
U045 Chloromethane (Methyl chloride) Chloromethane (Methyl chloride)	74-87-3	0.19	30
U046 Chloromethyl methyl ether Chloromethyl methyl ether	107-30-2	(WETOX or CHOXD) fb	INC

POLLUTION CONTROL BOARD

NOTICE OF PROPOSED AMENDMENTS

		CARBN; or INCIN	
U047 2-Chloronaphthalene			
2-Chloronaphthalene	91-58-7	0.055	5.6
U048 2-Chlorophenol			
2-Chlorophenol	95-57-8	0.044	5.7
U049 4-Chloro-o-toluidine hydrochloride			
4-Chloro-o-toluidine hydrochloride	3165-93-3	(WETOX or CHOXD) fb CARBN; or INCIN	INCIN
U050 Chrysene			
Chrysene	218-01-9	0.059	3.4
U051 Creosote			
Naphthalene	91-20-3	0.059	5.6
Pentachlorophenol	87-86-5	0.089	7.4
Phenanthrene	85-01-8	0.059	5.6
Pyrene	129-00-0	0.067	8.2
Toluene	108-88-3	0.080	10
Xylenes-mixed isomers (sum of o-, m-, and p-xylene concentrations)	1330-20-7	0.32	30
Lead	7439-92-1	0.69	0.37 mg/l TCLP
U052 Cresols (Cresylic acid)			
o-Cresol	95-48-7	0.11	5.6
m-Cresol (difficult to distinguish from p-cresol)	108-39-4	0.77	5.6
p-Cresol (difficult to distinguish from m-cresol)	106-44-5	0.77	5.6
Cresol-mixed isomers (Cresylic acid) (sum of o-, m-, and p-cresol concentrations)	1319-77-3	0.88	11.2

POLLUTION CONTROL BOARD

NOTICE OF PROPOSED AMENDMENTS

U053 Crotonaldehyde			
Crotonaldehyde	4170-30-3	(WETOX or CHOXD) fb CARBN; or INCIN	CMBST
U055 Cumene			
Cumene	98-82-8	(WETOX or CHOXD) fb CARBN; or INCIN	CMBST
U056 Cyohexane			
Cyclohexane	110-82-7	(WETOX or CHOXD) fb CARBN; or INCIN	CMBST
U057 Cyclohexanone			
Cyclohexanone	108-94-1	0.36	CMBST
Cyclohexanone; alternate(6) standard for nonwastewaters only	108-94-1	NA	0.75
U058 Cyclophosphamide			
Cyclophosphamide	50-18-0	CARBN; or INCIN	CMBST
U059 Daunomycin			
Daunomycin	20830-81-3	(WETOX or CHOXD) fb CARBN; or INCIN	INCIN
U060 DDD			
o,p'-DDD	53-19-0	0.023	0.087
p,p'-DDD	72-54-8	0.023	0.087
U061 DDT			
o,p'-DDT	789-02-6	0.0339	0.087

POLLUTION CONTROL BOARD

NOTICE OF PROPOSED AMENDMENTS

p,p'DDT	50-29-3	0.0039	0.087
o,p'-DDD	53-19-0	0.023	0.087
p,p'-DDD	72-54-8	0.023	0.087
o,p'-DDE	3424-82-6	0.031	0.087
p,p'-DDE	72-55-9	0.031	0.087

U062
Diallate
| Diallate | 2303-16-4 | (WETOX or CHOXD) fb CARBN; or INCIN | INCIN |

U063
Dibenz(a,h)anthracene
| Dibenz(a,h)anthracene | 53-70-3 | 0.055 | 8.2 |

U064
Dibenz(a,i)pyrene
| Dibenz(a,i)pyrene | 189-55-9 | (WETOX or CHOXD) fb CARBN; or INCIN | CMBST |

U066
1,2-Dibromo-3-chloro-propane 1,2-Dibromo-3O chloropropane
| | 96-12-8 | 0.11 | 15 |

U067
Ethylene dibromide (1,2-Dibromoethane)
Ethylene dibromide (1,2- Dibromoethane)
| | 106-93-4 | 0.028 | 15 |

U068
Dibromoethane
Dibromomethane)
| | 74-95-3 | 0.11 | 15 |

U069
Di-n-butyl phthalate
| Di-n-butyl phthalate | 84-74-2 | 0.057 | 28 |

U070
o-Dichlorobenzene
| o-Dichlorobenzene | 95-50-1 | 0.088 | 6.0 |

U071
m-Dichlorobenzend

POLLUTION CONTROL BOARD

NOTICE OF PROPOSED AMENDMENTS

| m-Dichlorobenzend | 541-73-1 | 0.036 | 6.0 |

U072
p-Dichlorobenzend
| p-Dichlorobenzene | 106-46-7 | 0.090 | 6.0 |

U073
3,3'-Dichlorobenzidine
| 3,3'-Dichlorobenzidine | 91-94-1 | (WETOX or CHOXD) fb CARBN; or INCIN | INCI |

U074
1,4-Dichloro-2-butene
| cis-1,4-Dichloro-2-butene | 1476-11-5 | (WETOX or CARBN; or INCIN | |
| trans-1,4-Dichloro-2-butene | 764-41-0 | (WETOX or CHOXD) fb INCIN | |

U075
Dichlorodifluoromethane
| Dichlorodifluoromethane | 75-71-8 | 0.23 | 7.2 |

U076
1,1-Dichloroethane
| 1,1-Dichloroethane | 75-34-3 | 0.059 | 6.0 |

U077
1,2-Dichloroethane
| 1,2-Dichloroethane | 107-06-2 | 0.21 | 6.0 |

U078
1,1-Dichloroethylene
| 1,1-Dichloroethylene | 75-35-4 | 0.025 | 6.0 |

U079
1,2-Dichloroethylene
| trans-1,2-Dichloro-ethylene | 156-60-5 | 0.054 | 30 |

U080
Methylene chloride
| Methylene chloride | 75-09-2 | 0.089 | 30 |

U081

POLLUTION CONTROL BOARD

NOTICE OF PROPOSED AMENDMENTS

2,4-Dichlorophenol			
2,4-Dichlorophenol	120-83-2	0.044	14
U082			
2,6-Dichlorophenol			
2,6-Dichlorophenol	87-65-0	0.044	14
U083			
1,2-Dichloropropane			
1,2-Dichloropropane	78-87-5	0.85	18
U084			
1,3-Dichloropropylene			
cis-1,3-Dichloro-propylene	10061-01-5	0.036	18
trans-1,3-Dichlorol propylene	10061-02-6	0.036	18
U085			
1,2;3,4-Diepoxybutane			
1,2;3,4-Diepoxybutane	1464-53-5	(WETOX or CHOXD) fb CARBN; or INCIN	CMBST
U086			
N,N'-Diethylhydrazine			
N,N'-Diethylhydrazine	1615-80-1	CHOXD; CHRED; CARBN; BIODG; or INCIN	CHOXD; CHRED; or CMBST
U087			
O,O-Diethyl S-methyldithiophosphate			
O,O-Diethyl S-methyl-dithiophosphate	3288-58-2	CARBN; or INCIN	CMBST
U088			
Diethyl phthalate			
Diethyl phthalate	84-66-2	0.20	28
U089			
Diethyl stilbestrol			
Diethyl stilbestrol	56-53-1	(WETOX or CHOXD) fb CARBN; or INCIN	CMBST
U090			

POLLUTION CONTROL BOARD

NOTICE OF PROPOSED AMENDMENTS

Dihydrosafrole			
Dihydrosafrole	94-58-6	(WETOX or CHOXD) fb CARBN; or INCIN	CMBST
U091			
3,3'-Dimethoxybenzidine			
3,3'-Dimethoxybenzidine	119-90-4	(WETOX or CHOXD) fb CARBN; or INCIN	INCIN
U092			
Dimethylamine			
Dimethylamine	124-40-3	(WETOX or CHOXD) fb CARBN; or INCIN	INCIN
U093			
p-Dimethylaminoazobenzene			
p-Dimethyl-aminoazobenzene	60-11-7	0.13	INCIN
U094			
7,12-Dimethylbenz(a) anthracene			
7,12-Dimethylbenz(a)-anthracene	57-97-6	(WETOX or CHOXD) fb CARBN; or INCIN	CMBST
U095			
3,3'-Dimethylbenzidine			
3,3'-Dimethylbenzidine	119-93-7	(WETOX or CHOXD) fb CARBN; or INCIN	INCIN
U096			
alpha, alpha-Dimethyl benzyl hydroperoxide			
alpha, alpha-Dimethyl benzyl hydroperoxide	80-15-9	CHOXD; CHRED; CARBN; BIODG; or INCIN	CHOXD; CHRED; or CMBST
U097			
Dimethylcarbamoyl chloride			
Dimethylcarbamoyl chloride	79-44-7	(WETOX or CHOXD) fb CARBN; or INCIN	INCIN

POLLUTION CONTROL BOARD

NOTICE OF PROPOSED AMENDMENTS

U098
1,1-Dimethylhydrazine
1,1-Dimethylhydrazine	57-14-7	CHOXD; CHRED; CARBN; BIODG; or INCIN	CHOXD; CHRED; or CMBST

U099
1,2-Dimethylhydrazine
| 1,2-Dimethylhydrazine | 540-73-8 | CHOXD; CHRED; CARBN; BIODG; or INCIN | CHOXD; CHRED; or CMBST |

U101
2,4-Dimethylphenol
| 2,4-Dimethylphenol | 105-67-9 | 0.036 | 14 |

U102
Dimethyl phthalate
| Dimethyl phthalate | 131-11-3 | 0.047 | 28 |

U103
Dimethyl sulfate
| Dimethyl sulfate | 77-78-1 | CHOXD; CHRED; CARBN; BIODG; or INCIN | CHOXD; CHRED; or CMBST |

U105
2,4-Dinitrotoluene
| 2,4-Dinitrotoluene | 121-14-2 | 032 | 140 |

U106
2,6-Dinitrotoluene
| 2,6-Dinitrotoluene | 606-20-2 | 0.55 | 28 |

U107
Di-n-octyl phthalate
| Di-n-octyl phthalate | 117-84-0 | 0.017 | 28 |

U108
1,4-Dioxane
| 1,4-Dioxane | 123-91-1 | (WETOX or CHOXD) fb CARBN; or INCIN | CMBST |
| 1,4-Dioxane; alternate (6) standard for nonwastewaters only | 123-91-1 | NA | 170 |

POLLUTION CONTROL BOARD

NOTICE OF PROPOSED AMENDMENTS

U109
1,2-Diphenylhydrazine
1,2-Diphenylhydrazine	122-66-7	CHOXD; CHRED; CARBN; BIODG; or INCIN	CHOXD; CHRED; or CMBST
1,2-Diphenylhydrazine; alternate(6) standard for wastewaters only	122-66-7	0.087	NA

U110
Dipropylamine
| Dipropylamine | 142-84-7 | (WETOX or CHOXD) fb CARBN; or INCIN | INCIN |

U111
Di-n-propylnitrosamine
| Di-n-propylnitrosamine | 621-64-7 | 0.40 | 14 |

U112
Ethyl acetate
| Ethyl acetate | 141-78-6 | 0.34 | 33 |

U113
Ethyl acrylate
| Ethyl acrylate | 140-88-5 | (WETOX or CHOXD) fb CARBN; or INCIN | CMBST |

U114
Ethylenebisdithiocarbamic acid salts and esters
| Ethylenebisdithio-Carbamic acid | 111-54-6 | (WETOX or CHOXD) fb CARBN; or INCIN | INCIN |

U115
Ethylene oxide
| Ethylene oxide; | 75-21-8 | (WETOX or CHOXD) fb CARBN; or INCIN | CHOXD; or INCIN |
| Ethylene oxide; alternate(6) standard for wastewaters only | 75-21-8 | 0.12 | NA |

POLLUTION CONTROL BOARD

NOTICE OF PROPOSED AMENDMENTS

U116
Ethylene thiourea
Ethylene thiourea   96-45-7   (WETOX or   INCIN
                                CHOXD) fb
                                CARBN; or
                                INCIN

U117
Ethyl ether
Ethyl ether   60-29-7   0.12   160

U118
Ethyl methacrylate
Ethyl methacrylate   97-63-2   0.14   160

U119
Ethyl methane sulfonate
Ethyl methane sulfonate 62-50-0 (WETOX or   INCIN
                                CHOXD) fb
                                CARBN; or
                                INCIN

U120
Fluoranthene
Fluoranthene   206-44-0   0.068   3.4

U121
Trichloromonofluoromethane
Trichloromonofluoro- 75-69-4   0.020   .30
methane

U122
Formaldehyde
Formaldehyde   50-00-0   (WETOX or   CMBST
                                CHOXD) fb
                                CARBN; or
                                INCIN

U123
Formic acid
Formic acid   64-18-6   (WETOX or   CMBST
                                CHOXD) fb
                                CARBN; or
                                INCIN

U124
Furan
Furan   110-00-9   (WETOX or   CMBST

POLLUTION CONTROL BOARD

NOTICE OF PROPOSED AMENDMENTS

                                CHOXD) fb
                                CARBN; or
                                INCIN

U125
Furfural
Furfural   98-01-1   (WETOX or   CMBST
                                CHOXD) fb
                                CARBN; or
                                INCIN

U126
Glycidylaldehyde
Glycidylaldehyde   765-34-4   (WETOX or   CMBST
                                CHOXD) fb
                                CARBN; or
                                INCIN

U127
Hexachlorobenzene
Hexachlorobenzene   118-74-1   0.055   10

U128
Hexachlorobutadiene
Hexachlorobutadiene 87-68-3   0.055   5.6

U129
Lindane
  alpha-BHC   319-84-6   0.00014   0.066
  beta-BHC)   319-85-7   0.00014   0.066
  delta-BHC   319-86-8   0.033   0.066
  gamma-BHC (Lindane) 58-89-9   0.0017   0.066

U130
Hexachlorocyclopentadiene
Hexachlorocyclopenta- 77-47-4 0.057   2.4
diene

U131
Hexachloroethane
Hexachloroethane   67-72-1   0.055   10

U132
Hexachlorophene
Hexachlorophene   70-30-4   (WETOX or   INCIN
                                CHOXD) fb
                                CARBN; or
                                INCIN

POLLUTION CONTROL BOARD

NOTICE OF PROPOSED AMENDMENTS

U133
Hydrazine

| Hydrazine | 302-01-2 | CHOXD; CHRED; CARBN; BIODG; or INCIN | CHOXD; CHRED; or CMBST |

U134
Hydrogen fluoride

| Fluoride (measured in wastewaters only) | 16964-48-8 | 35 | ADGAS fb NEUTR; or NEUTR |

U135
Hydrogen sulfide

| Hydrogen sulfide | 7783-06-4 | CHOXD; CHRED; or INCIN | CHOXD; CHRED; or INCIN |

U136
Cacodylic acid

| Arsenic | 7440-38-2 | 1.4 | 5.0 mg/l TCLP |

U137
Indeno(1,2,3-cd)pyrene

| Indeno(1,2,3-cd)pyrene | 193-39-5 | 0.0055 | 3.4 |

U138
Iodomethane

| Iodomethane | 74-88-4 | 0.19 | 65 |

U140
Isobutyl alcohol

| Isobutyl alcohol | 78-83-1 | 5.6 | 170 |

U141
Isosafrole

| Isosafrole | 120-58-1 | 0.081 | 2.6 |

U142
Kepone

| Kepone | 143-50-8 | 0.0011 | 0.13 |

U143
Lasiocarpine

| Lasiocarpine | 303-34-4 | (WETOX or CHOXD) fb CARBN; or INCIN | INCIN |

POLLUTION CONTROL BOARD

NOTICE OF PROPOSED AMENDMENTS

U144
Lead acetate

| Lead | 7439-92-1 | 0.69 | 0.37 mg/l TCLP |

U145
Lead phosphate

| Lead | 7439-92-1 | 0.69 | 0.37 mg/l TCLP |

U146
Lead subacetate

| Lead | 7439-92-1 | 0.69 | 0.37 mg/l TCLP |

U147
Maleic anhydride

| Maleic anhydride | 108-31-6 | (WETOX or CHOXD) fb INCIN | CMBST |

U148
Maleic hydrazide

| Maleic hydrazide | 123-33-1 | (WETOX or CHOXD) fb CARBN; or INCIN | INCIN |

U149
Malononitrile

| Malononitrile | 109-77-3 | (WETOX or CHOXD) fb CARBN; or INCIN | INCIN |

U150
Melphalan

| Melphalan | 148-82-3 | (WETOX or CHOXD) fb CARBN; or INCIN | INCIN |

U151
U151 (mercury) nonwastewaters that contain greater than or equal to 260 mg/kg total mercury.

| Mercury | 7439-97-6 | NA | RMERC |

U151
U151 (mercury) nonwastewaters that contain less than 260 mg/kg total mercury and that are residues from RMERC only.

POLLUTION CONTROL BOARD

NOTICE OF PROPOSED AMENDMENTS

Mercury	7439-97-6	NA	0.20 mg/l TCLP

U151
U151 (mercury) nonwastewaters that contain less than 260 mg/kg total mercury and that are not residues from RMERC only.

Mercury	7439-97-6	NA	0.025 mg/l TCLP

U151
All U151 (mercury) wastewater.

Mercury	7439-97-6	0.15	NA

U151
Element Mercury Contaminated with Radioactive Materials

Mercury	7439-97-6	NA	AMLGM

U152
Methacrylonitrile

Methacrylonitrile	126-98-7	0.24	84

U153
Methanethiol

Methanethiol	74-93-1	(WETOX or CHOXD) fb CARBN; or INCIN	INCIN

U154
Methanol

Methanol	67-56-1	(WETOX or CHOXD) fb CARBN; or INCIN	CMBST
Methanol; alternate(6) set of standards for both wastewaters and nonwastewaters	67-56-1	5.6	0.75 mg/l TCLP

U155
Methapyrilene

Methapyrilene	91-80-5	0.081	1.5

U156
Methyl chlorocarbonate

Methyl chlorocarbonate	79-22-1	(WETOX or CHOXD) fb CARBN; or INCIN	INCIN

POLLUTION CONTROL BOARD

NOTICE OF PROPOSED AMENDMENTS

U157
3-Methylcholanthrene

3-Methylcholanthrene	56-49-5	0.0055	15

U158
4,4'-Methylene bis(2-chloroaniline)

4,4'-Methylene bis(2-chloroaniline)	101-14-4	0.50	30

U159
Methyl ethyl ketone

Methyl ethyl ketone	78-93-3	0.28	36

U160
Methyl ethyl ketone peroxide

Methyl ethyl ketone peroxide	1338-23-4	CHOXD; CHRED; CARBN; BIODG; or INCIN	CHOXD; CHRED; or CMBST

U161
Methyl isobutyl ketone

Methyl isobutyl ketone	108-10-1	0.14	33

U162
Methyl methacrylate

Methyl methacrylate	80-62-6	0.14	160

U163
N-Methyl-N'-nitro-N-nitrosoguanidine

N-Methyl-N'-nitro-N-nitrosoguanidine	70-25-7	(WETOX or CHOXD) fb CARBN; or INCIN	INCIN

U164
Methylthiouracil

Methylthiouracil	56-04-2	(WETOX or CHOXD) fb CARBN; or INCIN	INCIN

U165
Naphthalene

Naphthalene	91-20-3	0.059	5.6

U166
1,4-Naphthoquinone

1,4-Naphthoquinone	130-15-4	(WETOX or	CMBST

POLLUTION CONTROL BOARD

NOTICE OF PROPOSED AMENDMENTS

		CHOXD) fb CARBN; or INCIN	
U167 1-Naphthylamine 1-Naphthylamine	134-32-7	(WETOX or CHOXD) fb CARBN; or INCIN	INCIN
U168 2-Naphthylamine 2-Naphthylamine	91-59-8	0.52	INCIN
U169 Nitrobenzene Nitrobenzene	98-95-3	0.068	14
U170 p-Nitrophenol p-Nitrophenol	100-02-7	0.12	29
U171 2-Nitropropane 2-Nitropropane	79-46-9	(WETOX or CHOXD) fb CARBN; or INCIN	INCIN
U172 N-Nitrosodi-n-butylamine N-Nitrosodi-n-butylamine	924-16-3	0.40	17
U173 N-Nitrosodiethanolamine N-Nitrosodiethanolamine	1116-54-7	(WETOX or CHOXD) fb CARBN; or INCIN	INCIN
U174 N-Nitrosodiethylamine N-Nitrosodiethylamine	55-18-5	0.40	28
U176 N-Nitroso-N-ethylurea			

POLLUTION CONTROL BOARD

NOTICE OF PROPOSED AMENDMENTS

N-Nitroso-N-ethylurea	759-73-9	(WETOX or CHOXD) fb CARBN; or INCIN	INCIN
U177 N-Nitroso-N-methylurea N-Nitroso-N-methylurea	684-93-5	(WETOX or CHOXD) fb CARBN; or INCIN	INCIN
U178 N-Nitroso-N-methylurethane N-Nitroso-N-methyl-urethane	615-53-2	(WETOX or CHOXD) fb CARBN; or INCIN	INCIN
U179 N-Nitrosopiperidine N-Nitrosopiperidine	100-75-4	0.013	35
U180 N-Nitrosopyrrolidine N-Nitrosopyrrolidine	930-55-2	0.013	35
U181 5-Nitro-o-toluidine 5-Nitro-o-toluidine	99-55-8	0.32	28
U182 Paraldehyde Paraldehyde	123-63-7	(WETOX or CHOXD) fb CARBN; or INCIN	CMBST
U183 Pentachlorobenzene Pentachlorobenzene	608-93-5	0.055	10
U184 Pentachloroethane Pentachloroethane	76-01-7	(WETOX or CHOXD) fb CARBN; or INCIN	INCIN

POLLUTION CONTROL BOARD

NOTICE OF PROPOSED AMENDMENTS

Pentachloroethane; alternate(6) standards for both wastewaters and nonwastewaters	76-01-7	0.055	6.0
U185 Pentachloronitrobenzene Pentachloronitrobenzene	82-68-8	0.055	4.8
U186 1,3-Pentadiene 1,3-Pentadiene	504-60-9	(WETOX or CHOXD) fb CARBN; or INCIN	CMBST
U187 Phenacetin Phenacetin	62-44-2	0.081	16
U188 Phenol Phenol	108-95-2	0.039	6.2
U189 Phosphorus sulfide Phosphorus sulfide	1314-80-3	CHOXD; CHRED; or INCIN	CHOXD; CHRED; or INCIN
U190 Phthalic anhydride Phthalic anhydride (measured as Phthalic acid or Terephthalic acid)	100-21-0	0.055	28
Phthalic anhydride	85-44-9	0.055	28
U191 2-Picoline 2-Picoline	109-06-8	(WETOX or CHOXD) fb CARBN; or INCIN	INCIN
U192 Pronamide Pronamide	23950-58-5	0.093	1.5

POLLUTION CONTROL BOARD

NOTICE OF PROPOSED AMENDMENTS

U193 1,3-Propane sultone 1,3-Propane sultone	1120-71-4	(WETOX or CHOXD) fb CARBN; or INCIN	INCIN
U194 n-Propylamine n-Propylamine	107-10-8	(WETOX or CHOXD) fb CARBN; or INCIN	INCIN
U196 Pyridine Pyridine	110-86-1	0.014	16
U197 p-Benzoquinone p-Benzoquinone	106-51-4	(WETOX or CHOXD) fb CARBN; or INCIN	CMBST
U200 Reserpine Reserpine	50-55-5	(WETOX or CHOXD) fb CARBN; or INCIN	INCIN
U201 Resorcinol Resorcinol	108-46-3	(WETOX or CHOXD) fb CARBN; or INCIN	CMBST
U202 Saccharin and salts Saccharin	81-07-2	(WETOX or CHOXD) fb CARBN; or INCIN	INCIN
U203 Safrole			

POLLUTION CONTROL BOARD

NOTICE OF PROPOSED AMENDMENTS

Safrole	94-59-7	0.081	22
U204 Selenium dioxide Selenium	7782-49-2	0.82	0.16 mg/l TCLP
U205 Selenium sulfide Selenium	7782-49-2	0.82	0.16 mg/l TCLP
U206 Streptozotocin Streptozotocin	18883-66-4	(WETOX or CHOXD) fb CARBN; or INCIN	INCIN
U207 1,2,4,5-Tetrachlorobenzene 1,2,4,5-Tetrachloro-benzene	95-94-3	0.055	14
U208 1,1,1,2-Tetrachloroethane 1,1,1,2-Tetrachloro-ethane	630-20-6	0.057	6.0
U209 1,1,2,2-Tetrachloroethane 1,1,2,2-Tetrachloro-ethane	79-34-5	0.057	6.0
U210 Tetrachloroethylene Tetrachloroethylene	127-18-4	0.056	6.0
U211 Carbon tetrachloride Carbon tetrachloride	56-23-5	0.057	6.0
U213 Tetrahydrofuran Tetrahydrofuran	109-99-9	(WETOX or CHOXD) fb CARBN; or INCIN	CMBST
U214			

POLLUTION CONTROL BOARD

NOTICE OF PROPOSED AMENDMENTS

Thallium (I) acetate Thallium (measured in wastewaters only)	7440-28-0	1.4	
U215 Thallium (I) carbonate Thallium (measured in wastewaters only)	7440-28-0	1.4	
U216 Thallium (I) chloride Thallium (measured in wastewaters only)	7440-28-0	1.4	
U217 Thallium (I) nitrate Thallium (measured in wastewaters only)	7440-28-0	1.4	
U218 Thioacetamide Thioacetamide	62-55-5	(WETOX or CHOXD) fb CARBN; or INCIN	
U219 Thiourea Thiourea	62-56-6	(WETOX or CHOXD) fb CARBN; or INCIN	INCIN
U220 Toluene Toluene	108-88-3	0.080	10
U221 Toluenediamine Toluenediamine	25376-45-8	CARBN; or INCIN	CMBST
U222 o-Toluidine hydrochloride o-Toluidine hydro-chloride	636-21-5	(WETOX or CHOXD) fb CARBN; or INCIN	INCIN

POLLUTION CONTROL BOARD

NOTICE OF PROPOSED AMENDMENTS

U223
Toluene diisocyanate

Toluene diisocyanate	26471-62-5	CARBN; or INCIN	CMBST

U225
Bromoform (Tribromomethane)

Bromoform (Tribromo-methane)	75-25-2	0.63	15

U226
1,1,1-Trichloroethane

1,1,1-Trichloroethane	71-55-6	0.054	6.0

U227
1,1,2-Trichloroethane

1,1,2-Trichloroethane	79-00-5	0.054	6.0

U228
Trichloroethylene

Trichloroethylene	79-01-6	0.054	6.0

U234
1,3,5-Trinitrobenzene

1,3,5-Trinitrobenzene	99-35-4	(WETOX or CHOXD) fb CARBN; or INCIN	INCIN

U235
tris-(2,3-Dibromopropyl)-phosphate

tris-(2,3-Dibromo-propyl)-phosphate	126-72-7	0.11	0.10

U236
Trypan Blue

Trypan Blue	72-57-1	(WETOX or CHOXD) fb CARBN; or INCIN	INCIN

U237
Uracil mustard

Uracil mustard	66-75-1	(WETOX or CHOXD) fb CARBN; or INCIN	INCIN

POLLUTION CONTROL BOARD

NOTICE OF PROPOSED AMENDMENTS

U238
Urethane (Ethyl carbamate)

Urethane (Ethyl carbamate	51-79-6	(WETOX or CHOXD) fb CARBN; or INCIN	INCIN

U239
Xylenes

Xylenes-mixed isomers (sum of o-,m-,and p-xylene concentrations)	1330-20-7	0.32	30

U240
2,4-D (2,4-Dichlorophenoxyacetic acid)

2,4-D (2,4-Dichloro-phenoxyacetic acid)	94-75-7	0.72	10
2,4-D (2,4-Dichloro-phenoxyacetic acid) salts and esters	NA	(WETOX or CARBN; or CHOXD)fb INCIN	INCIN

U243
Hexachloropropylene

Hexachloropropylene	1888-71-7	0.035	30

U244
Thiram

Thiram	137-26-8	(WETOX or CHOXD) fb CARBN; or INCIN	INCIN

U246
Cyanogen bromide

Cyanogen bromide	506-68-3	CHOXD; WETOX; or INCIN	CHOXD; WETOX; or INCIN

U247
Methoxychlor

Methoxychlor	72-43-5	0.25	0.18

U248
Warfarin, & salts, when present at concentrations of 0.3% or less

Warfarin	81-81-2	(WETOX or CHOXD) fb CARBN; or INCIN	CMBST

POLLUTION CONTROL BOARD

NOTICE OF PROPOSED AMENDMENTS

U249
Zinc phosphide, Zn(3)P(2), when present at concentrations of 10% or less

| Zinc Phosphide | 1314-84-7 | CHOXD; CHRED; or INCIN | CHOXD; CHRED; or INCIN |

U328
p-Toluidine

| o-Toluidine | 95-53-4 | INCIN; or CHOXD fb (BIODG or CARBN); or BIODG fb CARBN | INCIN; or Thermal Destruction |

U353
p-Toluidine

| p-Toluidine | 1-6-49-0 | INCIN; or CHOXD fb (BIODG or CARBN); or BIODG fb CARBN | INCIN; or Thermal Destruction |

U359
2-Ethoxyethanol

| 2-Ethoxyethanol | 110-80-5 | INCIN; or CHOXD fb (BIODG or CARBN); or BIODG fb CARBN | CMBST |

Notes:

1 The waste descriptions provided in this table do not replace waste descriptions in 35 Ill. Adm. Code 721. Descriptions of Treatment or Regulatory Subcategories are provided, as needed, to distinguish between applicability of different standards.

2 CAS means Chemical Abstract Services. When the waste code and/or regulated constituents are described as a combination of a chemical with its salts and/or esters, the CAS number is given for the parent compound only.

3 Concentration standards for wastewaters are expressed in mg/l are based on analysis of composite samples.

4 All treatment standards expressed as a Technology Code or combination of Technology Codes are explained in detail in 35 Ill. Adm. Code 728.Table C, "Technology Codes and Description of Technology-Based Standards". "fb" inserted between waste codes denotes "followed by", so that the

POLLUTION CONTROL BOARD

NOTICE OF PROPOSED AMENDMENTS

first-listed treatment is followed by the second-listed treatment. ";" separates alternative treatment schemes.

5 Except for Metals (EP or TCLP) and Cyanides (Total and Amenable) the nonwastewater treatment standards expressed as a concentration were established, in part, based upon incineration in units operated in accordance with the technical requirements of 35 Ill. Adm. Code 724.Subpart O or 35 Ill. Adm. Code 725.Subpart O, or based upon combustion in fuel substitution units operating in accordance with applicable technical requirements. A facility may comply with these treatment standards according to provisions in 35 Ill. Adm. Code 728.140(d). All concentration standards for nonwastewaters are based on analysis of grab samples.

6 Where an alternate treatment standard or set of alternate standards has been indicated, a facility may comply with this alternate standard, but only for the Treatment or Regulatory Subcategory or physical form (i.e., wastewater and/or nonwastewater) specified for that alternate standard.

7 Both Cyanides (Total) and Cyanides (Amenable) for nonwastewaters are to be analyzed using Method 9010 or 9012, found in "Test Methods for Evaluating Solid Waste, Physical or Chemical Methods", U.S. EPA Publication SW-846, as incorporated by reference in 35 Ill. Adm. Code 720.111, with a sample size of 10 grams and a distillation time of one hour and 15 minutes.

NA means not applicable.

(Source: Added at 19 Ill. Reg. _____, effective _____.)

POLLUTION CONTROL BOARD

NOTICE OF PROPOSED AMENDMENTS

Section 728.TABLE U Universal Treatment Standards (UTS)

Regulated Constituent-Common Name	CAS(1) No.	Wastewater Standard Concentration (in mg/l(2)	Nonwastewater Standard Concentration (in mg/kg(3) unless noted as "mg/l TCLP")
Acenaphthylene	208-96-8	0.059	3.4
Acenaphthene	83-32-9	0.059	3.4
Acetone	67-64-1	0.28	160
Acetonitrile	75-05-8	5.6	1.8
Acetophenone	96-86-2	0.010	9.7
2-Acetylaminofluorene	53-96-3	0.059	140
Acrolein	107-02-8	0.29	NA
Acrylamide	79-06-1	19	23
Acrylonitrile	107-13-1	0.24	84
Aldrin	309-00-2	0.021	0.066
4-Aminobiphenyl	92-67-1	0.13	NA
Aniline	62-53-3	0.81	14
Anthracene	120-12-7	0.059	3.4
Aramite	140-57-8	0.36	NA
alpha-BHC	319-84-6	0.00014	0.066
beta-BHC	319-85-7	0.00014	0.066
bis(2-Chloroethoxy)methane	111-91-1	0.036	7.2
bis(2-Chloroethyl) ether	111-44-4	0.033	6.0
Chloroform	67-66-3	0.046	6.0

POLLUTION CONTROL BOARD

NOTICE OF PROPOSED AMENDMENTS

bis(2-Chloro-isopropyl)ether	108-60-1	0.055	7.2
p-Chloro-m-cresol	59-50-7	0.018	14
2-Chloroethyl vinyl ether	110-75-8	0.062	NA
Chloromethane (Methyl chloride	74-87-3	0.19	30
2-Chloronaphthalene	91-58-7	0.055	5.6
2-Chlorophenol	95-57-8	0.044	5.7
3-Chloropropylene	107-05-1	0.036	30
Chrysene	218-01-9	0.059	3.4
o-Cresol	95-48-7	0.11	5.6
m-Cresol (difficult to distinguish from p-cresol)	108-39-4	0.77	5.6
p-Cresol (difficult to distinguish from m-cresol)	106-44-5	0.77	5.6
Cyclohexanone	108-94-1	0.36	0.75mg/l TCLP
1,2-Dibromo-3-chloro-propane	96-12-8	0.11	15
Ethylene dibromide (1,2-Dibromoethane)	106-93-4	0.028	15
Dibromomethane	74-95-3	0.11	15
2,4-D (2,4-Dichloro-phenoxyacetic acid)	94-75-7	0.72	10
p,p'-DDD	53-19-0	0.023	0.087
p,p'-DDD	72-54-8	0.023	0.087
o,p'-DDE	3424-82-6	0.021	0.087

POLLUTION CONTROL BOARD

NOTICE OF PROPOSED AMENDMENTS

p,p'-DDD	72-55-9	0.031	0.087
o,p'-DDT	789-02-6	0.0039	0.087
p,p'-DDT	50-29-3	0.0039	0.087
Dibenz(a,h)anthracene	53-70-3	0.055	8.2
Dibenz(a,e)pyrene	192-65-4	0.061	NA
m-Dichlorobenzene	541-73-1	0.036	6.0
o-Dichlorobenzene	95-50-91	0.088	6.0
p-Dichlorobenzene	106-46-7	0.090	6.0
Dichlorodifluoromethane	75-71-8	0.23	7.2
1,1-Dichloroethane	75-34-3	0.059	6.0
1,2-Dichloroethane	107-06-2	0.21	6.0
1,1-Dichloroethylene	75-35-4	0.025	6.0
trans-1,2-Dichloroethylene	156-60-5	0.054	30
2,4-Dichlorophenol	120-83-2	0.044	14
2,6-Dichlorophenol	87-65-0	0.044	14
1,2-Dichloropropane	78-87-5	0.85	18
cis-1,3-Dichloropropylene	10061-01-5	0.036	18
trans-1,3-Dichloropropylene	10061-02-6	0.036	18
Dieldrin	60-57-1	0.017	0.13
Diethyl phthalate	84-66-2	0.20	28
2,4-Dimethyl phenol	105-67-9	0.036	14
Dimethyl phthalate	131-11-3	0.047	28
Di-n-butyl phthalate	84-74-2	0.057	28

POLLUTION CONTROL BOARD

NOTICE OF PROPOSED AMENDMENTS

1,4-Dinitrobenzene	100-25-4	0.32	2.3
4,6-Dinitro-o-cresol	534-52-1	0.28	160
2,4-Dinitrophenol	51-28-5	0.12	160
2,4-Dinitrotoluene	121-14-2	0.32	140
2,6-Dinitrotoluene	606-20-2	0.55	28
Di-n-octyl phthalate	117-84-0	0.017	28
p-Dimethylaminoazobenzene	60-11-7	0.13	NA
Di-n-propylnitrosamine	621-64-7	0.40	14
1,4-Dioxane	123-91-1	NA	170
Diphenylamine (difficult to distinguish from diphenylnitrosamine)	122-39-4	0.92	13
Diphenylnitrosamine (difficult to distinguish from diphenylamine)	86-30-6	0.92	13
1,2-Diphenylhydrazine	122-66-7	0.087	NA
Disulfoton	298-04-4	0.017	6.2
Endosulfan I	939-98-8	0.023	0.066
Endosulfan II	33213-6-5	0.029	0.13
Endosulfan Sulfate	1-31-07-8	0.029	0.13
Endrin	72-20-9	0.0028	0.13
Endrin aldehyde	7421-93-4	0.025	0.13
Ethyl acetate	141-78-6	0.34	33
Ethyl cyanide (Propanenitrile)	107-12-0	0.24	360
Ethyl benzene	100-41-4	0.057	10

POLLUTION CONTROL BOARD

NOTICE OF PROPOSED AMENDMENTS

Ethyl ether	60-29-7	0.12	160
bis(2-Ethylhexyl) phthalate	117-81-7	0.28	28
Ethyl methacrylate	97-63-2	0.14	160
Ethylene oxide	75-21-8	0.12	NA
Famphur	52-85-7	0.017	15
Fluoranthene	206-44-0	0.068	3.4
Fluorene	86-73-7	0.059	3.4
Heptachlor	76-44-8	0.0012	0.066
Heptachlor epoxide	1024-57-3	0.016	0.066
Hexachlorobenzene	118-74-1	0.055	10
Hexachlorobutadiene	87-68-3	0.055	5.6
Hexachloro-cyclopentadiene	77-47-4	0.057	2.4
HxCDDs (All Hexachloro-dibenzo-p-dioxins)	NA	0.000063	0.001
HxCDFs (All Hexachloro-dibenzofurans)	NA	0.000063	0.001
Hexachloroethane	67-72-1	0.055	30
Hexachloropropylene	1888-71-7	0.035	30
Indeno (1,2,3-c,d) pyrene	193-39-5	0.0055	3.4
Iodomethane	74-88-4	0.19	65
Isobutyl alcohol	78-83-1	5.6	170
Isodrin	465-73-6	0.021	0.066
Isosafrole	120-58-1	0.081	2.6
Kepone	143-50-8	0.0011	0.13

POLLUTION CONTROL BOARD

NOTICE OF PROPOSED AMENDMENTS

Methacrylonitrile	126-98-7	0.24	84
Methanol	67-56-1	5.6	0.75 mg/l TCLP
Methapyrilene	91-80-5	0.081	1.5
Methoxychlor	72-43-5	0.25	0.18
3-Methylcholanthrene	56-49-5	0.0055	15
4,4-Methylene bis(2-chloroaniline)	101-14-4	0.50	30
Methylene chloride	75-09-2	0.089	30
Methyl ethyl ketone	78-93-3	0.28	36
Methyl isobutyl ketone	108-10-1	0.14	33
Methyl methacrylate	80-62-6	0.14	160
Methyl methansulfonate	66-27-3	0.018	NA
Methyl parathion	298-00-0	0.014	4.6
Naphthalene	91-20-3	0.059	5.6
2-Naphthylamine	91-59-8	0.52	NA
o-Nitroaniline	88-74-4	0.27	14
p-Nitroaniline	100-01-6	0.028	28
Nitrobenzene	98-95-3	0.068	14
5-Nitro-o-toluidine	99-55-8	0.32	28
o-Nitrophenol	88-75-5	0.028	13
p-Nitrophenol	100-02-7	0.12	29
N-Nitrosodiethylamine	55-18-5	0.40	28
N-Nitrosodimethylamine	62-75-9	0.40	2.3
N-Nitroso-di-n-butyl-amine	924-16-3	0.40	14

POLLUTION CONTROL BOARD

NOTICE OF PROPOSED AMENDMENTS

N-Nitrosomethylethyl-amine	10595-95-6	0.40	2.3
N-Nitrosomorpholine	59-89-2	0.40	2.3
N-Nitrosopiperidine	100-75-4	0.013	35
N-Nitrosopyrrolidine	930-55-2	0.013	35
Parathion	56-38-2	0.014	4.6
Total PCBs (sum of all PCB isomers, or all Aroclors)	1336-36-3	0.10	10
Pentachlorobenzene	608-93-5	0.055	10
PeCDDs (All Pentachloro-dibenzo-p-dioxins)	NA	0.000063	0.001
PECDFs (All Pentachloro-dibenzofurans)	NA	0.000035	0.001
Pentachloroethane	76-01-7	0.055	6.0
Pentachloronitrobenzene	82-68-8	0.055	4.8
Pentachlorophenol	87-86-5	0.089	7.4
Phenacetin	62-44-2	0.081	16
Phenanthrene	85-01-8	0.059	5.6
Phenol	108-95-2	0.039	6.2
Phorate	298-02-2	0.021	4.6
Phthalic acid	100-21-0	0.055	28
Phthalic anhydride	85-44-9	0.055	28
Pronamide	23950-58-5	0.093	1.5
Pyrene	129-00-0	0.067	8.2
Pyridine	110-86-1	0.014	16
Safrole	94-59-7	0.081	22

POLLUTION CONTROL BOARD

NOTICE OF PROPOSED AMENDMENTS

Silvex (2,4,5-TP)	93-72-1	0.72	7.9
2,4,5-T (2,4,5-Trichloro-phenoxyacetic acid)	93-76-5	0.72	7.9
1,2,4,5-Tetrachloro-benzene	95-94-3	0.055	14
TCDDs (All Tetrachloro-dibenzo-p-dioxins)	NA	0.000063	0.001
TCDFs (All Tetrachloro-dibenzofurans)	NA	0.000063	0.001
1,1,1,2-Tetrachloro-ethane	630-20-6	0.057	6.0
1,1,2,2-Tetrachloro-ethane	79-34-5	0.057	6.0
Tetrachloroethylene	127-18-4	0.056	6.0
2,3,4,6-Tetrachloro-phenol	58-90-2	0.030	7.4
Toluene	108-88-3	0.080	10
Toxaphene	8001-35-2	0.0095	2.6
Bromoform (Tribromo-methane)	75-25-2	0.63	15
1,2,4-Trichlorobenzene	120-82-1	0.055	19
1,1,1-Trichloroethane	71-55-6	0.054	6.0
1,1,2-Trichloroethane	79-00-5	0.054	6.0
Trichloroethylene	79-01-6	0.054	6.0
Trichloromonofluoro-methane	75-69-4	0.020	30
2,4,5-Trichlorophenol	95-95-4	0.18	7.4
2,4,6-Trichlorophenol	88-06-2	0.035	7.4

POLLUTION CONTROL BOARD

NOTICE OF PROPOSED AMENDMENTS

1,2,3-Trichloropropane	96-18-4	0.85	30
1,1,2-Trichloro-1,2,2-trifluoroethane	76-13-1	0.057	30
tris-(2,3-Dibromopropyl) phosphate	126-72-7	0.11	0.10
Vinyl chloride	75-01-4	0.27	6.0
Xylenes-mixed isomers (sum of o-, m-, and p-xylene concentrations)	1330-20-7	0.32	30
Antimony	7440-36-0	1.9	2.1 mg/l TCLP
Arsenic	7440-38-2	1.4	5.0 mg/l TCLP
Barium	7440-39-3	1.2	7.6 mg/l TCLP
Beryllium	7440-41-7	0.82	0.014 mg/l TCLP
Cadmium	7440-43-9	0.69	0.19 mg/l TCLP
Chromium (Total)	7440-47-3	2.77	0.86 mg/l TCLP
Cyanides (Total)(4)	57-12-5	1.2	590
Cyanides (Amenable)(4)	57-12-5	0.86	30
Fluoride	16964-48-8	35	NA
Lead	7439-92-1	0.69	0.37 mg/l TCLP
Mercury-Nonwastewater from Retort	7439-97-6	NA	0.20 mg/l TCLP
Mercury-All Others	7439-97-6	0.15	0.025 mg/l TCLP
Nickel	7440-02-0	3.98	5.0 mg/l TCLP
Selenium	7782-49-2	0.82	0.16 mg/l TCLP
Silver	7440-22-4	0.43	0.30 mg/l TCLP
Sulfide	8496-25-8	14	NA
Thallium	7440-28-0	1.4	0.078 mg/l TCLP

POLLUTION CONTROL BOARD

NOTICE OF PROPOSED AMENDMENTS

Vanadium(5)	7440-62-2	4.3	0.23 mg/l TCLP
Zinc(5)	7440-66-6	2.61	5.3 mg/l TCLP

1   CAS means Chemical Abstract Services. When the waste code or regulated constituents are described as a combination of a chemical with its salts or esters, the CAS number is given for the parent compound only.

2   Concentration standards for wastewaters are expressed in mg/l are based on analysis of composite samples.

3   Except for metals (EP or TCLP) and cyanides (total and amenable), the nonwastewater treatment standards expressed as a concentration were established, in part, based on incineration in units operated in accordance with the technical requirements of 35 Ill. Adm. Code 724.Subpart O or 35 Ill. Adm. Code 725.Subpart O or on combustion in fuel substitution units operating in accordance with applicable technical requirements. A facility may comply with these treatment standards according to provisions in 40 CFR 268.40(d). All concentration standards for nonwastewaters are based on analysis of grab samples.

4   Both Cyanides (Total) and Cyanides (Amenable) for nonwastewaters are to be analyzed using Method 9010 or 9012, found in "Test Methods for Evaluating Solid Waste, Physical/Chemical Methods", U.S. EPA Publication SW-846, incorporated by reference in 35 Ill. Adm. Code 729.111, with a sample size of 10 grams and a distillation time of one hour and 15 minutes.

5   Vanadium and zinc are not "underlying hazardous constituents" in characteristic wastes, according to the definition at 35 Ill. Adm. Code 268.2(i).

Note: NA means not applicable.

(Source: Added   at   19   Ill.   Reg. _____,   effective
_____)

POLLUTION CONTROL BOARD

NOTICE OF PROPOSED REPEALER

1) Heading of the Part: Outline of Waste Disposal Regulations

2) Code citation: 35 Ill. Adm. Code 700

3) Section numbers: Proposed action:

   700.106   Repealed

4) Statutory authority: 415 ILCS 5/13, 22.4 and 27.

5) A complete description of the subjects and issues involved:

   A more detailed description is contained in the Board's proposed opinion
   of March 2, 1995, in R95-4 and R95-6 (consolidated), which opinion is
   available from the address below. Sections 13(c) and 22.4(a) of the
   Environmental Protection Act [415 ILCS 5/13(c) & 22.4(a)] provides that
   Section 5-35 of the Administrative Procedure Act [5 ILCS 100/5-35] shall
   not apply. Because this rulemaking is not subject to Section 5-35 of the
   APA, it is not subject to first notice or to second notice review by JCAR.

   This rulemaking updates Parts 700, 702, 703, 705, 720, 721, 722, 723, 724,
   725, 726, 728, 730, 738, and 739 of the Illinois RCRA Subtitle C hazardous
   waste and underground injection control (UIC) rules to correspond with
   amendments adopted by U.S. EPA that appeared in the Federal Register
   during the period July 1 through December 31, 1994. During this period,
   U.S. EPA amended its regulations as follows:

Federal Action	Summary
59 Fed. Reg. 38536, July 28, 1994	Exclusion from definition of solid waste for certain in-process recycled secondary materials used by the petroleum refining industry
59 Fed. Reg. 43496, August 24, 1994	Withdrawal of exemption from Subtitle C regulation of slag residues from high temperature metal recovery (HTMR) of electric arc furnance dust (K061), steel finishing pickle liquor (K062), and electroplating sludges (F006) that are used in a manner constituting disposal
59 Fed. Reg. 47980, September 19, 1994	Restoration of text from 40 CFR 268.7(a) inadvertently omitted in the amendments of August 31, 1993, at 58 Fed. Reg. 46040

POLLUTION CONTROL BOARD

NOTICE OF PROPOSED REPEALER

59 Fed. Reg. 47982, September 19, 1994	Phase II land disposal restrictions (LDRs); universal treatment standards for organic toxicity wastes and newly-listed wastes (including underground injection control (UIC) amendments)
59 Fed. Reg. 62896, December 6, 1994	Organic material air emission standards for tanks, surface impoundments, and containers

In addition to these principal amendments that occurred during the update
period, the Board has included an additional, later action:

60 Fed. Reg. 242, January 3, 1995	Corrections to the Phase II land disposal restrictions (universal treatment standards)

This January 3 action was an amendment of the September 19, 1994 Phase II
LDRs (universal waste rule). U.S. EPA corrected errors and clarified
language in the universal treatment standards. The Board did not delay in
adding these amendments for three reasons:

1) The January 3, 1995 amendments are corrections and clarifications
   of the September 19, 1994 regulations, and not new substantive
   amendments;

2) Prompt action on the January 3, 1995 amendments will facilitate
   implementation of the Phase II LDRs; and

3) The Board has received a request from the regulated community that
   we add the January 3, 1995 amendments to those of September 19,
   1994. (See "Expedited Consideration" below.)

The Board also notes that the later amendments occurred within six months
of the earliest amendments included in this docket, even if they occurred
outside the nominal time-frame of the docket.

In addition to the federally-derived amendments, the Board used this
opportunity to undertake a number of housekeeping and corrective
amendments. We have effected the removal of all cross-references for
effective dates and repealed Part 700. We have converted equations and
formulae to the standard scientific format. We have tried to improve the
language and structure of various provisions, including correcting
grammar, punctuation, and spelling where necessary.

Specifically, the segment of the amendments involved in the repeal of Part
700 remove regulations that had become outdated and superfluous with time.
After recent amendments, the sole provision in this Part was Section
700.106, which set forth effective dates of segments of the Illinois UIC
and RCRA Subtitle C programs. Associated proposed amendments to 35 Ill.

POLLUTION CONTROL BOARD

NOTICE OF PROPOSED REPEALER

Statement of statewide policy objectives:

Adm. Code 703, 705, 720 through 723, 725, and 730 would now thoroughly remove all references to Section 700.106 and obviate its further use, thus clearing the way for the repeal of Part 700.

6) Will this proposed rule replace an emergency rule currently in effect? No.

7) Does this proposed repeal contain an automatic repeal date? No.

8) Do these proposed repeal contain incorporations by reference? No.

9) Are there any other amendments pending on this Part? No.

10) Statement of statewide policy objectives:
This rulemaking is mandated by Sections 1(c) and 22.4(a) of the Environmental Protection Act [415 ILCS 5/1(c) & 22.4(a)]. The statewide policy objectives are set forth in Section 20 of that Act. This rulemaking imposes mandates on units of local governments only to the extent that they may be involved in the generation, transportation, treatment, storage, or disposal of hazardous waste or they engage in underground injection of waste.

11) Time, place and manner in which interested persons may comment on this proposed rulemaking:
The Board will accept written public comment on this proposal for a period of 45 days after the date of this publication. Comments should reference Docket R97-4/R95-6 and be addressed to:

Ms. Dorothy M. Gunn, Clerk
Illinois Pollution Control Board
State of Illinois Center, Suite 11-500
100 W. Randolph St.
Chicago, IL 60601
312/814-6931

Address all questions to Michael J. McCambridge, at 312/814-6924.

12) Initial regulatory flexibility analysis:

A) Date rule was submitted to the Small Business Office of the Department of Commerce and Community Affairs: March 6, 1995.

B) Types of small businesses affected:
the existing rules and proposed amendments affect small businesses that generate, transport, treat, store, or dispose of

POLLUTION CONTROL BOARD

NOTICE OF PROPOSED REPEALER

hazardous waste or engage in underground injection of waste.

C) Reporting, bookkeeping or other procedures required for compliance:
The existing rules and proposed amendments require extensive reporting, bookkeeping, and other procedures, including the preparation of manifests and annual reports, waste analyses, and maintenance of operating records.

D) Types of professional skills necessary for compliance:
Compliance with the existing rules and proposed amendments may require the services of an attorney, certified public accountant, chemist, and registered professional engineer.

The full text of the proposed repealer begins on the next page.

POLLUTION CONTROL BOARD

NOTICE OF PROPOSED REPEALER

TITLE 35: ENVIRONMENTAL PROTECTION
SUBTITLE G: WASTE DISPOSAL
CHAPTER I: POLLUTION CONTROL BOARD
SUBCHAPTER a: GENERAL PROVISIONS

PART 700
OUTLINE OF WASTE DISPOSAL REGULATIONS (REPEALED)

SUBPART A: GENERAL

Section
700.101   Applicability (Repealed)
700.102   Other Regulations (Repealed)
700.103   Organization (Repealed)
700.104   Intent and Purpose (Repealed)
700.105   Interim Status (Repealed)
700.106   Effective Dates (Repealed)
700.107   Severability (Repealed)
700.108   References to Federal Rules (Repealed)
700.109   Permits Prior to Authorization (Repealed)

SUBPART B: DEFINITIONS

Section
700.201   Definitions (Repealed)
700.205   Act (Repealed)
700.210   Chapter 7 Operating Requirements (Repealed)
700.215   Chapter 7 Permits (Repealed)
700.220   Chapter 9 Operating Requirements (Repealed)
700.225   Chapter 9 Permits (Repealed)
700.230   Conflict (Repealed)
700.235   HWM (Repealed)
700.240   Operating Requirements (Repealed)
700.245   Permit Requirements (Repealed)
700.250   RCRA Operating Requirements (Repealed)
700.255   RCRA Permit (Repealed)
700.260   RCRA Rules (Repealed)
700.265   Subject To (Repealed)

SUBPART C: GENERATORS

Section
700.301   Permits (Repealed)
700.302   Operating Requirements (Repealed)
700.303   Manifests (Repealed)
700.304   Small Quantity Exemptions (Repealed)

SUBPART D: TRANSPORTERS

POLLUTION CONTROL BOARD

NOTICE OF PROPOSED REPEALER

Section
700.401   Permits (Repealed)
700.402   Operating Requirements (Repealed)
700.403   Manifests (Repealed)
700.404   Small Quantity Exemptions (Repealed)

SUBPART E: OWNERS AND OPERATORS OF HWM SITES

Section
700.501   Permits (Repealed)
700.502   Operating Requirements (Repealed)
700.503   Manifests (Repealed)
700.504   Small Quantity Exemptions (Repealed)

SUBPART F: HAZARDOUS (INFECTIOUS) HOSPITAL WASTE

Section
700.601   Hazardous (Infectious) Hospital Waste (Repealed)
700.602   General Rule (Repealed)
700.603   Generators (Repealed)
700.604   Transporters (Repealed)
700.605   Owners and Operators (Repealed)

Appendix A   Applicability Provisions (Repealed)

AUTHORITY: Implementing Sections 13 and 22.4 and authorized by Section 27 of the Environmental Protection Act [415 ILCS 5/13, 22.4 and 27].

SOURCE: Adopted in R81-22, 43 PCB 427, at 5 Ill. Reg. 9781, effective May 17, 1982; amended and codified in R81-22, 45 PCB 317, at 6 Ill. Reg. 4828, effective May 17, 1982; amended in R81-32, 47 PCB 93, at 6 Ill. Reg. 12655, effective May 17, 1982; amended in R82-18, 51 PCB 31, at 7 Ill. Reg. 2518 effective February 22, 1983; amended in R82-19, at 7 Ill. Reg. 14457, effective October 12, 1983; amended in R83-24, at 8 Ill. Reg. 200, effective December 27, 1983; amended in R94-5 at 18 Ill. Reg. 18244, effective December 20, 1994; repealed in R95-6 at 19 Ill. Reg. _____, effective _____.

SUBPART A: GENERAL

Section 700.106 Effective Dates (Repealed)

a) U.S. EPA granted interim authorization to the Illinois RCRA Subtitle C Program effective May 17, 1982, at 47 Fed. Reg. 21043 (May 17, 1982); U.S. EPA granted final authorization effective January 31, 1986, at 51 Fed. Reg. 3778 (January 30, 1986).

b) The effective date of 35 Ill. Adm. Code 720, 721, 722, 723, and 725 was May 17, 1982.

POLLUTION CONTROL BOARD

NOTICE OF PROPOSED REPEALER

2) ~~The effective date of 35 Ill. Adm. Code 702 and 705, to the
extent they apply to the issuance of RCRA permits, was May 17,
1982; however, RCRA permits were not to be issued prior to
January 31, 1986.~~

3) ~~The effective date of 35 Ill. Adm. Code 703 and 724 was October
12, 1983; however, RCRA permits were not to be issued prior to
January 31, 1986.~~

b) ~~U.S. EPA authorized the Illinois UIC program effective March 3, 1984,
at 49 Fed. Reg. 3991 (Feb. 1, 1984).~~

1) ~~The effective date of 35 Ill. Adm. Code 702, 704 and 705, to the
extent they apply to the issuance of UIC (Underground Injection
Control) permits, was March 3, 1984.~~

2) ~~The effective date of 35 Ill. Adm. Code 730 was March 3, 1984.~~

(Source: Repealed at 19 Ill. Reg. _____, effective
_____)

POLLUTION CONTROL BOARD

NOTICE OF PROPOSED AMENDMENTS

1) Heading of the Part: Procedures for Permit Issuance

2) Code citation: 35 Ill. Adm. Code 705

3) Section numbers: Proposed action:

705.128   Amended

4) Statutory authority: 415 ILCS 5/13, 22.4 and 27.

5) A complete description of the subjects and issues involved:

A more detailed description is contained in the Board's proposed opinion of
March 2, 1995, in R95-4 and R95-6 (consolidated), which opinion is available
from the address below. Sections 13(c) and 22.4(a) of the Environmental
Protection Act [415 ILCS 5/13(c) & 22.4(a)] provides that Section 5-35 of
the Administrative Procedure Act [5 ILCS 100/5-35] shall not apply. Because
this rulemaking is not subject to Section 5-35 of the APA, it is not subject
to first notice or to second notice review by JCAR.

This rulemaking updates Parts 700, 702, 703, 705, 720, 721, 722, 723, 724,
725, 726, 728, 730, 738, and 709 of the Illinois RCRA Subtitle C hazardous
waste and underground injection control (UIC) rules to correspond with
amendments adopted by U.S. EPA that appeared in the Federal Register during
the period July 1 through December 31, 1994. During this period, U.S. EPA
amended its regulations as follows:

Federal Action	Summary
59 Fed. Reg. 38536, July 28, 1994	Exclusion from definition of solid waste for certain in-process recycled secondary materials used by the petroleum refining industry
59 Fed. Reg. 43496, August 24, 1994	Withdrawal of exemption from Subtitle C regulation of slag residues from high temperature metal recovery (HTMR) of electric arc furnace dust (K061), steel finishing pickle liquor (K062), and electroplating sludges (F006) that are used in a manner constituting disposal
59 Fed. Reg. 47980, September 19, 1994	Restoration of text from 40 CFR 268.7(a) inadvertently omitted in the amendments of August 31, 1993, at 58 Fed. Reg. 46040

POLLUTION CONTROL BOARD

NOTICE OF PROPOSED AMENDMENTS

59 Fed. Reg. 47982, September 19, 1994		Phase II land disposal restrictions (LDRs); universal treatment standards for organic toxicity wastes and newly-listed wastes (including underground injection control (UIC) amendments)
59 Fed. Reg. 62896, December 6, 1994		Organic material air emission standards for tanks, surface impoundments, and containers

In addition to these principal amendments that occurred during the update period, the Board has included an additional, later action;

60 Fed. Reg. 242, January 3, 1995		Corrections to the Phase II land disposal restrictions (universal treatment standards)

This January 3 action was an amendment of the September 19, 1994 Phase II LDRs (universal waste rule). U.S. EPA corrected errors and clarified language in the universal treatment standards. The Board did not delay in adding these amendments for three reasons:

1) The January 3, 1995 amendments are corrections and clarifications of the September 19, 1994 regulations, and not new substantive amendments;

2) Prompt action on the January 3, 1995 amendments will facilitate implementation of the Phase II LDRs; and

3) The Board has received a request from the regulated community that we add the January 3, 1995 amendments to those of September 19, 1994. (See "Expedited Consideration" below.)

The Board also notes that the later amendments occurred within six months of the earliest amendments included in this docket, even if they occurred outside the nominal time-frame of the docket.

In addition to the federally-derived amendments, the Board used this opportunity to undertake a number of housekeeping and corrective amendments. We have effected the removal of all cross-references for effective dates and repealed Part 700. We have converted equations and formulae to the standard scientific format. We have tried to improve the language and structure of various provisions, including correcting grammar, punctuation, and spelling where necessary.

Specifically, the segment of the amendments involved in Part 705 are primarily corrective or clarifying in nature. The Board opened Section 705.128 for the purpose of deleting a cross-references to 35 Ill. Adm. Code 700.106 for effective dates. The Board then used the opportunity to make corrections and to clarify the language of this provision.

POLLUTION CONTROL BOARD

NOTICE OF PROPOSED AMENDMENTS

6) Will this proposed rule replace an emergency rule currently in effect? No.

7) Does this rulemaking contain an automatic repeal date? No.

8) Do these proposed amendments contain incorporations by reference? No.

9) Are there any other amendments pending on this Part? No.

10) Statement of statewide policy objectives:

This rulemaking is mandated by Sections 13(c) and 22.4(a) of the Environmental Protection Act [415 ILCS 5/13(c) & 22.4(a)]. The statewide policy objectives are set forth in Section 20 of that Act. This rulemaking imposes mandates on units of local government only to the extent that they may be involved in the generation, transportation, treatment, storage, or disposal of hazardous waste or they engage in underground injection of waste.

11) Time, place and manner in which interested persons may comment on this proposed rulemaking:

The Board will accept written public comment on this proposal for a period of 45 days after the date of this publication. Comments should reference Docket R95-4/R95-6 and be addressed to:

Ms. Dorothy M. Gunn, Clerk
Illinois Pollution Control Board
State of Illinois Center, Suite 11-500
100 W. Randolph St.
Chicago, IL 60601
312/814-6931

Address all questions to Michael J. McCambridge, at 312/814-6924.

12) Initial regulatory flexibility analysis:

A) Date rule was submitted to the Small Business Office of the Department of Commerce and Community Affairs: March 6, 1995.

B) Types of small businesses affected:

The existing rules and proposed amendments affect small businesses that generate, transport, treat, store, or dispose of hazardous waste or engage in underground injection of waste.

C) Reporting, bookkeeping or other procedures required for compliance:

POLLUTION CONTROL BOARD

NOTICE OF PROPOSED AMENDMENTS

The existing rules and proposed amendments require extensive
reporting, bookkeeping, and other procedures, including the
preparation of manifests and annual reports, waste analyses, and
maintenance of operating records.

D)   Types of professional skills necessary for compliance:

Compliance with the existing rules and proposed amendments may
require the services of an attorney, certified public accountant,
chemist, and registered professional engineer.

The full text of the proposed amendments begins on the next page:

POLLUTION CONTROL BOARD

NOTICE OF PROPOSED AMENDMENTS

TITLE 35: ENVIRONMENTAL PROTECTION
SUBTITLE G: WASTE DISPOSAL
CHAPTER I: POLLUTION CONTROL BOARD
SUBCHAPTER b: PERMITS

PART 705
PROCEDURES FOR PERMIT ISSUANCE

SUBPART A: GENERAL PROVISIONS

SUBPART B: PERMIT APPLICATIONS

SUBPART C: APPLICATION REVIEW

SUBPART D: PUBLIC NOTICE

SUBPART E: PUBLIC COMMENT

POLLUTION CONTROL BOARD

NOTICE OF PROPOSED AMENDMENTS

705.182   Public Hearings
705.183   Obligation to Raise Issues and Provide Information
705.184   Reopening of Public Comment Period

SUBPART F: PERMIT ISSUANCE

Section
705.201   Final Permit Decision
705.202   Stay upon Timely Application for Renewal
705.203   Stay for New Application or upon Untimely Application for Renewal
705.204   Stay upon Reapplication or for Modification
705.205   Stay Following Interim Status
705.210   Agency Response to Comments
705.211   Administrative Record for Final Permits or Letters of Denial
705.212   Appeal of Agency Permit Determinations

APPENDIX A   Procedures for Permit Issuance
APPENDIX B   Modification Process
APPENDIX C   Application Process
APPENDIX D   Application Review Process
APPENDIX E   Public Comment Process
APPENDIX F   Permit Issuance or Denial

AUTHORITY: Implementing Sections 13 and 22.4 and authorized by Section 27 of
the Environmental Protection Act [415 ILCS 5/13, 22.4 and 27].

SOURCE: Adopted in R81-32, 47 PCB 93, at 6 Ill. Reg. 12479, effective May 17,
1982; amended in R82-19, at 7 Ill. Reg. 14352, effective May 17, 1982; amended
in R84-9, at 9 Ill. Reg. 11894, effective July 24, 1985; amended in R89-2 at 14
Ill. Reg. 3682, effective February 20, 1990; amended in R94-5 at 18 Ill. Reg.
18265, effective December 20, 1994; amended in R95-6 at 19 Ill. Reg.
_____, effective _____.

SUBPART B: PERMIT APPLICATIONS

Section 705.128 Modification of Permits

a)   The Agency may modify a Permits permit may be modified either at the
     request of any interested person (including the permittee) or upon non
     the Agency's its own initiative. However, the Agency may only modify
     a permits permit may only be modified for the reasons specified in 35
     Ill. Adm. Code 704.261 through 704.263 or 35 Ill. Adm. Code 703.270
     through 703.273. All A requests request for permit modification shall
     must be made in writing, must be addressed to the Agency (Division of
     Land Pollution Control), and shall Must contain facts or reasons
     supporting the request.

b)   If the Agency decides determines that the a request for modification
     is not justified, it shall send the requester a brief written response

POLLUTION CONTROL BOARD

NOTICE OF PROPOSED AMENDMENTS

giving a reason for the decision determination. A Denials denial of a
requests request for modification are is not subject to public notice,
comment, or public hearings hearing requirements. The requester may
appeal a Denial denial of a request to modify a permit may be appealed
to the Board pursuant to 35 Ill. Adm. Code 105.

c)   Agency Modification Procedures

     1)   If the Agency tentatively decides to initiate steps to modify a
          permit under this section Section and 35 Ill. Code 704.261
          through 704.263 or 35 Ill. Adm. Code 703.270 through 703.273, it
          shall, after giving public notice pursuant to Section
          705.161(a)(1), as though an application had been received (See
          705.161(a)(1)), it shall prepare a draft permit under See
          Section 705.141 incorporating the proposed changes. The Agency
          may request additional information and may require the submission
          of an updated permit application. For reissued permits, the
          Agency shall require the submission of a new application.

     2)   In a permit modification proceeding under this section Section,
          only those conditions to be modified shall be reopened when a new
          draft permit is prepared. During any modification proceeding,
          including any appeals appeal if any to the Board, the permittee
          shall comply with all conditions of the its existing permit until
          a new final permit is reissued.

     3)   "Minor modifications", as defined in 35 Ill. Adm. Code 704.264,
          and "Class 1 and 2 modifications," as defined in 35 Ill. Adm.
          Code 703.281 and 703.282, are not subject to the requirements of
          this section Section. If the Agency makes a minor modification,
          the modified permit must be accompanied by a letter stating the
          reasons for the minor modification.

d)   To the extent that the Agency has authority to terminate or reissue
     permits, if it decides to do so it must prepare a draft permit or
     notice of intent to deny in accordance with Section 705.141 if it
     decides to do so.

e)   The Agency or any person may seek the revocation of a permit in
     accordance with Title VIII of the Environmental Protection Act and in
     accordance with the procedure of 35 Ill. Adm. Code 103. Revocation
     may only be sought only for those reasons specified in 35 Ill. Adm.
     Code 702.186(a) through (d).
     BOARD NOTE: Derived from 40 CFR 124.5 (1988 1993)--amended-at-13-Fed-
     Reg-37934-September-26,-1988.

(Source: Amended at   19   Ill.   Reg.   _____, effective
_____.)

POLLUTION CONTROL BOARD

NOTICE OF PROPOSED AMENDMENTS

1) **Heading of the Part:** RCRA and UIC Permit Programs

2) **Code Citation:** 35 Ill. Adm. Code 702

3) **Section Numbers:**   **Proposed Action:**

     702.181   Amended

4) **Statutory Authority:** 415 ILCS 5/13, 22.4 and 27.

5) **A complete description of the subjects and issues involved:**

A more detailed description is contained in the Board's proposed opinion of March 2, 1995, in R95-4 and R95-6 (consolidated), which opinion is available from the address below. Sections 13(c) and 22.4(a) of the Environmental Protection Act (415 ILCS 5/13(c) & 22.4(a)] provide that Section 5-35 of the Administrative Procedure Act (5 ILCS 100/5-35) shall not apply. Because this rulemaking is not subject to Section 5-35 of the APA, it is not subject to first notice or to second notice review by JCAR.

This rulemaking updates Parts 700, 702, 703, 705, 720, 721, 722, 723, 724, 725, 726, 728, 730, 738, and 739 of the Illinois RCRA Subtitle C hazardous waste and underground injection control (UIC) rules to correspond with amendments adopted by U.S. EPA that appeared in the Federal Register during the period July 1 through December 31, 1994. During this period, U.S. EPA amended its regulations as follows:

Federal Action	Summary
59 Fed. Reg. 38536, July 23, 1994	Exclusion from definition of solid waste for certain in-process recycled secondary materials used by the petroleum refining industry
59 Fed. Reg. 43496, August 24, 1994	Withdrawal of exemption from Subtitle C regulation of slag residues from high temperature metal recovery (HTMR) of electric arc furnace dust, (K061), steel finishing pickle liquor (K062), and electroplating sludges (F006) that are used in a manner constituting disposal
59 Fed. Reg. 47980, September 19, 1994	Restoration of text from 40 CFR 268.7(a) inadvertently omitted in the amendments of August 31, 1993, at 58 Fed. Reg. 46040

POLLUTION CONTROL BOARD

NOTICE OF PROPOSED AMENDMENTS

59 Fed. Reg. 47982, September 19, 1994	Phase II land disposal restrictions (LDRs): universal treatment standards for organic toxicity wastes and newly-listed wastes (including underground injection control (UIC) amendments)
59 Fed. Reg. 62896, December 6, 1994	Organic material air emission standards for tanks, surface impoundments, and containers

In addition to these principal amendments that occurred during the update period, the Board has included an additional, later action:

60 Fed. Reg. 242, January 3, 1995	Corrections to the Phase II land disposal restrictions (universal treatment standards)

This January 3 action was an amendment of the September 19, 1994 Phase II LDRs (universal waste rule). U.S. EPA corrected errors and clarified language in the universal treatment standards. The Board did not delay in adding these amendments for three reasons:

1) The January 3, 1995 amendments are corrections and clarifications of the September 19, 1994 regulations, and not new substantive amendments;

2) Prompt action on the January 3, 1995 amendments will facilitate implementation of the Phase II LDRs; and

3) The Board has received a request from the regulated community that we add the January 3, 1995 amendments to those of September 19, 1994. (See "Expedited Consideration" below.)

The Board also notes that the later amendments occurred within six months of the earliest amendments included in this docket, even if they occurred outside the nominal time-frame of the docket.

In addition to the federally-derived amendments, the Board used this opportunity to undertake a number of housekeeping and corrective amendments. We have effected the removal of all cross-references for effective dates and repealed Part 700. We have converted equations and formulae to the standard scientific format. We have tried to improve the language and structure of various provisions, including correcting grammar, punctuation, and spelling where necessary.

Specifically, the segment of the amendments involved in Part 702 are based on the December 6, 1994 federal air emissions regulations. The federal amendments broaden exceptions from the general federal rule that compliance with the conditions of a permit constitutes compliance with federal law. Since the rule in Illinois is that compliance with the

POLLUTION CONTROL BOARD

NOTICE OF PROPOSED AMENDMENTS

conditions of a permit constitutes compliance only with the requirements of the law to operate in compliance with the permit, the federal amendments were unnecessary to Section 702.181. Rather, the Board added a note that explains the corresponding federal provision and the differences between Illinois and federal law.

6) Will this proposed rule replace an emergency rule currently in effect? No

7) Does this rulemaking contain an automatic repeal date? No

8) Do these proposed amendments contain incorporations by reference? No

9) Are there any other amendments pending on this Part? No

10) Statement of statewide policy objectives: This rulemaking is mandated by Sections 13(c) and 22.4(a) of the Environmental Protection Act [415 ILCS 5/13(c) & 22.4(a)]. The statewide policy objectives are set forth in Section 20 of that Act. This rulemaking imposes mandates on units of local government only to the extent that they may be involved in the generation, transportation, treatment, storage, or disposal of hazardous waste or they engage in underground injection of waste.

11) Time, place and manner in which interested persons may comment on this proposed rulemaking: The Board will accept written public comment on this proposal for a period of 45 days after the date of this publication. Comments should reference Docket R95-4/R95-6 and be addressed to:

    Ms. Dorothy M. Gunn, Clerk
    Illinois Pollution Control Board
    State of Illinois Center, Suite 11-500
    100 W. Randolph St.
    Chicago, IL 60601
    (312) 814-6931

Address all questions to Michael J. McCambridge, at (312) 814-6924.

12) Initial regulatory flexibility analysis:

    A) Date rule was submitted to the Small Business Office of the Department of Commerce and Community Affairs: March 6, 1995.

    B) Types of small businesses affected: The existing rules and proposed amendments affect small businesses that generate, transport, treat, store, or dispose of hazardous waste or engage in underground injection of waste.

    C) Reporting, bookkeeping or other procedures required for compliance: The existing rules and proposed amendments require extensive

POLLUTION CONTROL BOARD

NOTICE OF PROPOSED AMENDMENTS

reporting, bookkeeping, and other procedures, including the preparation of manifests and annual reports, waste analyses, and maintenance of operating records.

    D) Types of professional skills necessary for compliance: Compliance with the existing rules and proposed amendments may require the services of an attorney, certified public accountant, chemist, and registered professional engineer.

The full text of the proposed amendments begins on the next page:

POLLUTION CONTROL BOARD

NOTICE OF PROPOSED AMENDMENTS

TITLE 35: ENVIRONMENTAL PROTECTION
SUBTITLE G: WASTE DISPOSAL
CHAPTER I: POLLUTION CONTROL BOARD
SUBCHAPTER b: PERMITS

PART 702
RCRA AND UIC PERMIT PROGRAMS

SUBPART A: GENERAL PROVISIONS

POLLUTION CONTROL BOARD

NOTICE OF PROPOSED AMENDMENTS

AUTHORITY: Implementing Sections 13 and 22.4 and authorized by Section 27 of
the Environmental Protection Act [415 ILCS 5/13, 22.4 and 27].

SOURCE: Adopted in R81-32, 47 PCB 93, at 6 Ill. Reg. 12479, effective May 17,
1982; amended in R82-19, at 53 PCB 131, 7 Ill. Reg. 14352, effective May 17,
1982; amended in R84-9 at 9 Ill. Reg. 11926, effective July 24, 1985; amended
in B85-23 at 10 Ill. Reg. 13274, effective July 29, 1986; amended in R86-1 at
10 Ill. Reg. 14083, effective August 12, 1986; amended in R86-28 at 11 Ill.
Reg. 6131, effective March 24, 1987; amended in R87-5 at 11 Ill. Reg. 19376,
effective November 12, 1987; amended in R87-26 at 12 Ill. Reg. 2579, effective
January 15, 1988; amended in R87-29 at 12 Ill. Reg. 6673, effective March 28,
1988; amended in R87-39 at 12 Ill. Reg. 13083, effective July 29, 1988; amended
in R89-1 at 13 Ill. Reg. 18452, effective November 13, 1989; amended in R89-2
at 14 Ill. Reg. 3089, effective February 20, 1990; amended in R89-9 at 14 Ill.
Reg. 6273, effective April 16, 1990; amended in R92-10 at 17 Ill. Reg 5769,
effective March 26, 1993; amended in R93-16 at 18 Ill. Reg. 6918, effective
April 26, 1994; amended in R94-5 at 18 Ill. Reg. 18284, effective December 20,
1994; amended at 19 Ill. Reg. _____, effective _____.

SUBPART D: ISSUED PERMITS

Section 702.181 Effect of a Permit

   a)   The existence of a RCRA or UIC permit does not constitute a defense to
        a violation of the Environmental Protection Act or this Subtitle,
        except for development, modification, or operation without a permit.
        However, a permit may be modified, reissued, or revoked during its
        term for cause as set forth in 35 Ill. Adm. Code 703.270 through
        703.273 (RCRA) or 35 Ill. Adm. Code 704.261 through 704.263 (UIC) and
        Section 702.186.

POLLUTION CONTROL BOARD

NOTICE OF PROPOSED AMENDMENTS

BOARD NOTE: 40 CFR 270.4(a) differs from this subsection (a) in two significant aspects: (1) it states that compliance with the permit is compliance with federal law, and (2) it enumerates exceptions when compliance with the permit can violate federal law. The exceptions are intervening (1) statutory requirements; (2) 40 CFR 268 land disposal restrictions; (3) 40 CFR 264 leak detection requirements; and (4) 40 CFR 266, subparts AA, BB, and CC air emissions limitations. By not codifying the federal exceptions, since they are not necessary in the Illinois program to accomplish the intended purpose, the Board does not intend to imply that compliance with a RCRA permit obviates immediate compliance with any of the event included in the federal exceptions.

b) The issuance of a permit does not convey any property rights of any sort, or any exclusive privilege.

c) The issuance of a permit does not authorize any injury to persons or property or invasion of other private rights, or any infringement of State or local law or regulations, except as noted in subsection (a) above.

BOARD NOTE: Derived from 40 CFR 144.35 (1993) and 40 CFR 270 (1992) (1994), as amended at 49 Fed. Reg. 62952 (Dec. 6, 1994). am+

POLLUTION CONTROL BOARD

NOTICE OF PROPOSED AMENDMENTS

1) Heading of the Part: RCRA Permit Program

2) Code Citation: 35 Ill. Adm. Code 703

3) Section numbers:

Section numbers:	Proposed action:
703.183	Amended
703.201	Amended
703.202	Amended
703.203	Amended
703.213	New Section

4) Statutory authority: 415 ILCS 5/22.4 and 27.

5) A complete description of the subjects and issues involved:

A more detailed description is contained in the Board's proposed opinion of March 2, 1995, in R95-4 and R95-6 (consolidated), which opinion is available from the address below. Section 22.4(a) of the Environmental Protection Act [415 ILCS 5/22.4(a)] provides that Section 5-35 of the Administrative Procedure Act [5 ILCS 100/5-35] shall not apply. Because this rulemaking is not subject to Section 5-35 of the APA, it is not subject to first notice or to second notice review by JCAR.

This rulemaking updates Parts 700, 702, 703, 705, 720, 721, 722, 723, 724, 725, 726, 728, 730, 738, and 739 of the Illinois RCRA Subtitle C hazardous waste and underground injection control (UIC) rules to correspond with amendments adopted by U.S. EPA that appeared in the Federal Register during the period July 1 through December 31, 1994. During this period, U.S. EPA amended its regulations as follows:

Federal Action	Summary
59 Fed. Reg. 38536, July 28, 1994	Exclusion from definition of solid waste for certain in-process recycled secondary materials used by the petroleum refining industry
59 Fed. Reg. 43496, August 24, 1994	Withdrawal of exemption from Subtitle C regulation of slag residues from high temperature metal recovery (HTMR) of electric arc furnace dust (K061), steel finishing pickle liquor (K062), and electroplating sludges (F006) that are used in a manner constituting disposal

POLLUTION CONTROL BOARD

NOTICE OF PROPOSED AMENDMENTS

59 Fed. Reg. 47980, September 19, 1994	Restoration of text from 40 CFR 268.7(a) inadvertently omitted in the amendments of August 31, 1993, at 58 Fed. Reg. 46040
59 Fed. Reg. 47982, September 19, 1994	Phase II land disposal restrictions (LDRs): universal treatment standards for organic toxicity wastes and newly-listed wastes (including underground injection control (UIC) amendments)

In addition to these principal amendments that occurred during the update period, the Board has included an additional, later action:

60 Fed. Reg. 242, January 3, 1995	Corrections to the Phase II land disposal restrictions (universal treatment standards)

This January 3 action was an amendment of the September 19, 1994 Phase II LDRs (universal waste rule). U.S. EPA corrected errors and clarified language in the universal treatment standards. The Board did not delay in adding these amendments for three reasons:

1) The January 3, 1995 amendments are corrections and clarifications of the September 19, 1994 regulations, and not new substantive amendments;

2) Prompt action on the January 3, 1995 amendments will facilitate implementation of the Phase II LDRs; and

3) The Board has received a request from the regulated community that we add the January 3, 1995 amendments to those of September 19, 1994. (See "Expedited Consideration" below.)

The Board also notes that the later amendments occurred within six months of the earliest amendments included in this docket, even if they occurred outside the nominal time-frame of the docket.

In addition to the federally-derived amendments, the Board used this opportunity to undertake a number of housekeeping and corrective amendments. We have effected the removal of all cross-references for effective dates and repealed Part 700. We have converted equations and formulae to the standard scientific format. We have tried to improve the language and structure of various provision, including correcting grammar, punctuation, and spelling where necessary.

Specifically, the segment of the amendments involved in Part 703

POLLUTION CONTROL BOARD

NOTICE OF PROPOSED AMENDMENTS

incorporate revisions made by U.S. EPA as part of the December 6, 1994 air emissions requirements. They update the RCRA permit application regulations to add the information necessary to demonstrate prospective compliance with the new air emissions rules.

6) Will this proposed rule replace an emergency rule currently in effect? No.

7) Does this rulemaking contain an automatic repeal date? No.

8) Do these proposed amendments contain incorporations by reference? No.

9) Are there any other amendments pending on this Part? No.

10) Statement of statewide policy objectives:

This rulemaking is mandated by Section 22.4(a) of the Environmental Protection Act (415 ILCS 5/22.4(a)). The statewide policy objectives are set forth in Section 20 of that Act. This rulemaking imposes mandates on units of local government only to the extent that they may be involved in the generation, transportation, treatment, storage, or disposal of hazardous waste or they engage in underground injection of waste.

11) Time, place and manner in which interested persons may comment on this proposed rulemaking:

The Board will accept written public comment on this proposal for a period of 45 days after the date of this publication. Comments should reference Docket R95-4/R95-6 and be addressed to:

Ms. Dorothy M. Gunn, Clerk
Illinois Pollution Control Board
State of Illinois Center, Suite 11-500
100 W. Randolph St.
Chicago, IL 60601
312/814-6931

Address all questions to Michael J. McCambridge, at 312/814-6924.

12) Initial regulatory flexibility analysis:

A) Date rule was submitted to the Small Business Office of the Department of Commerce and Community Affairs: March 6, 1995.

B) Types of small businesses affected:

The existing rules and proposed amendments affect small businesses that generate, transport, treat, store, or dispose of hazardous waste

POLLUTION CONTROL BOARD

NOTICE OF PROPOSED AMENDMENTS

or engage in underground injection of waste.

C) Reporting, bookkeeping or other procedures required for compliance:

The existing rules and proposed amendments require extensive
reporting, bookkeeping, and other procedures, including the
preparation of manifests and annual reports, waste analyses, and
maintenance of operating records.

D) Types of professional skills necessary for compliance:

Compliance with the existing rules and proposed amendments may
require the services of an attorney, certified public accountant,
chemist, and registered professional engineer.

The full text of the proposed amendments begins on the next page:

POLLUTION CONTROL BOARD

NOTICE OF PROPOSED AMENDMENTS

TITLE 35: ENVIRONMENTAL PROTECTION
SUBTITLE G: WASTE DISPOSAL
CHAPTER I: POLLUTION CONTROL BOARD
SUBCHAPTER b: PERMITS

PART 703
RCRA PERMIT PROGRAM

SUBPART A: GENERAL PROVISIONS

POLLUTION CONTROL BOARD

NOTICE OF PROPOSED AMENDMENTS

SUBPART E: SHORT TERM AND PHASED PERMITS

SUBPART F: PERMIT CONDITIONS OR DENIAL

POLLUTION CONTROL BOARD

NOTICE OF PROPOSED AMENDMENTS

SUBPART G: CHANGES TO PERMITS

APPENDIX A Classification of Permit Modifications

AUTHORITY: Implementing Section 22.4 and authorized by Section 27 of the Environmental Protection Act [415 ILCS 5/22.4 and 27].

SOURCE: Adopted in R82-19, 53 PCB 131, at 7 Ill. Reg. 14289, effective October 12, 1983; amended in R83-24 at 8 Ill. Reg. 206, effective December 27, 1983; amended in R84-9 at 9 Ill. Reg. 11899, effective July 24, 1985; amended in R85-22 at 10 Ill. Reg. 1110, effective January 2, 1986; amended in R85-23 at 10 Ill. Reg. 13284, effective July 28, 1986; amended in R86-1 at 10 Ill. Reg. 14093, effective August 12, 1986; amended in R86-19 at 10 Ill. Reg. 20702, effective December 2, 1986; amended in R86-28 at 11 Ill. Reg. 6121, effective March 24, 1987; amended in R86-46 at 11 Ill. Reg. 13543, effective August 4, 1987; amended in R87-5 at 11 Ill. Reg. 19383, effective November 12, 1987; amended in R87-26 at 12 Ill. Reg. 2584, effective January 15, 1988; amended in R87-39 at 12 Ill. Reg. 13069, effective July 29, 1988; amended in R88-16 at 13 Ill. Reg. 447, effective December 27, 1988; amended in R89-1 at 13 Ill. Reg. 18477, effective November 13, 1989; amended in R89-9 at 14 Ill. Reg. 6278, effective April 16, 1990; amended in R90-2 at 14 Ill. Reg. 14492, effective August 22, 1990; amended in R90-11 at 15 Ill. Reg. 9616, effective June 17, 1991; amended in R91-13 at 15 Ill. Reg. 14554, effective September 30, 1991; amended in R91-13 at 16 Ill. Reg. 9767, effective June 9, 1992; amended in R92-10 at 17 Ill. Reg. 5774, effective March 26, 1993; amended in R93-4 at 17 Ill. Reg. 20794, effective November 22, 1993; amended in R93-16 at 18 Ill. Reg. 6898, effective April 26, 1994; amended in R94-7 at 18 Ill. Reg. 12392, effective July 29, 1994; amended in R94-5 at 18 Ill. Reg. 18316, effective December 20, 1994; amended in R95-6 at 19 Ill. Reg. _____, effective

NOTE: In this Part, superscript numbers or letters are denoted by parentheses; subscript are denoted by brackets.

SUBPART D: APPLICATIONS

Section 703.183 General Information

POLLUTION CONTROL BOARD

NOTICE OF PROPOSED AMENDMENTS

The following information is required in the Part B application for all HWM
facilities; except as 35 Ill. Adm. Code 724.101 provides otherwise:
   a) A general description of the facility;
   b) Chemical and physical analyses of the hazardous wastes and hazardous
      debris to be handled at the facility. At a minimum, these analyses
      must contain all the information which must be known to treat, store
      or dispose of the wastes properly in accordance with 35 Ill. Adm. Code
      724;
   c) A copy of the waste analysis plan required by 35 Ill. Adm. Code
      724.113(b) and, if applicable, 35 Ill. Adm. Code 724.113(c);
   d) A description of the security procedures and equipment required by 35
      Ill. Adm. Code 724.114, or a justification demonstrating the reasons
      for requesting a waiver of this requirement;
   e) A copy of the general inspection schedule required by 35 Ill. Adm.
      Code 724.115(b). Include where applicable, as part of the inspection
      schedule, specific requirements in 35 Ill. Adm. Code 724.374,
      724.293(i), 724.295, 724.326, 724.354, 724.373, 724.403, 724.702,
      724.933, 724.952, 924.953, and 724.958, 724.988, and 724.991;
   f) A justification of any request for a waiver of the preparedness and
      prevention requirements of 35 Ill. Adm. Code 724.Subpart C;
   g) A copy of the contingency plan required by 35 Ill. Adm. Code
      724.Subpart D;
      BOARD NOTE: Include, where applicable, as part of the contingency
      plan, specific requirements in 35 Ill. Adm. Code 724.327 and 724.355.
      35 Ill. Adm. Code 724.355 has not yet been adopted.
   h) A description of procedures, structures, or equipment used at the
      facility to:
      1) Prevent hazards in unloading operations (for example, ramps, or
         special forklifts);
      2) Prevent runoff from hazardous waste handling areas to other areas
         of the facility or environment, or to prevent flooding (for
         example, berms, dikes, or trenches);
      3) Prevent contamination of water supplies;
      4) Mitigate effects of equipment failure and power outages;
      5) Prevent undue exposure of personnel to hazardous waste (for
         example, protective clothing); and
      6) Prevent releases to the atmosphere.
   i) A description of precautions to prevent Accidental ignition or
      reaction of ignitable, reactive, or incompatible wastes, as required
      to demonstrate compliance with 35 Ill. Adm. Code 724.117, including
      documentation demonstrating compliance with 35 Ill. Adm. Code
      724.117(c);
   j) Traffic pattern, estimated volume (number and types of vehicles), and
      control (for example, show turns across traffic lanes and stacking
      lanes, tif appropriate); describe access road surfacing and load
      bearing capacity; and show traffic control signals);
   k) Facility location information, as required by Section 703.184;
   l) An outline of both the introductory and continuing training programs

POLLUTION CONTROL BOARD

NOTICE OF PROPOSED AMENDMENTS

      by the owners owner or operators operator to prepare persons to
      operate or maintain the HWM facility in a safe manner, as required to
      demonstrate compliance with 35 Ill. Adm. Code 724.116. A brief
      description of how training will be designed to meet actual job tasks
      in accordance with requirements in 35 Ill. Adm. Code 724.116(a)(3);
   m) A copy of the closure plan and, where applicable, the post-closure
      plan required by 35 Ill. Adm. Code 724.212, 724.218, and 724.297.
      Include where applicable, as part of the plans, specific requirements
      in 35 Ill. Adm. Code 724.278, 724.297, 724.328, 724.358, 724.380,
      724.410, 724.451, 724.701, and 724.703;
   n) For hazardous waste disposal units that have been closed,
      documentation that notices required under 35 Ill. Adm. Code 724.219
      have been filed;
   o) The most recent closure cost estimate for the facility, prepared in
      accordance with 35 Ill. Adm. Code 724.242, and a copy of the
      documentation required to demonstrate financial assurance under 35
      Ill. Adm. Code 724.243. For a new facility, a copy of the required
      documentation may be submitted 60 days prior to the initial receipt of
      hazardous wastes, if it is later than the submission of the Part B
      permit application;
   p) Where applicable, the most recent post-closure cost estimate for the
      facility, prepared in accordance with 35 Ill. Adm. Code 724.244, plus
      a copy of the documentation required to demonstrate financial
      assurance under 35 Ill. Adm. Code 724.245. For a new facility, a
      copy of the required documentation may be submitted 60 days prior to
      the initial receipt of hazardous wastes, if it is later than the
      submission of the Part B permit application;
   q) Where applicable, a copy of the insurance policy or other
      documentation which comprises compliance with the requirements of 35
      Ill. Adm. Code 724.247. For a new facility, documentation showing the
      amount of insurance meeting the specification of 35 Ill. Adm. Code
      724.247(a) and, if applicable, 35 Ill. Adm. Code 724.247(b) that the
      owner or operator plans to have in effect before initial receipt of
      hazardous waste for treatment, storage, or disposal. A request for an
      alternative level of required coverage, for a new or existing
      facility may be submitted as specified in 35 Ill. Adm. Code
      724.247(c);
   r) A topographic map showing a distance of 1000 feet around the facility
      at a scale of 2.5 centimeters (1 inch) equal to not more than 61.0
      meters (200 feet). Contours must be shown on the map. The contour
      interval must be sufficient to clearly show the pattern of surface
      water flow in the vicinity of and from each operational unit of the
      facility. For example, contours with an interval of 1.5 meters (5
      feet), if relief is greater than 6.1 meters (20 feet), or an interval
      of 0.6 meters (2 feet), if relief is less than 6.1 meters (20 feet).
      Owners and operators of HWM facilities located in mountainous areas
      shall use larger contour intervals to adequately show topographic
      profiles of facilities. The map must clearly show the following:

POLLUTION CONTROL BOARD

NOTICE OF PROPOSED AMENDMENTS

1) Map scale and date;
2) 100-year floodplain area;
3) Surface waters including intermittent streams;
4) Surrounding land uses (e.g., residential, commercial, agricultural, recreational, etc.);
5) A wind rose (i.e., prevailing windspeed and direction);
6) Orientation of the map (north arrow);
7) Legal boundaries of the HWM facility site;
8) Access control (e.g., fences, gates, etc.);
9) Injection and withdrawal wells both on-site and off-site;
10) Buildings; treatment, storage, or disposal operations; or other structures (e.g., recreation areas, runoff control systems, access and internal roads, storm, sanitary and process sewage systems, loading and unloading areas, fire control facilities, etc.);
11) Barriers for drainage or flood control;
12) Location of operational units within the HWM facility site, where hazardous waste is (or will be) treated, stored, or disposed (include equipment cleanup areas);
BOARD NOTE: For large HWM facilities, the Agency shall allow the use of other scales on a case by case basis.
s) Applicants shall submit such information as the Agency determines is necessary for it to determine whether to issue a permit and what conditions to impose in any permit issued;
t) For land disposal facilities, if a case-by-case extension has been approved under 35 Ill. Adm. Code 728.105, or if a petition has been approved under 35 Ill. Adm. Code 728.106, a copy of the notice of approval of the extension or of approval of the petition is required.
BOARD NOTE: Derived from 40 CFR 270.14(b) (1988 1994), as amended at 59 59 Fed. Reg. 37881, August 18, 1992 62952 (Dec. 6, 1994).

(Source: Amended at 19 Ill. Reg. _____, effective _____)

Section 703.201 Containers

For facilities that store containers of hazardous waste, except as otherwise provided in 35 Ill. Adm. Code 724.270, the Part B application must include:
a) A description of the containment system to demonstrate compliance with 35 Ill. Adm. Code 724.275. Show at least the following:
1) Basic design parameters, dimensions, and materials of construction;
2) How the design promotes drainage or how containers are kept from contact with standing liquids in the containment system;
3) Capacity of the containment system relative to the number and volume of containers to be stored;
4) Provisions for preventing or managing run-on; and
5) How accumulated liquids can be analyzed and removed to prevent

POLLUTION CONTROL BOARD

NOTICE OF PROPOSED AMENDMENTS

overflow;
b) For storage areas that store containers holding wastes that do not contain free liquids, a demonstration of compliance with 35 Ill. Adm. Code 724.275(c), including:
1) Test procedures and results or other documentation or information to show that the wastes do not contain free liquids; and
2) A description of how the storage area is designed or operated to drain and remove liquids or how containers are kept from contact with standing liquids;
c) Sketches, drawings, or data demonstrating compliance with 35 Ill. Adm. Code 724.276 (location of buffer zone and containers holding ignitable or reactive wastes) and Section 724.277(c) (location of incompatible wastes), where applicable.
d) Where incompatible wastes are stored or otherwise managed in containers, a description of the procedures used to ensure compliance with 35 Ill. Adm. Code 724.117(b) and (c) and 724.277(a) and (b).
e) Information on air emission control equipment, as required in Section 703.213.
BOARD NOTE: Derived from 40 CFR 270.15 (1992 1994), as amended at 59 Fed. Reg. 62952 (Dec. 6, 1994).

(Source: Amended at 19 Ill. Reg. _____, effective _____)

Section 703.202 Tank Systems

Except as otherwise provided in 35 Ill. Adm. Code 724.290, owners and operators of facilities that use tanks to store or treat hazardous waste shall provide the following additional information:
a) A written assessment that is reviewed and certified by an independent, qualified, registered professional engineer as to the structural integrity and suitability for handling hazardous waste of each tank system, as required under 35 Ill. Adm. Code 724.291 and 724.292;
b) Dimensions and capacity of each tank;
c) Description of feed systems, safety cutoff, bypass systems, and pressure controls (e.g., vents);
d) A diagram of piping, instrumentation, and process flow for each tank system;
e) A description of materials and equipment used to provide external corrosion protection, as required under 35 Ill. Adm. Code 724.292(a)(3)(B);
f) For new tank systems, a detailed descriptions of how the tank system(s) will be installed in compliance with 35 Ill. Adm. Code 724.292(b), (c), (d), and (e);
g) Detailed plans and description of how the secondary containment system for each tank system is or will be designed, constructed and operated to meet the requirements of 35 Ill. Adm. Code 724.293(a), (b), (c), (d), (e), and (f);

b) For tank systems for which alternative design and operating practices are sought pursuant to 35 Ill. Adm. Code 724.293(g):

1) Detailed plans and engineering and hydrogeologic reports, as appropriate, describing alternate design and operating practices that will, in conjunction with location aspects, prevent the migration of any hazardous waste or hazardous constituents into the groundwater or surface water during the life of the facility, or

2) A detailed assessment of the substantial present or potential hazards posed to human health or the environment should a release enter the environment.

3) A copy of the petition for alternative design and operating practices or, if such have already been granted, a copy of the Board Order granting alternative design and operating practices;

i) Description of controls and practices to prevent spills and overflows, as required under 35 Ill. Adm. Code 724.294(b); and

j) For tank systems in which ignitable, reactive or incompatible wastes are to be stored or treated, a description of how operating procedures and tank system and facility design will achieve compliance with the requirements of 35 Ill. Adm. Code 724.298 and 724.299~;~ and

k) Information on air emission control equipment, as required in Section 703.213;

~[Board Note~ BOARD NOTE: ~See~ 40 CFR 270.16 (~1986~ 1994), as amended at 5~1~ 59 Fed. Reg. 9~54~73~, July 14, 1986~ 62952 (Dec. 6, 1994).~

(Source: Amended at 19 Ill. Reg. _____, effective
_____)

Section 703.203 Surface Impoundments

For facilities that store, treat, or dispose of hazardous waste in surface impoundments, except as otherwise provided in 35 Ill. Adm. Code 724.101, the Part B application must include:

a) A list of the hazardous wastes placed or to be placed in each surface impoundment;

b) Detailed plans and an engineering report describing how the surface impoundment is designed and is or will be constructed, operated, and maintained to meet the requirements of 35 Ill. Adm. Code 724.119, 724.321, 724.322 and 724.323, addressing the following items:

1) The liner system (except for an existing portion of a surface impoundment). If an exemption from the requirement for a liner is sought, as provided by 35 Ill. Adm. Code 724.321(b), submit a copy of the Board order granting an adjusted standard pursuant to 35 Ill. Adm. Code 724.321(b);

2) The double liner and leak (leachate) detection, collection and removal system, if the surface impoundment must meet the requirements of 35 Ill. Am. Code 724.321 (c). If an exemption from the requirements for double liners and a leak detection,

collection, and removal system or alternative design is sought as provided by 35 Ill. Adm. Code 724.321(d), (e), or (f), submit appropriate information;

3) If the leak detection system is located in a saturated zone, submit detailed plans and an engineering report explaining the leak detection system design and operations and the location of the saturated zone in relation to the leak detection system;

4) The construction quality assurance (CQA) plan if required under 35 Ill. Adm. Code 724.119; and

5) Proposed action leakage rate, with rationale, if required under 35 Ill. Adm. Code 724.322~; response action plan, if required under 35 Ill. Adm. Code 724.323~; and a proposed pump operating level, if required under 35 Ill. Adm. Code 724.326 (d)(3));

6) Prevention of overtopping; and

7) Structural integrity of dikes;

c) A description of how each surface impoundment, including the double liner system, leak detection system, cover system and appurtenances for control of overtopping will be inspected in order to meet the requirements of 35 Ill. Adm. Code 724.226(a), (b), and (d). This information must be included in the inspection plan submitted under Section 703.183(e);

d) A certification by a qualified engineer which attests to the structural integrity of each dike, as required under 35 Ill. Adm. Code 724.226(c). For new units, the owner or operator shall submit a statement by a qualified engineer that the engineer will provide such a certification upon completion of construction in accordance with the plans and specifications;

e) A description of the procedure to be used for removing a surface impoundment from service, as required under 35 Ill. Adm. Code 724.327(b) and (c). This information must be included in the contingency plan submitted under Section 703.183(g);

f) A description of how hazardous waste residues and contaminated materials will be removed from the unit at closure, as required under 35 Ill. Adm. Code 724.328(a)(1). For any wastes not to be removed from the unit upon closure, the owner or operator shall submit detailed plans and an engineering report describing how 35 Ill. Adm. Code 724.328(a)(2) and (b) will be complied with. This information must be included in the closure plan and, where applicable, the post-closure plan submitted under Section 703.183(m);

g) If ignitable or reactive wastes are to be placed in a surface impoundment, an explanation of how 35 Ill. Adm. Code 724.329 will be complied with;

h) If incompatible wastes, or incompatible wastes and materials, will be placed in a surface impoundment, an explanation of how 35 Ill. Adm. Code 724.330 will be complied with~and~;

i) A waste management plan for hazardous waste numbers F020, F021, F022, F023, F026, and F027 describing how the surface impoundment is or will be designed, constructed, operated, and maintained to meet the

POLLUTION CONTROL BOARD

NOTICE OF PROPOSED AMENDMENTS

requirements of 35 Ill. Adm. Code 724.331. This submission must address the following items as specified in that Section:

1) The volume, physical, and chemical characteristics of the wastes, including their potential to migrate through soil or to volatilize or escape into the atmosphere;

2) The attenuative properties of underlying and surrounding soils or other materials;

3) The mobilizing properties of other materials co-disposed with these wastes; and

4) The effectiveness of additional treatment, design or monitoring techniques.

5) Information on air emission control equipment, as required in Section 703.213.

BOARD NOTE: Derived from 40 CFR 270.17 (1991 1994), as amended at 57 59 Fed. Reg. 3485, January 29, 1992 62952 (Dec. 6, 1994).

(Source: Amended at 19 Ill. Reg. _____, effective _____)

Section 703.213 Air Emission Controls for Tanks, Surface Impoundments, and Containers

Except as otherwise provided in 35 Ill. Adm. Code 724.101, owners and operators of tanks, surface impoundments, or containers that use air emission controls in accordance with the requirements of 35 Ill. Adm. Code 724.Subpart CC shall provide the following additional information:

a) Documentation for each cover installed on a tank subject to 35 Ill. Adm. Code 724.984(b)(2) or 724.984(b)(3) that includes information prepared by the owner or operator or provided by the cover manufacturer or vendor describing the cover design, and certification by the owner or operator that the cover meets the applicable design specifications as listed in 35 Ill. Adm. Code 725.991(c).

b) Identification of each container area subject to the requirements of 35 Ill. Adm. Code 724.Subpart CC and certification by the owner or operator that the requirements of this Subpart are met.

c) Documentation for each enclosure used to control air emissions from containers in accordance with the requirements of 35 Ill. Adm. Code 724.986(b)(2)(A) that includes information prepared by the owner or operator or provided by the manufacturer or vendor describing the enclosure design, and certification by the owner or operator that the enclosure meets the specifications listed in 35 Ill. Adm. Code 725.987(b)(2)(B).

d) Documentation for each floating membrane cover installed on a surface impoundment in accordance with the requirements of 35 Ill. Adm. Code 724.985(c) that includes information prepared by the owner or operator or provided by the cover manufacturer or vendor describing the cover design, and certification by the owner or operator that the cover meets the specifications listed in 35 Ill. Adm. Code 725.986(e).

POLLUTION CONTROL BOARD

NOTICE OF PROPOSED AMENDMENTS

e) Documentation for each closed-vent system and control device installed in accordance with the requirements of 35 Ill. Adm. Code 724.987 that includes design and performance information as specified in 703.24(c) and (d).

f) An emission monitoring plan for both Method 21 and control device monitoring methods. This plan must include the following information: monitoring points, monitoring methods for control devices, monitoring frequency, procedures for documenting exceedances, and procedures for mitigating noncompliances.

g) When an owner or operator of a facility subject to 35 Ill. Adm. Code 725.Subpart CC cannot comply with 35 Ill. Adm. Code 724. Subpart CC by the date of permit issuance, the schedule of implementation required under 35 Ill. Adm. Code 725.982.

BOARD NOTE: Derived from 40 CFR 270.27, added at 59 Fed. Reg. 62952 (Dec. 6, 1994).

(Source: Added at 19 Ill. Reg. _____, effective _____)

POLLUTION CONTROL BOARD

NOTICE OF PROPOSED AMENDMENTS

1) **Heading of the Part:** Standards Applicable to Generators or Hazardous Waste

2) **Code citation:** 35 Ill. Adm. Code 722

3) **Section numbers:**   **Proposed action:**

   722.122   Amended
   722.134   Amended

4) **Statutory authority:** 415 ILCS 5/22.4 and 27.

5) **A complete description of the subjects and issues involved:**

A more detailed description is contained in the Board's proposed opinion of March 2, 1995, in R95-4 and R95-6 (consolidated), which opinion is available from the address below. Section 22.4(a) of the Environmental Protection Act [415 ILCS 5/22.4(a)] provides that Section 5-35 of the Administrative Procedure Act [5 ILCS 100/5-35] shall not apply. Because this rulemaking is not subject to Section 5-35 of the APA, it is r' subject to first notice or to second notice review by JCAR.

This rulemaking updates Parts 700, 702, 703, 705, 720, 721, 722, 723, 724, 725, 726, 728, 730, 738, and 739 of the Illinois RCRA Subtitle C hazardous waste and underground injection control (UIC) rules to correspond with amendments adopted by U.S. EPA that appeared in the Federal Register during the period July 1 through December 31, 1994. During this period, U.S. EPA amended its regulations as follows:

Federal Action	Summary
59 Fed. Reg. 38536, July 28, 1994	Exclusion from definition of solid waste for certain in-process recycled secondary materials used by the petroleum refining industry
59 Fed. Reg. 43496, August 24, 1994	Withdrawal of exemption from Subtitle C regulation of slag residues from high temperature metal recovery (HTMR) of electric arc furnace dust (K061), steel finishing pickle liquor (K062), and electroplating sludges (F006) that are used in a manner constituting disposal
59 Fed. Reg. 47980, September 19, 1994	restoration of text from 40 CFR 268.7(a) inadvertently omitted in the amendments of August 31, 1993, at 58 Fed. Reg. 46040

POLLUTION CONTROL BOARD

NOTICE OF PROPOSED AMENDMENTS

59 Fed. Reg. 47982, September 19, 1994	Phase II land disposal restrictions (LDRs): universal treatment standards for organic toxicity wastes and newly-listed wastes (including underground injection control (UIC) amendments)
59 Fed. Reg. 62896, December 6, 1994	Organic material air emission standards for tanks, surface impoundments, and containers

In addition to these principal amendments that occurred during the update period, the Board has included an additional, later action:

60 Fed. Reg. 242, January 3, 1995	Corrections to the Phase II land disposal restrictions (universal treatment standards)

This January 3 action was an amendment of the September 19, 1994 Phase II LDRs (universal waste rule). U.S. EPA corrected errors and clarified language in the universal treatment standards. The Board did not delay in adding these amendments for three reasons:

1) The January 3, 1995 amendments are corrections and clarifications of the September 19, 1994 regulations, and not new substantive amendments;

2) Prompt action on the January 3, 1995 amendments will facilitate implementation of the Phase II LDRs; and

3) The Board has received a request from the regulated community that we add the January 3, 1995 amendments to those of September 19, 1994. (See "Expedited Consideration" below.)

The Board also notes that the later amendments occurred within six months of the earliest amendments included in this docket, even if they occurred outside the nominal time-frame of the docket.

In addition to the federally-derived amendments, the Board used this opportunity to undertake a number of housekeeping and corrective amendments. We have effected the removal of all cross-references for effective dates and repealed Part 700. We have converted equations and formulae to the standard scientific format. We have tried to improve the language and structure of various provisions, including correcting grammar, punctuation, and spelling where necessary.

Specifically, the segment of the amendments involved in Part 722 incorporate revisions made by U.S. EPA as part of the December 6, 1994 air emissions requirements. The amendments indicate those segments of treatment, storage, and disposal facility air emissions standards that apply to a hazardous waste generator placing hazardous waste in tanks or

POLLUTION CONTROL BOARD

NOTICE OF PROPOSED AMENDMENTS

containers.

6) Will this proposed rule replace an emergency rule currently in effect? No.

7) Does this rulemaking contain an automatic repeal date? No.

8) Do these proposed amendments contain incorporations by reference? No.

9) Are there any other amendments pending on this Part? No.

10) Statement of statewide policy objectives:

This rulemaking is mandated by Section 22.4(a) of the Environmental Protection Act (415 ILCS 5/22.4(a)). The statewide policy objectives are set forth in Section 20 of that Act. This rulemaking imposes mandates on units of local government only to the extent that they may be involved in the generation, transportation, treatment, storage, or disposal of hazardous waste or they engage in underground injection of waste.

11) Time, place and manner in which interested persons may comment on this proposed rulemaking:

The Board will accept written public comment on this proposal for a period of 45 days after the date of this publication. Comments should reference Docket R95-4/R95-6 and be addressed to:

Ms. Dorothy M. Gunn, Clerk
Illinois Pollution Control Board
State of Illinois Center, Suite 11-500
100 W. Randolph St.
Chicago, IL 60601
312/814-6931

Address all questions to Michael J. McCambridge, at 312/814-6924.

12) Initial regulatory flexibility analysis:

A) Date rule was submitted to the Small Business Office of the Department of Commerce and Community Affairs: March 6, 1995.

B) Types of small businesses affected:

The existing rules and proposed amendments affect small businesses that generate, transport, treat, store, or dispose of hazardous waste or engage in underground injection of waste.

C) Reporting, bookkeeping or other procedures required for compliance:

POLLUTION CONTROL BOARD

NOTICE OF PROPOSED AMENDMENTS

The existing rules and proposed amendments require extensive reporting, bookkeeping, and other procedures, including the preparation of manifests and annual reports, waste analyses, and maintenance of operating records.

D) Types of professional skills necessary for compliance:

Compliance with the existing rules and proposed amendments may require the services of an attorney, certified public accountant, chemist, and registered professional engineer.

The full text of the proposed amendments begins on the next page:

POLLUTION CONTROL BOARD

NOTICE OF PROPOSED AMENDMENTS

TITLE 35: ENVIRONMENTAL PROTECTION
SUBTITLE G: WASTE DISPOSAL
CHAPTER I: POLLUTION CONTROL BOARD
SUBCHAPTER c: HAZARDOUS WASTE OPERATING REQUIREMENTS

PART 722
STANDARDS APPLICABLE TO
GENERATORS OF HAZARDOUS WASTE

SUBPART A: GENERAL

Section
722.110   Purpose, Scope and Applicability
722.111   Hazardous Waste Determination
722.112   USEPA Identification Numbers

SUBPART B: THE MANIFEST

Section
722.120   General Requirements
722.121   Acquisition of Manifests
722.122   Number of Copies
722.123   Use of the Manifest

SUBPART C: PRE-TRANSPORT REQUIREMENTS

Section
722.130   Packaging
722.131   Labeling
722.132   Marking
722.133   Placarding
722.134   Accumulation Time

SUBPART D: RECORDKEEPING AND REPORTING

Section
722.140   Recordkeeping
722.141   Annual Reporting
722.142   Exception Reporting
722.143   Additional Reporting
722.144   Special Requirements for Generators of between 100 and 1000 kilograms
            per month

SUBPART E: EXPORTS OF HAZARDOUS WASTE

Section
722.150   Applicability
722.151   Definitions

POLLUTION CONTROL BOARD

NOTICE OF PROPOSED AMENDMENTS

722.152   General Requirements
722.153   Notification of Intent to Export
722.154   Special Manifest Requirements
722.155   Exception Report
722.156   Annual Reports
722.157   Recordkeeping

SUBPART F: IMPORTS OF HAZARDOUS WASTE

Section
722.160   Imports of Hazardous Waste

SUBPART G: FARMERS

Section
722.170   Farmers

APPENDIX A   Hazardous Waste Manifest

AUTHORITY: Implementing Section 22.4 and authorized by Section 27 of the
Environmental Protection Act [415 ILCS 5/22.4 and 27].

SOURCE: Adopted in R81-22, 43 PCB 427, at 5 Ill. Reg. 9781, effective May 17,
1982; amended and codified in R81-22, 45 PCB 317, at 6 Ill. Reg. 4828,
effective May 17, 1982; amended in R82-18, 51 PCB 31, at 7 Ill. Reg. 2518,
effective February 22, 1983; amended in R84-9 at 9 Ill. Reg. 11950, effective
July 24, 1985; amended in R85-22 at 10 Ill. Reg. 1131, effective January 2,
1986; amended in R86-1 at 10 Ill. Reg. 14112, effective August 12, 1986;
amended in R86-19 at 10 Ill. Reg. 20709, effective December 2, 1986; amended in
R86-46 at 11 Ill. Reg. 13555, effective August 4, 1987; amended in R87-5 at 11
Ill. Reg. 19392, effective November 12, 1987; amended in R87-39 at 12 Ill. Reg.
13129, effective July 29, 1988; amended in R88-16 at 13 Ill. Reg. 452,
effective December 27, 1988; amended in R89-1 at 13 Ill. Reg. 18523, effective
November 13, 1989; amended in R90-10 at 14 Ill. Reg. 16653, effective September
25, 1990; amended in R90-11 at 15 Ill. Reg. 9644, effective June 17, 1991;
amended in R91-1 at 15 Ill. Reg. 14562, effective October 1, 1991; amended in
R91-13 at 16 Ill. Reg. 9833, effective June 9, 1992; amended in 92-1 at 16 Ill.
Reg. 17696, effective November 6, 1992; amended in R93-4 at 17 Ill. Reg. 20822,
effective November 22, 1993; amended in R95-6 at 19 Ill. Reg. _____,
effective _____ .

SUBPART B: THE MANIFEST

Section 722.122 Number of Copies

The manifest consists of at least the that number of copies which that will
provide the generator; each transporter; and the owner or operator of the
designated receiving treatment, storage, or disposal facility each with one

POLLUTION CONTROL BOARD

NOTICE OF PROPOSED AMENDMENTS

oopy ~~each~~ for their records, ~~and another~~ plus provide one copy to be returned
to the generator, ~~and~~ plus provide two oopies to be sent to the Agency, one by
each of the generator and by the HWM receiving treatment, storage, or disposal
facility owner or operator.

(Source: Amended   at   19   Ill.   Reg. _____, effective
                                    _____)

SUBPART C: PRE-TRANSPORT REQUIREMENTS

Section 722.134 Accumulation Time

a) Except as provided in subsections (d), (e), or (f), below, a generator
    is exempt from all the requirements in 35 Ill. Adm. Code 725.Subparts
    G and M, except for 35 Ill. Adm. Code 725.211 and 725.214, and may
    accumulate hazardous waste on-site for 90 days or less without a
    permit or without having interim status; provided that:
    I) The waste is placed:
        A) In containers and the generator complies with 35 Ill. Adm.
            Code 725.Subparts Subpart I, AA, BB, and CC; or
        B) In tanks and the generator complies with 35 Ill. Adm. Code
            725.Subparts Subpart J (except 35 Ill. Adm. Code 725.297(c)
            and 725.300), AA, BB, and CC; or
        C) On drip pads and the generator complies with 35 Ill. Adm.
            Code 725.Subpart W and maintains the following records at
            the facility:
            i) A description of the procedures that will be followed
                to ensure that all wastes are removed from the drip
                pad and associated collection system at least once
                every 90 days; , and
            ii) Documentation of each waste removal, including the
                quantity of waste removed from the drip pad and the
                sump or collection system and the date and time of
                removal; or
        D) In containment buildings and the generator complies with 35
            Ill. Adm. Code 725.Subpart DD (has placed its Professional
            Engineer (PE) certification that the building complies with
            the design standards specified in 35 Ill. Adm. Code 725.1101
            in the facility's operating record ~~no later than 60 days
            after~~ prior to the date of initial operation of the unit).
            ~~After February 19, 1993, the PE certification will be
            required prior to operation of the unit.~~ The owner or
            operator shall maintain the following records at the
            facility:
            i) A written description of procedures to ensure that
                each waste volume remains in the unit for no more than
                90 days. a written description of the waste generation
                and management practices for the facility showing that

POLLUTION CONTROL BOARD

NOTICE OF PROPOSED AMENDMENTS

            they are consistent with respecting the 90 day limit,
            and documentation that the procedures are complied
            with; or
        ii) Documentation that the unit is emptied at least once
            every 90 days.
            BOARD NOTE: The "in addition" hanging subsection
            ~~which~~ that appears in the Federal rules after 40 CFR
            262.34(a)(1)(iv)(B) is in the introduction to
            subsection (a), above.
    2) The date upon which each period of accumulation begins is clearly
        marked and visible for inspection on each container;
    3) While being accumulated on-site, each container and tank is
        labeled or marked clearly with the words, "Hazardous Waste", and
    4) The generator complies with the requirements for treatment,
        storage, and disposal facility owners or operators in 35 Ill.
        Adm. Code 725.Subparts C and D, and with 35 Ill. Adm .Code
        725.116 and 728.107(a)(4).
b) A generator who that accumulates hazardous waste for more than 90 days
    is an operator of a storage facility and is subject to the
    requirements of 35 Ill. Adm. Code 724 and 725 and the permit
    requirements of 35 Ill. Adm. Code 702, 703 and 705 unless the
    generator has been granted an extension of the 90-day period. If
    hazardous wastes must remain on-site for longer than 90 days due to
    unforeseen, temporary, and uncontrollable circumstances, the generator
    may seek an extension of up to 30 days by means of a variance or
    provisional variance, pursuant to Section 37 of the Environmental
    Protection Act and 35 Ill. Adm. Code 180 (agency procedural
    regulations).
c) Accumulation near the point of generation.
    I) A generator may accumulate as much as 55 gallons of hazardous
        waste or one quart of acutely hazardous waste listed in 35 Ill.
        Adm. Code 721.133(e) in containers at or near any point of
        generation where wastes initially accumulate which that is under
        the control of the operator of the process generating the waste,
        without a permit or interim status and without complying with
        subsection (a), above, provided the generator:
        A) Complies with 35 Ill. Adm. Code 725.271, 725.272 and
            725.273(a); and
        B) marks the generator's containers either with the words
            "Hazardous Waste" or with other words that identify the
            contents of the containers.
    2) A generator who that accumulates either hazardous waste or
        acutely hazardous waste listed in 35 Ill. Adm. Code 721.133(e) in
        excess of the amounts listed in subsection (c) (1), above at or
        near any point of generation must, with respect to that amount of
        excess waste, comply within three days with subsection (a),
        above or other applicable provisions of this chapter Chapter.
        During the three day period the generator must continue to comply

POLLUTION CONTROL BOARD

NOTICE OF PROPOSED AMENDMENTS

with subsection (c) (1); above. The generator must mark the container holding the excess accumulation of hazardous waste with the date the excess amount began accumulating.

d) A generator who that generates greater than 100 kilograms but less than 1000 kilograms of hazardous waste in a calendar month may accumulate hazardous waste on-site for 180 days or less without a permit or without having interim status provided that:

1) The quantity of waste accumulated on-site never exceeds 6000 kilograms;

2) The generator complies with the requirements of 35 Ill. Adm. Code 725.Subpart I; (except the generator need not comply with 35 Ill. Adm. Code 725.276 and 725.178);

3) The generator complies with the requirements of 35 Ill. Adm. Code 725.301;

4) The generator complies with the requirements of subsections (a)(2) and (c) (3); above, of 35 Ill. Adm. Code 725.Subpart C; and of 35 Ill. Adm. Code 728.107(a)(4); and

5) The generator complies with the following requirements;

A) At all times there must be at least one employee either on the premises or on call (i.e., available to respond to an emergency by reaching the facility within a short period of time) with the responsibility for coordinating all emergency response measures specified in subsection (d)(5)(D); below. The employee is the emergency coordinator.

B) The generator shall post the following information next to the telephone;

i) The name and telephone number of the emergency coordinator;

ii) Location of fire extinguishers and spill control material; and, if present, fire alarm; and

iii) The telephone number of the fire department, unless the facility has a direct alarm.

C) The generator shall ensure that all employees are thoroughly familiar with proper waste handling and emergency procedures, relevant to their responsibilities during normal facility operations and emergencies;

D) The emergency coordinator or designee shall respond to any emergencies that arise. The applicable responses are as follows:

i) In the event of a fire, call the fire department or attempt to extinguish it using a fire extinguisher;

ii) In the event of a spill, contain the flow of hazardous waste to the extent possible, and, as soon as is practicable, clean up the hazardous waste and any contaminated materials or soils;

iii) In the event of a fire, explosion, or other release which that could threaten human health outside the facility, or when the generator has knowledge that a

POLLUTION CONTROL BOARD

NOTICE OF PROPOSED AMENDMENTS

spill has reached surface water, the generator shall immediately notify the National Response Center (using its 24-hour toll free number 800/-424-8802). The report must include the following information: the name, address, and U.S.EPA identification number (35 Ill. Adm. Code 722.111) of the generator; the date, time, and type of incident (e.g., spill or fire); the quantity and type of hazardous waste involved in the incident; the extent of injuries, if any; and; the estimated quantity and disposition of recoverable materials, if any.

e) A generator who that generates greater than 100 kilograms but less than 1000 kilograms of hazardous waste in a calendar month and who that must transport the waste; or offer the waste for transportation; over a distance of 200 miles or more for off-site treatment, storage, or disposal may accumulate hazardous waste on-site for 270 days or less without a permit or without having interim status, provided that the generator complies with the requirements of subsection (d); above.

f) A generator who' that generates greater than 100 kilograms but less than 1000 kilograms of hazardous waste in a calendar month and who that accumulates hazardous waste in quantities exceeding 6000 kg or accumulates hazardous waste for more than 180 days (or for more than 270 days if the generator must transport the waste; or offer the waste for transportation; over a distance of 200 miles or more) is an operator of a storage facility and is subject to the requirements of 35 Ill. Adm. Code 724 and 725 and the permit requirements of 35 Ill. Adm. Code 703 unless the generator has been granted an extension to the 180-day (or 270-day if applicable) period. If hazardous wastes must remain on-site for longer than 180 days (or 270 days if applicable) due to unforeseen, temporary, and uncontrollable circumstances, the generator may seek an extension of up to 30 days by means of variance or provisional variance pursuant to Section 37 of the Environmental Protection Act.

(Source: Amended at 19 Ill Reg. _____, effective _____.)

POLLUTION CONTROL BOARD

NOTICE OF PROPOSED AMENDMENTS

1) Heading of the Part: Standards Applicable to Transporters of Hazardous Waste

2) Code citation: 35 Ill. Adm. Code 723

3) Section numbers: Proposed action:

   723.130   Amended

4) Statutory authority: 415 ILCS 5/22.4 and 27.

5) A complete description of the subjects and issues involved:

   A more detailed description is contained in the Board's proposed opinion of March 2, 1995, in R95-4 and R95-6 (consolidated), which opinion is available from the address below. Section 22.4(a) of the Environmental Protection Act (415 ILCS 5/22.4(a)] provides that Section 5-35 of the Administrative Procedure Act (5 ILCS 100/5-35] shall not apply.   Because this rulemaking is not subject to first notice or to second notice review by JCAR.

   This rulemaking updates Parts 700, 702, 703, 705, 720, 721, 722, 723, 724, 725, 726, 728, 730, 738, and 739 of the Illinois RCRA Subtitle C hazardous waste and underground injection control (UIC) rules to correspond with amendments adopted by U.S. EPA that appeared in the Federal Register during the period July 1 through December 31, 1994. During this period, U.S. EPA amended its regulations as follows:

Federal Action	Summary
59 Fed. Reg. 38536, July 28, 1994	Exclusion from definition of solid waste for certain in-process recycled secondary materials used by the petroleum refining industry
59 Fed. Reg. 43496, August 24, 1994	Withdrawal of exemption from Subtitle C regulation of slag residues from high temperature metal recovery (HTMR) of electric arc furnace dust (K061), steel finishing pickle liquor (K062), and electroplating sludges (F006) that are used in a manner constituting disposal
59 Fed. Reg. 47980, September 19, 1994	Restoration of text from 40 CFR 268.7(a) inadvertently omitted in the amendments of August 31, 1993, at 58 Fed. Reg. 46040

POLLUTION CONTROL BOARD

NOTICE OF PROPOSED AMENDMENTS

59 Fed. Reg. 47982, September 19, 1994	Phase II land disposal restrictions (LDRs): universal treatment standards for organic toxicity wastes and newly-listed wastes (including underground injection control (UIC) amendments)
59 Fed. Reg. 61896, December 6, 1994	Organic material air emission standards for tanks, surface impoundments, and containers

In addition to these principal amendments that occurred during the update period, the Board has included an additional, later action:

60 Fed. Reg. 242, January 3, 1995	Corrections to the Phase II land disposal restrictions (universal treatment standards)

This January 3 action was an amendment of the September 19, 1994 Phase II LDRs (universal waste rule). U.S. EPA corrected errors and clarified language in the universal treatment standards. The Board did not delay in adding these amendments for three reasons:

1) The January 3, 1995 amendments are corrections and clarifications of the September 19, 1994 regulations, and not new substantive amendments;

2) Prompt action on the January 3, 1995 amendments will facilitate implementation of the Phase II LDRs; and

3) The Board has received a request from the regulated community that we add the January 3, 1995 amendments to those of September 19, 1994. (See "Expedited Consideration" below.)

The Board also notes that the later amendments occurred within six months of the earliest amendments included in this docket, even if they occurred outside the nominal time-frame of the docket.

In addition to the federally-derived amendments, the Board used this opportunity to undertake a number of housekeeping and corrective amendments. We have effected the removal of all cross-references for effective dates and repealed Part 700. We have converted equations and formulae to the standard scientific format. We have tried to improve the language and structure of various provisions including correcting grammar, punctuation, and spelling where necessary.

Specifically, the segment of the amendments involved in Part 723 were for the express purpose of removing a reference to 35 III. Adm. Code 700.106 for an effective date. The Board opened the Section to make this change to the Section source note by making a number of corrective and clarifying changes. In the course of these revisions, we updated the name of the

POLLUTION CONTROL BOARD

NOTICE OF PROPOSED AMENDMENTS

state agency a transporter must notify in the event of a release of hazardous waste from the Emergency Services and Disaster Agency to the Illinois Emergency Management Agency.

6) Will this proposed rule replace an emergency rule currently in effect? No.

7) Does this rulemaking contain an automatic repeal date?: No.

8) Do these proposed amendments contain incorporations by reference? No.

9) Are there any other amendments pending on this Part? No.

10) Statement of statewide policy objectives:

This rulemaking is mandated by Section 22.4(a) of the Environmental Protection Act [415 ILCS 5/22.4(a)]. The statewide policy objectives are set forth in Section 20 of that Act. This rulemaking imposes mandates on units of local government only to the extent that they may be involved in the generation, transportation, treatment, storage, or disposal of hazardous waste or they engage in underground injection of waste.

11) Time, place and manner in which interested persons may comment on this proposed rulemaking:

The Board will accept written public comment on this proposal for a period of 45 days after the date of this publication. Comments should reference Docket R95-4/R95-6 and be addressed to:

Ms. Dorothy M. Gunn, Clerk
Illinois Pollution Control Board
State of Illinois Center, Suite 11-500
100 W. Randolph St.
Chicago, IL 60601
312/814-6931

Address all questions to Michael J. McCambridge, at 312/814-6924.

12) Initial regulatory flexibility analysis:

A) Date rule was submitted to the Small Business Office of the Department of Commerce and Community Affairs: March 6, 1995.

B) Types of small businesses affected:

The existing rules and proposed amendments affect small businesses that generate, transport, treat, store, or dispose of hazardous waste or engage in underground injection of waste.

POLLUTION CONTROL BOARD

NOTICE OF PROPOSED AMENDMENTS

C) Reporting, bookkeeping or other procedures required for compliance:

The existing rules and proposed amendments require extensive reporting, bookkeeping, and other procedures, including the preparation of manifests and annual reports, waste analyses, and maintenance of operating records.

D) Types of professional skills necessary for compliance:

Compliance with the existing rules and proposed amendments may require the services of an attorney, certified public accountant, chemist, and registered professional engineer.

The full text of the proposed amendments begins on the next page:

POLLUTION CONTROL BOARD

NOTICE OF PROPOSED AMENDMENTS

TITLE 35: ENVIRONMENTAL PROTECTION
SUBTITLE G: WASTE DISPOSAL
CHAPTER I: POLLUTION CONTROL BOARD
SUBCHAPTER c: HAZARDOUS WASTE OPERATING REQUIREMENTS

PART 723
STANDARDS APPLICABLE TO
TRANSPORTERS OF HAZARDOUS WASTE

SUBPART A: GENERAL

Section
723.110   Scope
723.111   USEPA Identification Number
723.112   Transfer Facility Requirements

SUBPART B: COMPLIANCE WITH THE MANIFEST
SYSTEM AND RECORDKEEPING

Section
723.120   The Manifest System
723.121   Compliance with the Manifest
723.122   Recordkeeping

SUBPART C: HAZARDOUS WASTE DISCHARGES

Section
723.130   Immediate Action
723.131   Discharge Clean Up

AUTHORITY: Implementing Section 22.4 and authorized by Section 27 of the
Environmental Protection Act [415 ILCS 5/22.4 and 27].

SOURCE: Adopted in R81-22, 43 PCB 427, at 5 Ill. Reg. 9781, effective May 17,
1982; amended and codified in R81-22, 45 PCB 17, at 6 Ill. Reg. 4828, effective
May 17, 1982; amended in R84-9, at 9 Ill. Reg. 11961, effective July 24, 1985;
amended in R86-19, at 10 Ill. Reg. 20718, effective December 2, 1986; amended
in R86-46 at 11 Ill. Reg. 13570, effective August 4, 1987; amended in R87-5 at
11 Ill. Reg. 19412, effective November 12, 1987; amended in R95-6 at 19 Ill.
Reg. _____, effective _____.

SUBPART C: HAZARDOUS WASTE DISCHARGES

Section 723.130 Immediate Action

a) In the event of a discharge of hazardous waste during transportation,
    the transporter must take appropriate immediate action to protect
    human health and the environment (e.g., notify local authorities, dike

---

POLLUTION CONTROL BOARD

NOTICE OF PROPOSED AMENDMENTS

the discharge area).

b) If a discharge of hazardous waste occurs during transportation and an
    official (of State state or local government or of a Federal Agency
    federal agency) acting within the scope of his or her official
    responsibilities determines that immediate removal of the waste is
    necessary to protect human health or the environment, that official
    may authorize the removal of the waste by transporters who that do not
    have U.S. EPA identification numbers and without the preparation of a
    manifest.

c) An air, rail, highway, or water transporter who that has discharged
    hazardous waste must:

    1) Give notice--if--required--by--49--CFR--171.15, to the National
        Response Center (800-424-8802 or 202-426-2675), if required by 49
        CFR 171.15; and

    2) Report in writing as-required-by-49-CFR-171.16 to the Director,
        Office of Hazardous Materials Regulations, Materials
        Transportation Bureau, Department of Transportation, Washington,
        D.C. 20590, as required by 49 CFR 171.16; and;

    3) give notice to:
        Emergency---Services---and---Disaster---Agency,---110--E.--Adams,
        Springfield,-Il-62706,-A/C-217-782-7860.
        Illinois Emergency Management Agency
        110 East Adams
        Springfield, Illinois 62706
        217-782-7860

d) A water (bulk shipment) transporter who that has discharged hazardous
    waste must give the same notice as required by 33 CFR 153.203 for oil
    and hazardous substances.

(Source: Amended at 19 Ill. Reg. _____, effective
_____.)

POLLUTION CONTROL BOARD

NOTICE OF PROPOSED AMENDMENTS

1) **Heading of the Part**: Standards for Owners and Operators of Hazardous Waste
   Treatment, Storage, and Disposal Facilities

2) **Code Citation**: 35 Ill. Adm. Code 724

3) **Section numbers**:

	Proposed Action:
724.101, 724.113, 724.115	Amended
724.156, 724.173, 724.177	Amended
724.279, 724.300, 724.332	New Section
724.701, 724.933, 724.963	Amended
724.980, 724.981, 724.982	New Section
724.983, 724.984, 724.985	New Section
724.986, 724.987, 724.988	New Section
724.989, 724.990, 724.991	New Section
724.1102	Amended

4) **Statutory Authority**: 415 ILCS 5/22.4 and 27

5) **A complete description of the subjects and issues involved**:

   A more detailed description is contained in the Board's proposed opinion
   of March 2, 1995, in R95-4 and R95-6 (consolidated), which opinion is
   available from the address below. Section 22.4(a) of the Environmental
   Protection Act [415 ILCS 5/22.4(a)] provides that Section 5-35 of the
   Administrative Procedure Act [5 ILCS 100/5-35] shall not apply. Because
   this rulemaking is not subject to Section 5-35 of the APA, it is not
   subject to first notice or to second notice review by JCAR.

   This rulemaking updates Parts 700, 702, 703, 705, 720, 721, 722, 723, 724,
   725, 726, 728, 730, 738, and 739 of the Illinois RCRA Subtitle C hazardous
   waste and underground injection control (UIC) rules to correspond with
   amendments adopted by U.S. EPA that appeared in the Federal Register
   during the period July 1 through December 31, 1994. During this period,
   U.S. EPA amended its regulations as follows:

Federal Action	Summary
59 Fed. Reg. 38536, July 28, 1994	Exclusion from definition of solid waste for certain in-process recycled secondary materials used by the petroleum refining industry
59 Fed. Reg. 43496, August 24, 1994	Withdrawal of exemption from Subtitle C regulation of slag residues from high temperature metal recovery (HTMR) of electric arc furnace dust (K061), steel finishing pickle liquor (K062), and electroplating

POLLUTION CONTROL BOARD

NOTICE OF PROPOSED AMENDMENTS

	sludges (F006) that are used in a manner constituting disposal
59 Fed. Reg. 47980, September 19, 1994	Restoration of text from 40 CFR 268.7(a) inadvertently omitted in the amendments of August 31, 1993, at 58 Fed. Reg. 46040
59 Fed. Reg. 47982, September 19, 1994	Phase II land disposal restrictions (LDRs): universal treatment standards for organic toxicity wastes and newly-listed wastes (including underground injection control (UIC) amendments)
59 Fed. Reg. 62896, December 6, 1994	Organic material emission standards for tanks, surface impoundments, and containers

In addition to these principal amendments that occurred during the update
period, the Board has included an additional, later action:

60 Fed. Reg. 242, January 3, 1995	Corrections to the Phase II land disposal restrictions (universal treatment standards)

This January 3 action was an amendment of the September 19, 1994 Phase II
LDRs (universal waste rule). U.S. EPA corrected errors and clarified
language in the universal treatment standards. The Board did not delay in
adding these amendments for three reasons:

1) The January 3, 1995 amendments are corrections and clarifications of
   the September 19, 1994 regulations, and not new substantive
   amendments;

2) Prompt action on the January 3, 1995 amendments will facilitate
   implementation of the Phase II LDRs; and

3) The Board has received a request from the regulated community that we
   add the January 3, 1995 amendments to those of September 19, 1994.
   (See "Expedited Consideration" below.)

The Board also notes that the later amendments occurred within six months
of the earliest amendments included in this docket, even if they occurred
outside the nominal time-frame of the docket.

In addition to the federally-derived amendments, the Board used this
opportunity to undertake a number of housekeeping and corrective
amendments. We have effected the removal of all cross-references for
effective dates and repealed Part 700. We have converted equations and
formulae to the standard scientific format. We have tried to improve the
language and structure of various provisions, including correcting

POLLUTION CONTROL BOARD
NOTICE OF PROPOSED AMENDMENTS

grammar, punctuation, and spelling where necessary.

Specifically, the segment of the amendments involved in Part 724 incorporate the major requirements of the federal air emissions regulations of December 6, 1994 and one federal air emissions standard for tanks, containers, and surface impoundments is in new 35 Ill.Subpart CC. The federal correction, made as part of the September 19, 1994 Phase II GBRs, is the correction at Section 724.101(g)(6) of the type of waste that is exempt from regulation if managed in an elementary neutralization unit from corrosive to reactive waste.

6) Will this proposed rule replace an emergency rule currently in effect? No

7) Does this rulemaking contain an automatic repeal date? No

8) Do these proposed amendments contain incorporations by reference? Yes. 35 Ill. Adm. Code 720.111 is the central listing of all documents incorporated by reference throughout the text of 35 Ill. Adm. Code 702 through 705, 721 through 726, 728, 730, 738, and 739. The present amendments update the documents incorporated by reference in a few ways. First, the Board has added the year code to the references to ASTM methods at Sections 724.931(b)(2) and 724.963(d)(1) and (h). We then add the methods references in 724,Subpart CC used by U.S. EPA in the December 6, 1994 air emissions requirements: the U.S. DOT hazardous materials transportation regulations of 49 CFR 1781 the use of Method II of 40 CFR 60, appendix A; and the 40 CFR 60, subpart VV and 61, subpart V equipment leaks air requirements.

9) Are there any other amendments pending on this Part? No

10) Statement of statewide policy objectives: This rulemaking is mandated by Section 22.4(a) of the Environmental Protection Act (415 ILCS 5/22.4(a)). The statewide policy objectives are set forth in Section 20 of that Act. This rulemaking imposes mandates on units of local government only to the extent that they may be involved in the generation, transportation, treatment, storage, or disposal of hazardous waste or they engage in underground injection of waste.

11) Time, place and manner in which interested persons may comment on this proposed rulemaking: The Board will accept written public comment on this proposal for a period of 45 days after the date of this publication. Comments should reference Docket R95-4/R95-6 and be addressed to:

Ms. Dorothy M. Gunn, Clerk
Illinois Pollution Control Board
State of Illinois Center, Suite 11-500

POLLUTION CONTROL BOARD
NOTICE OF PROPOSED AMENDMENTS

100 W. Randolph St.
Chicago, IL 60601
(312) 814-6931

Address all questions to Michael J. McCambridge, at (312) 814-6931.

12) Initial regulatory flexibility analysis:

A) Date the rule was submitted to the Small Business Office of the Department of Commerce and Community Affairs: March 6, 1995.

B) Types of small businesses affected: The existing rules and proposed amendments affect small businesses that generate, transport, treat, store, or dispose of hazardous waste or engage in underground injection of waste.

C) Reporting, bookkeeping or other procedures required for compliance: The existing rules and proposed amendments require extensive reporting, bookkeeping, and other procedures, including the preparation of manifests and annual reports, waste analyses, and maintenance of operating records.

D) Types of professional skills necessary for compliance: Compliance with the existing rules and proposed amendments may require the services of an attorney, certified public accountant, chemist, and registered professional engineer.

The full text of the proposed amendments begins on the next page.

POLLUTION CONTROL BOARD

NOTICE OF PROPOSED AMENDMENTS

TITLE 35: ENVIRONMENTAL PROTECTION
SUBTITLE G: WASTE DISPOSAL
CHAPTER I: POLLUTION CONTROL BOARD
SUBCHAPTER c: HAZARDOUS WASTE OPERATING REQUIREMENTS

PART 724
STANDARDS FOR OWNERS AND OPERATORS OF
HAZARDOUS WASTE TREATMENT, STORAGE, AND DISPOSAL FACILITIES

SUBPART A: GENERAL PROVISIONS

POLLUTION CONTROL BOARD

NOTICE OF PROPOSED AMENDMENTS

POLLUTION CONTROL BOARD

NOTICE OF PROPOSED AMENDMENTS

POLLUTION CONTROL BOARD

NOTICE OF PROPOSED AMENDMENTS

POLLUTION CONTROL BOARD

NOTICE OF PROPOSED AMENDMENTS

POLLUTION CONTROL BOARD

NOTICE OF PROPOSED AMENDMENTS

POLLUTION CONTROL BOARD

NOTICE OF PROPOSED AMENDMENTS

724.990   Reporting Requirements
724.991   Alternative Control Requirements for Tanks

SUBPART DD: CONTAINMENT BUILDINGS

Section
724.1100   Applicability
724.1101   Design and operating standards
724.1102   Closure and post-closure care

APPENDIX A   Recordkeeping Instructions
APPENDIX B   EPA Report Form and Instructions (Repealed)
APPENDIX D   Cochran's Approximation to the Behrens-Fisher Student's T-Test
APPENDIX E   Examples of Potentially Incompatible Waste
APPENDIX I   Groundwater Monitoring List

AUTHORITY: Implementing Section 22.4 and authorized by Section 27 of the Environmental Protection Act [415 ILCS 5/22.4 and 27].

SOURCE: Adopted in R82-19, 53 PCB 131, at 7 Ill. Reg. 14059, effective October 12, 1983; amended in R84-9 at 9 Ill. Reg. 11964, effective July 24, 1985; amended in R85-22 at 10 Ill. Reg. 1136, effective January 2, 1986; amended in R86-1 at 10 Ill. Reg. 14119, effective August 12, 1986; amended in R86-28 at 11 Ill. Reg. 6138, effective March 24, 1987; amended in R86-28 at 11 Ill. Reg. 8684, effective April 21, 1987; amended in R86-46 at 11 Ill. Reg. 13577, effective August 4, 1987; amended in R87-5 at 11 Ill. Reg. 19397, effective November 12, 1987; amended in R87-39 at 12 Ill. Reg. 13135, effective July 29, 1988; amended in R88-16 at 13 Ill. Reg. 458, effective December 28, 1988; amended in R89-1 at 13 Ill. Reg. 18527, effective November 13, 1989; amended in R90-2 at 14 Ill. Reg. 14511, effective August 22, 1990; amended in R90-10 at 14 Ill. Reg. 16658, effective September 25, 1990; amended in R90-II at 15 Ill. Reg. 9654, effective June 17, 1991; amended in R91-1 at 15 Ill. Reg. 14572, effective October 1, 1991; amended in R91-13 at 16 Ill. Reg. 9833, effective June 9, 1992; amended in R92-1 at 16 Ill. Reg. 17702, effective November 6, 1992; amended in R92-10 at 17 Ill. Reg. 5806, effective March 26, 1993; amended in R93-4 at 17 Ill. Reg. 20830, effective November 22, 1993; amended in R93-16 at 18 Ill. Reg. 6973, effective April 26, 1994; amended in R94-7 at 18 Ill. Reg. 12487, effective July 29, 1994; amended in R94-I7 at 18 Ill. Reg. 17601, effective November 23, 1994; amended in R95-6 at 19 Ill. Reg. _____, effective _____.

NOTE: In this Part, superscript numbers or letters are denoted by parentheses; subscript are denoted by brackets.

SUBPART A: GENERAL PROVISIONS

Section 724.101 Purpose, Scope and Applicability

POLLUTION CONTROL BOARD

NOTICE OF PROPOSED AMENDMENTS

a) The purpose of this Part is to establish minimum standards which that define the acceptable management of hazardous waste.

b) The standards in this Part apply to owners and operators of all facilities which that treat, store, or dispose of hazardous waste, except as specifically provided otherwise in this Part or 35 III. Adm. Code 72I.

c) The requirements of this Part apply to a person disposing of hazardous waste by means of ocean disposal subject to a permit issued under the Marine Protection, Research and Sanctuaries Act (16 U.S.C. 1431-1434, 33 U.S.C. I401) only to the extent they are included in a RCRA permit by rule issued to such a person under 35 III. Adm. Code 703.141. A "RCRA permit" is a permit required by Section 21(f) of the Environmental Protection Act and 35 Ill. Adm. Code 703.121.
    BOARD NOTE: This Part does apply to the treatment or storage of hazardous waste before it is loaded onto an ocean vessel for incineration or disposal at sea.

d) The requirements of this Part apply to a person disposing of hazardous waste by means of underground injection subject to a permit issued by the Agency pursuant to Section 12(g) of the Environmental Protection Act only to the extent they are required by 35 III. Adm. Code 704, Subpart F.
    BOARD NOTE: This Part does apply to the above-ground treatment or storage of hazardous waste before it is injected underground.

e) The requirements of this Part apply to the owner or operator of a POTW (publicly owned treatment works) which that treats, stores, or disposes of hazardous waste only to the extent included in a RCRA permit by rule granted to such a person under 35 III. Adm. Code 703.141.

f) This subsection corresponds with 40 CFR 264.1(f), which provides that the federal regulations do not apply to T/S/D activities in authorized states, except under limited, enumerated circumstances. This statement maintains structural consistency with U.S. EPA rules.

g) The requirements of this Part do not apply to:
    1) The owner or operator of a facility permitted by the Agency under Section 21 of the Environmental Protection Act to manage municipal or industrial solid waste, if the only hazardous waste the facility treats, stores, or disposes of is excluded from regulation under this Part by 35 III. Adm. Code 721.105.
        BOARD NOTE: The owner or operator may be subject to 35 III. Adm. Code 807 and may have to have a supplemental permit under 35 III. Adm. Code 807.210.
    2) The owner or operator of a facility managing recyclable materials described in 35 Ill. Adm. Code 721.106(a)(2), through (a)(4) (except to the extent that requirements of this Part are referred to in 35 III. Adm. Code 726.Subparts C, F, G, or H or 35 III. Adm. Code 739).
    3) A generator accumulating waste on-site in compliance with 35 III. Adm. Code 722.134.

POLLUTION CONTROL BOARD

NOTICE OF PROPOSED AMENDMENTS

4) A farmer disposing of waste pesticides from the farmer's own use in compliance with 35 Ill. Adm. Code 722.170.

5) The owner or operator of a totally enclosed treatment facility, as defined in 35 Ill. Adm. Code 720.110.

6) The owner or operator of an elementary neutralization unit or a wastewater treatment unit, as defined in 35 Ill. Adm. Code 720.110, provided that if the owner or operator is diluting hazardous ignitable (D001) wastes (other than the D001 High TOC Subcategory defined in 35 Ill. Adm. Code 728.Table 8[)] or corrosive (D002) reactive (D003) wastes to remove the characteristic before land disposal, the owner or operator must comply with the requirements set out in Section 724.117(b) of this part.

7) Immediate response:
    A) Except as provided in subsection [(i)(8)(B)] (g)(8)(B) below, a person engaged in treatment or containment activities during immediate response to any of the following situations:
        i) A discharge of a hazardous waste;
        ii) An imminent and substantial threat of a discharge of hazardous waste;
        iii) A discharge of a material that which when discharged, becomes a hazardous waste when discharged.
    B) An owner or operator of a facility otherwise regulated by this Part must comply with all applicable requirements of Subparts 724.Subparts C and D.
    C) Any person who that is covered by subsection [(i)(8)(A)] (g)(8)(A) above and who that continues or initiates hazardous waste treatment or containment activities after the immediate response is over is subject to all applicable requirements of this Part and 35 Ill. Adm. Code 702, 703, and 705 for those activities. Or;

8) A transporter storing manifested shipments of hazardous waste in containers meeting the requirements of 35 Ill. Adm. Code 722.130 at a transfer facility for a period of ten days or less.

9) The addition of absorbent materials to waste in a container (as defined in 35 Ill. Adm. Code 720) or the addition of waste to absorbent material in a container, provided these actions occur at the time waste is first placed in the container, and Sections 724.117(b), 724.271, and 724.272 are complied with.

h) This Part applies to owners and operators of facilities which that treat, store, or dispose of hazardous wastes referred to in 35 Ill. Adm. Code 728.

(Source: Amended at 19 Ill. Reg. _____, effective _____.)

SUBPART B: GENERAL FACILITY STANDARDS

POLLUTION CONTROL BOARD

NOTICE OF PROPOSED AMENDMENTS

Section 724.113 General Waste Analysis

a) Analysis:
    1) Before an owner or operator treats, stores, or disposes of any hazardous wastes, or non-hazardous wastes if applicable under Section 724.213(d), the owner or operator shall obtain a detailed chemical and physical analysis of a representative sample of the wastes. At a minimum, the analysis must contain all the information which that must be known to treat, store, or dispose of the waste in accordance with this Part and 35 Ill. Adm. Code 728.
    2) The analysis may include data developed under 35 Ill. Adm. Code 721, and existing published or documented data on the hazardous waste or on hazardous waste generated from similar processes. BOARD NOTE: For example, the facility's records of analyses performed on the waste before the effective date of these regulations, or studies conducted on hazardous waste generated from processes similar to that which generated the waste to be managed at the facility may be included in the data base required to comply with subsection (a)(1) above. The owner or operator of an off-site facility may arrange for the generator of the hazardous waste to supply part or all of the information required by subsection (a)(1) above, except as otherwise specified in 35 Ill. Adm. Code 728.107(b) and (c). If the generator does not supply the information, and the owner or operator chooses to accept a hazardous waste, the owner or operator is responsible for obtaining the information required to comply with this Section.
    3) The analysis must be repeated as necessary to ensure that it is accurate and up to date. At a minimum, the analysis must be repeated:
        A) When the owner or operator is notified, or has reason to believe, that the process or operation generating the hazardous waste, or non-hazardous waste if applicable under Section 724.213(d), has changed; and
        B) For off-site facilities, when the results of the inspection required in subsection (a)(4) below indicate that the hazardous waste received at the facility does not match the waste designated on the accompanying manifest or shipping paper.
    4) The owner or operator of an off-site facility shall inspect and, if necessary, analyze each hazardous waste movement shipment received at the facility to determine whether it matches the identity of the waste specified on the accompanying manifest or shipping paper.

b) The owner or operator shall develop and follow a written waste analysis plan which that describes the procedures which that it will carry out to comply with subsection (a) above. The owner or operator

shall keep this plan at the facility. At a minimum, the plan must specify:

1) The parameters for which each hazardous waste, or non-hazardous waste if applicable under Section 724.213(d), will be analyzed and the rationale for the selection of these parameters (i.e., how analysis for these parameters will provide sufficient information on the waste's properties to comply with subsection (a) above).

2) The test methods which that will be used to test for these parameters.

3) The sampling method which that will be used to obtain a representative sample of the waste to be analyzed. A representative sample may be obtained using either:
   A) One of the sampling methods described in 35 Ill. Adm. Code 721.Appendix A; or
   B) An equivalent sampling method.
      BOARD NOTE: See 35 Ill. Adm. Code 720.121 for related discussion.

4) The frequency with which the initial analysis of the waste will be reviewed or repeated to ensure that the analysis is accurate and up to date.

5) For off-site facilities, the waste analyses that hazardous waste generators have agreed to supply.

6) Where applicable, the methods which that will be used to meet the additional waste analysis requirements for specific waste management methods as specified in Sections 724.117, 724.414, 724.441, 724.934(d), and 724.963(d), and 724.983 and 35 Ill. Adm. Code 707. And:

7) For surface impoundments exempted from land disposal restrictions under 35 Ill. Adm. Code 728.104(a), the procedures and schedules for:
   A) The sampling of impoundment contents;
   B) The analysis of test data; and;
   C) The annual removal of residues which that are not delisted under 35 Ill. Adm. Code 720.122 or which exhibit a characteristic of hazardous waste; and either:
      i) Do not meet applicable treatment standards of 35 Ill. Adm. Code 728.Subpart D; or
      ii) Where no treatment standards have been established, Such such residues are prohibited from land disposal under 35 Ill. Adm. Code 728.132 or 728.139; or such residues are prohibited from land disposal under 35 Ill. Adm. Code 728.133(f).

8) For owners and operators seeking an exemption to the air emission standards of 724.Subpart CC in accordance with Section 724.982:
   A) The procedures and schedules for waste sampling and analysis and the analysis of test data to verify the exemption; and
   B) Each generator's notice and certification of the volatile

organic concentration in the waste if the waste is received from off site.

c) For off-site facilities, the waste analysis plan required in subsection (b) above must also specify the procedures which that will be used to inspect and, if necessary, analyze each movement shipment of hazardous waste received at the facility to ensure that it matches the identity of the waste designated on the accompanying manifest or shipping paper. At a minimum, the plan must describe:

1) The procedures which that will be used to determine the identity of each movement of waste managed at the facility; and

2) The sampling method which that will be used to obtain a representative sample of the waste to be identified, if the identification method includes sampling; and

3) The procedures that the owner or operator of an off-site landfill receiving containerized hazardous waste will use to determine whether a hazardous waste generator or treater has added a biodegradable sorbent to the waste in the container.
   BOARD NOTE: 35 Ill. Adm. Code 703; requires that the waste analysis plan be submitted with Part B of the permit application.

(Source: Amended at 19 Ill. Reg. _____, effective _____)

Section 724.115 General Inspection Requirements

a) The owner or operator shall conduct inspections often enough to identify problems in time to correct them before they harm human health or the environment. The owner or operator shall inspect the facility for malfunctions and deterioration, operator errors, and discharges which that may be causing; or may lead to:
   1) Release of hazardous waste constituents to the environment; or
   2) A threat to human health.

b) Inspection schedule.
   1) The owner or operator shall develop and follow a written schedule for inspecting monitoring equipment, safety and emergency equipment, security devices, and operating and structural equipment (such as dikes and sump pumps) that are important to preventing, detecting, or responding to environmental or human health hazards.
   2) The owner or operator shall keep this schedule at the facility.
   3) The schedule must identify the types of problems (e.g., malfunctions or deterioration) which that are to be looked for during the inspection (e.g., inoperative sump pump, leaking fitting, eroding dike, etc.).
   4) The frequency of inspection may vary for the items on the schedule. However, it should be based on the rate of deterioration of the equipment and the probability of an environmental or human health incident if the deterioration,

POLLUTION CONTROL BOARD

NOTICE OF PROPOSED AMENDMENTS

malfunction or any operator error goes undetected between inspections. Areas subject to spills, such as loading and unloading areas, must be inspected daily when in use. At a minimum, the inspection schedule must include the items and frequencies called for in Sections 724.274, 724.293, 724.295, 724.326, 724.354, 724.378, 724.403, 724.447, 724.702, 724.933, 724.952, 724.953, and 724.958, 724.988, and 724.991(b), where applicable.
BOARD NOTE: 35 Ill. Adm. Code 703 requires the inspection schedule to be submitted with Part B of the permit application. The Agency will must evaluate the schedule along with the rest of the application to ensure that it adequately protects human health and the environment. As part of this review, the Agency may modify or amend the schedule as may be necessary.

c) The owner or operator shall remedy any deterioration or malfunction of equipment or structures which that the inspection reveals on a schedule which ensures that the problem does not lead to an environmental or human health hazard. Where a hazard is imminent or has already occurred, remedial action must be taken immediately.

d) The owner or operator shall record inspections in an inspection log or summary. The owner or operator shall keep these records for at least three years from the date of inspection. At a minimum, these records must include the date and time of the inspection, the name of the inspector, a notation of the observations made and the date, and nature of any repairs or other remedial actions.

[Source: Amended at 19 Ill. Reg. _____, effective _____]

SUBPART D: CONTINGENCY PLAN AND EMERGENCY PROCEDURES

Section 724.156 Emergency Procedures

a) Whenever there is an imminent or actual emergency situation, the emergency coordinator (or the designee when the emergency coordinator is on call) shall immediately:
   1) Activate internal facility alarms or communication systems, where applicable, to notify all facility personnel; and
   2) Notify appropriate state or local agencies with designated response roles if their help is needed.

b) Whenever there is a release, fire, or explosion, the emergency coordinator shall immediately identify the character, exact source, amount, and areal extent of any released materials. The emergency coordinator may do this by observation or review of facility records or manifests; and, if necessary, by chemical analysis.

c) Concurrently, the emergency coordinator shall assess possible hazards to human health or the environment that may result from the release, fire, or explosion. This assessment must consider both direct and

POLLUTION CONTROL BOARD

NOTICE OF PROPOSED AMENDMENTS

indirect effects of the release, fire, or explosion (e.g., the effects of any toxic, irritating, or asphyxiating gases that are generated, or the effects of any hazardous surface water run-off from water or chemical agents used to control fire and heat-induced explosions).

d) If the emergency coordinator determines that the facility has had a release, fire, or explosion that could threaten human health or the environment outside the facility, the emergency coordinator shall report the findings as follows:
   1) If the assessment indicates that evacuation of local areas may be advisable, the emergency coordinator shall immediately notify appropriate local authorities. The emergency coordinator must be available to help appropriate officials decide whether local areas should be evacuated; and
   2) The emergency coordinator shall immediately notify either the government official designated as the on-scene coordinator for that geographical area (in the applicable regional contingency plan under 40 CFR Part 300); or the National Response Center (using their 24-hour toll free number 800-424-8802). The report must include:
      A) Name and telephone number of reporter;
      B) Name and address of facility;
      C) Time and type of incident (e.g., release, fire);
      D) Name and quantity of materials(s) material involved, to the extent known;
      E) The extent of injuries, if any; and
      F) The possible hazards to human health or the environment outside the facility.

e) During an emergency, the emergency coordinator shall take all reasonable measures necessary to ensure that fires, explosions, and releases do not occur, recur, or spread to other hazardous waste at the facility. These measures must include, where applicable, stopping processes and operations, collecting and containing release waste, and removing or isolating containers.

f) If the facility stops operations in response to a fire, explosion, or release, the emergency coordinator shall monitor for leaks, pressure buildup, gas generation, or ruptures in valves, pipes, or other equipment, wherever this is appropriate.

g) Immediately after an emergency, the emergency coordinator shall provide for treating, storing, or disposing of recovered waste, contaminated soil or surface water, or any other material that results from a release, fire, or explosion at the facility.
BOARD NOTE: Unless the owner or operator can demonstrate, in accordance with 35 Ill. Adm. Code 721.103(c) (d) or (d) (e), that the recovered material is not a hazardous waste, the owner or operator becomes a generator of hazardous waste and must manage it in accordance with all applicable requirements of 35 Ill. Adm. Code 722, 723, and 724.

h) The emergency coordinator shall ensure that, in the affected area(s)

POLLUTION CONTROL BOARD

NOTICE OF PROPOSED AMENDMENTS

areas of the facility:
   1) No waste that may be incompatible with the released material is
      treated, stored, or disposed of until cleanup procedures are
      completed; and
   2) All emergency equipment listed in the contingency plan is cleaned
      and fit for its intended use before operations are resumed.
   i) The owner or operator shall notify the Agency and appropriate state
      and local authorities, that the facility is in compliance with
      paragraph subsection (h) above before operations are resumed in the
      affected areas+) areas of the facility.
   j) The owner or operator shall note in the operating record the time,
      date, and details of any incident that requires implementing the
      contingency plan. Within 15 days after the incident, the owner or
      operator shall submit a written report on the incident to the Agency.
      The report must include:
      1) Name, address, and telephone number of the owner or operator;
      2) Name, address, and telephone number of the facility;
      3) Date, time, and type of incident (e.g., fire, explosion);
      4) Name and quantity of materials+ materials involved;
      5) The extent of injuries, if any;
      6) An assessment of actual or potential hazards to human health or
         the environment, where this is applicable; and
      7) Estimated quantity and disposition of recovered material that
         resulted from the incident.

(Source: Amended at   19   Ill.   Reg.   _____,   effective
   _____)

SUBPART E: MANIFEST SYSTEM, RECORDKEEPING AND REPORTING

Section 724.173 Operating Record

   a) The owner or operator shall keep a written operating record at the
      facility.
   b) The following information must be recorded, as it becomes available,
      and maintained in the operating record until closure of the facility:
      1) A description and the quantity of each hazardous waste received,
         and the method or methods and date or dates of its treatment,
         storage, or disposal at the facility, as required by Section
         724.Appendix A;
      2) The location of each hazardous waste within the facility and the
         quantity at each location. For disposal facilities, the location
         and quantity of each hazardous waste must be recorded on a map or
         diagram of each cell or disposal area. For all facilities, this
         information must include cross-references to specific manifest
         document numbers, if the waste was accompanied by a manifest:
         BOARD NOTE: See Section 724.219 for related requirements.
      3) Records and results of waste analyses and waste determinations

POLLUTION CONTROL BOARD

NOTICE OF PROPOSED AMENDMENTS

      performed as specified in Sections 724.113, 724.117, 724.414,
      724.441, 724.934, 724.963, and 724.983 and in 35 Ill. Adm. Code
      728.104(a) and 728.107;
   4) Summary reports and details of all incidents that require
      implementing the contingency plan, as specified in Section
      724.156(j);
   5) Records and results of inspections, as required by Section
      724.115(d) (except these data need to be kept only three years);
   6) Monitoring, testing, or analytical data and corrective action
      data where required by 724.Subpart F or Sections 724.119,
      724.291, 724.293, 724.295, 724.322, 724.323, 724.326, 724.352
      through 724.354, 724.376, 724.378, 724.380, 724.402 through
      724.404, 724.409, 724.447, 724.702, 734.934(c) through (f),
      724.935, 724.963(d) through (i), or 724.964, 724.988, 724.989,
      and 724.991;
   7) For off-site facilities, notices to generators as specified in
      Section 724.112(b);
   8) All closure cost estimates under Section 724.242 and, for
      disposal facilities, all post-closure cost estimates under
      Section 724.244;
   9) A certification by the permittee, no less often than annually,
      that the permittee has a program in place to reduce the volume
      and toxicity of hazardous waste that the permittee generates, to
      the degree the permittee determines to be economically
      practicable, and that the proposed method of treatment, storage,
      or disposal is that practicable method currently available to the
      permittee which that minimizes the present and future threat to
      human health and the environment;
   10) Records of the quantities (and date of placement) for each
       shipment of hazardous waste placed in land disposal units under
       an extension of the effective date of any land disposal
       restriction granted pursuant to 35 Ill. Adm. Code 728.105, a
       petition to 35 Ill. Adm. Code 728.106 or a certification under 35
       Ill. Adm. Code 728.108, and the applicable notice required of a
       generator under 35 Ill. Adm. Code 728.107(a);
   11) For an off-site treatment facility, a copy of the notice, and the
       certification and demonstration, if applicable, required of the
       generator or the owner or operator under 35 Ill. Adm. Code
       728.107 or 728.108;
   12) For an on-site treatment facility, the information contained in
       the notice (except the manifest number), and the certification
       and demonstration, if applicable, required of the generator or
       the owner or operator under 35 Ill. Adm. Code 728.107 or 728.108;
   13) For an off-site land disposal facility, a copy of the notice, and
       the certification and demonstration, if applicable, required of
       the generator or the owner or operator of a treatment facility
       under 35 Ill. Adm. Code 728.107 or 728.108, whichever is
       applicable; and

POLLUTION CONTROL BOARD

NOTICE OF PROPOSED AMENDMENTS

14) For an on-site land disposal facility, the information contained in the notice required of the generator or owner or operator of a treatment facility under 35 Ill. Adm. Code 728.107, except for the manifest number, and the certification and demonstration if applicable, required under 35 Ill. Adm. Code 728.108 whichever is applicable.

15) For an off-site storage facility, a copy of the notice, and the certification and demonstration if applicable, required of the generator or the owner or operator under 35 Ill. Adm. Code 728.107 or 728.108; and

16) For an on-site storage facility, the information contained in the notice (except the manifest number), and the certification and demonstration if applicable, required of the generator or the owner or operator under 35 Ill. Adm. Code 728.107 or 728.108.

(Source: Amended at 19 Ill. Reg. _____, effective _____)

Section 724.177 Additional Reports

In addition to submitting the annual report and unmanifested waste reports described in Sections 724.175 and 724.176, the owner or operator shall also report to the Agency:

a) Releases, fires, and explosions, as specified in Section 724.156(j);
b) Facility closures specified in Section 724.215; and
c) As otherwise required by 724.Subparts F, K through N, AA, and BB, and CC.

(Source: Amended at 19 Ill. Reg. _____, effective _____)

SUBPART I: USE AND MANAGEMENT OF CONTAINERS

Section 724.279 Air Emission Standards

The owner or operator shall manage all hazardous waste placed in a container in accordance with the requirements of 724.Subpart CC.

(Source: Added at 19 Ill. Reg. _____, effective _____)

SUBPART J: TANK SYSTEMS

Section 724.300 Special--Requirements--for-Hazardous-Wastes-F020,-F021,-F022, F023,-F026-and-F027 Air Emission Standards

In--addition--to--the--other--requirements--of--this--Subpart,--the---following Requirements---apply--to--tanks-storing-or-treating-hazardous-wastes-F020,-F021,

POLLUTION CONTROL BOARD

NOTICE OF PROPOSED AMENDMENTS

F022,-F023,-F026-and-F027.

a) Tanks--must-have-systems-designed-and-operated-to-detect-and-adequately contain-spills-or-leaks.--The-design-and-operation-of-any--containment system-must-reflect-consideration-of-all-relevant-factors,-including:
  1) Capacity-of-the-tank;
  2) Volumes--and--characteristics--of-wastes-stored-or-treated-in-the tank;
  3) Method-of-collection-of-spills-or-leaks;
  4) The-design-and-construction-materials-of-the-tank-and-containment system;-and
  5) The-need-to-prevent-precipitation-and-run-on-from--entering--into the-system.
b) As--part--of--the-contingency-plan-required-by-Subpart-B,-the-owner-or operator-shall-specify-such-procedures-for-responding-to--a--spill--or leak--from-the-tank-into-the-containment-system-as-may-be-necessary-to protect-human-health--and--the--environment.---These--procedures--must include--measures--for--immediate-removal-of-the-waste-from-the-system and-replacement--for--repair-of-the-leaking-tank.
The owner or operator shall manage all hazardous waste placed in a tank in accordance with the requirements of 724.Subpart CC.

(Source: Section repealed, new Section adopted at 19 Ill. Reg. _____, effective _____)

SUBPART K: SURFACE IMPOUNDMENTS

Section 724.332 Air Emission Standards

The owner or operator shall manage all hazardous waste placed in a surface impoundment in accordance with the requirements of 724.Subpart CC.

(Source: Added at 19 Ill. Reg. _____, effective _____)

SUBPART X: MISCELLANEOUS UNITS

Section 724.701 Environmental Performance Standards

A miscellaneous unit must be located, designed, constructed, operated, maintained, and closed in a manner that will ensure protection of human health and the environment. Permits for miscellaneous units are to contain such terms and provisions as are necessary to protect human health and the environment, including, but not limited to, as appropriate, design and operating requirements, detection and monitoring requirements, and requirements for responses to releases of hazardous waste or hazardous constituents from the unit. Permit terms and provisions must include those requirements of 724.Subparts I through O and AA through CC and of 35 Ill. Adm. Code 702, 703, and 730, that are appropriate for the miscellaneous unit being permitted.

POLLUTION CONTROL BOARD

NOTICE OF PROPOSED AMENDMENTS

Protection of human health and the environment includes, but is not limited to:

a) Prevention of any releases that may have adverse effects on human health or the environment due to migration of waste constituents in the groundwater or subsurface environment, considering:

1) The volume and physical and chemical characteristics of the waste in the unit, including its potential for migration through soil, liners, or other containing structures;

2) The hydrologic and geologic characteristics of the unit and the surrounding area;

3) The existing quality of groundwater, including other sources of contamination and their cumulative impact on the groundwater;

4) The quantity and direction of groundwater flow;

5) The proximity to and withdrawal rates of current and potential groundwater users;

6) The patterns of land use in the region;

7) The potential for deposition or migration of waste constituents into subsurface physical structures and into the root zone of food-chain crops and other vegetation;

8) The potential for health risks caused by human exposure to waste constituents; and

9) The potential for damage to domestic animals, wildlife, crops, vegetation, and physical structures caused by waste constituents.

b) Prevention of any releases that may have adverse effects on human health or the environment due to migration of waste constituents in surface water, or in wetlands, or on the soil surface, considering:

1) The volume and physical and chemical characteristics of the waste in the unit;

2) The effectiveness and reliability of containing, confining, and collecting systems and structures in preventing migration;

3) The hydrologic characteristics of the unit and surrounding area, including the topography of the land around the unit;

4) The quantity, quality, and direction of groundwater flow;

5) The proximity of the unit to surface waters;

6) The current and potential uses of the nearby surface waters and any water quality standards in 35 Ill. Adm. Code 302 or 303;

7) The existing quality of surface waters and surface soils, including other sources of contamination and their cumulative impact on surface waters and surface soils;

8) The patterns of land use in the region;

9) The potential for health risks caused by human exposure to waste constituents; and

10) The potential for damage to domestic animals, wildlife, crops, vegetation, and physical structures caused by exposure to waste constituents; and

c) Prevention of any releases that may have adverse effects on human health or the environment due to migration of waste constituents in

---

POLLUTION CONTROL BOARD

NOTICE OF PROPOSED AMENDMENTS

the air, considering:

1) The volume and physical and chemical characteristics of the waste in the unit, including its potential for the emission and dispersal of gases, aerosols, and particulates;

2) The effectiveness and reliability of systems and structures to reduce or present emissions of hazardous constituents to the air;

3) The operating characteristics of the unit;

4) The existing quality of the air, including other sources of contamination and their cumulative impact on the air;

5) The potential for health risks caused by human exposure to waste constituents; and

6) The potential for damage to domestic animals, wildlife, crops, vegetation, and physical structures caused by waste constituents.

(Source: Amended at 19 Ill. Reg. _____, effective _____)

SUBPART AA: AIR EMISSION STANDARDS FOR PROCESS VENTS

Section 724.933 Standards: Closed-vent Systems and Control Devices

a) Compliance Required.

1) Owners or operators of closed-vent systems and control devices used to comply with the provisions of this Part shall comply with the provisions of this Section.

2) The owner or operator of an existing facility who that cannot install a closed-vent system and control device to comply with the provisions of this Subpart on the effective date that the facility becomes subject to the provisions of this Subpart shall prepare an implementation schedule that includes dates by which the closed-vent system and control device will be installed and in operation. The controls must be installed as soon as possible, but the implementation schedule may allow up to 18 months after the effective date that the facility becomes subject to this Subpart for installation and startup. All units that begin operation after December 31, 1990, must comply with the rules immediately (i.e., must have control devices installed and operating on startup of the affected unit) until the 2-year implementation schedule does not apply to these units.

b) A control device involving vapor recovery (e.g., a condenser or adsorber) must be designed and operated to recover the organic vapors vented to it with an efficiency of 95 weight percent or greater unless the total organic emission limits of Section 724.932(a)(1) for all affected process vents is attained at an efficiency less than 95 weight percent.

POLLUTION CONTROL BOARD

NOTICE OF PROPOSED AMENDMENTS

c) An enclosed combustion device (e.g., a vapor incinerator, boiler, or
    process heater) must be designed and operated to reduce the organic
    emissions vented to it by 95 weight percent or greater; to achieve a
    total organic compound concentration of 20 ppmv, expressed as the sum
    of the actual compounds, and not in carbon equivalents, on a dry
    basis, corrected to 3 percent oxygen; or to provide a minimum
    residence time of 0.50 seconds at a minimum temperature of 760° C. If
    a boiler or process heater is used as the control device, then the
    vent stream must be introduced into the flame zone of the boiler or
    process heater.

d) Flares:
    1) A flare must be designed for and operated with no visible
        emissions, as determined by the methods specified in subsection
        (e)(1), except for periods not to exceed a total of 5 minutes
        during any 2 consecutive hours.
    2) A flare must be operated with a flame present at all times, as
        determined by the methods specified in subsection (f)(2)(e)
        (f)(2)(C) below.
    3) A flare must be used only if the net heating value of the gas
        being combusted is 11.2 MJ/scm (300 Btu/scf) or greater if and
        the flare is steam-assisted or air-assisted; or if the net
        heating value of the gas being combusted is 7.45 MJ/scm (200
        Btu/scf) or greater if and the flare is nonassisted. The net
        heating value of the gas being combusted must be determined by
        the methods specified in subsection (e)(2) below.
    4) Exit Velocity.
        A) A steam-assisted or nonassisted flare must be designed for
            an operated with an exit velocity, as determined by the
            methods specified in subsection (e)(3) below, less than 18.3
            m/s (60 ft/s), except as provided in subsections (d)(4)(B)
            and (e) (d)(4)(C) below.
        B) A steam-assisted or nonassisted flare designed for and
            operated with an exit velocity, as determined by the methods
            specified in subsection (e)(3) below, equal to or greater
            than 18.3 m/s (60 ft/s) but less than 122 m/s (400 ft/s) is
            allowed if the net heating value of the gas being combusted
            is greater than 37.3 MJ/scm (1000 Btu/scf).
        C) A steam-assisted or nonassisted flare designed for and
            operated with an exit velocity, as determined by the methods
            specified in subsection (e)(3) below, less than the
            velocity, V_L as determined by the method specified in
            subsection (e)(4) below and less than 122 m/s (400 ft/s) is
            allowed.
    5) An air-assisted flare must be designed and operated with an exit
        velocity less than the velocity, V_L as determined by the method
        specified in subsection (e)(5) below.
    6) A flare used to comply with this Section must be steam-assisted,
        air-assisted, or nonassisted.

POLLUTION CONTROL BOARD

NOTICE OF PROPOSED AMENDMENTS

e) Compliance determination and equations.
    1) Reference Method 22 in 40 CFR 60, incorporated by reference in 35
        Ill. Adm. Code 720.111, must be used to determine the compliance
        of a flare with the visible emission provisions of this Subpart.
        The observation period is 2 hours and must be used according to
        Method 22.
    2) The net heating value of the gas being combusted in a flare must
        be calculated using the following equation:

$$H[T] = K \times \sum_{i=1}^{n} C[i] \times H[i]$$

        Where:

        $H[T]$ is the net heating value of the sample in MJ/scm;
        where the net enthalpy per mole of offgas is, based on
        combustion at 25° C and 760 mm Hg, but the standard
        temperature for determining the volume corresponding to 1
        mole is 20° C.

        $K = 1.74 \ E\ -7$ (1/ppm)(g mol/scm)(MJ/kcal) where standard
        temperature for (g mol/scm) 20° C.

        SUM(Xi) means the sum of the values of X for each component
        i, from i=1 to n.

        $C[i]$ is the concentration of sample component i in ppm on a
        wet basis, as measured for organics by Reference Method 18
        in 40 CFR 60, and for carbon monoxide, by ASTM D1946
        D 1946-90, incorporated by reference in 35 Ill. Adm. Code
        720.111.

        $H[i]$ is the net heat of combustion of sample component i,
        kcal/gmol at 25° C and 760 mm Hg. The heats of combustion
        must be determined using ASTM D2382 D 2382, incorporated by
        reference in 35 Ill. Adm. Code 720.111, if published values
        are not available or cannot be calculated.
    3) The actual exit velocity of a flare must be determined by
        dividing the volumetric flow rate (in units of standard
        temperature and pressure), as determined by Reference Methods 2,
        2A, 2C, or 2D in 40 CFR 60, incorporated by reference in 35 Ill.
        Adm. Code 720.111, as appropriate, by the unobstructed (free)
        cross-sectional area of the flare tip.
    4) The maximum allowed velocity in m/s, V for a flare complying with
        subsection (d)(4)(C) must be determined by the following
        equation:
        Log(V) = (H-+-28.8)-/-31.7

$$\log[10] \ V[max] = \frac{H[T] + 28.8}{31.7}$$

POLLUTION CONTROL BOARD

NOTICE OF PROPOSED AMENDMENTS

31.7

Where:

Log means logarithm to the base 10

H is the net heating value as determined in subsection
(e)(2).

5) The maximum allowed velocity in m/s, V for an air-assisted flare
must be determined by the following equation:

V = 8.706 + 8.7084H

$$V = 8.706 + 0.7084 \times 10[T]$$

Where:

H(T) is the net heating value as determined in
subsection (e)(2) below.

f) The owner or operator shall monitor and inspect each control device
required to comply with this Section to ensure proper operation and
maintenance of the control device by implementing the following
requirements:
1) Install, calibrate, maintain, and operate according to the
manufacturer's specifications a flow indicator that provides a
record of stream flow from each affected process vent to the
control device at least once every hour. The flow indicator
sensor must be installed in the vent stream at the nearest
feasible point to the control device inlet but before the point
at which the vent streams are combined.
2) Install, calibrate, maintain and operate according to the
manufacturer's specifications a device to' continuously monitor
control device operation as specified below:
A) For a thermal vapor incinerator, a temperature monitoring
device equipped with a continuous recorder. The device must
have accuracy of +-½ ± ½ percent of the temperature being
monitored in ° C or +-e° ± 0.5° C, whichever is greater. the
The temperature sensor must be installed at a location in
the combustion chamber downstream of the combustion zone.
B) For a catalytic vapor incinerator, a temperature monitoring
device equipped with a continuous recorder. The device must
be capable of monitoring temperature at two locations and
have an accuracy of +-½ ± ½ percent of the temperature being
monitored in ° C or +-8.5-0 ± 0.5° C, whichever is greater.
One temperature sensor must be installed in the vent stream
at the nearest feasible point to the catalyst bed inlet and

POLLUTION CONTROL BOARD

NOTICE OF PROPOSED AMENDMENTS

a second temperature sensor must be installed in the vent
stream at the nearest feasible point to the catalyst bed
outlet.
C) For a flare, a heat sensing monitoring device equipped with
a continuous recorder that indicates the continuous ignition
of the pilot flame.
D) For a boiler or process heater having a design heat input
capacity less than 44 MW, a temperature monitoring device
equipped with a continuous recorder. The device must have
an accuracy of +-½ ± ½ percent of the temperature being
monitored in ° C or +-8.5-0 ± 0.5° C, whichever is greater.
The temperature sensor must be installed at a location in
the furnace downstream of the combustion zone.
E) For a boiler or process heater having a design heat input
capacity greater than or equal to 44 MW, a monitoring device
equipped with a continuous recorder to measure a
parameter(s) parameters that indicates good combustion
operating practices are being used.
F) For a condenser, either:
i) A monitoring device equipped with continuous recorder
to measure the concentration level of the organic
compounds in the exhaust vent stream from the
condenser; or
ii) A temperature monitoring device equipped with a
continuous recorder. The device must be capable of
monitoring temperature at two locations and have an
accuracy of +-½ ± ½ percent of the temperature being
monitored in ° C or +-8.5-0 ± 0.5° C, whichever is
greater. One temperature sensor must be installed at a
location in the exhaust vent stream from the condenser,
and a second temperature sensor must be installed at a
location in the coolant fluid exiting the condenser.
G) For a carbon adsorption system that regenerates the carbon
bed directly in the control device such as a fixed-bed
carbon adsorber, either
i) A monitoring device equipped with a continuous recorder
to measure the concentration level of the organic
compounds in the exhaust vent stream from the carbon
bed, or
ii) A monitoring device equipped with continuous recorder
to measure a parameter that indicates the carbon bed is
regenerated on a regular, predetermined time cycle.
3) Inspect the readings from each monitoring device required by
subsection (f)(1) and (2) (f)(2) at least once each operating day
to check control device operation and, if necessary, immediately
implement the corrective measures necessary to ensure the control
device operates in compliance with the requirements of this
Section.

POLLUTION CONTROL BOARD

NOTICE OF PROPOSED AMENDMENTS

g) An owner or operator using a carbon adsorption system such as a fixed-bed carbon adsorber that regenerates the carbon bed directly onsite in the control device shall replace the existing carbon in the control device with fresh carbon at a regular, predetermined time interval that is no longer than the carbon service life established as a requirement of Section 724.935(b)(4)(C)(vi).

h) An owner or operator using a carbon adsorption system such as a carbon canister that does not regenerate the carbon bed directly onsite in the control device shall replace the existing carbon in the control device with fresh carbon on a regular basis by using one of the following procedures:

   1) Monitor the concentration level of the organic compounds in the exhaust vent stream from the carbon adsorption system on a regular schedule, and replace the existing carbon with fresh carbon immediately when carbon breakthrough is indicated. The monitoring frequency must be daily or at an interval no greater than 20 percent of the time required to consume the total carbon working capacity established as a requirement of Section 724.935(b)(4)(C)(vii), whichever is longer.

   2) Replace the existing carbon with fresh carbon at a regular, predetermined time interval that is less than the design carbon replacement interval established as a requirement of Section 724.935(b)(4)(C)(vii).

i) An alternative operational or process parameter may be monitored if the operator demonstrates that the parameter will ensure that the control device is operated in conformance with these standards and the control device's design specifications.

j) An owner or operator of an affected facility seeking to comply with the provisions of this Part by using a control device other than a thermal vapor incinerator, catalytic vapor incinerator, flare, boiler, process heater, condenser, or carbon adsorption system is required to develop documentation including sufficient information to describe the control device operation and identify the process parameter or parameters that indicate proper operation and maintenance of the control device.

k) Closed vent systems.

   1) Closed-vent systems must be designed for an operated with no detectable emissions, as indicated by an instrument reading of less than 500 ppm background and by visual inspections, as determined by the methods specified at Section 724.934(b).

   2) Closed-vent systems must be monitored to determine compliance with this Section during the initial leak detection monitoring, which must be conducted by the date that the facility becomes subject to the provisions of this Section annually, and at other times as specified in the RCRA permit. For the annual leak detection monitoring after the initial leak detection monitoring, the owner or operator is not required to monitor those closed-vent system components that operate in vacuum service or

POLLUTION CONTROL BOARD

NOTICE OF PROPOSED AMENDMENTS

those closed-vent system joints, seams, or other connections that are permanently or semi-permanently sealed (e.g., a welded joint between two sections of metal pipe or a bolted and gasketed pipe flange).

   3) Detectable emissions, as indicated by an instrument reading greater than 500 ppm and visual inspections, must be controlled as soon as practicable, but not later than 15 calendar days after the emission is detected.

   4) A first attempt at repair must be made no later than 5 calendar days after the emission is detected.

l) Closed-vent systems and control devices used to comply with provisions of this Subpart must be operated at all times when emissions may be vented to them.

m) The owner or operator using a carbon adsorption system shall document that all carbon removed from a carbon adsorption system to comply with subsections (g) and (h) above is managed in one of the following manners:

   1) It is regenerated or reactivated in a thermal treatment unit that is permitted under 724.Subpart X.

   2) It is incinerated by a process that is permitted under 724.Subpart O, or

   3) It is burned in a boiler or industrial furnace that is permitted under 724.Subpart H.

(Source: Amended at 19 Ill. Reg. _____, effective _____.)

SUBPART BB: AIR EMISSION STANDARDS FOR EQUIPMENT LEAKS

Section 724.963 Test Methods and Procedures

a) Each owner or operator subject to the provisions of this Subpart shall comply with the test methods and procedures requirements provided in this Section.

b) Leak detection monitoring, as required in Sections 724.952 through 724.962, must comply with the following requirements:

   1) Monitoring must comply with Reference Method 21 in 40 CFR 60, incorporated by reference in 35 Ill. Adm. Code 720.111.

   2) The detection instrument must meet the performance criteria of Reference Method 21.

   3) The instrument must be calibrated before use on each day of its use by the procedures specified in Reference Method 21.

   4) Calibration gases must be:
      A) Zero air (less than 10 ppm of hydrocarbon in air).
      B) A mixture of methane or n-hexane and air at a concentration of approximately, but less than 10,000 ppm methane or n-hexane.

   5) The instrument probe must be traversed around all potential leak

POLLUTION CONTROL BOARD

NOTICE OF PROPOSED AMENDMENTS

interfaces as close to the interface as possible as described in Reference Method 21.

c) When equipment is tested for compliance with no detectable emissions, as required in Sections 724.952(e), 724.953(i), 724.954, and 724.957(f), the test must comply with the following requirements:
1) The requirements of subsections (b)(1) through ~~(4)~~ (b)(4) above apply.
2) The background level must be determined as set forth in Reference Method 21.
3) The instrument probe must be traversed around all potential leak interfaces as close to the interface as possible as described in Reference Method 21.
4) This arithmetic difference between the maximum concentration indicated by the instrument and the background level is compared with 500 ppm for determining compliance.

d) In accordance with the waste analysis plan required by Section 724.113(b), an owner or operator of a facility shall determine, for each piece of equipment, whether the equipment contains or contacts a hazardous waste with organic concentration that equals or exceeds 10 percent by weight using the following:
1) Methods described in ASTM Methods ~~D-2267,~~ ~~D-169,~~ ~~D-160,~~ ~~D-260~~ D 2267-88, E 168-88, E 169-87, and E 260-85, incorporated by reference in 35 Ill. Adm. Code 720.111;
2) Method 9060 or 8240 of SW-846, incorporated by reference in 35 Ill. Adm. Code 720.111; or
3) Application of the knowledge of the nature of the hazardous wastestream or the process by which it was produced. Documentation of a waste determination by knowledge is required. Examples of documentation that must be used to support a determination under this provision include production process information documenting that no organic compounds are used, information that the waste is generated by a process that is identical to a process at the same or another facility that has previously been demonstrated by direct measurement to have a total organic content less than 10 percent, or prior speciation analysis results on the same wastestream where it is also documented that no process changes have occurred since that analysis that could affect the waste total organic concentration.

e) If an owner or operator determines that a piece of equipment contains or contacts a hazardous waste with organic concentrations at least 10 percent by weight, the determination can be revised only after following the procedures in subsection (d)(1) or ~~(2)~~ (d)(2) above.

f) When an owner or operator and the Agency do not agree on whether a piece of equipment contains or contacts a hazardous waste with organic concentrations at least 10 percent by weight, the procedures in subsection (d)(1) or ~~(2)~~ (d)(2) above must be used to resolve the dispute.

g) Samples used in determining the percent organic content must be

POLLUTION CONTROL BOARD

NOTICE OF PROPOSED AMENDMENTS

representative of the highest total organic content hazardous waste that is expected to be contained in or contact the equipment.

h) To determine if pumps or valves are in light liquid service, the vapor pressures of constituents must either be obtained from standard reference texts or be determined by ASTM ~~D-2879~~ D 2879-86, incorporated by reference in 35 Ill. Adm. Code 720.111.

i) Performance tests to determine if a control device achieves 95 weight percent organic emission reduction must comply with the procedures of Section 724.934(c)(1) through ~~(4)~~ (c)(4).

(Source: Amended at 19 Ill. Reg. _____, effective _____)

SUBPART CC: AIR EMISSION STANDARS FOR TANKS, SURFACE IMPOUNDMENTS, AND CONTAINERS

Section 724.980 Applicability

a) The requirements of this Subpart apply to owners and operators of all facilities that treat, store, or dispose of hazardous waste in tanks, surface impoundments, or containers subject to 724.Subpart I, J, or K, except as Section 724.101 and subsection (b) below provide otherwise.

b) The requirements of this Subpart do not apply to the following waste management units at the facility:
1) A waste management unit that holds hazardous waste placed in the unit before June 5, 1995, and in which no hazardous waste is added to the unit on or after June 5, 1995.
2) A container that has a design capacity less than or equal to 0.1 m(3) (3.5 ft(3) or 26.4 gal).
3) A tank in which an owner or operator has stopped adding hazardous waste and the owner or operator has begun implementing or completed closure pursuant to an approved closure plan.
4) A surface impoundment in which an owner or operator has stopped adding hazardous waste (except to implement an approved closure plan) and the owner or operator has begun implementing or completed closure pursuant to an approved closure plan.
5) A waste management unit that is used solely for on-site treatment or storage of hazardous waste that is generated as the result of implementing remedial activities required pursuant to the Act or Board regulations or under the corrective action authorities of RCRA sections 3004(u), 3004(v) or 3008(h); CERCLA authorities; or similar federal or state authorities.
6) A waste management unit that is used solely for the management of radioactive mixed waste in accordance with all applicable regulations under the authority of the Atomic Energy Act (42 U.S.C. 2011 et seq.) and the Nuclear Waste Policy Act.

c) For the owner and operator of a facility subject to this Subpart and who received a final RCRA permit prior to June 5, 1995, the

POLLUTION CONTROL BOARD

NOTICE OF PROPOSED AMENDMENTS

requirements of this Subpart shall be incorporated into the permit when the permit is reissued, renewed, or modified in accordance with the requirements of 35 Ill. Adm. Code 703 and 705. Until such date when the owner and operator receives a final permit incorporating the requirements of this Subpart, the owner and operator is subject to the requirements of 35 Ill. Adm. Code 725.Subpart CC.

(Source: Added at 19 Ill. Reg. _____, effective _____)

Section 724.981 Definitions

As used in this Subpart, all terms shall have the meaning given to them in 35 Ill. Adm. Code 725.981, RCRA, and 35 Ill. Adm. Code 720.110.

(Source: Added at 19 Ill. Reg. _____, effective _____)

Section 724.982 Standards: General

a) This Section applies to the management of hazardous waste in tanks, surface impoundments, and containers subject to this Subpart.

b) The owner or operator shall control air emissions from each waste management unit in accordance with standards specified in Section 724.984 through 724.987, as applicable to the waste management unit, except as provided for in subsection (c) below.

c) A waste management unit is exempted from standards specified in Sections 724.984 through 724.987, provided that all hazardous waste placed in the waste management unit is determined by the owner or operator to meet either of the following conditions:

   1) The average VO concentration of the hazardous waste at the point of waste origination is less than 100 parts per million by weight (ppmw). The average VO concentration shall be determined by the procedures specified in Section 724.983(a).

   2) The organic content of the hazardous waste has been reduced by an organic destruction or removal process that achieves any one of the following conditions:

      A) The process removes or destroys the organics contained in the hazardous waste to a level such that the average VO concentration of the hazardous waste at the point of waste treatment is less than the exit concentration limit (C[t]) established for the process. The average VO concentration of the hazardous waste at the point of waste treatment and the exit concentration limit for the process shall be determined using the procedures specified in Section 724.983(b).

      B) The process removes or destroys the organics contained in the hazardous waste to a level such that the organic

---

POLLUTION CONTROL BOARD

NOTICE OF PROPOSED AMENDMENTS

reduction efficiency (R) for the process is equal to or greater than 95 percent, and the average VO concentration of the hazardous waste at the point of waste treatment is less than 50 ppmw. The organic reduction efficiency for the process and the average VO concentration of the hazardous waste at the point of waste treatment shall be determined using the procedures specified in Section 724.983(b).

C) The process removes or destroys the organics contained in the hazardous waste to a level such that the actual organic mass removal rate (MR) for the process is greater than the required organic mass removal rate (RMR) established for the process. The required organic mass removal rate and the actual organic mass removal rate for the process shall be determined using the procedures specified in Section 724.983(b).

D) The process is a biological process that destroys or degrades the organics contained in the hazardous waste so that either of the following conditions is met:

   i) The organic reduction efficiency (R) for the process is equal to or greater than 95 percent, and the organic biodegradation efficiency (R[bio]) for the process is equal to or greater than 95 percent. The organic reduction efficiency and the organic biodegradation efficiency for the process shall be determined in accordance with the procedures specified in Section 724.983(b).

   ii) The total actual organic mass biodegradation rate (MR(bio]) for all hazardous waste treated by the process is equal to or greater than the required organic mass removal rate (RMR). The required organic mass removal rate and the actual organic mass biodegradation rate for the process shall be determined using the procedures specified in Section 724.983(b).

E) The process removes or destroys the organics contained in the hazardous waste and meets all of the following conditions:

   i) All of the materials entering the process are hazardous wastes.

   ii) From the point of waste origination through the point where the hazardous waste enters the process, the hazardous waste is continuously managed in waste management units which use air emission controls in accordance with the standards specified in Sections 724.984 through 724.987, as applicable to the waste management unit.

   iii) The average VO concentration of the hazardous waste at the point of waste treatment is less than the lowest

POLLUTION CONTROL BOARD

NOTICE OF PROPOSED AMENDMENTS

average VO concentration at the point of waste
origination, determined for each of the individual
hazardous waste streams entering the process; or 100
ppmw, whichever value is lower. The average VO
concentration of each individual hazardous waste
stream at the point of waste origination shall be
determined using the procedure specified in Section
724.983(a). The average VO concentration of the
hazardous waste at the point of waste treatment shall
be determined using the procedure specified in Section
724.983(b).

F) A hazardous waste incinerator for which the owner or
operator has either:

1) Been issued a final permit under 35 Ill. Adm. Code 703
and 705, and designs and operates the unit in
accordance with the requirements of 724.Subpart O; or

ii) Has certified compliance with the interim status
requirements of 35 Ill. Adm. Code 725.Subpart O.

G) A boiler or industrial furnace for which the owner or
operator has either:

1) Been issued a final permit under 35 Ill. Adm. Code 703
and 705, and designs and operates the unit in
accordance with the requirements of 35 Ill. Adm. Code
726.Subpart H; or

ii) Has certified compliance with the interim status
requirements of 35 Ill. Adm. Code 726.Subpart H.

d) When a process is used for the purpose of treating a hazardous waste
to meet one of the sets of conditions specified in subsections
(c)(2)(A) through (c)(2)(E) above, each material removed from or
exiting the process that is not a hazardous waste but which has an
average VO concentration equal to or greater than 100 ppmw shall be
managed in a waste management unit in accordance with the requirements
of subsection (b) above.

e) The Agency may at any time perform or request that the owner or
operator perform a waste determination for a hazardous waste managed
in a tank, surface impoundment, or container that is exempted from
using air emission controls under the provisions of this Section as
follows:

1) The waste determination for average VO concentration of a
hazardous waste at the point of waste origination shall be
performed using direct measurement in accordance with the
applicable requirements of Section 724.983(a). The waste
determination for a hazardous waste at the point of waste
treatment shall be performed in accordance with the applicable
requirements of Section 724.983(b).

2) Where the owner or operator is requested to perform the waste
determination, the Agency may elect to have an authorized
representative observe the collection of the hazardous waste

POLLUTION CONTROL BOARD

NOTICE OF PROPOSED AMENDMENTS

samples used for the analysis.

3) Where the results of the waste determination performed or
requested by the Agency do not agree with the results of a waste
determination performed by the owner or operator using knowledge
of the waste, then the results of the waste determination
performed in accordance with the requirements of subsection
(e)(1) above shall be used to establish compliance with the
requirements of this Subpart.

4) Where the owner or operator has used an averaging period greater
than one hour for determining the average VO concentration of a
hazardous waste at the point of waste origination, the Agency may
elect to establish compliance with this Subpart by performing or
requesting that the owner or operator perform a waste
determination using direct measurement based on waste samples
collected within a one-hour period as follows:

A) The average VO concentration of the hazardous waste at the
point of waste origination shall be determined by direct
measurement in accordance with the requirements of Section
724.983(a).

B) Results of the waste determination performed or requested by
the Agency showing that the average VO concentration of the
hazardous waste at the point of waste origination is equal
to or greater than 100 ppmw shall constitute noncompliance
with this Subpart, except in a case as provided for in
subsection (e)(4)(C) below.

C) Where the average VO concentration of the hazardous waste at
the point of waste origination previously has been
determined by the owner or operator using an averaging
period greater than one hour to be less than 100 ppmw but
because of normal operating process variations the VO
concentration of the hazardous waste determined by direct
measurement for any given one-hour period may be equal to or
greater than 100 ppmw, information that was used by the
owner or operator to determine the average VO concentration
of the hazardous waste (e.g., test results, measurements,
calculations, and other documentation) and recorded in the
facility records in accordance with the requirements of
Section 724.983(a) and Section 724.989 shall be considered
by the Agency together with the results of the waste
determination performed or requested by the Agency in
establishing compliance with this Subpart.

(Source: Added   at   19   Ill.   Reg. _____,   effective
_____)

Section 724.983 Waste Determination Procedures

a) Waste determination procedure for average volatile organic (VO)

POLLUTION CONTROL BOARD

NOTICE OF PROPOSED AMENDMENTS

concentration of a hazardous waste at the point of waste origination.

1) An owner or operator shall determine the average VO concentration at the point of waste origination for each hazardous waste placed in waste management units exempted under the provisions of Section 724.982(c)(1) from using air emission controls in accordance with standards specified in Section 724.984 through Section 724.987, as applicable to the waste management unit.

2) The VO concentration at the point of waste origination for a hazardous waste shall be determined in accordance with the procedures specified in 35 Ill. Adm. Code 725.984(a)(2) through (a)(6).

b) Waste determination procedures for treated hazardous waste.

1) An owner or operator shall perform the applicable waste determinations for each treated hazardous waste placed in waste management units exempted under the provisions of Section 724.982(c)(2) from using air emission controls in accordance with standards specified in Section 724.984 through 724.987, as applicable to the waste management unit.

2) The waste determination for a treated hazardous waste shall be performed in accordance with the procedures specified in 35 Ill. Adm. Code 725.984(b)(2) through (b)(10), as applicable to the treated hazardous waste.

c) Procedure to determine the maximum organic vapor pressure of a hazardous waste in a tank.

1) An owner or operator shall determine the maximum organic vapor pressure for each hazardous waste placed in tanks using air emission controls in accordance with standards specified in Section 724.984(c).

2) The maximum organic vapor pressure of the hazardous waste shall be determined in accordance with the procedures specified in 35 Ill. Adm. Code 725.984(c)(2) through (c)(4).

(Source: Added at 19 Ill. Reg. _____, effective _____)

Section 724.984 Standards: Tanks

a) This Section applies to owners and operators of tanks subject to this Subpart into which any hazardous waste is placed, except for the following tanks:

1) A tank in which all hazardous waste entering the tank meets the conditions specified in Section 724.982(c); or

2) A tank used for biological treatment of hazardous waste in accordance with the requirements of Section 724.982(c)(2)(D).

b) The owner or operator shall place the hazardous waste into one of the following tanks:

1) A tank equipped with a cover (e.g., a fixed roof) that is vented through a closed-vent system to a control device in accordance

POLLUTION CONTROL BOARD

NOTICE OF PROPOSED AMENDMENTS

with the requirements specified in subsection (d) below;

2) A tank equipped with a fixed roof and internal floating roof in accordance with the requirements of Section 724.99);

3) A tank equipped with an external floating roof in accordance with the requirements of Section 724.99); or

4) A pressure tank that is designed to operate as a closed system such that the tank operates with no detectable organic emissions at all times that hazardous waste is in the tank except as provided for in subsection (g) below.

c) As an alternative to complying with subsection (b) above, an owner or operator may place hazardous waste in a tank equipped with a cover (e.g., a fixed roof) meeting the requirements specified in subsection (d)(1) below when the hazardous waste is determined to meet all of the following conditions:

1) The hazardous waste is not mixed, stirred, agitated, or circulated within the tank by the owner or operator using a process that results in splashing, frothing, or visible turbulent flow on the waste surface during normal process operations;

2) The hazardous waste in the tank is not heated by the owner or operator except during conditions requiring that the waste be heated to prevent the waste from freezing or to maintain adequate waste flow conditions for continuing normal process operations;

3) The hazardous waste in the tank is not treated by the owner or operator using a waste stabilization process or a process that produces an exothermic reaction; and

4) The maximum organic vapor pressure of the hazardous waste in the tank, as determined using the procedure specified in Section 724.983(c), is less than the following applicable value:

A) If the tank design capacity is equal to or greater than 151 m(3) (5333 ft(3) or 39,887 gal), then the maximum organic vapor pressure shall be less than 5.2 kPa (0.75 psia or 39 mm Hg);

B) If the tank design capacity is equal to or greater than 75 m(3) (2649 ft(3) or 19,810 gal) but less than 151 m(3) (5333 ft(3) or 39,887 gal), then the maximum organic vapor pressure shall be less than 27.6 kPa (4.0 psia or 207 mm Hg); or

C) If the tank design capacity is less than 75 m(3) (2649 ft(3) or 19,810 gal), then the maximum organic vapor pressure shall be less than 76.6 kPa (11.1 psia or 574 mm Hg).

d) To comply with subsection (b)(1) above, the owner or operator shall design, install, operate, and maintain a cover that vents the organic vapors emitted from hazardous waste in the tank through a closed-vent system connected to a control device.

1) The cover shall be designed and operated to meet the following requirements:

A) The cover and all cover openings (e.g., access hatches, sampling ports, and gauge wells) shall be designed to

POLLUTION CONTROL BOARD

NOTICE OF PROPOSED AMENDMENTS

operate with no detectable organic emissions when all cover openings are secured in a closed, sealed position; and

   B) Each cover opening shall be secured in a closed, sealed position (e.g., covered by a gasketed lid or cap) at all times that hazardous waste is in the tank except as provided for in subsection (f) below.

2) The closed-vent system and control device shall be designed and operated in accordance with the requirements of Section 724.987.

e) The owner and operator shall install, operate, and maintain enclosed pipes or other closed-systems to:

BOARD NOTE: U.S. EPA considers a drain system that meets the requirements of 40 CFR 61.346(a)(1) or (b)(1) through (b)(3) to be a "closed-system". The Board intends that this meaning be included in the use of that term for the purposes of this Subpart.

1) Transfer all hazardous waste to the tank from another tank, surface impoundment, or container subject to this Subpart except for those hazardous wastes that meet the conditions specified in Section 724.982(c); and

2) Transfer all hazardous waste from the tank to another tank, surface impoundment, or container subject to this Subpart except for those hazardous wastes that meet the conditions specified in Section 724.982(c).

f) Each cover opening shall be secured in a closed, sealed position (e.g., covered by a gasketed lid) at all times that hazardous waste is in the tank except when it is necessary to use the cover opening to:

1) Add, remove, inspect, or sample the material in the tank;

2) Inspect, maintain, repair, or replace equipment located inside the tank; or

3) Vent gases or vapors from the tank to a closed-vent system connected to a control device that is designed and operated in accordance with the requirements of Section 724.987.

g) One or more safety devices that vent directly to the atmosphere may be used on the tank, cover, closed-vent system, or control device provided each safety device meets all of the following conditions:

1) The safety device is not used for planned or routine venting of organic vapors from the tank or closed-vent system connected to a control device; and

2) The safety device remains in a closed, sealed position at all times, except when an unplanned event requires that the device open for the purpose of preventing physical damage or permanent deformation of the tank, cover, closed-vent system, or control device in accordance with good engineering and safety practices for handling flammable, combustible, explosive, or other hazardous materials. An example of an unplanned event is a sudden power outage.

(Source: Added at 19 Ill. Reg. _____, effective
_____)

POLLUTION CONTROL BOARD

NOTICE OF PROPOSED AMENDMENTS

Section 724.985 Standards: Surface Impoundments

a) This Section applies to owners and operators of surface impoundments subject to this Subpart into which any hazardous waste is placed except for the following surface impoundments:

1) A surface impoundment in which all hazardous waste entering the surface impoundment meets the conditions specified in Section 724.982(c); or

2) A surface impoundment used for biological treatment of hazardous waste in accordance with the requirements of Section 724.982(c)(2)(D).

b) The owner or operator shall place the hazardous waste into a surface impoundment equipped with a cover (e.g., an air-supported structure or a rigid cover) that is vented through a closed-vent system to a control device meeting the requirements specified in subsection (d) below.

c) As an alternative to complying with subsection (b) above, an owner or operator may place hazardous waste in a surface impoundment equipped with a floating membrane cover meeting the requirements specified in subsection (e) below when the hazardous waste is determined to meet all of the following conditions:

1) The hazardous waste is not mixed, stirred, agitated, or circulated within the surface impoundment by the owner or operator using a process that results in splashing, frothing, or visible turbulent flow on the waste surface during normal process operations;

2) The hazardous waste in the surface impoundment is not heated by the owner or operator; and

3) The hazardous waste is not treated by the owner or operator using a waste stabilization process or a process that produces an exothermic reaction.

d) To comply with subsection (b)(1) above, the owner or operator shall design, install, operate, and maintain a cover that vents the organic vapors emitted from hazardous waste in the surface impoundment through a closed-vent system connected to a control device.

1) The cover shall be designed and operated to meet the following requirements:

   A) The cover and all cover openings (e.g., access hatches, sampling ports, and gauge wells) shall be designed to operate with no detectable organic emissions when all cover openings are secured in a closed, sealed position;

   B) Each cover opening shall be secured in the closed, sealed position (e.g., covered by a gasketed lid or cap) at all times that hazardous waste is in the surface impoundment, except as provided for in subsection (g) below; and

   C) The closed-vent system and control device shall be designed and operated in accordance with Section 724.987.

e) To comply with subsection (c) above, the owner or operator shall

POLLUTION CONTROL BOARD

NOTICE OF PROPOSED AMENDMENTS

design, install, operate, and maintain a floating membrane cover that
meets all of the requirements specified in 35 Ill. Adm. Code
725.986(e)(1) through (e)(4).

f)   The owner or operator shall install, operate, and maintain enclosed
pipes or other closed-systems to:
BOARD NOTE: U.S. EPA considers a drain system that meets the
requirements of 40 CFR 61.346(a)(1) or (b)(1) through (b)(3) to be a
"closed-system". The Board intends that this meaning be included in
the use of that term for the purposes of this Subpart.
1)   Transfer all hazardous waste to the surface impoundment from
another tank, surface impoundment, or container subject to this
Subpart except for those hazardous wastes that meet the
conditions specified in Section 724.982(c); and
2)   Transfer all hazardous waste from the surface impoundment to
another tank, surface impoundment, or container subject to this
Subpart except for those hazardous wastes that meet the
conditions specified in Section 724.982(c).

g)   Each cover opening shall be secured in the closed, sealed position
(e.g., a cover by a gasketed lid or cap) at all times that hazardous
waste is in the surface impoundment except when it is necessary to use
the cover opening to:
1)   Add, remove, inspect, or sample the material in the surface
impoundment;
2)   Inspect, maintain, repair, or replace equipment located
underneath the cover;
3)   Remove treatment residues from the surface impoundment in
accordance with the requirements of 35 Ill. Adm. Code 728.4; or
4)   Vent gases or vapors from the surface impoundment to a
closed-vent system connected to a control device that is designed
and operated in accordance with the requirements of Section
724.987.

h)   One or more safety devices that vent directly to the atmosphere may be
installed on the cover, closed-vent system, or control device provided
each device meets all of the following conditions:
1)   The safety device is not used for planned or routine venting of
organic vapors from the surface impoundment or the closed-vent
system connected to a control device; and
2)   The safety device remains in a closed, sealed position at all
times, except when an unplanned event requires that the device
open for the purpose of preventing physical damage or permanent
deformation of the cover, closed-vent system, or control device
in accordance with good engineering and safety practices for
handling flammable, combustible, explosive, or other hazardous
materials. An example of an unplanned event is a sudden power
outage.

(Source: Added   at   19   Ill.   Reg. _____,   effective
_____)

POLLUTION CONTROL BOARD

NOTICE OF PROPOSED AMENDMENTS

Section 724.986 Standards: Containers

a)   This Section applies to the owners and operators of containers having
design capacities greater than 0.1 m(3) (3.5 ft(3) or 26.4 gal)
subject to this Subpart into which any hazardous waste is placed
except for a container in which all hazardous waste entering the
container meets the conditions specified in Section 724.982(c).

b)   An owner or operator shall manage hazardous waste in containers using
the following procedures:
1)   The owner or operator shall place the hazardous waste into one of
the following containers, except when a container is used for
hazardous waste treatment as required by subsection (b)(2) below:
A)   A container that is equipped with a cover which operates
with no detectable organic emissions when all container
openings (e.g., lids, bungs, hatches, and sampling ports)
are secured in a closed, sealed position. The owner or
operator shall determine that a container operates with no
detectable emissions by testing each opening on the
container for leaks in accordance with Method 21 in 40 CFR
Part 60, Appendix A, incorporated by reference in 35 Ill.
Adm. Code 720.111, the first time any portion of the
hazardous waste is placed into the container. If a leak is
detected and cannot be repaired immediately, the hazardous
waste shall be removed from the container and the container
not used to meet the requirements of this subsection until
the leak is repaired and the container is retested.
B)   A container having a design capacity less than or equal to
0.46 m(3) (16.2 ft(3) or 122 gal) that is equipped with a
cover and complies with all applicable Department of
Transportation regulations on packaging hazardous waste for
transport under 49 CFR Part 178, incorporated by reference
at 35 Ill. Adm. Code 720.111.
i)   A container that is managed in accordance with the
requirements of 49 CFR Part 178, incorporated by
reference at 35 Ill. Adm. Code 720.111, for the
purpose of complying with this Subpart, is not subject
to any exceptions to the 49 CFR Part 178 regulations,
except as noted in subsection (b)(1)(B)(ii) below.
ii) A lab pack that is managed in accordance with the
requirements of 49 CFR Part 178, incorporated by
reference at 35 Ill. Adm. Code 720.111, for the
purpose of complying with this Subpart, may comply
with the exceptions for combination packaging
specified in 49 CFR 173.12(b), incorporated by
reference at 35 Ill. Adm. Code 720.111.
C)   A container that is attached to or forms a part of any
truck, trailer, or railcar and that has been demonstrated
within the preceding 12 months to be organic vapor tight

when all container openings are in a closed, sealed position (e.g., the container hatches or lids are gasketed and latched). For the purpose of meeting the requirements of this subsection, a container is organic vapor tight if the container sustains a pressure change of not more than 0.75 kPa (0.11 psig or 5.6 mm Hg) within 5 minutes after it is pressurized to a minimum of 4.50 kPa (0.65 psig or 33.7 mm Hg). This condition is to be demonstrated using the pressure test specified in Method 27 of 40 CFR Part 60, Appendix A, and a pressure measurement device which has a precision of ± 2.5 mm water and which is capable of measuring above the pressure at which the container is to be tested for vapor tightness.

2) An owner or operator treating hazardous waste in a container by either a waste stabilization process, any process that requires the addition of heat to the waste, or any process that produces an exothermic reaction shall meet the following requirements:

A) Whenever it is necessary for the container to be open during the treatment process, the container shall be located inside an enclosure that is vented through a closed-vent system to a control device.

B) The enclosure shall be a structure that is designed and operated in accordance with the following requirements:

i) The enclosure shall be a structure that is designed and operated with sufficient airflow into the structure to capture the organic vapors emitted from the hazardous waste in the container and vent the vapors through the closed-vent system to the control device.

ii) The enclosure may have permanent or temporary openings to allow worker access, passage of containers through the enclosure by conveyor or other mechanical means, entry of permanent mechanical or electrical equipment, or to direct airflow into the enclosure. The pressure drop across each opening in the enclosure shall be maintained at a pressure below atmospheric pressure so that whenever an open container is placed inside the enclosure no organic vapors released from the container exit the enclosure through the opening. The owner or operator shall determine that an enclosure achieves this condition by measuring the pressure drop across each opening in the enclosure. If the pressure within the enclosure is equal to or greater than atmospheric pressure then the enclosure does not meet the requirements of this Section.

C) The closed-vent system and control device shall be designed and operated in accordance with the requirements of Section 724.987.

3) An owner or operator transferring hazardous waste into a container having a design capacity greater than 0.46 m(3) (16.2 ft(3) or 122 gal) shall meet the following requirements:

A) Hazardous waste transfer by pumping shall be performed using a conveyance system that uses a tube (e.g., pipe, hose) to add the waste into the container. During transfer of the waste into the container, the cover shall remain in place and all container openings shall be maintained in a closed, sealed position except for those openings through which the tube enters the container and as provided for in subsection (c) below. The tube shall be positioned in a manner so that:

i) The tube outlet continuously remains submerged below the waste surface at all times waste is flowing through the tube;

ii) The lower bottom edge of the tube outlet is located at a distance no greater than two inside diameters of the tube or 15.25 cm (6.0 in), whichever distance is greater, from the bottom of the container at all times waste is flowing through the tube; or

iii) The tube is connected to a permanent port mounted on the bottom of the container so that the lower edge of the port opening inside the container is located at a distance equal to or less than 15.25 cm (6.0 in) from the container bottom.

B) Hazardous waste transferred by a means other than pumping shall be performed such that during transfer of the waste into the container, the cover remains in place and all container openings are maintained in a closed, sealed position except for those openings through which the hazardous waste is added and as provided for in subsection (d) below.

c) Each container opening shall be maintained in a closed, sealed position (e.g., covered by a gasketed lid) at all times that hazardous waste is in the container except when it is necessary to use the opening to:

1) Add, remove, inspect, or sample the material in the container;

2) Inspect, maintain, repair, or replace equipment located inside the container; or

3) Vent gases or vapors from a cover located over or enclosing an open container to a closed-vent system connected to a control device that is designed and operated in accordance with the requirements of Section 724.987.

d) One or more safety devices that vent directly to the atmosphere may be used on the container, cover, enclosure, closed-vent system, or control device provided each device meets all of the following conditions:

1) The safety device is not used for planned or routine venting of

organic vapors from the container, cover, enclosure, or
closed-vent system connected to a control device; and

2)   The safety device remains in a closed, sealed position at all
     times except when an unplanned event requires that the device
     open for the purpose of preventing physical damage or permanent
     deformation of the container, cover, enclosure, closed-vent
     system, or control device in accordance with good engineering and
     safety practices for handling flammable, combustible, explosive,
     or other hazardous materials. An example of an unplanned event
     is a sudden power outage.

(Source: Added at 19 Ill. Reg. _____, effective
_____)

Section 724.987 Standards: Closed-vent Systems and Control Devices

a)   This Section applies to each closed-vent system and control device
     installed and operated by the owner or operator to control air
     emissions in accordance with standards of this Subpart.
b)   The closed-vent system shall meet the following requirements:
     1)   The closed-vent system shall route the gases, vapors, and fumes
          emitted from the hazardous waste in the waste management unit to
          a control device that meets the requirements specified in
          subsection (c) below.
     2)   The closed-vent system shall be designed and operated in
          accordance with the requirements specified in Section 724.933(k)
          of this Part.
     3)   If the closed-vent system contains one or more bypass devices
          that could be used to divert all or a portion of the gases,
          vapors, or fumes from entering the control device, the owner or
          operator shall meet the following requirements:
          A)   For each bypass device, except as provided for in subsection
               (b)(3)(B) below, the owner or operator shall either:
               i)   Install, calibrate, maintain, and operate a flow
                    indicator at the inlet to the bypass device that
                    indicates at least once every 15 minutes whether gas,
                    vapor, or fume flow is present in the bypass device;
                    or
               ii) Secure a valve installed at the inlet to the bypass
                    device in the closed position using a car-seal or a
                    lock-and-key type configuration. The owner or operator
                    shall visually inspect the seal or closure mechanism
                    at least once every month to verify that the valve is
                    maintained in the closed position.
          B)   Low leg drains, high point bleeds, analyzer vents,
               open-ended valves or lines, and safety devices are not
               subject to the requirements of subsection (b)(3)(A) above.
c)   The control device shall meet the following requirements:

1)   The control device shall be one of the following devices:
     A)   A control device designed and operated to reduce the total
          organic content of the inlet vapor stream vented to the
          control device by at least 95 percent by weight;
     B)   An enclosed combustion device designed and operated in
          accordance with the requirements of Section 724.933(c); or
     C)   A flare designed and operated in accordance with the
          requirements of Section 724.933(d).
2)   The control device shall be operating at all times when gases,
     vapors, or fumes are vented from the waste management unit
     through the closed-vent system to the control device.
3)   The owner or operator using a carbon adsorption system to comply
     with subsection (c)(1) above shall operate and maintain the
     control device in accordance with the following requirements:
     A)   Following the initial startup of the control device, all
          activated carbon in the control device shall be replaced
          with fresh carbon on a regular basis in accordance with the
          requirements of Section 724.933(g) or Section 724.933(h).
     B)   All carbon removed from the control device shall be managed
          in accordance with the requirements of Section 724.933(m).
4)   An owner or operator using a control device other than a thermal
     vapor incinerator, flare, boiler, process heater, condenser, or
     carbon adsorption system to comply with subsection (c)(1) above
     shall operate and maintain the control device in accordance with
     the requirements of Section 724.933(s).
5)   The owner or operator shall demonstrate that a control device
     achieves the performance requirements of subsection (c)(1) above,
     as follows:
     A)   An owner or operator shall demonstrate using either a
          performance test, as specified in subsection (c)(5)(C)
          below, or a design analysis, as specified in subsection
          (c)(5)(D) below, the performance of each control device
          except for the following:
          i)   A flare;
          ii)   A boiler or process heater with a design heat input
                capacity of 44 megawatts or greater;
          iii) A boiler or process heater into which the vent stream
                is introduced with the primary fuel;
          iv)   A boiler or process heater burning hazardous waste for
                which the owner or operator has been issued a final
                permit under 35 Ill. Adm. Code 703 and 705 and designs
                and operates the unit in accordance with the
                requirements of 35 Ill. Adm. Code 726.Subpart H; or
          v)   A boiler or process heater burning hazardous waste for
                which the owner or operator has certified compliance
                with the interim status requirements of 35 Ill. Adm.
                Code 726.Subpart H.
     B)   An owner or operator shall demonstrate the performance of

each flare in accordance with the requirements specified in Section 724.933(e).

C) For a performance test conducted to meet the requirements of subsection (c)(5)(A) above, the owner or operator shall use the test methods and procedures specified in Section 724.934(c)(1) through (c)(4).

D) For a design analysis conducted to meet the requirements of subsection (c)(5)(A) above, the design analysis shall meet the requirements specified in Section 724.935(b)(4)(C).

E) The owner or operator shall demonstrate that a carbon adsorption system achieves the performance requirements of subsection (c)(1) above based on the total quantity of organics vented to the atmosphere from all carbon adsorption system equipment that is used for organic adsorption, organic desorption or carbon regeneration, organic recovery, and carbon disposal.

6) If the owner or operator and the Agency do not agree on a demonstration of control device performance using a design analysis then the disagreement shall be resolved using the results of a performance test performed by the owner or operator in accordance with the requirements of subsection (c)(5)(C) above. The Agency may choose to have an authorized representative observe the performance test.

(Source: Added at 19 Ill. Reg. _____, effective _____)

Section 724.988 Inspection and Monitoring Requirements

a) This Section applies to an owner or operator using air emission controls in accordance with the requirements of Sections 724.984 through 724.987.

b) Each cover used in accordance with requirements of Sections 724.984 through 724.986 shall be visually inspected and monitored for detectable organic emissions by the owner or operator using the procedure specified in 35 Ill. Adm. Code 725.989(f)(1) through (f)(7), except as follows:

    1) An owner or operator is exempted from performing the cover inspection and monitoring requirements specified in 35 Ill. Adm. Code 725.989(f)(1) through (f)(7) for the following tank covers:

        A) A tank internal floating roof that is inspected and monitored in accordance with the requirements of Section 724.991; or

        B) A tank external floating roof that is inspected and monitored in accordance with the requirements of Section 724.991.

    2) If a tank is buried partially or entirely underground, an owner or operator is required to perform the cover inspection and

monitoring requirements specified in 35 Ill. Adm. Code 725.989(f)(1) through (f)(7) only for those portions of the tank cover and those connections to the tank cover or tank body (e.g., fill ports, access hatches, gauge wells, etc.) that extend to or above the ground surface and can be opened to the atmosphere.

3) An owner or operator is exempted from performing the cover inspection and monitoring requirements specified in 35 Ill. Adm. Code 725.989(f)(1) through (f)(7) for a container that meets all requirements specified in either Section 724.986(b)(1)(B) or (b)(1)(C).

4) An owner or operator is exempted from performing the cover inspection and monitoring requirements specified in 35 Ill. Adm. Code 725.989(f)(1) through (f)(7) for an enclosure used to control air emissions from containers in accordance with the requirements of Section 724.986(b)(2).

c) Each closed-vent system used in accordance with the requirements of Section 724.987 shall be inspected and monitored by the owner or operator in accordance with the procedure specified in Section 724.933(k).

d) Each control device used in accordance with the requirements of Section 724.987 shall be inspected and monitored by the owner or operator in accordance with the procedures specified in Section 724.933(f) and 724.933(j).

e) The owner or operator shall develop and implement a written plan and schedule to perform all inspection and monitoring requirements of this section. The owner or operator shall incorporate this plan and schedule into the facility inspection plan required under Section 724.115.

(Source: Added at 19 Ill. Reg. _____, effective _____)

Section 724.989 Recordkeeping Requirements

a) Each owner or operator of a facility subject to requirements in this Subpart shall record and maintain the following information as applicable:

    1) Documentation for each cover installed on a tank in accordance with the requirements of Section 724.984(b)(2) or 724.984(b)(3) that includes information prepared by the owner or operator or provided by the cover manufacturer or vendor describing the cover design, and certification by the owner or operator that the cover meets the applicable design specifications as listed in 35 Ill. Adm. Code 725.991(c).

    2) Documentation for each floating membrane cover installed on a surface impoundment in accordance with the requirements of Section 724.985(c) that includes information prepared by the owner or operator or provided by the cover manufacturer or vendor

POLLUTION CONTROL BOARD

NOTICE OF PROPOSED AMENDMENTS

describing the cover design, and certification by the owner or operator that the cover meets the specifications listed in 35 Ill. Adm. Code 725.986(e).

3) Documentation for each enclosure used to control air emissions from containers in accordance with the requirements of Section 724.986(b)(2)(A) that includes information prepared by the owner or operator or provided by the manufacturer or vendor describing the enclosure design, and certification by the owner or operator that the enclosure meets the specifications listed in Section 724.986(b)(2)(B).

4) Documentation for each closed-vent system and control device that is installed in accordance with the requirements of Section 724.987 that includes:

   A) Certification that is signed and dated by the owner or operator stating that the control device is designed to operate at the performance level documented by a design analysis as specified in subsection (a)(4)(B) below or by performance tests as specified in subsection (a)(4)(C) below when the tank, surface impoundment, or container is or would be operating at capacity or the highest level reasonably expected to occur.

   B) If a design analysis is used, then design documentation as specified in Section 724.935(b)(4). The documentation shall include information prepared by the owner or operator or provided by the control device manufacturer or vendor that describes the control device design in accordance with Section 724.935(b)(4)(C) and certification by the owner or operator that the control equipment meets the applicable specifications.

   C) If performance tests are used, then a performance test plan as specified in Section 724.935(b)(3) and all test results.

   D) Information as required by Section 724.935(c)(1) and (c)(2).

5) Records for all Method 27 tests performed by the owner or operator for each container used to meet the requirements of Section 724.986(b)(1)(C).

6) Records for all visual inspections conducted in accordance with the requirements of Section 724.988.

7) Records for all monitoring for detectable organic emissions conducted in accordance with the requirements of Section 724.988.

8) Records of the date of each attempt to repair a leak, repair methods applied, and the date of successful repair.

9) Records for all continuous monitoring conducted in accordance with the requirements of Section 724.988.

10) Records of the management of carbon removed from a carbon adsorption system conducted in accordance with Section 724.987(c)(3)(B).

11) Records for all inspections of each cover installed on a tank in accordance with the requirements of Section 724.984(b)(2) or

POLLUTION CONTROL BOARD

NOTICE OF PROPOSED AMENDMENTS

Section 724.984(b)(3) that includes information as listed in 35 Ill. Adm. Code 725.991(c).

b) An owner or operator electing to use air emission controls for a tank in accordance with the conditions specified in Section 724.984(c) shall record the following information:

   1) Date and time each waste sample is collected for direct measurement of maximum organic vapor pressure in accordance with Section 724.983(c).

   2) Results of each determination of the maximum organic vapor pressure of the waste in a tank performed in accordance with Section 724.983(c).

   3) Records specifying the tank dimensions and design capacity.

c) An owner or operator electing to use air emission controls for a tank in accordance with the requirements of Section 724.991 shall record the information required by Section 724.991(c).

d) An owner or operator electing not to use air emission controls for a particular tank, surface impoundment, or container subject to this Subpart in accordance with the conditions specified in Section 724.982(c) shall record the information used by the owner or operator for each waste determination (e.g., test results, measurements, calculations, and other documentation) in the facility operating log. If analysis results for waste samples are used for the waste determination, then the owner or operator shall record the date, time, and location that each waste sample is collected in accordance with applicable requirements of Section 724.983.

e) An owner or operator electing to comply with requirements in accordance with Section 724.982(c)(2)(E) or Section 724.983(c)(2)(F) shall record the identification number for the incinerator, boiler, or industrial furnace in which the hazardous waste is treated.

f) An owner or operator designating a cover as unsafe to inspect and monitor pursuant to 35 Ill. Adm. Code 725.989(f)(5) or difficult to inspect and monitor pursuant to 35 Ill. Adm. Code 725.989(f)(6) shall record in a log that is kept in the facility operating record the following information:

   1) A list of identification numbers for tanks with covers that are designated as unsafe to inspect and monitor in accordance with the requirements of 35 Ill. Adm. Code 725.989(f)(5), an explanation for each cover stating why the cover is unsafe to inspect and monitor, and the plan and schedule for inspecting and monitoring each cover.

   2) A list of identification numbers for tanks with covers that are designated as difficult to inspect and monitor in accordance with the requirements of 35 Ill. Adm. Code 725.989(f)(6), an explanation for each cover stating why the cover is difficult to inspect and monitor, and the plan and schedule for inspecting and monitoring each cover.

g) All records required by subsections (a) through (f) above, except as required in subsections (a)(1) through (a)(4), shall be maintained in

POLLUTION CONTROL BOARD

NOTICE OF PROPOSED AMENDMENTS

the operating record for a minimum of 3 years. All records required by subsections (a)(1) through (a)(4) above shall be maintained in the operating record until the air emission control equipment is replaced or otherwise no longer in service.

h) The owner or operator of a facility that is subject to this Subpart and to the control device standards in 40 CFR Part 60, Subpart VV or 40 CFR Part 61, Subpart V, incorporated by reference in 35 Ill. Adm. Code 720.111, may elect to demonstrate compliance with the applicable Sections of this Subpart by documentation either pursuant to this Subpart, or pursuant to the provisions of 40 CFR Part 60, Subpart VV or 40 CFR Part 61, Subpart V, to the extent that the documentation required by 40 CFR Part 60 or 61 duplicates the documentation required by this Section.

(Source: Added at 19 Ill. Reg. _____, effective _____)

Section 724.990 Reporting Requirements

a) Each owner or operator managing hazardous waste in a tank, surface impoundment, or container exempted from using air emission controls under the provisions of Section 724.982(c) shall report to the Agency each occurrence when hazardous waste is placed in the waste management unit in noncompliance with the conditions specified in Section 724.982(c)(1) or (c)(2), as applicable. Examples of such occurrences include placing in the waste management unit a hazardous waste having an average VO concentration equal to or greater than 100 ppmw at the point of waste origination or placing in the waste management unit a treated hazardous waste which fails to meet the applicable conditions specified in Section 724.982(c)(2)(A) through (c)(2)(E). The owner or operator shall submit a written report within 15 calendar days of the time that the owner or operator becomes aware of the occurrence. The written report shall contain the U.S. EPA identification number, the facility name and address, a description of the noncompliance event and the cause, the dates of the noncompliance and the actions taken to correct the noncompliance and prevent reoccurrence of the noncompliance. The report shall be signed and dated by an authorized representative of the owner or operator.

b) Each owner or operator using air emission controls on a tank in accordance with the requirements Section 724.984(c) shall report to the Agency each occurrence when hazardous waste is managed in the tank in noncompliance with the conditions specified in Section 724.984(c)(1) through (c)(4). The owner or operator shall submit a written report within 15 calendar days of the time that the owner or operator becomes aware of the occurrence. The written report shall contain the U.S. EPA identification number, the facility name and address, a description of the noncompliance event and the cause, the dates of the noncompliance, and the actions taken to correct the

POLLUTION CONTROL BOARD

NOTICE OF PROPOSED AMENDMENTS

noncompliance and prevent reoccurrence of the noncompliance. The report shall be signed and dated by an authorized representative of the owner or operator.

c) Each owner or operator using a control device in accordance with the requirements of Section 724.987 shall submit a semiannual written report to the Agency excepted as provided for in subsection (d) below. The report shall describe each occurrence during the previous 6-month period when a control device is operated continuously for 24 hours or longer in noncompliance with the applicable operating values defined in Section 724.935(c)(4) or when a flare is operated with visible emissions as defined in Section 724.933(d). The written report shall include the U. S. EPA identification number, the facility name and address, and an explanation why the control device could not be returned to compliance within 24 hours, and actions taken to correct the noncompliance. The report shall be signed and dated by an authorized representative of the owner or operator.

d) A report to the Agency in accordance with the requirements of subsection (c) above is not required for a 6-month period during which all control devices subject to this Subpart are operated by the owner or operator so that during no period of 24 hours or longer did a control device operate continuously in noncompliance with the applicable operating values defined in Section 724.935(c)(4) or a flare operate with visible emissions, as defined in Section 724.933(d).

(Source: Added at 19 Ill. Reg. _____, effective _____)

Section 724.991 Alternative Control Requirements for Tanks

a) This Section applies to owners and operators of tanks that elect to comply with Section 724.984(b)(2) or Section 724.984(b)(3).

1) The owner or operator that elects to comply with Section 724.984(b)(2) shall design, install, operate, and maintain a fixed roof and internal floating roof that meet the requirements specified in 35 Ill. Adm. Code 725.991(a)(1)(A) through (a)(1)(I).

2) The owner or operator that elects to comply with Section 724.984(b)(3) shall design, install, operate, and maintain an external floating roof that meets the requirements specified in 35 Ill. Adm. Code 725.991(a)(2)(A) through (a)(2)(C).

b) The owner or operator shall inspect and monitor the control equipment in accordance with the following requirements:

1) For a tank equipped with a fixed roof and internal floating roof in accordance with the requirements of subsection (a)(1) above, the owner or operator shall perform the inspection and monitoring requirements specified in 35 Ill. Adm. Code 725.991(b)(1).

2) For a tank equipped with an external floating roof in accordance

POLLUTION CONTROL BOARD

NOTICE OF PROPOSED AMENDMENTS

with the requirements of subsection (a)(2) above, the owner or operator shall perform the inspection and monitoring requirements specified in 35 Ill. Adm. Code 725.991(b)(2).

c) The owner or operator shall record the following information in the operating record in accordance with the requirements of Section 724.989(a)(1) and (a)(11):

1) For a tank equipped with a fixed roof and internal floating roof in accordance with the requirements of subsection (a)(1) above, the owner or operator shall record the information listed in 35 Ill. Adm. Code 725.991(c)(1).

2) For a tank equipped with an external floating roof in accordance with the requirements of subsection (a)(1) above, the owner or operator shall record the information listed in 35 Ill. Adm. Code 725.991(c)(2).

(Source: Added at 19 Ill. Reg. _____, effective _____)

SUBPART DD: CONTAINMENT BUILDINGS

Section 724.1102 Closure and post-closure care

a) At closure of a containment building, the owner or operator must remove or decontaminate all waste residues, contaminated containment system components (liners, etc.), contaminated subsoils, and structures and equipment contaminated with waste and leachate, and manage them as hazardous waste unless 35 Ill. Adm. Code 721.103(e) ~~721.103(e)~~ applies. The closure plan, closure activities, cost estimates for closure, and financial responsibility for containment buildings must meet all of the requirements specified in 739.Subparts G and H.

b) If, after removing or decontaminating all residues and making all reasonable efforts to effect removal or decontamination of contaminated components, subsoils, structures, and equipment as required in subsection (a) above, the owner or operator finds that not all contaminated subsoils can be practicably removed or decontaminated, he must close the facility and perform post-closure care in accordance with the closure and post-closure requirements that apply to landfills (35 Ill. Adm. Code 724.310). In addition, for the purposes of closure, post-closure, and financial responsibility, such a containment building is then considered to be a landfill, and the owner or operator must meet all the requirements for landfills specified in 739.Subparts G and H.

(Source: Amended at 19 Ill. Reg. _____, effective _____)

POLLUTION CONTROL BOARD

NOTICE OF PROPOSED AMENDMENTS

1) Heading of the Part: Standards for the Management of Specific Hazardous Waste and Specific Types of Hazardous Waste Management Facilities

2) Code citation: 35 Ill. Adm. Code 726

3) Section numbers:

	Proposed action:
726.120	Amended
726.123	Amended
726.200	Amended
726.App. A, 726.App. B, 726.App. C	Amended
726.App. E	Amended
726.App. M	New Section

4) Statutory authority: 415 ILCS 5/22.4 and 27.

5) A complete description of the subjects and issues involved:

A more detailed description is contained in the Board's proposed opinion of March 2, 1995, in R95-4 and R95-6 (consolidated), which opinion is available from the address below. Section 22.4(a) of the Environmental Protection Act [415 ILCS 5/22.4(a)] provides that Section 5-35 the Administrative Procedure Act [5 ILCS 100/5-35] shall not apply. Because this rulemaking is not subject to Section 5-35 the APA, it is not subject to first notice or to second notice review by JCAR.

This rulemaking updates Parts 700, 702, 703, 705, 720, 721, 722, 723, 724, 725, 726, 728, 730, 738, and 739 of the Illinois RCRA Subtitle C hazardous waste and underground injection control (UIC) rules to correspond with amendments adopted by U.S. EPA that appeared in the Federal Register during the period July 1 through December 31, 1994. During this period, U.S. EPA amended its regulations as follows:

Federal Action	Summary
59 Fed. Reg. 38536, July 28, 1994	Exclusion from definition of solid waste for certain in-process recycled secondary materials used by the petroleum refining industry
59 Fed. Reg. 43496, August 24, 1994	Withdrawal of exemption from Subtitle C regulation of slag residues from high temperature metal recovery (HTMR) of electric arc furnace dust (K061), steel finishing pickle liquor (K062), and electroplating sludges (F006) that are used in a manner constituting disposal

POLLUTION CONTROL BOARD

NOTICE OF PROPOSED AMENDMENTS

59 Fed. Reg. 47980, September 19, 1994	Restoration of text from 40 CFR 268.7(a) inadvertently omitted in the amendments of August 31, 1993, at 58 Fed. Reg. 46040
59 Fed. Reg. 47982, September 19, 1994	Phase II land disposal restrictions (LDRs); universal treatment standards for organic toxicity wastes and newly-listed wastes (including underground injection control (UIC) amendments)
59 Fed. Reg. 62896, December 6, 1994	Organic material air emission standards for tanks, surface impoundments, and containers

In addition to these principal amendments that occurred during the update period, the Board has included an additional, later action:

60 Fed. Reg. 242, January 3, 1995	Corrections to the Phase II land disposal restrictions (universal treatment standards)

This January 3 action was an amendment of the September 19, 1994 Phase II LDRs (universal waste rule). U.S. EPA corrected errors and clarified language in the universal treatment standards. The Board did not delay in adding these amendments for three reasons:

1) The January 3, 1995 amendments are corrections and clarifications of the September 19, 1994 regulations, and not new substantive amendments;

2) Prompt action on the January 3, 1995 amendments will facilitate implementation of the Phase II LDRs; and

3) The Board has received a request from the regulated community that we add the January 3, 1995 amendments to those of September 19, 1994. (See "Expedited Consideration" below.)

The Board also notes that the later amendments occurred within six months of the earliest amendments included in this docket, even if they occurred outside the nominal time-frame of the docket.

In addition to the federally-derived amendments, the Board used this opportunity to undertake a number of housekeeping and corrective amendments. We have effected the removal of all cross-references for effective dates and repealed Part 700. We have converted equations and formulae to the standard scientific format. We have tried to improve the language and structure of various provisions, including correcting grammar, punctuation, and spelling where necessary.

Specifically, the segment of the amendments involved in Part 726 results

POLLUTION CONTROL BOARD

NOTICE OF PROPOSED AMENDMENTS

from three of the federal actions involved in this docket. As a result of the July 28 exclusion of certain in-process recycled secondary materials used by the petroleum refining industry, certain cross-references were changed in Section 726.200(b)(3). As a result of the August 24, 1994 withdrawal of the exemption for certain HTMR slags, limiting language was added at Section 726.120(c). As a part of the September 19, 1994 Phase II LDR rules, U.S. EPA added a limited exemption for mercury recovery furnaces, which resulted in amendment to Section 726.200(c) and the addition of Section 726.Appendix M. Amendments to Sections 726.Appendix A through 726.Appendix C and 726.Appendix E are not based on federal actions; they are limited to converting the numbers set forth to standard decimal format.

6) Will this proposed rule replace an emergency rule currently in effect? No.

7) Does this rulemaking contain an automatic repeal date? No.

8) Do these proposed amendments contain incorporations by reference?

Yes. 35 Ill. Adm. Code 720.111 is the central listing of all documents incorporated by reference throughout the text of 35 Ill. Adm. Code 702 through 705, 721 through 726, 728, 730, 738, and 739. The present amendments are limited to reformatting the references to ASTM methods in Section 726.200(g) to include the year code, which is actually presented by ASTM as part of the method number.

9) Are there any other amendments pending on this Part? No.

10) Statement of statewide policy objectives:

This rulemaking is mandated by Section 22.4(a) of the Environmental Protection Act [415 ILCS 5/22.4(a)]. The statewide policy objectives are set forth in Section 20 of that Act. This rulemaking imposes mandates on units of local government only to the extent that they may be involved in the generation, transportation, treatment, storage, or disposal of hazardous waste or they engage in underground injection of waste.

11) Time, place and manner in which interested persons may comment on this proposed rulemaking:

The Board will accept written public comment on this proposal for a period of 45 days after the date of this publication. Comments should reference Docket R95-4/R95-6 and be addressed to:

Ms. Dorothy M. Gunn, Clerk
Illinois Pollution Control Board
State of Illinois Center, Suite 11-500

POLLUTION CONTROL BOARD

NOTICE OF PROPOSED AMENDMENTS

100 W. Randolph St.
Chicago, IL 60601
312/814-6931

Address all questions to Michael J. McCambridge, at 312-814-6924.

12) **Initial regulatory flexibility analysis:**

A) **Date rule was submitted to the Small Business Office of the Department of Commerce and Community Affairs:** March 6, 1995.

B) **Types of small businesses affected:**

The existing rules and proposed amendments affect small businesses that generate, transport, treat, store, or dispose of hazardous waste or engage in underground injection of waste.

C) **Reporting, bookkeeping or other procedures required for compliance:**

The existing rules and proposed amendments require extensive reporting, bookkeeping, and other procedures, including the preparation of manifests and annual reports, waste analyses, and maintenance of operating records.

D) **Types of professional skills necessary for compliance:**

Compliance with the existing rules and proposed amendments may require the services of an attorney, certified public accountant, chemist, and registered professional engineer.

The full text of the proposed amendments begins on the next page:

POLLUTION CONTROL BOARD

NOTICE OF PROPOSED AMENDMENTS

TITLE 35: ENVIRONMENTAL PROTECTION
SUBTITLE G: WASTE DISPOSAL
CHAPTER I: POLLUTION CONTROL BOARD
SUBCHAPTER c: HAZARDOUS WASTE OPERATING REQUIREMENTS

PART 726
STANDARDS FOR THE MANAGEMENT OF
SPECIFIC HAZARDOUS WASTE AND SPECIFIC TYPES
OF HAZARDOUS WASTE MANAGEMENT FACILITIES

SUBPART C: RECYCLABLE MATERIALS USED IN A
MANNER CONSTITUTING DISPOSAL

Section	
726.120	Applicability
726.121	Standards applicable to generators and transporters of materials used in a manner that constitutes disposal
726.122	Standards applicable to storers, who are not the ultimate users, of materials that are to be used in a manner that constitutes disposal
726.123	Standards applicable Applicable to users Users of materials Materials that are used Used in a manner Manner that constitutes—disposal Constitutes Disposal

SUBPART D: HAZARDOUS WASTE BURNED FOR ENERGY RECOVERY

Section	
726.130	Applicability (Repealed)
726.131	Prohibitions (Repealed)
726.132	Standards applicable to generators of hazardous waste fuel (Repealed)
726.133	Standards applicable to transporters of hazardous waste fuel (Repealed)
726.134	Standards applicable to marketers of hazardous waste fuel (Repealed)
726.135	Standards applicable to burners of hazardous waste fuel (Repealed)
726.136	Conditional exemption for spent materials and by-products exhibiting a characteristic of hazardous waste (Repealed)

SUBPART E: USED OIL BURNED FOR ENERGY RECOVERY (Repealed)

Section	
726.140	Applicability (Repealed)
726.141	Prohibitions (Repealed)
726.142	Standards applicable to generators of used oil burned for energy recovery (Repealed)
726.143	Standards applicable to marketers of used oil burned for energy recovery (Repealed)
726.144	Standards applicable to burners of used oil burned for energy recovery (Repealed)

POLLUTION CONTROL BOARD

NOTICE OF PROPOSED AMENDMENTS

SUBPART F: RECYCLABLE MATERIALS UTILIZED FOR
PRECIOUS METAL RECOVERY

Section
726.170   Applicability and requirements

SUBPART G: SPENT LEAD-ACID BATTERIES
BEING RECLAIMED

Section
726.180   Applicability and requirements

SUBPART H: HAZARDOUS WASTE BURNED IN BOILERS
AND INDUSTRIAL FURNACES

Section
726.200   Applicability
726.201   Management prior to Burning
726.202   Permit standards for Burners
726.203   Interim status standards for Burners
726.204   Standards to control Organic Emissions
726.205   Standards to control PM
726.206   Standards to control Metals Emissions
726.207   Standards to control HCl and Chlorine Gas Emissions
726.208   Small quantity On-site Burner Exemption
726.209   Low risk waste Exemption
726.210   Waiver of DRE trial burn for Boilers
726.211   Standards for direct Transfer
726.212   Regulation of Residues
726.219   Extensions of Time

APPENDIX A   Tier I and Tier II Feed Rate and Emissions Screening Limits for Metals
APPENDIX B   Tier I Feed Rate Screening Limits for Total Chlorine
APPENDIX C   Tier II Emission Rate Screening Limits for Free Chlorine and Hydrogen Chloride
APPENDIX D   Reference Air Concentrations
APPENDIX E   Risk Specific Doses
APPENDIX F   Stack Plume Rise
APPENDIX G   Health-Based Limits for Exclusion of Waste-Derived Residues
APPENDIX H   Potential PICs for Determination of Exclusion of Waste-Derived Residues
APPENDIX I   Methods Manual for Compliance with BIF Regulations
APPENDIX J   Guideline on Air Quality Models
APPENDIX K   Lead-Bearing Materials That May be Processed in Exempt Lead Smelters
APPENDIX L   Nickel or Chromium-Bearing Materials that may be Processed in Exempt Nickel-Chromium Recovery Furnaces

POLLUTION CONTROL BOARD

NOTICE OF PROPOSED AMENDMENTS

APPENDIX M   Mercury-Bearing Wastes That May Be Processed in Exempt Mercury Recovery Units
TABLE A   Exempt Quantities for Small Quantity Burner Exemption

AUTHORITY: Implementing Section 22.4 and authorized by Section 27 of the Environmental Protection Act [415 ILCS 5/22.4 and 27].

SOURCE: Adopted in R85-22 at 10 Ill. Reg. 1162, effective January 2, 1986; amended in R86-1 at 10 Ill. Reg. 14156, effective August 12, 1986; amended in R87-26 at 12 Ill. Reg. 2900, effective January 15, 1988; amended in R89-1 at 13 Ill. Reg. 18606, effective November 13, 1989; amended in R90-2 at 14 Ill. Reg. 14533, effective August 22, 1990; amended in R90-11 at 15 Ill. Reg. 9727, effective June 17, 1991; amended in R91-13 at 16 Ill. Reg. 9858, effective June 9, 1992; amended in R92-10 at 17 Ill. Reg. 5865, effective March 26, 1993; amended in R93-4 at 17 Ill. Reg. 20904, effective November 22, 1993; amended in R94-7 at 18 Ill. Reg. 12500, effective July 29, 1994; amended in R95-6 at 19 Ill. Reg. _____, effective _____.

SUBPART C: RECYCLABLE MATERIALS USED IN A
MANNER CONSTITUTING DISPOSAL

Section 726.120   Applicability

a)   The regulations of this Subpart apply to recyclable materials that are applied to or placed on the land:
   1)   Without mixing with any other substance(s); or
   2)   After mixing or combination with any other substance(s). These materials will be referred to throughout this Subpart as "materials used in a manner that constitutes disposal."
b)   Products produced for the general public's use that are used in a manner that constitutes disposal and that contain recyclable materials are not presently subject to regulation under this Subpart if the recyclable materials have undergone a chemical reaction in the course of producing the products so as to become inseparable by physical means and if such products meet the applicable treatment standards in 35 Ill. Adm. Code 728.Subpart D (or applicable prohibition levels in 35 Ill. Adm. Code 728.132 or 728.139, where no treatment standards have been established) for each recyclable material (i.e. hazardous waste) that they contain. Commercial fertilizers that are produced for the general public's use that contain recyclable materials also are not presently subject to regulation, provided they meet the same treatment standards or prohibitions levels for each recyclable material they contain. However, zinc-containing fertilizers using hazardous waste K061 that are produced for the general public's use are not presently subject to regulation under this Subpart.
c)   Anti-skid and deicing uses in a manner constituting disposal of slags that are generated from high temperature metals recovery (HTMR) processing of hazardous wastes K061, K062, and F006 are not covered by

POLLUTION CONTROL BOARD

NOTICE OF PROPOSED AMENDMENTS

the exemption in subsection (b) above, and such uses of these materials remain subject to regulation.

(Source: Amended at 19 Ill. Reg. _____, effective _____)

Section 726.123 Standards applicable Applicable to users Users of materials Materials that are used Used in a manner Manner that constitutes Constitutes disposal Disposal

a) Owners or operators of facilities that use recyclable materials in a manner that constitutes disposal are regulated under all applicable provisions of 35 Ill. Adm. Code 702, 703, and 705, 35 Ill. Adm. Code 724, Subparts A through N, and 35 Ill. Adm. Code 725, Subparts A through N, 35 Ill. Adm. Code 728, and 35 Ill. Adm. Code 702, 703 and 705, and the notification requirement under Section 3010 of the Resource Conservation and Recovery Act. (These requirements do not apply to products which that contain these recyclable materials under the provisions of Section 726.120(b)).

b) The use of waste or used oil or other material--which that is contaminated with dioxin or any other hazardous waste (other than a waste identified solely on the basis of ignitability) for dust suppression or road treatment is prohibited.

(Source: Amended at 19 Ill. Reg. _____, effective _____)

SUBPART H: HAZARDOUS WASTE BURNED IN BOILERS AND INDUSTRIAL FURNACES

Section 726.200 Applicability

a) The regulations of this Subpart apply to hazardous waste burned or processed in a boiler or industrial furnace (BIF) (as defined in 35 Ill. Adm. Code 720.110) irrespective of the purpose of burning or processing, except as provided by subsections (b), (c), (d), and (f), below. In this Subpart, the term "burn" means burning for energy recovery or destruction or processing for materials recovery or as an ingredient. The emissions standards of Sections 726.204, 726.205, 726.206, and 726.207 apply to facilities operating under interim status or under a RCRA permit, as specified in Sections 726.202 and 726.203.

b) The following hazardous wastes and facilities are not subject to regulation under this Subpart:

1) Used oil burned for energy recovery that is also a hazardous waste solely because it exhibits a characteristic of hazardous waste identified in 35 Ill. Adm. Code 721, Subpart C. Such used oil is subject to regulation under 35 Ill. Adm. Code 739, rather

POLLUTION CONTROL BOARD

NOTICE OF PROPOSED AMENDMENTS

than this Subpart;

2) Gas recovered from hazardous or solid waste landfills, when such gas is burned for energy recovery;

3) Hazardous wastes that are exempt from regulation under 35 Ill. Adm. Code 721.104 and 721.106(a)(3)(BD) through (a)(3)(F)(H), and hazardous wastes that are subject to the special requirements for conditionally exempt small quantity generators under 35 Ill. Adm. Code 721.105; and

4) Coke ovens, if the only hazardous waste burned is U.S. EPA USEPA Hazardous Waste No. hazardous waste no. K087, decanter tank tar sludge from coking operations.

c) Owners and operators of smelting, melting, and refining furnaces (including pyrometallurgical devices such as cupolas, sintering machines, roasters and foundry furnaces, but not including cement kilns, aggregate kilns, or halogen acid furnaces burning hazardous waste) that process hazardous waste solely for metal recovery are conditionally exempt from regulation under this Subpart, except for Sections 726.201 and 726.212.

1) To be exempt from Sections 726.202 through 726.211, an owner or operator of a metal recovery furnace or mercury recovery furnace shall comply with the following requirements, except that an owner or operator of a lead or a nickel-chromium recovery furnace, or a metal recovery furnace that burns baghouse bags used to capture metallic dust emitted by steel manufacturing, shall comply with the requirements of subsection (c)(3), below:

A) Provide a one-time written notice to the Agency indicating the following:

1) The owner or operator claims exemption under this subsection;

11) The hazardous waste is burned solely for metal recovery consistent with the provisions of subsection (c)(2), below;

111) The hazardous waste contains recoverable levels of metals; and

1v) The owner or operator will comply with the sampling and analysis and recordkeeping requirements of this subsection;

B) Sample and analyze the hazardous waste and other feedstocks as necessary to comply with the requirements of this subsection under procedures specified by Test Methods for Evaluating Solid Waste, Physical/Chemical Methods, SW-846, incorporated by reference in 35 Ill. Adm. Code 720.111, or alternative methods that meet or exceed the SW-846 method performance capabilities. If SW-846 does not prescribe a method for a particular determination, the owner or operator shall use the best available method; and

C) Maintain at the facility for at least three years records to document compliance with the provisions of this subsection

POLLUTION CONTROL BOARD

NOTICE OF PROPOSED AMENDMENTS

including limits on levels of toxic organic constituents and
Btu value of the waste, and levels of recoverable metals in
the hazardous waste compared to normal non-hazardous waste
feedstocks.

2) A hazardous waste meeting either of the following criteria is not
processed solely for metal recovery:

A) The hazardous waste has a total concentration of organic
compounds listed in 35 Ill. Adm. Code 721.Appendix H,
exceeding 500 ppm by weight, as fired, and so is considered
to be burned for destruction. The concentration of organic
compounds in a waste as-generated may be reduced to the 500
ppm limit by bona fide treatment that removes or destroys
organic constituents. Blending for dilution to meet the 500
ppm limit is prohibited, and documentation that the waste
has not been impermissibly diluted must be retained in the
records required by subsection (c)(1)(C), above; or

B) The hazardous waste has a heating value of 5,000 Btu/lb or
more, as-fired, and is so considered to be burned as fuel.
The heating value of a waste as-generated may be reduced to
below the 5,000 Btu/lb limit by bona fide treatment that
removes or destroys organic constituents. Blending for
dilution to meet the 5,000 Btu/lb limit is prohibited and
documentation that the waste has not been impermissibly
diluted must be retained in the records required by
subsection (c)(1)(C), above.

3) To be exempt from Sections 726.202 through 726.211, and owner or
operator of a lead, or nickel-chromium, or mercury recovery
furnace or a metal recovery furnace that burns a baghouse bags
used to capture metallic dusts emitted by steel manufacturing
must provide a one-time written notice to the Agency identifying
each hazardous waste burned and specifying whether the owner or
operator claims an exemption for each waste under this subsection
or subsection (c)(1), above. The owner or operator shall comply
with the requirements of subsection (c)(1), above, for those
wastes claimed to be exempt under that subsection and shall
comply with the following requirements below for those wastes
claimed to be exempt under this subsection:

A) The hazardous wastes listed in Sections 726.Appendices K,
and L, and M and baghouse bags used to capture metallic
dusts emitted by steel manufacturing are exempt from the
requirements of subsection (c)(1), above, provided that:

i) A waste listed in Appendix K must contain recoverable
levels of lead; A a waste listed in Appendix L must
contain recoverable levels of nickel or chromium; a
waste listed in Section 726.Appendix M must contain
recoverable levels of mercury and contain less that
500 ppm of 35 Ill. Adm. Code 261.Appendix H organic
constituents, and baghouse bags used to capture

POLLUTION CONTROL BOARD

NOTICE OF PROPOSED AMENDMENTS

metallic dusts emitted by steel manufacturing must
contain recoverable levels of metal; and

ii) The waste does not exhibit the Toxicity Characteristic
of 35 Ill. Adm. Code 721.124 for an organic
constituent; and

iii) The waste is not a hazardous waste listed in 35 Ill.
Adm. Code 721.Subpart D because it is listed for an
organic constituent, as identified in 35 Ill. Adm.
Code 721.Appendix G; and

iv) The owner or operator certifies in the one-time notice
that hazardous waste is burned under the provisions of
subsection (c)(1), above, and that sampling and
analysis will be conducted or other information will
be obtained as necessary to ensure continued
compliance with these requirements. Sampling and
analysis must be conducted according to subsection
(C)(1)(B), above, and records to document compliance
with Subsection (c)(3), above, must be kept for at
least three years.

B) The Agency may decide, on a case-by-case basis, that the
toxic organic constituents in a material listed in Appendix
K, or Section 726.Appendix L, or 726.Appendix M that
contains a total concentration of more than 500 ppm toxic
organic compounds listed in 35 Ill. Adm. Code 721.Appendix H
may pose a hazard to human health and the environment when
burned in a metal recovery furnace exempt from the
requirements of this Subpart. In that situation Under these
circumstances, after adequate notice and opportunity for
comment, the metal recovery furnace will become subject to
the requirements of this Subpart when burning that material.
In making the hazard determination, the Agency shall
consider the following factors:

i) The concentration and toxicity of organic constituents
in the material; and

ii) The level of destruction of toxic organic constituents
provided by the furnace; and

iii) Whether the acceptable ambient levels established in
Appendices D or E will be exceeded for any toxic
organic compound that may be emitted based on
dispersion modeling to predict the maximum annual
average off-site ground level concentration.

d) The standards for direct transfer operations under Section 726.211
apply only to facilities subject to the permit standards of Section
726.202 or the interim status standards of Section 726.203.

e) The management standards for residues under Section 726.212 apply to
any BIF burning hazardous waste.

f) Owners and operators of smelting, melting, and refining furnaces
(including pyrometallurgical devices such as cupolas, sintering

POLLUTION CONTROL BOARD

NOTICE OF PROPOSED AMENDMENTS

machines, roasters, and foundry furnaces) that process hazardous waste for recovery of economically significant amounts of the precious metals gold, silver, platinum, palladium, iridium, osmium, rhodium, or ruthenium, or any combination of these metals, are conditionally exempt from regulation under this Subpart, except for Section 726.212. To be exempt from Sections 726.202 through 726.211, an owner or operator shall:

1) Provide a one-time written notice to the Agency indicating the following:

A) The owner or operator claims exemption under this Section;
B) The hazardous waste is burned for legitimate recovery of precious metal; and
C) The owner or operator will comply with the sampling and analysis and recordkeeping requirements of this Section;

2) Sample and analyze the hazardous waste, as necessary, to document that the waste is burned for recovery of economically significant amounts of precious metal, using procedures specified by Test Methods for Evaluating Solid Waste, Physical/Chemical Methods, SW-846, incorporated by reference in 35 Ill. Adm. Code 720.111, or alternative methods that meet or exceed the SW-846 method performance capabilities. If SW-846 does not prescribe a method for a particular determination, the owner or operator shall use the best available method; and

3) Maintain, at the facility for at least three years, records to document that all hazardous wastes burned are burned for recovery of economically significant amounts of precious metal.

g) Abbreviations and definitions. The following definitions and abbreviations are used in this Subpart:

"APCS" means air pollution control system.

"BIF" means boiler or industrial furnace.

"Carcinogenic metals" means arsenic, beryllium, cadmium, and chromium.

"CO" means carbon monoxide.

"Continuous monitor" is a monitor which that continuously samples the regulated parameter without interruption, and that evaluates the detector response at least once each 15 seconds, and that computes and records the average value at least every 60 seconds.

"DRE" means destruction or removal efficiency.

"cu m" or "m(3)" means cubic meters.

"E" means "ten to the power". For example, "XE-Y" means "X times

POLLUTION CONTROL BOARD

NOTICE OF PROPOSED AMENDMENTS

ten to the -Y power".

"Feed rates" are measured as specified in Section 726.202(e)(6).

"Good engineering practice stack height" is as defined by 40 CFR 51.100(ii), incorporated by reference in 35 Ill. Adm. Code 720.111.

"HC" means hydrocarbon.

" HCl" means hydrogen chloride gas.

"Hourly rolling average" means the arithmetic mean of the 60 most recent kone-minute average values recorded by the continuous monitoring system.

"K" means Kelvin.

"kVA" means kilovolt amperes.

"MEI" means maximum exposed individual.

"MEI location" means the point with the maximum annual average off-site (unless on-site is required) ground level concentration.

"Noncarcinogenic metals" means antimony, barium, lead, mercury, thallium, and silver.

"One hour block average" means the arithmetic mean of the one minute averages recorded during the 60-minute period beginning at one minute after the beginning of preceding clock hour

"PIC" means product of incomplete combustion.

"PM" means particulate matter.

"POHC" means principal organic hazardous constituent.

"ppmv" means parts per million by volume.

"QA/QC" means quality assurance and quality control.

"Rolling average for the selected averaging period" means the arithmetic mean of one hour block averages for the averaging period.

"RAC" means reference air concentration: the acceptable ambient level for the noncarcinogenic metals for purposes of this

POLLUTION CONTROL BOARD

NOTICE OF PROPOSED AMENDMENTS

Subpart. RACs are specified in Appendix D.

"RSD" means risk-specific dose, the acceptable ambient level for the carcinogenic metals for purposes of this Subpart. RSDs are specified in Appendix E.

"SSU" means "Saybolt Seconds Universal", a unit of viscosity measured by ASTM D 88-87 or D 2161-87, incorporated by reference in 35 Ill. Adm. Code 720.111.

"TCLP test" means the toxicity characteristic leaching procedure of 35 Ill. Adm. Code 721.124.

"TESH" means terrain-adjusted effective stack height (in meters).

"Tier I". See Section 726.206(b).

"Tier II". See Section 726.206(c).

"Tier III". See Section 726.206(d).

"Toxicity equivalence" is estimated, pursuant to Section 726.204(e), using "Procedures for Estimating the Toxicity Equivalence of Chlorinated Dibenzo-p-Dioxin and Dibenzofuran Congeners" in Appendix I ("eye").

"ug" means microgram.

(Source: Amended at 19 Ill. Reg. _____, effective _____)

POLLUTION CONTROL BOARD

NOTICE OF PROPOSED AMENDMENTS

Section 726.APPENDIX A Tier I and Tier II Feed Rate and Emissions Screening Limits for Metals

I-A
Tier I and Tier II Feed Rate and Emissions Screening Limits for Noncarcinogenic Metals for Facilities in Noncomplex Terrain
(Values for urban areas)

TESH (m)	Antimony (g/hr)	Barium (g/hr)	Lead (g/hr)	Mercury (g/hr)	Silver (g/hr)	Thallium (g/hr)
4	6.0E+01	1.0E+04	2.0E+01	6.0E+01	6.0E+02	6.0E+01
6	6.0E+01	1.1E+04	2.0E+01	6.0E+01	6.0E+02	6.0E+01
8	7.6E+01	1.3E+04	2.3E+01	7.6E+01	7.6E+02	7.6E+01
10	8.6E+01	1.4E+04	2.6E+01	8.6E+01	8.6E+02	8.6E+01
12	9.6E+01	1.7E+04	3.0E+01	9.6E+01	9.6E+02	9.6E+01
14	1.1E+02	1.8E+04	3.4E+01	1.1E+02	1.1E+03	1.1E+02
16	1.2E+02	2.1E+04	3.6E+01	1.2E+02	1.3E+03	1.3E+02
18	1.4E+02	2.4E+04	4.3E+01	1.4E+02	1.4E+03	1.4E+02
20	1.6E+02	2.7E+04	4.6E+01	1.6E+02	1.6E+03	1.6E+02
22	1.8E+02	3.0E+04	5.4E+01	1.8E+02	1.8E+03	1.8E+02
24	2.0E+02	3.4E+04	6.0E+01	2.0E+02	2.0E+03	2.0E+02
26	2.3E+02	3.9E+04	6.8E+01	2.3E+02	2.3E+03	2.3E+02
28	2.6E+02	4.3E+04	7.8E+01	2.6E+02	2.6E+03	2.6E+02
30	3.0E+02	5.0E+04	9.0E+01	3.0E+02	3.0E+03	3.0E+02
35	4.0E+02	6.6E+04	1.1E+02	4.0E+02	4.0E+03	4.0E+02
40	4.6E+02	7.8E+04	1.4E+02	4.6E+02	4.6E+03	4.6E+02
45	6.0E+02	1.0E+05	1.8E+02	6.0E+02	6.0E+03	6.0E+02
50	7.0E+02	1.3E+05	2.3E+02	7.0E+02	7.0E+03	7.0E+02
55	9.6E+02	1.7E+05	3.0E+02	9.6E+02	9.6E+03	9.6E+02
60	1.2E+03	2.0E+05	3.6E+02	1.2E+03	1.2E+04	1.2E+03
65	1.5E+03	2.5E+05	4.3E+02	1.5E+03	1.5E+04	1.5E+03
70	1.7E+03	2.8E+05	4.7E+02	1.7E+03	1.7E+04	1.7E+03
75	1.9E+03	3.2E+05	5.5E+02	1.9E+03	1.9E+04	1.9E+03
80	2.2E+03	3.6E+05	6.4E+02	2.2E+03	2.2E+04	2.2E+03
85	2.5E+03	4.0E+05	7.6E+02	2.5E+03	2.5E+04	2.5E+03
90	2.0E+03	4.6E+05	9.0E+02	1.2E+03	2.0E+04	2.0E+03
95	3.2E+03	5.4E+05	9.6E+02	3.2E+03	3.2E+04	3.2E+03
100	3.6E+03	6.0E+05	1.1E+03	3.6E+03	3.6E+04	3.6E+03
105	4.0E+03	6.8E+05	1.1E+03	4.0E+03	4.0E+04	4.0E+03
110	4.6E+03	7.8E+05	1.4E+03	4.6E+03	4.6E+04	4.6E+03
115	5.4E+03	8.6E+05	1.5E+03	5.4E+03	5.4E+04	5.4E+03
120	6.0E+03	1.0E+06	1.8E+03	6.0E+03	6.0E+04	6.0E+03

TESH (m)	Antimony (g/hr)	Barium (g/hr)	Lead (g/hr)	Mercury (g/hr)	Silver (g/hr)	Thallium (g/hr)
4	60.	10000.	18.	60.	600.	60.

POLLUTION CONTROL BOARD

NOTICE OF PROPOSED AMENDMENTS

6	68.	11000.	20.	68.	680.	68.
8	76.	13000.	23.	76.	760.	76.
10	86.	14000.	26.	86.	860.	86.
12	96.	17000.	30.	96.	960.	96.
14	110.	18000.	34.	110.	1100.	110.
16	130.	21000.	36.	130.	1300.	130.
18	140.	24000.	41.	140.	1400.	140.
20	160.	27000.	46.	160.	1600.	160.
22	180.	30000.	54.	180.	1800.	180.
24	200.	34000.	60.	200.	2000.	200.
26	230.	39000.	68.	230.	2300.	230.
28	260.	43000.	78.	260.	2600.	260.
30	300.	50000.	90.	300.	3000.	300.
35	400.	66000.	110.	400.	4000.	400.
40	460.	78000.	140.	460.	4600.	460.
45	600.	100000.	180.	600.	6000.	600.
50	780.	130000.	230.	780.	7800.	780.
55	960.	170000.	300.	960.	9600.	960.
60	1200.	200000.	360.	1200.	12000.	1200.
65	1500.	250000.	430.	1500.	15200.	1500.
70	1700.	280000.	500.	1700.	17000.	1700.
75	1900.	320000.	580.	1900.	19000.	1900.
80	2200.	360000.	640.	2200.	22000.	2200.
85	2500.	400000.	742.	2500.	25000.	2500.
90	2800.	460000.	820.	2800.	28000.	2800.
95	3200.	540000.	960.	3200.	32000.	3200.
100	3600.	600000.	1100.	3600.	36000.	3600.
105	4000.	680000.	1200.	4000.	40000.	4000.
110	4600.	780000.	1400.	4600.	46000.	4600.
115	5400.	860000.	1600.	5400.	54000.	5400.
120	6000.	1000000.	1800.	6000.	60000.	6000.

I-B

Tier I and Tier II Feed Rate and Emissions Screening Limits for
Noncarcinogenic Metals for Facilities in Noncomplex Terrain
[Values for rural areas]

TRSH (m)	Antimony (g/hr)	Barium (g/hr)	Lead (g/hr)	Mercury (g/hr)	Silver (g/hr)	Thallium (g/hr)
~~4~~	~~3.1E+01~~	~~5.2E+03~~	~~9.4E+00~~	~~3.1E+01~~	~~3.1E+01~~	~~3.1E+01~~
~~6~~	~~3.6E+01~~	~~6.0E+03~~	~~1.1E+01~~	~~3.6E+01~~	~~3.6E+01~~	~~3.6E+01~~
~~8~~	~~4.0E+01~~	~~6.8E+03~~	~~1.2E+01~~	~~4.0E+01~~	~~4.0E+01~~	~~4.0E+01~~
~~10~~	~~4.6E+01~~	~~7.8E+03~~	~~1.4E+01~~	~~4.6E+01~~	~~4.6E+01~~	~~4.6E+01~~
~~12~~	~~5.8E+01~~	~~9.6E+03~~	~~1.7E+01~~	~~5.8E+01~~	~~5.8E+01~~	~~5.8E+01~~
~~14~~	~~6.8E+01~~	~~1.1E+04~~	~~2.1E+01~~	~~6.8E+01~~	~~6.8E+01~~	~~6.8E+01~~
~~16~~	~~8.6E+01~~	~~1.4E+04~~	~~2.6E+01~~	~~8.6E+01~~	~~8.6E+01~~	~~8.6E+01~~
~~18~~	~~1.1E+02~~	~~1.8E+04~~	~~3.2E+01~~	~~1.1E+02~~	~~1.1E+02~~	~~1.1E+02~~

POLLUTION CONTROL BOARD

NOTICE OF PROPOSED AMENDMENTS

~~20~~	~~1.3E+02~~	~~2.2E+04~~	~~4.0E+01~~	~~1.3E+02~~	~~1.3E+03~~	~~1.3E+02~~
~~22~~	~~1.7E+02~~	~~2.8E+04~~	~~5.0E+01~~	~~1.7E+02~~	~~1.7E+03~~	~~1.7E+02~~
~~24~~	~~2.2E+02~~	~~3.6E+04~~	~~6.4E+01~~	~~2.2E+02~~	~~2.2E+03~~	~~2.2E+02~~
~~26~~	~~2.8E+02~~	~~4.6E+04~~	~~8.2E+01~~	~~2.8E+02~~	~~2.8E+03~~	~~2.8E+02~~
~~28~~	~~3.5E+02~~	~~5.8E+04~~	~~1.0E+02~~	~~3.5E+02~~	~~3.5E+03~~	~~3.5E+02~~
~~30~~	~~4.3E+02~~	~~7.6E+04~~	~~1.3E+02~~	~~4.3E+02~~	~~4.3E+03~~	~~4.3E+02~~
~~40~~	~~1.1E+03~~	~~1.8E+05~~	~~3.2E+02~~	~~1.1E+03~~	~~1.1E+04~~	~~1.1E+03~~
~~45~~	~~1.5E+03~~	~~2.5E+05~~	~~4.6E+02~~	~~1.5E+03~~	~~1.5E+04~~	~~1.5E+03~~
~~50~~	~~2.0E+03~~	~~3.3E+05~~	~~6.0E+02~~	~~2.0E+03~~	~~2.0E+04~~	~~2.0E+03~~
~~55~~	~~2.6E+03~~	~~4.4E+05~~	~~7.8E+02~~	~~2.6E+03~~	~~2.6E+04~~	~~2.6E+03~~
~~60~~	~~3.4E+03~~	~~5.8E+05~~	~~1.0E+03~~	~~3.4E+03~~	~~3.4E+04~~	~~3.4E+03~~
~~65~~	~~4.6E+03~~	~~7.6E+05~~	~~1.4E+03~~	~~4.6E+03~~	~~4.6E+04~~	~~4.6E+03~~
~~70~~	~~5.4E+03~~	~~7.6E+05~~	~~1.6E+03~~	~~5.4E+03~~	~~5.4E+04~~	~~5.4E+03~~
~~75~~	~~6.4E+03~~	~~1.1E+06~~	~~1.9E+03~~	~~6.4E+03~~	~~6.4E+04~~	~~6.4E+03~~
~~80~~	~~7.6E+03~~	~~1.3E+06~~	~~2.3E+03~~	~~7.6E+03~~	~~7.6E+04~~	~~7.6E+03~~
~~85~~	~~9.4E+03~~	~~1.5E+06~~	~~2.9E+03~~	~~9.4E+03~~	~~9.4E+04~~	~~9.4E+03~~
~~90~~	~~1.1E+04~~	~~1.8E+06~~	~~3.3E+03~~	~~1.1E+04~~	~~1.1E+05~~	~~1.1E+04~~
~~95~~	~~1.3E+04~~	~~2.2E+06~~	~~3.9E+03~~	~~1.3E+04~~	~~1.3E+05~~	~~1.3E+04~~
~~100~~	~~1.5E+04~~	~~2.5E+06~~	~~4.6E+03~~	~~1.5E+04~~	~~1.5E+05~~	~~1.5E+04~~
~~105~~	~~1.9E+04~~	~~3.1E+06~~	~~3.2E+04~~	~~1.9E+04~~	~~1.9E+05~~	~~1.9E+04~~
~~115~~	~~2.2E+04~~	~~3.6E+06~~	~~6.6E+03~~	~~2.2E+04~~	~~2.2E+05~~	~~2.2E+04~~
~~120~~	~~2.6E+04~~	~~4.4E+06~~	~~9.3E+03~~	~~9.3E+04~~	~~9.3E+05~~	~~3.1E+04~~

TRSH (m)	Antimony (g/hr)	Barium (g/hr)	Lead (g/hr)	Mercury (g/hr)	Silver (g/hr)	Thallium (g/hr)
4	31.	5200.	9.4	31.	210.	31.
6	36.	6000.	11.	36.	360.	36.
8	40.	6800.	12.	40.	400.	40.
10	46.	7800.	14.	46.	460.	46.
12	58.	9600.	17.	58.	580.	58.
14	68.	11000.	21.	68.	680.	68.
16	86.	14000.	26.	86.	860.	86.
18	110.	18000.	32.	110.	1100.	110.
20	130.	22000.	40.	130.	1300.	130.
22	170.	28000.	50.	170.	1700.	170.
24	220.	34000.	64.	220.	2200.	220.
26	280.	46000.	82.	280.	2800.	280.
28	350.	58000.	100.	350.	3500.	350.
30	430.	76000.	130.	430.	4300.	430.
35	720.	120000.	210.	720.	7200.	720.
40	1100.	180000.	320.	1100.	11000.	1100.
45	1500.	250000.	460.	1500.	15000.	1500.
50	2000.	330000.	600.	2000.	20000.	2000.
55	2600.	440000.	780.	2600.	26000.	2600.
60	3400.	580000.	1000.	3400.	34000.	3400.

POLLUTION CONTROL BOARD

NOTICE OF PROPOSED AMENDMENTS

65	4600.	760000.	1400.	4600.	46000.	4600.
70	5400.	900000.	1600.	5400.	54000.	5400.
75	6400.	1100000.	1900.	6400.	64000.	6400.
80	7600.	1300000.	2300.	7600.	76000.	7600.
85	9400.	1500000.	2800.	9400.	94000.	9400.
90	11000.	1800000.	3300.	11000.	110000.	11000.
95	13000.	2200000.	3800.	13000.	130000.	13000.
100	15000.	2600000.	4600.	15000.	150000.	15000.
105	18000.	3000000.	5400.	18000.	180000.	18000.
110	22000.	3600000.	6600.	22000.	220000.	22000.
115	26000.	4400000.	7800.	26000.	260000.	26000.
120	31000.	5000000.	9200.	31000.	310000.	31000.

I-C
Tier I and Tier II Feed Rate and Emissions Screening Limits for
Noncarcinogenic Metals for Facilities in Complex Terrain

Values for urban and rural areas

TBSH (m)	Antimony (g/hr)	Barium (g/hr)	Lead (g/hr)	Mercury (g/hr)	Silver (g/hr)	Thallium (g/hr)
4	1.4E+01	8.4E+03	4.3E+00	1.4E+01	1.4E+02	1.4E+01
6	2.1E+01	3.5E+03	6.2E+00	2.1E+01	2.1E+02	2.1E+01
8	3.0E+01	5.0E+03	9.2E+00	3.0E+01	3.0E+02	3.0E+01
10	4.3E+01	7.6E+03	1.3E+01	4.3E+01	4.3E+02	4.3E+01
12	5.4E+01	9.0E+03	1.7E+01	5.4E+01	5.4E+02	5.4E+01
14	6.8E+01	1.1E+04	2.0E+01	6.8E+01	6.8E+02	6.8E+01
16	7.8E+01	1.3E+04	2.4E+01	7.8E+01	7.8E+02	7.8E+01
18	8.6E+01	1.4E+04	2.6E+01	8.6E+01	8.6E+02	8.6E+01
20	9.6E+01	1.6E+04	2.9E+01	9.6E+01	9.6E+02	9.6E+01
22	1.0E+02	1.8E+04	3.2E+01	1.0E+02	1.0E+03	1.0E+02
24	1.2E+02	1.9E+04	3.5E+01	1.2E+02	1.2E+03	1.2E+02
26	1.3E+02	2.2E+04	3.6E+01	1.3E+02	1.3E+03	1.3E+02
28	1.4E+02	2.4E+04	4.3E+01	1.4E+02	1.4E+03	1.4E+02
30	1.6E+02	2.7E+04	4.6E+01	1.6E+02	1.6E+03	1.6E+02
35	2.0E+02	3.3E+04	5.8E+01	2.0E+02	2.0E+03	2.0E+02
40	2.4E+02	4.0E+04	7.2E+01	2.4E+02	2.4E+03	2.4E+02
45	3.0E+02	5.0E+04	9.0E+01	3.0E+02	3.0E+03	3.0E+02
50	3.6E+02	6.0E+04	1.1E+02	3.6E+02	3.6E+03	3.6E+02
55	4.6E+02	7.6E+04	1.4E+02	4.6E+02	4.6E+03	4.6E+02
60	5.8E+02	9.4E+04	1.7E+02	5.8E+02	5.8E+03	5.8E+02
65	6.8E+02	1.1E+05	2.1E+02	6.8E+02	6.8E+03	6.8E+02
70	7.8E+02	1.3E+05	2.4E+02	7.8E+02	7.8E+03	7.8E+02
75	8.6E+02	1.4E+05	2.6E+02	8.6E+02	8.6E+03	8.6E+02
80	9.6E+02	1.6E+05	2.9E+02	9.6E+02	9.6E+03	9.6E+02
85	1.1E+03	1.8E+05	3.3E+02	1.1E+03	1.1E+04	1.1E+03
90	1.2E+03	2.0E+05	3.6E+02	1.2E+03	1.2E+04	1.2E+03

POLLUTION CONTROL BOARD

NOTICE OF PROPOSED AMENDMENTS

95	1.4E+03	2.3E+05	4.0E+02	1.4E+03	1.4E+04	1.4E+03
100	1.5E+03	2.6E+05	4.6E+02	1.5E+03	1.5E+04	1.5E+03
105	1.7E+03	2.8E+05	5.0E+02	1.7E+03	1.7E+04	1.7E+03
110	1.9E+03	3.2E+05	5.8E+02	1.9E+03	1.9E+04	1.9E+03
115	2.1E+03	3.6E+05	6.4E+02	2.1E+03	2.1E+04	2.1E+03
120	2.4E+03	4.0E+05	7.2E+02	2.4E+03	2.4E+04	2.4E+03

TBSH (m)	Antimony (g/hr)	Barium (g/hr)	Lead (g/hr)	Mercury (g/hr)	Silver (g/hr)	Thallium (g/hr)
4	14.	2400.	4.3	14.	140.	14.
6	21.	3500.	6.2	21.	210.	21.
8	30.	5000.	9.2	30.	300.	30.
10	43.	7600.	13.	43.	430.	43.
12	54.	9000.	17.	54.	540.	54.
14	68.	11000.	20.	68.	680.	68.
16	78.	13000.	24.	78.	780.	78.
18	86.	14000.	26.	86.	860.	86.
20	96.	16000.	29.	96.	960.	96.
22	100.	18000.	32.	100.	1000.	100.
24	120.	19000.	35.	120.	1200.	120.
26	130.	22000.	36.	130.	1300.	130.
28	140.	24000.	43.	140.	1400.	140.
30	160.	27000.	46.	160.	1600.	160.
35	200.	33000.	58.	200.	2000.	200.
40	240.	40000.	72.	240.	2400.	240.
45	300.	50000.	90.	300.	3000.	300.
50	360.	60000.	110.	360.	3600.	360.
55	460.	76000.	140.	460.	4600.	460.
60	580.	94000.	170.	580.	5800.	580.
65	680.	110000.	210.	680.	6800.	680.
70	780.	130000.	240.	780.	7800.	780.
75	860.	140000.	260.	860.	8600.	860.
80	960.	160000.	290.	960.	9600.	960.
85	1100.	180000.	330.	1100.	11000.	1100.
90	1200.	200000.	360.	1200.	12000.	1200.
95	1400.	230000.	400.	1400.	14000.	1400.
100	1500.	260000.	460.	1500.	15000.	1500.
105	1700.	280000.	500.	1700.	17000.	1700.
110	1900.	320000.	580.	1900.	19000.	1900.
115	2100.	360000.	640.	2100.	21000.	2100.
120	2400.	400000.	720.	2400.	24000.	2400.

I-D
Tier I and Tier II Feed Rate and Emissions Screening Limits for
Carcinogenic Metals for Facilities in Noncomplex Terrain

Values for use in urban areas

POLLUTION CONTROL BOARD

NOTICE OF PROPOSED AMENDMENTS

TESH (m)	Arsenic (g/hr)	Cadmium (g/hr)	Chromium (g/hr)	Beryllium (g/hr)
4	4.6B-0.46	1.1B+00	1.7B-0.17	8.2B-0.82
6	5.4B-2.54	1.3B+00	1.9B-0.19	9.4B-0.94
8	6.0B-0.60	1.4B+00	2.2B-0.22	1.1B+00
10	6.8B-0.68	1.6B+00	2.4B-0.24	1.2B+00
12	7.6B-0.76	1.8B+00	2.7B-0.27	1.4B+00
14	8.6B-0.86	2.1B+00	3.1B-0.31	1.5B+00
16	9.6B-0.96	2.3B+00	3.5B-0.35	1.7B+00
18	1.1B+00	2.6B+00	4.0B-0.40	2.0B+00
20	1.2B+00	3.0B+00	4.4B-2.44	2.2B+00
22	1.4B+00	3.4B+00	5.0B-0.50	2.5B+00
24	1.6B+00	3.9B+00	5.8B-0.58	2.8B+00
26	1.8B+00	4.3B+00	6.4B-0.64	3.2B+00
28	2.0B+00	4.8B+00	7.2B-0.72	3.6B+00
30	2.3B+00	5.4B+00	8.2B-0.82	4.0B+00
35	3.0B+00	6.8B+00	1.0B+00	5.4B+00
40	3.6B+00	9.0B+00	1.3B+00	6.0B+00
45	4.6B+00	1.1B+011	1.7B+00	8.0B+00
50	6.0B+00	1.4B+014	2.2B+00	1.1B+011
55	7.6B+00	1.8B+018	2.7B+00	1.4B+014
60	9.4B+00	2.2B+022	3.4B+00	1.7B+017
65	1.1B+011	2.8B+028	4.2B+00	2.1B+021
70	1.3B+013	3.1B+031	4.6B+00	2.4B+024
75	1.5B+015	2.6B+026	5.4B+00	2.7B+027

POLLUTION CONTROL BOARD

NOTICE OF PROPOSED AMENDMENTS

TESH (m)	Arsenic (g/hr)	Cadmium (g/hr)	Chromium (g/hr)	Beryllium (g/hr)
80	1.7B+017	4.0B+040	6.0B+00	3.0B+030
85	1.9B+019	4.6B+046	6.8B+00	3.4B+034
90	2.2B+022	5.0B+050	7.8B+00	3.9B+039
95	2.5B+025	5.8B+058	9.0B+00	4.4B+044
100	2.8B+028	6.8B+068	1.0B+010	5.0B+050
105	3.2B+032	7.6B+076	1.1B+011	5.6B+056
110	3.6B+036	8.6B+086	1.3B+013	6.4B+064
115	4.0B+040	9.6B+096	1.5B+015	7.2B+072
120	4.6B+046	1.1B+110	1.7B+017	8.2B+082

I-D (con't.

Values for use in rural areas

TESH (m)	Arsenic (g/hr)	Cadmium (g/hr)	Chromium (g/hr)	Beryllium (g/hr)
4	2.4B-0.24	5.8B-0.58	8.6B0.086	4.3B-0.43
6	2.7B-0.28	6.6B-0.66	1.0B-0.10	5.0B-0.50
8	3.2B-0.32	7.6B-0.76	1.1B-0.11	5.6B-0.56
10	3.6B-0.36	8.6B-0.86	1.3B-0.13	6.4B-2.64
12	4.3B-0.43	1.1B+00	1.6B-0.16	7.8B-0.78
14	5.4B-0.54	1.3B+00	2.0B-0.20	9.6B-0.96
16	6.8B-0.68	1.6B+00	2.4B-0.24	1.2B+00
18	8.2B-0.82	2.0B+00	3.0B-0.30	1.5B+00
20	1.0B+00	2.5B+00	4.0B-0.37	1.9B+00
22	1.3B+00	3.2B+00	4.8B-0.48	2.4B+00
24	1.7B+00	4.0B+00	6.0B-0.60	3.0B+00

POLLUTION CONTROL BOARD

NOTICE OF PROPOSED AMENDMENTS

			θ‡	
26	2.1E+00	5.0E+00	7.6E-0.76	3.9E+00
28	2.7E+00	6.4E+00	9.9E-0.98 θ‡	5.0E+00
30	3.5E+00	8.3E+00	1.2E+00 θ‡	6.2E+00
35	5.4E+00	1.3E+0<u>13.</u>	1.9E+00	9.6E+00
40	8.2E+00	8.0E+0<u>20.</u> ‡	3.0E+00	1.5E+0<u>15.</u> ‡
45	1.1E+0<u>11.</u> ‡	2.8E+0<u>28.</u> ‡	4.2E+00	2.1E+0<u>21.</u> ‡
50	1.5E+0<u>15.</u> ‡	3.7E+0<u>37.</u> ‡	5.4E+00	2.8E+0<u>28.</u> ‡
55	2.0E+0<u>20.</u> ‡	5.0E+0<u>50.</u> ‡	7.2E+00	3.6E+0<u>36.</u> ‡
60	2.7E+0<u>27.</u> ‡	6.4E+0<u>64.</u> ‡	9.6E+00	4.8E+0<u>48.</u> ‡
65	3.6E+0<u>36.</u> ‡	8.6E+0<u>86.</u> ‡	1.3E+0<u>13.</u> ‡	6.4E+0<u>64.</u> ‡
70	4.3E+0<u>43.</u> ‡	1.0E+0<u>100.</u> 0‡	1.5E+0<u>15.</u> ‡	7.6E+0<u>76.</u> ‡
75	5.0E+0<u>50.</u> ‡	1.2E+0<u>120.</u> 0‡	1.8E+0<u>18.</u> ‡	9.0E+0<u>90.</u> ‡
80	6.0E+0<u>60.</u> ‡	1.4E+0<u>149.</u> 0‡	2.2E+0<u>22.</u> ‡	1.1E+0<u>110.</u> 0‡
85	7.2E+0<u>72.</u> ‡	1.7E+0<u>170.</u> 0‡	2.6E+0<u>26.</u> ‡	1.3E+0<u>130.</u> 0‡
90	8.6E+0<u>86.</u> ‡	2.0E+0<u>200.</u> ‡	3.0E+0<u>30.</u> ‡	1.5E+0<u>150.</u> 0‡
95	1.0E+0<u>100.</u> 0‡	2.4E+0<u>240.</u> 0‡	3.6E+0<u>36.</u> ‡	1.8E+0<u>180.</u> 0‡
100	1.2E+0<u>120.</u> 0‡	2.9E+0<u>290.</u> 0‡	4.3E+0<u>43.</u> ‡	2.2E+0<u>220.</u> 0‡
105	1.4E+0<u>140.</u> 0‡	3.4E+0<u>340.</u> 0‡	5.0E+0<u>50.</u> ‡	2.6E+0<u>260.</u> 0‡
110	1.7E+0<u>170.</u> 0‡	4.0E+0<u>400.</u> 0‡	6.0E+0<u>60.</u> ‡	3.0E+0<u>300.</u> 0‡
115	2.0E+0<u>200.</u> ‡	4.8E+0<u>482.</u> ‡	7.3E+0<u>73.</u> ‡	3.6E+0<u>360.</u> 0‡
120	2.4E+0<u>240.</u>	5.8E+0<u>580.</u> ‡	8.6E+0<u>86.</u> ‡	4.3E+0<u>430.</u>

I-E
Tier I and Tier II Feed Rate and Emissions Screening Limits for
Carcinogenic Metals for Facilities in Complex Terrain
Values for use in urban and rural areas

POLLUTION CONTROL BOARD

NOTICE OF PROPOSED AMENDMENTS

TRSH (m)	Arsenic (g/hr)	Cadmium (g/hr)	Chromium (g/hr)	Beryllium (g/hr)
4	1.1E-01	2.6E-01	4.0E-02	8.0E-01
6	1.6E-01	3.9E-01	5.8E-02	2.9E-01
8	2.4E-01	5.8E-01	8.6E-02	4.3E-01
10	3.5E-01	8.2E-01	1.3E-01	6.2E-01
12	4.3E-01	1.0E+00	1.5E-01	7.6E-01
14	5.0E-01	1.3E+00	1.9E-01	9.4E-01
16	6.0E-01	1.6E+00	2.3E-01	1.1E+00
18	6.8E-01	1.8E+00	2.4E-01	1.2E+00
20	7.6E-01	2.0E+00	2.7E-01	1.3E+00
22	8.3E-01	1.9E+00	3.0E-01	1.5E+00
24	9.0E-01	2.1E+00	3.3E-01	1.6E+00
26	1.0E+00	2.4E+00	3.5E-01	1.8E+00
28	1.1E+00	2.7E+00	4.0E-01	2.0E+00
30	1.2E+00	3.0E+00	4.4E-01	2.2E+00
35	1.7E+00	4.0E+00	5.4E-01	2.7E+00
40	1.9E+00	4.6E+00	6.8E-01	3.4E+00
45	2.4E+00	5.4E+00	8.4E-01	4.2E+00
50	2.9E+00	6.4E+00	1.0E+00	5.0E+00
55	3.5E+00	8.4E+00	1.3E+00	6.4E+00
60	4.3E+00	1.0E+01	1.5E+00	7.8E+00
65	5.1E+00	1.3E+00	1.9E+00	9.6E+00
70	6.0E+00	1.4E+01	2.1E+00	1.1E+01
75	6.9E+00	1.5E+01	2.4E+00	1.2E+01
80	8.2E+00	1.9E+01	2.7E+00	1.3E+01
85	9.2E+00	2.1E+01	3.2E+00	1.5E+01
90	9.4E+00	2.3E+01	3.4E+00	1.7E+01
95	1.1E+01	2.5E+01	4.0E+00	1.9E+01
100	1.2E+01	2.9E+01	4.3E+00	2.1E+01
105	1.3E+01	3.2E+01	4.8E+00	2.4E+01
110	1.5E+01	3.5E+01	5.4E+00	2.7E+01
115	1.7E+01	4.0E+01	6.1E+00	3.0E+01
120	1.9E+01	4.4E+01	6.4E+00	3.3E+01

TRSH (m)	Arsenic (g/hr)	Cadmium (g/hr)	Chromium (g/hr)	Beryllium (g/hr)
4	0.11	0.26	0.040	0.20
6	0.16	0.39	0.058	0.29
8	0.24	0.58	0.086	0.43
10	0.35	0.82	0.13	0.62
12	0.43	1.0	0.13	0.76
14	0.50	1.3	0.19	0.94
16	0.60	1.4	0.23	1.1
18	0.68	1.6	0.24	1.2
20	0.76	1.8	0.27	1.3

POLLUTION CONTROL BOARD

NOTICE OF PROPOSED AMENDMENTS

22	0.82	1.9	0.20	1.5
24	0.90	2.1	0.22	1.6
26	1.0	2.4	0.26	1.8
28	1.1	2.7	0.40	3.0
30	1.2	3.0	0.44	2.2
35	1.5	3.7	0.54	2.7
40	1.9	4.6	0.68	3.4
45	2.4	5.4	0.84	4.2
50	2.9	6.8	1.0	5.0
55	3.5	8.4	1.3	6.4
60	4.3	10.	1.5	7.8
65	5.4	12.	1.9	9.6
70	6.0	14.	2.2	11.
75	6.8	16.	2.4	12.
80	7.6	18.	2.7	13.
85	8.2	20.	3.0	15.
90	9.4	23.	3.4	17.
95	10.	25.	4.0	19.
100	12.	28.	4.3	21.
105	13.	32.	4.8	24.
110	15.	35.	5.4	27.
115	17.	40.	6.0	30.
120	19.	44.	6.4	33.

(Source: Amended at 19 Ill. Reg. _____, effective _____)

POLLUTION CONTROL BOARD

NOTICE OF PROPOSED AMENDMENTS

Section 726.APPENDIX B Tier I Feed Rate Screening Limits for total Chlorine

Tier I Feed Rate Screening Limits for Total Chlorine

TESH (m)	Noncomplex Terrain Urban (g/hr)	Noncomplex Terrain Rural (g/hr)	Complex Terrain (g/hr)
4	8.2E+01 82.	4.2E+01 42.	1.9E+01 19.
6	9.1E+01 91.	4.8E+01 48.	2.8E+01 28.
8	1.0E+02 100.	5.3E+01 53.	4.1E+01 41.
10	1.2E+02 120.	6.2E+01 62.	5.8E+01 58.
12	1.3E+02 130.	7.7E+01 77.	7.2E+01 72.
14	1.5E+02 150.	9.1E+01 91.	9.1E+01 91.
16	1.7E+02 170.	1.2E+02 120.	1.1E+02 110.
18	1.9E+02 190.	1.4E+02 140.	1.2E+02 120.
20	2.1E+02 210.	1.8E+02 180.	1.3E+02 130.
22	2.4E+02 240.	2.3E+02 230.	1.4E+02 140.
24	2.7E+02 270.	2.9E+02 290.	1.6E+02 160.
26	3.1E+02 310.	3.7E+02 370.	1.7E+02 170.
28	3.5E+02 350.	4.7E+02 470.	1.9E+02 190.
30	3.9E+02 390.	5.8E+02 580.	2.1E+02 210.
35	5.3E+02 530.	9.6E+02 960.	2.4E+02 240.
40	6.2E+02 620.	1.4E+03 1400.	3.3E+02 330.
45	8.2E+02 820.	2.0E+03 2000.	4.0E+02 400.
50	1.1E+03 1100.	2.6E+03 2600.	4.8E+02 480.
55	1.3E+03 1300.	3.5E+03 3500.	6.2E+02 620.
60	1.6E+03 1600.	4.6E+03 4600.	7.7E+02 770.
65	2.0E+03 2000.	6.2E+03 6200.	9.1E+02 910.
70	2.3E+03 2300.	7.2E+03 7200.	1.1E+03 1100.
75	2.5E+03 2500.	8.6E+03 8600.	1.2E+03 1200.
80	2.9E+03 2900.	1.3E+04 13000.	1.3E+03 1300.
85	3.3E+03 3300.	1.4E+04 12000.	1.4E+03 1400.
90	3.7E+03 3700.	1.4E+04 14000.	1.6E+03 1600.
95	4.2E+03 4200.	1.7E+04 17000.	1.8E+03 1800.
100	4.8E+03 4800.	2.1E+04 21000.	2.0E+03 2000.
105	5.3E+03 5300.	2.4E+04 24000.	2.3E+03 2300.
110	6.2E+03 6200.	2.9E+04 29000.	2.5E+03 2500.
115	7.2E+03 7200.	3.5E+04 35000.	2.8E+03 2800.
120	8.2E+03 8200.	4.1E+04 41000.	3.2E+03 3200.

(Source: Amended at 19 Ill. Reg. _____, effective _____)

POLLUTION CONTROL BOARD

NOTICE OF PROPOSED AMENDMENTS

Section 726.APPENDIX C Tier II Emission Rate Screening Limits for Free Chlorine and Hydrogen Chloride

TRSH (m)	Noncomplex Terrain Urban-areas Chlorine		Noncomplex Terrain Rural-areas Chlorine		Complex Terrain Urban-and rural-areas Chlorine	
	Gas (g/hr)	HCl (g/hr)	Gas (g/hr)	HCl (g/hr)	gas (g/hr)	HCl (g/hr)
4	8.2E+02	1.4E+03	4.2E+01	7.3E+02	1.3E+01	2.3E+02
6	9.1E+01	1.6E+03	4.8E+01	8.3E+02	2.8E+01	4.9E+02
8	1.0E+02	1.8E+02	5.3E+01	9.2E+02	4.1E+01	7.1E+02
10	1.2E+02	2.0E+03	6.2E+01	1.1E+03	5.8E+01	1.0E+03
12	1.3E+02	2.3E+03	7.7E+01	7.3E+01	7.2E+01	1.3E+03
14	1.5E+02	2.6E+03	9.1E+01	1.6E+03	9.1E+01	1.6E+03
16	1.7E+02	2.9E+03	1.2E+02	2.0E+02	1.1E+02	1.8E+03
18	1.9E+02	3.3E+03	1.4E+02	2.5E+03	1.2E+02	2.0E+03
20	2.1E+02	3.7E+03	1.8E+02	3.1E+03	1.3E+02	2.3E+03
22	2.4E+02	4.2E+03	2.3E+02	3.9E+03	1.4E+02	2.4E+03
24	2.7E+02	4.8E+03	2.9E+02	5.0E+03	1.6E+02	2.8E+03
26	3.1E+02	5.4E+03	3.7E+02	6.5E+03	1.7E+02	3.0E+03
28	3.5E+02	6.0E+03	4.7E+02	8.1E+03	1.9E+02	3.4E+03
30	3.9E+02	6.9E+03	5.8E+02	1.0E+04	2.1E+02	3.7E+03
35	5.3E+02	9.2E+03	9.6E+02	1.7E+04	2.6E+02	4.6E+03
40	6.2E+02	1.1E+04	1.4E+03	2.5E+04	3.3E+02	5.7E+03
45	8.2E+02	1.4E+04	2.0E+03	3.5E+04	4.0E+02	7.0E+03
50	1.1E+03	1.8E+04	2.6E+03	4.6E+04	4.8E+02	8.4E+03
55	1.3E+03	2.3E+04	3.5E+03	6.1E+04	6.2E+02	1.1E+04
60	1.6E+03	2.9E+04	4.6E+03	8.1E+04	7.7E+02	1.3E+04
65	2.0E+03	3.4E+04	6.2E+03	1.1E+05	9.1E+02	1.6E+04
70	2.3E+03	3.9E+04	7.2E+03	1.3E+05	1.1E+03	1.8E+04
75	2.5E+03	4.5E+04	8.6E+03	1.5E+05	1.2E+03	2.0E+04
80	2.9E+03	5.0E+04	1.0E+04	1.8E+05	1.3E+03	2.3E+04
85	3.3E+03	5.8E+04	1.2E+04	2.2E+05	1.4E+03	2.5E+04
90	3.7E+03	6.6E+04	1.4E+04	2.5E+05	1.6E+03	2.9E+04
95	4.2E+03	7.4E+04	1.7E+04	3.0E+05	1.8E+03	3.2E+04
100	4.8E+03	8.4E+04	2.1E+04	3.6E+05	2.0E+03	3.5E+04
105	5.3E+03	9.2E+04	2.4E+04	4.2E+05	2.2E+03	3.9E+04
110	6.2E+03	1.1E+05	2.9E+04	5.1E+05	2.5E+03	4.3E+04
115	7.2E+03	1.3E+05	3.5E+04	6.1E+05	2.9E+03	5.0E+04
120	8.2E+03	1.4E+05	4.1E+04	7.2E+05	3.2E+03	5.6E+04

TRSN	Noncomplex Terrain Urban areas Chlorine		Noncomplex Terrain Rural areas Chlorine		Complex Terrain Urban and rural areas Chlorine	
	Gas	HCl	Gas	HCl	gas	HCl

(m)	(g/hr)	(g/hr)	(g/hr)	(g/hr)	(g/hr)	(g/hr)
4	82.	1400.	42.	730.	13.	230.
6	91.	1600.	48.	830.	28.	490.
8	120.	1800.	53.	920.	41.	710.
10	120.	2000.	62.	1100.	58.	1000.
12	130.	2300.	77.	1300.	72.	1300.
14	150.	2600.	91.	1600.	91.	1600.
16	170.	2900.	120.	2000.	110.	1800.
18	190.	3300.	140.	2500.	120.	2000.
20	210.	3700.	180.	3100.	130.	2300.
22	240.	4200.	230.	3900.	140.	2400.
24	270.	4800.	290.	5000.	160.	2800.
26	310.	5400.	370.	6500.	170.	3000.
28	350.	6000.	470.	8100.	190.	3400.
30	390.	6900.	580.	10000.	210.	3700.
35	530.	9200.	960.	17000.	260.	4600.
40	620.	11000.	1400.	25000.	330.	5700.
45	820.	14000.	2000.	35000.	400.	7000.
50	1100.	18000.	2600.	46000.	480.	8400.
55	1300.	23000.	3500.	61000.	620.	11000.
60	1600.	29000.	4600.	81000.	770.	13000.
65	2000.	34000.	6200.	110000.	910.	16000.
70	2300.	39000.	7200.	130000.	1100.	18000.
75	2500.	45000.	8600.	150000.	1200.	20000.
80	2900.	50000.	10000.	180000.	1300.	23000.
85	3300.	58000.	12000.	220000.	1400.	25000.
90	3700.	66000.	14000.	250000.	1600.	29000.
95	4200.	74000.	17000.	300000.	1800.	32000.
100	4800.	84000.	21000.	360000.	2000.	35000.
105	5300.	92000.	24000.	420000.	2200.	39000.
110	6200.	110000.	29000.	510000.	2500.	43000.
115	7200.	130000.	35000.	610000.	2900.	50000.
120	8200.	140000.	41000.	720000.	3200.	56000.

(Source: Amended at 19 Ill. Reg. _____, effective _____)

POLLUTION CONTROL BOARD

NOTICE OF PROPOSED AMENDMENTS

Section 726.APPENDIX E Risk Specific Doses

BOARD NOTE: These are risk specific doses (RSDs) based on a risk of 1 in 10,000(1x10(-5)).

Constituent	CAS No.	Unit risk (cu m(3)/ug)	RSD (ug/cu-m(3))
Acrylamide	79-06-1	0.0013 1+3B-03	0.0077 7+7B-03
Acrylonitrile	107-13-1	0.000068 6+8B-05	0.15 1+5B-01
Aldrin	309-00-2	0.0049 4+9B-03	0.0020 2+0B-03
Aniline	62-53-3	0.0000074 7+4B-06	1.4 1+4B-00
Arsenic	7440-38-2	0.0043 4+3B-03	0.0023 2+3B-03
Benz(a)anthracene	56-55-3	0.00089 8+9B-04	0.011 1+1B-02
Benzene	71-43-2	0.0000083 8+3B-06	1.2 1+2B-00
Benzidine	92-87-5	0.067 6+7B-02	0.00015 1+5B-04
Benzo(a)pyrene	50-32-8	0.0033 3+3B-03	0.0030 3+0B-03
Beryllium	7440-41-7	0.0024 2+4B-03	0.0042 4+2B-03
Bis(2-chloroethyl)ether	111-44-4	0.00033 3+3B-04	0.030 3+0B-02
Bis(chloromethyl)ether	542-88-1	0.062 6+2B-02	0.00016 1+6B-04
Bis(2-ethylhexyl)phthalate	117-81-7	0.00000024 2+4B-07	42. 4+2B-01
1,3-Butadiene	106-99-0	0.00028 2+8B-04	0.036 3+6B-02
Cadmium	7440-43-9	0.0018 1+8B-03	0.0056 5+6B-03
Carbon Tetrachloride	56-23-5	0.000015 1+5B-05	0.67 6+7B-01
Chlordane	57-74-9	0.00037 3+7B-04	0.027 2+7B-02
Chloroform	67-66-3	0.000023 2+3B-05	0.43 4+3B-01
Chloromethane	74-87-3	0.0000036 3+6B-06	2.8B-00
Chromium VI	7440-47-3	0.012 1+2B-02	0.00083 8+3B-04
DDT	50-29-3	0.000097 9+7B-05	0.10 1+0B-01
Dibenz(a,h)anthracene	53-70-3	0.014 1+4B-02	0.00071 7+1B-04
1,2-Dibromo-3-chloropropane	96-12-8	0.0063 6+3B-03	0.0016 1+6B-03
1,2-Dibromoethane	106-93-4	0.00022 2+2B-04	0.045 4+5B-02
1,1-Dichloroethane	75-34-3	0.000026 2+6B-05	0.38 3+8B-01
1,2-Dichloroethane	107-06-2	0.000026 2+6B-05	0.38 3+8B-01
1,1-Dichloroethylene	75-35-4	0.000050 5+0B-05	0.20 2+0B-01
1,3-Dichloropropene	542-75-6	0.25 2+5B-01	0.000022 2+2B-05
Dieldrin	60-57-1	0.0046 4+6B-03	0.0022 2+2B-03
Diethylstilbestrol	56-53-1	0.14 1+4B-01	0.000071 7+1B-05
Dimethylnitrosamine	62-75-9	0.014 1+4B-02	0.00071 7+1B-04
2,4-Dinitrotoluene	121-14-2	0.000088 8+8B-05	0.11 1+1B-01
1,2-Diphenylhydrazine	122-66-7	0.00022 2+2B-04	0.045 4+5B-02
1,4-Dioxane	123-91-1	0.000014 1+4B-05	7.1 B-00
Epichlorohydrin	106-89-8	0.0000012 1+2B-06	8.3 B-00
Ethylene Oxide	75-21-8	0.00010 1+0B-04	0.10 1+0B-01
Ethylene Dibromide	106-93-4	0.00022 2+2B-04	0.045 4+5B-02
Formaldehyde	50-00-0	0.000013 1+3B-05	0.77 7+7B-01

POLLUTION CONTROL BOARD

NOTICE OF PROPOSED AMENDMENTS

Heptachlor	76-44-8	0.0013 1+3B-03	0.0077 7+7B-03
Heptachlor Epoxide	1024-57-3	0.0026 2+6B-03	0.0038 3+8B-03
Hexachlorobenzene	118-74-1	0.00049 4+9B-04	0.020 2+0B-02
Hexachlorobutadiene	87-68-3	0.000020 2+0B-05	0.50 5+0B-01
Alpha-hexachlorocyclohexane	319-84-6	0.0018 1+8B-03	0.0056 5+6B-03
Beta-hexachlorocyclohexane	319-85-7	0.00053 5+3B-04	0.019 1+9B-02
Gamma-hexachlorocyclohexane	58-89-9	0.00038 3+8B-04	0.026 2+6B-02
Hexachlorocyclohexane, Technical		0.00051 5+1B-04	0.020 2+0B-02
Hexachlorodibenzo-p-dioxin(1,2 Mixture)		1.3 B+0	0.0000077 7+7B-06
Hexachloroethane	67-72-1	0.0000040 4+0B-06	2.5 B+00
Hydrazine	302-01-2	0.0029 2+9B-03	0.0034 3+4B-03
Hydrazine Sulfate	302-01-2	0.0029 2+9B-03	0.0034 3+4B-03
3-Methylcholanthrene	56-49-5	0.0027 2+7B-03	0.0037 3+7B-03
Methyl Hydrazine	60-34-4	0.00031 3+1B-04	0.032 3+2B-02
Methylene Chloride	75-09-2	0.0000041 4+1B-06	2.4 B+00
4,4'-Methylene-bis-2-chloroaniline	101-14-4	0.000047 4+7B-05	0.21 2+1B-01
Nickel	7440-02-0	0.00024 2+4B-04	0.042 4+2B-02
Nickel Refinery Dust	7440-02-0	0.00024 2+4B-04	0.042 4+2B-02
Nickel Subsulfide	12035-72-2	0.00048 4+8B-04	0.021 2+1B-02
2-Nitropropane	79-46-9	0.027 2+7B-02	0.00037 3+7B-04
N-Nitroso-n-butylamine	924-16-3	0.0016 1+6B-03	0.0063 6+3B-03
N-Nitroso-n-methylurea	684-93-5	0.086 8+6B-02	0.00012 1+2B-04
N-Nitrosodiethylamine	55-18-5	0.043 4+3B-02	0.00023 2+3B-04
N-Nitrosopyrrolidine	930-55-2	0.00061 6+1B-04	0.016 1+6B-02
Pentachloronitrobenzene	82-68-8	0.000073 7+3B-05	0.14 1+4B-01
PCBs	1336-36-3	0.0012 1+2B-03	0.0083 8+3B-03
Pronamide	23950-58-5	0.0000046 4+6B-06	2.2 B+00
Reserpine	50-55-5	0.0030 3+0B-03	0.0033 3+3B-03
2,3,7,8-Tetrachlorodibenzo-p-dioxin	1746-01-6	45. 4+5B+01	0.00000022 2+2B-07
1,1,2,2-Tetrachloroethane	79-34-5	0.000058 5+8B-05	0.17 1+7B-01
Tetrachloroethylene	127-18-4	0.00000048. 4+8B-07	21. 2+1B+01
Thiourea	62-56-6	0.00055 5+5B-04	0.018 1+8B-02
1,1,1-Trichloroethane	79-00-5	0.000016 1+6B-05	0.63 6+3B-01
Trichloroethylene	79-01-6	0.0000013 1+3B-06	7.7 B+00
2,4,6-Trichlorophenol	88-06-2	0.0000057 5+7B-06	1.8 B+00
Toxaphene	8001-35-2	0.00032 3+2B-04	0.031 3+1B-02
Vinyl Chloride	75-01-4	0.0000071 7+1B-06	1.4 B+00

(Source: Amended at 19 Ill. Reg. _____, effective _____)

POLLUTION CONTROL BOARD

NOTICE OF PROPOSED AMENDMENTS

Section 726.APPENDIX M Mercury-Bearing Wastes That May Be Processed in Exempt Mercury Recovery Units

The following materials are exempt mercury-bearing materials containing less than 500 ppm of 35 Ill. Adm. Code 721.Appendix H organic constituents, when generated by manufacturers or users of mercury or mercury products:

    Activated carbon
    Decomposer graphite
    Wood
    Paper
    Protective clothing
    Sweepings
    Respiratory cartridge filters
    Cleanup articles
    Plastic bags and other contaminated containers
    Laboratory and process control samples
    K106 and other wastewater treatment plan sludge and filter cake
    Mercury cell sump and tank sludge
    Mercury cell process solids
    Recoverable levels of mercury contained in soil

(Source: Added at 19 Ill. Reg. _____, effective
_____)

POLLUTION CONTROL BOARD

NOTICE OF PROPOSED AMENDMENTS

1) Heading of the Part: Standards for the Management of Used Oil

2) Code Citation: 35 Ill. Adm. Code 739

3) Section numbers: Proposed Action:

    739.110   Amended

4) Statutory Authority: 415 ILCS 5/22.4 and 27

5) A complete description of the subjects and issues involved:

A more detailed description is contained in the Board's proposed opinion of March 2, 1995, in R95-4 and R95-6 (consolidated), which opinion is available from the address below. Section 22.4(a) of the Environmental Protection Act [415 ILCS 5/22.4(a)] provides that Section 5-35 of the Administrative Procedure Act [5 ILCS 100/5-35] shall not apply. Because this rulemaking is not subject to Section 5-35 of the APA, it is not subject to first notice or to second notice review by JCAR.

This rulemaking updates Parts 700, 702, 703, 705, 720, 721, 722, 723, 724, 725, 726, 728, 730, 738, and 739 of the Illinois RCRA Subtitle C hazardous waste and underground injection control (UIC) rules to correspond with amendments adopted by U.S. EPA that appeared in the Federal Register during the period July 1 through December 31, 1994. During this period, U.S. EPA amended its regulations as follows:

Federal Action	Summary
59 Fed. Reg. 38536, July 28, 1994	Exclusion from definition of solid waste for certain in-process recycled secondary materials used by the petroleum refining industry
59 Fed. Reg. 43496, August 24, 1994	Withdrawal of exemption from Subtitle C regulation of slag residues from high temperature metal recovery (HTMR) of electric arc furnace dust (K061), steel finishing pickle liquor (K062), and electroplating sludges (F006) that are used in a manner constituting disposal
59 Fed. Reg. 47980, September 19, 1994	Restoration of text from 40 CFR 268.7(a) inadvertently omitted in the amendments of August 31, 1993, at 58 Fed. Reg. 46040

POLLUTION CONTROL BOARD

NOTICE OF PROPOSED AMENDMENTS

59 Fed. Reg. 47982,   Phase II land disposal restrictions (LDRs);
September 19, 1994   universal treatment standards for organic
                       toxicity wastes and newly-listed wastes
                       (including underground injection control
                       (UIC) amendments)

59 Fed. Reg. 62896,   Organic material air emission standards for
December 6, 1994   tanks, surface impoundments, and containers

In addition to these principal amendments that occurred during the update
period, the Board has included an additional, later action;

60 Fed. Reg. 242,   Corrections to the Phase II land disposal
January 3, 1995   restrictions (universal treatment standards)

This January 3 action was an amendment of the September 19, 1994 Phase II
LDRs universal waste rule). U.S. EPA corrected errors and clarified
language in the universal treatment standards. The Board did not delay in
adding these amendments for three reasons;

1) The January 3, 1995 amendments are corrections and clarifications of
    the September 19, 1994 regulations, and not new substantive
    amendments;

2) Prompt action on the January 3, 1995 amendments will facilitate
    implementation of the Phase II LDRs; and

3) The Board has received a request from the regulated community that we
    add the January 3, 1995 amendments to those of September 19, 1994.
    (See "Expedited Consideration" below.)

The Board also notes that the later amendments occurred within six months
of the earliest amendments included in this docket, even if they occurred
outside the nominal time-frame of the docket.

In addition to the federally-derived amendments, the Board used this
opportunity to undertake a number of housekeeping and corrective
amendments. We have effected the removal of all cross-references for
effective dates and repealed Part 700. We have converted equations and
formulae to the standard scientific format. We have tried to improve the
language and structure of various provision, including correcting grammar,
punctuation, and spelling where necessary.

Specifically, the segment of the amendments involved in Part 739 change
the reference from former 35 Ill. Adm. Code 721.103(c)(2)(A) to the new
location at 35 Ill. Adm. Code 721.103(e)(1), renumbered in this docket.

6) Will this proposed rule replace an emergency rule currently in effect? No

POLLUTION CONTROL BOARD

NOTICE OF PROPOSED AMENDMENTS

7) Does this rulemaking contain an automatic repeal date? No

8) Do these proposed amendments contain incorporations by reference? No.

9) Are there any other amendments pending on this Part? No

10) Statement of statewide policy objectives: This rulemaking is mandated by
    Section 22.4(a) of the Environmental Protection Act [415 ILCS 5/22.4(a)].
    The statewide policy objectives are set forth in Section 20 of that Act.
    This rulemaking imposes mandates on units of local government only to the
    extent that they may be involved in the generation, transportation,
    treatment, storage, or disposal of hazardous waste or they engage in
    underground injection of waste.

11) Time, place and manner in which interested persons may comment on this
    proposed rulemaking: The Board will accept written public comment on this
    proposal for a period of 45 days after the date of this publication.
    Comments should reference Docket R95-4/R95-6 and be addressed to:

        Ms. Dorothy M. Gunn, Clerk
        Illinois Pollution Control Board
        State of Illinois Center, Suite 11-500
        100 W. Randolph St.
        Chicago, IL 60601
        (312) 814-6931

    Address all questions to Michael J. McCambridge, at (312) 814-6924.

12) Initial regulatory flexibility analysis:

    A) Date rule was submitted to the Small Business Office of the Department
        of Commerce and Community Affairs: March 6, 1995.

    B) Types of small businesses affected: The existing rules and proposed
        amendments affect small businesses that generate, transport, treat,
        store, or dispose of hazardous waste or engage in underground
        injection of waste.

    C) Reporting, bookkeeping, or other procedures required for compliance:
        The existing rules and proposed amendments require extensive
        reporting, bookkeeping, and other procedures, including the
        preparation of manifests and annual reports, waste analyses, and
        maintenance of operating records.

    D) Types of professional skills necessary for compliance: Compliance
        with the existing rules and proposed amendments may require the
        services of an attorney, certified public accountant, chemist, and
        registered professional engineer.

POLLUTION CONTROL BOARD

NOTICE OF PROPOSED AMENDMENTS

The full text of the proposed amendments begins on the next page:

POLLUTION CONTROL BOARD

NOTICE OF PROPOSED AMENDMENTS

TITLE 35: ENVIRONMENTAL PROTECTION
SUBTITLE G: WASTE DISPOSAL
CHAPTER I: POLLUTION CONTROL BOARD
SUBCHAPTER c: SPECIFIC HAZARDOUS WASTE MANAGEMENT STANDARDS

PART 739
STANDARDS FOR THE MANAGEMENT OF USED OIL

SUBPART A: DEFINITIONS

POLLUTION CONTROL BOARD

NOTICE OF PROPOSED AMENDMENTS

739.146   Tracking
739.147   Management of residues

SUBPART F: STANDARDS FOR USED OIL PROCESSORS

Section
739.150   Applicability
739.151   Notification
739.152   General facility standards
739.153   Rebuttable presumption for used oil
739.154   Used oil management
739.155   Analysis plan
739.156   Tracking
739.157   Operating record and reporting
739.158   Off-site shipments of used oil
739.159   Management of residues

SUBPART G: STANDARDS FOR USED OIL BURNERS WHO BURN OFF-SPECIFICATION
USED OIL FOR ENERGY RECOVERY

Section
739.160   Applicability
739.161   Restriction on burning
739.162   Notification
739.163   Rebuttable presumption for used oil
739.164   Used oil storage
739.165   Tracking
739.166   Notices
739.167   Management of residues

SUBPART H: STANDARDS FOR USED OIL FUEL MARKETERS

Section
739.170   Applicability
739.171   Prohibitions
739.172   On-specification used oil fuel
739.173   Notification
739.174   Tracking
739.175   Notices

SUBPART I: STANDARDS FOR USE AS A DUST SUPPRESSANT DISPOSAL OF USED OIL

Section
739.180   Applicability
739.181   Disposal
739.182   Use as a dust suppressant

AUTHORITY: Implementing Section 22.4 and authorized by Section 27 of the

POLLUTION CONTROL BOARD

NOTICE OF PROPOSED AMENDMENTS

Environmental Protection Act [415 ILCS 5/22.4 and 27].

SOURCE: Adopted in R93-4 at 17 Ill. Reg. 20954, effective November 22, 1993;
amended in R93-16 at 18 Ill. Reg. 6931, effective April 26, 1994; amended in
R94-17 at 18 Ill. Reg. 17616, effective November 23, 1994; amended in R95-6 at
19 Ill. Reg. _____, effective _____.

SUBPART B: APPLICABILITY

Section 739.110 Applicability

This Section identifies those materials which are subject to regulation as used
oil under this Part. This Section also identifies some materials that are not
subject to regulation as used oil under this Part, and indicates whether these
materials may be subject to regulation as hazardous waste under Parts 702, 703,
720 through 726, and 728.

a) Used oil. U.S. EPA presumes that used oil is to be recycled unless a
    used oil handler disposes of used oil, or sends used oil for disposal.
    Except as provided in Section 739.111, the regulations of this Part
    apply to used oil, and to materials identified in this Section as
    being subject to regulation as used oil, whether or not the used oil
    or material exhibits any characteristics of hazardous waste identified
    in 35 Ill. Adm. Code 721.Subpart C.

b) Mixtures of used oil and hazardous waste.

    1) Listed hazardous waste.

        A) A mixture of used oil and hazardous waste that is listed in
            35 Ill. Adm. Code 721.Subpart D is subject to regulation as
            hazardous waste under 35 Ill. Adm. Code 703, 720 through
            726, and 728, rather than as used oil under this Part.

        B) Rebuttable presumption for used oil. Used oil containing
            more than 1,000 ppm total halogens is presumed to be a
            hazardous waste because it has been mixed with halogenated
            hazardous waste listed in 35 Ill. Adm. Code 721.Subpart D.
            Persons may rebut this presumption by demonstrating that the
            used oil does not contain hazardous waste (for example, by
            using an analytical method from SW-846, Edition III, to show
            that   the   used oil does not contain significant
            concentrations of halogenated hazardous constituents listed
            in 35 Ill. Adm. Code 721.Appendix H). U.S. EPA Publication
            SW-846, Third Edition, is available from the Government
            Printing Office, Superintendent of Documents. P.O. Box
            371954, Pittsburgh, PA 15250-7954, (202) 783-3238 (document
            number 955-001-00000-1).

            i)   The   rebuttable   presumption   does   not   apply to
                 metalworking oils or fluids containing chlorinated
                 paraffins, if they are processed, through a tolling
                 arrangement as described in Section 739.124(c), to
                 reclaim metalworking oils or fluids. The presumption

POLLUTION CONTROL BOARD

NOTICE OF PROPOSED AMENDMENTS

does apply to metalworking oils or fluids if such oils or fluids are recycled in any other manner, or disposed.

ii) The rebuttable presumption does not apply to used oils contaminated with chlorofluorocarbons (CFCs) removed from refrigeration units where the CFCs are destined for reclamation. The rebuttable presumption does apply to used oils contaminated with CFCs that have been mixed with used oil from sources other than refrigeration units.

2) Characteristic hazardous waste. A mixture of used oil and hazardous waste that exhibits a hazardous waste characteristic identified in 35 III. Adm. Code 721.Subpart C and a mixture of used oil and hazardous waste that is listed in Subpart D of this Part solely because it exhibits one or more of the characteristics of hazardous waste identified in 35 III. Adm. Code 721.Subpart C is subject to:

   A) Except as provided in subsection (b)(2)(C) of this Section, regulation as hazardous waste under 35 III. Adm. Code 703, 720 through 726, and 728 rather than as used oil under this Part, if the resultant mixture exhibits any characteristics of hazardous waste identified in 35 III. Adm. Code 721.Subpart C; or

   B) Except as provided in subsection (b)(2)(C) of this Section, regulation as used oil under this Part, if the resultant mixture does not exhibit any characteristics of hazardous waste identified under 35 III. Adm. Code 721.Subpart C.

   C) Regulation as used oil under this Part, if the mixture is of used oil and a waste which is hazardous solely because it exhibits the characteristic of ignitability (e.g., ignitable-only mineral spirits), provided that the resultant mixture does not exhibit the characteristic of ignitability under 35 III. Adm. Code 721.121.

3) Conditionally exempt small quantity generator hazardous waste. A mixture of used oil and conditionally exempt small quantity generator hazardous waste regulated under 35 III. Adm. Code 721.105 is subject to regulation as used oil under this Part.

c) Materials containing or otherwise contaminated with used oil.

1) Except as provided in subsection (c)(2) of this Section, a material containing or otherwise contaminated with used oil from which the used oil has been properly drained or removed to the extent possible such that no visible signs of free-flowing oil remain in or on the material:

   A) Is not used oil, and thus, it is not subject to this Part, and

   B) If applicable, is subject to the hazardous waste regulations of 35 III. Adm. Code 703, 705, 720 through 726, and 728.

2) A material containing or otherwise contaminated with used oil

---

POLLUTION CONTROL BOARD

NOTICE OF PROPOSED AMENDMENTS

that is burned for energy recovery is subject to regulation as used oil under this Part.

3) Used oil drained or removed from materials containing or otherwise contaminated with used oil is subject to regulation as used oil under this Part.

d) Mixtures of used oil with products.

1) Except as provided in subsection (d)(2) below, mixtures of used oil and fuels or other fuel products are subject to regulation as used oil under this Part.

2) Mixtures of used oil and diesel fuel mixed on-site by the generator of the used oil for use in the generator's own vehicles are not subject to this Part once the used oil and diesel fuel have been mixed. Prior to mixing, the used oil is subject to the requirements of Subpart C of this Part.

e) Materials derived from used oil.

1) Materials that are reclaimed from used oil that are used beneficially and are not burned for energy recovery or used in a manner constituting disposal (e.g., re-refined lubricants) are:

   A) Not used oil and thus are not subject to this Part, and

   B) Not solid wastes and are thus not subject to the hazardous waste regulations of Parts 35 III. Adm. Code 703, 720 through 726, and 728 as provided in 35 III. Adm. Code 721.103(c)(1)(A)(e)(1).

2) Materials produced from used oil that are burned for energy recovery (e.g., used oil fuels) are subject to regulation as used oil under this Part.

3) Except as provided in subsection (e)(4) below, materials derived from used oil that are disposed of or used in a manner constituting disposal are:

   A) Not used oil and thus are not subject to the hazardous waste regulations of 35 III. Adm. Code 703, 720 through 726, and 728 if the materials are listed or identified as hazardous waste.

   B) Are solid wastes and are thus subject to the hazardous waste regulations of 35 III. Adm. Code 703, 720 through 726, and 728 if the materials are listed or identified as hazardous waste.

4) Used oil re-refining distillation bottoms that are used as feedstock to manufacture asphalt products are not subject to this Part.

f) Wastewater. Wastewater, the discharge of which is subject to regulation under either Section 402 or Section 307(b) of the Clean Water Act (including wastewaters at facilities which have eliminated the discharge of wastewater), contaminated with de minimis quantities of used oil are not subject to the requirements of this Part. For purposes of this subsection, "de minimis" quantities of used oils are defined as small spills, leaks, or drippings from pumps, machinery, pipes, and other similar equipment during normal operations or small amounts of oil lost to the wastewater treatment system during washing or draining operations. This exception will not apply if the used oil is discarded as a result of abnormal manufacturing operations

POLLUTION CONTROL BOARD

NOTICE OF PROPOSED AMENDMENTS

resulting in substantial leaks, spills, or other releases, or to used oil recovered from wastewaters.

g) Used oil introduced into crude oil pipelines or a petroleum refining facility.

1) Used oil mixed with crude oil or natural gas liquids (e.g., in a production separator or crude oil stock tank) for insertion into a crude oil pipeline is exempt from the requirements of this Part. The used oil is subject to the requirements of this Part prior to the mixing of used oil with crude oil or natural gas liquids.

2) Mixtures of used oil and crude oil or natural gas liquids containing less than 1% used oil that are being stored or transported to a crude oil pipeline or petroleum refining facility for insertion into the refining process at a point prior to crude distillation or catalytic cracking are exempt from the requirements of this Part.

3) Used oil that is inserted into the petroleum refining process before crude distillation or catalytic cracking without prior mixing with crude oil is exempt from the requirements of this Part, provided that the used oil contains less than 1% of the crude oil feed to any petroleum refining facility process unit at any given time. Prior to insertion into the petroleum refining process, the used oil is subject to the requirements of this Part.

4) Except as provided in subsection (g)(5) below, used oil that is introduced into a petroleum refining process after crude distillation or catalytic cracking is exempt from the requirements of this Part only if the used oil meets the specification of Section 739.111. Prior to insertion into the petroleum refining facility process, the used oil is subject to the requirements of this Part.

5) Used oil that is incidentally captured by a hydrocarbon recovery system or wastewater treatment system as part of routine process operations at a petroleum refining facility and inserted into the petroleum refining facility process is exempt from the requirements of this Part. This exemption does not extend to used oil that is intentionally introduced into a hydrocarbon recovery system (e.g., by pouring collected used oil into the wastewater treatment system).

6) Tank bottoms from stock tanks containing exempt mixtures of used oil and crude oil or natural gas liquids are exempt from the requirements of this Part.

h) Used oil on vessels. Used oil produced on vessels from normal shipboard operations is not subject to this Part until it is transported ashore.

i) Used oil containing PCBs. In addition to the requirements of this Part, a marketer or burner of used oil that markets used oil containing any qualifiable level of PCBs is subject to the

POLLUTION CONTROL BOARD

NOTICE OF PROPOSED AMENDMENTS

requirements of 40 CFR 761.20(e).

(Source: Amended at 19 Ill. Reg. _____, effective _____)

POLLUTION CONTROL BOARD

NOTICE OF PROPOSED AMENDMENTS

1) Heading of the Part: Underground Injection Control Operating Requirements

2) Code Citation: 35 Ill. Adm. Code 730

3) Section numbers: Proposed action:
   730.104, 730.105, 730.110   Amended
   730.132, 730.133, 730.151   Amended

4) Statutory Authority: 415 ILCS 5/13, 22.4 and 27.

5) A complete description of the subjects and issues involved:

A more detailed description is contained in the Board's proposed opinion of March 2, 1995, in R95-4 and R95-6 (consolidated), which opinion is available from the address below. Sections 13(c) and 22.4(a) of the Environmental Protection Act [415 ILCS 5/13(c) & 22.4(a)] provides that Section 9-35 of the Administrative Procedure Act [5 ILCS 100/5-35] shall not apply. Because this rulemaking is not subject to Section 9-35 of the APA, it is not subject to first notice or to second notice review by JCAR.

This rulemaking updates Parts 700, 702, 703, 705, 720, 721, 722, 724, 725, 726, 728, 730, 738, and 739 of the Illinois RCRA Subtitle C hazardous waste and underground injection control (UIC) rules to correspond with amendments adopted by U.S. EPA that appeared in the Federal Register during the period July 1 through December 31, 1994. During this period, U.S. EPA amended its regulations as follows:

Federal Action	Summary
59 Fed. Reg. 38536, July 28, 1994.	Exclusion from the definition of solid waste for certain in-process recycled secondary materials used by the petroleum refining industry
59 Fed. Reg. 43496, August 24, 1994.	Withdrawal of exemption from Subtitle C regulation of slag residues from high temperature metals recovery (HTMR) of electric arc furnace dust (K061); steel finishing pickle liquor (K062); and electroplating sludges (F006) that are used in a manner constituting disposal
59 Fed. Reg. 47980, September 19, 1994.	Retraction of text from 40 CFR 268.7(a) inadvertently omitted in the amendments of August 31, 1993, at 58 Fed. Reg. 46040

POLLUTION CONTROL BOARD

NOTICE OF PROPOSED AMENDMENTS

59 Fed. Reg. 47982, September 19, 1994.	Phase II land disposal restrictions (LDRs) including underground injection control (UIC amendments)
59 Fed. Reg. 62896, December 6, 1994.	Organic material air emission standards for tanks, surface impoundments, and containers

In addition to these principal amendments that occurred during the update period, the Board has included an additional, later action:

60 Fed. Reg. 242, January 3, 1995.	Corrections to the Phase II land disposal restrictions (universal treatment standards)

This January 3 action was an amendment of the September 19, 1994 Phase II LDRs (universal waste rule). U.S. EPA corrected errors and clarified language in the universal treatment standards. The Board did not delay in adding these amendments for three reasons:

1) The January 3, 1995 amendments are corrections and clarifications of the September 19, 1994 regulations, and not new substantive amendments;

2) Prompt action on the January 3, 1995 amendments will facilitate implementation of the Phase II LDRs; and

3) The Board has received a request from the regulated community that we add the January 3, 1995 amendments to those of September 19, 1994. (See "Expedited Consideration," below.)

The Board also notes that the later amendments occurred within six months of the earliest amendments included in this docket, even if they occurred outside the nominal time-frame of the docket.

In addition to the federally-derived amendments, the Board used this opportunity to undertake a number of housekeeping and corrective amendments. We have effected the removal of all cross-references for effective dates and repealed Part 700. We have converted equations and formulae to the standard scientific format. We have tried to improve the language and structure of various provisions, including correcting grammar, punctuation, and spelling where necessary.

Specifically, the segment of the amendments involved in Part 730 involve correction and clarification of various provisions. The original intent was to open the Sections involved to remove reliance on references to 35 Ill. Adm. Code 700.106 for effective dates. The Board effected this by making the corrections and clarifications, so that the references to

POLLUTION CONTROL BOARD

NOTICE OF PROPOSED AMENDMENTS

Sections 700.106 would be removed from the Section source notes.

6) Will this proposed rule replace an emergency rule currently in effect? No

7) Does this rulemaking contain an automatic repeal date? No

8) Do these proposed amendments contain incorporations by reference? No

9) Are there any other amendments pending on this Part? No

10) Statement of statewide policy objectives:

This rulemaking is mandated by Sections 13(c) and 22.4(a) of the
Environmental Protection Act [415 ILCS 5/13(c) & 22.4(a)]. The statewide
policy objectives are set forth in Section 20 of that Act. This
rulemaking imposes mandates on units of local government only to the
extent that they may be involved in the generation, transportation,
treatment, storage, or disposal of hazardous waste or they engage in
underground injection of waste.

11) Time, place and manner in which interested persons may comment on this
proposed rulemaking:

The Board will accept written public comment on this proposal for a period
of 45 days after the date of this publication. Comments should reference
Docket R95-4/R95-6 and be addressed to:

Ms. Dorothy M. Gunn, Clerk
Illinois Pollution Control Board
State of Illinois Center, Suite 11-500
100 W. Randolph St.
Chicago, IL 60601
Telephone: 312/814-6931

Address all questions to Michael J. McCambridge, at 312/814-6924.

12) Initial regulatory flexibility analysis:

A) Date rule was submitted to the Small Business Office of the
Department of Commerce and Community Affairs: March 6, 1995.

B) Types of small businesses affected:

The existing rules and proposed amendments affect small businesses
that generate, transport, treat, store, or dispose of hazardous waste
or engage in underground injection of waste.

C) Reporting, bookkeeping or other procedures required for compliance:

POLLUTION CONTROL BOARD

NOTICE OF PROPOSED AMENDMENTS

The existing rules and proposed amendments require extensive
reporting, bookkeeping, and other procedures, including the
preparation of manifests and annual reports, waste analyses, and
maintenance of operating records.

D) Types of professional skills necessary for compliance:

Compliance with the existing rules and proposed amendments may
require the services of an attorney, certified public accountant,
chemist, and registered professional engineer.

The full text of the proposed amendments begins on the next page:

POLLUTION CONTROL BOARD

NOTICE OF PROPOSED AMENDMENTS

TITLE 35: ENVIRONMENTAL PROTECTION
SUBTITLE G: WASTE DISPOSAL
CHAPTER I: POLLUTION CONTROL BOARD
SUBCHAPTER d: UNDERGROUND INJECTION CONTROL AND
UNDERGROUND STORAGE TANK PROGRAMS

PART 730
UNDERGROUND INJECTION CONTROL OPERATING REQUIREMENTS

SUBPART A: GENERAL

POLLUTION CONTROL BOARD

NOTICE OF PROPOSED AMENDMENTS

SUBPART F: CRITERIA AND STANDARDS APPLICABLE
TO CLASS V INJECTION WELLS

AUTHORITY: Implementing Sections 13 and 22.4 and authorized by Section 27 of the Environmental Protection Act [415 ILCS 5/13, 22.4, and 27].

SOURCE: Adopted in R81-32, 47 PCB 93, at 6 Ill. Reg. 12479, effective March 3, 1984; amended in R82-19, 53PCB131, at 7 Ill. Reg. 14426, effective March 3, 1984; recodified at 10 Ill. Reg. 14174; amended at R89-2 at 14 Ill. Reg. 3130, effective February 20, 1990; amended in R89-11 at 14 Ill. Reg. 11959, effective July 9, 1990; amended in R93-6 at 17 Ill. Reg. 15646, effective September 14, 1993; amended in R94-5 at 18 Ill. Reg. 18391, effective December 20, 1994; amended in R95-6 at 19 Ill. Reg. _____, effective _____.

SUBPART A: GENERAL

Section 730.104 Criteria for Exempted Aquifers

An aquifer or a portion thereof which that meets the criteria for an "underground source of drinking water" in Section 730.103 may be determined by the Board under 35 Ill. Adm. Code 704.103, 704.123, and 702.105 to be an "exempted aquifer" if it meets the following criteria:

a) It does not currently serve as a source of drinking water; and

b) It cannot now and will not in the future serve as a source of drinking water because:

  I) It is mineral, hydrocarbon, or geothermal energy producing, or

POLLUTION CONTROL BOARD

NOTICE OF PROPOSED AMENDMENTS

ean--be--demenstrated--by--a permit applicant can demonstrate, as part of a permit application for a Class II or III operation injection well, that the aquifer to eentain contains minerals or hydrocarbons that eensidering--their--quantity--and--leeatien are expected to be commercially producible considering their quantity and location;

2) It is situated at a depth or location which that makes recovery of water for drinking water purposes economically or technologically impractical;

3) It is so contaminated that it would be economically or technologically impractical to render that water fit for human consumption; or

4) It is located over a Class III well mining area subject to subsidence or catastrophic collapse; or

c) The total dissolved solids content of the ground-water is more than 3,000 and less than 10,000 mg/l and the aquifer is not reasonably expected to supply a public water system.

(Source: Amended at 19 Ill. Reg. _____, effective _____)

Section 730.105 Classification of Injection Wells

Injection wells are classified as follows:

a) Class I.

1) Wells used by generators of hazardous wastes or owners or operators of hazardous waste management facilities to inject hazardous waste beneath the lowermost formation containing--within--402--meters--(1/4--mile)-of-the-well-bore; an underground source of drinking water within 402 meters (1/4 mile) of the well bore.

2) Other industrial and municipal disposal wells whieh that inject fluids beneath the lowermost formation containing--within-402 meters-(1/4-mile)-of-the-well--bore; an underground source of drinking water within 402 meters (1/4 mile) of the well bore.

b) Class II. Wells whieh that inject fluids:

1) Whieh That are brought to the surface in connection with conventional oil or natural gas production and which may be commingled with wastewaters from gas plants whieh that are an integral part of production operations, unless those waters are classified as a hazardous waste at the time of injection;

2) For enhanced recovery of oil or natural gas; and

3) For storage of hydrocarbons whieh that are liquid at standard temperature and pressure.

c) Class III. Wells whieh that inject for extraction of minerals, including:

1) Mining of sulfur by the Frasch process;

2) In situ production of uranium or other metals. This category

---

POLLUTION CONTROL BOARD

NOTICE OF PROPOSED AMENDMENTS

includes only in situ production from ore bodies whieh that have not been conventionally mined. Solution mining of conventional mines, such as stopes leaching, is included in Class Vv;

3) Solution mining of salts or potash.

(Beard--NeteBOARD NOTE: Class III wells include the recovery of geothermal energy to produce electric power but do not include wells used in heating or aquaculture whieh that fall under Class V.)

d) Class IV.

1) Wells used by generators of hazardous waste or of radioactive waste, by owners or operators of hazardous waste management facilities, or by owners or operators of radioactive waste disposal sites to dispose of hazardous waste or radioactive waste into a formation whieh that within-402-meters-(1/4-mile)-of-the well contains an underground source of drinking water within 402 meters (1/4 mile) of the well.

2) Wells used by generators of hazardous waste or of radioactive waste, by owners or operators of hazardous waste management facilities, or by owners or operators of radioactive waste disposal sites to dispose of hazardous waste or radioactive waste above a formation whieh that within-402-meters-(1/4-mile)-of--the well contains an underground source of drinking water within 402 meters (1/4 mile) of the well.

3) Wells used by generators of hazardous waste or owners or operators of hazardous waste management facilities to dispose of hazardous waste;--whieh that cannot be classified under 35-Ill; Adm.-Code-730.105 subsection (a)(1), er--730.105(d)(1), and or (d)(2) above (e.g., wells used to dispose of hazardous wastes into or above a formation whieh that contains an aquifer whieh that has been exempted pursuant to 35-Ill;-Adm;-Code Section 730.104).

e) Class V. Injection wells not included in Class I, Class II, Class III, or Class IV. Class V wells include:

1) Air conditioning return flow wells used to return the water used in a heat pump for heating or cooling to the supply aquifer the water-used-for-heating-or-cooling-in-a-heat-pump;

2) Cesspools, including multiple dwelling, community, or regional cesspools, or other devices that receive wastes;-whieh that have an open bottom and sometimes have perforated sides. The UIC requirements do not apply to single family residential cesspools or to non-residential cesspools whieh that receive solely sanitary wastes and have the capacity to serve fewer than 20 persons a day;

3) Cooling water return flow wells used to inject water previously used for cooling;

4) Drainage wells used to drain surface fluid; primarily storm runoff, into a subsurface formation;

5) Dry wells used for the injection of wastes into a subsurface

POLLUImON CONTROL BOARD

NOTICE OF PROPOSED AMENDMENTS

formation;
6) Recharge wells used to replenish the water in an aquifer;
7) Salt water intrusion barrier wells used to inject water into a fresh water aquifer to prevent the intrusion of salt water into the fresh water;
8) Sand backfill and other backfill wells used to inject a mixture of water and sand, mill tailings, or other solids into mined out portions of subsurface mines whether what is injected is a radioactive waste or not;
9) Septic system wells used to inject the waste or effluent from a multiple dwelling, business establishment, community, or regional business establishment septic tank. The UIC requirements do not apply to single family residential septic system wells, or to non-residential septic system wells which that are used solely for the disposal of sanitary waste and which have the capacity to serve fewer than 20 persons a day;;
10) Subsidence control wells (not used for the purpose of oil or natural gas production) used to inject fluids into a non-oil or gas producing zone to reduce or eliminate subsidence associated with the overdraft of fresh water;
11) Radioactive waste disposal wells other than Class IV wells;
12) Injection wells associated with the recovery of geothermal energy for heating, aquaculture or production of electric power;
13) Wells used for solution mining of conventional mines such as stopes leaching;
14) Wells used to inject spent brine into the same formation from which it was withdrawn after extraction of halogens or their salts; and
15) Injection wells used in experimental technologies.

(Source: Amended at 19 Ill. Reg. _____, effective _____)

Section 730.110 Plugging and Abandoning Class I and Class III Wells

a) Prior to abandoning a Class I or Class III well, the well shall be plugged with cement in a manner which that will not allow the movement of fluids either into or between underground sources of drinking water. The Agency may allow Class III wells to use other plugging materials if it is satisfied that such materials will prevent movement of fluids into or between underground sources of drinking water.
b) Placement of the cement plugs shall be accomplished by one of the following:
   1) The Balance Method;
   2) The Dump Bailer Method;—or
   3) The Two-Plug Method; or
   4) An alternative method approved by the Agency in the permit—which that will reliably provide a comparable level of protection to

POLLUTION CONTROL BOARD

NOTICE OF PROPOSED AMENDMENTS

underground sources of drinking water.
c) The well to be abandoned shall must be in a state of static equilibrium with the mud weight equalized top to bottom, either by circulating the mud in the well at least once or by a comparable method prescribed by the Agency, prior to the placement of the cement plug.
d) The plugging and abandonment required in 35 Ill. Adm. Code 704.188 and 704.187 shall must also demonstrate adequate protection of USDWs in the case of a Class III project well which that underlies or is in an aquifer which that has been exempted under Section 730.104,—also demonstrate—adequate—protection—of—USDWs. The Agency shall prescribe aquifer cleanup and monitoring where it deems it necessary and feasible to insure adequate protection of USDWs.

(Source: Amended at 19 Ill. Reg. _____, effective _____)

SUBPART D: CRITERIA AND STANDARDS APPLICABLE TO CLASS III WELLS

Section 730.132 Construction Requirements

a) All new Class III wells shall must be cased and cemented to prevent the migration of fluids into or between underground sources of drinking water. The Agency may waive the cementing requirements for new wells in existing projects or portions of existing projects where it has substantial evidence that no contamination of underground sources of drinking water would result. The casing and cement used in the construction of each newly drilled well shall must be designed for the life expectancy of the well. In determining and specifying casing and cementing requirements, the following factors shall must be considered:
   1) Depth to the injection zone;
   2) Injection pressure, external pressure, internal pressure, axial loading, etc.;
   3) Hole size;
   4) Size and grade of all casing strings (wall thickness, diameter, nominal weight, length, joint specification, and construction material);
   5) Corrosiveness of injected fluids and formation fluids;
   6) Lithology of injection and confining zones; and
   7) Type and grade of cement.
b) Appropriate logs and other tests shall must be conducted during the drilling and construction of new Class III wells. A descriptive report interpreting the results of such logs and tests shall must be prepared by a knowledgeable log analyst and submitted to the Agency. The logs and tests appropriate to each type of Class III well shall must be determined based on the intended function, depth, construction, and other characteristics of the well; availability of

POLLUTION CONTROL BOARD

NOTICE OF PROPOSED AMENDMENTS

similar data in the area of the drilling site, and the need for additional information that may arise from time to time as the construction of the well progresses. Deviation checks shall must be conducted on all holes where pilot holes and reaming are used, unless the hole will be cased and cemented by circulating cement to the surface. Where deviation checks are necessary they shall must be conducted at sufficiently frequent intervals to assure that vertical avenues for fluid migration in the form of diverging holes are not created during drilling.

c) Where the injection zone is a formation which that is naturally water-bearing, the following information concerning the injection zone shall must be determined or calculated for new Class III wells or projects:
   1) Fluid pressure;
   2) Fracture pressure; and
   3) Physical and chemical characteristics of the formation fluids.

d) Where the injection formation is not a water-bearing formation, the information in paragraph subsection (c)(2) above must be submitted.

e) Where injection is into a formation which that contains water with less than 10,000 mg/l TDS, monitoring wells shall be completed into the injection zone and into any underground sources of drinking water above the injection zone which that could be affected by the mining operation. These wells shall be located in such a fashion as to detect any excursion of injection fluids, process by-products, or formation fluids outside the mining area or zone. If the operation may be affected by subsidence or catastrophic collapse, the monitoring wells shall be located so that they will not be physically affected.

f) Where injection is into a formation which that does not contain water with less than 10,000 mg/l TDS, no monitoring wells are necessary in the injection stratum.

g) Where the injection wells penetrate an USDW in an area subject to subsidence or catastrophic collapse, an adequate number of monitoring wells shall must be completed into the USDW to detect any movement of injected fluids, process by-products, or formation fluids into the USDW. The monitoring wells shall must be located outside the physical influence of the subsidence or catastrophic collapse.

h) In determining the number, location, construction and frequency of monitoring of the monitoring wells the following criteria shall must be considered:
   1) The population relying on the USDW affected or potentially affected by the injection operation;
   2) The proximity of the injection operation to points of withdrawal of drinking water;
   3) The local geology and hydrology;
   4) The operating pressures and whether a negative pressure gradient is being maintained;
   5) The nature and volume of the injected fluid, the formation water, and the process by-products; and

POLLUTION CONTROL BOARD

NOTICE OF PROPOSED AMENDMENTS

   6) The injection well density.

(Source: Amended at 19 Ill. Reg. _____, effective _____)

Section 730.133 Operating, Monitoring, and Reporting Requirements

a) Operating Requirements. Operating requirements prescribed shall must, at a minimum, specify that:
   1) Except during well stimulation, injection pressure at the wellhead shall must be calculated so as to assure that the pressure in the injection zone during injection does not initiate new fractures or propagate existing fractures in the injection zone. In no case shall injection pressure initiate fractures in the confining zone or cause the migration of injection or formation fluids into an underground source of drinking water.
   2) Injection between the outermost casing protecting underground sources of drinking water and the well bore is prohibited.

b) Monitoring Requirements. Monitoring requirements shall, at a minimum, specify:
   1) Monitoring of the nature of injected fluids with sufficient frequency to yield representative data on its characteristics. Whenever the injection fluid is modified to the extent that the analysis required by Section 730.134 (a)(7)(C) is incorrect or incomplete, the owner or operator shall provide the Agency with a new analysis as required by Section 730.134 (a)(7)(C);
   2) Monitoring of injection pressure and either flow rate or volume semimonthly, or metering and daily recording of injected and produced fluid volumes, as appropriate;
   3) Demonstration of mechanical integrity pursuant to Section 730.108 at least once every five years during the life of the well for salt solution mining;
   4) Monitoring of the fluid level in the injection zone semi-monthly, where appropriate, and monitoring of the parameters chosen to measure water quality in the monitoring wells required by Section 730.132(e) semi-monthly; and
   5) Quarterly monitoring of wells required by Section 730.133(g).
   6) All Class III wells may be monitored on a field or project basis, rather than on an individual well basis, by manifold monitoring. Manifold monitoring may be used in cases of facilities consisting of more than one injection well, operating with a common manifold. Separate monitoring systems for each well are not required provided the owner or operator demonstrates that manifold monitoring is comparable to individual well monitoring.

c) Reporting Requirements. Reporting requirements shall, at a minimum, include:
   1) Quarterly reporting to the Agency on required monitoring;
   2) Results of mechanical integrity and any other periodic test

POLLUTION CONTROL BOARD

NOTICE OF PROPOSED AMENDMENTS

required by the Agency reported with the first regular quarterly report after the completion of the test; and

3) Monitoring may be reported on a project or field basis rather than individual well basis where manifold monitoring is used.

(Source: Amended at 19 Ill. Reg. _____, effective _____)

SUBPART F: CRITERIA AND STANDARDS APPLICABLE
TO CLASS V INJECTION WELLS

Section 730.151 Applicability

This Subpart sets forth criteria and standards for underground injection control programs to regulate all injection not regulated in 730.Subparts B, D, and E. Class II wells, however, are not regulated by this Subpart.

a) Generally, wells covered by this Subpart inject non-hazardous fluids into or above formations that contain underground sources of drinking water. It includes all wells listed in Section 730.105(e) but is not limited to those types of injection wells.

b) It also includes wells not covered in Class IV that inject radioactive materials listed in 10 CFR 20, Appendix B, Table II, Column 2.

(Source: Amended at 19 Ill. Reg. _____, effective _____)

DEPARTMENT OF PUBLIC AID

NOTICE OF PROPOSED AMENDMENTS

1) Heading of the Part: Hospital Reimbursement Changes

2) Code Citation: 89 Ill. Adm. Code 152

3)
Section Numbers:	Proposed Action:
152.100	Repeal
152.150	Amendment
152.200	Amendment
152.250	Amendment

4) Statutory Authority: Section 12-13 of the Illinois Public Aid Code (Ill. Rev. Stat. 1991, ch. 23, par. 12-13) [305 ILCS 5/12-13]

5) Complete Description of the Subjects and Issues Involved: The Department of Public Aid is proposing changes to 89 Ill. Adm. Code 152 to maintain rates of reimbursement for hospital services at the levels which have been effective since January 18, 1994. The maintenance of rates will continue through fiscal year 1996, and will affect rates calculated according to methodologies located in 89 Ill. Adm. Code 149, Diagnosis Related Grouping (DRG) Prospective Payment System (PPS), and 89 Ill. Adm. Code 148, Hospital Services. These cost containment measures are necessary to permit the Department to continue to purchase hospital services in a prudent and cost effective manner, and to prevent excessive and unnecessary expenditures, while maintaining adequate reimbursement levels.

Section 152.250 provides an appeal mechanism for any hospital that believes it is facing significant financial hardships by continuing to provide services according to this rate maintenance. Under these proposed amendments, the availability of this appeal process is also being extended through fiscal year 1996.

Section 152.100, which is being proposed for repeal, provides for the application of an adjustment factor to certain add-on payments for hospitals. Because of Public Act 88-554, the add-on payments must be eliminated at the end of fiscal year 1995 and the adjustment factors will no longer be applicable.

The proposed amendments to Sections 152.150, 152.200, and 152.250 are not expected to result in any budgetary changes. It is anticipated that the repeal of Section 152.100 will result in a reduction in Department expenditures of approximately $190.7 million for fiscal year 1996.

6) Will these proposed amendments replace emergency amendments currently in effect? No

7) Does this rulemaking contain an automatic repeal date? Yes. Sections 152.150(e), 152.200(c) and 152.250(g) contain an automatic repeal date of June 30, 1996.

DEPARTMENT OF PUBLIC AID

NOTICE OF PROPOSED AMENDMENTS

8) Do these proposed amendments contain incorporations by reference? No

9) Are there any other proposed amendments pending on this Part? No

10) Statement of Statewide Policy Objectives: These proposed amendments do not affect units of local government.

11) Time, Place, and Manner in which Interested Persons may comment on this proposed rulemaking: Any interested parties may submit comments, data, views, or arguments concerning this proposed rulemaking. All comments must be in writing and should be addressed to Joanne Jones, Bureau of Rules and Regulations, Illinois Department of Public Aid, 100 South Grand Ave. E., 3rd Floor, Springfield, Illinois 62762 (Phone: (217) 524-3215). The Department requests the submission of written comments within 30 days after the publication of this notice. The Department will consider all written comments it receives during the first notice period as required by Section 5-40 of the Illinois Administrative Procedure Act [5 ILCS 100/5-40].

These proposed amendments may have an impact on small businesses, small municipalities, and not for profit corporations as defined in Sections 1-75, 1-80 and 1-85 of the Illinois Administrative Procedure Act [5 ILCS 100/1-75, 1-80, 1-85]. These entities may submit comments in writing to the Department at the above address in accordance with the regulatory flexibility provisions in Section 5-30 of the Illinois Administrative Procedure Act [5 ILCS 100/5-30]. These entities shall indicate their status as small businesses, small municipalities, or not for profit corporations as part of any written comments they submit to the Department.

12) Initial Regulatory Flexibility Analysis:

A) Types of small businesses, small municipalities and not for profit corporations affected: Hospitals

B) Reporting, bookkeeping or other procedures required for compliance: None

C) Types of professional skills necessary for compliance: None

13) State reasons for this rulemaking if it was not included in either of the two most recent regulatory agendas: The reasons for this rulemaking are fully described above in the complete description of the subjects and issues involved. This rulemaking was not anticipated by the Department when the two most recent regulatory agendas were published.

The full text of the Proposed Amendments begins on the next page:

DEPARTMENT OF PUBLIC AID

NOTICE OF PROPOSED AMENDMENTS

TITLE 89: SOCIAL SERVICES
CHAPTER I: DEPARTMENT OF PUBLIC AID
SUBCHAPTER e: GENERAL TIME-LIMITED CHANGES

PART 152
HOSPITAL REIMBURSEMENT CHANGES

Section
152.100 Reimbursement Add-on Adjustments (Repealed)
152.150 Diagnosis Related Grouping (DRG) Prospective System (PPS)
152.200 Non-DRG Reimbursement Methodologies
152.250 Appeals

AUTHORITY: Implementing and authorized by Articles III, IV, VI and Section 12-13 of the Illinois Public Aid Code (Ill. Rev. Stat. 1991, ch. 23, pars. 3-1 et seq., 4-1 et seq., 5-1 et seq., 6-1 et seq., and 12-13) (305 ILCS 5/Arts. III, IV, V and VI and 12-13) and implementing Article III of the Illinois Health Finance Reform Act (Ill. Rev. Stat. 1991, ch. 111 1/2, par. 6503-1 et seq.) [20 ILCS 2215/Art. III].

SOURCE: Emergency rules adopted at 18 Ill. Reg. 2150, effective January 18, 1994, for maximum of 150 days; adopted at 18 Ill. Reg. 10141, effective June 17, 1994; amended at 19 Ill. Reg. _____, effective _____.

Section 152.100 Reimbursement Add-on Adjustments (Repealed)

a) Notwithstanding any provisions set forth in 89 Ill. Adm. Code 148, the changes in rule described in this Section will be effective January 18, 1994.

b) Outpatient indigent volume adjustments, as described in 89 Ill. Adm. Code 148.140(b)(3)(A) and (b)(3)(B), as calculated for rate year 1994, shall remain in effect through fiscal year 1995. Hospitals not qualifying in rate year 1994 (October 1, 1993, through September 30, 1994), must submit the data described in 89 Ill. Adm. Code 148.150 in order to qualify in rate year 1995 (October 1, 1994, through September 30, 1995).

c) Uncompensated care payment adjustments, as described in 89 Ill. Adm. Code 148.150(h), for the period of October 1, 1994, through June 30, 1995, shall be adjusted by a factor that will equalize aggregate payments made under 89 Ill. Adm. Code 148.150(h) during the period of July 1, 1994, through June 30, 1995, to the payments made under 89 Ill. Adm. Code 148.150(g) and (h) during the period of July 1, 1993, through June 30, 1994. The factor shall be a fraction, the numerator of which is the aggregate uncompensated care payments for the period of July 1, 1993, through June 30, 1994, and the denominator of which is the aggregate uncompensated care payments for the period of July 1, 1994, through June 30, 1995.

DEPARTMENT OF PUBLIC AID

NOTICE OF PROPOSED AMENDMENTS

d) Trauma--center--adjustments,--as--described--in--89--Ill.--Adm.---Code
148.290(c)(1),--(c)(2),--and-(c)(3),-for-the-period-of-October-1,-1994,
through-June-30,-1995,--shall--be--adjusted--by--a--factor--that--will
equalize---aggregate---payments--made--under--89--Ill.--Adm.--Code
148.290(c)(1),--(c)(2),--and-(c)(3),-during-the-period-of-July-1,-1994,
through--June--30,--1995,-to-the-payments-made-under-89-Ill.-Adm.-Code
148.290(c)(1),--(c)(2),--and-(c)(3),--during-the-period-of-July--1,--1993,
through-June-30,-1994.---The-factor-shall-be-a-fraction,-the-numerator
of-which-is-the-aggregate-trauma-center-adjustments-for-the-period--of
July--1,--1993,-through-June-30,-1994,-and-the-denominator-of-which-is
the-aggregate-trauma-center-adjustments-for--the--period--of--July--1,
1994,-through-June-30,-1995.

e) Rehabilitation-hospital-adjustments,-as-described-in-89-Ill.-Adm.-Code
148.290(d)(1),--for--the--period-of-October-1,-1994,-through-June-30,
1995,-shall-be-adjusted-by--a--factor--that--will--equalize--aggregate
payments--made--under-89-Ill.-Adm.-Code-148.290(d)(1)-during-the-period
of-July-1,-1994,-through-June-30,-1995,-to-the-payments-made-under--89
Ill.--Adm.--Code-148.290(d)(1)--during--the--period--of-July-1,-1993,
through-June-30,-1994.--The-factor-shall-be-a-fraction,-the--numerator
of--which-is-the-aggregate-rehabilitation-hospital-adjustments-for-the
period-of-July-1,-1993,-through-June-30,-1994,-and-the-denominator--of
which--is--the--aggregate--rehabilitation-hospital-adjustments-for-the
period-of-July-1,-1994,-through-June-30,-1995.

f) Perinatal-center-adjustments,--as--described--in--89--Ill.--Adm.--Code
148.290(e)(1),--for--the--period--of-October-1,-1994,-through-June-30,
1995,-shall-be-adjusted-by--a--factor--that--will--equalize--aggregate
payments--made--under-89-Ill.-Adm.-Code-148.290(e)(1)-during-the-period
of-July-1,-1994,-through-June-30,-1995,-to-the-payments-made-under--89
Ill.--Adm.--Code-148.290(e)(1)--during--the--period--of-July-1,-1993,
through-June-30,-1994.-The-factor-shall-be-a-fraction,-the--numerator
of--which-is-the-aggregate-perinatal-center-adjustments-for-the-period
of-July-1,-1993,-through-June-30,-1994,-and-the-denominator--of--which
is-the--aggregate-perinatal-center-adjustments-for-the-period-of-July
1,-1994,-through-June-30,-1995.

g) Obstetrical-care-adjustments,--as--described--in--89--Ill.--Adm.--Code
148.290(f)(1),--for--the--period--of-October-1,-1994,-through-June-30,
1995,-shall-be-adjusted-by--a--factor--that--will--equalize--aggregate
payments--made--under-89-Ill.-Adm.-Code-148.290(f)(1)-during-the-period
of-July-1,-1994,-through-June-30,-1995,-to-the-payments-made-under--89
Ill.--Adm.--Code-148.290(f)(1)--during--the--period--of-July-1,-1993,
through-June-30,-1994.-The-factor-shall-be-a-fraction,--the--numerator
of--which-is-the-aggregate-obstetrical-care-adjustments-for-the-period
of-July-1,-1993,-through-June-30,-1994,-and-the-denominator--of--which
is--the--aggregate-obstetrical-care-adjustments-for-the-period-of-July
1,-1994,-through-June-30,-1995.

h) Targeted-access-payment-adjustments,-as-described-in-89-Ill.-Adm.-Code
148.290(g)(1),--(g)(2),--(g)(3),--(g)(4),--(g)(5)-and-(g)(6),-for--the--period--of
October--1,-1994,-through-June-30,-1995,-shall-be-adjusted-by-a-factor

DEPARTMENT OF PUBLIC AID

NOTICE OF PROPOSED AMENDMENTS

that-will-equalize-aggregate-payments-made-under--89--Ill.,--Adm.,--Code
148.290(g)(1),--(g)(2),--(g)(3),-(g)(4),-(g)(5)-and-(g)(6)-during-the-period-of
July-1,-1994,-through-June-30,-1995,-to-the--payments--made--under--89
Ill.-Adm.-Code-148.290(g)(1),--(g)(2),--(g)(3),-(g)(4),-(g)(5)-and-(g)(6)-during
the--period--of-July-1,-1993,-through-June-30,-1994.--The-factor-shall
be-a-fraction,-the-numerator-of-which-is-the-aggregate-targeted-access
payment-adjustments-for-the-period-of-July-1-1993,--through--June--30,
1994,--and--the--denominator-of-which-is-the-aggregate-targeted-access
payment-adjustments-for-the-period-of-July-1,-1994,--through--June--30,
1995.

i) Targeted--access--payment--adjustments,-as-calculated-under-subsection
(h)-above,-for-the-period-of-October-1,-1994,-through-June--30,--1995,
shall--be--further--adjusted--by-a-factor-which-will-inversely-adjust
targeted-access-spending-in-an-amount-equal-to-the-updates--calculated
under--89-Ill.-Adm.-Code-148.290(h)(2)(C).---The
factor-shall-be-a-fraction,-the-numerator-of-which-is-the-amount-equal
to-the-updates-calculated-under-89-Ill.-Adm.-Code-148.290(h)(2)(C)-and
148.290(h)(2)(D)--and-the-denominator-of-which-is-the-aggregate-target
access-payment-adjustments-made-under-89--Ill.,--Adm.,--Code--152.150(h)
above-during-the-period-of-July-1,-1994,-through-June-30,-1995.

j) Medicaid--high--volume--adjustments,-as-described-in-89-Ill.-Adm.-Code
148.290(h)(2)(D),-for-the-period-of-October-1,-1994,-through-June--30,
1995,--shall--be--adjusted--by--a--factor-that-will-equalize-aggregate
payments-made-under-89-Ill.--Adm.--Code--148.290(h)(2)(D)--during--the
period--of--July-1,-1994,-through-June-30,-1995,-to-the-payments-made
under-89-Ill.-Adm.-Code-148.290(h)(2)(D)--during-the-period-of-July--1,
1993,--through--June--30,--1994.----The-factor-shall-be-a-fraction,-the
numerator-of-which-is-the-appropriate-Medicaid-high-volume-adjustments
for-the-period-of-July-1,-1993,--through--June--30,---and--the
denominator-of-which-is-the-aggregate-Medicaid-high-volume-adjustments
for-the-period-of-July-1,-1994,-through-June-30,-1995.

k) This-Section-shall-be-automatically-repealed-effective-June-30,-1995.

(Source: Repealed at 19 III. Reg. _____, effective
_____)

Section 152.150 Diagnosis Related Grouping (DRG) Prospective Payment System
(PPS)

a) Notwithstanding any provisions set forth in 89 Ill. Adm. Code 149, the
changes in rule described in this Section will be effective January
18, 1994.

b) For the rate periods, as described in 89 Ill. Adm. Code
148.25(g)(2)(B), the DRG weighting factors shall be adjusted by a
factor, the numerator of which is the statewide weighted average DRG
base payment rate in effect for the base period, as described in 89
III. Adm. Code 148.25(g)(2)(A), and the denominator of which is the
statewide weighted average DRG base payment rate for the rate period.

DEPARTMENT OF PUBLIC AID

NOTICE OF PROPOSED AMENDMENTS

as described in 89 Ill. Adm. Code 148.25(g)(2)(B). For this adjustment, DRG base payment rate means the product of the PPS base rate, as described in 89 Ill. Adm. Code 149.100(c)(3), and the indirect medical education factor, as described in 89 Ill. Adm. Code 149.150(c)(3).

c) All payments calculated under 89 Ill. Adm. Code 149.140 and 149.150(c)(1), (c)(2) and (c)(4), in effect on January 18, 1994, shall remain in effect until June 30, 1995.

d) For hospital inpatient services rendered on or after July 1, 1995, and prior to July 1, 1996, the Department shall reimburse hospitals using the relative weighting factors and the base payment rates calculated pursuant to the methodology described in this Section, that were in effect on June 30, 1995, less the portion of such rates attributed by the Department to the cost of medical education.

e) This Section shall be automatically repealed effective June 30, 1996 June 30, 1995.

(Source: Amended at 19 Ill. Reg. _____, effective _____)

Section 152.200 Non-DRG Reimbursement Methodologies

a) Notwithstanding any provisions set forth in 89 Ill. Adm. Code 148, the changes in rule described in this Section will be effective January 18, 1994.

b) All per diem payments calculated under 89 Ill. Adm. Code 148, except for those described in 89 Ill. Adm. Code 148.120, 148.160, 148.170, 148.175(d) and 148.290(d) 148.290(b)(1)(A) through (b)(1)(C), in effect on January 18, 1994, shall remain in effect until June 30, 1996 June 30, 1995.

c) This Section shall be automatically repealed effective June 30, 1996 June 30, 1995.

(Source: Amended at 19 Ill. Reg. _____, effective _____)

Section 152.250 Appeals

a) Right to appeal. Any hospital seeking to appeal its prospective payment rate for operating costs related to inpatient care or other allowable costs must submit a written request to the Department within 30 days after the date of the letter notifying the hospital of its prospective rate. The written request must contain the information as specified in subsection (c) below. The Department shall respond to the hospital's request for additional reimbursement within 30 days or after receipt of any additional documentation requested by the Department, whichever is later. The hospital shall bear the burden of proof throughout the appeal process.

DEPARTMENT OF PUBLIC AID

NOTICE OF PROPOSED AMENDMENTS

b) Non-appealable issue. The October 1, 1993, rates and reimbursement systems used to calculate the rates are not appealable.

c) Appeal documentation.

1) The hospital must submit an explanation of the circumstances creating the need for the appeal, including a detail of the hospital services that will be significantly curtailed if the hospital is not granted financial relief. The explanation must included a statement of attestation signed by the hospital's chief executive officer, chief financial officer, treasurer or its properly authorized agent. The signature verifies by written declaration, and under penalties of perjury, that the signing officer has personally examined the documentation and that the information is true, correct, and complete.

2) The hospital must file a cash position statement which is based upon current assets (including all unrestricted investments), current liabilities and other data for a date which is less than 60 days old. Any liabilities payable to owners or related parties must not be reported as current liabilities on the cash position statement.

3) The hospital must submit a copy of its last two financial statements audited by an external, independent certified public accountant. If the hospital is part of a group of entities which are related by common ownership or control or both, a consolidated financial statement audited by an external, independent certified public account is also required. If consolidated financial statements are not available, then the individual audited financial statements from each of the related entities may be submitted seperately. The Department will merge the information.

d) Appeal Process. In no event shall financial relief be awarded, unless the hospital demonstrates to the satisfaction of the Director that the Medicaid rate it receives under the Medicaid prospective payment system is insufficient to ensure Medicaid recipients reasonable access to sufficient inpatient hospital services of adequate quality. In making such demonstration the hospital must meet all of the following criteria:

1) The current Medicaid prospective payment rate jeopardizes the long-term financial viability of the hospital. In appropriate cases, financial jeopardy may be shown to exist if, by providing care to Medicaid recipients at the current Medicaid rate, the hospital can demonstrate that it is, in the aggregate, incurring a marginal loss. In appropriate cases, financial jeopardy may be shown to exist if the hospital is incurring a marginal gain but can demonstrate that it has unique and compelling Medicaid costs, which if unreimbursed by Medicaid, would clearly jeopardize the hospital's long-term financial viability.

2) The population served by the hospital seeking financial relief has no reasonable access to other inpatient hospitals.

DEPARTMENT OF PUBLIC AID

NOTICE OF PROPOSED AMENDMENTS

Reasonable access exists if most individuals served by the hospital seeking financial relief can receive inpatient hospital care within a 30 minute travel time at total cost which is less to the Department that the cost which would be incurred at the hospital seeking financial relief.

3) The ratio of current assets to current liabilities reflected on the cash position statement described in subsection (c)(2) above is less than 1.0.

4) The financial statements described in subsection (c)(3) above must reflect a net loss in each of the two years.

5) The most recent financial statement as described in subsection (g)(3) above must reflect a ratio of current assets to current liabilities of less than 1.3.

e) Financial relief. If the hospital demonstrates adequate financial jeopardy, the Department will determine the amount of the financial relief to be granted. The amount of the financial relief will be dependent upon the individual hospital's needs.

f) Definitions. For purposes of this Section, unless the context requires otherwise:

1) "Current assets" must follow Generally Accepted Accounting Principles, except for this purpose all unrestricted investments must be included as current assets.

2) "Current liabilities" must follow Generally Accepted Accounting Principles, except for this purpose any liabilities due to entities related by ownership or control must not be included as current liabilities.

3) "Marginal loss" is the amount by which total variable costs for each patient day exceeds the Medicaid payment rate. In calculating marginal loss, the hospital shall compute variable costs at 60 percent of total inpatient operating costs and fixed costs at 40 percent of total inpatient operating costs; however, the Director may accept a different ratio of fixed and variable operating costs if a hospital is able to demonstrate that a different ratio is appropriate for its particular institution.

4) "Ratio of current assets to current liabilities" means current assets divided by current liabilities, as defined above.

5) "Unrestricted investments" means funds which have not been restricted by the donors for use only for some purpose other than hospital operations. Also, investments which have been legally restricted against use for hospital operations, such as loan collateral, will be considered to be restricted. Funds restricted by the hospital's board of directors will be considered as unrestricted funds for the purpose of this analysis.

g) This Section shall be automatically repealed effective June 30, 1996 June 30, 1995.

(Source: Amended at 19 Ill. Reg. _____, effective

DEPARTMENT OF PUBLIC AID

NOTICE OF PROPOSED AMENDMENTS

_____)

DEPARTMENT OF PUBLIC AID

NOTICE OF PROPOSED AMENDMENTS

1) **Heading of the Part**: Long Term Care Reimbursement Changes

2) **Code Citation**: 89 Ill. Adm. Code 153

3) **Section Numbers**:   Proposed Action:

       153.100   Amendment
       153.150   Amendment

4) **Statutory Authority**: Section 12-13 of the Illinois Public Aid Code (Ill. Rev. Stat. 1991, ch. 23, par. 12-13) [305 ILCS 5/12-13]

5) **Complete Description of the Subjects and Issues Involved**: The Department of Public Aid is proposing changes to Section 153.100 to maintain rates of reimbursement for long term care services at the levels which have been effective since January 18, 1994. The maintenance of rates will continue through June 30, 1996, and will affect nursing homes, facilities for persons with developmental disabilities, and developmental training facilities. Several exceptions to the rate maintenance provisions are detailed in the rules. These cost containment measures are necessary to permit the Department to continue to purchase long term care services in a prudent and cost effective manner, and to prevent excessive and unnecessary expenditures.

The Department is also proposing amendments to Section 153.150 to continue quality assurance (QA) reviews in nursing facilities until June 30, 1996. The QA process provides a mechanism for reviewing and maintaining the quality of care delivered in Medicaid funded nursing facilities during a period of rate maintenance when Inspections of Care are not necessary for rate setting purposes. The QA process was established in conjunction with the stabilization of reimbursement levels for nursing homes for the period January 18, 1994 through June 30, 1995, to monitor quality of care and the continuance of program delivery necessary for resident services. According to these amendments, the QA process will be continued through June 30, 1996.

These proposed amendments are not expected to result in any budgetary changes.

6) **Will these proposed amendments replace emergency amendments currently in effect?** No

7) **Does this rulemaking contain an automatic repeal date?** Yes. Sections 153.100(l) and 153.150(g) contain an automatic repeal date of June 30, 1996.

8) **Do these proposed amendments contain incorporations by reference?** No

DEPARTMENT OF PUBLIC AID

NOTICE OF PROPOSED AMENDMENTS

9) **Are there any other proposed amendments pending on this Part?** No

10) **Statement of Statewide Policy Objectives**: These proposed amendments do not affect units of local government.

11) **Time, Place, and Manner in which Interested Persons may comment on this proposed rulemaking**: Any interested parties may submit comments, data, views, or arguments concerning this proposed rulemaking. All comments must be in writing and should be addressed to Joanne Jones, Bureau of Rules and Regulations, Illinois Department of Public Aid, 100 South Grand Ave. E., 3rd Floor, Springfield, Illinois 62762 (Phone: (217) 524-3215). The Department requests the submission of written comments within 30 days after the publication of this notice. The Department will consider all written comments it receives during the first notice period as required by Section 5-40 of the Illinois Administrative Procedure Act [5 ILCS 100/5-40].

These proposed amendments may have an impact on small businesses, small municipalities, and not for profit corporations as defined in Sections 1-75, 1-80 and 1-85 of the Illinois Administrative Procedure Act [5 ILCS 100/1-75, 1-80, 1-85]. These entities may submit comments in writing to the Department at the above address in accordance with the regulatory flexibility provisions in Section 5-30 of the Illinois Administrative Procedure Act [5 ILCS 100/5-30]. These entities shall indicate their status as small businesses, small municipalities, or not for profit corporations as part of any written comments they submit to the Department.

12) **Initial Regulatory Flexibility Analysis**:

     A) **Types of small businesses, small municipalities and not for profit corporations affected**: Long term care facilities

     B) **Reporting, bookkeeping or other procedures required for compliance**: None

     C) **Types of professional skills necessary for compliance**: None

13) **State reasons for this rulemaking if it was not included in either of the two most recent regulatory agendas**: The reasons for this rulemaking are fully described above in the complete description of the subjects and issues involved. This rulemaking was not anticipated by the Department when the two most recent regulatory agendas were published.

The full text of the Proposed Amendments begins on the next page:

DEPARTMENT OF PUBLIC AID

NOTICE OF PROPOSED AMENDMENTS

TITLE 89: SOCIAL SERVICES
CHAPTER I: DEPARTMENT OF PUBLIC AID
SUBCHAPTER e: GENERAL TIME-LIMITED CHANGES

PART 153
LONG TERM CARE REIMBURSEMENT CHANGES

Section
153.100   Reimbursement for Long Term Care Services
153.150   Quality Assurance Review

AUTHORITY: Implementing and authorized by Articles III, IV, V, VI and Section
12-13 of the Illinois Public Aid Code (Ill. Rev. Stat. 1991, ch. 23, pars. 3-1
et seq., 4-1 et seq., 5-1 et seq., 6-1 et seq., and 12-13) [305 ILCS 5/Arts.
III, IV, V and VI and 12-13] and implementing Article III of the Illinois
Health Finance Reform Act (Ill. Rev. Stat. 1991, ch. 111 1/2, par. 6503-1 et
seq.) [20 ILCS 2215/Art. III].

SOURCE: Emergency rules adopted at 18 Ill. Reg. 2159, effective January 18,
1994, for a maximum of 150 days; adopted at 18 Ill. Reg. 10154, effective June
17, 1994; emergency amendment at 18 Ill. Reg. 11380, effective July 1, 1994,
for a maximum of 150 days; amended at 18 Ill. Reg. 16669, effective November 1,
1994; amended at 19 Ill. Reg. _____, effective _____.

Section 153.100 Reimbursement for Long Term Care Services

a) Notwithstanding the provisions set forth in 89 Ill. Adm. Code 140, 144
   and 147 for reimbursement of long term care services, effective
   January 18, 1994, reimbursement rates for long term care facilities
   (SNF/ICF and ICF/MR) and day training providers will remain at the
   levels in effect on January 18, 1994, except as otherwise provided in
   this Section.
b) The results of Inspection of Care (IOC) surveys for which the exit
   conference is completed prior to January 18, 1994, will be processed
   and reflected in facility rates effective with the annual nursing rate
   adjustment date. The reconsideration process which is provided for in
   89 Ill. Adm. Code 147.100 remains in effect for these surveys and
   other surveys set forth in this Section.
c) Capital and support rates in effect on January 18, 1994, will be
   adjusted based on final audits of cost report data in accordance with
   89 Ill. Adm. Code 140.582(b) and 140.590.
d) Capital rates will be increased for major capital improvements in
   accordance with 89 Ill. Adm. Code 140.560(c) and (e).
e) New facilities which are assigned median rates in accordance with 89
   Ill. Adm. Code 140.560(b) will have rates recalculated based upon
   receipt of their first cost report and first IOC survey.
f) Rates may change based upon an interim IOC conducted at the facility's
   written request for any facility which changed ownership no earlier
   than 90 days prior to and not later than January 18, 1994. The

DEPARTMENT OF PUBLIC AID

NOTICE OF PROPOSED AMENDMENTS

interim IOC request must include justification and documentation which
supports one of the criteria set forth in 89 Ill. Adm. Code
147.150(d).
g) Requests for interim IOCs received through January 18, 1994, will be
   processed in accordance with 89 Ill. Adm. Code 147.150(d).
h) Interim IOCs may be conducted, at the facility's written request, if
   there has been a change in the Medicaid census since the last IOC
   survey in accordance with 89 Ill. Adm. Code 147.150(d), except that
   the requirement that the request must be made within 180 days after
   the last IOC need not be met. The written request must contain
   documentation supporting the change in Medicaid census.
i) The Department reserves the right to initiate interim IOC surveys, if
   necessary, based upon a significant reduction in the level of resident
   care or for the health and safety concerns of residents.
j) Any rate adjustments that result from an interim IOC conducted under
   this Section will have an effective date of the first day of the month
   following the exit date of the interim IOC.
k) Requests for IOCs upon which rate determinations are based upon a
   Medicaid resident being transferred from a State operated
   developmentally disabled facility to a community setting will be
   considered on a case-by-case basis.
l) This Section shall be automatically repealed effective June 30,
   1996 June 30, 1995.

(Source: Amended at 19 Ill. Reg. _____, effective
_____)

Section 153.150 Quality Assurance Review

a) Purpose - Notwithstanding the provisions set forth in 89 Ill. Adm.
   Code 147 for Inspection of Care (IOC) in nursing facilities, effective
   July 1, 1994 through June 30, 1996 June 30, 1995, quality assurance
   (QA) reviews will be conducted in nursing facilities to verify that
   programs scored during the last IOC and new programs established for
   Medicaid residents continue to meet criteria as described in 89 Ill.
   Adm. Code 147.
b) Review Process
   1) QA reviews will include the following 11 program areas from the
      IOC:
      A) Restorative Bathing/Grooming
      B) Restorative Clothing
      C) Restorative Eating
      D) Restorative Mobility
      E) Restorative Continence
      F) Psychosocial/Mental Status
      G) Pressure Ulcer Treatment
      H) Pressure Ulcer Prevention
      I) Psychotropic Med Reduction

DEPARTMENT OF PUBLIC AID

NOTICE OF PROPOSED AMENDMENTS

    J) Passive Range of Motion
    K) Restraint Reduction and Management
2) A random 30 percent sample of Medicaid clients residing in a facility will be selected for the review.
3) Wherever possible, the sample will only include residents surveyed during the last IOC.
4) When there is not a sufficient number of residents in the facility from the last IOC to derive a random 30 percent sample, the sample will be chosen from the entire Medicaid population of the facility.
5) No less than ten Medicaid residents will be reviewed, unless fewer than ten Medicaid residents reside in the facility.
6) In facilities with a Medicaid census of less than ten, all Medicaid residents will be reviewed.
7) Assessments, plans of care and implementation of programs will be reviewed as described in 89 Ill. Adm. Code 147.
8) Copies of completed QA modified Form DPA 2700, Illinois Assessment of Need for Care, will be presented to the facility daily.
9) Each QA review will be concluded with an exit conference.
c) Resolution
    1) There will be no formal negotiation or arbitration.
    2) There may be residents who are not receiving the same services now that they were receiving at the last IOC. Resident health status may change over time, either through improvement or deterioration, and the resident may no longer benefit from a program. Consequently, the resolution process will include a provision for scoring discontinued programs where there is documentation to support that the program was discontinued appropriately because the resident could no longer benefit from it. The facility is encouraged to discuss discontinued programs with Department staff and to present any documentation to support its position.
    3) Disagreement on any QA review findings that cannot be settled between the facility and QA team will be resolved at the Bureau of Long Term Care (BLTC) regional supervisor level.
d) Notification of QA Results
    1) Data gathered during the QA review will be evaluated by the Department.
    2) If the results of the QA review indicate the current service level is at least 90 percent of the service level of the last IOC, the facility will pass the QA review and no further action will be taken.
    3) To determine whether the 90 percent level has been maintained, the Department will compare the dollar amount calculated from the QA review for the 11 program areas to the reimbursed amount for the same 11 program areas from the latest IOC.
    4) If the QA review indicates a reduction of more than ten percent

DEPARTMENT OF PUBLIC AID

NOTICE OF PROPOSED AMENDMENTS

in the earned rate, the following procedures will be implemented:
    A) The facility will be notified, in writing, of the QA findings within 30 days after the QA review exit date.
    B) Upon request from the facility, consultation will be provided by BLTC field staff to assist the facility with correction of problems.
    C) A follow-up QA review will be conducted between 90 and 120 days after the first QA exit date.
        i) The procedure defined in subsection (b)(2) through (b)(6) of this Section will be used to select a 30 percent random sample for the follow-up QA review.
        ii) Resolution as defined in subsection (c) above is available during the follow-up QA review.
    D) The facility will be notified, in writing, of the follow-up QA findings within 30 days after the follow-up QA review exit date.
    E) If the follow-up QA review indicates a reduction after more than ten percent in earned rate from the last IOC, a full IOC on 100 percent of Medicaid residents will be initiated within 45 days after notification of the results from the follow-up QA review.
e) Rate Adjustments
    1) In any case where a 100 percent review is performed due to a reduction in services, rates will be recalculated and reduced, if indicated, based upon the full IOC results. The reduced rate will become effective on the first day of the month following the month that the full IOC exit took place.
    2) Rates will not be increased based upon IOC results.
f) The QA review process will be used during the rate maintenance period which ends June 30, 1996 June 30, 1995.
g) This Section shall be automatically repealed effective June 30, 1996 June 30, 1995.

(Source: Amended at 19 Ill. Reg. _____, effective _____)

DEPARTMENT OF PUBLIC AID

NOTICE OF PROPOSED AMENDMENTS

1) **Heading of the Part:** Medical Payment

2) **Code Citation:** 89 Ill. Adm. Code 140

3) **Section Numbers:**   Proposed Action:

140.80	Amendment
140.82	Amendment
140.84	Amendment

4) **Statutory Authority:** Section 12-13 of the Illinois Public Aid Code (Ill. Rev. Stat. 1991, ch. 23, par. 12-13) [305 ILCS 5/12-13]

5) **Complete Description of the Subjects and Issues Involved:** The Department of Public Aid is proposing changes to the rules pertaining to provider assessments for hospitals, long term care facilities for persons with developmental disabilities, and nursing homes. These changes are designed to extend the provider assessment programs beyond June 30, 1995. This proposed rulemaking responds to the Governor's initiative which is intended to enable Illinois to continue to maximize federal financing benefits to hospitals, long term care facilities and nursing homes, and thereby ensure the continuance of necessary care and services.

In fiscal year 1995, the provider assessment programs generated approximately $689.7 million in spending ($355.4 million in assessments and $334.3 million in federal matching funds). These proposed amendments will have a significant budgetary impact upon the Department, because if the assessment programs conclude on June 30, 1995, the expected loss of revenue for fiscal year 1996 is estimated at approximately $738.8 million ($380.7 million in assessments and $358.1 million in federal matching funds).

6) **Will these proposed amendments replace emergency amendments currently in effect?** No

7) **Does this rulemaking contain an automatic repeal date?** No

8) **Do these proposed amendments contain incorporations by reference?** No

9) **Are there any other proposed amendments pending on this Part?** Yes

Sections	Proposed Action	Illinois Register Citation
140.11	Amendment	January 13, 1995 (19 Ill. Reg. 165)
140.12	Amendment	January 13, 1995 (19 Ill. Reg. 165)
140.80	Amendment	March 17, 1995 (19 Ill. Reg. 3248)
140.82	Amendment	March 17, 1995 (19 Ill. Reg. 3248)
140.84	Amendment	March 17, 1995 (19 Ill. Reg. 3248)

DEPARTMENT OF PUBLIC AID

NOTICE OF PROPOSED AMENDMENTS

140.400	Amendment	February 10, 1995 (19 Ill. Reg. 1200)
140.413	Amendment	July 8, 1994 (18 Ill. Reg. 10637);
140.435	Amendment	February 10, 1995 (19 Ill. Reg. 1200)
140.523	Amendment	January 13, 1995 (19 Ill. Reg. 165)
140.645	Amendment	December 16, 1994 (18 Ill. Reg. 17865)

10) **Statement of Statewide Policy Objectives:** These proposed amendments do not affect units of local government.

11) **Time, Place, and Manner in which Interested Persons may comment on this proposed rulemaking:** Any interested parties may submit comments, data, views, or arguments concerning this proposed rulemaking. All comments must be in writing and should be addressed to Joanne Jones, Bureau of Rules and Regulations, Illinois Department of Public Aid, 100 South Grand Ave. E., 3rd Floor, Springfield, Illinois 62762 (Phone: (217) 524-3215). The Department requests the submission of written comments within 30 days after the publication of this notice. The Department will consider all written comments it receives during the first notice period as required by Section 5-40 of the Illinois Administrative Procedure Act (5 ILCS 100/5-40).

These proposed amendments may have an impact on small businesses, small municipalities, and not for profit corporations as defined in Sections 1-75, 1-80 and 1-85 of the Illinois Administrative Procedure Act (5 ILCS 100/1-75, 1-80, 1-85). These entities may submit comments in writing to the Department at the above address in accordance with the regulatory flexibility provisions in Section 5-30 of the Illinois Administrative Procedure Act (5 ILCS 100/5-30). These entities shall indicate their status as small businesses, small municipalities, or not for profit corporations as part of any written comments they submit to the Department.

12) **Initial Regulatory Flexibility Analysis:**

A) **Types of small businesses, small municipalities and not for profit corporations affected:** Hospitals, long term care facilities for persons with developmental disabilities, and nursing homes

B) **Reporting, bookkeeping or other procedures required for compliance:** None

C) **Types of professional skills necessary for compliance:** None

13) **State reasons for this rulemaking if it was not included in either of the two most recent regulatory agendas:** The reasons for this rulemaking are fully described above in the complete description of the subjects and issues involved. This rulemaking was not anticipated by the Department

DEPARTMENT OF PUBLIC AID

NOTICE OF PROPOSED AMENDMENTS

when the two most recent regulatory agendas were published.

The full text of the Proposed Amendments begins on the next page:

DEPARTMENT OF PUBLIC AID

NOTICE OF PROPOSED AMENDMENTS

TITLE 89: SOCIAL SERVICES
CHAPTER I: DEPARTMENT OF PUBLIC AID
SUBCHAPTER d: MEDICAL PROGRAMS

PART 140
MEDICAL PAYMENT

SUBPART A: GENERAL PROVISIONS

DEPARTMENT OF PUBLIC AID

NOTICE OF PROPOSED AMENDMENTS

DEPARTMENT OF PUBLIC AID

NOTICE OF PROPOSED AMENDMENTS

DEPARTMENT OF PUBLIC AID

NOTICE OF PROPOSED AMENDMENTS

DEPARTMENT OF PUBLIC AID

NOTICE OF PROPOSED AMENDMENTS

DEPARTMENT OF PUBLIC AID

NOTICE OF PROPOSED AMENDMENTS

DEPARTMENT OF PUBLIC AID

NOTICE OF PROPOSED AMENDMENTS

DEPARTMENT OF PUBLIC AID

NOTICE OF PROPOSED AMENDMENTS

DEPARTMENT OF PUBLIC AID

NOTICE OF PROPOSED AMENDMENTS

AUTHORITY: Implementing Article III of the Illinois Health Finance Reform Act
[Ill. Rev. Stat. 1993, ch. 111 1/2, par. 6503-1 et seq.] [20 ILCS 2215/Art.
III] and implementing and authorized by Articles III, IV, V, VI, VII and
Section 12-13 of the Illinois Public Aid Code [Ill. Rev. Stat. 1991, ch. 23,
pars. 3-1 et seq., 4-1 et seq., 5-1 et seq., 6-1 et seq., 7-1 et seq., and
12-13) [305 ILCS 5/Arts. III, IV, V, VI, VII, and 12-13].

SOURCE: Adopted at 3 Ill. Reg. 24, p. 166, effective June 10, 1979; rule
repealed and new rule adopted at 6 Ill. Reg. 8374, effective July 6, 1982;
emergency amendment at 6 Ill. Reg. 8508, effective July 6, 1982, for a maximum
of 150 days; amended at 7 Ill. Reg. 681, effective December 30, 1982; amended
at 7 Ill. Reg. 7956, effective July 1, 1983; amended at 7 Ill. Reg. 8308,
effective July 1, 1983; amended at 7 Ill. Reg. 8271, effective July 5, 1983;
emergency amendment at 7 Ill. Reg. 8354, effective July 5, 1983, for a maximum
of 150 days; amended at 7 Ill. Reg. 8540, effective July 15, 1983; amended at 7
Ill. Reg. 9382, effective July 22, 1983; amended at 7 Ill. Reg. 12868,
effective September 20, 1983; peremptory amendment at 7 Ill. Reg. 15047,
effective October 31, 1983; amended at 7 Ill. Reg. 17358, effective December
21, 1983; amended at 8 Ill. Reg. 294, effective December 21, 1983; emergency
amendment at 8 Ill. Reg. 580, effective January 1, 1984, for a maximum of 150
days; codified at 8 Ill. Reg. 2483; amended at 8 Ill. Reg. 3012, effective
February 22, 1984; amended at 8 Ill. Reg. 5262, effective April 9, 1984;
amended at 8 Ill. Reg. 6785, effective April 27, 1984; amended at 8 Ill. Reg.
6983, effective May 9, 1984; amended at 8 Ill. Reg. 7258, effective May 16,
1984; emergency amendment at 8 Ill. Reg. 7910, effective May 22, 1984, for a
maximum of 150 days; amended at 8 Ill. Reg. 7910, effective June 1, 1984;
amended at 8 Ill. Reg. 10032, effective June 18, 1984; emergency amendment at 8
Ill. Reg. 10062, effective June 20, 1984, for a maximum of 150 days; amended at
8 Ill. Reg. 13343, effective July 17, 1984; amended at 8 Ill. Reg. 13779,
effective July 24, 1984; Sections 140.72 and 140.73 recodified to 89 Ill. Adm.
Code 141 at 8 Ill. Reg. 16354; amended (by adding sections being codified with
no substantive change) at 8 Ill. Reg. 17899; peremptory amendment at 8 Ill.
Reg. 18151, effective September 18, 1984; amended at 8 Ill. Reg. 21629,
effective October 19, 1984; peremptory amendment at 8 Ill. Reg. 21677,
effective October 24, 1984; amended at 8 Ill. Reg. 22097, effective October 24,

DEPARTMENT OF PUBLIC AID

NOTICE OF PROPOSED AMENDMENTS

1984; peremptory amendment at 8 Ill. Reg. 22155, effective October 29, 1984; amended at 8 Ill. Reg. 23218, effective November 20, 1984; emergency amendment at 8 Ill. Reg. 23721, effective November 21, 1984, for a maximum of 150 days; amended at 8 Ill. Reg. 25067, effective December 19, 1984; emergency amendment at 9 Ill. Reg. 407, effective January 1, 1985, for a maximum of 150 days; amended at 9 Ill. Reg. 2697, effective February 22, 1985; amended at 9 Ill. Reg. 6235, effective April 19, 1985; amended at 9 Ill. Reg. 8677, effective May 28, 1985; amended at 9 Ill. Reg. 9564, effective June 5, 1985; amended at 9 Ill. Reg. 10025, effective June 26, 1985; emergency amendment at 9 Ill. Reg. 11403, effective June 27, 1985, for a maximum of 150 days; amended at 9 Ill. Reg. 11357, effective June 28, 1985; amended at 9 Ill. Reg. 12000, effective July 24, 1985; amended at 9 Ill. Reg. 12306, effective August 5, 1985; amended at 9 Ill. Reg. 13998, effective September 3, 1985; amended at 9 Ill. Reg. 14684, effective September 13, 1985; amended at 9 Ill. Reg. 15503, effective October 4, 1985; amended at 9 Ill. Reg. 16312, effective October 11, 1985; amended at 9 Ill. Reg. 19138, effective December 2, 1985; amended at 9 Ill. Reg. 19737, effective December 9, 1985; amended at 10 Ill. Reg. 338, effective December 27, 1985; emergency amendment at 10 Ill. Reg. 798, effective January 1, 1986, for a maximum of 150 days; amended at 10 Ill. Reg. 672, effective January 6, 1986; amended at 10 Ill. Reg. 1206, effective January 13, 1986; amended at 10 Ill. Reg. 3041, effective January 24, 1986; amended at 10 Ill. Reg. 6981, effective April 16, 1986; amended at 10 Ill. Reg. 7825, effective April 30, 1986; amended at 10 Ill. Reg. 8128, effective May 7, 1986; emergency amendment at 10 Ill. Reg. 8912, effective May 13, 1986, for a maximum of 150 days; amended at 10 Ill. Reg. 11440, effective June 20, 1986; amended at 10 Ill. Reg. 14714, effective August 27, 1986; amended at 10 Ill. Reg. 15211, effective September 12, 1986; emergency amendment at 10 Ill. Reg. 16729, effective September 18, 1986, for a maximum of 150 days; amended at 10 Ill. Reg. 18808, effective October 24, 1986; amended at 10 Ill. Reg. 19742, effective November 12, 1986; amended at 10 Ill. Reg. 21784, effective December 15, 1986; amended at 11 Ill. Reg. 698, effective December 19, 1986; amended at 11 Ill. Reg. 1418, effective December 31, 1986; amended at 11 Ill. Reg. 2323, effective January 16, 1987; amended at 11 Ill. Reg. 4002, effective February 25, 1987; Section 140.71 recodified to 89 Ill. Adm. Code 141 at 11 Ill. Reg. 4302; amended at 11 Ill. Reg. 4303, effective March 6, 1987; amended at 11 Ill. Reg.7664, effective April 15, 1987; emergency amendment at 11 Ill. Reg. 9342, effective April 20, 1987, for a maximum of 150 days; amended at 11 Ill. Reg. 9169, effective April 28, 1987; amended at 11 Ill. Reg. 10903, effective June 1, 1987; amended at 11 Ill. Reg. 11528, effective June 22, 1987; amended at 11 Ill. Reg. 12011, effective June 30, 1987; amended at 11 Ill. Reg. 12290, effective July 6, 1987; amended at 11 Ill. Reg. 14048, effective August 14, 1987; amended at 11 Ill. Reg. 14771, effective August 25, 1987; amended at 11 Ill. Reg. 16758, effective September 28, 1987; amended at 11 Ill. Reg. 17295, effective September 30, 1987; amended at 11 Ill. Reg. 18696, effective October 27, 1987; amended at 11 Ill. Reg. 20909, effective December 14, 1987; amended at 12 Ill. Reg. 916, effective January 1, 1988; emergency amendment at 12 Ill. Reg. 1960, effective January 1, 1988, for a maximum of 150 days; amended at 12 Ill. Reg. 5427, effective March 15, 1988; amended at 12 Ill. Reg. 6246,

DEPARTMENT OF PUBLIC AID

NOTICE OF PROPOSED AMENDMENTS

effective March 16, 1988; amended at 12 Ill. Reg. 6728, effective March 22, 1988; Sections 140.900 thru 140.912 and 140.Table H and 140.Table I recodified to 89 Ill. Adm. Code 147.5 thru 147.205 and 147.Table A and 147.Table B at 12 Ill. Reg. 6956; amended at 12 Ill. Reg. 6927, effective April 5, 1988; Sections 140.940 thru 140.972 recodified to 89 Ill. Adm. Code 149.5 thru 149.325 at 12 Ill. Reg. 7401; amended at 12 Ill. Reg. 7695, effective April 21, 1988; amended at 12 Ill. Reg. 10497, effective June 3, 1988; amended at 12 Ill. Reg. 10717, effective June 14, 1988; emergency amendment at 12 Ill. Reg. 11868, effective July 1, 1998, for a maximum of 150 days; amended at 12 Ill. Reg. 12509, effective July 15, 1988; amended at 12 Ill. Reg. 14271, effective August 29, 1988; emergency amendment at 12 Ill. Reg. 16921, effective September 28, 1988, for a maximum of 150 days; amended at 12 Ill. Reg. 16738, effective October 5, 1988; amended at 12 Ill. Reg. 17879, effective October 24, 1988; amended at 12 Ill. Reg. 18198, effective November 4, 1988; amended at 12 Ill. Reg. 19396, effective November 6, 1988; amended at 12 Ill. Reg. 19734, effective November 15, 1988; amended at 13 Ill. Reg. 125, effective January 1, 1989; amended at 13 Ill. Reg. 2475, effective February 1, 1989; amended at 13 Ill. Reg. 3069, effective February 28, 1989; amended at 13 Ill. Reg. 3351, effective March 6, 1989; amended at 13 Ill. Reg. 3917, effective March 17, 1989; amended at 13 Ill. Reg. 5175, effective April 3, 1989; amended at 13 Ill. Reg. 5718, effective April 10, 1989; amended at 13 Ill. Reg. 7025, effective April 24, 1989; Sections 140.850 thru 140.896 recodified to 89 Ill. Adm. Code 146.5 thru 148.225 at 13 Ill. Reg. 7040; amended at 13 Ill. Reg. 7786, effective May 20, 1989; Sections 140.94 thru 140.398 recodified to 89 Ill. Adm. Code 148.10 thru 148.390 at 13 Ill. Reg. 9572; emergency amendment at 13 Ill. Reg. 10977, effective July 1, 1989, for a maximum of 150 days; emergency expired November 28, 1989; amended at 13 Ill. Reg. 11516, effective July 3, 1989; amended at 13 Ill. Reg. 12119, effective July 7, 1989; Section 140.110 recodified to 89 Ill. Adm. Code 148.120 at 13 Ill. Reg. 12118; amended at 13 Ill. Reg. 12562, effective July 17, 1989; amended at 13 Ill. Reg. 14391, effective August 31, 1989; emergency amendment at 13 Ill. Reg. 15473, effective September 12, 1989; amended at 13 Ill. Reg. 16992, effective October 16, 1989; amended at 14 Ill. Reg. 190, effective December 21, 1989; amended at 14 Ill. Reg. 2564, effective February 9, 1990; emergency amendment at 14 Ill. Reg. 3241, effective February 14, 1990, for a maximum of 150 days; emergency expired July 14, 1990; amended at 14 Ill. Reg. 4543, effective March 12, 1990; emergency amendment at 14 Ill. Reg. 4577, effective March 6, 1990, for a maximum of 150 days; emergency expired August 3, 1990; emergency amendment at 14 Ill. Reg. 5575, effective April 1, 1990, for a maximum of 150 days; emergency expired August 29, 1990; emergency amendment at 14 Ill. Reg. 5865, effective April 3, 1990, for a maximum of 150 days; amended at 14 Ill. Reg. 7141, effective April 27, 1990; emergency amendment at 14 Ill. Reg. 7249, effective April 27, 1990; emergency amendment at 14 Ill. Reg. 10062, effective June 12, 1990; amended at 14 Ill. Reg. 10409, effective June 19, 1990; emergency amendment at 14 Ill. Reg. 12082, effective July 5, 1990, for a maximum of 150 days; amended at 14 Ill. Reg. 13262, effective August 6, 1990; emergency amendment at 14 Ill. Reg. 14184, effective August 16, 1990, for a

DEPARTMENT OF PUBLIC AID

NOTICE OF PROPOSED AMENDMENTS

maximum of 150 days; emergency amendment at 14 Ill. Reg. 14570, effective August 22, 1990, for a maximum of 150 days; amended at 14 Ill. Reg. 14826, effective August 31, 1990; amended at 14 Ill. Reg. 15366, effective September 12, 1990; amended at 14 Ill. Reg. 15981, effective September 21, 1990; amended at 14 Ill. Reg. 17279, effective October 12, 1990; amended at 14 Ill. Reg. 18057, effective October 22, 1990; amended at 14 Ill. Reg. 18508, effective October 30, 1990; amended at 14 Ill. Reg. 18813, effective November 6, 1990; amended at 14 Ill. Reg. 20478, effective December 7, 1990; amended at 14 Ill. Reg. 20729, effective December 12, 1990; amended at 15 Ill. Reg. 298, effective December 28, 1990; emergency amendment at 15 Ill. Reg. 592, effective January 1, 1991, for a maximum of 150 days; amended at 15 Ill. Reg. 1051, effective January 18, 1991; Section 140.569 withdrawn at 15 Ill. Reg. 1174; amended at 15 Ill. Reg. 6220, effective April 18, 1991; amended at 15 Ill. Reg. 6534, effective April 30, 1991; amended at 15 Ill. Reg. 8264, effective May 23, 1991; amended at 15 Ill. Reg. 8972, effective June 17, 1991; amended at 15 Ill. Reg. 10114, effective June 21, 1991; amended at 15 Ill. Reg. 10468, effective July 1, 1991; amended at 15 Ill. Reg. 11176, effective August 1, 1991; emergency amendment at 15 Ill. Reg. 11515, effective July 25, 1991, for a maximum of 150 days; emergency expired December 22, 1991; emergency amendment at 15 Ill. Reg. 12919, effective August 15, 1991, for a maximum of 150 days; emergency expired January 12, 1992; emergency amendment at 15 Ill. Reg. 16366, effective October 22, 1991, for a maximum of 150 days; amended at 15 Ill. Reg. 17318, effective November 18, 1991; amended at 16 Ill. Reg. 17733, effective November 22, 1991; emergency amendment at 16 Ill. Reg. 300, effective December 20, 1991, for a maximum of 150 days; amended at 16 Ill. Reg. 174, effective December 24, 1991; amended at 16 Ill. Reg. 1877, effective January 24, 1992; amended at 16 Ill. Reg. 3552, effective February 28, 1992; amended at 16 Ill. Reg. 4006, effective March 6, 1992; amended at 16 Ill. Reg. 6408, effective March 20, 1992; amended at 16 Ill. Reg. 6849, effective April 7, 1992; amended at 16 Ill. Reg. 7017, effective April 17, 1992; amended at 16 Ill. Reg. 10050, effective June 5, 1992; amended at 16 Ill. Reg. 11174, effective June 26, 1992; expedited correction at 16 Ill. Reg. 11348, effective March 20, 1992; emergency amendment at 16 Ill. Reg. 11947, effective July 10, 1992, for a maximum of 150 days; amended at 16 Ill. Reg. 12186, effective July 24, 1992; emergency amendment at 16 Ill. Reg. 13337, effective August 14, 1992, for a maximum of 150 days; emergency amendment at 16 Ill. Reg. 15109, effective September 21, 1992, for a maximum of 150 days; amended at 16 Ill. Reg. 15561, effective September 30, 1992; amended at 16 Ill. Reg. 17302, effective November 2, 1992; emergency amendment at 16 Ill. Reg. 18097, effective November 17, 1992, for a maximum of 150 days; amended at 16 Ill. Reg. 19146, effective December 1, 1992; amended at 16 Ill. Reg. 19879, effective December 7, 1992; amended at 17 Ill. Reg. 837, effective January 11, 1993; amended at 17 Ill. Reg. 1112, effective January 15, 1993; amended at 17 Ill. Reg. 2290, effective February 15, 1993; amended at 17 Ill. Reg. 2951, effective February 17, 1993; amended at 17 Ill. Reg. 3421, effective February 19, 1993; amended at 17 Ill. Reg. 6196, effective April 5, 1993; amended at 17 Ill. Reg. 6839, effective April 21, 1993; amended at 17 Ill. Reg. 7004, effective May 17, 1993; expedited correction at 17 Ill. Reg. 7078, effective December 1, 1992; emergency amendment at 17 Ill. Reg. 11201,

DEPARTMENT OF PUBLIC AID

NOTICE OF PROPOSED AMENDMENTS

effective July 1, 1993, for a maximum of 150 days; emergency amendment at 17 Ill. Reg. 15162, effective September 2, 1993, for a maximum of 150 days; emergency amendment at 17 Ill. Reg. 18152, effective October 1, 1993, for a maximum of 150 days; amended at 17 Ill. Reg. 18571, effective October 8, 1993; emergency amendment at 17 Ill. Reg. 18611, effective October 1, 1993, for a maximum of 150 days; emergency amendment suspended effective October 12, 1993; amended at 17 Ill. Reg. 20999, effective November 24, 1993; emergency amendment repealed at 17 Ill. Reg. 22583, effective December 20, 1993; amended at 18 Ill. Reg. 3620, effective February 28, 1994; amended at 18 Ill. Reg. 4250, effective March 4, 1994; amended at 18 Ill. Reg. 5951, effective April 1, 1994; emergency amendment at 18 Ill. Reg. 10922, effective July 1, 1994, for a maximum of 150 days; amended at 18 Ill. Reg. 11244, effective July 1, 1994; amended at 18 Ill. Reg. 14126, effective August 29, 1994; amended at 18 Ill. Reg. 16675, effective November 1, 1994; emergency amendment suspended, effective November 15, 1994; amended at 18 Ill. Reg. 18059, effective December 19, 1994; amended at 19 Ill. Reg. 1082, effective January 20, 1995; amended at 19 Ill. Reg. 2933, effective March 1, 1995; emergency amendment at 19 Ill. Reg. 3529, effective March 1, 1995, for a maximum of 150 days; amended at 19 Ill. Reg. _____, effective _____

SUBPART C: PROVIDER PARTICIPATION FEES

Section 140.80 Hospital Provider Fund

a) Purpose and Contents

1) The Hospital Provider Fund ("Fund") was created in the State Treasury upon enactment of Public Act 87-861 and Public Act 88-88. Interest earned by the Fund shall be credited to the Fund. The Fund shall not be used to replace any funds appropriated to the Medicaid program by the General Assembly.

2) The Fund is created for the purpose of receiving and disbursing monies in accordance with this Section and Public Act 87-861, as amended by Public Act 88-88.

3) The Fund shall consist of:

A) All monies collected or received by the Department under subsection (b) below;

B) All federal matching funds received by the Department as a result of expenditures made by the Department that are attributable to monies deposited in the Fund;

C) Any interest or penalty levied in conjunction with the administration of the Fund;

D) All other monies received for the Fund from any other source, including interest earned thereon;

E) All monies transferred from the Hospital Services Trust Fund; and

F) All monies transferred from the Tobacco Products Tax Act.

b) Provider Assessments

Effective July 1, 1994 Beginning-on-July-1,-1993,-and-ending-on-June

DEPARTMENT OF PUBLIC AID

NOTICE OF PROPOSED AMENDMENTS

30, 1994, an assessment is imposed upon each hospital provider in an amount equal to 1.88% of the provider's adjusted gross hospital revenue, as described in subsection (1)(1) of this Section, for the most recent calendar year ending before the beginning of that State fiscal year y--An-assessment-is-imposed-upon-each--hospital--provider for--the-fiscal-year-beginning-on-July-1,-1994,-and-ending-on-June-30, 1995,-in-an-amount-equal-to-the--provider's--adjusted--gross--hospital revenue,--as--described--in-subsection-(1)(1)-of-this-Section,-for-the most-recent-calendar-year-ending-before-the-beginning--of--that--State fiscal-year multiplied by the Provider's Savings Rate, as described in subsection (1)(10) of this Section. The Department reserves the right to audit the reported data. The Department shall notify hospital providers of the Provider's Savings Rate by mailing a notice to each provider's last known address as reflected by the records of the Department.

c) Payment of Assessment Due

1) The assessments imposed in subsection (b) above shall be due and payable in quarterly installments, each equalling one-fourth of the assessment for the year, on September 30, December 31, March 31, and May 31 of the year. Assessment payments postmarked on the due date will be considered as paid on time.

2) All payments received by the Department shall be credited first to unpaid installment amounts (rather than to penalty or interest), beginning with the most delinquent installments.

d) Reporting Requirements, Penalty, and Maintenance of Records

1) After December 31 of each year, and on or before March 31 of the succeeding year, every hospital provider subject to an assessment under subsection (b) above shall file a report with the Department. The report shall be on a form prepared by the Department. The report shall include the adjusted gross hospital revenue from the calendar year just ended and shall be utilized by the Department to calculate the assessment for the State fiscal year commencing on the next July 1. If a hospital provider conducts, operates, or maintains more than one hospital licensed by the Illinois Department of Public Health, a separate report shall be filed for each hospital. In the case of a hospital provider existing as a corporation or legal entity other than an individual, the report filed by it shall be signed by its president, vice-president, secretary, or treasurer or by its properly authorized agent.

2) If the hospital provider fails to file its report for a State fiscal year on or before the due date of the report, there shall be, unless waived by the Department for reasonable cause, added to the assessment imposed in subsection (b) above a penalty assessment equal to 25% of the assessment imposed for the year.

3) Every hospital provider subject to an assessment under subsection (b) above shall keep records and books that will permit the determination of adjusted gross hospital revenue on a calendar

DEPARTMENT OF PUBLIC AID

NOTICE OF PROPOSED AMENDMENTS

year basis. All such books and records shall be maintained for a minimum of three years following the filing date of the assessment report and shall, at all times during business hours of the day, be subject to inspection by the Department or its duly authorized agents and employees.

4) Amended Assessment Reports. With the exception of amended assessment reports filed in accordance with subsections (d)(5) or (6) below, an amended assessment report must be filed within 30 calendar days of the original report due date. The amended report must be accompanied by a letter identifying the changes and the justification for the amended report. The provider will be advised of any adjustments to the original annual assessment amount through written notification from the Department. Penalties may be applied to the amount underpaid due to a filing error.

5) Submission of Financial Audit Statements. All hospital providers are required to submit a copy of all financial statements audited by an external, independent auditor, to the Department within 30 days after the close of such externally performed financial audits. If the hospital's year end does not coincide with the December 31 ending date for the assessment report, the hospital must submit all financial audits covering the assessment report period. An amended assessment report must accompany such external financial audit statements if the data submitted on the initial assessment report changes based upon the findings of such external financial audits and as indicated in the audited external financial statements. Penalties may be applied to the amount underpaid due to a filing error.

6) Reconsideration of Adjusted Assessment. If the Department, through an audit conducted by the Department or its agent within three years after the end of the fiscal year in which the assessment was due, changes the assessment liability of a hospital provider, the hospital provider may request a review or reconsideration of the adjusted assessment within 30 days after the Department's notification of the change in assessment liability. Requests for reconsideration of the assessment adjustment shall not be considered if such requests are not postmarked on or before the end of the 30 day review period. Penalties may be applied to the amount underpaid due to a filing error.

e) Procedure for Partial Year Reporting/Operating Adjustments

1) Cessation of business during the fiscal year in which the assessment is being paid. If a hospital provider ceases to conduct, operate, or maintain a hospital for which the person is subject to assessment under subsection (b) above, the assessment for the State fiscal year in which the cessation occurs shall be adjusted by multiplying the assessment computed under subsection (d) by a fraction, the numerator of which is the number of days

DEPARTMENT OF PUBLIC AID

NOTICE OF PROPOSED AMENDMENTS

in the year during which the provider conducts, operates, or maintains the hospital and the denominator of which is 365. The person shall file a final, amended report with the Department not more than 30 calendar days after the cessation, reflecting the adjustment, and shall pay with the final return the assessment for the year as so adjusted, to the extent not previously paid.

2) Commencing of business during the fiscal year in which the assessment is being paid. A hospital provider who commences conducting, operating, or maintaining a hospital for which the person is subject to assessment under subsection (b) above, shall file an initial report for the State fiscal year in which the commencement occurs within 30 calendar days thereafter and shall pay the assessment under subsection (d) above as computed by the Department in equal installments on the due date of the initial assessment determination and on the regular installment due dates for the State fiscal year occurring after the due date of the initial assessment determination. In determining the annual assessment amount for the provider the Department shall develop hypothetical annualized revenue projections based upon geographic location, facility size and patient case mix. The assessment determination made by the Department is final.

3) Partial Calendar Year Operation Adjustment. For a hospital provider that did not conduct, operate, or maintain a hospital throughout the entire calendar year reporting period, the assessment for the following State fiscal year shall be annualized based on the provider's actual revenues for the portion of the reporting period the hospital was operational (dividing adjusted gross hospital revenue by the number of days the hospital was in operation and then multiplying the amount by 365). Revenues realized by a prior provider from the same hospital during the calendar year shall be used in the annualization equation, if available.

4) Change in Ownership and/or Operations. The full quarterly assessment must be paid on the designated due dates regardless of changes in ownership or operators. Liability for the payment of the assessment amount (including past due assessments and any interest or penalties that may have accrued against the amount) rest on the hospital provider currently operating or maintaining the hospital regardless if these amounts were incurred by the current owner or were incurred by previous owners. Collection of delinquent assessment fees from previous providers will be made against the current provider. Failure of the current provider to pay any outstanding assessment liability incurred by previous providers shall result in the application of penalties described in subsection (f)(1) of this Section.

f) Penalties

1) Any hospital that fails to pay the full amount of an installment when due shall be charged, unless waived by the Department for

DEPARTMENT OF PUBLIC AID

NOTICE OF PROPOSED AMENDMENTS

reasonable cause, a penalty equal to 5% of the amount of the installment not paid on or before the due date, plus 5% of the portion thereof remaining unpaid on the last day of each month thereafter, not to exceed 100% of the installment amount not paid on or before the due date.

2) Within 45 days from the due date, the Department may begin recovery actions against delinquent hospitals participating in the Medicaid Program. Payments may be withheld from the hospital until the entire assessment, including any penalties, is satisfied or until a reasonable repayment schedule has been approved by the Department. If a reasonable agreement cannot be reached or if a hospital fails to comply with an agreement, the Department reserves the right to recover any outstanding provider assessment, interest and penalty by recouping the amount or a portion thereof from the hospital's future payments from the Department. The provider may appeal this recoupment in accordance with Department rules contained in 89 Ill. Adm. Code 104. The Department has the right to continue recoupment during the appeal process. Penalties pursuant to subsection (f)(1) above will continue to accrue during the recoupment process. Recoupment proceedings against the same hospital two times in a fiscal year may be cause for termination from the Program. Failure by the Department to initiate recoupment activities within 45 days shall not reduce the provider's liabilities nor shall it preclude the Department from taking action at a later date.

3) If the hospital does not participate in the Medicaid Program, or is no longer doing business with the Department, or the Department cannot recover the full amount due through the claims processing system, within three months after the fee due date, the Department may begin legal action to recover the monies, including penalties and interest owed, plus court costs.

g) Delayed Payment - Groups of Hospitals
The Director may establish delayed payment of assessments and/or waive the payment of interest and penalties for groups of hospitals such as disproportionate share hospitals or all other hospitals when:

1) the State delays payments to hospitals due to problems related to State cash flow, or

2) a cash flow bond pool's, or any other group financing plans', requests from providers for loans are in excess of its scheduled proceeds such that a significant number of hospitals will be unable to obtain a loan to pay the assessment.

h) Delayed Payment - Individual Hospitals
In addition to the provisions of subsection (g) above, the Director may delay assessments for individual hospitals that are unable to make timely payments under this Section due to financial difficulties. No delayed payment arrangements shall extend beyond the last business day of the calendar quarter following the quarter in which the assessment

DEPARTMENT OF PUBLIC AID

NOTICE OF PROPOSED AMENDMENTS

was to have been received by the Department as described in subsection (c) above.

1) Criteria. Delayed payment provisions may be instituted only under extraordinary circumstances. Delayed payment provisions may be made only to qualified hospitals who meet all of the following requirements:

A) the provider has experienced an emergency which necessitates institution of delayed payment provisions. Emergency in this instance is defined as a circumstance under which institution of the payment and penalty provisions described in subsections (c)(1), (c)(2), (f)(1) and (f)(2) above would impose severe and irreparable harm to the clients served. Circumstances which may create such emergencies include, but are not limited to, the following:

   i) Department system errors (either automated system or clerical) which have precluded payments, or which have caused erroneous payments such that the provider's ability to provide further services to clients is severely impaired;

   ii) cash flow problems encountered by a provider which are unrelated to Department technical system problems and which result in extensive financial problems to a facility, adversely impacting on its ability to serve its clients.

B) the provider serves a significant number of clients under the medical assistance program. "Significant" in this instance means:

   i) a hospital that serves a significant number of clients under the medical assistance program; significant in this instance means that the hospital qualifies as a disproportionate share hospital under 89 Ill. Adm. Code 148.120(a)(1) through 148.120(a)(5); or qualifies as a Medicare DSH hospital under the current federal guidelines.

   ii) a government-owned facility, which meets the cash flow criterion under subsection (h)(1)(A)(ii) above.

   iii) a hospital which has filed for Chapter 11 bankruptcy, which meets the cash flow criterion under subsection (h)(1)(A)(ii) above.

C) the provider must file a delay of payment request as defined under subsection (h)(3)(A) below, and the request must include a, Cash Position Statement which is based upon current assets, current liabilities and other data for a date which is less than 60 days prior to the date of filing. Any liabilities payable to owners or related parties must not be reported as current liabilities on the Cash Position Statement. A deferral of assessment payments will be denied if any of the following criteria are met:

DEPARTMENT OF PUBLIC AID

NOTICE OF PROPOSED AMENDMENTS

   i) the ratio of current assets divided by current liabilities is greater than 2.0.

   ii) cash, short term investments and long term investments equal or exceed the total of accrued wages payable and the assessment payment. Long term investments which are unavailable for expenditure for current operations due to donor restrictions or contractual requirements will not be used in this calculation.

D) the provider must show evidence of denial of an application to borrow assessment funds through a cash flow bond pool or financial institution such as a commercial bank. The denial must be 90 days old or less.

E) the provider must sign an agreement with the Department which specifies the terms and conditions of the delayed payment provisions. The agreement shall contain the following provisions:

   i) specific reason(s) for institution of the delayed payment provisions:

   ii) specific dates on which payments must be received and the amount of payment which must be received on each specific date described;

   iii) the interest or a statement of interest waiver as described in subsection (h)(5) that shall be due from the provider as a result of institution of the delayed payment provisions;

   iv) a certification stating that, should the entity be sold, the new owners will be made aware of the liability' and any agreement selling the entity will include provisions that the new owners will assume responsibility for repaying the debt to the Department according to the original agreement; and

   v) a certification stating that all information submitted to the Department in support of the delayed payment request is true and accurate to the best of the signature's knowledge; and

   vi) such other terms and conditions that may be required by the Department. tfi2 2) A hospital which does not meet the above criteria may request a delayed payment schedule and/or the waiver of interest and penalties. The Director may approve the request, notwithstanding the hospital not meeting the above criteria, upon a sufficient showing of financial difficulties and good cause by the hospital. If the request for a delayed payment schedule and/or waiver of interest and penalties is approved, all other conditions of this subsection (h) shall apply.

3) Approval Process

A) In order to receive consideration for delayed payment

DEPARTMENT OF PUBLIC AID

NOTICE OF PROPOSED AMENDMENTS

provisions, providers must submit their request in writing (telefax requests are acceptable) to the Bureau of Program and Reimbursement Analysis. The request must be received as follows: delayed payment requests for installments due on September 30 of the year must be received on or before September 10 of the year; delayed payment requests for installments due on December 31 of the year must be received on or before December 10 of the year; delayed payment requests for installments due on March 31 of the year must be received on or before March 11 of the year; and delayed payment requests for installments due on May 31 of the year must be received on or before May 10 of the year. Requests must be complete and contain all required information before they are considered to have met the time requirements for filing a delayed payment request. All telefax requests must be followed up with original written requests, postmarked no later than the date of the telefax. The request must include:

   i)   an explanation of the circumstances creating the need for the delayed payment provisions;

   ii) supportive documentation to substantiate the emergency nature of the request including a cash position statement as defined in subsection (h)(1)(C) of this Section, a denial of application to borrow the assessment as defined in subsection (h)(1)(D) of this Section and an explanation of the risk of irreparable harm to the clients; and

   iii) specification of the specific arrangements requested by the provider.

B) The hospital shall be notified by the Department, in writing prior to the assessment due date, of the Department's decision with regard to the request for institution of delayed payment provisions. An agreement shall be issued to the provider for all approved requests. The agreement must be signed by the administrator, owner, chief executive officer or other authorized representative and be received by the Department prior to the first scheduled payment date listed in such agreement.

4) Waiver of Penalties. The penalties described in subsections (f)(1) and (f)(2) of this Section may be waived upon approval of the provider's request for institution of delayed payment provisions. In the event a provider's request for institution of delayed payment provisions is approved and the Department has received the signed agreement in accordance with subsection (h)(3)(B) above, such penalties shall be permanently waived for the subject quarter unless the provider fails to meet all of the terms and conditions of the agreement. In the event the provider fails to meet all of the terms and conditions of the agreement,

the agreement shall be considered null and void and such penalties shall be fully reinstated.

5) Interest. The delayed payments shall include interest at a rate not to exceed the State of Illinois borrowing rate. The applicable interest rate shall be identified in the agreement described in subsection (h)(1)(E) above. The interest may be waived by the Director if the facility's current ratio, as described in subsection (h)(1)(C) above, is 1.5 or less and the hospital meets the criteria in subsections (h)(1)(A) and (B) above. Any such waivers granted shall be expressly identified in the agreement described in subsection (h)(1)(E) above.

6) Subsequent Delayed Payment Arrangements. Once a provider has requested and received approval for delayed payment arrangements, the provider shall not receive approval for subsequent delayed payment arrangements until such time as the terms and conditions of any current delayed payment agreement have been satisfied or unless the provider is in full compliance with the terms of the current delayed payment agreement. The waiver of penalties described in subsection (h)(4) shall not apply to a provider that has not satisfied the terms and conditions of any current delayed payment agreement.

i) Administration and Enforcement Provisions
Pursuant to Section 5A-7 of P.A. 86-861, to the extent practicable, the Department shall administer and enforce P.A. 86-861, as amended by P.A. 88-88, and collect the assessments, interest, and penalty assessments imposed under the Law, using procedures employed in its administration of this Code generally and, as it deems appropriate, in a manner similar to that in which the Department of Revenue administers and collects the retailers' occupation tax under the Retailers' Occupation Tax Act ("ROTA").

j) Exemptions

1) A rural hospital, as defined in subsection (l)(11) below, shall be exempt from the assessment imposed under subsection (b), unless the exemption is a judged to be unconstitutional or otherwise invalid, in which case the provider shall pay the assessment imposed under subsection (b) above.

2) A hospital provider which is a county with a population of more than 3,000,000 that makes intergovernmental transfer payments as provided in Section 15-3 of P.A. 87-861, as amended by P.A. 88-85 and P.A. 88-88, shall be exempt from the assessment imposed by subsection (b) above, unless the exemption is adjudged to be unconstitutional or otherwise invalid, in which case the hospital shall pay the assessment imposed by subsection (b) above for all assessment periods beginning on or after July 1, 1992, and the assessment so paid shall be creditable against the intergovernmental transfer payments.

3) The Department is authorized to enter into an interagency agreement with a hospital organized under the University of

DEPARTMENT OF PUBLIC AID

NOTICE OF PROPOSED AMENDMENTS

Illinois Hospital Act exempt from the assessment imposed under subsection (b) of this Section, to make intergovernmental transfer payments to the Department. These payments shall be deposited into the General Revenue Fund.

4) The Department is also authorized to enter into agreements with publicly owned or operated hospitals not described in subsections (j)(1) through (j)(3) above to make intergovernmental transfer payments to the Department. These payments shall be deposited into the Hospital Provider Fund.

k) Nothing in P.A. 88-88 shall be construed to prevent the Department from collecting all amounts due under this Section pursuant to an assessment imposed before the effective date of P.A. 88-88.

l) Definitions
   As used in this Section, unless the context requires otherwise:
   1) "Adjusted gross hospital revenue" means the hospital provider's total gross patient charges less Medicare contractual allowances, but does not include gross patient revenue (and the portion of any Medicare contractual allowance related thereto) from skilled or intermediate long-term care services within the meaning of Title XVIII or XIX of the Social Security Act. Revenue generated from swing beds, as described in subsection (l)(12) below, is considered to be part of the provider's gross hospital revenue. Revenue not related to patient care, such as investment income, gift shop, cafeteria, or parking lot revenue, is not considered as patient revenue. Adjusted gross hospital revenue must be reported on an accrual basis for the assessment reporting period. All patient revenue accrued during the assessment reporting period must be included even though reimbursement may occur after the assessment reporting period. Patient revenue must be reported on a basis that is consistent with methods used on the hospital's last two cost reports.
   2) "Cigarette Tax Contribution" is the sum of the total amount deposited in the Hospital Provider Fund in the previous State fiscal year 1994 pursuant to Section 2(a) of the Cigarette Tax Act, plus the total amount deposited in the Hospital Provider Fund in the previous State fiscal year 1994 pursuant to Section 5A-3(c) of Public Act 88-88.
   3) "Department" means the Illinois Department of Public Aid.
   4) "Fund" means the Hospital Provider Fund.
   5) "Hospital" means an institution, place, building, or agency located in this State that is subject to licensure by the Illinois Department of Public Health under the Hospital Licensing Act, whether public or private and whether organized for profit or not-for-profit.
   6) "Hospital provider" means a person licensed by the Department of Public Health to conduct, operate, or maintain a hospital, regardless of whether the person is a Medicaid provider. For purposes of this definition, "person" means any political

DEPARTMENT OF PUBLIC AID

NOTICE OF PROPOSED AMENDMENTS

subdivision of the State, municipal corporation, individual, firm, partnership, corporation, company, limited liability company, association, joint stock association, or trust, or a receiver, executor, trustee, guardian, or other representative appointed by order of any court.

7) "Intergovernmental transfer payment" means the payments established under Section 15-3 of P.A. 87-861, as amended by P.A. 88-85 and P.A. 88-88, and includes without limitation payments payable under that Section for July, August and September of 1992.

8) "Maximum Section 5A-2 Contribution" is the total amount of tax imposed by Section 5A-2 of Public Act 88-88 in the previous State fiscal year 1994 on providers subject to the assessment imposed by subsection (b) above; multiplied by a fraction the numerator of which is adjusted gross hospital revenues reported to the Department by providers subject to the assessment imposed by subsection (b) for the previous State fiscal year 1994 and the denominator of which is adjusted gross hospital revenues reported to the Department by providers subject to the assessment imposed by subsection (b) for State fiscal year immediately preceding the previous State fiscal year 1993.

9) "Medicare Contractual Allowance" means the difference between charges at established rates and the amount estimated to be paid by Medicare, as appropriate, pursuant to agreements between the hospital and the Health Care Financing Administration.

10) "Provider's Savings Rate" is 1.88% multiplied by a fraction, the numerator of which is the Maximum Section 5A-2 Contribution minus the Cigarette Tax Contribution, and the denominator of which is the Maximum Section 5A-2 Contribution.

11) "Rural hospital" means a hospital that is:
    A) either located outside a metropolitan statistical area; or is
    B) located 15 miles or less from a county that is outside a metropolitan statistical area and that is licensed to perform medical/surgical or obstetrical services and had has a combined approved total bed capacity of 75 or fewer beds in these two service categories as of the effective date of P.A. 88-88 (July 14, 1993), as determined by the Illinois Department of Public Health; or
    C) qualified as a rural hospital according to subsection (l)(11)(A) or (B) above, on July 14, 1993.

12) The Illinois Department of Public Health must have been notified in writing of any changes to a facility's bed count on or before the effective date of P.A. 88-88 (July 14, 1993). Appeals of the geographic designation of hospital provider shall be in accordance with 89 Ill. Adm. Code 148.310(m).

12)13) "Swing-beds" means those beds for which a hospital provider has been granted an approval from the federal Health Care

Financing Administration to provide post-hospital extended care services (42 CFR 409.30, October 1, 1991) and be reimbursed as a swing-bed hospital (42 CFR 413.114, October 1, 1991).

[Source: Amended at 19 Ill. Reg. _____ , effective _____)

Section 140.82 Developmentally Disabled Care Provider Fund

a) Purpose and Contents
    1) The Developmentally Disabled Care Provider Fund was created in the State Treasury upon enactment of Public Act 87-861 and Public Act 88-88. Interest earned by the Fund shall be credited to the Fund. The Fund shall not be used to replace any funds Appropriated to the Medicaid program by the General Assembly.
    2) The Fund is created for the purpose of receiving and disbursing monies in accordance with this Section and Public Act 87-861, as amended by Public Act 88-88.
    3) The Fund shall consist of:
        A) All monies collected or received by the Department under subsection (b) below;
        B) All federal matching funds received by the Department as a result of expenditures made by the Department that are attributable to monies deposited in the Fund;
        C) Any interest or penalty levied in conjunction with the administration of the Fund;
        D) All other monies received for the Fund from any other source, including interest earned thereon; and
        E) All monies transferred from the Medicaid Developmentally Disabled Provider Participation Fee Trust Fund.

b) Provider Assessments
    Beginning on July 1, 1993, an An assessment is imposed upon each developmentally disabled care provider for the State fiscal year beginning on July 1, 1993, and ending on June 30, 1995, in an amount equal to six percent of its adjusted gross developmentally disabled care revenue for the prior State fiscal year. Adjusted gross developmentally disabled care revenue for the fiscal year beginning on July 1, 1993, will be based upon the provider's annualized State fiscal year 1993 revenue. Adjusted gross developmentally disabled care revenue for the fiscal year beginning on July 1, 1994, will be based upon the provider's annualized State fiscal year 1994 revenue. The revenue for each year will be reported on the Developmentally Disabled Care Provider Tax form to be filed by a date designated by the Department. The Department reserves the right to audit the reported data.

c) Payment of Assessment Due
    1) The assessment described in subsection (b) above shall be due and payable in quarterly installments, each equalling one-fourth of

the assessment for the year, on September 30, December 31, March 31, and May 31 of the year. Assessment payments postmarked on the due date will be considered paid on time.
    2) All payments received by the Department shall be credited first to unpaid installment amounts (rather than to penalty or interest), beginning with the most delinquent installments.

d) Reporting Requirements, Penalty, and Maintenance of Records
    1) After June 30 of each State fiscal year, and on or before September 30 of the succeeding State fiscal year, every developmentally disabled care provider subject to an assessment under subsection (b) above shall file a report with the Department. The report shall be on a form prepared by the Department. The report shall include the adjusted gross developmentally disabled care revenue from the State fiscal year just ended and shall be utilized by the Department to calculate the assessment for the State fiscal year commencing on the preceding July 1. If a developmentally disabled care provider operates or maintains more than one developmentally disabled care facility, a separate report shall be filed for each facility. In the case of a developmentally disabled care provider existing as a corporation or legal entity other than an individual, the report filed by it shall be signed by its president, vice-president, secretary, or treasurer or by its properly authorized agent.
    2) If the developmentally disabled care provider fails to file its report for a State fiscal year on or before the due date of the report, there shall be, unless waived by the Department for reasonable cause, added to the assessment imposed in subsection (b) above a penalty assessment equal to 25% of the assessment imposed for the year.
    3) Every developmentally disabled care provider subject to an assessment under subsection (b) above shall keep records and books that will permit the determination of adjusted gross developmentally disabled care revenue on a State fiscal year basis. All such books and records shall be maintained for a minimum of three years following the filing date of the assessment report and shall, at all times during business hours of the day, be subject to inspection by the Department or its duly authorized agents and employees.
    4) Amended Assessment Reports. With the exception of amended assessment reports filed in accordance with subsection (d)(5) or (6) below, an amended assessment report must be filed within 30 calendar days after the original report due date. The amended report must be accompanied by a letter identifying the changes and the justification for the amended report. The provider will be advised of any adjustments to the original annual assessment amount through a written notification from the Department. Penalties may be applied to the amount underpaid due to a filing

DEPARTMENT OF PUBLIC AID

NOTICE OF PROPOSED AMENDMENTS

error.

5) Submission of Financial Audit Statements.. All developmentally disabled care providers are required to submit a copy of all financial statements audited by an external, independent auditor to the Department within 30 days of the close of such externally performed financial audits. If the provider's year end does not coincide with the June 30th ending date for the assessment report, the provider must submit all financial audits covering the assessment report period. An amended assessment report must accompany such external financial audit statements if the data submitted on the initial assessment report changes based upon the findings of such external financial audits and as indicated in the audited external financial statements. Penalties may be applied to the amount underpaid due to a filing error.

6) Reconsideration of Adjusted Assessment. If the Department, through an audit conducted by the Department or its agent within three years after the end of the fiscal year in which the assessment was due, changes the assessment liability of a developmentally disabled care provider, the developmentally disabled care provider may request a review or reconsideration of the adjusted assessment within 30 days of the Department's notification of the change in assessment liability. Requests for reconsideration of the assessment adjustment shall not be considered if such requests are not postmarked on or before the end of the 30 day review period. Penalties may be applied to the amount underpaid due to a filing error.

e) Procedure for Partial Year Reporting/Operating Adjustments

1) Cessation of business during the fiscal year in which the assessment is being paid. For a developmentally disabled care provider who ceases to conduct, operate, or maintain a facility to which the person is subject to assessment under subsection (b) above, the assessment for the State fiscal year in which the cessation occurs shall be adjusted by multiplying the assessment computed under subsection (d) by a fraction, the numerator of which is the number of days in the year during which the provider conducts, operates, or maintains the facility and the denominator of which is 365. The person shall file a final, amended report with the Department not more than 30 calendar days after the cessation, reflecting the adjustment, and shall pay with the final report the assessment for the year as so adjusted, to the extent not previously paid.

2) Commencing of business during the fiscal year in which the assessment is being paid. A developmentally disabled care provider who commences conducting, operating, or maintaining a facility of which the person is subject to assessment under subsection (b) above, shall file an initial return for the State fiscal year in which the commencement occurs within 30 calendar days thereafter and shall pay the assessment under subsection (d)

DEPARTMENT OF PUBLIC AID

NOTICE OF PROPOSED AMENDMENTS

above as computed by the Department in equal installments on the due date of the initial assessment determination and on the regular installment due dates for the State fiscal year occuring after the due date of the initial assessment determination. In determining the annual assessment amount for the provider the Department shall develop hypothetical annualized revenue projections based upon geographic location, facility size and patient case mix. The assessment determination made by the Department is final.

3) Partial Fiscal-Year Operation Adjustment. For a developmentally disabled care provider that did not conduct, operate, or maintain a facility throughout the entire fiscal year reporting period, the assessment for the following State fiscal year shall be annualized based on the provider's actual developmentally disabled care revenue for the portion of the reporting period the facility was operational (dividing adjusted developmentally disabled care revenue by the number of days the facility was in operation and then multiplying that amount by 365). Developmentally disabled care revenue realized by a prior provider from the same facility during the fiscal year shall be used in the annualization equation, if available.

4) Changes in Ownership and/or Operators. The full quarterly assessment must be paid on the designated due dates regardless of changes in ownership or operators. Liability for the payment of the assessment amount (including past due assessments and any interest or penalties that may have accrued against the amount rests on the developmentally disabled care provider currently operating or maintaining the developmentally disabled care facility regardless if these amount were incurred by the current owner or were incurred by previous owners. Collection of delinquent assessment fees from previous providers will be made against the current provider. Failure of the current provider to pay any outstanding assessment liabilities incurred by previous providers shall result in the application of penalties described in subsection (f)(1) of this Section.

f) Penalties

1) Any facility that fails to pay the full amount of an installment when due shall be charged, unless waived by the Department for reasonable cause, a penalty equal to 5% of the amount of the installment not paid on or before the due date, plus 5% of the portion thereof remaining unpaid on the last day of each month thereafter, not to exceed 100% of the installment amount not paid on or before the due date.

2) Within 45 days from the due date, the Department may begin recovery actions against delinquent facilities participating in the Medicaid Program. Payments may be withheld from the facility until the entire assessment, including any penalties, is satisfied, or until a reasonable repayment schedule has been

DEPARTMENT OF PUBLIC AID

NOTICE OF PROPOSED AMENDMENTS

approved by the Department. If a reasonable agreement cannot be reached, or if the facility fails to comply with an agreement the Department reserves the right to recover any outstanding provider assessment. Interest and penalty by recouping the amount or a portion thereof from the provider's future payments from the Department. The provider may appeal this recoupment in accordance with Department rules contained in 89 Ill. Adm. Code 104. The Department has the right to continue recoupment during the appeal process. Penalties pursuant to subsection (f)(1) above will continue to accrue during the recoupment process. Recoupment proceedings against the same facility two times in a fiscal year may be cause for termination from the Program. Failure by the Department to initiate recoupment activities within 45 days shall not reduce the provider's liabilities nor shall it preclude the Department from taking action at a later date.

3) If the facility does not participate in the Medicaid Program, or is no longer doing business with the Department, or the Department cannot recover the full amount due through the claims processing system, within three months of the assessment due date, the Department may recover the monies, including penalties and interest owed, plus court costs.

g) Delayed Payment - Groups of Facilities.
The Director may establish delayed payment of assessments and/or waive the payment of interest and penalties for groups of facilities when:
1) the State delays payments to facilities due to problems related to State cash flow, or
2) a cash flow bond pool's or any other group financing plans' requests from providers for loans are in excess of its scheduled proceeds such that a significant number of facilities will be unable to obtain a loan to pay the assessment.

h) Delayed Payment - Individual Facilities
In addition to the provisions of subsection (g) above, the Director may delay assessments for individual facilities that are unable to make timely payments under this Section due to financial difficulties. No delayed payment arrangements shall extend beyond the last business day of the calendar quarter following the quarter in which the assessment was to have been received by the Department as described in subsection (C) above.
1) Criteria. Delayed payment provisions may be instituted only under extraordinary circumstances. Delayed payment provision shall be made only to qualified facilities who meet all of the following requirements:
A) the facility has experienced an emergency which necessitates institution of delayed payment provisions. Emergency in this instance is defined as a circumstance under which institution of the payment and penalty provisions described in subsections (c)(i), (c)(2), (f)(1), (f)(2) and (f)(3)

DEPARTMENT OF PUBLIC AID

NOTICE OF PROPOSED AMENDMENTS

above would impose severe and irreparable harm to the clients served. Circumstances which may create such emergencies include, but are not limited to, the following:
i) Department system errors (either automated system or clerical) which have precluded payments, or which have caused erroneous payments such that the facility's ability to provide further services to clients is severely impaired;
ii) cash flow problems encountered by a facility which are unrelated to Department technical system problems and which result in extensive financial problems to a facility adversely impacting on its ability to serve its clients.
B) the facility serves a significant number of clients under the Medical Assistance Program. Significant in this instance means:
i) 85 percent or more of their residents must be eligible for public assistance.
ii) a government-owned facility, which meets the cash flow criteria under subsection (h)(1)(A)(ii) above.
iii) a provider who has filed for Chapter 11 bankruptcy, which meets the cash flow criterion under subsection (h)(1)(A)(ii) above.
C) the facility must file a delay of payment request as defined in subsection (h)(3)(A) below, and the request must include a Cash Position Statement which is based upon current Assets, current liabilities and other data for a date which is less than 60 days prior to the date of filing. Any liabilities payable to owners or related parties must not be reported as current liabilities on the Cash Position Statement. A deferral of assessment payments will be denied if any of the following criteria are met:
i) the ratio of current assets divided by current liabilities is greater than 2.0;
ii) cash, short term investments and long term investments equal or exceed the total of accrued wages payable and the assessment payment. Long term investments which are unavailable for expenditure for current operations due to donor restrictions or contractual requirements will not be used in this calculation;
iii) cash or other assets have been distributed during the previous 90 days to owners or related parties in an amount equal to or exceeding the assessment payment for dividends, salaries in excess of those allowable under Section 140.541 or payments for purchase of goods or services in excess of cost as defined in Section 140.537.
D) the facility, with the exception of government owned

DEPARTMENT OF PUBLIC AID

NOTICE OF PROPOSED AMENDMENTS

facilities, must show evidence of denial of an application to borrow assessment funds through a cash flow bond pool or financial institution such as a commercial bank. The denial must be 90 days old or less.

E) the facility must sign an agreement with the Department which specifies the terms and conditions of the delayed payment provisions. The agreement shall contain the following provisions:

i) specific reason(s) for institution of the delayed payment provisions;

ii) specific dates on which payments must be received and the amount of payment which must be received on each ·specific date described;

iii) the interest or a statement of interest waiver as described in subsection (h)(5) that shall be due from the facility as a result of institution of the delayed payment provisions;

iv) a certification stating that, should the entity be sold, the new owners will be made aware of the liability and any agreement selling the entity will include provisions that the new owners will assume responsibility for repaying the debt to the Department according to the original agreement;

v) a certification stating that all information submitted to the Department in support of the delayed payment request is true and accurate to ·the best of the signature's knowledge; and

vi) such other terms and conditions that may be required by the Department.

2) A facility which does not meet the above criteria may request a delayed payment schedule and/or the waiver of interest and penalties. The Director may approve the request, notwithstanding the facility not meeting the above criteria, upon a sufficient showing of financial difficulties and good cause by the facility. If the request for a delayed payment schedule and/or waiver of interest and penalties is approved, all other conditions of this subsection (h) shall apply.

3) Approval Process

A) In order to receive consideration for delayed payment provisions, facilities must submit their request in writing (telefax requests are acceptable) to the Bureau of Program and Reimbursement Analysis. The request must be received as follows: delayed payment requests for installments due on September 30 of the year must be received on or before September 10 of the year; and delayed payment requests for installments due on December 31 of the year must be received on or before December 10 of the year; delayed payment requests for installments due on March 31 of the year must

DEPARTMENT OF PUBLIC AID

NOTICE OF PROPOSED AMENDMENTS

be received on or before March 11 of the year; delayed payment requests for installments due on May 31 of the year must be received on or before May 10 of the year. Requests must be complete and contain all required information before they are considered to have met the time requirements for filing a delayed payment request. All telefax requests must be followed up with original written requests postmarked no later than the date of the telefax. The request must include:

i) an explanation of the circumstances creating the need for the delayed payment provisions;

ii) supportive documentation to substantiate the emergency nature of the request and risk of irreparable harm to the clients; and

iii) specification of the specific arrangements requested by the facility.

B) The facility shall be notified by the Department, in writing prior to the assessment due date, of the Department's decision with regard to the request for institution of delayed payment provisions. An agreement shall be issued to the facility for all approved requests. The agreement must be signed by the administrator, owner or other authorized representative and be received by the Department prior to the first scheduled payment date listed in such agreement.

4) Waiver of Penalties. The penalties described in subsections (f)(1) and (f)(2) of this Section may be waived upon approval of the facility's request for institution of delayed payment provisions. In the event a facility's request for institution of delayed payment provisions is approved and the Department has received the signed agreement in accordance with subsection (h)(3)(B) above, such penalties shall be permanently waived for the subject quarter unless the facility fails to meet all of the terms and conditions of the agreement. In the event the facility fails to meet all the terms and conditions of the agreement, the agreement shall be considered null and void and such penalties shall be fully reinstated.

5) Interest. The delayed payments shall include interest at a rate not to exceed the State of Illinois borrowing rate. The applicable interest rate shall be identified in the agreement described in subsection (h)(1)(E) above. The interest may be waived by the Director if the facility's current ratio, as described in subsection (h)(1)(C) above, is 1.5 or less and the facility meets the criteria in (h)1)(A) and (B). Any such waivers granted shall be expressly identified in the agreement described in subsection (h)(1)(E) above.

6) Subsequent Delayed Payment Arrangements. Once a facility has requested and received approval for delayed payment arrangements, the facility shall not receive approval for subsequent delayed

DEPARTMENT OF PUBLIC AID

NOTICE OF PROPOSED AMENDMENTS

payment arrangements until such time as the terms and conditions
of any current delayed payment agreement have been satisfied or
unless the provider is in full compliance with the terms of the
current delay of payment agreement. The waiver of penalties
described in subsection (h)(4) shall not apply to a facility that
has not satisfied the terms and conditions of any current delayed
payment agreement.

i) Administration; enforcement provisions
    Pursuant to Section 5C-6 of P.A. 86-861, to the extent practicable,
    the Department shall administer and enforce P.A. 86-861, as amended by
    P.A. 88-88, and collect the assessments, interest, and penalty
    assessments imposed under the law, using procedures employed in its
    administration of this Code generally and, as it deems appropriate, in
    a manner similar to that in which the Department of Revenue
    administers and collects the retailers' occupation tax under the
    Retailers' Occupation Tax Act ("ROTA").

j) Nothing in P.A. 88-88 shall be construed to prevent the Department
    from collecting all amounts due under this Section pursuant to an
    assessment impose before the effective date of P.A. 88-88.

k) Definitions
    1) "Adjusted gross developmentally disabled care revenue" means the
        developmentally disabled care provider's total revenue for
        inpatient residential services, less contractual allowances and
        discounts on patients' accounts, but does not include non-patient
        revenue from sources such as contributions, donations or
        bequests, investments, day training services, television and
        telephone service, rental of facility space, or sheltered care
        revenue. Adjusted gross developmentally disabled care revenue
        must be reported on an accrual basis for the tax reporting
        period. All patient revenue accrued during the tax reporting
        period must be included even though reimbursement may occur after
        the tax reporting period. Patient revenue must be reported on a
        basis that is consistent with methods used on the facility's last
        two cost reports.
    2) "Contractual Allowance" means the difference between charges at
        established rates and the amount estimated to be paid by third
        party payors or patients, as appropriate, pursuant to
        agreements/contracts with the developmentally disabled care
        provider; courtesy and policy discounts provided to employees,
        medical staff and clergy; and charity care, but "contractual
        allowance" does not mean any Provider Participation fees/taxes
        paid to the Illinois Department of Public Aid.
    3) "Department" means the Illinois Department of Public Aid.
    4) "Developmentally disabled care facility" means an intermediate
        care facility for the mentally retarded within the meaning of
        Title XIX of the Social Security Act, whether public or private
        and whether organized for profit or not-for-profit, but shall not
        include any facility operated by the State.

DEPARTMENT OF PUBLIC AID

NOTICE OF PROPOSED AMENDMENTS

5) "Developmentally disabled care provider" means a person
    conducting, operating, or maintaining a developmentally disabled
    care facility. For this purpose, "person" means any political
    subdivision of the State, municipal corporation, individual,
    firm, partnership, corporation, company, limited liability
    company, association, joint stock association, or trust, or a
    receiver, executor, trustee, guardian or other representative
    appointed by order of any court.
6) "Facility" means all intermediate care facilities as defined
    under "Developmentally disabled care facility" above.
7) "Fund" means the Developmentally Disabled Care Provider Fund.

(Source: Amended at 19 Ill. Reg. _____, effective
          _____)

Section 140.84 Long Term Care Provider Fund

a) Purpose and Contents
    1) The Long Term Care Provider Fund was created in the State
        Treasury upon enactment of Public Act 87-861 and Public Act
        88-88. Interest earned by the Fund shall be credited to the
        Fund. The Fund shall not be used to replace any funds
        appropriated to the Medicaid program by the General Assembly.
    2) The Fund is created for the purpose of receiving and disbursing
        monies in accordance with this Section and Public Act 87-861, as
        amended by Public Act 88-88.
    3) The Fund shall consist of:
        A) All monies collected or received by the Department under
            subsection (b) below;
        B) All federal matching funds received by the Department as a
            result of expenditures made by the Department that are
            attributable to monies deposited in the Fund;
        C) Any interest or penalty levied in conjunction with the
            administration of the Fund;
        D) All other monies received for the Fund from any other
            source, including interest earned thereon;
        E) All monies transferred from the Medicaid Long Term Care
            Provider Participation Fee Trust Fund; and
        F) All monies transferred from the Tobacco Products Tax Act.

b) License Fee
    Beginning on July 1, 1993, a A nursing home license fee is imposed
    upon each nursing home provider for the State fiscal year beginning on
    July 1, 1993, and ending on June 30, 1995, in an amount equal to $1.50
    for each licensed nursing bed day for the calendar quarter in which
    the payment is due. All nursing home beds subject to licensure under
    the Nursing Home Care Act or the Hospital Licensing Act, with the
    exception of swing-beds, as defined in subsection (k)(8) of this
    Section will be used to calculate the licensed nursing bed days for

DEPARTMENT OF PUBLIC AID

NOTICE OF PROPOSED AMENDMENTS

each quarter. This license fee shall not be billed or passed on to
any resident of a nursing home operated by the nursing home providers.
Changes in the number of licensed nursing beds will be reported to the
Department quarterly, as described in subsection (d)(1) below. The
Department reserves the right to audit the reported data.

c) Payment of License Fee Due

   1) The license fee described in subsection (b) above shall be due
      and payable in quarterly installments, on September 10, December
      10, March 10, and June 10 of the year. License fee payments
      postmarked on the due date will be considered as paid on time.

   2) All payments received by the Department shall be credited first
      to unpaid installment amounts (rather than to penalty or
      interest), beginning with the most delinquent installments.

   3) County nursing homes directed and maintained pursuant to Section
      5-1005 of the Counties Code may meet their license fee obligation
      by the county government certifying to the Department that county
      expenditures have been obligated for the operation of the county
      nursing home in an amount at least equal to the amount of the
      license fee. County governments wishing to provide such
      certification must:

      A) Sign a certification form certifying that the funds
         represent expenditures eligible for federal financial
         participation under Title XIX of the Social Security Act (42
         U.S.C. 1396 et seq.), and that these funds are not federal
         funds, or are federal funds authorized by federal law to be
         used to match other federal funds;

      B) Submit the certification document to the Department once a
         year along with a copy of that portion of the county budget
         showing the funds appropriated for the operation of the
         county nursing home. These documents must be submitted
         within 30 days after the final approval of the county
         budget. The county budget and/or budgets covering the State
         fiscal year of July 1, 1993, through June 30, 1995, must be
         submitted by a date designated by the Department;

      C) Submit the monthly claim form in the amount of the rate
         established by the Department minus any third party
         liability amount. This amount will be reduced by an amount
         determined by the amount certified and the number of months
         remaining in the fiscal year, prior to payment because a
         certification statement was provided in lieu of an actual
         license fee payment; and

      D) Make records available upon request to the Department and/or
         the United States Department of Health and Human Services
         pertaining to the certification of county funds.

d) Reporting Requirements, Penalty, and Maintenance of Records

   1) On or before the due dates described in subsection (c)(1), each
      nursing home provider subject to a license fee under subsection
      (b) of this Section shall file a report with the Department

DEPARTMENT OF PUBLIC AID

NOTICE OF PROPOSED AMENDMENTS

reflecting any changes in the number of licensed nursing beds
occurring during the reporting quarter. The report shall be on a
form prepared by the Department. The changes will be reported
quarterly and shall be submitted with the revised quarterly
license fee payment. For the purpose of calculating the license
fee described in subsection (b) above, all changes in licensed
nursing beds will be effective upon approval of the change by the
Illinois Department of Public Health. Documentation showing the
change in licensed nursing beds, and the date the change was
approved by the Illinois Department of Public Health, must be
submitted to the Department of Public Aid with the licensed
nursing bed change form. If a nursing home provider operates or
maintains more than one nursing home, a separate report shall be
filed for each facility. In the case of a nursing home provider
existing as a corporation or legal entity other than an
individual, the report filed by it shall be signed by its
president, vice-president, secretary, or treasurer or by its
properly authorized agent.

   2) If the nursing home provider fails to file its report for a State
      fiscal year on or before the due date of the report, there shall,
      unless waived by the Department for reasonable cause, be added to
      the license fee imposed in subsection (b) above a penalty fee
      equal to 25% of the license fee imposed for the year.

   3) Every nursing home provider subject to a license fee under
      subsection (b) above shall keep records and books that will
      permit the determination of licensed nursing bed days on a
      quarterly basis. All such books and records shall be maintained
      for a minimum of three years following the filing date of the
      license fee report and shall, at all times during business hours
      of the day, be subject to inspection by the Department or its
      duly authorized agents and employees.

   4) Amended License Fee Reports. With the exception of amended
      license fee reports filed in accordance with subsection (d)(5)
      below, an amended license fee report must be filed within 30
      calendar days after the original report due date. The amended
      report must be accompanied by a letter identifying the changes
      and the justification for the amended report. The provider will
      be advised of any adjustments to the original annual license fee
      amount through a written notification from the Department.
      Penalties may be applied to the amount underpaid due to a filing
      error.

   5) Reconsideration of Adjusted License Fee. If the Department,
      through an audit conducted by the Department or its agent within
      three years after the end of the fiscal year in which the
      assessment/license fee was due, changes the license fee liability
      of a nursing home provider, the nursing home provider may request
      a review or reconsideration of the adjusted license fee within 30
      days of the Department's notification of the change in license

DEPARTMENT OF PUBLIC AID

NOTICE OF PROPOSED AMENDMENTS

fee liability. Requests for reconsideration of the license fee adjustment shall not be considered if such requests are not postmarked on or before the end of the 30 day review period. Penalties may be applied to the amount underpaid due to a filing error.

e) Procedure for Partial Year Reporting/Operating Adjustments

1) Cessation of business during the quarter in which the license fee is being paid and the closure date has been set. A nursing home provider who ceases to conduct, operate, or maintain a facility to which the person is subject to the license fee imposed under subsection (b) above, and for which the closure date for the facility has been set, shall file a final report with the Department on or before the due date for the quarter in which the closure is to occur. The report will reflect the adjusted number of days the facility is open during the reporting quarter, and shall be submitted with the final quarterly payment Example: A facility is set to close on September 24. On or before the due date of September 30, the facility will submit a final report reflecting 86 days of the operation (July 1 through September 24) and the corresponding quarterly license fee payment.

2) Cessation of business after the quarterly due date. A nursing home provider who ceases to conduct, operate, or maintain a facility for which the person is subject to the license fee imposed under subsection (b) above, and for which closure occurs after the due date for the reporting quarter, but prior to the last day of the reporting quarter, shall file an amended final report with the Department within 30 days after the closure date. The amended report will reflect the number of days the facility was operated during the reporting quarter and the revised license fee amount. Upon verifying the data submitted on the amended report, the Department will issue a refund for the amount overpaid. Example: On December 10 a facility pays the license fee for 92 days covering the reporting quarter of October 1 through December 31. The facility closed December 27. An amended report reflecting 88 days, the actual number of days the facility was operational during the quarter (October 1 through December 27) must be filed with the Department.

3) Cessation of business prior to the quarterly due date. A nursing home provider who ceases to conduct, operate, or maintain a facility for which the person is subject to the license fee imposed under subsection (b) above, and for which closure occurs prior to the due date for the reporting quarter, shall file a final report with the Department within 30 days after the closure date. The final report will reflect the number of days the facility was operational during the reporting during the quarter and the corresponding final license fee amount. Closure dates will be verified with the Department of Public Health, and if necessary adjustments will be made to the final license fee due.

DEPARTMENT OF PUBLIC AID

NOTICE OF PROPOSED AMENDMENTS

Example: Facility closes on January 17. On or before February 17, the facility must file a final report for the reporting quarter of January 1 through March 31. The report would reflect 17 days of operation (January 1 through January 17) during the quarter and must be accompanied by the final license fee payment for the facility.

4) Commencing of business during the fiscal year in which the license fee is being paid. A nursing home provider who commences conducting, operating, or maintaining a facility for which the person is subject to the license fee imposed under subsection (b) above, shall file an initial report for the reporting quarter in which the commencement occurs within 30 calendar days thereafter and shall pay the license fee under subsection (d) above.

5) Change in ownership and/or operators. The full quarterly assessment/license fee must be paid on the designated due date regardless of changes in ownership operators. Liability for the payment of the assessment/license fee amount (including past due assessment/license fees and any interest or penalties that may have accrued against the amount) rests on the nursing home provider currently operating or maintaining the nursing facility regardless if these amounts were incurred by the current owner or were incurred by previous owners. Collection of delinquent assessment/license fees from previous providers will be made against the current provider. Failure of the current provider to pay any outstanding assessment/license fee liabilities incurred by previous providers shall result in the application of penalties described in subsection (f)(1) of this Section.

f) Penalties

1) Any nursing home provider that fails to pay the full amount of an installment when due, or fails to report a change in licensed nursing beds approved by the Department of Public Health prior to the due date of installment, shall be charged, unless waived by the Department for reasonable cause, a penalty equal to 5% of the amount of the installment not paid on or before the due date, plus 5% of the portion thereof remaining unpaid on the last day of each month thereafter, not to exceed 100% of the installment amount not paid on or before the due date.

2) Within 45 days from the due date, the Department may begin recovery actions against delinquent nursing home providers participating in the Medicaid Program. Payments may be withheld from the provider until the entire license fee, including any penalties, is satisfied or until a reasonable repayment schedule has been approved by the Department. If a reasonable agreement cannot be reached, or if a provider fails to comply with an agreement, the Department reserves the right to recover any outstanding license fee, interest and penalty by recouping the amount or a portion thereof from the provider's future payments from the Department. The provider may appeal this recoupment in

DEPARTMENT OF PUBLIC AID

NOTICE OF PROPOSED AMENDMENTS

accordance with the Department rules contained in 89 Ill. Adm.
Code 104. The Department has the right to continue recoupment
during the appeal process. Penalties pursuant to subsection
(f)(1) above will continue to accrue during the recoupment
process. Recoupment proceedings against the same nursing home
provider two times in a fiscal year may be cause for termination
from the Program. Failure by the Department to initiate
recoupment activities within 45 days shall not reduce the
provider's liabilities nor shall it preclude the Department from
taking action at a later date.

3) If the nursing home provider does not participate in the Medicaid
Program, or is no longer doing business with the Department, or
the Department cannot recover the full amount due through the
claims processing system, within three months after the fee due
date, the Department may begin legal action to recover the
monies, including penalties and interest owed, plus court costs.

g) Delayed Payment - Groups of Facilities
The Director may establish delayed payment of fees and/or waive the
payment of interest and penalties for groups of facilities when:
1) the State delays payments to facilities due to problems related
to State cash flow, or
2) a cash flow bond pool's or any other group financing plans'
requests from providers for loans are in excess of its scheduled
proceeds such that a significant number of facilities will be
unable to obtain a loan to pay the license fee.

h) Delayed Payment - Individual Facilities
In addition to the provisions of subsection (g) above, the Director
may delay license fees for individual facilities that are unable to
make timely payments under this Section due to financial difficulties.
No delayed payment arrangements shall extend beyond the last business
day of the calendar quarter following the quarter in which the license
fee was to have been received by the Department as described in
subsection (c) above.
1) Criteria. Delayed payment provisions may be instituted only
under extraordinary circumstances. Delayed payment provisions
shall be made only to qualified facilities who meet all of the
following requirements:
A) the facility has experienced an emergency which necessitates
institution of delayed payment provisions. Emergency in
this instance is defined as a circumstance under which
institution of the payment and penalty provisions described
in subsections (c)(1), (c)(2), (f)(1), (f)(2) and (f)(3)
above would impose severe and irreparable harm to the
clients served. Circumstances which may create such
emergencies include, but are not limited to, the following:
i) Department system errors (either automated system or
clerical) which have precluded payments, or which have
caused erroneous payments such that the facility's

DEPARTMENT OF PUBLIC AID

NOTICE OF PROPOSED AMENDMENTS

ability to provide further services to clients is
severely impaired;
ii) cash flow problems encountered by a facility which are
unrelated to Department technical system problems and
which result in extensive financial problems to a
facility adversely impacting on its ability to serve
its clients.
B) the facility serves a significant number of clients under
the Medical Assistance Program. Significant in this
instance means:
i) 85 percent or more of their residents must be eligible
for public assistance.
ii) a government-owned facility, which meets the cash flow
criterion under subsection (h)(1)(A)(ii) above.
iii) a provider who has filed for Chapter 11 bankruptcy,
which meets cash flow criterion under subsection
(h)(1)(A)(ii).
C) the facility must file a delay of payment request as defined
under subsection (h)(3)(A) and the request must include a
Cash Position Statement which is based upon current assets,
current liabilities and other data for a date which is less
than 60 days prior to the date of filing. Any liabilities
payable to owners or related parties must not be reported as
current liabilities on the Cash Position Statement. A
deferral of license fee payments will be denied if any of
the following criteria are met:
i) the ratio of current assets divided by current
liabilities is greater than 2.0;
ii) cash, short term investments and long term investments
equal or exceed the total of accrued wages payable and
the license fee payment. Long term investments which
are unavailable for expenditure for current operations
due to donor restrictions or contractual requirements
will not be used in this calculation;
iii) cash or other assets have been distributed during the
previous 90 days to owners or related parties in an
amount equal to or exceeding the license fee payment
for dividends, salaries in excess of those allowable
under Section 140.541 or payment for purchase of goods
or services in excess of cost as defined in Section
140.537.
D) the facility, with the exception of government owned
facilities, must show evidence of denial of an application
to borrow license fee funds through a cash flow bond pool or
financial institutions such as a commercial bank. The
denial must be 90 days old or less.
E) the facility must sign an agreement with the Department
which specifies the terms and conditions of the delayed

DEPARTMENT OF PUBLIC AID

NOTICE OF PROPOSED AMENDMENTS

payment provisions. The agreement shall contain the following provisions:

i) specific reason(s) for institution of the delayed payment provisions;

ii) specific dates on which payments must be received and the amount of payment which must be received on each specific date described;

iii) the interest or a statement of interest waiver as described in subsection (h)(5) below that shall be due from the facility as a result of institution of the delayed payment provisions;

iv) a certification stating that, should the entity be sold, the new owners will be made aware of the liability and any agreement selling the entity will include provisions that the new owners will assume responsibility for repaying the debt to the Department according to the original agreement;

v) a certification stating that all information submitted to the Department in support of the delayed payment request is true and accurate to the best of the signature's knowledge; and

vi) such other terms and conditions that may be required by the Department.

2) A facility which does not meet the above criteria may request a delayed payment schedule and/or the waiver of interest and penalties. The Director may approve the request, notwithstanding the facility not meeting the above criteria, upon a sufficient showing of financial difficulties and good cause by the facility. If the request for a delayed payment schedule and/or waiver of interest and penalties is approved, all other conditions of this subsection (h) shall apply.

3) Approval Process

A) In order to receive consideration for delayed payment provisions, facilities must submit their request in writing (telefax requests are acceptable) to the Bureau of Program and Reimbursement Analysis. The request must be received as follows: delayed payment requests for installments due on September 10 of the year must be received on or before August 20 of the year; delayed payment requests for installments due on December 10 of the year must be received on or before November 22 of the year; delayed payment requests for installments due on March 10 of the year must be received on or before February 18 of the year; and delayed payment requests for installments due on June 10 of the year must be received on or before May 20 of the year. Requests must be complete and contain all required information before they are considered to have met the time requirements for filing a delayed payment request. All

DEPARTMENT OF PUBLIC AID

NOTICE OF PROPOSED AMENDMENTS

telefax requests must be followed up with original written requests by certified mail postmarked no later than the date of the telefax. The request must include:

i) an explanation of the circumstances creating the need for the delayed payment provisions;

ii) supportive documentation to substantiate the emergency nature of the request including a cash position statement as defined in subsection (h)(1)(C) a denial of application to borrow the license fee as defined in subsection (h)(1)(D) and an explanation risk of irreparable harm to the clients; and

iii) specification of the specific arrangements requested by the facility.

B) The facility shall be notified by the Department, in writing prior to the license fee due date, of the Department's decision with regard to the request for institution of delayed payment provisions. An agreement must be issued to the facility for all approved requests. The agreement must be signed by the administrator, owner or other authorized representative and be received by the Department prior to the first scheduled payment date listed in such agreement.

4) Waiver of Penalties. The penalties described in subsections (f)(1) and (f)(2) may be waived upon approval of the facility's request for institution of delayed payment provisions. In the event a facility's request for institution of delayed payment provisions is approved and the Department has received the signed agreement in accordance with subsection (h)(3)(B) above, such penalties shall be permanently waived for the subject quarter unless the facility fails to meet all of the terms and conditions of the agreement. In the event the facility fails to meet all of the terms and conditions of the agreement, the agreement shall be considered null and void and such penalties shall be fully reinstated.

5) Interest. The delayed payments shall include interest at a rate not to exceed the State of Illinois borrowing rate. The applicable interest rate shall be identified in the agreement described in subsection (h)(1)(B) above. The interest may be waived by the Director if the facility's current ratio, as described in subsection (h)(1)(C) above, is 1.5 or less and the facility meets the criteria in (h)(1)(A) and (B). Any such waivers granted shall be expressly identified in the agreement described in subsection (h)(1)(B) above.

6) Subsequent Delayed Payment Arrangements. Once a facility has requested and received approval for delayed payment arrangements, the facility shall not receive approval for subsequent delayed payment arrangements until such time as the terms and conditions of any current delayed payment agreement have been satisfied or unless the provider is in full compliance with the terms of the

current delay of payment' agreement. The waiver of penalties
described in subsection (h)(4) shall not apply to a facility that
has not satisfied the terms and conditions of any current delayed
payment agreement.

i) Administration; enforcement provisions

Pursuant to Section 5B-7 of P.A. 87-861, to the extent practicable,
the Department shall administer and enforce P.A. 86-861, as amended by
P.A. 88-88, and collect the license fees, interest, and penalty fees
imposed under the law, using procedures employed in its administration
of this Code generally and, as it deems appropriate, in a manner
similar to that in which the Department of Revenue administers and
collects the retailers' occupation tax under the Retailers' Occupation
Tax Act ("ROTA").

j) Nothing in P.A. 88-88 shall be construed to prevent the Department
from collecting all amounts due under this Section pursuant to an
assessment imposed before the effective date of P.A. 88-88.

k) Definitions

As used in this Section, unless the context requires otherwise:

1) "Department" means the Illinois Department of Public Aid.

2) "Fund" means the Long-Term Care Provider Fund.

3) "Hospital Provider" means a person licensed by the Department of
Public Health to conduct, operate, or maintain a hospital,
regardless of whether the person is a Medicaid provider. For
purposes of this definition, "person" means any political
subdivision of the State, municipal corporation, individual,
firm, partnership, corporation, company, limited liability
company, association, joint stock association, or trust, or a
receiver, executor, trustee, guardian, or other representative
appointed by order of any court.

4) "Licensed nursing bed days" means, with respect to a nursing home
provider, the sum for all nursing home beds, with the exception
of swing-beds, as described in subsection (k)(8) of this Section,
of the number of days during a calendar quarter on which each bed
is covered by a license issued to that provider under the Nursing
Home Care Act or the Hospital Licensing Act.

5) "Nursing home" means a skilled nursing or intermediate long-term
care facility, whether public or private and whether organized
for profit or not-for-profit, that is subject to licensure by the
Illinois Department of Public Health under the Nursing Home Care
Act, including a county nursing home directed and maintained
under Section 5-1005 of the Counties Code; and a part of a
hospital in which skilled or intermediate long-term care services
within the meaning of Title XVIII or XIX of the Social Security
Act. However, the term "nursing home" does not include a facility
operated solely as an intermediate care facility for the mentally
retarded within the meaning of Title XIX of the Social Security
Act.

6) "Nursing home provider" means a person licensed by the Department

of Public Health to operate and maintain a skilled nursing or
intermediate long-term care facility which charges its residents,
a third party payor, Medicaid, of Medicare for skilled nursing or
intermediate long-term care services; or a hospital· provider
that provides skilled or intermediate long-term care service
within the meaning of Title XVIII or XIX of the Social Security
Act.

7) "Person" means, in addition to natural persons, any political
subdivision of the State, municipal corporation, individual,
firm, partnership, corporation, company, limited liability
company, association, joint stock association, or trust, or a
receiver, executor, trustee, guardian, or other representative
appointed by order of any court.

8) "Swing-beds" means those beds for which a hospital provider has
been granted an approval from the federal Health Care Financing
Administration to provide post-hospital extended care services
(42 CFR 409.30, October 1, 1991) and be reimbursed as a swing-bed
hospital (42 CFR 413.114, October 1, 1991).

(Source: Amended at 19 Ill. Reg. _____, effective
_____)

DEPARTMENT OF REVENUE

NOTICE OF PROPOSED AMENDMENTS

1) Reading of the Part: Retailers' Occupation Tax

2) Code Citation: 86 Ill. Adm. Code 130

3) Section Numbers: Proposed Action:

   130.340   Amendment

4) Statutory Authority: 35 ILCS 120

5) A Complete Description of the Subjects and Issues Involved: This
   amendment changes the reference to an Illinois Commerce Commission
   Certificate of Authority to an Illinois Commerce Commission Certificate of
   Registration that recognizes interstate carriers for hire for
   documentation of the rolling stock exemption. This change in terminology
   does not change the type of documentation required to document this
   exemption. The use of the term "Certificate of Registration" is
   considered a more appropriate description of the certificate that the
   Illinois Commerce Commission has and currently continues to issue to
   certain interstate carriers for hire.

6) Will this proposed rule replace an emergency rule currently in effect? No

7) Does this rulemaking contain an automatic repeal date? No

8) Does this proposed amendment contain incorporations by reference? No

9) Are there any other proposed amendments pending on this Part? Yes

   Section Numbers   Proposed Action   IL Register Citation

   130.2007   Amendment   1/28/94, 18 Ill. Reg. 982
   130.501   Amendment   10/14/94, 18 Ill. Reg. 15383
   130.502   Amendment   10/14/94, 18 Ill. Reg. 15383
   130.510   Amendment   10/14/94, 18 Ill. Reg. 15383
   130.540   Amendment   10/14/94, 18 Ill. Reg. 15383
   130.331   Amendment   1/20/95, 19 Ill. Reg. 571

10) Statement of Statewide Policy Objectives: This rulemaking does not
    create a State Mandate, nor does it modify any existing State Mandates.

11) Time, Place and Manner in which interested persons may comment on
    this proposed rulemaking: Persons who wish to submit comments on this
    proposed rule may submit them in writing by no later than 45 days after
    publication of this notice to:

    Terry Charlton

DEPARTMENT OF REVENUE

NOTICE OF PROPOSED AMENDMENTS

Associate Counsel
Illinois Department of Revenue
Office of General Counsel
101 West Jefferson
Springfield, Illinois 62794
Phone: (217) 782-6996

12) Initial Regulatory Flexibility Analysis:

    A) Types of small businesses affected: Interstate carriers
       for hire recognized by the Illinois Commerce Commission and any
       small businesses that sell items that qualify for the rolling
       stock exemption.

    B) Reporting, bookkeeping or other procedures required for
       compliance: This rulemaking requires no new reporting,
       bookkeeping, or other procedure for compliance.

    C) Types of professional skills necessary for compliance: No new
       professional skills are required by this rulemaking.

The full text of the Proposed Amendment(s) begins on the next page:

DEPARTMENT OF REVENUE

NOTICE OF PROPOSED AMENDMENTS

TITLE 86: REVENUE
CHAPTER I: DEPARTMENT OF REVENUE

PART 130
RETAILERS' OCCUPATION TAX

SUBPART A: NATURE OF TAX

SUBPART B: SALE AT RETAIL

SUBPART C: CERTAIN STATUTORY EXEMPTIONS

SUBPART D: GROSS RECEIPTS

SUBPART E: RETURNS

SUBPART F: INTERSTATE COMMERCE

SUBPART G: CERTIFICATE OF REGISTRATION

DEPARTMENT OF REVENUE

NOTICE OF PROPOSED AMENDMENTS

130.1901   Addition Agents to Plating Baths
130.1905   Agricultural Producers
130.1910   Antiques, Curios, Art Work, Collectors' Coins, Collectors' Postage Stamps and Like Articles
130.1915   Auctioneers and Agents
130.1920   Barbers and Beauty Shop Operators
130.1925   Blacksmiths
130.1930   Chiropodists, Osteopaths and Chiropractors
130.1935   Computer Software
130.1940   Construction Contractors and Real Estate Developers
130.1945   Co-operative Associations
130.1950   Dentists
130.1951   Enterprise Zones
130.1955   Farm Chemicals
130.1960   Finance Companies and Other Lending Agencies - Installment Contracts - Repossessions
130.1965   Florists and Nurserymen
130.1970   Hatcheries
130.1975   Operators of Games of Chance and Their Suppliers
130.1980   Optometrists and Opticians
130.1985   Pawnbrokers
130.1990   Peddlers, Hawkers and Itinerant Vendors
130.1995   Personalizing Tangible Personal Property
130.2000   Persons Engaged in the Printing, Graphic Arts or Related Occupations, and Their Suppliers
130.2005   Persons Engaged in Nonprofit Service Enterprises and in Similar Enterprises Operated As Businesses, and Suppliers of Such Persons
130.2006   Sales by Teacher-Sponsored Student Organizations
130.2007   Exemption Identification Numbers
130.2008   Sales by Nonprofit Service Enterprises
130.2010   Persons Who Rent or Lease the Use of Tangible Personal Property to Others
130.2015   Persons Who Repair or Otherwise Service Tangible Personal Property
130.2020   Physicians and Surgeons
130.2025   Picture-Framers
130.2030   Public Amusement Places
130.2035   Registered Pharmacists and Druggists
130.2040   Retailers of Clothing
130.2045   Retailers on Premises of the Illinois State Fair, County Fairs, Art Shows, Flea Markets and the Like
130.2050   Sales and Gifts By Employers to Employees
130.2055   Sales by Governmental Bodies
130.2060   Sales of Alcoholic Beverages, Motor Fuel and Tobacco Products
130.2065   Sales of Automobiles for Use In Demonstration
130.2070   Sales of Containers, Wrapping and Packing Materials and Related Products
130.2075   Sales To Construction Contractors, Real Estate Developers and

DEPARTMENT OF REVENUE

NOTICE OF PROPOSED AMENDMENTS

       Speculative Builders
130.2080   Sales to Governmental Bodies, Foreign Diplomats and Consular Personnel
130.2085   Sales to or by Banks, Savings and Loan Associations and Credit Unions
130.2090   Sales to Railroad Companies
130.2095   Sellers of Gasohol, Coal, Coke, Fuel Oil and Other Combustibles
130.2100   Sellers of Feeds and Breeding Livestock
130.2105   Sellers of Newspapers, Magazines, Books, Sheet Music and Phonograph Records and Their Suppliers
130.2110   Sellers of Seeds and Fertilizer
130.2115   Sellers of Machinery, Tools and the Like
130.2120   Suppliers of Persons Engaged in Service Occupations and Professions
130.2125   Trading Stamps and Discount Coupons
130.2130   Undertakers and Funeral Directors
130.2135   Vending Machines
130.2140   Vendors of Curtains, Slip Covers, Floor Covering and Other Similar Items Made to Order
130.2145   Vendors of Meals
130.2150   Vendors of Memorial Stones and Monuments
130.2155   Vendors of Signs
130.2156   Vendors of Steam
130.2160   Vendors of Tangible Personal Property Employed for Premiums, Advertising, Prizes, Etc.
130.2165   Veterinarians
130.2170   Warehousemen
ILLUSTRATION A: Examples of Tax Exemption Cards

AUTHORITY: Implementing the Illinois Retailers' Occupation Tax Act [35 ILCS 120] and authorized by Section 39b3 of the Civil Administrative Code of Illinois [20 ILCS 2505/39b3].

SOURCE: Adopted July 1, 1933; amended at 2 Ill. Reg. 50, p. 71, effective December 10, 1978; amended at 3 Ill. Reg. 12, p. 4, effective March 19, 1979; amended at 3 Ill. Reg. 13, pp. 93 and 95, effective March 25, 1979; amended at 3 Ill. Reg. 23, p. 164, effective June 3, 1979; amended at 3 Ill. Reg. 25, p. 229, effective June 17, 1979; amended at 3 Ill. Reg. 44, p. 193, effective October 19, 1979; amended at 3 Ill. Reg. 46, p. 52, effective November 2, 1979; amended at 4 Ill. Reg. 24, pp. 520, 539, 564 and 571, effective June 1, 1980; amended at 5 Ill. Reg. 818, effective January 2, 1981; amended at 5 Ill. Reg. 3014, effective March 11, 1981; amended at 5 Ill. Reg. 12782, effective November 2, 1981; amended at 6 Ill. Reg. 2860, effective March 3, 1982; amended at 6 Ill. Reg. 6780, effective May 24, 1982; codified at 6 Ill. Reg. 8229; recodified at 6 Ill. Reg. 8999; amended at 6 Ill. Reg. 15225, effective December 3, 1982; amended at 7 Ill. Reg. 7990, effective June 15, 1983; amended at 8 Ill. Reg. 5319, effective April 11, 1984; amended at 8 Ill. Reg. 19062, effective September 26, 1984; amended at 10 Ill. Reg. 1937, effective January

DEPARTMENT OF REVENUE

NOTICE OF PROPOSED AMENDMENTS

10, 1986; amended at 10 Ill. Reg. 12067, effective July 1, 1986; amended at 10 Ill. Reg. 19538, effective November 5, 1986; amended at 10 Ill. Reg. 19772, effective November 5, 1986; amended at 11 Ill. Reg. 4325, effective March 2, 1987; amended at 11 Ill. Reg. 6252, effective March 20, 1987; amended at 11 Ill. Reg. 18284, effective October 27, 1987; amended at 11 Ill. Reg. 18767, effective October 28, 1987; amended at 11 Ill. Reg. 19138, effective October 29, 1987; amended at 11 Ill. Reg. 19696, effective November 23, 1987; amended at 12 Ill. Reg. 5652, effective March 15, 1988; emergency amendment at 12 Ill. Reg. 14401, effective September 1, 1988, for a maximum of 150 days, modified in response to an objection of the Joint Committee on Administrative Rules at 12 Ill. Reg. 19531, effective November 4, 1988, not to exceed the 150 day time limit of the original rulemaking; emergency expired January 29, 1989; amended at 13 Ill. Reg. 11824, effective June 29, 1989; amended at 14 Ill. Reg. 241, effective December 21, 1989; amended at 14 Ill. Reg. 872, effective January 1, 1990; amended at 14 Ill. Reg. 15463, effective September 10, 1990; amended at 14 Ill. Reg. 16028, effective September 18, 1990; amended at 15 Ill. Reg. 6621, effective April 17, 1991; amended at 15 Ill. Reg. 13542, effective August 30, 1991; amended at 15 Ill. Reg. 15757, effective October 15, 1991; amended at 16 Ill. Reg. 1642, effective January 13, 1992; amended at 17 Ill. Reg. 860, effective January 11, 1993; amended at 17 Ill. Reg. 18142, effective October 4, 1993; amended at 17 Ill. Reg. 19651, effective November 2, 1993; amended at 18 Ill. Reg. 1537, effective January 13, 1994; amended at 18 Ill. Reg. 16866, effective November 7, 1994; amended at 19 Ill. Reg. _____, effective

SUBPART C: CERTAIN STATUTORY EXEMPTIONS

Section 130.340 Rolling Stock

a) Notwithstanding the fact that the sale is at retail, the Retailers' Occupation Tax does not apply to sales of tangible personal property to interstate carriers for hire for use as rolling stock moving in interstate commerce, or lessors under leases of one year or longer executed or in effect at the time of purchase to interstate carriers for hire for use as rolling stock moving in interstate commerce.

b) The term "Rolling Stock" includes the transportation vehicles of any kind of interstate transportation company for hire (railroad, bus line, air line, trucking company, etc.), but not vehicles which are being used by a person to transport its officers, employees, customers or others not for hire (even if they cross State lines) or to transport property which such person owns or is selling and delivering to customers (even if such transportation crosses State lines). Railroad "rolling stock" includes all railroad cars, passenger and freight, and locomotives (including switching locomotives) or mobile power units of every nature for moving such cars, operating on railroad tracks, and includes all property purchased for the purpose of being attached to such cars or locomotives as a part thereof. The

DEPARTMENT OF REVENUE

NOTICE OF PROPOSED AMENDMENTS

exemption includes some equipment (such as containers called trailers) which are used by interstate carriers for hire, loaded on railroad cars, to transport property, but which do not operate under their own power and are not actually attached to the railroad cars. The exemption does not apply to fuel nor to jacks or flares or other items that are used by interstate carriers for hire in servicing the transportation vehicles, but that do not become a part of such vehicles, and that do not participate directly in some way in the transportation process. The exemption does not include property of an interstate carrier for hire used in the company's office, such as furniture, typewriters, office supplies and the like.

c) The rolling stock exemption cannot be claimed by a purely intrastate carrier for hire as to any tangible personal property which it purchases because it does not meet the statutory tests of being an interstate carrier for hire.

d) The exemption applies to vehicles used by an interstate carrier for hire, even just between points in Illinois, in transporting, for hire, persons whose journeys or property whose shipments, originate or terminate outside Illinois on other carriers. The exemption cannot be claimed for an interstate carrier's use of vehicles solely between points in Illinois where the journeys of the passengers or the shipments of property neither originate nor terminate outside Illinois.

e) When the rolling stock exemption may properly be claimed, the purchaser should give the seller a certification that the purchaser is an interstate carrier for hire, and that the purchaser is purchasing the property for use as rolling stock moving in interstate commerce. If the purchaser is a carrier, the purchaser must include its Interstate Commerce Commission Certificate of Authority number or must certify that it is a type of interstate carrier for hire (such as an interstate carrier of agricultural commodities for hire) that is not required by law to have an Interstate Commerce Commission Certificate of Authority. In the latter event, the carrier must include its Illinois Commerce Commission Certificate of Authority Registration number indicating that it is recognized by the Illinois Commerce Commission as an interstate carrier for hire. If the carrier is a type which is subject to regulation by some Federal Government regulatory agency other than the Interstate Commerce Commission, the carrier must include its registration number from such other Federal Government regulatory agency in the certification claiming the benefit of the rolling stock exemption. If the purchaser is a long term lessor (under a lease of one year or more in duration), the purchaser must give the seller of the property a certification to that effect, similarly identifying the lessee interstate carrier for hire. The giving of such a certification does not preclude the Department from going behind it and disregarding it if, in examining such purchaser's records or activities, the Department finds that the certification was

DEPARTMENT OF REVENUE

NOTICE OF PROPOSED AMENDMENTS

not true as to some fact or facts which show that the purchase was taxable and should not have been certified as being tax exempt. The Department reserves the right to require a copy of the carrier's Interstate Commerce Commission or other Federal Government regulatory agency Certificate of Authority Registration or Illinois Commerce Commission Certificate of Authority (or as much of the certificate as the Department deems adequate to verify the fact that the carrier is an interstate carrier for hire) to be provided whenever the Department deems that to be necessary.

(Source: Amended at 19   Ill.   Reg. _____, effective _____)

DEPARTMENT OF TRANSPORTATION

NOTICE OF ADOPTED AMENDMENTS

1) Heading of the Part: Administrative Requirements For Official Testing Stations

2) Code Citation: 92 Ill. Adm. Code 451

3)
Section Numbers:	Adopted Action:
451.Appendix A	Repeal
451.Appendix B	Repeal
451.Appendix C	Repeal
451.Appendix D	Repeal
451.Appendix E	Repeal
451.Appendix G	Repeal
451.Illustration A	Repeal
451.Illustration B	Repeal

4) Statutory Authority: 625 ILCS 5/Ch. 12, Art. VIII and 5/Ch. 13

5) Effective Date of Rulemaking: March 13, 1995

6) Does this rulemaking contain an automatic repeal date? No

7) Does this rulemaking contain incorporations by reference? No.

8) Date Filed in Agency's Principal Office: March 7, 1995

9) Notice of Proposal Published in Illinois Register: September 9, 1994, 18 Ill. Reg. 13729

10) Has JCAR issued a Statement of Objections to these rules? No

11) Difference(s) between proposal and final version:

The volume number in the Section Source Notes was updated.

The ILCS cite was corrected in the Authority Note.

The Section Headings of the Appendices were corrected.

12) Have all the changes agreed upon by the agency and JCAR been made as indicated in the agreement letter issued by JCAR? No changes were necessary.

13) Will this rulemaking replace an emergency rule currently in effect? No

14) Are there any amendments pending on this Part? No

15) Summary and Purpose of Rulemaking: By this Notice of Adopted Amendments, the Department is repealing the Appendices and Illustrations which are

DEPARTMENT OF TRANSPORTATION

NOTICE OF ADOPTED AMENDMENTS

applicable to school buses. Elsewhere in this *Illinois Register*, the Department is establishing three new Parts to replace the Appendices and Illustrations repealed by this rulemaking. Part 451 now addresses only the administrative requirements for operating an Illinois Official Testing Station. The school bus regulations are promulgated as separate Parts.

16) Information and questions regarding these adopted amendments shall be directed to:

    Ms. Cathy Allen
    Regulations and Training Unit
    Illinois Department of Transportation
    Division of Traffic Safety
    P.O. Box 19212
    Springfield, Illinois 62794-9212
    (217) 785-1181

17) State reasons for this rulemaking if it was not included in the two (2) most recent regulatory agendas:

The full text of the Adopted Amendment begins on the next page:

DEPARTMENT OF TRANSPORTATION

NOTICE OF ADOPTED AMENDMENTS

TITLE 92: TRANSPORTATION
CHAPTER I: DEPARTMENT OF TRANSPORTATION
SUBCHAPTER e: TRAFFIC SAFETY (EXCEPT HAZARDOUS MATERIALS)

PART 451
ADMINISTRATIVE REQUIREMENTS FOR OFFICIAL TESTING STATIONS

AUTHORITY: Implementing and authorized by Section 6-410 of the Illinois Driver Licensing Law [625 ILCS 5/6-410], Article VIII of the Illinois Vehicle Equipment Law [625 ILCS 5/Ch. 12, Art. VIII], and the Illinois Vehicle Inspection Law [625 ILCS 5/Ch. 13].

DEPARTMENT OF TRANSPORTATION

NOTICE OF ADOPTED AMENDMENTS

SOURCE: Adopted at 13 Ill. Reg. 19597, effective December 1, 1989; amended at 17 Ill. Reg. 12039, effective July 27, 1993; amended at 19 Ill. Reg. **4594** , effective OCT 10 1995 .

DEPARTMENT OF TRANSPORTATION

NOTICE OF ADOPTED AMENDMENTS

Section 451.APPENDIX A Inspection Procedures/Specifications for Type I School Buses (Repealed)

SUBJECT	PROCEDURES/SPECIFICATIONS	REJECT-VEHICLE-IF
a)--AIR-CLEANER	Any-type-is-acceptable.	No-air-cleaner-is-present.
b)--AISLE	Unobstructed-minimum clearance-leading-from service-door-to emergency-door-(or back--of--bus)--must--be-at least-12--inches--(305--mm) wide---------For-----buses manufactured-in-July-1989 or--later,--aisle--width-at two--inches--below--top--of seat-back-must-be-15-inches (380-mm)-Floor-to-ceiling height-must-be-a-minimum-of 68.9-inches-(1.75-m)-at-any location-within-the-aisle.	Does-not-meet-minimum standards-or-is obstructed.
c)--ALTERNATOR (GENERATOR)	The-generator,-or alternator-with rectifier,-shall-have a-minimum--capacity--rating of--60-amperes-and-shall-be capable--of---meeting---all electrical-requirements.	Does-not-meet-minimum standards-or-is-not functioning.
d)--AXLES	Must-meet-federal chassis-requirements as-indicated-on federal-certification label,--49-CFR-568	Visible-signs-of-apparent damage-or-not-firmly attached.
e)--BARRIER, GUARD	A-guard-barrier, constructed-and thickly-padded-so-as to-provide-head,-knee and-leg-protection, shall-be-installed-in-front of----each---forward--facing passenger--seat--that--does not-directly-face-the--rear surface------of-----another	Barrier-is-not-solidly attached.--Padding-or covering-shows-wear-and tear.--Does-not-meet requirements.

DEPARTMENT OF TRANSPORTATION

NOTICE OF ADOPTED AMENDMENTS

SUBJECT	PROCEDURES/SPECIFICATIONS	REJECT-VEHICLE-IF
	passenger----seat------The barrier--must--measure--the same----height----as----the passenger------seat----back directly------behind----that barrier-(i.e.,-24--inches), 49-CFR-571.222	
	In--a--bus--manufactured-in January--1988--or----later, guard-barriers-must-measure the-same-height-as-the-seat back--directly--behind-that barrier-(i.e.,-24-inches).	
Exception--in-a-bus-manufactured-from-July-1,-1987,-to-December-3 the-barrier-may-be-less-than-the-required-24-inch-seat-back.		
	Exception--In-a--bus--with chassis--------(incomplete vehicle)--manufactured--in March-1977-or-earlier,--the barrier--may--consist--of-a floor-to-ceiling--vertical stanchion,-padded-to-within three-inches-of-ceiling-and floor,------and------a stanchion-to-wall----fully padded,---horizontal--guard rail.--However,-if--located adjacent--to-stepwell,-this type-barrier-shall--include a-stepwell-guard-panel-that extends--from-the-stanchion to-the-wall--and--from--the guard-rail--to--within-two inches-of-the-floor.	
	Exception--All------buses manufactured---prior---to September-1974--are--exempt from--padding-on-stanchions and-guard-rails.	
f)--BATTERY-OR BATTERIES	One-or-more-batteries	Not--securely-mounted.

DEPARTMENT OF TRANSPORTATION

NOTICE OF ADOPTED AMENDMENTS

SUBJECT	PROCEDURES/SPECIFICATIONS	REJECT-VEHICLE-IF
	may-be-mounted-either in-engine-compartment or-on-outside-of passenger/driver area.--Battery-(or batteries-together)-in-a-12 volt-system-shall-be-rated when-new,--to--provide-the following:	excessively-corroded;-not rated-for-manufacturer's cold-cranking-current-and reserve-capacity-or ampere-hour-rating.
	Engine------manufacturer's recommended--Cold--Cranking Current----(amperes--for--30 seconds)-at--18--degrees--C (0--degree--F),-or,--at-the purchaser's-option,-at--29 degrees-C-(-20-degrees-F). The----battery(s)----shall provide-a-Reserve--Capacity (duration--of--25--ampere current-flow)-at-27-degrees C-(80--degrees--F)--for--no less-than-135-minutes; low-rate-discharge-capacity of--70-ampere-hours-or-more (20-hour-discharge-test--at 80-degrees-F). Exception--A--------bus manufactured-in-August-1974 or--earlier--may--have-a-70 ampere-hour-battery--in--a 12-volt-system.	
g)--BATTERY CABLES	Check-condition.	Cables-are-corroded; Not-securely-attached.
h)--BATTERY CARRIER	When-the-battery-is mounted-outside-the engine-compartment-it-shall be-welded--or--bolted-in-a closed,-weather-tighty--and vented--compartment-that-is located-and-arranged-so--as to--provide--for-convenient	Does-not-meet requirements.

DEPARTMENT OF TRANSPORTATION

NOTICE OF ADOPTED AMENDMENTS

SUBJECT	PROCEDURES/SPECIFICATIONS	REJECT VEHICLE IF
	~~routine---servicing----The battery--compartment--door; or-cover;-shall-be--secured by---a---manually--operated latch-or-other-fastener--A latch-or-fastener--must--be designed--in-such-a-fashion as-to-keep-the-door--closed when----in----the--latched position;--Each--electrical cable-----connecting----the battery-in-this-carrier--to the--body--or-chassis-shall be-one-piece--between--the terminal--connector-and-the first--body---or--chassis terminal-connector;~~	
~~i)--BRAKES~~	~~Every-motor-vehicle shall-be-equipped-with two--separate---means---of applying--the--brakes---and they-----shall----be---so constructed-that-failure-of any--one---part---of---the operating--mechanism--shall not-leave-the-motor-vehicle without--brakes;---(Section 12-301(a)--of--the-Illinois Vehicle-Equipment-Law;~~	~~Does-not-meet requirements;~~
~~i)--Backing Plate~~	~~Check-condition;~~	~~Backing-plate-is-in-poor condition;~~
~~2)--Drums/ Discs~~	~~Inspect-drums-and/or discs-for-cracks-or-for being-worn-or-reworked beyond-the-marked-discard limit;~~	~~Worn-or-reworked-beyond the-following-limits; i)--Drum-diameter--040 inch-(1mm)-under marked-discard-limit on-Type-I-bus; 2)--Drum-diameter--030 inch-(.75mm)-under marked-discard-limit $Non-Type-II-bus;~~

DEPARTMENT OF TRANSPORTATION

NOTICE OF ADOPTED AMENDMENTS

SUBJECT	PROCEDURES/SPECIFICATIONS	REJECT VEHICLE IF
		~~3)--Disc-thickness--030 inch------------(.75mm) over-marked discard-limit on-any-bus; 4)--Other-rework-(rebore; reface)-limit-specified by------------chassis manufacturer;~~
~~3)--Emergency /Parking Brake~~	~~Emergency/parking braking-system-must-apply brakes-to-at-least-two wheels;-(Section--12-301(a) of---the--Illinois--Vehicle Equipment-Law;~~	~~Does-not-meet requirements;~~
~~AGENCY-NOTE--~~	~~Micro-brakes-are-not considered-a-separate-means of-breaking-and-are-not acceptable; Procedures-for-testing;~~	
	~~i)--Apply-operating control-fully;~~	~~Not-equipped-with emergency/parking brakes;-----------Operating mechanism-does-not-hold--in the-applied-position;~~
	~~2)--Check-actuating mechanism-for-release;~~	~~Actuating-mechanism-does not-fully-release-when release-control-is-operated properly;~~
	~~Brake-Performance-Test;~~	
	~~Using-drive-on-pad-type tester;~~	
	~~i)--Drive-vehicle-onto brake-machine-pads-at 4-8-mph;~~	
	~~2)--Apply-emergency/parking brakes-to-bring-vehicle to-a-halt; Do-not-lock-wheels;~~	
	~~3)--Note-the-braking~~	~~Machine-does-not-register~~

DEPARTMENT OF TRANSPORTATION

NOTICE OF ADOPTED AMENDMENTS

SUBJECT	PROCEDURES/SPECIFICATIONS	REJECT VEHICLE IF
	forces registered by the brake machine.	a total braking force of at least 20% of vehicle empty weight. Braking forces at opposite wheels on same axle vary more than 20%.
	Using roller type tester.	
	1) Position axle with emergency brake onto roller.	
	2) Apply emergency brake but do not lock wheels.	Machine does not register a total braking force of at least 20% of vehicle empty weight. Braking forces at opposite wheels on same axle vary more than 20%.
4) Emergency Brake Ratchet (Pedal or lever)	Must be in proper adjustment.	Does not meet requirements.
5) Pedal Clearance (Service Brakes)	Minimum 1 1/2 inch clearance with pedal fully depressed.	Does not meet requirements.
6) Power Systems At Air	With air system fully charged compressor governor "cut out") run engine at low idle. Make one full (maximum) brake application and immediately record reservoir air pressure. Apply and release brakes until pressure is at least 18 psi (1.v.) pounds per square inch below governor "cut in" pressure. Run	Time required to raise air pressure from recorded to cut out is more than 30 seconds.

DEPARTMENT OF TRANSPORTATION

NOTICE OF ADOPTED AMENDMENTS

SUBJECT	PROCEDURES/SPECIFICATIONS	REJECT VEHICLE IF
	engine at high idle and determine seconds required to raise reservoir pressure from recorded pressure.	
B) Electric/ Hydraulic	Turn engine "off." Depress service brake pedal. Electric hydraulic pump must come "on" (listen).	Electric pump does not operate properly or is absent.
C) Hydraulic	Inspect booster system belts, supports, tubes, hoses, connections and general condition. Clean reservoir cover as necessary and check booster fluid level. Do not contaminate fluid. Turn engine "on." Warning signal must come on (look/listen). Depress brake pedal lightly. Start engine. Pedal must move down slightly (feel). Warning signal must go "off" (look/listen).	Belt is slack or worn, tube or hose is damaged, any part leaks or is cracked, booster fluid is low. Either booster or warning signal does not operate properly.
D) Vacuum/ Hydraulic	Inspect tank(s), chambers, hoses, tubes, connectors, clamps, and booster air cleaner. Inspect supports and attachments.	1) Any component is restricted, collapsed, scraped, cracked, loose, or broken. Booster air cleaner is clogged. 2) Any support or attachment is broken. Any connecting line or other

SUBJECT	PROCEDURES/SPECIFICATIONS	REJECT VEHICLE IF
		component is not attached or supported so as to prevent damage from scraping or rubbing.
	With engine off, repeatedly apply service brakes until vacuum is depleted with medium pressure on brake pedal, start engine; release brake and operate engine until maximum vacuum is established, stop engine. Apply service brakes hard. With brakes still applied, start engine after one minute of running engine, check "Low Vacuum" indicator.	3. Foot pedal does not fall away from foot when engine is started; insufficient vacuum reserve to permit one full service brake application after engine is off without actuating "Low Vacuum" indicator, valve or diaphragm leaking.
7. Service Brakes	Must be equipped with service brakes on all wheels. (Section 12-301(a)(1) of the Illinois Vehicle Equipment Law)	Do not meet requirements.
	Must be equipped with a "split system" on service brakes. 49 CFR 571.105	Do not meet requirements.
	Power assisted service brakes are required. 49 CFR 571.105	Do not meet requirements.
A. Brake Report and Certification Form (SB6)	Verify SB6 for following: 1. Proper completion. 2. Issued not more than 10 days before safety test.	Absent or invalid SB6.

SUBJECT	PROCEDURES/SPECIFICATIONS	REJECT VEHICLE IF
	3. Correct brake mileage.	
B. Brake Performance Test	Using Drive-On-Pad-Type Brake Tester.	
	Check vehicle's stopping ability before testing. Drive vehicle onto brake machine pads at 4-8 m.p.h. Apply service brakes to bring vehicle to a halt. Do not lock wheels. Note the braking forces register by the brake machine.	Machine does not register a total braking force of at least 50% of the vehicle empty weight.
	Using Roll-On-Type Tester.	
	When using roller-type tester each axle must be tested separately. Transmission must be in neutral when testing brakes on any drive axle. Drive front axle onto rollers. Start roller motor. Apply service brakes, but do not lock wheels. Repeat the above step for each axle.	Braking forces at opposite wheels on same axle vary more than 20%.
	The total braking force on a vehicle must be determined by adding the results of the test on each axle.	Machine does not register a total braking force of at least 50% of the vehicle empty weight. Braking forces at opposite wheels on same axle vary more than 20%.
8. BUMPER, FRONT	Either channel-type; formed of rolled steel at	Does not meet thickness, face-height and color

DEPARTMENT OF TRANSPORTATION

NOTICE OF ADOPTED AMENDMENTS

SUBJECT	PROCEDURES/SPECIFICATIONS	REJECT-VEHICLE-IF
	least--1/9-inch-(4.5-mm) (approximately-3/16-inch) thick,-of-approved-energy absorbing-type. Buses---manufactured---in August-1974-or--later--must have-9.9-inches-(200-mm)-or more-vertical-black-face. Bumper-must-extend-to-outer edges--of--fenders-and-other front---and---sheet---metal. Must---be--of--strength--to permit-pushing--vehicle--of equal----weight----without permanent-distortion. Exceptions:--Buses manufactured----prior----to September-1974--are--exempt from--bumper--thickness-and 9.9-inch-face-requirement.	requirements.--Must-be solidly-attached;-in-good condition;-free-from damage-and-sharp-edges.
k)---BUMPER, REAR	Channel-steel-at-least x10-inches--(4.55-mm) (approximately-3/16-inch) thick-with-a-minimum-0.9 inch-(225-mm)-black-face; full---wrap---around----and attached--so--as-to-prevent hitching----rides----five. *nonhitchable*. Shall-be-attached--so-that removal---is---possible--by commonly---available---hand tools. Shall--be--of--strength--to permit-bus-being-pushed--by another---vehicle---without permanent-distortion.	Does-not-meet requirements. Not-solidly-attached. Sharp-edges-are-present. Rear-bumper-is-hitchable.
AGENCY-NOTE:	*Nonhitchable*--is--defined as--the--rear--of--the--bus being designed-and-maintained-to prevent-or-discourage riding-or-grasping rear-of-bus-so-as	

DEPARTMENT OF TRANSPORTATION

NOTICE OF ADOPTED AMENDMENTS

SUBJECT	PROCEDURES/SPECIFICATIONS	REJECT-VEHICLE-IF
	to-"hitch"-rides.	
l)--CERTIFICATE-AND REGISTRATION CARD-HOLDER	At--least-one-card-holder with-a-transparent-face no--less-than-5x9-inches-by 3.9-inches-(150-mm--by--100 mm)--shall---be---securely affixed---to---the---inside header----panel----out---of students'-easy-reach.	Does-not-meet requirements.
m)--CERTIFICATION LABEL		
1)--Federal	Federal-rules-require-a permanently-affixed manufacturer's certification-label-in each-bus-either manufactured-on-or-after June-1,-1971,-or-built-up from-a-chassis manufactured-on-or-after June-1,-1971.--The manufacturer's certification-might-be supplemented-by-an alterer's-certification. The-manufacturer's-label must-contain-the following-information:	A-required-label-is absent,-defaced, destroyed,-not-riveted, or-not-permanently affixed,--"Permanently affixed"--means-the-label cannot-be-removed-without distroying-or-defacing-it. A-certification-label does-not-contain-the required-statement-and all-other-information required-for-that-label.
	1)--Name-of-vehicle-(bus) manufacturer-and-the month-and-year-in which-manufacture of-the-vehicle-was completed;	
	2)--Name---of----incomplete vehicle-(chassis) manufacturer-and-the month-and-year-in which-he-performed his-last-manufacturing	

DEPARTMENT OF TRANSPORTATION

NOTICE OF ADOPTED AMENDMENTS

SUBJECT   PROCEDURES/SPECIFICATIONS   REJECT VEHICLE IF

on the incomplete
vehicle;
3) Gross vehicle weight
rating or ratings
(GVWR);
4) Gross axle weight
ratings
(GAWR);
5) The statement, "This
vehicle conforms to all
applicable federal motor
vehicle safety standards
in effect in
(month/year)";
6) The vehicle
identification number
(VIN);
7) The vehicle's
classification (usually
"bus"); 49 CFR 567.5

Alterer's certification A
certified vehicle might
have been altered before
its purchase for use as a
school bus. The
alterations may have
included, but are not
limited to, classification
changes, gross weight
rating changes or changes
to the
application/effective date
of a federal motor vehicle
safety standard. If any
such alteration occurred,
the bus must carry an
additional federal label
that identifies the
alterer, shows when
alteration was completed,
as altered
GVWR, GAWR and classification
(if changed). It must also
state that the altered
vehicle conforms to all

DEPARTMENT OF TRANSPORTATION

NOTICE OF ADOPTED AMENDMENTS

SUBJECT   PROCEDURES/SPECIFICATIONS   REJECT VEHICLE IF

applicable federal motor
vehicle safety standards in
effect in (month/year). 49
CFR 567.7

8) State   The State of Illinois   The month shown on the
requires a certification   State of Illinois
label in each new Type I   certification label is
bus constructed upon a   earlier than the month
chassis   (incomplete   shown in the statement
vehicle)
that was manufactured   of conformance to federal
in April 1977 or later.   standards on the federal
This label may be displayed   certification label.
in earlier buses.   The Vehicle
Identification Number
When displayed, this   (VIN) on the state and
label must contain   federal certification
1) Name of vehicle (bus)   labels is not the same
manufacturer (usually   number.
same as on federal
label);
2) An identification of
the completed bus by
VIN; and
3) A statement that the
bus conforms to all
applicable Illinois
minimum safety
standards in effect on
the first day of the
same month shown in
the latest statement of
conformance to federal
standards, or on the
first day of a later
month.

New buses that have been
manufactured to meet other
than Illinois construction
standards, but have been
sold for use in Illinois,
must display a federal and
state certification label
certifying that all

DEPARTMENT OF TRANSPORTATION

NOTICE OF ADOPTED AMENDMENTS

SUBJECT	PROCEDURES/SPECIFICATIONS	REJECT-VEHICLE-IF
	Illinois--requirements-have been-met.	
	Used-buses-that--have--been manufactured--to-meet-other than-Illinois---construction standards--but--have--been sold--for--use-in-Illinois, must-either-display-federal and-state-labels-or--obtain a--letter--of-approval-from DOT----------administration personnel--verifying---all Illinois-------construction standards---have---been--met. Such-letter-must-remain--on the-bus-at-all-times.	
n)--DEFROSTERS	Using-heat-from-heaters and-circulation-from fans,--defrosting-equipment shall-keep-the--windshield, the--windows-to-the-left-of the-operator-and-the-glass in-the-service--door--clear of--fog,--frost,--and-snow. Auxiliary--fans---are---not considered----to---be----a defrosting---and--defogging system.---Must--conform--to federal-standards.--49--CFR 571.103	Defrosting-system-does not-function-properly.
o)--DRIVE-SHAFT GUARD	Shall-be-of-sufficient strength-to-protect-drive shaft-and-prevent--it-from going---through---floor--or dropping---to---ground---if broken.--Shall-be--required on-each-segment-on-shaft.	Drive-shaft-guard-is-not solid-and-is-not-firmly attached.
p)--ELECTRICAL SYSTEM		
1)--Circuits	Shall-be-arranged-in-at	Breaks-in-insulation-are

DEPARTMENT OF TRANSPORTATION

NOTICE OF ADOPTED AMENDMENTS

SUBJECT	PROCEDURES/SPECIFICATIONS	REJECT-VEHICLE-IF
	least-nine-regular circuits-as-follows: 1)--Heady-tail--stop (brake)-and-instrument panels-lamps. 2)--Clearance-lamps-and-any lamp-in-or-adjacent-to step-risers. 3)--Interior-lamps. 4)--Starter-motor. 5)--Ignition;----emergency exit alarm-signals-and other alarm-signals. 6)--Turn-signal-lamps. 7)--Alternately-flashing signal-lamps--and--stop signal-am-lamps. 8)--Horn. 9)--Heater-and-defroster.-- A-separate-fuse-or circuitbreaker-for-each circuit, except-starter-motor and-ignition.	present.--Not-on-proper circuit-or-properly-wired.
2)--Fuses	Two-extra-fuses-for-each size-fuse-used-on-the-bus shall-be-conveniently mounted-on-the-bus-body.	Fuses-are-not-present-or are-not-conveniently mounted.
3)--Switches	Check-operation-and condition.	Switches-not-operating properly-or-are-missing.
4)--Wiring	All-wires-shall-be properly-insulated-and securely-attached-at-not more--than--18½--inch-(460 mm)----intervals.----Check condition.	Insulation-is-frayed-or missing.--Wiring-not securely-attached.
q)--EMERGENCY EXITS	All-buses-must-be equipped-with-either-a rear-emergency--door--or-a left-side--emergency--door and---a--rear--emergency	Do-not-meet-requirements.

DEPARTMENT OF TRANSPORTATION

NOTICE OF ADOPTED AMENDMENTS

SUBJECT	PROCEDURES/SPECIFICATIONS	REJECT VEHICLE IF
	window--49-CFR-571.217	
1)--Left Side	Shall-be-hinged-on-front side-and-open-outward. Shall-be-equipped-with alarm-and-safety-glass (or-equivalent).--Glass shall-be-located-in-upper and-lower-portions-of-the door.--Door-shall-be-of at-least-the-same-gauge metal-as-the-body.--Shall be-24-inches-or-more clear--horizontal--opening with---forward--edge---of opening--in-line--with-the rearmost--edge-of-a--seat back.--Shall-have-45-inches or--more---clear--vertical opening.	Release-mechanism-is-not protected,-accessible,-or operable-(inside-and outside).--Unable-to-open easily.-hinge-is-located at-incorrect-location/ location-and-size-of opening-is-incorrect. Alarm-at-door-does-not function-(see-EMERGENCY EXIT---Alarms-and-Locks).
AGENCY-NOTE:	If-the-bus-is-equipped with-a-rear-emergency exit,-a side-exit-is-optional.	
2)--Rear	Shall-be-protected against-accidental release,-easily accessible,-readily operated-manually-without use-of-remote-controls, power-device,-or-tools. Shall-have-permanently attached-inside-and outside-release-handles. Outside-release-handle must-be-non-hitchable. Rear-exit-shall-hinge-on right,-open-outwards, have-a-24-inch-or-more clear---horizontal--opening and 45-inch-or-more-clear vertical-opening-above	Inside-and-outside release-mechanisms-are not-protected,-accessible or-do-not-operate properly.--Outside release-mechanism-is hitchable.--Door-does-not open-easily.--location-of hinge-is-incorrect.--Size of-opening-is-incorrect. Glazing-does-not-meet requirements.--General condition-of-door-(rubber and-seal)-is-poor.--Door alarm-does-not-operate properly-(see-EMERGENCY EXIT---Alarms-and-Locks).

DEPARTMENT OF TRANSPORTATION

NOTICE OF ADOPTED AMENDMENTS

SUBJECT	PROCEDURES/SPECIFICATIONS	REJECT VEHICLE IF
	floor.---Glazing--shall--be installed--in--upper--and lower----portions.----Alarm shall-be-audible-at-door when---door--is--not--fully latched--while--engine---is running-----(see--EMERGENCY EXIT---Alarms-and-Locks). Exception:--Buses manufactured---------before September-1974---are--exempt from---glazing---in---lower portion--of--rear-emergency door.	
3)--Emergency Window	When-the-emergency-door is-located-on-the-left-side not-function,--Alarm-does a-rear-emergency-window shall-be-provided.--- Minimum-16-inches-high and-48-inches-wide. Designed-to-be-opened-from the-inside-or-the-outside. Hinged-on-top,-designed and-operated-to-insure against-accidental--closing in--an--emergency.---Inside handle--shall--provide--for quick---release.---Outside handle-shall-be-nondetachable and-nonhitchable.-When--not fully-latched,-window-shall actuate--alarm--audible--to driver.--No--cutoff-switch allowed.	Operating-mechanisms-do not-function.--Glass-is cracked-or-broken-(see EMERGENCY-EXIT ---Alarms-and-Locks).
4)--Alarms-and locks	Audible-and-visual-alarms shall-alert-driver-when engine-is-running-and-any emergency-door-either: 1)--is-not--fully--latched, or 2)--is-locked-and-not readily-operated manually.	Alarms-do-not-alert driver-as-required. Locks-do-not-meet requirements.

DEPARTMENT OF TRANSPORTATION

NOTICE OF ADOPTED AMENDMENTS

SUBJECT	PROCEDURES/SPECIFICATIONS	REJECT-VEHICLE-IF
	Also----engine---starting system--shall--not--operate while-any-emergency-door-is locked-by-any-means-that prevents----ready----manual operation-without--using--a tool,-key,-or-combination. Alarm-cut-off-or-"squelch" control-is-prohibited. Exception:--On-a--bus--with chassis--------(incomplete vehicle)---manufactured--in March-1977-or-earlier---the "not--fully--latched"-alarm may-only-be-audible-to--the seated--driver.--The-engine starting-system-may-operate while-the-emergency-door-is locked.	
2)---ENTRANCE DOOR 1)--Physical Requirements	Minimum-24-inch horizontal-opening. Minimum-68-inch-vertical opening;--jack-knife-or split-type-door-required on-buses-purchased-after September-1974.--If-split type-door-is-used-and-one section-opens-inward-and the-other-outward--front section-shall-open-outward. Door-shall--be--located--on the--right--side--near--the front,--convenient--to--the seated------------driver's unobstructed----------vision. Entrance---door---shall--be power-or-manually--operated from--the--driver's-seat-and designed--to--afford--easy release-----and-----prevent accidental---opening.-----No	Binding-or-jamming-is evident;-malfunctions; not-equipped--over-ride device-on-power-operated door-does-not-function; control-not-accessible-by driver. Door-is-missing,-loose, or-torn.

DEPARTMENT OF TRANSPORTATION

NOTICE OF ADOPTED AMENDMENTS

SUBJECT	PROCEDURES/SPECIFICATIONS	REJECT-VEHICLE-IF
	parts--of--the--hand--lever shall--come--together-so-as to-shear-or-crush--fingers. Vertical----closing---edges shall--be--equipped--with flexible----material---to prevent-injury.-Lower--and upper--panels-of-door-shall be--of--safety---glass---or equivalent.---Bottom--of lower-panel-shall--be--not more--than--35--inches-from ground-when-unloaded.---Top of--upper-glass-panel-shall be-not-more-than--6--inches from--top-of-door.--No-door is-permitted--to--left--of driver. A--service--door---equipped with--power--shall--also-be capable-of-manual-operation in-case-of-power-failure. Exception:--All------buses purchased---prior-----to September--1974--are-exempt from-split-type-door.--They may--be--split;--sedan,--or jack-knife-type.	
2)--Locks and Alarms	A-service-door-lock-is not-required;-but-if-any type-of-service-door locking-system-is installed-on-the-bus;-the system-shall-conform-to the-following: 1)--The-locking-system-shall not-be-capable-of preventing-the-seated driver-from-easily-and quickly-opening-the service	Locks-and-alarms-do-not meet-requirements. Bent,-worn-or-dislocated parts-that-would-delay quick-door-release-and opening-are-present.

DEPARTMENT OF TRANSPORTATION

NOTICE OF ADOPTED AMENDMENTS

SUBJECT	PROCEDURES/SPECIFICATIONS	REJECT VEHICLE IF
	door.	
	2) The locking system shall include an audiovisual alarm. The alarm shall emit sound and light for other visual indications that demands attention and will alert the seated driver when the engine is running and the service door is locked. An alarm disconnect, "squelch control," or other alarm defeating or weakening device shall be prohibited. Exception: A bus with chassis incomplete vehicle, manufactured in March 1977 or earlier, is exempt from driver being seated, that is, the driver may move from driver's seat to interior side of service entrance to operate service door.	
3) EXHAUST SYSTEM	"Exhaust System" includes each component used to conduct gas from an engine exhaust port (manifold) to authorized exit point, including each seating, connecting, and supporting component. Exhaust system shall be outside body and attached to chassis. Size of tailpipe shall not be reduced after it leaves muffler. Any flexible component that contains exhaust gas shall be of stainless steel.	All parts of system are not securely fastened and supported. Any part is leaking, missing, or patched. Any part contains holes not made by manufacturer.

DEPARTMENT OF TRANSPORTATION

NOTICE OF ADOPTED AMENDMENTS

SUBJECT	PROCEDURES/SPECIFICATIONS	REJECT VEHICLE IF
	System shall not leak. System shall have an outlet at its discharge end, only.	
1) Shielding	Any flammable material, electrical wiring, brake hoses, or fuel system component containing fuel that is located within 13/16 inches (300 mm) of a component containing exhaust gas shall be safeguarded by a heat shield. Exhaust system shall be shielded from either accidental contact, "hitching toy" or "standing on," except at discharge end. A chassis or body component may provide required shield.	
2) Discharge	The exhaust system's discharge end (tailpipe) shall be within 78 inch (25 mm) of bus side, rear, or rear corner, but not to rear of rear bumper and not outside a side rub rail; however, it may be more than 78 inch (25 mm) below bumper or body skirt. Gas shall not be directed towards a door or other opening into bus body. In addition, the discharge end, or end, shall not be located in any prohibited zone shown in illustration B.	
3) FENDERS	Shall be properly braced and free from any body attachment.	Fenders are not solid or in bad condition. Sharp edges are evident.

DEPARTMENT OF TRANSPORTATION

NOTICE OF ADOPTED AMENDMENTS

SUBJECT	PROCEDURES/SPECIFICATIONS	REJECT-VEHICLE-IF
	There-shall-be approximately-one-inch located-between-front fenders-and-back-face-to cowl.	Fenders-are-loose or-protrude-out.
v.--FILTER,--OIL	Replaceable-element-or cartridge-type.--Minimum one-quart-capacity.	Does-not-meet requirements.
v.--FIRE EXTINGUISHER	Pressurized-dry-chemical gauge-type-approved-by Underwriters' Laboratories,-having rating-of-not-less-than 10-B,C,-mounted-in bracket-and-readily accessible.--Sealed-with a-type-of-seal-that-will not-interfere-with operation.----If-stored-in locked-compartment, compartment-must-be labelled.	Gauge-does-not-indicate in-the-calibrated-or marked-"Full-Charge" area.--Seal-is-broken. Extinguisher-is-not mounted,-not-in-a-quick release-holder-or-not labelled-in-compartment if-applicable.
v.--FIRST-AID KIT	Kit-shall-be-readily identifiable,-removable, and-mounted-in-readily accessible-place-in driver's-compartment--- either-in-full-view-or-in specified-secured compartment-(see-LOCKED COMPARTMENT).--If-not carried-in-compartment,-the case-shall--be--dust--tight and----------substantially constructed----of---durable material.----The---contents shall-include,-but--not--be limited----to,----either--the following-Type-1-or-Type-2. Type-1.--Unit-Type-(Minimum Contents)	Kit-is-not-complete. Dust-or-other-visible dirt-is-present-inside case.--Individual packages-are-not-sealed. Medicine-or-tourniquet-is present.--Locked compartment-containing kit-is-not-labelled.

DEPARTMENT OF TRANSPORTATION

NOTICE OF ADOPTED AMENDMENTS

SUBJECT	PROCEDURES/SPECIFICATIONS	REJECT-VEHICLE-IF
	4"--bandage--compress.--2 pkgs (May-be-1-package-in-bus with--chassis---(incomplete vehicle)--manufactured--in March-1977-or-earlier.) 2"--bandage--compress.--2 pkgs (May-be-1--package--in--bus with--chassis--(incomplete vehicle)--manufactured--in March-1977-or-earlier.) 1"--bandage---or--adhesive compress.--------------1-pkg 40"-triangle--bandage--with two-safety-pins.--1 Splint,-wire-or-wood.--1 Type---2.--Commercial--Type (Minimum-Contents) Sterile-gauze-pad 3"-x-3"------------------36 Gauze-bandage 2"-x-5-yds.------------10 Adhesive-tape,--1".--2-1/2 yds. (The--above--three--may-be longer-or-wider) 40"-triangle-bandage with-two-safety-pins.--1 Wire-or-wood-splint.--1 Scissors.-----------------1 A-tourniquet-or-any-type-of ointment---antiseptic--or other-medicine-shall-not-be included.	
v.--FLOORS-AND FLOOR COVERING	Covering-in-underseat area,-including-tops-of wheel-housings,-driver's compartment-and-toeboard shall-be-covered-with fire-resistant-floor	Abnormal-wear-and obstructions-are present.--Holes-or openings-are-present-in floors,-floor-covering or-boots.

DEPARTMENT OF TRANSPORTATION

NOTICE OF ADOPTED AMENDMENTS

SUBJECT	PROCEDURES/SPECIFICATIONS	REJECT VEHICLE IF
	~~covering of type commonly used in passenger transportation equipment. The floor covering in the aisle and entrance area shall be a nonskid, wear resistant, fire resistant and rth type commonly used in commercial passenger transportation vehicles. Covering must be permanently bonded to floor and must not crack when subjected to sudden changes in temperature. Bonding or adhesive material shall be waterproof. All seams must be sealed with waterproof sealer. All openings in floorboard or firewall between chassis and passenger carrying compartment must be solid and sealed. Boots and seals around shift levers and emergency brakes must be secure and solidly attached.~~	
~~y) FRAME AND BODY~~	~~Visually inspect: 1) Body mounts shall be attached and sealed to the chassis cowl so as to prevent the entry of water, dust or fumes through the joint between the chassis cowl and the body. 2) Cross member mounting bolts. 3) Engine mounting bolts. 4) Frame shall extend to some of body cross member.~~	~~1) Cracked, loose, missing bolts. Any repair done by welding body to frame, insulation strip missing. 2) Loose, cracked, broken or missing. 3) Missing, loose. 4) Cracked, broken, bent, rusted to a depth as to substantially weaken~~

DEPARTMENT OF TRANSPORTATION

NOTICE OF ADOPTED AMENDMENTS

SUBJECT	PROCEDURES/SPECIFICATIONS	REJECT VEHICLE IF
	~~5) Frame extension is permitted when alterations are behind rear hanger or rear springs and not for the purpose of extending wheel base.~~	~~frame welding except by body manufacturer. 5) Unless permitted, frame extends past wheel base.~~
~~z) FUEL STORAGE AND DELIVERY SYSTEM~~	~~Entire fuel system except extensions for driver control of air or fuel, must be outside passenger and driver compartment.~~	~~Any part of fuel system except extensions for driver control of air or fuel, is within passenger/driver compartment.~~
~~1) Fuel Filler Cap~~	~~Meets federal specifications. Must be the same as or equivalent to original equipment. 49 CFR 393.67~~	~~Defective or missing.~~
~~2) Fuel Lines~~	~~Firmly attached. No leakage, seepage, abrasion or chafing. Must be 11 13/16 inches (300 mm) from any part of exhaust system that contains exhaust gas or be safeguarded by a heat shield. Inside engine compartment the chassis manufacturer's standard shall govern separation and shielding between parts designed by chassis manufacturer.~~	~~Cracked, leaky, insecure mounting, damaged clamps missing, mount clips missing or not separated or not shielded properly.~~
~~3) Fuel Filler~~		

DEPARTMENT OF TRANSPORTATION

NOTICE OF ADOPTED AMENDMENTS

SUBJECT	PROCEDURES/SPECIFICATIONS	REJECT VEHICLE IF
Tube	Check condition.	Leaks or is not secure.
4. Fuel Pump	Check condition.	Leaks, damaged, or is not secure.
5. Fuel Tank(s)	Tank must be safeguarded by structure that protects from side or angular impact blows. 49 CFR 571.301 Exception: A bus with chassis incomplete vehicle manufactured in March 1977 or earlier is exempt from being equipped with a tank guard structure.	Leakage, seepage, or abrasion, hole, or crack that would leak or seep when tank is full.
6. Fuel tank mounting	Check condition.	Cracked, looser, bolts missing.
7. Fuel tank straps	Check condition.	Cracked, looser, or missing.
8. Propane relief valve/ piping	The relief valve discharge shall be vented to the left or driver's side of the vehicle and up the outside near or at the driver's station and then to the eave of the roof line. It must not reach above this point and must be nonhitchable. Where it is possible to do so, it is acceptable to run the discharge piping between the inner and outer walls of the bus.	Propane relief valve/piping system is not properly installed.

DEPARTMENT OF TRANSPORTATION

NOTICE OF ADOPTED AMENDMENTS

SUBJECT	PROCEDURES/SPECIFICATIONS	REJECT VEHICLE IF
	On existing installations, if the discharge pipe is run through the inside of the bus, the following criteria shall also apply: The pipe shall be galvanized. No connections may be made inside of the bus in other words, the pipe should be one length and threaded only on the exterior, both top and bottom. The pipe shall be covered with a material, such as foam rubber, to prevent a person from hurting themselves if they were pushed or fell against the post. The pipe must be securely clamped with a u bolt on the bottom to hold it in place. If the pipe goes through the vertical stanchion, the vertical stanchion shall be bolted both top and bottom as it was originally constructed. In all cases, the discharge piping shall terminate above the window line. An appropriate rain cap arrangement shall be provided to prevent the entry of water, too, stray into the discharge piping.	
aa. GRAB HANDLES		
1. Exterior	At least one step grab handle shall be located on each side at front of	Missing or loose.

DEPARTMENT OF TRANSPORTATION

NOTICE OF ADOPTED AMENDMENTS

SUBJECT	PROCEDURES/SPECIFICATIONS	REJECT-VEHICLE-IF
	body-so-as-to-provide easy-access-to-windshield,	
2)--Interior	Stainless-clad-steel-with measurements--not-less-than 20-inches-long--located--in unobstructed-------location inside-doorway.	Not-solidly-attached.
bb)--HEATERS	Nameplate-must-identify manufacturer-and-heater rating-capacity.--Must-be capable----of---maintaining inside--temperature--of--50 degrees.--The-heater--hoses shall-be-supported-to-guard against--excessive-wear-due to-vibration-and-shall--not interfere--with-or-restrict the-operation-of-any-engine function.--Any-hose-in--the passenger-compartment-shall be--protected--to--prevent injury-from--burns--in--the event-of-rupture.	Poor--working-condition, defective-hoses,-supports or-baffles.
cc)--HOOD	Open-hood-and-inspect safety-catch-and-hinges for-proper-operation. Close-hood-and-inspect for-proper-full-closure. Manually-inspect-latches or-remote-control-for proper-operation.	Hood-does-not-open-or hood-latches-do-not securely-hold-hood-in-its proper-fully-closed position.--Secondary-or safety-catch-does-not function-properly.--Hinge is--broken,-missing,-or-not attached-to-body.
dd)--HORN	At-least-one-horn-shall be-provided-giving-an audible--warning--at----a distance--of--200--feet-and shall----be---conveniently controlled----from----the operator's-seated-position. (Section--12-601---of---the Illinois-Vehicle-Equipment Law)	Horn--control-is-missing, defective-or-not-audible.

DEPARTMENT OF TRANSPORTATION

NOTICE OF ADOPTED AMENDMENTS

SUBJECT	PROCEDURES/SPECIFICATIONS	REJECT-VEHICLE-IF
ee)--INSTRUMENTS AND INSTRUMENT PANEL	Shall-be-equipped-with the-following-nonglare illuminated,-instruments and-gauges-mounted-for easy-maintenance-and repair-and-in-such-a-manner that--each--is----clearly visible--to--the--seated driver.--An-indicator-light instead--of--a--pressure-or temperature----gauge----is permissable----49---CFR 571.101 1)--Speedometer. 2)--Odometer. 3)--Fuel-Gauge. 4)--Oil-Pressure-Gauge. 5)--Water-Temperature Gauge. 6)--Ammeter-with-graduated charge-and-discharge indications. 7)--High-beam-headlight indicator. 8)--Directional-signal indicator. 9)--Air-pressure-or-vacuum gauge-(when-air-or vacuum-brakes-are used). 10)--Stop-light-flasher indicator.	Does-not-operate properly,-instruments-are missing,-inaccurate readings.
ff)--INSULATION	The-ceiling-and-sidewalls shall-be-thermally insulated------with------a fire-resistant-----material which---shall---reduce--the noise-level-and-vibration.	Does-not-meet requirements.
gg)--LETTERING 1)--Exterior	The-body-and-chassis	Does-not-meet

DEPARTMENT OF TRANSPORTATION

NOTICE OF ADOPTED AMENDMENTS

SUBJECT	PROCEDURES/SPECIFICATIONS	REJECT-VEHICLE-IF
	manufacturer's-name, emblem-or-other identification-may-be displayed-(colorless-or any-color)-on-any unglazed--surface--of---the bus.	requirements---lettering or-decals-are-not-black, distinct,-required-or allowed.
A,--Front	"SCHOOL-BUS"-in-black-at least-eight-inches-(200 mm)-high-placed-as-high as-possible-on-body-or sign-attached-thereto. Vehicle-number-assigned-for identification--shall--be--a minimum-of-four-inches-(100 mm)--high--and--located--as high----as----practicable, Decals---are----practicable, All---lettering---must---be black. (Section--12-802-of the----Illinois----Vehicle Equipment-Law)	Does-not-meet requirements---lettering is-not-black,-distinct, required-or-allowed.
B,--Left	Owner's-name-and-school district-number-must-be at-least-four-inches high,-approximately centered---and---as---high--as practicable---below---window line. (Section--12-802--of the----Illinois----Vehicle Equipment-Law) If--bus--is-equipped-with-a side--emergency--door---or emergency-windows-which-are knock-out-type,-they-are-to be---labeled---"EMERGENCY EXIT"-in-letters--at--least two--inches--high--directly below-window. Optional:---Vehicle---number assigned-for-identification may---be---displayed--at--a minimum--height---of---four inches-(100-mm).	Does-not-meet requirements---lettering is-not-black,-distinct, required,-or-allowed.

DEPARTMENT OF TRANSPORTATION

NOTICE OF ADOPTED AMENDMENTS

SUBJECT	PROCEDURES/SPECIFICATIONS	REJECT-VEHICLE-IF
	Decals---are---permissible. All---lettering---must---be black.	
C,--Rear	"SCHOOL-BUS"--in-black lettering-at-least-eight inches-(200-mm)-high placed-as-high-as possible--on--body--or-sign attached-thereto. (Section 12-802---of---the--Illinois Vehicle---Equipment----Law) "EMERGENCY----DOOR"----or "EMERGENCY----EXIT"-----in lettering---at---least--two inches--high--at---top---of emergency-door,-or-directly above,--or--on-door-glazing at-least-44-inches-(1.12-m) above-floor-level. "EMERGENCY--EXIT"-(for-buses without---rear---emergency door)--in--letters-at-least two--inches--high--directly below---rear----emergency window,--or-on-exit-glazing at-least--44---inches--above floor---level. An-arrow--at least-5.5-inches-in--length and--3/4--inches---in--width indicating--direction--each release-mechanism-should-be turned---to--open--door--or window-located---within--5.5 inch---of--release-handle in-black. Vehicle--number assigned-for-identification shall-be-a-minimum-4-inches (100-mm)-high. Decals-are permissible. All-lettering must-be-black. If-bus-uses-alternate fuel-(e.g.,-propane, CNG),-vehicle-must-be marked-with-identifying	Lettering-or-arrows-are not-black,-distinct, required,-or-allowed. Buses-using-alternate fuels-are-not-properly marked-with-decal.--Decal is-in-wrong-location.

DEPARTMENT OF TRANSPORTATION

NOTICE OF ADOPTED AMENDMENTS

SUBJECT	PROCEDURES/SPECIFICATIONS	REJECT VEHICLE IF
	decal. Such decal shall be diamond-shaped with white or silver scotchlite lettering one inch in height and a stroke of the brush at least 1/4 inch wide on a black background with a white or silver scotchlite border bearing either the words:	
	"PROPANE" if propelled by liquefied petroleum gas other than liquefied natural gas; or "CNG" if propelled by compressed natural gas. The sign or decal shall be maintained in good legible condition. The alternate fuel decal shall be displayed on or near the rear bumper and visible from the rear of vehicle. (Section 12 704.) of the Illinois Vehicle Equipment Law)	
2) Right	Owner's name and school district number must be at least four inches (100 mm) high; approximately centered and as high as possible below window line. (Section 12-802 of the Illinois Vehicle Equipment Law) The following lettering must be at least two inches (50 mm) high:	lettering or decals are not black, distinct, required; or allowed;
	a) The word "CAPACITY," or abbreviation "CAP.," and the rated passenger capacity followed by the word	

DEPARTMENT OF TRANSPORTATION

NOTICE OF ADOPTED AMENDMENTS

SUBJECT	PROCEDURES/SPECIFICATIONS	REJECT VEHICLE IF
	"PASSENGERS," or the abbreviation "PASS.;" shall be displayed on the outside of the body near the rear edge of the service entrance.	
	2) Empty weight in both pounds and newtons; must be shown. Empty weight is indicated by "EW" and newtons is indicated by "N." (Section 12-802 of the Illinois Vehicle Equipment Law)	
	3) If emergency window is installed, "EMERGENCY EXIT" shall be displayed on or immediately below emergency window; Manufacturer's identification name or emblem may be displayed, but not on service door glazing. Manufacturer's name or emblem must not interfere with required lettering. Decals are permissible; may be black; must be black; Exception: A bus with chassis incomplete vehicle; manufactured in March 1977 or earlier need not show empty weight in newtons.	
AGENCY NOTE:	Weight in newtons (N) = weight in pounds (lb) x 4.448222 (or 4.45).	
2) Interior		
A) Front	Each letter or numeral must be at least two inches (50 mm) high and	Does not meet requirements; lettering is not black, distinct;

DEPARTMENT OF TRANSPORTATION

NOTICE OF ADOPTED AMENDMENTS

SUBJECT	PROCEDURES/SPECIFICATIONS	REJECT VEHICLE IF
	contrasting-sharply-with background.--A---colorless background--strip--(such-as white,-aluminum-or--silver) may--be--used---Decals-are permitted.	required-or-allowed.
	On---right----side.--Either "CAPACITY"--or--"CAP."-plus numerals---showing----rated passenger---------capacity, followed------by-----either "PASSENGER"-or-"PASS." As--nearly--as--practicable opposite--the----center---of aisle,--but--to--right--of inside-mirror---either--"NO STANDEES"---or---"NO-STANDEES PERMITTED." A-red-cross-formed-of--five equal--squares--with--words "FIRST-AID-KIT"---shall--be displayed--------on--------the compartment-door,-or-cover if--the-first-aid-kit-is-to be-carried--in--the--locked compartment. The------words----"FIRE EXTINGUISHER"----shall--be displayed------on------the compartment-door,-or-cover if-the-fire-extinguisher-is to-be-carried-in-the-locked compartment. Exception--On--a--bus-with chassis--------(incomplete vehicle)--manufactured--in March--1977-or-earlier,--"NO STANDEES"--need--not--be opposite--center--of--aisle and-the-word--"PASSENGERS," or-"PASS.",-is-optional.	
By---Left	A-"Stop-line"-in contrasting-color-is required-between-5,9-and 5,6-inches-(150-mm-and	Does-not-meet requirements.--Line-or line-and-lettering-is-not distinctly-required-or

DEPARTMENT OF TRANSPORTATION

NOTICE OF ADOPTED AMENDMENTS

SUBJECT	PROCEDURES/SPECIFICATIONS	REJECT VEHICLE IF
	150-mm--below--the-top-of the--window--opening.---The line---shall--be---located between--each--window--that slides-downward.	allowed.
By---Rear	"EMERGENCY-DOOR"--or "EMERGENCY-EXIT"--in letters-at-least-two inches-(50-mm)-high painted----or---permanently affixed----either---directly above-each-emergency--exit or--on--top--metal--of-exit (door-or-window)--or-on-top of-exit-glazing-at-least--44 inches---(112---m)---above floor.--An-arrow-indicating the-direction-in--which--to move----release---mechanism handle(s)-to-open-emergency exit-shall--be--painted--or permanently-affixed-within six-inches-of-each---release handle.--All-lettering-and arrow(s)-must-contrast-with background.----Decals---are permitted.	Does-not-meet requirements.--Lettering is-not-black,-distinct, required,-or-allowed.
By---Right	A-"Stop-line"--in contrasting-color--is required-between-5,9-and 6,1-inches-(150-mm--and 150-mm)-below-the-top-of the--window--opening.--The line---shall--be---located between--each--window--that slides--downward.---Decals are-permitted. Instructions---for-emergency operation--of---power operated---door---shall--be affixed-permanently-on--the inside---of---the--door--in letters-at--least--,5--inch high--------Decals------are	Does-not-meet requirements.--Line-or line-and-lettering-is-not black,-distinct,-required or-allowed.

DEPARTMENT OF TRANSPORTATION

NOTICE OF ADOPTED AMENDMENTS

SUBJECT	PROCEDURES/SPECIFICATIONS	REJECT-VEHICLE-IF
	permitted.	
11)---LIGHTS		
1)---Back-Up	Two-white-lights-shall-be provided.--Must-meet federal-standards.--49 CFR-571.108 Exception.----All---buses purchased-----prior-----to September--1974-are-exempt; however.---for---any---unit equipped---with---back---up lamps---they---must----be operational.	Does-not-function; illegal-color;-broken glass.
2)---Clearance; Front	Two-clearance-lights (amber)-at-highest-and widest-portions-of-the body.----Must---conform-to federal-standards.--49--CFR 571.108.--May--be--combined with-side-marker-lamp.	Does-not-function; improper-color;-broken glass.
3)---Clearance; Rear	Two-clearance-lights (red)-mounted-at-highest and-widest-part-of-body. Must---conform--to--federal standards.--49-CFR-571.108	Does-not-function; improper-color;-broken glass
4)---Cluster; Front	Three-amber-lights mounted-at-center-front near-top-of-body-above "SCHOOL--BUS"--sign.---Must conform-----to-----federal standards.--49-CFR-571.108	Does-not-function properly;-improper-color; broken-glass.
5)---Cluster; Rear	Three-red-lights-mounted at-center-rear-near-top of-body-either-above-or	Does-not-function properly;-improper-color; broken-glass.

DEPARTMENT OF TRANSPORTATION

NOTICE OF ADOPTED AMENDMENTS

SUBJECT	PROCEDURES/SPECIFICATIONS	REJECT-VEHICLE-IF
	below--"SCHOOL--BUS"--sign. Must---conform---to--federal standards.--49-CFR-571.108	
6)---Flashing Lights	All-school-buses purchased-after-December 31,-1975,-shall-be equipped--with---an---eight light----flashing----signal system-with-two-red-and-two amber-flashing-signal-lamps mounted---above--windshield spaced-no-less---than--three feet---apart---and--at--same horizontal-level.--The-rear of--the--vehicle--shall--be equipped-with-two---red---and two---amber--flashing-signal lamps-mounted-and-spaced-no less-than-three-feet---apart and---at---same--horizontal level.----Minimum---diameter 5-1/2-inch-sealed-beam. Effective--December--31, 1975,---all---school--buses shall-be-equipped-with--the eight-light-flashing-signal system---described--in--the above--paragraph. (Section 12-805--of---the--Illinois Vehicle-Equipment-Law) A--separate-circuit-breaker and-a-master--switch--shall be-provided-for-this-signal system.--When-in-its-"off" position-this-master-switch shall-----prevent------the following: 1)--Operation-of-the-8-lamp system; 2)--Operation-of-any-lamps mounted-on-the-stop signal-arm; 3)--Operation-of-any	Does-not-function properly;-broken-lens-or improper-lens-color.

DEPARTMENT OF TRANSPORTATION

NOTICE OF ADOPTED AMENDMENTS

SUBJECT	PROCEDURES/SPECIFICATIONS	REJECT-VEHICLE-IF
	electrically controlled mechanism that would cause the stop-signal-arm to extend.	

The-controls-for-the--right lamp--flashing-signals,-the stop--signal--arm--and--the service-entrance-door-shall be--arranged---as---as---to provide--for--the-following sequence---of---operations while----the----engine--is running:

1) Place-the-alternately flashing-signal-system master-switch-in-its "off"-position.--Close and-secure-the--service entrance-door.
Actuate-the alternately-flashing signal-system-hand-or foot-controls.--The alternately-flashing signal-lamps-of-either yellow-(amber)-or-red color-shall-not-go-on.

2) With-the-master-switch "off"-and-the-hand-or foot-control-actuated, open-the-service door.--The-alternately flashing-signals-of either-color-shall-not go-on-and-the-stop signal-arm-shall-not extend.

3) Deactivate-the-hand-or foot-controls.--Place the-alternately flashing-signal-system master-switch-in-its "on"-position.--Close and-secure-the-service door.--Open-the

DEPARTMENT OF TRANSPORTATION

NOTICE OF ADOPTED AMENDMENTS

SUBJECT	PROCEDURES/SPECIFICATIONS	REJECT-VEHICLE-IF
	service-door.--The alternately-flashing signal-lamps-of-either color-shall-not-go-on and-stop-signal-arm shall-not-extend.	

4) Close-and-secure-the service-door.--Actuate the-alternately flashing-signal-system by-hand-or-foot controls.--A-yellow pilot-lamp-in-the-view of-the-driver-and-the yellow-alternately flashing-signals-shall go-on.

5) Resecure-but-do-not open-the-service door.--The-yellow pilot-and-the-yellow alternately-flashing signals-shall-go-off. A-red-pilot-lamp-in the-view-of-the-driver and-the-red alternately-flashing signals-shall-go-on. The-stop-signal-arm shall-extend.

6) Fully-open-the-service door.--The-red-pilot and-red-signals-shall remain-on-and-the-stop arm-shall--remain extended.

7) Close-but-do-not secure-the-service door.--The-red-pilot and-red-signals-shall remain-on-and-the-stop arm-shall-remain extended.

8) Open-the-service door.--The-red-pilot and-red-signals-shall

DEPARTMENT OF TRANSPORTATION

NOTICE OF ADOPTED AMENDMENTS

~~SUBJECT~~	~~PROCEDURES/SPECIFICATIONS~~	~~REJECT-VEHICLE-IF~~
	~~remain-on-and-the-stop arm-remain-extended.~~ ~~9.--Open-the-service door.--Alternately flashing-signals-of either-color-shall-not go-on-and-the-stop-arm shall-not-extend.~~	
~~7.--Headlights~~	~~Shall-have-at-least-two sealed-beam-headlamps--with at--least--one--mounted--on each--side--of-the-front-of the-bus.--Lamp-body-must-be securely-attached.--Lenses, reflectors,--bulbs,---etc, must--be-in-good-condition, properly-aimed-(see.--Aiming Procedures--below)-and-fill required-intensity.---Shall conform------to----federal standards.--49-CFR-571.108~~	~~Do-not-meet-requirements.~~
~~A.--Aiming~~	~~Use-approved-calibrated headlamp-tester-according to-----------manufacturer's instructions.---The-headlamp tester--shall--be--in--good repair-and-calibration. All---type---"2"-----lamps, regardless-of-size,-must-be aimed--and--tested--on--low beam. Check--for-bulb-burnout-and proper-beam-switching. Check-springs--for--sag--or broken-lenses, Clean-lenses.~~	~~Headlights-are-not-aimed properly.~~
~~B.--Test Procedures~~	~~1.--Upper-Beam-Aim Applies-only-to-5-3/4 inch--Type--"1"-sealed-beam headlamp-units, 2.--Lower-Beam-Aim~~	

DEPARTMENT OF TRANSPORTATION

NOTICE OF ADOPTED AMENDMENTS

~~SUBJECT~~	~~PROCEDURES/SPECIFICATIONS~~	~~REJECT-VEHICLE-IF~~
	~~The-following-type-headlamp units-are-to-be-tested-only on-the-lower-beam:~~ ~~5-3/4----inch---Type---"2" sealed-beam,-or 7--inch---Type--"2"--sealed beam.~~	
~~8.--Interior~~	~~Adequate-to-illuminate aisles,-step-well,-and emergency-passageways.~~	~~Does-not-provide-adequate lighting,-cracked-or broken-lenses,-improper color.~~
~~9.--License Plate~~	~~Adequate-white-light-to illuminate-license plate.--49-CFR-571.108. May-be-combined with--one---of--the--tail lights.~~	~~Does-not-provide-adequate lighting,-cracked-or broken-lenses,-improper color.~~
~~10.--Marker, Left~~	~~Two-lamps,--one--amber-at front-and-one-red-at rear,-mounted-as-high-as practicable.--Shall conform-to-federal standards.--49-CFR-571.108 Exception,--All------buses purchased-----prior-----to September-1974-are-exempt.~~	~~Does-not-meet requirements,-does-not function-properly, improper-color,-cracked or-broken-lenses.~~
~~11.--Marker, Right~~	~~Two-lamps,-one-amber-at front-and-one-red-at rear,-mounted-as-high-as practicable.--Shall conform----to----federal standards.--49-CFR-571.108 Exception,--All------buses purchased-----prior-----to September-1974-are-exempt.~~	~~Does-not-meet requirements,-improper color,-cracked-or-broken lenses.~~
~~12.--Parking Light~~	~~Shall-be-one-lamp-on-each side,-white-or-amber~~	~~Does-not-meet requirements,-improper~~

DEPARTMENT OF TRANSPORTATION

NOTICE OF ADOPTED AMENDMENTS

SUBJECT	PROCEDURE/SPECIFICATIONS	REJECT-VEHICLE-IF
	color,--49-CFR-571.108	color,-cracked-or-broken lenses.
	All-buses-80-or-more-inches in-overall-width-which--are equipped--with--side-marker lamps,-clearance-lamps,-and intermediate--side--marker lamps---are---exempt---from having----parking---lights. However,--if---vehicle--is equipped---with---parking lights,----they---must---be operational. (Section 12-208-of---the--Illinois Vehicle-Equipment-Law)	
13.--Step-Well	At-least-the-nosings-of the-service-entrance steps-and-the-floor around-the-step-well-shall be-automatically illuminated---with--white light--when--the-following occurs: 1)--Service-entrance-door is-opened. 2)--Clearance-lamps-are-on and-the-door-is-opened. 3)--Ignition-is-on-and-the door-is-opened. No-lamp-shall-be--installed so--as--to--shine--directly into--the--eyes--of-a-pupil moving-through-the--service entrance-and-looking-at-the service-steps. Exception:--On--a--bus-with chassis---------(incomplete vehicle)--manufactured---in March--1977--or--earlier,-a stepwell--light--that--does not-illuminate-all-the-step nosings---or---does---not illuminate-the-floor-around the-service-entranceway-may be-used.	Does-not-meet requirements,-improper color,-cracked-or-broken lenses.

DEPARTMENT OF TRANSPORTATION

NOTICE OF ADOPTED AMENDMENTS

SUBJECT	PROCEDURE/SPECIFICATIONS	REJECT-VEHICLE-IF
14.--Stop	Two-red-lights-mounted-at same-height-and-as-high as-practicable-below window-lines.--Seven-inch minimum-diameter-or-19 square---inches.---Not--less than---three--feet---apart laterally.--Must-conform-to federal--standards.--49-CFR 571.108	Does-not-meet requirements,-improper color,-cracked-or-broken lenses,-does-not-function properly.
15.--Strobe (optional)	If-installed,-lamp-must comply-with-following requirements: 1) One-per-bus. 2) Shall-emit-white-or bluish/white-light. 3) Shall-be-visible-from any-direction. 4) Shall-flash-60-to-120 times-per-minute. 5) Shall-be-visible-in normal-sunlight. 6) Mounted-at-or-behind center-of-rooftop-and equal-distance-from each---side. (Section 12-815-of---the--Illinois Vehicle-Equipment-Law) Distance--from-rear-will-be calculated---by--measuring height--of--filament---and multiplying---same---by-30 inches.---(i.e.,---Filament height-x-30-=-distance-from rear--of--bus-where-lamp-is to-be-located)	If-installed,-does-not meet-installation requirements,-does-not function-properly, improper-color,-cracked or-broken-lenses
16.--Tail	Two-red-lights-mounted with-centers-not-less than-15-inches-nor-more than-50-inches-from surface-on-which-vehicle	Does-not-meet requirements,-does-not function-properly, improper-color,-cracked or-broken-lenses

Shielding-is present.

DEPARTMENT OF TRANSPORTATION

NOTICE OF ADOPTED AMENDMENTS

SUBJECT	PROCEDURES/SPECIFICATIONS	REJECT-VEHICLE-IF
	stands---Must---conform--to federal-standards--49--CFR 571.108	
17)--Turn Signal, Left (armored)	Flush-mounted-"armored" type-amber-clearance-lamp mounted-behind-driver's seat-at-seat-level-and rub-rail-height. Functions-with-regular-turn signal. Exceptions:-All------buses purchased------prior----to September-1974--are--exempt from--having--left--armored turn-signals.	Does-not-meet requirements.-does-not function-properly. improper-color.-cracked or-broken-lenses.
18)--Turn Signal, Right (armored)	Flush-mounted-"armored" type-amber-clearance-lamp mounted-at-approximately seat-level-and-rub-rail height-just-to-rear-of service---door.---Functions with--regular--turn--signal lamp. Exceptions:-All------buses purchased----prior----to September-1974--are-exempt from-having-right--armored turn-signals.	Does-not-meet requirements.-does-not function-properly. improper-color.-cracked or-broken-lenses.
19)--Turn Signal, Front	One-amber-lamp-at-least four-inches-in-diameter or-12-1/2-square-inches, located-on-each-side-at or-near-the-front.--They shall--be--located--at--the same---height---and--as--far apart---as----practicable. lamps---must---conform--to	Does-not-meet requirements.-does-not function-properly. improper-color.-cracked or-broken-lenses.

DEPARTMENT OF TRANSPORTATION

NOTICE OF ADOPTED AMENDMENTS

SUBJECT	PROCEDURES/SPECIFICATIONS	REJECT-VEHICLE-IF
	federal-standards--49--CFR 571.108 Operate-turn-signals-and four-way-warning-hazards to---check--performance--of front-and-rear-lights.	Four-way-warning-hazards do-not-operate-properly.
20)--Turn Signal, Rear	Chassis-manufactured after-March-31,-1977, must-have-two-7-inch diameter-or-49-square inch,-amber-lenses mounted-on-the-rear-as--far apart---and--as--high--as practicable--below----rear window.-49-CFR-571.108 Exception:--Chassis manufactured-prior-to-April 1,-1977,-may-have-yellow-or red-turn-signals-with-arrow lenses.-49-CFR-571.108	Does-not-meet requirements.-improper color.-does-not-function properly.-cracked-or broken-lenses.
21)--LOCKED COMPARTMENT	Fire-extinguisher, first-aid-kit,-and warning-devices-may-be stored-either-in-a closed,-unlocked compartment-or-under-lock and-key-provided-the locking-device-is-connected with--an--automatic-warning signal---that---will--alert driver--when-compartment-is locked.---The---automatic alarm-shall-be-both-audible and--visible--to-the-seated driver.--The--alarm---shall alert-the-driver--when--the engine-is--running-and-the compartment-is--locked--and not-readily--opened-without using---a---tool,--key,--or combination.----An----alarm	Not-readily-accessible-to driver.-lettering-or identification-missing. alarm-does-not-function properly-when-compartment is-locked-and-vehicle-is running.

DEPARTMENT OF TRANSPORTATION

NOTICE OF ADOPTED AMENDMENTS

SUBJECT	PROCEDURES/SPECIFICATIONS	REJECT VEHICLE IF
	cut-off-----or----"squelch" control-is-prohibited. Each-safety-item-inside-the compartment-shall-be-named on---the---outside--of--the compartment-cover,-or-door. In-addition,--a--RED--CROSS formed----of---five---equal squares-shall-be--displayed on-the-cover-when-the-first aid--kit--is--inside--the compartment. Exception:--A--bus---with chassis----manufactured---in March--1977-or-earlier-need not-have-a-visible-alarm.	
777--MIRRORS	Every-required-mirror shall-be-of-reflecting material-protected-from abrasion,-scratching,-and corrosion.--Mirror-shall be-firmly-installed-on stable-supports--so--as--to give---a---clear---stable reflected---view.---Mirrors shall-be-adjustable--so--as to--give--and--maintain-its required-field-of-view.	Does-not-meet requirements:-defective, excessively-clouded,-not adjustable,-not-securely attached,-cracked-or broken-glass.
1)--Exterior A)--Rear View Driving	Shall-be-mounted outside.--Must-give seated-driver-a-view-to the-rear-along-each-side of-bus.--Must-be-at-least 50-square-inches-of usable--flat--rectangular reflecting-surface-on--each side--49-CFR-571.111. A-convex-driving-mirror-may be--installed-to-expand-the driving-view-to--the--rear, provided--the--usable--flat	Does-not-meet requirements:-defective, excessively-clouded,-not adjustable,-not-securely attached,-cracked-or broken-glass.

DEPARTMENT OF TRANSPORTATION

NOTICE OF ADOPTED AMENDMENTS

SUBJECT	PROCEDURES/SPECIFICATIONS	REJECT VEHICLE IF
	reflecting---surface---is rectangular-and-is-at-least 50-square-inches. Exception:--When--a--convex driving-mirror-is-installed on--a--bus--manufactured-in August-1974-or-earlier,-the usable---flat---reflecting surface---need---not---be rectangular-but-must-be--at least-50-square-inches.	
B)--Right Side Safety	An-outside-convex-mirror either-alone-or-in combination-with-the driving-mirror-system, shall-give-the-seated driver-a-view-of-the roadway---along--the--right side-of-the-bus-between the-most-forward-surface-of the-right--front--tire--and the---rear---of---the--rear bumper.--The----projected reflecting--surface-of-this convex-mirror-shall--be--at least---40---square--inches (7-1/8-inches-diameter-if-a circle). Extra-wide-angle----convex mirror------heads-------are permissible--on-right-front corner--only. Exception:--A-right--safety mirror-is-optional-on-a-bus manufactured-in-August-1974 or-earlier.	Does-not-meet requirements, defective,-excessively clouded,-not-adjustable, not-securely-attached, cracked-or-broken-glass.
C)--Left Side Safety	The-seated-driver-shall have-a-reflected-view-of the-roadway-along-the left-side-of-the-bus between-the-front-edge-of	Does-not-meet requirements:-defective, excessively-clouded,-not adjustable,-not-securely attached,-cracked-or

DEPARTMENT OF TRANSPORTATION

NOTICE OF ADOPTED AMENDMENTS

SUBJECT	PROCEDURES/SPECIFICATIONS	REJECT VEHICLE IF
	the driver's seat (in most forward position) and the rear of the rear bumper. If the left driving mirror system does not give that view, a convex mirror shall be installed, that, either alone or in combination with the driving mirror, does give the seated driver that view. Exception: A left safety mirror is optional on a bus with chassis manufactured in March 1977 or earlier.	broken glass.
1) Cross Over Mirror	An outside convex mirror shall give the seated driver a view of the front bumper and the area of roadway in front of the bus. The projected reflecting surface of this mirror shall be at least 40 square inches (7 1/8 inches diameter if a circle). 49 CFR 571.111 Exception: If the seated driver of a forward control bus has a direct view of the front bumper and the area of roadway in front of the bus, a cross over mirror is optional.	Does not meet requirements: defective; excessively clouded; not adjustable; not securely attached; cracked or broken glass.
2) Interior	Clear view safety glass, minimum 6 inches x 30 inches overall; framed with rounded and padded corners and edges. It shall afford good view of	Does not meet requirements: defective; excessively clouded; not adjustable; not securely attached; cracked or broken glass.

DEPARTMENT OF TRANSPORTATION

NOTICE OF ADOPTED AMENDMENTS

SUBJECT	PROCEDURES/SPECIFICATIONS	REJECT VEHICLE IF
	the bus interior and portions of the roadway to the rear. Exception: All buses manufactured prior to September 1974 are exempt from padding on the mirror.	
hh) PAINT REQUIREMENTS	The exterior of the body, excluding the required rails, shall be painted a uniform color, National School Bus Glossy Yellow. The front and rear bumpers, required rub rails and wheels shall be black. Additional rub rails may either be painted black or yellow. Grilles and hub caps may be a bright finish (e.g., chrome), anodized aluminum, etc. Retaining rings may be gray or aluminum. Manufacturer's name or emblem may be any color but must not interfere with required lettering, numbering or arrows. (Section 12-801 of the Illinois Vehicle-Equipment Law) Optional: Black areas around flashers are permitted. Must not interfere with "SCHOOL BUS" lettering. Exception: Fenders on buses manufactured prior to January 1976 may be painted black. (Section 12-801 of the Illinois Vehicle Equipment Law)	Does not meet color requirements: paint in poor condition (i.e., faded, peeling or rusted). Optional black area around flashers interferes with required lettering.

DEPARTMENT OF TRANSPORTATION

NOTICE OF ADOPTED AMENDMENTS

SUBJECT	PROCEDURES/SPECIFICATIONS	REJECT VEHICLE IF
	Exception--Hoods--may--be lusterless-----black-----or lusterless----school----bus yellow.	
ii)--PROJECTIONS		
1)--Exterior	Entire-rear-and-bumper area-of-bus-must-be nonhitchable. "Nonhitchable"-is-defined as---the--rear--of--the--bus being------designed-----and maintained--to--prevent--or discourage----riding-----or grasping--rear-of-bus-so-as to-"hitch"-rides.	Does-not-comply-with nonhitchable-projection requirements.
2)--Interior	Interior-shall-be-free-of all-unnecessary projections.--Remaining projections-shall-be padded-to-prevent injury.--This-includes inner-lining-of-ceiling and-walls.--Installation of--book--racks---is--not permissible. Exception:--All-buses purchased-prior-to September-1974-may-be equipped-with-book racks.--However--if--book racks---are--present--they shall-be-above-side-windows and---shall---not---extend forward--of--the-front-seat or--across--or--above---the emergency-door.--Racks-must be--free---of--projections likely-to-cause-injury.	Projections-are-not padded-(e.g.,-external speakers).--Book-racks are-present. Flush-mounted-speakers are-exempt-from-padding requirements. For-buses-purchased-prior to-September-1974,-book racks-do-not-meet requirements.
mm)--REFLECTORS		
1)--Front	Two-yellow-rigid-or sheet-type-(tape)-front reflex-reflectors-shall be-attached-securely-and	Missing-or-damaged reflective-materials-not located-or-positioned-as required.

DEPARTMENT OF TRANSPORTATION

NOTICE OF ADOPTED AMENDMENTS

SUBJECT	PROCEDURES/SPECIFICATIONS	REJECT VEHICLE IF
	as----far---forward-----as practicable. (Section 12-202--of--the--Illinois Vehicle-Equipment-Law)-They shall-be-located-between-15 and--60--inches--above--the roadway-at--either--fender cowly-or-body-and-installed no--as--to--mark--the-outer edge-of-the--maximum--width of-the-bus.--No-part-of-the required---------reflecting material-may-be-obscured-by a-lamp,-mirror,-bracket,-or any--other--portion--of-the bus.--No--part---of---the required---------reflecting material--may--be-more-than 15.0--inches---(380----mm) inboard--of--the-outer-edge of-the-nearest-rub-rail-(12 inches--on--a--bus--with chassis---manufactured---in March--1977--or--earlier). The-reflector--may--be--any shape----(e.g.,----square, rectangle,--circle)--oval, etc.).--A-rigid-type-reflex reflector--may--be-any-size if----permanently----marked either-DOT,-SAE-A,-or-SAE-B 594;--otherwise--it--shall display--at--least---seven square-inches-of-reflecting material---(about--3-inch diameter---if---a---solid circle).--A--sheet--type (tape)-reflex-reflector-may conform-to-the--surface--on which--it--is-installed-but its----forward----projected reflecting-area-shall-be-at least-eight-square-inches.	
2)--Left-Side	One-amber-at-or-near-the front-and-one-red-at-or	Missing-or-damaged reflective-materials,-not

DEPARTMENT OF TRANSPORTATION

NOTICE OF ADOPTED AMENDMENTS

SUBJECT	PROCEDURES/SPECIFICATIONS	REJECT VEHICLE IF
	near-the-rear---Mounted at-a-height-not-less-than 35-inches-and-not-more-than 60-inches-above-the-surface of-the-road---On--sides--of buses--20--feet--or-more-in length,-one-amber--as--near center--as-practicable-must also-be-provided.--(Section 12-202---of---the--Illinois Vehicle----Equipment---law) Minimum---three--inches---in diameter.	located-or-positioned-as required.
3.--Right-Side	One--amber-at-or-near-the front-and-one-red-at-or near-the-rear.--Mounted at-a-height-not-less-than 35-inches-and-not-more-than 60-inches-above-the-surface of--the--road.--On-sides-of buses-20-feet--or--more--in length,--one--amber-as-near center-as-practicable--must also-be-provided.--(Section 12-202---of---the--Illinois Vehicle---Equipment----law) Minimum---three--inches--in diameter.	Missing-or-damaged reflective-material;-not located-or-positioned-as required.
4.--Rear	Two-red-reflectors-on rear-body-within-12 inches-of-lower-right-and lower-left-corners. (Section-12-202---of---the Illinois--Vehicle-Equipment law)-Minimum---three--inches in-diameter.	Missing-or-damaged reflective-material;-not located-or-positioned-as required.
00.--RUB-RAILS	There-shall-be-one-rub rail-located approximately-at-seat level-which-shall-extend from---the---rear---of---the service-entrance-completely around-the-bus-body-without	Rub-rails-are-not-firmly attached;-incorrect color;-incorrect-number of-rails-or-missing.

DEPARTMENT OF TRANSPORTATION

NOTICE OF ADOPTED AMENDMENTS

SUBJECT	PROCEDURES/SPECIFICATIONS	REJECT VEHICLE IF
	interruptions-except--at--a rear--emergency--door--or--a rear--compartment,--to---a point-of-curvature-near-the front--of--the--body-on-the left-side. There-shall-be-one-rub-rail on---each--side---located approximately--at-the-floor line--which--shall---extend over--the-same-longitudinal distance-as--the--rub--rail located-at-the-seat-level. More-than-two-rub-rails-may be--installed--on-sides-and rear-of-body. Rub-rails-of-longitudinally corrugated-or-ribbed--steel at--least--3½--inches-(130 mm)-wide-shall-be-fixed--on the-outside-of-the-bus. Exceptions: 1)--Rub---rail---need---not extend across-wheel-housing. 2)--Rub-rail-may-terminate at-the-point-of curvature-at-the-right and-left-rear corners-of-the-body.	
00.--SEAT-BELTS	Must-be-installed-on driver's-seat.--(Section 12-807-of-the-Illinois Vehicle-Equipment-law) Belt-material;-buckle tongue,--etc.--shall-remain above--floor--when--not--in use.----All----retractors installed---shall---be---an automatic-locking-type. Exceptions:--On-a-bus manufactured-in-August 1974-or-earlier,-a retractor-must-be	Reject-if-dirty,-frayed, torn,-cracked-or-broken or-if-retractor-or-buckle does-not-operate-properly.
		In-buses-manufactured prior-to-September-1974, seat-belt-is-excessively dirty.

DEPARTMENT OF TRANSPORTATION

NOTICE OF ADOPTED AMENDMENTS

SUBJECT	PROCEDURES/SPECIFICATIONS	REJECT VEHICLE IF
	installed;--however,--the belt;-etc;-need-not-remain above-floor-but-must-not-be excessively-dirty.	
pp.--SEAT, DRIVER'S	The-driver's-seat-shall be-rigidly-positioned-and shall-afford-vertical, forward-and-backward adjustments---if--not--less than 9.9-inches-(100-mm)-without the--use--of--a--tool;--or non-attached--devices.---The shortest--distance--between the--steering-wheel-and-the back-rest-of-the-operator's seat-shall-be-no-less--than 15-inches-(380-mm). Seat--padding--and-covering shall-be-in-good-condition, free-from-holes-and--tears. Seat---cushions---shall--be securely--fastened--to--the seat-frame.	Not-securely-anchored-to floor,-in-poor-condition, adjustment--mechanism-does not-function-properly.
qq.--SEAT, PASSENGER	All-seats-shall-have-a minimum-front-to-rear depth-of-14-inches. In-determining-seating capacity-of-a-bus, individual-seating-width shall-be-13-inches-where 3-3-(three-pupils-on-both sides-of-aisle)-seating plan-is-used-and-15 inches-where-3-2-(three pupils-on-one-side-of aisle-and-two-pupils-on other-side-of--aisle)--plan is-used. All--seats-shall-be-forward facing---and----shall----be securely--fastened--to-that	Not-firmly-attached-to body,-broken-frame, cushions-not-firmly attached,-padding-and covering-not-fire resistant.---Padding-or covering-is-loose,-in poor-condition,-or missing;-seats-are-torn or-have-holes;-minimum seat-dimensions-or-seat spacing-are-not-in compliance.

DEPARTMENT OF TRANSPORTATION

NOTICE OF ADOPTED AMENDMENTS

SUBJECT	PROCEDURES/SPECIFICATIONS	REJECT VEHICLE IF
	part-or-parts-of--the--body which--support--them.---No jump-or-portable-seats--are allowed. The-forwardmost-seat-on-the right-side-of-the-bus-shall be--located--so--as--not-to interfere-with-the-driver's vision-and-not--be--farther forward--than--the--rear-of the--driver's--seat---when adjusted--to--its--rearmost position. The--center-to-center--seat spacing--shall--be--no-more than-24-inches,--measured-at cushion---height.---The distance----between---the rearmost--position--of--the driver's-seat-and-the-front face-of-the--seat--back--of the-forwardmost-seat-on-the left-side-shall-not-be-less than--24-inches-measured-at cushion-height. A-minimum-of-35--inches--of headroom--for--the--sitting position,--above--the-top-of the---undepressed---cushion line-of-all-seats-shall--be provided.---Measurement shall--be--made--vertically not-more-than-7-inches-from the--side--wall--or-cushion height-and-at-the-front-and rear-center-of-cushion. Seat-backs-of-similar--size shall--be-of-the-same-width at-the-top-and-of-the--same height--from--the-floor-and shall--slant--at--the--same angle-with-the-floor. Buses--manufactured---after June--30,--1987,--shall--be equipped--with-28-inch-seat backs. (Section--12-807.)	

DEPARTMENT OF TRANSPORTATION

NOTICE OF ADOPTED AMENDMENTS

SUBJECT	PROCEDURES/SPECIFICATIONS	REJECT VEHICLE IF

of the Illinois Vehicle
Equipment Law.
Buses manufactured after
December 31, 1987, shall
have 28 inch guard
barriers.
All buses manufactured
during and after September
1974 shall be equipped with
energy absorbing padding on
all exposed top and side
rails. The side rails
shall be padded in such a
manner to retain the 12
inch aisle (15 inches at
two inches below top of
seat back) for buses
manufactured after June 30,
1987. On the rear of a
seat back, the padding
shall extend from the top
of the seat back to the top
level of the seat cushion.
Seat padding and covering
shall be of fire resistant
material. Padding and
covering shall be in good
condition (i.e., free from
holes and tears). Seat
cushions shall be securely
fastened to the seat frame.
Optional: The rearmost
seats may be exempt from
seat back padding
requirement.
Exception: All buses
manufactured prior to
September 1974 are exempt
from padding on top and
side rails and seat back to
cushion level. Buses
purchased prior to
September 1974 may be
equipped with fiberglass
seats. If so equipped
they must meet or exceed

DEPARTMENT OF TRANSPORTATION

NOTICE OF ADOPTED AMENDMENTS

SUBJECT	PROCEDURES/SPECIFICATIONS	REJECT VEHICLE IF

the following
requirements:
1) Fiberglass seats must
meet all foregoing
provisions for seats
except those
concerning
construction of seat
cushions and seat
backs.
2) Fiberglass seats
shall combine rigid
construction of welded
tubular steel with
contoured matched
die formed or
hand sprayed molded
plastic shell.
Exposed steel shall be
stainless steel or
shell
be finished with baked
enamel.
3) Plastic shells shall
consist of good
commercially
fire resistant,
color pigmented resin
reinforced with glass
fibers in such manner
as to avoid resin rich
sections. Shells
shall be shaped to
provide maximum
comfort.
4) Both metal frames and
plastic shells shall
have rounded corners
and be free from sharp
edges.

SUBJECT	PROCEDURES/SPECIFICATIONS	REJECT VEHICLE IF
rr) STEERING SYSTEM		
1) Exterior		
A) King Pins	Raise vehicle so as to	Wheel bearing movement

DEPARTMENT OF TRANSPORTATION

NOTICE OF ADOPTED AMENDMENTS

SUBJECT	PROCEDURES/SPECIFICATIONS	REJECT VEHICLE IF
	unload kingpins (brakes should be applied to eliminate wheel bearing looseness). Either grasp wheel at top and bottom or use a bar for leverage. Attempt to rock wheel in and out. check movement at extreme top or bottom of tire. If movement exists, place a dial indicator, tape measure, or a fixed device at the wheel and measure amount of movement. Place leverage bar under tire. Raise bar to check for vertical movement between spindle and support axle.	exceed 1/4 inch, or kingpin movement exceeds. Wheel size --- Max Allowed 16" or less ---- 1/4 16x1" to 18" --- 3/8 over 18" ------- 1/2"
B) Linkage	For buses with single "I" beam or tube type front axle, hoist bus under axle. For buses with twin "I" beam type front axles or with "A" frame control arms, each axle or arm must be hoisted independently so as to load the ball joints. Grasp front and rear of tire and attempt to shake assembly right and left to determine linkage looseness. Measure movement of wheel. Inspect for damage to or looseness in the following linkage components:	Measurement is found to be in excess of: Maximum Allowable Pin Diameter Movement 16" or less ------ 1/4 17" and 18" ----- 3/8 over 18" ---------- 1/2"
	1) Ball Joints 2) Cotter Pins 3) Drag Link	Any linkage component is bent, welded, loose, insecurely mounted or

DEPARTMENT OF TRANSPORTATION

NOTICE OF ADOPTED AMENDMENTS

SUBJECT	PROCEDURES/SPECIFICATIONS	REJECT VEHICLE IF
	4) Idler Arm 5) Pitman Arm 6) Steering Box 7) Tie Rod 8) Tie Rod Ends	missing.
C) Power Steering	Manually and visually inspect.	Steering components are:
	1) Belts	1) Loose, frayed, cracked, missing, incorrect belts.
	2) Cylinders 3) Fluid Level 4) Hoses	2) Loose and/or leaking. 3) Low fluid level 4) Cracked, leaking, rubbed by moving parts.
	5) Mounting Brackets	5) Cracked, loose, or broken.
	6) Power Assist 7) Pump	6) No assist is evident. 7) Loose, leaking.
D) Toe In/ Toe Out	With wheels held in a straight ahead position, drive vehicle slowly over the approved drive on side slip indicator. Excessive toe in or toe out is a general indication that complete check should be made of all front wheel alignment factors (caster, camber, steering axis inclination).	More than 30 feet per mile on the approved side slip indicator.
E) Wheel Bearings	With the front end of the vehicle lifted so as to load any ball joints, grasp the front tire top and bottom, rock it in and out. Record movement. To verify that any looseness detected is in the wheel bearing, notice the relative movement between	Relative movement between drum and backing plate, measured at tire, is 1/4 inch or more.

DEPARTMENT OF TRANSPORTATION

NOTICE OF ADOPTED AMENDMENTS

SUBJECT	PROCEDURES/SPECIFICATIONS	REJECT VEHICLE IF
AGENCY NOTE;	the brake drum or disc and the backing plate or splash shield. Wheel bearing play can be eliminated by applying service brakes.	
2) Interior		
A) Column	Inspect to determine that column support bracket is properly tightened and all bolts are present.	Column support bracket is not properly tightened or bolts are missing.
B) Lash	With road wheels in straight ahead position, turn steering wheel until a turning movement can be observed at the left road wheel. Slowly reverse steering wheel motion and measure lash.	Lash exceeds following acceptable limits: Steering Acceptable wheel lash (inches) maximum measured at diameter maximum (inches) circumference 16 or less ... 2 18 ... 2 3/4 20 ... 2 3/4 22 ... 3 3/4
C) Shaft	Grasp steering wheel with both hands and attempt to move shaft up and down.	Steering shaft moves up and down.
D) Steering Wheel	Inspect steering wheel condition.	Steering wheel is damaged. Any spokes are missing or reinforcement ring is exposed.
E) Travel	Turn steering wheel through a full right and left turn checking for binding, jamming and complete travel left and right.	Binding or jamming is present. Does not complete full turn from left to right. Tire rubs on fender or frame during turn.
33) STEPS; ENTRANCE	Steps shall be enclosed and shall not protrude	Steps or risers are not solid. Steps, risers or

DEPARTMENT OF TRANSPORTATION

NOTICE OF ADOPTED AMENDMENTS

SUBJECT	PROCEDURES/SPECIFICATIONS	REJECT VEHICLE IF
	beyond side body line. Surface shall be of nonskid material with 1 1/2 to 3 inch white nosing as part of the nonskid material. Riser of upper step not more than 15 inches in height. When more than two steps are used, risers must be approximately of equal height, except when floor is plywood over steel (increase by thickness of plywood).	nonskid material covering is missing, loose, or not in good condition.
44) STOP ARM PANEL	A stop arm panel must be installed on the left side of the bus and may be operated either manually or mechanically. The arm shall be a hexagon shaped semaphore approximately 18 inches wide and 18 inches long and of 16 gauge metal. The stop arm signal shall have the "STOP" painted on both sides in white letters at least six inches high with a brush stroke approximately 7/8 inches wide. The word "STOP" shall be painted on a panel with red background of approximately 8 inches by 16 inches. Remaining area of stop arm blade is to be painted white with a band of white border at least 1/2 inch wide painted front and rear on both sides as contrast. White portion of stop arm signal shall be reflectorized or shall have	Stop arm panel is in poor condition (i.e., faded, peeling or rusted). Lights do not operate properly (if installed). Not securely attached. Not operating properly.

DEPARTMENT OF TRANSPORTATION

NOTICE OF ADOPTED AMENDMENTS

SUBJECT	PROCEDURES/SPECIFICATIONS	REJECT VEHICLE IF
	double-faced-lamps-with-red lens---approximately---four inches-in-diameter---located in---the---top-and-bottommost position---of---the---hidad. These-lamps-shall-light-and flash---when--stop--arm--is extended-and-likewise---turn off--and-stop-flashing-when arm-is-closed---Decals--may be---used---in---lieu---of painting. (Section---12-803---of---the Illinois--Vehicle-Equipment law)--(See--Illustration--A for-example.)	
ww)--STORAGE COMPARTMENT (optional)	Covered,-fire-resistant container-securely fastened---of----adequate strength---and---capacity-for tire-chains-and--tools--for minor-emergency-repairs.	If-installed,-does-not meet-requirements.
ww)--SUN-VISOR	Interior,-adjustable, transparent,-not-less than-6-inches-by-30-inches; installed-above-windshield. Must---not---interfere--with view-of-interior-rear--view mirror. Exemption:--Buses--purchased prior--to--August--1967-are exempt---from---having---a transparent-sun-shield.	Does-not-meet requirements.
ww)--SUSPENSION		
1)--shocks	Bus-shall-be-equipped with-front-and-rear double-acting-shock absorbers-compatible-with manufacturer's-rated-axle capacity.	Severe-leakage-(not slight-dampness)-occurs. Mounting-bolts-or-mounts are-broken-or-loose,-or rubber-bushing-is partially-or-completely

DEPARTMENT OF TRANSPORTATION

NOTICE OF ADOPTED AMENDMENTS

SUBJECT	PROCEDURES/SPECIFICATIONS	REJECT VEHICLE IF
	With-vehicle-on-a-hoist-or jacked-up,-visually-inspect shock---absorbers-----for excessive---------leakage, looseness---of---mounting brackets-and-bolts. Physically-grab--upper--and lower---portion---of--shock inspecting-for-looseness-in rubber--bushing,---mounting brackets-or-bolts.	missing.
2)--Springs		
A)--Coil	Visually-inspect:-- 1)--spring 2)--control-arms 3)--torque-arms-(rear)	Coil-is-missing, disconnected,-broken, loose-bushing,-welded-or damaged.
B)--leaf	With-use-of-a-pry-bar-and using-frame-as-a-pivot, attempt--to-pry-front-and rear-spring-attachments and-check-for-movement. Front-of-vehicle-must-be jacked-up-on-chassis-for checking-front suspension.--Visually inspect:-- 1)--Springs 2)--Shackles 3)--Hangers 4)--U-bolts 5)--Center-bolts 6)--Bushings-or-pivot	Springs-are-broken. Shackles-or-"U"-bolts worn-or-loose.--Center bolt-in-springs-sheared or-broken.--Steering stops-allow-tire-to-rub on-frame-or-metal.--Any leaves-are-cracked-or missing.--Any-shackle shackle-pins,-hangers-or "U"-bolts-are-worn, loose,-or-missing.
C)--Torsion Bar (Stabilizer Bar)	Visually-inspect: 1)--Torsion-bar 2)--Mounting-brackets 3)--Control-arms 4)--Torque-arms-(if applicable--rear) 5)--Stabilizer-bar(s)-(if applicable)	Missing,-disconnected, broken,-loose,-welded, damaged.

DEPARTMENT OF TRANSPORTATION

NOTICE OF ADOPTED AMENDMENTS

SUBJECT	PROCEDURES/SPECIFICATIONS	REJECT VEHICLE IF
xx) TOW HOOKS (optional)		
1) Front	A front tow hook must not extend beyond the front of the front bumper. Each front tow hook not fastened securely to the chassis frame shall be connected to the frame by suitable braces.	Tow hook(s) extend beyond bumper; not securely attached.
2) Rear	Any tow hook(s) installed on the rear shall be attached or braced to the chassis frame or to an equivalent structural member of an integral type bus. A tow hook must not extend beyond the rear face of the rear bumper.	Tow hook(s) extend beyond bumper; not securely attached.
yy) UNDERCOATING	Fire resistant undercoating material applied to entire underside of body front fenders, wheel wells, floor members, and side panels below floor level. Non metallic parts need not be coated.	Does not meet requirements.
zz) VENTILATION	Body must be equipped with ventilating system capable of supplying proper quantity of air under operating conditions.	Air is obstructed; not securely fastened; not covered.
aaa) WARNING DEVICES	Either three red cloth flags not less than 12 inches square and three red reflectors minimum of 3 inches in diameter or three bidirectional emergency triangles that conform to 49 CFR 571.125 (Section 12.702 of the Illinois	Required warning devices are not present or are in poor condition.

DEPARTMENT OF TRANSPORTATION

NOTICE OF ADOPTED AMENDMENTS

SUBJECT	PROCEDURES/SPECIFICATIONS	REJECT VEHICLE IF
	Vehicle Equipment Law). All shall be securely stored.	
bbb) WHEELS		
1) Housings	Pull open type attached to floor sheet to prevent water, fumes or dust entering the body. Inside height should not exceed 18 inches above floor liner. Housings shall allow for unimpeded wheel and tire service or removal. Housing shall provide clearance for installation and use of tire chains on the dual or single tires installed on the rear wheel. Inspect tire and road wheel assemblies.	Does not meet clearance requirement. Wheel housing is not firmly secured; holes are present. A tire or wheel is rubbing against any portion of the suspension, chassis or body.
2) Rim	Inspect all wheel and rim bolts, nuts, studs, lugs, locking rings, etc. Each cover, cap, or decorative ring that obscures any of these items must be removed prior to the inspection. Inspect for visible wheel damage.	Any wheel or rim securing device such as a nut, bolt, stud, lug, ring, or other type securing device is loose, missing or cracked. Wheel locating hole(s) are elongated, oversized, or "wallowed out." Any part of a wheel or rim is cracked, repaired by welding or rewelding, or damaged so as to cause unsafe operation of the vehicle.
3) Tires	A regrooved, retreaded,	Regrooved, retreaded or

DEPARTMENT OF TRANSPORTATION

NOTICE OF ADOPTED AMENDMENTS

SUBJECT	PROCEDURES/SPECIFICATIONS	REJECT VEHICLE IF
	or recapped tire shall not be on the front steering axle. A tire with restricted use marking is prohibited. (e.g. "NHS" or "SL" following size marking. "Off Highway." "Farm Use." "Racing Only." etc.) Inspect for tread wear. Check for the presence of tread wear indicators.	recapped tire is located on front steering axle. Restricted marking is present.
	1) Tires with tread wear indicators.	Tread wear indicators contact road in any two adjacent grooves at three equally spaced intervals around the circumference of the tire.
	2) Tires without tread wear indicators. Use tread depth gauge. Do not measure on a tie bar, groove hump fillet, or tread wear indicator.	On steering axle, tread groove depth is less than 4/32 inch (drive axle is 2/32 inch) in any two adjacent grooves at three essentially equally spaced intervals around the circumference of the tire.
	3) Tires without tread wear indicators and with noncircumferential grooves, or "spaces," between the tread elements (as in snow mud, lug, knob, or traction treads).	On steering axle, tread groove depth is less than 4/32 inch (drive axle is 2/32 inch) when measured in a major groove at a point half way between the center of the tire and the outside of the tread at three essentially equally spaced intervals around the circumference of the tire. The lateral width of any bald area measured across the tire between bordering grooves is 1/4 or more of the tread width (measured across the
	4) Tires with treads that are bald, partially bald, cupped, dished, or unevenly worn.	

DEPARTMENT OF TRANSPORTATION

NOTICE OF ADOPTED AMENDMENTS

SUBJECT	PROCEDURES/SPECIFICATIONS	REJECT VEHICLE IF
		tire between the outer edges of the outermost tread elements.
AGENCY NOTE:	"Bald" means without a groove. Inspect for visible cord damage and exposure of ply cords in sidewalls and treads, including belting material cords.	A broken or cut cord can be seen. Rubber is worn, cracked, cut or otherwise deteriorated or damaged so that a cord can be seen—either when the tire is not touched or when the edges of the crack, cut or damage are parted or lifted by hand.
	Inspect for evidence of tread or sidewall separation.	Tire has humpy, bulgy knot or other evidence of partial carcass failure, air seepage, or loss of adhesion between carcass and tread or sidewall.
	Inspect for regrooved or recut treads.	Tread has been regrooved or recut on a tire that does not have the word "REGROOVABLE" molded on or into both sides of the tire.
AGENCY NOTE:	49 CFR 369 require tires marked "REGROOVABLE" to have sufficient tread rubber that, after regrooving, cord material below the grooves shall have a protective covering of tread material at least 3/32 inch thick.	
	Inspect tires for legible markings showing size designation and carcass construction.	A tire on a road wheel does not exhibit a legible size marking and a legible construction marking.

DEPARTMENT OF TRANSPORTATION

NOTICE OF ADOPTED AMENDMENTS

SUBJECT	PROCEDURES/SPECIFICATIONS	REJECT-VEHICLE-IF
AGENCY-NOTE:--	"R"-in-size-designation shows-radial-construction. More-plies--at--tread--than sidewall----shows----belted construction.--Same-number of--plies--at--tread--and sidewall--without-a-belted or-radial-indication;-shows plain-bias-construction. Tires-on-same-axle-must be-of-same-construction.	Tires-on-same-axle are-not-of-same construction.
	Inspect-tires-for-size designation-and-for matched-construction.	A-tire-exceeds-the diameter-(not-width)-of its-mate-by-1/2-inch-(1/4 inch-radius);--or--mate;--or one-tire-touches-its-mate.
AGENCY-NOTE:--	"Construction"---refers--to bias;---bias---belted;---or radial arrangement-of-ply-cords-in the-tire-carcass. Inspect--each--single--dual tire-assembly. A-mixture-of-regular-and mud-and-snow-treads-must be-same-on-both-sides-of axle.	Does-not-meet-requirements.
	When------radial------and conventional tires-are-both--used--on--a vehicle;----one----of---the following-two--requirements shall-be-met--	Does-not-meet-requirements.
	1.--On-vehicles-with-one single-wheel-axle-and one-or-more-dual wheel-axle; radial-tires-shall be-used-on-the steering-(i.e. front)-axle-only. 2.--On-vehicles-having-two single-wheel	

DEPARTMENT OF TRANSPORTATION

NOTICE OF ADOPTED AMENDMENTS

SUBJECT	PROCEDURES/SPECIFICATIONS	REJECT-VEHICLE-IF
	axle;--radial tires-shall-be-used on-the-rear-axle-only. A-tube-built-only-for bias-tire-shall-not-be installed-in-a-radial tire.--Red-color-shall not be-added-to-stem-of a-"bias" tube---(Valve-stem of-tube for-radial-tire-is either marked-"radial" or-has-red-ring or-is-painted-red.)--A "radial"-tube-and-flap may-be used-in-a-bias-tire. Inspect-valve-stems.	Does-not-meet-requirements.
		A-valve-stem-leaks;-is cracked;-is-either-damaged or-positioned-so-as to-hamper-pressure checking-or-inflation; shows-evidence-of wear-because-of misalignment.
cccc).--WINDOWS	All-applicable-provisions of-49-CFR-571.205-apply to-the-optional-laminated safety--glass--and--also-to any---plastic---material(s) used-in-a--multiple--glazed unit.	Do-not-meet-requirements. Not-properly-identified.
	Glazing--shall-be-marked-as follows-pursuant-to-49--CFR 571.205:	
	1.--Windshield--AS-1-Glass 2.--Driver's-Window---AS-1 Glass-or-AS-2-Glass 3.--Driver's-door---As-1 Glass-or-AS-2-Glass.	

DEPARTMENT OF TRANSPORTATION

NOTICE OF ADOPTED AMENDMENTS

SUBJECT	PROCEDURES/SPECIFICATIONS	REJECT VEHICLE IF
	4) All other locations--- AS-1 Glass, AS-2 Glass, or AS-3 Glass.	
1) Emergency (Also see EMERGENCY EXITS)	The following provisions have been established in accordance with 49 CFR 571.217.	
	If the bus is not equipped with a rear emergency door, a rear emergency window shall be provided. The window shall be 16 inches in height and as wide as practicable. It shall open from the inside and the outside and be top hinged. It shall be devised and operated to insure against accidental closing. In an emergency, inside handle shall provide for quick release. Outside handle shall be nondetachable and nonhitchable. When not fully latched, window shall actuate signal audible to driver. No cutoff switch allowed.	Operating mechanisms do not function properly. Alarm signal does not function properly. Glass is cracked or broken.
2) Rear	Glazed panels or windows, except rear emergency windows, shall be of fixed type and installed in the rear of the bus so the seated driver has a reflected view through the rear of the bus as wide and as high as practicable. Such view shall be as low as allowed by the backs of the rear seats. When the aisle extends to a rear emergency	Visibility through rear windows is obstructed. Lettering is not at least 44 inches above floor level. Glass is cracked or broken.

DEPARTMENT OF TRANSPORTATION

NOTICE OF ADOPTED AMENDMENTS

SUBJECT	PROCEDURES/SPECIFICATIONS	REJECT VEHICLE IF
	door, an additional lower window panel shall be installed so the driver has an additional view through such panel at least the width of the required aisle and as low and high as practicable. Any authorized or required signs, letters or numerals displayed on the window in the rear of the bus shall be located at least 44 inches above floor line.	
3) Side	Each side window shall provide unobstructed emergency opening at least 9 inches high and 22 inches wide, obtained either by lowering window or by use of knock-out type split sash. A "Stop line" is required six inches from top of window on all windows. Safety glass with exposed edges shall be banded. Window latches must be in proper working order.	Does not meet emergency opening requirements. Window does not open easily. Glass is cracked or broken. Stop lines are missing. Latches do not operate properly.
4) Windshield	Shall be installed between front corner posts and designed not to obstruct driver's view (Section 12-501 of the Illinois Vehicle Equipment law). Windshield shall be slanted to reduce glare. Tinted safety glass shall only be allowed six inches below top of windshield.	Windshield is not firmly sealed or attached. Glass is broken, cracked or discolored (not including allowed tint).
5) WINDSHIELD WASHER	Windshield washer shall effectively clean entire	Washer does not effectively clean entire

DEPARTMENT OF TRANSPORTATION

NOTICE OF ADOPTED AMENDMENTS

SUBJECT	PROCEDURES/SPECIFICATIONS	REJECT-VEHICLE-IF
	area-covered-by-both wipers- Exception---All-------buses purchased----prior----to September--1974-are-exempt- However--if--bus---is---so equipped--washer-must-be-in good-operating-condition-	area-or-does-not-operate properly-
ccc7---WINDSHIELD WIPER	Two-automatic--variable speed-wipers-with nonglare-arms-and blades- Need-not-be individually-powered-	Wiper-does-not-cover entire-cleaning-area- Blades-are-damaged--torn- hardened--or-rubber wiping-element-has-broken down- Wiper-fails-to-park properly-when-shut-off-

MAR 13 1995 Repealed at 19 Ill. Reg. **4394**, effective

DEPARTMENT OF TRANSPORTATION

NOTICE OF ADOPTED AMENDMENTS

Section 451.APPENDIX B Inspection Procedures/Specifications for Type II School Buses (Repealed)

SUBJECT	PROCEDURES/SPECIFICATIONS
a)--AIR-CLEANER	Same-as-Section-451-Appendix-A(a)-
b)--AISLE	Unobstructed-minimum-clearance-leading-from-service door-to-emergency-door-or-back-of-bus-must-be-at--least--12 inches--wide- Floor-to-ceiling-height-must-be-a-minimum-of 58-1/2-inches-at-any-location-within-the-aisle- Reject-procedures-same-as-in-Section-451-Appendix-A(b)-
c)--ALTERNATOR (GENERATOR)	The-generator-or-alternator-with-rectifier-shall-have-a minimum-capacity-rating-of-55-amperes-and-shall-be--capable of-meeting-all-electrical-requirements- Reject-procedures-same-as-in-Section-451-Appendix-A(c)-
d)--AXLES	Meets-federal-chassis-requirements-as-indicated-on-federal certification--label- 49-CFR-568- Wheel-base-shall-not-be less-than-123-inches- Reject-procedures-same-as-in-Section-451-Appendix-A(d)-
e)--BARRIER- GUARD	Shall-be-either-the-following-Type-A-or-B- Type-A--Constructed-and-thickly-padded-to--give--head--and knee--impact--protection- Installed-at-the-rear-of-service entrance-at-least-22-inches-ahead-of-seat-back-and-no--more than-one-inch-from-right-hand-wall--bottom-shall-be-no-more than--two--inches--above--floor- Guard-barrier-shall-match width--and--above--floor---height---of---the---seat-back---on right-front--forward-facing--seat--provided--however--the barrier's-width-shall-be-reduced-as-necessary-to-maintain-a 12--inches-wide-service-entrance-way-and-aisle- Except-for a-grab-handle--the-guard-barrier-shall-not-extend-more-than one-inch-ahead-of-the-rear-of-service-door-opening-nor-more than-1-inch-into-the-space--above--any--service--step- No portion--of--the-barrier-shall-present-a-"snagging"-sharp- tripping--or-other--hostile--surface--to--a-person--moving through-aisle-or-service-entrance-way- Type--B--Stanchion-post-shall-be-installed-to-the-rear-and left-of-the--service--entrance--step--well--from---floor--to ceiling--with--guard--rail-installed-approximately-39-inches above-the-floor- A-step-well-guard--panel--installed--from stanchion--to-right-hand-wall-and-from-guard-rail-to-within two-inches-of-floor- Clearance-between-step-well-and-first

DEPARTMENT OF TRANSPORTATION

NOTICE OF ADOPTED AMENDMENTS

SUBJECT	PROCEDURES/SPECIFICATIONS
	seat-should-be-at-least-24-inches-measured--from--panel--to front--face--of--seat-back-at-cushion-height.--All--stanchion and-guard-rails-shall-be-padded.--Padding-on-the-stanchions shall-extend-to-within-3-inches-of-ceiling--and--floor.--on guard--rail-it-shall-extend-from-wall-to-stanchion.--49-CFR 568. Exception:--All-buses-manufactured-prior--to--September--1, 1974,--require--Type--A--or--B.--Buses--manufactured--from September-1,-1974,-to-March-31,-1977,-require-Type-A. Exception:--Buses-manufactured-after-April-1,-1977,-are-not required-to-have-guard-barriers. Reject-procedures-same-as-in-Section-451.Appendix-A(f).
2)--BATTERY-OR BATTERIES	Battery-may-be-mounted-either-in-engine-compartment-or-on outside--of--passenger/driver--areas.---Battery--shall-be-a nominal-12-volt-type.--It-shall-be-of--sufficient--capacity to--supply--all--electrical-requirements-but-shall-be-rated not--less--than--either--70-ampere--hours--at--the--20-hour discharge-rate-or-105-minutes-at--the--25-ampere--discharge rate. Reject-procedures-same-as-in-Section-451.Appendix-A(f).
g)--BATTERY CABLES	Same-as-Section-451.Appendix-A(g).
h)--BATTERY CARRIER	Same-as-Section-451.Appendix-A(h).
i)--BRAKES 1)--Backing Plate	Same-as-Section-451.Appendix-A(i). Same-as-Section-451.Appendix-A(i)(1).
2)--Drums/ Discs	Same-as-Section-451.Appendix-A(i)(2).
3)--Emergency/ Parking Brake	Same-as-Section-451.Appendix-A(i)(3).
4)--Emergency Brake Ratchet	Same-as-Section-451.Appendix-A(i)(4).
5)--Pedal Clearance	Same-as-Section-451.Appendix-A(i)(5).
6)--Power Systems	Same-as-Section-451.Appendix-A(i)(6).

DEPARTMENT OF TRANSPORTATION

NOTICE OF ADOPTED AMENDMENTS

SUBJECT	PROCEDURES/SPECIFICATIONS
7)--Service Brakes	Same-as-Section-451.Appendix-A(i)(7). Power-assisted-brakes-are-required.--49-CFR-571.105
j)--BUMPER, FRONT	Manufacturer's-standard-for-vehicle-or-an-equivalent-bumper which--meets--or--exceeds--manufacturer's-standard.--Black color-is-not-required. Reject-procedures-same-as-in-Section-451.Appendix-A(j).
k)--BUMPER, REAR	Manufacturer's-standard-for-vehicle-and-so-attached-or shielded-between-body-and-bumper--as--to--prevent--hitching rides-or-hows.--Black-color-is-not-required. Exception:--A-bus--manufactured-in-October-1978-or-earlier is-exempt-from-having-a-non-hitchable-bumper. Reject-procedures-same-as-in-Section-451.Appendix-A(k).
l)--CERTIFICATE-AND REGISTRATION CARD-HOLDER	Not-required-for-Type-II.
m)--CERTIFICATION LABEL	
1)--Federal	Inspect-federal-label-with-a-chassis-(incomplete-vehicle) manufactured-after-November-10,-1978. Inspection-procedures-are-same-as-in--Section--451.Appendix A(m)(2)-for-federal-label.
2)--State	Type-II-buses-are-exempt-from-State-certification-labels.
n)--DEFROSTERS	Defrosting-equipment-shall-keep-the-windshield-and-the window--to--the--left--of-the-operator-and-the-glass-in-the service-door-clear-of-fogy-frost-and-snow,-using-heat--from heaters-and-circulation-from-fans.--Must-conform-to-federal standard.--49---CFR---571.103.----(Auxiliary--fans--are--not considered-to-be-a-defrosting-and-defogging-system.) Reject-procedures-same-as-in-Section-451.Appendix-A(n).
o)--DRIVE-SHAFT GUARD	Same-as-Section-451.Appendix-A(o).
p)--ELECTRICAL SYSTEM 1)--Circuits	Circuits-arranged-to-manufacturer's-specifications-are acceptable.--An-additional-circuit-shall-be-added-for-the

DEPARTMENT OF TRANSPORTATION

NOTICE OF ADOPTED AMENDMENTS

SUBJECT	PROCEDURES/SPECIFICATIONS
	alternate-flashing-signal-lamps-and-the-stop-signal-lamps: Circuits-may-be-added-as-necessary: Reject-procedures-same-as-in-Section-451:Appendix-A{p}{2}:
2}--Fuses	Same-as-Section-451:Appendix-A{p}{2}:
3}--Switches	Same-as-Section-451:Appendix-A{p}{3}:
4}--Wiring	Same-as-Section-451:Appendix-A{p}{4}:
q}--EMERGENCY EXITS	
2}--Left Side	Same-as-Section-451:Appendix-A{q}{2}:
2}--Rear	Shall-open-outward-with-a-120-degree-minimum-swing: Upper-portion-of--each--door--shall--contain--fixed--safety glazing:---Shall--be--equipped--with--an--alarm:---Shall-be equipped--with--fastening--device--which--can--be--quickly released--from--inside--and--outside-the-body:--The-outside fastening-device-must-be-non-hitchable:-Shall-be-protected against-accidental-operation-and-must-be-easily--accessible from-the-inside:--Must-be-operated-only-by-moving-handle-as shown--by--arrow--and--without-use-of-remote-control:-power device:-keys:-tools-or-any--attached--or--unattached--object other-than-the-release-handle:-49-CFR-571:217: Exception:--On---a--bus--manufactured--in--August--1974--or earlier:-the-emergency-exit-shall-be-in-the-center--of--the rear--end:-exempt-from-120-degree-swing-and-may-open-either vertically-or-horizontally: Reject-procedures-same-as-in-Section-451:Appendix-A{q}{2}:
3}--Emergency Window	Same-as-Section-451:Appendix-A{q}{3}:
4}--Alarms and Locks	Audible-and-visible-alarms-shall-alert-driver-when the-engine-is-running-and-any-emergency-door-either: 1}-is-not-fully-latched:-or 2}--is-locked-and-not-readily-operated-manually: Also:-the-engine-starting-system-shall--not--operate--while any--emergency--door--is--locked-by-any-means-that-prevents ready-manual--operation--without--using--a--tool:--keys--or combination: An-alarm-cut-off-or-"squelch"-control-is-prohibited:

DEPARTMENT OF TRANSPORTATION

NOTICE OF ADOPTED AMENDMENTS

SUBJECT	PROCEDURES/SPECIFICATIONS
	On--a-van-conversion:-any-rear-cargo-door-inside-lock{s}-of the-type-installed-by-the--chassis--manufacturer--{such--as commonly--used--in--cars--push/pull--type}-shall-be-made inoperable:---The--mechanism---cannot---through---jarring: vibration:--etc:--cause--the--door--to-become-locked-and-be inoperable-from-the-inside-or-outside: Exception:--On-a--bus--with--chassis--{incomplete--vehicle: manufactured--in-March-1977-or-earlier:-the-engine-starting system-may-operate-while-the-emergency-door-is-locked:--The "Not-Stop-engine"-requirement-applies-to-every-bus: Exception:--On--a-bus--manufactured--in--August--1974---or earlier:--the--"Not--Fully-Latched"-alarm-is-optional:--The "Door-locked"-alarm-is-required-on-each-bus:-with-a-lockable emergency-door: Reject-procedures-same-as-in-Section-451:Appendix-A{q}{4}:
r}--ENTRANCE DOOR	
1}--Physical Require- ments	Door-shall-be-located-to-right-of-operator-and operated-by-an-over-center-control:-Upper-portions-of door-shall-be-safety-glass-or--equivalent:----Exposed--edges must-be-banded: Each--door--on--the--right--side--of-the-vehicle:-hinged-or sliding:-except-the-service-door-shall-be-made--permanently inoperable--by--means-other-than-the-rub-rail-on-the-outside of-the-body: Reject-procedures-same-as-in-Section-451:Appendix-A{r}{1}:
2}--Locks and Alarms	A-service-door-lock-is-not-required-but-if-any-type of-service-door-locking-system-is-installed-on-the-bus:-the system-shall-conform-to-one-of-the-following: 1}--The-locking-system-shall-not-be-capable-of preventing-the-seated-driver-from-easily-and quickly-opening-the-service-door: 2}--The-locking-system-shall-include-an-audiovisual alarm:--The-alarm-shall-emit-sound-and-light-for other-visual-indications:-that-demand-attention-and will-alert-the-seated-driver-when-the-engine-is running-and-the-service-door-is-locked:--An-alarm disconnect:-"squelch-control:"-or-other-alarm defeating-or-weakening-device-shall-not-be

DEPARTMENT OF TRANSPORTATION

NOTICE OF ADOPTED AMENDMENTS

SUBJECT	PROCEDURES/SPECIFICATIONS
	installed.
	Exception: On a bus manufactured in October 1978 or earlier, option #1 above is exempt from driver being seated. That is, the driver may move from driver's seat to interior of service entrance to release the door. Reject procedures same as in Section 451 Appendix A[1][2].
3) EXHAUST SYSTEM	Exhaust pipe, muffler and tail pipe shall meet manufacturer's standards and shall be outside the bus body and attached to chassis. Tail pipe shall not extend beyond rear bumper. Size of tail pipe shall not be reduced after it leaves muffler. The tail pipe shall exit the exhaust gases either to the right or left side behind the rear wheel well, or at the rear bumper. Exhaust system shall be insulated by metal shield when it is 12 inches or less from fuel tank or tank connections. No part of exhaust system shall pass within 12 inches of any flexible brake line or hose unless shielded. Reject procedures same as in Section 451 Appendix A[3].
4) FENDERS	Same as Section 451 Appendix A[1].
5) FILTER, OIL	Same as Section 451 Appendix A[4].
6) FIRE EXTINGUISHER	Same as Section 451 Appendix A[4].
7) FIRST AID KIT	Same as Section 451 Appendix A[4] with following exception.
	Type II First Aid Kits are required to have one package when two packages are required in Type I kits.
8) FLOORS AND FLOOR COVERINGS	A plywood of 5/8 inches exterior BB grade or equivalent material shall be applied over the existing steel floor and securely fastened. Covering in underseat area shall be of fire resistant floor covering of type commonly used in passenger transportation equipment and shall have a minimum thickness of .125 inches. The floor covering in the aisle shall be nonskid, wear resistant, fire resistant and rib type. The aisle floor covering shall have a minimum thickness of .140 inches.

DEPARTMENT OF TRANSPORTATION

NOTICE OF ADOPTED AMENDMENTS

SUBJECT	PROCEDURES/SPECIFICATIONS
	All floor coverings must be permanently bonded to the floor and must not crack when subjected to sudden changes in temperature. Bonding or adhesive material shall be waterproof. All seams must be sealed with waterproof sealer. All openings in floorboard or fire wall between chassis and passenger carrying compartment must be solid and sealed. Boots and seals around shift levers and emergency brakes must be secure and solidly attached. Reject procedures same as in Section 451 Appendix A[4].
9) FRAME AND BODY	Same as Section 451 Appendix A[7].
10) FUEL STORAGE AND DELIVERY SYSTEM	
1) Fuel Filler Cap	Same as Section 451 Appendix A[1][1].
2) Fuel Lines	Same as Section 451 Appendix A[1][2].
3) Fuel Filler Tube	Same as Section 451 Appendix A[z][3].
4) Fuel Pump	Same as Section 451 Appendix A[1][4].
5) Fuel Tank[s]	Minimum capacity of 24 gallons; mounted, fitted, and vented specifications; 49 CFR 571.301. Reject procedures same as in Section 451 Appendix A[1][5].
6) Fuel Tank Mount[s]	Same as Section 451 Appendix A[1][6].
7) Fuel Tank Straps	Same as Section 451 Appendix A[1][7].
8) Propane Relief	

DEPARTMENT OF TRANSPORTATION

NOTICE OF ADOPTED AMENDMENTS

SUBJECT   PROCEDURES/SPECIFICATIONS

Valve/Piping
Same-as-Section-451.Appendix-A(z)(8).

aa).--GRAB
HANDLES

1).--Exterior   Not-required.

2).--Interior   Shall-be-of-stainless-clad-steel,-installed-inside
doorway,-solidly-attached-on-left--side,--and--as--long--as
practicable.
Reject-procedures-same-as-in-Section-451.Appendix-A(aa)(2).

bb).--HEATERS   Must-be-capable-of-maintaining-inside-temperature-of
50-degrees.--The-heater-hoses-shall-be-adequately-supported
to--guard-against-excessive-wear-due-to-vibration-and-shall
not-interfere-with-or-restrict-the-operation-of-any--engine
function.--Any--hose-in-the-passenger-compartment-shall-be
adequately-protected-to-prevent-injury-from--burns--in--the
event--of--rupture.--Primary-heater-shall-be-a-high-output
fresh-air-type.
The-secondary--heater--may--be--a--recirculating--type--and
located-so-as-not-to-interfere-with-aisle-space.
Reject-procedures-same-as-in-Section-451.Appendix-A(bb).

cc).--HOOD   Same-as-Section-451.Appendix-A(cc).

dd).--HORN   Dual-electric-horns-shall-be-provided-giving-an
audible--warning--at--a--distance--of-200-feet-and-shall-be
conveniently--controlled--from---the---operator's--seated
position.
Reject-procedures-same-as-in-Section-451.Appendix-A(dd).

ee).--INSTRUMENTS
AND-INSTRUMENT
PANEL   Same-as-Section-451.Appendix-A(ee).

ff).--INSULATION Same-as-Section-451.Appendix-A(ff).

gg).--LETTERING

1).--Exterior   Same-as-Section-451.Appendix-A(gg)(1).

A).--Front   Same-as-Section-451.Appendix-A(gg)(1)(A)-with
following-exception.

DEPARTMENT OF TRANSPORTATION

NOTICE OF ADOPTED AMENDMENTS

SUBJECT   PROCEDURES/SPECIFICATIONS

Exception.--All-buses-purchased-prior-to-September-1994,
may--have--roof-mounted-"SCHOOL-BUS"-sign-with-flashing-red
lights.

B).--Left   Same-as-Section-451.Appendix-A(gg)(1)(B).

C).--Rear   Same-as-Section-451.Appendix-A(gg)(1)(C)-with
following-exception.

In-case-of-"push"-or-"pull"-type-of-release-mechanism-where
the-direction-of-movement-to-open-emergency-exit-cannot--be
shown--by--one--arrow,-either-three-or-four-straight-arrows
shall-be-placed-equally-spaced-as--practicable--around--the
object--to-be-pushed-or-pulled--with-the-head-of-each-arrow
adjacent--to-and-pointing-directly--at--that--object.--Each
arrow--shall--be--the-same-color-and--when-practicable--the
same-size-as-though-it-were-a-single-arrow.--In--addition,
the-pertinent-word-"PUSH"-or-"PULL"-shall-be-displayed-near
that-object.
AGENCY--NOTE.--If--adequate--space--is--not--available--in
required-positions-for-emergency-door-lettering,--lettering
may-be-immediately-below-window-level.

D).--Right   Owner's-name-and-number-of-school-district-must-be
as--least--four--inches-high,-approximately-centered-and-as
high-as-practicable-below-the-window-line.
(Section-12-802-of-the-Illinois-Vehicle-Equipment-Law)
The-following-lettering-must-be-at-least-two-inches-high.
1).--The-word-"CAPACITY,"-or-the-abbreviation-"CAP.,"
and-the-rated--passenger-capacity-followed-by
the-word-"PASSENGERS,"-or-the-abbreviation
"PASS.,"-shall-be-displayed-on-the-outside-of-the-body
near-the-rear-edge-of-the-service-entrance.
2)   Empty-weight-in-pounds-shall
be-shown-on-bus.
(Section-12-802-of-the-Illinois-Vehicle-Equipment
Law)
3).--"EMERGENCY-EXIT"-shall-be-on-or-immediately-below
emergency-window-(if-installed).--Manufacturer's
identification-name,-emblem,-or-number(s)-may-be
displayed-but-not-on-service-door-glazing.
Manufacturer's-name,-emblem,-etc.-must-not-interfere
with-required-lettering.--Decals-are-permissable.
All-lettering-must-be-black.--Reject-procedures-same-as
in-Section-451.Appendix-A(gg)(1)(D).

DEPARTMENT OF TRANSPORTATION

NOTICE OF ADOPTED AMENDMENTS

SUBJECT	PROCEDURES/SPECIFICATIONS
2)--Interior	
A)--Front	Same-as-Section-451.Appendix-A)gg))(2))(A).
B)--Left	Same-as-Section-451.Appendix-A)gg))(2))(B).
C)--Rear	"EMERGENCY-DOOR"-in-letters-at-least-two-inches-high directly--over--emergency--door--exit.----"Emergency"--door operating--instructions"--applied-to-door.--Arrow-or-arrows required-unless-"push-or-pull"-type-of-release-mechanism-is used. In-the-case-of-a-"push"-or-"pull"-type-of-release-mechanism where-the-direction-of-movement-to-open-the-emergency--exit cannot-be-shown-by-one-arrow.-either-three-or-four-straight arrows--shall--be--placed--as-equally-spaced-as-practicable around-the-object-to-be-pushed-or-pushed.-with-the-head--of each--arrow--adjacent--to--and--pointing--directly--at-that object.--Each-arrow-shall--be--the--same--color--and--when practicable.--the--same--size--as--though--it-were-a-single arrow.--In-addition.-the-pertinent-word--"PUSH"--or--"PULL" shall-be-displayed-near-that-object. Reject--procedures---same---as---in--Section--451.Appendix A)gg))(2))(C).
D)--Right	Same-as-section-451.Appendix-A)gg))(2))(D).
hh)--LIGHTS	
1)--Back-Up	Same-as-Section-451.Appendix-A)hh))(1).
2)--Clearance. Front	Same-as-Section-451.Appendix-A)hh))(2)-with-following exception. Buses-less-than-80-inches-wide-or-20-feet-long-are--exempt. (Section-12-202(a)-of-the-Illinois-Vehicle-Equipment-Law)
3)--Clearance. Rear	Same-as-Section-451.Appendix-A)hh))(3)-with-following exception. Buses--less-than-80-inches-wide-or-20-feet-long-are-exempt. (Section-12-202(a)-of-the-Illinois-Vehicle-Equipment-Law)
4)--Cluster. Front	Same-as-Section-451.Appendix-A)hh))(4)-with-following exception.

DEPARTMENT OF TRANSPORTATION

NOTICE OF ADOPTED AMENDMENTS

SUBJECT	PROCEDURES/SPECIFICATIONS
	Buses-less-than-80-inches-wide-or-20-feet-long-are--exempt. (Section-12-202(a)-of-the-Illinois-Vehicle-Equipment-Law)
5)--Cluster. Rear	Same-as-Section-451.Appendix-A)hh))(5)-with-following exception.
	Buses--less-than-80-inches-wide-or-20-feet-long-are-exempt. (Section-12-202(a)-of-the-Illinois-Vehicle-Equipment-Law)
6)--Flashing	Same-as-Section-451.Appendix-A)hh))(6).
7)--Headlights	Same-as-Section-451.Appendix-A)hh))(7).
8)--Interior	Same-as-Section-451.Appendix-A)hh))(8).
9)--License Plate	Same-as-Section-451.Appendix-A)hh))(9).
10)--Marker. Left	Same-as-Section-451.Appendix-A)hh))(10). Exception.--A-bus-manufactured-in-August-1974-or-earlier-is exempt. Buses-less-than-80-inches-wide-or-20-feet-long-are--exempt.
11)--Marker. Right	Same-as-Section-451.Appendix-A)hh))(11)-with-following exception. Exception.--A-bus-manufactured-in-August-1974-or-earlier-is exempt. Buses--less-than-80-inches-wide-or-20-feet-long-are-exempt.
12)--Parking	Same-as-Section-451.Appendix-A)hh))(12).
13)--Step-Well	Same-as-Section-451.Appendix-A)hh))(13).
14)--Stop	Same-as-Section-451.Appendix-A)hh))(14).
15)--Strobe (optional)	Same-as-Section-451.Appendix-A)hh))(15).
16)--Tail	Same-as-Section-451.Appendix-A)hh))(16).
17)--Turn	

DEPARTMENT OF TRANSPORTATION

NOTICE OF ADOPTED AMENDMENTS

SUBJECT	PROCEDURES/SPECIFICATIONS
Signal, Left (armored)	Same-as-Section-451,Appendix-A(hh)(17)-with following-exceptions:
	1)-Shall-be-located-behind-driver's-seat. 2)-Buses-with-capacity-rating-of-less-than-33 passengers-are-exempt.--Buses-manufactured-in August-1974-or-earlier-are-exempt.--Buses-that measure-less-than-88-inches-wide-or-20-feet-long are-exempt.
(8)--Turn Signal, Right (armored)	Same-as-Section-451,Appendix-A(hh)(18)-with-following exceptions:
	Exceptions:--Buses-with-capacity-rating--of--less--than--33 passengers--are--exempt.--Buses-manufactured-in-August-1974 or-earlier-are-exempt.--Buses-that--measure--less--than--88 inches-wide-or-20-feet-long-are-exempt.
(9)--Turn Signal, Front	One-amber-or-white-lens-on-each-side,-at-or-near the-front, at--the--same-height-and-as-far-apart-as-practicable.--Must meet-federal-standard-49-CFR-571,108. Reject-procedure-same-as-Section-451,Appendix-A(hh)(19).
(28)--Turn Signal, Rear	One-red-or-amber-lens-on-each-side-at-the-same-height-and as--far--apart--as--practicable--below--window.--Must--meet federal-standard-49-CFR-571,108. Reject-procedure-same-as-Section-451,Appendix-A(hh)(28).
(ii)--LOCKED COMPARTMENT	Same-as-Section-451,Appendix-A(iii).
(jj)--MIRRORS	Same-as-Section-451,Appendix-A(jjj).
1)-Exterior A)-Rear View	

DEPARTMENT OF TRANSPORTATION

NOTICE OF ADOPTED AMENDMENTS

SUBJECT	PROCEDURES/SPECIFICATIONS
Driving	Two-firmly-mounted,-adjustable,-exterior-rear-view mirrors-located-to-the-left-and-to-the-right-of-the-driver. Rectangular--five--inch--x--ten--inch-minimum.--The-outside mirror-mounts-shall-include-a-side-angle-adjustable--convex mirror--(no--less-than-three-inches-in-diameter)-to-provide an-additional-close-in-field-of-vision-located-so-as-not-to reduce-the-visual-field-of-the-flat-surface-mirror-below-50 square--inches.--49-CFR-571,111. Exceptions:--Buses-purchased-prior-to--September--1974--may have--the--three--inch--"stick--on"--type--convex--mirrors, provided--they-do-not-reduce-the-visual-field-of-the-mirror below-50-square-inches. Reject--procedures--same--as--in--Section--451,-Appendix A(jjj)(1)(A).
B)--Right Side Safety	Optional-Mirrors---Unless-otherwise-specified-by-the purchaser,--the--following--may--be-installed-on-the-right left-or-both-sides-of-the-bus-in-lieu-of-or-in-addition--to the-corresponding-convex-mirror(s)-required. An-outside-convex-mirror-may-be-installed-on-the-right-side that,--either-alone-or-in-combination-with-the-flat-driving mirror,-will-afford-any-seated-driver-a-reflected--view--of the-roadway--along-the-right-side-of-the-bus-from-at-least the-forwardmost-surface-of-the-right-front-tire-to-at-least the-rearmost-surface-of-the--rear--bumper.---The--projected reflecting-area-of-this-convex-mirror-shall-be-no-less-than 40-square-inches. Reject--procedures--same--as--in--Section--451,-Appendix A(jjj)(1)(B).
C)--Left Side Safety	An-outside-convex-mirror-may-be-installed-on-the-left-side that,-either-alone-or-in-combination-with-the-flat--driving mirror,-will--afford-any-seated-driver-a-reflected--view--of the-roadway-along-the-left-side-of-the-bus--from--at--least the--rear--edge--of--the--driver's-seat-in-its-most-forward position-to-at-least--the--rearmost--surface--of--the--rear bumper.---The--projected--reflecting--area--of--the-convex mirror-shall-be-no-less-than-18-square-inches. Reject--procedures--same--as--in--Section--451,-Appendix A(jjj)(1)(C).
D)--Cross Over	An-adjustable-convex-mirror-at-least-7-1/2-inches-in

DEPARTMENT OF TRANSPORTATION

NOTICE OF ADOPTED AMENDMENTS

SUBJECT PROCEDURES/SPECIFICATIONS

 diameter--firmly--mounted--at--the--left--front--corner--of--the
 vehicle.--The--mirror--shall--give--the--seated--driver--a--view--of
 the--front--bumper--and--the--area--of--roadway--in--front--of--the
 bus.
 If--the--seated--driver--of--a--forward-control--bus--has--a--direct
 view--of--the--front-bumper--and--the--area--of--roadway--in--front
 of--the--bus,--a--cross--over--mirror--is--optional.
 Reject---procedures---same---as---in---Section--45.--Appendix
 A.(j)(1)(B).

2)--Interior All--buses--purchased--during--and--after--September--1974--must
 have--a--clear--view--safety--glass,--metal--backed--and--framed
 with--rounded--corners--and--edges--which--shall--be--padded.
 Shall--afford--a--good--view--of--the--interior--and--roadway--to--the
 rear.
 All--buses--purchased--prior--to--September--1974--must--have--a
 rear-view-mirror.
 Reject-procedures-same-as-in-Section--45.-Appendix-A-(j)(1)(2).

kk)--PAINT
REQUIREMENTS *The--exterior--of--the--body,--excluding--required--rub--rail*
 and--lettering,--shall--be--painted--a--uniform--color.--National
 School-Bus-Glossy-Yellow.---Required-rub-rail-and--lettering
 must--be--black.---Additional--rub--rails--may--either--be--black--or
 yellow.---The--front--and--rear--bumpers--and--wheels--may--be--black
 or--manufacturer's--color.---Grilles--and--hub--caps--may--be--a
 bright--finish--(chrome,--anodized--aluminum,--etc.).---(Section
 12-801-of-the--Illinois-Vehicle-Equipment-Law)
 Optional:--Black--area--around--flashing--lights--is--permitted.
 Black--area--must--not--interfere--with--"SCHOOL--BUS"--lettering.
 Reject-procedures-same-as-in-Section--45.-Appendix-A(kk).

ll)--PROJECTIONS

 1)--Exterior Entire-rear-of-bus-must-be-nonhitchable.
 Exceptions:--A-bus--manufactured--in--October--1978--or--earlier
 is-exempt-from-nonhitchable-bumpers.--A-bus-manufactured-in
 August--1974---or--earlier---is--exempt---from--nonhitchable
 projections.---Every--school--bus,--however,--must--have--a
 nonhitchable-door-handle.
 Reject-procedures-same-as-in-Section--45.-Appendix-A(ll)(1).

 2)--Interior Same-as-Section-45.-Appendix-A(ll)(2)-with-following
exception:

 All-buses-purchased-prior-to-September-1974-are-exempt-from
 padding-on-interior-projections.

DEPARTMENT OF TRANSPORTATION

NOTICE OF ADOPTED AMENDMENTS

SUBJECT PROCEDURES/SPECIFICATIONS

mm)--REFLECTORS

 1)--Front Same-as-Section-45.-Appendix-A-(mm)(1)-with-following-exception:

 Buses--less--than--80--inches--wide--or--20--feet--long--are--exempt.
 (Section-12-202(b)-of-the-Illinois-Vehicle-Equipment-Law)

 2)--Left
 Side Same-as-Section-45.-Appendix-A(mm)(2).

 3)--Right
 Side Same-as-Section-45.-Appendix-A(mm)(3).

 4)--Rear Same-as-Section-45.-Appendix-A(mm)(4)-with-following-exception:

 Buses--less--than--80--inches--wide--or--20--feet--long--are--exempt.

nn)--RUB-RAILS There--shall--be--one--rub--rail--located--approximately--at--seat
 level--which--shall--extend--from--the--rear--of--the--entrance--door
 on--both--sides--to--a--point--of--curvature--at--the--rear--of--the
 body.----Rub---rails---shall---be---constructed---of---16-gauge
 longitudinally-corrugated-or-ribbed-steel,-ventilated--four
 inches--minimum--width,--and--securely--fastened--to--the--body--by
 bolts,-rivets,-or-welding.
 Exception:--Rub-rails-are-not-required-on-Type--II--service
 and--driver's--entrance--doors,--however,--if--installed,--they
 must-meet-same-requirements-as-above.
 Reject-procedures-same-as-in-Section-45.-Appendix-A(nn).

oo)--SEAT-BELTS *A-seat-belt-shall--be-installed--for--the-driver*
 (Section-12-807-of-the--Illinois--Vehicle--Equipment--Law).
 Seat-belts-shall-be-installed-for-each-pupil-as-required-by
 49--CFR--571.222.---At--all--times,--each--seat--belt--shall--be
 readily-available-for-quick-and-easy-use.---All--retractors
 installed--shall--be--automatic--locking--type.---Each-belt
 assembly--shall--be--clean.---Belt--material:--buckle,--tongue,
 etc.---of--each--driver's--belt--shall--remain--above--floor--when
 not-in-use.
 Exception:--On--a--bus--with--incomplete--vehicle--(chassis)
 manufactured--in--March--1977--or--earlier,--pupil--belts--are--not
 required.
 Exception:--On--a--bus--manufactured--in--August--1974--or
 earlier,--driver's--belts--may--need--not--remain--above--floor.
 Reject-procedures-same-as-in-Section-45.-Appendix-A(oo).

SUBJECT	PROCEDURES/SPECIFICATIONS
pp)--SEAT, DRIVER'S	The-driver's-seat-shall-be-rigidly-positioned-and-have-a forward-and-backward-adjustment-without-the-use-of-tools-or other-nonattached-devices;- Seat-padding-and-covering-shall-be-in-good-condition-(i;e;, free--from--holes--and--tears);---Seat--cushions--shall--be securely-fastened-to-the-seat-frame; Reject-procedures-same-as-in-Section-45);Appendix-A(pp);
qq)--SEAT, PASSENGER	For-buses-purchased-after-September-1974-all-seats shall--have-a-minimum-depth-of-14-inches-and-a-minimum-back rest-height-of-20-inches-with-a-12-inch--allowable--average hip--room-in-determining-seating-capacity;--All-seats-shall be-forward-facing-and-securely-fastened-to-part-or-parts-of bus-which-support-them;--No-bus-shall-be-equipped-with-jump seats-or--portable--seats;---The--center-to-center--spacing shall--be--no--more--than--24-inches;--Padding-and-covering shall-be-of-fire--resistant--material;---Minimum--35--inch headroom--for--sitting--position--above--top-of-undepressed cushion-line-on-all-seats--measured--vertically--not--more than--seven--inches-from-side-wall-at-cushion-height-and-at front--and-rear-center-of-cushion);--Backs-of-all--seats--of similar-size-shall-be-of-the-same-width-at-top-and-the-same height--from--floor--and-shall-slant-at-the-same-angle-with the-floor;--The-top-and-side-rails-and-seat-backs-shall--be padded--to--cushion-level;--Seat-padding-and-covering-shall be-in-good-condition-(i;e;,-free--from--holes--and--tears); Seat-cushions-shall-be-securely-fastened-to-the-seat-frame; 49-CFR-591;222 All--buses--purchased--prior--to--September--1974-and-after January-1;-1972,-shall-have-a-seating-plan--for--16--pupils consisting--of--four--rows--of-38-inch-forward-facing-seats with-a-minimum-12-inch-aisle-down-the-center;--No--jump--or portable--seats-allowed;--No-seat-or-other-object-placed-in the-bus-which-restricts-passageway--to--emergency--door--to less-than-12-inches; Those-vehicles-used-as-a-school-bus-by-school-districts-and private-contractors-prior-to-January-1;-1972;-and-are-still in-their-possession-that-had-previously-passed-a-school-bus safety-inspection-can-still-be-utilized-if-they-continue-to meet--the--inspection--requirements--that-were-in-effect-at that-time;--These-vehicles-will-not-have-to-be--brought--up to-the-above-standards; Reject-procedures-same-as-Section-45);Appendix-A(qq);
rr)--STEERING	

SUBJECT	PROCEDURES/SPECIFICATIONS
SYSTEM	
1)--Exterior	
A)--King Pins	Same--as-Section-45);Appendix-A(rr)(1))(A),
B)--Link-age	Same--as-Section-45);Appendix-A(rr)(1))(B),
C)--Power Steering	Same--as-Section-45);Appendix-A(rr)(1))(C),
D)--Toe-In/ Toe-Out	
E)--Wheel Bear- ings	Same--as-Section-45);Appendix-A(rr)(1))(E),
2)--Interior	
A)--Column	Same-as-Section-45);Appendix-A(rr)(2))(A),
B)--Lash	Same--as-Section-45);Appendix-A(rr)(2))(B),
C)--Shaft	Same--as-Section-45);Appendix-A(rr)(2))(C),
D)--Steering Wheel	Same--as-Section-45);Appendix-A(rr)(2))(D),
E)--Travel	Same-as-Section-45);Appendix-A(rr)(2))(E),
ss)--STEPS	The-first-service-entrance-step-shall-be-no-more-than 12-1/2--inches--off--the--ground;---If-necessary-a-step-of adequate-width-and-length-shall-be-installed-to--meet--this requirement;---Provision--shall--be--to--prevent-road splash-from-the-wheel-from--accumulating--on--the--step--if installed-outside-the-body; Risers-shall-be-approximately-equal-in-height;-upper-risers no-more-than-12-inches-in-height; The--surface--entrance--steps-shall-have-a-nonskid-material applied;--A-1-1/2--inch--to--three--inch--white--nosing--is required--as-an-integral-part-of-this-material-on-each-step and-on-the-floor-at-the-top-riser; Reject-procedures-same-as-in-Section-45);Appendix-A(ss);
tt)--STOP-ARM PANEL	Same-as-Section-45);Appendix-A(tt);
uu)--STORAGE COMPARTMENT (optional)	Same-as-Section-45);Appendix-A(uu);

DEPARTMENT OF TRANSPORTATION

NOTICE OF ADOPTED AMENDMENTS

SUBJECT	PROCEDURES/SPECIFICATIONS
vv)--SUN-VISOR inches	Shall-be-interior,-adjustable-and-not-less-than-five by-15-inches.--Must-be--installed--above--windshield.---Not required--to--be--transparent,--but-must-not-interfere-with view-of-interior-rear-view-mirror. Reject-procedures-same-as-in-Section-45),Appendix-A(vv).
ww)--SUSPENSION	
1)--Shocks	Equipped-with-front-and-rear-heavy-duty,-double-acting shock-absorbers. Reject-procedures-same-as-in-Section-45),Appendix-A(ww)(1).
2)--Springs	
A)--Coil	Same-as-Section-45),Appendix-A(ww)(2)(A).
B)--Leaf	Same-as-Section-45),Appendix-A(ww)(2)(B).
C)--Torsion (Stabilizer Bar)	Same-as-Section-45),Appendix-A(ww)(2)(C).
xx)--TOW-HOOKS (optional)	Same-as-Section-45),Appendix-A(xx).
yy)--UNDERCOATING	Fire-resistant-undercoating-material-applied-by-spray. Entire-underside-of-body,-front-fenders,-floor-members,-and side-panels-below-floor-level-must-be-covered. Reject-procedures-same-as-in-Section-45),Appendix-A(yy).
zz)--VENTILATION	Same-as-Section-45),Appendix-A(zz).
aaa)--WARNING DEVICES	Same-as-Section-45),Appendix-A(aaa).
bbb)--WHEELS	Same-as-Section-45),Appendix-A(bbb).
ccc)--WINDOWS	
1)--Emergency	Same-as-Section-45),Appendix-A(ccc)(1).
2)--Rear	Glazing-in-rear-of-bus-shall-be-of-fixed-type. Reject---procedures--same---as---in--Section--45),Appendix A(ccc)(2).

DEPARTMENT OF TRANSPORTATION

NOTICE OF ADOPTED AMENDMENTS

SUBJECT	PROCEDURES/SPECIFICATIONS
3)--Side	All-buses-purchased-after-September-1974-must-have-each side-window-as-an-unobstructed--emergency--opening--and--at least--a--nine--inch--by--22--inch-wide-opening-obtained-by lowering-the-window.--Six-inch-stop-line--required--on--all windows.---Safety--glass--or-equivalent--with-exposed-edges banded.--All-buses-purchased-prior-to--September--1974--and after--January--1,--1972,--must-have-approved-safety-glass-in all-windows-and-doors-and-all-exposed-edges--of--the--glass shall--be--banded.---These--vehicles-used-as-school-bus-by school-districts-and-private-contractors-prior--to--January 1,--1972,--and--are--still--in--their--possession--and--had previously--passed--the--school--bus--safety-inspection-can still-be-utilized-if-they-continue-to-meet--the--inspection requirements--that--were--in--effect--at--that-time.--These vehicles-will-not-have--to--be--brought--up--to--the--above standard. Reject--procedures---same---as---in--Section--45),Appendix A(ccc)(3).
4)--Windshield	Shall-be-installed-between-front-corner-posts-and-must nee--obstruct--driver's--view.--(Section--12-501--of--the Illinois-Vehicle-Equipment-Law) All--buses--purchased-on-and-after-September-1974-must-have tinted-safety-glass-six-inches-below-top-of--windshield--or equivalent-to-reduce-glare. All--buses--purchased--prior--to--September--1974-must-have safety-glass-and-shall-be-heat-resistant,-laminated-plate. Reject--procedures---same---as---in--Section--45),Appendix A(ccc)(4).
ddd)--WINDSHIELD WASHER	Windshield-washer-shall-effectively-clean-the-area covered-by-both-wipers. Reject-procedure-same-as-in-Section-45),Appendix-A(ddd).
eee)--WINDSHIELD WIPER	Wipers-shall-be-either-two-speed-or-variable-speed-with nonglare--arms-and-blades.--Blades-need-not-be-individually powered. Reject-procedure-same-as-in-Section-45),Appendix-A(eee).

(Source: Repealed-at 19 Ill. Reg. 4894 , effective
MAR 13 1995)

DEPARTMENT OF TRANSPORTATION

NOTICE OF ADOPTED AMENDMENTS

Section 451.APPENDIX C Inspection Procedures/Specifications for Type I Special
Education School Buses (Repealed)

SUBJECT	PROCEDURES/SPECIFICATIONS	REJECT VEHICLE IF
a) GENERAL REQUIREMENTS	Generally---a--school--bus used for--transporting--children declared----eligible----for Special--Education--services shall--comply---with---the applicable----------minimum standards-for-either-a-Type I--school--bus--(GVWR--more than-10,000-lbs.)--or-a-Type II--school-bus-(GVWR-10,000 lbs.---or---less)---However, due--to---the---nature---of certain-------handicapping conditions,------vehicles utilized-----for----special education----transportation shall--be--adapted---to---the specific--needs---of---the children--receiving---this service.--These--needs--may require-modification-of-the minimum-standards. The----interior----design-of these-vehicles-will-not--be a---cause---for---rejection provided---an----approval issued-by-the-Department-of Transportation,---------is presented--to-the-Certified Safety-Tester-at--the--time of-inspection.	
b) RESTRAINING OR SAFETY DEVICES	In-buses-manufactured-prior to-November-10,-1978, restraining-devices-or-safety belts-may-be-used-if-they are--securely--fastened--to the	Restraining-devices-or seat-belts-are-not securely-fastened-or-are missing-when-required.

DEPARTMENT OF TRANSPORTATION

NOTICE OF ADOPTED AMENDMENTS

SUBJECT	PROCEDURES/SPECIFICATIONS	REJECT VEHICLE IF
	seat--or--the--floor-of-the vehicle. In--buses--manufactured--on and--after--November---10, 1978,----each---handicapped passenger's--seat--must--be equipped.--with--restraining or-safety-devices.	
c) SPECIAL SERVICE DOOR	A-special-door-opening-may be-located-on-right-side-of bus-far-enough-to-rear-to prevent-door,-when-open, from-obstructing-front right-service--door.--Door opening-shall--be--adequate to------accommodate----wheel chairs. Door-shall-be-equipped-with device--that--will--actuate audible-or-visible--signal, located----in----driver's compartment,--when-doors-are not-securely-closed. Each---door---shall--contain-a fixed--or--movable---window aligned--with--and-of-same size----(as----nearly----as practicable)----as----other windows-on--right--side--of bus. Each--door-panel-shall-open outward--and---a---positive fastening--device--shall-be installed-to-hold--door--in open-position. Door--panels--shall---be constructed----to-----be equivalent-in-strength--and materials--to--other-school bus-doors. Door--posts---and---headers shall----be----reinforced sufficiently---to--provide	Does-not-operate-properly. Does-not-meet-requirements. Audible-or-visible-alarm does-not-work-or-is missing.

DEPARTMENT OF TRANSPORTATION

NOTICE OF ADOPTED AMENDMENTS

SUBJECT	PROCEDURES/SPECIFICATIONS	REJECT VEHICLE IF
	support----and----strength equivalent-to-area-of--side of-bus-not-used-for-service doors.-----Outriggers---from chassis-shall-be--installed at--front--and-rear-of-door openings-to--support--floor with-same-strength-as-other floor-portions.	
d)--BI-PARTING DOORS	Door-shall-be-made-of-two panels-of-approximately equal-width.--They-shall-be hinged-to-side-of-bus each---panel---shall---open outward. Forward---panel---shall--be provided--with--overlapping flange-to-close-space-where door---panels--meet---and weather---seal---shall---be provided--to-close-all-door edges. Door-shall-be-equipped-with at----least-------one-point fastening--device--on--rear panel--to--floor--or-header and---at---least----two-point fastening--device--to-floor and-header-on-forward--door panels-----both----manually operated. Sliding-----doors-----are acceptable--provided---they meet--------manufacturer's specifications.	Does-not-operate-properly. Does-not-meet-requirements. Door---does----not----seal properly. Weather-seal-is-cracked-or missing.
e)--LIFTS-AND --RAMPS	Floor-of-ramp-or-lift-shall be-covered-with-nonskid material. Protection-against-dust-and water-sufficient-to-ensure reliable-operation-must--be	Does-not-operate-properly. Does-not-meet-requirements.

DEPARTMENT OF TRANSPORTATION

NOTICE OF ADOPTED AMENDMENTS

SUBJECT	PROCEDURES/SPECIFICATIONS	REJECT VEHICLE IF
	present.	
f)--POWER-LIFT	If-power-lift-is-used,--it Does-not-operate-properly. shall-be-of-sufficient capacity---and--dimension-to lift-maximum-imposed--load. lift---at--top---and--bottom travel-limits-shall-provide easy-entrance-and-exit-from the-lift. If-electricity-is-used,-the alternator-or-generator-and battery---must----be----of increased-capacity. Controls-shall--be--operable from---both---interior---and exterior-of-vehicle. Device-shall--be--installed which---will---be--used--to prevent-operation--of--lift until-doors-are-opened. In---travel--position--the lift---must---be---in---its uppermost---position---and securely-fastened. Vehicles---of---less---than 14-passenger---capacity constructed------------for transportation----------of handicapped---children--may have-the-fuel-tank--located behind--rear-wheels--inside or-outside--chassis--frame, with--fill--pipe-located-on right-side-of-body.	Does-not-meet-requirements.
g)--RAMP	Ramp-shall-be-of-sufficient Does-not-operate-properly. strength-and-rigidity-to Does-not-meet-requirements. support-the-imposed-load. Shall--be--equipped---with protective--flange--on-each longitudinal-side--to--keep wheelchair-on-ramp.	Does-not-operate-properly. Does-not-meet-requirements.

DEPARTMENT OF TRANSPORTATION

NOTICE OF ADOPTED AMENDMENTS

SUBJECT	PROCEDURES/SPECIFICATIONS	REJECT-VEHICLE-IF
	Ramp--shall--be--equipped--with handles,--or--handles,--and--be of--sufficient---weight----to permit--one--person--to--put ramp-in-place-and-return-to storage-place. Ramp--shall--be--connected---to bus--at-floor-level-in-such manner-as--to--permit--easy access---of--wheelchair--to floor-of-bus. Ramp---length---shall----be sufficient---for---easy-entry and-exit.	
6,--FASTENING DEVICES	Positive-fastening-devices shall--be-provided-and attached-to-the-floor,-walls, or-both,-that-will-securely hold-wheelchair-in-position in-bus.	Does-not-securely-hold wheelchair-to-floor position.--Does-not-meet requirements.
g,--SPECIAL LIGHT	Light-shall-be-placed inside bus--over-special-service door-opening,-or-at-other location-if-shielded-to prevent--glare.---The--lamp shall-illuminate-the--floor inside---the---opening--and shall-be-operated-from-door area.	Does-not-operate-properly. Does-not-meet requirements.--Missing.
h,--GRAB-HANDLES	Grab-handles-shall-be provided-on-each-side-of front-right-service-door-only when-this-door-is-used--for entry-and-exit-of-children.	Not-securely-attached. Does-not-meet requirements.--Missing.
i,--OVER-CENTER DOOR-CONTROL	Over-center-door-control shall-be-provided-only-when this-door-is-used-for-entry and-exit-of-children.	If-installed,-does-not operate-properly.--Does not-meet-requirements. Missing-when-required.

DEPARTMENT OF TRANSPORTATION

NOTICE OF ADOPTED AMENDMENTS

(Source: Repealed at 19 Ill. Reg. 4394, effective
MAR 13 1995)

DEPARTMENT OF TRANSPORTATION

NOTICE OF ADOPTED AMENDMENTS

Section 451.APPENDIX D Inspection Procedures/Specifications for Type II Special Education School Buses (Repealed)

SUBJECT	PROCEDURES/SPECIFICATIONS
a)--GENERAL REQUIREMENTS	Same-as-in-Section-451.Appendix-C(a)
b)--RESTRAINING OR-SAFETY DEVICES	In-buses-manufactured-on-and-after-April-1,-1977, restraining--devices-or-seat-belts-are-mandatory-on all-seats.--In-buses-manufactured-prior-to-April-1, 1977,--restraining--devices--or--seat--belts--are optional.--If--restraining-devices-or-safety-belts are-furnished,-they-must-be--securely--fastened--to the-seat-or-the-floor-of-the-vehicle. Reject--procedures--same-as-in-Section-451.Appendix C(b).
c)--SPECIAL-SERVICE DOOR	Same-as-Section-451.Appendix-C(c).
d)--BI-PARTING DOORS	Same-as-Section-451.Appendix-C(d).
e)--LIFTS-AND RAMPS	Same-as-Section-451.Appendix-C(e).
f)--FASTENING DEVICES	Same-as-Section-451.Appendix-C(f).
g)--SPECIAL-LIGHT	Same-as-Section-451.Appendix-C(g).
h)--GRAB-HANDLES	Same-as-Section-451.Appendix-C(h).
i)--OVER-CENTER DOOR-CONTROL	Same-as-Section-451.Appendix-C(i).

(Source: Repealed at 19 Ill. Reg. 4394, effective MAR 13 1995)

DEPARTMENT OF TRANSPORTATION

NOTICE OF ADOPTED AMENDMENTS

Section 451.APPENDIX E Driver's Pre-Trip Inspection Requirements (Repealed)

As--required--in-Section-13-115-of-the-Illinois-Vehicle-Inspection-Law,-drivers must-complete-the-following-"Pre-trip-Inspection"-daily.

"Each-day-that-a-school-bus-is-operated-the--driver--shall--conduct--a pre-trip--inspection-of-the-mechanical-and-safety-equipment-on-the-bus as-prescribed-by-rule--or--regulation--of--the--Department." (Section 13-115-of-the-Illinois-Vehicle-Inspection-Law)

The-following-requirements-became-effective-August-1,-1975.

a)--The-driver-must-inspect-his-vehicle-each-day-prior-to-beginning-a-trip.

b)--The-driver-is-required-to-make-a-written-report-of-this-pre-trip inspection.--He-must-report-any-defects-found-to-the-proper-authority so-that-the-defects-can-be-corrected.

c)--The-pre-trip-inspection-report-shall-be-made-in-duplicate.

d)--As-designated-by-the-owner,-the-original-copy-shall-be-presented-to-the person-of-authority-on-a-daily-basis.--These-original-copies-shall-be retained-by-the-owner-for-one-hundred-and-eighty-days.

e)--The-duplicate-copy-shall-remain-in-the-bus-for-a-period-of-at-least thirty-days.

f)--The-form-shall-specify-items-to-be-checked-(see-subsection-(i))-and-the minimum-information-to-be-recorded.

g)--The-pre-trip-inspection-records-and-reports-will-be-made-available-for inspection-and-audit-by-authorized-representatives-of-the-Department-at any-time.

h)--It-is-the-responsibility-of-the-bus-owner-to-furnish-pre-trip inspection-report-forms-that-meet-the-minimum-requirements-of-this Section.

i)--Required-items-to-be-checked-during-the-driver's-Pre-Trip-Inspection-is due:

1)--Coolant:-oil.--battery,-washer-fluid-levels,-fan-belts--and--wiring.

2)--Steps:--cleanliness,--upholstery,--windows--warning-devices,-fuses,-first aid--kit.----fire--extinguisher,--emergency--door--(open--and--close), lettering.

3)--Odometer-reading-and-indication-of-whether-or-not-state-inspection--is due.

4)--Steering--wheel,--windshield-wipers-and-washers,-heater-and-defroster, horn,--service-door-(open-and-close),-all--mirrors--(adjustment),--door buzzer,--clutch,--brake--warning--buzzer,-stop-arm-control,-gear-shift lever,-neutral-safety-switch,-water-temperature,-fuel,--vacuum--or--air pressure,--gauges,--parking-brake,-seat-belt(s).

5)--Ammeter,-all-interior-lights,-headlights-(high/low-beams).

6)--Right-front-wheel-and-tire,--right-side-marker-lamps,-turn-signal-light and--reflectors,--right--rear--view-and-safety-mirror,-headlights,--turn signals,-cluster-clearance--and--I.D.--lights,--alternating--flashing lights,--windshield,-underside-of-chassis,-crossover-mirror,-left-rear view-mirror-and-safety-mirror,-left-front--wheel--and--tire,--driver's side--window,--stop-arm,-left-side-marker-lamp,-turn-signal-light-and

reflectors,--emergency--door--(open--and--close));---left--rear--wheels--and
tires;--exhaust--system--(tailpipe--clear);--clusters--clearance--and--2.0;
lights;--taillights;--turn--signals--and--reflectors;--alternating--flashing
lights;--rear--emergency--door--(open--and--close);--right--rear--wheels--and
tires;--fuel--tank--filler--cap;

7) Drain-air-brake-tank.--Record-condition-of-bus-tires;-satisfactory--or
unsatisfactory.

(Source: Repealed at 19 Ill. Reg. 4394 , effective
MAR 13 1995)

Section 451.APPENDIX G Illinois Minimum Standards for School Bus -, Van Type
Conversion 1-16 Passengers Purchased Prior to September 1974 [Repealed]

a) The-service-door-shall-be-located-to-the-right-of-the-operator-and-may
be--manually--controlled--from--the--operator's-seat-by-an-over-center
control.

b) The-emergency-doors-shall-be-located-in-the-center-of-the-rear-end--or
on--the-right-hand-side-of-the-school-bus.--The-door-shall-be-equipped
with-fastening-devices-for-opening-from-the--inside--and--the--outside
body--which--may--be--quickly--released--but--is--designed--to-offer
protection-against-accidental-release.

c) No-seat-or-other-object-shall-be-placed-in--the--bus--which--restricts
passageway-to-the-emergency-door-to-less-than-twelve-inches.

d) The--minimum--clearance-of-all-aisles;--including-between--the-seats-and
leading-to-the-emergency-door-shall-be-twelve-inches.

e) The-ceiling-and-walls-shall-be-insulated-with--fireproof--material--to
deaden-sound-and-reduce-vibration-to-a-minimum.

f) The--interior--of--the--school--bus--shall--be-free-of-all-unnecessary
projections-likely-to-cause-injury.--The-inner-lining-on-ceilings-and
walls-shall-be-fiberboard-or-metal.

g) All-glass-in-the-windshield;-windows-and-doors-shall-be--of--approved
safety--glass.--All-exposed-edges-of-glass-shall-be-banded.--The-glass
in-the-windshield-shall-be-heat-absorbent-laminated-plate.

h) 133-inch-wheelbase.

i) G.V.W.R.-7600-pounds.

j) 3300-lbs.-front-axle.

k) 5050-lbs.-rear-axle.

l) 1475-lbs.-front-springs.

m) 2200-lbs.-rear-springs.

n) 8:00-x-16.5;-8-ply-rating-tires.

o) 8-hole-disc-16.5"-x-6.00".

p) High-output-primary-heater.

q) Rear-heater-recirculating-type.

r) Two-moveable-glass-vents-or-windows.--One-located-on--the--right--side
and-one-on-the-left-side-of-the-driver's-area.--These-are-optional.

s) 240-cu.-in.-minimum-engine.

t) 55-amp-alternator.

u) 70-amp-battery.

v) Two--5"--x--10"-(minimum)-outside-rear-view-mirrors-(West-Coast-Type);
and-two-3"-convex-mirrors-(buses-purchased-prior-to--September--1974;
may-have-the-3"--"stick-on-type"-type-convex-mirrors-provided-they-do
not-reduce-the-visual-field-of-the-mirror-below-50-square-inches).
Inside-rear-view-mirror.

x) A-convex-crossover-mirror-7-1/2"-in-diameter,-mounted-on-left-front-to
give--the--seated-driver-a-view-of-the-roadway-immediately-in-front-of
the-front-bumper.

y) Seating-plan-must-allow-13-inches-of-seating-space-for-each-of--16--or
fewer--passengers;--exclusive--of--the--driver.---All--seats-must-face

DEPARTMENT OF TRANSPORTATION

NOTICE OF ADOPTED AMENDMENTS

forward--with--a--minimum--of--12"--aisle--down--the--center--or--down--the--right
side.--No--jump--or--portable--seats--allowed.
z) Manually--or--mechanically--operated--"Stop"--signal--arm.--Hexagon-shaped
semaphore--mandatory--on--all--vehicles--purchased--after--December--31,--1975.
aa) One--rub--rail--applied--to--each--side--operator's--door--and--service--door.
Rub--rail--may--be--omitted--on--operator's--door--if--"Stop"--signal--arm--is
mounted--on--it.
bb) Floor--must--be--covered--with--a--non-skid--type--material.
cc) Roof-mounted--"School--Bus"--sign--with--flashing--lights,--acceptable--until
December--31,--1976.--An--eight-light--system--is--then--mandatory.
dd) Color--of--bus--shall--be--National--School--Bus--Chrome--Yellow.
ee) All--required--lettering--shall--be--in--black.--Emergency--door--lettering
shall--be--two--inches.--Bus--Number,--School--Name,--District--or
Contractor's--name--on--both--sides--of--vehicle--shall--be--four--inches.
School--Bus--shall--be--eight--inches.
ff) Vehicles--may--not--be--altered--or--converted--to--carry--more--than--16
passengers.

(Source: ~~Amended~~ at 19 Ill. Reg. 4394 effective
MAR 13 1995)

DEPARTMENT OF TRANSPORTATION

NOTICE OF ADOPTED AMENDMENT(S)

Section 451.ILLUSTRATION A Stop Arm Panel (Repealed)

Hexagon.
This--arm--must--be--16--gauge--metal,--and--a--hexagon--shaped
semaphore--approximately--18--inches--wide--and--18--inches
long.

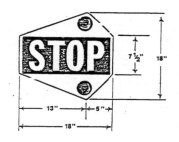

(Source: Repealed at 19 Ill. Reg. 4394 effective
MAR 13 1995)

Section 451.ILLUSTRATION B Exhaust Guidelines (Repealed)

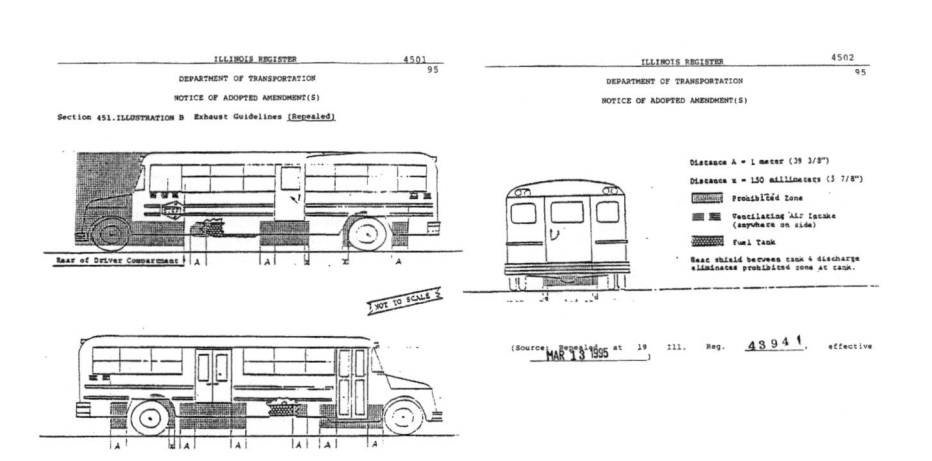

Rear of Driver Compartment

NOT TO SCALE

Distance A = 1 meter (39 3/8")
Distance x = 150 millimeters (5 7/8")

Prohibited Zone

Ventilating Air Intake
(anywhere on side)

Fuel Tank

Heat shield between tank & discharge
eliminates prohibited zone at tank.

(Source: Repealed at 19 Ill. Reg. 43941 , effective

MAR 13 1995)

DEPARTMENT OF TRANSPORTATION

NOTICE OF ADOPTED RULES

1) **Heading of the Part**: Inspection Procedures for Special Education School Buses

2) **Code Citation**: 92 Ill. Adm. Code 445

3) **Section Numbers**:

Section Numbers:	Adopted Action:
445.10	New Section
445.20	New Section
445.30	New Section
445.40	New Section
445.APPENDIX A	New Section
445.APPENDIX B	New Section

4) **Statutory Authority**: 625 ILCS 5/Ch. 12, Art. VIII and 5/Ch. 13

5) **Effective Date of Rulemaking**: March 13, 1995

6) **Does this rulemaking contain an automatic repeal date?** No

7) **Does this rulemaking contain incorporations by reference?** No

8) **Date Filed in Agency's Principal Office**: March 7, 1995

9) **Notice of Proposal Published in Illinois Register**: September 9, 1994, 18 Ill. Reg. 13835

10) **Has JCAR issued a Statement of Objections to these rules?** No

11) **Difference(s) between proposal and final version**:

The Department corrected the Authority Note.

The Department corrected the ILCS citation in Section 445.10(a).

In Section 445.30(c), the Department capitalized the word "state" on the first and second lines.

The Department deleted the labels in Section 445.40.

In Section 445.40, "Bus," the Department added a closed paren at the end of the sentence.

In Section 44.540, "Code," the Department inserted a period at the end of the sentence.

In Section 445.40, "Illinois Vehicle Equipment Law," the Department deleted the brackets and inserted a period.

DEPARTMENT OF TRANSPORTATION

NOTICE OF ADOPTED RULES

In the definition of "Manufacturer," the Department deleted the parentheses and inserted a comma after "use". The word "state" was also initially capped in this definition.

In Section 445.Appendix A(g), a slash was inserted after "PROCEDURES".

In Sections 445.Appendix A(g)(2)(B) and B(g)(2)(B), the commas were deleted after the word "and".

12) **Have all the changes agreed upon by the agency and JCAR been made as indicated in the agreement letter issued by JCAR?** Yes

13) **Will this rulemaking replace an emergency rule currently in effect?** No

14) **Are there any amendments pending on this Part?** No

15) **Summary and Purpose of Rulemaking**: By this Notice of Adopted Rules, the Department is establishing a new Part 445 which consists of the inspection requirements for special education school buses. Elsewhere in this issue of the Illinois Register, the Department is repealing Appendices C and D of 92 Ill. Adm. Code 451 which previously addressed the inspection requirements for special education school buses. Through reorganizing, the Department is making a number of substantive changes, providing clarification of, and correcting the regulations. This rulemaking also establishes Section 445.40, "Definitions," to define all necessary terms.

The following analysis identifies individual subsections within Appendices A and B which the Department has established for Type I and Type II special education school buses. These subsections have been reorganized in alphabetical order and rewritten to address and clarify the federal rule at 58 FR 4586, January 15, 1993.

This federal rule, which was promulgated by the National Highway Traffic Safety Administration, established new requirements for school buses used for special education transportation.

Appendices A and B both begin with an introduction which addresses the general requirement that school buses used for special education transportation must meet the minimum safety standards of all school buses. The introduction also includes a requirement for potential modification of special education school buses which may be necessary to meet the needs of special education students. Special modifications and equipment necessary to transport special educations students must be resolved in the student's Individualized Education Program.

Appendices A and B(d) - Seat Safety Belts

Appendix A - Adding provisions optional seat safety belts must meet if

DEPARTMENT OF TRANSPORTATION

NOTICE OF ADOPTED RULES

they are provided. Adding provisions for passenger seats which are
occupied only by a student's aid.

Appendix B - Adding requirements for seat safety belts on school buses
manufactured on or after April 1, 1977.

Appendices A and B(f) - Special Service Door

Adding a provision which allows the audible alarm to be deactivated
when the special door is completely open, when held by a fastening
device, and when used for the loading and unloading of passengers with
special needs.

Correcting language by moving bi-parting door requirements into
special service door subsection.

Appendices A and B(g) - Wheelchair Occupant Restraints

Establishing standards for wheelchair occupant restraints for school
buses manufactured on, before and after January 17, 1994 (the
effective date of 58 FR 4586, January 15, 1993).

Appendices A and B(h) - Wheelchair Securement Anchorages

Establishing standards for wheelchair securement anchorages for school
buses manufactured on, before, and after January 17, 1994.

16) Information and questions regarding these adopted rules shall be directed
to:

Ms. Cathy Allen
Regulations and Training Unit
Illinois Department of Transportation
Division of Traffic Safety
P.O., Box I9212
Springfield, Illinois 62794-9212
(217) 785-1181

17) State reasons for this rulemaking if it was not included in the two (2)
most recent regulatory agendas:

The full text of the Adopted Rule begins on the next page:

DEPARTMENT OF TRANSPORTATION

NOTICE OF ADOPTED RULES

TITLE 92: TRANSPORTATION
CHAPTER I: DEPARTMENT OF TRANSPORTATION
SUBCHAPTER e: TRAFFIC SAFETY (EXCEPT HAZARDOUS MATERIALS)

PART 445
INSPECTION PROCEDURES FOR SPECIAL EDUCATION SCHOOL BUSES

Section
445.10   Purpose and Scope
445.20   Application
445.30   Standards of Construction
445.40   Definitions

APPENDIX A   Procedures for Type I Special Education School Buses
APPENDIX B   Procedures for Type II Special Education School Buses

AUTHORITY: Implementing and authorized by Article VIII of the Illinois Vehicle
Equipment Law [625 ILCS 5/Ch. 12, Art. VIII] and the Illinois Vehicle
Inspection Law [625 ILCS 5/Ch. 13].

SOURCE: Adopted at   19   Ill. Reg. 4503 , effective
MAR 13 1995   .

Section 445.10 Purpose and Scope

This Part prescribes the requirements of the Illinois Department of
Transportation governing:
    a) Implementation of Article VIII of the Illinois Vehicle Equipment Law
        [625 ILCS 5/ch. 12, Art. VIII]; and
    b) Inspection procedures for special education school buses.

Section 445.20 Application

This Part applies to the following persons:
    a) Department personnel;
    b) Owners of Official Testing Stations;
    c) Employees of Official Testing Stations;
    d) School bus operation managers; and
    e) School bus drivers.

Section 445.30 Standards of Construction

    a) "Shall" and "must" are used in the imperative sense. "Shall" imposes
        an obligation to act. "Must" defines a condition that is to be
        satisfied. "May" allows permissiveness under terms specified in the
        standards. "Will" indicates intention, promise or willingness.
    b) Words imparting the masculine gender include the feminine.

DEPARTMENT OF TRANSPORTATION

NOTICE OF ADOPTED RULES

c) Changes in the administration of the State school bus inspection program and changes to federal and State law have caused the purchase or manufacture date of school buses to be critical in the application of these regulations. The effective dates for some of these standards will vary.

1) Exemptions to some standards are provided for school buses purchased prior to September 1974, the effective date of the Department's "Vehicle Inspection Stations Governing School Buses."

2) Exemptions to some standards are provided for school buses manufactured prior to March 1977, the date of the Department's Order "Minimum Safety Standards for Construction of Type I School Buses."

3) Exemptions are provided for Type II school buses manufactured prior to October 1978, the date of the Department's Order "Minimum Safety Standards for Construction of Type II School Buses."

4) Some standards are identified with other effective dates. These standards are applicable to all school buses manufactured or purchased after the identified date or during the time frame specified.

Section 445.40 Definitions

"Body" - Portion of vehicle that encloses the occupant and cargo spaces and separates those spaces from the chassis frame, engine compartment, driveline, and other chassis components, except certain chassis controls used by the driver.

"Body-on-Chassis" - Completed vehicle consisting of a passenger seating body mounted on a truck type chassis (or other separate chassis) so that the body and chassis are separate entities, although one may reinforce or brace the other.

"Bus" - Every motor vehicle, other than a commuter van, designed for carrying more than ten persons. (Section 1-107 of the Illinois Vehicle Code) [625 ILCS 5/1-107]

"Chassis" - Every frame or supportive element of a school bus that contains but is not limited to the axles, engine, drive train, steering components, and suspension which the body is attached to. (Section 1-110.1 of the Code)

"Code" - The Illinois Vehicle Code [625 ILCS 5].

"Commercial Vehicle Safety Section" (CVSS) - A section of the Bureau of Safety Programs of the Division of Traffic Safety of the Illinois Department of Transportation.

DEPARTMENT OF TRANSPORTATION

NOTICE OF ADOPTED RULES

"Department" - The Department of Transportation of the State of Illinois, acting directly or through its authorized agents or officers. (Section 13-100 of the Code)

"Empty Weight" - Unloaded vehicle weight; i.e., the weight of a vehicle with maximum capacity of all fluids necessary for operation of the vehicle but without cargo or occupant.

"Federal Motor Vehicle Safety Standards" (FMVSS) - The rules, regulations and standards set forth in 49 CFR 571.

"Illinois Vehicle Equipment Law" - 625 ILCS 5/Ch. 12.

"Individualized Education Program [IEP]" - A written statement for an exceptional child that provides at least a statement of the child's present levels of educational performance; annual goals and short-term instructional objectives; specific special education and related services (includes transportation); the extent of participation in the regular education program; the projected dates for initiation of services; anticipated duration of services; appropriate objective criteria and evaluation procedures; and a schedule for annual determination of short-term objectives. The following participants develop the child's IEP:

1) A representative of the local district, other than the child's teacher, who is authorized to commit services and who is qualified to provide or supervise the provision of special education.

2) The child's teacher.

3) One or both of the child's parents or guardians (if possible).

4) The child, where appropriate.

5) Other individuals at the discretion of the parent or local district.

"Manufacturer" - Unless otherwise indicated at the point of use, means the person or organization whose name follows "MANUFACTURED BY" or "MFD BY" on the federal and State certification label.

"Passenger" - Every occupant of the vehicle who is not the driver.

"Purchase Date" - Date when purchase transaction was completed, not when body or chassis was built.

"School Bus"

Type I School Bus - A School Bus with gross vehicle weight rating of more than 10,000 pounds.

Type II School Bus - A School Bus with gross vehicle weight

DEPARTMENT OF TRANSPORTATION

NOTICE OF ADOPTED RULES

rating of 10,000 pounds or less. (Section 12-800 of the Illinois
Vehicle Equipment Law)

*Every motor vehicle, except as provided below, owned or operated
by or for any of the following entities for the transportation of
persons regularly enrolled as students in grade 12 or below in
connection with any activity of such entity:*

> *Any public or private primary or secondary school;*

> *Any primary or secondary school operated by a religious
> institution; or*

> *Any public, private or religious nursery school.*

This definition shall not include the following:

> *A bus operated by a public utility, municipal corporation or
> common carrier authorized to conduct local or interurban
> transportation of passengers when such bus is not traveling
> a specific school bus route but is:*

> *On a regularly scheduled route for the transportation of
> other fare paying passengers;*

> *Furnishing charter service for the transportation of groups
> on field trips or other special trips or in connection with
> other special events; or*

> *Being used for shuttle service between attendance centers or
> other education facilities.*

A motor vehicle of the first division. (Section 1-182 of the
Code)

"Seat Safety Belt" - Any strap, webbing, or similar device designed to
secure a person in a motor vehicle in order to mitigate the results of
any accident, including all necessary buckles and other fasteners, and
all hardware designed for installing such seat belt assembly in a
motor vehicle.

"Special Education School Buses" - Vehicles constructed to transport
children with special needs which require the alteration of specific
component requirements (i.e., ramps, lifts, wheelchair
accommodations).

"Vehicle" -

DEPARTMENT OF TRANSPORTATION

NOTICE OF ADOPTED RULES

*First Division: Those motor vehicles which are designed for the
carrying of not more than ten persons.*

*Second Division: Those vehicles which are designed for carrying
more than ten persons, those designed or used for living quarters
and those vehicles which are designed for pulling or carrying
property, freight or cargo, those motor vehicles of the First
Division remodeled for use and used as motor vehicles of the
Second Division, and those motor vehicles of the First Division
used and registered as school buses.* (Section 1-217 of the Code)

"Wheelchair Occupant Restraints" - Any strap, webbing or similar
device designed to secure a person in a wheelchair in order to
mitigate the results of any accident, including all necessary buckles
and other fasteners, and all hardware designed for installing such
restraint in a school bus.

"Wheelchair Securement Anchorages" - The provision for transferring
wheelchair securement loads to the vehicle structure. Commonly
referred to as fastening devices. (58 FR 4586, January 15, 1993)

"Wheelchair Securement Device" - A strap, webbing or other device used
for securing a wheelchair to the school bus, including all necessary
buckles and other fasteners. (58 FR 4586, January 15, 1993)

DEPARTMENT OF TRANSPORTATION

NOTICE OF ADOPTED RULES

Section 445.APPENDIX A   Procedures for Type I Special Education School Buses

Generally, a school bus used for transporting children declared eligible for special transportation services shall comply with the applicable minimum standards for either a Type I school bus (see '92 Ill. Adm. Code 440) or a Type II school bus (see 92 Ill. Adm. Code 442). However, due to the nature of certain challenging conditions, vehicles utilized for special education transportation shall be adapted to the specific needs of the children receiving this service. These needs may require modification of the minimum standards. Equipment necessary for the transportation of special education students must be resolved in the student's Individualized Education Program.

The interior design of these vehicles will not be a cause for rejection provided an approval, issued by the Department, is presented to the Certified Safety Tester at the time of inspection.

a) Grab
   Handles   PROCEDURES/SPECIFICATIONS:

            Grab handles shall be provided on each side of front right service door only when this door is used for entry and exit of children.

            REJECT VEHICLE IF:

            Grab handles are not securely attached; do not meet requirements or are missing.

b) Lifts and
   Ramps   PROCEDURES/SPECIFICATIONS:

            Floor of ramp or lift shall be covered with nonskid material.

            Protection against dust and water sufficient to ensure reliable operation must be present.

            REJECT VEHICLE IF:

            Lifts and ramps do not operate properly or do not meet requirements.

   1) Power Lift

            PROCEDURES/SPECIFICATIONS:

DEPARTMENT OF TRANSPORTATION

NOTICE OF ADOPTED RULES

If power lift is used, it shall be of sufficient capacity and dimension to lift maximum imposed load, lift at top and bottom travel limits shall provide easy entrance and exit from the lift.

If electricity is used, the alternator or generator and battery must be of increased capacity.

Controls shall be operable from both interior and exterior of vehicle.

Device shall be installed which will be used to prevent operation of lift until doors are opened.

In travel position, the lift must be in its uppermost position and securely fastened.

Vehicles of less than 54-passenger capacity constructed for transportation of handicapped children may have the fuel tank located behind rear wheels, inside or outside chassis frame, with fill pipe located on right side of body.

REJECT VEHICLE IF:

Power lift does not operate properly or does not meet requirements.

   2) Ramp

            PROCEDURES/SPECIFICATIONS:

            Ramp shall be of sufficient strength and rigidity to support the imposed load. Shall be equipped with protective flange on each longitudinal side to keep wheelchair on ramp.

            Ramp shall be equipped with handle, or handles, and be of sufficient weight to permit one person to put ramp in place and return to storage place.

            Ramp shall be connected to bus at floor level in such manner as to permit easy access of wheelchair to floor of bus.

            Ramp length shall be sufficient for easy entry and exit.

            REJECT VEHICLE IF:

DEPARTMENT OF TRANSPORTATION

NOTICE OF ADOPTED RULES

Ramp does not operate properly; does not meet requirements.

c) Over Center
   Door
   Control   PROCEDURES/SPECIFICATIONS:

                  Over center door control shall be provided only when this
                  door is used for entry and exit of children.

                  REJECT VEHICLE IF:

                  If installed, does not operate properly. Does not meet
                  requirements. Missing when required.

d) Seat Safety
   Belts   PROCEDURES/SPECIFICATIONS:

                  Seat safety belts may be installed if they are securely
                  fastened to the seat or the floor of the vehicle.

                  Special education school buses may be equipped with
                  passenger seats that do not have guard barriers installed
                  in front of them. These passenger seats are to be used
                  only by student's aids and must be equipped with seat
                  safety belts at each location used by an aid. The school
                  bus driver must present a letter from the Commercial
                  Vehicle Safety Section approving this exception.

                  REJECT VEHICLE IF:

                  If installed, seat safety belts are not securely fastened
                  to the seat or the floor of the vehicle.

                  Barrier is not present in front of aids' seat and no seat
                  safety belts are provided. No letter of exception
                  provided.

e) Special
   Light   PROCEDURES/SPECIFICATIONS:

                  Light shall be placed inside bus over special service door
                  opening, or at other location if shielded to prevent glare.
                  The lamp shall illuminate the floor inside the opening and
                  shall be operated from door area.

                  REJECT VEHICLE IF:

DEPARTMENT OF TRANSPORTATION

NOTICE OF ADOPTED RULES

Special light does not operate properly; does not meet
requirements or is missing.

f) Special
   Service
   Door   PROCEDURES/SPECIFICATIONS:

                  A special door opening may be located on right side of bus
                  far enough to rear to prevent door, when open, from
                  obstructing front right service door. Door opening shall
                  be adequate to accommodate wheel chairs.

                  Door shall be equipped with device that will actuate
                  audible or visible signal, located in driver's compartment,
                  when special service door is not securely closed.

                  Each door shall contain a fixed or movable window aligned
                  with and of same size (as nearly as practicable) as other
                  windows on right side of bus.

                  Each door panel shall open outward and a positive fastening
                  device shall be installed to hold door in open position.
                  When the special service door is completely open for
                  loading and unloading passengers with special needs and
                  being held by the fastening device, the audible alarm can
                  be deactivated.

                  Door panels shall be constructed to be equivalent in
                  strength and materials to other school bus doors.

                  Door posts and headers shall be reinforced sufficiently to
                  provide support and strength equivalent to area of side of
                  bus not used for service doors. Outriggers from chassis
                  shall be installed at front and rear of door openings to
                  support floor with same strength as other floor portions.

                  Bi-parting doors must meet the following requirements:

                  Bi-parting doors shall be made of two panels of
                  approximately equal width. They shall be hinged to side of
                  bus and each panel shall open outward. Forward panels
                  shall be provided with overlapping flange to close space
                  where door panels meet and weather seal shall be provided
                  to close all door edges.

                  Bi-parting doors shall be equipped with at least one-point
                  fastening device on rear panel to floor or header and at
                  least two-point fastening device to floor and header on

DEPARTMENT OF TRANSPORTATION

NOTICE OF ADOPTED RULES

forward door panel, both manually operated.

Sliding doors are acceptable provided they meet manufacturer's specifications.

REJECT VEHICLE IF:

Special service door does not operate properly; does not meet requirements; audible or visible alarm does not work or is missing.

Bi-parting or sliding doors do not operate properly. Does not meet requirements. Door does not seal properly. Weather seal is cracked or missing.

g) Wheelchair Occupant Restraints

PROCEDURES/SPECIFICATIONS:

1) For buses manufactured prior to January 17, appropriate and adequate wheelchair occupant restraints must be installed at each wheelchair location which transports a student in a wheelchair. The restraints must be securely anchored to the wheelchair or the floor of the vehicle.

2) For buses manufactured on or after January 17, 1994, each wheelchair location which transports a student in a wheelchair must be equipped with:

A) Not less than one anchorage for the upper end of the upper torso restraint;

B) Not less than two floor anchorages for wheelchair occupant pelvic and upper torso restraint; and

C) Wheelchair occupant pelvic and upper torso restraints. (58 FR 4586, January 15, 1993)

REJECT VEHICLE IF:

Wheelchair occupant restraints do not meet requirements.

h) Wheelchair

DEPARTMENT OF TRANSPORTATION

NOTICE OF ADOPTED RULES

Securement Anchorages

PROCEDURES/SPECIFICATIONS:

In buses manufactured prior to January 17, 1994, positive wheelchair securement anchorages shall be provided and attached to the floor, walls, or both, that will securely hold wheelchair in position in bus.

In buses manufactured on or after January 17, 1994, each wheelchair location must be equipped with forward-facing wheelchair securement anchorages. Additional securement anchorages which allow other than forward-facing orientation can be added to a wheelchair location provided the forward-facing anchorages are not altered and the additional anchorages meet the same standards as the existing fastening devices. (58 FR 4586, January 15, 1993)

In buses manufactured on or after January 17, 1994, each wheelchair location must be equipped with two wheelchair securement anchorages in the rear and two anchorages in the front. Each securement device must be either of webbing or strap and provide means of adjustment or of a design that provides limited movement. (58 FR 4586, January 15, 1993)

REJECT VEHICLE IF:

In buses manufactured prior to January 17, 1994, wheelchair securement anchorages securely do not hold wheelchair to floor, walls or both.

In buses manufactured on and after January 17, 1994:

1) Each wheelchair location is not equipped with forward-facing wheelchair securement anchorages. Additional anchorages do not meet same standards as existing anchorages.

2) Wheelchair securement anchorages do not meet requirements.

DEPARTMENT OF TRANSPORTATION

NOTICE OF ADOPTED RULES

Section 445.APPENDIX B Procedures for Type II Special Education School Buses

Generally, a school bus used for transporting children declared eligible for special transportation services shall comply with the applicable minimum standards for either a Type I school bus (see 92 Ill. Adm. Code 440) or a Type II school bus (see 92 Ill. Adm. Code 442). However, due to the nature of certain challenging conditions, vehicles utilized for special education transportation shall be adapted to the specific needs of the children receiving this service. These needs may require modification of the minimum standards. Equipment necessary for the transportation of special education students must be resolved in the student's Individualized Education Program.

The interior design of these vehicles will not be a cause for rejection provided an approval, issued by the Department, is presented to the Certified Safety Tester at the time of inspection.

a) Grab
   Handles   PROCEDURES/SPECIFICATIONS:

                  Grab handles shall be provided on each side of front right
                  service door only when this door is used for entry and exit
                  of children.

                  REJECT VEHICLE IF:

                  Grab handles are not securely attached, do not meet
                  requirements or are missing.

b) Lifts and
   Ramps   PROCEDURES/SPECIFICATIONS:

                  Floor of ramp or lift shall be covered with nonskid
                  material.

                  Protection against dust and water sufficient to ensure
                  reliable operation must be present.

                  REJECT VEHICLE IF:

                  Lifts and ramps do not operate properly or do not meet
                  requirements.

   1) Power Lift

                  PROCEDURES/SPECIFICATIONS:

DEPARTMENT OF TRANSPORTATION

NOTICE OF ADOPTED RULES

If power lift is used, it shall be of sufficient capacity and dimension to lift maximum imposed load, lift at top and bottom travel limits shall provide easy entrance and exit from the lift.

If electricity is used, the alternator or generator and battery must be of increased capacity.

Controls shall be operable from both interior and exterior of vehicle.

Device shall be installed which will be used to prevent operation of lift until doors are opened.

In travel position, the lift must be in its uppermost position and securely fastened.

Vehicles of less than 54-passenger capacity constructed for transportation of handicapped children may have the fuel tank located behind rear wheels, inside or outside chassis frame, with fill pipe located on right side of body.

REJECT VEHICLE IF:

Power lift does not operate properly or does not meet requirements.

2) Ramp

   PROCEDURES/SPECIFICATIONS:

   Ramp shall be of sufficient strength and rigidity to support the imposed load. Shall be equipped with protective flange on each longitudinal side to keep wheelchair on ramp.

   Ramp shall be equipped with handle, or handles, and be of sufficient weight to permit one person to put ramp in place and return to storage place.

   Ramp shall be connected to bus at floor level in such manner as to permit easy access of wheelchair to floor of bus.

   Ramp length shall be sufficient for easy entry and exit.

   REJECT VEHICLE IF:

Ramp does not operate properly or does not meet requirements.

c) Over Center Door Control

PROCEDURES/SPECIFICATIONS:

Over center door control shall be provided only when this door is used for entry and exit of children.

REJECT VEHICLE IF:

If installed, does not operate properly, does not meet requirements or is missing when required.

d) Seat Safety Belts

PROCEDURES/SPECIFICATIONS:

In buses manufactured on or after April 1, 1977, seat safety belts are required at each designated seating position. (49 CFR 571.208)

In buses manufactured prior to April 1, 1977, seat belts are optional. If safety belts are installed, they must be securely fastened to the seat or the floor of the vehicle.

Special education school buses may be equipped with passenger seats that do not have guard barriers installed in front of them. These passenger seats are to be used only by students' aids and must be equipped with seat safety belts at each seating location used by an aid. The school bus driver must present a letter from the Commercial Vehicle Safety Section approving this exception.

REJECT VEHICLE IF:

If installed, seat safety belts are not securely fastened to the seat or the floor of the vehicle.

Barrier is not present in front of aid's seat and no seat safety belt is provided. No letter of exception provided.

e) Special Light

PROCEDURES/SPECIFICATIONS:

Light shall be placed inside bus over special service door opening, or at other location if shielded to prevent glare. The lamp shall illuminate the floor inside the opening and

shall be operated from door area.

REJECT VEHICLE IF:

Special light does not operate properly, does not meet requirements or is missing.

f) Special Service Door

PROCEDURES/SPECIFICATIONS:

A special door opening may be located on right side of bus far enough to rear to prevent door, when open, from obstructing front right service door. Door opening shall be adequate to accommodate wheel chairs.

Door shall be equipped with device that will actuate audible or visible signal, located in driver's compartment, when special service door is not securely closed.

Each door shall contain a fixed or movable window aligned with and of same size (as nearly as practicable) as other windows on right side of bus.

Each door panel shall open outward and a positive fastening device shall be installed to hold door in open position. When the special service door is completely open for loading and unloading passengers with special needs and being held by the fastening device the audible alarm can be deactivated.

Door panels shall be constructed to be equivalent in strength and materials to other school bus doors.

Door posts and headers shall be reinforced sufficiently to provide support and strength equivalent to area of side of bus not used for service doors. Outriggers from chassis shall be installed at front and rear of door openings to support floor with same strength as other floor portions.

Bi-parting doors (if installed) must meet the following requirements:

Bi-parting doors shall be made of two panels of approximately equal width. They shall be hinged to side of bus and each panel shall open outward. Forward panels shall be provided with overlapping flange to close space where door panels meet and weather seal shall be provided

DEPARTMENT OF TRANSPORTATION

NOTICE OF ADOPTED RULES

to close all door edges.

Bi-parting doors shall be equipped with at least one-point fastening device on rear panel to floor or header and at least two-point fastening device to floor and header on forward door panel, both manually operated.

Sliding doors are acceptable provided they meet manufacturer's specifications.

REJECT VEHICLE IF:

Special service door does not operate properly. Does not meet requirements. Audible or visible alarm does not work or is missing.

Bi-parting or sliding doors do not operate properly or do not meet requirements. Door does not seal properly. Weather seal is cracked or missing.

g) Wheelchair
   Occupant
   Restraints   PROCEDURES/SPECIFICATIONS:

1) For buses manufactured prior to January 17, 1994, appropriate and adequate wheelchair occupant restraints must be installed at each wheelchair location which transports a student in a wheelchair. The restraints must be securely anchored to the wheelchair or the floor of the vehicle.

2) For buses manufactured on or after January 17, 1994, each wheelchair location which transports a student in a wheelchair must be equipped with:

   A) Not less than one anchorage for the upper end of the upper torso restraint;

   B) Not less than two floor anchorages for wheelchair occupant pelvic and upper torso restraint; and

   C) Wheelchair occupant pelvic and upper torso restraints. (58 FR 4586, January 15, 1993)

REJECT VEHICLE IF:

DEPARTMENT OF TRANSPORTATION

NOTICE OF ADOPTED RULES

Wheelchair occupant restraints do not meet requirements.

h) Wheelchair
   Securement
   Anchorages   PROCEDURES/SPECIFICATIONS:

In buses manufactured prior to January 17, 1994, positive wheelchair securement anchorages shall be provided and attached to the floor, walls, or both, that will securely hold wheelchair in position in bus.

In buses manufactured on or after January 17, 1994, each wheelchair location must be equipped with forward-facing wheelchair securement anchorages. Additional securement anchorages, which allow other than forward-facing orientation can be added to a wheelchair location provided the forward-facing anchorages are not altered and the additional anchorages meet the same standards as the existing fastening devices. (58 FR 4586, January 15, 1993)

In buses manufactured on or after January 17, 1994, each wheelchair location must be equipped with two wheelchair securement anchorages in the rear and two anchorages in the front. Each securement device must be either of webbing or strap and provide means of adjustment or of a design that provides limited movement. (58 FR 4586, January 15, 1993)

REJECT VEHICLE IF:

In buses manufactured prior to January 17, 1994, wheelchair securement anchorages securely do not hold wheelchair to floor, walls or both.

In buses manufactured on and after January 17, 1994:

1) Each wheelchair location is not equipped with forward-facing wheelchair securement anchorages. Additional anchorages do not meet same standards as existing anchorages.

2) Wheelchair securement anchorages do not meet requirements.

DEPARTMENT OF TRANSPORTATION

NOTICE OF ADOPTED RULES

1) **Heading of the Part**: Inspection Procedures for Type I School Buses

2) **Code Citation**: 92 Ill. Adm. Code 441

3) **Section Numbers**:

Section Numbers:	Adopted Action:
441.10	New Section
441.20	New Section
441.25	New Section
441.30	New Section
441.40	New Section
441.APPENDIX A	New Section
441.APPENDIX B	New Section
441.APPENDIX C	New Section
441.APPENDIX D	New Section
441.APPENDIX E	New Section
441.APPENDIX F	New Section
441.APPENDIX G	New Section
441.APPENDIX H	New Section
441.APPENDIX I	New Section
441.APPENDIX J	New Section
441.APPENDIX K	New Section
ILLUSTRATION A	New Section
ILLUSTRATION B	New Section
ILLUSTRATION C	New Section
ILLUSTRATION D	New Section
ILLUSTRATION E	New Section

4) **Statutory Authority**: 625 ILCS 5/Ch. 12, Art. VIII and 5/Ch. 13

5) **Effective Date of Rulemaking**: March 13, 1995

6) **Does this rulemaking contain an automatic repeal date?** No

7) **Does this rulemaking contain incorporations by reference?** Yes. These conform to Section 5-75(a) of the Illinois Administrative Procedure Act.

8) **Date Filed in Agency's Principal Office**: March 7, 1995

9) **Notice of Proposal Published in Illinois Register**: September 9, 1994, 18 Ill. Reg. 13855

10) **Has JCAR issued a Statement of Objections to these rules?** No

11) **Differences between proposal and final version**:

On the Table of Contents at Section 441.25, the Department changed "Standards" to "Regulations."

DEPARTMENT OF TRANSPORTATION

NOTICE OF ADOPTED RULES

The Department corrected the ILCS citations in the Authority Note.

At Section 441.10, the Department corrected the word "Part" in the Section heading. Also, at Section 441.10(a), the ILCS citation was corrected.

In Section 441.25, the Department added the phrase "and as amended at 59 FR 22997, May 4, 1994" to the first sentence.

The Department further indented the definitions in Section 441.40.

In Section 441.Appendix A(b), the Department inserted "September 1, 1994" following the word "after" and deleted "May 2, 1994."

In Section 441.Appendix A(b)(4), the Department inserted "; as amended at 59 FR 22997, May 4, 1994" after "1992".

In Section 441.Appendix D(b), the Department inserted ";as amended at 59 FR 22997, May 4, 1994" after "1992."

In Section 441.Appendix I(c), the Department deleted "May 2, 1994" and inserted "September 1, 1994" in its place.

In Section 441.Appendix I(c)(7), the Department inserted ";as amended at 59 FR 2297, May 4, 1994" after "1992-"

In Section 441.Illustration A, the Department corrected the references to Section 441.Appendix 10(a).

12) **Have all the changes agreed upon by the agency and JCAR been made as indicated in the agreement letter issued by JCAR?** No changes were necessary.

13) **Will this rulemaking replace an emergency rule currently in effect?** No

14) **Are there any amendments pending on this Part?** No

15) **Summary and Purpose of Rulemaking**:
By this Notice of Adopted Rules, the Department is establishing a new Part 441 which consists of the inspection requirements and criteria for Type I school buses. Elsewhere in this issue of the *Illinois Register*, the Department is repealing Appendices A through G and Illustrations A and B in 92 Ill. Adm. Code 451 which previously addressed the inspection criteria for Type I school buses. Through reorganizing, the Department is clarifying, correcting, adding to and deleting some requirements.

The following analysis indicates changes made to individual components.

Air cleaner:

DEPARTMENT OF TRANSPORTATION

NOTICE OF ADOPTED RULES

Adding "not properly attached" as cause for rejection.

Aisle:

Adding criteria pursuant to 57 FR 49413, November 2, 1992 requiring additional emergency exits.

Battery:

Adding "insufficient capacity" as cause for rejection.

Brakes:

Renaming booster to master cylinder.

Adding inspection criteria for brake inspection report.

Adding exception from brake inspection report requirements for new buses.

Bumper:

Adding provisions for optional crossing arm.

Certification Label:

Deleting and removing State certification label as subject of inspection. (Implementation of this requirement proved difficult for buses manufactured for use in another State.)

Defroster:

Adding requirements for auxiliary fans to be securely mounted and have protected blades.

Drive Shaft Guard:

Clarifying protection of each segment of the drive shaft guard.

Emergency Exits:

Adding provisions for optional emergency roofhatches.
Correcting requirement for left emergency door to have glass only in lower portion of the door.
Correcting requirement for only inside release mechanism to be protected.

Adding provisions for optional emergency windows.

DEPARTMENT OF TRANSPORTATION

NOTICE OF ADOPTED RULES

Clarifying alarm requirements for optional and required exits.
Adding criteria pursuant to 57 FR 49413, November 2, 1992 requiring additional emergency exits.

Entrance Door:

Adding provisions for over-the-center-door control.
Adding requirements that door must seal properly.
Correcting error in locks and alarm requirements.
Deleting requirement that locking system be dependent on driver being seated to operate the door. (It is physically impossible and unnecessary for driver to remain seated.)

Exhaust System:

Amending requirements for shielding diesel powered engines.
Adding rejection criteria for shielding requirements.

Fire Extinguisher:

Adding approval of halon fire extinguisher.

First Aid Kit:

Clarifying requirement that minimum number of packages be sealed.
Adding approval of OSHA approved blood-borne pathogen kits.
Removing Commercial Type as a kit option.
(Commercial Type kits are no longer used by the industry.)

Floor Covering:

Adding metal floor stripping as subject to inspection.

Frame and Body:

Adding provisions for collision damage as subject to inspection.

Fuel Storage System:

Correcting language to require fuel filler cap to meet manufacturer's specifications.
Adding exception for shielding of some diesel powered engines.
Expanding alternate fuel inspection criteria for liquefied petroleum gas and compressed natural gas.

Heaters:

Adding padding requirement if heater is not protected by a seat.

DEPARTMENT OF TRANSPORTATION

NOTICE OF ADOPTED RULES

Instrument Panel:

Adding emergency/parking brake indicator light as subject to inspection.

Lettering:

Exterior:

Adding Agency Note regarding marking requirements for interstate operations.
Correcting language by moving emergency window lettering to interior.
Removing requirement for lettering to be located at least 44 inches above the floor level on the rear emergency door.
Correcting lettering requirements by adding "and/or."
Adding criteria pursuant to 57 FR 49413, November 2, 1992 requiring additional emergency exits.
Removing reference to "Newton Weight."

Interior:

Deleting black color requirement for front lettering.
Adding labeling requirements for left doors and windows for consistency with construction standards.
Adding provisions for optional route identification markers.
Adding criteria pursuant to 57 FR 49413, November 2, 1992 requiring additional emergency exits.

Lights:

Renaming cluster to identification lights.
Correcting error in eight light flashing system by adding instructions to close the door.
Eliminating headlight aiming requirement as subject to inspection.
Renaming marker to sidemarker lights.
Clarifying stepwell light requirements.
Adding exception for armored turn signal lights on buses which transport less than 33 passengers.

Mirrors:

Adding provisions for combining convex crossover mirrors with other mirrors.
Clarifying language for consistency with Type II school bus requirements.
Eliminating reference to vehicles which were manufactured prior to 1974.

DEPARTMENT OF TRANSPORTATION

NOTICE OF ADOPTED RULES

Paint:

Adding provisions for optional reflectorized tape.
Adding provisions for required reflectorized tape pursuant to 57 FR 49413, November 2, 1992.

Projections:

Adding provisions for eliminating dangerous projections.
Clarifying provisions for optional equipment installed in the bus.

Rub Rails:

Eliminating requirement for rub rail on all functioning doors.

Seat Belts:

Adding requirement for optional belts to meet federal standards.

Seat, Passenger:

Clarifying requirements for seat spacing measurements.
Deleting detailed requirements for fiberglass or plastic seating.
(Fiberglass and plastic seating are not longer being used by the industry.)
Adding criteria for flip-up seats pursuant to 57 FR 49413, November 2, 1992 requiring additional emergency exits.

Steering:

Adding Agency Note regarding steering shaft for Navistar chassis.

Steps:

Adding provisions for white nosing on steps.

Stop Arm Panel:

Adding language pursuant to 56 FR 20363, May 3, 1991 requiring stop arm panels.
Clarifying language pursuant to P.A. 88-415 which allows octagon-shaped semaphores on all school buses.
Approving optional strobe lamps.

Wheels/Tires:

Adding proper inflation of tires as subject to inspection.
Changing requirement for measuring tread groove depth on steering axle

DEPARTMENT OF TRANSPORTATION

NOTICE OF ADOPTED RULES

from three locations on the tire to one location. (Change is being made for consistency with 625 ILCS 5/12-405(d).)

Windows:

Adding an exception which states the requirements of this subsection do not apply to a window or glazed panel installed forward of a front passenger seat, and are optional for a window installed either beside a rear passenger seat, or in a side emergency exit. Exception is pursuant to 92 Ill. Adm. Code 440 - minimum Safety Standards for the Construction of Type I School Buses.

16) Information and questions regarding these adopted rules shall be directed to:

Name: Ms. Cathy Allen
Address: Regulations and Training Unit
Illinois Department of Transportation
Division of Traffic Safety
P.O. Box 19212
Springfield IL 62794-9212
Telephone: (217) 785-1181

17) State reasons for this rulemaking if it was not included in the two (2) most recent regulatory agendas:

The full text of the Adopted Rule begins on the next page:

DEPARTMENT OF TRANSPORTATION

NOTICE OF ADOPTED RULES

TITLE 92: TRANSPORTATION
CHAPTER I: DEPARTMENT OF TRANSPORTATION
SUBCHAPTER e: TRAFFIC SAFETY (EXCEPT HAZARDOUS MATERIALS)

PART 441
INSPECTION PROCEDURES FOR TYPE I SCHOOL BUSES

AUTHORITY: Implementing and authorized by Article VIII of the Illinois Vehicle Equipment Law [625 ILCS 5/Ch. 12, Art. VIII] and the Illinois Vehicle Inspection Law [625 ILCS 5/Ch. 13].

SOURCE: Adopted at 19 Ill. Reg. 4523, effective MAR 13 1995.

Section 441.10 Purpose and Scope

This Part prescribes the requirements of the Illinois Department of Transportation governing:
a) Implementation of Article VIII, the Illinois Vehicle Equipment Law [625 ILCS 5/Ch. 12, Art VIII];
b) Inspection procedures for Type I school buses; and
c) Performance of the daily pre-trip inspection by school bus drivers.

Section 441.20 Application

DEPARTMENT OF TRANSPORTATION

NOTICE OF ADOPTED RULES

This Part applies to the following persons:
   a) Department personnel;
   b) Owners of Official Testing Stations;
   c) Employees of Official Testing Stations;
   d) School bus operation managers; and
   e) School bus drivers.

Section 441.25 Incorporation by Reference of Federal Regulations

Whenever this Part refers to the Code of Federal Regulations and that reference incorporates the federal regulations by reference, the federal regulations incorporated shall be that which was effective as of October 1, 1992, as amended at 57 FR 49413, November 2, 1992; as amended at 57 FR 57000, December 2, 1992; as amended at 57 FR 57020, December 2, 1992 and as amended at 59 FR 22997, May 4, 1994 not including any later amendments or editions. Copies of appropriate federal regulations are available for inspection at the Department's Commercial Vehicle Safety Section.

Section 441.30 Standards of Construction

   a) "Shall" and "must" are used in the imperative sense. "Shall" imposes an obligation to act. "Must" defines a condition that is to be satisfied. "May" allows permissiveness under terms specified in the standards. "Will" indicates intention, promise or willingness.
   b) Words imparting the masculine gender include the feminine.
   c) Changes in the administration of the state school bus inspection program and changes to federal and state law have caused the purchase or manufacture date of school buses to be critical in the application of this Part. The effective dates for some of these standards will vary.
      1) Exemptions to some standards are provided for school buses purchased prior to September 1974, the effective date of the Department's "Vehicle Inspection Stations Governing School Buses."
      2) Exemptions to some standards are provided for school buses manufactured prior to March 1977, the date of the Department's Order "Minimum Safety Standards for Construction of Type I School Buses."
      3) Some standards are identified with other effective dates. These standards are applicable to all school buses manufactured or purchased after the identified date or during the time frame specified.

Section 441.40 Definitions

   "Body" - Portion of vehicle that encloses the occupant and cargo spaces and separates those spaces from the chassis frame, engine compartment, driveline, and other chassis components, except certain

DEPARTMENT OF TRANSPORTATION

NOTICE OF ADOPTED RULES

chassis controls used by the driver.

"Body-on-Chassis" - Completed vehicle consisting of a passenger - seating body mounted on a truck type chassis (or other separate chassis) so that the body and chassis are separate entities, although one may reinforce or brace the other.

"Bus" - Every motor vehicle, other than a commuter van, designed for carrying more than ten persons. (Section 1-107 of the Illinois Vehicle Code (the Code)) [625 ILCS 5/1-107]

"Chassis" - Every frame or supportive element of a school bus that contains but is not limited to the axles, engine, drive train, steering components, and suspension which the body is attached to. (Section 1-110.1 of the Code)

"Code" - The Illinois Vehicle Code [625 ILCS 5].

"Commercial Vehicle Safety Section" (CVSS) - A section of the Bureau of Safety Programs of the Division of Traffic Safety of the Illinois Department of Transportation.

"Department" - The Department of Transportation of the State of Illinois, acting directly or through its authorized agents or officers. (Section 13-100 of the Code)

"Empty Weight" - Unloaded vehicle weight; i.e., the weight of a vehicle with maximum capacity of all fluids necessary for operation of the vehicle but without cargo or occupant.

"Federal Motor Vehicle Safety Standards" (FMVSS) - The rules, regulations and standards set forth in 49 CFR 571.

"Gross Vehicle Weight Rating or GVWR" - The value specified by the manufacturer as the loaded weight of the school bus. (Section 12-800 of the Illinois Vehicle Equipment Law)

"Illinois Vehicle Equipment Law" - [625 ILCS 5/12-100 through 12-902]

"Manufacturer" - (unless otherwise indicated at the point of use) means the person or organization whose name follows "MANUFACTURED BY" or "MFD BY" on the federal and state certification label.

"Newton" (N) - Metric unit of force and weight. N = mass multiplied by the standard acceleration of free fall, or "gravity" (i.e., 9.8).

"Passenger" - Every occupant of the vehicle who is not the driver.

DEPARTMENT OF TRANSPORTATION

NOTICE OF ADOPTED RULES

"Purchase Date" - Date when purchase transaction was completed, not when body or chassis was built.

"School Bus" -

Type I School Bus - A School Bus with gross vehicle weight rating of more than 10,000 pounds.

Type II School Bus - A School Bus with gross vehicle weight rating of 10,000 pounds or less. (Section 12-800 of the Illinois Vehicle Equipment Law)

Every motor vehicle, except as provided below, owned or operated by or for any of the following entities for the transportation of persons regularly enrolled as students in grade 12 or below in connection with any activity of such entity:

Any public or private primary or secondary school; Any primary or secondary school operated by a religious institution; or

Any public, private or religious nursery school.

This definition shall not include the following:

A bus operated by a public utility, municipal corporation or common carrier authorized to conduct local or interurban transportation of passengers when such bus is not traveling a specific school bus route but is:

On a regularly scheduled route for the transportation of other fare paying passengers;

Furnishing charter service for the transportation of groups on field trips or other special trips or in connection with other special events; or

Being used for shuttle service between attendance centers or other educational facilities.

A motor vehicle of the first division. (Section 1-182 of the Code)

"Vehicle"

First Division: Those motor vehicles which are designed for the carrying of not more than ten persons.

DEPARTMENT OF TRANSPORTATION

NOTICE OF ADOPTED RULES

Second Division: Those vehicles which are designed for carrying more than ten persons, those designed or used for living quarters and those vehicles which are designed for pulling or carrying property, freight or cargo, those motor vehicles of the First Division remodelled for use and used as motor vehicles of the Second Division, and those motor vehicles of the First Division used and registered as school buses. (Section 1-217 of the Code)

DEPARTMENT OF TRANSPORTATION

NOTICE OF ADOPTED RULES

Section 441.APPENDIX A Air Cleaner,Through Barrier, Guard

a) AIR CLEANER

PROCEDURE/SPECIFICATIONS:

Any type is acceptable.

REJECT VEHICLE IF:

Air cleaner is not properly attached or is
missing.

b) AISLE

PROCEDURES/SPECIFICATIONS:

Unobstructed minimum clearance leading from
service door to emergency door (or back of
bus) must be at least 12 inches (305 mm)
wide. For buses manufactured in July 1987
or later, aisle width at two inches below top
of seat back must be 15 inches (380 mm).
Floor to ceiling height must be a minimum of
68.9 inches (1.75 m) at any location within
the aisle.

A dedicated aisle may be adjacent to any side
emergency door. For buses manufactured on or
after September 1, 1994, the following must be met:

1)   The aisle must be unobstructed at all
      times.

2)   No portion of a seat or barrier may
      extend past the door opening.

3)   No portion of the door latch mechanism
      can be obstructed by a seat.

4)   There must be at least 11.7 inches (30
      cm) measured from the door opening to the
      seat back in front. (57 FR 49413, November
      2, 1992); as amended at 59 FR 22997, May 4,
      1994

REJECT VEHICLE IF:

DEPARTMENT OF TRANSPORTATION

NOTICE OF ADOPTED RULES

Aisle does not meet minimum standards.

c) ALTERNATOR
   (GENERATOR)

PROCEDURES/SPECIFICATIONS:

The generator, or alternator with rectifier,
shall have a minimum capacity rating of 60
amperes and shall be capable of meeting all
electrical requirements.

REJECT VEHICLE IF:

Alternator does not meet minimum standards or
is not functioning.

d) AXLES

PROCEDURES/SPECIFICATIONS:

Must meet federal chassis requirements as
indicated on federal certification label. 49
CFR 568 (1992)

REJECT VEHICLE IF:

Axles show visible signs of apparent damage,
leaking fluids or are not firmly attached.

e) BARRIER,
   GUARD

PROCEDURES/SPECIFICATIONS:

A guard barrier, constructed and thickly
padded so as to provide head, knee and leg
protection, shall be installed in front of
each forward facing passenger seat that does
not directly face the rear surface of another
passenger seat. The barrier must measure the
same height as the passenger seat back
directly behind that barrier (i.e., 24
inches). 49 CFR 571.222

In a bus manufactured in January 1988 or
later, guard barriers must measure the same
height as the seat back directly behind that
barrier (i.e., 28 inches).

DEPARTMENT OF TRANSPORTATION

NOTICE OF ADOPTED RULES

Exception: In a bus manufactured from July 1,
1987, to December 31, 1987, the barrier
may be less than the required 28 inch seat
back.

Exception: In a bus with chassis (incomplete
vehicle) manufactured in March 1977 or
earlier, the barrier may consist of a
floor-to-ceiling vertical stanchion, padded
to within three inches of ceiling and floor,
and a stanchion-to-wall, fully padded,
horizontal guard rail. However, if located
adjacent to stepwell, this type barrier shall
include a stepwell guard panel that extends
from the stanchion to the wall and from the
guard rail to within two inches of the floor.

Exception: All buses manufactured prior to
September 1974 are exempt from padding on
stanchions and guard rails.

Exception: See 92 Ill. Adm. Code 445.Appendix
A (Inspection Procedures for Special
Education School Buses) for possible
exception.

REJECT VEHICLE IF:

Barrier is not solidly attached. Padding or
covering shows wear and tear. Barrier does
not meet requirements.

DEPARTMENT OF TRANSPORTATION

NOTICE OF ADOPTED RULES

Section 441.APPENDIX B Battery or Batteries Through Bumper, Front

a) BATTERY OR
   BATTERIES

PROCEDURES/SPECIFICATIONS:

One or more batteries may be mounted either in
engine compartment or on outside of
passenger/driver area. Battery (or batteries
together) in a 12 volt system shall be
rated, when new, to provide the following:

Engine manufacturer's recommended Cold
Cranking Current (amperes for 30 seconds) at
-18 degrees C (0 degree F) or, at the
purchaser's option, at -29 degrees C (-20
degrees F).

The battery(s) shall provide a Reserve
Capacity (duration of 25 ampere current flow)
at 27 degrees C (80 degrees F) for no
less than 135 minutes.

Low rate discharge capacity of 90 ampere-hours
or more (20 hour discharge test at 80
degrees F).

Exception: A bus manufactured in August 1974
or earlier may have a 70 ampere-hour battery,
in a 12 volt system.

REJECT VEHICLE IF:

Battery or batteries are not securely mounted;
excessively corroded; of insufficient
capacity.

b) BATTERY
   CABLES

PROCEDURES/SPECIFICATIONS:

Check condition.

REJECT VEHICLE IF:

Cables are corroded or are not securely
attached.

DEPARTMENT OF TRANSPORTATION

NOTICE OF ADOPTED RULES

c) BATTERY
CARRIER

PROCEDURES/SPECIFICATIONS:

When the battery is mounted outside the engine
compartment it shall be welded or bolted
in a closed, weather-tight, and vented
compartment that is located and arranged so
as to provide for convenient routine
servicing. The battery compartment door, or
cover, shall be secured by a manually
operated latch or other fastener. A latch or
fastener must be designed in such a
fashion as to keep the door closed when in
the latched position. Each electrical cable
connecting the battery in this carrier to the
body or chassis shall be one piece between the
terminal connector and the first body or
chassis terminal connector.

REJECT VEHICLE IF:

Battery carrier does not meet requirements.

d) BRAKES

PROCEDURES/SPECIFICATIONS:

*Every motor vehicle shall be equipped with two
separate means of applying the brakes and
they shall be so constructed that failure
of any one part of the operating
mechanism shall not leave the motor vehicle
without brakes.* (Section 12-301(a) of the
Illinois Vehicle Equipment Law)

REJECT VEHICLE IF:

Brakes do not meet requirements.

1) Backing
Plate

PROCEDURES/SPECIFICATIONS:

Check condition.

REJECT VEHICLE IF:

Backing plate is in poor condition.

DEPARTMENT OF TRANSPORTATION

NOTICE OF ADOPTED RULES

2) Drums/
Discs

PROCEDURES/SPECIFICATIONS:

Inspect drums and/or discs for cracks or for
being worn or reworked beyond the marked
discard limit.

REJECT VEHICLE IF:

Worn or reworked beyond the following limits:

1)   Drum diameter .040 inch (1mm) under
     marked discard limit on Type L bus.

2)   Drum diameter .030 inch (.75mm) under
     marked discard limit on Type II bus.

3)   Disc thickness .030 inch (.75mm) over
     marked discard limit on any bus.

4)   Other rework (rebore, reface) limit
     specified by chassis manufacturer.

3) Emergency
/Parking
Brake

PROCEDURES/SPECIFICATIONS:

*Emergency/parking brake system must apply
brakes to at least two wheels.* (Section
12-301(a) of the Illinois Vehicle Equipment Law)

AGENCY NOTE: Micro brakes are not considered a separate
means of braking and are not acceptable.

Procedures for testing:

1)   Apply operating control fully.

2)   Check actuating mechanism for release.

Brake Performance Test:

Using Drive-On Pad Type Tester:

DEPARTMENT OF TRANSPORTATION

NOTICE OF ADOPTED RULES

1) Drive vehicle onto brake machine pads at 4-8 m.p.h.

2) Apply emergency/parking brakes to bring vehicle to a halt. Do not lock wheels.

3) Note the braking forces registered by the brake machine.

Using Roll-On Type Tester:

1) Position axle with emergency brake onto roller.

2) Apply emergency brake but do not lock wheels.

REJECT VEHICLE IF:

Emergency/parking brake does not meet requirements.

Procedures for testing:

1) Not equipped with emergency/parking brakes. Operating mechanism does not hold in the applied position.

2) Actuating mechanism does not fully release when release control is operated properly.

Brake Performance Test:

Drive-On Tester:

Machine does not register a total braking force of at least 20% of vehicle empty weight. Braking forces at opposite wheels on same axle vary more than 20%.

Roll-On Tester:

Machine does not register a total braking force of at least 20% of vehicle empty weight. Braking forces at opposite wheels on same axle vary more than 20%.

DEPARTMENT OF TRANSPORTATION

NOTICE OF ADOPTED RULES

4) Emergency Brake Ratchet (Pedal or Lever)

PROCEDURES/SPECIFICATIONS:

Must be in proper adjustment. A warning light must be visible when emergency brake is activated.

REJECT VEHICLE IF:

Emergency Brake ratchet or warning light do not meet requirements.

5) Pedal Clearance (Service Brakes)

PROCEDURES/SPECIFICATIONS:

Minimum 1 1/2 inch clearance with pedal fully depressed.

REJECT VEHICLE IF:

Pedal clearance does not meet requirements.

6) Power Systems

A) Air

PROCEDURES/SPECIFICATIONS:

With air system fully charged (compressor governor "cut-out") run engine at low idle. Make one full (maximum) brake application and immediately record reservoir air pressure.

Apply and release brakes until pressure indicated on the air gauge is at least 10 psi (i.e. pounds per square inch) below governor "cut-in" pressure. Run engine at high idle and determine seconds required to raise reservoir pressure from recorded

DEPARTMENT OF TRANSPORTATION

NOTICE OF ADOPTED RULES

pressure.

REJECT VEHICLE IF:

Time required to raise air pressure from
recorded to cut-out is more than 30 seconds.
Air gauge is missing or does not operate.

B) Electric/
Hydraulic

PROCEDURES/SPECIFICATIONS:

Turn engine "off." Depress service brake
pedal. Electric hydraulic pump must come
"on" (listen).

REJECT VEHICLE IF:

Electric pump does not operate properly or is
absent.

C) Hydraulic

PROCEDURES/SPECIFICATIONS:

Inspect booster belt(s), supports, tubes,
hoses, connections and general condition.
Clean reservoir and cover as necessary and
check master cylinder fluid level. Do not
contaminate fluid.

Turn engine "on." Warning signal must come on
(look/listen). Depress brake pedal
lightly. Start engine. Pedal must move down
slightly (feel). Warning signal must go
"off" (look/listen).

REJECT VEHICLE IF:

Belt is slack or worn; tube or hose is
damaged; any part leaks or is cracked; master
cylinder fluid is below maximum level.

Either booster or warning signal does not
operate properly.

D) Vacuum/
Hydraulic

PROCEDURES/SPECIFICATIONS:

DEPARTMENT OF TRANSPORTATION

NOTICE OF ADOPTED RULES

Inspect tank(s), chambers, hoses, tubes,
connectors, clamps, and booster air cleaner.

Inspect supports and attachments.

With engine off, repeatedly apply service
brakes until vacuum is depleted, with medium
pressure on brake pedal, start engine;
release brake and operate engine until
maximum vacuum is established; stop engine;
apply service brakes hard.

With brakes still applied, start engine; after
one minute of running engine, check "Low
Vacuum" indicator.

REJECT VEHICLE IF:

Any component is restricted, collapsed,
scraped, cracked, loose, or broken. Booster
air cleaner is clogged.

Any support or attachment is broken. Any
connecting line or other component is not
attached or supported so as to prevent
damage from scraping or rubbing.

Foot pedal does not fall away from foot when
engine is started; insufficient vacuum reserve
to permit one full service brake
application after engine is off without
actuating "low vacuum" indicator; valve or
diaphragm leaking.

7) Service
Brakes

PROCEDURES/SPECIFICATIONS:

Must be equipped with service brakes on all
wheels. (Section 13-301(a)(9) of the Illinois
Vehicle Equipment Law)

Must be equipped with a "split system" on
service brakes. 49 CFR 571.105

Power-assisted service brakes are required.
49 CFR 571.105

DEPARTMENT OF TRANSPORTATION

NOTICE OF ADOPTED RULES

REJECT VEHICLE IF:

Service brakes do not meet requirements.

A) Brake
Inspection
Report

PROCEDURES/SPECIFICATIONS:

Verify Brake Inspection Report for following
(refer to Section 441.Illustration C for
example of form):

1. Vehicle Identification Number (VIN), make
and year must correspond to the bus
presented for inspection.

2. The Brake Inspection Report must indicate
the date and mileage at time the
brake inspection was performed. If
date is more than one year prior to
time of inspection or mileage has
exceeded 10,000 miles, a brake
inspection must be performed.

3. The form must be completed with all
required information. No blank lines
are acceptable.

Exception: If the bus has operated less than
10,000 miles and less than 12 months have
passed since the bus was manufactured, an SB6
form is not required. Write "Less than
10,000 miles and less than one year old" in
the remarks section on the Vehicle Inspection
Report.

REJECT VEHICLE IF:

Absent, invalid, or incomplete Brake
Inspection Report.

B) Brake
Performance
Test

PROCEDURES/SPECIFICATIONS:

DEPARTMENT OF TRANSPORTATION

NOTICE OF ADOPTED RULES

Using Drive-On Pad Type Brake Tester:

Check vehicle's stopping ability before testing.

Drive vehicle onto brake machine pads at 4-8 m.p.h.

Apply service brakes to bring vehicle to a
halt. Do not lock wheels.

Note the braking forces registered by the
brake machine.

Using Roll-On Type Tester:

When using roller-type tester each axle must
be tested separately. Transmission must be in
neutral when testing brakes on any drive
axle.

Drive front axle onto rollers. Start roller
motor. Apply service brakes but do not lock
wheels.

Repeat the above steps for each axle.

The total braking force on a vehicle must be
determined by adding the results of the test
on each axle.

REJECT VEHICLE IF:

Drive-On Tester:

Machine does not register a total braking
force of at least 60% of the vehicle empty
weight.

Roll-On Tester:

Braking forces at opposite wheels on same axle
vary more than 20%.

Machine does not register a total braking
force of at least 60% of the vehicle empty
weight. Braking forces at opposite wheels on
same axle vary more than 20%.

e) BUMPER,

DEPARTMENT OF TRANSPORTATION

NOTICE OF ADOPTED RULES

FRONT PROCEDURES/SPECIFICATION:

Either channel type, formed of rolled steel at least .177 inch (4.5 mm) (approximately 3/16 inch) thick, or approved energy absorbing type.

Buses manufactured in August 1974 or later must have 7.9 inches (200 mm) or more vertical black face.

Bumper must extend to outer edges of fenders and other front end sheet metal. Must be of strength to permit pushing vehicle of equal weight without permanent distortion.

Bumper may be equipped with a crossing control arm. Crossing control arms can only display yellow reflectors or yellow lamps.

Exception: Buses manufactured prior to September 1974 are exempt from bumper thickness and 7.9 inch face requirement.

REJECT VEHICLE IF:

Front bumper does not meet thickness, face height and color requirements. Must be solidly attached, in good condition, free from damage and sharp edges.

DEPARTMENT OF TRANSPORTATION

NOTICE OF ADOPTED RULES

Section 441.APPENDIX C Bumper, Rear Through Drive Shaft Guard

a) BUMPER,
REAR PROCEDURES/SPECIFICATIONS:

Channel steel at least .18 inch (4.55 mm) (approximately 3/16 inch) thick with a minimum 8.9 inches (225 mm) black face, full wrap around and attached so as to prevent hitching rides (i.e., "nonhitchable").

Shall be attached so that removal is possible by commonly available hand tools.

Shall be of strength to permit bus being pushed by another vehicle without permanent distortion.

AGENCY NOTE: "Nonhitchable" is defined as the rear of the bus being designed and maintained to prevent or discourage riding or grasping rear of bus so as to "hitch" rides.

REJECT VEHICLE IF:

Rear bumper does not meet requirements. Not solidly attached. Sharp edges are present. Rear bumper is hitchable.

b) CERTIFICATE AND
REGISTRATION
CARD HOLDER PROCEDURES/SPECIFICATIONS:

At least one card holder with a transparent face no less than 5.9 inches by 3.9 inches (150 mm by 100 mm) shall be securely affixed to the inside header panel out of students' easy reach.

REJECT VEHICLE IF:

Certificate and registration card holder does not meet requirements.

c) CERTIFICATION
LABEL (FEDERAL) PROCEDURES/SPECIFICATIONS:

DEPARTMENT OF TRANSPORTATION

NOTICE OF ADOPTED RULES

Inspect federal certification label if the chassis (incomplete vehicle) was manufactured on or after June 1, 1971. The certification label may be supplemented by an alterer's certification.

The manufacturer's label must contain the following information:

1) Name of vehicle (bus) manufacturer and the month and year in which manufacture of the vehicle was completed;

2) Name of incomplete vehicle (chassis) manufacturer and, the month and year in which he performed his last manufacturing operation on the incomplete vehicle;

3) Gross vehicle weight rating, or ratings (GVWR);

4) Gross axle weight ratings (GAWR);

5) The statement, "This vehicle conforms to all applicable federal motor vehicle safety standards in effect in (month/year)";

6) The vehicle identification number (VIN);

7) The vehicle's classification (usually "bus"). 49 CFR-567.5

Alterer's certification: A certified vehicle might have been altered before its purchase for use as a school bus. The alterations may have included, but are not limited to, classification changes, gross weight rating changes, or changes to the application/effective date of a federal motor vehicle safety standard. If any such alteration occurred, the bus must carry an additional federal label that identifies the alterer, shows when alteration was completed, "as altered" GVWR, GAWR and classification (if changed). It must also state that the altered vehicle conforms to all applicable federal motor vehicle safety

DEPARTMENT OF TRANSPORTATION

NOTICE OF ADOPTED RULES

standards in effect in (month/year). 49 CFR 567.7

REJECT VEHICLE IF:

A required label is absent, defaced, destroyed, not riveted, or not permanently affixed. "Permanently affixed" means the label cannot be removed without destroying or defacing it.

A certification label does not contain the required statement and all other information required for that label.

d) DEFROSTERS

PROCEDURES/SPECIFICATIONS:

Using heat from heaters and circulation from fans, defrosting equipment shall keep the windshield, the windows to the left of the operator, and the glass in the service door clear of fog, frost, and snow. Must conform to federal standards 49 CFR 571.103. (Auxiliary fans are not considered to be a defrosting and defogging system.)

REJECT VEHICLE IF:

Defrosting system does not function properly.

Auxiliary fans are not securely mounted or blades are not protected.

e) DRIVE SHAFT
   GUARD

PROCEDURES/SPECIFICATIONS:

Shall be of sufficient strength to protect each segment of the drive shaft and prevent it from going through the floor or dropping to the ground if broken.

REJECT VEHICLE IF:

Drive shaft guard is missing, not firmly attached, or does not properly protect each segment of the drive shaft.

DEPARTMENT OF TRANSPORTATION

NOTICE OF ADOPTED RULES

Section 441.APPENDIX D Electrical System Through Fenders

a) ELECTRICAL
   SYSTEM

1) Circuits

PROCEDURES/SPECIFICATIONS:

Shall be arranged in at least nine regular
circuits as follows:

1) Head, tail, stop (brake) and instrument
    panel lamps;

2) Clearance lamps and any lamp in or
    adjacent to step risers;

3) Interior lamps;

4) Starter motor;

5) Ignition, emergency exit alarm signals
    and other alarm signals;

6) Turn signal lamps;

7) Alternately flashing signal lamps and
    stop signal arm lamps;

8) Horn;

9) Heater and defroster.

A separate fuse or circuit breaker for each
circuit, except starter motor and ignition.

REJECT VEHICLE IF:

Breaks in insulation are present. Not on
proper circuit or properly wired.

2) Fuses

PROCEDURES/SPECIFICATIONS:

Two extra fuses for each size fuse used on the
bus shall be conveniently mounted on the
bus body.

REJECT VEHICLE IF:

DEPARTMENT OF TRANSPORTATION

NOTICE OF ADOPTED RULES

Fuses are not present or are not conveniently
mounted.

3) Switches

PROCEDURES/SPECIFICATIONS:

Check operation and condition.

REJECT VEHICLE IF:

Switches are not operating properly or are
missing.

4) Wiring

PROCEDURES/SPECIFICATIONS:

All wires shall be properly insulated and
securely attached at not more than 18.1
inches (460 mm) intervals. Check condition.

REJECT VEHICLE IF:

Insulation is frayed or missing. Wiring not
securely attached.

b) EMERGENCY
   EXITS

PROCEDURES/SPECIFICATIONS:

All buses must be equipped with either a rear
emergency door or a left side emergency door
and a rear emergency window. 49 CFR 571.217

Additional emergency exits, including roof
hatches, may be required on buses
manufactured on or after May 2, 1994. (57
FR 49413, November 2, 1992); as amended
at 59 FR 22997, May 4, 1994

For those buses manufactured on or after May
2, 1994, each opening for a required emergency
exit must be outlined around its outside
perimeter with a minimum 1 inch (2.54 cm) wide
yellow retroreflective tape. This yellow
retroreflective tape must be on the
exterior surface of the bus. (57 FR 49413,

DEPARTMENT OF TRANSPORTATION

NOTICE OF ADOPTED RULES

November 2, 1992)

Optional emergency roof hatches are allowed.
They must be installed according to
manufacturer's recommendations and no alarm
is required. Open and close roof hatches
(required or optional) to verify their
operation.

REJECT VEHICLE IF:

Emergency exits do not meet requirements.
Roof hatches do not open.

1) Side

PROCEDURES/SPECIFICATIONS:

Shall be hinged on front side and open
outward. Shall be equipped with safety glass
(or equivalent). Glass shall be located
in upper portion of the door. Door shall be
of at least the same gauge metal as the body.
Shall be 24 inches or more clear
horizontal opening, with forward edge of
opening in line with the rearmost edge of a
seat back. Shall have 45 inches or more
clear vertical opening. (See Alarms and
Locks in this subsection for requirements.)

REJECT VEHICLE IF:

Release mechanism is not protected,
accessible, or operable (inside and outside);
unable to open easily; hinge is located
at incorrect location; location and size of
opening is incorrect.

2) Rear

PROCEDURES/SPECIFICATIONS:

Inside release mechanism must be protected
against accidental release; readily
accessible;
operated manually without use of remote
control, power device, or tool.

Shall have permanently attached inside and

DEPARTMENT OF TRANSPORTATION

NOTICE OF ADOPTED RULES

outside release handles. Outside release
handle must be non-hitchable.

Rear exit shall hinge on right; open outwards;
have a 24 inch or more clear horizontal
opening and 45 inch or more clear vertical
opening above floor. Glazing shall be
installed in upper and lower portions. (See
Alarms and Locks in this subsection for
requirements.)

Exception: Buses manufactured before
September 1974 are exempt from glazing in
lower portion of rear emergency door.

REJECT VEHICLE IF:

Inside release mechanism is not protected.
Inside and outside release mechanisms are not
accessible or do not operate properly.
Outside release mechanism is hitchable. Door
does not open easily. Location of hinge
is incorrect. Size of opening is incorrect.
Glazing does not meet requirements. General
condition of door (rubber and seal) is poor.

3) Emergency
Window

PROCEDURES/SPECIFICATIONS:

When the emergency door is located on the left
side, a rear emergency window shall be
provided. Minimum 16 inches high and 48
inches wide. Designed to be opened from the
inside or the outside. Hinged on top,
designed and operated to insure against
accidental closing in an emergency. Inside
handle shall provide for quick release.
Outside handle shall be nondetachable and
nonhitchable. (See Alarms and Locks in this
subsection for requirements.)

Optional emergency windows are allowed. They
must be labelled "Emergency Exit" in letters
at least two inches high, of a color that
contrasts with its background, located at the
top of or directly above the window on
the inside surface of the bus.

DEPARTMENT OF TRANSPORTATION

NOTICE OF ADOPTED RULES

REJECT VEHICLE IF:

Operating mechanisms do not function. Glass
is cracked or broken.

4) Alarms and
   Locks   PROCEDURES/SPECIFICATIONS:

Audible and visual alarms shall alert driver
when engine is running and any required
emergency exit or optional emergency exit
door either:

1)   Is not fully latched, or

2)   Is locked and not readily operated
     manually.

Optional emergency exit windows must be
equipped with an audible alarm which is
activated when the above criteria is met.

The engine starting system shall not operate
while any emergency exit (optional or
required) is locked from either inside or
outside the bus. "Locked" means that the
release mechanism cannot be activated and
the exit opened by a person at the exit
without a special device such as a key or
special information such as a combination.

Alarm cut-off or "squelch" control is
prohibited.

Exception: On a bus with chassis (incomplete
vehicle) manufactured in March 1977 or
earlier, the "not fully latched" alarm may
only be audible to the seated driver. The
engine starting system may operate while the
emergency door is locked.

REJECT VEHICLE IF:

Alarms do not alert driver as required. Locks
do not meet requirements.

c) ENTRANCE DOOR

DEPARTMENT OF TRANSPORTATION

NOTICE OF ADOPTED RULES

1) Physical
   Requirements

PROCEDURES/SPECIFICATIONS:

Minimum 24 inch horizontal opening. Minimum
68 inch vertical opening. Jack-knife or split
type door required on buses purchased
after September 1974. If split type door is
used and one section opens inward and the
other outward, front section shall open
outward. Door shall be located on the right
side near the front convenient to the seated
driver's unobstructed vision. Entrance door
shall be power or manually operated from the
driver's seat and designed to afford easy
release and prevent accidental opening. No
parts of the over center door control shall
come together so as to sheer or crush fingers.
The over center door control must
operate properly and must not bind or jam.
Vertical closing edges shall be equipped with
flexible material for a proper seal and to
prevent injury. Lower and upper panels of
door shall be of safety glass or equivalent.
Bottom of lower panel shall be not more than
35 inches from ground when unloaded. Top of
upper glass panel shall be not more than 6
inches from top of door. No door is
permitted to left of driver.

A service door equipped with power shall also
be capable of manual operation in case of
power failure.

Exception: All buses purchased prior to
September 1974 are exempt from split type
door. They may be split, sedan, or
jack-knife type.

REJECT VEHICLE IF:

Binding or jamming is evident, malfunctions,
over-ride device on power operated door does
not function, control not accessible by driver.

Door is missing, loose, or damaged. Rubber
seal is missing or torn.

DEPARTMENT OF TRANSPORTATION

NOTICE OF ADOPTED RULES

2) Locks and
   Alarms

PROCEDURES/SPECIFICATIONS:

A service door lock is not required, but if
any type of service door locking system is
installed on the bus, the system shall
conform to at least one of the following:

1)   The locking system shall not be capable
     of preventing the driver from easily and
     quickly opening the service door from
     inside the vehicle; or

2)   A locking system that is capable of
     preventing the bus driver from easily
     and quickly opening the service door
     shall include an audiovisual alarm.
     The alarm shall be audible and visible
     and must alert the driver when the engine
     is running and the service door is
     locked. An alarm disconnect, "squelch
     control," or other alarm defeating or
     weakening device shall be prohibited.

REJECT VEHICLE IF:

Locks and alarms do not meet requirements.
Bent, worn, or dislocated parts that would
delay quick door release and opening are
present.

d) EXHAUST
   SYSTEM

PROCEDURES/SPECIFICATIONS:

"Exhaust System" includes each component used
to conduct gas from an engine exhaust port
(manifold) to authorized exit point,
including each sealing, connecting, and
supporting component. Exhaust system shall
be outside body and attached to chassis. Size
of tailpipe shall not be reduced after it
leaves muffler. Any flexible component
that contains exhaust gas shall be of
stainless steel. System shall not leak.
System shall have an outlet at its discharge
end(s) only.

DEPARTMENT OF TRANSPORTATION

NOTICE OF ADOPTED RULES

1) Shielding

PROCEDURES/SPECIFICATIONS:

Any flammable material, electrical insulation,
brake hose, or fuel system component
containing fuel that is located within 11
13/16 inches (300 mm) of a component
containing exhaust gas shall be safeguarded
by a heat shield.

Exhaust system shall be shielded from either
accidental contact, "hitching to," or
"standing on," except at discharge end. A
chassis or body component may provide required
shield.

Exception: Fuel system components on diesel
powered engines that are located within four
inches of a component containing exhaust gas
shall be shielded.

REJECT VEHICLE IF:

Shielding is not present (if applicable).

2) Discharge

PROCEDURES/SPECIFICATIONS:

The exhaust system's discharge end (tailpipe)
shall be within .98 inch (25 mm) of bus side,
rear, or rear corner. It must not extend past
a side rub rail or more than one inch
past the bumper. Gas shall not be directed
towards a door or other opening into bus
body. In addition, the discharge end, or
ends, shall not be located in any prohibited
zone shown in Illustration B.

REJECT VEHICLE IF:

All parts of system are not securely fastened
and supported.

Any part is leaking, missing, or patched.

Any part contains holes not made by

DEPARTMENT OF TRANSPORTATION

NOTICE OF ADOPTED RULES

manufacturer. Exhaust discharges into
prohibited zones (see Illustration B).

e) FENDERS

PROCEDURES/SPECIFICATIONS:

Shall be properly braced and free from any
body attachment.

There shall be approximately one inch located
between front fenders and back face to cowl.

REJECT VEHICLE IF:

Fenders are not solid or in bad condition.

Sharp edges are evident.

Fenders are loose or protrude out.

DEPARTMENT OF TRANSPORTATION

NOTICE OF ADOPTED RULES

Section 441.APPENDIX B Filter, Oil Through Frame and Body

a) FILTER, OIL

PROCEDURES/SPECIFICATIONS:

Replaceable element or cartridge type.
Minimum one-quart capacity.

REJECT VEHICLE IF:

Oil filter leaks or does not meet requirements.

b) FIRE
EXTINGUISHER

PROCEDURES/SPECIFICATIONS:

Pressurized dry-chemical gauge type approved
by Underwriters' Laboratories. Inc., rating of
not less than 10 B.C. mounted in bracket
and readily accessible. Sealed with a type of
seal that will not interfere with
operation. If stored in locked compartment,
compartment must be labelled. Halon fire
extinguishers (10 B.C.) are approved.

REJECT VEHICLE IF:

Gauge does not indicate in the calibrated or
marked "Full Charge" area. Seal is broken.
Extinguisher is not mounted, not in a quick
release holder or not labelled in compartment,
if applicable. Improper rating. Missing.

c) FIRST AID KIT

PROCEDURES/SPECIFICATIONS:

Kit shall be readily identifiable, removable,
and mounted in readily accessible place in
driver's compartment -- either in full view
or in specified secured compartment (see
LOCKED COMPARTMENT). If not carried in
compartment, the case shall be dust
tight and substantially constructed
of durable material. The contents
shall include, but not be limited
to, the following:

DEPARTMENT OF TRANSPORTATION

NOTICE OF ADOPTED RULES

Unit Type (Minimum Contents)

4" bandage compress - 2 packages (May be 1
package in bus with chassis [incomplete
vehicle] manufactured in March 1977 or
earlier.)

2" bandage compress - 2 packages (May be 1
package in bus with chassis [incomplete
vehicle] manufactured in March 1977 or
earlier.)

1" bandage or adhesive compress - 1 package

40" triangle bandage with two safety pins - 1

Splint, wire or wood - 1

A tourniquet or any type of ointment,
antiseptic, or other medicine shall not be
included.

AGENCY NOTE: OSHA approved blood-borne pathogen kits are
                 permitted.

REJECT VEHICLE IF:

Kit is not complete. Dust or other visible
dirt is present inside case. Minimum number
of individual packages are not sealed.
Medicine or tourniquet is present. Locked
compartment containing kit is not labelled.
Not mounted in readily accessible location.
Missing.

d) FLOORS AND
   FLOOR
   COVERING

PROCEDURES/SPECIFICATIONS:

Covering in underseat area, including tops of
wheel housings, driver's compartment, and
toeboard shall be covered with fire-resistant
floor covering of type commonly used in
passenger transportation equipment. The floor
covering in the aisle and entrance area
shall be a nonskid, wear-resistant,
fire-resistant, and rib type commonly used in commercial

DEPARTMENT OF TRANSPORTATION

NOTICE OF ADOPTED RULES

passenger transportation vehicles. Covering
and metal floor stripping must be permanently
bonded to floor and must not crack when
subjected to sudden changes in temperature.
Bonding or adhesive material shall be
waterproof. All seams must be sealed with
waterproof sealer.

All openings in floorboard or firewall between
chassis and passenger-carrying
compartment must be solid and sealed.

Boots and seals around shift levers and
emergency brakes must be secure and solidly
attached.

REJECT VEHICLE IF:

Abnormal wear and obstructions are present.
Holes or openings are present in floors, floor
covering, or boots. Metal floor stripping
is not securely attached or broken.

e) FRAME AND
   BODY

PROCEDURES/SPECIFICATIONS:

Visually inspect:

1)   Body mounts shall be attached and sealed
     to the chassis cowl so as to prevent the
     entry of water, dust or fumes through the
     joint between the chassis cowl and
     the body.

2)   Cross members and mounting bolts.

3)   Engine mounting bolts.

4)   Frame shall extend to rear of body cross
     member.

5)   Frame extension is permitted when
     alterations are behind rear hanger or
     rear springs and not for the purpose of
     extending wheel base.

6)   Collision damage which is detrimental to
     the safe operation of the vehicle.

DEPARTMENT OF TRANSPORTATION

NOTICE OF ADOPTED RULES

REJECT VEHICLE IF:

1) Cracked, loose, missing bolts. Any
    repair done by welding body to frame.
    Insulation strip missing.

2) Loose, cracked, broken or missing.

3) Missing, loose.

4) Cracked, broken, bent, rusted to a depth
    as to substantially weaken frame -
    welding except by body manufacturer.

5) Unless permitted, frame extends past
    wheel base.

6) Collision damage which is detrimental to
    the safe operation of the vehicle.

DEPARTMENT OF TRANSPORTATION

NOTICE OF ADOPTED RULES

Section 441.APPENDIX F   Fuel Storage and Delivery System Through Horn

a) FUEL STORAGE
   AND DELIVERY
   SYSTEM   PROCEDURES/SPECIFICATIONS:

                   Entire fuel system, except extensions for
                   driver control of air or fuel, must be
                   outside passenger and driver compartment.

                   REJECT VEHICLE IF:

                   Any part of fuel system, except extensions for
                   driver control of air or fuel, is within
                   passenger/driver compartment.

1) Fuel Filler
   Cap   PROCEDURES/SPECIFICATIONS:

                   Meets manufacturer's specifications. Must be
                   the same as or equivalent to original
                   equipment.

                   REJECT VEHICLE IF:

                   Fuel filler cap is defective or missing.

2) Fuel Lines   PROCEDURES/SPECIFICATIONS:

                   Firmly attached. No leakage, seepage,
                   abrasion, or chafing. Must be 11 13/16
                   inches (300 mm) from any part of exhaust
                   system that contains exhaust gas or be
                   safeguarded by a heat shield. Inside engine
                   compartment, the chassis manufacturer's
                   standard shall govern separation and shielding
                   between parts designed by chassis
                   manufacturer.

                   Exception: Fuel system components on diesel
                   powered engines that are located within four
                   inches of a component containing exhaust gas
                   must be shielded.

                   REJECT VEHICLE IF:

                   Fuel lines are cracked, leaking, insecure
                   mounting, damaged, clamps missing, mount

DEPARTMENT OF TRANSPORTATION

NOTICE OF ADOPTED RULES

clips missing or not separated or not
shielded properly (if applicable).

3) Fuel Filler
   Tube   PROCEDURES/SPECIFICATIONS:

   Check condition.

   REJECT VEHICLE IF:

   Fuel filler tube leaks or is not secure.

4) Fuel Pump   PROCEDURES/SPECIFICATIONS:

   Check condition.

   REJECT VEHICLE IF:

   Fuel pump leaks, is damaged or is not secure.

5) Fuel
   Tank(s)   PROCEDURES/SPECIFICATIONS:

   Tank must be safeguarded by structure that
   protects from side or angular impact blows.
   49 CFR 571.301

   Exception: A bus with chassis (incomplete
   vehicle) manufactured in March 1977 or
   earlier is exempt from being equipped with a
   tank guard structure.

   REJECT VEHICLE IF:

   Fuel tank(s) have leakage, seepage, or
   abrasion; hole or crack that would leak or
   seep when tank is full.

6) Fuel tank
   mount(s)   PROCEDURES/SPECIFICATIONS:

   Check condition.

   REJECT VEHICLE IF:

   Fuel tank mount(s) are cracked, loose, or
   bolts are missing.

DEPARTMENT OF TRANSPORTATION

NOTICE OF ADOPTED RULES

7) Fuel tank
   straps   PROCEDURES/SPECIFICATIONS:

   Check condition.

   REJECT VEHICLE IF:

   Fuel tank straps are cracked, loose, or
   missing.

8) Alternate
   Fuel Systems
   (LPG or CNG)
               An alternate fuel system which is no
               longer in use must be completely removed
               from the vehicle.

   A) Carburetion
      Equipment
               A fuel filter is required on alternate
               fuel systems.

   B) Container
      Installation

               i)   Compressed or liquefied gas containers
                     shall not be mounted in the passenger or
                     driver's compartment.

               ii)   Container valves, appurtenances and
                     connections shall be mounted in an
                     enclosed compartment.

               iii) Containers shall be located at least 36
                     inches from the entrance door and any
                     emergency exit. Due to the smaller
                     size of Type II school buses, space
                     limitations may sometimes make it
                     impossible to locate a fuel tank
                     further than 36 inches from an exit. A
                     Type II school bus has a gross vehicle
                     weight rating of 10,000 pounds or less as
                     defined in Section 12-800 of
                     the Illinois Vehicle Equipment Law (625
                     ILCS 5/12-800]. If the original fuel
                     tank for a Type II bus was located
                     within 36 inches from any exit, the
                     alternate fuel container may be located

AMW"

DEPARTMENT OF TRANSPORTATION

NOTICE OF ADOPTED RULES

in the same location as the original tank.

C) Identification

The fuel identification decal (see Section 441.Illustration E) shall be displayed on the rear of the school bus not more than 12 inches above the top of the rear bumper and within 39 inches of the left side. The decal shall not be placed on any black portion of the bus body.

D) Pipe and Hose Installation

i) No fuel supply line shall pass through the driver or passenger's compartment.

ii) The pressure relief device shall be fabricated so that in the event of stress, the pipe or adaptor will break away without impairing the function of the relief valve.

iii) If installed, the adaptor connecting the piping system to the pressure relief device shall neither touch nor restrict any movable part of the pressure relief valve.

iv) The relief valve discharge piping system (piping system) must not be reduced at any point from the relief valve to the point of release into the atmosphere.

v) The piping system shall be routed to minimize sharp elbows or bends. Installation of any commercially available piping installed to meet the manufacturer's specifications is acceptable. Any fittings that restrict the flow of discharge are prohibited. From the pressure relief device adaptor to the atmosphere, the minimum inside diameter of the piping must measure at least 3/4 of an inch.

DEPARTMENT OF TRANSPORTATION

NOTICE OF ADOPTED RULES

vi) The piping system shall neither block nor hamper the operation of any window or door. The piping system shall preserve widths of passageways, aisles and emergency exits.

vii) Every portion of the piping system shall be gas tight (except the outlet) and shall be able to withstand forces from the discharge when the relief valve is in full open position. If for any reason the discharge outlet becomes blocked, the piping system must be capable of holding the full system pressure.

viii) To facilitate the removal of accumulated water, a drain cock shall be installed at the lowest point of the piping system. The drain must be capable of being held open manually and close automatically to prevent expelling LPG if discharged through the relief valve. A weep hole, or other opening that may result in discharged LPG flaming beneath the bus is prohibited.

ix) The portion of the piping system that leads upward to the atmosphere shall be installed either inside the passenger compartment, on the outside of the bus, or in the body wall between the inner and outer "skins" of the bus body.

x) Piping on the outside of the body shall be shielded below the window line to prevent "grabbing hold" or "hitching to." However, discharge piping that is located between the windshield and the vent window at the left front corner of the body need not be shielded.

xi) Any portion of the piping system that is installed either inside the passenger compartment or inside the body wall shall consist of one piece originating below the bus floor and exiting outside

DEPARTMENT OF TRANSPORTATION

NOTICE OF ADOPTED RULES

the bus roof. Every hole where piping
passes through the floor or roof shall be
sealed.

xii) The piping system must terminate above
the eave lines of the bus body.

xiii) The outlet of the piping system shall be
located at least 36 inches from the air
inlet or outlet of a ventilator or
similar device installed on or near the
roof. A "similar device" includes the
fresh air intake of a heating,
ventilating or air conditioning system.
It does not include a side window that
opens near the roof.

xiv) A rain cap is required where the piping
system exits into the atmosphere to
minimize water or dirt from entering
into either the relief valve or its
discharge piping. Installation of any
commercially available rain cap
installed to meet the manufacturer's
specifications is acceptable. The cap
shall remain in place except when the
relief valve operates. The cap shall
be installed to minimize the entrance of
water or dirt while the vehicle is in
motion.

xv) The discharge piping system on a special
education school bus shall conform to all
provisions of this Part.

REJECT VEHICLE IF:

Alternate fuel system does not meet
requirements listed above.

b) GRAB HANDLES

1) Exterior

POCEDURES/SPECIFICATIONS:

At least one step grab handle shall be located
on each side at front of body so as to

DEPARTMENT OF TRANSPORTATION

NOTICE OF ADOPTED RULES

provide easy access to windshield.

REJECT VEHICLE IF:

Exterior grab handles are missing or loose.

2) Interior

PROCEDURES/SPECIFICATIONS:

Stainless clad steel with measurements not
less than 10 inches long located in
unobstructed location inside doorway.

REJECT VEHICLE IF:

Interior grab handles are missing or are not
solidly attached.

c) HEATERS

PROCEDURES/SPECIFICATIONS:

Nameplate must identify manufacturer and
heater rating capacity. Must be capable of
maintaining inside temperature of 50 degrees.
The heater hoses shall be supported to
guard against excessive wear due to vibration
and shall not interfere with or restrict the
operation of any engine function. Any hose in
the passenger compartment shall be
protected to prevent injury from burns in the
event of rupture. If heater is not
protected by a seat, it must be padded.

REJECT VEHICLE IF:

Heater is missing; in poor working condition;
defective hoses, supports or baffles; not
firmly attached or not padded when required.

d) HOOD

PROCEDURES/SPECIFICATIONS:

Open hood and inspect safety catch and hinges
for proper operation. Close hood and inspect
for proper full closure. Manually inspect

latches or remote control for proper operation.

REJECT VEHICLE IF:

Hood does not open or hood latches do not securely hold hood in its proper fully-closed position. Secondary or safety catch does not function properly. Hinge is broken, missing, or not attached to body.

e) HORN

PROCEDURES/SPECIFICATIONS:

At least one horn shall be provided giving an audible warning at a distance of 200 feet and shall be conveniently controlled from the operator's seated position. (Section 12-601 of the Illinois Vehicle Equipment Law)

REJECT VEHICLE IF:

Horn control is missing, defective or not audible.

Section 441.APPENDIX G   Instruments and Instrument Panel Through Locked Compartment

a) INSTRUMENTS
   AND INSTRUMENT
   PANEL

PROCEDURES/SPECIFICATIONS:

Shall be equipped with the following nonglare illuminated instruments and gauges mounted for easy maintenance and repair and in such a manner that each is clearly visible to the seated driver. An indicator light instead of a pressure or temperature gauge is permissable. 49 CFR 571.101

1) Speedometer;
2) Odometer;
3) Fuel Gauge;
4) Oil Pressure Gauge;
5) Water Temperature Gauge;
6) Ammeter with graduated charge and discharge indications;
7) High beam headlight indicator;
8) Directional signal indicator;
9) Air pressure or vacuum gauge (when air or vacuum brakes are used);
10) Eight light flasher indicator.;
11) Emergency/service brake indicator.

REJECT VEHICLE IF:

Instruments or instrument panel do not operate properly; instruments are missing; inaccurate readings.

b) INSULATION

PROCEDURES/SPECIFICATIONS:

The ceiling and sidewalls shall be thermally insulated with a fire-resistant material which shall reduce the noise level and vibrations.

REJECT VEHICLE IF:

Insulation does not meet requirements.

DEPARTMENT OF TRANSPORTATION

NOTICE OF ADOPTED RULES

c) LETTERING

I) Exterior   PROCEDURES/SPECIFICATIONS:

The body and chassis manufacturer's name,
emblem, or other identification may be
displayed (colorless or any color) on any
unglazed surface of the bus.

AGENCY NOTE: School buses with interstate
authority may display the company's name,
city and state of its base and the interstate
"MC" number. This lettering must be
black in color.

REJECT VEHICLE IF:

Exterior lettering does not meet requirements.
Lettering or decals are not distinct,   .
required or allowed. Lettering is obstructed.

A) Front

PROCEDURES/SPECIFICATIONS:

*"SCHOOL BUS" in black at least eight inches
(200 mm) high placed as high as possible on
body or sign attached thereto. Vehicle number
assigned for identification shall be a
minimum of four inches (100 mm) high and
located as high as practicable. Decals are
permissable. All lettering must be black.*
(Section 12-802 of the Illinois Vehicle
Equipment Law)

REJECT VEHICLE IF:

Lettering does not meet requirements.
Lettering is not distinct, required or
allowed. Lettering is obstructed.

B) Left

PROCEDURES/SPECIFICATIONS:

*Either the owner's name or the school district
number or both must be at least four
inches high, approximately centered and as
high as practicable below window line.*
(Section 12-802 of the Illinois Vehicle

DEPARTMENT OF TRANSPORTATION

NOTICE OF ADOPTED RULES

Equipment Law) The above required lettering
must be located on one line.

If the bus is equipped with a side emergency
door, it must be labelled "EMERGENCY EXIT" in
letters at least two inches high directly at
the top of the emergency door, or directly
above, or on door glazing.

Optional: Vehicle number assigned for
identification may be displayed at a minimum
height of four inches (100 mm).

Decals are permissable. All lettering must be
black.

For buses manufactured on or after May 2, :
1994, "EMERGENCY DOOR" in letters at least
1.95 inches (5 cm) high must be located at
the top of, or directly above, any emergency
exit door. For any emergency window exit,
"EMERGENCY EXIT" must be located at the top
of, or directly above, or at the bottom of
the emergency window exit in letters at least
1.95 inches (5 cm) high. The labelling must
be of a color that contrasts with its
background. (57 FR 49413, November 2, 1992)

REJECT VEHICLE IF:

Lettering does not meet requirements.
Lettering is not distinct, required, or
allowed. Lettering is obstructed.

C) Rear

PROCEDURES/SPECIFICATIONS:

*"SCHOOL BUS" in black lettering at least eight
inches (200 mm) high placed as high as
possible on body or sign attached thereto.*
(Section 12-802 of the Illinois Vehicle
Equipment Law) "EMERGENCY DOOR" or
"EMERGENCY EXIT" in lettering at least two
inches high at top of emergency door, or
directly above, or on door glazing.

"EMERGENCY EXIT" (for buses without rear
emergency door) in letters at least two

GALLO"

DEPARTMENT OF TRANSPORTATION

NOTICE OF ADOPTED RULES

inches high directly below rear emergency window, or on exit glazing. An arrow, at least 5.9 inches in length and 3/4 inch in width indicating direction each release mechanism should be turned to open door or window located within 5.9 inches of release handle, in black. Vehicle number assigned for identification shall be a minimum 4 inches (100 mm) high. Decals are permissible. All lettering must be black.

If bus uses alternate fuel (e.g., propane, CNG), vehicle must be marked with identifying decal. Such decal shall be diamond shaped with white or silver scotchlite letters one inch in height and a stroke of the brush at least 1/4 inch wide on a black background with a white or silver scotchlite border bearing either the words or letters:

"PROPANE" = If propelled by liquefied petroleum gas other than liquefied natural gas; or

"CNG" = If propelled by compressed natural gas. The sign or decal shall be maintained in good legible condition.

The alternate fuel decal shall be displayed near the rear bumper and visible from the rear of vehicle. (see Appendix 6 (a)(8)) (Section 12-704.3 of the Illinois Vehicle Equipment Law)

For buses manufactured on or after May 2, 1994, "EMERGENCY DOOR" in letters at least 1.95 inches (5 cm) high must be located at the top of, or directly above, any emergency exit door. For any emergency window exit, "EMERGENCY EXIT" must be located at the top of, or directly above, or at the bottom of the emergency window exit in letters at least 1.95 inches (5 cm) high. The labelling must be of a color that contrasts with its background. (57 FR 49413, November 2, 1992)

REJECT VEHICLE IF:

DEPARTMENT OF TRANSPORTATION

NOTICE OF ADOPTED RULES

Lettering does not meet requirements. Lettering or arrows are not distinct, required, or allowed. Lettering is obstructed.

Buses using alternate fuels are not properly marked with decal. Decal is in wrong location.

D) Right

PROCEDURES/SPECIFICATIONS:

Either the owner's name or the school district number or both must be at least four inches (100 mm) high, approximately centered and as high as possible below window line. (Section 12-802 of the Illinois Vehicle Equipment Law) The above required lettering must be located on one line.

The following lettering must be at least two inches (50 mm) high:

1. *The word "CAPACITY," or abbreviation "CAP.," and the rated passenger capacity followed by the word "PASSENGERS," or the abbreviation "PASS.," shall be displayed on the outside of the body near the rear edge of the service entrance.*

2. *Empty weight in pounds must be shown. Empty weight is indicated by "EW."* (Section 12-802 of the Illinois Vehicle Equipment Law)

Manufacturer's identification name or emblem may be displayed, but not on service door glazing. Manufacturer's name or emblem must not interfere with required lettering. Decals are permissible. All lettering must be black.

Optional route identification markers (numbers or symbols) are allowed. They must be located in either the first window or on the bus body directly behind the service entrance door. Route markers affixed to the bus body must meet paint requirements and must not

obscure any required lettering.

For buses manufactured on or after May 2, 1994, "EMERGENCY DOOR" in letters at least 1.95 inches (5 cm) high must be located at the top of, or directly above, any emergency exit door. For any emergency window exit "EMERGENCY EXIT" must be located at the top of, or at the bottom of the emergency window exit in letters at least 1.95 inches (5 cm) high. The labelling must be of a color that contrasts with its background. [57 PA 49413, November 2r 1992]

REJECT VEHICLE IF:

Lettering does not meet requirements. Lettering or decals are not distinct, required, or allowed. Lettering is obstructed.

2) Interior:

A) Front:

PROCEDURES/SPECIFICATIONS:

Each letter or numeral must be at least two inches (50 mm) high and contrasting sharply with background. A colorless background strip may be used. Decals are permitted.

On right side: Either "CAPACITY" or "CAP." plus numerals showing rated passenger capacity, followed by either "PASSENGER" or "PASS."

As nearly as practicable opposite the center of aisle, but to right of inside mirror, either "NO STANDEES" or "NO STANDEES PERMITTED."

A red cross formed of five equal squares with words "FIRST-AID KIT" shall be displayed on the compartment door, or cover, if the first-aid kit is to be carried in the locked compartment.

The words "FIRE EXTINGUISHER" shall be displayed on the compartment door, or cover, if the fire extinguisher is to be carried in the locked compartment.

Exception: On a bus with chassis (incomplete vehicle) manufactured in March 1977 or earlier, "NO STANDEES" need not be opposite center of aisle and the word "PASSENGERS," or "PASS.," is optional.

REJECT VEHICLE IF:

Lettering does not meet requirements. Lettering is not distinct, required or allowed. Lettering is obstructed.

B) Left:

PROCEDURES/SPECIFICATIONS:

A "Stop Line" in contrasting color is required between 5.9 and 6.1 inches below the top of the window opening. The line shall be located between each window that slides downward.

If bus is equipped with a side emergency door or emergency windows which are knock-out type, they are to be labelled "EMERGENCY EXIT" in letters at least two inches high directly below window.

An arrow indicating the direction in which to move release mechanism handle(s) to open emergency exit and operating instructions shall be painted or permanently affixed within six inches of each release handle.

For buses manufactured on or after May 2, 1994, "EMERGENCY DOOR" in letters at least 1.95 inches (5 cm) high must be located at the top of, or directly above, any emergency exit door. For any emergency window exit, "EMERGENCY EXIT" must be located at the top of, or directly above, or at the bottom of the emergency window exit in letters at least 1.95 inches (5 cm) high. The labelling must be of a color that contrasts with its

DEPARTMENT OF TRANSPORTATION

NOTICE OF ADOPTED RULES

background. Concise operating instructions
describing the motions necessary to unlatch
and open the door must be located within 5.85
inches (15 cm) of the release mechanism on the
inside surface of the bus. These operating
instructions shall be in letters at least
.39 inches (1 cm) high and of a color that
contrasts with its background. (57 FR 49413,
November 2, 1992)

REJECT VEHICLE IF:

Lettering does not meet requirements. Line or
line and lettering is not distinct,
required, or allowed. Lettering is
obstructed.

C) Rear

PROCEDURES/SPECIFICATIONS:

"EMERGENCY DOOR" or "EMERGENCY EXIT" in
letters at least two inches (50 mm) high
painted or permanently affixed either
directly above each emergency exit, or on
top metal of exit (door or window), or on top
of exit glazing. An arrow indicating the
direction in which to move release
mechanism handle(s) to open emergency exit
and operating instructions shall be painted
or permanently affixed within six inches of
each release handle. All lettering and
arrow(s) must contrast with background.
Decals are permitted.

For buses manufactured on or after May 2,
1994, "EMERGENCY DOOR" in letters at least
1.95 inches (5 cm) high must be located at the
top of, or directly above, any emergency
exit door. For any emergency window exit,
"EMERGENCY EXIT" must be located at the top
of, or directly above, or at the bottom of
the emergency window exit in letters at least
1.95 inches (5 cm) high. The labelling must
be of a color that contrasts with its
background. Concise operating instructions
describing the motions necessary to unlatch
and open the door must be located within 5.85
inches (15 cm) of the release mechanism on the

DEPARTMENT OF TRANSPORTATION

NOTICE OF ADOPTED RULES

inside surface of the bus. These
operating instructions shall be in letters at
least .39 inches (1 cm) high and of a
color that contrasts with its background.
(57 FR 49413, November 2, 1992)

REJECT VEHICLE IF:

Lettering does not meet requirements.
Lettering is not distinct, required, or
allowed. Lettering is obstructed.

D) Right

PROCEDURES/SPECIFICATIONS:

A "Stop line" in contrasting color is required
between 5.9 and 6.1 inches below the top
of the window opening. The line shall be
located between each window that slides
downward. Decals are permitted.

If emergency window is installed, "EMERGENCY
EXIT" shall be displayed on or immediately
below emergency window.

Instructions for emergency operation of a
power operated door shall be affixed
permanently on the inside of the door in
letters at least .5 (one half) inch high.
Decals are permitted.

Optional route identification markers (numbers
or symbols) are allowed. They must be
located in either the first window or on the
bus body directly behind the service entrance
door. If route identification markers are
installed in permanent holder or bracket,
the holder or bracket must have rounded edges
or be padded.

For buses manufactured on or after May 2,
1994, "EMERGENCY DOOR" in letters at least
1.95 inches (5 cm) high must be located at
the top of, or directly above, any side
emergency door. For any emergency window
exit "EMERGENCY EXIT" in letters at least
1.95 inches (5 cm) high must be located at
the top of, or directly above, or at the
bottom of the emergency window exit. The

DEPARTMENT OF TRANSPORTATION

NOTICE OF ADOPTED RULES

labelling must be of a color that contrasts
with its background. Concise operating
instructions describing the motions necessary
to unlatch and open the exit must be
located within 5.85 inches (15 cm) of the
release mechanism on the inside surface of
the bus. These instructions shall be in
letters at least .39 inches (1 cm) high and
of a color that contrasts with its background.
(57 FR 49413, November 2, 1992)

REJECT VEHICLE IF:

Right interior lettering does not meet
requirements. Line or line and lettering is
not distinct, required, or allowed.
Lettering is obstructed.

E) Ceiling

PROCEDURES/SPECIFICATIONS

For buses manufactured on or after May 2,
1994, any roof exit must be labelled
"EMERGENCY EXIT" in letters at least 1.95
inches (5 cm) high, of a color that contrasts
with its background. The labelling must
be located on an inside surface of the exit,
or within 11.7 inches (30 cm) of the roof exit
opening. Concise operating instructions
describing the motions necessary to unlatch
and open the emergency exit shall be located
within 5.85 inches (15 cm) of the release
mechanism. These instructions shall be in
letters at least .39 inches (1 cm) high and
of a color that contrasts with its background.
(57 FR 49413, November 2, 1992)

d) LIGHTS

1) Back Up

PROCEDURES/SPECIFICATIONS:

Two white lights shall be provided. Must meet
federal standards. 49 CFR 571.108

Exception: All buses purchased prior to
September 1974 are exempt; however, for any
unit equipped with back up lamps, they must be

DEPARTMENT OF TRANSPORTATION

NOTICE OF ADOPTED RULES

operational.

REJECT VEHICLE IF:

Back-up lights do not function; illegal color;
broken lens.

2) Clearance,
   Front   PROCEDURES/SPECIFICATIONS:

Two clearance lights (amber) at highest and
widest portions of the body. Must conform to
federal standards. 49 CFR 571.108   May be
combined with side marker lamp.

REJECT VEHICLE IF:

Front clearance lights do not function;
improper color; broken lens.

3) Clearance,
   Rear   PROCEDURES/SPECIFICATIONS:

Two clearance lights (red) mounted at highest
and widest parts of body. Must conform to
federal standards. 49 CFR 571.108

REJECT VEHICLE IF:

Rear clearance lights do not function;
improper color; broken lens.

4) Identification,
   Front   PROCEDURES/SPECIFICATIONS:

Three amber lights mounted at center front
near top of body above "SCHOOL BUS" sign.
Must conform to federal standards. 49 CFR
571.108

REJECT VEHICLE IF:

Front cluster lights do not function properly;
improper color; broken lens.

5) Identification,
   Rear   PROCEDURES/SPECIFICATIONS:

DEPARTMENT OF TRANSPORTATION

NOTICE OF ADOPTED RULES

Three red lights mounted at center rear near
top of body either above or below "SCHOOL BUS"
sign. Must conform to federal standards.
49 CFR 571.108

REJECT VEHICLE IF:

Rear cluster lights do not function properly;
improper color; broken lens.

6) Flashing   PROCEDURES/SPECIFICATIONS:
Lights

*All school buses purchased after December 31,
1975, shall be equipped with an eight light
flashing signal system with two red and two
amber flashing signal lamps mounted above
windshield spaced no less than three feet
apart and at same horizontal level. The
rear of the vehicle shall be equipped with
two red and two amber flashing signal lamps
mounted and spaced no less than three feet
apart and at same horizontal level. Minimum
diameter 5 1/2 inch sealed beam.*

*Effective December 31, 1978, all school buses
shall be equipped with the eight light
flashing signal system described in the above
paragraph. (Section 12-805 of the
Illinois Vehicle Equipment Law)*

A separate circuit breaker and a master switch
shall be provided for this signal system.
When in its "off" position this master
switch shall prevent the following:

1) Operation of the 8 lamp system;

2) Operation of any lamps mounted on the
stop signal arm;

3) Operation of any electrically controlled
mechanism that would cause the stop
signal arm to extend.

The controls for the eight lamp flashing
signals, the stop signal arm and the service
entrance door shall be arranged so as to

DEPARTMENT OF TRANSPORTATION

NOTICE OF ADOPTED RULES

provide for the following sequence of
operations while the engine is running.

1) Place the alternately flashing signal
system master switch in its "off"
position. Close and secure the service
entrance door. Actuate the
alternately flashing signal system hand
or foot control. The alternately
flashing signal lamps of either yellow
(amber) or red color shall not go on.

2) With the master switch "off" and the hand
or foot control actuated, open the
service door. The alternately flashing
signals of either color shall not go on
and the stop signal arm shall not extend.

3) Deactivate the hand or foot control.
Place the alternately flashing signal
system master switch in its "on"
position. Open the service door. The
alternately flashing signal lamps of
either color and stop signal arm shall
signal arm shall not extend.

4) Close and secure the service door.
Actuate the alternately flashing signal
system by hand or foot control. A
yellow pilot lamp in the view of the
driver and the yellow alternately
flashing signals shall go on.

5) Desecure but do not open the service
door. The yellow pilot and the yellow
alternately flashing signals shall go
off. A red pilot lamp in the view of
the driver and the red alternately
flashing signals shall go on. The stop
signal arm shall extend.

6) Fully open the service door. The red
pilot and red signals shall remain on
and the stop arm shall remain extended.

7) Close but do not secure the service door.
The red pilot and red signals shall

DEPARTMENT OF TRANSPORTATION

NOTICE OF ADOPTED RULES

remain on and the stop arm shall
remain extended.

8)   Open the service door. The red pilot and
red signals shall remain on and the
stop arm remain extended.

9)   Close and secure the service door. The
red pilot and red signals shall go off ·
and the stop arm shall retract.

10)   Open the service door. Alternately
flashing signals of either color shall
not go on and the stop arm shall not
extend.

REJECT VEHICLE IF:

Flashing Lights do not function properly;
broken lens or improper lens color.

7) Headlights   PROCEDURES/SPECIFICATIONS:

Shall have at least two headlamps with at least
one mounted on each side of the front of the bus.
Lamp body must be securely attached.
Lenses, reflectors, bulbs, etc., must be in
good condition, properly aimed and fill
required intensity. Check for bulb burn out.
Verify high and low beams are
functioning. Shall conform to federal
standards. 49 CFR 571.108

REJECT VEHICLE IF:

Headlights do not meet requirements.

8) Interior   PROCEDURES/SPECIFICATIONS:

Adequate to illuminate aisles, step well, and
emergency passageways.

REJECT VEHICLE IF:

Interior lights do not provide adequate
lighting; cracked or broken lenses; improper
color.

DEPARTMENT OF TRANSPORTATION

NOTICE OF ADOPTED RULES

9) License Plate
PROCEDURES/SPECIFICATIONS:

Adequate white light to illuminate license
plate. 49 CFR 571.108 May be combined with
one of the tail lights.

REJECT VEHICLE IF:

License plate light does not provide adequate
lighting; cracked or broken lenses; improper
color.

10) Parking
Lights   PROCEDURES/SPECIFICATIONS:

Shall be one lamp on each side; white or amber
color. 49 CFR 571.108

All buses 80 or more inches in overall width
which are equipped with side marker lamps,
clearance lamps, and intermediate side
marker lamps are exempt from having parking
lights. However, if vehicle is equipped with
parking lights, they must be
operational. (Section 12-202 of the Illinois
Vehicle Equipment Law)

REJECT VEHICLE IF:

Parking lights do not meet requirements;
improper color; cracked or broken lenses.

11) Sidemarker,
Left
PROCEDURES/SPECIFICATIONS:

Two lamps: one amber at front and one red at
rear, mounted as high as practicable. Shall
conform to federal standards. 49 CFR 571.108

Exception: All buses purchased prior to
September 1974 are exempt.

REJECT VEHICLE IF:

Left marker lights do not meet requirements;
does not function properly; improper color;

DEPARTMENT OF TRANSPORTATION

NOTICE OF ADOPTED RULES

cracked or broken lenses.

12) Sidemarker,
Right

PROCEDURES/SPECIFICATIONS:

Two lamps: one amber at front and one red at
rear, mounted as high as practicable. Shall
conform to federal standards. 49 CFR 571.108

Exception: All buses purchased prior to
September 1974 are exempt.

REJECT VEHICLE IF:

Right marker lights do not meet requirements;
improper color; cracked or broken lenses.

13) Step Well

PROCEDURES/SPECIFICATIONS:

At least the nosings of the service entrance
steps and the floor around the stepwell shall
be automatically illuminated with white light
when the ignition is on and the service
entrance door is open.

No lamp shall be installed so as to shine
directly into the eyes of a pupil moving
through the service entrance and looking at
the service steps.

Exception: On a bus with chassis (incomplete
vehicle) manufactured in March 1977 or
earlier, a stepwell light that does not
illuminate all the step nosings or does not
illuminate the floor around the service
entranceway may be used.

REJECT VEHICLE IF:

Step well light does not meet requirements;
improper color; cracked or broken lenses.

14) Stop

PROCEDURES/SPECIFICATIONS:

Two red lights mounted at same height and as

DEPARTMENT OF TRANSPORTATION

NOTICE OF ADOPTED RULES

high as practicable below window line. Seven
inch minimum diameter or 19 square inches.
Not less than three feet apart laterally.
Must conform to federal standards. 49 CFR
571.108

REJECT VEHICLE IF:

Stop lights do not meet requirements; improper
color; cracked or broken lenses; do not
function properly.

15) Strobe
(optional)

PROCEDURES/SPECIFICATIONS:

If installed, lamp must comply with following
requirements:

1)   *One per bus;*

2)   *Shall emit white or bluish/white light;*

3)   *Shall be visible from any direction;*

4)   *Shall flash 60 to 120 times per minute;*

5)   *Shall be visible in normal sunlight;*

6)   *Mounted at or behind center of rooftop
and equal distance from each side.*
(Section 12-815 of the Illinois Vehicle
Equipment Law)

Distance from rear will be calculated by
measuring height of filament and multiplying
same by 30 inches. (i.e., Filament height x
30 = distance from rear of bus where lamp is
to be located)

REJECT VEHICLE IF:

If installed, strobe light does not meet
installation requirements; does not function
properly; improper color; cracked or broken
lenses.

Shielding is present.

DEPARTMENT OF TRANSPORTATION

NOTICE OF ADOPTED RULES

16) Tail

PROCEDURES/SPECIFICATIONS:

Two red lights mounted with centers not less
than 40 inches nor more than 90 inches from
surface on which vehicle stands. Must conform
to federal standards. 49 CFR 571.108

REJECT VEHICLE IF:

Tail lights do not meet requirements; do not
function properly; improper color; cracked or
broken lenses.

17) Turn
Signal,
Left
(armored)   PROCEDURES/SPECIFICATIONS:

Flush mounted "armored" type amber clearance
lamp mounted behind driver's seat at seat
level and rub rail height. Functions with
regular turn signal.

Exception: All buses purchased prior to
September 1974 are exempt from having left
armored turn signals.

Exception: Buses with capacity rating of less
than 33 passengers are exempt. Buses manufactured
in August 1974 or earlier are exempt. Buses that
measure less than 80 inches wide or 20
feet long are exempt.

REJECT VEHICLE IF:

Left turn signal light does not meet
requirements; does not function properly;
improper color; cracked or broken lenses.

18) Turn
Signal,
Right
(armored)   PROCEDURES/SPECIFICATIONS:

Flush mounted "armored" type amber clearance
lamp mounted at approximately seat level and
rub rail height just to rear of service door.

DEPARTMENT OF TRANSPORTATION

NOTICE OF ADOPTED RULES

Functions with regular turn signal lamps.

Exception: All buses purchased prior to
September 1974 are exempt from having right
armored turn signals.

Exception: Buses with capacity rating of less
than 33 passengers are exempt. Buses
manufactured in August 1974 or earlier are
exempt. Buses that measure less than 80
inches wide or 20 feet long are exempt.

REJECT VEHICLE IF:

Right turn signal light does not meet
requirements; does not function properly;
improper color; cracked or broken lenses.

19) Turn
Signal,
Front   PROCEDURES/SPECIFICATIONS:

One amber lamp at least four inches in
diameter, or 12 1/2 square inches, located on
each side at or near the front. They
shall be located at the same height and as
far apart as practicable. Lamps must conform
to federal standards. 49 CFR 571.108

Operate turn signals and four-way warning
hazards to check performance of front and
rear lights.

REJECT VEHICLE IF:

Front turn signal lights do not meet
requirements; do not function properly;
improper color; cracked or broken lenses.

Four-way warning hazards do not operate
properly.

20) Turn
Signal,
Rear   PROCEDURES/SPECIFICATIONS:

Chassis manufactured after March 31, 1977,
must have two 7 inch diameter, or 19 square

DEPARTMENT OF TRANSPORTATION

NOTICE OF ADOPTED RULES

inch, amber lenses mounted on the rear as far
apart and as high as practicable below
rear window. 49 CFR 571.108

Exception: Chassis manufactured prior to
April 1, 1977, may have yellow or red turn
signals with arrow lenses. 49 CFR 571.108

REJECT VEHICLE IF:

Rear turn signal lights do not meet
requirements; improper color; do not function
properly; cracked or broken lenses.

e) LOCKED
   COMPARTMENT   PROCEDURES/SPECIFICATIONS:

Fire extinguisher, first-aid kit, and warning
devices may be stored either in a closed,
unlocked compartment or under lock and key,
provided the locking device is connected with
an automatic warning signal that will alert
driver when compartment is locked. The
automatic alarm shall be both audible and
visible to the seated driver. The alarm
shall alert the driver when the engine is
running and the compartment is locked and
cannot be readily opened without using a
tool, key, or combination. An alarm cut-off
or "squelch" control is prohibited.

Each safety item inside the compartment shall
be named on the outside of the compartment
cover, or door. In addition, a RED CROSS
formed of five equal squares shall be
displayed on the cover when the first aid kit
is inside the compartment.

Exception: A bus with chassis manufactured in
March 1977 or earlier need not have a
visible alarm.

REJECT VEHICLE IF:

Locked compartment is not readily accessible
to driver; lettering or identification
missing; alarm does not function properly
when compartment is locked and vehicle is

DEPARTMENT OF TRANSPORTATION

NOTICE OF ADOPTED RULES

running.

DEPARTMENT OF TRANSPORTATION

NOTICE OF ADOPTED RULES

Section 441.APPENDIX H Mirrors Through Rub Rails

a) MIRRORS

PROCEDURES/SPECIFICATIONS:

Every required mirror shall be of reflecting material protected from abrasion, scratching, and corrosion. Mirror shall be firmly installed on stable supports so as to give a clear, stable, reflected view. Mirrors shall be adjustable so as to give and maintain its required field of view.

Convex crossover mirrors can be combined with either the right or left side safety mirrors provided the convex mirror meets the field of view and side requirements established in this subsection or in 49 CFR 571.111.

REJECT VEHICLE IF:

Mirrors do not meet requirements; defective; excessively clouded; not adjustable; not securely attached; cracked or broken glass.

1) Exterior

A) Rear View
Driving PROCEDURES/SPECIFICATIONS:

Shall be mounted outside on the left and right sides of the bus. Must give seated driver a view to the rear along each side of the bus. Must be at least 50 square inches of usable flat rectangular reflecting surface on each side. 49 CFR 571.111.

If the rear view driving mirror does not provide the required field of view, a convex driving mirror must be installed to expand the driving view to the rear. However, the usable flat reflecting surface must be rectangular and must maintain at least 50 square inches.

REJECT VEHICLE IF:

Rear view driving mirror does not meet

DEPARTMENT OF TRANSPORTATION

NOTICE OF ADOPTED RULES

requirements; defective; excessively clouded; not adjustable; not securely attached; cracked or broken glass.

B) Right
Side
Safety PROCEDURES/SPECIFICATIONS:

An outside convex mirror, either alone or in combination with the crossover mirror system, shall give the seated driver a view of the roadway along the right side of the bus between the most forward surface of the right front tire and the rear of the rear bumper. The projected reflecting surface of this convex mirror shall be at least 40 square inches (7 1/8 inches diameter if a circle).

Extra-wide-angle convex mirror heads are permissible on right front corner only.

Exception: A right safety mirror is optional on a bus manufactured in August 1974 or earlier.

REJECT VEHICLE IF:

Right side safety mirror does not meet requirements; defective; excessively clouded; not adjustable; not securely attached; cracked or broken glass.

C) Left Side
Safety
(Optional)

PROCEDURES/SPECIFICATIONS:

A convex mirror is required if the left rear view driving mirror system does not give the seated driver a reflected view of the roadway along the left side of the bus between the front edge of the driver's seat (in most forward position) and the rear of the rear bumper. The convex mirror shall be installed so that either alone or in combination with the rear view driving mirror gives the seated driver the proper view.

DEPARTMENT OF TRANSPORTATION

NOTICE OF ADOPTED RULES

Exception: A left safety mirror is optional
on a bus with chassis manufactured in March
1977 or earlier.

REJECT VEHICLE IF:

Left side safety mirror does not meet
requirements; defective; excessively
clouded; not adjustable; not securely
attached; cracked or broken glass.

D) Crossover

PROCEDURES/SPECIFICATIONS:

An outside convex mirror shall give the seated
driver a view of the front bumper and the
area of roadway in front of the bus. The
projected reflecting surface of this
mirror shall be at least 40 square inches (7
1/8 inch diameter if a circle). 49 CFR
571.111

Exception: If the seated driver of a forward
control bus has a direct view of the front
bumper and the area of roadway in front of
the bus, a crossover mirror is optional.

REJECT VEHICLE IF:

Crossover mirror does not meet requirements;
defective; excessively clouded; not
adjustable; not securely attached; cracked or
broken glass.

2) Interior PROCEDURES/SPECIFICATIONS:

Clear view safety glass, minimum 6 inches x 30
inches overall; framed with rounded and
padded corners and edges. It shall afford
good view of the bus interior and portions
of the roadway to the rear.

Exception: All buses manufactured prior to
September 1974 are exempt from padding on the
mirror.

REJECT VEHICLE IF:

DEPARTMENT OF TRANSPORTATION

NOTICE OF ADOPTED RULES

Interior mirror does not meet requirements;
defective; excessively clouded; not
adjustable; not securely attached; cracked or
broken glass.

b) PAINT
REQUIREMENTS

PROCEDURES/SPECIFICATIONS:

*The exterior of the body, excluding the
required rails, shall be painted a uniform
color, National School Bus Glossy Yellow.
The front and rear bumpers, required rub rails
and wheels shall be black. Additional
rub rails may either be painted black or
yellow. Grilles and hub caps may be a bright
finish (e.g., chrome, anodized aluminum,
etc.). Retaining rings may be gray or
aluminum.*

*Manufacturer's name or emblem may be any color
but must not interfere with required
lettering, numbering, or arrows.* (Section
12-801 of the Illinois Vehicle Equipment Law)

For buses manufactured on or after May 2,
1994, each opening for a required emergency
exit must be outlined around its outside
perimeter with a minimum 1 inch (2.54 cm.)
wide yellow retroreflective tape. This
yellow retroreflective tape must be on the
exterior surface of the bus. (57 FR 49413,
November 2, 1992)

Optional: Black areas around flashers are
permitted, but must not interfere with
"SCHOOL BUS" lettering.

Optional: Reflectorized tape is permitted
provided it reflects the same color that it
is applied to and is not located on any
bumper.

Exception: *Fenders on buses manufactured
prior to January 1976 may be painted black.*
(Section 12-801 of the Illinois Vehicle
Equipment Law)

DEPARTMENT OF TRANSPORTATION

NOTICE OF ADOPTED RULES

Exception: Hoods may be lusterless black or lusterless school bus yellow.

REJECT VEHICLE IF:

Paint does not meet color requirements or is in poor condition (i.e., faded, peeling or rusted).

Optional black area around flashers interferes with required lettering.

Optional reflectorized tape does not meet color requirements or is located on the bumper.

c) PROJECTIONS

1) Exterior   PROCEDURE/SPECIFICATIONS:

Entire rear and bumper area of bus must be nonhitchable.

AGENCY NOTE: "Nonhitchable" is defined as the rear of the bus being designed and maintained to prevent or discourage riding or grasping rear of bus so as to "hitch" rides.

REJECT VEHICLE IF:

Projections do not comply with nonhitchable requirements.

2) Interior   PROCEDURES/SPECIFICATIONS:

Interior shall be free of all dangerous projections.

Optional equipment (e.g., video camera) that is located in the bulkhead area of the bus and not flush with the interior walls must meet the following requirements:

1)   Must not interfere with occupants entering or exiting the bus.

2)   Must not be located in driver's head impact zone.

DEPARTMENT OF TRANSPORTATION

NOTICE OF ADOPTED RULES

3)   Must not obstruct required lettering.

Additional projections (e.g., external speakers) in the head impact zone shall be padded to prevent injury. This includes inner lining of ceiling and walls. Installation of book racks is not permissible.

Exception: All buses purchased prior to September 1974 may be equipped with book racks. However, if book racks are present, they shall be above side windows and shall not extend forward of the front seat or across or above the emergency door. Racks must be free of projections likely to cause injury.

REJECT VEHICLE IF:

Optional equipment in bulkhead does not meet requirements.

Remaining projections are not padded (e.g., external speakers). Book racks are present.

Flush mounted speakers are exempt from padding requirements.

For buses purchased prior to September 1974, book racks do not meet requirements.

d) REFLECTORS

1) Front   PROCEDURES/SPECIFICATIONS:

Two yellow rigid or sheet type (tape) front reflex reflectors shall be attached securely and as far forward as practicable. (Section 12-202 of the Illinois Vehicle Equipment Law) They shall be located between 15 and 60 inches above the roadway at either fender, cowl, or body and installed so as to mark the outer edge of the maximum width of the bus. No part of the required reflecting material may be obscured by a lamp, mirror, bracket, or any other portion of the bus. No part of the required reflecting material may

DEPARTMENT OF TRANSPORTATION

NOTICE OF ADOPTED RULES

be more than 11.8 inches (300 mm) inboard of the outer edge of the nearest rub rail (12 inches on a bus with chassis manufactured in March 1977 or earlier). The reflector may be any shape (e.g., square, rectangle, circle, oval, etc.). A rigid type reflex reflector may be any size if permanently marked either DOT, SAE A, or SAE J 594; otherwise, it shall display at least seven square inches of reflecting material (about 3 inch diameter if a solid circle).

A sheet type (tape) reflex reflector may conform to the surface on which it is installed but its forward projected reflecting area shall be at least eight square inches.

REJECT VEHICLE IF:

Missing or damaged reflective material; not located or positioned as required.

2) Left Side   PROCEDURES/SPECIFICATIONS:

One amber at or near the front and one red at or near the rear. Mounted at a height not less than 15 inches and not more than 60 inches above the surface of the road. On sides of buses 20 feet or more in length, one amber as near center as practicable must also be provided. (Section 12-202 of the Illinois Vehicle Equipment Law) Minimum three inches in diameter.

REJECT VEHICLE IF:

Missing or damaged reflective material; not located or positioned as required.

3) Right Side   PROCEDURES/SPECIFICATIONS:

One amber at or near the front and one red at or near the rear. Mounted at a height not less than 15 inches and not more than 60 inches above the surface of the road. On sides of buses 20 feet or more in length, one

DEPARTMENT OF TRANSPORTATION

NOTICE OF ADOPTED RULES

amber as near center as practicable must also be provided. (Section 12-202 of the Illinois Vehicle Equipment Law) Minimum three inches in diameter.

REJECT VEHICLE IF:

Missing or damaged reflective material; not located or positioned as required.

4) Rear   Two red reflectors on rear body within 12 inches of lower right and lower left corners. (Section 12-202 of the Illinois Vehicle Equipment Law) Minimum three inches in diameter.

REJECT VEHICLE IF:

Missing or damaged reflective material; not located or positioned as required.

e) RUB RAILS

PROCEDURES/SPECIFICATIONS:

There shall be one rub rail located approximately at seat level which shall extend from the rear of the service entrance completely around the bus body without interruption, except at functioning doors or a rear engine compartment, to a point of curvature near the front of the body on the left side.

There shall be one rub rail on each side located approximately at the floor line which shall extend over the same longitudinal distance as the rub rail located at the seat level.

More than two rub rails may be installed on sides and rear of bus.

Rub rails of longitudinally corrugated or ribbed steel at least 3.9 inches (100 mm) wide shall be fixed on the outside of the bus.

Exceptions:

DEPARTMENT OF TRANSPORTATION

NOTICE OF ADOPTED RULES

1) Rub rail need not extend across wheel housing.

2) Rub rail may terminate at the point of curvature at the right and left rear corners of the body.

REJECT VEHICLE IF:
Rub rails are missing; not firmly attached; incorrect color; or incorrect number of rails.

DEPARTMENT OF TRANSPORTATION

NOTICE OF ADOPTED RULES

Section 441.APPENDIX I   Seat Belts Through Steps, Entrance

a) SEAT BELTS

PROCEDURES/SPECIFICATIONS:

Must be *installed* on *driver's seat*. (Section 12-807 of the Illinois Vehicle Equipment Law) Belt material, buckle, tongue, etc. shall remain above floor when not in use. All retractors installed shall be an automatic locking type.

Optional: Passenger seats may be equipped with adjustable seat belts. The securement of these belts must conform to 49 CFR 671.222. At all times, each seat belt shall be readily available for quick and easy use. All retractors installed shall be automatic locking type. Each belt assembly shall be clean.

Exception: On a bus manufactured in August 1974 or earlier, a retractor must be installed; however, the belt need not remain above floor but must not be excessively dirty.

REJECT VEHICLE IF:

Driver's seat belt is dirty, frayed, torn, cracked or broken or if retractor or buckle does not operate properly.

Optional belts are not secured, not adjustable, cracked, broken, frayed, torn or dirty.

b) SEAT,
   DRIVER'S   PROCEDURES/SPECIFICATIONS:

The driver's seat shall be rigidly positioned and shall afford vertical, forward and backward adjustments of not less than 3.9 inches (100 mm) without the use of a tool or non-attached device. The shortest distance between the steering wheel and the back rest of the operator's seat shall be no less than 11 inches (280 mm).

DEPARTMENT OF TRANSPORTATION

NOTICE OF ADOPTED RULES

Seat padding and covering shall be in good
condition, free from holes and tears. Seat
cushions shall be securely fastened to the
seat frame.

REJECT VEHICLE IF:

Driver's seat is not securely anchored to
floor; in poor condition; adjustment
mechanism does not function properly.

c) SEAT,
   PASSENGER

PROCEDURES/SPECIFICATIONS:

All seats shall have a minimum front to rear
depth of 14 inches.

In determining seating capacity of a bus,
individual seating width shall be 13 inches
where 3-3 (three pupils on both sides of
aisle) seating plan is used and 15 inches
where 3-2 (three pupils on one side of aisle
and two pupils on other side of aisle)
plan is used.

All seats shall be forward facing and shall be
securely fastened to that part or parts
of the body which support them. No jump or
portable seats are allowed.

The forwardmost seat on the right side of the
bus shall be located so as not to interfere
with the driver's vision and not be farther
forward than the rear of the driver's seat
when adjusted to its rearmost position.

The seat spacing shall be no more than 24
inches, measured from the seating reference
point to the seat back or guard barrier in
front of the seat. The distance between the
rearmost position of the driver's seat
and the front face of the seat back of the
forwardmost seat on the left side shall not
be less than 24 inches measured at cushion
height.

A minimum of 36 inches of headroom for the
sitting position above the top of the

DEPARTMENT OF TRANSPORTATION

NOTICE OF ADOPTED RULES

undepressed cushion line of all seats shall
be provided. Measurement shall be made
vertically not more than 7 inches from
the side wall at cushion height and at the
front and rear center of cushion.

Seat backs of similar size shall be of the
same width at the top and of the same height
from the floor and shall slant at the
same angle with the floor.

*Buses manufactured after June 30, 1987, shall
be equipped with 28 inch seat backs. (Section
12-807.1 of the Illinois Vehicle
Equipment Law)*

Buses manufactured after December 31, 1987,
shall have 28 inch guard barriers.

All buses manufactured during and after
September 1974 shall be equipped with energy
absorbing padding on all exposed top and side
rails. The side rails shall be padded in
such a manner to retain the 12 inch aisle
(15 inches at two inches below top of
seat back for buses manufactured after June
30, 1987). On the rear of a seatback, the
padding shall extend from the top of the seat
back to the top level of the seat cushion.
Seat padding and covering shall be of fire
resistant material. Padding and covering
shall be in good condition (i.e., free from
holes and tears). Seat cushions shall be
securely fastened to the seat frame.

Optional: The rearmost seats may be exempt
from seatback padding requirement.

Exception: All buses manufactured prior to
September 1974 are exempt from padding on top
and side rails and seat back to cushion level.

A flip-up seat may be located only adjacent to
any side emergency door. For buses
manufactured on or after September 1, 1994, the
flip-up seat must conform to the following:

1)   The seat must be designed so that, when

DEPARTMENT OF TRANSPORTATION

NOTICE OF ADOPTED RULES

In the folded position, the seat cushion
is flat against the seat back to prevent
a child's limb from becoming lodged
between the seat cushion and seat back.

2)   The seat must be designed to discourage a
     child from standing on the seat
     cushion when in the folded position.

3)   The working mechanism under the seat must
     be covered to eliminate any tripping
     hazard.

4)   All sharp metal edges on the seat must be
     padded to prevent any snagging
     hazard.

5)   No portion of a seat frame or seat bottom
     may extend past door opening.

6)   No portion of the door latch mechanism
     can be obstructed by a seat.

7)   There must be at least 11.7 inches (30
     cm) measured from the door opening to the
     seat back in front. (57 FR 49413,
     November 2, 1992); as amended at 59 FR
     22997, May 4, 1994

REJECT VEHICLE IF:

Passenger seats are not firmly attached to
body; broken frame; cushions not firmly
attached; padding and covering not fire
resistant. Padding or covering is loose, in
poor condition, or missing; seats are
torn or have holes; minimum seat dimensions
or seat spacing is not in compliance.

d) STEERING SYSTEM

   1) Exterior

      A) King
         Pins   PROCEDURES/SPECIFICATIONS:

Raise vehicle so as to unload kingpins (brakes
should be applied to eliminate wheel

DEPARTMENT OF TRANSPORTATION

NOTICE OF ADOPTED RULES

bearing looseness). Either grasp wheel at
top and bottom or use a bar for leverage.
Attempt to rock wheel in and out. Check
movement at extreme top or bottom of tire.
If movement exists, place a dial indicator,
tape measure, or a fixed device at the wheel
and measure amount of movement.

Place leverage bar under tire. Raise bar to
check for vertical movement between spindle
and support axle.

REJECT VEHICLE IF:

Wheel bearing movement exceeds 1/4 inch; or
kingpin movement exceeds:

Wheel size	Max allowed
16" or less	1/4"
16.1" to 18"	3/8"
over 18"	1/2"

B) Linkage PROCEDURES/SPECIFICATIONS:

For buses with single "I" beam or tube type
front axle, hoist bus under axle. For buses
with twin "I" beam type front axles or with "A
frame" control arms, each axle or arm
must be hoisted independently so as to load
the ball joints. Grasp front and rear of
tire and attempt to shake assembly right and
left to determine linkage looseness.
Measure movement of wheel.

Inspect for damage to or looseness in the
following linkage components:

1)   Ball Joints
2)   Cotter Pins
3)   Drag Link
4)   Idler Arm
5)   Pitman Arm
6)   Steering Box
7)   Tie Rod
8)   Tie Rod Ends

REJECT VEHICLE IF:

DEPARTMENT OF TRANSPORTATION

NOTICE OF ADOPTED RULES

Measurement is found to be in excess of:

Rim Diameter	Maximum Allowable Movement
16" or less	1/4"
17" and 18"	3/8"
over 18"	1/2"

Any linkage component is bent; welded; loose; insecurely mounted or missing.

C) Power
   Steering
           PROCEDURES/SPECIFICATIONS:

           Manually and visually inspect:

           1)   Belts
           2)   Cylinders
           3)   Fluid Level
           4)   Hoses
           5)   Mounting Brackets
           6)   Power Assist
           7)   Pump

           REJECT VEHICLE IF:

           Steering components are:

           1)   Loose, frayed, cracked, missing; incorrect
                belts
           2)   Loose and/or leaking
           3)   Low fluid level
           4)   Cracked, leaking, rubbed by moving parts
           5)   Cracked, loose, or broken
           6)   No assist is evident
           7)   Loose, leaking.

D) Toe-In/
   Toe-Out   PROCEDURES/SPECIFICATIONS:

           With wheels held in a straight ahead position,
           drive vehicle slowly over the approved
           drive-on side slip indicator.

           Excessive toe-in or toe-out is a general
           indication that complete check should be made
           of all front wheel alignment factors

DEPARTMENT OF TRANSPORTATION

NOTICE OF ADOPTED RULES

(caster, camber, steering axis inclination).

REJECT VEHICLE IF:

More than 30 feet per mile on the approved
side slip indicator.

E) Wheel
   Bearings
           PROCEDURES/SPECIFICATIONS:

           With the front end of the vehicle lifted so as
           to load any ball joints, grasp the front
           tire top and bottom, rock it in and out.
           Record movement. To verify that any
           looseness detected is in the wheel bearing,
           notice the relative movement between the
           brake drum or disc and the backing plate or
           splash shield.

AGENCY NOTE: Wheel bearing play can be eliminated by
                applying service brakes.

           REJECT VEHICLE IF:

           Relative movement between drum and backing
           plate, measured at tire, is 1/4 inch or more.

2) Interior

A) Column   PROCEDURES/SPECIFICATIONS:

           Inspect to determine that column support
           bracket is properly tightened and all bolts
           are present.

           REJECT VEHICLE IF:

           Column support bracket is not properly
           tightened or bolts are missing.

B) Lash   PROCEDURES/SPECIFICATIONS:

           With road wheels in straight ahead position,
           turn steering wheel until a turning movement
           can be observed at the left road wheel.
           Slowly reverse steering wheel motion and
           measure lash.

DEPARTMENT OF TRANSPORTATION

NOTICE OF ADOPTED RULES

REJECT VEHICLE IF:

Lash exceeds following acceptable limits:

Steering wheel maximum diameter (inches)	Acceptable lash (inches) measured at maximum circumference
16 or less	2
18	2 1/4
20	2 1/2
22	2 3/4

C) Shaft   PROCEDURES/SPECIFICATIONS:

Grasp steering wheel with both hands and attempt to move shaft up and down.

REJECT VEHICLE IF:

Steering shaft moves up and down.

AGENCY NOTE: Steering shafts on International-Navistar vehicles will move up and down but must be within manufacturer's tolerances.

D) Steering Wheel   PROCEDURES/SPECIFICATIONS:

Inspect steering wheel condition.

REJECT VEHICLE IF:

Steering wheel is damaged. Any spokes are missing or reinforcement ring is exposed.

E) Travel   PROCEDURES/SPECIFICATIONS:

Turn steering wheel through a full right and left turn checking for binding, jamming and complete travel left and right.

REJECT VEHICLE IF:

Binding or jamming is present. Does not complete full turn from left to right. Tire rubs on fender or frame during turn.

DEPARTMENT OF TRANSPORTATION

NOTICE OF ADOPTED RULES

e) STEPS, ENTRANCE   PROCEDURES/SPECIFICATIONS:

Steps shall be enclosed and shall not protrude beyond side body line. Surface shall be of nonskid material with I 1/2 to 3 inch white nosing as part of the nonskid material. Riser of upper step not more than 15 inches in height. When more than two steps are used, risers must be approximately of equal height, except when floor is plywood over steel. (Increase by thickness of plywood.)

REJECT VEHICLE IF:

Steps or risers are not solid. Steps, risers or nonskid material covering is missing, loose, or not in good condition. White nosing is missing or in poor condition.

DEPARTMENT OF TRANSPORTATION

NOTICE OF ADOPTED RULES

Section 441.APPENDIX J   Stop Arm Panel Through Tow Hooks

a) STOP ARM
   PANEL   PROCEDURES/SPECIFICATIONS:

A stop arm panel must be installed on the left
side of the bus and may be operated
either manually or mechanically. Decals may
be used in lieu of painting.

Buses manufactured on or after September 1,
1992 must be equipped with an octagon-shaped
semaphore which meet the requirements listed
below under "Octagon."

Buses manufactured prior to September 1, 1992
may either be equipped with an octagon-shaped
semaphore which meets the requirements listed
below under "Octagon" or a hexagon shaped
semaphore which meets the requirements listed
below under "Hexagon."

Octagon - The arm shall be an octagon-shaped
semaphore which measures at least 450 mm x 450
mm (17.72 inches x 17.72 inches) in
diameter. The arm shall be red on both sides
with a white border at least 12 mm (.47
inches) wide on both sides. The arm shall
have the word "STOP" displayed in white
uppercase letters on both sides. The letters
shall be at least 150 mm (5.9 inches) in
height and have a stroke width of at least 20
mm (.79 inches).

The octagon-shaped stop signal arm shall
comply with either (a) or (b) below:

a)   The entire surface of both sides of the
      arm can be reflectorized to meet 49 CFR
      571.131; or

b)   Each side of the arm shall have at least
      two red lamps centered on the vertical
      centerline of the stop arm. One lamp
      shall be located at the extreme top of the
      arm and the other at its extreme bottom.
      The lamps shall light and flash
      alternately when stop arm is extended

DEPARTMENT OF TRANSPORTATION

NOTICE OF ADOPTED RULES

and likewise turn off and stop flashing
when arm is closed. (49 CFR 571.131)
(See Section 441.Illustration A for
examples.)

Hexagon - The arm shall be a hexagon shaped
semaphore approximately 18 inches wide and 18
inches long and of 16 gauge metal. The stop
arm signal shall have the "STOP" painted on
both sides in white letters at least six
inches high with a brush stroke approximately
7/8 inch wide. The word "STOP" shall be
painted on a panel with red background of
approximately 8 inches by 16 inches.
Remaining area of stop arm blade is to be
painted white with a band of white border at
least 1/2 inch wide painted from and rear on
both sides as contrast. White portion of stop
arm signal shall be reflectorized or
shall have double-faced lamps with red lens
approximately four inches in diameter located
in the top and bottommost position of the
blade. These lamps shall light and flash
alternately when stop arm is extended and
likewise turn off and stop flashing when arm
is closed. (Section 12-803 of the Illinois
Vehicle Equipment Law) (See Section
441.Illustration A for examples.)

Optional: Strobe lamps are acceptable on stop
arm panels.

REJECT VEHICLE IF:

Stop arm panel is in poor condition (i.e.,
faded, peeling, or rusted); lights do not
operate properly (if installed); is not
securely attached; is not operating properly;
does not meet requirements; is missing.

b) STORAGE
   COMPARTMENT
   (optional)   PROCEDURES/SPECIFICATIONS:

Covered, fire-resistant container securely
fastened of adequate strength and capacity
for tire chains and tools for minor emergency
repairs.

DEPARTMENT OF TRANSPORTATION

NOTICE OF ADOPTED RULES

REJECT VEHICLE IF:

If installed, does not meet requirements.

c) SUN VISOR   PROCEDURES/SPECIFICATIONS:

Interior, adjustable, transparent, not less than 6 inches by 30 inches, installed above windshield. Must not interfere with view of interior rear view mirror.

Exemption: Buses purchased prior to August 1967 are exempt from having a transparent sun shield.

REJECT VEHICLE IF:

Sun visor does not meet requirements.

d) SUSPENSION

1) Shocks   PROCEDURES/SPECIFICATIONS:

Bus shall be equipped with front and rear double-acting shock absorbers compatible with manufacturer's rated axle capacity.

With vehicle on a hoist or jacked up, visually inspect shock absorbers for excessive leakage, looseness of mounting, brackets, and bolts.

Physically grab upper and lower portion of shock inspecting for looseness in rubber bushing, mounting brackets or bolts.

REJECT VEHICLE IF:

Shocks are missing or severe leakage (not slight dampness) occurs. Mounting bolts or mounts are broken or loose, or rubber bushing is partially or completely missing.

2) Springs   PROCEDURES/SPECIFICATIONS:

A) Coil   Visually inspect:
1) Spring
2) Control arms

DEPARTMENT OF TRANSPORTATION

NOTICE OF ADOPTED RULES

3) Torque arms (rear)

REJECT VEHICLE IF:

Coil is missing, disconnected, broken, loose bushings, welded or damaged.

B) Leaf   PROCEDURES/SPECIFICATIONS:

With use of a pry bar and using frame as a pivot, attempt to pry front and rear spring attachments and check for movement. Front of vehicle must be jacked up on chassis for checking front suspension. Visually inspect:

1) Springs
2) Shackles
3) Hangers
4) U-bolts
5) Center bolts
6) Bushings or pivot

REJECT VEHICLE IF:

Springs are missing or broken. Shackles or "U" bolts worn or loose. Center bolt in springs sheared or broken. Steering stops allow tire to rub on frame or metal. Any leaves are cracked or missing. Any shackle, shackle pins, hangers, or "U" bolts are worn, loose, or missing.

C) Torsion Bar (Stabilizer Bar)   PROCEDURES/SPECIFICATIONS:

Visually inspect:

1) Torsion bar
2) Mounting brackets
3) Control arms
4) Torque arms (if applicable - rear)
5) Stabilizer bar(s) (if applicable)

REJECT VEHICLE IF:

Torsion bar is missing, disconnected, broken,

DEPARTMENT OF TRANSPORTATION

NOTICE OF ADOPTED RULES

loose, welded, damaged.

e) TOW HOOKS
   (optional)

   1) Front   PROCEDURES/SPECIFICATIONS:

               A front tow hook must not extend beyond the
               front of the front bumper. Each front tow
               hook not fastened securely to the chassis
               frame shall be connected to the frame by
               suitable braces.

               REJECT VEHICLE IF:

               Tow hook(s) extend beyond bumper; not securely
               attached.

   2) Rear   PROCEDURES/SPECIFICATIONS:

               Any tow hook(s) installed on the rear shall be
               attached or braced to the chassis frame
               or to an equivalent structural member of an
               integral type bus. A tow hook must not extend
               beyond the rear face of the rear bumper.

               REJECT VEHICLE IF:

               Tow hook(s) extend beyond bumper; not securely
               attached.

DEPARTMENT OF TRANSPORTATION

NOTICE OF ADOPTED RULES

Section 441.APPENDIX K Undercoating Through Windshield Wipers

a) UNDERCOATING
                    PROCEDURES/SPECIFICATIONS:

                    Fire resistant undercoating material applied
                    to entire underside of body, front fenders,
                    wheel wells, floor members, and side panels
                    below floor level. Non-metallic parts need
                    not be coated.

                    REJECT VEHICLE IF:

                    Undercoating does not meet requirements.

b) VENTILATION   PROCEDURES/SPECIFICATIONS:

                    Body must be equipped with ventilating system
                    capable of supplying proper quantity of air
                    under operating conditions.

                    REJECT VEHICLE IF:

                    Air is obstructed; not securely fastened; not
                    covered.

c) WARNING
   DEVICES   PROCEDURES/SPECIFICATIONS:

                    Either three red cloth flags not less than 12
                    inches square and three red reflectors minimum
                    of 3 inches in diameter or three
                    bidirectional emergency triangles that
                    conform to 49 CFR 571.125 (Section 12-702
                    of the Illinois Vehicle Equipment Law) Kit
                    shall be securely stored.

                    REJECT VEHICLE IF:

                    Required warning devices are not present or
                    are in poor condition.

d) WHEELS

   1) Housings   PROCEDURES/SPECIFICATIONS:

                    Full open type attached to floor sheet to

DEPARTMENT OF TRANSPORTATION

NOTICE OF ADOPTED RULES

prevent water, fumes or dust entering the
body. Inside height should not exceed 10
inches above floor line. Housings shall
allow for unimpeded wheel and tire service or
removal. Housing shall provide clearance
for installation and use of tire chains
on the dual or single tires installed on the
rear wheels.

Inspect tire and road wheel assemblies.

REJECT VEHICLE IF:

Wheel housings do not meet clearance
requirement; wheel housings are not firmly
secured; holes are present.

A tire or wheel is rubbing against any portion
of the suspension, chassis, or body.

2) Rim   PROCEDURES/SPECIFICATIONS:

Inspect all wheel and rim bolts, nuts, studs,
lugs, locking rings, etc. Each cover, cap, or
decorative ring that obscures any of
these items must be removed prior to the
inspection.

Inspect for visible wheel damage.

REJECT VEHICLE IF:

Any wheel or rim securing device such as a
nut, bolt, stud, lug, ring, or other type
securing device is loose, missing, or cracked.

Wheel locating hole(s) are elongated,
oversized, or "wallowed out." Any part of a
wheel or rim is cracked, repaired by
welding or rewelding, or damaged so as to
cause unsafe operation of the vehicle.

3) Tires PROCEDURES/SPECIFICATIONS:

Inspect tire for proper inflation (i.e., flat
tire).

A regrooved, retreaded, or recapped tire shall

DEPARTMENT OF TRANSPORTATION

NOTICE OF ADOPTED RULES

not be on the front steering axle.

A tire with restricted use marking is
prohibited. (e.g., "NHS" or "SL" following
size marking, "Off Highway," "Farm Use,"
"Racing Only," etc.)

No school bus shall be equipped with any tire
which has been so worn that tread
configuration is absent on any part of the
tire in contact with the road surface.

Inspect for tread wear:

1) Check for the presence of tread wear
   indicators.

2) For tires without tread wear indicators,
   use tread depth gauge to measure groove
   depth.
   Steering (Front) Axle: Measure groove
   depth at any point on a major tread
   groove.

   Drive (Rear) Axle: Measure groove depth
   in any two adjacent grooves at three
   equally spaced intervals around the
   circumference of the tire.

   Do not measure on a tie-bar, groove hump,
   or fillet.

3) For tires without tread wear indicators
   and with noncircumferential grooves, or
   "spaces," between the tread elements (as
   in snow, mud, lug knob, or traction
   treads):

   Steering (Front) Axle: Measure in a
   major groove at a point halfway
   between the center of the tire
   and the outside of the tread at any
   point on a major tread groove.

   Drive (Rear) Axle: Measure in a
   major groove at a point halfway
   between the center of the tire and
   the outside of the tread at three

DEPARTMENT OF TRANSPORTATION

NOTICE OF ADOPTED RULES

       equally spaced intervals around the
       circumference of the tire.

    4)   Inspect tire for bald, partially bald,
       cupped, dished or unevenly worn areas.

AGENCY NOTE: "Bald" means without a groove.

Inspect for visible cord damage and exposure
of ply cords in sidewalls and treads,
including belting material cords.

Inspect for evidence of tread or sidewall
separation.

Inspect for regrooved or recut treads.

AGENCY NOTE: 49 CFR 369 requires tires marked "REGROOVABLE"
to have sufficient tread rubber that,
after regrooving, cord material below the
grooves shall have a protective covering of
tread material at least 3/32 inch thick.

Inspect tires for legible markings showing
size designation and carcass construction.

AGENCY NOTE: "R" in size designation shows radial
construction. More plies at tread than
sidewall shows belted construction. Same
number of plies at tread and sidewall,
without a belted or radial indication, shows
plain bias construction.

Tires on same axle must be of same
construction.

Inspect tires for size designation and for
matched construction.

AGENCY NOTE: "Construction" refers to bias, bias belted, or
radial arrangement of ply cords in the
tire carcass.

Inspect each single dual tire assembly.

A mixture of regular and mud-and-snow treads
must be the same on both sides of axle.

DEPARTMENT OF TRANSPORTATION

NOTICE OF ADOPTED RULES

When radial and conventional (i.e., bias)
tires are both used on a vehicle, one of the
following two requirements shall be met:

    1)   On vehicles with one single wheel axle
       and one or more dual wheel axles, radial
       tires shall be used on the steering
       (i.e., front) axle only.

    2)   On vehicles having two single wheel
       xles, radial tires shall be used on the
       rear axle only.

A tube built only for bias tire shall not be
installed in a radial tire. Red color shall
not be added to stem of a "bias" tube. (Valve
stem of tube for radial tire is either
marked "radial" or has red ring or is painted
red.) A "radial" tube and flap may be used in
a bias tire.

Inspect valve stems.

REJECT VEHICLE IF:

Improper inflation (flat tire).

Regrooved, retreaded or recapped tire is
located on front steering axle.

Restricted marking is present.

Any part of tire which is in contact with road
surface is absent of tread configuration.

    1)   Tread wear indicators contact road in any
       two adjacent grooves at three
       equally spaced intervals around the
       circumference of the tire.

    2)   On steering (front) axle: Tread groove
       depth is less than 4/32 inch when
       measured at any point on a major tread
       groove.

       On drive (rear) axle: Tread groove depth
       is less than 2/32 inch when measured
       in any two adjacent grooves at three

DEPARTMENT OF TRANSPORTATION

NOTICE OF ADOPTED RULES

essentially equally spaced intervals
around the circumference of the tire.

3) On steering axle: Tread groove depth is
less than 4/32 inch when measured in a
major groove at a point halfway between
the center of the tire and the outside of
the tread at any point on a major
tread groove.

On drive axle: Tread groove depth is
less 2/32 when measured in a major
groove at a point halfway between the
center of the tire and the outside of
the tread at three essentially equally
spaced intervals around the circumference
of the tire.

4) The tire has bald, partially bald,
cupped, dished or unevenly worn areas. A
broken or cut cord can be seen. Rubber is
worn, cracked, cut or otherwise deteriorated
or damaged so that a cord can be seen -
either when the tire is not touched or when
the edges of the crack, cut or damage are
parted or lifted by hand.

Tire has bump, bulge, knot or other evidence
of partial carcass failure, air seepage, or
loss of adhesion between carcass and tread or
sidewall.

Tread has been regrooved or recut on a tire
that does not have the word "REGROOVABLE"
molded on or into both sides of the tire.

A tire on a road wheel does not exhibit a
legible size marking and a legible
construction marking.

Tires on the same axle are not of same
construction.

A tire exceeds the diameter (not width) of
its mate by 1/2 inch (1/4 inch radius) or
more; or one tire touches its mate.

DEPARTMENT OF TRANSPORTATION

NOTICE OF ADOPTED RULES

A mixture of regular and mud-and-snow treads
are not the same on both sides of the axle.

Requirements for using both radial and
conventional tires on a vehicle are not met.

A tube built only for bias tire but installed
in a radial tire.

A valve stem leaks; is cracked; is either
damaged or positioned so as to hamper
pressure checking or inflation; shows
evidence of wear because of misalignment.

e) WINDOWS   PROCEDURES/SPECIFICATIONS:

All applicable provisions of 49 CFR 571.205
apply to the optional laminated safety glass
and also to any plastic material(s) used in a
multiple glazed unit.

Glazing shall be marked as follows pursuant to
49 CFR 571.205:

1) Windshield - "AS 1" Glass

2) Driver's Window - "AS 1" Glass or "AS 2"
Glass

3) Driver's door - "AS 1" Glass or "AS 2"
Glass

4) All other locations - "AS 1" Glass, "AS
2" Glass, or "AS 3" Glass.

REJECT VEHICLE IF:

Windows do not meet requirements or are not
properly identified.

1) Emergency
(Also see
EMERGENCY
EXITS)

PROCEDURES/SPECIFICATIONS:

When the emergency door is located on the left
side, a rear emergency window shall be

DEPARTMENT OF TRANSPORTATION

NOTICE OF ADOPTED RULES

provided. Minimum dimensions are 16 inches
high and 48 inches wide. Designed to be
opened from the inside or the outside.
Hinged on top, designed and operated to
insure against accidental closing in an
emergency. Inside handle shall provide for
quick release. Outside handle shall be
nondetachable and nonhitchable. When locked
or not fully latched, window shall actuate
alarm audible and visible to driver. No
cutoff switch allowed.

Optional emergency windows are allowed. They
must be labelled "Emergency Exit" in letters
at least two inches high, of a color that
contrasts with its background, located at the
top of or directly above the window on
the inside surface of the bus. Optional
emergency windows must be equipped with an
audible alarm activated when window is locked
or not fully latched.

REJECT VEHICLE IF:

Operating mechanisms do not function. Alarm
does not function. Glass is cracked or broken
(see EMERGENCY EXIT - Alarms and Locks).

2) Rear   PROCEDURES/SPECIFICATIONS:

Glazed panels, or windows, (except rear
emergency window) shall be of fixed type.
Any authorized or required signs, letters or
numerals displayed on the window in the rear
of the bus shall be located so as not to
obstruct the driver's view.

REJECT VEHICLE IF:

Glass is cracked or broken. Visibility
through rear windows is obstructed.

3) Side   PROCEDURES/SPECIFICATIONS:

Each side window shall provide unobstructed
emergency opening at least 9 inches high and
22 inches wide, obtained either by lowering
window or by use of knock-out type split sash.

DEPARTMENT OF TRANSPORTATION

NOTICE OF ADOPTED RULES

A "Stop Line" is required six inches
from top of window on all windows. Safety
glass with exposed edges shall be banded.

Window latches must be in proper working order.

Exception: The requirements of this
subsection do not apply to a side window or
glazed panel installed forward of a front
passenger seat; and are optional for a side
window installed either beside a rear
passenger seat, or in a side emergency exit.

Note: For information regarding optional
route identification markings, see Lettering.

REJECT VEHICLE IF:

Side windows do not meet emergency opening
requirements. Window does not open easily.
Glass is cracked or broken. Stop lines
are missing.

Window latches do not operate properly.

4) Windshield   PROCEDURES/SPECIFICATIONS:

Shall be installed between front corner posts
and designed not to obstruct driver's view.
(Section 12-501 of the Illinois Vehicle
Equipment Law) Windshield shall be slanted
to reduce glare. Tinted safety glass shall
only be allowed six inches below top of
windshield.

REJECT VEHICLE IF:

Windshield is not firmly sealed or attached.
Glass is broken, cracked, or discolored (not
including allowed tint).

f) WINDSHIELD
WASHER   PROCEDURES/SPECIFICATIONS:

Windshield washer shall effectively clean
entire area covered by both wipers.

Exception: All buses purchased prior to

DEPARTMENT OF TRANSPORTATION

NOTICE OF ADOPTED RULES

September 1974 are exempt. However, if bus
is so equipped, washer must be in good
operating condition.

REJECT VEHICLE IF:

Windshield washer does not effectively clean
entire area or does not operate properly.

g) WINDSHIELD
   WIPERS

PROCEDURES/SPECIFICATIONS:

Two automatic, variable speed wipers with
nonglare arms and blades. Need not be
individually powered.

REJECT VEHICLE IF:

Windshield wipers do not cover entire cleaning
area.. Blades are damaged, torn,
hardened, or rubber wiping element has
broken down. Wiper fails to park properly
when shut off.

DEPARTMENT OF TRANSPORTATION

NOTICE OF ADOPTED RULES

Section 441.ILLUSTRATION A Stop Arm Panels

Octagon Shaped Semaphore (see Section 441.APPENDIX J(a))

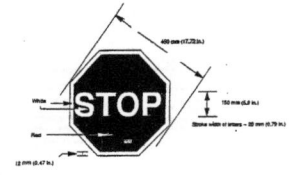

Hexagon Shaped Semaphore (see Section 441.APPENDIX J(a))

DEPARTMENT OF TRANSPORTATION

NOTICE OF ADOPTED RULES

Section 441.ILLUSTRATION B Exhaust Guidelines

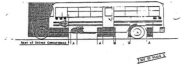

Distance A = 1 meter (39 3/8")

Distance a = 150 millimeters (3 7/8")

▦ Prohibited Zone

▨▩ Ventilating Air Intake (anywhere on side)

▦ Fuel Tank

* Heat shield between tank & discharge eliminates prohibited zone at tank.

DEPARTMENT OF TRANSPORTATION

NOTICE OF ADOPTED RULES

Section 441.ILLUSTRATION C Brake Inspection Report

[IDOT LETTERHEAD]   SCHOOL BUS BRAKE
                                            INSPECTION REPORT

District of Contractor:

Name_____
Address_____
City/State_____ Zip_____ Telephone(__)_____
School Bus Unit Number_____Chassis Make_____
Chassis Year_____Chassis V.I.N._____

Illinois law requires all school buses to be safety inspected at least once every six months or 10,000 miles, whichever occurs first. In addition, the Illinois Department of Transportation requires that a visual brake inspection be performed on every school bus operated in Illinois at least once a year or every 10,000 miles, whichever occurs first.

A completed School Bus Brake Inspection Report must be presented to the Certified Safety Tester each time a school bus is taken to an Official Testing Station for a safety inspection.

I attest that the entire brake system on the school bus listed above was inspected and found to be operating in accordance with the manufacturer's specifications or was repaired to perform in accordance with the manufacturer's specifications. The visual inspection of the brake system was performed on _____ by a qualified mechanic employed by
                           (date)
_____. The mileage on this school bus
(business/school district where
brake inspection was completed)
was_____when the visual brake inspection was performed.
       (mileage)

_____   _____
(name of authorized school   (date)
district official or contractor)
Please print or type

DEPARTMENT OF TRANSPORTATION

NOTICE OF ADOPTED RULES

Section 441.ILLUSTRATION D Propane Decal

DEPARTMENT OF TRANSPORTATION

NOTICE OF ADOPTED RULES

Section 441.ILLUSTRATION E Driver's Pre-Trip Inspection Requirements and Sample Form

As required in Section 13-115 of the Illinois Vehicle Inspection Law, drivers must complete the following "Pre-trip Inspection" daily:

"Each day that a school bus is operated the driver shall conduct a pre-trip inspection of the mechanical and safety equipment on the bus as prescribed by rule or regulation of the Department." (Section 13-115 of the Illinois Vehicle Inspection Law)

The following requirements became effective August 1, 1975:

a) The driver must inspect his vehicle each day prior to beginning a trip.

b) The driver is required to make a written report of this pre-trip inspection. He must report any defects found to the proper authority so that the defects can be corrected.

c) The pre-trip inspection report shall be made in duplicate.

d) As designated by the owner, the original copy shall be presented to the person of authority on a daily basis. These original copies shall be retained by the owner for one hundred and eighty days.

e) The duplicate copy shall remain in the bus for a period of at least thirty days.

f) The form shall specify items to be checked (see subsection (i)) and the minimum information to be recorded.

g) The pre-trip inspection records and reports will be made available for inspection and audit by authorized representatives of the Department at any time.

h) It is the responsibility of the bus owner to furnish pre-trip inspection report forms that meet the minimum requirements of this Chapter.

i) Required items to be checked during the driver's Pre-Trip Inspection:

1) Coolant; oil; battery; washer fluid levels; fan belts; and wiring.

2) Steps; cleanliness; upholstery; windows; warning devices; fuses; first aid kit; fire extinguisher; emergency door (open and close); lettering.

DEPARTMENT OF TRANSPORTATION

NOTICE OF ADOPTED RULES

3) Odometer reading and indication of whether or not state inspection is due.

4) Steering wheel; windshield wipers and washers; heater and defroster; horn; service door (open and close); all mirrors (adjustment); door buzzer; clutch; brake warning buzzer; stop arm control; gear shift lever; neutral safety switch; water temperature; fuel; vacuum or air pressure; gauges; parking brake; seat belt(s).

5) Ammeter; all interior lights; headlights (high/low beams).

6) Right front wheel and tire; right side marker lamps; turn signal light and reflectors; right rear view and safety mirror; headlights; turn signals; cluster; clearance and I.D. lights; alternating flashing lights; windshield; underside of chassis; crossover mirror; left rear view mirror and safety mirror; left front wheel and tire; driver's side window; stop arm; left side marker lamps; turn signal light and reflectors; emergency door (open and close); left rear wheels and tires; exhaust system (tailpipe clear); cluster; clearance and I.D. lights; taillights; turn signals and reflectors; alternating flashing lights; rear emergency door (open and close); right rear wheels and tires; fuel tank filler caps.

7) Drain air brake tank. Record condition of bus (i.e., satisfactory or unsatisfactory).

DEPARTMENT OF TRANSPORTATION

NOTICE OF ADOPTED RULES

COMPANY NAME OR SCHOOL DISTRICT NAME

Bus _____ Odometer _____ Date _____ Time _____

Open Hood and Check:
☐ Coolant, Oil, Battery, Washer Fluid Levels, Fan Belts and Wiring

Enter Bus and Check:
☐ Stops, Cleanliness, Upholstery, Windows, Warning Devices, Fuses, First Aid Kit, Fire Extinguisher and Emergency Door (open and close), Lettering

Record Odometer Reading _____
(Circle if State Inspection is due shortly)

Start Engine and Check:
☐ Steering Wheel
☐ Windshield Wipers and Washers
☐ Heater and Defroster
☐ Horn
☐ Service Door (open and close)
☐ All Mirrors (Adjustment)
☐ Door Buzzer
☐ Clutch
☐ Brake Warning Buzzer
☐ Stop Arm Control
☐ Gear Shift Lever
☐ Neutral Safety Switch
☐ Water Temp., Fuel, Vacuum or Air Pressure Gauges
☐ Parking Brake
☐ Seat Belt

Drive Bus Forward and Apply Brakes
Activate All Lights and Check:
☐ Ammeter, All Interior Lights, Headlights (high/low beams)

With Engine Running and All Lights On, Check Following Equipment Outside Bus:
☐ Rt. Front Wheel and Tire
☐ Rt. Side Marker Lamps, Turn Signal Light and Reflectors
☐ Rt. Rear View and Safety Mirror
☐ Headlights, Turn Signals
☐ Cluster, Clearance and I.D. Lights
☐ Alternating Flashing Lights
☐ Windshield
☐ Look under bus for leaks
☐ Crossover Mirror
☐ Left Rear View Mirror & Safety Mirror
☐ Left Front Wheel and Tire
☐ Driver's Side Window
☐ Stop Arm
☐ Left Side Marker Lamps, Turn Signal Light and Reflectors
☐ Emergency Door (open and close)
☐ Left Rear Wheels and Tires
☐ Exhaust System (tailpipe clear?)
☐ Cluster, Clearance and I.D. Lights
☐ Taillights, Turn Signals and Reflectors
☐ Alternating Flashing Lights
☐ Rear Emergency Door (open and close)
☐ Rt. Rear Wheels and Tires
☐ Fuel Tank Filler Caps

Drain Air Brake Tank
Condition of this Bus is:
☐ Satisfactory
☐ Unsatisfactory

REMARKS _____
_____
_____
_____

Signature of Driver making Report _____

Signature of Mechanic making Repairs _____

Date Repairs Completed _____

DEPARTMENT OF TRANSPORTATION

NOTICE OF ADOPTED RULES

1) **Heading of the Part:** Inspection Procedures for Type II School Buses

2) **Code Citation:** 92 Ill. Adm. Code 443

3) **Section Numbers:**   **Adopted Action:**

Section Numbers	Adopted Action
443.10	New Section
443.20	New Section
443.25	New Section
443.30	New Section
443.40	New Section
443.Appendix A	New Section
443.Appendix B	New Section
443.Appendix C	New Section
443.Appendix D	New Section
443.Appendix E	New Section
443.Appendix F	New Section
443.Appendix G	New Section
443.Appendix H	New Section
443.Appendix I	New Section
443.Appendix J	New Section
443.Appendix K	New Section
443.Appendix L	New Section
443.Illustration A	New Section
443.Illustration B	New Section
443.Illustration C	New Section
443.Illustration D	New Section
443.Illustration E	New Section

4) **Statutory Authority:** 625 ILCS 5/Ch. 12, Art. VIII and 5/Ch. 13

5) **Effective Date of Rulemaking:** March 13, 1995

6) **Does this rulemaking contain an automatic repeal date?** No

7) **Does this rulemaking contain incorporations by reference?** Yes. These conform to Section 5-75(a) of the Illinois Administrative Procedure Act.

8) **Date Filed in Agency's Principal Office:** March 7, 1995

9) **Notice of Proposal Published in Illinois Register:** September 9, 1994, 18 Ill. Reg. 13965

10) **Has JCAR issued a Statement of Objections to these rules?** No

11) **Difference(s) between proposal and final version:**

     The Department added an "s" to "Conversion" at "Appendix L" of the

DEPARTMENT OF TRANSPORTATION

NOTICE OF ADOPTED RULES

Table of Contents.

The Department corrected the ILCS citations throughout the rule.

At Section 443.10, the Department corrected the Section heading.

At Section 443.25, the Department inserted "and as amended at 59 FR 22997, May 4, 1994."

The Department indented all definitions in Section 443.40.

At Section 443.Appendix A(b), the Department deleted "May 2, 1994" and inserted "September 1, 1994" in its place.

At Section 443.Appendix A(b)(4), the Department inserted "; as amended at 59 FR 22997, May 4, 1994)" after "1992-"

At Section 443.Appendix D(b), the Department inserted "; as amended at 59 FR 22997, May 4, 1994)."

At Section 443.Appendix I(c), the Department deleted "May 2, 1994" and inserted "September 1, 1994" in its place.

At Section 443.Appendix K(d)(3), the Department deleted the period after "prohibited" and inserted a period after "etc." "etc.").

12) Have all the changes agreed upon by the agency and JCAR been made as indicated in the agreement letter issued by JCAR? Yes

13) Will this rulemaking replace an emergency rule currently in effect? No

14) Are there any amendments pending on this Part? No

15) Summary and Purpose of Rulemaking:
By this Notice of Adopted Rules, the Department is establishing a new Part 443 which consists of the inspection requirements and criteria for Type II school buses. Elsewhere in this issue of the *Illinois Register*, the Department is repealing Appendices A through G and Illustrations A and B in 92 Ill. Adm. Code 451 which previously addressed the inspection criteria for Type II school buses. Through reorganizing, the Department is clarifying, correcting, adding to and deleting some requirements.

The following analysis indicates changes made to individual components.

Air cleaner:

Adding "not properly attached" as cause for rejection.

DEPARTMENT OF TRANSPORTATION

NOTICE OF ADOPTED RULES

Aisle:

Adding criteria pursuant to 57 FR 49413, November 2, 1992 requiring additional emergency exits.

Battery:

Adding "insufficient capacity" as cause for rejection.

Brakes:

Renaming booster to master cylinder.
Adding inspection criteria for brake inspection report.
Adding exception from brake inspection report requirements for new buses.

Bumper:

Adding provisions for optional crossing arm.

Defroster:

Adding requirements for auxiliary fans to be securely mounted and have protected blades.

Drive Shaft Guard:

Clarifying protection of each segment of the drive shaft guard.

Emergency Exits:

Adding provisions for optional emergency roof hatches.
Correcting requirement for left emergency door to have glass only in lower portion of the door.
Correcting requirement for only inside release mechanism to be protected.
Adding provisions for optional emergency windows.
Clarifying alarm requirements for optional and required exits.
Adding criteria pursuant to 57 FR 49413, November 2, 1992 requiring additional emergency exits.

Entrance Door:

Clarifying language.
Deleting requirement that locking system be dependent on driver being seated to operate the door. (It is physically impossible and unnecessary for driver to remain seated.)

DEPARTMENT OF TRANSPORTATION

NOTICE OF ADOPTED RULES

Exhaust System:

Reorganizing and rewriting subsection for consistency with Type I School Bus Standards.

Fire Extinguisher:

Adding approval of halon fire extinguisher.

First Aid Kit:

Clarifying requirement that minimum number of packages be sealed.
Adding approval of OSHA approved blood-borne pathogen kits.
Removing Commercial Type as a kit option.
(Commercial Type kits are not longer used by the industry.)

Floor Covering:

Adding metal floor stripping as subject to inspection.

Frame and Body:

Adding provision for collision damage as subject to inspection.

Fuel Storage System:

Adding exception for shielding of some diesel powered engines.

Expanding alternate fuel inspection criteria for liquefied petroleum gas and compressed natural gas.

Heaters:

Adding padding requirement if heater is not protected by a seat.

Instrumental Panel:

Adding emergency/parking brake indicator light as subject to inspection.

Lettering:

Adding Agency Note regarding marking requirements for school buses operated under interstate authority.
Correcting language by moving emergency window lettering to interior.
Removing requirement for lettering to be located at least 44

DEPARTMENT OF TRANSPORTATION

NOTICE OF ADOPTED RULES

inches above the floor level on the rear emergency door.
Adding criteria pursuant to 57 FR 49413, November 2, 1992 requiring additional emergency exits.

Lights:

Renaming cluster to identification lights.
Correcting error in eight light flashing system by adding instructions to close the door.
Eliminating headlight aiming requirement as subject to inspection.
Renaming marker to sidemarker lights.
Clarifying stepwell light requirements.

Mirrors:

Rewriting subsection for consistency with Type I School Bus Standards.
Adding provisions for combining convex crossover mirrors with other mirrors.

Paint:

Adding provisions for optional reflectorized tape.
Adding provisions for required reflectorized tape pursuant to 57 FR 49413, November 2, 1992.

Projections:

Adding provisions for eliminating dangerous projections.
Clarifying provisions for optional equipment installed in the bus.

Rub Rails:

Eliminating requirement for rub rail on all functioning doors.

Seat, Passenger:

Clarifying requirements for seat spacing measurements.
Adding criteria for flip-up seats pursuant to 57 FR 49413, November 2, 1992 requiring additional emergency exits.

Steps:

Adding provisions for white nosing on steps.

Stop Arm Panel:

DEPARTMENT OF TRANSPORTATION

NOTICE OF ADOPTED RULES

Adding language pursuant to 56 FR 20363, May 3, 1991 requiring stop arm panels
Clarifying language pursuant to P.A. 88-415 which allows octagon-shaped semaphores on all school buses.
Approving optional strobe lamps.

Wheels/Tires:

Adding proper inflation of tires as subject to inspection.
Changing requirement for measuring tread groove depth on steering axle from three locations on the tire to one location.
(Change is being made for consistency with 625 ILCS 5/12-405(d).)

Windows:

Clarifying language for consistency with Type I School Bus Standards.

16) Information and questions regarding these adopted rules shall be directed to:

Name: Ms. Cathy Allen
Address: Regulation and Training Unit
Illinois Department of Transportation
Division of Traffic Safety
P.O. Box 19212
Springfield, Illinois 62794-9212
Telephone: (217)785-1181

17) State reasons for this rulemaking if it was not included in the two (2) most recent regulatory agendas:

The full text of the Adopted Rule begins on the next page:

DEPARTMENT OF TRANSPORTATION

NOTICE OF ADOPTED RULES

TITLE 92: TRANSPORTATION
CHAPTER I: DEPARTMENT OF TRANSPORTATION
SUBCHAPTER e: TRAFFIC SAFETY (EXCEPT HAZARDOUS MATERIALS)

PART 443
INSPECTION PROCEDURES FOR TYPE II SCHOOL BUSES

AUTHORITY: Implementing and authorized by Article VIII of the Illinois Vehicle Equipment Law [625 ILCS 5/Ch. 12, Art. VIII] and the Illinois Vehicle Inspection Law [625 ILCS 5/Ch. 13].

SOURCE: Adopted at 19 Ill. Reg. 4634, effective
MAR 13 1995

Section 443.10 Purpose and Scope

This Part prescribes the requirements of the Illinois Department of Transportation governing:
a)   Implementation of Article VIII, the Illinois Vehicle Equipment Law [625 ILCS 5/Ch. 12, Art. VIII];
b)   Inspection procedures for Type II school buses; and
c)   Performance of the daily pre-trip inspection by school bus drivers.

DEPARTMENT OF TRANSPORTATION

NOTICE OF ADOPTED RULES

Section 443.20 Application

This Part applies to the following persons:
a) Department personnel;
b) Owners of Official Testing Stations;
c) Employees of Official Testing Stations;
d) School bus operation managers; and
e) School bus drivers.

Section 443.25 Incorporation by Reference of Federal Regulations

Whenever this Part refers to the Code of Federal Regulations and that reference incorporates the federal regulations by reference, the federal regulations incorporated shall be that which was effective as of October 1, 1992, as amended at 57 FR 49413, November 2, 1992; as amended at 57 FR 57000, December 2, 1992; as amended at 57 FR 57020, December 2, 1992; and as amended at 59 FR 22997, May 4, 1994, not including any later amendments or editions. Copies of appropriate federal regulations are available for inspection at the Department's Commercial Vehicle Safety Section.

Section 443.30 Standards of Construction

a) "Shall" and "must" are used in the imperative sense. "Shall" imposes an obligation to act. "Must" defines a condition that is to be satisfied. "May" allows permissiveness under terms specified in the standards. "Will" indicates intention, promise or willingness.
b) Words imparting the masculine gender include the feminine.
c) Changes in the administration of the state school bus inspection program and changes to federal and state law have caused the purchase or manufacture date of school buses to be critical in the application of this Part. The effective dates for some of these standards will vary.
    1) Exemptions to some standards are provided for school buses purchased prior to September 1974, the effective date of the Department's "Vehicle Inspection Stations Governing School Buses."
    2) Exemptions are provided for Type II school buses manufactured prior to October 1978, the date of the Department's Order "Minimum Safety Standards for Construction of Type II School Buses."
    3) Some standards are identified with other effective dates. These standards are applicable to all school buses manufactured or purchased after the identified date or during the time frame specified.

Section 443.40 Definitions

"Body" - Portion of vehicle that encloses the occupant and cargo

DEPARTMENT OF TRANSPORTATION

NOTICE OF ADOPTED RULES

spaces and separates those spaces from the chassis frame, engine compartment, driveline, and other chassis components, except certain chassis controls used by the driver.

"Body-on-Chassis" - Completed vehicle consisting of a passenger seating body mounted on a truck type chassis (or other separate chassis) so that the body and chassis are separate entities, although one may reinforce or brace the other.

"Bus" - *Every motor vehicle, other than a commuter van, designed for carrying more than ten persons.* (Section 1-107 of the Illinois Vehicle Code (the Code)) [625 ILCS 5/1-107]

"Chassis" - *Every frame or supportive element of a school bus that contains but is not limited to the axles, engine, drive train, steering components, and suspension which the body is attached to.* (Section 1-110.1 of the Code)

"Code" - The Illinois Vehicle Code [625 ILCS 5]

"Commercial Vehicle Safety Section" (CVSS) - A section of the Bureau of Safety Programs of the Division of Traffic Safety of the Illinois Department of Transportation.

"Department" - *The Department of Transportation of the State of Illinois, acting directly or through its authorized agents or officers.* (Section 13-100 of the Code)

"Empty Weight" - Unloaded vehicle weight; i.e., the weight of a vehicle with maximum capacity of all fluids necessary for operation of the vehicle but without cargo or occupant.

"Federal Motor Vehicle Safety Standards" (FMVSS) - The rules, regulations and standards set forth in 49 CFR 571.

"Gross Vehicle Weight Rating" or *GVWR" - The value specified by the manufacturer as the loaded weight of the school bus.* (Section 12-800 of the Illinois Vehicle Equipment Law)

"Illinois Vehicle Equipment Law" - [625 ILCS 5/Ch. 12]

"Manufacturer" - (unless otherwise indicated at the point of use) means the person or organization whose name follows "MANUFACTURED BY" or "MFD BY" on the federal and state certification label.

"Newton" (N) - Metric unit of force and weight. N = mass multiplied by the standard acceleration of free fall, or "gravity" (i.e., 9.8).

DEPARTMENT OF TRANSPORTATION

NOTICE OF ADOPTED RULES

"Passenger" - Every occupant of the vehicle who is not the driver.

"Purchase Date" - Date when purchase transaction was completed, not when body or chassis was built.

"School Bus"

Type I School Bus - A School Bus with gross vehicle weight rating of more than 10,000 pounds.

Type II School Bus - A School Bus with gross vehicle weight rating of 10,000 pounds or less. (Section 12-800 of the Illinois Vehicle Equipment Law)

Every motor vehicle, except as provided below, owned or operated by or for any of the following entities for the transportation of persons regularly enrolled as students in grade 12 or below in connection with any activity of such entity:

Any public or private primary or secondary school;

Any primary or secondary school operated by a religious institution; or

Any public, private or religious nursery school.

This definition shall not include the following:

A bus operated by a public utility, municipal corporation or common carrier authorized to conduct local or interurban transportation of passengers when such Bus is not traveling a specific school bus route but is:

On a regularly scheduled route for the transportation of other fare paying passengers;

Furnishing charter service for the transportation of groups on field trips or other special trips or in connection with other special events; or

Being used for shuttle service between attendance centers or other educational facilities.

A motor vehicle of the first division. (Section 1-182 of the Code)

"Vehicle"

DEPARTMENT OF TRANSPORTATION

NOTICE OF ADOPTED RULES

First Division: Those motor vehicles which are designed for the carrying of not more than ten persons.

Second Division: Those vehicles which are designed for carrying more than ten persons, those designed or used for living quarters and those vehicles which are designed for pulling or carrying property, freight or cargo, those motor vehicles of the First Division remodeled for use and used as motor vehicles of the Second Division, and those motor vehicles of the First Division used and registered as school buses. (Section 1-217 of the Code)

DEPARTMENT OF TRANSPORTATION

NOTICE OF ADOPTED RULES

Section 443.APPENDIX A Air Cleaner Through Barrier, Guard

a) AIR CLEANER

PROCEDURE/SPECIFICATIONS:
Any type is acceptable.

REJECT VEHICLE IF:

Air cleaner is not properly attached or is
missing.

b) AISLE

PROCEDURES/SPECIFICATIONS:

Unobstructed minimum clearance leading from
service door to emergency door or back of bus
must be at least 12 inches wide. Floor to ceiling
height must be minimum of 58.9 inches at any
location with the aisle.

A dedicated aisle may be present adjacent to any side
emergency door. For buses manufactured on or after
September 1, 1994, the following must be met:

1) The aisle must be unobstructed at all times.

2) No portion of a seat or barrier may extend past
the door opening.

3) No portion of the door latch mechanism can be
obstructed by a seat.

4) There must be at least 11.7 inches (30 cm)
measured from the door opening to the seat back
in front. (57 FR 49413, November 2, 1992; as
amended at 59 FR 22997, May 4, 1994)

REJECT VEHICLE IF:

Aisle does not meet minimum standards.

c) ALTERNATOR
(GENERATOR)

PROCEDURES/SPECIFICATIONS:

The generator, or alternator with rectifier,
shall have a minimum capacity rating of 55
amperes and shall be capable of meeting all

DEPARTMENT OF TRANSPORTATION

NOTICE OF ADOPTED RULES

electrical requirements.

REJECT VEHICLE IF:

Alternator does not meet minimum standards or
is not functioning.

d) AXLES

PROCEDURES/SPECIFICATIONS:

Meets federal chassis requirements as
indicated on federal certification Label.
(49 CFR 568) Wheel base shall not be less
than 123 inches.

REJECT VEHICLE IF:

Axles show visible signs of apparent damage,
leaking fluids or are not firmly attached.

e) BARRIER,
GUARD

PROCEDURES/SPECIFICATIONS:

Shall be either the following Type A or B:

TYPE A: Constructed and thickly padded to
give head and knee impact protection.
Installed at the rear of service entrance at
least 23 inches ahead of seat back and no
more than one inch from right hand wall,
bottom shall be no more than two inches above
floor. Guard barrier shall match width and
above-floor height of the seat-back on
right-front forward-facing seat; provided,
however the barrier's width shall be reduced
as necessary to maintain a 12 inch wide
service entrance way and aisle. Except for a
grab handle, the guard barrier shall not
extend more than one inch ahead of the rear of
service door opening nor more than one
inch into the space above any service step.
No portion of the barrier shall present a
"snagging," sharp, tripping, or other hostile
surface to a person moving through aisle
or service entrance way.

TYPE B: Stanchion post shall be installed to
the rear and left of the service entrance step
well from floor to ceiling with guard

DEPARTMENT OF TRANSPORTATION

NOTICE OF ADOPTED RULES

rail attached approximately 30 inches above
the floor. A step well guard panel installed
from stanchion to right hand wall and
from guard rail to within two inches of
floor. Clearance between step well and first
seat should be at least 24 inches
measured from panel to front face of seat
back at cushion height. All stanchion and
guard rails shall be padded. Padding on the
stanchions shall extend to within three inches
of ceiling and floor; on guard rail it
shall extend from wall to stanchion. (49 CFR
568)

Exception: All buses manufactured prior to
September 1, 1974, require Type A or B. Buses
manufactured from September 1, 1974, to
March 31, 1977, require Type A.

Exception: Buses manufactured on and after
April 1, 1977, are not required to have guard
barriers.

Exception: See 92 Ill. Adm. Code 445.APPENDIX
B (Inspection Procedures for Type II
Special Education School Buses) for other
possible exceptions.

REJECT VEHICLE IF:

Barrier is not solidly attached. Padding or
covering shows wear and tear. Barrier does
not meet requirements.

DEPARTMENT OF TRANSPORTATION

NOTICE OF ADOPTED RULES

Section 443.APPENDIX B Battery or Batteries Through Bumper, Front

a) BATTERY OR
   BATTERIES   PROCEDURES/SPECIFICATIONS:

                    Battery may be mounted either in engine
                    compartment or on outside of passenger/driver
                    area. Battery shall be a nominal 12-volt
                    type. It shall be of sufficient capacity to
                    supply all electrical requirements but shall
                    be rated not less than either 70-ampere hours
                    at the 20-hour discharge rate or 105-minutes
                    at the 25-ampere discharge rate.

                    REJECT VEHICLE IF:

                    Battery or batteries are not securely mounted;
                    excessively corroded; of insufficient
                    capacity.

b) BATTERY
   CABLES   PROCEDURES/SPECIFICATIONS:

                    Check condition.

                    REJECT VEHICLE IF:

                    Cables are corroded or are not securely
                    attached.

c) BATTERY
   CARRIER   PROCEDURES/SPECIFICATIONS:

                    When the battery is mounted outside the engine
                    compartment it shall be welded or bolted
                    in a closed, weather-tight, and vented
                    compartment that is located and arranged so
                    as to provide for convenient routine
                    servicing. The battery compartment door, or
                    cover, shall be secured by a manually
                    operated latch or other fastener. A latch or
                    fastener must be designed in such a fashion
                    as to keep the door closed when in the
                    latched position. Each electrical cable
                    connecting the battery in this carrier to the
                    body or chassis shall be one piece between
                    the terminal connector and the first body or
                    chassis terminal connector.

DEPARTMENT OF TRANSPORTATION

NOTICE OF ADOPTED RULES

REJECT VEHICLE IF:

Battery carrier does not meet requirements.

d) BRAKES   PROCEDURES/SPECIFICATIONS:

*Every motor vehicle shall be equipped with two
separate means of applying the brakes and
they shall be so constructed that failure
of any one part of the operating
mechanism shall not leave the motor vehicle
without brakes. (Section 12-301(a)of the
Illinois Vehicle Equipment Law)*

REJECT VEHICLE IF:

Brakes do not meet requirements.

1) Backing
    Plate   PROCEDURES/SPECIFICATIONS:
Check condition.

REJECT VEHICLE IF:

Backing plate is in poor condition.

2) Drums/
    Discs   PROCEDURES/SPECIFICATIONS:

Inspect drums and/or discs for cracks or for
being worn or reworked beyond the marked
discard limit.

REJECT VEHICLE IF:

Worn or reworked beyond the following limits:

1)   Drum diameter .040 inch (1mm) under
marked discard limit on Type I bus.

2)   Drum diameter .030 inch (.75mm) under
marked discard limit on Type II bus.

3)   Disc thickness .030 inch (.75mm) over
marked discard limit on any bus.

4)   Other rework (rebore, reface) limit
specified by chassis manufacturer.

DEPARTMENT OF TRANSPORTATION

NOTICE OF ADOPTED RULES

3) Emergency
/Parking
Brake   PROCEDURES/SPECIFICATIONS:

*Emergency/parking brake system must apply
brakes to at least two wheels. (Section
12-301(a) of the Illinois Vehicle Equipment Law)*

AGENCY NOTE: Micro brakes are not considered a separate
means of braking and are not acceptable.

Procedures for testing:

1)   Apply operating control fully.

2)   Check actuating mechanism for release.

Brake Performance Test:

Using Drive-On Pad Type Tester:

1)   Drive vehicle onto brake machine pads at
4-6 m.p.h.

2)   Apply emergency/parking brake to bring
vehicle to a halt. Do not lock wheels.

3)   Note the braking forces registered by the
brake machine.

Using Roll-On Type Tester:

1)   Position axle with emergency brake onto
roller.

2)   Apply emergency brake but do not lock
wheels.

REJECT VEHICLE IF:

Emergency/parking brake does not meet requirements.

Procedures for testing:

1)   Not equipped with emergency/parking
brakes. Operating mechanism does not
hold in the applied position.

DEPARTMENT OF TRANSPORTATION

NOTICE OF ADOPTED RULES

2) Actuating mechanism does not fully
release when release control is operated
properly.

Brake Performance Test;

Drive-On Tester:

Machine does not register a total braking
force of at least 20% of vehicle empty
weight. Braking forces at opposite wheels on
same axle vary more than 20%.

Roll-On Tester:

Machine does not register a total braking
force of at least 20% of vehicle empty
weight. Braking forces at opposite wheels on
same axle vary more than 20%.

4) Emergency
Brake
Ratchet
(Pedal or
Lever)

PROCEDURES/SPECIFICATIONS:

Must be in proper adjustment. A warning light
must be visible when emergency brake is
activated.

REJECT VEHICLE IF:

Emergency brake ratchet or warning light do
not meet requirements.

5) Pedal
Clearance
(Service
Brakes)

PROCEDURES/SPECIFICATIONS:

Minimum 1 1/2 inch clearance with pedal fully
depressed.

REJECT VEHICLE IF:

DEPARTMENT OF TRANSPORTATION

NOTICE OF ADOPTED RULES

Pedal clearance does not meet requirements.

6) Power
Systems

A) Air

PROCEDURES/SPECIFICATIONS:

With air system fully charged (compressor
governor "cut-out") run engine at low idle.
Make one full (maximum) brake application and
immediately record reservoir air
pressure.

Apply and release brakes until pressure
indicated on the air gauge is at least 10 psi
(i.e, pounds per square inch) below
governor "cut-in" pressure. Run engine at
high idle and determine seconds required to
raise reservoir pressure from recorded
pressure.

REJECT VEHICLE IF:

Time required to raise air pressure from
recorded to cut-out is more than 30 seconds.
Air gauge is missing or does not operate.

B) Electric/
Hydraulic

PROCEDURES/SPECIFICATIONS:

Turn engine "off." Depress service brake
pedal. Electric hydraulic pump must come
"on" (listen).

REJECT VEHICLE IF:

Electric pump does not operate properly or is
absent.

C) Hydraulic

PROCEDURES/SPECIFICATIONS:

Inspect booster belt(s), supports, tubes,
hoses, connections and general condition.
Clean reservoir and cover as necessary and
check master cylinder fluid level. Do not
contaminate fluid.

DEPARTMENT OF TRANSPORTATION

NOTICE OF ADOPTED RULES

Turn engine "on." Warning signal must come on (look/listen). Depress brake pedal lightly. Start engine. Pedal must move down slightly (feel). Warning signal must go "off" (look/listen).

REJECT VEHICLE IF:

Belt is slack or worn; tube or hose is damaged; any part leaks or is cracked; master cylinder fluid is below maximum level. Either booster or warning signal does not operate properly.

D) Vacuum/
Hydraulic
   PROCEDURES/SPECIFICATIONS:

Inspect tank(s), chambers, hoses, tubes, connectors, clamps, and booster air cleaner.

Inspect supports and attachments.

With engine off, repeatedly apply service brakes until vacuum is depleted, with medium pressure on brake pedal, start engine; release brake and operate engine until maximum vacuum is established; stop engine; apply service brakes hard.

With brakes still applied, start engine; after one minute of running engine, check "LOW Vacuum" indicator.

REJECT VEHICLE IF:

Any component is restricted, collapsed, scraped, cracked, loose, or broken. Booster air cleaner is clogged.

Any support or attachment is broken. Any connecting line or other component is not attached or supported so as to prevent damage from scraping or rubbing.

Foot pedal does not fall away from foot when engine is started; insufficient vacuum reserve to permit one full service brake

DEPARTMENT OF TRANSPORTATION

NOTICE OF ADOPTED RULES

application after engine is off without actuating "low vacuum" indicator; valve or diaphragm leaking.

7) Service
Brakes

   PROCEDURES/SPECIFICATIONS:

Must be equipped with service brakes on all wheels. (Section 12-301(a)(5) of the Illinois Vehicle Equipment Law)

Must be equipped with a "split system" on service brakes. (49 CFR 571.105)

Power-assisted service brakes are required. (49 CFR 571.105)

REJECT VEHICLE IF:

Service brakes do not meet requirements.

A) Brake
Inspection
Report

   PROCEDURES/SPECIFICATIONS:

Verify Brake Inspection Report for following (refer to Section 443.Illustration C for example of form):

1. Vehicle Identification Number (VIN), make and year must correspond to the bus presented for inspection.

2. Brake Inspection Report must indicate the date and mileage at the time the brake inspection was performed. If date is more than one year prior to time of inspection or mileage has exceeded 10,000 miles, a brake inspection must be performed.

3. The form must be completed with all required information. No blank lines are acceptable.

DEPARTMENT OF TRANSPORTATION

NOTICE OF ADOPTED RULES

Exception: If the bus has operated less than
10,000 miles and less than 12 months have passed
since the bus was manufactured, an brake
inspection report is not required. Write
"Less than 10,000 miles and less than one
year old" in the remarks section on the
Vehicle Inspection Report.

REJECT VEHICLE IF:

Absent, invalid, or incomplete brake
inspection report.

B) Brake
   Performance
   Test

PROCEDURES/SPECIFICATIONS:

Using Drive-On Pad Type Brake Tester:

Check vehicle's stopping ability before testing.

Drive vehicle onto brake machine pads at 4-8
m.p.h.

Apply service brakes to bring vehicle to a
halt. Do not lock wheels.

Note the braking forces registered by the
brake machine.

Using Roll-On Type Tester:

When using roller-type tester each axle must
be tested separately. Transmission must be in
neutral when testing brakes on any drive
axle.

Drive front axle onto rollers. Start roller
motor. Apply service brakes but do not lock
wheels.

Repeat the above steps for each axle.

The total braking force on a vehicle must be
determined by adding the results of the test
on each axle.

DEPARTMENT OF TRANSPORTATION

NOTICE OF ADOPTED RULES

REJECT VEHICLE IF:

Drive-On Tester:

Machine does not register a total braking
force of at least 60% of the vehicle empty
weight.

Braking forces at opposite wheels on same axle
vary more than 20%.

Roll-On Tester:

Machine does not register a total braking
force of at least 60% of the vehicle empty
weight.

Braking forces at opposite wheels on same axle
vary more than 20%.

e) BUMPER,
   FRONT

PROCEDURES/SPECIFICATIONS:

Manufacturer's standard for vehicle or an
equivalent bumper which meets or exceeds
manufacturer's standards. Black color is not
required.

REJECT VEHICLE IF:

Bumper must be solidly attached, and free from
damage or sharp edges.
Bumper may be equipped with a crossing control
arm. Crossing control arms can only
display yellow reflectors or yellow lamps.

DEPARTMENT OF TRANSPORTATION

NOTICE OF ADOPTED RULES

Section 443.APPENDIX C Bumper, Rear Through Drive Shaft Guard

a) BUMPER,
REAR

PROCEDURES/SPECIFICATIONS:

Manufacturer's standard for vehicle and so
attached or shielded between body and bumper
as to prevent hitching rides or tows.
Black color is not required.

Exception: A bus manufactured in October 1978
or earlier is exempt from having a non-hitchable
bumper.

REJECT VEHICLE IF:

Rear bumper does not meet requirements.
Bumper is not solidly attached. Sharp edges
are present. Rear bumper is hitchable.

b) CERTIFICATE AND
REGISTRATION
CARD HOLDER   Not required for Type II.

c) CERTIFICATION
LABEL (FEDERAL)   PROCEDURES/SPECIFICATIONS:

Inspect federal certification label if the
chassis (incomplete vehicle) was
manufactured after November 10, 1978.
The manufacturer's label must contain the
following information:

1) Name of vehicle (bus) manufacturer and
the month and year in which manufacture
of the vehicle was completed;

2) Name of incomplete vehicle (chassis)
manufacturer and the month and year in
which he performed his last manufacturing
operation on the incomplete vehicle;

3) Gross vehicle weight rating, or ratings
(GVWR);

4) Gross axle weight ratings (GAWR);

5) The statement, "This vehicle conforms to

DEPARTMENT OF TRANSPORTATION

NOTICE OF ADOPTED RULES

all applicable federal motor vehicle
safety standards in effect in
(month/year)";

6) The vehicle identification number (VIN);

7) The vehicle's classification (usually
"bus"). (49 CFR 567.5)

Alterer's certification: A certified vehicle
might have been altered before its purchase
for use as a school bus. The alterations may
have included, but are not limited to,
classification changes, gross weight rating
changes, or changes to the application/
effective date of a federal motor vehicle
safety standard. If any such alteration
occurred, the bus must carry an additional
federal label that identifies the alterer,
shows when alteration was completed, "as
altered" GVWR, GAWR and classification (if
changed). It must also state that the
altered vehicle conforms to all applicable
federal motor vehicle safety standards in
effect in (month/year). (49 CFR 567.7)

REJECT VEHICLE IF:

A required label is absent, defaced,
destroyed, not riveted, or not permanently
affixed. "Permanently affixed" means the
label cannot be removed without destroying
or defacing it.

A certification label does not contain the
required statement and all other information
required for that label.

d) DEFROSTERS

PROCEDURES/SPECIFICATIONS:

Defrosting equipment shall keep the windshield
and the window to the left of the
operator and the glass in the service door
clear of fog, frost and snow, using heat from
heaters and circulation from fans. Must
conform to federal standard 49 CFR 571.103.

DEPARTMENT OF TRANSPORTATION

NOTICE OF ADOPTED RULES

(Auxiliary fans are not considered to be a
defrosting and defogging system.)

REJECT VEHICLE IF:

Defrosting system does not function properly.
Auxiliary fans are not securely mounted
or blades are not protected.

e) DRIVE SHAFT
   GUARD   PROCEDURES/SPECIFICATIONS:

Shall be of sufficient strength to protect
each segment of the drive shaft and prevent
it from going through the floor or dropping
to the ground if broken.

REJECT VEHICLE IF:

Drive shaft guard is missing, not firmly
attached, or does not properly protect each
segment of the drive shaft.

DEPARTMENT OF TRANSPORTATION

NOTICE OF ADOPTED RULES

Section 443.APPENDIX D Electrical System Through Fenders

a) ELECTRICAL
   SYSTEM

1) Circuits   PROCEDURES/SPECIFICATIONS:

Circuits arranged to manufacturer's
specifications are acceptable. An additional
circuit shall be added for the alternate
flashing signal lamps and the stop signal
lamps. Circuits may be added as necessary.

REJECT VEHICLE IF:

Breaks in insulation are present. Not on
proper circuit or properly wired.

2) Fuses

PROCEDURES/SPECIFICATIONS:

Two extra fuses for each size fuse used on the
bus shall be conveniently mounted on the
bus body.

REJECT VEHICLE IF:

Fuses are not present or are not conveniently
mounted.

3) Switches

PROCEDURES/SPECIFICATIONS:

Check operation and condition.

REJECT VEHICLE IF:

Switches not operating properly or are missing.

4) Wiring   PROCEDURES/SPECIFICATIONS:

All wires shall be properly insulated and
securely attached at not more than 18.1
inches (460 mm) intervals. Check condition.

REJECT VEHICLE IF:

DEPARTMENT OF TRANSPORTATION

NOTICE OF ADOPTED RULES

Insulation is frayed or missing. Wiring not securely attached.

b) EMERGENCY EXITS

PROCEDURES/SPECIFICATIONS:

All buses must be equipped with either a rear emergency door or a left side emergency door and a rear emergency window. (49 CFR 571.217)

Additional emergency exits, including roof hatches, may be required on buses manufactured on or after May 2, 1994. (57 FR 49413, November 2, 1992)

For those buses manufactured on or after May 2, 1994, each opening for a required emergency exit must be outlined around its outside perimeter with a minimum 1 inch (2.54 cm) wide yellow retroreflective tape. This yellow retroreflective tape must be on the exterior surface of the bus. (57 FR 49413, November 2, 1992; as amended at 59 FR 22997, May 4, 1994)

Optional emergency roof hatches are allowed. They must be installed according to manufacturer's recommendations and no alarm is required. Open and close roof hatches (required or optional) to verify their operation.

REJECT VEHICLE IF:

Emergency exits do not meet requirements. Roof hatches do not open.

1) Side

PROCEDURES/SPECIFICATIONS:

Shall be hinged on front side and open outward. Shall be equipped with safety glass (or equivalent) located in upper portion of the door. Door shall be of at least the same gauge metal as the body. Shall be 24

DEPARTMENT OF TRANSPORTATION

NOTICE OF ADOPTED RULES

inches or more clear horizontal opening, with forward edge of opening in line with the rearmost edge of a seat back. Shall have 45 inches or more clear vertical opening. Inside release mechanism must be protected against accidental release; easily accessible; readily operated manually without the use of remote control, power device or tool. (See Alarms and Locks in this subsection for requirements.)

REJECT VEHICLE IF:

Inside release mechanism is not protected. Inside and outside release mechanisms are not accessible, or operable; unable to open easily; hinge is located at incorrect location; location and size of opening is incorrect.

2) Rear

PROCEDURES/SPECIFICATIONS:

Shall open outward with a 120 degree minimum swing. Upper portion of each door shall contain fixed safety glazing. Shall be equipped with a fastening device which can be quickly released from inside and outside the body. The outside fastening device must be non-hitchable. (See Alarms and Locks in this subsection for requirements.)

Inside release mechanism must be protected against accidental operation and must be easily accessible from the inside. Must be operated only by moving handle as shown by arrow and without use of remote control, power device, key, tool, or any attached or unattached object other than the release handle. (49 CFR 571.217)

Exception: On a bus manufactured in August 1974 or earlier, the emergency exit shall be in the center of the rear end, exempt from 120 degree swing and may open either vertically or horizontally.

REJECT VEHICLE IF:

DEPARTMENT OF TRANSPORTATION

NOTICE OF ADOPTED RULES

Inside release mechanism is not protected.
Inside and outside release mechanisms are not
accessible or do not operate properly.
Outside release mechanism is hitchable. Door
does not open easily. Location of hinge
is incorrect. Size of opening is incorrect.
Glazing does not meet requirements. General
condition of door (rubber and seal) is poor.

3) Emergency
Window

PROCEDURES/SPECIFICATIONS:

When the emergency door is located on the left
side, a rear emergency window shall be
provided. Minimum 16 inches high and 48
inches wide. Designed to be opened from the
inside or the outside. Hinged on top,
designed and operated to insure against
accidental closing in an emergency. Inside
handle shall provide for quick release.
Outside handle shall be nondetachable and
nonhitchable. (See Alarms and Locks in this
subsection for requirements.)

REJECT VEHICLE IF:

Operating mechanisms do not function. Glass
is cracked or broken.

4) Alarms and
Locks

PROCEDURES/SPECIFICATIONS:

Audible and visible alarms shall alert driver
when the engine is running and any required
emergency exit or optional emergency exit door
either:

1) Is not fully latched, or

2) Is locked and not readily operated manually.

Optional emergency exit windows must be
equipped with an audible alarm which is
activated when the above criteria is met.
The engine starting system shall not operate
while any emergency exit (optional or
required) is locked from either inside or
outside the bus. "Locked" means that the

DEPARTMENT OF TRANSPORTATION

NOTICE OF ADOPTED RULES

release mechanism cannot be activated and
the exit opened by a person at the exit
without a special device such as a key or
special information such as a combination.

An alarm cut-off or "squelch" control is
prohibited.

On a van conversion, any rear cargo door
inside lock(s) of the type installed by the
chassis manufacturer (such as commonly used in
cars - "push/pull" type) shall be made inoperable.
The mechanism cannot, through jarring,
vibration, etc. cause the door to become
locked and be inoperable from the inside or
outside.

Exception: On a bus with chassis (incomplete
vehicle) manufactured in March 1977 or
earlier, the engine starting system may
operate while the emergency door is locked.
The "Not Stop Engine" requirement applies
to every bus.

Exception: On a bus manufactured in August
1974 or earlier, the "Not Fully Latched" alarm
is optional. The "Door Locked" alarm is
required on each bus with a lockable emergency
door.

REJECT VEHICLE IF:

Alarms do not alert driver as required. Locks
do not meet requirements.

c) ENTRANCE DOOR

1) Physical
Requirements

PROCEDURES/SPECIFICATIONS:

Door shall be located to right of operator and
operated by an over-center control.
Upper portions of door shall be safety glass
or equivalent. Vertical closing edges shall
be equipped with flexible material for a
proper seal and to prevent injury.

Each door on the right side of the vehicle, hinged or sliding, except the service door shall be made permanently inoperable by means other than the rub rail on the outside of the body.

REJECT VEHICLE IF:

Binding or jamming is evident, malfunctions, over-ride device on power operated door does not function, control not accessible by driver. Door is missing, loose, or damaged. Rubber seal is missing or torn.

2) Locks and Alarms

PROCEDURES/SPECIFICATIONS:

A service door lock is not required but if any type of service door locking system is installed on the bus, the system shall conform to one of the following:

1) The locking system shall not be capable of preventing the driver from easily and quickly opening the service door from inside the vehicle.

2) A locking system that is capable of preventing the bus driver from easily and quickly opening the service door shall include an audiovisual alarm. The alarm shall be audible and visible and must alert the driver when the engine is running and the service door is locked. An alarm disconnect, "squelch control," or other alarm defeating or weakening device shall not be installed.

REJECT VEHICLE IF:

Locks and alarms do not meet requirements. Bent, worn, or dislocated parts that would delay quick door release and opening are present.

d) EXHAUST SYSTEM

PROCEDURES/SPECIFICATIONS:

"Exhaust System" includes each component used

to conduct gas from an engine exhaust port (manifold) to authorized exit point, including each sealing, connecting, and supporting component. Exhaust system shall be outside body and attached to chassis. Size of tailpipe shall not be reduced after it leaves muffler. Any flexible component that contains exhaust gas shall be of stainless steel. System shall not leak. System shall have an outlet at its discharge end(s) only.

1) Shielding

PROCEDURES/SPECIFICATIONS:

Any flammable material, electrical insulation, brake hose, or fuel system component containing fuel that is located within 11 13/16 inches (300 mm) of a component containing exhaust gas shall be safeguarded by a heat shield.

Exhaust system shall be shielded from either accidental contact, "hitching to," or "standing on," except at discharge end. A chassis or body component may provide required shield.

REJECT VEHICLE IF:

Shielding is not present (if applicable).

Exception: Fuel system components on diesel powered engines that are located within four inches of a component containing exhaust gas shall be shielded.

2) Discharge

PROCEDURES/SPECIFICATIONS:

The exhaust system's discharge end (tailpipe) shall be within .98 inch (25 mm) of bus side, rear, or rear corner. It must not extend past a side rub rail or more than one inch past the bumper. Gas shall not be directed towards a door or other opening into bus body. In addition, the discharge end, or ends, shall not be located in any prohibited zone shown in Section 443.Illustration B.

DEPARTMENT OF TRANSPORTATION

NOTICE OF ADOPTED RULES

REJECT VEHICLE IF:

All parts of system are not securely fastened
and supported.

Any part is leaking, missing, or patched.

Any part contains holes not made by
manufacturer.

e) FENDERS

PROCEDURES/SPECIFICATIONS:

Shall be properly braced and free from any
body attachment.

There shall be approximately one inch located
between front fenders and back face to cowl.

REJECT VEHICLE IF:

Fenders are not solid or in bad condition.

Sharp edges are evident.

Fenders are loose or protrude out.

DEPARTMENT OF TRANSPORTATION

NOTICE OF ADOPTED RULES

Section 443.APPENDIX E Filter, Oil Through Frame and Body

a) FILTER, OIL

PROCEDURES/SPECIFICATIONS:

Replaceable element or cartridge type.
Minimum one-quart capacity.

REJECT VEHICLE IF:

Oil filter leaks or does not meet requirements.

b) FIRE
   EXTINGUISHER   PROCEDURES/SPECIFICATIONS:

Pressurized dry-chemical gauge type approved
by Underwriters' Laboratories, Inc., rating of
not less than 10 B.C. mounted in bracket
and readily accessible. Sealed with a type of
seal that will not interfere with
operation. If stored in locked compartment,
compartment must be labelled. Halon fire
extinguishers (10 B.C.) are approved.

REJECT VEHICLE IF:

Gauge does not indicate in the calibrated or
marked "Full Charge" area. Seal is broken.
Extinguisher is not mounted, not in a quick
release holder or not labelled in compartment,
if applicable. Improper rating. Missing.

c) FIRST AID KIT   PROCEDURES/SPECIFICATIONS:

Kit shall be readily identifiable, removable,
and mounted in readily accessible place in
driver's compartment -- either in full view
or in specified secured compartment (see
LOCKED COMPARTMENT). If not carried in
compartment, the case shall be dust tight
and substantially constructed of durable
material. The contents shall include, but
not be limited to the following:

Unit Type (Minimum Contents)

4"   bandage compress - 1 package

DEPARTMENT OF TRANSPORTATION

NOTICE OF ADOPTED RULES

2"   bandage compress - I package

I"   bandage or adhesive compress - I package

40"   triangle bandage with two safety pins - 1

Splint, wire or wood - I

A tourniquet or any type of ointment, antiseptic, or other medicine shall not be included.

AGENCY NOTE: OHSA approved blood-borne pathogen kits are permitted.

REJECT VEHICLE IF:

Kit is not complete. Dust or other visible dirt is present inside case. Minimum number of individual packages are not sealed. Medicine or tourniquet is present. Locked compartment containing kit is not labelled. Not mounted in readily accessible location. Missing.

d) FLOORS AND
   FLOOR COVERING   PROCEDURE/SPECIFICATIONS:

A plywood of 5/8 inch exterior BB grade or equivalent material shall be applied over the existing steel floor and securely fastened. Covering in underseat area shall be of fire resistant floor covering of type commonly used in passenger transportation equipment and shall have a minimum thickness of .125 inch. The floor covering in the aisle shall be nonskid, wear resistant, fire resistant and rib type. The aisle floor covering shall have a minimum thickness of .140 inch.

All floor coverings and metal floor stripping must be permanently bonded to the floor and must not crack when subjected to sudden changes in temperature. Bonding or adhesive material shall be waterproof. All seams must be sealed with waterproof sealer. All openings in floorboard or fire wall between chassis and passenger carrying compartment

DEPARTMENT OF TRANSPORTATION

NOTICE OF ADOPTED RULES

must be solid and sealed.

Boots and seals around shift levers and emergency brakes must be secure and solidly attached.

REJECT VEHICLE IF:

Abnormal wear and obstructions are present. Holes or openings are present in floors, floor covering, or boots. Metal floor stripping is not securely attached or broken.

e) FRAME AND
   BODY   PROCEDURES/SPECIFICATIONS:

Visually inspect:

1)   Body mounts shall be attached and sealed to the chassis cowl so as to prevent the entry of water, dust or fumes through the joint between the chassis cowl and the body.

2)   Cross members and mounting bolts.

3)   Engine mounting bolts.

4)   Frame shall extend to rear of body cross member.

5)   Frame extension is permitted when alterations are behind rear hanger or rear springs and not for the purpose of extending wheel base.

6)   Collision damage which is detrimental to the safe operation of the vehicle.

REJECT VEHICLE IF:

1)   Cracked, loose, missing bolts. Any repair done by welding body to frame, insulation strip missing.

2)   Loose, cracked, broken or missing.

3)   Missing, loose.

DEPARTMENT OF TRANSPORTATION

NOTICE OF ADOPTED RULES

4)   Cracked, broken, bent, rusted to a depth
     as to substantially weaken frame -
     welding except by body manufacturer.

5)   Unless permitted, frame extends past
     wheel base.

6)   Collision damage which is detrimental to
     the safe operation of the vehicle.

DEPARTMENT OF TRANSPORTATION

NOTICE OF ADOPTED RULES

Section 443.APPENDIX F   Fuel Storage and Delivery System Through Horn

a) FUEL STORAGE
   AND DELIVERY
   SYSTEM   PROCEDURES/SPECIFICATIONS:

                   Entire fuel system, except extensions for
                   driver control of air or fuel, must be
                   outside passenger and driver compartment.

                   REJECT VEHICLE IF:

                   Any part of fuel system, except extensions for
                   driver control of air or fuel, is within
                   passenger/driver compartment.

1) Fuel Filler
   Cap   PROCEDURES/SPECIFICATIONS:

                   Meets manufacturer's specifications. Must be
                   the same as or equivalent to original
                   equipment.

                   REJECT VEHICLE IF:

                   Fuel filler cap is defective or missing.

2) Fuel Lines   PROCEDURES/SPECIFICATIONS:

                   Firmly attached. No leakage, seepage,
                   abrasion, or chafing. Must be 11 13/16
                   inches (300 mm) from any part of exhaust
                   system that contains exhaust gas or be
                   safeguarded by a heat shield. Inside engine
                   compartment, the chassis manufacturer's
                   standard shall govern separation and shielding
                   between parts designed by chassis
                   manufacturer.

                   Exception: Fuel system components on diesel
                   powered engines that are located within four
                   inches of a component containing exhaust gas
                   shall be shielded.

                   REJECT VEHICLE IF:

                   Fuel lines are cracked, leak, insecure
                   mounting, damaged, clamps missing, mount

DEPARTMENT OF TRANSPORTATION

NOTICE OF ADOPTED RULES

clips missing or not separated or not
shielded properly (if applicable).

3) Fuel Filler
   Tube   PROCEDURES/SPECIFICATIONS:

                   Check condition.

                   REJECT VEHICLE IF:

                   Fuel filler tube leaks or is not secure.

4) Fuel Pump   PROCEDURES/SPECIFICATIONS:
                   Check condition.

                   REJECT VEHICLE IF:

                   Fuel pump leaks, is damaged or is not secure.

5) Fuel Tank(s)

                   PROCEDURES/SPECIFICATIONS:

                   Minimum capacity of 24 gallons, mounted,
                   filled, and vented entirely outside body.
                   Must meet manufacturer's specifications. (49
                   CFR 571.301)

                   REJECT VEHICLE IF:

                   Fuel tank(s) have leakage, seepage, or
                   abrasion; hole or crack that would leak or
                   seep when tank is full.

6) Fuel tank
   mount(s)   PROCEDURES/SPECIFICATIONS:

                   Check condition.

                   REJECT VEHICLE IF:

                   Fuel tank mount(s) are cracked, loose, or
                   bolts are missing.

7) Fuel tank
   straps   PROCEDURES/SPECIFICATIONS:

                   Check condition.

DEPARTMENT OF TRANSPORTATION

NOTICE OF ADOPTED RULES

REJECT VEHICLE IF:

Fuel tank straps are cracked, loose, or
missing.

8) Alternate
   Fuel Systems
   (LPG or CNG)
                   An alternate fuel system which is no longer
                   in use must be completely from the bus.

   A) Carburetion
      Equipment
                   A fuel filter is required on alternate
                   fuel systems.

   B) Container
      Installation
            i)   Compressed or liquefied gas containers
                    shall not be mounted in the passenger or
                    driver's compartment.

            ii)   Container valves, appurtenances and
                    connections shall be mounted in an
                    enclosed compartment.

            iii)   Containers shall be located at least 36
                    inches from the entrance door and any
                    emergency exit. Due to the smaller
                    size of Type II school buses, space
                    limitations may sometimes make it
                    impossible to locate a fuel tank
                    further than 36 inches from an exit. A
                    Type II school bus has a gross vehicle
                    weight rating of 10,000 pounds or less as
                    defined in Section 12-800 of the
                    Illinois Vehicle Equipment Law (625
                    ILCS 5/12-800). If the original fuel
                    tank for a Type II bus was located within
                    36 inches from any exit, the
                    alternate fuel container may be located
                    in the same location as the original tank.

   C) Identification
                   The fuel identification decal (see Section
                   443.Illustration E) shall be delayed on the
                   rear of the school bus not more than 12 inches
                   above the top of the rear bumper and within 39

95

DEPARTMENT OF TRANSPORTATION

NOTICE OF ADOPTED RULES

inches of the left side. The decal shall not be placed on any black portion of the bus body.

D) Pipe and Hose
Installation

i) No fuel supply line shall pass through the driver or passenger's compartment.

ii) The pressure relief device shall be fabricated so that in the event of stress, the pipe or adaptor will break away without impairing the function of the relief valve.

iii) If installed, the adaptor connecting the piping system to the pressure relief device shall neither touch nor restrict any movable part of the pressure relief valve.

iv) The relief valve discharge piping system (piping system) must not be reduced at any point from the relief valve to the point of release into the atmosphere.

v) The piping system shall be routed to minimize sharp elbows or bends. Installation of any commercially available piping installed to meet the manufacturer's specifications is acceptable. Any fittings that restrict the flow of discharge are prohibited. From the pressure relief device adaptor to the atmosphere, the minimum inside diameter of the piping must measure at least 3/4 of an inch.

vi) The piping system shall neither block nor hamper the operation of any window or door. The piping system shall preserve widths of passageways, aisles and emergency exits.

vii) Every portion of the piping system shall be gas tight (except the outlet) and shall be able to withstand forces from the discharge when the relief valve is in full

DEPARTMENT OF TRANSPORTATION

NOTICE OF ADOPTED RULES

open position. If for any reason the discharge outlet becomes blocked, the piping system must be capable of holding the full system pressure.

viii) To facilitate the removal of accumulated waste, a drain cock shall be installed at the lowest point of the piping system. The drain must be capable of being held open manually and close automatically to prevent expelling LPG if discharged through the relief valve. A weep hole, or other opening that may result in discharged LPG flaming beneath the bus is prohibited.

ix) The portion of the piping system that leads upward to the atmosphere shall be installed either inside the passenger compartment, on the outside of the bus, or in the body wall between the inner and outer "skins" of the bus body.

x) Piping on the outside of the body shall be shielded below the window line to prevent "grabbing hold" or "hitching to." However, discharge piping that is located between the windshield and the vent window at the left front corner of the body need not be shielded.

xi) Any portion of the piping system that is installed either inside the passenger compartment or inside the body wall shall consist of one piece originating below the bus floor and exiting outside the bus roof. Every hole where piping passes through the floor or roof shall be sealed.

xii) The piping system must terminate above the eave lines of the bus body.

xiii) The outlet of the piping system shall be located at least 36 inches from the air inlet or outlet of a ventilator or similar device installed on or near the

DEPARTMENT OF TRANSPORTATION

NOTICE OF ADOPTED RULES

roof. A "similar device" includes the fresh air intake of a heating, ventilating or air conditioning system. It does not include a side window that opens near the roof.

xiv) A rain cap is required where the piping system exits into the atmosphere to minimize water or dirt from entering into either the relief valve or its discharge piping. Installation of any commercially available rain cap installed to meet the manufacturer's specifications is acceptable. The cap shall remain in place except when the relief valve operates. The cap shall be installed to minimize the entrance or water or dirt while the vehicle is in motion.

xv) The discharge piping system on a special education school bus shall conform to all provisions of this Part.

REJECT VEHICLE IF:

Propane relief valve/piping system is not properly installed. Alternate fuel system does not meet requirements listed above.

b) GRAB HANDLES

1) Exterior   Not required.

2) Interior   PROCEDURES/SPECIFICATIONS:

Shall be of stainless clad steel, installed inside doorway, solidly attached on left side, and as long as practicable.

REJECT VEHICLE IF:

Missing or not solidly attached.

c) HEATERS   PROCEDURES/SPECIFICATIONS:

Must be capable of maintaining inside temperature of 50 degrees. The heater hoses

DEPARTMENT OF TRANSPORTATION

NOTICE OF ADOPTED RULES

shall be supported to guard against excessive wear due to vibration and shall not interfere with or restrict the operation of any engine function. Any hose in the passenger compartment shall be protected to prevent injury from burns in the event of rupture. Primary heater shall be a high output fresh air type. Heater must be padded if not protected by seat.

The secondary heater may be a recirculating type and located so as not to interfere with aisle space.

REJECT VEHICLE IF:

Heater is missing; in poor working condition; defective hoses, supports or baffles; not firmly attached or padded when required.

d) HOOD

PROCEDURES/SPECIFICATIONS:

Open hood and inspect safety catch and hinges for proper operation. Close hood and inspect for proper full closure. Manually inspect latches or remote control for proper operation.

REJECT VEHICLE IF:

Hood does not open or hood latches do not securely hold hood in its proper fully-closed position. Secondary or safety catch does not function properly. Hinge is broken, missing, or not attached to body.

e) HORN   PROCEDURES/SPECIFICATIONS:

Dual electric horns shall be provided giving an audible warning at a distance of 200 feet and shall be conveniently controlled from the operator's seated position. (Section 12-601 of the Illinois Vehicle Equipment Law)

REJECT VEHICLE IF:

DEPARTMENT OF TRANSPORTATION

NOTICE OF ADOPTED RULES

Horn control is missing, defective or not audible.

DEPARTMENT OF TRANSPORTATION

NOTICE OF ADOPTED RULES

Section 443.APPENDIX G Instruments and Instrument Panel Through Locked Compartment

a) INSTRUMENTS
   AND INSTRUMENT
   PANEL   PROCEDURES/SPECIFICATIONS:

                    Shall be equipped with the following nonglare
                    illuminated instruments and gauges mounted for
                    easy maintenance and repair and in such a
                    manner that each is clearly visible to
                    the seated driver. An indicator light instead
                    of a pressure or temperature gauge is
                    permissible. (49 CFR 571.101)

                    1)   Speedometer;

                    2)   Odometer;

                    3)   Fuel Gauge;

                    4)   Oil Pressure Gauge;

                    5)   Water Temperature Gauge;

                    6)   Ammeter with graduated charge and
                         discharge indications;

                    7)   High beam headlight indicator;

                    8)   Directional signal indicator;

                    9)   Air pressure or vacuum gauge (when air or
                         vacuum brakes are used);

                    10) Eight light flasher indicator;

                    11) Emergency/Service Brake Indicator.

                    REJECT VEHICLE IF:

                    Instrument and/or instrument panel does not
                    operate properly; instruments are missing;
                    inaccurate readings.

b) INSULATION   PROCEDURES/SPECIFICATIONS:

DEPARTMENT OF TRANSPORTATION

NOTICE OF ADOPTED RULES

The ceiling and sidewalls shall be thermally insulated with a fire-resistant material which shall reduce the noise level and vibrations.

REJECT VEHICLE IF:

Insulation does not meet requirements.

c) LETTERING

1) Exterior   PROCEDURES/SPECIFICATIONS:

The body and chassis manufacturer's name, emblem, or other identification may be displayed (colorless or any color) on any unglazed surface of the bus.

AGENCY NOTE: School buses with interstate authority may display the company's name, city and state of its base and the interstate "MC" number. This lettering must be black in color.

REJECT VEHICLE IF:

Exterior lettering does not meet requirements. Lettering or decals are not distinct, required or allowed. Lettering is obstructed.

A) Front   PROCEDURES/SPECIFICATIONS:

"SCHOOL BUS" in black at least eight inches (200 mm) high placed as high as possible on body or sign attached thereto. Vehicle number assigned for identification shall be a minimum of four inches (100 mm) high and located as high as practicable. Decals are permissable. All lettering must be black. (Section 12-802 of the Illinois Vehicle Equipment Law)

Exception: All buses purchased prior to September, 1974, may have roof mounted "SCHOOL BUS" sign with flashing red lights.

REJECT VEHICLE IF:

DEPARTMENT OF TRANSPORTATION

NOTICE OF ADOPTED RULES

Lettering does not meet requirements. Lettering is not distinct, required or allowed. Lettering is obstructed.

B) Left   PROCEDURES/SPECIFICATIONS:

Either the owner's name or the school district number or both must be at least four inches high, approximately centered and as high as practicable below window line. (Section 12-802 of the Illinois Vehicle Equipment Law). The above required lettering must be located on one line.

If bus is equipped with a side emergency door, it must be labelled "EMERGENCY EXIT" in letters at least two inches high at the top of the emergency door, or directly above, or on the door glazing.

Optional: Vehicle number assigned for identification may be displayed at a minimum height of four inches (100 mm).

Decals are permissible. All lettering must be black.

For buses manufactured on or after May 2, 1994, "EMERGENCY DOOR" in letters at least 1.95 inches (5 cm) high must be located at the top of, or directly above, any emergency exit door. For any emergency window exit, "EMERGENCY EXIT" must be located at the top of, or directly above, or at the bottom of the emergency window exit in letters at least 1.95 inches (5 cm) high. The labelling must be of a color that contrasts with its background. (57 FR 49413, November 2, 1992)

REJECT VEHICLE IF:

Lettering does not meet requirements. Lettering is not distinct, required, or allowed. Lettering is obstructed.

C) Rear   PROCEDURES/SPECIFICATIONS:

"SCHOOL BUS" in black lettering at least eight

DEPARTMENT OF TRANSPORTATION

NOTICE OF ADOPTED RULES

inches (200 mm) high placed as high as
possible on body or sign attached thereto.
(Section 12-802 of the Illinois Vehicle
Equipment Law) "EMERGENCY DOOR" or
"EMERGENCY EXIT" in lettering at least two
inches high at top of emergency door, or
directly above, or on door glazing.

"EMERGENCY EXIT" (for buses without rear
emergency door) in letters at least two
inches high directly below rear emergency
window, or on exit glazing. An arrow, at
least 5.9 inches in length and 3/4 inch in
width indicating direction each release
mechanism should be turned to open door or
window located within 5.9 inches of release
handle, in black. Vehicle number assigned for
identification shall be a minimum 4
inches (100 mm) high. Decals are
permissible. All lettering must be black.

If bus uses alternate fuel (e.g., propane,
CNG), vehicle must be marked with
identifying decal. Such decal shall be
diamond shaped with white or silver
scotchlite letters one inch in height and a
stroke of the brush at least 1/4 inch wide on
a black background with a white or silver
scotchlite border bearing either the words or
letters:

  "PROPANE" = If propelled by liquefied
  petroleum gas other than liquefied natural
  gas; or

  "CNG" = If propelled by compressed natural
  gas. The sign or decal shall be
  maintained in good legible condition.

The alternate fuel decal shall be displayed
near the rear bumper and visible from the rear
of vehicle. (See Section 443.Appendix
6(a)(8)) (Section 12-704.3 of the Illinois
Vehicle Equipment Law)

Exception: In case of "push" or "pull" type
of release mechanism where the direction of
movement to open emergency exit cannot be

DEPARTMENT OF TRANSPORTATION

NOTICE OF ADOPTED RULES

shown by one arrow, either three or four
straight arrows shall be placed equally
spaced as practicable around the object to
be pushed or pulled, with the head of each
arrow adjacent to and pointing directly at
that object. Each arrow shall be the same
color and, when practicable, the same size as
though it were a single arrow. In addition,
the pertinent word "PUSH" or "PULL" shall be
displayed near that object.

AGENCY NOTE: If adequate space is not available in required
positions for emergency door lettering,
lettering may be immediately below window
level.

For buses manufactured on or after May 2,
1994, "EMERGENCY DOOR" in letters at least
1.95 inches (5 cm) high must be located at
the top of, or directly above, any emergency
exit door. For any emergency window exit,
"EMERGENCY EXIT" must be located at the top
of, or directly above, or at the bottom of
the emergency window exit in letters at least
1.95 inches (5 cm) high. The labelling must
be of a color that contrasts with its
background. (57 FR 49413, November 2, 1992)

REJECT VEHICLE IF:

Lettering does not meet requirements.

Lettering or arrows are not distinct,
required, or allowed. Lettering is
obstructed.

Buses using alternate fuels are not properly
marked with decal. Decal is in wrong location.

D) Right   PROCEDURES/SPECIFICATIONS:

Either the owner's name or the school district
number or both must be at least four
inches high, approximately centered and as
high as practicable below the window line.
(Section 12-802 of the Illinois Vehicle
Equipment Law) The above required lettering
must be located on one line.

DEPARTMENT OF TRANSPORTATION

NOTICE OF ADOPTED RULES

The following lettering must be at least two inches high:

1) *The word "CAPACITY," or the abbreviation "CAP.," and the rated passenger capacity followed by the word "PASSENGERS," or the abbreviation "PASS.," shall be displayed on the outside of the body near the rear edge of the service entrance.*

2) *Empty weight in pounds shall be shown on bus.* (Section 12-802 of the Illinois Vehicle Equipment Law)

Manufacturer's identification name, emblem, or number(s) may be displayed but not on service door glazing. Manufacturer's name, emblem, etc. must not interfere with required lettering. Decals are permissable. All lettering must be black.

Optional route identification markers (numbers or symbols) are allowed. They must be located in either the first window or on the bus body directly behind the service entrance door. Route markers affixed to the bus body must meet paint requirements and must not obstruct any required lettering.

For buses manufactured on or after May 2, 1994, "EMERGENCY DOOR" in letters at least 1.95 inches (5 cm) high must be located at the top of, or directly above, any emergency exit door. For any emergency window exit "EMERGENCY EXIT" must be located at the top of, or directly above, or at the bottom of the emergency window exit in letters at least 1.95 inches (5 cm) high. The labelling must be of a color that contrasts with its background. (57 FR 49413, November 2, 1992)

REJECT VEHICLE IF:

Lettering does not meet requirements. Lettering or decals are not distinct, required, or allowed. Lettering is obstructed.

DEPARTMENT OF TRANSPORTATION

NOTICE OF ADOPTED RULES

2) Interior

A) Front

PROCEDURES/SPECIFICATIONS:

Each letter or numeral must be at least two inches (50 mm) high and contrasting sharply with background. A colorless background strip (such as white, aluminum or silver) may be used. Decals are permitted.

On right side: Either "CAPACITY" or "CAP." plus numerals showing rated passenger capacity, followed by either "PASSENGER" or "PASS."

As nearly as practicable opposite the center of aisle, but to right of inside mirror, either "NO STANDEES" or "NO STANDEES PERMITTED."

A red cross formed of five equal squares with words "FIRST-AID KIT" shall be displayed on the compartment door, or cover, if the first-aid kit is to be carried in the locked compartment.

The words "FIRE EXTINGUISHER" shall be displayed on the compartment door, or cover, if the fire extinguisher is to be carried in the locked compartment.

Exception: On a bus with chassis (incomplete vehicle) manufactured in March 1977 or earlier, "NO STANDEES" need not be opposite center of aisle and the word "PASSENGERS," or "PASS.," is optional.

REJECT VEHICLE IF:
Lettering does not meet requirements. Lettering is not black, distinct, required or allowed.

B) Left   PROCEDURES/SPECIFICATIONS:

A "Stop Line" in contrasting color is required between 5.9 and 6.1 inches below the top

DEPARTMENT OF TRANSPORTATION

NOTICE OF ADOPTED RULES

of the window opening. The line shall be located between each window that slides downward.

If bus is equipped with a side emergency door it is to be labelled "EMERGENCY EXIT" in letters at least two inches high directly above the door.

If bus is equipped with side emergency windows, they are to be labelled "EMERGENCY EXIT" in letters at least two inches high directly below the window.

An arrow indicating the direction in which to move release mechanism handle(s) to open emergency exit and operating instructions shall be painted or permanently affixed within six inches of each release handle.

For buses manufactured on or after May 2, 1994, "EMERGENCY DOOR" in letters at least 1.95 inches (5 cm) high must be located at the top of, or directly above, any emergency exit door. For any emergency window exit, "EMERGENCY EXIT" must be located at the top of, or directly above, or at the bottom of the emergency window exit in letters at least 1.95 inches (5 cm) high. The labelling must be of a color that contrasts with its background. Concise operating instructions describing the motions necessary to unlatch and open the door must be located within 5.85 inches (15 cm) of the release mechanism on the inside surface of the bus. These operating instructions shall be in letters at least .39 inches (1 cm) high and of a color that contrasts with its background. (57 FR 49413, November 2, 1992)

REJECT VEHICLE IF:

Lettering does not meet requirements. Line or line and lettering is not distinct, required, or allowed.

C) Rear   PROCEDURES/SPECIFICATIONS:

DEPARTMENT OF TRANSPORTATION

NOTICE OF ADOPTED RULES

"EMERGENCY DOOR" in letters at least two inches high directly over emergency door exit. "Emergency door operating instructions" applied to door. Arrow or arrows required unless "push or pull" type of release mechanism is used.

In the case of a "push" or "pull" type of release mechanism where the direction of movement to open the emergency exit cannot be shown by one arrow, either three or four straight arrows shall be placed as equally spaced as practicable around the object to be pushed or pulled, with the head of each arrow adjacent to and pointing directly at that object. Each arrow shall be the same color and, when practicable, the same size as though it were a single arrow. In addition, the pertinent word "PUSH" or "PULL" shall be displayed near that object.

For buses manufactured on or after May 2, 1994, "EMERGENCY DOOR" in letters at least 1.95 inches (5 cm) high must be located at the top of, or directly above, any emergency exit door. For any emergency window exit, "EMERGENCY EXIT" must be located at the top of, or directly above, or at the bottom of the emergency window exit in letters at least 1.95 inches (5 cm) high. The labelling must be of a color that contrasts with its background. Concise operating instructions describing the motions necessary to unlatch and open the door must be located within 5.85 inches (15 cm) of the release mechanism on the inside surface of the bus. These operating instructions shall be in letters at least .39 inches (1 cm) high and of a color that contrasts with its background. (57 FR 49413, November 2, 1992)

REJECT VEHICLE IF:

Lettering does not meet requirements. Lettering is not distinct, required, or allowed.

D) Right

DEPARTMENT OF TRANSPORTATION

NOTICE OF ADOPTED RULES

PROCEDURES/SPECIFICATIONS:

A "Stop Line" in contrasting color is required
between 5.9 and 6.1 inches below the top
of the window opening. The line shall be
located between each window that slides
downward. Decals are permitted.

"EMERGENCY EXIT" shall be on or immediately
below emergency window (if installed).

Instructions for emergency operation of a
power operated door shall be affixed
permanently on the inside of the door in
letters at least .5 inch high. Decals are
permitted.

Optional route identification markers (numbers
or symbols) are allowed. They must be
located in either the first window or on the
bus body directly behind the service entrance
door. If route identification markers are
installed in permanent holder or bracket,
the holder or bracket must have rounded edges
or be padded.

For buses manufactured on or after May 2,
1994, "EMERGENCY DOOR" in letters at least
1.95 inches (5 cm) high must be located at
the top of, or directly above, any side
emergency door. For any emergency window
exit "EMERGENCY EXIT" in letters at least
1.95 inches (5 cm) high must be located at
the top of, or directly above, or at the
bottom of the emergency window exit. The
labelling must be of a color that contrasts
with its background. Concise operating
instructions describing the motions necessary
to unlatch and open the exit must be
located within 5.85 inches (15 cm) of the
release mechanism on the inside surface of
the bus. These instructions shall be in
letters at least .39 inches (I cm) high and
of a color that contrasts with its background.
(57 FR 49413, November 2, 1992)

REJECT VEHICLE IF:

DEPARTMENT OF TRANSPORTATION

NOTICE OF ADOPTED RULES

Lettering does not meet requirements. Line or
line and lettering is not distinct, |
required, or allowed. Lettering is |
obstructed.

E) Ceiling

PROCEDURES/SPECIFICATIONS

For buses manufactured on or after May 2,
1994, any roof exit must be labelled
"EMERGENCY EXIT" in letters at least 1.95
inches (5 cm) high, of a color that contrasts
with its background. The labelling must
be located on an inside surface of the exit,
or within II.7 inches (30 cm) of the roof exit
opening. Concise operating instructions
describing the motions necessary to unlatch
and open the emergency exit shall be located
within 5.85 inches (15 cm) of the release
mechanism. These instructions shall be in
letters at least .39 inches (I cm) high and
of a color that contrasts with its background.
(57 FR 49413, November 2, 1992)

d) LIGHTS

1) Back Up

PROCEDURES/SPECIFICATIONS:

Two white lights shall be provided. Must meet
federal standards. (49 CFR 571.108)

Exception: All buses purchased prior to
September 1974 are exempt; however, for any
unit equipped with back up lamps, they must be
operational.

REJECT VEHICLE IF:

Back up lights do not function; illegal color;
broken lens.

2) Clearance,
   Front

PROCEDURES/SPECIFICATIONS:

Two clearance lights (amber) at highest and
widest portions of the body. Must conform to

DEPARTMENT OF TRANSPORTATION

NOTICE OF ADOPTED RULES

federal standards. 49 CFR 571.108 May be
combined with side marker lamp.

Exception: Buses less than 80 inches wide or
20 feet long are exempt. (Section 12-202(a)
of the Illinois Vehicle Equipment Law)

REJECT VEHICLE IF:

Front clearance lights do not function;
improper color; broken lens.

3) Clearance,
   Rear   PROCEDURES/SPECIFICATIONS:

Two clearance lights (red) mounted at highest
and widest parts of body. Must conform to
federal standards. 49 CFR 571.108

Exception: Buses less than 80 inches wide or
20 feet long are exempt. (Section 12-202(a)
of the Illinois Vehicle Equipment Law)

REJECT VEHICLE IF:

Rear clearance lights do not function;
improper color; broken lens.

4) Identification,
   Front   PROCEDURES/SPECIFICATIONS:

Three amber lights mounted at center front
near top of body above "SCHOOL BUS" sign.
Must conform to federal standards. 49 CFR
571.108

Exception: Buses less than 80 inches wide or
20 feet long are exempt. (Section 12-202(a)
of the Illinois Vehicle Equipment Law)

REJECT VEHICLE IF:

Front cluster lights do not function properly;
improper color; broken lens.

5) Identification,
   Rear

DEPARTMENT OF TRANSPORTATION

NOTICE OF ADOPTED RULES

PROCEDURES/SPECIFICATIONS:

Three red lights mounted at center rear near
top of body either above or below "SCHOOL BUS"
sign. Must conform to federal standards.
49 CFR 571.108

Exception: Buses less than 80 inches wide or
20 feet long are exempt. (Section 12-202 (a)
of the Illinois Vehicle Equipment Law)

REJECT VEHICLE IF:

Rear cluster lights do not function properly;
improper color; broken lens.

6) Flashing
   Lights   PROCEDURES/SPECIFICATIONS:

*All school buses purchased after December 31,
1975, shall be equipped with an eight light
flashing signal system with two red and two
amber flashing signal lamps mounted above
windshield spaced no less than three feet
apart and at same horizontal level. The
rear of the vehicle shall be equipped with
two red and two amber flashing signal lamps
mounted and spaced no less than three feet
apart and at same horizontal level. Minimum
diameter 5 1/2 inches sealed beam.*

*Effective December 31, 1978, all school buses
shall be equipped with the eight light
flashing signal system described in the above
paragraph. (Section 12-805 of the
Illinois Vehicle Equipment Law)*

A separate circuit breaker and a master switch
shall be provided for this signal system.
When in its "off" position this master
switch shall prevent the following:

1)   Operation of the 8 lamp system;

2)   Operation of any lamps mounted on the
      stop signal arm;

DEPARTMENT OF TRANSPORTATION

NOTICE OF ADOPTED RULES

3) Operation of any electrically controlled mechanism that would cause the stop signal arm to extend.

The controls for the eight lamp flashing signals, the stop signal arm and the service entrance door shall be arranged so as to provide for the following sequence of operations while the engine is running.

1) Place the alternately flashing signal system master switch in its "off" position. Close and secure the service entrance door. Actuate the alternately flashing signal system hand or foot control. The alternately flashing signal lamps of either yellow (amber) or red color shall not go on.

2) With the master switch "off" and the hand or foot control actuated, open the service door. The alternately flashing signals of either color shall not go on and the stop signal arm shall not extend.

3) Deactivate the hand or foot control. Place the alternately flashing signal system master switch in its "on" position. Close and secure the service door. Open the service door. The alternately flashing signal lamps of either color shall not go on and the stop signal arm shall not extend.

4) Close and secure the service door. Actuate the alternately flashing signal system by hand or foot control. A yellow pilot lamp in the view of the driver and the yellow alternately flashing signals shall go on.

5) Desecure but do not open the service door. The yellow pilot and the yellow alternately flashing signals shall go off. A red pilot lamp in the view of the driver and the red alternately flashing signals shall go on. The stop signal arm shall extend.

DEPARTMENT OF TRANSPORTATION

NOTICE OF ADOPTED RULES

6) Fully open the service door. The red pilot and red signals shall remain on and the stop arm shall remain extended.

7) Close but do not secure the service door. The red pilot and red signals shall remain on and the stop arm shall remain extended.

8) Open the service door. The red pilot and red signals shall remain on and the stop arm remain extended.

9) Close and secure the service door. The red pilot and red signals shall go off and the stop arm shall retract.

10) Open the service door. Alternately flashing signals of either color shall not go on and the stop arm shall not extend.

REJECT VEHICLE IF:

Flashing lights do not function properly; broken lens or improper lens color.

7) Headlights

PROCEDURES/SPECIFICATIONS:

Shall have at least two headlamps with at least one mounted on each side of the front of the bus. Lamp body must be securely attached. Lenses, reflectors, bulbs, etc., must be in good condition, properly aimed and fill required intensity. Check for bulb burnout. Verify high and low beams are functioning. Shall conform to federal standards. (49 CFR 571.108)

REJECT VEHICLE IF:

Headlights do not meet requirements.

8) Interior PROCEDURES/SPECIFICATIONS:

Adequate to illuminate aisles, step well, and emergency passageways.

DEPARTMENT OF TRANSPORTATION

NOTICE OF ADOPTED RULES.

REJECT VEHICLE IF:

Interior lights do not provide adequate
lighting; cracked or broken lenses; improper
color.

9) License
Plate

PROCEDURES/SPECIFICATIONS:

Adequate white light to illuminate license
plate. (49 CFR 571.108) May be combined
with one of the tail lights.

REJECT VEHICLE IF:

License plate light does not provide adequate
lighting; cracked or broken lenses; improper
color.

10) Parking
Lights

PROCEDURES/SPECIFICATIONS:

Shall be one lamp on each side; white or amber
color. (49 CFR 571.108)

*All buses 80 or more inches in overall width
which are equipped with side marker lamps,
clearance lamps, and intermediate side marker
lamps are exempt from having parking
lights. However, if vehicle is equipped with
parking lights, they must be operational.*
(Section 12-202 of the Illinois Vehicle
Equipment Law)

REJECT VEHICLE IF:

Parking lights do not meet requirements;
improper color; cracked or broken lenses.

11) Sidemarker, *Left*

PROCEDURES/SPECIFICATIONS:

Two lamps: one amber at front and one red at
rear, mounted as high as practicable. Shall
conform to federal standards. (49 CFR 571.108)

DEPARTMENT OF TRANSPORTATION

NOTICE OF ADOPTED RULES

Exception: A bus manufactured in August 1974
or earlier is exempt.

Buses less than 80 inches wide or 20 feet long
are exempt. (Section 12-202(a) of the
Illinois Vehicle Equipment Law)

REJECT VEHICLE IF:

Left marker lights do not meet requirements;
do not function properly; improper color;
cracked or broken lenses.

12) Sidemarker, Right

PROCEDURES/SPECIFICATIONS:

Two lamps: one amber at front and one red at
rear, mounted as high as practicable. Shall
conform to federal standards. (49 CFR 571.108)

Exception: A bus manufactured in August 1974
or earlier is exempt.

*Buses less than 80 inches wide or 20 feet long
are exempt.* (Section 12-202(a) of the
Illinois Vehicle Equipment Law)

REJECT VEHICLE IF:

Right marker lights do not meet requirements;
improper color; cracked or broken lenses.

13) Step Well

PROCEDURES/SPECIFICATIONS:

At least the nosings of the service entrance
steps and the floor around the stepwell shall
be automatically illuminated with white light
when the ignition is on and the service door
is open.

No lamp shall be installed so as to shine
directly into the eyes of a pupil moving
through the service entrance and looking at
the service steps.

Exception: On a bus with chassis (incomplete

DEPARTMENT OF TRANSPORTATION

NOTICE OF ADOPTED RULES

vehicle) manufactured in March 1977 or
earlier, a stepwell light that does not
illuminate all the step nosings or does not
illuminate the floor around the service
entranceway may be used.

REJECT VEHICLE IF:

Step well light does not meet requirements;
improper color; cracked or broken lenses.

14) Stop PROCEDURES/SPECIFICATIONS:

Two red lights mounted at same height and as
high as practicable below window line. Seven
inch minimum diameter or 19 square inches.
Not less than three feet apart laterally.
Must conform to federal standards. (49 CFR
571.108)

REJECT VEHICLE IF:

Stop lights do not meet requirements; improper
color; cracked or broken lenses; do not
function properly.

15) Strobe
(optional) PROCEDURES/SPECIFICATIONS:

If installed, lamp must comply with following
requirements:

1) One per bus;

2) Shall emit white or bluish/white light;

3) Shall be visible from any direction;

4) Shall flash 60 to 120 times per minute;

5) Shall be visible in normal sunlight;

6) Mounted at or behind center of rooftop
and equal distance from each side.
(Section 12-815 of the Illinois Vehicle
Equipment Law)

Distance from rear will be calculated by

DEPARTMENT OF TRANSPORTATION

NOTICE OF ADOPTED RULES

measuring height of filament and multiplying
same by 30 inches. (i.e., Filament height x
30 = distance from rear of bus where lamp is
to be located)

REJECT VEHICLE IF:

If installed, strobe does not meet
installation requirements; does not function
properly; improper color; cracked or broken
lenses.

Shielding is present.

16) Tail PROCEDURES/SPECIFICATIONS:

Two red lights mounted with centers not less
than 40 inches nor more than 50 inches from
surface on which vehicle stands. Must conform
to federal standards. 49 CFR 571.108

REJECT VEHICLE IF:

Tail lights do not meet requirements; do not
function properly; improper color; cracked or
broken lenses.

17) Turn
Signal,
Left
(armored) PROCEDURES/SPECIFICATIONS:

Flush mounted "armored" type amber clearance
lamp mounted behind driver's seat. Functions
with regular turn signal.

Exception: All buses purchased prior to
September 1974 are exempt from having left
armored turn signals.

Exceptions: Buses with capacity rating of
less than 33 passengers are exempt. Buses
manufactured in August 1974 or earlier are
exempt. Buses that measure less than 80
inches wide or 20 feet long are exempt.

REJECT VEHICLE IF:

DEPARTMENT OF TRANSPORTATION

NOTICE OF ADOPTED RULES

Left turn signal does not meet requirements;
does not function properly; improper color;
cracked or broken lenses.

18) Turn
Signal,
Right
(armored) PROCEDURES/SPECIFICATIONS:

Flush mounted "armored" type amber clearance
lamp mounted at approximately seat level and
rub rail height just to rear of service door.
Functions with regular turn signal lamps.

Exception: All buses purchased prior to
September 1974 are exempt from having right
armored turn signals.

Exceptions: Buses with capacity rating of
less than 33 passengers are exempt. Buses
manufactured in August 1974 or earlier are
exempt. Buses that measure less than 80
inches wide or 20 feet long are exempt.

REJECT VEHICLE IF:

Right turn signal does not meet requirements;
does not function properly; improper color;
cracked or broken lenses.

19) Turn
Signal,
Front PROCEDURES/SPECIFICATIONS:

One amber or white lens on each side, at or
near the front, at the same height and as far
apart as practicable. Must meet federal
standard 49 CFR 571.108.

Operate turn signals and four-way warning
hazards to check performance of front and
rear lights.

REJECT VEHICLE IF:

Front turn signal does not meet requirements;
does not function properly; improper color;
cracked or broken lenses.

DEPARTMENT OF TRANSPORTATION

NOTICE OF ADOPTED RULES

Four-way warning hazards do not operate
properly.

20) Turn
Signal,
Rear PROCEDURES/SPECIFICATIONS:

One red or amber lens on each side at the same
height and as far apart as practicable
below window. Must meet federal standard 49
CFR 571.108.

REJECT VEHICLE IF:

Rear turn signal does not meet requirements;
improper color; does not function properly;
cracked or broken lenses.

e) LOCKED
COMPARTMENT PROCEDURES/SPECIFICATIONS:

Fire extinguisher, first-aid kit, and warning
devices may be stored either in a closed,
unlocked compartment or under lock and key,
provided the locking device is connected with an
automatic warning signal that will alert driver when
compartment is locked. The automatic alarm
shall be both audible and visible to the
seated driver. The alarm shall alert the
driver when the engine is running and the
compartment is locked and cannot be readily
opened without using a tool, key, or
combination. An alarm cut-off or "squelch"
control is prohibited.

Each safety item inside the compartment shall
be named on the outside of the compartment
cover, or door. In addition, a RED CROSS
formed of five equal squares shall be
displayed on the cover when the first aid kit
is inside the compartment.

Exception: A bus with chassis manufactured in
March 1977 or earlier need not have a
visible alarm.

REJECT VEHICLE IF:

DEPARTMENT OF TRANSPORTATION

NOTICE OF ADOPTED RULES

Locked compartment is not readily accessible
to driver; lettering or identification
missing; alarm does not function properly
when compartment is locked and vehicle is
running.

DEPARTMENT OF TRANSPORTATION

NOTICE OF ADOPTED RULES

Section 443.APPENDIX H Mirrors Through Rub Rails

a) MIRRORS

PROCEDURES/SPECIFICATIONS:

Every required mirror shall be of reflecting
material protected from abrasion, scratching,
and corrosion. Mirror shall be firmly
installed on stable supports so as to give a
clear, stable, reflected view. Mirrors shall
be adjustable so as to give and maintain
its required field of view.

Convex crossover mirrors can be combined with
either the right or left side safety mirrors
provided the convex mirror meets the field of
view and size requirements established in this
subsection or in 49 CFR 571.111.

REJECT VEHICLE IF:

Mirrors do not meet requirements; defective;
excessively clouded; not adjustable; not
securely attached; cracked or broken glass.

1) Exterior

A) Rear
View
Driving

PROCEDURES/SPECIFICATIONS:

Shall be mounted outside on the left and right
sides of the bus. Must give seated
driver a view to the rear along each side of
the bus. Must be at least 50 square inches
of usable flat rectangular reflecting surface
on each side. (49 CFR 571.111)

If the rear view driving mirror does not
provide the required field of view, a convex
driving mirror must be installed to expand
the driving view to the rear. However, the
usable flat reflecting surface must be
rectangular and must maintain at least 50
square inches.

REJECT VEHICLE IF:

DEPARTMENT OF TRANSPORTATION

NOTICE OF ADOPTED RULES

Rear view driving mirror does not meet
requirements; defective; excessively clouded;
not adjustable; not securely attached;
cracked or broken glass.

**B) Right
Side
Safety**   PROCEDURES/SPECIFICATIONS:

An outside convex mirror, either alone or in
combination with the crossover mirror system,
shall give the seated driver a view of the
roadway along the right side of the bus
between the most forward surface of the right
front tire and the rear of the rear
bumper. The projected reflecting surface of
this convex mirror shall be at least 40
square inches (7 1/8 inches diameter if a
circle).

Extra-wide-angle convex mirror heads are
permissible on right front corner only.

Exception: A right safety mirror is optional
on a bus manufactured in August 1974 or
earlier.

REJECT VEHICLE IF:

Right side safety mirror does not meet
requirements; defective; excessively clouded;
not adjustable; not securely attached;
cracked or broken glass.

**C) Left
Side
Safety**   PROCEDURES/SPECIFICATIONS:

A convex mirror is required if the left rear
view driving mirror system does not give the
seated driver a reflected view of the roadway
along the left side of the bus between the
front edge of the driver's seat (in most
forward position) and the rear of the rear
bumper. The convex mirror shall be installed
so that either alone or in combination with
the rear view driving mirror gives the seated
driver the proper view.

DEPARTMENT OF TRANSPORTATION

NOTICE OF ADOPTED RULES

Exception: A left safety mirror is optional
on a bus with chassis manufactured in March
1977 or earlier.

REJECT VEHICLE IF:

Left side safety mirror does not meet requirements;
defective; excessively clouded; not adjustable; not
securely attached; cracked or broken glass.

D) Crossover   PROCEDURES/SPECIFICATIONS:

An outside convex mirror shall give the seated
driver a view of the front bumper and the
area of roadway in front of the bus. The
projected reflecting surface of this
mirror shall be at least 40 square inches (7
1/8 inch diameter if a circle). (49 CFR
571.111)

Exception: If the seated driver of a forward
control bus has a direct view of the front
bumper and the area of roadway in front of
the bus, a crossover mirror is optional.

REJECT VEHICLE IF:

Crossover mirror does not meet requirements;
defective; excessively clouded; not
adjustable; not securely attached; cracked or
broken glass.

2) Interior   PROCEDURES/SPECIFICATIONS:

All buses purchased during and after September
1974 must have a clear view safety glass,
metal backed and framed with rounded
corners and edges which shall be padded.
Shall afford a good view of the interior and
roadway to the rear.

All buses purchased prior to September 1974
must have a rear view mirror.

REJECT VEHICLE IF:

Interior mirror does not meet requirements;
defective; excessively clouded; not

DEPARTMENT OF TRANSPORTATION

NOTICE OF ADOPTED RULES

adjustable; not securely attached; cracked or broken glass.

b) PAINT REQUIREMENTS

PROCEDURES/SPECIFICATIONS:

The exterior of the body, excluding required rub rail and lettering, shall be painted a uniform color: National School Bus Glossy Yellow. Required rub rail and lettering must be black. Additional rub rails may either be black or yellow. The front and rear bumpers and wheels may be black or manufacturer's colors. Grilles and hub caps may be a bright finish (chrome, anodized aluminum, etc.). (Section 12-801 of the Illinois Vehicle Equipment Law)

For buses manufactured on or after May 2, 1994, each opening for a required emergency exit must be outlined around its outside perimeter with a minimum 1 inch (2.54 cm.) wide yellow retroreflective tape. This yellow retroreflective tape must be on the exterior surface of the bus. (57 FR 49413, November 2, 1992)

Optional: Black area around flashing lights is permitted. Black area must not interfere with "SCHOOL BUS" lettering.

Optional: Reflectorized tape is permitted provided it reflects the same color that is applied to and cannot be located on any bumper.

Exception: Hoods may be lusterless black or lusterless school bus yellow.

REJECT VEHICLE IF:

Paint does not meet color requirements; paint in poor condition (i.e., faded, peeling or rusted).

Optional black area around flashers interferes with required lettering.

Optional reflectorized tape does not meet color requirements or is located on the bumper.

c) PROJECTIONS

1) Exterior

PROCEDURES/SPECIFICATIONS:

Entire rear of bus must be nonhitchable.

Exceptions: A bus manufactured in October 1978 or earlier is exempt from nonhitchable bumpers. A bus manufactured in August 1974 or earlier is exempt from nonhitchable projections. Every school bus, however, must have a nonhitchable door handle.

REJECT VEHICLE IF:

Exterior projections do not comply with nonhitchable projection requirements.

2) Interior

PROCEDURES/SPECIFICATIONS:

Interior shall be free of all dangerous projections.

Optional equipment (e.g., video camera) that is located in the bulkhead area of the bus and not flush with the interior walls must meet the following requirements:

1) Must not interfere with occupant's entering or exiting the bus.

2) Must not be located in driver's head impact zone.

3) Must not obstruct required lettering.

Additional projections (e.g., external speakers) in the head impact zone shall be padded to prevent injury. This includes inner lining of ceiling and walls. Installation of book racks is not permissible.

Exception: All buses purchased prior to September 1974 may be equipped with book

DEPARTMENT OF TRANSPORTATION

NOTICE OF ADOPTED RULES

racks. However, if book racks are present,
they shall be above side windows and shall not
extend forward of the front seat or
across or above the emergency door. Racks
must be free of projections likely to cause
injury.

Exception: All buses purchased prior to
September 1974 are exempt from padding on
interior projections.

REJECT VEHICLE IF:

Optional equipment in bulkhead does not meet
requirements.

Remaining interior projections are not padded
(e.g., external speakers). Book racks are
present.

Flush mounted speakers are exempt from padding
requirements.

For buses purchased prior to September 1974,
book racks do not meet requirements.

d) REFLECTORS

   1) Front   PROCEDURES/SPECIFICATIONS:

*Two yellow rigid or sheet type (tape) front
reflex reflectors shall be attached securely
and as far forward as practicable.* (Section
12-202 of the Illinois Vehicle Equipment Law)
*They shall be located between 15 and 60
inches above the roadway at either fender,
cowl, or body and installed so as to mark
the outer edge of the maximum width of the
bus.* No part of the required reflecting
material may be obscured by a lamp, mirror,
bracket, or any other portion of the bus. No
part of the required reflecting material may
be more than 11.8 inches (300 mm) inboard of
the outer edge of the nearest rub rail (12
inches on a bus with chassis manufactured in
March 1977 or earlier). The reflector may be
any shape (e.g., square, rectangle, circle,
oval, etc.). A rigid type reflex reflector

DEPARTMENT OF TRANSPORTATION

NOTICE OF ADOPTED RULES

may be any size if permanently marked either
DOT, SAE A, or SAE J 594; otherwise, it shall
display at least seven square inches of
reflecting material (about 3 inch diameter if
a solid circle).

A sheet type (tape) reflex reflector may
conform to the surface on which it is
installed but its forward projected
reflecting area shall be at least eight
square inches.

Exception: *Buses that measure 80 inches wide
or less or that measure 25 feet long or less
are exempt.* (Section 12-202(a) of the
Illinois Vehicle Equipment Law)

REJECT VEHICLE IF:

Missing or damaged reflective material; not
located or positioned as required.

   2) Left Side   PROCEDURES/SPECIFICATIONS:

*One amber at or near the front and one red at
or near the rear. Mounted at a height not
less than 15 inches and not more than 60
inches above the surface of the road.* On
sides of buses 20 feet or more in length, one
amber as near center as practicable must
also be provided. (Section 12-202 of the
Illinois Vehicle Equipment Law) Minimum
three inches in diameter.

REJECT VEHICLE IF:

Missing or damaged reflective material; not
located or positioned as required.

   3) Right Side   PROCEDURES/SPECIFICATIONS:

*One amber at or near the front and one red at
or near the rear. Mounted at a height not
less than 15 inches and not more than 60
inches above the surface of the road.* On
sides of buses 20 feet or more in length, one
amber as near center as practicable must
also be provided. (Section 12-202 of the

DEPARTMENT OF TRANSPORTATION

NOTICE OF ADOPTED RULES

Illinois Vehicle Equipment Law) Minimum three
inches in diameter.

REJECT VEHICLE IF:

Missing or damaged reflective material; not
located or positioned as required.

4) Rear   PROCEDURES/SPECIFICATIONS:

*Two red reflectors on rear body within 12
inches of lower right and lower left corners.*
(Section 12-202 of the Illinois Vehicle
Equipment Law) Minimum three inches in
diameter.

Exception: *Buses that measure 80 inches wide
or less or that measure 25 feet long or less
are exempt.* (Section 12-202(a) of the
Illinois Vehicle Equipment Law)

REJECT VEHICLE IF:

Missing or damaged reflective material; not
located or positioned as required.

e) RUB RAILS

PROCEDURES/SPECIFICATIONS:

There shall be one rub rail located
approximately at seat level which shall
extend from the rear of the entrance door on
both sides, except at functioning doors,
to a point of curvature at the rear of the
body. Rub rails shall be constructed of
16-gauge longitudinally corrugated or ribbed
steel, ventilated four inches minimum
width, and securely fastened to the body by
bolts, rivets, or welding.

Rub rails are not required on Type II service
and driver's entrance doors; however, if
installed, they must meet same requirements
as above.

REJECT VEHICLE IF:

DEPARTMENT OF TRANSPORTATION

NOTICE OF ADOPTED RULES

Rub rails are missing; not firmly attached;
incorrect color; or incorrect number of rails.

DEPARTMENT OF TRANSPORTATION

NOTICE OF ADOPTED RULES

Section 443.APPENDIX I Seat Belts Through Steps

a) SEAT BELTS

PROCEDURES/SPECIFICATIONS:

A seat belt shall be installed for the driver (Section 12-807 of the Illinois Vehicle Equipment Law). Seat belts shall be installed for each pupil as required by 49 CFR 571.222. At all times, each seat belt shall be readily available for quick and easy use. All retractors installed shall be automatic locking type. Each belt assembly shall be clean. Belt material, buckle, tongue, etc., of each driver's belt shall remain above floor when not in use.

Exception: On a bus with incomplete vehicle (chassis) manufactured in March 1977 or earlier, pupil belts are not required.

Exception: On a bus manufactured in August 1974 or earlier, driver's belts, etc., need not remain above floor.

REJECT VEHICLE IF:

Seat belts are not secured, not adjustable, cracked, broken, frayed, torn or dirty. Retractor or buckle does not operate properly.

b) SEAT, DRIVER'S   PROCEDURES/SPECIFICATIONS:

The driver's seat shall be rigidly positioned and have a forward and backward adjustment without the use of tools or other nonattached devices.

Seat padding and covering shall be in good condition (i.e., free from holes and tears). Seat cushions shall be securely fastened to the seat frame.

REJECT VEHICLE IF:

DEPARTMENT OF TRANSPORTATION

NOTICE OF ADOPTED RULES

mechanism does not function properly.

c) SEAT, PASSENGER

PROCEDURES/SPECIFICATIONS:

For buses purchased after September 1974 all seats shall have a minimum depth of 14 inches and a minimum back rest height of 20 inches with a 13 inch allowable average hip room in determining seating capacity. All seats shall be forward facing and securely fastened to part or parts of bus which support them. No bus shall be equipped with jump seats or portable seats. The center-to-center seat spacing shall be no more than 24 inches, measured from the seating reference point to the seat back or guard barrier in front of the seat. Padding and covering shall be of fire resistant material. Minimum 36 inch headroom for sitting position above top of undepressed cushion line on all seats (measured vertically not more than seven inches from side wall at cushion height and at front and rear center of cushion). Backs of all seats of similar size shall be of the same width at top and the same height from floor and shall slant at the same angle with the floor. The top and side rails and seat backs shall be padded to cushion level. Seat padding and covering shall be in good condition (i.e., free from holes and tears). Seat cushions shall be securely fastened to the seat frame. (49 CFR 571.222)

Exception: All buses purchased prior to September 1974 and after January 1, 1972, shall have a seating plan for 16 pupils consisting of four rows of 30 inch forward facing seats with a minimum 12 inch aisle down the center. No jump or portable seats allowed. No seat or other object placed in the bus which restricts passageway to emergency door to less than 12 inches.

Exception: Those vehicles used as a school bus by school districts and private

DEPARTMENT OF TRANSPORTATION

NOTICE OF ADOPTED RULES

previously passed a school bus safety
inspection can still be utilized if they
continue to meet the inspection requirements
that were in effect at that time. These
vehicles will not have to be brought up to the
above standards.

A flip-up seat may be located only adjacent to
any side emergency door. For buses
manufactured on or after September 1, 1994 the
flip-up seat must conform to the following:

1)   The seat must be designed so that, when
     in the folded position, the seat cushion
     is flat against the seat back to prevent
     a child's limb from becoming lodged
     between the seat cushion and seat back.

2)   The seat must be designed to discourage a
     child from standing on the seat
     cushion when in the folded position.

3)   The working mechanism under the seat must
     be covered to eliminate any tripping
     hazard.

4)   All sharp metal edges on the seat must be
     padded to prevent any snagging
     hazard.

5)   No portion of a seat frame or seat bottom
     may extend past door opening.

6)   No portion of the door latch mechanism
     can be obstructed by a seat.

7)   There must be at least 11.7 inches (30
     cm) measured from the door opening to the
     seat back in front.

REJECT VEHICLE IF:

Passenger seats are not firmly attached to
body; broken frame; cushions not firmly
attached; padding and covering not fire
resistant. Padding or covering is loose, in
poor condition, or missing; seats are
torn or have holes; minimum seat dimensions

DEPARTMENT OF TRANSPORTATION

NOTICE OF ADOPTED RULES

or seat spacing is not in compliance.

d) STEERING
   SYSTEM

   1) Exterior

      A) King
         Pins   PROCEDURES/SPECIFICATIONS:

                   Raise vehicle so as to unload kingpins (brakes
                   should be applied to eliminate wheel
                   bearing looseness). Either grasp wheel at
                   top and bottom or use a bar for leverage.
                   Attempt to rock wheel in and out. Check
                   movement at extreme top or bottom of tire.
                   If movement exists, place a dial indicator,
                   tape measure, or a fixed device at the wheel
                   and measure amount of movement.

                   Place leverage bar under tire. Raise bar to
                   check for vertical movement between spindle
                   and support axle.

                   REJECT VEHICLE IF:

                   Wheel bearing movement exceeds 1/4 inch; or
                   kingpin movement exceeds:

Wheel size	Max allowed
16" or less	1/4"
16.1" to 18"	3/8"
over 18"	1/2"

      B) Linkage   PROCEDURES/SPECIFICATIONS:

                   For buses with single "I" beam or tube type
                   front axle, hoist bus under axle. For buses
                   with twin "I" beam type front axles or with "A
                   frame" control arms, each axle or arm
                   must be hoisted independently so as to load
                   the ball joints. Grasp front and rear of
                   tire and attempt to shake assembly right and
                   left to determine linkage looseness.
                   Measure movement of wheel.

DEPARTMENT OF TRANSPORTATION

NOTICE OF ADOPTED RULES

Inspect for damage to or looseness in the following linkage components:

1) Ball Joints

2) Cotter Pins

3) Drag Link

4) Idler Arm

5) Pitman Arm

6) Steering Box

7) Tie Rod

8) Tie Rod Ends

REJECT VEHICLE IF:

Measurement is found to be in excess of:

Rim Diameter	Maximum Allowable Movement
16" or less	1/4"
17" and 18"	3/8"
over 18"	1/2"

Any linkage component is bent; welded; loose; insecurely mounted or missing.

C) Power Steering

PROCEDURES/SPECIFICATIONS:

Manually and visually inspect:

1) Belts

2) Cylinders

3) Fluid level

4) Hoses

5) Mounting Brackets

DEPARTMENT OF TRANSPORTATION

NOTICE OF ADOPTED RULES

6) Power Assist

7) Pump

REJECT VEHICLE IF:

Steering components are:

1) Loose, frayed, cracked, missing; incorrect belts

2) Loose and/or leaking

3) Low fluid level

4) Cracked, leaking, rubbed by moving parts

5) Cracked, loose, or broken

6) No assist is evident

7) Loose, leaking.

D) Toe-In/ Toe-Out

PROCEDURES/SPECIFICATIONS:

With wheels held in a straight ahead position, drive vehicle slowly over the approved drive-on side slip indicator.

Excessive toe-in or toe-out is a general indication that complete check should be made of all front wheel alignment factors (caster, camber, steering axis inclination).

REJECT VEHICLE IF:

More than 30 feet per mile on the approved side slip indicator.

E) Wheel Bearings

PROCEDURES/SPECIFICATIONS:

With the front end of the vehicle lifted so as to load any ball joints, grasp the front tire top and bottom, rock it in and out. Record movement. To verify that any

DEPARTMENT OF TRANSPORTATION

NOTICE OF ADOPTED RULES

looseness detected is in the wheel bearing, notice the relative movement between the brake drum or disc and the backing plate or splash shield.

AGENCY NOTE: Wheel bearing play can be eliminated by applying service brakes.

REJECT VEHICLE IF:

Relative movement between drum and backing plate, measured at tire, is 1/4 inch or more.

2) Interior

A) Column PROCEDURES/SPECIFICATIONS:

Inspect to determine that column support bracket is properly tightened and all bolts are present.

REJECT VEHICLE IF:

Column support bracket is not properly tightened or bolts are missing.

B) Lash PROCEDURES/SPECIFICATIONS:

With road wheels in straight ahead position, turn steering wheel until a turning movement can be observed at the left road wheel. Slowly reverse steering wheel motion and measure lash.

REJECT VEHICLE IF:

Lash exceeds following acceptable limits:

Steering wheel maximum diameter (inches)	Acceptable lash measured at maximum circumference
16 or less	2
18	2 1/4
20	2 1/2
22	2 3/4

C) Shaft PROCEDURES/SPECIFICATIONS:

DEPARTMENT OF TRANSPORTATION

NOTICE OF ADOPTED RULES

Grasp steering wheel with both hands and attempt to move shaft up and down.

REJECT VEHICLE IF:

Steering shaft moves up and down.

D) Steering Wheel PROCEDURES/SPECIFICATIONS:

Inspect steering wheel condition.

REJECT VEHICLE IF:

Steering wheel is damaged. Any spokes are missing or reinforcement ring is exposed.

E) Travel PROCEDURES/SPECIFICATIONS:

Turn steering wheel through a full right and left turn checking for binding, jamming and complete travel left and right.

REJECT VEHICLE IF:

Binding or jamming is present. Does not complete full turn from left to right. Tire rubs on fender or frame during turn.

e) STEPS

PROCEDURES/SPECIFICATIONS:

The first service entrance step shall be no more than 13 1/2 inches off the ground. If necessary, a step of adequate width and length shall be installed to meet this requirement. Provision shall be made to prevent road splash from the wheel from accumulating on the step if installed outside the body.

Risers shall be approximately equal in height, upper risers no more than 12 inches in height.

The surface entrance steps shall have a

DEPARTMENT OF TRANSPORTATION

NOTICE OF ADOPTED RULES

nonskid material applied. A 1 1/2 inch to
three inch white nosing is required on the
floor at the top riser.

REJECT VEHICLE IF:

Steps or risers are not solid. Steps, risers
or nonskid material covering is missing,
loose, or not in good condition. White
nosing is missing or in poor condition.

DEPARTMENT OF TRANSPORTATION

NOTICE OF ADOPTED RULES

Section 443.APPENDIX J Stop Arm Panel Through Tow Hooks

a) STOP ARM PANEL

PROCEDURES/SPECIFICATIONS:

A stop arm panel must be installed on the left
side of the bus and may be operated
either manually or mechanically. Decals may
be used in lieu of painting.

Buses manufactured on or after September 1,
1992 must be equipped with an octagon-shaped
semaphore which meet the requirements listed
below under "Octagon."

Buses manufactured prior to September 1, 1992
may either be equipped with an octagon-shaped
semaphore which meets the requirements listed
below under "Octagon" or a hexagon shaped
semaphore which meets the requirements listed
below under "Hexagon."

Octagon - The arm shall be an octagon-shaped
semaphore which measures at least 450 mm x 450
mm (17.72 inches x 17.72 inches) in
diameter. The arm shall be red on both sides
with a white border at least 12 mm (.47
inches) wide on both sides. The arm shall
have the word "STOP" displayed in white
uppercase letters on both sides. The letters
shall be at least 150 mm (5.9 inches) in
height and have a stroke width of at least 20
mm (.79 inches).

The stop signal arm shall comply with either
(a) or (b) below:

a)   The entire surface of both sides of the
     arm can be reflectorized to meet 49 CFR
     571.131; or

b)   Each side of the arm shall have at least
     two red lamps centered on the vertical
     centerline of the stop arm. One lamp
     shall be located at the extreme top of
     the arm and the other at its extreme
     bottom. The lamps shall light and

DEPARTMENT OF TRANSPORTATION

NOTICE OF ADOPTED RULES

flash alternately when stop arm is
extended and likewise turn off and stop
flashing when arm is closed. (49
CFR-571.131) (See Section
443.Illustration A for examples.)

Hexagon - The arm shall be a hexagon shaped
semaphore approximately 18 inches wide and 18
inches long and of 18 gauge metal. The stop
arm signal shall have the "STOP" painted on
both sides in white letters at least six
inches high with a brush stroke approximately
7/8 inch wide. The word "STOP" shall be
painted on a panel with red background of
approximately 8 inches by 16 inches.
Remaining area of stop arm blade is to be
painted white with a band of white border at
least 1/2 inch wide painted from and rear on
both sides as contrast. White portion of stop
arm signal shall be reflectorized or
shall have double-faced lamps with red lens
approximately four inches in diameter located
in the top and bottommost position of the
blade. These lamps shall light and flash
alternately when stop arm is extended and
likewise turn off and stop flashing when arm
is closed. (Section 12-803 of the Illinois
Vehicle Equipment Law) (See Section
443.Illustration A for examples.)

Optional: Strobe lamps are acceptable on stop
arm panels.

REJECT VEHICLE IF:

Stop arm panel is in poor condition (i.e.,
faded, peeling, or rusted); lights do not
operate properly (if installed); is not
securely attached; is not operating properly;
does not meet requirements; is missing.

b) STORAGE
COMPARTMENT
(optional)   PROCEDURES/SPECIFICATIONS:

Covered, fire-resistant container securely
fastened of adequate strength and capacity
for tire chains and tools for minor emergency

DEPARTMENT OF TRANSPORTATION

NOTICE OF ADOPTED RULES

repairs.

REJECT VEHICLE IF:

If installed, storage compartment does not
meet requirements.

c) SUN VISOR

PROCEDURES/SPECIFICATIONS:

Shall be interior, adjustable and not less
than five inches by 16 inches. Must be
installed above windshield.

Not required to be transparent, but must not
interfere with view of interior rear view
mirror.

REJECT VEHICLE IF:

Sun visor does not meet requirements.

d) SUSPENSION

1) Shocks   PROCEDURES/SPECIFICATIONS:

Equipped with front and rear heavy-duty,
double acting shock absorbers.

REJECT VEHICLE IF:

Shocks are missing or severe leakage (not
slight dampness) occurs. Mounting bolts or
mounts are broken or loose, or rubber bushing
is partially or completely missing.

2) Springs

A) Coil   PROCEDURES/SPECIFICATIONS:

Visually inspect:

1)   Spring

2)   Control arms

3)   Torque arms (rear)

DEPARTMENT OF TRANSPORTATION

NOTICE OF ADOPTED RULES

REJECT VEHICLE IF:

Coil is missing, disconnected, broken, loose
bushings, welded or damaged.

B) Leaf   With use of a pry bar and using frame as a
           pivot, attempt to pry front and rear spring
           attachments and check for movement. Front of
           vehicle must be jacked up on chassis for
           checking front suspension. Visually inspect:

           1)   Springs

           2)   Shackles

           3)   Hangers

           4)   U-bolts

           5)   Center bolts

           6)   Bushings or pivot

           REJECT VEHICLE IF:

           Springs are missing or broken. Shackles or
           "U" bolts worn or loose. Center bolt in
           springs sheared or broken. Steering stops
           allow tire to rub on frame or metal.

           Any leaves are cracked or missing. Any
           shackle, shackle pins, hangers, or "U" bolts
           are worn, loose, or missing.

C) Torsion
   Bar (Stab-
   ilizer
   Bar)   PROCEDURES/SPECIFICATIONS:

           Visually inspect:

           1)   Torsion bar

           2)   Mounting brackets

           3)   Control arms

           4)   Torque arms (if applicable - rear)

DEPARTMENT OF TRANSPORTATION

NOTICE OF ADOPTED RULES

           5)   Stabilizer bar(s) (if applicable)

           REJECT VEHICLE IF:

           Torsion bar missing, disconnected, broken,
           loose, welded, or damaged.

e) TOW HOOKS
   (optional)

   1) Front   PROCEDURES/SPECIFICATIONS:

           A front tow hook must not extend beyond the
           front of the front bumper. Each front tow
           hook not fastened securely to the chassis
           frame shall be connected to the frame by
           suitable braces.

           REJECT VEHICLE IF:

           Tow hook(s) extend beyond bumper; not securely
           attached.

   2) Rear   PROCEDURES/SPECIFICATIONS:

           Any tow hook(s) installed on the rear shall be
           attached or braced to the chassis frame
           or to an equivalent structural member of an
           integral type bus. A tow hook must not extend
           beyond the rear face of the rear bumper.

           REJECT VEHICLE IF:

           Tow hook(s) extend beyond bumper; not securely
           attached.

Section 443.APPENDIX K Undercoating Through Windshield Wipers

a) UNDERCOATING

PROCEDURES/SPECIFICATIONS:

Fire resistant undercoating material applied by spray. Entire underside of body, front fenders, floor members and side panels below floor level must be covered.

REJECT VEHICLE IF:

Undercoating does not meet requirements.

b) VENTILATION

PROCEDURES/SPECIFICATIONS:

Body must be equipped with ventilating system capable of supplying proper quantity of air under operating conditions.

REJECT VEHICLE IF:

Air is obstructed; not securely fastened; not covered.

c) WARNING DEVICES

PROCEDURES/SPECIFICATIONS:

Either three red cloth flags not less than 12 inches square and three red reflectors minimum of 3 inches in diameter or three bidirectional emergency triangles that conform to 49 CFR 571.125 (Section 12-702 of the Illinois Vehicle Equipment Law) Kit shall be securely stored.

REJECT VEHICLE IF:

Required warning devices are not present or are in poor condition.

d) WHEELS

1) Housings PROCEDURES/SPECIFICATIONS:

Full open type attached to floor sheet to prevent water, fumes or dust entering the body. Inside height should not exceed 10 inches above floor line. Housings shall allow for unimpeded wheel and tire service or removal. Housing shall provide clearance for installation and use of tire chains on the dual or single tires installed on the rear wheels.

Inspect tire and road wheel assemblies.

REJECT VEHICLE IF:

Wheel housings do not meet clearance requirement; wheel housings are not firmly secured; holes are present.

A tire or wheel is rubbing against any portion of the suspension, chassis, or body.

2) Rim PROCEDURES/SPECIFICATIONS:

Inspect all wheel and rim bolts, nuts, studs, lugs, locking rings, etc. Each cover, cap, or decorative ring that obscures any of these items must be removed prior to the inspection.

Inspect for visible wheel damage.

REJECT VEHICLE IF:

Any wheel or rim securing device such as a nut, bolt, stud, lug, ring, or other type securing device is loose, missing, or cracked.

Wheel locating hole(s) are elongated, oversized, or "wallowed out." Any part of a wheel or rim is cracked, repaired by welding or rewelding, or damaged so as to cause unsafe operation of the vehicle.

3) Tires PROCEDURES/SPECIFICATIONS:

Inspect tire for proper inflation (i.e., flat tire).

DEPARTMENT OF TRANSPORTATION

NOTICE OF ADOPTED RULES

A regrooved, retreaded, or recapped tire shall
not be on the front steering axle.

A tire with restricted use marking is
prohibited (e.g., "MHS" or "SL" following
size marking, "Off Highway," "Farm Use,"
"Racing Only," etc.).

No school bus shall be equipped with any tire
which has been so worn that tread
configuration is absent on any part of the
tire which is in contact with the road
surface.

Inspect for tread wear:

1) Check for the presence of tread wear
    indicators.

2) For tires without tread wear indicators,
    use tread depth gauge to measure groove
    depth.

    Steering (Front) Axle: Measure groove
    depth at any point on a major tread
    groove.

    Drive (Rear) Axle: Measure groove depth
    in any two adjacent grooves at three
    equally spaced intervals around the
    circumference of the tire.

    Do not measure on a tie-bar, groove hump,
    or fillet.

3) For tires without tread wear indicators
    and with noncircumferential grooves, or
    "spaces," between the tread elements (as
    in snow, mud, lug knob, or traction
    treads):

        Steering (Front) Axle: Measure in a
        major groove at a point halfway
        between the center of the tire
        and the outside of the tread at any
        point on a major tread groove.

        Drive (Rear) Axle: Measure in a

DEPARTMENT OF TRANSPORTATION

NOTICE OF ADOPTED RULES

        major groove at a point halfway
        between the center of the tire and
        the outside of the tread at three
        equally spaced intervals around the
        circumference of the tire.

4) Inspect tire for bald, partially bald,
    cupped, dished, or unevenly worn areas.

AGENCY NOTE: "Bald" means without a groove.

    Inspect for visible cord damage and exposure
    of ply cords in sidewalls and treads,
    including belting material cords.

    Inspect for evidence of tread or sidewall
    separation.

    Inspect for regrooved or recut treads.

AGENCY NOTE: 49 CFR 369 requires tires marked "REGROOVABLE"
    to have sufficient tread rubber that,
    after regrooving, cord material below the
    grooves shall have a protective covering of
    tread material at least 3/32 inch thick.

    Inspect tires for legible markings showing
    size designation and carcass construction.

AGENCY NOTE: "R" in size designation shows radial
    construction. More plies at tread than
    sidewall shows belted construction. Same
    number of plies at tread and sidewall,
    without a belted or radial indication, shows
    plain bias construction.

    Tires on same axle must be of same
    construction.

    Inspect tires for size designation and for
    matched construction.

AGENCY NOTE: "Construction" refers to bias, bias belted, or
    radial arrangement of ply cords in the
    tire carcass.

    Inspect each single dual tire assembly.

DEPARTMENT OF TRANSPORTATION

NOTICE OF ADOPTED RULES

A mixture of regular and mud-and-snow treads must be same on both sides of axle.

When radial and conventional (i.e., bias) ply tires are both used on a vehicle, one of the following two requirements shall be met:

1. On vehicles with one single wheel axle and one or more dual wheel axles, radial tires shall be used on the steering (i.e., front) axle only.

2. On vehicles having two single wheel axles, radial tires shall be used on the rear axle only.

A tube built only for bias tire shall not be installed in a radial tire. Red color shall not be added to stem of a "bias" tube. (Valve stem of tube for radial tire is either marked "radial" or has red ring or is painted red.) A "radial" tube and flap may be used in a bias tire.

Inspect valve stems.

REJECT VEHICLE IF:

Improper inflation (flat tire).

Regrooved, retreaded or recapped tire is located on front steering axle.

Restricted marking is present.

Any part of tire which is in contact with road surface is absent of tread configuration.

1) Tread wear indicators contact road in any two adjacent grooves at three equally spaced intervals around the circumference of the tire.

2) On steering (front) axle: Tread groove depth is less than 4/32 inch when measured at any point on a major tread groove.

DEPARTMENT OF TRANSPORTATION

NOTICE OF ADOPTED RULES

On drive (rear) axle: Tread groove depth is less than 2/32 inch in any two adjacent grooves at three essentially equally spaced intervals around the circumference of the tire.

3) On steering axle: Tread groove depth is less than 4/32 inch when measured in a major groove at a point halfway between the center of the tire and the outside of the tread at any point on a major tread groove.

On drive axle: Tread groove depth is less than 2/32 inch when measured in a major groove at a point halfway between the center of the tire and the outside of the tread at three essentially equally spaced intervals around the circumference of the tire.

4) The tire has bald, partially bald, cupped, dished or unevenly worn areas.

A broken or cut cord can be seen. Rubber is worn, cracked, cut or otherwise deteriorated or damaged so that a cord can be seen - either when the tire is not touched or when the edges of the crack, cut or damage are parted or lifted by hand.

Tire has bump, bulge, knot or other evidence of partial carcass failure, air seepage, or loss of adhesion between carcass and tread or sidewall.

Tread has been regrooved or recut on a tire that does not have the word "REGROOVABLE" molded on or into both sides of the tire.

A tire on a road wheel does not exhibit a legible size marking and a legible construction marking.

Tires on the same axle are not of same construction.

A tire exceeds the diameter (not width) of its

DEPARTMENT OF TRANSPORTATION

NOTICE OF ADOPTED RULES

mate by 1/2 inch (1/4 inch radius) or
more; or one tire touches its mate.

A mixture of regular and mud-and-snow treads
are not the same on both sides of the axle.

Requirements for using both radial and
conventional tires on a vehicle are not met.

A tube built only for bias tire but installed
in a radial tire.

A valve stem leaks; is cracked; is either
damaged or positioned so as to hamper
pressure checking or inflation; shows
evidence of wear because of misalignment.

e) WINDOWS   PROCEDURES/SPECIFICATIONS:

All applicable provisions of 49 CFR 571.205
apply to the optional laminated safety glass
and also to any plastic material(s) used in a
multiple glazed unit.

Glazing shall be marked as follows pursuant to
49 CFR 571.205:

1)   Windshield - "AS 1" Glass

2)   Driver's window - "AS 1" Glass or "AS 2"
      Glass

3)   Driver's door - "AS 1" Glass or "AS 2"
      Glass

4)   All other locations - "AS 1" Glass, "AS
      2" Glass, or "AS 3" Glass.

REJECT VEHICLE IF:

Windows do not meet requirements or are not
properly identified.

1) Emergency
(Also see
EMERGENCY
EXITS)   PROCEDURES/SPECIFICATIONS:

DEPARTMENT OF TRANSPORTATION

NOTICE OF ADOPTED RULES

When the emergency door is located on the left
side, a rear emergency window shall be
provided. Minimum dimensions are 16 inches
high and 48 inches wide. Designed to be
opened from the inside or the outside.
Hinged on top, designed and operated to
insure against accidental closing in an
emergency. Inside handle shall provide for
quick release. Outside handle shall be
nondetachable and nonhitchable. When locked
or not fully latched, window shall actuate
alarm audible and visible to driver. No
cutoff switch allowed.

Optional emergency windows are allowed. They
must be labelled "Emergency Exit" in letters
at least two inches high, of a color that
contrasts with its background, located at the
top of or directly above the window on
the inside surface of the bus.

REJECT VEHICLE IF:

Operating mechanisms do not function. Alarm
does not function. Glass is cracked or broken
(see EMERGENCY EXIT - Alarms and Locks).

2) Rear   PROCEDURES/SPECIFICATIONS:

Glazing in rear of bus shall be of fixed type.
Any authorized or required sign, letters
or numerals displayed on the window in
the rear of the bus shall be located so as not
to obstruct the driver's view.

REJECT VEHICLE IF:

Visibility through rear windows is obstructed.
Glass is cracked or broken.

3) Side   PROCEDURES/SPECIFICATIONS:

All buses purchased after September 1974 must
have each side window as an unobstructed
emergency opening and at least a nine inch by
22 inch wide opening obtained by lowering
the window. Six inch stop line required
on all windows. Safety glass, or equivalent,

with exposed edges banded.

All buses purchased prior to September 1974
and after January 1, 1972, must have approved
safety glass in all windows and doors and all
exposed edges of the glass shall be banded.

Those vehicles used as a school bus by school
districts and private contractors prior to
January 1, 1972, and are still in their
possession and had previously passed the
school bus safety inspection can still be
utilized if they continue to meet the
inspection requirements that were in effect
at that time. These vehicles will not have to
be brought up to the above standards.

Note: For information regarding optional
route identification markings, see Lettering.

REJECT VEHICLE IF:

Windows do not meet emergency opening
requirements. Window does not open easily.
Glass is cracked or broken. Stop lines
are missing.

Window latches do not operate properly.

4) Windshield   PROCEDURES/SPECIFICATIONS:

*Shall be installed between front corner posts
and must not obstruct driver's view.* (Section
12-501 of the Illinois Vehicle Equipment Law)

All buses purchased after September 1974 must
have tinted safety glass six inches below top
of windshield or equivalent to reduce glare.

All buses purchased prior to September 1974
must have safety glass and shall be heat
resistant, laminated plate.

REJECT VEHICLE IF:

Windshield is not firmly sealed or attached.
Glass is broken, cracked, or discolored (not
including allowed tint).

f) WINDSHIELD
WASHER   PROCEDURES/SPECIFICATIONS:

Windshield washer shall effectively clean the
area covered by both wipers.

REJECT VEHICLE IF:
Windshield washer does not effectively clean
entire area or does not operate properly.

g) WINDSHIELD
WIPERS   PROCEDURES/SPECIFICATIONS:

Wipers shall be either two speed or variable
speed with nonglare arms and blades. Blades
need not be individually powered.

REJECT VEHICLE IF:

Windshield wipers do not cover entire cleaning
area. Blades are damaged, torn,
hardened, or rubber wiping element has
broken down. Wiper fails to park properly
when shut off.

DEPARTMENT OF TRANSPORTATION

NOTICE OF ADOPTED RULES

Section 443.APPENDIX L Illinois Minimum Standards for School Bus - Van Type
Conversions 1-16 Passengers Purchased Prior to September 1974

    a) The service door shall be located to the right of the operator and may be manually controlled from the operator's seat by an over center control.

    b) The emergency doors shall be located in the center of the rear end or on the right-hand side of the school bus. The door shall be equipped with fastening devices for opening from the inside and the outside body, which may be quickly released, but is designed to offer protection against accidental release.

    c) No seat or other object shall be placed in the bus which restricts passageway to the emergency door to less than twelve inches.

    d) The minimum clearance of all aisles, including between the seats and leading to the emergency door shall be twelve inches.

    e) The ceiling and walls shall be insulated with fireproof material to deaden sound and reduce vibration to a minimum.

    f) The interior of the school bus shall be free of all unnecessary projections likely to cause injury. This inner lining on ceilings and walls shall be fiberboard or metal.

    g) All glass in the windshield, windows, and doors shall be of approved safety glass. All exposed edges of glass shall be banded. The glass in the windshield shall be heat-absorbent laminated plate.

    h) 123 inch wheelbase.

    i) G.V.W.R. 7600 pounds.

    j) 3300 lbs. front axle.

    k) 5050 lbs. rear axle.

    l) 1475 lbs. front springs.

    m) 2200 lbs. rear springs.

    n) 8:00 x 16.5, 8 ply rating tires.

    o) 6 hole disc 16.5" x 6.00".

) High output primary heater.

DEPARTMENT OF TRANSPORTATION

NOTICE OF ADOPTED RULES

    q) Rear heater recirculating type.

    r) Two moveable glass vents or windows. One located on the right side and one on the left side of the driver's areas. These are optional.

    s) 240 cu. in. minimum engine.

    t) 55 amp alternator.

    u) 70 amp battery.

    v) Two 5" x 10" (minimum) outside rear view mirrors (West Coast Type), and two 3" convex mirrors (buses purchased prior to September, 1974, may have the 3" "stick on type" convex mirrors, provided they do not reduce the visual field of the mirror below 50 square inches).

    w) Inside rear view mirror.

    x) A convex crossover mirror 7 1/2" in diameter, mounted on left front to give the seated driver a view of the roadway immediately in front of the front bumper.

    y) Seating plan must allow 13 inches of seating space for each of 16 or fewer passengers, exclusive of the driver. All seats must face forward with a minimum of 12" aisle down the center or down the right side. No jump or portable seats allowed.

    z) Manually or mechanically operated "Stop" signal arm. Hexagon shaped semaphore mandatory on all vehicles purchased after December 31, 1975.

    aa) One rub rail applied to each side operator's door and service door. Rub rail may be omitted on operator's door if "Stop" signal arm is mounted on it.

    bb) Floor must be covered with a non-skid type material.

    cc) Roof mounted "School Bus" sign with flashing lights, acceptable until December 31, 1976. An eight light flashing system is then mandatory.

    dd) Color of bus shall be National School Bus Chrome Yellow.

    ee) All required lettering shall be in black. Emergency door lettering shall be two inches. Bus Number, School Name, District or Contractor's name on both sides of vehicle shall be four inches. "School Bus" shall be eight inches.

    ff) Vehicles may not be altered or converted to carry more than 16

Section 443.Illustration A Stop Arm Panels

Octagon Shaped Semaphore (see Section 443.APPENDIX J (a))

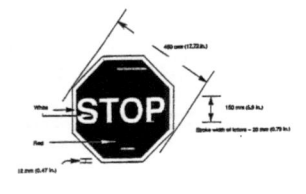

Hexagon Shaped Semaphore (see Section 443.APPENDIX J (a))

Section 443.Illustration B Exhaust Guidelines

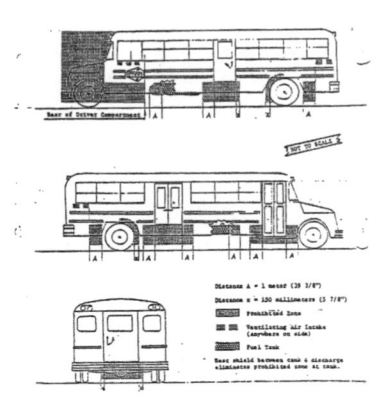

DEPARTMENT OF TRANSPORTATION

NOTICE OF ADOPTED RULES

Section 443.ILLUSTRATION C Brake Inspection Report

[IDOT Letterhead]   School Bus Brake
                                          Inspection Report

District of Contractor:

Name_____
Address_____
City/State_____ . Zip_____ Telephone(   )_____
School Bus Unit Number_____ Chassis Make_____
Chassis Year_____ Chassis V.I.N._____

Illinois law requires all school buses to be safety inspected at least once
every six months or 10,000 miles, whichever occurs first. In addition, the
Illinois Department of Transportation requires that a visual brake inspection
be performed on every school bus operated in Illinois at least once a year or
every 10,000 miles, whichever occurs first.

A completed School Bus Brake Inspection Report must be presented to the
Certified Safety Tester each time a school bus is taken to an Official Testing
Station for a safety inspection.

I attest that the entire brake system on the school bus listed above was
inspected and found to be operating in accordance with the manufacturer's
specifications or was repaired to perform in accordance with the
manufacturer's specifications. The visual inspection of the brake system
was performed on _____ by a qualified mechanic employed by
                      (date)
_____. The mileage on this school bus
(business/school district where
brake inspection was completed)
was_____when the visual brake inspection was performed.
      (mileage)

_____
  (name of authorized school   (date)
   district official or contractor)
      Please print or type

DEPARTMENT OF TRANSPORTATION

NOTICE OF ADOPTED RULES

_____
(signature of authorized school
 district official or contractor)
_____
              (title)

DEPARTMENT OF TRANSPORTATION

NOTICE OF ADOPTED RULES

Section 443.Illustration D Propane Decal

DEPARTMENT OF TRANSPORTATION

NOTICE OF ADOPTED RULES

Section 443.ILLUSTRATION E Driver's Pre-Trip Inspection Requirements and Sample Form

As required in Section 13-115 of the Illinois Vehicle Inspection Law, drivers must complete the following "Pre-trip Inspection" daily:

"Each day that a school bus is operated the driver shall conduct a pre-trip inspection of the mechanical and safety equipment on the bus as prescribed by rule or regulation of the Department." (Section 13-115 of the Illinois Vehicle Inspection Law)

The following requirements became effective August 1, 1975:

a) The driver must inspect his vehicle each day prior to beginning a trip.

b) The driver is required to make a written report of this pre-trip inspection. He must report any defects found to the proper authority so that the defects can be corrected.

c) The pre-trip inspection report shall be made in duplicate.

d) As designated by the owner, the original copy shall be presented to the person of authority on a daily basis. These original copies shall be retained by the owner for one hundred and eighty days.

e) The duplicate copy shall remain in the bus for a period of at least thirty days.

f) The form shall specify items to be checked (see subsection (i)) and the minimum information to be recorded.

g) The pre-trip inspection records and reports will be made available for inspection and audit by authorized representatives of the Department at any time.

h) It is the responsibility of the bus owner to furnish pre-trip inspection report forms that meet the minimum requirements of this Chapter.

i) Required items to be checked during the driver's Pre-Trip Inspection:

1) Coolant; oil; battery; washer fluid levels; fan belts; and wiring.

2) Steps; cleanliness; upholstery; windows; warning devices; fuses; first aid kit; fire extinguisher; emergency door (open and close) lettering.

3) Odometer reading and indication of whether or not state inspection is due.

DEPARTMENT OF TRANSPORTATION

NOTICE OF ADOPTED RULES

4) Steering wheel; windshield wipers and washers; heater and defroster; horn; service door (open and close); all mirrors (adjustment); door buzzer; clutch; brake warning buzzer; stop arm control; gear shift lever; neutral safety switch; water temperature; fuel; vacuum or air pressure; gauges; parking brake; seat belt(s).

5) Ammeter; all interior lights; headlights (high/low beams).

6) Right front wheel and tire; right side marker lamps; turn signal light and reflectors; right rear view and safety mirror; headlights; turn signals; cluster; clearance; and I.D. lights; alternating flashing lights; windshield; underside of chassis; crossover mirror; left rear view mirror and safety mirror; left front wheel and tire; driver's side window; stop arm; left side marker lamps; turn signal light and reflectors; emergency door (open and close); left rear wheels and tires; exhaust system (tailpipe clear); cluster; clearance and I.D. lights; taillights; turn signals and reflectors; alternating-flashing lights; rear emergency door (open and close); right rear wheels and tires; fuel tank filler caps.

7) Drain air brake tank. Record condition of bus (i.e., satisfactory or unsatisfactory).

DEPARTMENT OF TRANSPORTATION

NOTICE OF ADOPTED RULES

COMPANY NAME OR SCHOOL DISTRICT NAME
_____

Bus _____ Odometer _____ Date _____ Time _____

Open Hood and Check:
- ☐ Coolant, Oil, Battery, Washer Fluid Levels, Fan Belts and Wiring

Enter Bus and Check:
- ☐ Steps, Cleanliness, Upholstery, Windows, Warning Devices, Fuses, First Aid Kit, Fire Extinguisher and Emergency Door (open and close), Lettering

Record Odometer Reading _____
(Circle if State Inspection is due shortly)

Start Engine and Check:
- ☐ Steering Wheel
- ☐ Windshield Wipers and Washers
- ☐ Heater and Defroster
- ☐ Horn
- ☐ Service Door (open and close)
- ☐ All Mirrors (Adjustment)
- ☐ Door Buzzer
- ☐ Clutch
- ☐ Brake Warning Buzzer
- ☐ Stop Arm Control
- ☐ Gear Shift Lever
- ☐ Neutral Safety Switch
- ☐ Water Temp., Fuel, Vacuum or Air Pressure
- ☐ Gauges
- ☐ Parking Brake
- ☐ Seat Belt

Drive Bus Forward and Apply Brakes Activate All Lights and Check:
- ☐ Ammeter, All Interior Lights, Headlights (high/low beams)

With Engine Running and All Lights On, Check Following Equipment Outside Bus:
- ☐ Rt. Front Wheel and Tire
- ☐ Rt. Side Marker Lamps, Turn Signal Light and Reflectors
- ☐ Rt. Rear View and Safety Mirror
- ☐ Headlights, Turn Signals
- ☐ Cluster, Clearance and I.D. Lights
- ☐ Alternating Flashing Lights
- ☐ Windshield
- ☐ Look under bus for leaks
- ☐ Crossover Mirror
- ☐ Left Rear View Mirror & Safety Mirror
- ☐ Driver's Side Window
- ☐ Stop Arm
- ☐ Left Side Marker Lamps, Turn Signal Light and Reflectors
- ☐ Emergency Door (open and close)
- ☐ Left Rear Wheels and Tires
- ☐ Exhaust System (tailpipe clear?)
- ☐ Cluster, Clearance and I.D. Lights
- ☐ Taillights, Turn Signals and Reflectors
- ☐ Rear Emergency Door (open and close)
- ☐ Rt. Rear Wheels and Tires
- ☐ Fuel Tank Filler Caps

Drain Air Brake Tank
Condition of this Bus is:
- ☐ Satisfactory
- ☐ Unsatisfactory

REMARKS _____
_____
_____

Signature of Driver making Report _____

Signature of Mechanic making Repairs _____

Date Repairs Completed _____

DEPARTMENT OF TRANSPORTATION

NOTICE OF ADOPTED RULES

1) Heading of the Part: School Bus Brake Inspections

2) Code Citation: 92 Ill. Adm. Code 447

3) Section Numbers: Adopted Action:
   447.1000   New Section
   447.1010   New Section
   447.1020   New Section
   447.1030   New Section
   447.Illustration A   New Section

4) Statutory Authority: 625 ILCS 5/12-812

5) Effective Date of Rulemaking: March 13, 1995

6) Does this rulemaking contain an automatic repeal date? No

7) Does this rulemaking contain incorporations by reference? No.

8) Date Filed in Agency's Principal Office: March 7, 1995

9) Notice of Proposal Published in Illinois Register: September 2, 1994, 18 Ill. Reg. 13367

10) Has JCAR issued a Statement of Objections to these rules? No

11) Differences between proposal and final version:

The Department deleted the left parentheses at the labeled subsections in Sections 447.1010 and 447.1030.

The Department indented all definitions an addition 5 spaces.

At Section 447.1020, "Code," the ILCS citation was shortened and corrected.

A period was inserted between "447" and "Illustration" in Section 447.1020.

At Section 447.1030(j)(1), "Person or Person's name" has been changed to "Person(s).

At Section 447.1030(j)(4), "Identification" has been changed to "identification".

12) Have all the changes agreed upon by the agency and JCAR been made as indicated in the agreement letter issued by JCAR? Yes

13) Will this rulemaking replace an emergency rule currently in effect? No

DEPARTMENT OF TRANSPORTATION

NOTICE OF ADOPTED RULES

14) Are there any amendments pending on this Part? No

15) Summary and Purpose of Rulemaking: By this Notice of Adopted Rules, the Department is establishing standards for the Department's school bus brake inspection program. The Department requires brakes on school buses to be inspected once a year or every 10,000 miles, whichever occurs first.

16) Information and questions regarding these adopted rules shall be directed to:

Ms. Cathy Allen
Regulations and Training Unit
Illinois Department of Transportation
Division of Traffic Safety
P.O.. Box 19212
Springfield. Illinois 62794-9212
(217) 785-1811

17) State reasons for this rulemaking if it was not included in the two (2) most recent regulatory agendas:

The full text of the Adopted Rule begins on the next page:

DEPARTMENT OF TRANSPORTATION

NOTICE OF ADOPTED RULES

TITLE 92: TRANSPORTATION
CHAPTER I: DEPARTMENT OF TRANSPORTATION
SUBCHAPTER e: TRAFFIC SAFETY (EXCEPT HAZARDOUS MATERIALS)

PART 447
SCHOOL BUS BRAKE INSPECTIONS

Section
447.1000   Purpose
447.1010   Applicability
447.1020   Definitions
447.1030   Administrative Requirements

ILLUSTRATION A   School Bus Brake Inspection Report

AUTHORITY: Implementing and authorized by Section 12-812 of the Illinois
Vehicle Equipment Law [625 ILCS 5/12-812].

SOURCE: Adopted at 19 Ill. Reg. **4745**, effective
MAR 13 1995

Section 447.1000 Purpose

This Part prescribes the requirements and procedures used to implement the
Department's annual or 18,000 mile, whichever occurs first, school bus brake
inspection program.

Section 447.1010 Applicability

This Part applies to the following persons:
   a) Department personnel;
   b) School bus owners or operators;
   c) Mechanics performing school bus brake inspections; and
   d) Certified Safety Testers at Illinois School Bus Official Testing
       Stations.

Section 447.1020 Definitions

   "Brake components" - Any component the manufacturer has determined
   necessary to satisfy regulations or standards (FMVSS or SAE) governing
   braking operations.

   "Certified Safety Tester"(CST) - An individual employed by an Official
   Testing Station who has passed a written exam and has demonstrated
   proficiency in the operation of authorized safety test equipment and
   has been issued evidence and authority by the Department to safety
   test vehicles in Illinois.

DEPARTMENT OF TRANSPORTATION

NOTICE OF ADOPTED RULES

   "Code" - The Illinois Vehicle Code [625 ILCS 5].

   "Department" - The Department of Transportation of the State of
   Illinois, acting directly or through its authorized agents or
   officers. (Section 13-100 of the Code)

   "Federal Motor Vehicle Safety Standards" (FMVSS) - The rules,
   regulations and standards set forth in 49 CFR 571.

   "Officer" - An employee of the Illinois Department of Transportation.

   "Official Testing Station" - All contiguous real and personal property
   which houses the testing lane(s) and any and all equipment and
   supplies relating to the safety inspection of vehicles.

   "Society of Automotive Engineers"(SAE) - Society responsible for
   establishing industry standards which manufacturers follow in design
   and construction of motor vehicles.

   "School Bus" - *Every motor vehicle, except as provided below, owned or
   operated by or for any of the following entities for the
   transportation of persons regularly enrolled as students in grade 12
   or below in connection with any activity of such entity:*

      Any public or private primary or secondary school;

      *Any primary, or secondary school operated by a religious
      institution; or*

      Any public, private or religious nursery school.

   This definition shall not include the following:

      *A bus operated by a public utility, municipal corporation or
      common carrier authorised to conduct local or interurban
      transportation of passengers when such bus is not traveling a
      specific school bus route but is:*

         *On a regularly scheduled route for the transportation of
         other fare paying passengers;*

         *Furnishing charter service for the transportation of groups
         on field trips or other special trips or in connection with
         other special events; or*

         *Being used for shuttle service between attendance centers or
         other educational facilities.*

DEPARTMENT OF TRANSPORTATION

NOTICE OF ADOPTED RULES

A motor vehicle of the first division. (Section 1-182 of the Code.)

"School Bus Brake Inspection Report" (see Section 447.Illustration A) - The form established by the Department to be used by school bus owners/operators to record school bus brake inspection requirements. The Brake Inspection Report is presented to the CST at the Official Testing Station at the time of the safety inspection required by Section 13-101 of the Code.

"Vehicle Inspection Report" - The form prescribed by the Department which is completed at the Official Testing Station when a vehicle is presented for a safety inspection.

Section 447.1030 Administrative Requirements

a) The Department requires brakes on school buses operated in Illinois to be visually inspected every 10,000 miles or once a year (whichever occurs first).

b) This brake inspection is separate from and in addition to the 10,000 mile or semi-annual safety inspection required by Section 13-101 of the Code.

c) The brake components (e.g., linings, drums, hydraulic or air lines, wheel cylinders) must be visually inspected on each school bus. This inspection usually requires the wheels to be pulled from the school bus. Some manufacturers have provided inspection ports on the wheels which can be used in lieu of pulling the wheels provided all applicable brake components can be properly inspected.

d) The brake components must be inspected to verify the manufacturer's specifications are being met or exceeded at the time of the brake inspection.

e) A school bus brake inspection report must be completed for each school bus inspected to document compliance with the manufacturer's specifications.

f) The school bus brake inspection report (Section 447.Illustration A) contains the following information. An original or photocopy of Section 447.Illustration A must be used to comply with this subsection.
  1) Name, address and phone number of the bus owner/operator;
  2) District or school served;
  3) School bus unit number;
  4) School bus chassis make;
  5) School bus chassis year;
  6) Vehicle Identification Number;
  7) Date and location of brake inspection; and
  8) Mileage on school bus at the time of brake inspection.

g) The Brake Inspection Report must be signed and dated by an authorized official of the contractor or school district. The authorized

DEPARTMENT OF TRANSPORTATION

NOTICE OF ADOPTED RULES

official takes full responsibility for the inspection of the braking system.

h) A valid, properly completed Brake Inspection Report (see Section 447.Illustration A) must be presented to the CST at the time of the safety inspection required by Section 13-101 of the Illinois Vehicle Code. This report must be retained at the Official Testing Station attached to the corresponding Vehicle Inspection Report.

i) If the school bus has been driven less than 10,000 miles and less than 12 months have passed since the bus was manufactured, a brake inspection report is not required. The CST should write "Less than 10,000 miles and less than one year old" in the Remarks Section on the Vehicle Inspection Report.

j) For each school bus inspected, a separate maintenance record must be maintained which contains the following:
  1) Person(s) name performing the brake inspection and repairs, if necessary;
  2) Owner/operator of the school bus;
  3) Date of the brake inspection/repairs;
  4) Vehicle identification (i.e., year, make, model), Vehicle Identification Number);
  5) Mileage on the school bus at the time of the brake inspection; and
  6) Record of work performed on the bus in order to meet manufacturer's specifications (e.g., specific components repaired, replaced, adjusted, etc.).

k) The maintenance records required in subsection (k) shall be retained where the vehicle is either housed or maintained for a period of one year and for six months after the school bus leaves the owner/operator's control.

l) The maintenance records shall be available for inspection and audit by officers of the Department at any time.

DEPARTMENT OF TRANSPORTATION

NOTICE OF ADOPTED RULES

Section 447.ILLUSTRATION A School Bus Brake Inspection Report

Illinois Department
of Transportation   School Bus Brake
Division of Traffic Safety   Inspection Report
3215 Executive Park Drive
P.O. Box 19212
Springfield, Illinois 62794-9212

District or Contractor:

Name_____
Address_____
City/State_____ Zip_____ Telephone(__)_____
School Bus Unit Number_____ Chassis Make_____
Chassis Year_____Chassis V.I.N._____

Illinois law requires all school buses to be safety inspected at least once
every six months or 10,000 miles, whichever occurs first. In addition, the
Illinois Department of Transportation requires that a visual brake inspection
be performed on every school bus operated in Illinois at least once a year or
every 10,000 miles, whichever occurs first.

A completed School Bus Brake Inspection Report must be presented to the
Certified Safety Tester each time a school bus is taken to an Official Testing
Station for a safety inspection.

I attest that the entire brake system on the school bus listed above was
visually inspected and found to be operating in accordance with the
manufacturer's specifications or was repaired to perform in accordance with the
manufacturer's specifications. The visual inspection of the brake system was
performed on _____ by a qualified mechanic employed by
                    (date)
_____. The mileage on this school bus was
 (business/school district where
 brake inspection was completed)
_____when the visual brake inspection was performed.
   (mileage)

_____   _____
 (name of authorized school   (date)
 district official or contractor)
     Please print or type

DEPARTMENT OF TRANSPORTATION

NOTICE OF ADOPTED RULES

_____
 (signature of authorized school
 district official or contractor)

_____
           (title)

DEPARTMENT OF CHILDREN AND FAMILY SERVICES

NOTICE OF EMERGENCY AMENDMENTS

1) Heading of Part: Background Check of Foster Family Home Applicants

2) Code Citation: 89 Ill. Adm. Code 380

3)

Section Numbers	Emergency Action
380.1	Amend
380.2	Amend
380.3	Amend
380.4	Amend
380.5	Amend
380.6	Amend
380.8	Amend
380.11	Amend
380.12	Amend
380.13	Amend
380.14	Amend
Appendix A	New

4) Statutory Authority: Section 4 of the Child Care Act of 1969 [225 ILCS 10/4]

5) Effective Date of Amendments: March 24, 1995

6) If the emergency amendment is to expire before the end of the 150-day period, please specify the date on which it is to expire: Not applicable

7) Date filed in Agency's Principal Office: March 14, 1995

8) Reason for the Emergency: The Department has proposed amendments to 89 Ill. Adm. Code 385, Background Checks, to impose similar requirements on all child care facilities subject to licensure by the Department. Those proposed amendments continue to undergo review and refinement in response to the public comments received.

There has been an alarming number of tragedies in foster family and relative home care within the past few months, including three child deaths in foster family or relative care. Therefore, the Department is proceeding with emergency amendments to this Part, which is limited to foster family or relative care, until the issues in 89 Ill. Adm. Code 385 can be resolved fully.

9) A complete description of the subjects and issues involved: The Child Care Act of 1969 requires criminal background checks of all applicants for licensure as a foster family home and gives the Department the authority to require by rule criminal background checks of other adult members of the household. In addition, the Child Care Act of 1969 requires that persons who have been convicted of committing or attempting to commit

---

DEPARTMENT OF CHILDREN AND FAMILY SERVICES

NOTICE OF EMERGENCY AMENDMENTS

certain sections may not be granted a foster parent license and allows the Department to establish standards for how to consider crimes not specifically identified in the Child Care Act. The Department has identified the crimes in Appendix A as a sufficiently serious section to prevent licensure as a foster family home.

Nearly one fourth of child abuse and neglect reports involve other members of the foster family's household, rather than the foster parents themselves. Therefore, the Department is proposing that criminal background investigations be completed for all adult members of the foster parents(') household and that a check of the State Central Registry be completed for any member of the household age 13 or older. This will increase the safety of children placed in foster care and insure that all the safety of the foster home has been thoroughly evaluated.

10) Are there any proposed amendments to this Part pending? Yes

Section	Proposed Action	Illinois Register Citation
380.1	Repeal	June 17, 1994 (18 Ill. Reg. 8779)
380.2	Repeal	June 17, 1994 (18 Ill. Reg. 8779)
380.3	Repeal	June 17, 1994 (18 Ill. Reg. 8779)
380.4	Repeal	June 17, 1994 (18 Ill. Reg. 8779)
380.5	Repeal	June 17, 1994 (18 Ill. Reg. 8779)
380.6	Repeal	June 17, 1994 (18 Ill. Reg. 8779)
380.7	Repeal	June 17, 1994 (18 Ill. Reg. 8779)
380.8	Repeal	June 17, 1994 (18 Ill. Reg. 8779)
380.9	Repeal	June 17, 1994 (18 Ill. Reg. 8779)
380.10	Repeal	June 17, 1994 (18 Ill. Reg. 8779)
380.11	Repeal	June 17, 1994 (18 Ill. Reg. 8779)
380.12	Repeal	June 17, 1994 (18 Ill. Reg. 8779)
380.13	Repeal	June 17, 1994 (18 Ill. Reg. 8779)
380.14	Repeal	June 17, 1994 (18 Ill. Reg. 8779)

11) Statewide Policy Objectives: These rules do not create or expand a State mandate as defined in Section 3(b) of the State Mandates Act [30 ILCS 805/3].

12) Information and questions regarding these amendments shall be directed to:

Jacqueline Nottingham, Chief
Office of Rules and Procedures
Department of Children and Family Services
406 East Monroe Street, Station # 222
Springfield, Illinois 62701-1498

Telephone: (217) 524-1983
TTY: (217) 524-3715

DEPARTMENT OF CHILDREN AND FAMILY SERVICES

NOTICE OF EMERGENCY AMENDMENTS

The full text of the emergency amendments begins on the next page:

DEPARTMENT OF CHILDREN AND FAMILY SERVICES

NOTICE OF EMERGENCY AMENDMENTS

TITLE 89: SOCIAL SERVICES
CHAPTER III: DEPARTMENT OF CHILDREN AND FAMILY SERVICES
SUBCHAPTER d: LICENSING ADMINISTRATION

PART 380
BACKGROUND CHECK OF FOSTER FAMILY HOME APPLICANTS

Section
380.1   Purpose
EMERGENCY
380.2   Definitions
380.3   Authorization for Criminal History Check
EMERGENCY
380.4   Fingerprinting of Applicants and Adult Members of the Household
EMERGENCY
380.5   Notice to Foster Family Home Applicant
EMERGENCY
380.6   Confidentiality of Information Received
380.7   Standard of Review Concerning Criminal History
EMERGENCY
380.8   Suspension of Application When Criminal Charges Are Pending
EMERGENCY
380.9   Denial of or Refusal to Renew a License
380.10   Applicant Appeal of Denial of or Refusal to Renew a License
380.11   Destruction of Criminal History Information
380.12   Return to Applicant Individual of Materials Provided
EMERGENCY
380.13   Applicant Request for Information Obtained
EMERGENCY
380.14   Check With State Central Register

APPENDIX A   Criminal Convictions Which Prevent Licensure
EMERGENCY

AUTHORITY: Implementing and Authorized by Section 4 of the Child Care Act of
1969 [225 ILCS 10/4].

SOURCE: Adopted and codified at 5 Ill. Reg. 5501, effective May 27, 1981;
emergency amendment at 19 Ill. Reg. **4753**, effective March 24, 1995, for
a maximum of 150 days.

Section 380.1 Purpose
EMERGENCY

The purpose of this rule is to detail the process that the Department uses to

DEPARTMENT OF CHILDREN AND FAMILY SERVICES

NOTICE OF EMERGENCY AMENDMENTS

check foster family home applicants to determine if ~~the foster parent~~ any adult member of the household has any criminal history. The primary focus of the criminal background check is to consider criminal charges as ~~they might affect the applicant's ability to perform responsibly as a foster parent~~ they might affect the foster children's safety in the home. In addition, the Department shall conduct checks of the State Central Register on all members of the household age 13 or over to determine whether they have been involved in a child abuse/neglect report.

(Source: Emergency amendment at 19 Ill. Reg. ____**4753**____, effective March 24, 1995, for a maximum of 150 days)

Section 380.2 Definitions
EMERGENCY

"Adult" means any person who is eighteen (18) years of age or older.

"Foster family home applicant" means those individuals applying directly to the Department of Children and Family Services or through a licensed child welfare agency for a license to provide full-time care for children ~~not related to them.~~

~~"Foster parent(s)" means either a single person or a man and woman who are married to each other and who are licensed to operate a foster family home.~~

"Member of the household" means a person who resides in the household as evidenced by maintaining clothing and personal effects at the household address, receiving mail at the household address, or using identification with the household address.

(Source: Emergency amendment at 19 Ill. Reg. ____**4753**____, effective March 24, 1994, for a maximum of 150 days)

Section 380.3 Authorization for Criminal History Check
EMERGENCY

Each applicant for a foster family home license, whether applying directly to the Department of Children and Family Services or through a licensed child welfare agency, shall provide written authorization for the Department to request and receive information about the applicant from the United States Department of Justice, the Illinois ~~Department of Law Enforcement~~ State Police, or other named law enforcement agency. In addition, other adult members of the applicant(s)' household are required to authorize the Department to request and receive information about any criminal history background.

(Source: Emergency amendment at 19 Ill. Reg. ____**4753**____, effective March 24, 1995, for a maximum of 150 days)

DEPARTMENT OF CHILDREN AND FAMILY SERVICES

NOTICE OF EMERGENCY AMENDMENTS

Section 380.4 Fingerprinting of Applicants and Adult Members of the Household
EMERGENCY

Each applicant for a foster family home license and each adult member of the household shall submit to a fingerprinting process administered by the Department or its agent. Fingerprints shall be transmitted to the Illinois ~~Department of Law Enforcement~~ State Police or other law enforcement agency named by the Department of Children and Family Services ~~on Department forms provided for the purpose of obtaining criminal history information about a foster parent applicant.~~ in accordance with the process outlined by the Department for obtaining background information on these persons.

(Source: Emergency amendment at 19 Ill. Reg. ____**4753**____, effective March 24, 1995, for a maximum of 150 days)

Section 380.5 Notice to Foster Family Home Applicant
EMERGENCY

Each applicant for foster home licensure shall be informed in writing of the Department's requirement that the applicant and each adult member of the household consent to a criminal history check and submit to fingerprinting procedures as part of the foster home licensing process. Applicants shall be informed of their right to recover the identity materials submitted and to receive a copy of ~~all~~ criminal history information about the applicants obtained by the Department.

(Source: Emergency amendment at 19 Ill. Reg. ____**4753**____, effective March 24, 1995, for a maximum of 150 days)

Section 380.6 Confidentiality of Information Received
EMERGENCY

a) All information received by the Department of Children and Family Services from a law enforcement agency which concerns an applicant for foster family home licensure or any member of the household is confidential. It may be released only as authorized by this ~~rule~~ Part.

b) All information received pursuant to this ~~rule~~ Part shall be maintained in a single ~~manual~~ information system under the sole control of the Director of the Department of Children and Family Services or his designee.

c) All criminal history information shall be used solely for the purpose of evaluating ~~an applicant's suitability as a foster parent~~ the suitability of the foster home and shall be accessible only to those ~~Department of Children and Family Services'~~ employees directly involved in the foster home licensing process for the applicant or specifically designated by the Director of the Department to review criminal history information.

DEPARTMENT OF CHILDREN AND FAMILY SERVICES

NOTICE OF EMERGENCY AMENDMENTS

d) Any employee of the Department of Children and Family Services who
    gives or causes to be given in a manner not authorized by this rule
    any confidential information concerning any criminal charges and their
    disposition pertaining to a foster parent applicant shall be guilty of
    a Class A misdemeanor pursuant to Section 4 of the Child Care Act of
    1969, amended 1977 (Ill. Rev. Stat., ch. 23, Sec. 2214). [225 ILCS
    10/4].

(Source: Emergency amendment at 19 Ill. Reg. __4753__, effective
March 24, 1995, for a maximum of 150 days)

Section 380.7 Standard of Review Concerning Criminal History
EMERGENCY

a) In assessing the suitability of an applicant for foster parent
    licensure, the Department may consider prior criminal charges and
    their disposition (including convictions), criminal charges pending at
    the time of application, and criminal charges filed during review of
    the application.
b) When a criminal history has been discovered Department employees,
    designated by the Director of the Department, shall review the
    materials focusing on the relationship between the offense which was
    the basis for the conviction and the applicant's ability to perform
    responsibility as a foster parent. The following shall be considered:
    1) the type of crime for which the individual was convicted;
    2) the number of crimes for which the individual was convicted;
    3) the nature of the offense;
    4) the age of the individual at the time of the conviction;
    5) the length of time that has elapsed since the last conviction;
    6) the relationship of the crime and the ability to care for
        children;
    7) evidence of rehabilitation; and
    8) opinions of community members concerning the individual in
        question.
c) Persons with certain serious criminal convictions shall not receive a
    license to serve as a foster parent or be an adult member of the
    household of a foster family home. These serious crimes are listed in
    Appendix A of this Part.

(Source: Emergency amendment at 19 Ill. Reg. __4753__, effective
March 24, 1995, for a maximum of 150 days)

Section 380.8 Suspension of Application When Criminal Charges Are Pending
EMERGENCY

If criminal charges are pending against an applicant or adult member of the
household when the application for foster family home licensure is filed, the
application process for that particular individual foster family home shall be

DEPARTMENT OF CHILDREN AND FAMILY SERVICES

NOTICE OF EMERGENCY AMENDMENTS

suspended until some official disposition of the charges is submitted to the
Department by appropriate officials.

(Source: Emergency amendment at 19 Ill. Reg. __4753__, effective
March 24, 1995, for a maximum of 150 days)

Section 380.12 Return to Applicant Individual of Materials Provided
EMERGENCY

After the Criminal history check has been completed, all identity materials
obtained from the applicant or any adult member of the household by the
Department of Children and Family Services, or its agent, shall be returned in
its original form to the applicant upon written request to the Department of
Children and Family Services. No copies of the identity materials shall be
made or retained by the Department of Children and Family Services or by any
agency to which such identity materials were transmitted.

(Source: Emergency amendment at 19 Ill. Reg. __4753__, effective
March 24, 1995, for a maximum of 150 days)

Section 380.13 Applicant Request for Information Obtained
EMERGENCY

All information obtained from the criminal history check, including the source
of the information, and any conclusions or recommendations derived from this
information by the Department of Children and Family Services, shall be
provided to the applicant, individual, or his designee, upon written request to
the Director of the Department, prior to any final action on the application by
the Department of Children and Family Services.

(Source: Emergency amendment at 19 Ill. Reg. __4753__, effective
March 24, 1995, for a maximum of 150 days)

Section 380.14 Check With State Central Register
EMERGENCY

a) Applicants shall be informed that the Department's State Central
    Register of child abuse and neglect will be queried concerning
    indicated child abuse or neglect reports concerning them and any
    member of the household 13 years of age and older.
b) When an indicated report is discovered Department employees designated
    by the Director of the Department shall assess the information in
    accordance with the criteria established in 89 Ill. Adm. Code 385,
    Background Checks. materials focusing on the relationship between the
    abuse or neglect and the applicant's ability to perform responsibly as
    a foster parent. The following shall be considered:
    1) the type of indicated abuse and neglect;
    2) the age of the individual at the time of the report;

DEPARTMENT OF CHILDREN AND FAMILY SERVICES

NOTICE OF EMERGENCY AMENDMENTS

3) the--length--of--time--that--has--elapsed--since--the--most--recent
indicated--report;

4) the--relationship-of-the--report--and--the--ability--to--care--for
children;-and

5) evidence-of-successful-parenting.

c) An--applicant--shall--be--notified--in--writing--if-the-Department-decides-to
deny--a--foster--family-home-license-application-or-refuses-to-renew-a
foster-home-license-application-based-on-an-indicated-child--abuse--or
neglect-report-and-of-their-right-to-appeal-the-decision;

d) An--applicant--may--appeal--a--decision--to-deny-or-refuse--to-renew-a
license--because--of--an--indicated--child--abuse--or--neglect--report
according-to-the-process-in-Section-388.18.

(Source: Emergency Amendment at 19 Ill. Reg. **4753**, effective
March 24, 1995, for a maximum of 150 days)

DEPARTMENT OF CHILDREN AND FAMILY SERVICES

NOTICE OF EMERGENCY AMENDMENTS

Section 380.APPENDIX A Criminal Convictions Which Prevent Licensure
EMERGENCY

If the foster parent applicant(s) or any adult member of the household has been
convicted of committing or attempting to commit one or more of the following
serious criminal offenses under the Criminal Code of 1961 [720 ILCS 5] or under
any earlier Illinois criminal law or code or an offense in another state, the
elements of which are similar and bear a substantial relation to any of the
criminal offenses specified below, this conviction will serve as a bar to
receiving a foster home license or permit.

OFFENSES DIRECTED AGAINST THE PERSON

HOMICIDE

Murder
Solicitation of murder
Solicitation of murder for hire
Intentional homicide of an unborn child
Voluntary manslaughter of an unborn child
Involuntary manslaughter
Reckless homicide
Concealment of a homicidal death
Involuntary manslaughter of an unborn child
Reckless homicide of an unborn child

KIDNAPPING AND RELATED OFFENSES

Drug induced kidnapping
Kidnapping
Aggravated kidnapping
Unlawful restraint
Aggravated unlawful restraint
Forcible detention
Child abduction
Aiding and abetting child abduction

SEX OFFENSES

Indecent solicitation of a child
Sexual exploitation of a child
Sexual relations within families
Prostitution
Soliciting for a prostitute
Soliciting for a juvenile prostitute
Pandering
Felony keeping a place of prostitution
Patronizing a juvenile prostitute

DEPARTMENT OF CHILDREN AND FAMILY SERVICES

NOTICE OF EMERGENCY AMENDMENTS

Felony pimping
Juvenile pimping
Exploitation of a child
Felony obscenity
Child pornography
Felony harmful material

BODILY HARM

Felony aggravated assault
Vehicular endangerment
Felony domestic battery
Aggravated battery
Heinous battery
Aggravated battery with a firearm
Aggravated battery of a child or institutionalized mentally
retarded person
Aggravated battery of an unborn child
Tampering with food, drugs, or cosmetics
Aggravated battery of a senior citizen
Drug induced infliction of great bodily harm
Intimidation
Compelling organization membership of persons
Hate crime
Stalking
Aggravated stalking
Threatening public officials
Home invasion
Vehicular invasion
Criminal sexual assault
Aggravated sexual assault
Felony criminal sexual abuse
Aggravated sexual abuse
Criminal transmission of HIV
Abuse and gross neglect of a long term care facility resident
Criminal neglect of an elderly or disabled person
Child abandonment
Endangering the life or health of a child
Felony violation of an order of protection
Ritual mutilation
Ritualized abuse of a child

OFFENSES DIRECTED AGAINST PROPERTY

Felony theft
Robbery
Aggravated robbery
Aggravated vehicular hijacking

DEPARTMENT OF CHILDREN AND FAMILY SERVICES

NOTICE OF EMERGENCY AMENDMENTS

Burglary
Possession of burglary tools
Residential burglary
Criminal fortification of a residence or building
Arson
Aggravated arson

OFFENSES AFFECTING PUBLIC HEALTH, SAFETY AND DECENCY

Felony unlawful use of weapons
Aggravated discharge of a firearm
Reckless discharge of a firearm
Unlawful use of metal piercing bullets
Unlawful sale or delivery of firearms on the premises of any
school
Disarming a police officer
Obstructing justice
Concealing or aiding a fugitive
Armed violence
Felony contributing to the criminal delinquency of a juvenile

DRUG OFFENSES

Possession of more than thirty grams of cannabis
Manufacture of more than 10 grams of cannabis
Cannabis trafficking
Delivery of cannabis on school grounds
Unauthorized production of more than five cannabis sativa plants
Calculated criminal cannabis conspiracy
Unauthorized manufacture or delivery of controlled substances
Controlled substance trafficking
Manufacture, distribution, advertisement of look-alike substances
Calculated criminal drug conspiracy
Permitting unlawful use of a building
Delivery of controlled, counterfeit or look-alike substances to
persons under age 18, or at truck stops, rest stops, safety rest
areas, or on school property
Using, engaging, or employing persons under 18 to deliver
controlled, counterfeit or look-alike substances
Delivery of controlled substances
Sale or delivery of drug paraphernalia
Felony possession, sale or exchange of instruments adapted for use
of controlled substance or cannabis by subcutaneous injection

(Source: Emergency amendment at 19 Ill. Reg. __4753__, effective
March 24, 1995, for a maximum of 150 days)

DEPARTMENT OF AGRICULTURE

NOTICE OF PEREMPTORY AMENDMENTS

1) Heading of the Part: Meat and Poultry Inspection Act

2) Code Citation: 8 Ill. Adm. Code 125

3) Section Numbers: Peremptory Action:
   125.10   Amended
   125.270   Amended
   125.380   Amended

4) Reference to the Specific State or Federal Court Order, Federal Rule or Statute which requires this Peremptory Rulemaking: Section 16 of the Meat and Poultry Inspection Act (Ill. Rev. Stat. 1991, ch. 56 1/2, par. 316) [225 ILCS 650/16]; the Federal Meat Inspection Act (21 U.S.C.A. 661); the Federal Poultry Inspection Act (21 U.S.C.A. 454); 60 FR 5762 60 FR 10304.

5) Statutory Authority: The Meat and Poultry Inspection (Ill. Rev. Stat. 1991, ch. 56 1/2, par. 301 et seq.) [225 ILCS 650]. 10304.

6) Effective Date: March 13, 1995

7) A Complete Description of the Subjects and Issues Involved:

In order to maintain an "equal to" status with the federal meat and poultry products inspection program as required by the Federal Meat Inspection Act, the Federal Poultry Inspection Act, and in compliance with Section 16 of the Meat and Poultry Inspection Act, changes in the federal rules relative to meat and poultry inspection are hereby adopted.

The Food Safety and Inspection Service (FSIS) of the United States Department of Agriculture is correcting amendments to nutrition labeling regulations which were published in the Federal Register on January 3, 1995 (60 FR 174) and adopted by this agency on January 27, 1995. The sections of the federal rules being corrected are: 9 CFR 381.461 (refer to January 30, 1995 issue of the Federal Register, page 53621) and 9 CFR 381.409 (refer to February 24, 1995 issue of the Federal Register, page 10304).

The FSIS is also correcting an amendment to update references to an incorporation by reference in 9 CFR Part 318.19 which was published in the June 30, 1994 issue of the Federal Register (59 FR 33641) and adopted by this agency on July 29, 1994. The correction appears in the February 24, 1995 issue of the Federal Register, page 10304.

8) Does this rulemaking contain an automatic repeal date? No

9) Date Filed in Agency's Principal Office: March 14, 1995

10) This rule is in compliance with Section 9-50 of the Illinois

DEPARTMENT OF AGRICULTURE

NOTICE OF PEREMPTORY AMENDMENTS

Administrative Procedure Act, Peremptory Rulemaking.

11) Are there any proposed amendments pending to this Part? Yes, peremptory amendments to Sections 125.10, 125.100, 125.260, 125.270, and 125.380, 19 Ill. Reg. 1342, February 10, 1995.

12) Statement of Statewide Policy Objectives: Rulemaking does not affect units of local government.

13) Information and questions regarding this adopted amendment shall be directed to:

Name: Debbie Wakefield
Address: Illinois Department of Agriculture
            State Fairgrounds
            Springfield, Illinois 62794-9281
Telephone: 217/785-5713   FAX: 217/785-4505

The full text of the peremptory amendments begins on the next page.

DEPARTMENT OF AGRICULTURE

NOTICE OF PEREMPTORY AMENDMENTS

TITLE 8: AGRICULTURE AND ANIMALS
CHAPTER I: DEPARTMENT OF AGRICULTURE
SUBCHAPTER c: MEAT AND POULTRY INSPECTION ACT

PART 125
MEAT AND POULTRY INSPECTION ACT

SUBPART A: GENERAL PROVISIONS FOR BOTH MEAT AND/OR
POULTRY INSPECTION

DEPARTMENT OF AGRICULTURE

NOTICE OF PEREMPTORY AMENDMENTS

AUTHORITY: Implementing and authorized by the Meat and Poultry Inspection Act
(Ill. Rev. Stat. 1991, ch. 56 1/2, par. 301 et seq.) [225 ILCS 650] and Section
16 of the Civil Administrative Code of Illinois (Ill. Rev. Stat. 1991, ch. 127,
par. 16) [20 ILCS 5/16].

SOURCE: Adopted at 9 Ill. Reg. 1782, effective January 24, 1985; peremptory
amendment at 9 Ill. Reg. 2337, effective January 28, 1985; peremptory amendment
at 9 Ill. Reg. 2980, effective February 20, 1985; peremptory amendment at 9
Ill. Reg. 4856, effective April 1, 1985; peremptory amendment at 9 Ill. Reg.
9240, effective June 5, 1985; peremptory amendment at 9 Ill. Reg. 10102,
effective June 13, 1985; peremptory amendment at 9 Ill. Reg. 11673, effective
July 17, 1985; peremptory amendment at 9 Ill. Reg. 13748, effective August 23,
1985; peremptory amendment at 9 Ill. Reg. 15575, effective October 2, 1985;
peremptory amendment at 9 Ill. Reg. 19759, effective December 5, 1985;
peremptory amendment at 10 Ill. Reg. 447, effective December 23, 1985;
peremptory amendment at 10 Ill. Reg. 1307, effective January 7, 1986;
peremptory amendment at 10 Ill. Reg. 3318, effective January 24, 1986;
peremptory amendment at 10 Ill. Reg. 3880, effective February 7, 1986;
peremptory amendment at 10 Ill. Reg. 11478, effective June 25, 1986; peremptory
amendment at 10 Ill. Reg. 14858, effective August 22, 1986; peremptory
amendment at 10 Ill. Reg. 15305, effective September 10, 1986; peremptory
amendment at 10 Ill. Reg. 16743, effective September 19, 1986; peremptory
amendment at 10 Ill. Reg. 18203, effective October 15, 1986; peremptory
amendment at 10 Ill. Reg. 19818, effective November 12, 1986; peremptory
amendment at 11 Ill. Reg. 1696, effective January 5, 1987; peremptory amendment
at 11 Ill. Reg. 2930, effective January 23, 1987; peremptory amendment at 11
Ill. Reg. 9645, effective April 29, 1987; peremptory amendment at 11 Ill. Reg.
10321, effective May 15, 1987; peremptory amendment at 11 Ill. Reg. 11184,

DEPARTMENT OF AGRICULTURE

NOTICE OF PEREMPTORY AMENDMENTS

effective June 5, 1987; peremptory amendment at 11 Ill. Reg. 14830, effective August 25, 1987; peremptory amendment at 11 Ill. Reg. 18799, effective November 3, 1987; peremptory amendment at 11 Ill. Reg. 19805, effective November 19, 1987; peremptory amendment at 12 Ill. Reg. 2154, effective January 6, 1988; amended at 12 Ill. Reg. 3417, effective January 22, 1988; peremptory amendment at 12 Ill. Reg. 4879, effective February 25, 1988; peremptory amendment at 12 Ill. Reg. 6313, effective March 21, 1988; peremptory amendment at 12 Ill. Reg. 6819, effective March 29, 1988; peremptory amendment at 12 Ill. Reg. 13621, effective August 8, 1988; peremptory amendment at 12 Ill. Reg. 19116, effective November 1, 1988; peremptory amendment at 12 Ill. Reg. 20894, effective December 21, 1988; peremptory amendment at 13 Ill. Reg. 228, effective January 11, 1989; peremptory amendment at 13 Ill. Reg. 2160, effective February 13, 1989; amended at 13 Ill. Reg. 3696, effective March 13, 1989; peremptory amendment at 13 Ill. Reg. 15853, effective October 5, 1989; peremptory amendment at 13 Ill. Reg. 16838, effective October 11, 1989; peremptory amendment at 13 Ill. Reg. 17495, effective January 18, 1990; amended at 14 Ill. Reg. 3424, effective February 26, 1990; peremptory amendment at 14 Ill. Reg. 4953, effective March 23, 1990; peremptory amendment at 14 Ill. Reg. 11401, effective July 6, 1990; peremptory amendment at 14 Ill. Reg. 13355, effective August 20, 1990; peremptory amendment at 14 Ill. Reg. 16064, effective September 24, 1990; peremptory amendment at 14 Ill. Reg. 21060, effective May 29, 1991; peremptory amendment at 15 Ill. Reg. 620, effective January 2, 1991; peremptory amendment withdrawn at 15 Ill. Reg. 1574, effective January 2, 1991; peremptory amendment at 15 Ill. Reg. 3117, effective September 3, 1991; peremptory amendment at 15 Ill. Reg. 8714, effective May 29, 1991; amended at 15 Ill. Reg. 8801, effective June 7, 1991; peremptory amendment at 15 Ill. Reg. 13976, effective September 20, 1991; peremptory amendment at 16 Ill. Reg. 1899, effective March 2, 1992; amended at 16 Ill. Reg. 8349, effective May 26, 1992; peremptory amendment at 16 Ill. Reg. 11687, effective July 10, 1992; peremptory amendment at 16 Ill. Reg. 11963, effective July 22, 1992; peremptory amendment at 16 Ill. Reg. 12234, effective July 24, 1992; peremptory amendment at 16 Ill. Reg. 16337, effective October 19, 1992; peremptory amendment at 16 Ill. Reg. 17165, effective October 21, 1992; peremptory amendment at 17 Ill. Reg. 2063, effective February 12, 1993; peremptory amendment at 17 Ill. Reg. 15725, effective September 7, 1993; peremptory amendment at 17 Ill. Reg. 16238, effective September 8, 1993; peremptory amendment at 17 Ill. Reg. 18215, effective October 5, 1993; peremptory amendment at 18 Ill. Reg. 304, effective December 23, 1993; peremptory amendment at 18 Ill. Reg. 2164, effective January 24, 1994; amended at 18 Ill. Reg. 4622, effective March 14, 1994; peremptory amendment at 18 Ill. Reg. 6442, effective April 18, 1994; peremptory amendment at 18 Ill. Reg. 8493, effective May 27, 1994; amended at 18 Ill. Reg. 11489, effective July 7, 1994; peremptory amendment at 18 Ill. Reg. 12546, effective July 29, 1994; peremptory amendment at 18 Ill. Reg. 14475, effective September 7, 1994; amended at 18 Ill. Reg. 14924, effective September 26, 1994; peremptory amendment at 18 Ill. Reg. 15452, effective September 27, 1994; peremptory amendment at 19 Ill. Reg. 1342, effective January 27, 1995; peremptory amendment at 19 Ill. Reg. 4765, effective

MAR 13 1995

DEPARTMENT OF AGRICULTURE

NOTICE OF PEREMPTORY AMENDMENTS

SUBPART B: MEAT INSPECTION

Section 125.270   Entry   into   Official   Establishment;   Reinspection   and Preparation of Product

a) The Department incorporates by reference 9 CFR 318.1(c) through 318.7, 318.9 through 318.10, 318.14 through 318.20, 318.22, 318.28, 318.24, 318.300 through 318.311 (1990) 54 FR 43041, effective January 18, 1990; 55 FR 7294, effective August 28, 1990; 55 FR 34678, effective September 24, 1990, as amended by 55 FR 49991, December 4, 1990; 57 FR 27870, effective July 22, 1992; 57 FR 42885, effective October 19, 1992; 58 FR 4067, effective February 12, 1993; 58 FR 41138, effective September 1, 1993; 58 FR 42188, effective September 8, 1993; 58 FR 45238 and 58 FR 45240, effective September 27, 1993; 58 FR 59934, effective December 13, 1993; 58 FR 63521, effective January 3, 1994; 59 FR 12536, effective April 18, 1994; 59 FR 33641, effective June 30, 1994; 59 FR 41640, effective September 14, 1994; 59 FR 62551, effective January 5, 1995; 60 FR 10304, effective February 24, 1995).

b) No meat or meat product shall be brought into an official establishment unless it is inspected or has been prepared in an official establishment or in a federally licensed establishment and is identified by an official inspection legend as set forth in Section 125.99, a federal inspection legend, or is exempt from inspection as stated in Section 125.110. Meat and meat products received in an official establishment during the absence of the inspector shall be identified as set forth in Section 125.200 and, unless exempt from inspection, shall not be used or prepared until they have been reinspected. Any meat and meat product originally prepared at any official establishment may not be returned to any part of such establishment other than the receiving area until it has been reinspected by the inspector and passed. Wild game carcasses shall comply with Section 5(8)(4) of the Act. The official establishment shall maintain an inventory of non-meat items (e.g., spices, preservatives) which are received at the official establishment. Any product that is brought on the premises of an official establishment contrary to the provisions of this Section shall be removed immediately from such establishment by the operator of the establishment.

c) Reinspections of meat and/or meat products within the official establishment shall be performed through the use of a random digit table.

d) Docks and receiving rooms for meat and/or meat products or other articles used by the establishment in the preparation of meat products entering an official establishment shall be approved by the inspector if the location of such docks or receiving rooms will not permit such product or article to pass through rooms containing inspected and passed products.

e) The manner of defrosting frozen products and methods of treating to

DEPARTMENT OF AGRICULTURE

NOTICE OF PEREMPTORY AMENDMENTS

preserve products shall be in accordance with procedures as set forth in the "Meat and Poultry Inspection Manual" as adopted in Section 125.20.

f) Casings or weasand shall be inspected and passed if it is in compliance with the specific provisions as stated in 9 CFR 318.5(i) for passage of such articles.

g) The Department does not approve new substances to be used on meat or in meat products, their uses or the levels of use of an approved substance. Such substances will be permitted to be used and artificial flavorings may be used if they do not adulterate the meat and/or meat product in accordance with Section 2.11 of the Act and are in compliance with the provisions of this Section.

h) References to exemptions from slaughter and custom slaughter shall mean those exemptions set forth in Section 125.110.

i) Reference to 9 CFR 327 are not applicable to the Department in its enforcement of the rules of this Part. References to the federal Poultry Inspection Act, Section 403 of the Act, Section 7 of the Act, 9 CFR 303, and paragraph 23(a) of the Act shall be interpreted to mean in accordance with The Meat and Poultry Inspection Act and the rules of this Part.

j) The Department does not approve thermometers for use in smokehouses, dry rooms and other compartments that are used in the treatment of pork.

k) Disinfectants shall be those as set forth in Section 125.180.

l) Adequate vacuum shall be determined through the use of vacuum gauges.

m) Canned products which may be processed without steampressure cooking shall be those products as stated in the "Meat and Poultry Inspection Manual" as adopted by the Department in Section 125.20.

n) The inspector shall permit lots of canned product to be shipped from the official establishment prior to the completion of the incubation period on the representative samples in accordance with the specific provisions in 9 CFR 318.309.

o) The standards and procedures for determining when ingredients of finished products are in compliance with this Section shall be as set forth in the "Meat and Poultry Inspection Manual" as adopted by the Department in Section 125.20.

(Source: Peremptory amendment at 19 Ill. Reg. **4 7 6 5** , effective ___MAR 1 3 1995___)

SUBPART C: POULTRY INSPECTION

Section 125.380 Labeling and Containers

a) The Department incorporates by reference 381.115 through 381.127, 381.129 through 381.132(b)(1), 381.133 through 381.144(d), 381.400, 381.402, 381.408, 381.409, 381.412, 381.413, 381.443, 381.444, 381.445, 381.454, 381.456, 381.460, 381.461, 381.462, 381.469,

DEPARTMENT OF AGRICULTURE

NOTICE OF PEREMPTORY AMENDMENTS

381.480, 381.500 (1990; 55 FR 5976, effective March 23, 1990; 55 FR 7289, effective August 28; 1990; 55 FR 49826 and 50081, effective May 29, 1991; 56 FR 1359, effective September 3, 1991; 56 FR 22638, effective January 2, 1992; 56 FR 67485, effective March 2, 1992; 57 FR 24542, effective July 10, 1992; 57 FR 43598, effective October 21, 1992; 58 FR 38046, effective August 16, 1993; 59 FR 14528, effective May 27, 1994; 58 FR 632, 58 FR 43787, 58 FR 47624, and 59 FR 12157, effective July 6, 1994; 59 FR 40209, effective August 8, 1994; 59 FR 45189, effective September 1, 1994; 60 FR 174 and correction printed at 60 FR 5762, effective January 3, 1995; 60 FR 10304, effective February 24, 1995).

b) Each shipping container and each immediate container containing inspected and passed poultry and/or poultry products shall be identified in accordance with the labeling provisions of this Section.

c) Immediate containers of poultry products packed in, bearing or containing any chemical additive shall bear a label naming the additive and the purpose of its use.

d) Labels for consumer packages shall be approved if the label is not misbranded in accordance with Section 2.20 of the Act and is in compliance with this Section.

e) The specific statements listed in 9 CFR 381.121 may be added to the label for the shipping container at the option of the licensee.

f) The quantity of contents as shown on the label shall be in compliance with the Weights and Measures Act and the rules adopted thereto (8 Ill. Adm. Code 600.120).

g) No labeling or containers that have not been approved shall be used until a final decision is rendered at an administrative hearing in accordance with Section 19 of the Act and Section 125.60.

h) The Department shall approve the manufacture of a device or label containing an official mark of inspection provided the device or label is in compliance with Section 125.90.

i) Labeling and sketch labeling shall be approved by the Department if the label is in compliance with the provisions of this Section and the label is not misbranded in accordance with Section 2.20 of the Act. All labels and sketch labels shall be submitted to the Springfield office of the Department for approval.

j) The Department shall approve temporary labeling as stated in 9 CFR 381.132(b)(1). Labeling which has received temporary approval shall not be used beyond the temporary approval period unless the printer or manufacturer of the label is unable to provide the official establishment with the permanent labels before the expiration of the temporary approval.

k) A copy of each label submitted for approval shall be accompanied by a statement showing the common or usual names, the kinds and percentages of the ingredients comprising the poultry product and a statement indicating the method or preparation of the product with respect to which the label is to be used. Laboratories used for chemical analysis shall be any approved laboratory as defined in 8 Ill. Adm.

DEPARTMENT OF AGRICULTURE

NOTICE OF PEREMPTORY AMENDMENTS

Code 20.1.

1) The Department does not approve terms for generic labeling and considers the approval of terms as generic to be the responsibility of the federal government.

m) The Department does not issue a list of approved packaging materials and will permit for use any packaging material which has been approved by the U.S. Department of Agriculture (see 49 FR 2235, effective July 17, 1984).

n) Labels and devices approved for use pursuant to Section 125.90 and this Section shall be disposed of only when such labels or devices have been mutilated or damaged or when the establishment ceases to do business. Such labels and devices shall be given to the inspector for disposition.

o) The inspector shall grant authorization to transport labels, wrappers and containers bearing official marks from one official establishment to another official establishment provided the official establishment provides to the inspector the information required in 9 CFR 381.138 so that the inspector can notify the inspector at the destination point.

p) Labels to be used for the relabeling of inspected and passed product shall be permitted to leave the official establishment when the product must be relabeled because the original labels have become mutilated or damaged. The official establishment shall reimburse the Department for any overtime costs, if applicable, involved for the inspector to supervise the relabeling of a product. The overtime charges shall be as set forth in Section 125.80.

q) Labeling of custom slaughtered and/or custom processed poultry and/or poultry products and the containers containing custom slaughtered and/or custom processed poultry products shall be as set forth in Section 5 of the Act.

r) The Department shall approve only those abbreviations for marks of inspection as specifically stated in Section 2.26(j)(3), (4), (5) and (9) of the Act.

(Source: Peremptory amendment at 19 Ill. Reg. **4765**, effective **MAR 13 1995**)

JOINT COMMITTEE ON ADMINISTRATIVE RULES
ILLINOIS GENERAL ASSEMBLY

SECOND NOTICES RECEIVED

The following second notices were received by the Joint Committee on Administrative Rules during the period of March 7, 1995 through March 13, 1995, and have been scheduled for review by the Committee at its April 18, 1995 meeting. Other items not contained in this published list may also be considered. Members of the public wishing to express their views with respect to a rule should submit written comments to the Committee at the following address: Joint Committee on Administrative Rules, 700 Stratton Bldg., Springfield, IL 62706.

Second Notice Expires	Agency and Rule	Start of First Notice	JCAR Meeting
4/20/95	State Board of Elections, Practice and Procedures (26 Ill Adm Code 125)	5/6/94 18 Ill Reg 6509	4/18/95
4/20/95	Department of Nuclear Safety, Licensing Requirements for Source Material Milling Facilities (32 Ill Adm Code 332)	12/16/94 18 Ill Reg 17806	4/18/95
4/20/95	Department of State Police Merit Board, Procedures of the Department of State Police Merit Board (80 Ill Adm Code 150)	11/14/94 18 Ill Reg 16536	4/18/95
4/22/95	Department of Insurance, Tax Allocation (50 Ill Adm Code 942)	12/2/94 18 Ill Reg 17068	4/18/95
4/26/95	Department of Corrections, Chaplaincy (20 Ill Adm Code 425)	1/13/95 19 Ill Reg 152	4/18/95
4/26/95	Department of Professional Regulation, Illinois Dental Practice Act (68 Ill Adm Code 1220)	12/30/94 18 Ill Reg 18196	4/18/95
4/26/95	Department of Labor, Repeal of Illinois Minimum Wage Law (56 Ill Adm Code 200)	11/18/94 18 Ill Reg 16770	4/18/95
4/26/95	Department of Labor, Minimum Wage Law (56 Ill Adm Code 210)	11/18/94 18 Ill Reg 16787	

JOINT COMMITTEE ON ADMINISTRATIVE RULES
ILLINOIS GENERAL ASSEMBLY

SECOND NOTICES RECEIVED

Second Notice Expires	Agency and Rule	Start of First Notice	JCAR Meeting
4/26/95	Department of Labor, Illinois Child Labor Law (56 Ill Adm Code 250)	1/6/95 19 Ill Reg 19	4/18/95

PROCLAMATIONS

95-092
MOTORCYCLE AWARENESS MONTH

Whereas, Illinois is a national leader in motorcycle education; and

Whereas, the Illinois Department of Transportation has been conducting the Illinois Cycle Rider Safety Training Program since 1976; and

Whereas, the program is supported by state motorcycle registration fees and has been responsible for training more than 121,000 Illinois cyclists; and

Whereas, there is a need to enhance public awareness of the increased presence of motorcyclists on our roadways;

Therefore, I, Jim Edgar, Governor of the State of Illinois, proclaim May 1995 as MOTORCYCLE AWARENESS MONTH in Illinois in recognition of efforts to improve motorcycle safety and the continuing leadership role that our state has taken in promoting motorcycle safety training.

Issued by the Governor March 1, 1995.
Filed by the Secretary of State March 9, 1995.

95-093
BUILDING SAFETY WEEK

Whereas, the well-being of every citizen of Illinois depends on the safety of the buildings in which they live, work, and play; and

Whereas, code compliance in these buildings is the joint responsibility of building owners, building operators, architects, engineers, contractors, and building officials; and

Whereas, the general public should recognize the importance of building-safety codes, which protect the public's health and safety by regulating the structural, electrical, plumbing, mechanical, fire-safety, energy efficiency, accessibility, and other aspects of both newly constructed and existing buildings; and

Whereas, units of state and local government throughout the United States are joining in expressing appreciation to the conscientious members of the building industry who ensure the safety of buildings throughout our state and the nation;

Therefore, I, Jim Edgar, Governor of the State of Illinois, proclaim April 915, 1995, as BUILDING SAFETY WEEK in Illinois. I urge our citizens to take heed of the theme FEBuilding Safety is NO Accident," and to recognize the importance of modern building- safety codes.

Issued by the Governor March 2, 1995.
Filed by the Secretary of State March 9, 1995.

95-094
DANVILLE HIGH SCHOOL DAY

Whereas, the Freedom Shrine was inspired by the Freedom Train, a traveling exposition of American historical documents which toured the United States shortly after World War II; and

Whereas, in 1949, the Exchange Clubs of America agreed to install permanent displays of the best of these historical documents in communities throughout the nation so that Americans would have easy access to the rich

heritage of their past; and

Whereas, the Freedom Shrine has contributed to the great structure of our government and the rights that we have today; and

Whereas, American citizenship is a valuable honor every American shares and one which the Danville High School Library has taken great pride in sharing with its students; and

Whereas on March 23, 1995, the Danville High School PTA will present their library with the Freedom Shrine;

Therefore, I, Jim Edgar, Governor of the State of Illinois, proclaim March 23, 1995, as DANVILLE HIGH SCHOOL DAY in Illinois.

Issued by the Governor March 2, 1995.
Filed by the Secretary of State March 9, 1995.

95-095
TIBETAN NATINAL DAY

Whereas, in 1992 and 1993, nearly 100 Tibetans immigrated to Chicago from India and Nepal and currently live and work in Chicago; and

Whereas, hundreds of Illinois residents have assisted the Tibetan immigrants in finding jobs and housing, have served as volunteer sponsors and English language tutors, and have contributed financially to support the project to resettle Tibetans in Illinois; and

Whereas, on March 10, 1959, the Tibetan people rose up in resistance to the Chinese occupation of Tibet after nine years of mistreatment. This uprising continues to be memorialized by Tibetans and their supporters around the world to commemorate the struggle of Tibetans to reclaim their own country; and

Whereas, since the invasion of Tibet, more than one million Tibetans have died of unnatural causes, more than 6,000 Buddhist monasteries have been destroyed, political prisoners have been tortured and murdered by Chinese authorities, the Tibetan environment has been systematically destroyed by Chinese settlers, and massive numbers of ethnic Chinese have been encouraged by their government to resettle in Tibet, thus making the Tibetans an ethnic minority in their own country and threatening the very existence of Tibetan language and culture; and

Whereas, His Holiness the Dalai Lama was awarded the 1989 Nobel Peace Prize for his persistent promotion of peace and justice; and

Whereas, the United States Congress recognized Tibet as an occupied country through the State Department Authorization Act on October 28, 1991; and

Whereas, the worsening human rights conditions in Tibet threaten the continued existence of the Tibetan people;

Therefore, I, Jim Edgar, Governor of the State of Illinois, proclaim March 10, 1995, as TIBETAN NATIONAL DAY in Illinois to honor the Tibetan community in Illinois and the Tibetan Alliance of Chicago in its efforts to help promote human rights for Tibetans and its effort to help the Tibetan people preserve the culture.

Issued by the Governor March 2, 1995.
Filed by the Secretary of State March 9, 1995.

95-096
CASIMIR PULASKI DAY

Whereas, Polish war hero Casimir Pulaski fought and died valiantly, helping colonial America win its battle for independence during the Revolutionary War; and

Whereas, born in Warka, Poland, on March 4, 1747, Casimir Pulaski symbolizes the courage, patriotism, and determination of Polish American and Slavic Americans who have worked and fought to help make the United States the great country it is; and

Whereas, in as much as this individual was willing to make the supreme sacrifice through his death in battle while defending our nation, it is fitting that we, in Illinois, set aside the first Monday of each March to honor him as early Illinois settlers did by the naming of Pulaski County in Southern Illinois and Mt. Pulaski in Central Illinois after this great man; and

Whereas, the Polish American community of Illinois has contributed greatly to the rich ethnic diversity of the state in the areas of education, arts and science, agriculture, government, architecture, music, and sports; and

Whereas, many observances are being held in honor of Casimir Pulaski, including ceremonies at the Polish Museum of America and at Truman College;

Therefore, I, Jim Edgar, Governor of the State of Illinois, proclaim March 6, 1995, as CASIMIR PULASKI DAY in Illinois.

Issued by the Governor March 6, 1995.
Filed by the Secretary of State March 9, 1995.

95-097
FOREIGN LANGUAGE WEEK

Whereas, learning foreign languages opens the doors to understanding cultures around the world; and

Whereas, Alpha Mu Gamma was established in 1931 as the National Collegiate Foreign Language Honor Society of the United States and has grown to include nearly 300 chapters in colleges and universities across the nation; and

Whereas, Alpha Mu Gamma seeks to recognize achievement in the field of foreign language study and encourage the study of foreign languages, literatures, and cultures; and

Whereas, in 1957, President Eisenhower proclaimed the observance of National Foreign Language Week to emphasize the importance of foreign language study. Since that time, National Foreign Language Week has been recognized by each president, and the event has been celebrated annually by Alpha Mu Gamma;

Therefore, I, Jim Edgar, Governor of the State of Illinois, proclaim March 5-11, 1995, as FOREIGN LANGUAGE WEEK in Illinois.

Issued by the Governor March 3, 1995.
Filed by the Secretary of State March 9, 1995.

95-098
CHILDREN OF THE AMERICAN REVOLUTION DAY

Whereas, the National Society Children of the American Revolution was organized on Friday, April 5, 1895, in the City of Washington in the District of Columbia by Mrs. Harriet M. Lothrop; and

Whereas, the National Society Children of the American Revolution was incorporated under the Laws of the District of Columbia on April 11, 1895, and by such incorporation the headquarters of said National Society was fixed in

the City of Washington in the District of Columbia and perpetually incorporated on April 2, 1919; and

Whereas, the National Society Children of the American revolution is an organization for the training of young people in true patriotism and love of country in order that they shall be better fitted for American citizenship; and

Whereas, the members of the National Society Children of the American Revolution believe it is their duty to use their influence to create a deeper love of country, a loyal respect for its Constitution, and reverence for its flag among the young people with whom they come in contact; and

Whereas, the National Society Children of the American Revolution has enjoyed an organized society in the State of Illinois with the organization of the Richard Lord Jones Society in 1895 and 90 succeeding local societies;

Therefore, I, Jim Edgar, Governor of the State of Illinois, proclaim April 5, 1995, as CHILDREN OF THE AMERICAN REVOLUTION DAY in Illinois and urge all citizens, especially the children, to join with me in recognizing the 100th anniversary of the National Society Children of the American Revolution.

Issued by the Governor March 6, 1995.
Filed by the Secretary of State March 9, 1995.

95-099
DENTAL ASSISTANTS RECOGNITION WEEK

Whereas, dental assistants, working with the dental profession, play an important part in maintaining the dental health of the citizens of Illinois and of the United States; and

Whereas, dental assistants, through their skills and knowledge, make dental care possible for increasing numbers of our citizens; and

Whereas, for more than 70 years, the American Dental Assistants Association has encouraged and made possible continuing education for dental assistants in order to enhance the delivery of dental health care to the public; and

Whereas, the American Dental Assistants Association and the State of Illinois have designated the week of March 6-11, 1995, as Dental Assistants Recognition Week in Illinois and throughout the United States;

Therefore, I, Jim Edgar, Governor of the State of Illinois, proclaim March 6-11, 1995, as DENTAL ASSISTANTS RECOGNITION WEEK in Illinois and bring its importance to the attention of the citizens of our state.

Issued by the Governor March 6, 1995.
Filed by the Secretary of State March 9, 1995.

95-100
PROFESSIONAL SECRETARIES WEEK/PROFESSIONAL SECRETARIES DAY

Whereas, professional secretaries contribute to the strong economic climate throughout Illinois; and

Whereas, professional secretaries in business, education, and government ensure work-force productivity; and

Whereas, the professionalism and leadership of these secretaries enhance commerce in our state;

Therefore, I, Jim Edgar, Governor of the State of Illinois, proclaim April 24-28, 1995, as PROFESSIONAL SECRETARIES WEEK and April 26, 1995, as PROFESSIONAL SECRETARIES DAY in Illinois in recognition of these hard-working

individuals and the contributions they make to the business community.
Issued by the Governor March 6, 1995.
Filed by the Secretary of State March 9, 1995.

95-101
SMILES FOR LITTLE CITY DAYS

Whereas, for 36 years, Little City Foundation has been a nationally recognized leader in providing programs and services for persons with developmental challenges; and

Whereas, on October 5-7, 1995, Little City Foundation will hold its annual "Smiles for Little City" Tag Days throughout the state; and

Whereas, this annual tradition is made possible through the efforts of hundreds of Illinois residents who unselfishly volunteer their time and effort; and

Whereas, they are ably supported by governmental, business, and labor leaders across the state;

Therefore, I, Jim Edgar, Governor of the State of Illinois, proclaim October 5-7, 1995, as SMILES FOR LITTLE CITY DAYS in Illinois.

Issued by the Governor March 6, 1995.
Filed by the Secretary of State March 9, 1995.

95-102
ILLINOIS EYE FUND/UIC EYE CENTER DAY

Whereas, the month of May 1995 marks the 137th anniversary of the University of Illinois at Chicago Eye and Ear Infirmary (formerly the Chicago Charitable Eye and Ear Infirmary); and

Whereas, the Eye and Ear Infirmary has continued to make a major contribution to Chicago's health care and since 1858 has treated hundreds of thousands of people with conditions that threaten vision and hearing; and

Whereas, the Eye and Ear Infirmary is the oldest constituent unit of the University of Illinois at Chicago College of Medicine, the largest medical school in the nation; and

Whereas, the University of Illinois at Chicago Eye Center, housed in the Eye and Ear Infirmary, created the Illinois Eye Fund in 1986 to support its vision research, patient care, and educational programs; and

Whereas, the Illinois Eye Fund will hold its Ninth Annual Spring Benefit on April 8, 1995;

Therefore, I, Jim Edgar, Governor of the State of Illinois, proclaim April 8, 1995, as ILLINOIS EYE FUND/UIC EYE CENTER DAY in Illinois and encourage all Illinois residents to recognize the historical significance of the University of Illinois at ChicagoFEs Eye and Ear Infirmary.

Issued by the Governor March 7, 1995.
Filed by the Secretary of State March 9, 1995.

94-103
U.S. SAVINGS BOND CAMPAIGN MONTH

Whereas, the United States Savings Bonds Program has been making significant contributions to the well-being of Americans for more than 50 years by helping to build savings for the future; and

Whereas, the program has helped the economy of this state by giving our citizens an extra reserve of buying power; and

Whereas, the people of this state have shown through their purchase of savings bonds that they believe in the purposes of the program;

Therefore, I, Jim Edgar, Governor of the State of Illinois, proclaim April, 1995 as U.S. SAVINGS BOND CAMPAIGN MONTH in Illinois, and I urge all citizens to help themselves, their state, and their nation by purchasing United States Savings Bonds.

Issued by the Governor March 7, 1995.

Filed by the Secretary of State March 9, 1995.

94-104
WILLIAM MCCARTEY DAY

Whereas, William McCarty has tirelessly served the Tuscola National Bank of Tuscola for 30 years; and

Whereas, he began his career with the Tuscola National Bank in 1956 as a teller and escalated to President of Illinois Bankers Association, Group 7 in 1969; and

Whereas, he has been an outstanding citizen and contributed greatly to the prosperity of Douglas County;

Whereas, he has shown tremendous leadership and dedication to his profession and community and it to be highly commended; and

Therefore, I, Jim Edgar, Governor of the State of Illinois proclaim March 14, 1995, as WILLIAM MCCARTY DAY in Illinois in honor of 30 years of success and wish his entire family continued success in the future.

Issued by the Governor March 7, 1995.

Filed by the Secretary of State March 9, 1995.

95-105
YOUTH ART MONTH

"To have an appreciation of art is to have immeasurable wealth."
—Otto M. Rann

Whereas, the arts serve an important role in the educational development of our youth; and

Whereas, during the month of March, the Illinois Art Education Association will be sponsoring special events and exhibits in conjunction with a nationwide effort to highlight the accomplishments of art teachers and their students; and

Whereas, community organizations are encouraged to take advantage of this opportunity to emphasize the enjoyment that can be derived through the creation and appreciation of art;

Therefore, I, Jim Edgar, Governor of the State of Illinois, proclaim March 1995 as YOUTH ART MONTH in Illinois.

Issued by the Governor March 7, 1995.

Filed by the Secretary of State March 9, 1995.

95-106
LICENSED PRACTICAL NURSE WEEK

Whereas, the maintenance of good health care is of primary concern to everyone; and

Whereas, the role of the licensed practical nurse in caring for people's health needs has advanced in responsibility and complexity; and

Whereas, the Licensed Practical Nurse Association of Illinois encourages the continuance of education to ensure competency among its members; and

Whereas, the Licensed Practical Nurse Association of Illinois is holding its annual convention April 23-29, 1995 in Bloomingdale. This year's theme is "LPN's the needed Link in the Health Care Team;"

Therefore, I, Jim Edgar, Governor of the State of Illinois, proclaim April 23-29, 1995, as LICENSED PRACTICAL NURSE WEEK in Illinois in recognition of these dedicated men and women.

Issued by the Governor March 8, 1995.

Filed by the Secretary of State March 9, 1995.

ACTION CODES	
A - Adopted Rule	P - Proposed Rule
AR - Adopted Repealer	PF - Prohibited Filing Order by JCAR*
C - Notice of Corrections	PP - Peremptory or Court Ordered Rules
CC - Codification Changes	PR - Proposed Repealer
E - Emergency Rule	R - Refusal to meet JCAR* Objection
ER - Emergency Repealer	RC - Statement of Recommendation
M - Modification to meet JCAR* Objections	S - Suspension ordered by JCAR*
O - JCAR* Statement Of Objections	W - Withdrawal to meet JCAR* Objections
RQ - Request for Correction	MR - Modification and Refusal
EC - Expedited Corrections	
	*Joint Committee on Administrative Rules

ALL RULES ARE LISTED BY PART NUMBER AND HEADING ONLY. (FOR ACTION ON SPECIFIC SECTIONS, PLEASE REFER TO THE SECTIONS AFFECTED INDEX.) IF THERE ARE ANY QUESTIONS, PLEASE CONTACT THE ADMINISTRATIVE CODE DIVISION AT (217) 782-7017.

3

4

9

10

17

18

This Sections Affected Index lists, by title, each Section of a Part on which Rule Making has occurred in this volume (calendar year) of the Illinois Register. The columns indicate the type of rulemaking activity and the action taken along with the page number on which the first page of the notice of rulemaking activity appeared. If a Section on which action is being taken in the current volume of the Register is proposed in a previous volume, the last two digits of the previous volume's year appear immediately after the page number separated by a slash (e.g. 11 Ill. Adm. Code 465.115 was proposed last year and adopted this year. The action entry reads: (P-15655/94; A-6520). The codes are listed below.

TYPE OF RULE MAKING	ACTION CODE	
am = amend to existing Section	A = Adopted Rule	PF = Prohibited Filing
cc = codification changes	E = Emergency	S = Suspension
n = New section	P = Proposed Rule	O = JCAR Objection
r = repeal of existing Section	PE = Peremptory	F = Failure to Remedy Objections
re = recodified	M = Modification	Objection
# = renumbered	W = Withdrawl	RC = Recommendations
	CC = Codification Changes	EC = Expedited Correction
	RQ = Request for Correction	C = Correction
	R = Refusal	

TITLE 1			TITLE 9 (CONT'D)			TITLE 14 (CONT'D)		
100.100	am	(P-7087/A-13087)	600.1	am	(P-2303)	165.10	n	(P-14698/94; A-1915)
			600.300	am	(P-2356)	165.20	n	(P-14698/94; A-1915)
TITLE 2			600.320	am	(P-2360)	165.30	n	(P-14698/94; A-1915)
1236.10	am	(A-1334)	600.970	am	(P-2090)	165.40	n	(P-14698/94; A-1915)
1236.30	am	(A-1334)	600.Tb.E	am	(P-2088)	165.50	n	(P-14698/94; A-1915)
1236.110	am	(A-1334)	1400.148	am	(P-1164)	165.60	n	(P-14698/94; A-1915)
1236.120	am	(A-1334)	1400.147	am	(P-1164)	165.70	n	(P-14698/94; A-1915)
1236.310	am	(A-1334)				165.80	n	(P-14698/94; A-1915)
1236.380	am	(A-1334)	TITLE 11			165.90	n	(P-14698/94; A-1915)
1236.420	am	(A-1334)	311.15	n	(P-559)	550.40	am	(P-14155/94; A-1503)
1236.As.5	am	(A-1334)	311.25	n	(P-559)	550.50	am	(P-14155/94; A-1503)
			311.35	n	(P-559)	550.30	am	(P-14155/94; A-1503)
TITLE 8			311.40	am	(P-559)			
80.10	am	(P-754)	508.85	am	(P-12043/94; A-2405)	TITLE 57		
80.20	am	(P-754)	508.130	am	(P-13043/94; A-2405)	110.4	am	(P-1287)
80.30	am	(P-754)	1418.80	am	(P-15731/94; A-2471)	110.40	am	(P-1287)
80.40	am	(P-754)	1770.10	am	(P-751)	110.100	am	(P-1287)
80.60	am	(P-754)	1770.80	am	(P-751)	110.160	am	(P-1387)
80.70	am	(P-754)	1770.170	am	(P-751)	130.40	am	(P-1378)
80.80	r	(P-754)	1770.180	am	(P-751)	130.50	am	(P-1378)
125.10	am	(PP-1342)	1770.200	am	(P-751)	130.60	am	(P-1378)
125.100	am	(PP-1342)				130.70	am	(P-1378)
125.260	am	(PP-1342)	TITLE 14			130.65	am	(P-1378)
125.270	am	(PP-1342; PP-4785)	130.100	am	(P-2733)	130.100	am	(P-1378)
125.360	am	(PP-1342; PP-4785)	130.130	n	(P-2733)	850.10	am	(P-1414)
255.10	am	(P-1)	130.200	am	(P-2733)	850.20	am	(P-1414)
255.60	am	(P-1)	130.441	am	(P-2733)	850.21	am	(P-1414)
255.110	am	(P-1)	130.830	am	(P-2733)	850.22	am	(P-1414)
255.170	am	(P-1)	130.631	am	(P-2733)	850.23	am	(P-1414)
255.30	am	(P-13)	130.811	am	(P-2733)	850.40	am	(P-1414)
255.60	am	(P-13)	130.820	am	(P-2733)	850.50	am	(P-1414)
255.70	am	(P-13)	130.840	am	(P-2733)	850.60	am	(P-1414)

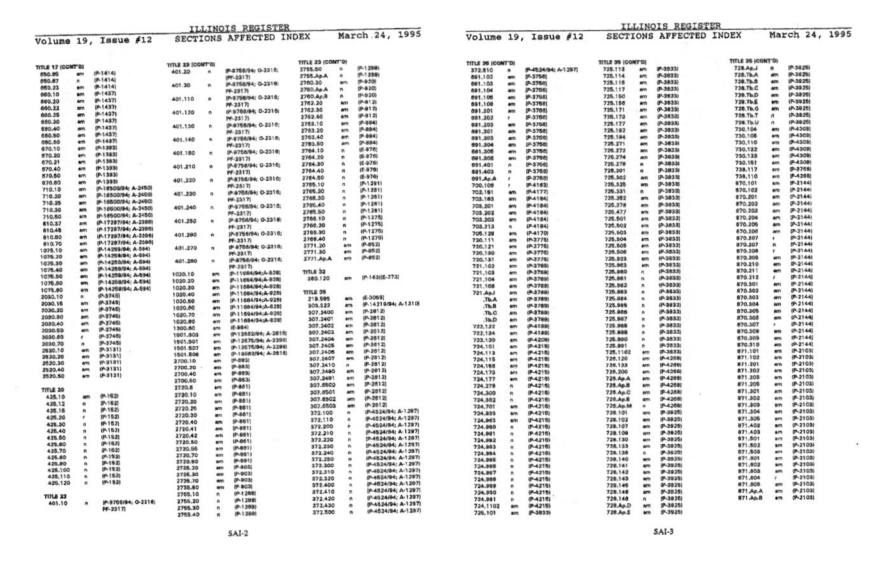

9 780260 932440